Alan R. Fischer
2.12.94
St. Mark's Bookstore
N.Y.C.

NICHOLAS RAY

An American Journey

NICHOLAS RAY

An American Journey

Bernard Eisenschitz
translated by Tom Milne

faber and faber

LONDON · BOSTON

First published in Great Britain in 1993
by Faber and Faber Limited
3 Queen Square London WC1 3AU

Originally published in 1990
as *Roman Américain: Les vies de Nicholas Ray*
by Christian Bourgois Éditeur et Longue Distance

Phototypeset by Intype, London
Printed in England by Clays Ltd, St Ives plc

© Bernard Eisenschitz, 1990
English translation © Tom Milne, 1993

Tom Milne is hereby identified as translator of this work in
accordance with Section 77 of the Copyright, Designs and
Patents Act 1988

A CIP record for this book is available from the British
Library

ISBN 0-571-14086-6

2 4 6 8 10 9 7 5 3 1

Contents

List of Illustrations

Nicholas Ray

Acknowledgements

It was Susan Ray who told me about the lines from *Moby Dick* which Nicholas Ray quoted to his doctor. That was when we met again in Paris (by way of the Rotterdam Festival) in 1980, ten months after the filming of *Lightning Over Water*; and it was then that the idea for this book was born. As the book itself testifies, she granted me free access to her archives, and, even more importantly, entrusted me with what she had learned of Nick Ray.

In 1982, John M. Hall, West Coast manager of RKO Pictures, Inc., had just inaugurated an open-door policy towards researchers wishing to consult the company archives, kept in admirable order by Vernon Harbin since the studio's demise in 1957. Without his help and trust, I would have been left in the dark concerning nearly half of Ray's creative output. John Hall died on 5 September 1987.

From beginning to end (even before the first word was written), Jean Narboni was my first reader.

All three were indispensable throughout those years of research and writing. Without them, there would have been no book.

My thanks are due to those who answered my questions – be it directly, into a tape recorder, or by telephone or letter – and who often generously entrusted me with precious documents:

Corey Allen; Rodney Amateau; Hanna Axmann-Rezzori; Tom Badal; Gerry Bamman; Ben Barzman (1911–89); Jean-Pierre Bastid; Andrés Berenguer; Manuel Berenguer; Howard Berk; John Berry; Connie Bessie (1917–85); A. I. Bezzerides; Charles Bitsch; Richard L. Bock; Charles Bornstein; Janet (Lou) Brandt; Harry Bromley-Davenport; Alan Brown; Joseph Brun; Stuart Byron (d. 1991); Dr Barrington Cooper; Joseph Cotten; Pierre Cottrell; Royal Dano; Howard Da Silva (1909–86); Jacques Doniol-Valcroze (1920–89); Roger Donoghue; David Dortort; Alfred Drake; Dan Edelman; Lotte H. Eisner (1896–1983); Jean Evans; William Fadiman; Daniel L. Fapp; Tom Farrell; Mary Losey Field; William Fitelson; Max Fischer; Milos Forman; Johnny Friedkin; Samuel Fuller; Hermine Garcia; Bernard Gordon; Max Gordon (d. 1989); Farley Granger; Mike Gray; Guy Green; Roland Gross (1909–89); José Luis Guarner; Burnett Guffey (1905–83); James C. Gutman; John Hammond (1910–87); Vernon Harbin (1909–88); Robert Herman; Helen Kienzle

Hiegel; Abbie Hoffman (1936–89); Dennis Hopper; Gretchen Hiegel Horner; Harry Horner; John Houseman (1902–88); Burl Ives; Jim Jarmusch; Jerry Jones; Barney Josephson (1902–88); Elia Kazan; Michel Kelber; Gene Kelly; Tony Kent; Bert Kleiner; Georges Klotz; Milton Krasner (1901–88); Robert La Cativa; Gavin Lambert; Jennings Lang; Jesse Lasky Jr (1908–88); Tom Lea; James Leahy; Will Lee (d. 1982); Maurice Le Roux (1923–92); Leslie Levinson; Lucie Lichtig; Renée Lichtig; Viveca Lindfors; Norman Lloyd; Alan Lomax; Edouard Luntz; Ida Lupino; Mercedes McCambridge; Charles H. Maguire; James Mason (1909–84); Walter Matthau; Claudio Mazzatenta; Myron Meisel; John Melson (1930–83); Jean-Claude Missiaen; Simon Mizrahi (1940–92); Sheri Nelson-McLean; H. Vladimir Novotny; Marcel Ophuls; Terry Ork; Gene Palmer; Robert Parrish; Vladimir Pozner (1905–92); Ellen Ray; Susan Schwartz Ray; Tim Ray; Silvia Richards; Martin Ritt (1920–90); Earl Robinson (1910–91); Jane Russell; Volker Schlöndorff; Barbet Schroeder; Henry Schubart Jr; Barbara Schulberg; Budd Schulberg; Betty Utey Schwab; Walter M. Scott (1905–89); Pete Seeger; Sam Shepard; Sidney Solow (1910–85); Andrew Solt (1916–90); Lenore T. Straus; Edgar Tafel; Daniel Taradash; Harry Tatelman; Stéphane Tchalgadjieff; Studs Terkel; David Turecamo; Ethel Tyne; Gore Vidal; Peter von Bagh; George Voskovec (1905–81); Charles Wagner; Tom Weitzner; Wim Wenders; Cornel Wilde (1915–89); Alice Kienzle Williams; Sumner Williams; Robert Wise; Philip Yordan.

My patient hosts, and listeners, were Ed Lachman, Beverly Walker, Philippe and Liz Garnier, Natacha Arnoldi, Monte Hellman, Carlos Clarens, Bérénice Reynaud, David and Barbara Stone, Florence Dauman, Fabiano Canosa, Laurie Frank, Adolfo Arrieta, Jackie Raynal, Susan Fenn, Jonathan Richards, Gretchen and Gary Horner.

I owe a great deal to conversations, sometimes unique, sometimes carried on over the course of years (and not necessarily relevant to the subject in any strict sense), with Blaine Allan, Thom Andersen, Patrick Brion, Kevin Brownlow, Noël Burch, Robert Carringer, Shirley Clarke, Jean-Louis Cohen, Vincent Curcio, Serge Daney, Pascale Dauman, Emile De Antonio, Jacques Demy, Jean Douchet, Jean-André Fieschi, Greg Ford, Anne Head, Anabel Herbout, Paul Falkenberg, Marilyn Goldin, Laurence Gavron-Schäfer, Philippe Haudiquet, Louella Intérim, Otar Iosseliani, Anna Karina, Bill Krohn, Jay Leyda, Robert Louit, Jacques Lourcelles, Eugène Lourié, Annette Michelson, Tom Milne, Todd McCarthy, Jos Oliver, Abraham Polonsky, Pierre Rissient, Bob Rosen, Jonathan Rosenbaum, Jean-Pierre Sarrazac, Martin Schäfer, Helen Scott,

Chris and Lilyan Sievernich, Noël Simsolo, Wieland Schulz-Keil, Elliott Stein, Howard Suber.

With special thanks to Anne Preiss.

My debt to archivists, *cinémathèques*, libraries and institutions is great:

American Film Institute, Louis B. Mayer Library, Los Angeles; British Film Institute (Ian Christie, John Gillett, Markku Salmi, Jackie Morris); Cekoslovensky Filmovy Ustav, Filmovy Archiv (Jiri Levy); Cinemateca Portuguesa (Luis de Pina, Joao Bénard Da Costa); Cinémathèque Française (Noëlle Giret, Marianne de Fleury, Dominique Brun, Vincent Pinel, Alain Marchand, Catherine Ficat); Cinémathèque royale de Belgique (Jacques Ledoux); Cinémathèque du Luxembourg (Fred Junck); Directors' Guild of America West (David Shepard); Filmoteca Española (Caterine Gautier, José-Maria Prado); George Mason University, Fenwick Library, Fairfax, Virginia; La Crosse Public Library (Amy Groskopf); Library of Congress (Archive of Folk Music, Joseph C. Hickerson, Marcia Maguire; Motion Picture, Broadcasting and Recorded Sound Division, Edwin M. Matthias); Museum of Modern Art, Department of Film, New York (Eileen Bowser); National Archives and Records Administration, Washington; Princeton University Library (Mary Ann Jensen); RKO Pictures, Inc. (John M. Hall, Vernon Harbin, David Chierichetti); University of California at Los Angeles, Theater Arts Library (Audree Malkin); University of Southern California, Los Angeles, Doheny University Library, Department of Special Collections (Leith Adams, Ned Comstock); University of Wisconsin-La Crosse (Eleanor M. Kennedy).

Nor should be forgotten what I gleaned from articles and other writings about Ray not mentioned in the main body of the text: by Joao Bénard Da Costa, Victor Erice and Jos Oliver, Thomas Elsaesser, Marco Giusti and Adriano Aprà, Douglas Gomery, Frieda Grafe, José Luis Guarner, Gérard Legrand, Myron Meisel, Jonathan Rosenbaum, François Truchaud, etc.

This book, finally, is a reminder of too many conversations sadly cut short: Carlos, Martin, D., already cited, Isabella Guermanovna, A.-M. R . . . Speak, memory.

Stills and illustrations appear courtesy of: Area Research Center (UW-La Crosse) (1); Bernard Eisenschitz collection (2, 3, 6, 17, 26–7, 36–9, 46, 71); Nicholas Ray Archive (4, 5, 7, 11, 12, 68); New York Public Library at Lincoln Center (8–9, 15); Jean Evans (10, 13); Museum of Modern Art, New York (14, 49, 52); BFI Stills, Posters and Designs (16, 19, 20,

22, 31–2, 34–5, 42–3, 47–8, 50–51, 57–8, 62–4); Academy of Motion Picture Arts and Sciences (18, 28, 30); Archéo Pictures, Paris (21); Cinémathèque Française (23–4, 29, 64–5, 70a–b); Carlos Clarens collection, Photothèque, New York (25); Filmoteca Española (33); Jim Damour (36–9); James Leahy (40–41, 69); Simon Mizrahi collection (53–5, 59, 78); National Film Archive (56); Lucie and Renée Lichtig collection (60–61, 65–7); P. Michael O'Sullivan (68); Martin Schäfer (71); Wim Wenders (72, 76a–b); Claudio Mazzatenta (73–5); Road Movies, Berlin (77); Pari Films, Paris (79).

Voyage

A very long loft apartment, white-painted brick, bare floor, two large window surfaces, one at each end, two double beds, one at each end. Facing me, two unframed paintings, greenish-brown tones, shadowy figures, anguished, divergent perspectives. Director's chairs, one with a name on it. Bookshelves: Conrad, Dostoevsky, Camus, Sartre, *You Can't Go Home Again*, Joyce, Mann, Colette, Scott Fitzgerald, Eliot, Brecht, children's books, a biography of Emily Dickinson. Two fine expressionist sketches in Indian ink, signed in dedication by Beverley Pepper. In one corner, an Academy Award nomination certificate ('best story, *Rebel Without a Cause*'). Strange movements 30 feet away, my reflection in the window. Green plants, knick-knacks, several books about alcoholism and a large chart listing twelve resolutions for former alcoholics.

A call-sheet: '29 March to 12 April, *Nicks Movie*, Actors. Gerry Bamman, Larry Pine, Nick Ray, Susan Schwartz, Tom Farrell, Caroline Cox, Kate Manheim.'

A week earlier, 22 March 1979. A telephone call from Pierre Cottrell: 'Nicholas Ray and Wim Wenders are co-directing a film, starting on Monday. They're going to shoot a feature in two weeks; it's to cost 200,000 francs, no more; we're going to see if it's possible.' During the weekend, confirmation comes that shooting will in fact start on Wednesday or Thursday, with Wenders arriving from San Francisco on the 28th. I decided to go and have a look.

Probably the last chance to watch Ray filming. I recalled a couple of meetings several years before – three or four if you count personal appearances at the Cinémathèque Française; in particular, one when he arrived during a screening of *In a Lonely Place* with a crimson-lined cape draped over his shoulders. Another time, Barbet Schroeder summoned me to come at once to act as interpreter for Ray, whom Jacques Perrin and the latter's business manager were going to see. Ray was living in a large attic room in a hotel near the Champs-Elysées. His habit of stooping was undoubtedly accentuated by the bizarre dimensions of the room. Perrin had come to discuss a film from Dino Buzzati's novel *Desert of the Tartars*, a copy of which Ray had managed to find in, and steal from, a public library in England. Eventually, it became apparent that the stumbling-block was the matter of a cash advance. Ray drew himself up to his full height, announced that he had paintings stored by a friend in the rue de Seine, and that he would go and sell one tonight, as he had done in the past. It was obvious that the money was needed to pay the hotel bill. The other two Frenchmen having left first, we talked briefly about Humphrey Bogart: Ray had not answered a letter I had sent him while preparing a book about the actor. He explained, more or less, that he avoided talking about relationships which had really meant something to him.

The next occasion is easier to date, early in 1973: a screening at the Palais de Chaillot Cinémathèque of a film Nick was in the process of finishing. Strange equipment was set up in the balcony; it soon appeared that the film was in 16, 35 and Super–8 mm. Ray was setting up and starting different projectors in a multi-screen pyrotechnic display. It was all pretty enigmatic, especially as the brilliance of the 35-mm projector made the other images look very pallid. The words of the title, *We Can't Go Home Again*, zoomed on to the screen; it all seemed very lively and incomprehensible, a sort of psychodrama about the relationship between Ray and his pupils. He himself, surrounded by friends and enjoying being the centre of attraction, was in great form, full of energy and the delight of someone working and able to talk about his work.

These were some of the motives behind the voyage to America. There was the desire to recapture the spell that his movie-making had created, but also to understand the betrayal that had followed. How he had moved from one compromise to another (like Robert Taylor in *Party Girl*), how the faculty of seeing had become progressively paralysed. And then, how he had rejected everything that cinema had become, moving from *55 Days at Peking* to . . . nothing at all. Followed by this film after the fact, *We Can't Go Home Again*, which left one with only the confused feeling that, whatever else, there was no longer any possible coming to terms with the film-maker and the surroundings in which he had worked for fifteen years.

I arrived in New York at night, while the company was away. The next morning was Friday, 30 March 1979. Nick Ray has cancer; he is dying. After the night shooting, this is a day of idleness, accompanying Ray to the hospital, reading a new outline of the film in the making, looking at the video recording that Tom Farrell has done of the Vassar university conference. Nick's face, the past superimposed on those marked features: 'The closer I get to my ending, the closer I am getting to rewriting my beginning. And certainly, by the last page, the climax has reconditioned the opening, and the opening usually changes.' In the evening, a screening of the film I saw in 1973 when it still required several projectors. Images explode on the fractured screen, and Nick talks about himself. Sometimes there are four images within a black frame on a background image, sometimes the entire screen is filled. The use of video here is like the invention of cinema, all over again. From the first minutes – a rapid, violent montage on the trial of the Chicago Seven in 1969 and the radical movement – you find more seeds of fiction than in any number of films. On screen, a girl in close-up tells Nick she wants to prostitute herself in order to get the money to finish the film. Ray, in the loft, to Wenders: 'All this really happened.'

The next day. Reverse angles of Wim's arrival in the loft and Nick in bed are alternately directed by Ray and Wenders. Nick is at the viewfinder, giving specific instructions for lighting. Wenders takes over; the relationship is easy. Calm preparations. Rehearsal called by Nick at the camera. Wim performs. Nick talks to him gently, precisely. Ready to shoot. Nick gets into bed with Susan. Between takes, everyone speaks softly, the dominant sound being the script-girl's electric typewriter. Nick talks to Wim, relaxed. He makes the crew laugh. Then calls action (Wim's arrival in the loft). Suddenly, his voice is twenty years younger. 'Once more please.'

During the night, a talk with Wim. Another view of the happening, which I didn't suspect from merely watching it. 'He's afraid of filming, because he hasn't shot anything for ten years, not of his own, at least. The story he wrote no longer satisfies him. There have been five versions of the script, we've abandoned them all. Now the only way to make a film about Nick is to make it about me too, and I don't want that. To show him as he is, that's exploitation. I'm not in the same situation as he is: that's his home.

'The crew has an enormous respect for him. They're very fond of him, and they were terribly upset to find him in this state. This morning, he bawled out Tom after the first take, correcting him, directing him in fact. Then, on the next take, he let him do what he liked. Actually, he was really talking to himself. He's more interested in the idea, in analysing something, than in directing. I'm just the opposite. In *We Can't Go Home Again* there's nothing left of *Johnny Guitar*. I evolved in the opposite direction. I still film him as he did Sterling Hayden.

'Maybe, instead of bringing all these people in, we should be making a documentary in 16 mm or Super–8. I don't know; I'm unable to do this any other way. If you made it without all this technique, you'd see exactly the same thing, and you'd see that it's a documentary. Maybe what we should be doing is showing that it's a documentary. Today I was constantly tempted to turn the camera round and film the crew.'

My feeling, I tell Wim, is that he'll find himself doing this anyway.

Sunday 1st. In the night, Wim has gone back to work and written five pages of dialogue, which he's now filming with very simple camera set-ups. Wim: 'I want to talk to you, Nick.' Nick: 'What about? Dying?' (the word has been added shakily in red on the page.) He rasps the word, in keeping with his performance throughout. Nick blames Wim for overacting. 'Shame on you!' Wim: 'I was only overacting because you were underacting.'

Murmurings on the 'set'. Director of photography Ed Lachman checks the final details: camera, clapperboard . . . Scene 20, take one. The alarm clock goes off shrilly. Nick tells it to shut up. He groans, contentedly. Coughs. 'I had a dream about a goddamn musical in Venezuela . . .' He hums softly for some time. Before Wim says 'cut', he howls. He repeats this terrifying howl between takes, and on each take of this very long (almost six minutes) travelling shot.

Scene 20/2 is a short, light conversation. Nick tells Wim he's trying to find prints of his films. In take one, Wim: 'I know where I could find a print of *Johnny Guitar* with Arabic subtitles.' Nick acts delighted: 'He talks about oil!' Then they rehearse a short dialogue about *Hammett* and its ten-million-dollar budget. Nick has trouble memorizing the lines: 'That's very unpretentious. For one per cent of that I could make a film on my budgets.' Scene 20/3, take one. Everything goes fine until 'I could make . . .' A sixteen-second silence, then he concludes, '. . . lightning over water'. After the 'cut', everyone laughs and relaxes. Wim: 'We'll do another take, but I know we can use that one.' On takes two and three, Nick is lost again: 'What the hell was the next clincher in that?' It becomes ten per cent, then ten films for one per cent . . . Wim: 'Don't overdo it. One or two, I guess.' Nick: 'Well, I'm a very modest fellow.'

On the evening of the 2nd, there's another screening of *We Can't Go Home Again* and an attempt at a discussion of the film with friends, which soon degenerates into a sort of TV round-table: it is as difficult to define the film as it is to communicate with Ray, who is exhausted by the screening and the delays in setting up the shot. When he reaches too far out, no one understands. 'I had dreams of being able to tell all of Charles Dickens in one film, all of Dostoevsky in one film. I wondered if it was possible for one film to contain all the aspects of human personality: needs, desires, expressions, wants . . .' He soon tires of this. 'I relate very much to *We Can't Go Home Again*, but I'm putting a hell of a lot more effort into relating to Wim's new film. And that is really where my effort is. If *We Can't Go Home Again* is going to become part of this effort, it'll be an honour.'

*

Back in Paris, I received a postcard from Cottrell, dated 13 April, LA: 'We stopped after twelve days. Wim had to work on *Hammett*. Nick went to hospital, his stomach was bad. We're going to start shooting again after Easter. What I've seen is really good. We have nine-and-a-half hours of rushes – probably 60 minutes we can use.'

15 June, another note: 'Nick is coming out of hospital in a few days. They've treated him with radiation too much in the past to use the same treatment on his swollen right arm. Susan told me it was the cancer starting up as before, and that the right side of the chest (which they opened up a few months ago) is ravaged again. He has difficulty spitting. Otherwise he is alert and amusing/amused, except that he doesn't say much. We are looking for a house by the sea near New York to shoot the last scene (The Junk).'

The next day, Nick Ray died. So too John Wayne, a few days earlier, also from cancer – a grotesque statement of the American cinema's impossible unity. On the same front page as Wayne, *France-Soir* announced that novelist Jean-Louis Bory had committed suicide: my first teacher, who had awakened his pupils, long ago, to the excitement behind the craft of writing, of composing, to the value of every trick, of every note, provided it was towards an end.

I wrote this about Nicholas Ray in *l'Humanité* of 19 June:

He had incredibly limpid eyes. ('Nobody can change the colour of a man's eyes' – Chandler.) His voice, slow, parsimonious, precise. You saw and heard the thought, the attention, the reaction to everything, the capacity for wonder. Physically, he was destroyed . . . The film – first called, simply, *Nicks Movie*, then *Lightning Over Water* – is a race against the clock, and it deals with just that: with death, the films Ray never made, his care for those who care for him, those close to him, those who love him in Europe. Making the film involved not so much any physical effort, which a devoted crew spared him, as a constant interchange with Wenders, which went far beyond the verbal.

This is the first Ray film in years. But he hadn't stopped filming. When someone escapes our modes of understanding or ways of life, escapes the image we had fashioned of him, we say that he is trying to destroy himself. It's an old story, and one that fills institutions. It was said of Ray that he had turned himself into a down-and-out: years of bumming around in Europe, alcohol, drugs. Having reached a point where the kind of cinema he had worked in now seemed no more than moneymaking, he set about severing all ties with that world – no matter what the risk. He was the only film-maker to have started again entirely from scratch, to have got his teeth (or his whole body) into the troubled America of the late 1960s: hippies and radicals, the resurgence of political awareness in the young, the Chicago Conspiracy trial . . . The notion of the finished film, the well-made artefact, no longer concerned him. He didn't give a damn, of course, about being just another American film-maker. The striking thing about those films of his which we love, viewed again today, is not their traditional qualities, but the extent to which they were aberrant . . . Among Ray's books there was one with an inscription from an Englishman: 'To Nick, who will never really know how much we owe him.' Nick knew.

That trip to New York had left more questions asked than answered. The ones concerning Ray's death-on-film, Wim Wenders had to deal with alone, and struggled stubbornly with for two years without – unsurprisingly – really being able to satisfy any of the witnesses. Questions about Ray's films, questions it was no longer the right time to ask during those last days in March, which had elicited in response from Nick only a joke or shrug of the shoulders, were left open. Supposing I had the right questions, then the answers had to be sought elsewhere. Hence the impossibility of the biographer's task, so often described, but to my mind never better than by Dashiell Hammett: 'The chief difference between the exceptionally knotty problem confronting the detective of fiction and that facing a real detective is that in the former there is usually a paucity of clues, and in the latter altogether too many.'

Bernard Eisenschitz

1
Wisconsin Boy

1   The Mississippi and La Crosse at the beginning of the century

His grandfather dropped dead on Main Street while carrying the first deer of the season on his shoulders (the first Kienzle to cause a scene at the heart of the town he had partly built), outside the consulting rooms of a doctor whom the Indians called White Beaver, not far from the cathedral on 6th and Main Street (builder, Raymond Nicholas Kienzle, his father), not far from the ready-to-wear Continental store on 4th and Pearl (builder, Raymond Nicholas Kienzle), not far from the Casino cinema, a dark and narrow building on Main between 3rd and 4th where Ruth Kienzle took her brother Raymond Nicholas Kienzle Jr to see his first film (it was *The Birth of a Nation*), 4th and Main where he tried to run over Doc Rhodes, the physician who had attended his dying father, not far from the Stoddard Hotel which, like the town's four other establishments in 1932, refused a room to James Ford, a black, the Communist candidate for the Vice-Presidency of the United States, leaving it up to Raymond Nicholas Jr to invite him to spend the night at the family home, variously remembered as having twelve or seventeen or twenty-two rooms (and four garages), formerly the residence of a man called MacDonald, a self-made lumber millionaire, and embellished by Raymond Nicholas Sr with a red brick wall separating it from the street, 226 West Avenue North, parallel to Losey Boulevard which bounded the town on the east side under the 570 feet of Grandad Bluff, which

2   The Kienzle family house in La Crosse

Nicholas Ray would later point out to his third wife, explaining how, in exhibitions of barnstorming, he skimmed these cliffs which had prevented any further spreading of this agglomeration, born in time and space, out to the west, at the junction of the Black River and the Mississippi, a prairie where French settlers had seen the Winnebago Indians playing a game similar to the one they called *la crosse*, and where in 1842 Nathan Myrick, a New Yorker, had established the first log cabin and the first trading post on the present site of the town.

La Crosse was a product of the river, and the river made its fortune: in the wake of the settlers, tree-trunks came down the Black River, were sorted, and organized into timber-rafts to be sent downstream to St Louis. Edna Ferber and Howard Hawks, who had both grown up in Wisconsin, told the story of these fortunes in *Come and Get It*, the Ferber novel filmed by Hawks in 1936. The years 1850 to 1900 saw the rise of the sawmills, subsequently ruined within seven years by the depletion of the forests. In between times came breweries and cement factories, and always there was the river.

Between 1840 and 1860 numerous immigrants, some of them driven from Europe by the failure of the revolutions of 1848, had been drawn to La Crosse Prairie, which was developing rapidly and became a town with 3,000 inhabitants in 1856. The Germans, the main group, were Catholic or Lutheran, the Norwegians were Lutheran; then came the Catholic

Bohemians and Irish, the Syrians and Orthodox Greeks, among others. In 1890, half the population had been born abroad; in 1900, a third.[1] The German Catholics had established a diocese in 1868, and the following year laid the foundation stone for the Cathedral of St Joseph the Workman, one of the first to the north of the Mississippi. The builder was one of their own, Kienzle the deerhunter. His son, Raymond Nicholas, was six years old. He was twenty when his father died, and took over the latter's work in progress, building landing stages for the paddle-steamers, flood barriers, dairies, brothels, breweries and cathedrals.

The first Kienzle came from southern Germany. The Kinzig is a river in the lower Black Forest, with its 'buzzing sawmills', its world-famous makers of clocks and barrel-organs; Kienzle (the root *Kien* means pine-wood) was probably a relative of Jakob Kienzle, the miller's son who founded the watch factory of the same name.[2] He had settled initially in Milwaukee, along with the first wave of liberal exiles which included a future Secretary of State for Indian Affairs, Carl Schurz (played by Edward G. Robinson in Ford's *Cheyenne Autumn*). He married a Miss Mueller, by whom he had seven children, five boys and two girls; the two youngest, Raymond and Joe, grew up following his removal to La Crosse and a red brick house at 1313 South 3rd Street. This house still stands whereas the private and public buildings on which his son served as contractor, supplying bricks and cement blocks, have all been razed or rebuilt.

Raymond Nicholas married (a church wedding) and had two daughters. Contracted to build a school at Galesville, a village 24 miles from La Crosse where European names, Norwegian in particular, were similarly replacing the Indian ones, he met Olene Toppen, eleven years his junior, obtained a divorce, and married her. Lena, as she came to be called, had been born of Norwegian parents in a log cabin in the Wisconsin Midwest, where the Menominee Indians still raided now and then.

Excommunicated following his divorce, Raymond Nicholas Kienzle joined the Congregational Church. Completing the break with his community, he also joined the Freemasons, then seen as the armed wing of Protestantism (as the Knights of Columbus were for Catholicism). Raymond Jr remembered his father swimming in the Mississippi, floating on his back, cigar in mouth. A great horse fancier, he presented his wife with a splendid animal and a two-seater cart; bent on artistic education, he decided to have her learn the violin. He appears to have played a real political role in the community, although written traces of the Kienzle family are as rare as they are abundant concerning the Losey family of La Crosse – pre-Revolutionary Americans and public benefactors.

3 The first Christmas of Raymond Nicholas Kienzle Jr, surrounded
by his three sisters

Kienzle lived in Galesville with the two daughters of his first marriage, who both wed early and lived near by. He had three other daughters: Alice, Ruth and Helen. Finally a son, named Raymond Nicholas after him, was delivered at 5 o'clock on the morning of 7 August 1911 (the parents were then aged forty-eight and thirty-seven) by Dr K. E. Berquist.[3]

Galesville (altitude 700 feet, population 1,069 in 1940), on the crest of a hill overlooking Lake Marinuka, was built around a shady village square. 'La Crosse was the city that we'd always go to to shop,' Alice Kienzle-Williams, Nicholas Ray's sister, recalls. 'A nice drive through sand that was *this* deep, where you'd have to take straw and shovels along to get your wheels out of the sand. We had Indians that lived quite close to us, a place called Black River, where you crossed the bridge, before you got to the Mississippi. Near Black River, there were always Indians living in their regular old teepees, weaving baskets and blankets, and they were really friends of ours for years and years. In those days the Indians were still carrying their babies as papooses on their backs. My father used to look after them a lot. If he felt that the winter was hard, he'd look in on them to see that they had enough to eat, and he would order flour and sugar, and see that the dogs were fed.'

Kienzle built – or rebuilt – Gale College, as well as a number of churches in the area, including one for the Lutheran Synod which he gave to the town, and where his wife would take the children, in black patent leather shoes and white socks, to Sunday School. Alice was confirmed, and Ruth, Helen and Raymond Jr baptized there. According to Alice: 'He was the first man there that had his crew build sidewalks and silos and cement block homes and things for the farmers. We were the first or second in that little town to have a car. Most people went around in one-seater horse and buggies, or the surreys with the fringe on top. We had one of those. The first car we had was an Imperial. Father didn't even drive it; he had one of his men from the factory come up on a Saturday or Sunday and drive us into the country or to the farm where Grandpa and Grandma lived. And that was a real thrill; it was beautiful country, the trout streams and the beavers . . .'

The Kienzle house, on a street corner, was painted beige, surrounded by a porch on all four sides. Lena would emerge in her nightdress at dawn to tend to the garden, barefoot in the mud. Described as a 'magnificent seamstress, ready quick wit, sharp', she was also 'of the old school. *He* was head of the family. His word was law', according to Helen Kienzle-Hiegel, Ray's youngest sister. But, as Alice pointed out, it was also the patriarch who worried incessantly over the children's health, 'much more than our mother'.

With 120,000 mobilized, Wisconsin played its part along with the other states in the First World War. Only the socialists of Milwaukee and Senator La Follette were opposed to the war; the former governor, champion of direct democracy, was denounced as a traitor and burned in effigy. In Galesville and La Crosse there are memories of stones being thrown through windows, of German names being Americanized: what happened to the Burgermeisters, Doerres, Tausches, Grunds, still to be

4   Raymond Nicholas Kienzle
(photo Johnson, Galesville)

5   Raymond Nicholas Kienzle,
1928/9

6   The Kienzle family, Christmas 1952: Helen, Alice, Raymond Nicholas
(Nicholas Ray, by then), Lena, Ruth

seen on the façades of buildings today, to the Lieberts, Hackners, Lie-bigs? Here Ray himself takes up the story in a small red-bound book, typewritten by his son Tim in 1968:

The first song I learned on the mandolin was the 'Ballad of Sam Hall.'

> Oh my name it is Sam Hall, it is Sam Hall.
> Well my name it is Sam Hall, it is Sam Hall.
> Well my name it is Sam Hall.
> And I hate you one and all.
> Yes I hate you one and all.
> Goddamn your eyes!

(Twenty years later I sang it for Carl Sandburg.)

At age three I changed my name to Sam Hall. At the outbreak of World War One, German names became unpopular in the United States, so I changed my name back to Raymond Nicholas Kienzle Jr, which my father seemed to approve since that is what appeared on my birth certificate. Thus my future and present views on prejudices and bigotry were built on a solid foundation. Having accomplished this, my father disappeared.

World War One began when I was three years old, so I wasn't much of an authority on it. It took me about three more years before I knew less. My ignorance continues to progress.

I heard my father'd gone South, wherever that was. South could have been down to the lower flats of the town, where the floods hit. We lived on the upper level, naturally. But he went a little further South. He went to North Carolina. I think Eugene Gant's father cut some stone for him. He was quite a fellow. He didn't get his second contract because he refused to stop negro children from playing on his sandpiles.

Eugene Gant, the son of a robust, hard-drinking stone-cutter, is the hero of the first two novels of Thomas Wolfe (*Look Homeward, Angel* and *Of Time and the River*), a native of North Carolina whose affinities with Nicholas Ray extend beyond a title in common, *You (We) Can't Go Home Again*.

Kienzle had tried to enlist, but was turned down because of cardiac weakness (as his son would be later), and leased his own services and those of his employees to the government to build air bases. His youngest daughter, Helen, went to visit him: 'I was angry because when the black men came along they would get off the sidewalk and walk into the gutter, and they'd say to my father, "Mo'nin', Cap'n!" And I thought that was terrible. But he tried to explain it, didn't do a very good job.'

7

From the red book again:

We played a game at school called 'Farmer in the Dell'. You know the tune? They changed the lyrics, too:

> The Hun is in the dell
> The Hun is in the dell
> hi ho the merry ho
> The Hun is in the dell.

I was always the Hun.

Since birth and the mumps the only time I remember crying until I got to Hollywood was then. I cried with such rage that I'd break through that circle, run over to the highest point on the school grounds, get on top of it and say 'Let's play King of the Mountain! I'm King of the Mountain!' And any one of those sons of bitches got close to me first, got it right square in the eyes from my right foot. Didn't make me very popular at the age of seven. The next fifty years didn't help much, either. I still feel the same way, I still want to be king of the mountain. And I still kick.

In 1918 we had a two lunger Cadillac and an Imperial. That two lunger was being repaired down in the lower flats. So we used the Imperial with those nice leather straps and gold buckles (brass), that fit right straight to headlamps. My oldest sister, Alice, drove my youngest sister, myself and the rest of the women thru the town of Galesville on the night of 8 November 1918 and we all beat pots and pans and lit red torches, honked the two horns and yelled out 'PEACE PEACE PEACE!! ARMISTICE ARMISTICE PEACE PEACE!!!'

The next morning my oldest sister came in to my room to say with heavy doom that it had been a false Armistice. I hadn't yet observed that that was the nature of life so I got goddamned Norwegian mad and ran slamming doors thru the house to the front porch. The walls were covered with antler heads, the floor with the tears of my mother and the Beizers, the old white-haired people who'd been our closest neighbours since ever ever was, now called Beezer, like Koehler was called Koller, and we, the Kienzles, were called Kenzel. Their house had been painted yellow during the night to show that they were still dirty yellow Huns.

After the war, Kienzle Sr decided to retire and return to La Crosse, where his mother was living. The new family residence no longer had to be in the centre of town. The pearl grey building on West Avenue, near State Street, housed the entire family, along with nieces from Galesville attending the Teachers' College. At its heart was a dining-room 30 x 15 feet, with parquet floor and a fireplace in Italian marble, and a music room. The house had two entrances, and it was generally by the back door that Kienzle came in, late for dinner (it was out of the question to start in his absence), going up the back stairs to the first floor, where his wife would have run his bath and laid out shoes, socks, underclothes, shirt, tie and suit, then dressing and coming down the front stairs to the hall, where he would call '*Leena*' – in the kitchen with the maid – never having learned to knot his tie and having once again 'become putty in my mother's hands' as Helen commented, before everyone could finally sit down to table.

'We would sit at the table the same place every time,' Helen said, 'a white linen tablecloth and dinner-size napkins. He wouldn't even have eaten lunch on a coloured tablecloth. Now my father had great preferences. One was German potato salad. And my mother spent her life trying to make the German potato salad like his mother made it, which was always . . . lacking.

'He was a very . . . what they were known as in those days . . . "high German". He was very erect in his stature, 5 ft 11, but he looked taller because of the way he carried himself. Shoulders back, head erect, and dared anyone of us to walk slouchy, he would have corrected it. He was very much the disciplinarian. He tried not to spoil any of us – other than my older sister and my brother. But he did a very good job. We must read: he loved to read, we all liked to read. And he loved music. So we were all in turn put through the process of the scales. And then, when I seemed to have shown a little ability in oratory – debate, declamatory – I was allowed speech lessons.

'And then returning home, I would sit Nick down, who was six years younger than I, and I'd make him learn. We used to play a lot of jokes on Father, which he didn't take very nicely. In fact, he resented them. But I don't recall ever being punished for them. And then, after Alice left home, he became my good friend.' In 1923, Alice married an accountant with General Motors, and went to live in Oshkosh, in the eastern part of the state. Helen was eighteen, Ruth nineteen. Both enjoyed much closer though different relationships with their little brother. Ruth, in revolt against her father, protected the two younger ones; Helen, reconciled with Raymond Sr, remained in alliance with her brother.

1924. 'Fighting Bob' La Follette, the former governor who had made Wisconsin the best governed state in the union, with one of the best educational systems, ran for President as a Progressive candidate, and obtained five million votes, including a majority in Wisconsin. The automobile. The radio. In Sinclair Lewis's novel *Main Street*, published in 1920, the streets of the town – a small town in neighbouring Minnesota twice the size of Galesville – had in four years become paved with cement, golf links had sprung up, with an occasional aeroplane on the fringes, young girls had learned 'the preferability of listening to radio instead of humming Czech folk songs . . . developing their own pretty ankles, buying their own pretty silk stockings, and learning their own gay manners . . . You hear 'em talking about Leopold and Loeb, about Kid McCoy, about the round-the-world fliers, about Tommy Gibbons's battle in England, about their flivvers and their radios'.[4]

Childhood years: Raymond the voracious reader. The lasting influence of American poetry, Thomas Hardy, translations of foreign literature, *Jean-Christophe* especially, Romain Rolland's fictionalized version of the life of Beethoven, with its humanitarian heroism and its belief in the artist's mission: 'A man must earn his living doing what he wants to do.' Discovery of the theatre, as he told the *La Crosse Tribune* in 1954, when 'the late Guy Beach had a stock company here' (Beach can be seen in three of Ray's early films).[5] First dream ambition: to be an orchestra conductor. The guide to Wisconsin published in 1940 by the Federal Writers' Project describes La Crosse as a musical centre: 'Steamboats and the railroad often brought large crowds from the surrounding territory to attend music festivals there.' Another experience of music was one to which Ray would give the chapter heading 'Runaway to Jazzdom' in his projected autobiography. In North Carolina, Helen had seen blacks. But there were none in La Crosse; Alice recalls only a laundress who used to come to the house.

'Runaway to Jazzdom', Nicholas Ray wrote in 1968. 'First time I saw a negro was at the age of nine. I ran away from home – about fourteen-and-a-half city blocks to the waterfront of the Mississippi River and got on board a Streckfus Line Steamboat. That afternoon I heard the most wonderful music since *Dardanella Blues*. It was being played by a group of black people; a woman was at the piano, her name was Lil Hardin. Trumpet was Louis Armstrong, fresh from the reformatory, etc.' (This meeting must have taken place in 1920–1.)

Helen was given a car by her father. 'So every evening, my duty after dinner was: "Tell your mother that we will be waiting in the car for her, for a ride down to the river." And I was allowed to drive. He taught me at the age of fourteen. They would sit in the back seat, he with the most beautiful cigar, that permeated everything in the house, always, and Mother was always airing things out . . . an *El Producto*.' Helen also used the car to take her brother to the river, to swim from the floating wooden stage, where the current would carry them down one or two blocks. When central heating was installed in the West Avenue house, brother and sister baptized it: 'We took a bottle of Father's brandy and christened it Leo, because it ate so much.' (Raymond, himself born under the sign of Leo, attached a certain significance to this animal.) The presence of the bottle in the house was not mere chance. For years, wine had been forbidden at table. 'Then all of a sudden,' (Helen again) 'maybe business wasn't any good, he would go off on a little binge and became very very ill, and my mother worried, oh how she worried.'

'I have been under the lash of alcoholism since I was born,' Nicholas Ray wrote towards the end of his life. 'My mother was fond of saying, "Lips that touch liquor shall never touch mine." Who cared when there were so many younger lips? In my most vivid memories of their relationship they slept in separate bedrooms.

'All during childhood and Prohibition there was booze in the house – and on the street. In my home it was for stealing – first pint at ten. On the street it was for buying with money stolen in the home. Grain alcohol mixed with sugar and hot water. One day a schoolmate downed a bottle of wood alcohol and died horribly – we held a drunken ritual.

'During Prohibition there were twenty-one saloons and speakeasies on one street and I was known in all by the time I was sixteen. I learned to drive when I was thirteen and I could get my father home safely from his nightly rounds of speakeasies and bootleggers. At the age of fourteen I learned of his mistress. At fifteen I made an unsuccessful pass at her. At sixteen I went hunting for her one night – my father could not be found. I found her in a speakeasy across from a brewery my father had built – she led me to a hotel room where he was lying in sweat and puke with puke pans on the floor at the side of the bed. I took him home and nursed him through the night. In the morning the doctor came and before I left for school I watched him heat some substance in a spoon and draw it into a hypodermic. In Latin class I alternated between dozing off and hypertension. I asked to be excused and was. I went to the pool hall and practised three-cushion billiards. A phone call. My mother had trailed me – my father was dying. He was dead when I arrived. I had never been in a Catholic church but I genuflected at his side, kissed him and spent the night in a Turkish bath.

'My mother and I got the doctor into court but I was so pissed on home brew I couldn't testify, so we lost. The next day I tried to run Doc Rhodes down. A shoeshine boy ran in front of me and I hit a fire hydrant so I'd miss the kid. Doc Rhodes left town. I got my first ticket for reckless driving.'

The *La Crosse Tribune*, Saturday 12 November 1927:

Raymond Nicholas Kienzle, 64, died at his home, 226 West Avenue North, Friday. He is survived by his wife, five daughters, Mrs Louis Rall and Mrs Carl Anderson of Galesville, Mrs Porter A. Williams of Oshkosh, Miss Ruth and Miss Helen of La Crosse: one son, Raymond, of La Crosse: and a brother, Joe Kienzle, La Crosse. Funeral services will be held from the residence on Monday, November 14, at 2:00 o'clock p.m. with Masonic services and Rev Charles Leon Mears officiating.

Ray Kienzle was now head of the family. In an episode entitled *Autobiography* from one of his last projects (*New York After Midnight*), he recalls his reluctance to sit in his father's chair during the meal for which all the relatives foregathered after the funeral. His sister Helen remembers simply that 'he missed his father terribly', and that he 'spent two years finishing up his high school and wrecking a couple of automobiles'. His schooldays were indeed troubled latterly; he dropped out of high school after only one year, in June 1929. *Booster*, the Central High School yearbook, lists the following activities under his name: Junior League football and basketball; Falstaff (one of the school's drama clubs). Along with these activities, the yearbook generally quotes a remark by the student. His: 'I got an A−− [double minus] once – in slumber.'[6] Despite the engaging smile in his photograph, he wasn't appreciated by all. Joseph Losey, two years his senior, said later that his sister Mary was a school friend of Ray's. But at the time Losey had already left La Crosse for Dartmouth, and his sister has insisted on denying it, describing 'Ray Kinzel' as 'a rather unattractive boy whom I had no desire to know'. Asked to be more specific, she used the adjective *pestiferous*.[7]

Helen said: 'Father's death didn't change anything at first. It didn't change that we could remain in the house, always. We had everything we needed. Then, after the crash of 1929, La Crosse was hit very badly, and Father had money in two banks instead of one. He owned some land, and of course some stock in a bank, and Mother was responsible. My mother knew nothing about finance. I thought, "Now I know what it is to go to the poorhouse." But not Mother. She managed beautifully, never had a mortgage on the home, never borrowed a cent, cashed in the stock . . . and paid her due share. We came out of it.'

During this time, Ruth had broken with the family, crossing Wisconsin by bus to arrive in Chicago. She married a chemist. Helen had artistic ambitions. While their father was still alive, she had been invited to join a group of travelling players – 'Father threw them out so fast that it wasn't even funny,' Alice remembers. But for some months she was able to work on a children's radio programme for the local station, WKBH. Accompanied by one of her teachers, she read Maupassant, Poe, A. A. Milne. Some little theatre ensued. Following in her footsteps, Raymond's first job was on radio. 'He had a very nice speaking voice,' Helen said, 'well-modulated, and it'd carry all over an auditorium, it boomed up.' He soon won a prize in a radio competition organized by three states (Iowa, Minnesota and Wisconsin). With a friend, Russ Huber (later to work professionally in local radio and television), he produced a radio adaptation of George Bernard Shaw's *Candida*, a favourite of little theatre groups. A college English teacher, Helen Dyson, a 'benefactress' of Nick and Helen, played the role of Candida. One of the members of the jury was a professor of dramatic arts at the University of Wisconsin, Rusty Lane (whose students over the years included Don Ameche, Tom Ewell and Uta Hagen). Ray would meet up with him again in Hollywood in 1956.[8]

Ray recalled this prize as 'a scholarship for any university in the world', his choice being the University of Chicago, which he appears to have been attending irregularly already. It is more likely that the prize (as a biographical note issued by CBS in 1940 suggests) involved an announcing scholarship for one year at the La Crosse radio station, while he concurrently studied with more indifferent results at the state Teachers' College.[9]

The following summer, Ray got himself hired by a travelling troupe of stunt fliers. 'I thought I could learn how to fly. I didn't make much money, but I got free instruction for selling tickets.' (He spoke elsewhere of bootlegging by air with a man called Barney Root; or again, claimed that he 'learned to fly' at fifteen 'with Floyd Pengar.') Then, still according to the CBS biography, 'He joined a photographic expedition recording "Steamboat Gothick" architecture along the Ohio and Mississippi rivers. "Steamboat Gothick" is a little something strictly American. When steamboat builders built homes along river, they modelled them after boats, with uniquely beautiful results.'

The inevitable departure from home, in the summer of 1931, saw him head for Chicago, a magnet for the whole Midwest, a symbol of the twentieth-century metropolis for the entire world. Even though Ray Kienzle – who was starting in his letters to ask his sisters to call him Nick – was to return often to La Crosse, family reunions would be marked, according to witnesses, by tensions 'visible to the naked eye', with temperaments on each side exacerbated by the encounters. It was into the 1930s before Nick Ray wrote: 'I talk with my mother for the first time. I like her.' But it was back there that the taciturn Nick Ray, impervious to all except in flashes of work or intimacy, had his roots. A close friend, Connie Bessie, retained from his descriptions an image of his mother sitting by the window, waiting for him to come home: 'I had a feeling of women overwhelmingly strong in that family.' And his third wife, Betty Utey, herself the daughter of Finnish immigrants: 'That's also the generation, and coming from a place like he did, the cold hard snow of Wisconsin, the cold hard folk who said when he was but ashes in a film case, "Don't bring him here, nobody wants him!" They didn't want him to be buried there. I had gone to his mother's funeral with him; it was very Germanic, a very frosty affair, very austere, very formal . . . a lot of conflict going on. *That* was "back where he came from".'[11]

Alice settled in California, where she saw Nick most frequently at the time of his marriage to Gloria Grahame and the birth of Tim. Alice's son, Sumner Williams, was to be associated with Nick throughout his career, from Hollywood to Madrid. Helen gave up the idea of being an actress to take up teaching, and in 1933 she married a Freemason, Ernest Hiegel, a native of Iowa. Like Alice, she felt that Hollywood was the ruin of her brother, and judged the family harshly: 'A little talent, not enough to get on top, too sensitive to fit into the mediocre life of an average citizen, you have to always do something different . . . It is an awful place to be.' Ruth, the most sophisticated of the three sisters, probably remained the closest to Nick, the most tormented, with staggering bursts of energy (she was a formidable businesswoman) alternating with periods of depression. She died in a fire in 1965.

2
The Apprentice

Chicago: three-and-a-half million inhabitants, the junction between the two coasts, the world's foremost railroad centre, the meat-market at the heart of the rich Midwestern states. The most signal expression of American democracy, this city, which had witnessed the bloody repression of the anarchist movement, was living then under a mayor, Big Bill Thompson, a benevolent dictator and social reformer, who tolerated gangsterism on an industrial scale, thriving on the embargoes of Prohibition. It was a juxtaposition of opulence, with its heart all skyscrapers, and the poverty of the industrial areas begrimed by factories. This was the city of Al Capone and of Utopian architecture, whose prophet Louis Sullivan died a down-and-out in 1924; a city of boxers, jazzmen and writers.

It was to Chicago that Nick's sister Ruth fled in a deliberate breakaway from the Kienzle family. Her husband was working, or had worked, with Lee De Forest, one of the pioneers in the photographic reproduction of sound. Ray lodged for a time with the couple, sleeping on a mattress on the floor above the Swedish Institute for Developmental Studies.

Ray came to Chicago for its university, where Robert Hutchins, recently appointed, was experimenting with modern educational methods. Hutchins brought in Thornton Wilder, whose *The Bridge of San Luis Rey* had been awarded the Pulitzer Prize in 1927. Wilder's classes – English, literary composition, classics in translation – filled lecture halls seating 160 students. The small, bespectacled man of thirty-three was accepted by them as 'one of the gang', and alcohol flowed freely.[1] Ray saw a good deal of Wilder, though not enrolled for his classes, and attracted the latter's attention sufficiently to be recommended, a little later on, for an experience which would leave its mark on the young man.

But neither Hutchins's new teaching methods nor Wilder's friendship brought Nick all he hoped from an education: 'I became a refugee from higher education,' he said in 1957 (and the phrase was to recur frequently in his conversation). 'I had a sense that anything that I might learn in university academic education, I would have to unlearn in order to make a living in the theatre, in my field, and I found this to be true.'[2] It didn't take him long to reach this conclusion: he was enrolled at the university only for the fall term of 1931, taking three classes and achieving a favourable report only in one, 'The Staging of Shakespeare's Plays'.[3] He filled 1932 with American football and wanderings. The CBS biography places him in California: at Carmel 'to write', in Hollywood 'to try his luck as an extra,' before returning to the Midwest 'to write a play'. None of this is attested, but much later (1973), Nick Ray did recall an encounter at Carmel:

'I will never understand about my youth how the hell I ever learned about and fell in love with Robinson Jeffers and his poetry. He had not been published; he wasn't in any school books; and yet my first hitchhike to California was to see Dick Caldron walking on the beach one day with Robinson Jeffers.'[4] A poet who combined a philosophy inspired by Nietzsche, Heraclitus and Schopenhauer, with themes of self-destruction borrowing the modes of Greek tragedy, and contemporary American settings, Jeffers had built himself a small castle at Carmel overlooking the Pacific. He left it only for visits to New Mexico, to a house in Taos where Nick would live almost forty years later.

The next step for Ray in these years of apprenticeship was New York, the theatre capital.

1933: the year in which the economic situation, national and individual, was at its lowest ebb. A backdrop of bloodily repressed strikes. The first hundred days of Roosevelt's presidency, with their succession of laws and urgent measures designed to patch up capitalism. But there were fifteen million unemployed, only six million of them receiving any form of benefit. Nick Ray left Chicago – where people were throwing themselves off bridges, where apples were being sold at street corners – for New York: the soup kitchens, the breadlines. New York was still 'an agglomeration of villages, in any one of which you might live out your life without ever leaving.'[5] In Greenwich Village – centre of the artistic renaissance, of political radicalism, 'of sex freedom or of sex licence depending upon the point of view'[6] – you learned to live without money.

Jean Abrams was born in Canada in September 1912, of parents Russian by origin; her mother died in the same year as Nick's father.[7] She left home and came to the metropolis in July 1933 to become a writer, taking the pen name of Jean Evans: 'Nick had just arrived from Wisconsin, me from California. I had met a woman named Esther Merrill who lived in the Village, and she sort of kept open house. She was the only rich person we knew: she was getting alimony. We were all starving, and used to hang out at Esther's. Nick was living in this broken-down place on Greenwich Street with two artists, one a painter, Danny Revsen, and

7 Nicholas Ray and Jean Evans

Lonnie Hauser was a sculptor from Wisconsin. Nick used to come over to Esther's to take a bath, and that was when I met him. We fell in love and became inseparable. We were poor, but it was a happy time. We were both rebelling against middle-class respectability. We lived together for three years without getting married.'

Nick and Jean were soon sharing an apartment on 11th Street: box-mattress, card-table, and apple-boxes for sitting on. Much of their time was spent out, in the Village coffee-houses: Hubert's Cafeteria (on West 4th Street), which stayed open all night, Paul's Rendezvous (Wooster Street), The 5th Circle (Varick Street), or Steward's Cafeteria on Sheridan Square, where you could linger for four hours over a single coffee.[8] ' "Bohemians" were on one side, what we called "tourists" on the other,' says Jean Evans. 'Sometimes we'd pick up a tourist: "Do you want to go to a real Greenwich Village party?" And we'd have him buy dinner! Every penny was important. Nick would sometimes be posing for 50 cents an hour for artists, for the Arts Students League or the John Reed art schools, and he'd go buy me flowers with the money!'

When Ray wrote the scenario in 1947 for what was to become his first film, *They Live by Night*, he took it to Jean, who was back living in the

Village: 'There was a lot of our relationship in the characterization of the girl, the description . . . "You're like a little kitten, soft and warm . . . and you purr, too." He was a very tender man. Emotional. Chaotic emotions.'

In 1933 Nick received an invitation from Frank Lloyd Wright to join his Taliesin Fellowship. 'We had a very young and tragic parting,' Jean recalls, 'with Nick saying "Wait for me", and he was gone. I don't know how long, whether it was six or eight months . . . I felt very unhappy at that period.' It was another native of Wisconsin, Thornton Wilder, who had recommended Ray to Wright, to whom the young man was evidently not unknown. While still living in La Crosse, Nick apparently used to visit him from time to time; and in New York went to hear him lecture at Columbia University, going to see him afterwards: 'We had a walk together, [and] he asked me to become one of his first students.'[9]

Frank Lloyd Wright was sixty-four years old. A rebel since his youth, he drew from the Bible a missionary sense of affirmation. He proclaimed the 'truth against the world', and championed a passionate and provocative conception of life, for which architecture – 'mother of the arts' – was in his view simply the most appropriate expression. In 1932, with his wife, he founded the Taliesin Fellowship. This educational set-up formalized the relationships he had long entertained with disciples from all over the world. He wanted to put forward a new way of thinking about architecture, indissociable from his conception of the world. The aim of Taliesin, the Utopian life in microcosm, was – as Wright wrote in a preliminary circular sent to friends and various universities, including Chicago – 'to develop a well-correlated human being: since correlation between hand and the mind's eye in action is most lacking in modern education.'[10]

The Fellowship established itself on a farm forty miles west of Madison, on State Highway 23 near the Wisconsin River, four miles from the nearest village. In 1911, Wright rechristened this place (Spring Green, where he had spent his childhood), giving it the Welsh name of Taliesin. He remodelled and enlarged the complex, transforming a school founded by his aunts. He added new elements: a refectory, kitchens, rooms for the apprentices, as well as exhibition rooms. But the main innovation was the Playhouse, a theatre/recreation hall replacing the school gymnasium. It was here that Nick Ray, one of several apprentices not involved with architecture (there were always some around Wright: weavers, musicians, sculptors), was to pursue his activities. The place itself reflected the great architect's philosophy, his openness to the other arts, his quest for a new relationship between creator and spectator.[11] The

Fellowship had no money, and the Playhouse was constructed over the years. Its essential equipment included a Bechstein concert grand on the ground floor, and upstairs a 35mm screening room. The stage curtains were the Fellowship's first artistic creation. Other noteworthy features included: 'Reflex seating arrangement, instead of seating on centerline with eyes directly front'; 'The stage, part of the audience room'; 'The sound track playing through beside the picture on a red band'; 'Sound magnifiers beneath stage floor – directed against rear wood wall of stage – sound thus becoming part of the room instead of directed at the ear'.[12]

At Taliesin, Nick found himself back in the rural landscapes of his childhood, their contours softened by erosion. Sometimes his sister Helen came from the other end of the state to spend a sunny weekend at Taliesin, listening to Wright's daughter play the piano. Nick shared with the great architect an attraction-repulsion for the city, which he gladly abandoned at the height of the Depression. Like him, the patriarch set great store by his immigrant origins – Welsh in his case – finding there a unique form of Americanism. Wright represented an elective father, and for Nick the communal life at Taliesin was the first avatar of many elective families, not least those ephemeral film units where he would assume the role of father in his turn.

When Nick arrived, the Playhouse was on its way to completion. Henry Schubart, a fellow disciple at this time, remembers 'seeing fine early films of Man Ray, Eisenstein, etc., and performances by Uday Shan-Kar'. All the apprentice need do was observe, listen, understand. Another apprentice, Edgar Tafel, chronicler of the Taliesin years, says of Nick: 'Mr Wright thought that he had a great future. There was a great mystery, I remember, as to what he was there for and what he was doing.' Young Henry Schubart, who had just finished high school, shared a room with Nick during part of the year: 'He was tempestuous, to say the least. One night we had a great fist fight out in the snow . . . and we were both fairly drunk on moonshine, so the reasons for the fight are absolutely blank. He loved poetry and literature, but I always had the feeling that he was internally nihilistic, defensive, and not basically productive.' His participation in the community life in fact seems questionable, or at any rate of no great significance, apart from the acquisition of experience, of 'an attitude toward looking at things', traces of which are not difficult to find after Ray had himself become an organizer of space and time. 'Architecture is a very spinal art, you know,' Ray was to say in 1957, 'it embraces everything if it's true architecture. Just "architecture", as a word, can be applied to a play, a score, a way of life.'[13]

It was over a word that the dispute arose between Ray and Wright which was to cut short his stay at Taliesin. 'A battle with Mr Wright over the word "organize" ', Ray noted, offering no further details. For the architect, who refused to let himself be influenced by events going on in the world, regretting rather that his work 'did not have more influence on these events', there was no question of acknowledging the syndicalist connotation of the word 'organize'. For the twenty-two-year-old apprentice, who had experienced urban depression, it was impossible to ignore. Nick left. He wrote to Jean Evans: 'I have felt the hand of genius, and it's a heavy hand.'

Another version. When Jean Evans met Wright a few years later for an interview, she found the latter 'very moralistic and vindictive, and he said that Nick was a homosexual.' Youthful escapade, or more fundamental tendency – as John Houseman thought? Houseman, who became one of his closest and staunchest friends, indulges a bit of psychological analysis in the fine portrait he sketches of Ray in his autobiography *Front and Center*:

> Reared in Wisconsin in a household dominated by women, he was a potential homosexual with a deep, passionate and constant need for female love in his life. This made him attractive to women, for whom the chance to save him from his own self-destructive habits proved an irresistible attraction of which Nick took full advantage and for which he rarely forgave them. He left a trail of damaged lives behind him – not as a seducer, but as a husband, lover and father.

Another friend, Elia Kazan, doesn't give much credence to this supposed homosexuality, much more scandalous for the puritans of Wisconsin than it probably was for Ray himself – whose only public statement on the subject was an impatient shrug of the shoulders in reply to a question about James Dean's bisexuality: 'What does that mean, bisexual? He was normal, that's all.'[14]

But Nick was often to relive this break with his first master. The sense of a wound barely healed was evident, even in 1958, to his third wife one evening when they met Wright (a year before his death) in a Los Angeles restaurant. 'Wright asked Nick if he had picked a plot of ground yet . . . I didn't know what he was talking about. Wright had promised to design a house for him. But Nick never did build, couldn't pick out a plot of ground.'[15]

Once the break with Wright was final, instead of returning to New York, Nick left in a ramshackle old car for a Mexico still shaken, in those early months of 1934, by the last tremors of the revolutions endemic to the country throughout the 1920s. He was accompanied by Fred Dupee, his elder by seven years. (Frederick W. Dupee, a literary critic later responsible for the American edition of Proust's *Plaisirs et les Jours*: he also edited the letters of E. E. Cummings and the autobiography of Henry James.)[16] The only account we have of this trip is Ray's own, in telegraphese: 'To Mexico in a Ford with $100.00. I live for a year in San Angel, Mexico D. F. In Taxco, work in the jewel mine during the week. Become friend of three miners. When I leave, they come to the bus and ask for 50 pesos. I had only 15. They said, Take this little memory of us, and gave me a little leather pouch full of colourful rocks. Christmas was coming and I didn't have any money for gifts. I sent these little rocks, I didn't know what they were. I got all these thank-you notes. 5 onyx, 5 sapphire.'

3

Theatre of Action

In 1934, when Nick Ray returned to New York, the cover of a prominent arts magazine carried a black border with the words, 'The Theatre is Dead. Let's Give It a Decent Burial'. For someone dreaming about the stage, the stilted Broadway style, holding out no hope of change, could hardly be considered ideal. Nick was offered a part in a play called *Her Man of Wax*. 'There was a hook in it,' he wrote. 'A sexual one. I rejected it and walked to a theatre housed in a loft at 42 East 12th Street, which I had heard was "real", "sincere".' Not exactly a theatre, but a group of actors working and storing their sets in this apartment. Upstairs was the Workers Film and Photo League. Not far away, on 13th Street, was a five-room apartment where the company's permanent nucleus of a dozen members lived. Nick passed an audition and was admitted to the Shock Troupe, the permanent collective: this was militant theatre. He moved into the 13th Street apartment. 'My eating habits changed from meals three times a day to tea and dark bread for breakfast, a cream cheese sandwich for lunch, and whatever remained of a $17-a-week food budget provided for dinner. And I began to enjoy a full life.'

The company had been formed in 1929, under the proletarian name of Workers' Laboratory Theatre. It gave performances at the request of trade unions, strike committees and political organizations, acting on makeshift stages in every imaginable sort of location: churches, street corners, docks, factory gates, the backs of trucks, assembly halls, Coney Island fairgrounds, meetings in Central Park, sometimes using megaphones like their French or German counterparts, drawing their themes from current topics, devising a free and flexible form. In four years, a penniless, impassioned group – 'We grew like amoebae' one member, Will Lee, said – had become a respected professional company. At the start of the 1933–4 season, the Workers' Lab took the name Theatre of Action, implying a mobile theatre as opposed to a 'stationary theatre' tied to a fixed stage.

The company had an ambitious work programme: communal life, collective elaboration of productions. A group of playwrights worked on a given theme, exchanging ideas with the actors, one writer being responsible for the final conception. The plays lasted fifteen or twenty

8 *The Young Go First*: 'Nik' Ray (top, on stack) with (left to right, one actor not identified) Earl Robinson, Perry Bruskin, Ben Berenberg, Will Lee, Harry Lessin, Curt Conway (straw hat)

minutes, and could be performed anywhere. Their best known work was *Newsboy*, dramatizing a poem by V. J. Jerome.[1]

The company's interest in film montage – in the Soviet sense of the term – was one of the basics of their style. As Earl Robinson describes it: 'Perry Bruskin would be on an unemployed line, and Harry Lessin was the newsboy. He was trying to sell newspapers: "Marlene Dietrich gets legs insured for a million dollars!" That kind of headline. And all of a sudden Harry would go up to Perry: "Got a nickel? Nickel? For a cup of coffee?" Perry would go on as a capitalist and answer [unctuous voice], "No, I don't believe in that kind of thing." So fast, so quick. Well, Nick fitted right into that. Partly he was a great director because he could really appreciate something like this, this kind of fast change in action.'

A remarkable amount of time was devoted to study. There was no longer any question of despising a suspect 'bourgeois' technique, but rather of assimilating it in its most progressive forms.[2] 'We advanced step by step,' Will Lee says, 'and people from Broadway began to want to join us. The method we followed influenced a lot of people. As for us, we were a very disciplined group, and we were lucky that such prominent people came to give us the benefit of their teaching. They profited by it, too; they were experimenting with us like surgeons.' Mornings were devoted to classes, five days a week; voice, body movement, stagecraft.[3] Visiting teachers followed in succession: the choreographer Anna Sokolow, volunteers from the Martha Graham company, Doris Dudley, Laura Elliott, Elsa Findlay (eurhythmics), various members of the Group Theater: Sanford Meisner, Elia Kazan, Morris Carnovsky, Bobby Lewis, Roman Bohnen, Leroi Leverett, J. Edward Bromberg; Harold Clurman, one of the founders of the group, came once or twice. Afternoons were devoted to rehearsals, but more particularly to 'special performances', strictly militant and offered at nominal rates to any organization that asked. In the evenings, more rehearsals or a performance in the loft with charges for admission to earn a little money, sometimes a beer party or hours of conversation in the Sheridan Square café. 'We were not innocent in what we did; we were young, with serious intent. We didn't feel superior to each other. We didn't compel people. The important thing was to get people to remember what they were doing to each other. We were close to each other, which means being able to talk to each other. There was a spirit inherent to the situation. I have a feeling Nick retained it.'[4]

Nick immediately felt at home in this new ambience. 'I didn't even think he had a father or a mother,' says Perry Bruskin. 'He kind of sprung full-fleshed upon the world.' And Earl Robinson: 'I don't remember the exact circumstances of how he got in. He just showed up, was just there. Tremendous energy. Nick was sometimes almost more energy than art. I remember this powerhouse on wheels getting into a scene ... I remember him most as a marvellous, what we call Jimmie Higgins, a person who does all the odd jobs. Broad, strong shoulders. Nick would always be lifting, carrying the whole set – we used to travel with our sets on the subway. My memory of him is of Nick being strong enough to carry all this stuff.' Will Lee remembers his attentiveness, his seriousness. There was more, too: for Nick had his own experience to share with the group. 'He would speak about Frank Lloyd Wright, of whom we knew nothing. He was so way ahead of us in this area. It affected us with a freedom of expression; we had to go out and learn. We were amazed at this tall, strong western type full of vigorous ideas, very alive in terms of the time itself. It was like a fresh wind blowing. Here I was, a Brooklyn kid, observing all this, and Nick brought with him another part of America.'

In this atmosphere of collective dynamism, Nick formed friendships which were to last all his life: Will Lee, Perry Bruskin (one of the youngest members of the group, taken on because he looked like a 'working class Joe'), Curt Conway (an actor whose parents were vaudevillians), Earl Robinson. He was to work with all of them again later, directing the first three; on his return from Europe, around 1969–70, he renewed his ties with them. But the most marked influence was probably that of Al Saxe, co-founder of the group with Will Lee. Himself a man of the Midwest, born Alfred Sachse, son of a Chicago rabbi, Saxe – stockily built, shaggy-haired – was the first to moderate the group's most radical conceptions. For Perry Bruskin, 'Al Saxe could stand up straight next to Kazan. He was much more ambiguous in his language, had a very intellectual quality in approach. There were very few meetings that we had or plays that we did, or just doing something social with Al, at which there wasn't a kind of pleasant or dramatic explosiveness. His level of participating in almost anything was very stimulating. Nick worshipped him, and was frightened of him.' Others speak highly of Saxe's intuition 'for movement, action, colour'. Ray himself, comparing him to Kazan, noted that 'Al's method was less articulate, more loving, more fanciful; he helped me use affective memory correctly'[5] – qualities which would not be out of place in a description of Nicholas Ray the film-maker. As for affective memory, it is interesting that Ray mentions this notion, elaborated by Stanislavsky, not in connection with the teachings of the Group Theater – which represented for him, as we shall see, the great revelation of 'The Method' – but with the work of one of the founders of the Workers' Lab. The Group Theater had not yet become the sole repository for the Stanislavsky tradition, and many there were during the 1920s who had attended classes by Boleslavsky, the master's authorized disciple in the United States.

Of American rural stock like Nick, joining the group shortly before him, Earl Robinson had arrived in New York in 1934 to complete his studies in classical music at a college such as Juilliard. Instead of which, he fell in with 'this little backward amateur bunch of singer-actors and had to work with them on getting two-part harmony. Well, I did, we got some marvellous effects. And the experience of taking the theatre out to ten thousand people was worth ten Juilliards!' The Theater of Action had always incorporated songs in its performances, but Robinson brought a change of direction. 'They were directed more toward the Europeans. Hanns Eisler was a god then. I simply strengthened it with a little Americana. I got American folk material in.' Before becoming famous with *Joe Hill* and *Ballad for Americans*, Robinson attracted attention as the Theatre of Action's composer, with workers' songs like *Flying Squadron* (dealing with flying pickets) and *Death House*, which broadened the scope of militant music. He organized a group specializing in singing. 'We sang *Casey Jones*, the Joe Hill Wobbly version: *Workers on the S. P. line to strike sent out a call*. We worked it out musically and it was very clever, very smart, my first high level arrangement, because I picked the six best singers in the group in order to do it instead of trying to deal with Willie [Lee] and others who sometimes would sing at a pitch and sometimes wouldn't. I stood in front of them and conducted them, and gradually we worked them into a dramatic thing, like a song-and-dance act. I remember Nick being marvellous. He was used as a bass member of that group. We didn't have any basses, so we used two baritones, two who acted as tenors 'cause they could sing higher, and then the two gals, Rhoda [Rammelkamp] and Greta Karnot.'

The latter was the wife of Stephen Karnot, the company's theorist and one of its directors. He had been a pupil of Boleslavsky, had worked with Charles Dullin in Paris, and above all, with Vsevolod Meyerhold in Moscow (which may be one of the origins of the strict study disciplines in the morning classes). It was doubtless thanks to Stephen Karnot that the name of that champion of 'theatrical theatre' and constructivism on the stage – for years consigned to obscurity – never faded from Nicholas Ray's memory, resurfacing vividly in the 1970s.[6] Karnot read Russian (Lenin in the original!), and it was he who instilled the first rudiments of dialectical materialism into Earl Robinson and others.

'We were a Communist theatre,' says Robinson. 'Absolutely, no question about it. I mean, the *quality* of the material was anti-capitalist. And we put out these musicals satirizing La Guardia, who would be called a liberal mayor, but he was far to the right of what we were.'[7] For all, or almost all, the question of commitment was simple. 'In those days we were all marching in the May Day parade and doing all that kind of thing,' says Elia Kazan. 'Everybody was reacting to the Depression by becoming part of the left movement.' 'America was boiling inside,' Will Lee recalls. 'The unemployment situation, the Veterans' March on Washington – MacArthur killed a few of them – the formation of the CIO. People were expressing their unions by using their feet. You felt it in New York – and elsewhere too, undoubtedly – that they were demanding the right to express themselves as to what they wanted the country to be.'

When the group moved at the end of 1934 and set up in a brownstone at 234 East 27th Street, couples became entitled to separate quarters. Jean Evans came to live with Nick. Unlike the members of the Theatre of Action, she had never been involved in militant activities: 'I was sympathetic, because the only people to take a family along to the welfare office and pound on the desk until they got something to eat were Communists. Nick himself was truly committed, like the rest of the group.' Within this context, he even joined the Communist Party – an episode undiscovered later by any official inquiry. For Perry Bruskin, 'Nick, politically, was just a romantic. I don't think he was deeply political even when he was with this deeply political group. I think the combination of theatre and politics interested him, not politics itself.'

Nick, a late arrival in the group, took part only in revivals of *Newsboy*; he was involved in another short play which followed that great Theatre of Action success, demonstrating the company's progress under the influence of its various teachers and its musical director. *Free Thaelmann* combined mime, dance and recitative. Eight members of the Shock Troupe made up the cast.[8] According to Earl Robinson: 'They all wore grey, sweatpants and shirts, everybody was dressed the same; there was a lot of dance, almost the whole thing was danced. And we took it out on the goddamn streets! We were doing steps on about an eight feet by eight feet section of the sidewalk. The only music was a gong, which could be hit at certain strategic times. That gong was hit, they were flat on the ground, and would slowly rise up chanting, counting off the strikes in the United States at this time of the formation of the CIO: "50,000 men in Akron, Ohio . . . STRIKE! 75,000 in Detroit . . . STRIKE!" Agit-prop, that was an honourable word. We never even thought of anything else in the world except that, agitation and propaganda.'

In another play about a seamen's strike, Nick – as chance would have it – played a Norwegian. Perry Bruskin remembers his 'bearing' and his 'dignity' in these street-corner scenes where two or three actors would be standing on a makeshift stage, or perhaps on a small packing-case, while others remained at the side or in front, mingling with the audience and intervening. 'He liked being big,' says Bruskin.

'On many of these bookings we would play a sketch or so, and then, after we finished one of these very dramatic, very left wing, pro-union sketches, we would sing some of Earl's songs written specially for these bookings. And short as I am, somehow very frequently I would end up next to Nick, right alongside this big guy. And every once in a while I would feel his arm come around me and give me a hug while we were singing. I would look up and we would kind of wave to each other, and we would get a little laugh from the audience because of the Mutt-and-Jeff look . . . I always remembered that feeling about him, of standing next to him singing, and how reassuring he was, how interesting he was. An English-Jewish phrase would put it well: an ordinary guy he was not. He was unusual. That's why it was frequently difficult to get him to do certain acting things. If you needed a character that was quite ordinary, an American Joe . . . well, Nick couldn't play Joe. What I'm saying fits together with what I saw in *The American Friend*. And the General in *Hair*. I liked that strange performance of his, but again, it was *strange*. It was not Joe.'

The Theatre of Action occupies an undisputed place in the revolutionary theatre of America; its reputation was high enough to rate the presence of such writers as Moss Hart, Erskine Caldwell, Albert Maltz, Michael Gold and Joseph Freeman on its advisory committee, and the occasional appearance of distinguished visitors like Bertolt Brecht and Hanns Eisler, when they arrived to work on the first American production of *Mother* in November-December 1935. The Group Theater at this time had undertaken a theatrical revolution of a different sort. It, too, had known poverty, its members putting the same passion into their work, the same purpose into their communal life. 'The Group Theater members' according to Elia Kazan, 'all lived in a house in those days, where we all took turns cooking. I would cook once a week, some other members would cook once a week, the then Mrs Strasberg would cook once a week. And the Theatre of Action collective, which was downtown, did have the same process, except they were more crowded, in a crummier house. Our house, our apartment wasn't bad.'

The Group Theater concentrated on an analysis of theatrical methods, primarily through the actor. From the Soviet experience in theatre and cinema, from the agit-prop of Western Europe, from Meyerhold's 'Theatrical October', the Theatre of Action learned montage, the effectiveness of juxtaposing incompatible forms, the assimilation of extraneous elements, of popular forms, the demolition of the proscenium arch, an examination of the very function of theatre and of the relationship between stage and audience. The Group, faithful to Stanislavsky's teachings, engaged in a consideration of textual meanings and the actor's own resources. A twofold experience by which each profited. If the Group rejected commitment in its practice, it could not ignore the commitment of the period (Strasberg himself belonged to the Theatre of Action's advisory committee) which informed its most vital plays.

On the first Sunday in 1935, the Group's actors, on stage and scattered among the audience at the Civic Repertory Theater, launched for the first time the call to strike with which *Waiting for Lefty* ends, and which was echoed by the entire audience in a frenzy of enthusiasm. Kazan remembers this as the most overwhelming reaction he ever witnessed in a theatre. The Theatre of Action's Shock Troupe were present, and spent the night discussing this turning point in political theatre, which was also the revelation of a dramatist, Clifford Odets, to whom they sent a congratulatory telegram.[9] Will Lee and his colleagues realized that the members of the Group, as young as themselves, were more advanced on a creative level. The Method, through their skill in applying it, was also a revelation, for Nick Ray especially. At the end of his life, re-reading the final chapters of *An Actor Prepares*[10] 'for the first time in 25 years', he noted that he had 'been working according to the principles of this book for 40 years', and credits his discovery, in particular, to Elia Kazan among the members of the Group.

Born in Istanbul, the son of Greek immigrants, two years older than Ray, Kazan had worked as a waiter and dishwasher to finance his studies. He was still only an actor and stage manager with the Group, but his dynamism had earned him the nickname of 'Gadget' (shortened to Gadge or Gadg). Very busy with the Group, he took the time to look in on the Theatre of Action, where he soon gained an ascendancy he did not have in his own company, dominated as it was by the powerful personalities of Lee Strasberg and Harold Clurman. At this militant theatre, he became identified with Agate Keller, the proletarian revolutionary he played in *Waiting for Lefty*, fist raised in Communist salute or an upper-cut. He made the identification himself: cap and leather jacket. 'We were imbued with the spirit of the working class,' Perry Bruskin recalls. 'Left-wing philosophy, that was more important than people or working-class persons; and here he was, a successful professional theatre *worker*, he kind of combined that image. Kazan's made of iron, he always has been. His muscularity, his macho was all there, and genuinely there. We believed every word he ever said. Nick and I idolized him. My version is that if we were on the second floor (I'm saying this *almost* seriously), if Kazan had said. "Nick, Perry, jump out that window!", we'd have done it. Or we'd have gotten awfully close to opening that window.'

Ray was cyclothymic [i.e. manic depressive] and a dreamer; Kazan was the opposite. His inexhaustible energy was concentrated entirely on self-assertion: 'ruthless' is the word he would use, in the presence of Jean Evans, to define this attitude in defending his own self and those near to him. Ray, far from being fixed on an immutable goal, shared with him the determination to become a director, and to learn how through acting. For him, Kazan was a mentor as well as a friend. Ray saw a good deal of him outside the theatre, along with his wife, Molly Day Thacher, play reader and writer, critic on occasion, teacher of playwriting, in a sense the puritan conscience of the Group. Ray quickly became convinced – and he was to change very little on this point – that Kazan would become the greatest director of actors of his generation. It was Kazan, he further noted in 1977, who 'brought the essence of these last four chapters of *An Actor Prepares* to me long before they were in print'.

Kazan was to be active in the affairs of the Theatre of Action for a period corresponding to his membership of the Communist Party, which lasted from the summer of 1934 to the autumn or spring of 1936.[11] During this year and a half, he appeared in five plays for the Group, stage managed two more, wrote and directed *Dimitroff* (his first professional production) with Art Smith, directed two other plays for the Theatre of Action, and took his first steps in cinema, acting in two semi-amateur short films, the second of which, *Pie in the Sky*, is an astonishing pre-figuration of the New York underground of the 1960s.[12]

Three days after the first public screening of *Pie in the Sky*, the Theatre of Action's first production in a legitimate theatre opened at the Park Theater on Columbus Circle, at the far end of Broadway. *The Young Go First* was directed by Alfred Saxe and Elia Kazan. The play was commissioned by the collective. Its authors were Peter Martin, George Scudder and Charles Friedman.[13]

'Time: the present.' The action takes place in a Civilian Conservation Corps camp. The CCC camps had been one of the Roosevelt administration's first measures: open-air labour camps, offering work to the young and the unemployed. The play, inspired by the personal experiences of one of the authors, Arthur Vogel (George Scudder), was critical less of their charitable and reformist nature than of their paramilitary organization: overseen by the army, the camps were described as instrumental in preparations for war (to which the young are the first to go, hence the title).[14]

Kazan, frustrated in his ambitions at the Group, saw this play as an opportunity to venture beyond their usual exercises in improvisation. The Workers' Lab was familiar with improvisation, which it employed in polishing up sketches like *Newsboy*. It was even more effective applied to a play episodic in structure and featuring a group of young people, especially since the authors were novices and the text was still unfinished when rehearsals began. Improvisation was thus a stage in rehearsal, subsequently resolved into definitive form. Ray would never work in any other way, frequently stressing that the improvisation 'must be as meticulously structured as a three-act play'.[15]

On the first night, the house was packed. The actors ran up and down the iron stairs in the wings to pump up their energy. 'We came on strong,' is how Ray remembered the performance. Instead of skeleton sets which could be carried on the subway, the company had secured the services of the distinguished designer Mordecai Gorelik, much more politicized than the Group Theater management. 'Nik' Ray (as he was known for a short time) played the part of Glenn Campbell, the camp barber, in a cast which included the principal members of the company and another future film-maker, Jack Arnold.[16] The high standard of the performances was generally recognized, but the few critics who ventured to the Park Theater, though respectful, lacked enthusiasm.

On Broadway, the length of run depended directly on the takings, and it was soon clear that they would be low. It was a big setback for the company, which had banked on success, borrowing from a number of not very wealthy friends. Despite a party given by th. stage-hands when the decision was taken to close, held in the offices of this theatre built by W. R. Hearst for one of his mistresses, it was not a new beginning for the collective, but the beginning of the end. For many, the cumulative weariness of years without sleep and without food was beginning to make itself felt.

One last play was produced, however, for a series of performances organized by *New Theater* magazine at the Civic Repertory Theater (where *Waiting for Lefty* had been premiered). The starkness of the production harked back to the collective's early days: skeleton sets, roneoed programmes, three performances (Sunday 1, 8 and 15 March 1936). *The Crime*, like *The Young Go First*, was specially written for the company, drawn from actuality, and again directed by Saxe and Kazan. The author this time was a professional jack-of-all-trades in the theatre, Michael Blankfort (who later scripted *Broken Arrow*).[17] The action is 'based on actual occurrences in Sioux Falls, S. D. and Omaha, Nebraska', and takes place 'in any town of 25,000, anywhere in the United States'. The opening quotation is a remark by a delegate to the American Federation of Labor's convention in 1935, out of which rose the dissidence of the Committee for Industrial Organization: 'You men may have had years of experience in the labour movement. That is the trouble – your experience goes back too far.' The play joins in this fray between 'craft' unionism (the AFL) and 'industrial' unionism (the CIO). The caution of the union leader, opposing the violent, united action of the workers in a meat cannery, causes the strike to fail, but the youthful agitators have understood the reason for their failure. There were again some twenty-five roles, and as many actors; first and foremost among them was Norman Lloyd, sent along to the Theatre of Action by his friend Joseph Losey. He represented the AFL. 'I was a good villain,' Lloyd comments, 'because I really was closer to being a bourgeois than they were.'

For Perry Bruskin, *The Crime* marked the point at which the company assimilated the Method, instead of retaining only isolated elements. 'Robert Garland remarked that you saw the wheels going round in our acting. It was true, we weren't yet capable of concealing the works.' And the critic of the *New York Times* felt that *The Crime* 'is not good theatre, as *Waiting for Lefty* was, but it is an efficient play of its kind'. Kazan put actors at the back of the auditorium, to fire at the stage over the audience's heads. 'Nicholas' (on this occasion) Ray had a small part in *The Crime* as Larry Nelson. Few have any recollection of him in the cast, which also included Martin Ritt, too young to be part of the 27th Street community: the future film-maker was still living at home with his parents.

Thanks to *The Young Go First*, most of the members of the company now had their Equity cards, which threatened to change the way their ensemble functioned. Furthermore, the emergence of the Federal Theater seemed to open new perspectives, allowing them to profit from the achievements of the Workers' Lab without betraying it. Immediately after *The Crime*, the company dissolved and merged into the Federal Theater; Ray had already been a member since November 1935. Stephen Karnot took over the organization of the Federal Theater Project's units in Manhattan; Al Saxe and Will Lee formed the One-Act Experimental Theater (Saxe was later to be assistant director on one of the *Living Newspapers*). Most of the group continued to live in their communal quarters, pending settlement of their debts. When they left the house on 27th Street, they could pride themselves on no longer owing anyone a cent. Nick and Jean Evans moved into an apartment at 72 West 52nd Street; that year, 1936, they got married.

4

Federal Theater

By the time *The Crime* appeared, groups like the Theatre of Action had outlived their function, henceforth taken over by the only experience of subsidized theatre in American history, the Federal Theater Project. The Works Progress Administration, an essential tool of Roosevelt's policy, had been voted by Congress in April 1935. $4,800 million of Federal funds were allocated to change the status of the country's twenty million wholly or partially unemployed from welfare cases to workers, paid directly by the government, in the exercise of their own skills and trades. Less than 1 per cent of this sum, $27 million, was to be devoted to the arts, but it was to be one of the New Deal's most enduring and thrilling successes. Within three months, under the guidance of Harry Hopkins, five arts projects were under way: Writers, Music, Plastic Arts, History, and Theatre. Hallie Flanagan, director of the last-named project, was not a Broadway celebrity but an intellectual who had become talked about as head of the Experimental Theater at Vassar College. It was thanks to her that the Federal Theater, among its various concerns, was as interested in the avant-garde as in playing safe with audiences. In four years, productions whose motto was 'free, adult, uncensored' were to reach over 30 million spectators on more than 200 stages all over the country. This Utopian prefiguration of an American National Theater gave their chance to subsequently famous names; Howard Da Silva, John Huston, E. G. Marshall, Joseph Cotten, Arthur Kennedy, Will Geer, Sidney Lumet, Vincent Sherman, Jules Dassin, Harold Hecht, Arthur Miller, Virgil Thomson, Howard Bay, and of course Joseph Losey, John Houseman and Orson Welles.[1]

At the time the Federal Theater started its activities, Losey recalled, there were 17,000 unemployed members of the theatrical profession in New York alone (the Federal Theater would employ in all only some 15,000 from over the entire country). 'To be able to apply for a job as a shop assistant, you had to show your university degrees. The decision to create subsidized theatres answered a determination to combat unemployment; it was also the first time a government had attempted to develop the popular culture of the American community.'[2] Employment was restricted to professionals already earning their living through theatrical skills (precluding encouragement of amateurs and, incidentally, the development of any real decentralization). Ray could lay claim to the title: thanks to *The Young Go First*, he was on relief.[3] Now, as Jean Evans put it, 'Bohemians suddenly were making $23.86 a week, fifty-two weeks a year. Artists had enough to eat. It was a Renaissance, a confused and rich time.'

Nick Ray was engaged as dramatic coach on Project 65–169, 11 8th Avenue (just above the Village), under the supervision of John Askling. For not quite three months, following the final performance of *The Crime*, he was officially assigned to the Minneapolis branch, which was in fact inactive.[4] Then, in New York, he took part in one of the Federal Theater's most notable ventures: *The Living Newspaper*. The concept involved a theatrical presentation of current events. In this, *The Living Newspaper* pursued the same goals and methods as agit-prop and the Workers' Lab sketches. Here, however, a complete show would be built around a given subject, with sizeable teams of writers to do research (among them Jean Evans), under the supervision of Morris Watson, a journalist who had been fired by the United Press for trying to establish a union there. Right from the first *Living Newspaper, Triple-A Plowed Under*, Joseph Losey (who collaborated on the direction with Gordon Graham) emerged as the mainspring. Leaving La Crosse at an early age, he became involved in theatre while a student at Dartmouth and Harvard, and made his début as a stage director in 1933. The year before that, he had taken a lengthy trip to Russia.[5] He hired Ray as stage manager (his official function with the Theatre of Action towards the end) on the third *Living Newspaper*: *Injunction Granted*.

Injunction Granted set out to retrace the history of the American Labor movement, from Charles II to modern times, through its relations with the law and the courts. As publicized, thirty-five researchers and fifteen writers worked on the text, under the supervision of Arthur Arent. Essentially, the dialogue was composed of quotations from authentic texts (in direct line with the Soviet avant-garde's rejection of fiction). The concluding passage was a speech by John L. Lewis, founder of the CIO, which left no doubt as to the attitude of the authors.

Nick Ray was, then, the general stage manager on this compact production (two hours, reduced to an hour and a half without interval in performance) which represented a technical tour de force: so much so that the first night had to be postponed twice (that, at least, was the reason given). There were over 500 lighting cues during the show, 140 music cues (Virgil Thomson's score, with an orchestra comprising sixteen percussionists, made abundant use of concrete sounds, including sirens), lantern slides with eight variously located projectors, and 125 actors,

9 *Injunction Granted*: in the centre, the Demagogue (Herbert Dobbins) and
the Clown (Norman Lloyd)

many of them duplicating roles (when one of them, William Roselle, left
the cast, he vacated no fewer than nine villain roles; Ray himself filled in
as a trade unionist), in about 100 separate scenic groupings.[6] Hjalmar
Hermanson's single unit set was in fact a composite of platforms, curving
ramps and steps, forming ten separate acting areas which could be individually lit. Losey used this fluid space to create violent contrasts –
juxtaposing an empty space with a crowd – or transitions in the manner
of cinematic dissolves. The mime and rhythmic movements of the actors,
reflecting the monotony of modern life – groupings expressive of collective power, crescendos of movement and sound emphasizing the toil and
stress of the workers – all this was attributed to the influence of Meyerhold and Okhlopkov (*New Theater* kept enthusiasts pretty well informed
about Soviet theatre); and Losey's visit to Russia was often referred to,
although Losey himself, reacting against 'the idea that the proletarian
masses are visually dreary, that the worker only likes grey', sometimes
dressed his workers in 'fuchsia and pink'.

'Stereopticon and lights are rather effective, with whatever story there
is aided by placards of identification, an amateurish device,' noted the
condescending *Variety* review (American showbiz hadn't yet digested
Brecht's dictates when *Mother* was first performed in New York). The
whole thing was actually more reminiscent of the influences Jean Evans
was thinking of when she described *The Living Newspaper* as 'Piscator,

with a touch of Brecht'. But it was also a culmination of the experiments conducted by the American theatre of political agitation. Losey recalled that in these productions 'every medium' was used: mime, dance, cabaret, cinema. 'An attempt to break with traditional theatre practice, to establish a new relationship between the play and the public.' Not the least effective of his ideas was to have the action of *Injunction Granted* commented on by a silent clown, played by Norman Lloyd, who, 'without taking sides', would pop up to accompany certain moments with gestures, mime, and even conjuring tricks.

As for the material itself, it lagged little behind the Theatre of Action, to judge by the review in the *Herald Tribune*:

> Most of its scorn seemed to be devoted to Hugh S. Johnston, the Supreme Court and William Randolph Hearst, but it also had harsh words for Donald Richberg, the president of the University of California, the Pinkerton Detective Agency, Judge Grosscup and other Tories. It championed the side of the industrial, as opposed to craft, unionism, and its heroes included the Molly Maguires, Mayor La Guardia, John L. Lewis, Oliver Wendell Holmes, Sacco and Vanzetti, Heywood Broun and, of all people, the late King Charles II . . . A bitter and sardonic cartoon chronicle . . . in short, stylized episodes . . . : the dispatching of indentured servants to the colonies, the first uprising of workers in Bacon's rebellion, the early eighteenth-century efforts at forming unions, the revolt and suppression of the Molly Maguires, the Haymarket Affair, the Pullman strike . . . and such recent events as the rise and fall of the Blue Eagle, the Newspapers Guild's controversy with Hearst, and the matter of relief in New Jersey.[7]

The show was a spectacular success: it played to full houses all through the summer, almost three months in all. But *The Living Newspaper* was explosive stuff: Liberty Leaguers physically threatened the technicians, there was sabotage, mounted police sometimes had to protect the theatres. In 1936, the start of Roosevelt's second presidential term marked a swing to the left, and accusations of extremist propaganda were hurled at the government's ventures, all the more so in the case of a show extolling trade unionism. *Injunction Granted* was the object of constant polemic between its prime movers, Morris Watson and Losey, and the Federal Theater's administrator, Hallie Flanagan, who was herself faced by bitter criticism. She was opposed to what she considered partisan use of a subsidized theatre, and called *Injunction Granted* 'bad journalism and hysterical theatre'. Losey, whose political commitment was somewhat vague, thought these accusations absurd. But from 7 August some episodes were cut; and when the run ended, Morris Watson and Losey left the Project, signalling the beginning of the end for the Federal Theater (many others, like Orson Welles and Earl Robinson, would leave soon after in similar circumstances).

Ray did the same. The last performance took place on 20 October. The following day, he took a leave of absence without pay from the Project to accept a job at Brookwood Labor College in Katonah, New York, for eight months at a monthly salary of $120. With him he took Earl Robinson: 'Nick comes to me one day, he says, "How would you like to work with a real labour theatre?" I had to be interested, although I was getting a chance to write some full scores with an orchestra on the Project. But . . . Nick's enthusiasm carried the day.' Brookwood Labor College, socialist in orientation, ran a six-month course of studies for union officers. It was financed by socialist-run unions, in particular the rubber workers. The work done by Ray and Robinson suffered from the effects of a conflict between partisans of Norman Towne, advocating a peaceful

10   Nicholas Ray

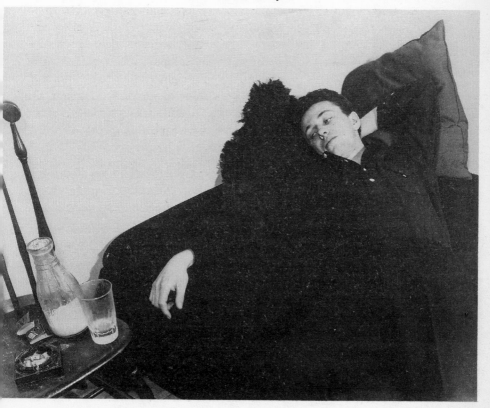

passage to socialism, and of Earl Browder and the American Communist Party, with Robinson and Ray among the latter. 'Norman Towne was more respected by the Establishment than Earl Browder or Communist leaders, and we were proud about that; we didn't want to be respected in those days,' Robinson recalls. 'I became respectable in spite of myself! Marxism was taught from the socialist standpoint. We looked down our noses at it.

'Nick was to be in charge of the theatre. We had two hours a day. He was allowed to put together a group of performers, and I would be integral part of it as music director. Nick was to build a show to take touring through the unions in the spring. We worked with improvisation – all the things he'd learned during the Theatre of Action he was applying here as the director. We had rehearsals, we worked with the union members in production stuff and had music classes, which I conducted. So it should have been good, have worked better. We stayed there only about three months. In that incredibly short time, what we did! But Nick found that it wasn't the place for him to do all the things he wanted to do. And part of the conflict could have been the problem between Communists and Socialists. Nick left by Christmas. I left after him. This was the year I met my wife – on an unemployment line on the Project.'

5

Washington

From January 1937, Ray was put in charge of local theatre activities by the Department of Agriculture's Resettlement Administration, and together with Jean Evans, went to live in Washington. Working for the government might seem a strange step in his somewhat unpredictable progress, but circumstance and friendly relations played their part in his decision. The Special Skills Division, run by the writer Adrian J. Dornbush with the musicologist Charles Seeger as his assistant, was the artistic branch of the Resettlement Administration.

The situation had been critical for America's farmers long before the Depression. The Depression itself was attended by natural disasters which brought ruin, evictions, mass exodus. 'The "great black blizzard" of 11 November 1933 – which darkened the sky of Chicago the following day and as far east as Albany, N.Y., the day after that – was only a prelude to disaster. During 1934 and 1935 thousands of square miles were to be laid waste and their inhabitants set adrift upon desperate migrations across the land.'[1] Under the inspired guidance of Rexford Tugwell, the purpose of the Resettlement Administration (which became the Farm Security Administration at the end of 1937) was to help farmers evicted from their land to start again from scratch, to acquire new land, to form co-operatives. According to Alan Lomax, 'It was Tugwell's idea that we should begin to build a new kind of community in America over the makeshift communities that had been run up in the factory towns and in shanty towns around the country. He invited artists to come down to help him give these new communities a living culture.' The Special Skills Division was a seed-bed of talent, observed from the fringes by an interested adolescent, Pete Seeger, son of the musicologist Charles Seeger: 'Curiously, this division was made up of artists, photographers, musicians like my father. You may wonder why, but my father would put out a song sheet, Ben Shahn would make a poster, Nick Ray would direct a play, and in a way they helped.' The little group also included the painter Jackson Pollock and his brother Charles, Eric Appleberger, who reproduced antique furniture, Margaret Valiant, a singer, etc.

It was a happy time. Nick Ray was not isolated in his work. Jean was pregnant; their son, Anthony, was born on 24 November 1937.

With the New Deal, America opened up on itself. Hitherto, cultural development had been slow and stamped with the puritanism of the pioneers. People had little idea what was happening in the rest of the country: communications were almost non-existent. Intellectuals, turned towards Europe, remained cut off from the heartlands of America. Only the literature of the previous generation – the novels of Sinclair Lewis, Sherwood Anderson – countered this situation. Within a few months, the Roosevelt administration was, as Alan Lomax put it, 'a line drawn across the development of the country'.

'The New Deal was the time the American Revolution began again. It wasn't just dealing with the Depression, it was dealing with all the problems we had accumulated in the hundred years between the time of the American Revolution and then, through selfishness and greed and exploitation, in killing the Indians and enslaving the Blacks and excluding the poor White. We knew what the problems were, we had been to school and this had been our training: I was an anthropologist, Nick was a remarkable intellectual from the Frank Lloyd Wright school, and there were tens of thousands of us in that city, all related to the problem and given a go-ahead signal, *do* something. It was made possible thanks to the enormous forward thrust of the New Deal. We had the ear of the common man.[2] All intellectuals were involved; everybody was in it. The Roosevelts were marvellous orchestrators. We unionized America, we set the base for integration, we set it free from European snobbery. It was a time of exhilaration, a dizzy feeling. By God! We Americans were pretty marvellous.'

This 'exhilaration' came not unaccompanied by a sense of urgency in face of the America thus discovered. The photographers despatched for Tugwell by Roy Stryker to every corner of the country brought back, not a picture of impressive achievements, but one of tragic backwardness.

Ever since Roosevelt's arrival at the White House, his policy – usually symbolized by his measures within the field of agriculture – had been the object of violent attacks and frenzied accusations of Communism. With the Fascist menace abroad and the Civil War in Spain, the American Communist Party, like its European counterparts, had moved towards a Popular Front policy since 1935, and supported the New Deal. It is probable that its members, swayed by the spirit of the times, would have done so anyway. The days when the Theatre of Action criticized the CCC camps as militaristic were long gone. 'Everybody who had knowledge of what was going on was a Communist,' says a witness in the documentary *The New Deal for Artists*,[3] where Ben Shahn also remarks that Party orders in cultural matters were 'happily ignored'.

The Special Skills Division was no exception. According to sculptress

Lenore Thomas, the sculptor Alonzo (Lonnie) Hauser, who had known Nick Ray in Wisconsin and in New York, had recommended him to Dornbush: 'Lonnie wanted Nick to join us because they were friends and because Nick was also a member of the Communist Party. We had a small underground cell in Washington. None of us carried cards. Mostly we sat around and talked and studied Marxism-Leninism, dialectic materialism, etc. We were not very dangerous, but very earnest. Our political convictions obviously affected whatever work we did and I know it affected what Nick was doing, although it could not be too overt.'

In this work, 'the planning wasn't formal. In fact, there seems to have been no planning other than what we did for ourselves. Each of us decided what he wanted to do, and did it. Charles Seeger travelled through the country making recordings and studying folk songs, Ben Shahn travelled through the country with his camera and painted frescoes in certain communities, I did sculptures for different communities, and lived in one of them, in Tennessee, for several months. That gives the impression of an artists' paradise, and I suppose it was one.'

Lenore Thomas (later Lenore Straus) deposited three aluminium discs with the Library of Congress on which Nick Ray, and mostly Charles Seeger, can be heard rehearsing musical sketches. Ray had sent Seeger some lines he wanted set to music, for a play he was staging in a Pennsylvanian community:

> Look, here we have our hands
> Our hands don't bring us much
> But with our hearts and with our hands
> We'll make this world our own, our own
> We'll make this world our own.

On the first disc, accompanying himself on the guitar, Seeger proposes three different melodies, each with a stirring rhythm (saying, 'If you don't like any of them let me know. I like them all!'). On the second disc, a ballad to piano accompaniment, in the syncopated style of the Brecht-Weill songs, tells the story of 'a big man and a little man' in a company town where everything belongs to the employer: what he pays in wages, he recoups in rents and purchases from his stores. The scarcely audible tracks give some idea what Nick Ray did for the community theatres for which he was responsible. He would go to the place, listen to the people, get them to talk about their lives, write a play based on this material, and stage the play with the people who had lived it in reality.

This activity took Ray to mining communities, among lumberjacks, smallholders, farm labourers, 'wherever the earth was ruined and the people were hungry,' as Jean Evans puts it. The latter often accompanied Nick to these backwoods, which people were becoming aware of through the photographs of Walker Evans, Russell Lee, Dorothea Lange, and through the films Pare Lorentz made for the Resettlement Administration (*The Plow That Broke the Plains, The River*). North and South Carolina, Arkansas, Alabama, Tennessee. 'Some of these people lived in such remote and undeveloped areas that when houses were built to resettle them, they didn't know what the bathtub was for.' With Jean pregnant, they spent several weeks on a North Carolina farm: 'Wonderful people, very warm-hearted simple, good people.' Other trips were more dangerous. In a journal started in Mexico, Ray made notes during his travels. He drove by car from Danville (Arkansas) to Penderlea Farms (North Carolina), to Somerfield, Tracy City and Palmer (Tennessee). *En route*, he picked up some negroes who had been beaten up, attended nocturnal union meetings among lumberjacks. 'I spoke on the right to organize, backed my Federal government, and spoke of Judas as scab. Very corny.'

Contrasting with this atmosphere of clandestinity, the Penderlea annual fair was organized with the assistance of Margaret Valiant and the Special Skills Division. Ray staged a pageant written by the inhabitants – even the words for the songs – who called it *Settlement and Resettlement*. Six thousand spectators attended, and a guest of honour, Eleanor Roosevelt, joined in the square dance which followed.

A month later Ray further noted in his journal: '27/7/37. Pennsylvania, not far from Pittsburgh. At Tink Queer's. Tink is a fiddler. His wife is a witch. Two daughters – tubercular. The third sings *Is it true what they say about Dixie* at the age of six. She is not married. Their home seems to have slid into place about three quarters down the mountain.

'Cabbage soup with a piece of pork and canned corn had been the evening meal. On the wall facing the entrance was a shotgun. Behind the gun-barrel was a bank account book. A memory. Below the gun, two pictures of the Dionne quintuplets. One a calendar, the other a cut-out. On the wall opposite was an enlarged photograph of Tink in First World War uniform. Saluting – very proudly. To the right of the picture was the chimney pipe for the coal stove which had possession of the room. Aside the stove was a bucket and a pan, and into either one was permitted to spit.

'When Tinker clanked into the room he cursed his wife, lit the lamp, set two curtains across the sink and said: "Has you'uns eaten? My wife's the god damdest one – don't suppose she's ast ye. How ye bin? Didya ast 'em has they et? I'm a workin' now. Where's my new pants, wife?"

' "Where ye thinkin' they'd be?"

' "I get new pants and she don't keep no count of 'em. She's runnin' out a spirit. Guess you'uns can see that." And Tinker turned to ask us again were we sure we'd et. We said, "Yes, plenty" again. We pulled out a bottle of Bourbon.

'Tinker turned the coal bucket on its open end and stood on the closed end as he pulled off his work clothes. His wife: "Get out and git some coal in that bucket afore ye slam thru it with a hoof."

' "I ain't freezin'," said Tinker. "Do ya mind when ye was last up here and the music we had? Guess near twenty people in this room cuttin' out some tunes."

' "An' near fifteen of 'em did we have for supper."

' "We did not," contradicted Tinker.

' "Do you mind?" the Mrs asked us. 'Do you mind, was it fifteen or more we had for supper?"

' "We had not a one," Tinker insisted. "Hand me down my fiddle and hand me up another drink of the city likker."

' "*We played all night to the break of day*, etc." '

Another time, Nick and Jean drove down from Washington to New Orleans, accompanied by Elia Kazan. Then, hitchhiking, Ray and Kazan went back up towards the pinewoods of eastern Texas. 'The first thing that I felt about him that I thought was novel or unusual,' Kazan recalled, 'was that he had a great interest in American folk music. We were both kids, down East Texas in the pine tree country, and we bummed around together. Then I got a job on a ranch there – I worked building a well for two weeks – and he went on. I don't know where he went. But in those days we just wandered here and there.' Few books or films have described this exploration of the country, the dangers, the resistance, the incomprehension, the different life-styles experienced in face-to-face encounters. Little comes to mind other than Kazan's *Wild River*, a film in making which, Kazan has said, he had his travels with Nick very much in mind. Actually, this film had a precursor: during the summer of 1937, Kazan had co-directed a short film with Ralph Steiner for Frontier Films in Monteagle, Tennessee: *People of the Cumberland*.[4] He also used to go frequently to Chattanooga, in the same state, to see a friend of his, a Communist organizer.

Yet another trip took Nick and Jean not far from the Cumberland Plain: 'We went,' Jean Evans says, 'to a place outside of Scottsboro, Alabama, called Skyline Farms, up on top of a mountain, where some of the people had never been down to the bottom. Relations between them were such that there were only two family names in the whole community. Nick prepared a programme of their folk music and folk dancing

11   Nicholas Ray rehearsing with non-professionals

and a play, and they performed on the White House lawn. Eleanor Roosevelt was a very interested person as far as the Resettlement Administration was concerned.' Nick's sister, Helen Hiegel, visited him and attended another of these shows: 'Nick was the only Democrat in the family, the rest were Republicans. He was a dear friend of the La Follettes and of Eleanor Roosevelt. He said his sister was here from Wisconsin, and Mary La Follette insisted that I come for this showing of the work of these people. They'd made these beautiful dolls of all the nations, and they were costumed beautifully, authentically. "WPA" was printed on the doll's foot underneath. Nick said, "I want the Norwegian doll." He got it and gave it to our mother.'[5]

Nick's already long-standing interest in music was stimulated by another encounter. Alan Lomax, the son of John A. Lomax, who was one of the first to undertake the collecting of American folk songs, started working with his father while still very young (he was born in 1915), travelling, recording, publishing, laying the foundations for the collection of American folk music in the Library of Congress.

'When I met Nick in Washington in the 1930s,' Alan Lomax says, 'he was certainly one of the most splendid young men in the whole world. He seemed to me to be the person I'd always dreamed of being. He was very powerful and gentle and wonderful to look at. He had a kind of a grin and a laughter that were the same thing. They were always playing on his face when he was discussing the most serious matters. And I think I represented something equally splendid for him, the whole America that he didn't know anything about and I had already explored by then, while he was just beginning, because he was in charge of starting theatre in rural America. He was just starting to think about what it was like, but I'd already been to all those places and knew what kinds of music there were. So we could talk immediately about common problems; where he was far ahead of me was in thinking that you could restore or support all of these many American working-class structures with the techniques and the dreams of sophisticated theatre people.

'I was the only person who had been out there with the Blacks, the Mexicans, the Cajuns, and all the rest. And Nick was one of the people who came and listened and took it seriously. Very seriously, and in ways that I wasn't aware were possible. His colleague Charles Seeger, who was a musicologist, added another level of seriousness in it for me, and we became a sort of trio of cultural workers in the city. So Nick and I were like Damon and Pythias, like brothers. He always understood without having to be told all the things that I was experiencing; and he was feeding me back all the richness of a theatrical tradition and the sophistication of New York, which I didn't have . . . and Frank Lloyd Wright, this whole marvellous monument.'

Thereafter on his travels, Nick sometimes took with him a Presto recording machine with a crystal microphone, heavy but manageable by one person. The new model, marketed in 1937–8, replaced the aluminium discs with acetate, and cutting instead of embossing. The machines were mechanically very touchy; the acetate wasn't constant in thickness, but the frequency response curve was better than on earlier models, and it was more practical (the first machines used by John and Alan Lomax in 1933 weighed 350 lbs).[6]

The Archive of Folk Music at the Library of Congress preserves only one series of recordings by Ray: eleven 12-inch records made in Mitchell, South Dakota, in October 1939. Thirty-eight tracks with a great variety of music and tales: variations on military songs, square dances, derivations – with spicy lyrics – from English ballads, songs of the West, fiddlers, a miners' song from the sierras of California which the singer had heard in Canada, a fine Western song – 'transcribed from the French' – from Glasswood Lake in northern Minnesota, and a sizeable number of obscene songs and stories, some of them devoted to the time-honoured antipathy between cowboys and sheepmen, the latter invariably depicted as copulating with their charges. Ray himself requests certain songs, asks questions, breaks into loud laughter: at least once a fit of giggles forces him to switch off. Paul Martin, of White River, declares that he doesn't like the cowboy songs sung on the radio, because they're sung 'through the nose'. Then he says, 'In 1919 I went to Chicago. I hated the city. I came back and wrote that song.' Someone called Indian Tom introduces himself, and plays a love song and a war song: 'My name is Straight Arrow. This ain't my violin so I don't think my love song will come all right.' Accompanied on the harmonium, fiddle and banjo, Ray himself sings *Irish Washerwoman* and *Turkey in the Straw*. Mitchell is not very far from La Crosse, to which it is linked by Interstate 90, crossing Minnesota from east to west.

Lomax describes Ray's collecting as poor: 'But it showed me that his heart was in the right place. He didn't know how to do it, but he was interested in the *real* raw guts at the bottom of the grass roots, where the shit piles up!' Ray's own regrets were that he was confined to Mitchell by his official responsibilities, instead of being able to explore the 'river rats' of the Jim [the James River], west of the Missouri, or the whole western region of South Dakota, with its mining industries and its stock farming, as well as an Indian reservation and a Mennonite colony, to both of which he had access: 'I hope that in the near future someone will be able to cover this untouched area of America which still contains much of the lore and spirit of the frontier.'[7]

Soon, left alone while his wife Elizabeth went on a trip to Mexico, Lomax went to stay with Nick and Jean at their home in Alexandria (in the state of Virginia, just outside the federal capital). The house would fill with singers he had met on his travels, about whom Nick and Jean became enthused in their turn, including startling invasions like that of Aunt Molly Jackson, a midwife from the Kentucky mining country. 'I left for the weekend,' Lomax says, 'and by the time I got back, Aunt Molly, who was a great ballad singer and a kind of witch, had that house completely in turmoil. Nick and Jean and Tony [sic] weren't speaking to each other; and I had to send Aunt Molly back home to her house in New York.' Huddie Ledbetter – 'Leadbelly' – a black singer discovered by the Lomaxes in a Southern penitentiary where he was serving a sentence for murder, was a frequent visitor. He would introduce himself to an audience by saying: 'My name is Leadbelly. I'm the king of the twelve-string guitar. When I come into town, all the girls come running with their skirts up over their heads.' A guest in the house, Leadbelly did the cooking. 'Rice and beans, rice and beans,' Kazan recalled. 'He sang *Washington Water Tastes Like Turpentine*. He impressed me. It was a time when all blacks were not defiant. He was defiant.'

On his arrival in the federal capital, Nick had brought, by way of visiting card, Earl Robinson's *Ballad of Joe Hill*, which he proceeded to introduce to Lomax and all Washington. Robinson, very active with the Federal Theater (he had written the scores for its last two shows), visited the capital. He ran through some of his cantatas on the piano. 'When I finally did the record in three-part harmony,' he says, 'Nick didn't like my harmony! He thought it was too full. He had heard me sing it at the piano very simply. Nick was like a lonely voice in the left-wing wilderness calling for more simplicity.' Robinson thought Leadbelly a wonderful discovery, and took him along to a Communist Party summer school. The militants were scandalized by his songs about gamblers and loose-living women; but he had no problem in recapturing his audience by singing *Bourgeois Blues*, which he had composed in Washington, and his ballad on the Scottsboro case.

Nick set up a political cabaret similar to Losey's in New York. The WPC (Washington Political Cabaret) presented its first (and only) 'topical revue' in the spring of 1938. This ambitious show, 'entire production staged by Nicholas Ray', comprised no fewer than thirteen scenes with two intervals. It was performed on the first floor of a restaurant. There were several sketches, including a one-act play by Jean Evans about the *Anschluss*, *Message from a Refugee*, and *Castaways*, a sketch written by Ray and Bernard C. Schoenfeld (later a screenwriter and 'friendly' witness before the House Un-American Activities Committee); dances and songs – Jean Evans remembers one entitled *What's My Civil Service Rating With You*, which was a great success ('Half of Washington was civil service jobs').[8]

At home, there were often musical evenings. Jean and Nick loved the blues, the lyrics grave and insinuating by turn. Jean: 'There was one blues called *Louise Louise*, and one of the lines was, "You may be beautiful, but you've got to die some day", which I thought was wonderful.' The evenings often ended with a song which Lomax had learned from a convict in Florida. 'It told us,' Lomax later said at Ray's memorial service, 'about the anger and the sorrow which Americans were just beginning to express openly.' Nick and Alan often sang it together:

> Go down, go down, you little red
> Red and ruby risin' sun
> And don't you never bring day,
> O God almighty, no more
> To the pine, to the pine,
> Where the Sun and God almighty don't shine

You gotta shiver when the cold,
O Lord almighty, rain blow . . .
I killed no man, I robbed,
Lord almighty, no train,
And I did no man, O Lord almighty, no crime.
I wish to my soul that old bald,
Bald-headed judge was dead
And green grass growing round,
O Lord almighty, his head,
So go down, go down,
You little red, red and ruby risin' sun
And don't you never bring day,
O Lord almighty, no more.

One day, at the Library of Congress, Alan Lomax was visited by one of the great New Orleans musicians. Jelly Roll Morton, the self-styled 'inventor of jazz', had been forgotten during the Depression, and was reduced to playing in a seedy Washington club. For a month Lomax recorded him, laying the foundations for what he would describe as the 'first oral history', his book *Mister Jelly Roll*, published in 1949, and for the rediscovery of the pianist-composer. Morton became a regular visitor to the house. 'He used to introduce himself by saying,' according to Jean, ' "My name is Jelly Roll Morton. I've got a stovepipe in my pants, and all the girls are dying to turn the damper down".'

In 1938, the funds allocated to the Farm Security Administration were cut back, and Nick, while continuing to work unofficially with the Lomaxes, was assigned to a new job. From July, he came under the direct authority of the WPA – as the Federal Theater already did – with the title of drama supervisor of the Recreation Division. The purpose of the Recreation Division was to encourage amateur or semi-professional ventures on a state-wide basis, taking specific requirements into account and helping these amateurs to become professional. Collaboration with other governmental authorities took shape as the Joint Committee for Folk Arts, resulting from informal discussions among friends. The idea was to systematize research into and the recording of the country's musical heritage. The official listing of the members of the committee gives an idea of the wide variety of cultural interests involved: 'Chairman B. A. Botkin, of the Federal Writers' Project; Vice-Chairman Charles Seeger, of the Federal Music Project; Herbert Halpert, of the Federal Theater Project; C. Adolph Glassgold, of the Federal Art Project; Ernestine L. Friedman, of the WPA Education Divison: S. B. Child, of the Historical

Records Survey; and Nicholas Ray, of the WPA Recreation Division.'⁹
The most concrete result was an expedition into the South with a sound
truck, from which Herbert Halpert brought back more than 400 discs in
1939. Nick was not concerned exclusively with folk music; together with
another friend, the psychiatrist Les Farber (brother of the painter and
film critic Manny Farber, himself involved at the time with the WPA
Toys Project), he was experimenting with psychodrama at St Elizabeth
Hospital.

But the Recreation Division, while pursuing activities similar to those
of Ray's previous assignment, was distinctly more bureaucratic in
character. Nick reacted with equally bureaucratic discontent, complaining of his grading, which put a ceiling on his salary at $3,200 a year.
His only consolation lay in his travels all over the country, for which he
now had to lodge a written request each time.

November 1938: Tennessee.
January 1939: Ohio.
23 February–4 March: Kentucky and Tennessee.
24–30 April: New York, for the opening of the World Fair.
1–6 May: Connecticut.
27 May–12 June: New Orleans, Texas (Kirbyville, Dallas, Amarillo,
   Stratford).
21–30 July: North Carolina, then Florida (Nagshead, Jacksonville,
   Tampa, Miami, Southwood).
7–19 August: New York, Albany, Boston, New Jersey.
4 October–8 November: Madison, Wisconsin; Nebraska (Grandis-
   land, Lincoln), South Dakota, St Louis, Jefferson City, Kansas City,
   Indianapolis.

Lacking funds, Ray did his best to encourage WPA organizations at
state level to suggest solutions, contacts, examples, to establish relations
between employees of the various organizations created under the New
Deal, to overcome rivalries between agencies. More often than not, his
work was blocked by ill-feeling between private and public concerns, and
he was forced to spend a good deal of his time on questions of procedure.
In New York for the preparations for the World Fair, in which the
Recreation Program was involved, he sat in on and supervised rehearsals
for two shows, but was also obliged without fail to present himself in
person at the offices of various administrators, and to make mention of
this in his report.

In practical terms, the only form of action open to him was personal
intervention. In Tennessee, he took the initiative for a play about the war

in China, *I Saw a Newsreel*, which was successfully performed a little later in the International Ladies' Garment Workers' hall in Chattanooga: 'On a bare little platform, scarcely elevated above the floor of the hall – without curtain, without scenery, with only suggestions of stage properties . . .', a local paper noted. In New York, he attempted to step in and simplify the show introducing visitors at the World Fair to the activities of the Recreation Division. He was more successful in more distant states such as Florida or North Carolina, where the black novelist Zora Neale Hurston was among the contacts he made.

In an appendix to his report on Kentucky, Ray describes the genesis of a short play. During a discussion on ways of creating theatre within and with communities, a 'gentleman who had been a small town circuit wrestler, and who had two tremendous cauliflower ears' launched into an old folk tale he had known for years. It told of a squire at loggerheads with the inhabitants of a small town, and ended in marriage to an ass. Even as the gentleman with the cauliflower ears told the story, the people present started acting it out, cutting asses' ears, props and bits of decor out of yellow paper. 'This atmosphere of general improvisation continued throughout the performance.'

Such moments were not to be repeated often; 1939 was a difficult year for the New Deal. Another economic crisis, the worst in six years; a political atmosphere of bitter opposition to Roosevelt; determination to turn the Republican victories at the 1938 legislative elections into a presidential victory in 1940; rivalry among Democratic candidates for the presidential nomination, until Roosevelt announced his decision to seek a third term in office. The Roosevelt administration was targeted in particular through its cultural ventures, automatically suspected of Communism. Under pressure, it gave less weight to programmes born of the great crisis and designed to cope with it, and in various areas initiated a withdrawal of the federal government in favour of state support or private enterprise.

In the last days of August, news of the Nazi-Soviet pact, and the immediate volte-face by American Communist Party leaders, seemed to vindicate the 'Red-hunters' and Senator Martin Dies, definitively putting an end to the possibility of a united leftist movement. The war in Europe brought this period to a close in America as well. It was against this backdrop that 'the notion of neanderthalism won out again . . . and made zombies of us,' as Studs Terkel remarked of the termination of artistic projects in *The New Deal for Artists*.

For months, the Federal Theater had been under attack by the Woodrum and Dies Congressional committees (for Dies, read House Un-

American Activities Committee, here making its first significant mark).
Colonel Harrington, successor to Harry Hopkins as head of the WPA,
was not interested in artistic programmes. In April, Roosevelt revoked
the independent status of the WPA, which became subordinate to
another agency, the Federal Works Administration. In June, through the
Emergency Relief Act, the Senate suppressed the Federal Theater, and
authorized the WPA's four other Arts Projects (Writers, Music, Plastic
Arts and History) to continue their activities only provided that state
(rather than federal) funds were secured, comprising a sizeable proportion of private investment. Furthermore, the Emergency Relief Act
imposed a considerable cutback in personnel, all redeployment to be
effected within two months. Although Nicholas Ray retained his job –
provisionally – the summer of 1939 was, for him as for all the Washington survivors, a period of confusion and discouragement.

In a report dispatched on 31 July, he once again reviewed the conditions which had to be met in order to establish theatres across the
country, stressing the lesson to be learned from the Federal Theater, and
the advantages to be had in collaborating with its former members. The
recommendation was hardly opportune. In her memoirs, Hallie Flanagan
noted that the WPA was 'so affected by the measures taken against the
Federal Theater that our members found themselves being told, in one
place after another, that "instructions from Washington" prohibited
them from being given work.'

Ray also did his best to impose ideas such as on-the-spot surveys of
local needs for community drama, the development of forms of children's
theatre and youth drama, the use of material drawn from the realms of
folklore and labour, marionette theatres and pageants. These proposals,
formulated on Ray's return from a trip to North Carolina, were doomed
in advance. Festivals and large open-air pageants, the answer came back,
'would seem to be beyond our range of activity at this time'. As for
technically qualified theatre personnel who had been transferred from the
Federal Theater to the Recreation Division, 'their aptitudes in fields other
than the drama should be cultivated'. Although Ray continued to work
for the WPA for nine months, he no longer had much to do. Lenore
Thomas sums it up: 'I didn't see very much of Nick when he worked for
the WPA. I don't think he was very happy there. He sat at a small desk in
a small office and kept a pint of whisky in a handy drawer.'

In October 1939, the trip to the Midwestern states, South Dakota and
Missouri, where his intervention had been expressly requested, and
which was the most carefully prepared of his field trips, was also something of a farewell to arms. Ray wanted to 'try to make of these thirteen

days [subsequently curtailed] a practical project demonstration of how arts and crafts, music, dance and drama can be integrated'.

In actuality, things were very different, and Ray could only complain: 'I have made several attempts to outline and develop, in a rather comprehensive way, my ideas on the origin, development, and the decline of the Folk Theatre in America. I cannot do it while I am constantly interrupted by making train schedules and carrying on my other duties.' If no trace remains of this project, this is less a reflection of Ray's vacillating nature than of the failure of so many other projects at a time when the revolutionary dream the New Deal held out for three or four years was finally coming to an end.

Although the upshot of Ray's involvement with popular theatres was thus one long frustration, he found ample compensation in his work with Lomax. Paradoxically, it was in this same year of 1939 that CBS asked the latter to do a radio series on folk music. Lomax: 'I thought this was a joke. I didn't know that anybody could be seriously interested in working on the radio, a pile of crap. Then I heard Corwin's broadcasts and I did a flip, I realized that radio was a great art of the time, there was a way to do it quick and straight, and with a few sounds you could evoke . . . Well, I took the job, partly because Nick encouraged me and said it would be an opportunity. He was always a good writer, he had a sense of theatre and drama, so it was with his encouragement that I learned how to write a script. It was the first time that America had ever heard itself, and it went into all the schools. But I don't think I could have done it without Nick's support and belief in me. Every week was a mad adventure. The people used to come and stay with me, and we worked on the script in my house. I was working at the Library of Congress, and Woody [Guthrie] stayed two weeks, Pete [Seeger] stayed four months, and inevitably Nick was swimming in it. That was part of his life, and a very important part.'

The crucial revelation came with Woody Guthrie. Here was a real-life character out of *The Grapes of Wrath*, a child of the Dust Bowl – the Great Plains of the South ravaged by the 'black blizzard' and drought, whose ruined farmers became migrants to California. At once singer, storyteller, improviser, humorist and fabulist, a storehouse of popular songs, Guthrie was also a radical, a committed revolutionary who had no qualms about writing a column in a Communist paper. The actor Will Geer had brought him to New York, where Alan Lomax heard him for the first time at a benefit concert.[10] At once he saw in Guthrie everything he had been looking for: a popular expression of the times, a wide-ranging artist. A few days later Guthrie was in Washington, and he stayed for a fortnight in the house shared by the Lomaxes and the Rays at Arlington. Woody didn't want to 'get soft', and preferred the turf (Will Lee, on tour in Washington with the Group Theater, was surprised to learn that 'the guy sleeping on the lawn' was the singer he admired), the floor or a couch to a bed, so as to be ready at any moment to take off on the road again – as he in fact did. Ray assured Guthrie's biographer that not once during those two weeks did he take his boots off. He listened to the same records all the time, especially the Carter family (*John Hardy*). Lomax did not miss the chance to record him for the Library of Congress (issued commercially, these recordings remain the finest existing testimony to Guthrie and his music). He also introduced him on his CBS programme, *The American School of the Air*.

New York, too, had its music; black music first and foremost, which spread from Harlem to the downtown clubs of Greenwich Village, to records, and to the radio. Nick's visits to New York, and the contacts he still had there, made him a connecting link between this music and the kind Lomax and a few others had gone to the far corners of the country to find. In New York, the movement picked up momentum with the New Deal; this was largely the work of three men, with whom Ray became friendly.

John Hammond, scion of one of New York's great families, was a knowledgeable jazz-lover and a militant in the black cause. He had recorded Bessie Smith and Billie Holiday, whom he virtually discovered, organized concerts, brought jazz to Carnegie Hall, and served as musical mentor to Joseph Losey as well as to Barney Josephson. Max Gordon, Lithuanian by birth, opened the Village Vanguard in February 1934 during the coldest winter of the Depression, and his club was an indispensable venue for music-lovers. Barney Josephson, the son of Latvian immigrants, came to New Jersey in 1938–9 and opened his first club in New York, the Café Society. Typical of the New Deal, it was a big place, seating 220 at modest prices: admission $2 and $2.50 at weekends, beer 65 cents, liquor 70 cents. On the walls, frescoes painted by WPA artists. But the novelty of the Café Society lay elsewhere: it was the first inter-racial night-club in the United States.

'Up to that time,' Josephson recalls, 'there wasn't a night-club or restaurant that offered entertainment in the entire country to have blacks and whites together on the same programme. In addition to that, black people were not permitted to come into these white places. For example, the Cotton Club in its heyday: Duke Ellington had his orchestra playing there, but his own mother wouldn't be permitted to come in as a customer; she would have to be working in the band. I opened the first place that also put black and white talent together. Billie Holiday was my first singer, and I had a very funny comedian-entertainer named Jack Gilford, a white man. The political climate was such that you could attempt to do it with some measure of success. And a year later I opened another Café Society, off Park Avenue and 58th St.' The club was frequented by black intellectuals – Paul Robeson, Langston Hughes, Richard Wright – as well as by music enthusiasts.

'So I got to know Nick and all these people. Nick was a lover and connoisseur of jazz, and particularly American folk music. My place presented jazz, plus folk and blues and some comedy, which usually had to do with satirizing the Establishment, Café Society people and so forth. Of course Nick and such people gravitated to my place. This was their kind of thing; they were at home there. Nick was quite active with the folk singers. He developed a closeness to all of them, he socialized with them. I was in a different position. For the black artists, I was the white-man-boss, so they would incline to keep their distance, and rightly so, for all that they knew I was left and progressive. Although I got Billie Holiday to sing a song like *Strange Fruit*, Billie and I were never intimate in any sense that Nick could be with her. Mostly these people were apolitical, not aware even of their own plight. And it was people like Nick who would talk to them and develop them into people with a viewpoint – which helped them become greater artists, no doubt.'

April 1940. The first separation for Nick Ray and Jean Evans. The immediate cause was Nick's alcoholism. For Jean, Nick was 'a wonderful man, not to be married to', not prepared to assume the responsibilities conventionally expected in a marriage. 'How he managed to accomplish what he did – it took him a wonderful discipline; for years he managed not to drink.' The inner violence, the chaotic emotions, had regained the upper hand. The break was not for the moment considered to be definitive. It was understood between them that Nick would start analysis, to confront the problem of his alcoholism. 'He had a stab at it, but his resistance was so great that he lost his voice.' The analysis was discontinued after a few weeks.

Jean left Washington and returned to New York, initially leaving their son Tony for a while with friends in the country. Her relations with Nick would always remain friendly, tinged with tenderness. She was hired as a special reporter by a new paper, *PM*, which was a daily, carrying no advertising, financed by the Chicago millionaire Marshall Field, editorially liberal or leftist. Jean started work even before the first issue appeared on 18 July 1940. She soon became famous for her 'portrait-interviews' in the Sunday magazine section. Nick particularly liked her portrait of a boxer, *Bummy Davis, Who Yearned for Glory*, and put her in touch with a dramatist with a view to turning it into a play. He soon followed her to New York, where they spent the summer together and brought Tony to be with them. Nick was officially dismissed from the WPA Community Service in July 1940.

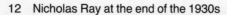

12   Nicholas Ray at the end of the 1930s

6

New York 1940–1

Almost immediately, a new opportunity presented itself. Following the success of Lomax's programme, CBS offered him a regular evening slot. Lomax accepted, provided Nick Ray was hired as director.

Lomax's morning programme for *American School of the Air* involved practically no direction: he simply presented a series of songs. Its merit lay in the voices and the authentic accompaniments that were heard – which didn't prevent it from being widely listened to: in 1934, *CBS School of the Air* was heard by an audience of 6 million; out of 32 million American families, 27,500,000 had radio sets. The effectiveness of the medium had been proved less than two years before by Orson Welles's adaptation of *The War of the Worlds*, which panicked millions of listeners. With Welles, Norman Corwin and a few others, the new broadcasting medium had already won its titles of distinction. For an evening programme, some form more dynamic than Lomax's very didactic approach had to be found.

CBS did a test for the Ray-Lomax project with a 28-minute pilot, forming part of a series, *Forecast*, whose purpose was in fact to try out new ideas, with the coming year's programming in mind. *Back Where I Come From* was the tenth out of seventeen in this series: it was broadcast on 19 August 1940. Lomax recalls: 'We wrote a script about the weather with all the members of the cast. We had Adam, we had Noah, we had the busboy, we had all the American folklore of the weather in this one show, and it had an all-star cast of the greatest singers in the US.'

The team assembled for the *Forecast* programme was headed, of course, by Woody Guthrie, who – with the backing of Alan Lomax – had just made his first record. There was also the Golden Gate Quartet, a group of black singers from Shallotte, North Carolina, whom Nick had admired at the second annual jazz concert organized by John Hammond at Carnegie Hall in 1939; he lost no time in bringing them to Washington and having them recorded for the Library of Congress. Then Josh White, a black singer from South Carolina, who had served as a guide to the blind when he was a child: it was thus he met 'Blind Lemon' Jefferson, a singer who also exercised a considerable influence on Leadbelly. After a five-year eclipse, White had recently begun singing and playing again. Finally there was Burl Ives, a son of the Great Crisis from the heartlands

of America, southern Illinois, where he grew up on Irish ballads. A radio
star for the past year, he still preferred to spend the night in a sleeping-
bag in Central Park rather than in his luxury apartment on Riverside
Drive. He shared with Nick the sense of being a stranger passing through,
as well as a fondness for Thomas Wolfe.[1] Together, they got mixed up in
a number of street brawls. Despite his weighty physique, Ives's voice was
delicately modulated, and his preference was always for the old ballads.

Master of Ceremonies was Clifton Fadiman, a literary critic and New
York personality. The programme, he announced at the beginning,
would talk of things about which every American has an opinion. 'I like
talking things over, what things are like, back where the other fellow
comes from.' After the announcement of the topic of the day, a babble of
voices saying 'Back where I come from . . .', 'We always say . . .', and
offering old saws, then the Golden Gate concludes this introductory
come-on in song. Fadiman takes the listener down South, home of the
Golden Gate Quartet, into New York houses, and to the other end of the
state in 1820, during the building of the Erie Canal. Woody Guthrie then
intervenes, telling in his sing-song voice of his amazed discovery of the
New York subway: 'I believe there's more of New York underground
than on top . . . Trains were so crowded today you couldn't even fall
down. I had to change stations twice, and every time I came out with a
different pair of shoes on.' Len Doyle, a comedian with a drawling voice,
talks of the weather in the Midwest, and gets excited about the Petrified
Forest in Arizona, pronouncing it 'all putrified!'. And Woody talks of the
Dust Bowl: 'Back where I come from – Okema, Oklahoma.' The whis-
tling of the wind leads in to one of his most famous songs, *Dusty Old
Dust*, best known for its chorus:

> So long, it's been good to know you
> So long, it's been good to know you
> So long, it's been good to know you
> This dusty old dust is a-gettin' my home
> And I've got to be drifting along . . .

Telling with bitter irony the reactions of the folk 'back where Guthrie
comes from' to the great dust storm of 1935, it is punctuated with his
characteristic improvised asides and a few enacted scenes: a telephone
call from Woody to his mother, his parting farewell to a girl-friend.

Next comes Burl Ives with a tender ballad. With the Golden Gate
Quartet, and Josh White providing guitar backing, Willie Johnson tells
the story of Noah, the 'granddaddy of all meteorologists'. In conclusion,
all join in a reprise of 'So long, it's been good to know you'.

The series was programmed for the autumn. It was on for fifteen minutes, three times a week: Mondays, Wednesdays and Fridays, at 10.30 p.m. Len Doyle, planned as the regular announcer, luckily dropped out. The announcer's role varied from simple speaker – an anonymous CBS staff member – to the very active compering Woody Guthrie could provide. The signature tune, *I'll Dance with the Girl with the Golden Braids*, was sung at a lively tempo by the Golden Gate Quartet. To Guthrie, White, Ives and the Golden Gate Quartet were added, naturally enough, Leadbelly and Pete Seeger, whose adolescence had been steeped in folk music.

'Alan would pick a subject,' Pete Seeger says, 'and ask various singers to comment on it in songs of various traditions: Afro-American, Irish . . . sometimes Woody Guthrie would make up a song. The subject could be anything: 'Who knows a song about . . . animals, food, workers and bosses, travelling?' Alan would weave in a great variety of songs with a certain amount of continuity, there was a narration . . . Nick was behind a glass window telling us to speed up or to slow down, pointing up cues. I was very impressed with Nick's skill. It took a ruthless genius to cut in 15 seconds here, one minute there, and make an exciting hour. It was a single-minded directorial control.'

Earl Robinson, who served as announcer a little later, adds: 'We never got sponsored and worked for minimum rates, something like 17, 18, maybe 21 dollars a night, not much more. We told stories, the material was absolutely unlimited and it was fun! We talked about versions of songs and we'd keep mixing up the word with "virgins" . . . "There's a virgin I knew down there . . ." Nick would always be sure, clear about the simple, direct way to do it. He'd been part of a thing in the South, along with Pete Seeger's father. There he did a lot of directing of ordinary people. You could say it was a lifelong conflict of Nick's, working with "real people" as against the pros.'

'By then I was writing four radio shows a week,' Lomax says, 'three for Nick and one for myself, and commuting between New York and Washington, so I'd just send him the material or telephone it in. And I ransacked the Library of Congress. I would go up with a sack, strip a whole section, and put it into one of those *Back Where I Come From* scripts. We tried to give it a poetic form in the Sandburgian fashion.'

The formula for the programmes was not so very different from Lomax's didactic broadcasts: selected themes like 'Children', 'Sailors', 'Courtin'', 'Nonsense Songs', 'Work Songs of the City', 'Love True and Careless', 'Railroad'. What distinguished the series was its liveliness, its lightness, the way the participants had of keeping the ball going, of reacting with pleasure to what the others did. The Sound Reference Room at the Library of Congress has not preserved a copy of the programme Ray remembers most fondly: on the anniversary of the 13th Amendment to the Constitution (18 December 1865), Guthrie read the text, to the background accompaniment of the Golden Gate Quartet singing *Oh Freedom*: 'Neither slavery nor involuntary servitude, except as a punishment for a crime whereof the party shall have been duly convicted, shall exist within the United States, or any place subject to their jurisdiction.'[2]

The intimacy of the team assembled for *Back Where I Come From* was not without its hazards, and Woody Guthrie's intransigent radicalism created explosive situations. He had given up his column in the Communist *Daily Worker* to become a radio star. After the *Forecast* pilot, CBS put him under contract at $150 a week, and according to his biographer Joe Klein, 'he was trying to exorcise his sense of guilt by redoubling his integrity in other areas'; protesting, for instance, that Ray gave too much prominence to Josh White at the expense of the less 'crowd-pleasing' Leadbelly. The rivalry between the two singers seems to have been somewhat exaggerated by Klein. Woody Guthrie's presence on the programme nevertheless soon engendered a malaise: some got the feeling that he was drinking (untrue), others that he was ill (true). 'Woody was hard to control,' Jean Evans says, 'he would seem to string things out.' For Pete Seeger, 'Woody had a genius of his own. He would tell Nick, "You point that finger at me and I'm struck dumb, I freeze, I cannot do anything." '

The break came in October, a quarrel with Ray, and Guthrie left the programme. Lomax wrote to him: 'I wish there was some way you and Nick could get together again. The first programme that you failed to appear on just about broke my heart . . . I'd like to hear your side of the story and I'd like to try to do something about the situation.'[3] Guthrie in fact did come back after a while, and his role in *Back Where I Come From* grew, until the end of the year, when he suddenly left New York; determined not to 'get soft', he had seen enough of the big city for the time being.

Like so many ventures at the heart of which Nick Ray played a crucial role, this one was brief and intense. Earl Robinson, for example, remembers the programme as having run throughout the season. Among listeners, too, *Back Where I Come From* left an indelible memory: in a family of Finnish immigrants in Duluth, Minnesota, it was the only programme that little Elizabeth Uitti, aged five, was allowed to listen to, glued to the radio with her brother when it was repeated on Saturday mornings. Eighteen years later, she would become Nick Ray's third wife.

But in fact CBS cancelled the programme as early as February. 'The show was sensational,' Alan Lomax says. 'Our agent William Morris told us we were set for life. And then the great paw of America reached out and stopped it: Mister William B. Paley said that he didn't want any of that goddamn hillbilly music on his network. And that was that.' Informed by Ray, Guthrie wrote to Lomax from Los Angeles: 'Too honest again I suppose? Maybe not purty enough. O well, this country's a getting to where it cain't hear its own voice. Someday the deal will change.'[4]

In 1941, Nicholas Ray was for the first time the subject of an FBI investigation. 'While engaged in another investigation, Special Agent [deleted] contacted [deleted] who advised that subject had moved into that building on 15 June 1941. Subject [several words deleted] stored some boxes in the basement storeroom for a friend. Subject and another person carried three large cardboard boxes in the basement storeroom from an automobile, which [deleted] later learned were Communistic in content. Special Agent [deleted] stated that he examined the contents of an open box and found various Communist Party publications therein. [Several words deleted] subject is unemployed and spends most of the night in his room typewriting [deleted] believed to be Communist propaganda. Subject receives approximately seven or eight telephone calls per day, and is constantly going out and coming in with books and pamphlets. Subject has had numerous, well-dressed, coloured visitors who come with bundles of leaflets. Subject's wife is employed by *PM* newspaper as a reporter, writing under the name of Jean Evans . . . In the neighbourhood of 338 East 15th Street, New York City, inquiry showed that subject moved to the adjoining building, 342 East 15th Street, Apartment 3D, on 15 August 1941. The mail box bears the names Nicholas Ray and Jean Evans, and also Abrahams.'[5]

In the autumn, Nick moved again. He sublet a room at 130 West 10th Street, corner of 6th Avenue, from the Almanac Singers, a new group whose nucleus comprised Pete Seeger, Lee Hays, Millard Lampell and Woody Guthrie. The Almanac Singers revived the Theatre of Action tradition of communal living, and their political activism left nothing to be desired in comparison (this was the time when Guthrie's guitar carried the inscription, 'This machine kills Fascists'). Like Alan Lomax's place in Washington, the house was open to any singer passing through, and evening sessions of music were a regular thing when the Almanac Singers, very much in demand since the summer, were there. Nick spent his evenings at Max Gordon's club, the Village Vanguard. Established in the heart of Greenwich Village, in a small basement on 7th Avenue (where it was still to be found in 1980), it was a rendezvous for artists and bohemians, and there, according to Max Gordon, Nick was 'waiting for something to happen'. For some months at the Vanguard, a youthful group, led by a former switchboard operator from the Mercury Theater, had been presenting what were effectively shows comprising satirical musical sketches about New York. The 'Revuers' were Judy Holliday (the ex-telephonist), Betty Comden and Adolph Green (future authors of *On the Town* and many other musicals), plus John Frank and Alvin Hammer. Nick and Judy became close: 'He was like one of the regulars coming in, you know, didn't have to pay,' Max Gordon recalls. When 'Judy and the kids', as the latter called them, received an offer from a fashionable night-club, Nick couldn't understand their reason for accepting. Gordon remembers Nick saying, 'They've got a long way to go, and if they'd asked me I'd have told 'em, Stay where you are and learn your business.'

Leadbelly and Josh White were both in New York and out of work. Nick met them at the Almanac Singers' apartment, and thought the time had come to introduce them to a new audience. With Max Gordon looking for replacements for the Revuers, he suggested presenting the two singers together, offering to prepare their show. For a week, Nick, Leadbelly and Josh White met Max Gordon at the Vanguard every afternoon (he had the only key to the premises), and they worked while emptying a bottle of rye whiskey. 'And one day, twenty bottles later,' Gordon recalls, 'Nick said he thought they were ready, and when did I want them to open?'

On the opening night, Max Gordon wrote, 'there was in the place a feeling that something important was going to happen. I never saw so many guitars in the place: Pete Seeger, Burl Ives, Richard Dyer-Bennett, Millard Lampell, The Almanac Singers, five strong, and Woody Guthrie – all present, with guitars slung over their shoulders. Josh – smooth, handsome and bare-throated; and Leadbelly, in high "yaller" shoes, his power frame immaculately attired in a powder blue suit.'

Josh White sang *Great God A'mighty Folks a'Feelin' Bad*, *The Jack Rabbit That Had the Habit*; Leadbelly, *Boll Weevil*, *Bottle Up and Go*, *Bourgeois Blues*, *Take This Hammer*; and both together, *Don't Lie Buddy* and *Grey Goose*, on which the audience joined in. They finished up confronting each other on guitar in a 'carving contest'. Max Gordon: 'Nick came over and said to me, "Woody thinks we need a mike for Leadbelly. I don't think so. Huddie's got enough power in his own voice to move a mountain." I was glad Nick felt that way, because the Van-guard owned one mike and Josh was using it. Nobody moved when intermission came. They were waiting for the second show.'[6]

A few days later, Guthrie sent a lengthy missive to Max Gordon, also for the attention of Nick, even though they were sharing the same apartment. In it he talked of the blues, 'Blind Lemon' Jefferson, blacks, publicity and propaganda, Hitler and the Red Army, the strengths and weaknesses of the show. Josh, like Leadbelly, Guthrie wrote, came from the same background as he did, and both were continuing the tradition of 'Blind Lemon' Jefferson, the Texan singer-guitarist memorable equally for his freedom as a musician and the vividness of his vision. 'Leadbelly is a regular philosopher of chain gangs, prisons, wardens, and hard times in the country, the country where there's more of it under corn than under concrete [. . .] Huddie says, My people has got the blues about every-thing, about clothes, about money, about places to stay, and places that ain't worth the rent you got to pay – use to be lots of people had the blues; nowadays everybody's got the blues; but the white folks blues quit where the Negro blues starts in . . . I've never heard the Negro situation said any clearer or easier than that.'

Among the spectators at the Village Vanguard was Libby Holman. An actress and singer, she remained associated with one song, *Moanin' Low*. At thirty-seven, she had not been on a Broadway stage for three years, and had recorded nothing for seven. Fully alive to the power of black music, she was excited by Josh White and asked Nick, whom she knew, to make the introductions. Ray let himself be persuaded to arrange an audition in Libby Holman's Manhattan apartment. 'It was worse than any audition I ever had on Broadway,' she said. Josh White was won over, and during the following months, they appeared and recorded the blues together.[7] Ray was not involved in this venture, although he was to re-encounter Libby Holman some years later. On 7 December, a fort-night after the White and Leadbelly opening at the Village Vanguard, as Jean Evans was finally making the decision to obtain a divorce, the Japanese attacked Pearl Harbor.

7

The Voice of America

13   Nicholas Ray and John Houseman, New York

Shortly after the United States entered the war, the writer Robert E.
Sherwood, a close adviser to Roosevelt, invited John Houseman to create
a national radio propaganda. In a country which had become acutely
sensitive to the problem of communication, radio had become the prime
medium, reaching a wider audience than even the cinema. The President's 'fireside chats', the revelation of live reportage with the Hinden-
burg disaster, the Welles and Houseman programme about the invasion
of the Martians, are only a few examples. Houseman's task was therefore
to create *The Voice of America*, addressed to the American people and,
above all, to a world at war.

Before he was twenty-two, John Houseman had known three national-
ities: Romanian (he was born in Bucharest in 1902), French (his parents
lived in Paris), English (he had a public school education, an affinity
with Raymond Chandler which the latter did not fail to appreciate).

63

Established in the United States since 1924, he had turned to the theatre after the crash in 1929, becoming known primarily as a producer.[1] As director of the Federal Theater's Negro Theater Project, his career became linked for several years with that of Orson Welles; he was the mainspring (if not the creative power) of the Mercury Theater and of the same team's radio broadcasts, then left for Hollywood with Welles, and having quarrelled with the latter, was working for David Selznick when Sherwood's invitation came along. He soon drew Nick Ray into the venture.

Ray had been rejected for military service (because of rheumatoid arthritis, and the congenital cardiac malformation from which his father and grandfather had both suffered). The two men had known each other since the days of the Theatre of Action and the Federal Theater. A European man of culture, Houseman had an impressive capacity for work. As a producer, he was capable of loyalty and devotion; he was a man given to enthusiasms, inclined to idolize his friends. His encounter with Ray was one of the few not to end, for the latter, in a sense of betrayal or desertion. 'Of the many people with whom I have collaborated over the years,' Houseman wrote in his autobiography, 'Ray, Welles, [Herman] Mankiewicz, [Joseph] Barnes and Virgil Thomson are the five of whom I can attest without qualification, that they gave me more than I gave them.' For six years, they were to work together almost without interruption.

Appointed head of the Overseas Programming Bureau, Houseman came under the Foreign Information Service, a government agency headed by Colonel William ('Wild Bill') Donovan, an already somewhat legendary figure, soon to enter history with the creation of OSS (the ancestor and anti-Nazi version of the post-war CIA). In a few months, with a nucleus of collaborators already assembled by Sherwood, he had made his first programmes. The first, in German (on 11 February 1942, two weeks after his arrival), was followed by versions in different languages, principally English, French and Italian. A year later, 3,000 people were working for the New York bureau of the Overseas Branch of the Office of War Information (OWI), yet another new agency created to make Sherwood independent of Donovan. These 3,000 employees were producing 1,000 broadcasts daily, in 27 languages.

As the length of the broadcasts gradually increased, Houseman soon began to feel the need to go beyond mere information. In these first months of the war, while the United States were losing in the Pacific, an image of life in America needed to be presented to audiences. Trying to avoid the monotony of the British news services as well as the German

64

bombast, Houseman created an English Feature Desk, which became the pivot of his activities and to which he enticed all possible talent. Under the supervision of Dorothy Van Doren, its regular members included writers of repute (Howard Fast, Robert Ardrey, Jerome Weidman, Bessie Breuer, Claude McKay, Arthur Arent . . .). Outside contributors were numerous, ranging from John Steinbeck to Paul Robeson, Norman Corwin, Carson McCullers, John Latouche, Wendell Willkie (the luckless Presidential candidate in 1940), and Archibald MacLeish. 'All this,' Houseman wrote, 'was recorded and used in many versions on different English language broadcasts, before being translated and incorporated into our foreign language programmes.'

One series of programmes presented the States of the Union, inspired by the guides produced by the Federal Writers' Project. The series was to include a great deal of music, and this was entrusted to Nick Ray. 'We discovered that folk music is international,' Houseman recalled, 'and, more and more, we used to use a lot of folk music in order to convince everybody – our allies, our enemies – that we were brothers under the skin, that Americans were not remote barbarians. We needed somebody to organize all that and to bring in people to execute these things, and Nick was in charge of that department.' Nick brought in all the participants from *Back Where I Come From*: Burl Ives, Earl Robinson, Woody Guthrie, Pete Seeger, Leadbelly, Josh White, the Golden Gate Quartet, and the Lomax family – Alan's wife Elizabeth, and his sister Bess, a folk music librarian: 'I was only twenty myself, supervising little girls who weren't over fifteen and had lied nobly about their age . . . What I really recall about those crazy days was the sense of dedication I felt in the people I dealt with – the elevator operators, the errand runners, the truck drivers and the library clerks. I think many of them felt that for once in their lives they were doing something important.'[2] Connie Ernst, a woman scarcely older than Bess Lomax, called this group 'Nick's barefoot guitar players', and the name stuck. For her, it was an exalting time, 'an ingrown and incestuous time. The Office was like a family. It was a good war, we were clear what it was about, we had a place that we believed in, there was leadership. Wartime meant that you were doing the most you could.'

Connie Ernst, whom Houseman had known at the Mercury Theater, was the daughter of a famous lawyer, Morris L. Ernst, a specialist in matters of censorship (it was he who pleaded the case for lifting the ban on *Ulysses* in the United States). At twenty-four, this 'dark, vital Bennington girl' as Houseman called her – for women were still defined by the colleges they attended, like Hallie Flanagan and Vassar – had worked at the Mercury, for the political cabaret TAC, for the radio (with Norman Corwin) and on Roosevelt's re-election campaign in 1940. On *The Voice of America* she was a producer, one of her jobs being to assemble answers to English questions about the United States (questions collated by the BBC; in reply, she interviewed Americans, celebrities or unknowns).

'Nick and I met at the OWI,' Connie Ernst recalls, 'and became "friends". We were very close, very supportive of each other. He had just gotten a divorce, it must have been 1942, Tony was seven. We went on to live together.

'After work we went to see films at eleven at night. We then used to go and eat (very well) at Louisa's, a restaurant on the East Side. Later, when I was sent to London to do a programme from there for D-Day, he took me to see *Lifeboat* the night before I left! Another time, he gave a party for me at Sardi's with nothing but men, the wives had to wait downstairs. He had that playfulness. When I left for London, he went to Hollywood, but it was not because I went off. There was no talk of getting married. We were intimate in a very real sense.

'He had this problem with drinking. Sometime or other we went to Florida for two or three days. We took trains filled with soldiers. Once we were there, he disappeared gambling. It was very tricky, being with Nick.'

Houseman describes an incident arising from the partiality of 'Nick's barefoot guitar players' in favour of the CIO, which roused the wrath of the head of the AFL's Federation of Musicians. James Caesar Petrillo had launched a recording strike which continued throughout this period.[3] It was thanks to an arrangement with his union that the OWI had free access to all recordings, including those specially produced for *The Voice of America*. The series on the States of the Union incorporated a march by CIO strikers. Faced with Petrillo's fury, Nick's team pointed out that the AFL didn't even have a march, but offered to improvise one right away. Sent to Petrillo that very afternoon, the record delighted him.

The broadcasts came in all shapes and forms. John Berry recalls having played a pilot under Ray's direction. In 1972, the Finnish critic Peter von Bagh listened to some 78 rpm records the film-maker had kept of his programmes: 'Pete Seeger singing the Russian national anthem . . . in Russian. A hard-line pro-Communist speech by Dos Passos. In another, the announcer read a statement by Goebbels on the degenerate art of jazz, followed by seven top jazz musicians, in an extraordinary version of *Indiana*.' In addition to broadcasting, the OWI produced records destined for Allied radio services. Connie Ernst played the lead in one of these, under the direction of Nick Ray: *White Collar Girl*, number 10 in the series *Meet an American*. After a musical-style evocation of the early morning stir and rush hour in American cities, the commentator (Norman Rose) focuses on a girl employed in a large government office in Washington, and the dialogue starts. The life of the white collar girl is described, supported by statistics brought into the conversation. We visit the apartment she shares with two other girls, she telephones her family in Indiana, and finally, in a monologue, she dreams about what she will do after the war, when she can go back home. A routine product, without ambition, *White Collar Girl* nevertheless does have (perhaps thanks to Connie Ernst's own speech rhythms) a fresh, natural tone far removed from that of official propaganda.

Ray's work also included some activity as a producer. In an inconsistent account, Connie Ernst states that he was attached to the English staff, and that he produced programmes in twenty-six languages. Houseman is equally imprecise, probably due to departmental overlapping in the daily work-load. Ray worked with a variety of people: a trio in charge of the British desk, Russell Paige, Leonard Miall and Mark Abrams (the last-named specializing in the analysis of enemy propaganda), Pierre Lazareff, head of the French staff.

'The scripts were written, they'd pass the Control Desk,' Connie Ernst recalls. 'Then there would be a 15-minute rehearsal and we'd be on the air or recording. We had two people reading news [in fact more, according to Houseman]. We did essays with name persons. We had no right to change the text in the various languages. And one of the announcers was André Breton, who refused to read any item having to do with the Church. Imagine working there, of all places, with André Breton!'

One of the OWI's best-loved teams was the Czech one, thanks to a pair of comedians: Jiri Voskovec and Jan Werich. In their Prague theatre and in the few films they made, they created a new form of politico-intellectual musical comedy, combining Dadaism, the circus, jazz, Chaplin, Keaton and American vaudeville. 'To say the Prague cultural atmosphere of the thirties is almost equal to saying Voskovec and Werich,' wrote Josef Skvorecky.[4] When the Germans invaded Czechoslovakia, theatre circles worried about them. On their arrival in America, Ray tried to find work for them. 'At that time,' Norman Lloyd says, 'I was closer to Houseman than Nick. Nick asked me to dinner one night, and he tried to get me to get them together with Houseman. I remember that night very well. I think Nick passed out. Or someone did.'

Settled into the Village, the two actors regained their professional stride only with *The Voice of America*, where they were generally admired. Houseman, like Ray, attended their rehearsals purely for pleasure, without understanding a word of the language. According to George Voscovec (he Americanized his first name when he decided to remain in the United States), 'We had regular programmes that we wrote ourselves, and they were naturally based on factual material coming from the American government's information service. So we did have certain directives under which to work. But otherwise we were extremely free, and we would do more or less what we wanted. We did satirical dialogue and gags and funny sketches, which were beamed in Czech to occupied Czechoslovakia, and were of course very violently anti-Nazi. As far as Nick's part was concerned, it was strictly technical since the whole thing was in Czech, and in any case we mostly improvised.

'Working with Nick was nice, very agreeable and great fun. We all had the same ideas about art and, needless to say, about the war. So it was a joyous and productive companionship. Nick was as I always knew him; he had that sort of vague quality about him, extremely talented, extremely inspired and imaginative, but tending to sort of drift into vagueness. The war was still on and we were still broadcasting, but I think that he, at that time, switched to movies under the influence of Gadge Kazan. And later our work was not so much fun; it was censored and "approved".'

Houseman also talked about another of Ray's activities: 'Nick did much more than just the folk stuff. He did a lot of "man in the street" work in New York – in fact, he was sort of "general features". On the night of the invasion of North Africa, Nick was very busy, and brought in French sailors for interviews, things like that. He did a lot of that mobile stuff, all on discs.'

The night of 7–8 November 1942 was one of *The Voice of America*'s great moments. Eight transmitters broadcast the news of the landings, along with Roosevelt's appeal to the French armed forces and the population to welcome the Allies as friends. Lazareff and the French desk surpassed themselves. The Quebec premier, hauled out of bed, commented on the news in French; he was followed by an old recording of Foch paying tribute to the USA. As for Nick Ray, he had gone to the gates of a foundry in the Navy yards, to wait for some workers and French sailors. 'When the guys came off shift at midnight,' according to Connie Ernst, 'he did interviews, telling them that we'd landed in North Africa. Then he came back to broadcast this along with the news. Great production. That's the kind of thing he did for us; he was allowed to use his own imagination and ideas to enhance what we were doing. We all thought it was terrific, because we were broadcasting the news and Nick was coming with the colour, so to speak.'

But *The Voice of America*, as might now be expected of any Rooseveltian venture, was in the middle of increasingly bitter political conflicts. The adoption of personal stances on the air, forbidden by official regulation but inevitable in work of this nature, became a favourite political target. The first serious instance came with the landings in North Africa, over the compromise effected between Eisenhower and Darlan; this was openly disapproved by Sherwood's team, thus giving the impression of a divergence between the policies of the President and those of the military commander-in-chief. 'It sometimes seemed,' Houseman wrote, 'as if there were two wars being fought – one officially declared, national war against the Axis, and that other bloodless, continuing conflict between Roosevelt's New Deal and its enemies, who had grown increasingly frustrated and embittered during the ten years of his presidency. There was also a third, unspoken war; [what many saw as] our final, inevitable war against the Russians.'

In the elections of 1942 the Republicans regained control of both Houses, thanks to an alliance with the Southern Democrats. Twice a year, Houseman and the OWI team appeared before the Congressional Appropriations Committee, which was concerned not only with the allocation of funds, but also with the background and ideology of employees. In 1943, the Overseas Branch received $24 million, but the Domestic Branch was eliminated shortly afterwards by a vote in the House. Hunting for Reds, or what were now called 'premature anti-facists', was starting again. At the beginning of the war, the American civil and secret services had deliberately turned a blind eye to the political affiliations of those they hired. Many Communists had even been signed up advisedly by Donovan at the OWI, members of the Communist Party being considered as patriots, very useful to the war effort.[5] A year later a team of investigators, many of them trained in the fight against social unrest in the 1930s, undertook a screening of personnel at the OWI, specifying that 'an earmark of an American Communist today is an advanced degree of patriotism. This makes it difficult to distinguish friend from foe'.[6]

Communists were far from being the only victims of this turnabout, which resulted in incessant petty harassment for the entire organization, not to mention interrogations (since, as Houseman remarked, 'it took them years to dig up the past'). In April 1943, amid a flurry of resignations, Houseman handed in his and prepared to return to Hollywood, where a contract as a producer awaited him at Paramount.

In November, a week after the House had approved an additional grant of $5 million for the Overseas Branch, the Republican senator from Illinois, Fred A. Busbey, made public a list of twenty-two OWI employees with allegedly Communistic ideologies.[7] Heading this alphabetical list was a close friend of Houseman's, Joseph Barnes, Moscow correspondent for the *Herald Tribune* from 1937 to 1939 (which was enough to point the finger), who was Sherwood's deputy and director of Atlantic operations in the latter's absence. Also on the list were names as diverse as Mitchell Grayson, the Austrian (socialist) writer Leo Lania, Tony Kraber ('member of the executive board of the Theater Arts Committee – TAC – popularly known as "Stalin's Fifth Column on Broadway"', and a member of the League of American Writers'), the black actor Canada Lee, Irving Lerner, Alfred Saxe and, in seventeenth place, 'Nicholas K. Ray, Eastern press and radio programme director, salary $3,800 a year. Discharged from the WPA community service of Washington, DC, for Communist activity. Member of the League of Writers.'

It was in May 1943 that a 'confidential source' had informed the FBI that this was the reason for Ray's dismissal from the WPA. Neither the Dies Committee nor Hoover's agents had been able to find confirmation for the charge, and by July had given up pursuing their inquiries. At this same period, moreover, the Attorney General was rescinding the 'Special Case procedure' in wartime classifications established by the FBI, who had drawn from them a list of suspects to be placed under custodial detention in case of emergency. Nicholas Ray appeared on the list, under the classification B–2, as a Communist.[8] As for his membership of the League of American Writers, it automatically put him, at the very least, in the extremely elastic category of 'sympathizers'. The League, accused of being a front organization for the American Communist Party, had in reality covered a much wider political spectrum, especially during the Spanish Civil War. But its adherence between 1939 and 1941 (latterly under the presidency of Dashiell Hammett) to a strictly pro-Soviet line, with the vacillations that implied, had drained it of all content and left it dying, if not defunct. Until when was Ray a member, if indeed he was? No other source, not even the FBI dossier, mentions the matter. (In other respects, membership of the League would imply writing ambitions unfulfilled, at this time at least, in Ray's activities.)

Barely four days after Senator Busbey's scoop, an FBI official wrote to his director, J. Edgar Hoover, that the case of Nicholas K. Ray was considered 'as not warranting investigation'. In nine other cases, inquiries were under way, or else the OWI, informed, had already traversed the

claim. The information relating to the twelve remaining names was too
unspecific to warrant investigation!

Connie Ernst has remained very discreet on this subject: 'We never
really discussed politics.' She tends to see his commitment as limited to
his barefoot guitar players. 'He lived his life very much in compartments
– he was very masculine in that.' But she was struck by the ability
Nick had 'to walk *across*, not *through*, the most personal problems and
survive, where others wouldn't have taken it . . . I wasn't seeing him
during the witch hunts, but I can readily imagine, on the one hand the
terror it could mean for people in their daily lives, and on the other, how
Nick would have walked around the experience. That's something that
protected him all his life.'

The failure to press actual charges did not ease the general situation.
The days of *The Voice of America*, in the form that Houseman had
given it, were numbered. In January 1944 three of Sherwood's immediate
subordinates – Joseph Barnes, Deputy Director of Atlantic Operations,
James Warburg, Deputy Director in charge of Psychological Warfare,
and Edd Johnson, Head of the Overseas Editorial Board – were forced to
resign. Ray followed soon after. He and Houseman have given diverging
accounts of his dismissal, which beg rather more questions than they
answer. Ray has described how 'I was queried at length by the government intelligence. The final question of the fourth hour was stated thusly:
"On the night of so and so, such a young lady was seen to enter your
apartment at 8.30 at night, and not to leave until 8 the next morning.
What do you have to say to that?" – "It was a delightful evening."

'There were lots of questions like that. Finally, I said: "Gentlemen,
when I volunteered to serve the US in this war, I was not asked to take an
oath of celibacy." And so my connection with the government service
was subtly ended with the co-operation of courageous Lou Cowan
[Houseman's successor].'⁹

In the version Houseman gives of the episode, he sees it as an illustration of one of his theories about Ray, which he nevertheless refrains
from developing: 'He was thrown out of OWI after I left, I always
thought on political grounds, swept out along with the rest of us. But in
fact the ostensible reason was homosexuality, and only because when
Nick went to the Draft Board (he wouldn't have got into the army
anyway because of his bad heart), he told them of his homosexual experiences as a young man. And he was actually fired from OWI for this
remote homosexual connection.'

It is probable that Ray hung on to his job so long only because of the
presence of Connie Ernst. But at the OWI, she had met a young editor,

Michael Bessie (blows were exchanged, on at least one occasion, between him and Nick). The OWI moreover sent Connie to London to prepare a live broadcast with D-Day in mind. According to Houseman, Nick tried to accompany her, but was refused a passport (just as Houseman had been a year earlier; in Ray's case, for the political reasons already mentioned). His little black joke, taking Connie to see *Lifeboat* on the eve of her departure (it's about survivors from a ship sunk by a German U-Boat in the Atlantic), fixes the earliest possible date for their separation: Hitchcock's film opened in New York on 12 January 1944.

At OWI, Nick had renewed acquaintance with Kazan's wife, Molly Day Thacher – she became Houseman's assistant – and this led to a revival of his friendship with 'Gadge', now one of Broadway's most noted directors. In the interim, Kazan had gained some experience in cinema, both in documentary and in the studios. He was about to embark on his first feature as a director for a major studio. Encouraged by his wife, who spoke highly of Ray's work on radio, Kazan suggested that Nick follow him out to the West Coast to learn about film-making.[10]

8

First Stay in Hollywood

Prior to this departure in March 1944, Hollywood and the cinema seemed a logical step in Ray's somewhat somnambulistic progress, though little different from any of the others through which he was accumulating experience in every field; it was logical, after everything else, that he should also try films. His interest seemed to be in new methods of communication, in neglected means of expression, rather than in artistic forms. Of course he dreamed, like those who preceded him, Kazan and Losey, of becoming a director. But why not in the theatre? Possible points of contact with the cinema had not been lacking in the past; why the Theatre of Action and not Frontier Films? Why community theatre and radio, rather than documentary, with the Resettlement Administration, with WPA, with OWI? Losey, Kazan, Houseman, Irving Lerner, almost all the members of the Group Theater (not to mention Orson Welles) had some experience of cinema in one guise or another – marginal, independent, documentary, or even major studio – before choosing between Broadway and Hollywood.

Apart from one offer of a role in a film following his first stage appearances (which, it went without saying given the spirit of the times, he could only refuse; and so, following Kazan's advice, he did),[1] the evidence suggests that Nick Ray had hitherto remained no more than a filmgoer, and an occasional – though not uninformed – one at that. He certainly shared the tastes and interests of his friends; in the 1930s, their great passion was for foreign films, not so much the Soviet cinema, whose last great eye-openers, *The Road to Life* or *Aerograd*, dated from the early sound period, as the French, admired as avant-garde art (*Le Sang d'un poète*), a cinema of actors (Raimu) and directors (Renoir). If Ray's personal preferences were in any way divergent, we have only one piece of evidence: one of his favourite films, if not his favourite, was Leo McCarey's *Ruggles of Red Gap*, released in 1933.[2] This satire of middle American manners was one of the first films to reveal McCarey as a master of emotional ambiguity.

In January 1944 the New York attorney William ·H. Fitelson had recommended Ray to an RKO executive, Peter Rathvon. His departure with Kazan was therefore not entirely a matter of impulse. Fitelson wrote that Ray was 'anxious to go to Hollywood as a dialogue or assistant director'.[3] There was no reaction from RKO. Despite his reputation in broadcasting and in the folk music field, the studios had no reason to be interested in him. They were interested, on the other hand, in Kazan, now one of the most brilliant directors on Broadway. His latest productions had been impressive box-office successes: 359 performances for Thornton Wilder's *The Skin of Our Teeth*, 348 for *Harriet*, 567 for the musical comedy *One Touch of Venus* (S.J. Perelman, Ogden Nash and Kurt Weill). Following the disbanding of the Group Theater, Kazan had no further ties in New York; and with both Warner Brothers and Darryl F. Zanuck's 20th Century-Fox bidding for his services, he chose the latter.

So Kazan took Nick with him when he left for Hollywood after the première of *Jacobowsky and the Colonel* on 14 March. Awaiting him at Fox was *A Tree Grows in Brooklyn*, an adaptation of a weighty novel by Betty Smith about first-generation immigrants. The reasons why Kazan agreed to direct it are easy to understand, especially in retrospect: affinities with the themes of many of his later and more personal films may be found in it. But he had no hand in either the preparation of the script (credited to Tess Slesinger and Frank Davis, it was considered sufficiently prestigious to figure as the only Fox film represented in the collection *Best Film Plays of 1945*), or in decisions about the production, costumes, sets or make-up. 'The clothes were always clean, the mother was too pretty, and the father too nice.'[4]

Ray's contract started on 30 March. He followed the filming of tests, and was present throughout the shooting: he watched the producer struggling with an unfilmable script, saw the director of photography Leon Shamroy, secure in his two Oscars, suggest to the producer, a few days after filming began, that he should co-direct. Professional lessons that did not go unheeded: when Ray made his own début as a director, he would choose a tyro cameraman, even though aware that he would make the same exacting demands on him as Kazan had.[5]

'He was ... hanging around,' Kazan recalled. 'He was on the set taking notes. He made a notebook of things I'd said, a little *cahier*,[6] which he'd expand on or elaborate. He was wonderful; he was on the set every day and very devoted. Nick was also very impressed by the producer of that picture, Bud Lighton – Louis D. Lighton – who was an extreme right-winger and a fine man. Nick was impressed with his ideas about film, so some of his notes came from Lighton. I would parrot what Lighton said too.'

Was Ray under the influence of Lighton or of Kazan? During the making of this film, Ray defined some of his ideas about cinema in a fairly precise way, and in terms which were to remain unchanged. At the beginning of his copy of the script, for example, he noted: 'Find the tension in each scene – what breaks it and what movement sets it free. Close-ups when life – changes – reactions occur.' In an interview during the 1960s, he said: 'Kazan was the first to point out to me the validity of the hero in terms of audience identification: that a hero has sometimes to be shown just as confused or screwed up as you. But regardless of that, you have to be able to say that if you were at that particular moment and in that particular situation you would do as he has done, whether it's right or wrong. I think that's the dynamic investigation of the hero.' Kazan, in conversation with Michel Ciment, described this idea as stemming from Lighton.[7]

Ray's function on *A Tree Grows in Brooklyn* remains unclear; an assistant content merely to assist, according to Kazan; according to others, sketch artist. His subsequent habit of sketching shots for his films (often to end up with something different) tends to confirm this. Nick's copy of the script, at all events, is covered with notes concerned exclusively with the performances of the two children, analogous to his marginal notes for Gloria Grahame on the script for *In a Lonely Place*.

Kazan also put his knowledge of music to use. After the director's departure, Ray worked (around 20 November) with Alfred Newman on putting the finishing touches to the music track, which is remarkably rich.[8] For Houseman, there is no doubt that 'Gadge and Nick' learned cutting together on *A Tree Grows in Brooklyn*. Kazan mentions a more basic apprenticeship: 'I think he was learning an unsentimental attitude towards material. The custom there was to deal with heroes and villains, and I think Nick learned . . . well, I guess what I tried to learn: to be realistic about the emotional values of something.'

Ray also learned the paradoxical ways in which a studio functioned, and watched Kazan at work, discovering with him the differences between stage and screen acting. 'During the casting,' he noted, 'some incredible tests were shot. For instance, a test of a remarkable actress who later went through a long period of institutionalization. She must have been twenty-three or twenty-four and very sophisticated at the time, with a fabulous body. At the request of the studio heads, they taped over her tits to give her a flat chest, so that she could appear for rehearsal and eventually an expensive test for the role of Francie, a twelve-year-old girl. We ended up with Peggy Ann Garner, a child actress with no stage experience, who could not be loaded down with any theories of acting. But she did have the experience of a broken family, a mother who was a lush and a bad cheque passer. [As the mother] Dorothy McGuire, from a fairly elegant background, well-educated, married into a Northeastern blue-blood family. And Jimmy Dunn, who could have been a vaudeville comic, associated mostly with gamblers and musicians and burlesque people. He had all of the realistic qualities of the [father's] character. He was a drunk, drank himself out of the business. He was a constant risk in the minds of everybody. He was also a beautiful human being. And he gave an Academy Award-winning performance. Kazan's extraordinary technique brought them all together in a unit. He got them all in the same key, they all belonged together, not one note jarring. After the test with these three people, I made a note: "When you find the real thing, fuck acting." At the moment you start with that and you've said "Fuck acting", then begins the most subtle kind of direction with a non-actor.

'Another of my notes was: Working with an actor direct from the theatre, one who has not had experience of the camera but has had the experience of projecting what he is doing into row Z of the balcony . . . the actor, if he has a method of work at all, must be encouraged in his method of work so that he can arrive at the same truth of emotion, and then you must help him sit on it, because the camera is a microscope and an enlarger.'

After completing *A Tree Grows in Brooklyn*, Kazan moved back to the East Coast and other directing jobs, while Ray spent some more time at Fox with the vaguest possible status: technical supervisor and director.[9] His only credited job was as dialogue director on a minor B thriller, *A Caribbean Mystery*. This was the third version of the same story produced by the studio in twelve years. James Dunn, despite his Oscar-winning success with Kazan, was embarked on a descent into B movies, repeating what had happened during his first career with Fox in 1931–5. Here he played the lead, a Brooklyn detective handling an investigation on an island, amid quicksands and alligators. 'Less shooting here means more shooting there – save film!' was the motto heading studio documents. Director Robert D. Webb, whose first film this was, wrapped up *A Caribbean Mystery* in twenty-five days (17 January–14 February 1945). Three scriptwriters followed one after another, and Ray made revisions to the dialogue (officially recorded at least twice) during shooting.

During 1944, an election year, militancy on behalf of the war effort was pretty strenuous on the West Coast, and Ray immediately joined the movement, which was spearheaded by the vast Hollywood Writers' Mobilization Group. No sooner had he arrived than, on 22 March 1944, he was presenting a report on the Folk Festival Committee to a meeting of the Continuations Committee. The folk music connection was also to lead, indirectly, to his next job.

The Writers' Mobilization was already the target of attacks by an evocatively titled pressure group, the Motion Picture Alliance for the Preservation of American Ideals, one of whose pillars was none other than Louis D. Lighton. Also in March, the Alliance called on the Dies Committee, the first version of the House Un-American Activities Committee, to come and investigate Hollywood (an unprecedented instance of an appeal for outside intervention from within an industry). In May, under the aegis of the Screen Writers' Guild, a coalition of professional and trade union organizations pledged loyalty to Roosevelt during the electoral campaign which was starting.[10]

Ray was also in touch again with the OWI, whose West Coast branch was producing documentaries intended as an introduction to the United States for foreign audiences. As on the East Coast, the watchdogs in Congress were suspicious of any critical views concerning the country and of any Rooseveltian propaganda, thus limiting the films in what they could say. As a result, produced under the supervision of the writer Philip Dunne, they tended to be at their best when sticking to generalized topics: between 1941 and 1944, for instance, *The Town* (Sternberg), *Valley of the Tennessee, Autobiography of a Jeep, Swedes in America* (with Ingrid Bergman), *Salute to France* (Renoir), *Hymn of the Nations* (with Toscanini). In June, Ray was assigned to a project on American folk music. In October, he was one of fifty writers from the Mobilization who were working on fourteen scripts under preparation (it was in this same month that the two-day hearings triggered by the Alliance's initiative took place).

John Houseman was in Hollywood, working as a producer at Paramount. He and Dunne, with the approval of Robert Riskin, who was in charge of the entire project, decided to make a film for the Overseas Branch, drawing on Mobilization and Paramount studio technicians for assistance.

Dunne wanted to make a film which would explain the democratic electoral system in terms simple enough to be understood the world over. For a relatively abstract description of the three powers, Houseman and Dunne resorted to animation, which they entrusted to John Hubley, a refugee from the Disney studios (and later 'pre-designer' on Losey's early films). Around this didactic section, the process is illustrated by way of voting day in Riverton, a fictional small town in California. Then the horizon broadens, incorporating newsreel footage. This part was written by Howard Koch (who, after his radio script for *The War of the Worlds*, had become one of Warner Brothers' star writers). John Berry, also a former member of the Mercury Theater (and like Houseman, a client of

Nicholas Ray

MCA and Lew Wasserman), directed the staged scenes in three days. Virgil Thomson, an old friend of Houseman's, composed and directed the score, which was recorded in New York. Ray was Houseman's 'general assistant'.

Tuesday in November, whose titles list no names, runs for seventeen minutes. A travelling shot from a car takes us through an as yet deserted small town, where the shops and the school are closed for election day. A woman gets out of a car: she is the school's headmistress, and she opens up the classroom which has been transformed into a polling station. The other officials, representing 'the major political parties' (not once does the commentary refer to the American two-party system), arrive and are sworn in (direct sound). The first voter is the milkman. In front of the polling booth, the camera stops: 'That's as far as we go' declares the commentary (which constantly stresses the strict observation of procedure, the secrecy of the vote, respect for the law and the Constitution). Assuming 'miraculous powers', the camera nevertheless enters the booth.

14   *Tuesday in November*

Thus begins the animation sequence: starting with the complicated ballot paper, it illustrates the distinction between the three powers.

A new segment of the film then begins. In documentary footage alternating with staged scenes (involving some Hollywood supporting actors), voters are seen throughout the country, from the Riverton polling station to presidential candidate Dewey and soldiers fighting on other continents.

Over an evocation of the national conventions, the campaign, and 'the great debate', the commentary notes that 'for the first time in American history, organized labour takes an active part in the campaign'. It then focuses on the role played by radio: 'Time on the air is paid for by all parties [sic] and distributed evenly among them; even the party in power has no advantage over its opponents.' More than 70 million Americans heard the electoral speeches by the candidates on the radio (staged and documentary shots of people listening).

'Now all that is over': electors leave the polling stations. The teacher telephones the results (direct sound). At a radio station, a man comes in with a sheet of paper. In Times Square, a huge crowd waits in the night beneath the *New York Times'* illuminated sign which displays the results. 'A nation of 140 million has elected a government,' the commentary concludes. The music, which accompanies the film without interruption, is an arrangement of choral or fugal forms, folk themes or dances, and developments of chords or scales, answering between wood and strings. A fugue in single flow accompanies the two-and-a-half minute closing sequence.[11] The harmonic movement is dominated by a sense of serenity, totally unstressed, which is largely responsible for the film's success.

Ray was present throughout filming, his contribution mainly involving work on the post-production stages of cutting and sound editing, crucial to the successful completion of a film of this kind: *Tuesday in November* may be thought of as Ray's first film, according to John Houseman. 'There was a good deal of music and sound, and Nick was very, very good at it. He knew a great deal about sound editing, and while it's not absolutely the same as film cutting, it is essentially the same. He was an absolutely brilliant sound editor in all those montages and things that we used to do at the OWI.' *Tuesday in November* was distributed in more than twenty foreign language versions, and Houseman considers it 'one of the few films I have made about which I have absolutely no regrets or second thoughts'.

Continuing his civic activities with the Writers' Mobilization, Ray shortly became involved with a tribute to Roosevelt, on Monday 23 April 1945, eleven days after the President's death. Initiated by Mayor Fletcher

Bowron, this Civic Tribute took place at the Hollywood Bowl. The veteran actor Jean Hersholt was chairman, Dore Schary the producer, Joseph Losey and Nick Ray the co-directors, Franz Waxman the musical director. It comprised a series of invocations, addresses, prayers, pledges and songs (one of them by Earl Robinson), in which many stars took part: Walter Huston, Edward G. Robinson, Orson Welles, Ingrid Bergman, Eddie Cantor, Frank Sinatra, James Cagney; plus a fine collection of accents in evocation of the United Nations: Charles Boyer, Ronald Colman, Philip Dorn, Jean Hersholt, Alexander Knox, Dame May Whitty.[12] Again for Dore Schary, Losey and Ray were also to collaborate on staging the Academy Award ceremony (then a public occasion, but relayed only by radio).[13]

Despite this catalogue of activities, the months Ray spent on the West Coast were dominated by unemployment, financial problems and frustration. Connie Ernst had been sent to Los Angeles from London by the OWI in August-September 1944. Apart from this period of reunion, Ray had several affairs, mostly unhappy: with the Fox actress who had tested for *A Tree Grows in Brooklyn*, with Doris Dowling and with Judy Holliday.[14] According to Norman Lloyd, 'Nick always had much charm and was most inarticulate. I never knew how he ever got anything done, because you'd wait for a long time for that sentence to come out. You didn't know what the hell he was thinking about. He had many of the mannerisms of Joe Losey, but Joe was more articulate, Joe would get it out. Nick seemed to be in deep thought, nearly always. And one never knew whether he was or not.'

On his arrival, he lived in an apartment at 1304½ North Harper. A villa in Californian baroque style, a tree in the middle of a patio, a little terrace leading to this and out to the street, overlooking the crossing with Fountain Street and an apartment block.[15] The place was summarily reconstructed as a studio set for *In a Lonely Place*, and one of the rare exterior shots in the film offers a glimpse of its perspective on the street. Soon Ray found a bungalow in Santa Monica, 207 Ocean Front, where he had Houseman as a neighbour. He spent the rest of this first stay there. Houseman ironically mentions Ray's double suicide attempt with Judy Holliday in Santa Monica Bay. Ray was a frequent visitor to Gene Kelly's house, which was always full of visitors from the East Coast. 'He'd come to my house and just be one of the gang,' Kelly says. 'We all came from New York and we were theatre people, but we became very much in love with pictures. So everybody in that group was thinking about movies and ideas. Nick would tend to disappear from time to time, but when he'd come back every once in a while he'd always drop in and say hello. As if he'd just gone down to the corner.' Silvia Richards, then an aspiring screenwriter married to a radio writer, made his acquaintance at this time:

'I think he was a friend of George Rosenberg, who was a friend of Natalie Talmadge, and I lived next door to Natalie Talmadge's beach house. And Nick began to wander in and out of my house. He was madly in love with a wonderful, tall, dark-haired girl, who later married Artie Shaw. I didn't know him to have any jobs; he was very impecunious, so I have no idea how he was living. He was always trying to sell ideas. Then he would come and talk about writing. He was sort of brooding. Very emotional. I thought he was brilliant but would never make it as a writer, because he had no sense of structure, no discipline. I think that he really didn't know anything about the emotional life of people, because he certainly didn't know anything about his own. I don't think he had much of a sense of story structure; but later on, when he was directing, I do think he had a way of creating mood in a picture, a richness of mood and emotion. Without ever having to define it.'

The *Los Angeles Daily News* of 25 April 1945 noted one of Ray's 'ideas': 'The first penetrating study of the Nazi mind has come in screenplay form, from actor Howard Da Silva in collaboration with Nick Ray. Doctors in the screenplay hope to learn from the patient's reaction to insulin shock just what makes a Nazi tick. What they do discover is the way the "master race" virus is injected into each generation.'[16] Ray's meeting with Da Silva evidently took place during his activities with the Writers' Mobilization.

The only trace of an idea he may have sold is in the files of the Writers' Guild, crediting him with collaboration on 'the original story' of a Monogram film, *Swing Parade of 1946*. Directed by Phil Karlson, this was a collection of songs, comedy sketches and similar material linked by a minimal plot. Gale Storm sang *On the Sunny Side of the Street* and *Oh, Brother*; Connee Boswell, *Stormy Weather* and *Just a Little Fond Affection*; the ragbag cast included the Three Stooges and Ed Brophy. The film was reviewed in the *Motion Picture Daily* on 28 January 1946. By then, Nick Ray had been in New York for several months.

9

New York Interlude

Houseman had preceded Ray to the East Coast. Although he had produced two successful films at Paramount (*Miss Susie Slagle's* and *The Blue Dahlia*), he left to accept an offer of a non-exclusive contract at RKO for one film a year from head of production William Dozier. In New York, the summer of 1945 loomed workless.

'I was sort of hanging around,' Houseman recalled, 'and an old friend of mine, who had been at CBS at the time Orson and I were doing our radio there, said one day, "Would you like to try your hand at television?" I said sure, I talked to Nick about it right then and there, and we wondered what we could do. There'd been a very successful radio show called *Sorry, Wrong Number*, written by Bernard Herrmann's wife, Lucille Fletcher, a very close friend. So we thought, if we can get permission, why don't we do that as a television show, because the limitations were two cameras, and we had about a thousand bucks for the set, which was nothing at all. I asked Nick if he would direct it while I produced, and that's what happened.'

Sorry, Wrong Number was virtually a monologue for a bed-ridden woman, dependent on her telephone, who overhears plans for a murder in which it gradually becomes evident that she is the intended victim.[1] Broadcast on 25 May 1943, this 27-minute episode in the *Suspense* radio series was so successful that it was repeated seven times (and translated into fifteen languages) before being adapted several years later – by Lucille Fletcher herself, for Hal B. Wallis – as a movie directed by Anatole Litvak and starring Barbara Stanwyck. So it was a hot property when Houseman and Ray decided to turn it into a half-hour television programme. They did the adaptation together.

In 1945, television meant some 10,000 sets in the USA. CBS, one of the two big networks, did its best to create its own production units, brought together from all over the place, by sending them to improvise shows in studios set up in the huge empty mezzanine at Grand Central Station. There, television cameramen, designers and technicians were trained. The average production cost in those days was $1,000 a minute, as against $10,000 in the cinema. Agnes Moorehead, who had created the *Sorry, Wrong Number* role on radio, was now working in Hollywood. To bring her right across the country would be too expensive. Instead,

Houseman chose Mildred Natwick, whom he had directed in a radio adaptation of Euripides' *The Trojan Women*, and who worked more often on the stage than in films. After a week of rehearsals, the filming took two days.

'It was electronic, live,' Houseman recalled. 'The cameras were enormous, absolutely unmanageable, lighting was totally primitive. I did get an old friend of mine, Millie Natwick, to play it, and so that part of it was all right. It was the sort of thing that worked very well. It was a big success, we got wonderful reviews, but there was no great temptation at that moment to stay in television. But I think Nick probably learned quite a bit from it. He probably added just a little bit of expertise, but he learned to produce, he learned something about framing. But it was all done so quickly; I don't remember theorizing much about it.'

In his memoirs, Houseman quotes the *Variety* comment: 'The most successful instance of the blending of top drawer film artistry with a live video performance. The show was tops . . . However, one Houseman does not make a summer.'

To have worked in television was no passport to fame in Hollywood, and it was only the success of the programme (as noted in *Variety*, which did not yet carry television reviews) that made Ray's very first *mise en scène* memorable. Nevertheless, at a time when television was a prime target for movie jokes (the exchange between Marilyn Monroe and George Sanders in *All About Eve*: 'Do they have auditions in television too?' – 'That's all television is, my dear . . . nothing but auditions'), Ray persisted in thinking of it as a possibility, not as a last resort. Years later, he would recall his first words, as a director, to his cameraman on *They Live By Night*: 'Every mistake in this film is going to be mine. I want to find out if film is for me or not, and if it's not, I'm going back to Broadway, and there's a little thing called television coming up.'

The producer Michael Myerberg invited Houseman to direct a stage production: a musical comedy based on a Chinese classic, *Pipa ji*, which had itself been successfully staged in America a few years earlier (as *Pi-Pa-Ki*). Myerberg, still in search of backing, had a star: Mary Martin, made famous by the song *My Heart Belongs to Daddy*.[2] He had also selected several creative collaborators, most notably the great designer Robert Edmond Jones. Contracts with Houseman and Ray, the latter engaged as assistant, were signed in August. At that stage, Myerberg had made up his mind to finance the show himself, a decision for which Ray was always to remain grateful to him.

The cast for the musical, called *Lute Song*, included a virtually unknown actor of Russian-Chinese origin – Yul Brynner – in the role of the heroine's husband. According to the programme, he had seen *Pipa ji* performed by Mei Lan Fang in Peking, and had fought on the Republican side in Spain. Brought to the USA by Michael Chekhov, he had appeared on Broadway only in one of the latter's productions. Houseman vaguely remembered him as an occasional announcer on French programmes for *The Voice of America*. The hero's second wife, the Princess who elevates him to a position of importance in the Imperial court, was played by Helen Craig, who had made her debut in Orson Welles's production of *Julius Caesar*. Supporting roles were entrusted to Augustin Duncan, Isadora's blind brother, and to Nancy Davis (the future Nancy Reagan).

Rehearsals started in October. Houseman worked alone on the dramatic scenes, which were more complex than in traditional musicals. With the composer Raymond Scott at the piano, he took the principals through their solos and duets. The big musical numbers and the crowd scenes were rehearsed under the joint direction of the choreographer Yeichi Nimura, Nick, and Houseman himself. 'Nick's unselfish collaboration,' Houseman wrote, 'was of inestimable value: between us we were able to watch and control every aspect of the production and to maintain the unity of style without which it would have fallen apart.'[3] On one occasion, Ray sought the advice of Gene Kelly, who was charmed by what he saw.[4] According to Broadway custom, the production went the break-in route before opening: New Haven (Shubert Theater), Boston, Philadelphia (Forrest Theater from 17 December). *Lute Song* toured slightly in advance of a Garson Kanin comedy, *Born Yesterday*, whose star was replaced at a moment's notice by Judy Holliday. The two companies crossed paths in Philadelphia, and at the Warwick Hotel, Houseman and Ray coached Judy in her lines for the role that was to make her famous overnight.

After seven weeks of polishing, *Lute Song* opened on Broadway at the Plymouth Theater on Saturday, 2 February 1946.[5] Houseman notes a number of compromises resulting from this break-in route. Mary Martin's impresario husband insisted on modifications in the lighting and in Robert Edmond Jones's costumes, and he had the ending changed: originally, torn in his love for two women, the hero was allowed, by special imperial decree, to remain married to both. In the bowdlerized version, the Princess gave up the hero to his village sweetheart.

As one might imagine, and as the original cast recording confirms, *Lute Song* was an extremely pleasant oriental spectacle. The composer stressed the exotic elements, the strong dramatic situations of the play did the rest. The tastefulness exercised by Houseman and his collaborators kept it far removed from standard Broadway kitsch, but equally remote from the ironies of Hanns Eisler in his 'chinoiseries' for Brecht or the new spirit soon to be imposed on the musical by young composers, dancers, writers and choreographers with *On the Town*.

The reviews were generally very favourable. *Lute Song* was enough of a success to run until June, and to be revived in Chicago in the autumn. Houseman nevertheless estimates Michael Myerberg's loss to have been over a quarter of a million dollars.

A few months later, a repeat of the *Lute Song* episode seemed on the cards: Houseman and Ray, returning from California with a sense of discouragement, became involved with another musical. It started as a project brought to Houseman by the black designer Perry Watkins: a musical inspired by John Gay's *The Beggar's Opera*, which was to be Broadway's first 'integrated' show, with a mixture of black and white in both cast and orchestra. Watkins's idea was to bring together the black composer Duke Ellington and the white writer John Latouche, author of the lyrics for *Ballad for Americans* and a successful black musical, *Cabin in the Sky* (directed by George Balanchine on stage, Vincente Minnelli on film).

Houseman accepted, closing his eyes to all the auguries of failure: Latouche's libretto was far from finished, and Ellington's continuing availability to work on the score was unlikely. This time, Nick Ray was to serve as associate director. Or at any rate, that was how Houseman introduced him to Alfred Drake, who had shot to stardom with *Oklahoma!* According to Perry Bruskin, who played a small part, Houseman contented himself with supervising Ray's direction, and the latter found the responsibility too heavy. It soon became clear that it would be a very costly production, and that the backing was intermittent and unreliable. It also became apparent that Latouche was incapable of finishing the libretto. Houseman and Ray managed to get the first act together, and the other two were improvised somehow or other in rehearsal – the last virtually during the première. As for Duke Ellington, busy with tours, he left it to his arranger, Billy 'Swee'Pea' Strayhorn, to assemble some existing pieces he hadn't used yet.[6] But the lack of a structured score made itself cruelly felt. Billy Strayhorn impressed Houseman and Ray by more than once saving the day.

The excitement roused by the project, the enthusiasm of the cast, put the permanent state of crisis out of mind. Besides Alfred Drake the cast included Libby Holman, Zero Mostel (a Café Society discovery) as Peachum, Avon Long (from the original cast of *Porgy*), and the black singer and dancer Marie Bryant (from Katherine Dunham's company). Among the dancers, the twenty-five-year-old choreographer Valerie Bettis selec-

15   *Beggars' Holiday*: sets by Oliver Smith

ted two unknowns: Herbert Ross and Marjorie Bell (later to become Marge Champion).

At the end of November, the first try-out performances of *Beggars' Holiday* took place in Connecticut, at Hartford, then at New Haven, and finally, three weeks at the Opera House in Boston, where the crisis came. The day after the première, the *Boston Herald*'s judgement was that, 'There is such a raft of material unorganized that it is difficult to sort the good from the indifferent and to understand what it is all about'. In conclusion, the review noted that: '*Twilight Alley* will have a new title, *Beggars' Holiday*, when it opens in New York. At the present time it is probably superfluous to say that what it needs more than a different name is serious editing, pruning and a sense of direction.'

The role of director no longer counted for much, an associate director even less. A few days later, the producers and backers made the logical – and radical – decisions: a well-known Broadway director, George Abbott, was urgently called in to do a complete overhaul on *Beggars' Holiday* and make it presentable for Broadway. Houseman withdrew (or was fired). Libby Holman, nervous and not at her best – only her sardonic *Lullaby for Junior*, sung to Macheath in jail, received favourable notice – was replaced by Bernice Parks.[7] Perry Bruskin felt that 'all Libby Holman had to do was walk on stage to reveal more presence than that poor soul'. He also described Nick Ray's reaction:

'There was a big furore going on on stage and the set was being moved around, didn't fit properly on the stage. Oliver Smith was very upset, everybody was running around, and Nick was in front of the theatre . . . playing craps with some of the stagehands who weren't working at that moment and some of the front of house people! One of the reasons was that he knew nobody else would dare to do that, and *because* no one would dare, he wanted to do it. He tried to make it seem absolutely normal, but the excitement that he engendered was too great to let you feel that. That stood out in my mind as representative of how unique and how different he wanted to be all his life. In the middle of an out-of-town situation with a new play trying out, all the problems that were involved, the script not in the best shape, here he is, the director of the play, playing dice in front of the theatre!'

Houseman stayed in Boston while the reins were being handed over. He suggested to Abbott that he should keep Ray on, to make the transition easier. Abbott 'gratefully' accepted, Houseman wrote, but it seems that Ray's continuing presence was not universally appreciated. In Hartford, the writers Paul and Jane Bowles, old friends of Latouche and Oliver Smith, attended one of the first performances. They made the acquaintance of Libby Holman and Ray; the start of a long friendship in the first case, but not the second. A year later, Jane Bowles wrote, with reference to Ray, of 'the general disinterest we showed him' and of 'Oliver's rudeness' towards him: reactions doubtless provoked by his retention in the company while Libby Holman was replaced.[8] From then on, however, Nick himself was more or less pushed aside. According to Alfred Drake, 'Nick, while he was still being kept on, disappeared, because Mr Abbott didn't feel the need for a co-director. The show was in terrible trouble. Once Mr Abbott came in, we hardly heard a peep out of Nick any longer, because he was put in such a subordinate position. He made a joke about it at some rehearsal when Mr Abbott wasn't there and he had been asked to give some notes or something. He said he seemed to have lost his voice for quite a long time during the out-of-town.'

'Lines and whole scenes have been cut, new lyrics have been added and the material has been worked over to such an extent that even the members of the cast don't recognize it as the same show,' a journalist wrote on 23 December. Houseman himself felt that the New York version opened 'with relatively few changes or improvements'.[9] He nevertheless decided, a few days before the opening night, to have his name removed. Abbott, whose involvement meant that the necessary backing was once more forthcoming, didn't want to lend his name to the production either. Paradoxically, Nick Ray – not mentioned in the Boston programme –

found himself the only director credited in New York, for the dramatic scenes: 'Book directed by Nicholas Ray.'

When *Beggars' Holiday* opened at the Broadway Theater on 26 December 1946, its costs were over $300,000, and it had become the most expensive musical show of the season.[10] Despite the gloomy predictions and the sense of discouragement shared by everyone concerned (reflected in the general recollection of it as a resounding flop), it ran for a full three months, and was then revived in Chicago – though that wasn't enough to make it break even financially. The critics were agreeably surprised, too. The star of the show seems to have been Oliver Smith's sets, stylized cityscapes which prefigured his own designs, years later, for *West Side Story*.[11] Latouche and Ellington also drew compliments. Perry Bruskin has his own view of *Beggars' Holiday*: 'Houseman felt he had the coming together of his own feelings about theatre, the kind of theatre he enjoyed doing because it was a unique original statement. I think it reflected Houseman's attitude towards the theatre of the 1930s, because those were his most exciting days, and Nick and I came from that same background. He and Latouche represented that same period. There was a dynamic reason for the grouping of those people. The only thing they did *not* anticipate was that the play wasn't that good.'

No matter; a few weeks later, Nick Ray left once more for Hollywood, this time to stay.

10

They Live by Night

A few days after the first night of *Lute Song*, Ray left by car for California in the company of Houseman and screenwriter Herman J. Mankiewicz. On arrival, Houseman had him hired, at $200 a week, as his personal assistant on a project called *That Girl from Memphis* (21 February 1946). The argument Houseman put up to executive producer William Dozier involved Ray's work with Alan Lomax and his knowledge of the milieu in which the film was set, as well as his active participation in 'conferences' with Mankiewicz in New York and during the trip west. He wrote to Dozier: 'I think of him no less highly than I did of Jack Berry as potential for a film director.' (John Berry, whose directing début had been with Houseman as producer, was making a film with Dozier at the time.)

The Hollywood to which Nicholas Ray came, and where he was to work for twelve years, was determined by the power of the studios, for whom 1946 marked a high tide of prosperity. Production for the majors was a closed circuit: everything from original idea to cinema auditorium belonged to them, by long-term contract in the case of human assets. Any other form of production was precluded. But prosperity creates its own antibodies: the late 1940s saw the rising importance of Poverty Row studios, the increasing power of the guilds and unions, a sharpening urge to independence among stars, most of whom were prepared to take the risk, and the eventual emergence of a new voice: the agent, hitherto simply a business manager, but fast taking secret control of the industry.

After eleven weeks of work on *That Girl from Memphis* (leaving no one remembering a thing about it), Houseman took Ray and Mankiewicz to the Campbell Ranch, on a *mesa* near Victorville, where Mankiewicz had written the first draft of *Citizen Kane*. There Nick Ray began work on adapting a novel by Edward Anderson, *Thieves Like Us*. Houseman didn't buy it, he found it: a studio property which had become something of a recurring nightmare.

This novel of the Depression (of which John Ford said that although he hated the expression 'social significance', that's what it was about) had been bought from its author, a Texan journalist-adventurer, by Rowland Brown.[1] Writer-director of an incisive trio of films suggesting an intimate knowledge of gangsterdom – which he depicts as a cog in the capitalist machine – Brown was not in good odour with the studios. In 1941, having bought the rights from the author for $500, he resold them to RKO for $10,000, along with a script he had prepared. There was no question of Brown directing, but the project was reconsidered in turn by Robert D. Andrews, Dudley Nichols and Brown again, without getting anywhere. In March 1946, Dozier finally noted that 'Houseman works on it himself'. Houseman was in fact covering for the novice Ray, who submitted a 196-page 'screen treatment (first draft)' to the studio, dated 23 April.

According to Houseman, 'I found the book and gave it to Nick to read, and he fell madly in love with it – as indeed I did, but Nick particularly was very familiar with that territory [the South in the 1930s]. He'd been there when he worked with the Lomaxes, he'd been there when he worked with the Department of Agriculture, and so on. And that whole Depression thing was terribly his stuff. So he sat down and wrote this treatment. I'd come home at night and we'd go over it; I'd edit it a little, that's all, and it was very, very good. I don't know that Nick could ever have been a good writer, because his sense of organization, which was very strong as a director, was not so strong when he wrote. He was able to do *They Live by Night* simply because the book was there, and he was able to move within the book.'

Still in the role of godfather, Houseman then asked for Ray to be signed up with the status of scriptwriter (and corresponding salary increase to $300 a week) on *Thieves Like Us*. 'I expect to work on it myself with Nick Ray,' he reassured Dozier on 19 June. On 24 June, Ray was therefore moved from *That Girl from Memphis* to *Thieves Like Us*.

From the outset, there was never any question for Nick Ray but that he would direct *Thieves Like Us* himself. Memory and imagination have done their work, with Ray and Houseman each claiming credit for the other's involvement. It doesn't really matter: the project was Ray's alone, and only Houseman (who exercised considerable authority, despite having produced few films) could secure the beginner his chance.

Living at Houseman's place in the Hollywood hills just above Sunset Strip (Doheny Drive), Ray drafted two slightly different versions of the 196-page treatment of 23 April: one dated 1 August (175 pages), the other 6 August (176 pages).[2] A punctilious prefatory note headed the latter: 'This is *not* an underworld movie – no lurid tale of blood or squalor. It is tender, not cynical; tragic, not brutal. It is a Love Story; it is also a Morality Story – in the tempo of our time.' Two threads were to run through the film, 'the chase' and 'the romance of two lost kids, who have never been properly introduced to the world. Their need for each other is as deep and ill-starred as was the love of Romeo and Juliet, and their span of happiness runs just about as long.' In an astonishing narrative aside, the finished film, *They Live by Night*, similarly opens with a visual declaration of intent: a close-up of the two lovers, with subtitles announcing, in almost the same words as the treatment, that 'This boy . . . and this girl . . . were never properly introduced to the world we live in . . .' They look up, startled, and the title of the film appears.

The cinema began telling this tale of lovers on the run, hounded by society, with Fritz Lang's *You Only Live Once*, a film contemporary with Anderson's novel but which Ray hadn't seen; and in other re-tellings, culminating in *Bonnie and Clyde*, it became the stuff of legend. Here, the story of Bowie and Keechie is the story of a love threatened by Bowie's loyalty to T-Dub and Chickamaw, his companions in escape from prison, and by an omnipresent corruption that emerges in counterpoint: the corruption of Chickamaw's brother Mobley, small-time crook and blackmailer; of a justice of the peace, fence for stolen goods on the side; of T-Dub's sister-in-law Mattie, turning informer to secure her husband's parole.

In the treatment, at least one version of which he titled *I'm a Stranger Here Myself*, Ray defines the characters. He notes that 'the girl' is part-Indian. 'She has retained her virginity for no other reason than apathy induced by witnessing her own mother's actions [. . .] You believe her when she says she was never sexually alive until now: "Who's your fellow, Keechie?" – "I never did see any use of it." ' At times he adds to the novel, inventing fragments of family history, for example, which the film happily reduces to mere mentions (Bowie's mother moving in with the man who killed his father). The burden of hypocritical parents redoubles the indignation against society, which is one of the novel's main thrusts. He toys with a few formal devices which he was to abandon: a hallucinatory vision in the rearview mirror of a car, a stream-of-consciousness monologue for Bowie as Keechie sleeps beside him. He sketches out an updating: 'Three men who have been incarcerated during the entire period of war, re-enter "society" and find it changed. Black markets and Bonus thievery add fuel to their own beliefs and rationalizations that they're not such bad guys after all.' The idea is retained in the film, but the world in which Anderson and Ray's characters evolve is unequivocally that of the 1930s and not the 1940s.

'The time is the present,' says the first sentence on the first page of the treatment. An old black prisoner is seen singing *The Midnight Special*, accompanying himself on guitar – a recollection of Leadbelly and the visits Ray and Lomax made to penitentiaries in the South.[3] The escape is suggested, within the prison, by sound alone. Then the fugitives appear on board a train (rather than in a stolen car). Next comes the episode with the farmer, corresponding to the first chapter of the novel.

It is Mobley (and not his daughter Keechie, as in the film) who comes to collect the injured Bowie. But as soon as Keechie appears (heard, in the treatment, before she is seen), the text focuses on the relationship between the two young people. Ray sticks fairly closely to the sequence of events in the novel, highlighting lines like 'Banks, that's us' or 'It sure takes money to make money'. The whole social aspect is stressed, indeed amplified, through the character of Hawkins, the sleazy justice of the peace, who delivers a lengthy diatribe on the corruption of society.

After the car accident, Bowie rambles deliriously about his mother, the men she took up with, the various names she adopted. As the idyll with Keechie develops, he tells her he has 'all the blues rolled up in one', softly singing:

> I'm a stranger here,
> I'm a stranger everywhere,
> I would go home, but
> I'm a stranger there.

The bus trip and the wedding – interpolations not in the novel – are described just as they appear in the film. Later on, in the night-club scene, the treatment specifies a Mexican dancer (as in the book), whereas the role would in fact be magnificently filled by a black *chanteuse*, with the lyrics of her song echoing the action. Another invention: the scene in the night-club toilets, where Bowie is disarmed by a man in a dinner-jacket, and which draws the dividing line between organized urban crime and the confused defiance of the hillbilly outlaw. The fruitless attempt to escape to Mexico is also an interpolation: as the *I'm a Stranger Here* blues is heard again, Keechie and Bowie realize that they are 'trapped': 'Not just here – everywhere! People don't even know us, and they don't want us . . .'

Chickamaw's escape, which heralds the end in the novel, is still present in the treatment; when Bowie forces him to get out of the car, he is choosing Keechie rather than his former associates (this scene is placed much earlier in the film). Ray then introduces a sequence in which Mattie is making a deal with the police, and a conversation between Mattie and Bowie before the latter heads for the cabin and is shot down. The awakened Keechie screams and rushes to his body. These three crucial scenes appear in the film as described in the treatment, even to Keechie being swallowed up in darkness in the last shot.

This treatment is much less disciplined than the finished film, but it is already infused with the characteristic tone Ray lent to Anderson's material, with the film's textures of light and sound, the intimism and the distaste for violence that set it apart from the thriller genre, the oscillation between sympathetic identification with characters and poor South milieu on the one hand, and elegance of execution on the other.

The film was not to be made in 1946, however. For the moment, it fell victim to a power struggle within the studio. RKO, one of the most unstable of the majors, had discovered something like a sense of direction in the early 1940s under the successive presidencies of George Schaefer (responsible for *Citizen Kane*) and Charles Koerner. The latter's sudden death at the beginning of the year heralded a period of *coups d'état* by the various interests controlling the company outside the film industry. Koerner was succeeded by a man from the Atlas Corporation, Peter Rathvon, who had brought in William Dozier as head of production, but who also got rid of him in the summer.

When management of a studio changes hands, the preceding administration's projects are automatically set aside or viewed with suspicion. And this particular project, upsetting genre rules and conventions, ran into a whole string of objections and negative opinions which offered ample justification for sidelining it. Dudley Nichols felt that reading the script was like reading the book. The head of the Censorship Department (each studio had one, since the Breen Office was set up by the studios themselves), felt that 'one very objectionable, inescapable flavour of this story is the general indictment of Society which justifies the title'. The Breen Office decreed the project 'enormously dangerous from the standpoint of political censorship, generally' (in other words, censorship beyond the industry's self-regulation, in particular from local authorities). As far as other departments were concerned, they were simply convinced that the project had no commercial value. It also stirred enthusiasm in unexpected places. Mark Robson, for example, hoped that 'Nick Ray breaks his leg before production' (so that he could take his place: even then, Ray was the only director envisaged), and suggested an unknown, Michael Steele, for the lead.

Houseman declared himself 'deeply upset at the realization of the Studio's indifference to the project'. Since he was contracted on a film by film basis, he returned with Ray to New York, taking along copies of the treatment (which Ray showed to those close to him: Jean, Connie, Lomax). The *Beggars' Holiday* venture kept both of them busy until the end of 1946, but Houseman continued negotiating to get *Thieves Like Us* under way again, insisting on the fact that he had 'shown in the past an almost monolithic obstinacy in wanting to make this picture'.[4]

Early in 1947, Dore Schary was appointed head of production at RKO. Houseman immediately had him read the treatment and returned to Hollywood. And on 10 February Ray signed a contract for one year, with renewable options (at the studio's discretion).[5] 'It is the intention,' Schary specified in a memo, 'to have him direct as his first assignment *Thieves Like Us*'.

Schary, who moved over from the Selznick organization, had been very active in the Screen Writers' Guild and various civic enterprises; he had the reputation of being a cultivated, intelligent and liberal producer. His job was to get production going again after several months of stagnation, and for the next year RKO was to become the most adventurous studio in Hollywood, both in its choice of subjects and in its faith in directors who were often beginners: Losey, Ray, Norman Panama and Melvin Frank, Ted Tetzlaff, Mark Robson, Robert Wise.[6] It was also a year particularly rich in *films noirs* from the studio, and Ray's career got started thanks to a slight misconception here. But the years of profit were already over for RKO.

Ray's agents, Berg and Allenberg, had him prepare an official document listing (so that he could retain the rights) everything he had written prior to employment by the studio. The list, although sketchy to say the least, is nevertheless revealing:

- a 3-act play tentatively called *Stranger Here Myself*;[7]
- the outline of a radio series of 39 suggested programmes in collaboration with Dwight Whitney and John Houseman, *Show Time*;
- a screenplay outline registered last year, *Jazz Man*, the story of a band;
- a stage adaptation and a screen adaptation of the novel by David Garnett, *Man in the Zoo*;
- a musical review in preparation, *After Hours*.

On 7 March he became a Hollywood film-maker: he directed a test with the actress Joan Chandler (who was to appear in *Rope*). Behind the camera was Nick Musuraca, a studio veteran with whom he would work again. 'I just want to express my appreciation,' Ray wrote to Schary, 'of the efficiency of your staff and at the co-operation received, last Friday, during my first production experience on this lot.' Schary circulated this note, 'which speaks for itself, and very nicely'. Other tests followed, including one with Helen Craig, from *Lute Song*, who was to play Mattie ('a tough woman in her middle thirties, once handsome, now beginning to fade, to get hard'), and also with two young contract players: Guy Madison and Jane Greer.

Meanwhile, Houseman had brought in a novice but brilliant screenwriter, Charles Schnee, to turn Ray's treatment into an Estimating Script. This was finished early in May. Houseman recalled: 'It was so tricky anyway, such an offbeat property, that when Dore came in on it, simply for everybody's security – including my own – I felt we should have a proven professional scriptwriter. But this was a great problem, because I didn't want them fucking around with what Nick had done. I wanted really to do a transfer job, to transfer the treatment into a screenplay. Charlie Schnee was an old friend, and when I talked to him about it, I made it absolutely clear that I didn't want any original creative work, simply an effective job with anything he could contribute. He behaved very well and generously, and Nick was around, and there were no problems. It was a very quick job, done in a few weeks. But the whole feeling about it, as you can tell from comparing it with Altman's picture[8] . . . *that* was Nick talking.'

Schnee completed a 117-page script with Ray, dated 2 May 1947. The year of enforced reflection had been to the film-maker's advantage; it was in a discussion with Jean Evans that the idea for the pre-credit sequence took shape. He also came up with a new title, since neither the censors nor the studio wanted to use *Thieves Like Us*: *Your Red Wagon*, borrowed from an expression native to the New Orleans region. The meaning ('It's your business') was explained by a young couple in a scene which was shot but cut. It is also the title of the song sung in the night-club. In the long run, censorship considerations helped Schnee and Ray to find a unity by encouraging stylization (no reference to real places, allusive rather than direct action) and dramatic compression (the elision of two hold-ups out of three); the violence was now shown only in counterpoint, the story of the two lovers clearly becoming the focus of the film.

In the script, as opposed to the treatment, the hold-up is now seen only from outside the bank, from Bowie's point of view (as suggested in the novel); the escape from the prison camp just before the end having been removed, Bowie forces Chickamaw to leave much earlier, immediately after the armed robbery in which T-Dub is killed (brilliantly elided: another improvement due to censorship); the marriage scene loses all sense of equivocality, manifestly seen from the lovers' point of view and stressing their apartness from the world in which they live; the deal Mattie makes with the police is vindicated by the police commissioner, whose role is to point the moral of the film. But Ray also has Mattie's husband present in this scene where she turns informer to buy his free-

dom. He turns away from her, and she, complimented by the commissioner on saving 'a lot of people a lot of grief', comments, 'I don't
think that's going to help me sleep nights,' a line which subverts the
meaning of the scene.

While preproduction was already under way, the Breen Office surprised everyone by again objecting to the modified script. Skirmishes
went on right up until shooting started, leading to the provisional elimination of some factual names and details, and of a few moments of violence, at least one of which was judiciously transformed: Chickamaw
must not 'strike Mattie brutally' but push or shake her, and Mattie's
gesture in seizing a fragment of mirror to defend herself must be eliminated. Ray substituted a fine piece of business for Helen Craig: in the
film, it is Mattie who breaks the mirror, hurling it away in fury.

'Except for our young lovers,' Houseman wrote, 'the casting was easy.
Mostly Nick and I used our friends – men and women we had worked
with before.' Several Ray films suffer, more than is usual with other film-
makers since this was the point at which a movie crystallized for him,
from coercion exercised at the casting stage or from his own tendency to
conciliation. Here, he scarcely hesitated. Two Goldwyn players were
jointly contracted to play Bowie and Keechie. According to Farley Granger, 'I had met Nick at Gene Kelly's house. Then somebody told me he
wanted me in a film. That's nice, I thought, only he hasn't said anything
about it. But RKO wanted me to do a test, which I did.' Granger had in
fact appeared in only two films, a few years earlier, before being drafted.
'Nick asked me who I'd feel most comfortable with, and I said Cathy
O'Donnell, because I knew her at Goldwyn. So we did the test with
Cathy, and it was very good. Then, of course, he had to test with all the
RKO actors under contract! He and John Houseman were among the
few people who fought for me in my career. They said no, we will not
make the film without him. When Nick believed in you, he was very
loyal.' Cathy O'Donnell had only one film behind her, and the contract
binding the pair of them to Sam Goldwyn was seriously impeding their
careers. It was Ray who insisted on casting them: 'I thought she was
beautiful – beautiful because she wasn't beautiful.' They prefigure all of
Ray's youthful protagonists, down to the weakness and confusion of the
boy, the innocent, boyish characteristics of the girl. The notes for casting
specify: 'Acts like she's "Queen of Rumania" one minute and the frightened child she really is, the next. Smart, wary, alert to danger, due to her
life among thieves, she has a withdrawn innocence that becomes apparent in her touching and deep love for Bowie.' One can see Natalie Wood
not too far away, right down to the earnest way Keechie says, 'You want

to live your life fast' – a line from the novel, but one which heralds so many other Ray characters.

At RKO, Ray met a contract player, Robert Mitchum: studio star, but also a troublemaker, a child of the Depression who knew about riding the boxcars and serving time on chain gangs. Mitchum told Philippe Garnier: 'I knew all about that picture, because it was about Oklahoma bank robbers, and I wanted to play the Indian bank robber. So I shaved my hair and dyed it black. I took the idea to the studio. They said, "No, no, you can't do that because you're the hero, you can't play a bank robber, you can't die." Anyway, they got Farley Granger, and so [Nick] was pissed off because I didn't do it. It was not the same film as it would have been if we had done it.'[9] Granger was undoubtedly Ray's choice (he claims he even gave the treatment to Granger before returning to New York in 1946), and the 'Indian bank robber' is Chickamaw, the role in fact played by Howard Da Silva. The only established name in the cast, borrowed from Paramount, Da Silva had appeared in the memorable Welles-Houseman production of *The Cradle Will Rock*.[10] Chickamaw is no longer an Indian, as he was in the treatment, but Ray wanted to have him blind in one eye. Da Silva recalls animated discussions on the best way to mask the eye.

Ray called on his New York friend Marie Bryant (from *Beggars' Holiday*) to play the night-club singer. Also from New York, remembered from the Theatre of Action, came Curt Conway (the man in the tuxedo at the night-club), Will Lee (the jeweller) and Erskine Sanford (the doctor, cut out in the editing). Jay C. Flippen (T-Dub), known as a comedian on stage, had just appeared in Jules Dassin's *Brute Force*, embarking on a busy Hollywood career at the age of forty-seven. Ray even brought in Pete Seeger for a test, but without success.[11] Hollywood character actors made up the rest of the cast. Ian Wolfe played Hawkins, the corrupt judge, reduced by the Breen Office to being merely in charge of a seedy wedding parlour; the actor was to become a mascot in Houseman productions. The Californian Will Wright replaced the New Yorker Art Smith, originally slated to play Mobley. The all-round professionalism of the cast underlined the isolation and inexperience of the two young protagonists.

Early in June, matte shots were filmed by a second unit. On Monday 23 June 1947, shooting started on what was probably the least troubled production of Ray's career. Houseman was deep in an engrossing venture in Los Angeles: the first production in English of Bertolt Brecht's *Galileo*, featuring Charles Laughton. The first night took place on 30 July while Ray was in the middle of filming; but Houseman still managed to lend

16 *They Live by Night*: the first day of the shoot

the tyro his support. On that first day of shooting, Houseman wrote, 'I
realized that our association had undergone a subtle but drastic change
[. . .] Suddenly there was a new balance. Until then, though I had complete faith in his taste and talent and frequently accepted his judgements,
Nick had functioned as my assistant. Overnight this was changed. From
the first instant of shooting, Nick Ray emerged as an autonomous creator
with a style and work patterns that were entirely and fiercely his own.'

Ray and Houseman had planned the schedule so as to be able to shoot
in continuity as much as possible. For his first shot – 'Ext. highway –
early morning. Full shot. Car' – Ray decided to use not a crane but a
helicopter: a double or quits gamble on which a beginner might be stak-
ing his film and his career. Helicopters had been used before, and still
were, for establishing shots, panoramic views of cities and landscapes,
but never for an action shot. Recalling his job with the barnstormers in
Wisconsin, Ray used that to persuade Houseman. To do the scene, they
brought in a Marine pilot and a veteran cameraman of French origin,

17 *They Live by Night:* Nicholas Ray with Cathy O'Donnell and
Farley Granger

Paul Ivano, who had worked with Stroheim, Vidor, Murnau and
Sternberg. At Canoga Park, near Newhall, north-east of Los Angeles,
Ray spent an afternoon in the helicopter. The next day, a little after 9
a.m., he again took the cameraman's place to set up the shot, then let
Ivano climb in beside the pilot.

'The first take was a dud,' Houseman wrote. 'Over the walkie-talkie
the pilot announced he was coming down and, as soon as he'd landed,
everyone came running and gathered for a conference clear of the slowly
revolving blades. Ivano said he needed more time to change his focus as
the car passed beneath him. Nick gave new instructions to Da Silva, who
was driving. The car went back to its starting mark as the helicopter
blades began to turn. This time, as it rose, it barely avoided a scrub oak.
It was a few minutes before noon and it was getting hot. Once again the
helicopter hovered noisily overhead. The assistant gave the cue and the
Model A bounced past us, gathering speed as the camera came down to
meet it. This time it worked. The Frenchman reported a perfect take all

99

the way. For protection Nick made two more – neither as good as the first – then broke for lunch.'

During the rest of the day, 'drunk with power', Ray used the helicopter to shoot fifteen more set-ups, including the one of the roadside poster under which Bowie waits, his ankle sprained (Farley Granger really did injure it a few days later), for his confederates to collect him. These roadside posters are indissolubly linked to the iconography of the Depression years: a celebrated photograph by Dorothea Lange, in which a poster sings the joys of travelling by train to a couple of hoboes, lent them a mythical dimension.[12] For Ray, and for American audiences, the film is talking, without emphasis but without ambiguity, about the 1930s, the Depression and the South. The radio and the naked light bulbs are there too, but without the stress laid on them in Altman's version.

At the RKO ranch, in the days that followed, other shots were filmed from early in the script: close-ups of the poster, a railway line, a freight train (manifest in the film mainly through its whistle), then the scenes in the kitchen of the young farmer who is taken hostage by the fugitives: an episode drawn from the book, later cut as being redundant before the helicopter shots, which provided a much stronger opening. Next, on Stage 11 at the studio, came the interior of Mobley's shack, his scene with the three fugitives, and the first appearance in the room of his daughter Keechie. These scenes, deliberately fragmented, were rehearsed for two days, a month before shooting. 'With the first week's rushes,' Houseman wrote, 'it became clear that we had an unusual film here. Nick maintained his tempo and, after a few days, even the production department came around. He was working with actors now – mostly with the Boy and the Girl.' Ray also took great liberties with the script, reshaping the dialogue, allowing room for improvisation, eliminating, reorganizing. As the shooting drew to an end, he was sure enough of himself to take the time to add a five-page scene for Helen Craig. Filming continued until 21 August in the RKO studios and in the Los Angeles area. Howard Da Silva spoke of him as a director: 'Nick was atypical, there was nothing violent about him. He was in love with film-making, enamoured of lyricism. The sadism of someone like John Farrow was completely lacking in him. He had the capacity to win people's affection; the helicopter shot made the admiration of technicians.' And Farley Granger had an early experience of his very individual way of directing: 'He was very private. He'd sort of take you aside and talk to you. He'd never direct you in front of the others, so it became very personal.'

Ray had learned his lesson from *A Tree Grows in Brooklyn*. 'I made my associates there [in Hollywood] the editors, projectionists and writers

– to hell with the stars. I wanted to learn. I spent my time there with the guys who were doing it, who were making the films. I wasn't afraid of making mistakes. I had learned that from Kazan, I think – to be bold.' While making tests, he had chosen George E. Diskant as his director of photography.[13] Only recently credited as a lighting cameraman, he showed a willingness to take risks that one couldn't fail to notice.

'For the first shot we did together, I told him I wanted the lens as close to the stage floor as possible. He said, "I'll have to saw a hole in the stage floor." I said, "I don't care what you do." He said, "It'll take me 40 minutes." It took him twenty, and we made the next three films together. I like *They Live by Night* because all the mistakes are mine.'[14]

His editor was Sherman Todd, who had cut *For Whom the Bell Tolls*. Todd worked on few films, got highly paid, and refused to get hung up over editing. He was present during shooting, as editors often were with first-time directors. 'We didn't see much of Houseman during that time,' Todd's assistant Gene Palmer says, 'but Nick Ray'd call him on the phone and keep him informed. [Soon] we saw scenes that we hadn't seen before, because he'd put cameras right in a car and drive around when they went to rob the bank . . . Did a lot of things with sound; great creating mood, too. He made everybody part of a team, we felt like we contributed something. He would listen to what you had to say, whether he used it or not; and he was very compassionate with people too, even if they were new or inexperienced.' As Ray recalled in 1977, Todd encouraged him to 'try things' – like bad 'matches' – in defiance of the rules. ' "Go ahead," he'd say, "do it. Screw them." '[15]

Houseman had created ideal conditions, availing himself of his every prerogative – and Schary's benevolent attitude – to protect Ray and leave him unaware of the institutional power of the studio and of the producer over the director: an apprenticeship which Ray was to undergo, to his cost, on his next film.

A few scenes were eliminated in the editing: the one from the beginning involving the farmer and his wife; a botched robbery at a dance-hall, where the expression 'your red wagon' was heard for the first time; the last traces of the relationship between T-Dub and his woman, Lula; a scene with a beggar. But it was in putting the soundtrack together that Ray revealed his mastery, adding to the visual texture an evocative world of sound: a stylized echo of ordinary, everyday noises, using haunting elements like train whistles, themes drawn from folk music. Even Ray's original treatment was already conspicuously different from other scripts of the period in its wealth of references to sound. Only Welles similarly tried to define acoustic and even verbal textures as much as the visual –

often to change everything later. Ray's style structured itself not only around a dramatic nucleus of events drawn more or less faithfully from the novel, but also – in the manner of a musical composition – around songs, annotations, and counterpoints to the action. In the film, the original themes contributed by the composer Leigh Harline[16] are interwoven with the three songs chosen by the director: *I Know Where I'm Going* is introduced in the opening sequence, and returns no fewer than nine times, often barely identifiable; Woody Guthrie's *Going Down the Road Feeling Bad* is heard, in ironic counterpoint, on the radio of the escape car which the fugitives set on fire; *Your Red Wagon*, after a first snatch on the radio in Mobley's car, is sung at the night-club. As well as bits directly reinforcing the action, Harline himself composed three pieces: a total of 10 minutes 51 seconds out of the 29 minutes 32 seconds of music used in the film.[17]

The aural effects suggested in the treatment were in fact whittled down. As Ray commented, 'If you've done musicals on Broadway, and you go out on the road with eighteen songs, knowing you're going to come in with fourteen, you make your selection on the basis of whether the song advances the story or not.' As was the case with *Your Red Wagon*, sung by Marie Bryant: 'That night-club scene is the climax of their being real people.'[18]

> Your business is your red wagon
> What's in it is all your own
> So don't load it up with trouble
> 'Cause you're draggin' it all alone
> If you stick your nose some place it don't belong
> Don't you come to me if things go wrong
> That's your red wagon
> That's your red wagon
> So just keep draggin'
> Your red wagon along.

(Ray quotes it differently: 'The arrangement was a little square for us, so we juiced it up a bit. "If you get loaded and act the clown, be the laughing stock of all the town, it's your red wagon . . ."')

Completed in October 1947, *Your Red Wagon* had an excellent preview, and Ray made a few minor changes, mostly in the soundtrack. Bantam Books republished the novel under that title in an edition of 270,000 copies. The first, very favourable reviews appeared in the trade papers. But the studio didn't really know what to do with a property like this. In April 1948, with the release set for July, an argument broke out over the title. Schary chose *The Twisted Road*.

In the midst of all this, Howard Hughes took control of RKO, and for two months interminable lists of titles (filling eight pages in double column) were circulating between executives fearful of losing their jobs. It was an audience research poll which finally settled on *They Live by Night*, a title favoured by Hughes (but which outraged Selznick, who had meantime put Cathy O'Donnell under contract).[19]

They Live by Night was finally released in November 1949, with a publicity campaign playing up the juvenile violence angle. Failing to reach its audience, the film chalked up an estimated loss of $445,000 on its total cost of $775,000. In between times, it had led to Farley Granger being hired by Hitchcock for *Rope*, and to Ray directing Maureen O'Hara and – more notably – Humphrey Bogart; MGM had repeated the Granger-O'Donnell pairing in Anthony Mann's *Side Street*; and the King Brothers had set up a film with a similar subject, *Gun Crazy*. In that month of November 1949, Ray was already directing his fourth film, *In a Lonely Place*; he had married Gloria Grahame and was in the process of separating from her. 'A short career,' as a friend remarked, 'very short but very violent. He attracted disaster.'[20]

While making *Your Red Wagon*, Ray could still dream about cinema in terms much like those Thomas Wolfe used about his first novel: 'I had no literary experience. I had never had anything published before. My feelings towards writers, publishers, books, that whole fabulous far-away world, was almost as romantically unreal as when I was a child. And yet my book, the characters with which I had peopled it, the colour and the weather of the universe which I had created, had possessed me, and so I wrote and wrote with that bright flame with which a young man writes who never has been published, and who yet is sure all will be good and must go well. This is a curious thing and hard to tell about, yet easy to understand in every writer's mind. I wanted fame, as every youth who ever wrote must want it, and yet fame was a shining, bright, and most uncertain thing.'[21]

What Ray was not to know – and perhaps made all the difference for him – was that contact with his audience. The experience of being an author who was read (or seen) was to be denied the author of *They Live by Night*, in America at least.

In Britain, presented in the spring of 1949 as a semi-experimental effort ('If the director had taken the trouble to be French, we would be licking his boots in ecstasy,' wrote the *Spectator*), the film was enthusiastically received by two critics: the young Gavin Lambert, later a scriptwriter for Ray and acid chronicler of Hollywood, in the magazine *Sequence*; and Richard Winnington in the *News Chronicle*.[22]

In France, as *Les Amants de la nuit*, the film was presented in 1950 at the 'Rendez-vous de Biarritz' (under the sponsorship of the film society Objectif 49) 'before a totally indifferent audience who saw it as just another of the gangster movies that were going the rounds' (Jacques Doniol-Valcroze).[23] It then opened in Paris in September 1951, in one single cinema, the Broadway. 'A *film maudit* if ever there was one,' André Bazin wrote later, 'since it couldn't even run for a week on the Champs-Elysées. Patrons emerged red with anger and advising others not to go in. It left an indelible memory on the manager of the cinema.'[24] This was nevertheless the first contact between Ray's work and a generation of French filmgoers. In the fifth issue of *Cahiers du Cinéma*, in a piece titled 'Paul and Virginie Marry at Night', Jacques Doniol-Valcroze made the first reference to Bresson in connection with Ray. 'I was seeing it then for the third time. It impressed me even more than it had on previous viewings, stirring me emotionally in a way no other film did until I saw *Journal d'un curé de campagne*.' François Truffaut, too, in his first article for *Cahiers du Cinéma*, wrote of 'the most Bressonian of American films,' coupling *They Live By Night* with Robert Wise's *Born to Kill*.[25] For Jean Douchet, in retrospect, the Biarritz screening represented 'the first shock intimation of what was happening to American movies. The classical cinema was going out the window, a new cinema was being born. From that moment on, he became one of our two poles, along with Rossellini: Ray was feeling, offsetting, as it were, Rossellini's intelligence.'[26]

Careless of the conventions of *film noir* (but sometimes encountering them along the way), Ray drew on his own experience of America, communicating the wealth of his intimacy with the land in every gesture and every line. 'Some day I'd like to see some of this country we've been travellin' through.' But he did so without leaving the studio, concentrating on looks and faces: the conflict is emotional rather than social, expressed through a dramatic manipulation of space rather than through a documentary approach. Nicholas Ray's discovery of the cinema went hand in hand – perhaps for the first time in America since the silent days came to an end – with an investment in intimacy.

11
A Woman's Secret

18   *A Woman's Secret*: Nicholas Ray with Gloria Grahame and
Maureen O'Hara

Serialized in *Collier's* magazine as 'The Long Denial', Vicki Baum's novel was published in book form as *Mortgage on Life* and immediately bought by RKO. Herman J. Mankiewicz was to produce and script this 'modern and sophisticated drama with a music business background.'[1] Co-author of *Citizen Kane*, a friend of Houseman's, Mankiewicz was, according to the latter, 'largely resigned to making his living as a well-paid, occasionally brilliant studio hack'.[2] On *A Woman's Secret*, he received his first screen credit since 1945. Given that he saw his dual function as a chance to get more money, this was one of the final *coups* of an ageing, embittered writer. As director, the studio originally slated Jacques Tourneur, whom Dore Schary had offered a two-year contract to make two films per year. But Tourneur, busy finishing *Berlin Express*, indicated on 19 November 1947 that he didn't want to make the film, and on the same day Ray was assigned to take his place. In Ray's version of what happened: 'It was my second picture, and Dore Schary asked me to do it. I read the script and said, "No, Dore, no please, you can't make a film like this." And he said, "I guess you're right." So I went out of the office very happy; I'd finished my first film, I didn't have to do this one, and I went up into the mountains to relax for ten days with Gene Kelly, Stanley Donen, and Gene's daughter Kerry. I got back to the studio and was having lunch when there was a call from Dore Schary: "How do you feel?" – "I feel great." I was feeling so grateful for the non-interference that when he said, "Ready to go to work?" I said, "Hell, yes, anything you want." He said, "Brother, you've got it." So I had to do *A Woman's Secret*.'

In a later, more politic explanation, Ray compared the film to his last Hollywood production, *Party Girl*: the studio needed a product which would serve to justify the salaries of actors and technicians under contract. 'RKO didn't care if the picture was good or not; they were acting compulsively in response to their bookkeeping, which controls so much of our art.' Unsatisfactory the reason may be, but it does help one to understand why this 'Dore Schary Presentation' is mostly so uncharacteristic of the producer who had sanctioned films like Dmytryk's *Crossfire*, Losey's *The Boy with Green Hair*, Wise's *The Set-Up* and Nichols's *Mourning Becomes Electra*. Schary was here relegating Ray to the position of studio hack, at the same time not neglecting to profit by the reputation which *Your Red Wagon* was already beginning to attract. It seemed unthinkable for a beginner not to be eager to obey orders, to play his part in a collective of skills expected to produce a given number of products each year. One may wonder why Ray did not make good use of the breathing space after finishing his film to promote a project to which

Schary might have proved receptive. The only one for which traces remain seems distinctly suicidal: his proposal to adapt David Garnett's novel *Man in the Zoo*, which is about a young man, disappointed in love, who has himself shut away in a cage as a specimen of humankind.[3]

In a second mistake – perhaps out of sympathy for Herman Mankiewicz – he accepted. The star, Maureen O'Hara, was on loan from Fox; on 7 January 1948 she viewed *Your Red Wagon*. The male lead, Melvyn Douglas, was at forty-six on the way down from a career as a man of the world in Lubitsch comedies. The part of Estrellita went to a contract player, Gloria Grahame. Aged twenty-two, the daughter of a British actress who had settled in California, she had made her début on Broadway while very young. Then came contracts with MGM in 1944, RKO in 1947. She had just attracted attention in a supporting role in *Crossfire* which brought her an Oscar nomination. She was earning $750 a week. Among his friends, Ray was able to find parts for Jay C. Flippen and Curt Conway.

Filming on *The Long Denial*, entirely on studio stages, began on 16 February; Diskant was again on camera. Proceeding smoothly, shooting was completed on 30 March, four days ahead of schedule. Some of the rushes had caused misgivings about Maureen O'Hara's 'extremely revealing' postures, expressed in a memo from Harold Melniker to Mankiewicz on 31 March: 'Postures [which] could reasonably attract resistance by the Breen Office . . . in view of past unfortunate experiences with the Breen Office bearing on Miss O'Hara's postures.' The film was ready in May, and with the arrival of Howard Hughes, the re-titling merry-go-round started up again until, in November, Hughes himself chose *A Woman's Secret*. Following a preview in June, Ray shot a new scene, with Gloria Grahame in a hospital room. A victim of the studio upheavals, the film was not released until 5 March 1949, to be greeted by a sarcastic press. The president of RKO, Ned Depinet, immediately wrote to executive producer Sid Rogell, 'It looks as though we will take a very heavy loss on this film'. Estimated loss, $760,000 on a direct budget of $853,000.

'The settings of *The Long Denial* fall into the natural category for Ray,' the studio announced. The music business background is not noticeably present in *A Woman's Secret*, except for a fine opening sequence: the closing moments of a live radio broadcast. A smarmy announcer introduces the last song. As Gloria Grahame sings it, her voice shifts, by way of a slow dissolve, into an apartment where Maureen O'Hara looks at her watch, moves around the room, switches off the sound-on-disk recorder connected to the radio, then sits down to await her protégée.

In an unambitious product, the absurd settings – an Algeria even more artificial than the Morocco of *Casablanca*, the ballroom of a liner lifted out of a Fred Astaire movie – not to mention the dated performance of Melvyn Douglas, would be less embarrassing. The Mankiewicz script is at once contemptuous and slapdash, pretentious and pitiful, in its attempt to reconstruct the truth in its many facets through a number of overlapping stories. There are no fewer than five flashbacks, two of them contradictory, with the same scene seen from different points of view, as in *Citizen Kane*; but here – preceding *Stage Fright* by a year – one of the flashbacks lies. Mankiewicz is on the one hand relying on *Kane* as testimony to his virtuosity, and on the other showing his contempt for cinema in an irritating welter of trademark flourishes and empty witticisms.

Making a film like this implies a depressing lack of ambition, and Ray adds to the silliness, for example in the depiction of Jay C. Flippen and his wife. It is the latter, a policeman's wife but a devotee of detective stories, who offers a solution to the mystery, even though previously presented as a fool: she spills sugar over her husband, prevents him from listening to the radio, fusses around his guests. It is difficult to imagine characters and relationships more unlike those in *They Live by Night*. If one may assume that Ray had, even unconsciously, the slightest interest in *A Woman's Secret*, it lies in this gratuitous malice, this excessively cruel treatment of the minor characters; as far as the two stars are concerned, there is nothing to distinguish the scenes between them from dozens of other movies.

The Gloria Grahame character is revealing of Ray's misogynist streak. He had few kind things to say about her: the film was 'a disastrous experience, among other things because I met her . . . I was infatuated with her but I didn't like her very much.' This 'encounter film' more than confirms the appraisal he expressed; it is difficult to imagine, only months after Gloria Grahame's touching portrayal in *Crossfire*, any treatment of Estrellita more devoid of sympathy. The role is, of course, conceived as a foil for Maureen O'Hara, in a situation which to some extent prefigures – but inverts – the Margo Channing-Eve relationship in *All About Eve* (written and directed by another Mankiewicz): a natural talent is discovered and moulded by a singer who has lost her voice, while the pupil remains less interested in her career than in her sordid intrigues. Susan Caldwell, later known as Estrellita, starts out as a small-town girl in New York who skips on meals, saving up to consult a fortune-teller. Ray has her noisily drinking a glass of water before singing *Paradise*, an old Pola Negri number. He stresses her scandalous past back home in California, parades her in a ridiculous Algeria. Scheming and stupid, she tries without success to worm her way into the relationship between Maureen O'Hara and Melvyn Douglas.

A Woman's Secret, the film and the fact that Ray agreed to make it (it wasn't to be the only time), is perhaps revealing of another side to the romantic who made *They Live by Night*: cynicism and compromise. With this in mind, the end of the film – a series of lies designed to protect some social climbing – offers one of its rare points of interest.

At the end of May, Gloria Grahame went to Las Vegas, and on 1 June at 1.30 p.m., obtained her divorce from actor Stanley Clements, putting an end to a stormy marriage. At 6.30, in her lawyer Paul Ralli's office, she married Nicholas Ray.[4] A press photograph shows the latter 'radiant, with his white handkerchief and polka-dot tie; less ravishing, though, than Gloria, in her generously low-cut Mexican dress'.[5] His sister Alice Williams, who had come to Las Vegas for the ceremony, saw Nick as 'disappearing and gambling away all his money. They never stopped bringing him drinks'.[6] He himself commented: 'Something vindictive about me made me stay at the crap tables while she was still spending the last few days waiting for her divorce to become final. I was at the crap table when my best man Jay C. Flippen came to tell me it was time to go to the church in the grounds of the El Rancho Vegas. I think I wanted to be absolutely broke; I didn't want this dame, who proved to be as shrewd as she had threatened to be, to have anything of mine. I had lost a bundle. Now here we were, two people starting out fresh. The reason I went ahead with the marriage was because she was pregnant and I had promised I would marry her. A nice, Midwestern boy who goes by the credo: my word is better than my bond. How little that means in this business.' The studio prudently announced that the actress had met the director after her separation from Clements – and that it was Ray's first marriage. When their son Tim was born on 12 November, the RKO press office similarly had to announce that he arrived 'almost four months before the date he was expected' (in fact, Grahame had been on maternity leave since 17 September).[7]

These two people, as ill-prepared for family life as it is possible to be, did their best to live up to it for several months. The birth of Tim helped more than anything. In their Malibu home, they were away from Hollywood but close to friends: Houseman, Gene Kelly, James Stewart were their neighbours. Nick's elder son Tony, aged twelve, and his niece Gretchen, aged thirteen, visited them; Gloria Grahame's family was there too: her mother, and her sister who was married to Robert Mitchum's brother.[8] Since his arrival in Hollywood, Nick was seeing his eldest sister, Alice, who had been living in California since the 1930s. 'I had never seen such tenderness in a father,' she says. 'If Timmy had a sore leg, he at once feared infantile paralysis and called a doctor. He was very like our father, who was always worrying about our health, much more than our mother.'

12

Knock on Any Door

Hardly surprising, after *A Woman's Secret*, that the possibility of working elsewhere than at RKO seemed welcome. The studios were almost completely sealed off from each other: standard operating conditions might vary greatly, and professional secrets were jealously guarded. Coming from Humphrey Bogart, the invitation to direct him in his first independent production was flattering professional testimony, given that neither of Ray's first two films had yet been released, and the second had clearly indicated the limits of his autonomy.

From RKO's point of view, their stable of young directors was a feather in the studio's cap (particularly during the Schary regime), producing films which were themselves not very highly rated within the industry. *Your Red Wagon* had done the round of private screenings in Beverly Hills, and for a few months Ray was the studio's white-haired boy. But the fact that Hitchcock, Selznick, Maureen O'Hara or Bogart liked his work was no reason to offer Ray better films. Rather, it transformed him into a possible source of profit: RKO paid him exactly half of what they received for the loan-out of his services.

It may seem surprising that Humphrey Bogart – in 1948 the most highly paid actor of the fiscal year – should have chosen Willard Motley's hefty novel *Knock on Any Door* for his first production. Motley, a black writer who emerged (like Richard Wright) from the Federal Writers' Project in Chicago, was soon to become a victim of the witch hunts and emigrate to Mexico, where he lived until his death. He had made this novel the work of a lifetime; published in 1947, compared by critics to Dreiser, it was hailed as a new American classic. In its ninety crowded chapters, the book contains enough dramatic situations for several films. Its documentary accuracy is impressive.

The novel had been bought by Mark Hellinger for his company, in association with Selznick and Bogart.[1] But Hellinger died on 21 December 1947; and Bogart, determined to leave Warner Brothers, founded his own company along with his business manager, A. Morgan Maree, and Robert Lord, an enterprising writer-producer from Warners' social conscience days.[2] Five days after Santana was officially set up (12 April 1948), Ray's loan-out was agreed: he was hired for a maximum of twenty weeks starting on 29 May, with an option for a second film.

111

These were the weeks during which he was having money wired to him in Las Vegas by the studio and by his agent, contracting a glamorous marriage, and trying to find a loophole in his contract which would allow him to work for television: all too clearly a naïve attempt to deal from a position of strength so relative that he inevitably got trumped. In the meantime, it is true, Howard Hughes had taken control of the studio, and Ray had good reason to want to be elsewhere.

He was, it seemed, going to be working under favourable conditions at Columbia, which was giving Santana house room: it was an independent production, even if Harry Cohn remained the boss. All the same, Ray was to discover limits to his status. He had been chosen, but had chosen neither the subject (even if, in some respects, it chose him) nor the broad outlines along which the novel would be adapted, already sketched out in a first treatment by John Monks Jr.[3] Between censorship and marketing requirements, there weren't too many options open in adapting the book: eliminating what was unacceptable to the Production Code; developing Bogart's role within reasonable proportions; giving the social criticism (no longer in fashion) a legalistic form, culminating (unlike the book) in a courtroom plea; and reducing to 100 minutes, of course, the 504 pages and the 'grand form' adopted by Willard Motley.[4] It is difficult to see what other possibilities remained open, unless one happened to be Abraham Polonsky.

Daniel Taradash, a staunch liberal, was the man for the job; Robert Lord hired him. Ray was consulted very little over the script. Taradash, much more involved at the time in an adaptation of Sartre's *Les Mains Sales* (*Red Gloves*) for Broadway, was hired after Ray but worked mostly with Robert Lord. He stayed within the flashback structure established by Monks. Ray became involved mainly through script conferences, and seemed to Taradash 'a very quiet, rather withdrawn man; he was not a vehement man, and did not seem to have any particular demands in any area including the script. He had a slight sense of humour, but – this seems like an odd thing to say about Nicholas Ray – he was almost colourless.' Taradash, *en route* from New York, stopped off in Chicago to visit the areas described in the novel. He confirms that Bogart had no reservations about not being the film's real lead.

What Bogart had in mind can be seen a little more clearly in his choice of director: a desire to get as far away as possible from the studio formulas which most Warner stars found terribly stale and constricting. His decision to use a director noted for his work with young actors, on a film where the juveniles were quite likely to steal his thunder, was not without courage (a courage that did not balk at the choice of a 'big subject'). Work on the production, however, proceeded along highly traditional lines in the Warner manner: the scriptwriter scripts, the director directs.

The director of photography, Burnett Guffey, had spent seventeen years at Columbia. 'I was kind of a captive. Whoever they assigned me to, if it was agreeable with the director, I went and I did the picture. They might alter a few fronts and have different signs, but it was a standing street.' For everyone in the crew it was just another film: art director Robert Peterson, set decorator William Kiernan, associate producer Henry S. Kesler, costume designer Jean Louis.

One or two personalities stand out here, most notably the editor, Viola Lawrence. In the business since 1916, at Columbia since 1934, she had been schooled by Stroheim, and more recently had acted as midwife to Welles in his labours over *The Lady from Shanghai* (finished two years earlier, but only recently released). At fifty-three, Viola Lawrence was a sort of mandarin of the cutting-rooms – rather like Margaret Booth at MGM, Dorothy Spencer at Fox, or later on, at the time of *Wind Across the Everglades*, Rudi Fehr at Warners. Also worthy of note is the composer, George Antheil, who had not long before published a witty autobiography full of condescension for the cinema. Once the composer on *Ballet mécanique*, he now worked purely for his weekly paycheque, but had not lost his talent.

Ray's contribution was therefore in the casting. First and foremost he had to assemble a gang of kids, more homogeneous than in the novel, where the action spreads over seven years. He picked Mickey Knox (a small part in Brecht's *Galileo* and four films), Cara Williams (directed by Kazan in *Boomerang*), Pepe Hern, Dewey Martin (his début), the young black Robert A. Davis (début the previous year), and finally his nephew Sumner Williams, who was in between school years. Everyone has his own version of the discovery of John Derek: one of those Hollywood searches (Taradash), personal recommendation from Rodney Amateau, etc. The son of silent film-maker Lawson Harris, he had been demobilized two years earlier, and had been hanging around under contract to Fox. As for the two girls in the film, Allene Roberts and Susan Perry, they reveal little in common with the heroines usually favoured by Ray.

Finally, and most importantly, there was the Ray-Bogart encounter – two generations and two different worlds – which was not without its prickles and ironies, but also marked a mutual recognition. According to Rodney Amateau's sarcastic account: 'The first day's shooting, the first scene, Bogart's supposed to be coming to the door, there's a close-up of him, he looks, says "Hello", and he walks out of the scene. So Nick

19 *Knock on Any Door*. 'father and son' – Humphrey Bogart and John Derek

walks up to Bogart, he says, "Listen, when you come in, really give me that certain . . ." Bogart says to me, "Jesus, the man's crazy." I say, "No, that's just the way he works, don't make judgement until you realize . . ." Nick would be smoking and pacing up and down, lots of dramatics. Bogart would come in and say, "What the hell is the matter with him?" – "Nothing, nothing, he's thinking" – "So what is he thinking about?" – "Everything. Very important stuff, you and I don't even know what he's thinking about." Because Bogart used to come in and read the paper, read the lines twice, have a beer, and be ready for work. He didn't suffer. Nick suffered for everybody. He was so emotionally charged that he couldn't turn it off and on like a light switch. Every film was a difficult film for him to make. He couldn't direct somebody crossing a street without getting involved.'

Years later, Ray quoted this first day as an example of bad direction: 'But this speaks of Bogie's sense of himself. He would probably let me go all the way through the take, and then afterwards Bogie would come to

20 *Knock on Any Door*: Bogart's courtroom plea

me – as the young director, and he was president of the company and the producer – and he would say, "Look, Nick, you know, I just don't think that's the best way for me to do it," in his offhand manner of speaking. But that wasn't necessary because I knew from his tone, and as soon as he put his arm around my shoulder, what to do.'

Another story illustrates the extent to which Ray didn't know how to work 'the easy way': the one which tells how he filmed the courtroom plea in a single take against the wishes of Bogart, who claimed that he hadn't had to say more than three lines at a time for the past fifteen years. Ray repeated the story several times, but a look at the film itself shows that it isn't really true. The sequence doesn't last nearly as long as the nine minutes Ray claimed, and it is broken up into twelve shots, ten of them on Bogart. These ten shots represent at least six set-ups, although a fairly complex camera movement, tracking back and then laterally, does support Ray's description. Contrary to standard professional practice, carried to extremes by film-makers like Wyler and Stevens, Ray's set-ups

115

are all given equal weight: the final cut contradicts the hierarchy of master shot and 'matches', the ideology of 'covering'.[5] The story is also of interest for Bogart's show of reluctance, hiding his pleasure in breaking his own professional habits. He and Ray were drawn together by a number of things in common, in both their work and their private lives: a show of rebelliousness not proof against the demands of social life, honesty in their work, antipathy towards the studios . . . and also alcoholism, marriage to younger women. Their children were born around the same time: Tim Ray on 12 November 1948, Steve Bogart on 6 January 1949.

Filming ended on 17 September. General satisfaction: Columbia handed Ray a bonus of $5,000. The information was relayed to Hughes, who let it be known that he 'approved'. And Santana decided to exercise its option for a second film. This news arrived on 17 December, while Ray was passing what were probably his worst moments at RKO: he had just been assigned to direct *I Married a Communist*, and would do everything he could to get out of his contract.

Knock on Any Door looks like a throwback to the socially conscious gangster movie of the 1930s, but one from which all the original material – even down to the choice of vocabulary – has been carefully eliminated. Bogart had chosen Ray for the tone of *Your Red Wagon*, the intimist treatment beneath which a teeming social activity could be glimpsed. What we find here is not the abstract territory often favoured by Ray in his later work, but the resurrection of a dying genre.

The film is structured in three parts around a criminal case: the crime, the arrest of Nick Romano; Morton, in court, describes Nick's life in four long flashbacks; the legal battle and the outcome. Ray didn't want flashbacks. He would have preferred to follow the novel in tracing Nick Romano through his adolescence, culminating in the crime and the trial. The structure was set in the original treatment, and his hopes of changing it at the editing stage were unrealistic. As for the Bogart character, Andrew Morton, about whom the novel tells us little, the scriptwriters (Taradash, probably) gave him the same background as the John Derek character, Nick Romano: he escaped from poverty and crime through hard work and determination, not through revolt. The film develops and enriches this echo effect, turning Morton into a father figure, and carrying the resonance even further in a scene quite near the beginning where Morton recognizes himself in an old man.

In the grey light of dawn, in a Skid Row street reminiscent of the Bowery as photographed by Weegee, Morton is walking along after seeing Nick in prison, revisiting the streets he left behind him long ago.

From a truck which doesn't slow down, a bundle of newspapers is thrown to an old man in a doorway. As Morton comes up, the old man says:

- 'What are you doing, Andy? Slumming?'
- 'How's it, Junior? You look just the same.'
- 'A little older, a little more tired, a little more confused . . .'

Morton sits with him on the kerb to ask his help. Then he gets up with the parting advice, 'Stay away from squirrels.' Junior calls after him, 'In my day, comedians had style!' This last crack (more Broadway than Chicago) was an addition to the script, as was the name Junior (originally, he was simply called 'Pop'). The line 'A little older, a little more tired, a little more confused' (which was in the script though not the novel) was later appropriated by Ray for another paternal situation in which he was both the senior and the 'junior', opposite Dennis Hopper in *The American Friend*.

Bogart and John Derek are brought face to face in a number of scenes, but few of them really develop this theme, which is expressed mostly through the dialogue; few scenes attempt, as Ray himself might have put it, to explore the dynamics of the relationship. Apart from the meeting with Junior, only one sequence shows Morton on Skid Row. Having been robbed by Nick, he hangs around the local bars looking for him, accosts him politely, drags him into an alleyway, and knocks him down to go through his pockets. Nick watches with a certain admiration as he leaves. In a 'rewriting' process that he was to become partial to, Ray later faced John Derek with a similar situation, this time opposite Cagney, in *Run for Cover*.

The description of Skid Row is simple and straightforward, lacking visual subtlety by comparison with *They Live by Night* or the later *On Dangerous Ground*. 'Walk through the slum section of any American city some evening. Pause at the poolrooms, the gyms, the dingy bars, the candy stores, and certain street corners where boys and young men gather. Any one of them might be a Johnny Rocco.' Rocco rather than Nick Romano, because this description is not from the script or from Willard Motley's book, but from a documentary narrative written by Jean Evans in 1947. 'Johnny Rocco' forms part of her book *Three Men, an Experiment in the Biography of Emotion*, published in 1950: three inquiries into the social psychology of so-called pathological 'lives'.[6] The sources – cultural, emotional, visual – were common to Jean Evans and Ray. Johnny Rocco's story is typical, with his rejection of the 'chicken-hearted', his motto 'Everybody's out for himself', his determination finally to change, which sets him against everyone – parents, friends, authorities – and it helps in understanding Nick Romano's.

Paradoxically, it is in the trial scene that Ray is most at ease. His direction is designed to support Bogart, eliminating camera trickery or showy acting effects. Ray simply has him play off good actors and carefully chosen small-part players. George Macready, who had attracted attention two years earlier, playing a role with strong homosexual overtones in *Gilda*, invests the district attorney, Kerman, with all the hatred that drives him in the novel: class contempt, racism, careerist competition with Morton, physical envy of Nick Romano. Here Ray brings off one of his finest caricatures, transcending the dated sociological thesis which meant that he could merely hint at themes later much more satisfactorily explored. 'I wish Buñuel had made *Los Olvidados* before I made *Knock on Any Door*,' Ray said later, 'because I would have made a hell of a lot better film.' As it is, its semi-success is due to the contradiction between its overt concerns and those of the director: the ballet of movement for the young actors, the gestures he invents, like Dewey Martin describing the barman, or a girl in a backyard tossing her hair.

13

Howard Hughes

With filming completed on *Knock on Any Door* by mid-September, Ray returned to RKO, where important changes had once more been taking place. The financier Floyd Odlum had acquired half of RCA's shares in 1935, and the rest, plus Rockefeller's interests, in 1943. To this business-man, who was neither in nor of the cinema, circumstances seemed unfavourable in 1947, the future for production restricted. Foreign markets had become protectionist, television had just caused a first appreciable drop in attendances. At the studio itself, Dore Schary's ambitious programme was no guarantee of short-term profits.

Then, too, the political crisis and the first stirrings of the witch-hunts were threatening to tear the cinema apart. Meeting at the Waldorf in New York under the chairmanship of Eric Johnston, the heads and chief executives of the studios took a stand against 'The Hollywood Ten', and pledged themselves not to employ Communists or subversives. RKO was represented by Ned Depinet and Dore Schary, who described his own attitude as ambiguous. He was a member of the committee which drafted the 'Waldorf Statement'. Two of 'The Ten' – Adrian Scott and Edward Dmytryk – had produced and directed *Crossfire*, the studio's most prestigious film of 1947, and one of the most profitable. Floyd Odlum, disgusted and discouraged, felt that 'Hollywood wouldn't be long in foundering', and was looking to withdraw, if not from the cinema, at least from his majority holding in the studio.[1]

By May 1948, he had found a buyer: Howard Hughes. The eccentric millionaire had already been producing films over the years, and had himself directed two. He was just emerging from a series of setbacks: after a single test flight, his Hercules Flying Boat (the 'Spruce Goose'), the largest aircraft ever built, had proved to be a dead end, and he had been involved in a tough battle with a Special Senate Committee. Although he emerged victorious in the eyes of public opinion, the fact remained that, having freely spent government funds during and after the war years, he had accomplished nothing of note in his pet field of aeronautics.

Hughes was in the process of reorganizing his personal staff, with the first Mormons making their appearance. In his Hollywood offices, at 7000 Romaine Street and a few blocks away at the Goldwyn Studios (Formosa Street, at the corner of Romaine), he was being captivated by the cinema all over again, while the public figure was disappearing completely.

Between January and May 1948, Hughes was negotiating in the highest secrecy with Odlum. The businessman, himself married to an aviatrix, Jacqueline Cochran, was doubtless fascinated by the aviator-film-maker. 'He must have been to our house sixty times,' she later recalled. 'He just loved to deal.'[2] By 16 May,[3] after complicated negotiations, Hughes had bought the 929,020 shares owned by Odlum's Atlas Corporation, at $9.50 a share (slightly above the market price), representing a transaction of $8,825,690. With 24 per cent of the shares, he became the studio's principal stockholder.

Hughes had insisted that he would not interfere with the running of RKO. Schary, whose contract stipulated that he could leave the studio if control changed hands, lasted only a month and a half.[4] He resigned when Hughes announced the cancellation of three of his favourite projects, including what was to become Ray's fourth film: *Bed of Roses*, a production which various film-makers had been trying to set up for years. Immediately after this, Hughes fired a sizeable percentage of the studio's personnel.[5] Increasingly, the management at RKO was coming to resemble the government of one of those banana republics dear to comic strips.

Hughes the eccentric. He came to look over the studio, and had only one thing to say: 'Paint the place.' This was the first – costly – undertaking of the new management. Hughes was to sell the studio Jane Russell's contract with the Hughes Tool Company, as well as films he had personally produced but been unable to release. From his office at Goldwyn's, a mile away from the studios in which he never again set foot, he insisted on controlling everything.

Hughes the boss was undoubtedly a disaster: placing his yes-men in key positions; terrorizing a staff severely depleted by July's mass dismissals; allowing no independence to any of the producers he wrested away from other studios by bidding higher for their services, and who were forced to leave (either fired or resigning) without having brought any of their projects to fruition. According to Vernon Harbin, a studio employee since 1931, 'He set up a "security office" whose job was to screen the background of all studio personnel for subversive inclinations.'[6]

Nicholas Ray was to start playing for time. On his return to the studio, two projects were awaiting him. Rumours of success were circulating around his Bogart film, and various studios were interested in him. Earlier, when CBS had contacted him in June, vice-president J.J. Nolan had refused him permission to work for television. On 9 September, Hal B. Wallis of Paramount asked for him to direct Barbara Stanwyck in *The File on Thelma Jordon*. Featuring a big star, this *film noir*, sired by *Double Indemnity*, would have been at least a plus for him. On the 17th, Sid Rogell lunched with Ray to tell him he would not be making *The File on Thelma Jordon* (which was directed by Robert Siodmak) but *Operation Malaya* for Robert Sparks at the studio. Rogell, a long-time executive turned man-of-straw under Hughes, had agreed to take charge of production following the resignations of Schary and, two weeks later, his successor, Peter Rathvon. For Ray, the humiliation was all the more bitter when, on 8 October, Columbia sought him to direct Paulette Goddard, and Walter Wanger for Joan Bennett ('We suggest Losey,' J. J. Nolan noted). His reputation within professional circles might well have had something to do with this victimization.

Ray must have got out of *Operation Malaya* (which was never made) without too much difficulty. A few weeks later he found himself in a more serious situation. Joseph Losey, who had made his feature début the previous year thanks to Schary, had preceded Ray in this plight. As Losey put it: 'I was offered a film called *I Married a Communist*, which I turned down categorically – I was the first. I later learned this was a touchstone for establishing who was not "a red": you offered *I Married a Communist* to anybody you thought was a Communist, and if they turned it down, they were. It was turned down by thirteen directors before it was made, but in the meantime, somewhere before the thirteenth of us, round about the eighth or ninth in fact, it was offered to Nick Ray.'[7]

John Cromwell, suspected of leftist sympathies, is the first name to appear in the production files, the first director officially announced, though certainly not the first to have been approached. His version of what happened confirms Losey's. Convinced that the script was so bad that it could never be made, he didn't refuse, and let Art Cohn, writer of *The Set-Up*, battle on with an impossible script. After a certain time, Cromwell's salary was to go up to $7,500 a week, so the studio released him.[8]

A script did in fact exist at this stage, and forms had been prepared for sending to Picasso and Chastakovitch [sic] asking for permission to use their names in a dialogue passage: 'Only one thing bothers me . . . some of these phoney intellectuals and black tie Pinkos . . . they're worrying about the social significance of the ballet, Picasso's latest painting or a Chastakovitch symphony . . . there's *work* to be done . . . NOW . . . but *not* with a paint brush or a ballet slipper.'

On 8 December, the *New York Times* announced that Cromwell 'withdrew last week', and that Art Cohn was working on the script. On the 17th, an internal memo noted that Ray and Jack Gross had been assigned as director and producer respectively. According to Losey: 'Nick Ray and I used to walk in empty lots in order to stay out of offices, not to be seen together, and not to be in cars so that we wouldn't incriminate each other. In the political situation, I mean. There was one famous time when Nick came to me and said that he'd been offered *I Married a Communist* [. . .] It was a kind of test. He asked my advice about it, and we walked and walked and walked. Then we got into his car and he dropped me at my house. Just a very short time after, he rang me on the phone and said: "I've had a call from Hughes, who knows I've talked to you, so for God's sake don't say anything about it." Even the precautions we took weren't good enough, you know.'[9]

In 1974, Ray recalled the episode with more bravado. 'It was so ludicrous – like a 1917 Hearst editorial, with the bomb-throwing Communist – I thought we might make a comedy out of it. I got calls from my friends on the left: "Nick, what are you doing? Are you out of your mind?" I'd say "Shut up!" and hang up the phone.'[10]

Actually, he did not handle the matter with the irony and detachment he pretends. When he was assigned to the film, he had his agents Berg and Allenberg intervene to try to secure his release from his contract. Four days later, the studio replied by registered letter, requiring acknowledgement of receipt: 'Each of you has been told repeatedly that we have no intention of giving Mr Ray a release from his agreement of employment with us and we are repeating this in this letter so that there will be no misunderstanding on your part and so that you will be under no misapprehension concerning this.' Ray, the letter further states, 'has been assigned by us to render his services in connection with the photoplay *I Married a Communist*'.

In the absence of further evidence (the political files are missing from the RKO archives), only the tone of this letter remains to suggest the atmosphere during those weeks. Berg and Allenberg were Hollywood's most reputable (if not most powerful) agents; Frank Capra was among their clients. Ray must have been truly cornered to persuade them to make such persistent representations with no legal foundation. They introduced him to Edward G. Robinson, harassed by anti-Semitic smears from the witch-hunters, who was facing a similar decision: he had been offered the lead on Broadway in an anti-Stalinist play adapted from *Darkness at Noon*. 'Should he accept and survive?'[11] It is difficult, however, to compare Arthur Koestler and *I Married a Communist*. All the indications suggest that at this stage Ray had not met Hughes. On 31 December Ray sent him a telegram from Indio, in the Californian desert: 'Believe it will be important we talk before I begin my first assignment for you. Time, place or manner at your convenience. Am at the La Quinta Hotel for the next few days. Happy New Year.'

Early in January, the studio publicity department announced *I Married a Communist*, starring Jane Greer and Paul Lukas, directed by Nicholas Ray. And the latter ended up writing to his producer, Jack Gross, not yet back from holiday: 'Dear Jack, No one could ask for more consideration or co-operation than I have received from you. I had hoped our first association in work would produce something of which we could both be proud. My regret that it could not be so on this picture is eased somewhat by the knowledge that bowing out of it is the fairest thing I could do for all concerned. Until your return to the studio I will act for you on this project in your best interest, if you so desire. Yours, Nick.'

On 13 January 1949, he advised Sid Rogell as to the steps he had taken in 'Jack's' absence: meeting with the various departments, discussing the plans and sketches on hand, cautioning them 'to refrain from any construction' until the producer's return. He had also prepared a list of suggestions for the head of casting, Schuessler, and he had not let slip the occasion to offer friends a few weeks' work: Herman Mankiewicz (6 weeks at $2,250 a week), Rodney Amateau, Sherman Todd.

On the 20th, in a memorandum addressed to Sid Rogell, Ross Hastings considered the 'several remedies' possible 'because Nick Ray refused to direct *I Married a Communist*': terminate his contract; place him under suspension; extend his contract by a term equivalent to the term of suspension; or demand compensation from him. 'It can be contended that he has wasted the time since [*Knock on Any Door*] while assigned to *Operation Malaya* and *I Married a Communist*, to both of which he objected. As of 20 January, we paid him for 16 weeks at $1,000 during which he has not performed.'

The most surprising thing about this memorandum is its conclusion: 'Both Joe Nolan and I feel that in consideration for not suspending and seeking to recover damages, we should ask for an additional option, possibly asking for one additional year at $2,000 and a second additional year at $2,250, and perhaps settling for $2,500 for both years.' These two additional years 'will take us to the limit of the 7-year law, computing this from 7 February 1949.'

Why did this refusal not cost Ray his career? On several occasions, in his autobiographical notes and even on his last public appearance (Museum of Modern Art, New York, on 6 May 1979), he reiterated his gratitude and his admiration for Howard Hughes, 'who saved me from blacklisting'. Losey's reminiscences seem to confirm this. William Fadiman, a story editor brought in by Dore Schary who became head of the literary department under Hughes, felt that Hughes had the necessary power, thanks to his connections outside the cinema, not in Hollywood but in Washington. 'No one else could have done it.' For the tycoon to have reacted in such a way is nevertheless surprising. At the time, RKO became the most reactionary of all the studios. Hughes had no hesitation in removing subversive names from his films (scriptwriter Paul Jarrico, eliminated from the credits of *The Las Vegas Story*, lost all his legal appeals; actor Lloyd Gough's name vanished from *Rancho Notorious* when the studio bought the film for distribution). Professor Howard Suber, an expert on the blacklist, considers the studios to have been very careful in preparing their lists of undesirables;[12] but Ray's membership of the Communist Party, and more openly of various leftist organizations, was not in any doubt.

One can only conclude that Hughes did indeed protect Ray after his refusal to direct *I Married a Communist*, keeping him on at the studio and extending his contract (unlike Cromwell and Losey). That protection was tantamount to saving him from the blacklist, and sparing him a summons to testify in public. His case was not important enough for the investigators to make a show of force, as they did with established names (John Garfield, Larry Parks, Edward G. Robinson).

What is certain is that he must have had to either testify in private or write a letter explaining his past associations, or both. In his memoirs, Houseman reports that he himself wrote such a letter, which he reproduces; he does not appear to feel that there was any humiliation involved in having done so.[13] With these private statements, the studios protected themselves against outside investigation and kept their employees under control.

A little later on, Ray made a curious admission to Jean Evans: 'He told me that when he had to testify, he said I was the one who brought him to the Communist Youth League, which wasn't true at all.'[14] Despite her connection with the liberal paper *PM*, Jean, on the East Coast, was not harassed in any way. Nick, in Hollywood, was deep in the hysteria of the witch-hunts; but besides small treacheries such as this, he maintained his distances. His immediate circle were people indifferent to politics. Later, some of the victims claimed that 'he wasn't one of us'.[15] He certainly remained circumspect. Others, however – Pete Seeger, for example – attested that his house always remained open to them.[16] And in October 1950, he was one of the twenty-five members of the Directors' Guild who signed a petition demanding a meeting in defence of the Guild president, Joseph L. Mankiewicz, against the attacks of Cecil B. DeMille.[17] Politics, in any case, seemed less to interest Ray than to stimulate him at times, and these times were not exactly stimulating. That was how Perry Bruskin saw it in retrospect: 'There were a lot of things that were lying there for many years. But he let them lie, he had no reason to let his feelings go in any direction politically. He could be friends with everybody. He could be friends with his old radical friends, because he hadn't done anything to hurt them. He could be friends with the Howard Hugheses and . . . *anybody!*'[18]

To return to *I Married a Communist*: Ray had not, as Losey thought, reached a point 'about three or four days before shooting'. Far from it. At the end of January, with the project in mind, Hughes was viewing films by John Brahm, Byron Haskin, Ted Tetzlaff, Edward Ludwig; it was no longer only contract directors who were under consideration. Other names followed. But were their services ever requested? Following the Ray episode, the project may have ceased being a test to become a book-keeping necessity. In the end it was a Selznick employee, the British director Robert Stevenson − no more suspect of subversive tendencies than the names considered before him − who finally made *I Married a Communist* months later.[19]

Once extricated from this pickle, Ray did his best to appear constructive by proposing subjects: 'I'd be enthusiastic about directing either or both of these stories as well as collaborating on the scripts.' He tried to push them in a telegram to Hughes: 'Have developed two original story ideas which would meet RKO budget requirements and cast commitments. The first is a drama loaded with music and based on the wreck of the old 97. The second is a warm-hearted western comedy. Not satiric. Presentations are brief. Hope you will have time to read them personally.' Despite the bit of nudging, it was Sid Rogell who, a few days later, turned down *Wreck of the Old 97* by Mindret Lord, and *Evening Sun* by Rodney Amateau.[20]

So as not to waste any more of the studio's money, Ray was finally loaned out. Far from being a promotion, the job involved was entirely thankless: patching up an unreleasable film, tailoring it to the wishes of an ageing, cranky producer. Sam Goldwyn still had Farley Granger under contract; aside from periods when he was bringing in money out on loan, Goldwyn shoved him into mediocre parts. *Roseanna McCoy* was a variation on *Romeo and Juliet*, updated to a rural American setting, in which Granger appeared opposite Joan Evans, a short-lived Goldwyn discovery. The journeyman director was Irving Reis, who had made the biggest success of Schary's regime at RKO, *The Bachelor and the Bobby-Soxer*.

'It was such a mess,' Farley Granger recalls. 'We had a wonderful script [by John Collier] that Sam Goldwyn threw away. So we were shooting day by day and getting the scenes hot from the typewriter. We had done location work early on in the Sierra Madre. But poor Irving Reis didn't know what the story was about. So after it was finished, Nick said he'd do it, and we had to go up to the Sierra Madre again. He didn't do much.'[21]

Goldwyn had a distribution deal with RKO, and it seemed natural to lend him Ray's services to direct the actor he had first brought to prominence. It was also a disciplinary measure of sorts, but at least *Roseanna McCoy* introduced Ray to a great cameraman, Lee Garmes. 'Goldwyn asked me to make the love scenes look very "soft", as George Barnes used to do for him,' Garmes recalled, 'he wanted gauzes. I did what he wanted, and the scenes were very beautiful, but they didn't cut right. The change from hard to soft focus was too abrupt; I should have *slid* into them. Goldwyn kept saying, "The love scenes are too soft," after he'd asked for them, too!'[22]

Nick Ray worked on *Roseanna McCoy* from 23 February to 4 April 1949. From the Goldwyn studio, he wrote again to Hughes after finishing: 'Can we get together and talk about my future activities at your convenience?' Whether or not he then met Hughes, the outcome remained the same: he would be assigned to house projects, dear to Hughes but not to him. The first of them, about which the great man was 'red hot' according to Sid Rogell, had been trailing around the studio for four years.

14

Born to Be Bad

21   *Born to Be Bad*: Joan Fontaine and Zachary Scott

Bed of Roses, it will be remembered, was one of the films in preparation which Hughes cancelled in June 1948, thereby provoking Dore Schary's departure. Seven screenwriters and five directors assigned to the project (Edmund Goulding, John Hambleton, John Berry, the actor Paul Stewart, and Shepard Traube) had already worked on it. In January 1949, Joan Fontaine, originally lined up as the star after buying the rights to the book on publication, was approached again by Hughes. She felt that Hughes's interest was an old romance backfiring. Returning the script, her husband, William Dozier, wrote, 'I'm afraid Joan's enthusiasm for this project has not heightened any with the passage of time.' Hughes's money did the trick; and once again, the balance-sheets made the film's existence a necessity.

At the beginning of May, Robert Sparks and Ray were assigned to produce and direct *Bed of Roses*. Sparks, responsible for *Out of the Past*, was a respected and well-liked producer, but lacked the prestige of someone like Houseman which might have impressed Hughes. Married to actress Penny Singleton, he taught Ray a lesson borrowed from Oscar Wilde: 'Never be rude to someone you meet on your way up, you might cross him again on your way down.' For both of them, the film was a commercial chore.

First, the casting. Three men are involved with Christabel Caine, the heroine 'born to be bad'. For the role of the honest millionaire she dupes into marrying her, Sparks was considering Ronald Reagan, David Niven, Dan Duryea, Vincent Price, George Sanders, Alan Marshal or Franchot Tone.[1] Hughes's choice had neither the Britannic charm nor the ambiguity of several of those named: he picked the dreary Zachary Scott, who specialized in suave villainy. As the ambitious painter, Mel Ferrer was also a Hughes choice, having just been hired by him in a triple capacity as writer-director-actor.[2] Joan Leslie, an *ingénue* with Warners some ten years back, was hired by Hughes for this one film (Ray would have preferred Jane Wyatt). Ray, for his part, insisted from the outset on the casting of Robert Ryan, a contract player. It was the start of a lasting friendship.

Born in Chicago in 1911, the son of a Black Irish immigrant who became the head of a contracting company, Ryan had been a boxing champion at Dartmouth College for four years. He studied acting at Max Reinhardt's Hollywood workshop, as well as with European actors like Vladimir Sokoloff and Michael Chekhov. On his return from the war (he served in the Marines), he played the traumatized coastguard in Renoir's *The Woman on the Beach*. The success of *Crossfire* and *The Set-Up* made him one of the studio's biggest names, classifying him among neurotic or criminal types. 'A disturbing mixture of anger and tenderness,' Houseman wrote, '[. . .] married to a beautiful, gentle, Quaker-educated Jungian scholar and novelist.'[3] Ray did not fail to take note of him in Losey's *The Boy with Green Hair*.

Bed of Roses was shot in 35 days (20 June – 30 July), with an attention to economy and budget restrictions in which Sparks took much pride.[4] Ray, too, seems to have brought rather more to the film than conscientious professionalism.

'Robert Sparks', according to Rodney Amateau, 'was the perfect Hollywood producer, terrific guy, red face, very Irish, and every day he'd go and have lunch with a Martini, a real gentleman, he didn't want all the suffering. Just wanted to make a nice picture with RKO, and instead Nick would say to him: "I hate this scene" – "What's wrong with it?" – "I don't know, I can't get into this scene" – "But you liked it when the guy wrote it" – "No, I'm gonna change the whole scene" – "Wait a minute, you can't change . . ." It was a major studio system, and I'd say, "Nick, don't do that, don't get involved with this thing, why don't you shoot the scene, it's just Joan Fontaine, it's just a fucking picture" – "No-ooo, this picture shows the turmoil inside a woman's heart." I said, "The only turmoil inside Joan Fontaine's heart is whether her dressing room is heated in the morning. You're the only one who's got any turmoil." "You're insensitive," he'd say, "you're absolutely insensitive, you don't understand." ' Meanwhile (18 July), Joan Fontaine was inquiring as to the possibility of acquiring her wardrobe from the film at half-price.

The film was finished, passed by the Breen Office (full approval withheld pending consideration of their request to 'tone down the kiss at the end of the scene in Ryan's apartment'), and previewed. While Ray was away filming at Columbia, Hughes decided to change the ending. Edith Sommers (who had worked on *Bed of Roses* over the years) and her husband, Bob Soderberg, wrote some scenes with Sparks: among them a reconciliation between Zachary Scott and Joan Leslie on an airfield. Rewritten by Hughes himself, this becomes a confessional monologue for Scott that is revealing in its naïvety: 'I made a big mistake when I gave up flying. Maybe I'm one of those people that has to back away from things to see them clearly. Because once I'm in that plane, all by myself, I can look down and see things as they really are, in their true proportions. The big and important things look big. The little dirty things look like . . . just that.'

This scene was followed by: Joan Fontaine's departure from Scott's house, in the presence of Ferrer and Ryan (written by Soderberg; Sparks felt that it 'finishes off the story for Ryan and Fontaine in terms of comedy, which would give the end of the picture a bright "lift" '); a car accident; a scene in hospital, with Fontaine and Ferrer; a scene at a lawyer's office. Ray filmed these scenes in January 1950.

In May, Robert Stevenson reshot the hospital scene; and in July Richard Fleischer shot a scene in a prison hospital with actors new to the cast. All these scenes except one were rejected by the Legion of Decency on 28 August 1950. Hughes, it seems, established two versions, one for home consumption and one for export. The former ends with the scene on the airfield (all reference to a divorce eliminated), Christabel's departure from the house in the company of Ferrer (but not Ryan), and a brief scene

with Ferrer alone. In the export version, Fontaine still has time to steal a
doctor and a lawyer from their wives.[5]

For the first time in his career, Ray raised the question of the director's
right to final cut, stirring up some slight unease in his employers. As Ross
Hastings wrote to Rogell on 5 August, no relevant clause existed in the
Basic Agreement, the collective contract signed with the Screen Directors'
Guild. It all depended on specific clauses in the personal contracts of
certain highly-rated directors.

> Under the Basic Agreement, section B, the director:
> - shall be permitted to view the rushes at such times as not to interfere
>   with photographing;
> - shall be permitted to see cut sequences and make changes, providing
>   this doesn't cause delay. Before the producer re-edits these
>   sequences, the director shall have the option of either showing or
>   explaining them as cut by him to the producer;
> - when the rough cut is completed, the director shall be invited to
>   view it and to discuss with the producer any changes the director
>   wishes.
>
> Nicholas Ray's contract does not contain any provisions giving him
> rights in addition to those with respect to cutting.

The collective contract, moreover, made no mention of remuneration for,
or the time to be spent on, assisting at the editing stage.

It seems incredible that Ray should not have asked himself this question before reaching his fourth film. Was it some effect of his blend of
naïvety and subtlety that made him try to steal a march on his employers,
without seeing that they held all the cards and that he could only win by
guile? On *Your Red Wagon*, the 'everything is possible' innocence had
been carefully sheltered by Houseman. The meeting and friendship with
a creative editor like Sherman Todd had completed an apprenticeship
begun on radio and with *Tuesday in November*. Todd had not played the
role of supervisor (even to keeping an eye on the direction) which the
studios expected of an editor working with a first-time director. He had
shared Ray's enthusiasm for the material in *Your Red Wagon*. On *A
Woman's Secret*, Ray had Todd again. The question he asked in August
1949 implies frustration over the editing of *Born to Be Bad* by Frederick
Knudtson. Hughes had time on his side, not just the law; in May 1950,
he was still sending out eight pages of notes about the editing.

Schooled in a manner not unlike Orson Welles (stage and radio), Ray
was moving into an exclusive domain where his presence was merely
tolerated. Film-makers from the silent days – Ford, Hitchcock – edited

'in the camera', leaving the editor a purely technical job to do. Welles, on his third film, could no longer venture to shoot in long takes. As for the other rising generation in Hollywood – Wise, Robson, John Sturges, Dmytryk, Robert Parrish – all had learned to direct through editing, not through the direction of actors or the orchestration of sound.

The opening sequence of *Born to Be Bad*, as the film was finally called, is a strange exercise in *mise en scène*. Coming down a corridor with doors leading off to various rooms on one side, and on the other a staircase down to a lower level of the apartment, Donna (Joan Leslie) is moving around preparing for a party: she uses an automatic buzzer to open the door downstairs, answers the telephone, says goodbye to an older woman who leaves, gives instructions to a black couple who come up with groceries, lets in Gobby (Mel Ferrer), takes him into the kitchen with her. Returning to the corridor with an armful of flowers, she trips over a suitcase left at the top of the stairs and falls heavily. A visitor, Christabel (Joan Fontaine) is sitting there on a divan. After her first exchange with Gobby, it is all too clear that she is a cheat and a charmer. The sequence ends with a close-up of Christabel.

The two long scenes that follow, introducing the other characters, also take place in this complex setting, at different times during the evening. The gradual exploration of this space, of rooms opening one off another and off the corridor, together with Nick Musuraca's perfectly balanced lighting (superb compositions, zones of light and shadow created by natural light sources), makes up for characters of little interest except for Robert Ryan, first seen in close-up as his head appears from behind the door of a refrigerator to launch a verbal sparring match with Christabel.[6] The collaboration between Ray and Musuraca, who passed on the maxims he learned from Sternberg, is seen at its best here. Active since the 1920s, this RKO cameraman had worked on many atmospheric movies to which his low-key lighting made a considerable contribution.[7] Fritz Lang was to speak highly of his feeling for camera movement on *Clash by Night* and *The Blue Gardenia*. But apart from these opening sequences, a starchy script and indifferent sets offered him fewer opportunities on *Born to Be Bad* than he found in his *films noirs*.

Christabel, niece of a wealthy publisher, embarks on an affair with Nick (Ryan), a writer. She has her portrait painted by Gobby, who has an eye on her uncle's money. Then she takes the millionaire Curtis (Zachary Scott) away from his fiancée, Donna, a reader for the uncle's firm. For Christabel, her marriage to Curtis is a business proposition; at the first opportunity she slips away to meet Nick. Caught out in her lies, thrown out by her husband, she leaves the house with her furs ('I wouldn't want anything that belonged to Curtis . . . [but as far as the furs are concerned] I'll simply have to force myself'). Gobby retrieves his painting of her; with the scandal enhancing its value as she proceeds to seduce first her doctor and then her lawyer away from their wives, he doubles its price tag each time in a gallery window. The cynicism is hard to beat in suggesting the main point of interest of a film open to two complementary interpretations, depending upon whether you attribute it to Hughes the tycoon or to Ray the employee.

15

In a Lonely Place

Relations between Ray and Bogart during *Knock on Any Door* had been better than the film itself might lead one to suppose. Santana – Bogart and Lord, in other words – insisted on exercising their option for a second loan-out of the director, despite the incompatibility of dates pleaded by RKO, who had assigned Ray to direct *Carriage Entrance*, another typical Howard Hughes concoction. On 2 August 1949, Santana's determination prevailed over Hughes. Lord sent a one-word note to Rogell: 'Dear Sid, Thanks'.

The production circumstances for *In a Lonely Place* were the same as on *Knock on Any Door*, but the film, as enigmatic as the other is explicit, is very different. It explores many facets of the title, borrowed by Dorothy B. Hughes from J. M. Synge, and one of the few things to survive from her novel.[1] It refers not just to the violence, but equally to the depiction of Hollywood, which remains one of the finest in literature or film. We never see a sound stage, but the central character is an ageing scriptwriter, tacitly blacklisted by producers as an alcoholic with a taste for brawling; and the film emerges closer to Nathanael West or Scott Fitzgerald than to the first *A Star is Born* (one of Bogart's favourite movies).

The first paradox is that *In a Lonely Place* was scripted by a writer charmed by Hollywood. Arriving from Budapest shortly before the war, thanks to having sold a play to Columbia, Andrew Solt worked mostly with establishment film-makers like Mervyn LeRoy or Victor Fleming. He was hired through the instrumentality of his agent Lew Wasserman when Ray was already engaged in pre-production work. The decision had been taken earlier to set the action within the film world. So the months of August, September and October were devoted to writing the script with the director and producer. According to Solt, Ray did not take much of a hand in the writing, while the film did not stray much from his script. Bogart seemingly insisted on filming it 'without changes' after a reading at his house in the presence of Ray, Lord and Lauren Bacall.[2]

'I can't say that [Ray] was a director like some of the directors, who really become collaborators and know what's going on in my head. I never had that with him. It wasn't a close thing; he was the director and I would write the scenes, and we would discuss it, that's all. He gathered what I had in mind, otherwise he couldn't have made it so well. The scene was written, then I would take it to him and he would make suggestions, most of the time through his mouthpiece Amateau. And after the reading in the Bogart house, he couldn't touch it anyway, because the boss said, "This is it." '

A glance at the script suggests another version of the facts. This is dated 18 October, only one week before shooting started; and pages of revisions continued to be dictated until the end of November. Even more striking, of the 140 pages in the script, only four reached the shooting stage *without* revisions. In comparison, the 132-page *Knock on Any Door* script has 62 revised pages, all of them done within the week following the date on the script. The changes may have been made by Solt, although he had (by his own account) been kept off the set by a momentary falling-out with Bogart.[3] More important, they were occasioned by the bond between the director and the two leading actors.

The set-up was straightforward: apart from three days of location work in Los Angeles at the end of the production schedule, the whole film was shot on the Columbia sound stages, starting on Tuesday, 25 October. Ray had no lack of opportunity to do as he wanted. He even turned the restrictions on time and budget to his advantage, knowing he had to be back at RKO for another film early in December. So improvisation and the vagaries of chance play their part in the direction of *In a Lonely Place*; but they are carefully prepared for by the way the script is structured and by a strategic choice of actors.

The film centres on a relationship between scriptwriter Dixon Steele (Bogart) and a young woman, Laurel Gray. Late in his life, Ray offered an account of how Gloria Grahame came to be cast, which is fantastic enough to be true, featuring as it does Howard Hughes and Harry Cohn.[4]

' "I hear you're having a problem with the leading lady," [Cohn said to him]. I said, "I don't have a problem. I just don't want Ginger Rogers." "Who do you want?" "Gloria Grahame." "You're married to her, huh?" "What the hell does that have to do with it? She's right for the part." He said, "Well, ask your man Hughes to call me." I said, "Why don't you call him?" Somehow or other, I got a call from Howard saying, "Have Harry Cohn meet me at the corner of Santa Monica and Formosa at midnight in the filling station."

'Apparently Harry met him, because he called me about two o'clock in the morning and said, "What the hell are you trying to do to me? You know what I did with that maniac all night? I drove in that dirty Chevrolet of his up and down the alleys of Bennett and Santa Monica. All night long!" I wish I'd been there. Because here were two tycoons, two robber barons, who hadn't talked to each other in five years. And he said, "You tell him the next time we have a meeting, we have it in my home."

'The next time they had it in Harry's home. He called me the next day and said, "You know what that crazy son of a bitch did last night?" – "No, what'd he do, Harry?" – "Well, he saw this window over on the far right side of my room. It was open about a foot. The only one outside was my watchman. He goes over and pushes down the damn window so we won't be overheard by anybody." "What happened?" "Well, I made a deal." And my wife got a job.' (Just try imagining *In a Lonely Place* with Ginger Rogers.)[5]

Ray attached a particular importance to the character of Mel, Dix/ Bogart's agent from a long way back. He noted in the margin of his script: 'Relationship with him must be *warm* – endure everything – friend to the death. They [Laurel and Mel] both protect [Dix].' In the role, Ray cast Art Smith, who had been one of the earliest members of the Group Theater. Around 1934 he was writing agitational plays like *Dimitroff* (with Kazan) and *The Tide Rises*. Moving to the West Coast at the time of *A Tree Grows in Brooklyn*, he had been constantly in work. Two-and-a-half years after *In a Lonely Place*, Art Smith's career was stopped short when first Elia Kazan, then Clifford Odets, named him as one of the members of the Group Theater's Communist cell.

Ray drew up a list of sequences and of character developments, showing what he wanted to stress: the relationship between Dix and Laurel and the process of its destruction by forces both exterior (professional pressures, police harassment) and interior. 'What Dix wants no one girl can supply. He's a sick man.' The same dread words were to be applied often enough to Ray himself. Rodney Amateau says of him at this time: 'He always felt that people were out to get him, and nobody was out to get him, you know? But if you feel somebody's out to get you long enough, they become . . . they play the part.'[6] The circles in which the characters move are hostile in their indifference. It is out of this indifference, as much as from Dix himself, that the violence is born. In its ambiguities and its reticences, the film is as far removed from genre formula as it is from sociological statements.

A *film noir* credits sequence combines two images within the frame: a nocturnal drive through Beverly Hills, and Bogart's eyes framed in the rearview mirror of a car – a first instance of the fragmentation of the screen that was to assume obsessional forms in Ray's work. The first scene is an addition to the script, dated 8 November, after filming had already started. At a red light, greeted by a woman in a car pulled up alongside his (an actress who had appeared in a film he scripted), Dix denies knowing her, and when her husband intervenes, cracks back at her, 'You shouldn't have done it, honey, no matter how much money that pig's got.' He's raring for a fight, but the man accelerates away. The deliberate rudeness establishes a sense of unease characteristic of Ray (and perhaps of Bogart), and strips the inner violence of any romantic aura (along self-destructive artist lines) one may be tempted to read into it.

The second scene, rewritten on 21 October a few days before filming began (it was one of the first scenes in the schedule) introduced two new characters in its revised version. Concerning the first of these, the alcoholic old actor Charlie Waterman (played by Robert Warwick), Andrew Solt claims that Bogart asked him to write a part for an actor who was slipping, and who had helped him in his early days. Robert Warwick did indeed appear in the cast of Bogart's first Broadway play, but could hardly be said to be slipping. In movies since the silent days, he appeared in several films every year; recently he had been in Kazan's *Gentleman's Agreement* and in *A Woman's Secret*.

The second new character is 'Junior', some bigshot producer's 'son-in-law' who comes into the bar boasting about 'his' preview, insults the old actor, and is knocked down by Dix. The first two moments of violence thus surface very early in the film, both linked to the Hollywood environment and stressing the rage it arouses in Dix Steele. Hardly surprising that Solt (assuming he even wrote it) did not much care for this sequence in the film: 'I didn't like too well the way he directed the first reel. Romanoff's was the Mecca of Hollywood, but the feeling here was cheap, the set was cheap, there weren't enough elegant people in there.'

Elegance and sumptuousness of setting are neither the strong point nor the purpose of the scenes at 'Paul's' – directly inspired by Romanoff's restaurant. What we see is characters meeting and engaging in commonplace small-talk, beyond which their real concerns – money, malice, hustling – can be read. Steele's dealings with women are suggested in a brief scene with a former lover, Fran, who sits down beside him after the fight with Junior: 'I was pretty nice to you,' he protests. 'No,' she says, 'not *to* me. But you were pretty nice.' Similarly with his fairly open pick-up – though the conventions are adhered to (each pretending to think the other is asking or accepting only what is proper) – of the hat-check girl, Mildred Atkinson, who has been reading the novel Dix is supposed to adapt. He takes her back to his place on the pretext of having her tell him the story, but discouraged by her silliness, packs her off home again.

While he and Mildred are crossing the patio leading to his apartment, they are overtaken by Laurel, who passes between them. Wearing a light-coloured coat, her hands in the pockets, she glances up at him, half-smiling as she apologizes. 'Definite interest – not first time she's seen him – he looks interesting – liked his face,' Ray noted of this scene. Later, we twice see Laurel at her window, watching Dix: 'Strategy – seeming indifference.'

Early next morning, Dix is woken by an old friend, a detective, and taken down to headquarters: after she left his place, Mildred Atkinson was murdered. Under questioning, he remembers his neighbour watching from her apartment. She is sent for.

The script specified a police stenographer. Instead, Dix offers another insolent crack: 'How are you fellows recording this, tape or wire?' Ray's interest in the techniques of recording and surveillance restricts the scene to four people; Laurel Gray, Dix, Brub Nicolai (Frank Lovejoy) – the detective who served with Dix during the war – and Captain Lochner

22   *In a Lonely Place*: in the police headquarters: Gloria Grahame, Frank Lovejoy, Carl Benton Reid and Humphrey Bogart

(Carl Benton Reid). This intimist tendency, the *Kammerspiel* effect of the film, becomes increasingly pronounced.

In directing Gloria Grahame – and the film – Ray tried to uncover the deeper meaning behind scenes, words and gestures.[7] Two aspects of the Method – improvisation and affective memory – were put to use here, not literally but in that the material itself invited elaboration of that sort. At the beginning of his script, Ray noted: 'The simpler, more direct, more honest, better it will create Laurel, flesh and blood. She's the same girl in her reactions to different situations.' Elsewhere, one of the keys to the film: 'Nobody saying what they think.'

In the script, the scene at police headquarters covers six pages, four of which are dated 9 November (second and third revisions), one each 26 and 27 October. Laurel says she doesn't know Dix, but has seen him a few times and knows who he is: 'When I moved in a few days ago, Mr Steele was pointed out to me by the manager. She was very proud of having a celebrity for a tenant.' She confirms Steele's alibi, and explains that she was watching 'because he looked interesting. I like his face.' She leaves. Dix joins her in the corridor, but she has the cop who brought her drive her home. The script comprises almost five pages of dialogue, with no business indicated other than entries and exits, Captain Lochner miming the killer's actions, and Steele's 'broad, victorious smile' (sic) at Laurel's remark about his face. Neither of these stage directions is observed in the scene, shot on 18 and 19 November. Alongside Laurel's dialogue on her entry, Ray noted: 'Scan room, alert but not defensive.' Against her remark about the manager: 'Amused.' When she says she saw Dix with Mildred Atkinson: 'Doesn't want to say [she] was watching.'

Laurel is wearing slacks and a checked jacket. She sits down, spots a carton of coffee, tilts a paper cup to see if there's any in it. Solt was shocked by the vulgarity of her gesture ('It's wrong. A real floozie will do that, she never would'), failing to recognize either its primary meaning (Laurel was woken by the police and it's still very early) or its secondary one (her frankness, her way of making what she wants quite clear).

Sitting in front of the desk facing the two policemen, with Dix remaining seated behind her, Laurel has to turn round when asked if she knows him. She turns round again, startled but not suspicious, when she is told about the murder. 'You know . . . mugged,' says Dix, sketching a gesture illustrating Lochner's statement that Mildred was strangled. Lochner crosses and sits down beside Dix. Calmly – slight smile, eyebrows raised, voice lightly inflected – she looks at Lochner and answers his questions, but the dialogue is in fact taking place between her and Dix. Each line spoken marks a shift in the balance of their respective positions.

In the corridor, Laurel is standing by a drinking-fountain. Playing by the same rules, Dix speaks not to her but to a waiting policeman: 'Oh, I'll see that Miss Gray gets home.' In response, she addresses him directly: 'Thank you, but I always go home with the man who brought me.' Ray's marginal note: 'Don't take it for granted, you don't handle me that way.'

Another example of elaboration using the script as a springboard is the scene with the nightclub singer. Unknown to everyone (except Mel), Dix and Laurel have started living together, happily so far: Dix is working on a script and Laurel is typing it, not telling him that she has again been questioned by the police, who still suspect him. The scene is dated 25 November, an extremely concise '2nd revision'; including the lyrics, it takes up one page of the script. It was filmed on 29 and 30 November. The script describes the feature characteristic of the setting: 'A copper-toned piano. Around it are Dix, Laurel and a few other people seated on high bar stools, using the piano top as a table. At the piano an entertainer is singing.' According to the script, the policeman Barton enters with a woman on his arm, Dix gives him a sign of recognition, Laurel tenses when she sees him, and Dix jokes in 'parody-gangster's intonation' (the self-mockery of Bogart also featured in an earlier scene, abbreviated during editing).

Interviewed in 1983, the singer Hadda Brooks described how she was helped by Bogart, who tried to put her at her ease by telling stories.[8] She also recalled the director's irritability when she couldn't synchronize with her own playback, and claimed that this was why the camera cut away to a shot of Bogart as she started singing, until she was able to get into synch. This, of course, is much more an editing problem than one of filming, and is an example of a memory at fault: in the film, the blues does in fact start on the singer. The incident does perhaps evoke a Ray much less sure of his margin of freedom for manoeuvre than he later became, and impatient to clear the ground to work with his two stars. The lyrics, moreover, do feature in the script (just as they did with *They Live by Night*), which gives some idea of the importance given to the counterpoint between the blues (*I Hadn't Anyone 'til You*) and the action. The lyrics and the description of the setting are in fact the only elements that survive from the script.

As filmed, the scene is virtually reversed. Starting out as a moment of serenity and poise (as expressed by the open, symmetrical frame compositions), it pivots on a change of angle bizarre even by *film noir* standards.[9] Laurel and Dix have been shown face-to-face with the singer in

23   *In a Lonely Place*: Hadda Brooks at the piano

24   *In a Lonely Place*: Dix and Laurel see the policeman in the nightclub

reverse angle shots. A huge lateral close-up of them isolates Dix and (behind him) Laurel, who leans in close to whisper lovingly in his ear. In so doing, she looks up, her expression changing as she sees Barton. Dix turns and looks in the same direction. Furiously he stubs out his cigarette, startling the singer, and they leave, passing the policeman in the doorway. 'Suspicion made tangible', Ray noted. At this point, reality reflects Dix's 'sickness': he does not know, though the spectator does, that he is still the police's most likely suspect, and that Laurel is still being questioned.

Dissolving into the next scene, we find Laurel contaminated by the spreading suspicion. She is dominated (low-angle shot, the woman's bulk) by her masseuse, Martha, who complacently warns her about Dix's history of violence. Laurel reacts angrily ('combating her [own] suspicions'). Martha ('the only thing left of Laurel's movie career'), reminding her of the security she once enjoyed as a kept woman, insists that she is her only real friend. Martha is the last link in a chain of Hollywoodian rumours and ostracisms. In the two years since 'The Great Fear' started in Hollywood (to borrow David Caute's phrase), no other film had captured the atmosphere so sharply. Perhaps this is why *In a Lonely Place* was so admired by film-makers like Abraham Polonsky, Samuel Fuller or Anthony Mann, for whom success was not the sole criterion.

At the same time, Ray lets scenes be guided by the characters' moods, by the revelation of imperceptible shifts in their relationships. For instance, in the series of brief episodes during which Dix's violence breaks out. Towards the end of a picnic with the Nicolais on Santa Monica beach, Brub's wife, Sylvia, inadvertently reveals that Laurel has been questioned again by the police. Dix, realizing both that she lied to him and that he is still suspected of murder, stalks angrily away to his car. Laurel follows. Dix runs straight through a halt sign and side-swipes another car. The young driver rushes up, very upset. Almost without provocation, Dix knocks him down, goes on hitting him brutally, then picks up a big stone. A cry from Laurel stops him, and he gets back into the car.

In the margins of the script, Ray notes on three occasions that the perturbed Laurel 'doesn't anticipate Dix's violence'. As they drive away from the beach, she takes a 'quick look to see [his] mood' (eliminated and replaced by a disdainful look from Bogart as she offers him a cigarette). During the fight, she 'cries out' her 'horror of seeing what he's capable [sic].' When they drive off again, she 'sinks back, numb, chest heaving'. 'Not sullen, subjecting.' The 'basic situation' is her 'terrible upset'. She isn't able to talk, Ray also notes. According to the script, she offers Dix a cigarette, 'really saying, I have nothing to say'. Another note says 'thoughts of Randolph – Mildred' (the police told Laurel that Dix could be Mildred Atkinson's killer; her lesbian masseuse stressed the injuries he inflicted on Frances Randolph, a former girl-friend). Ray's direction of the scene reverses the bits of business: she talks, he takes the initiative over the cigarette. The marginal notes are not used to rewrite the script or to predetermine gestures, but to give the director himself a better springboard than mere directions in a written text, to help the scene evolve in one direction or another without losing sight of the underlying implications of the film and of the characters. The last of these notes ('thoughts of Randolph – Mildred') pinpoints the convergence of two motifs: police/professional persecution and inner violence.

Faced with Dix's efforts to explain – he speaks as though to himself – Laurel says to him: 'You weren't really angry with him. You've been wanting to slug somebody ever since you left the beach.' The line carries the annotation: 'Taken out on first person – upset comes through – don't try to kid me [and] blame him.' Pensive, still almost in an aside, Dix quotes four lines he has written:

> I was born when she kissed me
> I died when she left me
> I lived a few weeks
> While she loved me.

He says to Laurel: 'I want to put it in the script' (annotation: 'Secretary'). She: 'The farewell note?' (annotation: 'Mind elsewhere'). He: 'Yes. Can you remember it?' (annotation: 'So you can type it'). In the film, this line is replaced by: 'I don't know, maybe. Say it back to me, let's hear how it sounds.' Then she (annotation: 'Remembering') repeats the poem, starting in a toneless voice, but she cannot finish it. All this dialogue is delivered in a neutral tone: to talk about themselves, they have to talk about something else.

Overall, these very simple suggestions, ranging from textual analysis to probing for underlying meanings in the dialogue, comprised direction for Gloria Grahame as well as memory-joggers for Ray's own use. Here, they define the function of this pivotal sequence. (The poem did not make its appearance until filming had started, in revisions dated 9 November, and the scenes comprising the sequence were the last to be shot.)

Contrasting with the virtuosity of this fragmented sequence, the disintegration of the love affair is achieved in a very simply structured scene: first one unbroken medium shot as Dix enters Laurel's living-room, then a series of set-ups from the same angle (as in the scenes at police headquarters). Only the close-ups of the two protagonists are out of key with the normality of their movements around the three-room apartment, the matter-of-factness of their words and gestures. Coming into Laurel's apartment, Dix finds her cleaning-woman, Effie, at work there. He unplugs the vacuum-cleaner in case she wakes Laurel. Effie says Laurel is taking pills. Dix goes into Laurel's bedroom, switches off the alarm clock as she turns over sleepily, looks at the bottle of sleeping pills, kisses her on the shoulder, and goes out.

Preparing breakfast in the kitchen, he straightens the curved grapefruit knife. His manner is ostensibly casual as the still sleepy Laurel comes in, smiles on seeing the straightened knife. They talk about the love scene she has typed for the script, which she likes. Dix: 'That's because they're not always telling each other how much in love they are. A good love scene should be about something else beside love. For instance, this one: me fixing grapefruit, you sitting over there, dopey, half asleep. Anyone looking at us could tell we were in love.' He pauses, pretending casualness: 'Effie wants us to get married.' A close-up of Laurel, alarmed, then the rest of the scene shows Dix, intense, closely observing her reactions, asking about the pills, and Laurel trying to back off: 'It's only lately that you've wanted to know everything about me.' In reality escaping from the room, she makes the excuse of going to attend to the coffee; he follows, takes her in his arms; a slow track-in ends with the 'Yes' extracted by Dix from the cornered Laurel, and with a kiss that carries the chill of terror.

All the themes converge in the disastrous engagement party at Paul's restaurant: Dix's past (Frances butting in), the professional constraints (Dix being offered opinions on his script, barely finished and circulated without his knowledge by Laurel and Mel), friendship (he insults and hits Mel, immediately seeking reconciliation with him), the inevitable end in Laurel running away. Tersely, the film pursues its thread: jealousy, violence, the final break-up.

What you notice in *In a Lonely Place* is the swiftness and sureness of gesture and movement, the sureness of the risks taken with the two actors in deliberately putting the skids under them. Bogart, a physical presence – ageing, stripped of his aura, in pyjamas or with shirt-sleeves rolled up over hairy forearms – and no longer the icon in the inevitable immaculate white shirt of his last Warner films (*Key Largo*); Grahame, a variety of striking clothes ('No fluff, please', the script notes) both erotic and very time-bound, awareness of her body (in the alarm clock scene, her bare shoulder suggests that she is nude under the covers), the frankness of her desire, the ambiguity nevertheless of her eroticism. To say that they are both playing themselves is a truism. But this re-creation of the Hollywood environment on Columbia's sound stages (showing none of the fascination with the studios evident even in films as caustic as *Sunset Boulevard*) produces a situation on the verge of psychodrama; a verge that would soon be crossed. Bogart is here credited with the scandalous behaviour that became part of his legend (a legend he himself encouraged, and which was in fact at variance with his nature as a fairly solid citizen), and with a bitterness towards 'the system' that must have delighted him; Grahame is presented as a negotiable asset (her former lover built her a swimming-pool 'to increase the value of his property'), passed from hand to hand and trying to take decisions which aren't hers to make.

Strategically, this was not without its dangers, and another 'engagement' took place concurrently on the set. Ray took extreme precautions: with the consent of the producers, he had Grahame sign a separate agreement whereby she was contractually bound to submit to the director's wishes.[10] *In a Lonely Place* was not shot in continuity, and filming of the ending as envisaged in the script was set for about half-way through the schedule: Dix discovers that Laurel is getting ready to run out on him, and strangles her; Brub arrives to arrest him as he is typing the end of his script, the four lines heard earlier. As Ray explained in the documentary *I'm a Stranger Here Myself*, the circumstances in which he came to this point in the schedule were unusual:

'In the meantime I had separated from my wife. And if I had let the producer Bobby Lord or Bogie know that, they would have gone crazy, or Harry Cohn would have gone crazy. So I said, "Look, I'm having trouble with the third act. Make an apartment for me in a couple of dressing-rooms, 'cause I don't want to drive to Malibu every night. I want to get downstage and work at night.' Which I did. And Gloria behaved beautifully. Nobody knew that we were separated. And I just couldn't believe the ending that Bundy [Solt] and I had written. I shot it because it was my obligation to do it. Then I kicked everybody off stage except Bogart, Art Smith and Gloria. And we improvised the ending as it is now. In the original ending we had ribbons so it was all tied up into a very neat package, with Frank Lovejoy coming in and arresting him as he was writing the last lines, having killed Gloria. Huh! And I thought, shit, I can't do it, I just can't do it! Romances don't have to end that way. Marriages don't have to end that way, they don't have to end in violence. Let the audience make up its own mind about what's going to happen to Bogie when he goes outside of the apartment area – which was the first apartment I lived in in Hollywood, by the way.'

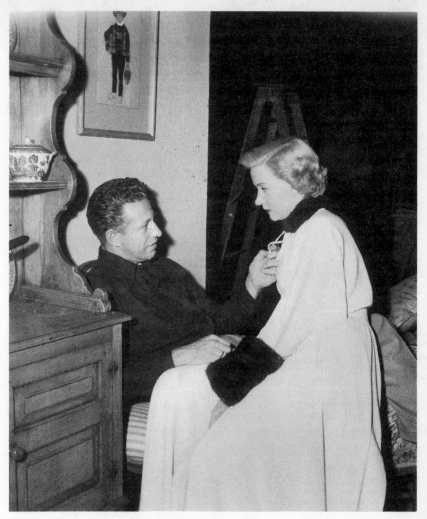

25   Nicholas Ray and Gloria Grahame

The final sequence, in both versions, was shot between 15 and 17 November.[11] The pages alluding to the killer's confession (in a curious hint of panic, he was given the same name as the associate producer, Henry Kesler) were dictated on the 15th. Brub's telephone call on the 18th, along with a note, 'The other end of telephone conversation has already been photographed.' Ray used as much of the first version as credibility permitted: Dix, trembling with rage, wild-eyed, starts strangling Laurel. He is stopped by the ringing of the telephone, but also by the fact – suggested by his movements and his delivery of the line, 'A man

145

wants to apologize to you' – that he is completely drained. Then he goes out and, in discordant diagonals, down the steps. A close-up of Laurel, murmuring the last line of the poem; and a final high-angle shot of Dix crossing the patio.

A film both prescriptive (the constraints of filming in studio sets, scenes dictated by the genre to which it purportedly belongs) and eccentric, *In a Lonely Place* is thus predicated on the forcing gambit which transforms the final murder into an equally harrowing separation. 'Portrait of a future killer,' says Solt. A narrow squeak, is the film's rather different view, twice showing Dix in the act of murder: lifting the stone to hit the young driver, and strangling Laurel. Commenting on the final scene, Ray said: 'You do not know whether the man is going to go out, to get drunk, have an accident in his car, or whether he is going to go to a psychiatrist for help. And that's the way it should be; either one of the two things could happen to him because now the pressure is off, but now there is an internal pressure. He has a problem about himself.'[12]

Ray's later observation in *Lightning Over Water* that 'the closer I get to my ending, the closer I am getting to rewriting my beginning' – perhaps more relevant to *In a Lonely Place* than to any of his other films – suggests another reading. The disorientation, the unease induced by this ending, spreads back through earlier scenes where the spectator is seeing something he shouldn't that doesn't ring quite right: the excessively crude provocations in the opening sequence, Dix's gloating reconstruction of the murder for Brub and his wife, the obsessiveness of his affair with Laurel, the touch of equivocality in the latter's relationship with her masseuse, the grapefruit knife being straightened under the impression that it was bent, all of the love scenes.

Around a conventional nucleus, a clear formal structure is developed, both plastically and rhythmically: its dominant notes nocturnal or twilit. The intimist nature of the drama does not preclude a bold visual conception, determined by the rare exteriors that punctuate the film. For these, Ray made a particular architectural choice, using Californian baroque, a Hispanic style known as 'neo-Leo Carrillo': the Beverly Hills civic hall and post office, the corner of Fountain and Harper. These are scenes in counterpoint, never head on, in which the main dramatic theme is developed in space and time. Ray always swore by this conception of *mise en scène*, but perhaps never employed it with such sureness and spontaneity as here. It was a conception which, shorn of its context in other circumstances, could lead to chaos and lack of finish.

16

On Dangerous Ground

Ray came across the English novelist Gerald Butler's *Mad With Much Heart* in June 1949, during the six weeks of preparatory work on *Born to Be Bad*. It was the story of a policeman, on the trail of a retarded boy, killer of a three-year-old girl, who falls in love with the boy's blind sister. Ray gave it to Sid Rogell to read, and sent it to Houseman in New York. The RKO readers turned in negative reports, Houseman wasn't enthusiastic.[1] But Houseman had to fulfil his contract with RKO, and he knew that working under the Hughes regime wouldn't be easy. He therefore drove back down to Hollywood (Ray cabled him the money necessary to make the last few miles from Victorville). It was largely thanks to the personal involvement of Robert Ryan, anxious to work again with Ray after the frustrating *Born to Be Bad*, that Houseman managed to have the novel bought.[2] Faced with the trio's resolution, the front office reluctantly started preparing the project; on 14 December, when he arrived back from Columbia, Ray was officially assigned as director on *Mad With Much Heart*, although a memo added: 'We want to make it clear that we do assign him to the picture with our right to revoke the assignment at any time at our discretion.'

Houseman wrote of these months at RKO as 'among the darkest and most arid of my life': 'It was a distasteful and unproductive atmosphere – one to which I developed an intense and debilitating allergy.' However, in return for producing *The Company She Keeps*, Houseman was able to get *Mad With Much Heart* under way. Since Charles Schnee wasn't free – Ray and Houseman's first choice as scriptwriter – William Fadiman suggested 'an able, hard-hitting writer', A. I. Bezzerides, as an alternative.

A. I. Bezzerides came to the United States at the age of nine months. Armenian on his father's side, Greek on his mother's ('They spoke Turkish to each other'), he grew up among the Fresno immigrants, truckers, produce haulers – the characters who people his two novels, *Long Haul* and *Thieves' Market*. He knew the seedy neighbourhoods, the darker urban recesses. If Charles Schnee was a professional, Bezzerides was a real writer: Ray got on with him from the start.

They began work on a treatment more than a hundred pages in length (dictated starting from 17 October) which bears the unmistakable stamp of the writer. In the manner of his novels, his scripts[3] – indeed, of his

147

correspondence or his conversation – it is a breathless narrative studded with dialogue: a wild, vigorous flood of words, with sudden surges of emotion reinforcing or enriching the central theme. Here, for instance, is a digression, a by-product of the police investigation which never reached the screen:

'A man is standing, with proprietary air, in the doorway of the ultimate bar. Here no music plays. The street is quiet. There are only the endless disturbing sounds of night life. Jim crosses to the man. He asks him a question, and the man answers, pointing off. Jim gestures thanks. An eagerness runs through his face. He walks purposefully as he wades through the crowd across the street.

'. . . There is a sign in the café which says, JESUS SAVES. Near the door a man dressed in a kind of Salvation Army uniform is handing out printed matter. "Do you believe in the True Salvation?" he asks Jim in an exalted voice, holding out a pamphlet. "Have you confessed your sins? Is your place in heaven waiting?" Jim flashes his badge and passes into the café.

'Within the café, men are standing in line, waiting for a free dinner. After they are served, they walk with their trays to the tile-surfaced tables that fill the room. As Jim walks about, we get a view of the hungry men. The old ones prong at the food with forks, held in faltering, clumsy hands. They eat greedily, their lips smacking as the fork catches at the food, carries it up, hoists at the mouth. Too much food, too few teeth. Choking. There is one man with a tremendous vegetation of beard. He eats expertly, and it is like eating through a bush.'[4]

This night-time city of bums, cops, pimps, snitches, winos and too-young girls was common ground for the writer and the director (it was the subject of one of Ray's last projects, *New York After Midnight*, in 1970). But it had nothing to do with the novel. Ray developed an opening section comprising prowlings, acts of violence, what he describes in the preface to the first draft continuity (here the tone and vocabulary are more his than Bezzerides's) as 'numerous apparently unrelated and anonymous incidents in the course of Jim Wilson's duties on the Special Squad of a big city police force. This is the life that has made Jim the man he is'. Jim's violence is not, and would not be, explained. 'His mouth contains a twist of anger, and his eyes squint with a kind of inner rage. But the rage is focusless, inexpressed. All it requires is a victim.' In this treatment, it is the intensity of the emotions that is foregrounded: so much so that when Jim talks to the young killer, the murder doesn't come into it.

This was a scene that meant a lot to Bezzerides: 'I remembered when I wrote it . . . in high school there were two girls who lived near me. They came out of a very rich family, and I lived in a kind of background where the girls simply wouldn't be attracted to me, because when they saw the house and my people, it was repulsive to them. And I loved them, I admired them. But I was a little bit too eager and they sensed it. So one day when I was walking down the narrow street, there were the two girls, and I thought, now they'll have to look at me, and then I can talk to them. And as they came near, they ran. I got so upset, it hurt me like I was a murderer. I saw them run into the house, slam the door, and then look through the curtains to see if I was still there. I used this in the script, and Nick got very touched by it. He understood. So when he shot the scene – the cop's trying to talk to the kid, but the kid's afraid of the cop, and he backs away and backs away and falls over a cliff – he did it fabulously.' (The memory in fact surfaces twice in the film, since it inspires not only the death of Danny, the young killer, but also what he tells Jim earlier about the murder he committed.)

The treatment ends with Jim leaving the blind girl, who tells him not to come back, and closing the door behind him. Jim stands for a long moment on the porch, is about to open the door. 'Then he goes slowly down the steps and heads away across the frozen yard.'

The first draft continuity, which Bezzerides started dictating concurrently on 21 November, and which was finished much later, on 14 February 1950, tacks a third part on to this ending reminiscent of *In a Lonely Place*: 'a brutal, garish echo of part one', as the preface already quoted puts it. Houseman and Bezzerides never got over the feeling of having been conned, without ever really knowing how or why. Bezzerides felt that there were three stories instead of one. Houseman was of much the same opinion: 'The character played by Bob Ryan was really essentially Nick's creation. So we had two pictures. We had the business of a good cop given to violence, and then we had the perfectly ridiculous plot about the blind girl and the boy, and all that. I always rather disliked it. And the two never blended. Al Bezzerides is a good writer, but I think he was always a little bewildered by that picture, as indeed I was. I just wanted Nick to get what he wanted and to do what he wanted, but I never really quite understood what the hell he was doing.'

It was precisely this that gave the film its impact and meaning, however: the radical dichotomy, both narrative and visual, between the two plots. The first, adopting all the formal attributes of the thriller genre, is keyed to an unremitting darkness: describing a character, it is virtually plotless. The second is bathed in white light, its narrative drive the idea of a quest for lost innocence.

When the list of screen credits was eventually prepared, Houseman requested a separate credit for Ray as author of the story: 'Part of the story on which the picture is based is entirely original with Nicholas Ray, being an enlarged portion of the story which was not contained in the basic novel by Gerald Butler.' He suggested the wording: 'Based on a Screen Story by Nicholas Ray, and the Novel by Gerald Butler.' (In the end, Ray and Bezzerides received co-credit for the adaptation, Bezzerides alone for the script.)

Houseman has remarked on how the two men spent their nights in squad cars from the Los Angeles Police Department. Bezzerides insists that he was alone: 'Anyway, there wouldn't have been room for two in those cars.' And in fact Ray had gone east, away from the Gloria Grahame split-up, to pursue his own research, to spend Christmas and New Year in Wisconsin with his mother and sisters, and to scout – possibly film – some snowy locations around Boston.

From 29–31 December, then again from 10–12 January 1950, he was

26　*On Dangerous Ground*: unremitting darkness – Robert Ryan, Anthony Ross, Charles Kemper and Cleo Moore

in New York, at the Algonquin. At the theatre, accompanied by the distinguished reporter John Bartlow Martin,[5] he saw Sidney Kingsley's *Detective Story*, a play very similar in theme to the Ray-Bezzerides script.[6] Early in January, Ray went to Boston, where he watched Irish cops at work (Thomas Sullivan, Tom Reilly, John Preston, Frank Mulvey), riding in squad cars, living in the same place as they did. It was probably there that the film took shape for him.[7] 'The particular man that I modelled a great deal of the physical surroundings and the behaviour on was a member of the Boston Violence Squad [sic] police desk whom I went out on his assignments with. He was a bachelor who began being a police officer in order to put his brother through college and to make it possible for him to study for the priesthood. By the time his brother was a priest, he'd be a police officer who was going to remain a police officer unless he got kicked out for being too violent, which he almost was.'[8]

In Bezzerides's treatment, we followed Jim Wilson through the city's

27 *On Dangerous Ground*: lost innocence – Sumner Williams

lower depths without learning anything about him other than his violence, born of the contact with violence. We never saw the cops off duty, or relaxing together. The film has an entirely different centre of gravity, and shows the city only as the scene of their activities.

Following the credits, a woman's hands pick up a gun in a shoulder-holster and buckle it on to a man. The woman snuggles up to him from behind. She doesn't like being left on her own. Pete pulls himself away. Another apartment, a Western playing on the TV. Shabby kids sit watching it. A car horn blares. The father, a fat, middle-aged man, gets up and goes to the bedroom. His wife hands him his gun. 'Thanks, mother.' The car horn. Close-up of a series of police mug-shots. Jim Wilson has them spread out like a pack of cards by his plate. He scrapes his dishes into the dustbin, gets his jacket, pockets the mug-shots. At police headquarters, the men check in like workers. The captain urges them to redouble their efforts in the search for a pair of cop-killers. The squad cars race away. A rain-wet street. Lucky, an informer, attaches himself to Jim, follows him into a bar. A blonde accosts Jim, who asks how old she is. The barman and a bag-lady joke about this. From a booth at the back, a man (Bezzerides himself) calls him over, mockingly holding out some money: 'Look, you won!' 'I didn't bet on any horse,' Jim says. Back in the squad car again; a radio message sends them after a man running along a busy street. Caught, frisked and released, the suspect protests: 'Dumb cops, I was only runnin'!' Jim turns back threateningly, is restrained by Pete. Hostile mutterings from the bystanders.

Later, in a drugstore. A woman smiles at Jim; someone says her boyfriend wouldn't like it. 'That's all he'd need to know, me going out with a cop!' she says. Jim turns away. A newspaper vendor gives Jim the address of a girl, Myrna, who may be a lead to the cop-killers. Jim and Pete sent the old cop, Pop, home in a taxi. 'Seven kids, what a mob to come home to!' They go to Myrna's, look round her B-girl apartment. Jim asks about the man in a photograph tucked into the mirror. 'He was real cute. You want to see how cute he was? (She shows him the bruises on her arm.) You're cute too.' She punches him, not very hard. Close-up. 'If I don't, you'll make me talk. You'll squeeze it out of me with those big, strong arms . . . won't you?' Pete has already left. Dissolve to Jim coming slowly down the stairs.

Early morning. The squad car pulls up at a hotel. Pete and Jim go upstairs, bursting in on the startled Burney in his room. People crowding in from neighbouring rooms are ushered out by Pete. Pete goes out himself. Jim: 'We're alone now. You can't talk, huh?' Dolly in on Burney's face, expressionistically lit. Low-angle shot of Jim. He lunges for the taunting Burney: 'Why do you make me do it?' He beats him up. Later, Jim crosses the police parking lot alone. He goes up the steps leading to his apartment, catches a newspaper thrown at him by a delivery boy, makes a couple of football passes with the kid. He switches the light on in his one-room apartment, looks at an athletic trophy on the bureau along with a photograph, a lamp, a small crucifix. He puts coffee on to heat, washes his hands at the sink, drying them compulsively.

Jim receives a warning from his captain. Immediately after, in the squad car, he hears a woman screaming, makes a U-turn. On a fire escape, women are shouting. In a pool of light below, two men beating up a blonde run off. It is Myrna. Jim chases one of the men, corners him and starts beating him up. Pop hauls him off, bawls him out. Jim: 'Garbage, that's all we handle, garbage! How do you do it? How do you live with yourself?' Pop: 'I don't, I live with other people.' This ends the city section in the film as shot, with the captain sending Jim away on a job upstate to avoid the consequences of his brutality.

In mid-January, Ray was back at the studio, and very reluctantly confirmed as assigned to this project while pages of the script were still being turned out. But relations with the front office were at a new low. Offered a bigger office by Sid Rogell, Ray replied: 'While the larger office would suit my purposes quite nicely, I know that by depriving the present incumbent of its benefits I would be embarrassed and engender a feeling of antagonism toward me which would make me feel far more uncomfortable than any physical inconvenience . . . Until then, forget it.' Rogell sent a basket of fruit to Ray, who thanked him: 'I hope you won't have to shop for a basket of rotten tomatoes to throw at me when the picture is finished. Gratefully.' Rogell commented: 'I wish there was something we could do to keep him happy.'

The various versions of the script were wrapped up and submitted to Fadiman.[9] On 8 March Houseman reported to Rogell: 'I trust you have been regularly receiving the final pages as we turn them out. We have a few days more, working for even greater intensity and depth in the scenes between Jim and the girl.' Houseman also reported 'extraordinary reactions', perhaps to reassure Rogell as well as himself. 'At no time,' he in fact wrote in his autobiography, 'did it manage to engender the creative enthusiasm or the deep personal involvement that had illuminated my first film with Nick Ray.'

On that same 8 March, the latter departed for Durango, Colorado, leaving several problems to his producer. Closer than Boston, Colorado offered suitable climatic conditions this late in the year for the snow scenes. Filming would have to follow quickly after the locations were scouted, before the thaw. Except for Ryan, of course, none of the leading players had been selected yet. For the other two principal male roles, candidates were: as Bond, father of the murdered girl, 'Lee Cobb, Howard Da Silva, Ward Bond, Albert Dekker, Rhys Williams, James Bell' (the part was eventually played by Ward Bond, with the name changed to Brent): as Pop Daly, 'Wallace Ford, Ward Bond, Ray Collins, Jay Flippen' (Charles Kemper, fresh from *Where Danger Lives*, got the part).

The choices listed for the role of the young blind woman are rather more surprising. For 'the crux of our casting', Houseman put forward no fewer than twelve names, annotated by Rogell under instructions from Hughes: Jane Wyman, Susan Hayward, Olivia de Havilland . . . 'Of the more accessible girls', Houseman notes Ida Lupino ('OK' comments Rogell), Deborah Kerr ('No'), Janet Leigh (Houseman adds question mark, and Rogell confirms 'No'), Wanda Hendrix ('No'); 'a very remote possibility that something could be done with Betty [Lauren] Bacall' ('OK, possible'), Teresa Wright ('No'), Margaret Sullavan ('No'), Faith Domergue ('Possible'). Rogell made no comment on the whole paragraph devoted to a commendation of Margaret Phillips, a rising Broadway star then playing the part of a handicapped wife in Cukor's *A Life of Her Own*, and about whom Houseman and Ray seemed enthusiastic.[10]

Ida Lupino, one of the most intense actresses around in the 1940s, had founded her own production company, Filmakers, a year earlier. Alone or in collaboration, she had scripted, produced and directed *Not Wanted* (released in July 1949) and *Never Fear* (January 1950). Howard Hughes, impressed by these low-budget movies, offered Filmakers a deal with RKO. *Outrage*, the first production under this new contract, was due for release in August 1950. So it was the studio that cast Ida Lupino, in Ray's absence, with the idea of profiting by the star in return for the risks she presented as a producer.

In his memo, Houseman remained very discreet about the identity of the actor being considered for the part of the young killer, the blind girl's brother, simply announcing 'an interesting discovery'. This was Ray's nephew, Sumner Williams, who had played a small role in *Knock on Any Door*.

At Granby, over 4,000 metres up in Colorado's Rocky Mountains, Ray found locations boasting late seasonal snow. He and Houseman managed to secure as their cameraman George Diskant, who – having left RKO for Columbia – had to be 'borrowed' at $750 a week. His willingness to take risks was to prove a great boon to Ray yet again (and to Ryan): scenes shot in near-darkness, the camera sometimes hand-held.[11]

28   *On Dangerous Ground*: Nicholas Ray, Robert Ryan, Ward Bond
and Ida Lupino on location

On 29 April, Ryan, Ward Bond and Ian Wolfe left for Denver, joined
the next day by character actor Frank Ferguson. Ryan was in a scene as
soon as he arrived, at 4.30 in the afternoon. The next day, shooting
started outside Brent's farm. The late afternoons, from 4 to 5, were
devoted to scouting locations and setting up for the next day. Location
filming far from Hollywood permitted a certain relaxation in union rules.
In response to a query from the Screen Actors' Guild concerning the use
of local extras and the 'right to continuity in the role', assistant director
Lloyd Richards wrote a short report on the location shooting.

30 March. We used local men as hunters, and one as a Bit hunter
(Birdsill).

31 March. Ext. Willows Farm. As you know, this was scheduled for
stage 9, being a big night sequence calling for a bonfire and other light
effects which we could not possibly shoot on location with no
adequate light equipment. Nick and George Diskant tried to get
around the problem by shooting it Day-for-Night. The fact that the
principal character, Ida Lupino, was not on location at all did not
appear to matter. A dolly shot key was made to take care of her part in
the sequence, with a double (Spencer) used in the long shots.

Instead of bringing up any of the Denver theatre group whom we had
interviewed before leaving Denver for Granby, Nick decided he would
see what he could get out of the locals [. . .] I wired the studio their
names and paid them the Guild minimum – fifty-five dollars.

6 April. Retake at the Willows Farm location. Nick wanted to go back
there now that Ida was with us just to tie her in with the location. No
matching of the original scene had been contemplated, but when I
reached the location during the afternoon, Bill and Max [the assist-
ants] told me that many shots had been taken and that the quintet [of
extras] had repeated their lines. That the quintet was there at all was a
stroke of luck.

Back at the studio, after a day of rehearsals, filming resumed on the
11th (with the crew observing a minute of silence in memory of Walter
Huston), starting with Ida Lupino's scenes. Ray worked closely with
Diskant and the actors. Sumner Williams, still self-conscious in front of
the camera, felt that he was helped without being directed: 'Nick had a
way of instilling a feeling for a moment in a character. He knew that I
had the character down, we didn't work on it together. Just at rehearsal,
he would suggest very subtly, never pushed you in any direction. You
never felt as if he were pulling you around on a chain like a dancing
bear.'

Ryan agreed: 'He directs very little . . . I hate film-makers who want
long discussions with actors over a scene. An actor who doesn't know
what a scene he's going to play is all about is in the wrong profession.
Nick had, I think, great respect for me. Right from the start of our
collaboration, he only offered me a very few suggestions. He took a lot of
trouble to get a certain reality. During shooting, he talked to me [about
cops] as if he were telling me a story: "At one moment they did so and so,
at another moment they did such and such." He never told me what to
do. He was never specific about anything at all.'

As for Ida Lupino, she was a star and playing up to it, so a duet was
improvised for the benefit of Darr Smith, who arrived to report on the

production for the *Los Angeles Daily News*. 'She has been intently observing the technique of Ray, who just happens to be one of the best directors in the directing dodge. According to the star, "He's wonderful, but he's also a bum. He read the script for Filmakers' next picture – which just happens to be called *The Lowdown* – and said there was a part he'd like to play. And he was so right! It is perfect for him – a guy who's tall, suave and bad. So every time we thought of the part we thought of Nick Ray. Then we started to do some rewrites on the script and we did them thinking of the lug.

' "Now the part is tailored to him and he's being coy. He won't say yes or no. His agent says Nick will cost a lot of money as an actor. I say he won't because, even though his salary is established as a director, it's not established as an actor. I say we should get him for peanuts because of all the trouble he's already cost us."

'Nick broke in with: "When do you start?" – "You know very well when we start, but you've said you'd be cutting the picture then. Besides, I don't know whether I want to direct you as an actor. You'd probably sit back and think, There she goes, lousing it up again!" "No," said Nick, "I'd probably be thinking, what a great actress she is." From Miss Lupino, "Drop dead!"

'Ray, a quiet man, practically whispers directions to his actors. He took Robert Ryan aside and solemnly whispered in his ear. Ryan nodded. Then Ray went to Miss Lupino and whispered to her. She nodded. Ray moved behind camera, and the scene was shot. They did it again. More whispering. Miss Lupino took more preparation, and it was done.

'Miss Lupino threw her arms around Ray's neck again and said, "Darling, how was it? Will you play the part?" Ray said, "Let's move over in front of the fan where I can think." '[12]

A few days later, Lupino did in fact direct Ray in a test for her film, now known as *Mother of a Champion* The part of the elegant, cynical promoter was eventually played by Carleton G. Young, and the film was released in March 1951 under the title *Hard, Fast and Beautiful*.

Aside from this, the legend that Ida Lupino directed one or more scenes is not confirmed by the production files or by Lupino herself. 'In a way Bob Ryan and I did: we did it our way,' was all Lupino herself claimed when asked about the final scene. 'The end was nothing like the way we had it in the script. It ended with me standing alone in the doorway and crying. I said to Bob, "I don't like it". He said, "Neither do I." And we decided we'd end the picture the way you see it now. When he comes back at night, she feels her way downstairs, and Bob is standing there. We told our cameraman[13] that Bob's hand would reach out and touch hers. She smiles and says, "Oh, you're back." He says, "Yes, I never wanted to leave you." And as the camera comes in to those two faces tight, then we have the camera go down to our two hands clenched together, and it says *The End*.' Ray similarly had no objections when Ward Bond interrupted filming, 'rehearsing a new speech which he personally rewrote many times' (as the continuity script notes).

Filming was completed on 10 May. The editor, Roland Gross, already had a rough cut of the studio scenes.[14] Ray spent his time watching the footage with him, in long discussions over the editing of the exteriors (complicated, Gross recalled, by the loss of part of the continuity script). In August, complex sound editing ensued, and by 9 November the film was ready for viewing – without music – by the Breen Office.

Maddened by Howard Hughes's whims, Sid Rogell had resigned in May, and the power was now shared by heads of departments, William Fadiman in particular, and by producers new to the studio. The most prestigious acquisition was undoubtedly Jerry Wald. He and Norman Krasna had just signed an agreement with Hughes as producers 'with complete autonomy'. Wald in fact acted as head of production at the studio for a time.

Against the advice of Wald and the studio, Houseman insisted on hiring the composer Bernard Herrmann, whom he had known since Mercury Theater days. In November, Herrmann (who was offered an unusual contract to compose, orchestrate and conduct the score) wrote to Houseman, who had left for New York: 'Beginning tomorrow morning I am plunging in on the score of your picture. It certainly needs a lot of music and I hope that I can do everything that I can to add to the story. I think that Nicholas Ray did a superb job; however, I must say that I don't think much of your writer. I feel, as I always have, that the excellence of a picture still depends on the words on the written page.'[15] Herrmann composed a series of pieces for full orchestra (65 musicians) and viola d'amore, played by the soloist Virginia Majewski. The instrument is associated with the Ida Lupino character, contrasting with the unusual orchestration of the 'death hunt': eight horns (in two octave groups), suggesting the baying of hounds, augmented brass – six trumpets, six trombones, two tubas – and percussion.[16]

On 2 March 1951 the finished film (negative cut) ran 89 minutes 19 seconds. On 27 April several cuts were made in the last reels:[17] in particular, 2 minutes 55 seconds of dialogue between Lupino and Ryan before the latter's departure for the city. On 6 June Hughes's viewing notes led to further cuts in three sequences.[18] Hughes didn't recognize the girl being beaten up in the 'return to the city' sequence as Myrna, the one questioned by the cops at the beginning of the film. Fadiman and Lewis Rachmil, a producer recently arrived at RKO, set about suggesting how to make the film presentable (in the eyes of their boss) without spending money: explain Ryan's violence by the fact that his father, also a cop, had been killed by a gangster; start the film with the beating-up, without identifying the girl; eliminate the return to the city, replacing it with voice-overs; reduce the film to the minimum length required for a feature. Rachmil barely restrained himself from suggesting the elimination of Ida Lupino's blindness: it would be too expensive. Fadiman suggested a continuity for the ending which was adopted.

On 11 July, Wald, Fadiman, Rachmil, Ray, Hughes's representative Jim Wilkinson, and the editor were present at a screening. Rachmil and Fadiman had already had the beating-up scene moved from the third part to the end of the first. This brought continuity to the disconnected vignettes involving the girl-informer, thus remedying the fundamental discontinuity of the film which bothered them so much. With reference to the cuts already made, Ray and Wald wanted some more work done on the rhythm: Roland Gross made note of 'a general tightening throughout the first three reels'. They strenuously – and successfully – opposed the psychological explanation for the Ryan character, and the final kiss demanded by Hughes.[19] Wald, on the other hand, put in his own two cents' worth by demanding a close-up of Ida Lupino praying over her dead brother's body. The additional scenes were shot a week later. Diskant, who was working on a Filmakers' production with Lupino and Ryan at RKO (*Beware, My Lovely*) was on camera. A dialogue scene between Ryan and Ed Begley was shot and in the can between 10.30 and 12.45; Ida Lupino was kept only an hour and a half doing a scene in her bedroom.[20] The film was finished in September. It ran 81 minutes 49 seconds. It was released in February 1952. Manny Farber (*The Nation*, 22 March) saw it as 'a treadmill of stumbling, fumbling, smooching, hurtling movement', and as a story 'told with the camera' which 'is often late to the scene and not sure of what is about to happen'. Distributed and received with indifference, it chalked up a loss of $425,000.[21] The accounts department dated the director's 'services rendered' as ending on 15 July 1950; on the 17th, he started work on *Flying Leathernecks*.

17

Flying Leathernecks

The Cold War was on the point of hotting up over the 38th parallel: during a period of several weeks after 25 June 1950, the world thought that it was on the brink of the Third World War. For some months now, the threat of armed conflict had revived Hollywood's interest in the war movie: 20th Century-Fox told the story of the Marines and their Pacific campaign in *Halls of Montezuma* (directed by Lewis Milestone, three years earlier one of the 'Hollywood Nineteen'); Pine-Thomas productions showed the same Marines, early in the nineteenth century, fighting Barbary pirates on the Libyan coast in *Tripoli*.

Howard Hughes saw the opportunity to indulge one of his great passions while boosting the foundation of his industrial empire: aviation, already the subject of his first great success in the cinema (*Hell's Angels*, 1930). Since late in 1949, Josef von Sternberg, Jules Furthman, John Wayne and many more had been floundering about on his behalf, working interminably on *Jet Pilot*, a big aerial and anti-Communist spectacle.

A war-movie specialist, Edmund Grainger had produced several films featuring John Wayne and written by James Edward Grant or Kenneth Gamet.[1] Early in 1950 Hughes grabbed him from Republic, where he had just produced *Sands of Iwo Jima*, an Allan Dwan film, which looked like being one of the year's big box-office successes. Grainger set to work at once on two subjects, one about submarines, the other (*Flying Devil Dogs*) about Marine aviation. The second project was approved by the army's Pictorial Branch in Washington, who asked to see a shooting script. It was never to arrive.

During the summer, at the time Ray was assigned to direct the film – now known as *Flying Leathernecks* – Grainger was preparing a lengthy list of film material to look for in the Pictorial Branch's archives. As the assistant editor Bob Belcher, working first in Washington and then in Quantico, was to put it: 'This has been a lot harder than *Stromboli*' (referring to the American version of Rossellini's film, entirely reworked – under instructions from Hughes – by director Alfred Werker and editor Roland Gross). It was Grainger himself who did the pre-selection of the archive footage at Pathé studios. Hitherto, the tendency had been to use black-and-white for war movies, whether to preserve a documentary tone (*Sands of Iwo Jima*) or to drain the conflict of spectacle (*Twelve*

O'Clock High). Such films, though, were focused on past battles and not evocative of wars to come. Times had changed; like *Halls of Montezuma*, this film was to be shot in Technicolor.

The Marine Corps authorized filming to proceed on the El Toro air base, at Camp Joseph H. Pendleton, Oceanside, about 125 miles south of Hollywood; Grainger had already made *Sands of Iwo Jima* there. Anxious to get John Wayne, who was under contract to Republic, Grainger had Kenneth Gamet's script rewritten by James Edward Grant (the actor's regular scriptwriter and friend). Beirne Lay Jr, co-author of Henry King's austere *Twelve O'Clock High*, was meanwhile injecting a watered down and repetitive version of that film's conflict between two kinds of military authority. While Grainger continued with his viewings, confusion reigned as the starting date approached. On 7 November, Harold Melniker wrote to the Washington representative, Hardie Meakin:

'Changed pages by the dozen come in daily and we try to keep up with them. As to sending in a script, at this point you might at least post Wilkinson on the fact that considerable rewriting is under way. What they will do as to sending the final script is not clear to me. I know, for your private information, they are reluctant about having the script attacked by all the Pentagon writers and have pages of criticism come back. It is a never-ending process. At some point, perhaps there will really be a *final* script, and they may decide to send it along. I believe the cast will be headed by John Wayne and Bob Ryan (an ex-Marine).'

Shortly after filming started, Rodney Amateau – estranged from Ray by a quarrel after *In a Lonely Place* – found himself involved again: 'I was at my aunt's house having dinner, Nick tracked me. On the phone he says, "I'm in big trouble. I need your help." I say, "OK, what can I do?" "I'm in the middle of a picture, down here at Camp Pendleton. I'm shooting from three different scripts," he says. I ask why. "Well, I like some things in this script and some things in that . . . but it's not all going together, it doesn't make sense. Can you come down and put the three scripts together, because there's no continuity?" I went down there – I was already directing second units by then – and he had a whole tent city; it was a mess. Because he really had shot as he said . . . like at one point a guy has died, and at another he's still alive. So it takes me about five days just to get this script together. I made him a new script. I cut and pasted and looked at the film, threw an assembly of what he had made together. I stayed there for the whole shooting and did dialogue director on it.'

Ray's dislike of the project was, of course, not unconnected with this state of affairs. Like a replay of the *I Married a Communist* episode, *Flying Leathernecks* was an assignment – or an imposition – designed to

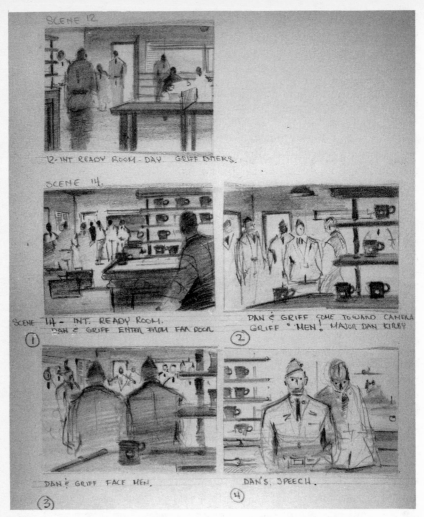

29 *Flying Leathernecks*: storyboard of the opening scene

test his political and professional loyalty.[2] Robert Ryan told Rui
Nogueira that Ray might have indulged in some over-directing on the
film purely out of disgust: 'We often asked ourselves what we were doing
on a film like this. I hate war films.'[3] None of which stood in the way of a
good relationship with Wayne. As with Bogart and later Cagney, Ray
could appreciate one of the great professionals and his modesty with
regard to directors.

'Nick Ray and Robert Ryan were very liberal,' says Amateau (who
places himself 'a little to the right of Attila the Hun'). 'Very, very liberal.
Wayne and Flippen and the rest of the guys were not. Which made for

some very interesting political arguments. Wayne would close all political discussion with "You're full of shit!" and that was the end of it. Wayne was always a very prudent, careful man. He was kind to everybody. And he felt sorry that Nick made a lot of enemies. The reason Nick made enemies wasn't because he was a bad person, he honestly wasn't, he was a good, decent person. But he was so intense about his work. If nothing matters but the work, you're going to make enemies.'

Overall, the film is unmistakably the product of a single-minded plan, ideology and crew. It isn't often one sees any hireling efface himself to this extent: Ray directs with the anonymous competence he would shortly display in filming additional material for other Hughes films (*Flying Leathernecks* was the first of his RKO films to which the millionaire put his name). The result, on the one hand, of a scissors-and-paste job involving several scripts, and on the other of scenes written around remarkable documentary footage of aerial combat (a crash-landing, a parachute escape from an aircraft that has just blown up), the film alternates routine military situations and battle scenes, fragmented in the extreme by Sherman Todd's editing.

The cameraman, William Snyder, uses colour with a delicacy rare in such films, and rare for Technicolor at that time. Not only do the hills of California (standing in for Guadalcanal), the khaki uniforms, the aircraft, the lightly overcast skies suggest the green and beige tones associated with images of war; but also these colours are echoed in Wayne's home, where certain scenes are played out in semi-darkness or against a single splash of brightness. Similarly worthy of note is a strategic manoeuvre, signposted by garishly-coloured flags – red, yellow and violet. It was on this film, incidentally, that Ray discovered another useful medium, 16 mm. On 9 January 1951 he issued notice that it was 'most important that nobody under any circumstances run any prints of any 16 mm Kodachrome film shot on this location unless or until duplicate prints have been made.'[4]

A first cut was ready in March; a few modifications in May; the film finished in June–July; it opened in New York on 19 September. In La Crosse, Wisconsin, the première took place in the presence of the National Guard.[5] Ray, who a little while before had put his job on the line by refusing to execute an order, had restored his reputation within the company: he had delivered the goods as required. The production files reveal no trace of impatience concerning the muddle over the various scripts or the delays in filming (which were actually no fault of Ray's: in December, Hughes was still debating between half-a-dozen actresses for the part of Wayne's wife).

So it was that Ray enhanced his prestige with the owner of the studio. A picturesque interlude was to ensue, but as one may imagine, he had little to gain by the new relationship.

18

The Racket and Macao

The year of *Flying Leathernecks*, 1951, saw RKO becoming increasingly isolated among the major studios. Despite the influx of distinguished producers, Hughes was concentrating the power in his own hands, intervening directly in production. The foundations of his empire lay elsewhere, but Hughes was passionately interested in cinema, insisting on looking at everything, checking the slightest detail, fortifying his view of the world, one might say, through the films he caused to be made. Paradoxically, the mystery in which he shrouded himself nevertheless won him the loyalty of some studio executives and stars. Mitchum has talked of his affection for Hughes, Ray his admiration. William Fadiman, engaged as a literary expert by Dore Schary, survived the change of regime to work for Hughes:

'Although he owned RKO, he only worked at the Samuel Goldwyn studios; he never entered RKO, which is the truth. I was his executive assistant for many years then, and I saw him five times in my entire career, literally. Always under those strange, theatrical circumstances that he engendered. It is true that we were picked up at two, three or four in the morning, it is true that we were shuttled from one car to another, usually a total of three cars, to avoid knowing precisely where we were going.

'It is true that there are very few memos in the RKO files from Howard Hughes; there's a reason for that. The memos would come in typed at the bottom, as a signature, H. H. These were pre-Xerox days. About four, four-thirty, one of his numerous personal secretaries would appear at the office of the man or woman to whom the memo was addressed and ask for the original copy back. He obviously didn't want anyone to know how he was running the company. And the memos may have been trivial, they may have been vital, but the secretary always got the original back.'

There was nothing unusual about the fact that most of the employees in a large enterprise had never seen their boss, but the tycoon's working habits, the sense of omnipresence, the constant interference over the slightest details, sowed panic: 'Nick spent Christmas not in Palm Springs but in a little village on the coast, and Hughes found him or had him found there,' Sumner Williams recalls. This trivial incident fascinated Ray, obsessed as he was by methods of remote control.

Hughes the film-maker was another matter. Before he was thirty (he was born in 1905), he had produced several important films (including *Scarface*) and directed the best passages in one of them (*Hell's Angels*). His return to the cinema had been less happy. One can only deplore his personal takeover on *The Outlaw*, begun by Hawks.[1]

But it wasn't through directing that he chose to take a hand in RKO's output when he assumed the title of 'Managing Director – Production'. According to William Fadiman: 'He was determined to learn to be a film-maker, *despite* being front office. And he did – not successfully, but he learned about films, he worked hard at learning the craft, largely of editing, which was his major interest in films. He would labour for an untouchable number of hours and days over individual frames or shots to make what *he* thought was right.

'But he lived remotely, he lived eccentrically, he tried to change the world to his way of living. The other tycoon-giants tried to change their way of living to the world; each of them, L.B. Mayer, Jack Warner, Harry Cohn, felt that he automatically would react as would the ordinary American average citizen. But Howard, since he had little contact with human beings except on brief occasions, was never able to arrive at an area where he could understand completely what Mr Smith and Mr Jones wanted in Oklahoma City. And that's what made him a failure corporately.'

Editors Roland Gross and Gene Palmer were among the first to be involved in these late night appointments at the Goldwyn Studios, Formosa Avenue. Gross felt that Hughes 'knew all the functions of making a picture and all the technical end. He was the nearest thing to a genius as far as I was concerned. He wouldn't care if he'd spend days and money, money, money. He was like a perfectionist, he wanted everything just so.' Gene Palmer, impressed by the histrionics attending Hughes's appearances, noted that 'he worried not so much about the cutting of the film or the changing of angles, but about technical details, in the sound for instance. He knew something about blooping. When you had an optical track, you had hot splices, so you'd take ink and paint them; because if you left any split in the splice, the light would go through and make snaps in the sound. So he'd say "Those tracks aren't blooped." We never argued with him about anything: "Fine, we'll check it out."[2] That's what he was concerned about – or the actresses' hair. He recast one show because he didn't like the hairdo.'

It was in this spirit that Hughes sent for Ray. One of his most celebrated memos deals with Jane Russell's brassière in *Macao*.[3] In the 1970s, Ray offered highly-coloured versions of his pact with the tycoon:

'He says, "Would you mind sitting down on this side? I'm a little deaf." – "Well, we have friends in common, Mr Hughes, who tell me that if you're standing at the stern of a boat and a dollar bill floats to the deck at the bow, you'll hear it fall." Hughes says, "Why can't you make the film [*I Married a Communist*], Nick?" – "I can't make a good one for you, Mr Hughes." – "Why not?" – "Mr Hughes," I say, "I learned to fly when I was fifteen, sixteen years old. I used to barnstorm country fairs. A few years after that I read one of the most poetic sentences I ever read – it was in the *Time Magazine* account of your flight around the world where you saw five sunsets in four days. I thought that was beautiful. I know about your first film attempt, and the subsequent one. And I know your will: when you crashed into two houses in Beverly Hills, and the doctor got there, you asked about your chances and he said fifty-fifty. You spent the next 45 minutes dictating all your observations about what was wrong with the plane, before you turned to the doctor and said, "OK, knock me over." I know about you taking the same airplane you crashed and trying to get the bugs out of it. You couldn't, you built a building round it, tried to get the bugs out, you couldn't, and finally you destroyed the airplane" [. . .] A year later, he asked me to run the studio for him.'[4]

'When the legend becomes fact, print the legend,' Ford's *The Man Who Shot Liberty Valance* concluded. The studio archives tell a story considerably different from Ray's. But archives can't reckon with the more than slightly macho relationships forged between such tall men as Hughes, Ray, Ryan, Mitchum. Sumner Williams recalls going with his uncle to a dinner at Hughes's place. The details confirm the legend: the tennis shoes, the absolutely empty house, without a stick of furniture, books all over the floor.[5] Of the four men, Ray was the only one with something to lose in these affairs of honour and loyalty, of words worth more than a hundred contracts, etc. Hughes may have saved Ray from the blacklist, but in return he received services faithfully and more effectively rendered on pointless chores than by yes-men like Robert Stevenson. Interminable retakes, additional scenes of tearful emotion or violence, incessant revisions, releases delayed for one, two or three years. It was perhaps a rather heavy price to pay for one single film in all these years – *The Lusty Men* – since *In a Lonely Place* and *On Dangerous Ground* would have been made without Hughes, and were made in spite of him.

The Racket was a remake of one of the earliest gangster movies, one of Hughes's first successes as a producer, dealing – not without courage for 1929 – with corruption in the administration of certain big cities. The director of this remake, John Cromwell, had acted with Edward G. Robinson in the original stage play. Hughes wanted to update the new version to a context of post-war crime: the Kefauver investigations had just started at the time.[6] He commissioned a script first from Samuel Fuller,[7] then (having rejected this) from William Wister Haines and W.R. Burnett, who were amenable to updating, though not too much. Having shot it quickly (in thirty-two days) in the spring of 1951, a 'very old and sick' Cromwell, according to Robert Ryan, quit Hollywood in disgust and returned to New York. Burnett put in another week's work against a cheque for $2,250, and Ray was called in to film these additional scenes. Awaiting him was a familiar team: producer Edmund Grainger, cameraman George Diskant, editor Sherman Todd. Five days from 18–22 June; no fewer than eleven sets, and eleven or twelve actors a day.

The following scenes, or bits of scenes, were shot by Ray:

1 An expository dialogue between the go-between Connolly (Don Porter) and the gang's lawyer Davis (Ralph Peters).

2 A long, static, expository dialogue in the governor's office, a statutory scene much favoured by Hughes (since *Scarface*).[8]

3 In the police locker room, the men talk about their new captain, the hard and honest McQuigg (Mitchum). The latter puts in an appearance (his first in the film), the men come to attention, he delivers a tough speech about their duty (delivered with all the platitude Mitchum could muster), then congratulates Officer Johnson (William Talman).

4 After a bomb goes off at his home, McQuigg, informed by his men, sets off in a police car after the men who did it, who are cornered in a garage.

5 All of the next sequence, in which he arrives at the garage and chases one of the criminals (Ed Parker) to the roof, where the latter falls. Looking at the body, McQuigg says, 'That's not the man I want.'

6 A close shot of Irene (Lizabeth Scott) singing, cut in as four segments (Cromwell's continuity, using camera movement, left her in the background).

7 A conversation between the reporter Ames (Robert Hutton) and Johnson, a friend from the services; Johnson, realizing that McQuigg is offering himself as bait by having his name put in the paper, asks Ames to do the same for him by publishing his address.

8 Johnson's death and McQuigg's tribute to him in the presence of the doctor.

9 Picked up, Nick Scanlon (Ryan) arrives at headquarters. McQuigg places him under arrest, tears up his habeas corpus while the cops rough up the shyster lawyer Davis a little. Nick goes mad with rage (in the first version he kept his cool), exchanges blows with McQuigg, who advises him not to complain about police brutality.

10 Irene walking in the street, Ames catches up with her, they go off together.[9]

In the ensuing months, further brief scenes or matches were shot; one day's work was directed by Sherman Todd, another by Tay Garnett.[10] In all, Ray's contribution adds up to a little over ten minutes of film: scenes which hardly stand out against the overall dreariness, although they do a little to counter the slow, stagy pacing. Their purpose was to stress Nick Scanlon's psychotic nature, to show Lizabeth Scott to a little more advantage, and to inject a decently filmed action sequence into a tedious movie. Most of all, of course, the idea was to justify, indeed glorify, police methods. On 11 September the film was 'approved enthusiastically' and 'under all its aspects' by the Breen Office. André Bazin, comparing it to *On Dangerous Ground*, described it as 'despicable'.[11]

Macao, Ray's second doctoring job, deserves rather more attention, both because the director was Josef von Sternberg, and because of the high mimetic quality of Ray's contribution, which makes the attribution of individual scenes rather difficult. With no exaggeration, Sternberg could write of his two films for Howard Hughes that 'the controlling factors were a dozen assorted and constantly shifted producers – never the director'.[12] Jane Russell, as a mere actress, confirmed this: 'We were kind of trying to fight our own battles and rewrite scripts, because there was nobody at the head that was creative. They were businessmen, that's all, and they made no bones about it.'

After *Jet Pilot*, Sternberg approached the second film required by the contract he had 'foolishly accepted' with no illusions. The project seemed unpromising from the start, with a script[13] designed to promote Jane Russell in the role of a bird of passage, a Dietrich-style singer, and to exploit two *film noir* stars, one a contract actor (Mitchum), the other a loan-out (William Bendix). Of this concoction not unmindful of *Casablanca*, Sternberg might well have said – as of *Jet Pilot* – 'I just followed instructions'. He even directed a photographic test of Gina Lollobrigida, certainly of more benefit to Howard Hughes than to the film.

Samuel Bischoff, at the age of sixty, had taken over from Sid Rogell as executive producer. Sternberg was responsible to him, rather than to the nominal producer, Alex Gottlieb. Two weeks after filming started, Gloria

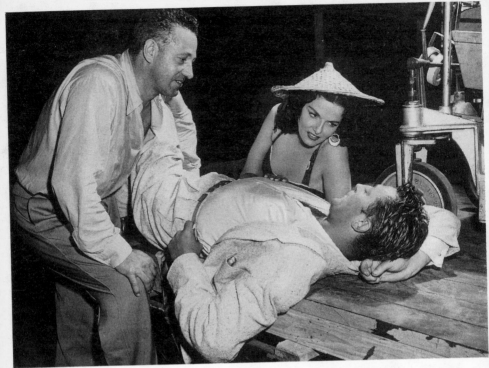

30 *Macao*: Nicholas Ray, Jane Russell and Robert Mitchum

Grahame, who was to be the fourth member of the cast, sent Howard Hughes a telegram indicative of the atmosphere at the studio: 'Dear Mr Hughes, I have a thing to tell you. You were misinformed that I liked a part designated for me in a picture called *Macao*. At this writing there is no part in this picture for me. Also as described by one of your representatives the part itself varied in interpretation from Eurasian to White Russian to "Marge" in a mere fifteen minutes of laborious discussion. In the meantime all I asked for was a release or a good part. No executive in your studio has admitted seeing my performance opposite Bogart, a loan-out which you so kindly sanctioned. Now, according to a Mr Bischoff, the part I am requested to play in *Macao* has not been written – this is true – his statement that I am happy with this unwritten part is misrepresentation' (5 September 1950).

Macao was the consequence of chaos at the studio. Sternberg, pretending no show of interest in the chore, amused himself by provoking the hatred of the cast. Jane Russell, for instance: 'The director was

Dieterle . . . oh, Sternberg, yeah. He was . . . German! That was a nightmare because he wouldn't talk to any of the crew . . . He would try to butter me up and talk about Mitchum, and then he would go to Mitchum and butter him up and talk about me. He didn't want anybody eating on the set, so Mitch had a whole lunch prepared and brought it over and sat right down.' Robert Mitchum: 'He was very short. He wore suede trousers and scarves. He used to stand on a box. And our cameraman, Harry Wild, when he lost patience, would throw down his hat and kick out. Once he kicked the apple box and Joe fell off backwards. I think Joe sort of lost heart at that point.'[14]

Sternberg had no liking for the ersatz repartee the two stars increasingly took to improvising, drawing on recollections of better-written previous roles. Rather than fake it, he preferred to devote himself to what Borges called his 'fads'.[15] He introduced a number of picturesque subsidiary characters, of some of whom the only remaining trace is in the list of cast and characters: rickshaw man, Russian doorman, bus driver, barman, Sikh policeman, Portuguese pilot, old fisherman, coolie, captain, Dutch tourist, female barber, Arab. He had the night-club pianist play *Pavane for a Dead Infanta* and an unpublished piece by Granados.[16] He asked the editor to remind him to shoot inserts like 'a lizard moving on a wall', to record a Chinese version of the line 'Where am I?' spoken by the Russian actor Vladimir Sokoloff. He also introduced a pair of Biblical references, which Bischoff hated, but one of which survived in the finished film.[17]

Most of these details, designed to bring some colour and atmosphere to the film, were to be eliminated by Bischoff, who was brought up on more direct narrative styles at Warners and Columbia, and felt (in keeping with Hughes's tastes) that any digression must be a fault. Notes have survived concerning two screenings of a rough cut shortly after shooting ended on 19 October. Present at the first (2–3 November) were Bischoff, Sternberg, and the editor, Samuel Beetley; at the second, Bischoff, Wilkinson and Beetley. These notes are helpful (much more so than the composite script published in 1980)[18] in attempting to reconstruct the original version of the film (prior even to the version first previewed, which had – as we shall see – already been tampered with) before, as Sternberg put it, 'instead of fingers in that pie, half a dozen clowns immersed various parts of their anatomy in it'. Nicholas Ray agreed to be one of those clowns.

At these two screenings, Bischoff objected to everything that might slow down the action. Sternberg justified himself without conviction. By the end of the year, the Sternberg cut was completed. On 12 and 13

February 1951, Robert Stevenson reshot some scenes with Russell, Mitchum and Philip Ahn.[19] The film, then running 85 minutes 18 seconds, was previewed in Pasadena on 4 April. The scenes most liked were the 'Chase thru fish nets', 'Chinaman being thrown out', 'Boat scenes', 'All Bendix scenes'. The preview audience felt that the action was too slow or that there wasn't enough of it, didn't care much for either Mitchum or Russell, and thought that Gloria Grahame deserved a better part. In June, Jerry Wald took the production in hand and prepared a careful estimate of sets to be built and scenes that were actually needed, noting that they would only be brief scenes. Mitchum said: 'So they turned it over to Nick. Nick, Jane and I looked at each other, and finally Jane handed me a pencil and a piece of paper. I wrote one line and ad-libbed it from there. They had said the picture needed three days, they didn't say what part of it. We worked about three weeks . . .'

These retakes were estimated at around $100,000. Two new scriptwriters worked on them: Norman Katkov (who was paid $3,000) and Walter Newman ($500). The actors involved were Russell, Mitchum, Bendix, Brad Dexter and Thomas Gomez. Ray insisted on informing the Screen Directors' Guild and telling Sternberg – as he had failed to do in Cromwell's case[20] – that if he (Sternberg) disapproved he wouldn't touch it. '[Sternberg] said, "Oh no, Nick. I'm here in New Jersey with my rose garden, I'm close to Wall Street and my art gallery. Go ahead." '[21]

Changes proved necessary in the scene, already partially reshot by Stevenson, in which Mitchum gets away from Gloria Grahame's house. Ten days before the filming was scheduled, however, Ray and Grahame separated for the second time, this time permanently. He later claimed that she told him, 'If you cut me out of the picture entirely, you won't have to pay me alimony.'

On 18 July, now under contract to Paramount, the actress arrived on the neighbouring RKO lot, where it was Mel Ferrer who directed her scenes. After that Ray did twelve days filming, then supervised with Jerry Wald (and a new editor) the editing, writing and recording of the narration, and the selection of stock shots (fairly plentiful, as was often the case in Hughes productions). On 26 February 1952, the film was completed, and released two months later in a version running exactly 80 minutes.

Although it had been publicly screened, and there is no certificate of destruction in the *Macao* files, it seems certain that the print of the first version was dismantled during the re-editing, with the cuts and outtakes destroyed according to custom. Rule of thumb estimates as to the respective contributions of Ray and Sternberg have varied, depending on the commentator's whim, from one third to a film 'almost entirely re-shot'.[22] The lower estimate is closer to the truth. But although the great majority of the scenes technically remain directed by Sternberg, what we see is material whose meaning has been changed by the editing and the sound. Sternberg didn't shoot *Macao* in the same way as his films in the early 1930s, but more like *Sergeant Madden* (where he had greater resources at his disposal): he covered himself more, cut into scenes more (he had himself had occasion to film additional material for other directors, on *The Great Waltz* and *Duel in the Sun*). One can imagine his version as having a balance – at least in the obsessive repetition of images and places – that no longer exists. The longer takes are fragmented or moved around, while scenes extraneous to the plot, and shots showing neither the actors nor what they are directly concerned with, have been removed. The Howard Hughes aesthetic[23] lay in confronting a normal, sober, healthy world (Bendix, Interpol) with an aggressively gaudy eroticism-exoticism (the reason why Sternberg had been hired: for his images, not for their logic) without ever losing sight of the characters.

Here Ray was a faithful interpreter. He has described how much he enjoyed the challenge of imitating Sternberg's style; and the night scene which opens the film confirms how well he met it. He was also responsible (as was Sternberg) for several scenes very flatly played against two-dimensional sets. His main concern was with the unexpected, making use of contingencies in filming, and working with actors whom he would direct again. It is not certain whether all the scenes he directed appear in the finished film.

'It meant nothing to us, except craftsmanship, that's all,' said Walter Newman.[24] It doubtless meant no more to Sternberg, who later told Kevin Brownlow: 'Nicholas Ray is an idiot. He did terrible things to *Macao*, he cut it and ruined it. His name did not appear but mine did. It was a great injustice.' On 16 August Ray let it be known that he did not wish to be credited for the work he had done on *The Racket* and *Macao*.[25]

19

The Lusty Men

The very title *The Lusty Men* – a real Howard Hughes title – betrays its probable source and reflects on the film. This, of course, was not how the people who made the film thought of it; during production it was *Cowpoke* (later, *This Man Is Mine*). Though accidental, the relevance of this title to the film is (like other contingencies arbitrarily integrated into it) none the less real.[1]

Along with Fritz Lang's *Clash by Night*, *The Lusty Men* was one of the rare projects brought to fruition by Jerry Wald and Norman Krasna during their association with Howard Hughes. Enlisted to produce sixty films in five-and-a-half years ('The biggest independent transaction in industry history,' *Hollywood Reporter* wrote), they insisted at the time that Hughes would give them 'even more autonomy than Zanuck'. They came to sing a different tune.

Wald and Krasna at first thought of entrusting Ray with the direction of *Clash by Night*, based on the play by Clifford Odets, with whom he had been friendly since the days of the Group Theater. Then being planned as a Bette Davis vehicle, the project called for a specialist in female melodrama: Curtis Bernhardt, Irving Rapper . . . or Nicholas Ray, who had delivered the goods with Maureen O'Hara and Joan Fontaine. He was, in point of fact, already becoming the man to turn to in a crisis; and he was on hand to help Wald and Krasna out of a fix.

Wald was generally recognized as the driving force in the partnership, with Krasna simply a brilliant screenwriter. A New York journalist, he learned his trade as a scriptwriter, then producer, at Warner Brothers. Robert Parrish, the director originally slated for the film, said: 'Jerry Wald's idea of making a picture was to get a title from the headlines – he was from that old Warner school – or from a story that somebody tells him, and then take a half-page in the *Hollywood Reporter*, in *Variety*, and announce the production; that's the first thing, before you do anything else. He would have maybe ten pictures announced – "ready to go, so-and-so's writing on them". And then he worked on the law of averages. Out of these ten pictures would come one *Johnny Belinda*.

'He saw a piece in *Life* magazine by a very good writer named Claude Stanush, and he wanted to make a picture about rodeo cowboys. So I was employed to direct the picture. I spent about six weeks with Stanush. A new writer came in named David Dortort. Then Dortort's script was not what they wanted to shoot, nor was it what I wanted to shoot, so I got another job and the picture went back on the shelf.'

Stanush was hired at the same time as David Dortort, a young writer from Brooklyn, who had himself submitted ideas for a similar subject. As contractually agreed, Stanush supplied a wealth of documentation and helped Dortort out with his erudition. Together with Parrish, Dortort drafted a 137-page treatment called *Cowpoke* during the closing months of 1950. After Parrish left, Wald and Krasna thought for a while of having John Huston direct *Reminiscences of a Cowboy*, a project of Huston's for Horizon Pictures. In May-June 1951, Richard Wormser did a new treatment of a rodeo subject, on the basis of which Wald and Krasna tried unsuccessfully to sign up Raoul Walsh, banking on getting Gary Cooper if Walsh was directing. But that spring, three majors were announcing rodeo movies: the Wald-Krasna one, *Tophands* (an MGM project), and *Bronco Buster* (which Budd Boetticher directed for Universal). After considering Anthony Mann, Wald and Krasna turned to Ray, who by the end of the summer was starting to plan filming in arenas a long way away from Hollywood.

As with all his films, no sooner had Ray started work than he was immersed in the copious documentation provided by Stanush: 50 pages on 'Western dialogue and colloquialisms', 75 on 'drought and grass problems', 120 on 'general research, ranching and rodeo', plus a collection of notes, amassed over a period of more than ten years, on the modern cowboy.

There was no vestige of plot in all this: which is doubtless what Robert Mitchum was thinking of when he claimed to have thought up the story and presented Wald with it: 'So Wald puts two writers on the project, completely unbeknownst to each other, and eventually they write themselves right past each other, right off the lot. Wald hires Nicholas Ray to direct, but he still doesn't have any kind of a script. Tom Lea [*sic*, actually Stanush] has written a thing in *Life* magazine about rodeo. So we call Tom Lea and he writes us a seven-page letter.[2] Nick and I say, "Fuck! We'll shoot the letter." We had a script from the letter.

'Meanwhile Howard Hughes is calling and keeps telling me, "Will you please tell Jerry Wald you don't want to do the picture with him so I can get him off my back?" "No," I told him, "I *want* to do the picture." So Hughes says, "Well, at least you have a good script?" I say, "We don't even *have* a script. Just let me have Nick Ray to direct it, and Eddie Killy as a production manager, and we'll come up with a script."[3] OK, this is Friday. So Jerry Wald calls me on Monday and he says, "Bob, guess what? Howard has given a go-ahead on the picture, and guess who we have as a director?" And I said, "Tell me." He said, "Nick Ray" – "No shit!" – "And we've got Eddie Killy as production manager." I said, "Marvellous!"[4]

At the beginning of September, Horace McCoy was hired. 'As a former Texas sports writer and long-time rodeo fan,' he said at the time, 'I go way back to "Foghorn" Clancy's show in 1924.' Originally from the South, born in 1897, McCoy had turned his hand to every kind of job since he was twelve. An impassioned, macho, harsh writer, he wrote several novels more highly rated in Europe than in America. As a script-writer, McCoy worked to order ('I used to do fifteen to twenty scripts a year for Universal'), often for Poverty Row studios, with a few exceptions: in particular, two collaborations with Raoul Walsh (*Gentleman Jim, The World in His Arms*), which give some idea of the sort of characters he felt at home with. Early in 1951, he had pulled off one of the best deals in his career, by selling Hal Wallis a treatment called *Scalpel* (which he also turned into a novel).[5]

In the screenwriters' file kept by Fadiman, McCoy was listed under the category of 'masculine relationships'; and that, for the moment, was the trouble with this script. The writer was tempted by the money, and by the free hand promised him by Wald and Krasna. 'For once I have a chance to do a script exactly as I want, with no interference from the front office at all,' he ingenuously told the *L.A. Daily News*.

So McCoy set to work with Ray, and on 9 November delivered a script still entitled *Cowpoke*, which stops at the beginning of the third part, just as the role played by Wes's wife Louise (almost non-existent in the earlier versions) becomes central. Many of the best scenes in the film were already laid out here, notably the whole of the beginning and the scene continuity until about two-thirds of the way through.

'My only objection,' wrote Stanush after reading it, 'was that there was a lot of dialogue that was Southern negro dialect rather than cowboy Western: items like "What kind of manners is them?", "I didn't figure nobody lived here", etc.'[6] In *Lightning Over Water*, the second of these lines (slightly modified) can be heard concluding an extract from *The Lusty Men*, whereupon Wim Wenders comments, 'It's more about coming home than anything I've seen.' The scene follows McCoy's script fairly closely:

43 *MED.SHOT* – low set up, shooting under the house. Obviously Jeff knows exactly what he is looking for. He reaches up under the joists somewhere and takes down an old Prince Albert can. He opens it to

31   *The Lusty Men*: coming home – Robert Mitchum

whiff the tobacco and a couple of nickels fall out. Jeff regards these memorabilia; then between him and the camera there strides a pair of legs clad in worn old trousers and on his feet are worn and battered work shoes. We see only the legs and the barrel of a rifle; but Jeff does not yet see these. The rifle barrel is lifted up out of scene as the man cradles it.

177

MAN'S VOICE (with hostility): All right, you under there. Back out nice and slow.

Jeff reacts with dumbfoundment, does as he is told, scrounging out feet first. He looks up.

44 *MED.SHOT* from his angle up on Jeremiah Watrous. He is an old man of sixty or sixty-five, his hair sparse and stringy, and his eyes narrow and suspicious. His rifle is at the ready, and it is noteworthy that in all this desolation and dry-rot the rifle is one single thing that looks well-kept and efficient.

JEREMIAH: What're you up to?

45 *MED.SHOT* across Jeremiah down on Jeff. Jeff has made no effort to rise.

JEFF: Nothing, mister. Not a thing. I didn't figure nobody lived here.

Jeff still makes no move to get up. He knows that you never can tell about these old codgers.

JEREMIAH: Somebody lives here. What're you doing crawling around under my house?

Jeff shows the tobacco tin and the two nickels.

JEFF: Wanted to see if it was still there. Used to be my home place – this did. Was born here. (Starts to get up).

46 *MED.SHOT* – Jeremiah. Some of the hostility leaves his face and it relaxes a little.

JEREMIAH: You Connie McCloud's boy?

JEFF: Name's Jeff.

JEREMIAH: Howdy.

JEFF: Howdy.

JEREMIAH: I'm Jeremiah Watrous.

Jeff nods and they shake hands perfunctorily.

JEFF: Did you know my old man?

JEREMIAH: Not personal. (They look at each other.) You care to have some coffee?

JEFF: That'd be nice.

He follows the old man around the house, towards the porch.

But soon relations with McCoy became difficult. Preoccupied with writing *Scalpel*, McCoy's mind was elsewhere. He was also becoming less and less the man for the job, as the film turned into one about a woman. For so Hughes – interested in Susan Hayward – had decreed. Mitchum has described how he had to improvise a non-existent storyline for Susan Hayward's benefit, and how he and Ray had to commit that improvisation to paper, then write scenes every night for the next day.

On 17 November McCoy submitted a new script, now called *This Man Is Mine* to stress the feminine angle. This script is marked 'Temporary' (indicating that it was not yet ready to be used as a basis for preproduction: breakdown, lining-up, construction of sets, etc.). By 30 November the production department had 55 pages of 'final' script. This was not enough to prepare a breakdown and shooting schedule, since the 'second act' had not yet arrived (McCoy's script, a note states, 'hasn't been rewritten to match characters' to changes made at the beginning). One of Wald's assistants pointed out that preparations hinged on 'the requirement of concentrating on Susan Hayward's work. There is very little of Susan in this first portion of the script and much of it will be scheduled in back of Susan Hayward's work in the second act.' The dates between which the actress would be available had indeed been categorically fixed by her studio, 20th Century-Fox.

The production files give only a faint idea of the panic that ensued. Missing, for instance, are the famous memos with which Jerry Wald inundated everyone; Horace McCoy, disgusted, stuck them up on the wall in their order of arrival and lost all interest in the film. David Dortort, whose first script this was to reach production, had stayed on to observe. He typed up the improvisations of Mitchum and Ray. 'The basic concept of my story and the resulting film', he wrote, 'were a source of constant argument between Nicholas Ray and Jerry Wald. I must say that Mr Ray invariably understood what I was trying to do, whereas Mr Wald never quite understood what the story was about, or which story to tell. This difference of opinion went on all through the shooting and even grew worse during the editing.'

Ray and Mitchum were thus embarked on a film being scripted from day to day. In selecting the rest of the cast, Ray showed the same sure eye as on his first film. Arthur Hunnicutt was discovered by Howard Hawks, who had used him in *The Big Sky*; after reading the script, Hawks recommended him to Wald and Ray.[7] Burt Mustin had been spotted by Wyler on stage in *Detective Story* – where Ray also saw him – and made his movie début at the age of sixty-seven. As so often, Ray does not so much 'discover' an actor as reveal his true face; the old farmer who has bought the McCloud home remains as unforgettable as Ian Wolfe in *They Live by Night* or Houseley Stevenson in *Knock on Any Door*. The rodeo women are remarkable too. Carol Nugent (the tomboyish girl who travels with Hunnicutt), Maria Hart (Rosemary, a former lover of Jeff's), Lorna Thayer (whose husband is killed in the arena), Karen King.

Ray fought to get Lee Garmes hired, having met him on *Roseanna McCoy*. 'They didn't like him. He did unorthodox things.'[8] Garmes, who made his début in 1918, had shot *Morocco* and *Scarface*. Not for nothing did Ray call him 'a renegade'. Tied to no studio, he had no hesitation in committing himself to offbeat ventures like the films made by Ben Hecht and Charles MacArthur (on which he was credited as co-director). 'The camera', Hecht wrote, 'was a brush with which he painted, but in his painting was the knowledge of the hundred hazards of a movie set. Nothing I ever encountered in the movies was as uniquely talented as the eyes of Lee Garmes. I prided myself on being an acute observer, but beside Lee I was almost a blind man.'[9]

Filming, scheduled to start on 20 December, was postponed for a week, and the exteriors involving Susan Hayward were eliminated, except for those which could be shot in the vicinity of Los Angeles. The first scenes were those in and around the house where Jeff was born. Talking to Vassar students on the evening of 29 March 1979, as the *Lightning Over Water* venture was just starting, Ray compared the challenges presented by the two films: 'We are starting this film of ours with about the same amount of head start that we had on *Lusty Men* [. . .] We had about twenty-five or thirty pages of script [. . .] I like it that way. Keeps the show fresh and spontaneous. And your imagination works overtime. We wrote every night. So there wasn't much beside instinct and the reactions of my actors to what we had done the day before. There was no possibility of meticulous, Henry James type of construction.'

Working like this, Ray happened – by chance if not by design (at least for the moment) – on a method practised in the European cinema (by Renoir, for example), constructing each scene as a separate entity. He knew how to find what he later called 'a common language with actors'. To begin with, he had difficulty communicating with Susan Hayward, who was not his choice in the part. According to one of his students, reporting what he told them in 1977: 'Nick saw that she had a book of poems by Thomas Wolfe, talked to her about them, gave her other Wolfe poems, which they read together, and on the basis of this contact he was able to build something else, which he needed.'[10] He filmed in long takes, later fragmented in the editing, or if pressed for time, in reverse angle shots. The fluid structure of the sequence at the farm derives partly from its basis in a carefully prepared, written script; in these two scenes, comprising a long dialogue passage with Burt Mustin, done in a single take, one can sense the personal involvement of Mitchum as a rootless child of the Depression. Similarly with the scenes in which Mitchum joins Arthur Kennedy and Susan Hayward in the cabin where they live, with groupings of either two or three figures simultaneously defining the cramped space and the dynamics of their changing relationships. By contrast,

32   *The Lusty Men*: cramped together – Susan Hayward, Arthur Kennedy
and Robert Mitchum

the scene in which Louise comes to ask Jeff to discourage her husband
from continuing in rodeo – ending with a final soliloquy on redheads
from Jeff – is shot in reverse angles (the naked light bulb hanging
between them is a fine touch). Very successful in its suggestion of sexual
antagonism, the meaning of the scene is reversed by the revelation of
Louise's past and her need for social roots.

This scene was the work of yet another scriptwriter. On 17 December,
Alfred Hayes – an ex-GI who had served in Italy, and who had adapted
Clash By Night for Wald and Krasna – dictated fourteen pages of dialogue, relating to five scenes, at least three of which (roughed out in
McCoy's version) found their way into the film: Wes and Jeff chatting
outdoors after dinner, talking of the best horse Jeff ever rode, until
Louise comes out to tell them it's time to go to bed; Wes coming home
after his first rodeo, showing Louise a cheque, and telling her they are
both leaving with Jeff; and the scene between Louise and Jeff in the barn.

181

Hayes was not the only writer called in to help the director and his star. Andrew Solt was also at RKO: 'I was writing the life of, I forget who, either Johann Strauss or Franz Liszt, it was never made. And one day in came Johnny Meyer, who was Howard's right hand in those days. He said, "We are shooting a picture with Mitchum, and Nick suggested that you could fix it." I said, "Fine, I'll do what I can, let me have the script and I'll let you know tomorrow." He said, "There's no time for that, come now with me." I went down on the set where sat, pouting, Susan Hayward. This woman had the foulest mouth that I've ever heard in my life. She sat there and she said, "No, I'm not going to say these lines, they insult me." And there sat Mr Mitchum, who couldn't care less, and Nick blowing his top. We went into Meyer's office, and he said, "We're in the worst fix in the world, because she's loaned from 20th Century-Fox, she has a return date because she's starting a week from Monday *The Snows of Kilimanjaro* with Gregory Peck, and we are out! If we don't finish this picture this week, we have no finished picture. And you can fix it."

'So I said, "OK, but let me read the script." Meyer said again, "You *can't* read the script, you have to start working now." I said I didn't know what the story was about. He says, "I don't care, Susan Hayward is sitting there and we're paying for it. You must start now. Nick, tell him what you shot so far." So we sat down and he told me the story of these rodeo riders. It was a steal from *Test Pilot* [directed by Victor Fleming]: the two guys, dangerous work, one woman in the middle, and then I remembered what I learned from Fleming. We wrote the scene [in *Joan of Arc*] where Ingrid's hair is cut by her mother, a marvellous Communist actress called Anne Revere, and Fleming said, "If Anne Revere cries, the audience just watches: Anne Revere will not cry and the audience will cry. That's what I did in *Test Pilot*. Make Anne Revere a Russian mother: angry." So I could start writing the thing because of what I learned from Fleming, and remembering *Test Pilot*.'[11]

In addition to this, there were scenes written by Wald himself, sent in the form of memos. 'Wald's scenes we'd always shoot after six o'clock,' according to Mitchum, 'when we went into overtime.' Soon there were other reasons for shooting overtime. After three days, Susan Hayward was laid up with a cold, and shooting was suspended on New Year's Eve. When it started again on 8 January 1952, Mitchum was suffering from a bowel infection, and Arthur Kennedy from an upper respiratory infection. Often at night, on the old Pathé studio stages, Lee Garmes had to shoot daylight exteriors with Susan Hayward.[12]

On 29 January it was Ray who was suffering: a punctured wound on his heel. His foot swelled up alarmingly. He finished off Susan Hayward's scenes, notably – the following day – the one in which Louise gives Babs a violent shove ('Beat it, sister, he's got a horse!') when she gets too friendly with her husband. Eleanor Todd, playing Babs, had to be lassooed by Chuck Roberson, then pushed by Hayward; during a take, she hit her head and had to be X-rayed.[13] After a few days, Ray suffered a reaction to his anti-tetanus injections, and had to be hospitalized at the Cedars of Lebanon.

Jerry Wald then called in Robert Parrish to take over direction for three or four days. The latter shot the interiors at the Jackhammer ranch and in the bunkhouse: the scene where Wes has Jeff hired by Rig Ferris, and the turn-out for work in the morning.[14] Parrish was a rarity among film-makers in that he was interested in the working methods of his colleagues. He didn't miss much where Ray was concerned.

'To this day I don't know what was wrong with him. I think it was exhaustion, because he worked at the top of his physical capacities at all times; every time I've seen him in my whole life, I always wondered if he wasn't just about ready to crack up. Right from the beginning . . .

'After he came back to work, there was a sequence that I had shot part of and he was going to pick up. So he asked me to come back and be on the set with him, to tell him what I had in mind. It was all very friendly. I was impressed, because I came up as a technician, and Nick was from the New York theatre . . . television, I don't know where the hell he'd been . . . but he was the first guy that I watched working where everything was about relationship between the actors rather than technique. If he had a certain kind of cameraman, that's what the picture would look like; but he dealt with the actors.

'This was the first time I'd worked with Mitchum. Some years later, when we'd become friends, I asked him what it was like working with Nick. Mitchum, who had his own cynical, sardonic style even then – it came at birth, I think – said, "Well, not very good at putting marks on the floor." I asked what he meant by that. He said, "Well, you know, a lot of directors will give you the marks. When I act, I come in and say: what page is it and where are the marks?" (This is a lie, by the way, because he's one of the best movie actors in the world.) "While the director is talking to the other actors, I check out the marks, and I hit 'em. But Nick is a fellow who likes to discuss the scenes with the actors, what they mean, what my background was, what the background of the rodeo bulls and horses was, and about my relationships. So while he would talk to me about those things, I'd be looking for my marks. He would usually end up these speeches by saying, *And also, improvise*. But I couldn't improvise the marks. Since Nick usually told the cameraman to be on the actor who had listened the most when he was telling them about their background, about Stanislavsky and those people, a lot of times I wasn't in the scene . . ."

'That's a Mitchum anecdote, of course; it's the kind of thing he said. But in fact I was impressed with Ray as having an intense interest in pinpointing performance, in character and in the actors, quite opposed to my background in technique; John Ford did both, but people like Bobby Wise, Mark Robson, Johnny Sturges and I had come up through being cutters. We were technicians, and that had a tendency to condition my reaction to Nick Ray: the difference in the way that he would direct and that I would direct.'

As the end of January approached – Hayward had to return to Fox, and the crew go off to shoot rodeos – Jerry Wald thought up a new ending. The Dortort and Wormser treatments and McCoy's synopsis all had Jeff die, but Wald thought he could do better. In the version he wrote, Jeff was reunited with an old girl-friend. According to Mitchum, 'She says, "Time heals all wounds." And I say – it's written, written! – "And wounds all heal. I'll see you later, Rosemary." Jerry says, "Who wrote that?" – "You, asshole!" And all on overtime!' Mitchum claims that he sent his secretary to steal the last reel and throw it into an incinerator, while the crew shot the real ending: Jeff's death, and Wes leaving with Louise. As Ray commented: 'They had all lived up to what they were supposed to live up to.'

Long after the exteriors were shot – two weeks in Tucson, San Angelo and Pendleton, where Mitchum and Kennedy briefly rode bulls and wild broncs – Ray and Wald took time tinkering with the film, adding shots and inserts.[15] McCoy, a former sports writer, returned during April and May, and amused himself writing newspaper headlines and commentaries for the rodeo announcers.

The flatness of the images depicting the rodeo context[16] is echoed by Roy Webb's music, which foregrounds the fanfares and flourishes of the arenas. These stereotypes are incorporated into a film whose thrust (although an amiable hack like Andrew Solt could readily see it, as planned, as just another movie like dozens before or since) was directly opposed to their rabble-rousing excitement. 'I guess we all have a little of that wildness in us,' Ray said at Vassar. Describing Lee Garmes's camerawork, Ray coined a word 'loininess': a sensuality in the landscapes (which, with their long shadows, all look as though they had been shot early or very late in the day, in the manner of silent movies) contrasting with the total artifice of the studio and second unit scenes. If Garmes's lighting sometimes recalls Walker Evans or the Farm Administration photographers, it is not just in the sense of a dated social realism. There is also a hint of hyper-realism before its time, in the caravan trailer interiors, for example. 'Looks like a hotel,' as a dialogue exchange puts it: 'It *is* a hotel.'

The background of the 1930s remained very potent for Ray, and he referred to it almost automatically in his Vassar lecture a few months before his death: 'This film is not a Western. This film is really a film about people who want a home of their own. That was the great American search at the time this film was made. I had gone through all the social rolls in Washington that asked for that kind of data – "What is your principal drive in life?" – and over 90 per cent was, "To own a house of my own." And that's what it was all about.' The film thus moves from nostalgic Americana to a mood of crisis and anxiety, not immediately apparent as the trio first arrive in the camp of tents and trailers, its roof open to the painted skies.

The whole production history of *The Lusty Men* was a headlong rush, a chapter of accidents (which a strictly professional point of view would deem unfortunate). Out of this consciously controlled panic there emerged, for those with eyes to see, not just a film but the potential for a new kind of film-making. This may have been difficult to perceive, right then and there, but that makes no difference. Jacques Rivette wrote at the time: 'We should cherish this cavalier attitude, this very gratifying lack of concern for sets, composition, lighting, continuity, the suitability of a bit player, and recognize this impetuosity, even in its excesses, not as caricature, but as the youthful exaggeration of a kind of cinema we value, in which everything is sacrificed to the expression, the effectiveness, the incisiveness of a look or a reaction . . . The fact that the inventiveness lies first and foremost in the pure pleasure of film-making, as a brush finds creative freedom on a canvas, means that there is little chance of it being taken seriously here.'[17]

Neither here, nor there. Shoved out as just another product in a poor year for RKO, Ray's film, like so many others, was a bottle in the sea.

20

Last Year at RKO

After finishing *Flying Leathernecks*, Ray had taken a trip to New York. Jean Evans, out of a job (*PM* had ceased publication in 1949; its successor, *The Star*, the following year), had begun researching a book on American gypsies, building up a unique documentation. Out of this, Ray concocted a two-page synopsis, *No Return*, which he offered to the studio. He got Jane Russell interested, and a young screenwriter, Walter Newman, who had worked on *Macao*.[1] Newman had read a lot about gypsies, and could speak the language a little. Jean Evans was engaged as a technical adviser, on what for her were fabulous terms; from New York, she answered questions by letter or telephone. Between March and June 1951, Newman and Ray wrote a first draft, then a 130-page treatment, summarized for Hughes by William Fadiman as follows:

'A young Gypsy, returning to his tribe after a year in jail, is reluctantly forced into a traditional marriage with a beautiful Gypsy girl. He tries to persuade the Gypsies that they must change their way of life, live as other people do. He refuses to consummate their marriage. The girl sticks by him as he tries to prove his point. Eventually they become husband and wife in fact and, after a number of setbacks, he is forced to conclude that he can't change the tribal ways when the Gypsy King announces that the time has come to move to a beautiful spot in the West for which they have been paying for years. Actually, the King knows there is no such spot. The young man learns this, beats the King in combat and becomes the new King, but learns that he, too, must pretend for the tribe that there is a place to go to.'

Fadiman and other readers reported on the treatment with an enthusiasm rare in studio correspondence: 'If well cast (ideal casting would be Marlon Brando and Ava Gardner), should make a profitable and arresting picture. There is a slight – but existent – risk of this turning into an "art" picture but if the emphasis is placed on the sex, the brawling, and humour and the hero-heroine personal conflict *rather* than on the philosophic old-v.-new concept, this can be avoided' (Fadiman). 'An exceptionally well-written screenplay with a rather wonderful grasp of an entirely new American background and a wonderful role for Jane Russell.' 'One of the most refreshing and original screenplays I've read in a long, long time.' 'This is a gem – a once-in-a-life-timer, and has all the potentialities of an Academy Award picture. I cannot muster a single criticism.' 'As far as I'm concerned it's something [. . .] to film with an absolute minimum of changes.'[2]

The novice producer Harry Tatelman, a former agent with MCA, seized on the project with enthusiasm, and while making *The Lusty Men*, Ray had Jean Evans employed for a further eight weeks. But the project became mired in the end-of-regime atmosphere gripping the studio.

Whereas Hughes Aircraft underwent phenomenal expansion during these Cold War years, the tycoon's erratic management of his cinematic affairs put the studio in a difficult situation. Fanatically tracking down Communists, Hughes even tangled with the Screen Writers' Guild over the Jarrico affair.[3] The studio personnel was reduced to a minimum, and so was its product. In December 1951 Vernon Harbin received instructions not to exercise Ray's annual option. The latter was granted an extension of his contract to finish *The Lusty Men*, for which he was (theoretically) on loan to Wald-Krasna productions. But once the film was finished on 19 February – with the editing and some continuity shots to follow in the ensuing months – a new contract was negotiated, under the benevolent eye of Hughes and Ray's new agents, MCA. This one-year contract was signed on 10 June. Ray's salary was raised to $1,500 a week; he became a producer and/or scriptwriter and/or director. In the event of renewal, he would have a choice between serving as producer or as director. An interesting clause features in it: he was authorized to terminate the contract 'if Howard Hughes ceases to be Managing Director – Production'.

As soon as the contract was signed, Ray discussed a project with Wald entitled *Size 12* (based on a short story by Jerome Weidman, 'I Knew What I Was Doing'), and asked for a loan of $15,000, personally authorized by Hughes. Like *No Return*, *Size 12* was destined to get nowhere. After *The Lusty Men*, Wald couldn't manage to get a single film into production, and contented himself with supervising retakes and work in progress. Ray was in the same boat. That year, fewer than half of the thirty-two films released by RKO were their own product.

For a few months thereafter, Nicholas Ray found himself the tycoon's right-hand man. Among the producers and directors Hughes had got his hands on, by way of juicy contracts and promises of independence, was Gabriel Pascal. This Hungarian, born in 1894, had followed a predictable trail through picaresque ups-and-downs by way of Berlin (UFA) and London. A gift for sweet-talking persuaded George Bernard Shaw to entrust him with the rights to his plays. His canned versions were so extravagant that he had to leave England after *Caesar and Cleopatra*, and was unable to set up *Androcles and the Lion* on his own in America.[4]

Androcles therefore came to RKO. After several false starts, the producers realized that, according to terms agreed with Shaw's estate (he had died in 1950), the film had to be released before 1 November 1952. It was therefore put into production under the direction of Chester Erskine, who ran twenty days over the forty-five-day schedule. At which point, the Hughes machinery took over: in April 1952, RKO assistant director Ed Killy did eight days' shooting with the lions and two English actors, Alan Mowbray and Robert Newton.

In July, it was Nicholas Ray's turn to do two-and-a-half days' filming, preceded by one of rehearsals: a scene with 7 minutes 35 seconds usable footage ('Exterior Arena')[5] and inserts in the forest. Nothing deserving more than a mention, except for what happened next.

A week later, Ray was executing one of Hughes-the-erotomaniac's most notorious ideas. Did Ray prompt it, spontaneously or otherwise? On 19 July he wrote to C. J. Tevlin, one of Hughes's assistants, mentioning in passing, 'in addition to the scenes already outlined, one more which I wish to discuss with you in more detail than when I first mentioned it. I think it will help the picture as well as our publicity campaign, but I think you might consider making it a publicity department charge.'

On 1 August he described the scene to the censor's representative, who responded apoplectically: 'You propose to have a group of girls clad in tight-fitting, flesh-coloured leotards over which are loosely fitted garments engaged in an intriguing ballet, which winds up with the girls divesting themselves of the outer garments before going into a pool enveloped in some sort of an effect of steam. The impression you conveyed to me is that the effect on the screen would be either that of nude women quickly enveloped in steam or at least the effect of the nude silhouette. *This is definitely a violation of the code.*'

Ray wrote to assure him that precautions had been taken, 'since the girls taking part are all prominent members of ballet troupes and the entire piece is to be choreographed by Carmelita Maracci and I assure you that we will try to keep the scene within as good taste as the nature of the times will allow.' On 4 August the censor further insisted that it should be clearly established that the dancer Shirley Lewis 'is not nude under her costume. The leotard looks like flesh'.

The scene was shot that day and the next. One of the dancers was sixteen years old, and on that day she was meeting Ray for the first time. She was called Betty Uitti, a Finnish name Americanized to Utey.

'I was a professional dancer very early. I didn't know I was professional until I was fifteen and was engaged to do a concert, then a film and so on, and just kept working. In those years there was one big musical after another for anyone who had ballet training and could also work in a jazz way. So by virtue of being one of maybe fifty trained dancers, I worked from film to film. I was rehearsing for a concert with Carmelita Maracci. She and Nick were friends and he needed to do some excerpts for *Androcles and the Lion*. Hughes wanted more sex. The whole troupe of us were told to wear bikinis and report to RKO. I'd never worn a bikini before and I felt really funked out. I stood there in this line-up, and Nick selected very voluptuous kinds of bodies. I wanted to run off the sound stage, because he was a very piercing personality and I felt like a fool. He walked over to me and he said, "What's your favourite fruit?" I told him I liked peaches. So a prop man appeared with a peach and I ate it full out, it dripped all over me. He featured me in the scene.'

The dancer from the Carmelita Maracci company was to see Ray again from time to time: before *Johnny Guitar*, before *Rebel Without a Cause*, during *Party Girl*. They would marry in 1958.

Ray set to work on the editing with Roland Gross, while Hughes, still anxious to add to the film's spectacular qualities, had Ned Depinet intervene personally to persuade a very reluctant Cecil B. DeMille to authorize the use of a 15-second clip from *The Sign of the Cross*.

Gabriel Pascal (flanked by a Hughes man, producer Lewis Rachmil) kept an eye on the editing. He was often distracted, because he was trying to interest Mary Martin in a musical adapted from Shaw's *Pygmalion*; he even put the project up to Ray (years later, it was to become *My Fair Lady*).[6] Ray was fascinated by his colourful personality, and decided he should play the King of the Gypsies in *No Return*. Walter Newman remembers Pascal exclaiming: 'Gypsies! I love them! I *am* a Gypsy – I ran away from home as a boy and lived with Gypsies!'[7]

On 26 September Pascal and Ray agreed on the final cut of *Androcles*. On 13 October Pascal gave his written consent for the 'Bath of the Vestal Virgins' to be included in the film in the United States, but not in the United Kingdom, Canada or Australia. The day after that, Ray had a curious change of heart. 'My final responsibility for RKO,' he wrote, 'has been to act for Mr Hughes in the matter of assisting Mr Pascal and Mr Rachmil to get *Androcles and the Lion* ready for presentation to the public.

'Among the various tasks I performed, I added a sequence taking place in the "steam room of the vestal virgins". The purpose of putting such a scene into the picture was obvious, but it has been so emasculated by the censors that it emerges only as a sour note and a piece of very bad taste in a picture which, for the most part, has considerable distinction.

'I cannot pretend to know the problems of exhibition. I try to be aware of them and this was an honest attempt to fill an expressed need. Still, I believe it can only bring discredit upon the Company as a piece of vulgarity typical of the "Hollywood disregard for the classic line", and provide local as well as foreign publics and critics with a target which cannot be missed; thus cancelling out much of whatever value it may give the 24-sheet.

'In all matters concerning this production I have had the complete trust and authority of Mr Hughes. I cannot faithfully execute that trust to its completion without requesting that a piece of my own handiwork be eliminated from the picture. Unless I hear to the contrary from you, I shall instruct the editor accordingly. Mr Pascal concurs.'

This note was addressed to a certain Sherrill Corwin. In September, Hughes had decided (with Ned Depinet following suit) to sell his shares in RKO to a Chicago-based 'syndicate'. The latter took over the studio on 2 October. Two weeks later, the *Wall Street Journal* exposed this syndicate's links with gangsterism and the questionable past history of some of its members. On 14 October, with characteristic timeliness, Ray's new agents, MCA, informed the studio that he was invoking the clause (the departure of Hughes) permitting him to withdraw from his contract.[8]

This was why, in writing to one of the members of the syndicate, Ray made reference to his 'final responsibility'. On 20 October, Pascal signed a formal agreement accepting the final cut, and Corwin decided that the sequence with the vestal virgins should be retained. On the 31st, the director Chester Erskine protested in his turn about the scenes 'depicting the Vestal Virgins as prostitutes. Vulgar, inaccurate and clumsily incorporated, they reflect so badly on all of us it would be to our considerable credit to remove them'.

Roland Gross had spent the month of October at Fort Lee, New Jersey, re-editing the film according to decisions taken from day to day; its running-time was reduced from 98 minutes 26 seconds to 97 minutes 38 seconds. On 6 November Austin Grant, new president of the board of directors, agreed to the elimination of the sequence. With some final changes by Pascal, the film opened on 3 January 1953, in a version running 95 minutes.

Ray had worked for 'Howard' on another occasion that summer of 1952, on one of Hughes's pet projects: *Pilate's Wife*. This started as a story by Clare Booth Luce (whose connections with the press and the political world must have intrigued the tycoon). It had been announced in March 1951 as a Wald-Krasna production, to be directed by René Clair. The latter had returned to Hollywood and written a script with Mrs Luce. He was long gone by the time Betty London and Ray were assigned to help the authoress in July 1952. While Mrs Luce viewed Fleming's *Joan of Arc*, Ray viewed *Come to the Stable*, which she had written. Despite a news item from the ever-willing Hedda Hopper ('Susan Hayward in *Pilate's Wife*, directed by Nick Ray'), there was never any question of Ray doing more than help on the script. A memo of his, dated 13 August, confirms this:

> Dear Howard, I believe I have a practical suggestion [. . .] Put Betty London, who has been working with Mrs Luce, in an office adjoining me for the next week or ten days, during which time we will work on the script together, and at the end of which time she will rejoin Mrs Luce in Connecticut with the major part of the construction job completed [. . .] I understand you are willing to wait until November for Mr Hitchcock. Since to have begun shooting before October under present circumstances would have been unwise, I think waiting for a director about whom we are all highly enthusiastic is a very wise decision.

On 11 September, a list of available directors included neither Hitchcock nor Ray; at the foot of the page was King Vidor. A few pages in the latter's autobiography describe what happened to the project, written at a time when he still had hopes of making the film.[9] Hopes that came to nothing, since Hughes shut himself away in 1953 – for the first but not the last time – in a bungalow in Las Vegas.

Ray's notes concerning his work on *Pilate's Wife* anticipate some of the problems he encountered while making *King of Kings*. A Jesuit suggested to 'Clare' that she follow 'the chronology of events' in the 'trial scene', which would thus unfold in two phases: the first dominated by the political accusation, the second by the religious accusation. The washing of hands would thus occur in the middle of the scene and not at the end. The trial in *King of Kings*, one of the scenes Ray was fondest of, respects this point. The Jesuit claimed that his version was more correct historically, adding that it would 'also serve to diminish objections from the Jewish community'.[10] This combined concern for drama and diplomacy was to be a feature of Ray's Bronston years.

In December, Louella Parsons announced that Humphrey Bogart had agreed to do an original story, *Round Trip*, written by Ray with him in mind. The story had been bought by Jack L. Warner, who had assigned

Henry Blanke as producer, and Ray would probably be invited to direct when Bogart had finished *Beat the Devil* in Europe.[11] But the actor was never again to set foot in the studio he hated: in 1953 he terminated his contract with Warner Brothers. As busy as Ray – three films in 1954, three in 1955 – Bogart was to die of cancer before he could work with Ray again.

'We were going to do other films together,' Ray told Rui Nogueira and Nicoletta Zalaffi in 1966. 'Sam Spiegel even asked us to make *The Bridge On the River Kwai* for him! [. . .] Then he became ill. I was one of the first of his friends to know about it. After his first operation [March 1956] I was there, waiting for the results, but after that I didn't want to go back to see Bogie again. Later, before going off to Libya to make *Bitter Victory*, I decided to go and see him. I called his wife and asked if I could see him or not. She told me: "He's unconscious right now. How long will you be away?" – "About six months." "He will be dead by then," she told me.'[12] (Bogart died on 14 January 1957.)

On 7 February 1953, the seven-year term of Ray's contract with RKO came to an end.

Ray's private life had been no happier. He had been separated from Gloria Grahame since July 1951 (at the end of 1950, RKO had not exercised their option, and she had gone on to a more profitable career with DeMille, then Minnelli, Kazan and Fritz Lang).

On 15 August 1952, a divorce was granted. Gloria Grahame simply told Judge Samuel R. Blake, 'My husband hit me twice: once at a party without provocation, once at our home when I locked my bedroom door. He was sullen and morose and he would go into another room when my friends came to the house.'[13] Being in a position to provide for herself, she sought no alimony, but was awarded $300 monthly in child support for her son, Tim. A lot was left unsaid by both parties about this marriage, which Ray referred to only as 'a very expensive experience'.[14] On 13 May 1960, Gloria Grahame married Anthony Ray, Nick's elder son.

Shortly after the divorce, Nick met a woman who was to become important to him. Hanna Axmann was German; half-Jewish, through the war she had lived in hiding in Germany, then came to the United States. She was married to Ed Tierney, brother of the actors Scott Brady and Lawrence Tierney, and knew everyone in Hollywood: she was a friend of Max Ophüls, appeared in a film (*The Red Menace*), wrote a script with Howard Koch about her experience in Germany (*An Ordinary Spring*)[15]. Carol Saroyan, the writer's wife, said to her at a party: 'If you want to meet somebody who is *more* complicated even than your husband, then I'll introduce you to Nick Ray.' 'It was like two magnets at that party,' Hanna Axmann recalled, 'the way we just didn't leave each other any more.'

Hanna Axmann soon left her husband and came to live for several months with Nick, who was going through a dark time. 'The hundreds of nights I spent, with Nick drinking . . . At four or five in the morning he'd start talking nonsense; by seven he'd be more or less fresh, contemplating his feet a bit to get back to earth. Then he would go off every morning to his psychoanalyst, Dr Vanderhyde, come back and start drinking. The black maid prepared meals for us: sometimes I did the cooking, badly. Then we would go and play cards – Nick played a lot of gin rummy. I already knew all the people he played cards with . . . John Huston, Billy Wilder . . . I met nobody through Nick. This famous Dr Vanderhyde insisted on meeting me, looked like a perfect devil. He talked about the drinking, and said: "Do you think Nicholas Ray is the solution to your life?" I don't know whether he helped Nick very much.'

While starting to prepare *Johnny Guitar*, Ray asked Hanna Axmann to return to Germany, promising to join her there soon.

21

MCA

No longer bound by a term contract, Nicholas Ray could dream of autonomy. From the end of 1953, he periodically announced independent projects.[1] Independence would come in other forms, or not at all, but his career was now dependent on another organization, as powerful as any studio could be: his agents. After Berg and Allenberg, he moved to William Morris in 1950, then (prior to June 1952) to MCA.

In 1953, one could no longer conceive of a Hollywood agent in the terms used by Raymond Chandler in his article *10% of Your Life*: a mere business manager, patterned on the literary model. The character played by Art Smith in *In a Lonely Place* was plausible only because his client was a screenwriter on the way down. Over the years, the agencies had become organizations combining bureaucratic procedures with personal relations. Before incorporating with MCA, the Myron Selznick agency was already declaring an annual turnover of $15 million.[2] But while the majors were still operating a closed circuit, the agent intervened only at certain strategic moments: the renewal of a contract, securing the services of an important director from outside the studio. Even in such cases, the balance of power was not all in the agent's favour. 'In the old days,' Richard Zanuck said in 1967, 'my father could staff and cast a picture in minutes from the card file listing everyone under contract.'[3]

After the war, however, the balance slowly shifted. The emergence of independent production, the stars growing older or more determined to choose their own roles, the quest for freedom among young film-makers: none of this would have had much effect on the majors had it not coincided with the anti-trust decisions which forced them to divorce production/distribution from exhibition. These were the 'Paramount decrees'; paradoxically, it was Hughes the trustee's RKO which was the first to apply them. The House Un-American Activities Committee investigations definitively destroyed the image of the studio as a family: employers and employees each discovered that they had higher commitments. The emergence of television opened possibilities – and created needs – to which the film industry long remained blind; the intervention of outside capital, glaringly obvious in the case of Hughes and the Chicago 'syndicate' episode, was increasing. At which point the old-style agents, with Berg and Allenberg among the most reputable, slowly gave way to William Morris, and above all MCA, whose origins were not bound up with Hollywood.

Music Corporation of America was founded in Chicago in 1924 by Jules Stein to handle orchestral engagements. During the 1930s it represented more than half of the country's big orchestras. In 1937, MCA established itself in Hollywood, opening a theatrical agency, MCA Artists Ltd. As in music, the new agency was less interested in promoting new talent than in exploiting established names, wresting them away from rival organizations. The first of these names was Bette Davis, followed by a great many more: Joan Crawford, John Garfield, Betty Grable, Jane Wyman. In 1945 MCA absorbed the two Leland Hayward agencies and their 300 clients, ranging from Alfred Hitchcock to Shirley Temple, Greta Garbo and Fred Astaire.

In 1946, a Los Angeles federal court found the agency guilty (in its musical activities) of violating the Sherman antitrust law. The judge described the agency then as 'the Octopus . . . with tentacles reaching out to all phases and grasping everything in show business'. Shortly afterwards, Lew R. Wasserman became the company's president. Born in Cleveland, Ohio, on 15 March 1913, Wasserman had enjoyed a very American success story: cinema usher, confectionery salesman in strip-clubs, he joined MCA as an errand boy ten years to the day before becoming president. On the West Coast, he turned the agency into a giant conglomerate, in the forefront of the film industry. At the same time, he earned the lasting personal trust of his clients, whose interests he ably defended against the all-powerful studios. When Dore Schary left MGM in 1943, abandoned by his agent, Wasserman arranged three meetings with studio heads in four hours, and Schary was hired by Selznick. After *They Died With Their Boots On*, he had Errol Flynn's salary doubled. With John Garfield anxious to appear in *Tortilla Flat*, he persuaded Jack L. Warner to loan the actor out for the first time in his career. His other personal clients included Alfred Hitchcock (he was one of the film-maker's rare friends, and would play a decisive role towards the end of his career), Davis, Crawford, Houseman, Montgomery Clift, James Stewart, Jerry Lewis, Jean Arthur, Frank Sinatra, Gene Kelly and Kirk Douglas.[4]

MCA established an image of the agent as a businessman, in contrast to the cliché of the truculent hustler. Tall, thin and soft-spoken, usually appearing on the fringes of photographs, Wasserman surrendered to publicity only for rare items featuring his house or the charitable works of his wife, Edie.[5] He did not give interviews.[6] Dore Schary sketched one of the rare portraits of him: 'He has always been a good listener, eyeing you intently, making sure that you are telling him the truth. Sometimes he has the disconcerting habit of watching your lips as you talk. Always, he had and has . . . an air of complete confidence with a penumbra of wisdom and assurance that impels you to place your career in his hands.'[7]

Wasserman and Stein had detected and were able to exploit the declining power of the studios. As early as 1946–7, the sociologist Hortense Powdermaker mentioned a big agency's interest in one or more major studios in which it was a shareholder, noting that the practice of the package deal was spreading.[8] The agency was MCA, and the studio Paramount: a *Saturday Evening Post* inquiry in 1946 had revealed that Jules Stein was Paramount's second leading stockholder. In 1948, Wasserman advised Dore Schary, as he was about to return to MGM through the front door: 'Get rid of the whole bunch of executives – if you don't, they'll kill you – insist on cleaning house or don't take the job.'

In 1951 he proposed to buy out Louis B. Mayer's interests in MGM to use as 'investments in future transactions' (with Selznick and Harry Cohn also entering the lists, Mayer preferred to sell to MGM's parent company, Loew's).[9] In 1952 MCA formed a television company, Revue Productions, obtaining from the Screen Actors' Guild – presided over by a Wasserman client, Ronald Reagan – a special waiver on the clause forbidding agents from any production activity.[10] Revue soon became the world's principal producer and distributor of television series. MCA's rise to power had begun. It marked the first steps in the subjection of production to external factors: the machine no longer ran on its own. In many respects, the studio head simply became a traffic cop: 'Instead of assembling a package – story, talent, director, producer – he is more apt to be presented with one, take it or leave it,' John Gregory Dunne wrote. In a second stage, the agents would take control of the studios, with the great conglomerates over them. In 1962, MCA gained control of Universal International, and chose to abandon its agency activities. Wasserman remained in charge until 1991, the last tycoon, or as Dalton Trumbo put it as early as 1959, 'the most powerful single person in the business'.[11] And not just in the business, perhaps, since there are those who say that MCA played a key – and continuing – role in Ronald Reagan's career.

Ray was one of the instruments of this mutation: his career was dependent on it, was maintained by it, and was broken by it. Wasserman's support enabled him to go on working as a director, but never to be his own master. A firm friendship existed between him and Wasserman, perhaps reaching beyond the fascination with men of wealth and power which made Wasserman a natural successor to Hughes. 'What made life very difficult for Nick in regard to Hollywood,' John Housemen felt, 'is the fact that there was a side to Nick that loved all that. I used to give him hell all the time for being so terribly concerned with the sordid and destructive part of Hollywood. Nick was always telling you how much he'd been offered and how much he'd refused and what so-much was getting. He played that game and his friendship with Lew Wasserman was purely insane. Nick had no business being friend to Lew.'

There was also the brotherhood of gamblers. Games of poker and gin rummy were frequent at Lew's place or involving him; and Ray, a compulsive gambler, sat in with the tycoons. Susan Ray recalled one of his anecdotes. A session with Wasserman, Nick, Al Bloomingdale. Nick remarked that it would be nice if you could play with a card, like the chips in casinos. Al Bloomingdale noted the idea, and the credit card was born.

There was a friendship, too, with Edie Wasserman, who had arrived in Hollywood with her husband and made a brilliant success of their social life. Edie continued to champion Nick enthusiastically, long after Lew had given up acting in his interests.

Ray had been with RKO for years, Joan Crawford with MGM and then Warner Brothers. In 1953 they were 'with' MCA, as was screen-writer Philip Yordan. According to the latter: 'Lew Wasserman was packaging for a few studios, like Paramount, and he was packaging for Republic.' So it was that Ray's next film came about.

22

Johnny Guitar

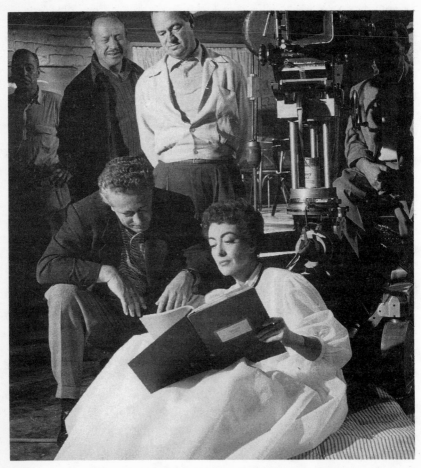

33 *Johnny Guitar*. Nicholas Ray and Joan Crawford

Johnny Guitar started out as a package: four Lew Wasserman clients and a story, sold to a studio. The first was Roy Chanslor, a former journalist turned hack screenwriter and novelist (he sold three to the cinema that year). When his *Johnny Guitar* was published in May 1953,[1] he immediately turned it into a sceenplay made to measure for Joan Crawford, the second client: the novel is dedicated to the star. After her 'second career' at Warners, launched by *Mildred Pierce* – a role she won thanks to Jerry Wald and Wasserman – Crawford went from studio to studio, film by film: her career was in fact being managed by MCA. Wasserman banked a great deal on Ray, who had left RKO on a high with *The Lusty Men*. But it was said of him, as of the director Cliff Harriston in Gavin Lambert's novel *The Slide Area*, 'He's good but you have to watch him'. In the chapter entitled 'The Closed Set', the star – transparently modelled on Crawford – has decided that 'All that man needs is a good picture, and I'm going to give it to him.' The director accepts because he needs the money.[2]

The conditions under which Ray approached his new film were much more favourable and flattering. The contract was with one of the smallest of the major studios, Republic, but it was a contract for a single film, and with his dual role as producer and director, it was a first step towards the independence he sought. Moreover, it was the studio's biggest production that year, and the Western was then far from 'finished'. Quite apart from the boost brought to the genre by 'Scope and 3-D, these were the years of the 'adult' and 'super-Western', to use André Bazin's term. *The Big Sky* and *High Noon* both came in 1952. The next year saw *The Naked Spur, Shane, Ride Vaquero*, not to mention films ignored by the American critics: *Rancho Notorious* (1952) and *Silver Lode* (1953). *Hondo*, a John Wayne production, *Apache*, a Burt Lancaster production directed by Ray's junior Robert Aldrich, and Otto Preminger's *River of No Return* were made at the same time as *Johnny Guitar*. The widescreen format orginally planned was abandoned, but the budget was generous, and colour was still a luxury for the studio long run by Herbert J. Yates.

Roy Chanslor's script[3] established the settings and basic situations for the film – or, more strictly, the Western clichés which the film then put to use. Faithfully adapted from the novel, it was a collection of unlikely platitudes (Chanslor ran a production line in B Western scripts for Universal): the town is Powderville, the saloon is called The Bills (to show that Vienna is grasping about money). No ambiguity, no past relationship between the characters. Johnny is a seducer and a tinhorn gambler, Vienna is interested only in money but her femininity will be revealed by love, Emma seeks revenge simply for her husband (not her brother), the Dancing Kid's gang has indeed robbed the stagecoach. The incidents – robbery, suspicions, fire, lynching, chase, bandit's hideout, chase – follow one another with no build-up, no differentiation in the secondary characters. Only two lines of dialogue survived from this script: 'The sun was shinin' in my eyes' and 'I'm not the fastest draw west of the Pecos.'

But their context and resonance are very different in the film. The first is given to a 'witness' not 'friendly' enough to please the interrogators; the second eases the tension during another interrogation, and places Johnny between the two camps (a witness neither 'hostile' nor 'friendly', in an analogy to which we shall return), at the same time establishing his personal ambivalence (we soon discover that he is lying).

Between June and the start of shooting in September, Ray took the time to fashion an entirely new script with a fourth MCA client. During a party at Bogart's, he had met a writer two years younger than himself, Philip Yordan. 'Somebody got into an argument with me, some big guy,' Yordan recalled. 'All of a sudden, somebody tall moved in behind me, took this guy and shoved him against the wall, and it was Nick. He just happened to be there and he intervened. That's how I met him.' Originally from Chicago, a lawyer by training, Yordan landed in Hollywood thanks to the success of his play *Anna Lucasta*, which transposed the plot of O'Neill's *Anna Christie* to a black milieu. He already had a number of robust scripts to his credit, especially for low-budget action films, and had begun a fruitful collaboration with Anthony Mann. He also had the reputation of serving as a front for blacklisted writers.[4] As Yordan, a staunch liberal, explains: 'We all [sic] helped blacklisted writers. Most of these guys were our friends, and as long as a guy had talent we didn't care about his politics. But the studios did the screening. Sometimes in picking guys we'd run into trouble with the studio, but if it wasn't important we got away with it.' The tone of *Johnny Guitar* at times comes quite close to that of Yordan's preceding film, *The Naked Jungle*; that script, however, was written by Ben Maddow, his 'ghost' on several other films. On the strength of this, *Johnny Guitar* is sometimes attributed to Maddow.[5] Maddow himself, who made no bones about claiming authorship of *The Naked Jungle*, *Men in War*, etc., denied that he had any hand in Ray's film.[6] No one has ever explained how Yordan could have had such a long career, and lent his name to such a coherent body of work, if he wrote nothing himself. His anonymous collaborators in fact thought of him as an administrator: just as Lew Wasserman sold film packages, Yordan's more modest operation sold script packages, with a guarantee of quality and finish which it was doubtless his responsibility to supply.

There can be little doubt that Yordan worked alone with the director, writing *Johnny Guitar* in two bursts: during August-September in Hollywood, then during shooting. After getting rid of Roy Chanslor and his initial script, Ray moved into a house neighbouring Yordan's, to make sure that it was indeed Yordan he was getting as a collaborator.[7] Their script ran to 200 pages. Ray deposited about thirty of these pages with the Cinémathèque Française. In the absence of a complete copy,[8] these scattered fragments offer a few surprises. Emma is still the wife – not the sister – of Len Small; it is only in the blue revised pages, dated 9 October (just before shooting started), that any reference is made to her repressed love for the Dancing Kid. As in Chanslor's script, Vienna and Johnny (who is called Pogue, not Logan) did not know each other before. Out of their first love scene, only the two italicized lines reached the screen:

JOHNNY: Can I kiss you again?
VIENNA: If you want.
    Who was she, Mr Pogue?
JOHNNY: Just a girl. It's so long I don't even remember. It could have been you.
VIENNA: It could have been.
JOHNNY: *How many men have you forgotten?*
VIENNA: *As many women as you've remembered.*
JOHNNY: Why are you being nice to me?
VIENNA: It's time someone was.
JOHNNY: But we're strangers. Why you?
VIENNA: Maybe it's because I don't want you to go. I need your help.
JOHNNY: You can buy me – cheap.

The scene is clearly indebted to Hawks's *To Have and Have Not* – and indeed to Sternberg.[9] But throughout, as here, little of the dialogue written for Vienna was retained, especially in her scenes with Johnny. The Mittel-European ambience, on the other hand, is rather clumsily stressed. The attentive viewer of *Johnny Guitar* will have noticed a bust of Beethoven in Vienna's room. This is not a prop man's quirk: it is linked with the heroine's father, and her choice of Vienna as a nickname, in a line of dialogue – eliminated during shooting – in the scene with Mr Andrews. Other important scenes, on the other hand, mostly without Vienna, were shot as written here. Johnny's arrival in the saloon and his first encounter with the employees ('Don't rush the night'); the McIvers-Emma-Vienna confrontation in the saloon (when Vienna refuses to help the leader of the posse, Ray notes: 'Play off Emma – Emma smiles'); the harassment of Turkey by McIvers and Emma ('all from Turkey's point of view', Ray notes) and his betrayal of Vienna; and the whole of the ending from the arrival of Johnny and Vienna in the Dancing Kid's hideout, the Lair (at most, a few lines of dialogue were eliminated). All these scenes figured in the script prior to shooting.

While writing in the Coldwater Canyon house and working on certain visual aspects of the film ('He collaborated with me', according to Yordan, 'less on the dramatic than the architectural level, creating settings like the saloon, working on the geometrical relationships between places'), Ray picked a powerful cast in support of his star. The male lead and title role went to Sterling Hayden. A sailor turned actor, OSS agent in Yugoslavia during the war, traumatized by the deposition he had been induced to make before the House Un-American Activities Committee, troubled by a marriage on the verge of breakdown, Hayden no longer gave a damn about his career and moved from one mediocre film to the next. Though declaring his professional admiration for Ray, Hayden had no reason to be interested in a role to which he brings so much, precisely through his air of having lost all his illusions and the dreamy detachment with which he delivers his most lyrical lines. 'Never direct a natural': Hayden has told of how he didn't know how to ride a horse, play the guitar or shoot:[10] these actions become archetypal in the film, an impression reinforced by the choice of supporting players, some of them from Republic's roster, others from Ford, André De Toth or Anthony Mann movies. Ward Bond's role was similar to the one he played in *On Dangerous Ground*. Royal Dano, as the tubercular outlaw, Corey, had appeared in Mann's *Bend of the River*.

At Sedona, Arizona, Republic had a Western street, a permanent set abutting on a cliff. It was here that shooting started in October, an early scene being the night of the fire. The other exteriors were shot in the vicinity at Oak Creek Canyon, which, after a flat desert road between Phoenix and Sedona, connects the latter town to Flagstaff. The rock here is reddish: instead of attenuating this, Ray laid it on in great slabs, in keeping with the very stylized colours of the film. Sedona had been the setting for several films, but was as yet untouched by tourism and developers.

'At the time,' Royal Dano recalled, 'there was a small hotel, which was used for our stars, and the rest of us stayed at a CCC camp of the 1930s [cf. *The Young Go First*]. It was like an army camp with barracks and a big mess hall, and the recreational areas were practically non-existent: a few small cowboy-type bars, a Legion Hall, and beyond that, not very much. And every night, after we had come home, we'd set up our own bar where the guys would all gather for a pre-dinner drink, and people would swap stories. We'd go off to dinner, and maybe after we came back there might be a little kidding around or a little hell-raising around the camp . . . and to bed and up the next morning. We had a foursome, the four bad guys, it consisted of Ernie Borgnine, Scott Brady, Ben Cooper and myself, all New Yorkers. We had a grand time together.

Other people may have had problems, but we were a happy lot. And we became a little gang of our own. [The production] went first class as far as we were concerned. Nick didn't scamp the shots, he didn't say, "Oh, the hell with it, I didn't like it but print it." If he felt that it wasn't right, he went back to get it right. I found him a very easy man to get along with.'

Herbert Yates is said to have told Yordan that his only concern was that 'Crawford should be happy during the filming'. This wasn't so easy to ensure. The overbearing, unbalanced personality of the star – the film's *raison d'être* – was to weigh heavily over the production. Nominally the producer, Ray in fact had no authority, which was shared by Herbert Yates in absentia and by a star whose $200,000 salary alone comprised the budgets of four of the 'Jubilee' Western series currently in production at Republic. In Gavin Lambert's novel, the star, Julia Forbes, is her own producer; but the studio head and agent hover in the background. Even before shooting starts, she whittles down the director's field of action in a series of skirmishes, and at a given point the latter loses interest in the film. In real life, the crucial incident happened a little later on.

Mercedes McCambridge found herself playing the principal villain, Emma Small – Crawford's antagonist – through a quirk of casting which was to prove a determining factor in the film. 'I felt I had a certain edge,' McCambridge recalled in her memoirs, 'because a gentleman with whom [Crawford] had, not long before, had some association, to the degree that she had given him gold cuff-links, was now my husband.'[11]

The story has often been told by Ray: 'That morning, after I shot her scenes, I had sent Joan back to camp because I didn't want her around while I was doing the scene where Mercedes addresses the posse. I had done two or three takes with Mercedes, and the third one went very well. I was pleased, and so was everybody else; cast and crew alike burst into applause. The moment they did, I looked over my shoulder and saw Miss Crawford sitting up on the hill, watching. I should have known some hell was going to break loose.'[12]

That night, Ray found the star telephoning for a limousine after having strewn McCambridge's clothes all over the road. She demanded 'five more scenes'. He called Yordan, who arrived in Sedona twenty-four hours later, along with Arthur Park, the MCA agent who looked after Crawford as well as Ray, Yordan and Mercedes McCambridge.[13] As Yordan told it: 'They were on location and Joan Crawford just decided that she wasn't going to make the picture. They were shooting about two weeks without her. So Wasserman called me up, and they chartered

34 *Johnny Guitar:* Mercedes McCambridge

a plane and flew me out there. When I saw Nick, he said he didn't know what the hell was going on, but he said she was nuts. So I said, "What's the problem?" He said, "She's got some crazy idea." So I went to see her and asked what her problem was, and . . . she said that she wanted to play the man's role. She said, "I'm Clark Gable, it's Vienna that's gotta be the leading part." Otherwise, she had ordered a limousine to pick her up and she was going to drive back the next morning to Los Angeles, and the picture would be abandoned. If this picture had been abandoned, I don't know if Republic Pictures at that time could have survived, because it was about a $2½ million picture [*sic*] when they were making pictures for $50,000.

'So this is her idea, I listened to it, and she said, "What do you think of it?" Well, my instructions were to keep the project afloat, so I said, "I think it's great." She said, "Nobody else likes it." I saw Nick, he says, "Yeah, she told me the same thing, she's nuts." "Well, what do you want to do, Nick?" I said, "If she walks, the picture folds, you lose your job, like I do. Wasserman'll be really pissed off." He says, "Well, what do you think? Can you do it?" – "Sure I can do it" – "Jesus, how the hell am I going to direct her?" I say, "Well, why don't you do this, Nick? It'll only be another six weeks. Get up every morning, look in the mirror, and when you shave, say, Look, I've only got five more weeks and I'll never have to see Joan Crawford again. Each day, just keep telling yourself you'll never have to see her again, till the six weeks is over." He looked at me for a long time – I'll never forget this – and he said, "You know, *never* is a long time." So I just wrote it the way she wanted: she shot it out with Mercedes McCambridge at the end, we got Sterling Hayden to play her part. She was Clark Gable, that's all. Every time, you thought of her as a man; you don't think of her as Joan Crawford. And that's the way Nick directed her, very masculine.'

For Yordan, it was a matter of confection. *Johnny Guitar* draws on *Casablanca*, just as his script for *Blowing Wild* (like the *Johnny Guitar* dialogue quoted above) borrowed from *To Have and Have Not*. Curtiz's film plays a not inconsiderable role in the masculinization of Crawford: the action centring on a song that is taboo, the devotion of the employees in the threatened saloon, and the nocturnal meetings in the deserted establishment, make Bogart rather than Gable the model for Vienna's character.

For Ray, it meant finding a new balance for the whole film. Nowhere in the novel, or in the Chanslor and Yordan scripts, was it suggested that Vienna and Johnny had known each other before the action starts. In the completed film, their meeting is a reunion, adding the weight of a past affair to their relationship, with each viewing the other as filtered through memory. This 'embitterment' makes *Johnny Guitar* another facet of Ray's treatment of love. Sentimentality transformed into lyricism: the choice of words, the forms of address, the moments of mutual understanding, even the repressed self-pity, were the very weft of the relationships in *They Live by Night*, *In a Lonely Place* and *On Dangerous Ground*. Hayden's rootlessness, Crawford's desire for independence, the couple trying to escape the world, the hopelessness of the outlaw and the vengeful persistence of the upright citizen, haunt and transform these films (as well as *The Lusty Men*). Even the production history of *Casablanca* finds an echo in Ray's direction. During the Vassar lecture in 1979, he referred to Michael Curtiz: 'He's a favourite personality [of mine]. And a very, very talented craftsman. When he made *Casablanca*, he had five scripts around his chair. And he was shooting it from each one of the five scripts. And keeping it all together.'

205

The tension between the two actresses had an immediate effect on the production. 'Quite a few times,' Ray claimed, 'I would have to stop the car and vomit before I got to work in the morning.' The Arizona press picked up on it, and so did the Hollywood gossips when the cast and crew returned to the studio for the interiors. Bob Thomas, in his biography of Crawford, goes into some detail; and Crawford herself, in her autobiography,[14] attributes responsibility to 'an actress who hadn't worked in ten years' (Mercedes McCambridge had won an Oscar two years earlier for *All the King's Men*), and to 'an actor with an equally dubious reputation' (Hayden), accusing the director of trying to capitalize on the crisis through the scandal sheets. In an interview book she is more concise: 'There is no excuse for making such a bad film.'[15]

Mercedes McCambridge also wrote an autobiography. When I tracked her down to the centre for alcoholic rehabilitation which she runs, she stuck to strictly technical detail: 'I was in the picture for a total of, I think, three weeks of shooting time. I tried terribly hard to stay clear of anything that is not my business in my profession, and I really had little to do with the Hollywood community. Joan Crawford and I hated each other, but that's been written about so many times that it bores me stiff. I thought he [Ray] was a fine director, because he just . . . gave me my head, that was really all. I went from what was written on the page, but I had a very small part in that film, really. So my long speech outside, up against the tree, was really the one big scene I had. The rest of the time I was running in and out, shooting up things and getting on and off the stupid horses and blowing the place. You took direction if you were an actor, you'd do what you were told. But I was not led into that speech; everybody was amazed when I did it in one take, and they all applauded. Nick Ray and I never discussed the character from any viewpoint whatsoever. I was cast in the part, it must have been that they thought I could play it.'

There were at least three takes, from three different angles, of Emma's tirade – but no more, since Republic was tight with film stock. In the film, these three set-ups are fragmented into six shots (ten with reaction shots), totalling 76 seconds. The disenchantment tinged with humour with which the actress recalls the scene belies Ray's recollection of it in 1974 as inspired, purposeful direction. 'Mercedes,' he supposedly said to her, 'I want you to play this all the way through – unremittingly – as the sulphuric acid that cuts through Crawford's sweetness and light. Without any let-up.' Factitious as memory, but a fine description of the performance.

For the rest of the cast and crew, these incidents would have passed almost unnoticed but for the rumours in the press, and brought few consequences. Royal Dano did not recall much improvisation. 'There seemed to be a problem just prior to the shooting of the sequence where Sterling Hayden and Ernie Borgnine have a fight. Joan went back to her dressing room. A little while later, our writer and director followed. And then Mr Yates appeared. In the end, there were changes made so that Joan – rather than some other subsidiary character – now ensured the fairness of the fight. It was story-lined out, but there was no new scene, just writing in the change of viewpoint. There was no explosion on set, as I've seen happen with other people. It was all handled very quietly. And just about everything that our little group was involved in was not subject to any major changes in structure.'

Comparison between the finished film and the surviving fragments of the script enable one to see how constructive such changes in viewpoint were. The masculinization of Crawford, already adumbrated in the script (contrary to what Yordan says, the final duel between the two women did figure in it), and the romantic dimension which takes over from a cynical conflict of interests, are grafted on to a solidly structured basis.

The original schedule allowed for thirty-four days of shooting, top limit for the studio.[16] With the changes to the script, this was extended to forty-four (excluding second unit), finishing in mid-December. Four to six weeks later,[17] Ray completed a very fragmented cut (the film contains 1090 shots).[18]

The experience had been traumatic for him. While shooting his next film, he wrote to Hanna Axmann: 'The atrocity *Johnny Guitar* is finished and released, to dreadful reviews and great financial success. Nausea was my reward, and I'm glad for you that you were not there to share the suffering.' Scandal was still to come from Sterling Hayden, who declared, at a première party which was broadcast on television: 'I've had all I want to do with working with Miss Crawford, and don't care to continue the contact.'

For the director, this film left a bitter taste, although he had seen it through successfully to the end. Part of it was injured self-esteem at seeing himself assigned the title of associate producer for the credits. He rejected this as being 'an office boy equivalent', and the film was released without a producer credit.[19] The reviews for *Johnny Guitar* were cold and negative (especially in the trade press), which seems to have wounded Ray. Many of them mentioned the film's baroque, psychoanalytical, self-parodic aspects: in the American press these were not a matter for praise. But with laudatory reviews in some of the periodicals (*Fortnight* and *Cue* in particular), opinions were not entirely unanimous.

It was in Europe that Ray was to change his mind after meeting admirers of the film. Gavin Lambert had written that 'the shadow of Krafft-Ebing hangs heavily over this preposterous Western', with an effect of 'fascinating, portentous lunacy'. Truffaut, in *Arts*, spoke of 'The *Belle et la Bête* of the Western genre'.[20] The comments are ambiguous, as was the director's aversion, given his disappointment at having won relative freedom only to see it thwarted. But as Sumner Williams put it, in connection with this detested film: 'Filming was always an unhappy time for Nick. I don't remember one occasion during which he felt good. During preparation, yes, and afterwards too.' The crisis had come through no fault of Ray's: there was a sizeable external factor. But he had brought the factors together. Crisis increasingly became the very condition of the film.

Films come to resemble their history. In this case, the casting helped. Ward Bond plays McIvers, leader of the posse, and Yordan describes his casting as a 'good trick' played on the actor, who thought he was playing a positive role. Ray's tactics with actors stopped at nothing, even to making use of their images – in other words, their past both on and off-screen. But there is no manipulation about this. 'It was not my intention to hit him with a surprise,' Ray explained. The character played by Bond remains ambivalent, very different from the unadulterated nastiness represented by Emma. The portrayal draws equally on Bond's private reputation as a 'witch-hunter' and on his screen image as a Ford pioneer (*Wagon Master* especially). The latter, as a matter of fact, literally made his presence felt on the actor. 'Ward', Royal Dano recalls, 'had this sequence where he wound up taking a bottle and throwing it against the saloon wall. Having played football in his youth, he threw it like a football, on spiral and with a lot of force. Naturally it just drilled a hole right through the papier-mâché wall. It took several takes to try to get Ward to throw the damn thing sideways. In the midst of all this, a face appeared from behind the camera, with an eye-patch, and it was John Ford. From that moment, Ward had trouble connecting one word to the next. One of the older boys had known Ward for years, and said that whenever Ford showed up, he was just terrified. He managed to get through it, but it didn't have the flow . . .'

Johnny Guitar is a long way from Ford. Its raw material is not the West, but a cinematic vision of the West. 'I had decided to violate all the rules of the Western': the platitude was used in justification only after the event. Yordan, doing his usual job, and Ray, in sheer desperation, exploited the crassness of the material supplied by Chanslor. They incorporated a number of decorative, dramatic or verbal stereotypes. Exchanges like 'You don't have the nerve' – 'Try me,' or 'Luck had nothing to do with it,' proliferate throughout. The excess breeds irony: dialogue rarely reveals so much about stereotypes and the ambiguity that may lie behind them as it does here, in a welter of lines like, 'I never shake hands with a left-handed draw,' not forgetting Ray's personal watchword, 'I'm a stranger here myself.' Stylization followed naturally from these options. As often with Ray, the action is precisely located in place and time: three days, from Friday afternoon to Sunday morning. Ray insisted that credit was due to Yordan and himself for this concern with the passing of time in daily life and with the lives of characters burdened with their pasts.

The extremely stylized colour and geometrical treatment of oppositions have been noted more often. In 1957, having changed his mind about the film, Ray talked about this to Charles Bitsch: 'I like my use of colour in it. I thought that ideas such as using the black and white costumes of the posse, and so on, were . . . all right. All the more credit to us in that the colour process at our disposal wasn't up to much: for example, to cover its defects, we filmed a lot of dissolves directly in camera. When the technical means at your disposal are inadequate, you always go back to the early methods of filming.'[21] *Johnny Guitar* was his second film in colour, and the first over which he retained relative control, subject to the limitations of the process. All Republic films were handled in a laboratory belonging to the studio, Consolidated Film Industries, and those in colour bore the trademark Trucolor. In this case, the Eastmancolor monopack was used;[22] it was not the nature of the process but the laboratory work that imposed limitations. 'Harry Stradling was a big help. We carefully avoided having blues in the field. My art director and camera operator sometimes felt that my worries about blue were becoming a bit of an obsession, but thanks to this, the film did not suffer from the defect inherent in the process.' No such originality is apparent in Harry Stradling's previous career as a distinguished studio craftsman. Ray had been able to judge his work from *Androcles and the Lion* (without actually working with him), but it was probably Kazan's *A Streetcar Named Desire* which won him the job.[23]

The composer, Victor Young, was also a prolific and talented craftsman.[24] His music confirms all the film's intentions: an extreme stylization, a touch of self-parody underlining the 'super-Western' element. Young, much more interested in melody than in harmony, is a far cry from the dissonances of Antheil, Herrmann's blocks of sound, the experimentation of Leigh Harline or, a little later on, Leonard Rosenman. Working in the same Hispanic register as his score for *For Whom the Bell Tolls*, he came up with a theme (borrowed from Granados) which defines

209

the film and underlines its flamboyant tone; all the more so in that the title song (reduced to a minimum, over the closing images) is entrusted to a lush torch singer, Peggy Lee.

The same purpose is evident in the handling of the performances. Royal Dano recalled a 'scene played by John Carradine which was a soliloquy. John was sweeping the floor and he was talking to himself. To the effect that "If I was as tall and if I was as strong as that stranger . . ." And dammit, when he finished that thing, it was one of the few times I wanted to applaud. A beautifully done job, and Carradine really laid into it. Yet in the final version of the film it was gone.'

The monologue came just after the bank robbery, when Vienna is paying off her employees and leaves money for Old Tom (Carradine), whose absence is not explained. It was included in a first rough cut viewed on 9 December (before filming was completed) by a representative of the front office, Jason Lindsey. He suggested that it should be cut: 'The scene would not be missed, and if it is retained I think there'll be some confusion in the mind of the audience as to Old Tom's reasons for his questions and answers. It's just barely possible to get the notion that Old Tom is in cahoots with the bank robbers.' Old Tom's secret love for Vienna (which costs him his life) adds to the mystery, but not to the plot.[25]

Two scenes which were not cut confirm and reinforce the theatrical slant. The first is a speech direct to camera (probably comparable to Carradine's monologue) by Vienna's croupier, Sam (Robert Osterloh): 'I've never seen a woman who was more a man. She thinks like one, acts like one, and sometimes makes me feel like I'm not.' A lateral cutaway eventually reveals that he is addressing, not the audience, but Johnny and Old Tom, framed in the service-hatch to the kitchen, which serves as a second proscenium for the little theatre in which he is appearing. The second is the death of Old Tom himself. In the script, he is killed instantly. Ray's marginal note reads: 'A dying moment'; and Carradine is given these final words: 'Everybody's looking at me. It's the first time I ever felt important.' It is difficult not to be reminded of the dialogue and situations in To Be or Not To Be, a film about actors; specifically, the moment where Felix Bressart's spear-carrier delivers Shylock's great tirade to an audience of real Nazis. The echo is undoubtedly not so much a direct steal from Lubitsch's film as the result of a common theatrical experience, in Ray's case stored in his memory since his days on Broadway.

Another death scene, flatly described in the script, adds to the resonance. When Bart (Ernest Borgnine) approaches Corey (Royal Dano) to suggest betraying the Dancing Kid, Ray notes: 'This is Bart's conception of decency.' It was he who elaborated the dialogue up to the moment when Bart stabs Corey, including his aside, 'Some people just won't listen'. When asked in an interview if Vienna represented Nick Ray, the latter replied (evading the point, of course): 'Only in the sense of a line I wrote for Ernie Borgnine. Scott Brady says to him, "What *do* you like?" And Bart says, "Me. I like me".'[26]

In a persuasive analysis, Michael Wilmington sees the theatre as the film's dominant metaphor, with this surreal quality becoming its only reality because it is true to the emotions.[27] The Sternbergian role-swapping (Joan Crawford's stroke of genius, according to Yordan) stands in contrast to actors – an actress – showing their age, their wrinkles, dissociating themselves from the dramatic artifice and formal visual effects. It is this interaction between artifice and nakedness – rather than any message (much debated) – that lies at the heart of the film.

In its description of the techniques of repression and persecution, *Johnny Guitar* clearly belongs with the liberal films of the day, those using genre plots to impart pluralist messages (*The Day the Earth Stood Still*, *Silver Lode*, etc.). Yordan sees this as the heart of the matter. He talks of problems with the censors, of an 'essentially modern theme, a situation created by the rise of a middle-class morality which encouraged this policy of terror. You're living peacefully in some quiet place, when suddenly someone appears and tells you, "You've no right to live here for such-and-such a reason, so get out, or else . . ." Why, I ask you, why haven't I the right to live where I want?'[28]

Unless Yordan used a ghost for this interview as well, he sums up the intentions of *Johnny Guitar* quite well – intentions which became the subject of startling polemics during the 1970s. Some saw Vienna above all as a continuation of the Crawford character in *Mildred Pierce*, with a final victory won over matriarchy (because Vienna prepares breakfast for Johnny at the end of the film); for others, the character is informed by the personality of the actress, who 'refused aid' (a claim nowhere substantiated) to the House Un-American Activities Committee. Vienna is 'a materialist', Johnny 'a Marxist ready to overthrow his oppressors by going outside the limits of the system'![29] Ray himself was not entirely innocent of these wild critical fancies. He told *Take One* that 'in Barcelona, the film split the city in two on political lines'.[30]

Yet the film carries the parallels to considerable lengths: two characters speak for the rest, one (Emma) in hysterical mode, the other (McIvers) more realistic. They begin by rejecting the outsiders, and when some of these (the Dancing Kid and his boys, innocent in the film of the wrong-

211

doing which the Chanslor script credited them with) are driven in fact to become outlaws, they are pressured to denounce the others. The dialogue between Johnny and Vienna about the posse reflects a particular climate, but also genre conventions:

JOHNNY: I've got a hunch the posse will be dropping in on you before night. The same people who paid you a visit yesterday. Only they won't be the same. A posse isn't people. I've ridden with them, and I've ridden against them. A posse is an animal. It moves like one and thinks like one.

VIENNA: They're men with itchy fingers and a coil of rope around their saddle horns, looking for somebody to hang. And after riding a few hours, they don't care much who they hang. You haven't told me a thing I don't know.

No spectator, however, could misread the scene of Turkey's interrogation by Emma and McIvers, given Vienna's earlier ironical comment about Emma's inability to produce 'any more witnesses':

EMMA: Tell us. Don't be afraid. We'll protect you . . . Just tell us Vienna was one of your bunch and we'll give you a chance.

MCIVERS: We might even let you ride out of here.

EMMA: You're only a boy. We don't want to hurt you.

MCIVERS: The truth, son, that's all we want . . . You don't have to say anything. Just nod.

Was Vienna one of you?

TURKEY shakes his head, no.

EMMA (sharply): Well, was she?

TURKEY nods in assent, and hangs his head.

The reference to a practice evolved during the witch-hunting years, whereby certain witnesses hoped to escape both the blacklist and the shame of being an informer, is clear.[31] This mistrust of the mob and the silent majority, the distinct bias towards the outsider, was not new in Ray's work. Emma's harangue to the posse clearly marks the convergence of this obsession (an integral part of Yordan's liberal purpose) with the Freudian emotional current which surfaced, almost inadvertently on the part of Yordan and Ray, during shooting.

In 'The Closed Set' chapter of Gavin Lambert's *The Slide Area*, the director Cliff Harriston insults the star at the end-of-filming party. She throws a drink in his face and slaps him. Lambert concludes: 'Cliff told me he wasn't going to the première. He is working on a new story, and is very excited about it. "This one's going to be really good." It will be for a different studio, as J. B. [the fictional producer] didn't renew his contract. Cliff looks better now than at the end of shooting *Every Inch a Lady* [the fictional film], but I always find a deep and almost fearful tiredness in his face. When he talks, he often looks away from you; his eyes are gazing out of a window, through an open door. I suppose they see a thin line stretching away, growing thinner.'

Though Mercedes McCambridge claims she didn't have much to do with her director, she nevertheless understood him: 'Nick Ray was a very tortured man. But you would have to write the analysis of his character. I think his films probably showed his great restlessness, his moroseness, his vulnerability, the rawness of his nature, the occasional tenderness, which was very profound – but that's just my observation of watching a man walk around the set.'

23

Run for Cover

After finishing his job at Republic, in mid-January 1954, Nicholas Ray announced two projects. The first was *Gypsy Story*, a reworking of *No Return*, which he hoped to produce in association with Jane Russell and Robert Mitchum, forgetting that the subject still belonged to RKO.[1] Then there was *Passport*, a project he carried around with him for years, trying to interest Eric Ambler in it during a trip to England. Ray felt strongly enough about it to talk of it as late as August 1961: '[It was] about an American whose passport is stolen, and who finds that the loss of a piece of paper is also a loss of identity. Searching for it, he would come one day upon a thief: a child, sitting by the sea, tearing up the passport pages and throwing them into the water. The child's question: "Where does the tide become national?" '[2] On both projects, Ray hoped to produce and direct.

Then, for the second time running, MCA proposed that he direct a big star from the 1930s: James Cagney, whose career was on the wane. The producers, William H. Pine and William C. Thomas, headed a B-movie unit at Paramount. They generally produced Westerns and exotic adventure films, directed by Edward Ludwig or Lewis R. Foster, and featuring second-rank actors like John Payne or Ronald Reagan. Their bad name was legendary; with Ray, Cagney and VistaVision (it was only the third film shot in the process), *Run for Cover* represented a promotion for them. Their relationship with the director nevertheless seems to have been relatively good, although one can sense the Paramount routine weighing heavily. The entire crew was under yearly contract: the cameraman (Daniel L. Fapp, thirty-six years in all with Paramount), the art director (Henry Bumstead, twenty-four years), and the editor (Howard Smith). The scriptwriter too, Winston Miller, was one of the studio's regular workhorses.[3] As authors of the original story, the writing team of Irving Ravetch and Harriet Frank Jr probably played a more important role: they were to make a name for themselves during the 1960s with 'realistic' or contemporary scripts set in the West or the American heartlands (*Home from the Hill, Hud, The Reivers*).

The final script for *Run for Cover* was written in the three weeks preceding shooting: the pages are dated from 6 to 20 May, and filming began on the 25th. Ray's copy bears numerous annotations, and includes

214

a storyboard, covering only the exterior sequences (and the one in the Aztec ruins).[4] This was probably the work of Henry Bumstead, who accompanied the director while locations were being scouted. In Colorado, Ray and Bumstead found Western streets which scarcely needed to be adapted to the requirements of the film.

The cameraman, Daniel Fapp, was not involved in the scouting, and had had no preparation when shooting began at over 10,000 feet (3,000 metres), above Silverton, then moved to Durango, at a more comfortable altitude of 6,000 feet (1,800 metres). Fapp: 'We had about equal amounts of work in both places, and they did the worst thing possible: they went to Silverton first. The crew was almost ready to fall on their faces, working hard, fast, and not used to that altitude.' Ray, because of his cardiac malformation, was not the least affected.

Far from the studio, it was a happy production. Ray got on well with Cagney. The latter's doctor brother had accompanied him to Colorado, and in the evenings they would invite the director and members of the crew to a barbecue. The pleasure of working with Cagney did not make up for the lack of time: time 'to be inventive as I would have liked', time to find the best solution for scenes.

The two producers were in Colorado, and there was some friction with the director. According to Fapp: 'Thomas would stand behind me and say, "You tell him, don't let him do that, don't let him do this." For example, there was one scene with a fight between Borgnine and Cagney on horseback. Ray wanted to do it in heavy woods. Well, that's okay if you've got six months to make a picture, but when you make a picture in thirty days, you can't go into heavy woods and try to shoot a fight. So that was one of the things that I had to argue him out of, and Thomas of course backed me up, because he knew enough about pictures to know it was wrong.' The script and storyboard set the scene in open ground; in the film, it takes place among a scattering of trees. On this occasion, Ray seemingly won his case.

But the director could do nothing about shooting day-for-night at crazy hours, or about dialogue delivered against a background of rocks. Unlike Losey (who described them as 'monsters'), Ray had no quarrel with Pine and Thomas, feeling that he had been trapped by a weak script. Cagney shared his disappointment: 'We had tried to make as offbeat a Western as possible, but whoever cut the film was evidently revolted by anything but clichés. As a consequence, little things that the director, Nick Ray (a good man), and actors put in to give the story added dimension were excised very proficiently. The result was just another programmer.'[5]

No important scene from the script has been cut in its entirety. As one might expect, the 'little things' that were eliminated had to do with the elaboration of details extraneous to the action: in particular, aspects of farm life which Ray wanted to stress. Only two shots remain from a planned montage sequence showing Matt Dow (Cagney) at work at the farm. The Easter sermon, another way of rooting the story in daily life, is also reduced to its bare bones. After shooting had begun, Ray devised a sequence in which the Indians, unaware of the presence of two white men, are playing games among themselves. He had wondered about Indians: 'What do they do when they're *not* being Indians?' Reading in a book, *The Comanche Indian*, about the Comanches and their skill on their mustangs – they could pick up a coin from the ground at the gallop – he created a kind of polo (lacrosse?) played with a boot instead of a ball. All that survives is three brief shots.

Thus the 'unusual freedom compared to Hollywood's conveyor-belt methods' which André Bazin praised in *Run for Cover*[6] was hampered by the Pine-Thomas formula. Ray's refusal to play fast and loose with genre (evident virtually nowhere else in his work except *Party Girl*) entails certain weaknesses: sluggish interior scenes, conventional acting (Jean Hersholt in particular).

Given the outcome of the *Johnny Guitar* venture – disastrous in his view – this second Western was an opportunity for Ray to wipe out the first: all the options exercised in *Run for Cover* are the opposite of those adopted in *Johnny Guitar*. Ray's procedure was sometimes to work through successive drafts, revising one film through another: *Knock on Any Door* with *Rebel Without a Cause, Wind Across the Everglades* with *The Savage Innocents*. *Run for Cover* is not a refinement of *Johnny Guitar*, but rather a sort of negation of it.

In the earlier film, Ray had pushed the clichés of the Western to extremes; here, almost to the point of taking the easy way out, he accepts stock solutions. Instead of subverting the star's image – an easier relationship with Cagney than with Crawford helped here – he brought out the private personality behind it. 'Jimmy has not only a great serenity,' Ray said, 'such as I've not seen in an actor, outside of Walter Huston at times, he has a great love of the earth and his fellow man, an understanding of loneliness. I wanted to try and use all that.'[7] The yearning for serenity in Matt Dow, contrasting with the explosive image associated with Cagney, lends resonance to the plot, in itself rather reminiscent of *Knock on Any Door* when reduced to essentials – with John Derek playing an almost identical role – but weighted in favour of the father-figure. The few psychological touches Ray added to the script –

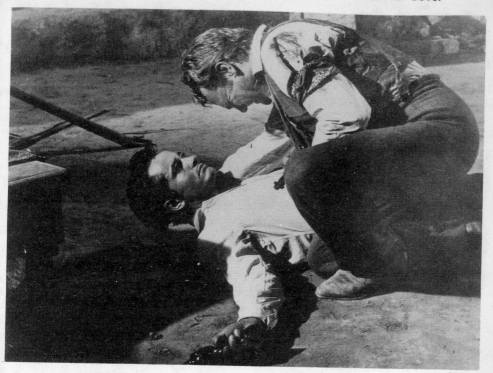

35   *Run for Cover*: 'father and son' – James Cagney and John Derek

stressing, in a nocturnal conversation, that Cagney sees Derek as a repetition of the failure he experienced with his own dead son – serve only to underline the younger man's weakness and his compulsion towards betrayal.

External action is given less importance: the lynching, and the killing of the bandits by Comanches, are elided; shots exchanged between the two protagonists and the Indians were eliminated during shooting. After the striking dissection of a miscarriage of justice that opens the film, Ray – as though negating the message of *Johnny Guitar* – seems to share his hero's desire to accept, morally speaking, the community he has entered. 'I was gonna look your town over,' Matt says, 'see if it was the kind of place I'd want to live in. You sure answered that question.' He nevertheless decides to live there. Along with the Western conventions comes a nostalgic look back at the rural Midwest and its immigrant pioneers. Where *Johnny Guitar* was fragmented, Ray's editing here is fluid. He links separate sequences from the script set in different places, different times. The rhythm he was after could scarcely survive intact, given the demand for linear action. We know he liked the rhythm of the sequences

217

at the farm belonging to Scandinavian immigrants, 'a rhythm I know well'. The music of the Nordic accents survives: no fuss, no caricature. Concerning Helga, for instance, the character played by Viveca Lind-fors,[8] Ray noted: 'Keep the dialogue going while she's out of the room for more warm water and clean towel.' He keeps her hands busy all the time, with flowers, some domestic article; even while playing chess, she is sewing. Her relationship with her father (Jean Hersholt, who had pre-sided over the tribute to Roosevelt staged by Ray in 1945) is taciturn. A year or two later, Ray considered adapting Willa Cather's *My Antonia*, which would doubtless have provided richer material for a similar remembrance of the past.

But it was two other books whose titles Ray scribbled in the margin at the beginning of the script: Thomas Wolfe's *You Can't Go Home Again* and Thomas Hardy's *Jude the Obscure*. This takes us deep into *Bildungs-roman* territory, and the film, much less provocative than its predecessor, undoubtedly picks up on the elements of novelistic romance detectable in *The Lusty Men*: this is what makes French critics feel so close to Ray.[9]

A fine opening sequence, shot in exteriors, heralds a film very different from *Johnny Guitar*. Two men, one middle-aged and the other young, meet and size each other up in an arena which seems as open as the one in the earlier film was closed. Provocation, object lesson, comprehension, obligation and reconciliation follow one upon the other in the space of a few moments.[10] All relationships require a certain formalism: their friendship is sealed by a lesson from Matt, talking to Davey (John Derek) about youth and the dangers of sneaking up on people from behind. Each relationship establishes its own moral code, and no morality exists in the abstract. The film therefore deals with this interchange and this mould-ing, which ends with Matt having succeeded, in an infinitesimal way, in channelling Davey's rage (his last line is 'Davey did fine') and having himself made progress. The code established by Matt at the beginning is later referred to several times. 'I made him ride in front,' says Matt (a line added by Ray), blaming himself for the shot that cripples Davey. In the final confrontation, several role reversals lead to the outcome. Tempted by the bandit Morgan (Ernest Borgnine), who promises to share the loot, Davey is surprised with him by Matt. The latter shoots Morgan and gets the drop on Davey. When the wounded Morgan tries to shoot Matt in the back, Davey shoots him. Matt, thinking that Davey is firing at him, kills him.

These mirror relationships ('trying several times to kill him, in show then in deed, [Davey] nevertheless cannot let anyone else do it,' Philippe Demonsablon wrote)[11] are rooted in the logic of the Western. Just as the community is shown as capable of change, so nature is presented as a sphere for reconciliation and harmony (unlike Anthony Mann's Western landscapes, places of toil and suffering). The photography, much less structured than in *Johnny Guitar*, favours the prevalent blues and greens, making good use of VistaVison's scope and definition.[12]

The treatment of the final confrontation differs from the rest of the film in being more geometrical: first in real ruins (at Aztec, New Mexico), then in a high-walled set with narrow raised windows, doorways and different levels to be negotiated. Ray grew increasingly fond of constructing sets to serve as arenas for conflict, for moments of abstraction from society and from history, emphasizing that the conflicts he staged there were, though never abstract in themselves, primarily inner-directed.

24

High Green Wall

Nicholas Ray had completed his tenth film. *Johnny Guitar* had been released, to good audience response, in June. Jennings Lang, a former agent who had known Ray a long time, was now working for MCA as an executive producer on television. It was he who invited Ray to contribute to the *G.E. [General Electric] Theater* series, a showcase for the new MCA-Revue production company, which was currently heading the ratings.[1]

Ray talked very little about his second directing job for TV, mentioning it (without even giving the title) on only one occasion: when he, along with Otto Preminger, was a guest of the New York Chamber of Commerce in the summer of 1976. He said then that he had placed one condition on his acceptance: 'That neither crew nor cast had worked for TV before. I was hoping for something new, accidental or planned, to happen. But it didn't. We shot it on film.'

The sense of retrospective disappointment implied by the last sentence is warranted only by Ray's preoccupations in 1976: he had by then left traditional narrative far behind him, and a digression in his speech brought up a name as yet unfamiliar to his audience: 'the immensely talented, inventive Nam June Paik.'

High Green Wall, directed by Ray with full mastery of his medium, is no disappointment when seen now. It was not, of course, a pioneer venture like *Sorry, Wrong Number*. By 1954 television was churning out series cheaper and faster than the cinema. The novelty lay in managing to attract a front-rank director. From this point of view, Lew Wasserman's master-stroke was to persuade Alfred Hitchcock to embark on his first series in January 1955. It was very much in the interests of MCA and other producers to ensure a high standard for the new medium. Which was why 1954–5 became a sort of golden age of television. Working there were well-known film-makers (their star sometimes on the wane), persuaded to succumb to temptation and collaborating once or twice on a relatively distinguished series, *Directors' Playhouse*, then later *Playhouse 90*; Hollywood professionals waiting to make their first features (Robert Aldrich), or New Yorkers (Sidney Lumet, Delbert Mann, John Frankenheimer) who brought with them the novelty and comparative

220

boldness of subjects tackled on the stage, as well as actors as yet unseen in movies (this was where the James Dean persona began to take shape).

G.E. Theater was a series of half-hour dramas produced for Revue Productions by Leon Gordon, a veteran from MGM. Universal Studios, which housed Revue, lent their logistical knowhow to these productions. *High Green Wall* was shot in 35mm, in fast, highly-concentrated conditions which suited the highly-charged theme. The most important members of the company were indeed new to television. The cameraman was the great Franz Planer (one of the few Ray ever wanted to work with again). The two leads were Joseph Cotten, still an established star; and Thomas Gomez, a Shakespearean actor by training, now one of Hollywood's top supporting players (*Force of Evil*): Ray had worked with him for three days on *Macao*.

'It was the first television show I'd ever worked in,' Joseph Cotten recalled, 'and I was frightened to death by television. I was working in a play, on the stage in La Jolla, so Nick Ray, Mr Gomez and the producer, Gordon, came down to La Jolla, and we rehearsed for a week. As you know, half-hour shows are now done in three days with no rehearsal. But we had a week to rehearse and three or four days to shoot: I felt that television could be exciting if it could be done that way. There was time for preparation, there was time for experiment, and there was time for change, if we'd guessed wrong.'

The source for *High Green Wall* was a short story written by Evelyn Waugh in 1933, 'The Man Who Liked Dickens', incorporated the following year into his novel *A Handful of Dust* (it forms the penultimate chapter, headed '*Du côté de chez Todd*'). The teleplay, which retains the title of the short story, and is distinguished by the tone and quality of the writing (the dialogue is almost entirely original), is by Charles Jackson (evidently the same Charles Jackson who wrote the novel *The Lost Weekend*, filmed by Billy Wilder in 1945).[2] It is dated 20 July 1954, so rehearsals must have started very shortly after (a slightly revised version, dated 8 August, incorporates the changes made during shooting). Jennings Lang does not recall whether the subject was suggested by Ray, or whether he simply agreed to direct it. Only internal evidence permits one to assume that Ray may have had a hand in the teleplay, or at least felt a rapport with Waugh, whether or not he was familiar with his novels.

The Charles Jackson text opens with two long shots of a limitless jungle, offering the aspect of an impenetrable wall. The film – as so often with Ray – dispenses with this rhetorical preamble: in medium shot, Henty (Joseph Cotten) stumbles out into a clearing. Instead of the script's subjective shots from the exhausted Henty's point of view, Ray cuts to McMaster (Thomas Gomez) getting up, then to the two men coming face to face. Henty collapses, and a tracking shot follows as two Indians help him along, the first of many such camera movements through this jungle in miniature, inhabited by exotic, unfathomable people.

When Henty comes to, four days have passed but his watch is still going: his saviour explains that he kept it rewound. An exposition scene introduces the two protagonists. McMaster, born of an American father and Indian mother, has lived all his life in the jungle. 'Some of the men and women in this savannah are my relations,' he says. 'All of them consider themselves my children.' The gun he carries maintains his authority. As to Henty, he was 'fed up with the jungle of the civilized world, so I thought I'd explore the real jungle.'

McMaster doesn't know how to read: he wouldn't let his father teach him (a detail not in the script), preferring to listen to him read. His father, and after him a 'visitor from Venezuela', read all of Dickens's work to him. While explaining this, McMaster climbs up to a high shelf and excitedly hands the volumes down to Henty. The latter has no choice but to offer himself as a reader. McMaster eagerly comes down the ladder: 'It takes a long time to read them all. More than two years.' 'They're bound to outlast my visit here,' says Henty. They go out on the verandah, where McMaster helps Henty into a hammock, and settles down at his feet. Henty reads the opening words of *A Tale of Two Cities*: 'It was the best of times, it was the worst of times, it was the age of wisdom, it was the age of foolishness, it was the season of Light, it was the season of Darkness, it was the spring of hope, it was the winter of despair . . .'

In the second reading scene, the places have changed: McMaster is in the hammock, Henty sitting on the steps. The latter is now reading a passage from *Oliver Twist* (which the script placed later): 'He was alone in a strange place . . .' The intervening sequence and the one following outline the mousetrap: we very soon realize that McMaster will never let Henty go. They stress the silent, inscrutable presence of the Indians, and prepare for one of the twists. Henty discovers the grave of his predecessor, the visitor from Venezuela, and McMaster says he thinks he'll put up a cross, 'to commemorate his death – and your arrival'. Later (as in *Run for Cover*, Ray telescopes sequences in the shooting, eliminating conventional transitions), Henty looks at the sky, hoping for the rains he believes will set him free.

In the scene immediately following this, an oil-lamp has been lit; McMaster is sitting drowsily, leaning on his gun as Henty reads, then starts soliloquizing: now, he says, he feels better equipped to face civiliz-

222

ation again. A clap of thunder interrupts him. The two men (with the camera dollying out) rush outside exultantly. The rain is pouring down. McMaster tells Henty that now he can't leave until the rainy season ends. Henty grabs him by the shirt. Watched by an Indian, the two men go inside, their heated conversation continuing behind the screen door. McMaster presses a book into Henty's hands: 'You must humour me. Read me another chapter.' 'I have read for the last time,' says Henty, hurling the book at the door after McMaster leaves.

After the caesura marked by the end of this crucial scene (in which characteristic Ray effects are deployed: ruptures of tone, physical conflict, dynamic exploitation of the setting), the game of cat and mouse continues. McMaster stops feeding Henty (the passage of time indicated by the rains ending: drops falling from a leaf) until he resumes reading. He starts with the words: 'And I have been seized with great violence and indignity, and brought a great journey on foot. Now held here against my will, I suffer beyond hope.' At a gesture from McMaster, an Indian goes to fetch food for Henty, who continues reading: 'For the love of heaven, of justice, of generosity, I supplicate you to succour and release me from this prison of horror . . .'

The transposition of this passage (in the script, this quotation and the one from *Oliver Twist* are reversed) lends greater cohesion to the dramatic development. It is precisely at this moment of Dickensian supplication that a hope of deliverance manifests itself: a lone prospector seeking shelter. Unable to talk in McMaster's presence, Henty tears a page from the book he was reading and presses it into the stranger's hand.

In the cabin, Henty is reading again, from *David Copperfield*: 'I took my leave of Mr Micawber for the time, charging him with my best remembrances to all at home. As I left him, I clearly perceived that there was something interposed between him and me . . .' McMaster interrupts to comment that he seems to be reading with pleasure again. 'I live in hope, Mr McMaster,' Henty says. 'Ah, yes,' says McMaster, 'Dickens does that to one.' The Indian comes in and whispers something. Aware of Henty's tension, McMaster asks if he was expecting news, then explains that the Indians are planning a celebration that night to which they are invited.

An Indian woman is dancing round a fire. The camera dollies past her and up to the two men, who are being served drinks. Exchange of glances; the dance becomes faster. Henty, under the influence of a drugged drink, muses aloud about the civilization he'll be so happy to see again. He falls into a narcotic stupor. The sounds of merry-making cease; only the birds can be heard. In the night, Indians stealthily approach him.

223

McMaster welcomes two explorers who are looking for Henty. The prospector had given them the torn-out page (with its printed appeal: 'Release me from this prison of horror'). McMaster is shocked: 'He tore a page from one of my books? Of course, it isn't surprising. Toward the end, the fever drove him to such odd things. He even imagined himself to be a character out of Dickens.'

When Henty wakes, McMaster tells him to put the page back in the book. The explorers, he says, told that Henty died from jungle fever, took photographs of the cross erected on the grave to commemorate his arrival. 'They were very easily pleased.' He also gave them Henty's watch (they, like Henty when he first arrived, were surprised to find it still going; McMaster explained that he 'kept it wound daily in poor Mr Henty's memory').

'We'll not have any Dickens today. But tomorrow, and the day after that, and the day after that, and the day after that . . .' (Close-up of Henty as McMaster continues, off.) 'And then we'll begin *A Tale of Two Cities* again. There are certain passages in that book I can never hear without the temptation to weep.' With these words, the camera cranes up to reveal the whole clearing. Henty's face appears in superimposition, and we hear him reading the opening of the novel again, ending with 'it was the winter of despair'. A rapid dissolve to a tree. Lightning strikes it, and riven asunder, a branch falls (this last shot is not mentioned in the script). The end.

It is interesting to see Ray working in this restricted format – brief running time, unity of place and action – yet unable to resist calling upon the forces of nature: monsoon, lightning, and of course the high green wall of the title, which – against all expectations – puts in a tangible appearance in the spectacular penultimate shot. Ray does not play the surprise twist game endemic to short films and TV segments, but there are plenty of surprises. 'It is a story of irony,' as Jennings Lang put it, 'where by helping him [Gomez] more, Cotten's wall would get larger so he couldn't get out.'

Above and beyond its ironic commentary on civilization (Waugh's contribution, and what sold the project), one can see here what the Portuguese critic A. P. Vasconcelos called 'a work full of cruelty and despair' that 'foreshadows the climate of madness in which the characters become immersed, which was to mark the next phase in Ray's work, especially if one remembers that those next films were *Bigger Than Life*, *Bitter Victory* and *Wind Across the Everglades*.'[3]

Without going so far (other films intervened before those three), one might see *High Green Wall* as an extension of the preceding films, with

36   *High Green Wall*: 'alone in a strange place' – Joseph Cotten reading
to Thomas Gomez

37   *High Green Wall*: the rains that Henty (Cotten) believes will set him free

38   *High Green Wall*: the confrontation

39   *High Green Wall*: the celebration

their mistrust of a society haunted by denunciations and lynchings. But it is true that Thomas Gomez, in his nimble corpulence, his domination (at once paternal and tyrannical) over 'his' natives, even his favourite posture enthroned on the verandah with his gun as his sceptre, foreshadows Cottonmouth as played by Burl Ives in *Wind Across the Everglades*; while the slim and hesitant Cotten, disillusioned with civilization for reasons which remain unclear (even more so in the film than in the script) and defeated by nature, is akin to Christopher Plummer's Walt Murdock. Here the protagonists are already driven and rent by two forces, the rejection of civilization and the trap set by nature.

The performances of both actors evolve from ironic detachment (the teleplay still described them as English) to impassioned grandiloquence. Both camera and actors perform complex movements within the restricted set, a jungle-hacienda-Indian village whose artificiality, with the director making no attempt to disguise the cheapness, is obvious. Ray relished an aspect of unreality like this, and the abstraction it encouraged: the Aztec city in *Run for Cover*, the gaudy settings of *Hot Blood*, the cliffside saloon in *Johnny Guitar*, or Crown City in *Bitter Victory*.

Polishing up the script, he enhanced the counterpoint between the plot development and the Dickens quotations (not featured at all in Waugh's story). The first of these passages, which also brings the film to a close, is the celebrated opening paragraph of Dickens's story of the French Revolution. Ray omits the last sentence, irresistibly evocative of the element of fable in *High Green Wall*: 'In short, the period was so far like the present period, that some of its noisiest authorities insisted on its being received, for good or for evil, in the superlative degree of comparison only.' Waugh mentioned six Dickens novels, but not *A Tale of Two Cities*.

When *High Green Wall* was broadcast by CBS on 3 October 1954, Ray was already installed in an office next door to Elia Kazan at Warner Brothers. The project whose basic idea he had just committed to paper was still known as *The Blind Run* or *The Juvenile Story*; it was to become *Rebel Without a Cause*, a film in many respects just the opposite of *High Green Wall*.

'I liked working with Ray,' Joseph Cotten commented. 'I thought he needed time to prepare, time to form a concept. I don't think he would ever have been happy in today's land of television.' This may be the reason why other projects put forward by Jennings Lang – and discussed during a trip to Las Vegas – never came to anything. This was the last likely trace of contact with the world of television. As Ray said, 'I was hoping for something new, accidental or planned, to happen. But it didn't.' He was doubtless dreaming of other images, which Nam June Paik would give him, too late, for *We Can't Go Home Again.*

25

Rebel Without a Cause

40 *Rebel Without a Cause*: Nicholas Ray and James Dean

1 *A Park—Night*

A man aflame is running directly toward camera. An officer and a
bench sitter run toward him, taking off their coats, then begin smoth-
ering the flames. As they do, we cut to: A wide-eyed youth of fourteen
or fifteen who has been staring at the scene and who now runs behind
the trees and disappears.

2 *Waterfront – night*

A girl, sixteen, stripped to the waist, is surrounded by and being whipped by three teenagers. There is a scream and a police whistle, and the
boys disappear.

3 *Int. car – Sepulveda Boulevard – night*

Two boys, two girls – half way up the hill going away from the valley.
The lights are out on the car and they are moving very rapidly.

Interior second car

Three boys, one girl – half way down the Sepulveda incline, going
toward the valley. The lights are out on their car. Both cars approach
the tunnel and the faces of both groups of kids are tense with anticipation. They crash head-on.

This is the first page of *The Blind Run*, a 17-page 'original story idea' by
Ray, dated 18 September 1954. The whole theme is reflected in these
opening vignettes: oneiric, tenebrous, filled with hallucinatory shock
images, unstructured and unfilmable at that time. It was this theme,
however, this story that is no story, which was to be enriched and given
shape through numerous collaborations and borrowings.

The essential features of each of the three main characters are already
laid out: Jerome, or 'Squint', son of rather shadowy parents, the Demos,
about whom all that is known is that 'they just move a lot'; Jimmy, the
leader of the gang, son of a teacher, who takes a jacket and a knife with
him when he leaves the house; Eve, consort to the gang, who tells her
parents she is spending the night at a girl-friend's house while preparations for the 'blind run' get under way. For this initiation night,
Jimmy has two cars stolen.

Waiting for the run, behind the school yard, two boys fight with
knives. The run does not involve driving towards the edge of a cliff, as in
the film's chicken run: the two cars race towards each other in a tunnel,
all lights off, avoiding collision at the last possible moment. Demo wins,
and a bond is established between him, Jimmy and Eve. After Eve goes
home, where she witnesses a quarrel between her parents, Ray indicates
the end of the first reel: we are already on page ten out of seventeen.
Before continuing, he interjects a few remarks: 'This provides enough
background without going into any of the slum area rationalizations
which have provided background for *Dead End*, *Knock on Any Door*,
and more recently the Filmakers' type of picture [the films produced by
the Ida Lupino company]. As a matter of approach, it should be kept in
mind that the youth is always in the foreground and adults are for the

most part to be shown only as the kids see them. The same is true of the normal activities available to the kids – the church, the playground, the 'Y's, the Scouts, the community centre dances, school functions – for some reason they don't reach the kids they are concerned with. They are only starting points, meeting places from where to carry on.'

From this point on, there is not so much a plot as impulse and motivation. Demo, Jimmy and Eve become an inseparable trio. After the failure of an attempt to come to terms with their parents, Demo turns to more serious, brutal delinquency. The others begin to avoid him: 'All [he] has dared for approval, stolen for, been brave for, begins to disappear again and, as it does, he becomes a savage leading other boys and girls into a series of frightening, bizarre, almost grotesque crimes. He believes he can never win anybody except for the moment of thrill and even the approbation of a lunatic seems to satisfy him. But the sad thing is: he wants to be caught.'

Demo is duly arrested and – with Eve pregnant – condemned to death. He escapes, and goes to talk to the gang: 'He just talks, kid to kid, beautifully, simply and humorously, about himself, and even parents and officers begin to understand a little.' The epilogue takes place in a corner of the drugstore, where another gang is meeting, as at the beginning. One says to the others, 'in the tone of nervous impatience we have heard so often, "What are we going to do tonight?" '

This draft was the result of a dinner with Lew and Edie Wasserman at Ray's house in September, after he had attended a preview of *Run for Cover*. 'We were old enough friends to have agreed that once we'd left the office, we wouldn't talk business. This evening, though, was to be an exception. After dinner, we watched *Dragnet* on television. Then I said to Lew: "I really have to want to do the next one." "What do you want to do?" he asked. "I have to believe in it," I said, "or feel that it's important. *War and Peace* is out of the running; there are four different versions now in preparation." "Well, what else is important?" said Lew. After a moment, I said, "Kids. Young people growing up. Their problems." And we started to talk about that . . .'

The next day, Wasserman sent Ray to Warner Brothers, where it was suggested that he should adapt *Rebel Without a Cause*, a non-fiction book published in 1944 by Dr Robert M. Lindner and subtitled *The Story of a Criminal Psychopath*. He refused, 'because the case was too abnormal. It was neither the psychopath nor the son of a poor family I was interested in now.' The astonishment with which this was received called for an explanation. 'But I didn't have any clear idea as yet what I wanted. I only knew that my newspaper clippings and the things I had seen were drawing me in a different direction. I was trying to dramatize the position of "normal" delinquents. Of one thing I was convinced: for all those adolescents from "ordinary" families, delinquency was a way of drawing attention to themselves. For three-quarters of an hour, I told all sorts of stories . . .'

Out of this improvisation for the benefit of Steve Trilling, Jack L. Warner's right-hand man and head of production, came the original story idea described above. *The Blind Run* sets down only the essentials for a film-maker: a point of view, images. The three vignettes which were to feature as a credit sequence (the first two having no direct connection with the action) suggest above all an urgency, a personal conviction. Scarred by his experience at Republic, Ray thus assured himself of credit for the 'original story', unusual in a period when adaptations were predominant. When the film was released, one of the scriptwriters complained bitterly about being denied this credit; but it isn't the plot, it's the point of view that makes the film what it is. In any case, Ray was not particular where he found his material. He hung around with the gangs in the Valley, which was not without its risks (one gang, some of whose members he had recorded on tape, trashed his house); and he drew on his own memories (what the kids get up to, in the father's absence, owes something to La Crosse). Yet another indirect source has been suggested by the screenwriter Silvia Richards:

'A friend of mine, Esther McCoy, was always broke, and so was I. We sold a few little things for radio, and we wrote an original story called *Main Street Heaventown*, which was about juvenile delinquency in Los Angeles. We haunted the juvenile court, taking notes, and we went out to the juvenile farms and reform schools, talked to the boys and ate with them. After weeks and weeks of research, we finally came up with a story. This property was shown to a lot of studios who liked it; Nick liked it particularly and tried to get Universal [*sic*] to buy it. They didn't. Subsequently he made *Rebel Without a Cause*; my friend and I went to see it, and she burst into tears because he had swiped our story . . . several distinct elements, like the planetarium, though he had developed the relationship between the boy and the girl, and added the automobile stuff. Our story was a little more involved with the downtown area of Los Angeles, his had more of the suburban flavour, but there's no doubt in the world that his springboard was *Main Street Heaventown*. I must say I think ours stimulated Nick, and he lifted from it either consciously or unconsciously. He didn't deny it when I accused him . . . The thing is, there's an awful lot of stuff takes place just below the conscious level; we always steal a little . . . That's probably what happened with Nick. I think he was trying to enrich his original idea, and on an unconscious or almost unconscious level, took pieces of our thing, pieces of something else, and came up with his final story, or got writers to do it. '

Doing a great deal of work himself, and not just with successive script-writers, Ray did indeed add scenes and touches of his own, incorporating or rejecting the material he was given. Shortly after the seventeen pages of *The Blind Run*, for instance, he noted three possible lines of develop-ment for a plot involving three characters: Jim or Jimmy, Eve, and the Professor (a variant on Demo, who was no longer the protagonist and became Plato). In the first, Jim and Eve – the boy and the girl – are substitute parents for the Professor: 'the conclusion could be classic tragedy', wherein the Professor interprets their need for each other as a rejection and, finding he is an intruder again, destroys them. Second possibility: the social integration of Jim. Or, lastly, guilty of a murder, the three kids run away from home. Pursued by the police, 'Jimmy and Eve meet and run together until they are caught, before they are able to play Romeo and Juliet to the death'. Another undated note adds to the affinities with *They Live by Night*: 'What about first title introducing the three kids all at the time that they are dreaming the common dream.'[1]

The studio allowed Ray his choice of producer from among those under contract. At Warner Brothers, one of Hollywood's feudal strong-holds, this was a sign of goodwill. He hit it off with the youngest of them: David Weisbart, thirty-nine-years-old, with two adolescent children, a former editor (*A Streetcar Named Desire* for Kazan, who recommended him to Ray) and producer of several genre films. 'Not the least valuable thing he did for me', Ray wrote, 'was to accept, with patience and under-standing, the two false starts over finding a writer, and allow the search for the right one to continue.'

The project continued to be called *Rebel Without a Cause*: along with the book, the studio had purchased free disposal of the title, which it could use on any story whatsoever (Ray was in fact to make a point of meeting Lindner). Ray's reason for keeping the title went deeper than mere sensationalism: 1954 had seen the American publication of *The Rebel*, a translation of *L'Homme révolté* which marked the revelation of Camus for two generations of intellectuals.[2] The word 'rebel' stood as a programme for the director: no more, perhaps, but at least that much. In a consensus society, Camus's 'I revolt, therefore I am,' seemed a radical transgression. It confirmed the film-maker's stance: definitively on the side of the kids.

In one of his rare published articles, *Story Into Script*, Ray described the evolution of his film from the original story outline. Along with another chapter on James Dean, this is all that survives of an unfinished book, *Rebel: Life Story of a Film*. 'I started writing a book about the film two weeks before I started shooting,' he told Derek Marlowe in 1974, 'because I had that feeling about it, that it was probably going to be a failure, but that I knew damn well the experience was not going to be a failure.'[3] His first choice as a scriptwriter was Clifford Odets, whose plays had dealt with youthful unrest in the 1930s, but the studio assigned Leon Uris, whose *Battle Cry*, scripted from his own novel, was the big Warner film of the year. In October, Uris and Ray embarked on documentary research similar to the preparatory work done for *On Dangerous Ground*. They also met with policemen, members of the California Youth Authority, a child psychoanalyst (pupil of Anna Freud), probation officers, university criminologists. Ray compared notes with Richard Brooks,[4] who was working on an adaptation of *The Blackboard Jungle*, hurriedly rushed into production by MGM in the wake of the sensation created by Evan Hunter's novel (the film would be released in March 1955). Both were confident that there was no risk of the two projects conflicting or being too similar. And on 18 October Ray wrote to Weisbart: 'At this point we have provided Lee [Uris] with incident, contact, theory and practice, characters and situations. He should feel free enough to drop the intellectual approach from this point and just write the story.' Was he harking back to the hallucinating images of his original outline? Or was it mistrust of a collective sociological approach in the manner of *Battle Cry*? Already at this time he was asking Weisbart 'not to involve Uris' in meetings with the West Los Angeles police. It is also possible that Ray's remarks may have been prompted by seeing *Los Olvidados*, having had it screened for himself a few days earlier.[5] (In Madrid during the 1960s, he insisted on meeting Buñuel.)

Uris began by describing 'one of those quiet "normal" communities now astonished by the number of juvenile delinquents in its midst' (*Story Into Script*). In a condescending flourish which would not be forgiven him, he called his 'normal community' Rayfield ('which made me vomit . . . I didn't read the rest of it,' Ray said in 1974). Uris then returned obediently to Ray's original point of departure, but any working relationship had become impossible.[6] By the end of October or early in November, several crucial elements were in place: Los Angeles as the setting; the 'chicken run' (replacing the blind run); the three main characters being at the same school; the living-room as the heart of the family. The parental relationships were already established too: Jim's father serves meals on trays to his mother, Eve's father is her hero. As for Jim, according to Ray, 'the character as I then imagined him was emerging from an angle which was to dominate the successive stages of the script'. Jim, anxious to fit in, invites the other pupils to his home, where he develops films in a darkroom. This hobby, the framed photographs and the classical records (Mahler, Beethoven) in his room, already suggest the influence on the character of James Dean.

Since moving into an office next door to Kazan, Ray had been hearing talk of the actor his neighbour had discovered. But Kazan was not recommending him: 'I got fed up with Dean at the very end of *East of Eden*. He began to abuse people and just throw his weight around.'[7] Even viewing a rough cut of the film left Ray uncertain. Dean sometimes came to see him in his office, and it was after several visits like the one Ray often described that he decided Dean should play Jim:

'Late one evening he arrived at my house. He was with Vampira, the television personality, and Jack Simmons, at this point a young unemployed actor. On entering the room, he turned a back somersault; then from the floor, looked keenly at me.

"Are you middle-aged?"

I admitted it.

"Did you live in a bungalow on Sunset Boulevard, by the old Clover Club?"

"Yes," I said.

"Was there a fire in the middle of the night?"

"Yes," I said.

"Did you carry a Boxer puppy out of your house in your bare feet and walk across the street with it and cut your feet?"

"Yes," I said.

He seemed to approve. Vampira had told him the story. He had come to find out if it were true.'[8]

They continued 'like a couple of Siamese cats sniffing each other out,' (as Ray described it), while Dean's entourage, with success looming for *East of Eden*, advised him to seek safer ground: adaptation of a best-seller, selection of a prestige director (Stevens-Huston-Wyler, in other words). Dean, however, never failed to attend the 'Sunday afternoons' to which Ray would invite friends ('We played music, sang and talked').[9] Ray was living in a bungalow at the Chateau Marmont, which became the hub of preparations for the film. The Chateau Marmont, built in 1927–9 as an apartment block, in Norman style (turrets, spires, arched windows, buttresses), dominated Sunset Strip; in the heart of Hollywood, it guaranteed privacy, indeed a monastic existence, to its distinguished tenants. It was surrounded by bungalows of the same period, looking like beach houses set apart from the hotel. Ray occupied Bungalow No. 2, beside the swimming-pool. 'He liked the Marmont,' according to Sumner Williams, 'he liked the bungalow, old shingle, wood, with an upstairs and three bedrooms, big kitchen, big fireplace, it was just comfortable. It was not really a hotel service. We did our own cooking. We did have maids for cleaning up, and that was it.' During these 'Sunday afternoons', many of the film's key scenes were conceived.

After many meetings, Ray chose a new scriptwriter, Irving Shulman. Born in Brooklyn in 1913, Shulman had written the first novel to deal with modern juvenile delinquency, *The Amboy Dukes* (1947), and devoted a thesis to *The Juvenile Delinquent in the American Novel*. The hack churning out best-sellers about *Harlow* or *Valentino* still lay in the future. He did what he was contracted to do, dealing with the very real but limited problem of structuring the plot with a particular viewpoint – and actor – in mind.[10] A year later, with the Oscars approaching, Shulman could in all sincerity claim to be the author of the original story.[11] Ray, however, attributed a good deal of the work to David Weisbart and himself. According to *Story Into Script*, it was they who suggested the Planetarium scene (prompted by the Silvia Richards-Esther McCoy project); and Weisbart, a native of Los Angeles, immediately made arrangements for filming at the one in Griffith Park.

The Planetarium is mentioned for the first time in a scene written by Ray himself, marginal to the plot as it then stood: *Jim at home* (2 December). He added handwritten queries ('Where do they move from? What do they do?', and 'They are using him as a punching bag. Don't realize it but they do'), and rewrote a long speech of Jim's: 'We had field study in the observatory. I got lost in the phoney stars [. . .] By that time the real stars were out (he starts laughing).'[12] Then on the 4th, he wrote the scene itself, with the lecturer's speech, as he uses an illuminated arrow to indicate the positions of the stars, heard over the easy banter of the pupils. Buzz and the gang wonder who the 'new guy' is; Plato gives the lecturer the right answers; Jimmy congratulates him ironically. Later, Ray got the idea of staging the climax at the Planetarium: 'When Plato believes that Jim, his only friend, has deserted him, I thought he should return to the deserted Planetarium at night, seeking shelter under its great dome and artificial sky. It was the kind of unexpected dramatic reference I felt the story should contain; there was for me a suggestion of classical tragedy about it. Discussing the scene with Jim [Dean] and with Leonard Rosenman – who, after seeing *East of Eden*, I had decided should be the composer for the film – I was encouraged that they agreed, and thought it would be one of the best scenes in the story.' Shulman disagreed: in his view, Plato should seek refuge in his own home. Ray continues: 'This was a crucial point for me, because it symbolized the more violent statement, the more sweepingly developed conflict that I was searching for and that Shulman seemed unable to accept. It was a gesture of anger and desperation that matched the kind of thing I had heard at Juvenile Hall.' A further wedge: Shulman, despite his interest in sports cars, established no contact with Dean when they met at the Chateau Marmont. Having solved the major structural problems, he lost no time in asking the studio for permission to turn his version of the script into a novel.[13] In the end, he dictated a 164-page script, dated 26 January. In the last memo Ray sent him, on 16 December, he insisted that Plato's act of violence should be prepared for on a narrative level: hence the revolver under the pillow. Whatever Plato's crime of violence should be, 'once it has been accomplished, we must know it was inevitable'. But 'none of the group should anticipate Plato's participation in any violent act, and it should be exposed by Plato within a given situation.' This radical surprise produced by violence had already featured in *In a Lonely Place*.

At this point, Ray was concentrating on the cast, Dean especially, whom he joined in New York in mid-December. Dean was living in an apartment in the brownstone district, on the fifth floor of an old building on 68th Street. Ray introduced him to his son Tony, 'a Plato of sorts', so as to see Dean through the eyes of his own generation.[14] 'Tony told me later he saw Jimmy several times, mainly at parties – at the 68th Street apartment or the rooms of one of the half-dozen young actors and actresses who were his most frequent companions. The same group was always there. Nobody ever wanted to go home. There were bongo drums, which Jimmy played. A negro dancer did calypso and imitations of Gene Kelly. Conversation ranged from new plays and movies to (as dawn broke) Plato and Aristotle. They read stories and plays, going right through *Twenty-Seven Wagon Loads of Cotton* one night, while people took turns to sleep.'

On 27 December Ray met some young New York actors, many of them pupils of Strasberg: John Cassavetes, Lee Remick, Brian Hutton, Geoffrey Horne, Scott Marlowe and Carroll Baker, among others.[15] In the end, not one of these actors he saw in New York was to appear in the film, which is indicative of the real motive for the trip. When he left to return to the West Coast, Ray knew that Dean had decided to do the film – despite his hatred of Warner Brothers, which symbolized all institutions for him. Abiding by their conception of honour, they 'shook hands on the basis of fifteen pages', the only portion of the script Ray was fully satisfied with. The studio was getting worried, and at this stage the project was on the verge of being abandoned.

A number of external factors led to the next scriptwriter, Stewart Stern. A New Yorker born in 1922, he had written only one film, Fred Zinnemann's *Teresa*, and some teleplays, including the recent *Thunder of Silence*, starring Paul Newman.[16] At MGM, he had worked with Houseman. And he got on well with Dean: they had become acquainted at the home of his cousin, Arthur Loew Jr, imitating animal cries (a bit of business that found its way into the film).[17] Stern met Ray at Gene Kelly's place, whereupon Ray spoke warmly and in detail about *Teresa*. When Leonard Rosenman, a friend of Dean's, also recommended him, Stern was quickly signed up.[18] Working against the clock, writer and director embarked on all-night sessions running through until breakfast, during which they began by talking about themselves. According to Stern: 'Nick was in agony, a kind of private hell, at that time. A creative hell. He had a concept and a vision of what he wanted to say, but he had not found a way to say it through the writers he had had. He was almost inarticulate about what he wanted and why he was not satisfied. Nick, like most artists, is part child. His child-part talked to my own. His bewildered adult talked to my bewildered adult, and out of the horns of our own private dilemmas, I began to get a picture of what we both wanted to say through a story about chidren.'

In his turn, Stern spent ten days and nights at the juvenile court, passing himself off as a welfare worker, staying with the kids in isolation or when they were confronted with their parents: 'One was thirteen years old and had spent six of these years in institutions!' The first pages written by Stern (21 January 1955) convey, even more strongly than the film, this sense of despair. A passer-by is jumped and beaten up by a gang of youths, who fade away singing a carol. Jim, drunk, is picked up at the scene of the assault; he sticks his tongue out at the camera as the words 'Starring James Dean' are superimposed on the screen. The following scene, at the police station, involves a number of Mexicans. This first scene, in definitive form, is followed by a 120-page provisional version, dated 31 January.[19]

Finally persuaded that the film could be made, the studio confirmed a not-too-distant starting date with Dean: 10 March. To reassure himself – or the front office – Ray sought the advice of Dr Douglas M. Kelley, a sociologist and criminologist (who had been the chief psychiatrist at the Nuremberg trials).

The script was now going well for Stern. He saw *Rebel* as a modern version of *Peter Pan*: three kids inventing a world of their own. 'From the beginning, Nick, Jimmy and I were aware *Rebel* was a unique opportunity in our lives to say something about the nature of loneliness and

love. Although our elements were "real", the thing we strove for had a
kind of mythic scope. Even the conception of the story told in a single
day, from dawn to dawn, was mythic rather than real.' He and Ray
agreed on the essential thing (to which he may have opened Ray's eyes):
that the sociological aspect was an alibi. By tacit consent, the juvenile
delinquency was relegated to the background. On 8 February, Stern
delivered 72 pages of an 'unfinished' first part, going up to the chicken
run, but followed by a more or less definitive synopsis of the rest; on 5
March, a 'revised estimating, not final' of 130 pages; and on 18 March, a
screenplay now requiring only minor cuts and adjustments. It was this
version that Ray worked with (he deposited his annotated copy at the
Cinématèque Française); the 'final' of 26 March was simply a shooting
script.

The action takes place during the Christmas period: on the morning
following the long introductory sequence at the police station, some kids
burn a Christmas tree. The chicken run scene is more developed than in
the film. It is staged at the edge of a cliff overlooking a busy road (in the
film, at the censor's insistence, this became a deserted rocky shore). On
the road below, passers-by stare at the burning cars. After the accident,
Judy, Jim and Plato leave in the same car. Jim and Plato are seized by
uncontrollable laughter. The realignment of the gang against Judy, Jim
and Plato is followed by a split-screen sequence intended to show Ray
Framek, the sympathetic cop, with the parents of Plato, Moose (another
member of the gang), Judy and Jim, whose kids have all disappeared.
Stern has told how, at Ray's request, he wrote another scene using the
same technique to show the reality alongside a fantasy of Jim's about his
parents.[20] After the scene at the villa and the flight to the Planetarium,
Jim's father, summoned by Framek, finds his son in the darkness; a
reconciliation is adumbrated between them, and Jim's father, shielding
his son from the police, helps him get to Plato. The scene in the Planetarium ends with Plato escaping to the roof, where he is shot down by the
police.

It is curious (and probably revealing, given the film's success) that the
growth to maturity coincides with a betrayal. Jim coaxes Plato into
handing over his gun, secretly removes the bullets, and gives it back,
saying, 'Friends always keep their promises.' Then he persuades Plato to
come out, and when Plato is shot down by an over-edgy cop, Jim yells, 'I
got the bullets!' This line – treachery appalled by its consequences – was
supplied by Clifford Odets. Unable to engage his services, Ray turned to
him for advice on several occasions. Odets enjoyed an almost legendary
prestige: to Dean, for example, meeting him was like meeting Ibsen or

41 *Rebel Without a Cause*: Clifford Odets, Nicholas Ray and Natalie Wood

Shaw. He was also the man who best represented what Ray thought of as the betrayal of his generation, the generation of the 'Red Thirties': the man who, to everyone's surprise, turned friendly witness and named names for the House Un-American Activities Committee, and who wrote a month later, shocked by the incomprehension he encountered: 'Personal clarity, in my opinion, is the first law of the day – that plus a true and real search for personal identity.'[21] Meeting Stewart Stern, Odets explained: 'Nobody can write now [. . .] because we all understand the other person's point of view now.'[22]

As the starting date for filming approached, Ray worked on his casting, pivoting around James Dean's personality. The Sunday afternoon gatherings alternated with days making tests at the studio. Corey Allen, a law student at UCLA who had appeared with a little theatre company and played two bit parts in movies, was among the young actors. He was not quite twenty-one.

'He cast very carefully. He had about two weeks of improvisations –

42 *Rebel Without a Cause*: James Dean and Corey Allen

mass improvisations – I'd never seen this before. First he saw me in a play in one of those little theatres. Then he called me up to talk to me. Then he said: "Will you do some trying-out?" I met him at the backlot at Warners', in a big amphitheatre, with bleachers and what seemed to me, conservatively, to have been 300 boys. He said, "Okay, we're gonna do some exercises. Do what you want. First of all, everybody get up and get to the top of the bleachers as fast as you can, and then come back down." Then he ran us through a game we call King of the Mountain, where there's a platform, and you battle to get on the platform and knock everybody else off. All very physical things. Towards the end, those of us who were the remaining candidates for that role were to bounce a ball; the bad guy – who was Frank Mazzola – was to come and try to steal the ball; that was to cause a fight, then everybody would pile in and try to get the ball. I was not a physical young man at all, I hated violence, and thought okay, we'll see what happens. That's how he cast that role. Not the reading but the attitude. It didn't matter whether you hung on to the

241

ball, got to the top of the bleachers or were the king of the mountain; what mattered was the attitude in the effort, the thinking, the psychology. That was a very personal piece of work. I was not the king of the mountain. I couldn't hang on to the ball. I ended up at the bottom of a pile – I think Frank was right on top of me, and that's how we got to know each other. But the thing was, when Nick did the exercise on the bleachers, everybody stampeded up there and came back down; I thought nuts, and just turned around and walked up there. I hadn't figured that out, it was just instinct, what I felt like doing as I couldn't beat the others anyway. I know that from that moment on Nick and I related to each other. It didn't have to do with getting along, it had to do with our psychology. Very personal casting . . .'

In the last week in February, tests were filmed at the studio with the short-listed actors: Corey Allen, Nick Adams, Dennis Hopper, Frank and Tony Mazzola, Steffi Sidney, Beverly Long (all of whom were cast), and others like Gloria Castillo, Jayne Mansfield, John Saxon, Pat Crowley ('Star of Tomorrow', 1954) and Kathryn Grant. In Dean's absence, it was Dennis Hopper who cued them. A further purpose of these tests was to experiment with CinemaScope in black-and-white – to be used here for the first time – and to become acquainted with Ernest Haller, the cameraman assigned by the studio. Ray would have preferred to work with someone he knew; very disappointed when Franz Planer was signed by Fox, he exchanged sharpish notes with David Weisbart, and also tried to get Lee Garmes. 'I favour situations which expose weakness,' he specified concerning these tests, 'rather than demonstrate positive qualities we already know.'[23]

For the role of Plato, he was still undecided at this point between Jeff Silver and Billy Gray – or possibly Dennis Hopper (the latter 'only after a test with James Dean'). The son of Bronx immigrants, a child actor on Broadway, Sal Mineo was first invited to the Chateau Marmont. 'I went to Nick Ray's hotel,' Mineo explained, 'and he introduced me to Jimmy. It was on a Sunday afternoon. He said: "I'd just like to go over a couple of scenes." But he hadn't told me ahead of time what role he wanted me to read. So we were sitting on the floor and he said, "Okay, let's read the scene now." I think the first one was where I ask Jimmy to go home with me after the chicken run. I was very embarrassed and said, "I don't know which role you want me to read." He was puzzled and said, "Which role would you like to read?" I said, "Definitely you want a Plato." They were both surprised, because Jimmy had more lines. I said, "Well, I just think it's a better role." So I started reading the scene with Jimmy. Then Nick said, "All right. Now let's put the script away. Can you do improvisation?" Of course I said yes – I had no idea what he was talking about, but I wanted that role very badly. I picked it up from Jimmy, realized that he was doing the scene but making up his own dialogue, and that that's what improvisations are. So we "improvised" the sequence.'[24]

In the role of Judy, Warner Brothers wanted a star, and considered borrowing Debbie Reynolds from MGM. Ray's candidates were Carroll Baker and Natalie Wood (whom he originally saw as playing Judy's friend, 'a schemer'). Wood was under contract to the studio (a child actress, she had at fifteen appeared in twenty-one films), and for this reason was not really in the running. To get the part, she put herself through another kind of test. 'The big problem,' she said (in the documentary *I'm a Stranger Here Myself*), 'was that up to that point I had really only played children. Although I was fifteen, I was finding it difficult – and Nick was finding it difficult – to convince the studio that I was out of pigtails. One day I came on an interview with a boyfriend who had cuts on his face, and Nick said, "Where did he get that?" Then shortly after that I actually was in a bad car accident with Dennis Hopper. I was in hospital, sort of semi-conscious, the police were asking me my parents' phone number, and I kept saying "Nick Ray, call Nick Ray, the number is . . ." I just kept repeating the number of the Chateau Marmont, so that's who they did call. Nick sent his doctor down to the hospital, then he came down, and I said, "Nick, they called me a goddam juvenile delinquent, *now* do I get the part?" And I got it.'

This was another feature of Ray's work: his ability to extract elements for a film out of real-life emotional conflicts. As James Leahy noted, 'There is no doubt that Nick did get very close to his actors and actresses, and this closeness enabled him to incorporate in his films facets of their psychology they would not otherwise have revealed.'[25] Improvisation, the most frequently stressed aspect of his work, does not simply involve reinventing on set during shooting, but rather working over a period of time, drawing on a variety of aspects of one's innermost self. Natalie Wood had never worked like this before. James Dean's biographers have reported numerous examples, but the most specific description was given by Ray himself in 1957, in connection with the scene where Jim returns home after the chicken run:

'I was worried about the scene. It had been written [by Shulman] to take place in the mother's bedroom, and it was static to me. So one night, Jimmy stopped in and I started talking about the scene. I sent him out to the back of the house, while I played the father in my living-room, pretending to be asleep with the television set turned to a dead channel, and gave Jimmy an action. Two contradictory actions: one, to get upstairs without being detected; and the contradictory action, that he had to talk to somebody. So he comes in, and he has to get by me to go upstairs. Then the contradictory action took over, and he flopped down on the couch with the bottle of milk, waiting until I woke up. At that point I called, "Now your mother comes downstairs". And then I knew I had the dynamics of the scene; I called the art director in, and the set that we used in *Rebel* was designed on the basis of my living-room where we did the improvisation. This is the most satisfactory way of working. It also gave me the idea for the point of view shot, the mother coming down the stairs as seen by Jimmy.'

As the reference to the art director suggests, this episode preceded shooting by some time; the scene is accurately described in the 18 March script, even down to the shot in which the mother is seen upside-down. Work on the scene nevertheless did not stop: Dean's business with the bottle of milk, and all of the ensuing dialogue, remained to be patiently improvised.

Ray took risks in casting the parents, too: Jim Backus (Jim's father), Marsha Hunt (his mother) and William Hopper (Judy's father) had to submit to filmed tests. Jim Backus is the most obvious instance of casting against type: he was best known as the voice of Mr Magoo and for comedy roles.[26] The soft-spoken Marsha Hunt cried off at the last minute.[27] Her replacement, Ann Doran, older and more inflexible, brought a note of harshness and hysteria to the part of the mother which definitively tipped the parents over into the area of caricature. This impression is strengthened by the casting of empty-eyed actors as Judy's parents, and of stage actress Virginia Brissac as Jim's grandmother.

On Wednesday, 30 March, the first of thirty-six days set for the shooting schedule, the crew was outside the Griffith Park Planetarium, and the knife duel between Jim and Buzz (Corey Allen) was staged with the aid of Frank Mazzola. For months, Mazzola had been setting up meetings for Ray (and later, Dean) with the gangs, while also acting as a 'glossary' for Ray and Stern. By the Friday, the studio's worries were apparent. Weisbart noted that the voices of some of the young actors didn't carry enough; as a good editor, he wanted to be sure that the director was covering himself with close shots. Jack L. Warner, who viewed the rushes and followed every stage of the production, was fussing about Natalie Wood's delivery; Ray had already taken the initiative and sent her to a voice coach, his friend Nina Moise. Like Weisbart, Warner thought the black-and-white rushes were excellent.

On the Saturday, however, the studio decided to switch to colour. Officially, the CinemaScope company, a subsidiary of 20th Century-Fox, had refused to hire out its process for films in black-and-white.[28] It may also have been that Jack L. Warner, after watching the knife fight, wanted to embellish what he was now calling 'a very important film'.[29] In an outline for his projected book about the making of the film, probably written in 1956, Ray gives a quite different explanation, which can be neither confirmed nor denied from other sources: 'After a week, the studio wanted to stop the film. I asked for twenty-four hours to arrange to take it over. In the meantime, the projectionist who was screening the rushes told the top brass it was the best film currently being made at the studio. We carried on.'[30] On 4 April (Stewart Stern had completed his job on 25 March), a series of revised pages adapted the script to colour, switching the Christmas period to Easter, necessitating fewer changes to the sets (any reference to a particular date eventually disappeared from the film), and incorporating dialogue revisions resulting from rehearsals with the actors, as well as censorship demands (no longer any intention to kill, knives during the chase to be replaced by bicycle chains which must not be whirled about, no doubts about the innocent nature of the cigarettes furtively palmed or about Judy's chastity, etc.). These further simplifications made themselves felt on the film, already sidetracked towards fairy-tale while Stewart Stern worked on it.

After two days at the City College of Santa Monica (where Dean had been a student), the first group of scenes to be shot in the studio followed: four days in the police station, on sound stage 6 at Burbank. On 11 April, the beginning of the third week, the unit was at Griffith Park again for four days, reshooting the knife fight in colour, before moving on the 16th to the deserted mansion. The schedule was again reshuffled because the mansion was to be demolished two days earlier than expected.[31] To the two days lost over the switch to colour, a two-day delay was added. And the hitches kept coming. On the Saturday night, Ray noted: 'In the master shot of the kids at the swimming pool which was made on Satur-day night, I had less than two minutes with which to complete a boom shot when the principal actor, whose time ran out at 11.00 promptly, folded on me. I had to keep rolling while he revived in order to save the time absorbed by resetting and all the other mish-mash that goes on after a cut. Having had less than ten minutes to work with the boom – since it was an hour late in arrival – and having had only one rehearsal of the action with camera, I was forced to complete the shot so I could go into my closer angles tonight without any major delay due to lighting.'

Up against studio logistics, too inflexible for a schedule involving numerous and scattered locations (the noise of the generators was a constant worry), Ray learned to appreciate both his crew and Ernest

Haller, with whom he spent three hours on the Sunday, exploring the lighting problems for 'the remainder of the mansion, the planetarium, and the chicken run'.

He maintained the concentration and unity of performance thanks to the relationships established with his cast. Corey Allen: 'I was so frightened in that film about my performance: I was twenty years old, had a very high kind of voice, and I always felt unmasculine. So, to clear away my doubts before a take, I would scream as loud as I could; that was my assertion of my rights, and the sound man had to take his earplugs out. Then we'd go to work. Jimmy had his ways, too, mostly involving staying in his dressing room until he was ready to come out. And we all respected each other. One day, somebody mocked one of us, I don't remember whether it was Jim or me; I was the easier target because you could scream, but how do you mock someone who stays in his dressing room? After lunch that day, Nick gathered everybody around and said, "Now, look, I just want it understood that you can walk off this film right now. Everybody has his way of working. I don't care what it is. If it contributes to his performance and therefore to our project, he is to do it. Anybody who wants to make it difficult for anybody else, leave. That's it." That's what I learned from Nick. A project depends on the security and the output of its artists, and that is to be cherished and protected. I loved him for that. He was that way with everybody, all these newcomers. He knew that I was very vulnerable, very frightened, and there was always that sense of "we will not go until you're ready". It was the same with Jimmy. Nick wouldn't go until Jimmy said so. And all Jimmy would ever do was nod his head; sometimes he wouldn't go, with the crew standing around, maybe becoming angry.'

Dennis Hopper: 'I got into terrible problems with him because we were both fucking Natalie Wood. Her parents were starting to figure it out, and Nick snitched on me! I was furious with him: the studio came down on me, and he came out of it as pure as snow. So, on the chicken run, I took him aside and told him we were going to get into a fight on the set. He said, "You know, some day you're gonna have to figure out how to do things without using your fists, you're gonna have to start using your mind." At that point, I lost my aggressiveness.'

Ray was sure enough of himself, and the risks he took were calculated enough, to make most of his inexperienced cast forget that they were acting, that they were being directed. As Dennis Hopper put it, 'I always thought . . . I always just assumed that Dean directed that movie. So it's hard for me to think of it another way, even though I know, logically, that he didn't. He did certainly control all the scenes he was in, and he's in almost every scene. I remember, in the knife fight, Corey Allen cut Jimmy's shirt or something. Nick called "Cut! Cut!", and Jimmy said, "Don't you ever say fucking Cut, man, I'm the only one who says Cut here. If I get that close, I want it on film. I don't want you cutting it.'

'Jimmy trusted Nick a great deal,' according to Natalie Wood. 'And I think Nick was very fatherly towards Jimmy. He really was to Sal and myself as well. But I think Nick just absolutely understood Jimmy, they were just completely in tune, their personalities. I guess maybe Jimmy reminded Nick of himself a great deal. So there was never any friction, as there was between Jimmy and other directors that he worked with. It was just a wonderful blend. Nick brought up this feeling of trust in Jimmy.'[32] Roger Donoghue, a young boxer who was present during the filming, says: 'Kazan had a lot of problems with Dean; and Nick could handle him. Dean told me once: "This man does not know what he's doing, Kazan did." I couldn't figure it out. Nick knew exactly what he was doing, because Nick was getting out of him exactly what he wanted.'

In Dean, Ray had found his ideal actor, not because of his association with the Method and the Actors' Studio, but because of their mutual understanding of codes of conduct or morality: Dean's 'urgent, inquisitive curiosity', his 'kind of pathological desire for tension' (as Leonard Rosenman put it), the actor's very arrogance, in which Ray recognized his own defence mechanism against the Hollywood circus. Dean had the capacity, in a backfire effect from direction, to lead the film-maker into areas of which Ray himself was unaware. Dean is said to have improvised the opening shot, remembering a painting by Manet; and the format of this painting unmistakably suggests the CinemaScope screen.[33] A toy monkey clashes mechanical cymbals; behind it, a young man falls to the ground, plays with the monkey, puts it to bed under a newspaper, and curls up beside it, while the credits unfold in red letters over the nocturnal street. Ray fills the frame with this mannered mime, which suggests an adolescent Emil Jannings as much as the Method. Dean the actor himself becomes an element in the making of the film, the movement that carries it along.

In the police station, the area is divided by desks and glass partitions. Pans and dollies link the trio who are to become the protagonists, switching attention from one to the other. A splash of red in a corner of the screen catches the eye: a pan reveals Judy, heavily made up and wearing a red coat over a red dress. A sound brings attention back to Jim, imitating a police siren and playfully firing an imaginary gun. Jim offers Plato his jacket: a pan takes us back to Judy; a pick-up on Judy from a different angle introduces a new scene. And so on. Over and above the dialogue

247

which serves simultaneously as exposition and manifesto, this first sequence, drawing connections between characters who are brittle, trembling, tearful, withdrawn from contact with adults, reveals Ray's purpose through colour and 'scope.

Group scenes, indeed, provide the film's best moments: a paradox when one considers the progressive elimination, from one version of the script to the next, and from each scene, of any confrontation with the outside world. A world scaled down, palpably a totality: this is the principle of the musical (a never-realized dream of Ray's). The knife fight, with saxophone theme suggestive of jazz, plays off a rapid flow of counter movements; the fight itself is merely the culmination of a series of complex gyrations through the multi-levelled area of the observatory terrace. The chicken run, another form of choreography, relies more on structure and editing to reveal the evolution of the characters: the relationships between Jim, Judy, Buzz and Plato are all transformed during the preparation, execution and aftermath of the run. In both cases, there is a constant interplay between the closest personal relationships and vast space.[34]

Ray's inspiration was not always so happy. Carried away by the excitement of filming, systematically reworking the dialogue, he did not realize that some of these amendments, added to the concessions made to censorship, were leading him into the Warner 'social conscience' movie territory of ten or twenty years before; in other words, into what had become the conformism of 1955. For the scene at the mansion, his copy of the script contains no fewer than four different handwritten lines spelling out that Judy and Jim are substitute parents for Plato. They were not used, of course. But Stewart Stern became worried by rumours he heard, and warned against this scarcely conscious process. 'We say, "Cut this, it's only a line" – "Shorten this scene, the point still gets across" – "You don't have to play this part of it here, another location would serve just as well" – "*State* this, don't *imply* it, it'll make everyone know what's going on." ' Stern was particularly annoyed by the elimination of the scene between Jim and Plato, returning home by car after the death of Buzz. 'It showed a reaction to tragedy which is not only bare and honest, but a reaction which, though probably the truest, has not been seen on the screen before, at least to my knowledge. It was a scene with which everyone who has come close to tragedy and felt the guilty impulse to laugh in celebration of their own relief at being alive, may fully identify. Beyond that, it is only because of the hysteria gripping him that Plato gets the nerve to invite Jim to his house and express his real need for companionship. I think that under no credible circumstance would he, even *in* hysteria, refer to Jim as his "father" here. By changing this scene, though it may seem just another small point, is to rob ourselves very substantially of the thing which can make this film. By changing this scene we are attempting to make the story conform, which it can never do because of its very nature – and we should be glad of it. By changing this and other things, minor things, we may be in grave danger of having that half-tamed, half-disciplined thing, a sad and compromised and violated effort.'[35]

Stern's justifiable remarks fail to take into account the dynamics of film-making, the urgency expressed by the central character. The scenes at Jim's home were shot in the studio, and Jim Backus had a taste of Dean's 'desire for tension'[36] when the latter grabbed him on the stairs and dragged him through the living-room. On 13 May, four days of night exteriors remained: the chicken run and the Planetarium. Ray was restricted by the crew, by the working hours prescribed for under-age actors, by police protecting the neighbourhood from noise, by Jack L. Warner's recommendation that inserts be filmed in the studio to save

43 *Rebel Without a Cause*: Dean's desire for tension – Jim Backus, James Dean and Ann Doran

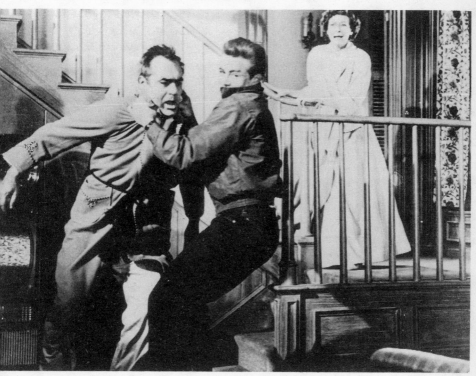

44 *Rebel Without a Cause*: storyboard for the final sequence at the
Planetarium: a) *Full shot. Dome.* b) *Plato is hit.* c) *Plato plummets down the
dome.* d) *Plato plummets down past Jim.* e) *Close-up Jim: But I've got
the bullets!*

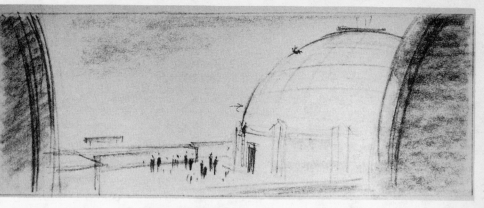

stock; and he asked Weisbart to help him make the best use of the time available.

In the first version of the final sequence, meticulously pre-designed, Plato climbed to the roof of the Planetarium, Jim and the police followed, Jim persuaded him to surrender his gun. Plato was shot as he stood up to throw the gun to Jim. Ray abandoned this ending, writing to Weisbart – who was busy assembling a rough cut – to explain: 'It is terribly important for us to end the picture with the beginning of a new day.' Filming with Plato on the roof, he would be forced to fill in too much at the studio, against walls or backdrops. After all, Ray continued, 'the film is shot in such a way that the business of the lights can be eliminated; and the combination of the visual effect of the planetarium auditorium sky, plus Plato's lines of "it's morning", plus the fact that cuts where the sky is shot will be very brief and incidental in the opening of the sequence, will certainly in total effect be acceptable and will not lose tension.'[37]

On 26 May filming was completed, eleven days behind schedule.[38] Roger Donoghue recalled that evening: 'It was on the Warner Brothers lot, and there were some catch-up scenes from the run where the car goes over the cliff, just car scenes out of context, and it was the last night of shooting. There was Natalie, Jimmy Dean, Dennis Hopper, Perry Lopez, who wasn't on the film, and myself. We're standing around, it's like midnight, it's all over, *Rebel* is finished. So Nick says, "Well, we'll all go to Googie's," a pancake and hamburger place diagonally across the street from the Chateau Marmont, next to Schwab's Drugstore. Nick had an old '50 or '51 Cadillac that he had bought from Robert Taylor for something like 800 bucks. We all got in the car, Jimmy went ahead on his motorcycle, and we went up over the Cahuenga Pass from Burbank to Hollywood, to Sunset Boulevard. Everyone was kind of sad because it was all over, and as we got four or five blocks from Googie's, Jimmy put his legs up over the back of the machine and rode like that. Nick turned round – he was driving – and said, "That should be the end of the film!" Because he didn't like the end, he was arguing with Warner Brothers. Anyway, we all ended up at Googie's, and it was like all the kids didn't want it to end, and Nick didn't want it to end, and it was probably the end of Nick that night, too . . .'

A lot of post-synch sessions remained to be done, and Ray still had a great deal of work to do on the editing. He had to start preparing *Hot Blood*, however, and Dean was awaited by George Stevens in Texas for *Giant*. On 7 June, a few days after the last dubbing session he directed, he wrote to Jack Warner: 'Dear Jack, My name is Nick Ray and I just finished making a picture for you called *Rebel Without a Cause*. I thought maybe you'd forgotten my name because the last time we met any closer than bowing distance was in your office late at night and you wished you'd never met me and I thought you should have felt just the opposite. At that time you threatened me with another such meeting if anything else went wrong, and while I *know* you must have been pissed off at me at least once – and strongly enough to have called another meeting – there hasn't been another such meeting. So either you've forgotten my name or else you have the kind of understanding a director dreams about.'

What he actually wanted to know was, not whether he might have more time for the editing – which he had really only started working on the previous evening, with Weisbart and editor William Ziegler – but whether the screening for Warner himself could be postponed: 'I know every important frame of it as if it had been printed on my skin, including the out-takes and the unprinted prints. I've seen a couple of sequences slapped together for an expediency of one sort or another (with takes in wrong places and the wrong parts of takes in other places, etc., etc.) and yet, because I do know what we have, I come out of the projection room feeling better than the law allows.'

Jack L. saw the film on 1 July. 'Picture itself is excellent,' he noted, 'Dean is beyond comprehension.' And, addressing Weisbart with reference to Ray and Rosenman: 'Do not let them go "arty" on us.' Weisbart duly eliminated the montage sequence in which the parents of the kids who have disappeared call policeman Ray Framek. He finally decided *not* to cut the moment where Plato shows off the mansion, an instance of Ray being 'arty' but inspired. On 12 June, a week away from his starting date on *Hot Blood*, Ray was still scribbling notes about the editing. He now saw the danger of 'over-explaining' the characters, and the changes he suggested mostly involved matters of detail (sometimes technical or anecdotal: the director's voice cueing Natalie Wood, Sal Mineo's Brooklyn accent). He worked on the nuances on which the film's delicate balance rested: a less static take should be substituted for the one used, a line should be heard over one character rather than another; at the Planetarium, the words 'man existing alone' should be 'on the lecturer', corrected to 'on the pupils' reaction'. He cut down the scene of the gang leaving the Planetarium, restricting it to Plato's point of view.[39] He switched scenes around in the chicken run, and continued to seek a balance in the love scene between Judy and Jim behind their houses, which was subjected to incessant modification. 'We must not cut the context of this show, for sake of time and smoothness,' he wrote.

The film was finished, as far as Ray was concerned. Eight days of dubbing still remained to be done during the summer, the last on 12 September. On that day, Dennis Hopper and James Dean both arrived from the *Giant* set. On the 30th, Dean died crashing his car. The film was released four days later, immediately becoming one of Warners' biggest hits of the year. In Europe at the time, Ray was aware only of the favourable audience response; the critical reception was no better than for *Johnny Guitar*.[40] It was at least the only one of his films to achieve official recognition, however small: Oscar nominations for Natalie Wood, Sal Mineo, and the 'original story'. Over the years, the lingering imprint left by *Rebel Without a Cause* on the collective memories of filmgoers and film-makers was to become more deeply ingrained.

The price of this success was that *Rebel Without a Cause* is more explicit, less mysterious than any other Ray film. No sooner had filming started than Ray, normally reticent about articulating his ideas, was ready to reveal the name of the game: look for the father. 'In one sentence,' he told a journalist visiting the set,[41] 'he fails to provide the adequate father image, either in strength or authority.' Jim's father is ridiculous because he wears an apron, and he finally lives up to his role by silencing his wife with a look. Immediately after Plato is killed, Jim introduces Judy to his father, who instantly rediscovers his lost dignity. This conclusion, which it would be nice to think of as imposed (like all those other happy endings so common in Hollywood, and so obviously pure convention that they fail to undermine the films themselves), completes the cyclical logic of *Rebel Without a Cause*, closing the twenty-four hours Jim wanted to live as 'one day when I didn't have to be all confused'. It is even 'signed': in the last shot, Ray himself enters the frame, back to camera, and heads towards the Planetarium. The omniscient film-maker is stealing a march on his characters, pointing out from his superior position what they don't know. When Judy's mother sighs, 'It's just the age', neither film-maker nor scriptwriter can resist having Judy's kid brother say, 'The atomic age!'[42] In this year of conformism, the film thus ended up by conforming – in part, at least – as Stewart Stern had feared, a share of the responsibility being his.

None of which prevents the film from compelling attention, and in terms of cinema: the fusion of the everyday and the 'mythical' wrought by expansive CinemaScope gestures, the dissonances of Leonard Rosenman's score, the cries and whispers of the kids. Not least, an image of the hero whose novelty is not easy for the spectator of today to perceive. Dean's character, as Stewart Stern put it, 'depicted a kind of manhood that did not need violence to assert its power. A manhood that announced itself in the willingness to be against the pack, therefore brave, and also unpopular. It was an attempt to define masculinity in a different way at a time when it seemed all to be leather and boots. The kids caught that. They caught the undercurrent of sweetness in Jim Stark and in the actor who portrayed him and the longing for a lost, loving world, where people could drop their bravado and treat each other gently.'[43]

26

Hot Blood

No Return, the project about gypsies, had finally been bought back from RKO. Fidelity Pictures, Howard Welsch's company (*Rancho Notorious*), had agreed a pick-up deal with Columbia: using the studio's technicians and equipment, the finished film was to be delivered in exchange for a fixed sum. As producer, Jane Russell wanted Harry Tatelman, who had already fought for the Walter Newman script in 1952. Ray, who had hoped to produce the film himself, was engaged to direct it after *Rebel Without a Cause*. But the context had changed by 1955, and development of the production took a curious turn.

Tatelman had only one film to his credit, *Underwater!*: 'Very frankly, I knew very little about producing at the time. I was working for Hughes [in 1953], so I got a call from Tevlin, the head of the studio, to come down to his office. Hughes was on the phone, and said to me: "I want to do a picture with Jane Russell in a bathing-suit." I said, "Yessir." He says, "So find a story." Then I said, "Sir, who do you want to produce the picture?" There was a pause, and he said, "Hell, you might as well do it." That's how I became a producer! I didn't know a medium shot from . . . So I went to Nick and asked him if he'd direct *Underwater!* I told him about it, he started laughing. And right after that I got a call from Tevlin saying that Hughes wanted John Sturges to direct it. So I went up to see Sturges, and the idea of doing a picture with Jane Russell in a bathing-suit appealed to him – isn't that strange? He was a hot talent at the time. He got in on it, so I told Nick, and Nick was very happy. One thing about Nick: he would never put down a fellow director. Never had a bad thing to say – which is very uncharacteristic in this business, and always has been.'

Tatelman, after MCA and Hughes, was now working for Jane Russell and her colourful husband-manager, the football pro Bob Waterfield. His personal relationship with Ray remained excellent. Like the director, Jane Russell was obliged to undertake this new film with little respite, still exhausted from the preceding one: she had just finished *Gentlemen Marry Brunettes*, expensively produced in Europe by herself and her husband.

The amorality and the open-endedness of Walter Newman's script, daring for 1952, seemed hardly acceptable in 1955: the gypsies blithely ignore American law; the hero, attempting to integrate them, tries to turn them into a pressure group during municipal elections; the heroine practises fraud in marriage. By way of conclusion, the gypsy caravan turns its back on the American home and sets off for a chimerical promised land, a lie deliberately maintained by the protagonists. Walter Newman told Rui Nogueira: 'Nick called me and said, "Look, we've got to take this from RKO with Janie over to Columbia, and they want these changes made." I said: "Nick, you and I discussed this at great length, we know what *we* want, and if they want something else, I don't want to do it. Go with God, it's up to you." '[1]

According to Tatelman, the decision to rewrite the script was a perversity typical of Ray. A former literary agent, Tatelman brought in a friend as scriptwriter: Jesse Lasky Jr, only middling as a writer but personally likeable.[2] As Lasky describes it: 'I was interviewed by Jane and her husband, who was also acting as executive producer. They said: "Nick wants to meet you informally, would you mind going up to his apartment tonight?" So that night, I drove up to Nick's apartment. I heard jazz coming out as I approached the door, and it sounded like a party. I went in, and the first time I saw Nick, he was dancing with another man. The other man was a young prizefighter, and the two of them were dancing cheek-to-cheek around the room to jazz. Nick waved me to sit down and waved the servant up with a drink, and I sat there and watched the two of them dance . . . They danced beautifully, very graceful guys, and I didn't for an instant think they were homosexual. This was just having a good time. When it was over, we talked for quite a while and had a lot of drinks. He said: "What are you doing tomorrow, Jesse? I want you to start on the story tomorrow." "You mean you've okayed me?" I asked. He said: "Yeah, I knew the minute you sat down in that chair that you were the right writer for me." '

Roger Donoghue had given up a boxing career to coach Marlon Brando during the filming of *On the Waterfront*. He had accompanied the actor and Budd Schulberg to Hollywood in the days before the Oscar ceremony in March, and had met Ray at the home of Joan Fontaine and Collier Young. Ray became interested in *Eighth Avenue*, a boxing story Donoghue had written with Schulberg, having James Dean and either Bogart or Cagney in mind; he took Donoghue on as an assistant for *Rebel Without a Cause* and *Tambourine* (the new title for *No Return*). Donoghue recalled the new film without enthusiasm: 'He said to me one night: "I only want to make pictures with kids, young people." I said: "Well, goddammit, why don't you do it? Why are you making this with forty-year-old Cornel Wilde and thirty-five-year-old Jane Russell? What are we doing here?" He said: "I'm committed. Lew Wasserman and MCA put the package together, Jane's a friend, I owe it to my ex-wife who wrote that thing, and . . ." I said: "Nick, if you make this picture, you're crazy!" I didn't care. I wasn't some guy trying to be an actor or anything, I'd go back and sell beer.'

Nobody seems to have wanted to make 'that thing'. According to Ray: 'Lew Wasserman turned pale when I said I wished to honour my word to Jane Russell that I would make this film with her.' Russell remembers only her own exhaustion. Jean Evans, who had been handsomely paid by RKO, had abandoned any idea of turning her researches into a book and lost interest in the subject. 'The tragedy and the flaws of the film,' Ray added, 'can be attributed to my overestimation of my own capacities and my underestimation of my involvement in *Rebel Without a Cause*.'

Jean Evans had spent weeks gaining the confidence of the store front gypsies on First, Second and Third Avenues on the Lower East Side. Her research was not only better than anything Ray could have hoped for; it was also, according to him, virtually unique.[3] Scorning this material, he doggedly started again, using intermediaries since he was so wrapped up in *Rebel Without a Cause*: a travesty of his own investigations into the youth scene before starting to construct the previous film. With the co-operation of the Los Angeles police, he packed Jesse Lasky Jr off to meet the King of the Gypsies: 'Nick said, "Hell, no books. Talk to him, get all those ideas, watch what you see, make your mental notes, don't pull anything out of your pocket, don't make a note, because he's a funny guy, he's a shifty guy. Remember, you're *not* a screenwriter." So I went down the next day and there was a big caravan, huge thing, without anything to pull it. A man came along, a big, fat, jolly man, he looked like an Italian restaurateur, with a moustache. I talked to him at length. I had to get out of the car for some reason; I went to the door, and he'd taken the doorknob off. He showed it to me and said, "Nobody leaves until I have finished talking to them." He told me the history of the gypsies. The next day I came back to Nick, and we began work together – he didn't write with me, but he had lots of talks with me. I found him a wonderful guy, we worked very well.'

Ray similarly sent Roger Donoghue to New York, seeking a quality that Jean Evans's research would have guaranteed but which fails to emerge as one of the film's prime merits: authenticity. Donoghue recalled: 'I asked Jim McShane, a New York cop who went on to be Chief Marshal of the US under John Kennedy, to find me a fallen gypsy, who would tell me exactly what happens at the wedding scenes, at the death scenes, and so forth. So I met this gypsy on Second Avenue, and I

taped him. Nick wired me $200 from California, and every ten minutes I
would give him ten dollars. Then Nick and I, we wrote the wedding
scene.' Weddings and funerals were in fact among the customs documented by Jean Evans, who had taken the time to win acceptance by the
gypsies and had attended both ceremonies. She describes a corpse lying
there 'with his hands full of money to help him pay the way to the other
world.' Or a marriage where 'they give the bride and groom a loaf of
bread, the inside scooped out and stuffed with money. But with this
modern touch: the bread is a loaf of Bond bread with the trademark
wrapper still on it.'

The improvised research brought some bizarre results. 'Just before we
started shooting,' according to Donoghue, 'Nick decided: "We've got to
make a musical." "Jesus Christ," I said, "we're really in trouble. You
should have walked away." He said, "Look, you keep telling me that, but
I'm in, I've got to do it." So he got Ross Bagdasarian, an Armenian
composer,[4] and Les Baxter, who did sweet stuff. Now I'm persuading the
King of the Gypsies of Los Angeles, setting it up so he'll be technical
adviser on the film, telling him: "Nick Ray is going to show what it is to
be gypsy, you're the last ethnic group who fights everything, you stay
together, and he's going to give the true story of it." Les Baxter, Ross
Bagdasarian, the choreographer and I go to see the King, Frank Morano
or Moreno, to hear the music they play at their weddings. So off we go in
the limousine to this little Archie Bunker kind of house. Frank Morano
has his family there, the girls come out to do the dance, and they put the
record on. All of a sudden everyone looks at each other: it was Mickey
Katz's Bar-Mitzvah Band.[5] That's the gypsy music! We went to the end of
Los Angeles to listen to Mickey Katz! Nick said, "Roger, thanks for the
trip!" I said, "You wanted me to research, we got the authentic music!" '

The casting of Cornel Wilde was the result of a compromise with the
Jaffe agency. Ray remembered having 'given way' because he was pressed
for time. Jane Russell recalled that 'we'd looked for months, way before
he made the other picture [*Rebel Without a Cause*]. He was looking for
an unknown, and we even had a boy flown up from Mexico City. We
never found one, and then we picked Cornel Wilde because at least he
looked like a gypsy.' 'I was a fairly obvious choice,' Wilde commented,
'because I speak several foreign languages, I have a mixed-up ethnic
background [Czech and Hungarian], and I easily looked gypsy.' His forty
years were not too evident against Jane Russell's thirty-four. But there
was no common language between actor and director, and Wilde's remi-
niscence of Ray – complete with uncharitable reference to doping –
reflects what professional circles felt about him after 1955:

'We had one rehearsal at his hotel suite with Jane Russell. He was always in control on the set, but at this rehearsal his speech was somewhat broken and slurred. A lot of what he said was incomprehensible, or at least it was way up on cloud nine as far as I was concerned. I know that Nick drank some, but I think he was on something else too. I was a pre-med student, I've been around a lot, so I understand these things . . . His expressions were so vague that frequently I didn't know what he was getting at. And then he would illustrate, which is really not a good thing for a director to do. On that film I really don't think he was much help to me. He might have helped Jane some. It wasn't that I needed help – by

45 *Hot Blood*: Cornel Wilde, Jane Russell and Nicholas Ray

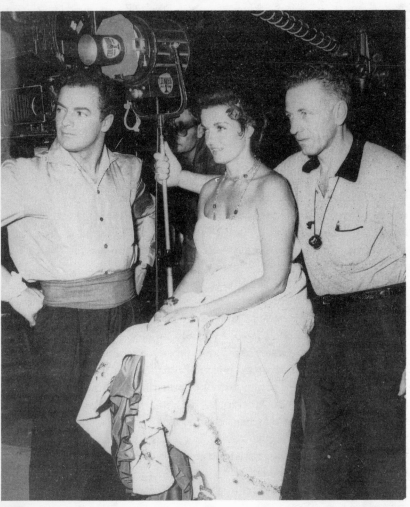

then I was a very experienced and confident actor – it's just that when he expressed himself, it was in rather vague, large-wordy terms. He did some fine films before that. I don't think *Hot Blood* was a fine film.' (When I suggested that it wasn't a failure, Wilde retorted with the ultimate proof: 'It wasn't a success.')

This first rehearsal with Wilde was to remain the only one. Other aspects were no less bizarre: the casting of the King of the Gypsies, for example. After the death of his ideal choice, Gabriel Pascal, Ray considered (according to Jesse Lasky) Edward G. Robinson, whose status matched that accorded to the character in the various scripts. It seems that Luther Adler, the Group Theater veteran who finally played the part, was indeed Ray's choice. Jane Russell insists that the ideal actor had been found, but that Ray wouldn't have him: 'A big, tall man, very dark and swarthy, and he looked like a gypsy. Nick said, "No! I'd never cast him in the part, I'd cast him as a faggot or something." Just because *that* would not fit his character at all, and he was the obvious choice for the Gypsy King. Instead Nick gets Luther Adler, who is short and doesn't look like a gypsy at all. It was kind of a *pot-pourri*; he would just decide that something, because it was obvious, shouldn't be done – he'd do the absolute opposite. He would do that with the script, too. He was not very disciplined, and I think possibly that's what Mitch meant when he described him as a very talented sophomore. He had all the ideas and the enthusiasm and the "we'll do it", but it just wasn't laid out and planned. What came out in the end *might* have been what he started out with, but could very possibly be something quite different.'

Busy with the editing of *Rebel Without a Cause*, Ray had an unpleasant surprise when he saw what Tatelman and Lasky had been doing. During the last few weeks, he still tried to patch up the script, working on it with Luther Adler, among others. Shooting started, with a rickety script, on this ill-prepared production on 18 July 1955. According to Jane Russell, 'Nick wanted to "get together and talk", and I was going, "Oh Nick, will you just give me the damn script!" He'd want me to come in early and look at the sets, but I just wasn't up to it, and it was disappointing for him. I was taking steam cabinets in my lunch hours, because I ached all over sometimes. I'd just come off a musical and he wanted me to dance. "You're out of your mind," I said, "I'm never going to learn that dance." He was very intense, and he really liked to get into characters . . . Columbia was a dreadful lot. The others were kind of civilized, with a little park in the middle or something, and the dressing-rooms were nice. Over there the dressing rooms were dreadful. I've heard stories of a secret passageway that Harry Cohn used to use. I could believe it at that studio, the way it was built; it was like an old haunted house.'

For weeks Ray had to struggle against the tide, pretending enthusiasm, battling his own weariness, meeting Donoghue on the set at 5.30 in the morning to set up the day's work. 'We thought that faith and love and everything would overcome,' Ray said later, 'and it doesn't. You must have the energy for imagination.' Tatelman remained ineffectual: 'I can just see that grin on Nick's face. I said, "Will you stop changing the script and go back to the original?" He said, "Oh no, we're going to make it better." Just no story discipline at all. And certainly I wasn't a proper producer for him, because I wasn't a proper producer for myself. I knew nothing about producing. Welsch couldn't care less; he was just interested in making the picture for x number of dollars, because when he turned the picture over he'd get x number of dollars, so whatever he made it for less than that was productive.' Cornel Wilde remained unconcerned: 'On the bigger scenes, there was a lot of rehearsal . . . a lot of improvisation around the scene, using any words you like, or doing scenes away from the script, improvising scenes that got people into a certain kind of mood, hate or laughter, whatever. And then, when they were relaxed, or really immersed in the emotion, he would go to the scene. I like to do that, too.'

The collaboration with cameraman Ray June was a happy one. Ray found this MGM veteran 'very tolerant of me, and also very appreciative of the almost intolerable situation in making the film.' Used to flamboyant colour at MGM, June took the film to the opposite pole from *Rebel Without a Cause*, away from any realistic reference, and gambled so successfully with stylized bad taste ('the gaudiest colours to be seen in the cinema,' Jean-Luc Godard wrote) that Ray, in retrospect, could describe him as 'better than Shamroy'.[6]

At the end of these five or six weeks, fatigue won out: Ray left for Europe, returning only after the post-production was finished. Luc Moullet, in his 1958 filmography, reports the director's version: 'Ray left the set on the last day of filming for *Hot Blood*, then known as *Tambourine*, and did not collaborate on the editing.'[7] Harry Tatelman remembered it differently: 'Nick did it all [the editing]. To the best of my knowledge. I know *I* didn't screw around with it, because I wouldn't know how to do it. And I don't think Welsch was around. Harry Cohn was; he may have screwed around with it.' Jane Russell denies this: 'We even asked Harry Cohn if he would oversee the cutting, and he didn't. He saw the film, he wasn't interested.' It is more likely that Ray left it to the Fidelity Pictures editor, Otto Ludwig, to assemble the material – deviating more than a little from the script – as he saw fit. His stay in Europe prolonged when he learned of James Dean's death, Ray returned only at the end of October, when the film had already been mixed and the negative cut (it was to be released in March 1956, the fifth Jane Russell in thirteen months). There was no conflict, since Ray, through tiredness rather than indifference, had by his own admission 'let down my standards of acceptance' before filming even began; abandoning the editing was merely the consequence of this premise, not a sudden loss of interest.

Contrary to the opinion of all concerned, there are many reasons for liking *Hot Blood*. First and foremost, those mentioned by Ray himself: 'Within that film, and the terribly bad foot that it gets off on, are things worthy of attention. I think the photography of Ray June is extraordinary. I think the folklore of the gypsies is as extraordinary as the folklore of any minority group that you can find any place in the world outside of the Aborigines. Some of the dancing by Matt Mattox, who danced the Cornel Wilde part, some of the orchestration which was concocted by Les Baxter, Ross Bagdasarian and myself – also the uncorrupted version of the song in the streets, ending up in the alley with Mikhail Rasumny, a wonderful old actor giving his last performance, taking over the song in his dying voice.[8] The detail of the "Keep off the grass" sign in Central Park, showing that the gypsies do not understand this kind of thing because they hold their dance and fiesta there, is still good theatre, I think. The stuff that takes place in the gypsy headquarters, the trial and the marriage, should go to the Library of Congress, because that's the way it was and there is no other record of it in our film history.'[9]

Right from the opening scene – still close to Walter Newman's script – the film overflows with gaiety and energy. The tribal king, Marco,[10] describes the Promised Land to the gypsies: a land of plenty with no *gajos* (outsiders) that recalls a painting hanging on the wall. In return, he collects money from them. In the street, a little man with glasses – a familiar type from musicals – passes the illuminated sign announcing 'Phrenology: 50 cents – Complete Psychoanalysis: 75 cents'. He has come to enquire about Stefano, Marco's brother, who has asked him for a job as a dance teacher. The film is instantly in collusion with the gypsies in the trick they play on the little man, as they tell him that Stefano is a habitual thief and a ladykiller. It adopts its characters' standpoint concerning both situations and coloration; it accepts their belief in certain magics and the importance of dreams. A time and a space are created, existing only within the film, out of key with any verisimilitude. Objects and colours (setting up only discordancies) are accumulated in every shot: striped curtains, carpets, astrological charts on the walls.

At the mock wedding contrived between Stefano (Wilde) and Annie (Russell), he is wearing a yellow shirt with an orange cravat, she a pink dress striped in red; Marco sports a carnation on his shirt, another gypsy (Nick Dennis) a red scarf. The confrontation between the newly-weds takes place by a bed with a red and purple canopy. The gypsies' rooms resemble tents; they are divided by drapes, one with light green horizontal stripes, another a diaphanous mauve. When Stefano leaves on tour to get away from Annie but remains haunted by her, he "sees" her superimposed on posters. The artlessness of such devices matters little; it also makes for fine scenes like the one (devised during filming) in which Stefano returns to change his shirt. Annie offers him mulled wine with peaches, and sings to herself, the simple words ('I could learn to love you . . .') continuing off as he changes, and ending with a line of dialogue addressed to him that picks up on the action again. In his determination to follow through on the idea of a musical, Ray had consulted Frank Loesser (whose *Guys and Dolls* had just been filmed). It was he who suggested the idea of a 'subconscious approach' to the song, meaning that the song should be heard over unmoving lips. The effect here is not really very different. (Ray had already considered using this device in the police station scene in *Rebel Without a Cause*, in particular for Jim's retort to his grandmother: 'You tell one more lie, and you're going to get turned to stone.')

A little later, when Stefano has changed his vermilion shirt for an orange one, the camera literally assumes his place. He is stretched out, drunk, a glass of wine held to his forehead, talking to Annie, who is undressing behind a screen. The CinemaScope image turns upside-down, and the audience sees – 'through his eyes' – Annie returning upside-down. Then, in a strange aberration, the camera changes its viewpoint by turning right side up to frame, in the same shot, Stefano himself and Marco as he comes in.

With an eye to this idea of a musical, Ray steered the film away from the 'authenticity' which was its guarantee of seriousness. Another sort of authenticity took its place: an intimacy with a way of life. This may not have been the sort of document suitable for deposit at the Library of Congress; but it is understandable that Ray, given the total isolation in which he made the film, should have felt the need to justify it on a documentary level.

In *Hot Blood*, his love for outsiders, for a life governed by aesthetic considerations, meshes with the richness and diversity of American life as described by Alan Lomax, all those aspects overlooked and obliterated in the US during the 1950s. Ray wove them into a movie dream: sketchily developed characters, projecting their feelings and desires through colour and dance. Regrets over never having made a great film musical (expressed by Ray's first words in *Lightning Over Water*) may perhaps be compounded by regrets for a career which let him pursue so few of the possibilities he saw in the cinema.

'I've been fooling around with film ever since,' Harry Tatelman concluded. 'I've done a lot of stuff. Some good, some not so good, but they've all made money. With the exception of *Hot Blood*, I guess.' For the filmgoer not bound by such criteria, the film is readily enjoyable. The future film-makers of the *Nouvelle Vague* made no mistake – and no extravagant interpretations – in recognizing it as an example of the kind of cinema they wanted to create.[11] 'After *Rebel Without a Cause*, Ray gives us his cause for living with this intelligent, devil-may-care film, bursting with health and life,' wrote François Truffaut in *Arts*.[12] Nowadays, whenever this rarely screened film is shown, the healthy laughter of audiences faced with its joy and vitality, its delight in these artful and artless characters (hammy performances notwithstanding), vindicates its tale of a group of people untouched by corruption other than sickness and old age.

27

European Parenthesis, 1955

With the shooting schedule for *Tambourine* barely completed, Ray fled to Europe: it was his first trip outside the American continent. The occasion: helping the Warner affiliates with publicity and release campaigns for *Rebel Without a Cause*. Serious difficulties were anticipated with national censorships: the presence of the director, with his charisma and his reputation in Europe, might help in ironing out problems. He also wanted to see Hanna Axmann, who had returned to Germany. And, now that he felt in a strong enough position to tackle independent production, he was curious to explore circles which seemed to react to his films more favourably than the American press or industry.

He had firm projects with James Dean: 'I got a bonus for the film [*Rebel Without a Cause*], and I took a 300 SL Mercedes. Jimmy and I had decided to form our own company together, and I bought two stories. One was called *Heroic Love*, and the other was a film about a Mexican road race. We were going to chart the course of the race in the Mercedes, then put cameras on the car . . . We had our holiday place to stay in Nicaragua all picked out. The Mercedes arrived in Hollywood while Jimmy was finishing the dubbing on *Giant*.'[1]

The author of *Heroic Love* was an Arizona teacher, Edward Loomis. The project was to resurface on several occasions right up to the end of Ray's life, with different casting ranging from Robert Wagner to David Carradine. 'The story follows the actions and destiny of a fatherless son and a sonless father – both heroes in the estimation of each other.'[2] The setting: a little town out West in the present. Jayboy returns ingloriously from the war (Korea in this first version, Vietnam in later ones). He wants to study law with Judge Cassius Martin, a prominent citizen who still thinks well of him. Cassius is married to a woman twenty-five years his junior, who is deceiving him with a dandified lawyer. She makes advances to Jayboy, which he rejects; but, disturbed, he begins running after all the girls in town. Thanks to his combat training, Jayboy disarms a Chinese who runs amok, afterwards helping the judge to protect the man from a lynch mob. An alliance is formed between the wife, the lecherous lawyer, and another of the latter's mistresses. They allege that Jayboy has seduced the wife. The judge publicly insults Jayboy in the town square, and whips him. Rather than humiliate him further, Jayboy says nothing. Cassius collapses and dies; Jayboy proclaims his innocence to the crowd; then he leaves town.

Towards the end of September 1955, it was in Paris, then London, that Ray learned of the enthusiastic reactions of both studio and audience when *Rebel Without a Cause* was previewed. It was to open in America on 3 October. On Friday, 30 September at 5.45 in the afternoon, driving a Porsche Spyder bought eleven days earlier, James Dean killed himself at the intersection of Routes 466 and 41, at Cholame, California. The news was announced on Saturday morning.

Roger Donoghue: 'I'm the one that called Nick in London. I was in Pleasantville, New York, and it came over the air that Dean was killed, so I called the AP or the UP, whatever it was, and they said, "No, he's dead, definitely dead". So I put through a call to London and got him, and said, "Have you heard anything?" "No, what's the matter, Rog?" he said. "Jimmy's dead," I said. There was a Nick Ray pause for about a minute, then he said, "Are you sure?" – "Yeah, I checked through UP and AP, and . . ." He said, "I'll talk to you tomorrow." That was it.'

Ray then left to see Hanna Axmann, who was living with her family near Frankfurt: 'For ever indelible in my mind is this sentence when he got out of the plane. "Hi, darling," then, "Jimmy's dead," and then he cried and cried. Living in a little village among the oak trees, I hadn't heard of James Dean's death then. Jimmy is dead? Can't be his son. I didn't dare ask, but I caught on after a while when he talked more about it. I had come to pick him up with the driver and with a nephew of mine, a little boy. From Frankfurt we had to drive quite a way to this country house, about 45 miles (80 km) or so, and we stopped at every inn, where he had to have a Steinhäger or something to drink, and it was always "Jimmy is dead, Jimmy is dead," and so he told me about everything. Then he stayed almost two weeks.'

On 13 October he went to West Germany's eastern border, and spent the day 'watching the first batch of German PoWs being returned. Quite an experience.'[3] That same evening, he returned to London, where he had to see *Rebel Without a Cause* with the censor Arthur Watkins. 'Much as I love the picture, though, it's a little like going to a funeral, as you can imagine,' he wrote to Steve Trilling from the Savoy. His presence did not have the desired effect: before even considering an X certificate (banned to under-sixteens), the British Board of Film Censors demanded four significant cuts. 'The less we have of this whole unpleasant idea of young people meeting together to witness a contest which could end in the death of one of the participants, the better.' Until 1968, British audiences saw *Rebel Without a Cause* shorn of six minutes.

46   The boxer Rocky Marciano surrounded by (left to right) his trainer
Charley Goldman, Elia Kazan, Nicholas Ray, Budd Schulberg and
Roger Donoghue (1955)

On Monday, 25 October Ray returned to New York, where he was
met by Roger Donoghue: 'Nick sent me a telegram from London, asking
me to pick him up. He came off the plane – it was Sunday morning [*sic*],
about ten o'clock – and it was the first time I'd ever seen him drunk. He
said, "Come on, we'll get a drink." "Nick, it's Sunday morning . . ." I
said, "Oh well, OK." But I was in shock because that whole summer of
1955 he was in good shape, he had it all going, and he had been taking
care of himself for three years, I guess . . . He had fallen off the wagon
before that, but I think it was all over on that September night of 1955.'
He stayed at the St Moritz, then sought refuge with Connie Bessie.
Early November saw him back at the Chateau Marmont, but by the end
of the year he was in Europe again. In London, he met Gavin Lambert,
with whom he had corresponded when the latter reviewed *They Live by
Night* in *Sequence*: 'I met Nick at a New Year's Eve party in London, at
the house of some mutual friends. We got to talking, and we had a sort of
instant click. I'd been away from writing about films at that time; I'd
been to Morocco, and had written and directed a little avant-garde film,
Another Sky, which Nick saw and liked very much.' A little later, Ray
was in Paris, then back in London again for the opening of *Rebel With-*

268

out a Cause. (He sent Trilling a cable: 'Reviews *Rebel* creating more sensation by quality and space than any other pic here in years.') Then Munich, where he spent two weeks with Hanna Axmann at the hotel Vier Jahreszeiten, before returning to California.

28

Bigger Than Life

During his stay in Paris, Ray had read an article by Berton Roueché entitled *Ten Feet Tall* in the *New Yorker* of 10 September 1955. Roueché, more than just the magazine's medical correspondent, was a great journalist. Lillian Ross praised 'the beautiful, limpid prose, simple and perfectly clear' he used in 'describing obscure people who exercise useful or fascinating professions' or 'unusual instances of medical discoveries'.[1] Among these last was cortisone, a hormone whose clinical application won a Nobel Prize for Dr Philip S. Hench in 1950. Roueché's article describes a case where the new drug caused side effects in the treatment of a teacher, a family man suffering from periarthritis nodosa (a degenerative and almost invariably fatal inflammation of the arteries). The cortisone alleviated the pain and induced in the teacher a new perception of the world, 'a new level of existence' in which 'a few minutes was as good as an hour'. Alternating between states of exaltation and despair, he played havoc with his domestic life, buying far too expensive clothes for his wife, scorning the pettiness in his life, and – in the belief that he had been invested with an educational mission – radically changing his conception of the teacher-pupil relationship. He terrorized his wife and son. Hospitalized again, he was relieved of his physical symptoms as well as his manic-depressive psychosis through treatment with another hormone, ACTH.

There was enough here to stimulate Ray, given his obsessive concern with anything permitting the manipulation of individuals, and his curiosity about medical services and their incursions into private lives. He informed Lew Wasserman of his interest in the subject, and a firm offer was transmitted to him in Germany by MCA.

This new film was another agent's deal. Darryl F. Zanuck, head of 20th Century-Fox since its inception, wanted to hand over the reins. One of the reasons for his lassitude was the increasing power assumed by middlemen, the growth of the package system. Wasserman was not alone in practising it: another well-known agent was Charles K. Feldman, who was credited as co-producer on *The Seven Year Itch*.[2] Feldman was James Mason's agent, and the latter was duly offered a contract at Fox. 'It was slightly mystifying to me,' Mason commented, 'because I never got the impression that anybody really exulted in having me work with them, and most of the films that I got involved in were not particularly success-ful. So it was a bit of a surprise that I was offered this very gratifying three-way contract by Fox, that they could use me either as a director or a producer or an actor. Because I'm always looking for a motive other than the obvious one, in this case I thought that probably Zanuck, before he went away to become this great international independent producer based in France . . . it looked as if he was doing good turns to old friends. Not that I was an old friend, but Charlie Feldman was my agent and Charlie Feldman was a very popular figure among the tycoons of Holly-wood. He used to have this habit of buying properties and having some of his clients work on them, and then the properties would be worth three or four times as much as they were when he bought them.'

Zanuck made way for his chosen successor, Buddy Adler, whom Ray had often met playing cards. Adler offered Ray a contract for two films of his choice: the first would therefore be an adaptation of *Ten Feet Tall*. James Mason was equally enthusiastic about the subject, and had made considerable progress in getting a script together when the director arrived on the West Coast. Cyril Hume and Richard Maibaum, a veteran screenwriting partnership whose routine product left no reason for sup-posing they had anything to bring to the subject, had already written a screenplay. Passing Gavin Lambert off as a cortisone specialist, Ray had him hired as a technical adviser. To win Mason over, Ray described how he himself had been given his start by Kazan. According to Lambert, 'It really meant working on every stage, from the script through the cutting. And I was in a mood – well, I had just stopped being a film critic, and I had to get out of England. So it was a very happy moment. I came to Hollywood and stayed in Nick's house for the first two films, *Bigger Than Life* and *The True Story of Jesse James*. Nick told me, before I arrived, that he had reservations about the script. When I read it, I understood why; it was a sort of very slick journalistic script, on a subject that could have taken much more.'

In so far as it stuck fairly closely to Berton Roueché's article, the Hume and Maibaum version, on which Ray and Lambert started working, complied with what Ray felt about the subject: '[The article] hit a couple of points of indignation with me – our national sense of values. It always offended me, even when I was in school, that teachers were the most poorly paid professionals in our society. In "trying to keep up with the Joneses" – the false central idea of much of our activity in this country – he [the teacher protagonist] attempts to overcome his economic position by doubling up on the use of his energy with a second job, as a lowly cab dispatcher, of which he is ashamed.' This first version nevertheless remained a little passé, in the manner of the films Fox was turning out after the war with a 'documentary approach' or 'important subjects'. The project was following in the wake of *The Man in the Gray Flannel Suit*, Zanuck's last personal production at Fox and the big hit of the year. In the script, the everyday dialogue (subject to particular attention from Ray) is extremely flat, never reflecting the ramifications of the illness. It invests Ed Avery right from the outset with a sense of his own importance. When he leaves for the hospital (the start of the story in this version), he displays a forced, morbid humour, which defines him as an intellectual, an exception to the norm, and therefore ready-made as a victim for a crisis of non-conformism. Ray's *mise en scène*, throughout, expresses the exact opposite of this attitude.

James Mason was aware of Ray's reservations, but had difficulty understanding what they were. Gavin Lambert commented: 'Mason wrote in his autobiography that Nick only began to talk about it when I arrived. And in fact I became quite known as Nick's interpreter, because as you know, Nick had an articulation problem. He could obviously have something on his mind, and have great problems getting it off his mind. I remember one of the executives at Fox saying to me quite early on, "Well, you know Nick Ray very well. We don't understand his silences, we're so intimidated by them." I'd tell people, "Don't be intimidated. When Nick is silent it means he's got nothing to say. It's really as simple as that." '

Mason further commented: 'He put up a fight at the beginning to have another writer – perhaps Clifford Odets – do another version of the script, and I said very firmly that I didn't want this to be done, because I had worked with the two writers, in tandem, and I'd come to the conclusion that this was the shape that I wanted the film to take. And if he objected, or if he could see any ways in which we could improve various sequences and so forth, well, he was welcome and he would have all my assistance, because I had done some screenwriting and so had he . . . He also took it above my head, directly to Buddy Adler, who told me that Nick had approached him, and Adler fortunately had given him more or less the same answer that I had.'

Despite this incident, the relationship between Ray and Mason remained one of respect and sympathy. According to Gavin Lambert, 'They got on as well as people who really don't have a great deal in common can get on.' Lambert (in 1958, at least) saw this refusal to disrupt the structure of the script as the reason for the film's failure. As he explained it in 1980: 'It did transpire that Nick felt that the relationship between the husband and wife – the basic fault in the script – was not there; the marriage, its past and general set-up, was not explored, and the characters were shallow. Mason felt it was too late to change anything except little things here and there. "Anything you want to change within the structure, fine, *but* . . ." They already had a shooting date.'

Opposition from Mason and Adler notwithstanding, Ray took Gavin Lambert off to see Clifford Odets. According to Lambert: 'We had two meetings with Clifford. At the first one, Nick had one of those tiny portable tape recorders that had just come out concealed in his vest pocket, so he recorded Odets's monologue on the whole thing, which was extraordinary. Of not much help, because what Clifford was doing was talking about marriage from his point of view and as he'd written about it, and he was really giving us a new version of a famous play of his called *The Country Girl*. He was trying to make out that the wife was the real villain; that she was charming and devoted and all that, but was pushing this man to work too hard, draining him of too much money, and she had social ambitions, etc., so she was a kind of villain. Afterwards, I said to Nick, "It's fascinating in a way, but we can't do it." '

Having become a well-paid Hollywood hack, torn between a boundless egocentricity and a guilty conscience which he transferred on to others – principally women – Odets nevertheless did provide a fresh angle through his scathing criticism of the middle classes.[3] Here is a page from the transcription of his monologue: 'Something that always struck me: as we get older, there is a shrinkage of idealism. When we're younger, we yearn to attach ourselves to and serve some great cause outside of ourselves – that's idealism. Then when we get older, full of cares and woes, or even of a position that we have to keep, a position we have to maintain – or, in the case of this man, he has to maintain a household on $4,500 a year – you unconsciously begin to take a great cause and try to make it serve you. This is where the death – this is where the creeping paralysis comes in. Frequently, this is very unconscious. And it happens to nine out of ten people. Yeats said, "Self-interest and self-preservation are the death of the poet." It's true. But here, where the man had ideals and a great cause to serve [. . .] – learning, pedagogy in its most contemporary modern sense – [. . .] he has begun now to make this thing serve him. It pays him forty-five or fifty-five hundred dollars a year he needs for what? For this petty life? And now the struggle of the teacher is to get more money and not to serve something better. Because, he says, by getting more money he will serve the students better.'[4]

Even if the film does not share this overall pessimism, it does bear the stamp of Odets's thinking – shared, for the most part, by Ray. One might well feel that Odets had worked fairly extensively on *Bigger Than Life*.

One might also wonder whether Ray was not thinking of him in his depiction of an intellectual; the character's vanity, his mistrust of his wife and conviction that she is depriving him of something, his obsession with the secret motives of the people he deals with, his arrogant affirmation of his own talent, his unhappy awareness of being able to express that talent only in part, through his own fault and that of America; even his insomnia – all this might well add up to a portrait of Odets.

Following this visit, the only changes made to the script by Ray and Lambert were, according to the latter, 'very minor': 'All we did, until right at the end, was to work together on the scenes the day before they had to be shot. Nick would say, "What do you think of that?", and I would maybe have some idea, or he would have some idea, and I would just type out the slightly changed version.' This rather underrates the work done. Hume and Maibaum presented the story strictly as a dramatized medical case history; their script opened with a pseudo-documentary preamble complete with test-tubes, narrator's voice and date ('1954'), and made little or nothing of the hero's financial problems (mentioned in passing in Roueché's article). The actual exposition was devised much later: the opening has not yet been drafted in the revisions 'by Mason and Ray' of 8 March ('*One in a Million*, Second Temporary'), appearing only in the 'Final' script of 3 April. The emergency is no longer centred on the home, it starts at work. Here we have one of those incipient crises that so fascinated Ray: after the credits unfold over kids happily leaving school, the opening shot shows Ed's hand clenching as he is suddenly stabbed by pain. This new beginning places Ed Avery at the centre of a knot of social contradictions, victim of an irrational malady: the malady is the film's postulate, and no longer its subject.

Originally set for 26 March, the starting date was put back to allow the director time to work on the script and to complete his casting. The film was shot, entirely on the Fox lot, between 16 April and 29 May; this production, A–770, carried little weight compared to A–769, *Bus Stop*. James Mason's producer credit was not purely honorary. But in making decisions, such as whether to re-shoot day-for-night scenes in real night conditions, he had to obtain the permission of Sid Rogell (an enemy of Ray's from RKO, the 'competent hack' described by Houseman, now with Fox): the one brief night exterior scene that survives shows that this request was refused.[5] When it came to increasing the budget for music by $3,200 so as to be able to extend the score to a 40-minute length, permission had to be sought even higher, from Buddy Adler.[6]

The studio publicity made much of the fact – pretty rare for a production like this – that no visitors were allowed on the closed set, and the even more unusual circumstance that the last fifteen pages of the script were not delivered to members of the unit until the last moment. There were reasons for this: dealing with a medical topic remained potentially explosive, no matter what advance precautions were taken by the studio hierarchy. And Ray – Mason, too, in point of fact – was dissatisfied by these final pages, as resumed by assistant director Eli Dunn in his production schedule: 'Int. Hospital – Ed's room and corridor. Scene 178. Trio enter hospital chapel for fade-out – 5 pages.'

As Gavin Lambert put it: 'There was a big problem at the end, in that when the James Mason character had his final, drastic breakdown and almost killed his son, and he wakes up in the hospital, this was totally underwritten; there was nothing there, and there had to be a bigger scene. Nick and I first talked about various things that didn't satisfy either of us. Then Nick said, "Let's go and see Clifford again." So he calls up Odets and says – this is the night before we had to shoot the scene – "We're in trouble and we need to talk to you." Odets says, "I can't see you, I've just taken a heavy sleeping pill." But Nick said, "Well, you gotta wake up." We went round there, and Odets somehow roused himself, in spite of the sleeping pill, and was extraordinary. He came up with the idea – never in the original script – of Mason confusing Abraham and Abraham Lincoln. He made this connection, and had an idea for a scene based on that. So Clifford and I went to the studio at six o'clock in the morning, and Clifford began talking about the scene. He wrote 90 per cent of it, I wrote maybe 10 per cent of it, and it was shot that day.'

Mason, who had worked with Lambert on this same scene the previous evening, was surprised to find Odets on the set. He instantly assumed that the writer had been secretly working on the script throughout filming. In his autobiography, Mason describes the panic caused by this development, which he himself accepted. Shortly after lunch, Lew Schreiber, Frank McCarthy and Sid Rogell (respectively, Buddy Adler's right-hand man, director of public relations, and studio manager) appeared on the set:

'They were moving fast, clearly intent on mischief, so I bounced out of my box and stood in their way.

"Where are you going?"

"I understand," said Lew, "that Nick is shooting some material that has not been approved. He can't do that. You know perfectly well that you can't go ahead . . ."

'I then went into one of my shouting acts – well, almost shouting.

"You're not going on that stage," I said, "they're working in there.

Nick is rehearsing a very difficult scene, and I won't have him upset. We will listen to your complaints later but not now. You can come in here and discuss it with me if you want."

'Somebody should have said to me, "Who do you think you are?" But they chose not to pick up that cue. To my surprise they dispersed.'

As one may imagine, Ray considered his relationship with his producer (who presents his own reaction to the crisis as perfectly natural) to have been among the happiest in his career.

The Hume and Maibaum script already had Ed Avery, at the height of his delirium, citing the story of Abraham and Isaac in justification of his decision to kill his son. When his wife protests that God stayed Abraham's hand, Ed retorts: 'God was wrong.' The original script had no hesitation in dropping the story of Abraham's sacrifice into the sermon at the church earlier on. And the final reminder of this Abraham connection, indicating Avery's recovery, was equally heavy-handed. A loudspeaker in the hospital corridor was heard summoning a certain Dr Abraham to the telephone . . . which provoked a 'change of expression' on Ed's face! One of the writers responsible for this brainwave, Richard Maibaum (better known for his hand in scripting the James Bond movies), later complained: 'Ray exaggerated some scenes and diluted others. Some directors don't realize that there are scenes that are like music: if you knock out a few notes, it becomes discordant.'[7] Yes, indeed.

Odets refocused Ed's recovery on a definition of Americanism: the first name to surface from his sleep, before he recognizes his wife, son and doctors, is that of Abraham Lincoln, to his mind his only possible interlocutor. Having asked for someone to 'turn out the sun' (a light that is blinding him), he tells his doctor he is 'a poor substitute for Abraham Lincoln', then explains: 'I was dreaming I walked with Lincoln . . . Abraham . . . Abraham.'[8] The reference is to his megalomaniac delirium and his fantasy of being another 'great emancipator'; only when he repeats the name 'Abraham' does the memory of his attempted murder resurface. The film then ends with the American family reunited. Even if Odets took this 'going home' very seriously, the direction reveals the fragility of the reconciliation, and with much greater conciseness than the original script.

Another sequence was improvised. Ray had become friendly with Marilyn Monroe after his slack period at the end of 1952, when he went to see Jane Russell on the set of *Gentlemen Prefer Blondes*. Marilyn used to visit the Chateau Marmont bungalow, and before too long the scandal sheet *Confidential*, specializing in 'revelations' about the stars (Monroe being one of their regular targets), gave their relationship the full treatment. Roger Donoghue: 'They had this big write-up of Nick and Marilyn balling on the way to Nick's Malibu house in the back of a limousine or something. So Nick's really teed off about it, and he says, "I'll sue the sonofabitch" and so forth. When you're a kid you don't think too much, and I said, "Hey, it's not a bad article. There's thirty million guys in America who want to go to bed with Marilyn Monroe, and you're written up!" Nick could be very humorous at times. "I'll still sue the sonofabitch" he said, "but now that you mention it . . ."'9

Bus Stop and *Bigger Than Life* were shooting on adjoining stages. Gavin Lambert recalled: 'Nick said, "Wouldn't it be amusing to have Marilyn as the nurse?" Mason had a dream before he woke up in the hospital, and Nick wanted Marilyn to come in as a nurse in the dream sequence. He put it to her and she said yes, she'd do it. Then, it was interesting, when it came to it, she froze with terror. Completely dried up, said, "I can't do it, what am I supposed to do?" All she had to do was wear a nurse's uniform and carry a tray with a glass of milk, a syringe or hypodermic or something like that, nothing more. She finally did it, but she was in terror about it for fifteen minutes.' What Lambert was referring to was probably not a dream sequence, but the montage sequence (added by Ray) resuming Ed's clinical progress under treatment. For contractual reasons (the studio was afraid that Monroe might chalk up this appearance as the second film she owed 20th Century-Fox), there was never any question of using it in the film.

Filming proceeded untroubled by any serious conflicts, yielding one of Ray's most intense films. His method, partially adumbrated in the earlier films, sometimes through the intervention of chance, is deployed here in its entirety: immersion in a subject; sociological data absorbed, simply to provide a springboard and nothing more; rejection of an existing source, and recourse to it; multiplication of points of view, with contributions from various quarters (Mason, Lambert, Odets); *mise en scène* resolved architecturally and spatially; improvisation applied on the basis of a solid foundation; and the focus on crisis, its power stemming from the speed and concentration of the filming (thirty-two days).

In this film, composite in its materials, calculated in its risks, each effect has a precise function: every remark is of consequence (like Ed's undergraduate or barrack-room humour at the hospital, much of it added by Ray), and so are appearances (the doctors, arriving in twos and threes, have the air of gangsters; Ed, dressed in black to attend mass, is transformed into the homicidal preacher of *Night of the Hunter*).10 Above all, there is the colour, dense, opaque, splashed against neutral or even colourless backgrounds: the reds of the schoolchildren's jackets and shirts, Ed's green waistcoat 'against' his wife's yellow blouse or, more especially, the orange dress he buys her, in one of the first manifestations of his mania, at a luxury department store that epitomizes the bad taste of the 1950s (and Fox). He makes Lou try on dresses of increasing garishness, finally settling on the orange. 'I began to feel the need for some extra kick for Barbara Rush,' Ray explained, 'so I had to find one or two significant things ensuring that attention was being paid to her. In that sense, the orange was inevitable. Later, when the highway departments began using orange instead of red for the protection of road workers and for important danger signs, I felt my psychology had been verified. Strange that it took us so long to wake up to that colour.

47   *Bigger Than Life*: James Mason at the staircase

Perhaps because of the literary strength of red. No significant orange literature. The use of green in *Bigger Than Life* was indicative of life, opposite of the use of green in *Party Girl*, where it's sinister and jealous, envious. With Barbara it was grass and hospital walls.'

Reverting to the cinema's classical tradition, Ray let the characters and their relationships predominate, signified through looks, attitudes and gestures as much as through events. The Averys' two-storey house is built around a staircase leading from the ground floor – hallway, living room, kitchen and study, all communicating and permitting various routes – to an upstairs comprising two bedrooms and a bathroom. Just as the film as a whole revolves around the Easter vacation period, so the final crisis, played out around the staircase, is anchored within the space of a week-end. The Saturday morning routine – father and son playing ball behind the house, the milkman calling, then a bank employee, a visit from the family friend Wally (Walter Matthau), a physical education teacher – becomes a series of foreboding signs: Lou telephones the family doctor, but he is away for the weekend. The evening, with endless homework inflicted on the boy, ends with an outburst from Ed, announcing to his wife and son that he considers the marriage to be over. On Sunday morning, attendance at church, then home again, where Ed tries to kill his son but is overpowered by Wally. The final sequence is equally pre-cisely dated: thirty hours later. In other words, Monday evening.

Interviewed by Charles Bitsch in February 1957, Ray talked about his practice as a film-maker: 'It changes. I shoot according to the way I feel, and trying, as I said, to hunt for the truth of the scene. Sometimes I may start with a master shot, and do it only in order to give the actors the sense of performance. Sometimes I may carry it all the way through, and I have done this for scenes running as long as there is film in the camera. The staircase scene in *Bigger Than Life*, lasting nine minutes, I shot without a break. It was very exciting, and the people in the projection room said, "Don't break it up, it's the greatest scene we've ever seen!" And this was the scene which a playwright had looked at on paper and said, "I don't see how you can ever play this." However, had I listened to the people who said, "Don't break it up," the dynamics would have been lost and I would not have been using film properly. Because I think they were looking at a technical achievement; and what had happened was that the actors, after all the rehearsals, had just begun to get the truth of the scene.'

These remarks explain the wherefore of the hypothetical shot-sequence Ray said he filmed with Bogart for the trial scene in *Knock on Any Door*: not as a deliberate structural choice, but as one strategy of approach among others, designed to test the dramatic effect of the scene and the degree of involvement of the actors. The decision had no more to do with filming a shot-sequence than it had to do with respecting traditional editing techniques. The staircase scene uses three different angles of view, not markedly different in size. Choices (as we shall see with *Bitter Victory*) are made at the editing stage. If the line 'God was wrong' provides one of the most powerful moments in all Ray's films – films which used words, their music as well as their weight, without ever letting dialogue take over – it is both because actor and director refuse to distance this 'unplayable' scene, and because they find a precise expression of its 'dynamic'.

A film about crisis, obsessional in manner, *Bigger Than Life* pursues the internal logic of madness. But its power derives less from its paroxystic nature than from its fundamental ambiguity. Each dramatic unit, each shot, confronts normality with the derangement that normality itself secretes. Ed Avery's sickness is also a very strong and very vital need for

48   *Bigger Than Life*: the derangement of normality

health. His delirium has connections with the bigotry often denounced by Ray, but also reflects certain remarks made by Ray himself. For example: 'We should get rid of the school system for kids over six, before they lose their "ESP", their instincts for learning. Let them live a little in society before we fill 'em with bullshit.'[11] This delirium is also the perspicacity of paranoia, very familiar to Ray. Truffaut noted the ambiguity: 'When [Ed Avery] feels most lucid, he really is so, and like a drunk he speaks many truths. The admirable thing is that he is never entirely right or wrong.' And when another critic, Robert Benayoun, espousing the simplistic Odets thesis, wrote of 'the stupidity of the model wife, indulging fits of jealousy while her husband is killing himself to pay for her every whim', he was blind to a magnificent movie character, well beyond the Paddy Chayefsky naturalism then much in vogue.[12] In connection with this film, Ray said that one of the few things he respected in Arthur Miller's play *Death of a Salesman* was the line 'Attention must be paid'. *Bigger Than Life* is one of the few works from that time to pay such attention to characters who are by self-definition 'dull'. The subject matter of the film is not so much illness as daily life, revealed through the manic lucidity of the illness.

'Social criticism' is only part of Ray's purpose (a point of departure), even if it is the most obvious aspect. The fact that the catastrophe is caused by abuse of medicaments rather than simply by their use, the fact that cortisone is named, thus limiting the denunciation to a particular drug, was deplored by Ray and Lambert, but in no way detracts from the film. It may seem compromised if considered from the point of view of content; but a contrary approach better reveals its riches. Eric Rohmer noted how close Ray came to classical cinema in form, how imponderables are resolved through *mise en scène*: 'The dullness of daily life, as revealed by art, interests us little, and yet it is also what interests us, what concerns us most in the world, for without this dullness, in which we are all more or less involved in one form or another, we should be unable to gauge the extraordinary. The greatest works of literature have indeed contrived to depict this zone, this borderline area between life and drama. But the camera, like a microscope, perceives a large surface where all we had ever seen before was a line. I do not say this because Ray shows a woman in the kitchen, a man in the bathroom, a boy watching television, things that many others had done before him – most of them succeeding only in boring us. What matters is the *tone* he uses in showing them, a tone which, *mutatis mutandis*, is not unreminiscent of *Voyage to Italy*: that very precise attention to little things and the refusal to dwell merely on their picturesqueness, those looks more revealing of the agonies of love than curiosity, fear or any other particular feeling, that very strong sense of man's earthly ties and simultaneously of his freedom.'[13]

Rohmer found in Ray, in this film in particular, an *élan*, a generosity akin to the Rossellini or the Dreyer of those years; without the spiritual certainty he saw in the other two, but analogous in attitude. The camera as microscope, inward emotions expressed through gestures, through space; this gave the film its coherence, and the reaction of French critics granted it a life it had been denied in America. 'To ask a paying audience to sit for almost an hour and watch somebody go through a painfully slow routine of becoming intoxicated from taking too much cortisone,' Bosley Crowther wrote in the *New York Times*, 'is adding a tax of tedium to the price of admission.'[14]

29

The True Story of Jesse James

While filming *Bigger Than Life*, Ray announced the founding of his own production company, Rexray (the Rex came from an associate, Rex Cole). At the time he was planning to embark on *Passport* (which he was negotiating with Eric Ambler to script) and *Heroic Love* immediately after *Bitter Victory*, which was to be a European production for producer Paul Graetz: he had projects taking him into 1958.[1] Meanwhile, he still had a film to make for 20th Century-Fox. Under Buddy Adler's management, the studio was functioning without any particular policy, relying among other things – the start of another sweeping change in trends – on what the exhibitors wanted. They asked for a remake of *Jesse James*, one of the big hits of 1939, directed by Henry King, and starring Tyrone Power and Henry Fonda. Adler suggested it to Ray.

Ray's response: 'I said, "Shit, I don't want to make any remakes." Buddy said, "Well, help me out, do it for me anyway." I said, "Let me think about it, Buddy. If I do it for you, you may not want me to make it the way I want to." I thought about it quite a while, and talked to Gavin about it.' According to Lambert: 'By that time he'd already read *Bitter Victory* and had the offer, and he was very excited about doing it. But he couldn't until he'd done the second Fox film. This was for him the most promising thing that was around – I think they'd offered him several other things which he felt he couldn't do at all. He was interested mainly because what he wanted was to have Elvis Presley play Jesse James. He saw Presley as another kind of James Dean. And met him, and was fascinated by him.'

Presley had in fact tested for Fox on 1 April, and that summer appeared in his first film: a Western directed by Robert D. Webb for David Weisbart, who had left Warner Brothers. That Ray should have seen him as a hero in the same mould as James Dean was hardly surprising: in 1956, Presley was twenty-two years old, a rebel, and had a powerful sexual magnetism (too powerful for the cinema, as was soon to become apparent). Ray must also have been very struck by him as a musician, with his background in gospel and rhythm'n'blues. Furthermore, as Ray saw it, Jesse James was not simply 'a sort of rebel without a cause' (Lambert), but above all a farmer's son, a country boy swept by circumstance into the limelight: which Elvis Presley was (born in Tupelo,

Mississippi), which James Dean from Indiana was, and certainly would have been in *Heroic Love*, more so than in any of his three films.

But the Fox administration had little flair. Weisbart and Robert Webb successfully did their best to tame Presley, and after *Love Me Tender* he made his next films for Paramount. Ray was saddled with a handsome young man, Robert Wagner, under contract to the studio and expressive of nothing but Californian physical culture. Gavin Lambert explained: 'Probably Fox tricked him and pretended to be interested in Presley, but always wanted to use their contract players, Robert Wagner and Jeffrey Hunter . . . who were fine. Then he was very happy with Wagner.' In retrospect, Ray himself was more equivocal: 'An all American laughing boy as Robert Wagner was – he wasn't too far from the legitimate concept of Jesse. He needed the work; not the money, but the work. His style reminded me of Joan Fontaine; very proud of his efficiency in changing wardrobe and always knowing where the key light was. It was the times I got through that that I thought he was good. And he was very good at times, except not real. The only times he was real was when he would be overcome by something at the moment and lose his self-consciousness about the external appearance of it. I don't know whether he really had anything inside that was interesting enough to reveal. But each man has the infinite in his soul, so keep on looking for it.'

The other reason why Ray became interested in the project was of a stylistic order. He was considering an unusual visual style that would take the film into areas of folk art: 'I'd do it entirely as a ballad, stylized in every aspect, all of it shot on the stage, including the horses, the chases, everything, and do it in areas of light.' The studio naturally rejected this proposal, and also rejected the one Ray fell back on: to film it in James brothers territory – Missouri and Arkansas – where he had gone scouting locations.

All efforts to impose a new conception thus foundered on studio routine. Brushing aside an initial script (Russell S. Hughes, May 1956), Ray had Walter Newman hired. Since their abortive collaboration on the script about gypsies, Newman had written *The Man with the Golden Arm* for Otto Preminger. He told Rui Nogueira: 'Both Nick and I were psychoanalytically oriented, and in doing research were struck by the fact that Jesse was unmistakably self-destructive. His exploits were increasingly more hazardous, and – surely it was unconscious on his part – he kept making disastrous mistakes. For example, he *gave* the man who killed him the gun with which it was done, as a *gift* – like an invitation to murder him. And to make it easier, he turned his back on the man to straighten a "God Bless Our Home" chromo on the wall. We thought that was a novel angle of attack for the story. Then, in telling the story, we moved back and forth through time – the way people did several years later in other films. This was Nick's concept. In my pedestrian way, I used flashbacks – some character talking about an experience with Jesse, and then we'd flash back, the conventional approach. Nick said, "Why the prologue? Let's just flash back and forth with no explanation at all. Write it conventionally and I'll shoot it that way, but then I'll try to convince the studio to do it my way. If I succeed, all right, and if I don't, we'll use the prologues.' If this is true, then Ray in his naïvety courted the disappointment that lay in wait.

A first script was completed on 20 July. The front office immediately complained that it was terribly difficult to read, and objected that it failed to arouse sympathy for Jesse James. The 'particular style' adopted for the flashbacks caused Buddy Adler some concern: he was keeping as close an eye on the production as the nominal producer, Herbert B. Swope Jr, a novice described by Gavin Lambert as 'a producer of singular lack of talent or imagination or anything'. Adler immediately asked for a lot of cutting and tightening in the Civil War scenes: the very area in which, to Ray's way of thinking, the answer essentially lay to the question posed by the journalist Wiley at the beginning of the film, 'What makes him Jesse James?' For Ray, the odyssey of the James brothers had its roots in the history of the land, and the devastated Confederate South directly evoked the America of the Depression. Adler objected to the reference (historically attested) to Frank's taste for Shakespeare, and categorically rejected various manifestations of a 'death wish' in Jesse.

The revisions in the 'Temporary Script' of 4 September were by Ray (and Lambert). They developed and improved several scenes, notably one of the best in the film: neighbours, Northern sympathizers, have denounced Jesse's family; he is whipped in front of his mother, and with the family expelled from Missouri by Union soldiers, he immediately leaves to join Quantrill's Raiders, with whom his brother is already fighting. Adler and Swope pointed out that the audience would be lost if they saw a family accused by their neighbours of twenty years' standing: in Ray's view, the James-Samuels had always been rootless. The scene was shot very early on, but Adler insisted that it be rewritten and reshot, because (among other things) he felt that Agnes Moorehead was excessively hysterical as the mother.

The 'Final' script is dated 14 September, but blue pages (revisions) are in the majority: in other words, considerable changes were still being made during filming, which started on 6 September. To play Zee, Ray picked the young and inexperienced Hope Lange (*Bus Stop*) in preference

49 *The True Story of Jesse James*: the revival meeting (cut scene) –
Hope Lange, John Carradine and Robert Wagner

to Joanne Woodward, the studio's choice. He was wary of getting too
much technical expertise from both sides if he brought Moorehead and
Woodward together. Adler thought that 'Zee in the footage shot looks
terrible'. He asked Ray to cover himself so that 'these very, very long
speeches' between Jesse and the preacher Bailey, played by John Carradine, could be cut down. It was Swope who then recalled Walter Newman
to rewrite the dialogue and work on the construction, under the supervision of the studio's executive story editor, David Brown. The producer
had a scene cut in which Quantrill puts the adolescent Jesse to the test
with a variation on Russian roulette. As seen by Ray, the guerrilla leader
was very different from the traditional Butcher of Kansas, as played by
Walter Pidgeon in Walsh's *The Dark Command*: 'Quantrill, 28, small,
slender, exquisite, with romantic features, pale complexion, long black
hair and fine apparel. He might be strolling a promenade for all the
impression his surroundings have upon him.'[2] Scenes were restructured,
the break between the two brothers transformed. For Adler, Jesse's principal motivation was vanity: 'Jesse became a hero to the people of his
community; he loved this; he liked being talked about and written about.
He became more and more reckless; he gave no thought to the lives of

50   *The True Story of Jesse James*: the Baptism

others; he was Jesse James, the man everybody was talking about.' Ray, without neglecting this aspect (historically validated), was more interested in the contemporary resonances: Jesse comes to believe his own publicity.

Towards the end of September, Adler brought in another writer, Arthur Kramer, to work with Newman on tightening the scenes he didn't like, in particular an important sequence at a revivalist meeting, which he felt was too verbose and overwritten. Shot anyway (prior to 28 September), the scene was left on the cutting-room floor: the most serious mutilation perpetrated on the film.

In the revivalist tent where the Reverend Bailey is preaching, the inhabitants of Clay County are side-by-side with Union soldiers, a veritable army of occupation: martial law is in force. Bailey exhorts his audience to repent publicly of their sins, raising his voice against hatred and greed. Jesse has noticed a Union soldier making eyes at Zee. He gets up and unburdens himself: 'These hands have been stained with blood! Federal soldiers are here tonight and the power is theirs. But in the war I killed them by the tens and by the scores! I repent! (*The admission has been uttered with pleasure. The repentance lacks conviction.*) At Centralia the prisoners we took grovelled on their knees, they kissed our feet, they begged for mercy – but we slaughtered them. I repent. They stand here now as conquerors, but at Riverfield, I smote them as David smote Goliath, scourging them in my wrath until they turned tail and fled the field. I repent. (*The audience response grows.*) Even now, there are times when I feel like killing a bluecoat. And what's more, I'm likely to do it if they don't watch out, martial law or no martial law. (*This is all he wanted to tell the soldier.*) So pray for me, all of you.'[3]

Jesse continues, carried away. Bailey exhorts him to receive baptism; dissolve to the river baptism, a fine scene in the film. Elimination of the revival sequence leaves unexplained a dialogue exchange between Cole Younger and Jesse after the baptism: 'That was rousin' testimony, Cousin Jesse. How's it feel to have all eyes upon you?' – 'Why, in my fervour, Cousin Cole, I never noticed.'

On 12 November, with filming completed, Buddy Adler viewed two rough cuts: one chronological, the other in flashbacks. 'Neither gives us clarity of story,' he noted. 'Our story as told now is very confusing.' A week later, Adler listed a dozen scenes to be shot or reshot. Chief among these were the scene in which Jesse is whipped in front of his mother and Union soldiers,[4] and some of the transitions between flashbacks. Originally, the step into delinquency took place fortuitously, almost innocently, after the baptism: Jesse, the Younger brothers and some others, walking around drinking and singing, gradually getting worked up and egging each other on, ended up by wrecking the main street of a nearby town. A new scene replaced this: after the attack on the Samuels's farm and the lynching of the hired hand, Hughie, Jesse persuades the Younger brothers and others to rob banks and use Northern carpetbaggers' funds to get their farms back into shape.

The murderous attack on the Samuels's house by Remington's men was also modified, stressing Remington's personal responsibility. Above all, the breach between the two brothers while hiding out in a cave was reshot in a colourless way. Ray commented: 'I think some of the best scenes I ever directed were in that film but were cut out. They were a little too bizarre. One was the fight between Frank and Jesse in the cave, with very straight dialogue in a good heavy sense. The action was also a little too violent. For taste, I reshot it.' With this scene watered down, removing Frank's charge that Jesse *wants* to die, the only motivations left for Jesse are vanity and (to a lesser extent) affection betrayed. One can imagine (indeed, one can *see* in the perfunctory quality of this scene, in the transitions, in the poor performances of Hope Lange, Moorehead and Carradine) how Ray lost interest. 'By the end,' according to Gavin

Lambert, 'he was simply wanting to finish. I remember during the last two weeks I would say, "We could do this, we could do that – *that* would be a little better, don't you think?"; and he'd say, "Yeah, but why bother?" It got to that. And Nick was drinking very heavily during that picture.'

Soon after shooting the additional footage, Ray left for Europe. The final touches – swirling mists heralding the flashbacks (which he repudiated especially), a tired score by Leigh Harline, a few inserts or perhaps retakes (probably done by Robert D. Webb) slotted in by the studio – threw the film even further off balance.

Jesse James, released as *The True Story of Jesse James*, survives as the broken fragments of a film. Listing the things that don't work, checking for signs of surrender, is an easy but thankless task. Deprived of any overall rhythm, the film nevertheless contains stunning moments. Ray took it upon himself to aggrandize a standing set on the studio backlot, here serving as the main street of Northfield. As with so many of his other films, this one opens in violence, filling the entire CinemaScope screen. In shots carefully predesigned but devoid of any pictorial affectation, marksmen appear on balconies, wagons are dragged across the street. The scene describes a collective action, with no protagonist as yet singled out. The sheriff is a local citizen, Hillstrom (John Doucette), one of several names with a Scandinavian ring in the film. The confusion in the little town is conveyed through unexpected movement, like the scene where Hillstrom is bombarded with additional information as he sends out his report in the telegraph office, and when someone mentions the name of the James Brothers, the frame opens out to take in the street outside (and the credits).

Towards the end, the Northfield bank raid – this same gun battle in the street – and the gang's escape are shown in a sequence which repeats some of the same images, but this time adopts the viewpoint of the raiders: a tactic rarely employed other than in *Citizen Kane, The Barefoot Contessa* and . . . *A Woman's Secret*. This second sequence goes even further in its majestic depiction of violence, showing the town as L-shaped (rather than the single straight street of tradition), and culminating in Frank and Jesse leaping on horseback through a storefront window.[5] That this shot, like the twin leap on horseback made by the brothers into a river and the nocturnal attack on a train, should in fact be images from Henry King's film blown up into CinemaScope, in no way diminishes their aptness. The jumps through the window and into the river echo the mirror relationship between the two brothers, while the raid on the train turns into something very different from King's good-humoured, Robin Hoodish hold-up.

The film remains faithful to its intended title: not *the true story* but *the ballad* of Jesse James. Western outlaws and Depression gangsters are linked in time (an uninterrupted genealogy of gangs had been traced from Quantrill's Raiders down to the Kansas City Massacre of 1933)[6] and in space: the James Brothers travel the same territory as Bowie and Keechie, the South-Southwest of Missouri, Kansas, Oklahoma, Texas. Above all they are linked by myth.[7] Ray drew less on the main reference work on the outlaws, James T. Horan's *Desperate Men* (based on the Pinkerton archives, and inclined to vindicate the agency), than on American folklore as brought to light by Carl Sandburg, the Lomaxes or Ben Botkin, his friends and colleagues when he was working in Washington.[8]

Three scenes in the film are drawn from the three texts about Jesse James published by Botkin in *A Treasury of American Folklore*, the fruit of his work for the Federal Writers' Project.[9] Firstly, the ballad itself, which – despite its celebrity – was used neither in King's film nor in Fritz

51 *The True Story of Jesse James*: playing at 'shooting Jesse James'

Lang's sequel, *The Return of Frank James*. One had to wait for it until Samuel Fuller's post-war *I Shot Jesse James*, more innovatory in every respect than Ray's wayward film, but sharing the same awareness of different levels: the psychoanalytical and theatrical aspects, the overturning of myth, etc. Ray uses the ballad only at the end of the film, but with a precise purpose: to show the incident and, simultaneously, what transformed it into legend, the murder and the popular account of it. The second text from the *Treasury*, 'Jesse James and the Poor Widow', is concisely staged in the scene where Jesse pays off Mrs Keevey's mortgage, to which Ray adds a preamble showing Jesse being careful to maintain his own image, and coming to believe in it. The third text was the first article ever published about Jesse's death, basis of the legend for all the films. Ray turns it into a scene with several entries and exits.

Jesse gives his revolvers to the two Ford brothers: 'I won't be needing these any more.' He goes out into the yard, where his children are playing at 'Jesse James'. When he returns, his conversation with the Ford brothers (who look like delinquents left over from *Rebel Without a*

52 *The True Story of Jesse James*: 'I just killed Jesse James'

Cause) reveals the ambiguity of his renunciation of violence, convinced as he is that his friends will turn against him, but vain enough to know the exact price on his head. 'And if you don't think I expect someone to try to put a bullet in me, you're wrong.' So saying, he deliberately turns his back on Bob Ford to take down the framed sampler that reads 'Hard Work Spells Success', and the latter shoots him. The murder thus does in fact conform to the traditional imagery, though with more complex implications.

Jesse's wife rushes down from the first floor (again the setting for a precarious domestic stability) into the room. The Ford Brothers run out into the street, and Bob excitedly starts shouting: 'I just killed Jesse James! Me, Robert Ford!' A crowd invades the house, and Frank, who has just arrived, pushes all the intruders out. Two shots show souvenirs being stolen. Outside, an old black street singer, blind and wearing a 'Help the Poor' sign around his neck, sings two stanzas of the ballad, rewritten by Ray:

> Jesse James was a man who lived outside the law
> And no one knew his face
> He was killed one day in the county of Clay[10]
> And he came from a solitary race
> Jesse came to the end with his back turned to a friend
> A friend he thought was brave
> But the dirty little coward who shot Mister Howard
> Has laid poor Jesse in his grave.

30
Bitter Victory

The story of *Bitter Victory* started in Paris, while Ray was looking for opportunities and work away from Hollywood. Anxious to meet French writers, he made the acquaintance of René Hardy, whom he invited to work with him. A while later, Paul Graetz sent a typescript translation of Hardy's third novel (and first success), *Amère Victoire*, to Ray in California. Interested in international productions, the producer of *Monsieur Ripois* (*Knave of Hearts*) had made no mistake. Born in Germany in 1899, Paul Graetz held American nationality and ran the Transcontinental companies in Paris, London, Hollywood and New York. He was able to get this war film off the ground thanks to majority financing from Columbia. The budget was estimated at a million and a half dollars: average for the American cinema, considerable for Europe.

As soon as he read it, Ray was fascinated by the book, finding in it, he said, 'statements which coincided very deeply with some of my feelings about war, what it does to people and how they expose themselves within the crucible of war, under pressure'.[1] Gavin Lambert, who was to act officially as co-scriptwriter for the first time, recalled: 'We talked mainly about the conflict between the two principal characters, something he felt very close to. Because ... basically he was both of them. And I think that was the mainspring of the film for him. It wasn't a war film, nor was it an anti-war film; it was a private psychological duel. I liked the idea that the outcome of the mission was really nothing to do with how they performed it, but with what they felt about each other. That, in a way, said something about war. That it was an example of people's neuroses coming out. And that if people could discover how neurotic they were in a war – and in peace – it might never have happened.'

During the summer of 1956, René Hardy arrived in Hollywood to work on the adaptation with Ray and Lambert. Born in 1910, a graduate of Saint Cyr military academy, Hardy was implicated in the betrayal of Jean Moulin, the Resistance leader tortured and killed by the Gestapo in 1942. Twice acquitted, he became a novelist. 'Not a movie writer,' Lambert said. 'A rather intelligent, cold character who really just wanted his novel to be filmed and tried to establish a kind of alliance with me, as a European, against Nick, and would say things like, "I suppose there's got to be a romance . . ." [Actually, the character of Brand's wife, and her affair with Leith before she married, figure prominently in the novel.] I don't think that Hardy was fundamentally interested. He was curious to see Hollywood, about which he had made up his mind in advance. He was prepared to think Nick an idiot from the start, on principle. He also used to complain to me that Nick was not very articulate, that he never quite understood what Nick meant, and so on. I think he came, if not to like him, to have a certain respect for him. But I don't think he ever had any very strong personal response to him. His main interest lay in seeing that we didn't do anything that he might feel violated the book. He never came up with ideas for transferring it on to the screen. When we were working out the structure, he would just say, "Well, you write that scene as it is in the book." That was really his approach to doing it. René didn't speak English. So he and I discussed in French, and I translated to Nick. It was slow and tricky the whole time that René was here, because everything had to be translated back and forth. It took quite some while.'

Graetz came to Los Angeles as the adaptation was being completed, and novelist, scriptwriter, director and producer were in agreement over this first script, a rough draft dated 13 August 1956. During the filming of *The True Story of Jesse James*, Ray and Lambert converted it into a 'Temporary Revised' (6 November).

Already the project was remarkably different from the novel: while adhering to its broad outlines (more so than the completed film did) and some narrative incidents (including one in an Arab village, looking for camel thieves), almost none of the dialogue was retained. The affair between Leith and Jane is handled in rather clumsy flashbacks, with a recurring background motif – a fable about a sphinx – which disappeared in subsequent versions of the script, but was to reappear sixteen years later in *We Can't Go Home Again*. A good deal of the dialogue, however, in the first part at least, made it to the shooting stage.

In September, *Le Film Français* announced that *Bitter Victory* was to be shot 'in North Africa' with Curd Jürgens, a German actor recently shot to prominence by clever publicity (*The Devil's General*), and Raymond Pellegrin (Sacha Guitry's Napoleon): the 'international stars' had yet to be cast. When Ray arrived in Paris in December, accompanied by Lambert, he had made his choice. For the role of Brand – the soldier who lives by and for regulations, the coward and the survivor – a young Welsh actor, a rising star in Hollywood: Richard Burton. As Leith, the archaeologist and dreamer who wants to die, Montgomery Clift, recent survivor, somewhat disfigured, of a serious car crash. Clift elected to appear in *The Young Lions* instead, and Ray's second choice was Paul

Newman, who had just made his name in *Somebody Up There Likes Me* (in a part originally slated for James Dean).

Graetz had assembled some of the finest French technicians: cameraman Michel Kelber (*French Cancan*), art director Jean d'Eaubonne (*Lola Montès*), sound engineer Joseph de Bretagne, assistant directors Christian Ferry and Edouard Luntz, continuity girl Lucie Lichtig. Ray was to film in the black-and-white Scope he wanted for *Rebel Without a Cause*; saving on colour still made a difference for a European producer, and Graetz must have felt that the spectacular aspects would be taken care of by the anamorphic process.[2]

Filming, it was decided, would take place in Libya, where the action is set. A constitutional monarchy closely supervised by the victors of the Second World War, it was safer than Algeria, still under French rule (filming coincided with the Battle of Algiers). Kelber left to scout locations: in the Roman city of Leptis Magna, where Henry Hathaway was shooting *Legend of the Lost*, and at Ghadames, an oasis on the Tunisian, Libyan and Algerian borders (two exteriors discarded by the director). Then Ray, Lambert, Keller, d'Eaubonne and Christian Ferry went to make a final selection. They discovered in the desert, 68 miles from Tripoli on the road to Jefren, the circular ruins of a fortified Berber town, which Ray christened Crown City: inside they found letters or signs in an unknown Berber script. Crown City took a strong hold on Ray's imagination, resurfacing in at least one later project (*The Children's Crusade*).

Lambert: 'We got to Paris, and then Nick said to me, "I'm not quite happy about this script as it is." The usual thing began to happen. It was a pattern of Nick's, and this time I couldn't get out of him what was wrong with it. He said, "I don't know, it's fine and yet I feel there's something I want, but I can't tell you what I want." This kind of thing. Then he said, "Would you mind meeting an old friend of mine called Vladimir Pozner? I think he might have some ideas." ' It is probable that at this point Ray was already working with Pozner, who had been one of the writers on the Roosevelt memorial programme directed by Losey and Ray. A cosmopolitan polyglot, the novelist had worked in Hollywood, then returned to France during the witch-hunts.[3] Ray called him soon after his arrival in Paris.

According to Pozner: 'He was staying in one of those hotels around the Bois de Boulogne where scriptwriters and film-makers work, mostly foreign ones because it's too expensive for the French or their producers. He wanted to change some of the dialogue – as much as possible – and also elements in the story. But the producer and the other writer were not to know that anyone else was working on it. Graetz especially, with his American connections, mustn't know about me, because of the blacklist. Even the secretary doing the typing! All the work was done in that hotel; so I could go there when I wanted, after giving him a call. I wrote the revisions, and he would take them to the secretary on another floor to type. Then he would show them to the other scriptwriter, saying he'd written them himself. I had left America in the autumn of 1947 before all the fuss in Washington. He stayed, he'd lived under McCarthyism. He knew how you had to lie, as so many people did in Hollywood, and we did the same thing in Paris. I changed a lot of things in the story; the ending was completely new. But it wasn't my story. I was like a mechanic repairing a broken-down car. I read the whole thing through carefully, then we talked for hours about what we disliked or didn't dislike, and why – and basically we thought pretty much alike. I would make suggestions, we'd talk some more, then he'd say, 'OK, let's do it." '

Lambert readily accepted Pozner's contribution. Hardy was a different matter: told about the changes, he threatened to veto the script – a veto Ray and Lambert only then discovered he had the right to exercise. During the weeks preceding filming, Graetz turned out, according to Lambert, to be 'one of those producers who hated directors. Loathed them. But he was cunning. He would be nice at first, enthusiastic and encouraging. Then the knife came out.'⁴

After his ban on changes to the script, another Graetz intervention shook up the casting. A third major character was Lutze, the German officer taken prisoner by the commando unit. Almost non-existent in the novel, he served in the November script – even more so than Lieutenant Barton – as a reflection of the clash between Leith and Brand, opposing his commitment to Leith's lack of it, his militarism to Brand's. Lambert: 'As you can imagine, Curd Jürgens was going to play the Nazi. It was a perfectly valid part for Jürgens to play, and Graetz had said from the start, "I want Curd Jürgens to play the Nazi." Fine. We came to Paris and he approved the casting of the two men: Burton and Clift at first, then Burton and Newman. Then Graetz announced that Jürgens was going to play Brand. We said it was impossible, that you couldn't have a German playing in a picture where the Germans were the other side. Graetz says, "Oh, I've thought about that, it's all right. You explain that he's South African, a Boer. That explains his accent." '

The release of *Et Dieu ... créa la femme* and *Michel Strogoff*, one after the other in the closing weeks of 1956, must certainly have influenced Graetz's decision. Jürgens was now a big European star; he would appear in four films within a year (*Œil pour œil, Les Espions, Bitter*

Victory and *Tamango*), and then try Hollywood. There were some (Michel Kelber, for instance) who felt that this switching of roles had disastrous consequences. Claiming that it was impossible for him to go to Libya, Graetz delegated authority to his 'pretty blonde wife', Janine, who, Jürgens wrote in his autobiography, 'helped me to fight fatigue'.[5] Their relationship gave the German actor inordinate influence over the script. As for Burton, originally cast as Brand, he found himself playing Leith.

At the same time, the producer got rid of Gavin Lambert: 'When we got back from looking at the locations, Graetz called me in and said, "How was it?" I said, "Fine. It's perfect, there's everything we want there." He said, "No, I'm not asking you that. How was Nick Ray? Was he drinking? What was he taking? What did he do in the evening?" I said I wasn't talking about that, and he said if I didn't I was off the picture. So I said, "Okay, I'm off the picture." He said, "It's a great pity. It'd be very useful for you, and I would like to have you around during the shooting, because I think you're a great help to Nick. But if you're not on my side and I can't have confidence in you, I just don't want to see you again." Naturally I told Nick about this. Nick, of course, hits the roof, insists that I'm brought back on the picture. Graetz says no. Nick says that he won't do the picture. Graetz says, "Then I'll sue you." So in fact they go to Libya and I'm not allowed to go.'

So for Lambert the film was doomed, and he could write in all sincerity in 1958: 'The story from there on was one of blighted hopes, threats of litigation, incessant battles; and the "free" film an American director had come to Europe to make turned into a straitjacket like the most hidebound Hollywood studio product.' This was true, but not the whole truth. The unit that left for Tripoli on Sunday, 10 February 1957 (effectively at double strength, not for efficiency but for reasons of co-production with Italy) was selected entirely by Graetz. Ray, however, found some allies – indeed, friends – in it.

Filming started on Friday, 15 February at 'Crown City', in the desert. Then the unit returned to Tripoli for the scenes of the attack on the German HQ. This was represented by a police station near the Arch of Marcus Aurelius, the only remaining Roman ruin in town. 'Everything was going well,' according to Michel Kelber, 'the script was very good, we'd had enough time to prepare. Nicholas had rehearsed all the scenes of the commando attack. He was very fond of rehearsing, and he was in good form. In the dunes [around Tripoli] we filmed by both night and day. For night scenes, I had an enormous number of arcs and generator units, all I could have hoped for: I was never refused anything in the

53　*Bitter Victory*: shooting in Tripoli

equipment line.' Very soon, the difficulties of filming in the desert made themselves felt. The locations were within a radius of about 120 miles from the capital, but not easy to get to. 'You had to leave the hotel at about four in the morning, drive for an hour and a half or two hours in an ordinary car, then switch to jeeps because the going got too rough for light cars, and still you had another hour's drive before getting there. We'd arrive around 8.30 a.m. and start filming; then at night, the same trip back. We slept very little. It was awful. Overtime run mad. In the desert, there's sand everywhere. At the least breath of wind, it gets under your eyelids, into car engines. So we had a van which used to be vacuumed twice a day and which sealed hermetically; we'd load and unload the magazines in there, otherwise the film would have been scratched.'

Yet another intervention rocked the production. Jürgens, sharing a suite at the Grand Hotel with the 'executive producer on location' (as she is credited on the film), objected to the character quite beyond redemption which Ray had turned Brand into, precisely in order to adapt the role to an actor devoid of any ambiguity. Janine Graetz conveyed his wishes to her husband in Paris. The latter brought in a new scriptwriter: Paul Gallico, Hungarian by origin, resident in Liechtenstein, working for the British cinema. Gallico came to Paris and began to 'clean up' the script, totally ignorant of the context or the terrain. His pages were telexed to Ray. 'He used to receive three-page cables, entire novels describing the new scene for the script,' according to Kelber, who has never forgotten some of Gallico's suggestions. 'At one point, Burton is stung by a scorpion. In one of these new scenes, he is woken by the sound the scorpion makes moving on the sand . . . It's true, honestly!'

The script approved by the producer often arrived after the scenes so rewritten had been shot. As Ray noted on his copy: 'Script received in three instalments with dictum from Graetz, "Not one word to be changed." ' Ray added exclamatory comments to the margins of Gallico's scenes. The one in which Leith is woken by the sound the scorpion makes on the sand is indeed there: to leave a doubt as to whether Brand is guilty, Leith notices the scorpion a moment before it stings him. His task being to vindicate Brand, Gallico hastened to underline Leith's self-destructive nature. Elaborating the fine dialogue between the two men as they trudge through the desert, he asserts that he has 'indicated strongly Leith's death wish and that he considers his life has come to an end through what he has done as well as failed to do' – as though that death wish had not already been indicated perfectly clearly enough (and had not been one of the turning points in the character of Jesse James in Ray's previous film). Gallico also laced his dialogue with unintentional humour, as in the exchange which concludes the walk in the desert:

BRAND (thinking hard): The intimate way she called you Jimmy . . .
LEITH: Happens to be my name.
BRAND (something dawns at last): Leith! You knew Jane . . . before . . .
LEITH (looks at Brand with mock admiration): Home in one, old boy!
[Ray's marginal note: 'Wow!']

Ray was now spending every night rewriting the scenes that were to be shot the next day, based on the script and the Jürgens-Gallico changes. He communicated once a week with Gavin Lambert, who was wary enough of Graetz not to use the telephone at the Hotel Raphaël, and would go to wait for Ray's calls at the post office on the Champs-Elysées.

Filming started to fall behind schedule. Edouard Luntz: 'With the producer absent, there were contradictory views about everything, there was a Columbia executive who could only see the practical side . . .' 'At this point,' according to Kelber, 'Nicholas started to drink. He had lost confidence in himself. Since he'd had a big emotional problem just before this, it all got on top of him. He suffered psychoses [*sic*]. He'd suddenly lose the use of one of his legs, for instance, and have to use a stick; or he'd lose his voice, open his mouth and be unable to speak, and so on.'

'Nick went through hell on that film,' Lucie Lichtig said. 'But what was hard for us was that at night, while we were typing away or working, he'd be gambling.' (The casino was situated in the hotel itself.) 'He used to gamble like a crazy man,' Kelber recalled, 'betting on all the numbers at roulette, forgetting what numbers he was playing, losing everything; the croupiers soon tumbled to him and pocketed everything. It really was a disaster.' Ray was accompanied by a young woman, Manon, a Moroccan Cherifian he had met in Saint-Germain-des-Prés, and with whom he had a stormy relationship. 'First they'd quarrel until one or two in the morning,' according to Lucie Lichtig, 'then he'd go to the casino. He wouldn't get any sleep except in the jeep taking him on location in the morning.'[6]

The problem of communicating with the unit didn't help matters, although as a matter of fact Ray got on better with the Libyans than the crew did, especially the Italians. As Luntz saw it: 'He was a man who had his films inside his head; but most of the time, when he arrived on set and people were waiting for him to tell them what to do, he was incapable of saying, "I want this, or that". He could explain what he *didn't* want. He could talk about the set or the performances and say he didn't want this or that, but he couldn't say what he wanted. I had just been working with Grémillon, who was a bit like him, and who always had terrible production problems, so I was used to it.'

Yet amid all this confusion, the film was taking shape. Steeped in the various contradictory versions, familiar with every facet of his characters, confronted by the desert and by confused but malleable actors (Jürgens excepted), Ray took decisions which radically altered the film's direction. Lucie Lichtig: 'I've never met anyone like him where directing actors is concerned. Sometimes I'd say to him, "But, Nick, this isn't exactly what you wanted"; and he'd say, "I know, but I'll use the best bit. Let it go, the next take will be for me, but I'll use that little bit." He'd know that little bit he needed as soon as he saw it. He would never go against the actor, claiming to be right, never. But if he wasn't satisfied, you did it again until he was. And rehearsals, rehearsals, rehearsals. He felt that actors were under no pressure so long as they were rehearsing, and the crew didn't have to be present; so there was no wear on people's nerves. He often said to me, "You can't expect everybody to be equally

54   *Bitter Victory*: Nicholas Ray and Richard Burton

involved in the film. You have to leave them free until you need them.''
That was how he got the best out of them, and why actors often didn't
realize they were being directed.

'He and Burton got on very well together. It's odd, actually, because
they talked more about art and the theatre than about the cinema or the
film itself. The film meant rehearsals, essentially, but in-between times
they would talk about art, music or the theatre. They understood each
other from the moment they met, but it was something the young English
actors in the cast couldn't buy, they couldn't make him out at all. Nigel
Green was terrific, but hated being directed by Nick. He was acting in a
fury all the time, raging at what Nick was making him do.' According to

301

Luntz, 'Nick very soon realized that Nigel Green was extraordinary. The mad scene, that was Green; he was twice as drunk as Ray when he did it.'

The more perceptive technicians realized what Ray was doing (a tactic admittedly out of order from a professional or practical point of view) without being able to take part. 'His improvisations with the actors were always a great success,' Kelber remarked. 'He used to improvise when he was in good form. That said, it was hard working with Nick, because he often changed his mind, and sometimes made transitions difficult . . . Sometimes the results were pretty unexpected, because Nicholas would say, "We'll shoot here," and I'd only have one arc. We'd roll anyway, and got astonishing results, because I'd have no other lights to hand and it had to be done quickly. "Shoot it under protest," he'd say to me.'

From this derives the dynamic of scenes like the nocturnal battle in the desert, or speeches like Leith's reaction to Crown City ('Tenth century . . . Too modern for me'), elaborated from day to day. Thus one of the few lines of dialogue originally retained from the novel – 'I polish off the wounded and save the dead' – forgotten in subsequent revisions, resurfaced to become 'I kill the living and I save the dead,' transforming the whole scene in which the wounded are killed. What was filmed is far from faithful to the version authorized by the producer. Each stage, completing the work begun on paper, served to develop the relationship between the protagonists, paring down incidents external to the theme.

In the novel, Brand refuses to lend Barton a hand when he is engaged by Germans, so Leith goes to his aid, asking Brand to go on ahead with the documents. In the 'temporary' script, Brand lets Leith go to help, with no mention of not waiting, but gives the order to leave as soon as Leith is gone; as in the book, Leith kills the wounded in Barton's presence. In the script, the commando unit has already regrouped; Brand *asks* Leith to remain behind with the wounded. Gallico's suggestion was that Barton should turn up alone with Lutze, Leith having stayed behind with the wounded. Brand thus assumes that Leith means to rejoin them later under his own steam, and does not wait for him. In the scene as shot, Barton, Lutze and the wounded are with the main squad. Brand tells Leith, who immediately accepts, that he is to stay with the wounded. Wilkins (who offers his services to finish the wounded off) and Dunnigan are detailed to stay with him; but Leith declines their company, and is left alone with the dying men.

The relative importance assumed by any particular character, of course, also had to do with relations with the actor. Barton was played by a South African actor who, according to Sumner Williams, 'carried a swagger stick through the towns of Libya, beating the Arabs out of the way, only it wasn't for the film!' His role was cut down in favour of Wilkins. Edouard Luntz: 'There were extraordinary things about Ray if you listened to him. You had to try to understand. I learned a lot of things from him that I never learned from anyone else. Where to put the camera: for him, it was where you could best see people's eyes. I noticed that whenever he had people playing a scene, he'd be below them, the better to see their eyes.'

The reckoning to be met – going over-schedule – was not excessive in Kelber's opinion, given the scale of the production and the location contingencies. The production office in Paris decreed differently. Two or three weeks before the anticipated wrap on location filming, they were given a week to finish. Luntz again: 'For all the scenes that remained to be filmed, he was obliged to do establishing shots, then pick up the scene in detail at the Victorine Studio in Nice. You can tell . . . more or less. Sometimes the desert, the real thing, looks like a set, you know.'

Libya (finishing on 22 March) was followed by the Victorine Studio. Still to be filmed for the desert sequences were the scene at the well (except for establishing shots), almost all of the scorpion scene (16 set-ups), and the final exchange between Brand and Leith as the *ghibli* (sand-storm) blows up. One planned scene, after Wilkins's fit of madness, in which he and Brand watch a scorpion crawl over Wilkins's foot and 'commit suicide' in the fire, was eliminated. In addition to these, all the interior scenes remained to be done in Nice, and a few exteriors with Jane. For this role, Ray had considered Moira Shearer, the young English ballerina, because she was 'very innocent-looking and very English' (Lambert). Graetz chose Ruth Roman, who boasted neither of these qualities, but whom he took to be a star.

During these weeks, scenes crucial to the relationship between Leith and Brand remained to be done, as well as the ending, about which there was still no agreement. 'It was hard going,' according to Luntz. 'There was a lot of tension, and they kept on rushing Nick, especially as the end came in sight. At some point, they must have realized that this wasn't going to be a very commercial film, and decided to keep the costs down. I saw just what sort of terrible pressure could be put on a director by people who didn't give a damn. Enough to make anybody crack.'

On a personal level, those weeks at the Victorine were as chaotic as before. According to Sumner Williams: 'We went to Monte Carlo one night and he lost about $60,000 at the table. I was writing the cheques. On the way back he stopped on the beach, and went and washed his face in the water.'[7] He nevertheless managed to film the relationship between Jane and Leith, their exclusion of the outside world, their secret feelings, exactly as he wanted to. Furthermore, according to Lucie Lichtig: 'He managed to pull a fast one on Jürgens: he made him think he was playing the hero, but showed by the way he filmed Burton and Pellegrin that the character was a coward. Jürgens never caught on. The only thing he did against his will was the ending, when he pins the medal on the dummy. Jürgens didn't want to do it. It was the thing there was most trouble about in Nice, but since we were in France, Mme Graetz couldn't get her own way.'

On 10 April, Ray eliminated the long dialogue scene preceding Leith's death, instead borrowing from Walt Whitman for Leith's last words as he saves Brand's life by sheltering him from the sandstorm with his own body: 'I contradict myself! I always contradict myself!' As for the ending, a compromise was made affecting what mattered to the producers, but not to Ray: the militaristic aspect.

To summarize the evolution of the ending: in the novel, Lutze burns the documents, and Brand, blamed for his conduct of the operation, is abandoned by Jane, condemned by his men. In the first script, Brand refuses the decoration General Paterson proposes to award him in order to create the impression that the operation was a success. It was Pozner who subsequently introduced the idea that he should, on the contrary, accept the medal, only to pin it on one of the training dummies in the final shot. Gallico's idea was that Brand should confess his cowardice to Jane ('No balls!', Ray notes in the margin), but the operation has been a success, and he accepts the decoration while his men look on ironically. As he receives the medal, Brand's eyes meet Jane's, and Gallico suggested shooting three endings – the look on his face indicates that she has forgiven him, that she is leaving him, or that she (along with the audience) is undecided – leaving the choice up to 'the producer and the director', or indeed to different countries!

In the completed film, 'clumsy' direction leaves it unclear how successful Lutze is in burning the documents. Ray has Brand lie once more: he tells Jane that he wanted to save Leith, who died, he says, before completing a message for her: 'I suppose he would have said . . . Tell Jane I love her.' When the General comes in with the men, Jane walks out of the scene and out of the film. The General's congratulatory speech, announcing that 'General Rommel is shortly going to find himself in a very delicate situation' (spoken off, and possibly added during post-production), while contradicting the original conception (the failure of the mission), is played over the watching faces of the men, stressing its hollowness. The men turn away from Brand and leave, Wilkins last of all, grinning enigmatically at him. Left alone, Brand pins the medal on to a dummy, and walks out of frame.

Not only did Ray fail to respect the suggestions (or obligations) represented by Gallico's revisions, he also made distinct departures from both the novel and the script he wrote with Gavin Lambert. There had come a point, therefore, in which the collaboration with Lambert was no longer dominant, and Ray had gone off in a different direction, first with Pozner, and then – under the stimulus of filming – alone, though still consulting Lambert. This explains the disappointment Lambert expressed over compromises which, on the screen, emerge primarily as an elaboration markedly diverging from his own conception.

Filming was completed (or once again cut short, according to Kelber, who had to spend two or three days doing continuity bits 'in a corner of a studio' back in Paris); from 15 February to 23 April, it had taken nine-and-a-half weeks – a week-and-a-half less than originally scheduled. Gavin Lambert saw Ray return to Paris 'a wreck. Ravaged, traumatized. It had obviously been horrendous. And I think the film was more or less taken out of his hands. To me, *Bitter Victory* was a crucial point in his life, because he was very excited about the European adventure. I must admit that at first I was taken in by Graetz; it wasn't until it was too late to get out that one realized one was dealing with some kind of psychopath. But as I say, I think this was a disaster for Nick, because he was disappointed by the whole thing. His personal problems, the drinking . . . and he got seriously into drugs in Paris, too . . . that's when it started. So I really think it was a turning-point; if the film had gone well, his whole life might have been quite different.'

Lambert – who had started writing his first novel, *The Slide Area*, during his forced inactivity in Paris – backed off: 'I thought I'd gone as far as I could go in that sort of collaboration, and he was in very bad shape. We were extremely good friends, but I thought perhaps we should stop working together for a while.'[8] When Ray received an offer from MGM (this was *Party Girl*, one year and one film later), Lambert decided not to work on it. Nor was he involved in the post-production work on *Bitter Victory*, about which there can be no dispute: no matter what his disagreements with Graetz, Ray supervised the editing, music and mixing (at Venice, he said he had 'done exactly what he wanted').[9]

He had an excellent team to work with: the editor Léonide Azar, also a compulsive gambler, and Renée Lichtig, the continuity girl's sister, who had discovered Ray during the first brief run of *They Live by Night* at the Broadway in Paris. 'One day – I was already an editor – Lucie said to me, "Do you want to do the sound editing on *Bitter Victory*?" I said yes, right away. He got me down to Nice, and I waited there for the unit to return. I had no idea what Nicholas Ray would be like physically: he might have been small, fat, thin . . . and then I saw this extraordinary man, with greying, curly hair and violet eyes, who limped slightly, using a stick.' Renée Lichtig, who had worked with Henri Langlois, introduced the two of them, thus initiating a lifelong friendship with the founder of the Cinémathèque Française and with Mary Meerson.

The composer Maurice Le Roux remembers Azar (Russian by origin, he was a brother of the directors Alexander Granovsky and Boris Ingster) editing the film as it used to be done in the silent days. 'He would hold the strips of film in his hand and say, "I'm going to cut here," then snip away, judging by eye. The bits he cut out, he just threw away. I was appalled, thinking of the loss of maybe twenty usable frames. Actually, there are shots missing: you feel the need of a reaction shot . . . but it couldn't be found. Every time this was pointed out to him, Azar would say, "It's not my fault. It was never filmed." Renée put things right; she more or less saved the film.' According to Renée Lichtig: 'Azar had no confidence in Nick, accusing him of drinking. One day Azar announced to me, "We'll do the mixing in three weeks." "I'm sorry," I said, "I'm in charge of the sound, and nothing's ready yet." I went to see Nick, who said, "Don't worry. He only works until eight o'clock anyway. I'll come and work through the night with the assistants." So that's what I did for three weeks, and that was how the film got finished. Azar never found out.

'Nick would always intervene on the screen [during projection], never in the cutting-room. Like Renoir, actually. Nick would choose what he wanted, and he had plenty to choose from. If it wasn't there in one set-up, it would be there in another. But he didn't take what he wanted just from the angle he wanted. Because it wasn't the angle that interested him, it was the performance. There was always a take which contained the phrase, the little bit he wanted. And that was his strength; even while filming, he could see that this line had something he needed.'

In May, Ray took a rough cut to the Cannes Festival to show the Soviet delegation; he wanted Dimitri Shostakovich to compose the score. The idea would certainly have been considered a provocation by a producer interested in the American market; it was also taken as such by the Soviets, who let it be known that they would never be party to such an exercise in the demythification of the hero.[10]

It was through Pierre Lazareff, formerly an associate on *The Voice of America* and now editor of *France-Soir*, that Ray met Maurice Le Roux. 'In those days,' according to Le Roux, 'Lazareff and his wife used to give lunches and dinners every Sunday at Louveciennes, to which everybody who was anybody in the political and artistic worlds was invited. People knew very well that when they were invited, it was because something was going to happen during the week, because Lazareff had a genius for knowing three days or a week in advance what was going to be happening everywhere in the world. Every weekend he'd have a list of the comings-and-goings of important political figures, and he knew how to get hold of ministers on the telephone.' Maurice Le Roux had composed very little film music, but he was an orchestra conductor, had written a book on Monteverdi, and was considered to be precocious and talented. He had not escaped the attention of Lazareff, who brought Ray to see him. 'I didn't know a word of English. He came here, I played the piano a bit, but he didn't seem much interested. I went to see his film, and loved it. But it seemed like an enormous job to me, long and hard, and I'd have a month and a half to two months to do it in. Graetz wanted a big orchestration – people made decisions like that in those days.

'I tried to ask Nicholas what he thought, which parts he felt should be scored. "Don't worry, we can talk about that, but come on, we're going out tonight." I hate nightclubs, restaurants . . . He took me to the Catalan, a little nightclub near the Palais-Royal, castanets, songs, flamenco, Spanish dancing, all that. He was in love with a girl who sang or danced. We'd go out in the evening, hang around till three in the morning, the same again the next day, and that went on for at least two weeks, maybe three. I started to do a little work, I saw his film twice, I went to the cutting-rooms . . .'

After this 'trial period', the slightly panicky Le Roux finally realized that, during these encounters, the director had come to accept him and extend his trust. 'Respect for a creative talent like his own, no great knowledge of classical music, great sensibility, responsibility – laziness too! So he didn't interfere. I wrote what everybody says is my best film score because I was able to do exactly what I wanted. I found a dramatic progression. In the credit sequence, it starts with *musique concrète*: over the dummies and close-combat training, I used only percussion sounds, objects, with a little high-pitched trumpet imitating the military style, but so remotely that it was just another sound. After which we have strictly dodecaphonic music for a little while, then atonal music a little later on. Then suddenly, halfway through the film, in the scene in the desert where Leith carries the dying soldier on his back, a tonal theme in G flat major develops, gradually prepared for but emerging only now, and not – as in a lot of films – over the credits or soon after. It emerges here, late in the film, and after that this theme remains constant to the end. But I made

307

sure – one of my ideas about film music – that the theme should be in tiny fragments, linked by silences inhabited by the accompaniment, which meant that it could be strung out over a lengthy period, meanwhile allowing the characters to talk. You were being led, and the silences formed part of the sound.'[11]

Le Roux suffered only two disappointments: the same recording of one of his themes was used over two sequences instead of one, and Graetz tried to compensate for the pessimism of the ending by forcing him to finish on conventional upbeat chords, whereas what he had written was 'music still blowing from the desert', slowing in tempo over the shot of the dummy. This ending was in any case eliminated in most countries. In its original version, the film ran for 103 minutes; it was reduced to 87 minutes for the version dubbed into French; it ran for 90 minutes in Great Britain, where it ended when help arrived; and 82 minutes in the United States.[12]

Over the last few weeks, Ray was physically exhausted, and had to go into hospital after the mixing was finished. He had just been invited to direct a film in the US, but this time for an independent producer, Budd Schulberg, which delighted him. He continued to envisage projects in Europe: *Passport* again, a film with Ingrid Bergman, another ('the drama of an American woman abroad') with Betsy Blair, who was living in Paris.[13] The rumours circulating about the filming of *Bitter Victory* probably helped to prevent them from materializing. Gavin Lambert claimed that 'Graetz wrote to people here [in the States] saying, "I want you to know that Nicholas Ray is a drunkard and you should never employ him." He wrote to Fox (he was a great friend of Spyros Skouras), he wrote to Warners.'

Bitter Victory was one of the four films (out of fifteen) invited to the Venice Festival by the selection committee (the rest being nominated by participating countries). Meeting with a baffled reception, it was not among the prizewinners (the main award went to another Ray, Satyajit, for *Aparajito*). Heading his comments in *Arts*, 'The only intelligent film shown at the Festival', Eric Rohmer noted: 'Ray is more likely to perplex because the schematism is even more extreme than in his earlier work. Scarcely has one move been hinted at than the next is under way, and the audience naturally gets winded trying to keep up. I must confess to having been somewhat disconcerted myself, failing to experience before the screen the same sense of complaisance that enveloped me as I read the book. I was expecting a film that surprised and resisted me, but it doesn't resist me quite as I would have thought. I was expecting a "delirious" film, but the delirium is not quite what I anticipated.'[14]

Meeting Ray in Venice, Jean Domarchi remarked that 'problems of form don't seem to interest him overmuch', any more than questions of external logic; asked about improbabilities during the commando raid on the German HQ, Ray responded by saying, 'Material details should always be subordinate to the rhythm of the film.'[15] It would be difficult to establish a narrative model, a formal system applicable to all of Ray's work. This particular film nevertheless establishes a narrative mode quite distinct from any of his earlier work. The tendency to abstraction is quite deliberate. Even though the elimination of certain scenes may be attributed to production circumstances, those circumstances are given purpose; most important, they lead to a distillation of dialogue, which interiorizes the duel over Jane (brought out into the open in the various versions of the script), leaving the conflict between Leith and Brand to revolve around existential questions.

For the first time, one can see a film taking shape along lines that are suggested but left unexplored, amidst unlikely military manoeuvres. Another film-maker would have tried to paper over these holes in the logic, or to make them acceptable. Nothing like that happens here, where the military operation simply fades into the background. Rohmer again, writing from Venice: 'The property of an achieved work of art is that it yields (examples abound in modern painting) a sense of incompleteness. The essence seems barely touched upon, the accessories to be treated as unduly important.'

The progression here follows the relationship between the three protagonists, seconded by a few other characters: Paterson, Callander, Wilkins, Mokrane. The images are tightly framed, determined by eyes *looking*; so too are movements in space. Waiting at the beginning for General Paterson to see him, Brand makes nervous, desultory gestures, crushing out his cigarette. Leith, similarly waiting, is first seen standing on a table, repairing a fan – for no reason except that his position is higher (and more unstable) than Brand's, who sees and talks to him as he emerges from the General's office. The positions are reversed in their final confrontation, when the dying Leith voices his contempt for Brand: 'You're an empty uniform, starched by authority so that it can stand up by itself.' 'But I *am* standing' is all Brand can find to say. 'Yes, you're right,' Leith concludes. 'For the first time, I almost have some respect for you.'

The sequence in which the wounded men are killed demonstrates the extent to which the actions of the two men are governed less by military reasons than by the film-maker's need to clarify their relationship at this point. Even a magnificently spare action scene, like the attack on the German HQ, is thematically concerned only with the respective attitudes of the two officers. In the scene preceding the actual attack, seeing Brand hesitate, Leith takes the initiative in stabbing the sentry; but it is not the German, it is Leith himself who utters a groan of pain. During the attack, each German killed echoes this murder, and what we witness is a series of professional killings, one set-up for each action. The moral is drawn when Wilkins (a burglar in civilian life) gets the safe open. 'Wilkie's won the war!' says one of the sergeants (Christopher Lee). 'So crime doesn't pay, eh?' Wilkins comments ironically. Brand, kneeling in front of the open safe, looks round as Leith comes in, as though caught in a shameful act. This two-handed game, with each trying to discover what the other knows without asking directly, began when Brand made a jealous scene with Jane. It continues during the march through the desert. From the moment Brand asks him to stay with the wounded, Leith knows what to expect, but Brand also knows. Mokrane sees Leith try to save a man who is already dead. Brand doesn't know whether Wilkins's fit of madness, when he mutters 'Jimmy and Jane, Jane and Jimmy . . .', is simulated or not. Barton considers Leith's violation of orders, uncertain whether or not he is a model to be copied ('I don't know enough to break the rules'). Brand sees that the men think he is too much of a coward to drink the possibly poisoned water from the well, so he drinks. Leith has seen that Brand is a coward, Brand knows that Leith wants to die. Mokrane sees (in a deliberately ambiguous scene) that Brand has seen what he, Mokrane, does not yet realize is a scorpion heading towards Leith.

It is evident both how much Ray's approach owes to his interest in psychoanalysis, and how his explorations draw on Camus. But with *Bitter Victory*, what one sees is a conception of cinema as a means to total expression starting to formulate. This, being no Eisenstein and no master of the latter's speculative methods, Ray could achieve only by risking everything he knew, surrendering some ground to make advances elsewhere, losing overall control. *Bigger Than Life*, the film *The True Story of Jesse James* might have been, *Bitter Victory*, then *Wind Across the Everglades*: films dragging anchor both in the object of their strategy – paranoia, death wish, hysteria – and in the strategy itself. Difficulty in communication becomes opaqueness, provoking puzzlement or active dislike. *Mise en scène* becomes *mise en crise*, first with the closed set and daily revisions on *Bigger Than Life*; then, as with Penelope's never-ending web, the constant questioning of the work in hand, the refusal to make definitive decisions – initially provoked by circumstances, a way of coping with enforced compromises, as on *The Lusty Men*, then a challenge accepted, indeed forced on him by his increasing unease in talking to people. He had a dream inside him, as Luntz put it, which he couldn't bring out. 'We don't get excited enough about the medium of cinema itself,' Ray declared in a press release before embarking on *Bitter Victory*. 'We must heighten the sense of entertainment. Perhaps we should all study our medium more thoroughly. After all, it should remain a "moving picture".'

Were this dream of an *other* cinema simply hypothetical or pure pretence, a mere anecdote in his career or his life, were it not that glimpses of it make themselves forcefully felt in these perhaps imperfectly achieved films, it would be of no great interest. Catastrophe becomes the film's momentum, but also its instrument – so hazardous, so indefinable that it is no great surprise to find technicians and actors beginning to write Ray off, or praising only his other work, never the film on which they themselves had collaborated.

Alert filmgoers, themselves budding film-makers, took up the challenge. Writing about Ray's films, they were soon not alone; Jean-Luc Godard's review of *Bitter Victory* was headed 'Beyond the Stars', and began with the now celebrated dictum, 'The cinema is Nicholas Ray.'[16]

Just prior to his departure for Libya, Ray had his first encounter with a writer from *Cahiers du Cinéma*. Charles Bitsch, commissioned to write a short piece for the weekly *Arts*, seized the opportunity to ask him for an interview. Since 1954, the magazine, still very cloistered, had undertaken an unprecedented series of taped interviews (recorded on wire in Ray's case), systematically covering the career of a film-maker: Becker, Renoir, Buñuel, Rossellini, Gance. Hollywood directors would come later, because the editorial staff were very isolated, having virtually no contact with the foreign trade press. The only way to find out where a film-maker might be staying was to ring round the hotels to which Americans usually went.

Although Ray knew the magazine, having received several issues, Bitsch's request stunned him at first. 'He was obviously rather panicky at the thought of this interview, which he felt was something both very important and very novel. As I recall, I saw him once at his hotel, the Raphaël, just for a drink – having prepared a number of questions – before the interview proper. He finally agreed to quite a short meeting, and I went to see him with the *Cahiers* recorder almost on the eve of his departure. It must have been late afternoon, and we carried on long after the allotted time, because the most vivid memory I have of that interview is the number of silences that cropped up, totally unpredictably, and might last maybe two or three minutes by the clock. Furthermore, he never looked at the person he was talking to; he'd either be looking down or up above your head, eyes lost somewhere beyond the horizon. So the interview limped along, and when he came to the end, I got the feeling that he'd grown quite to enjoy himself as time went by. I think it was the first time he'd been confronted with someone who had seen all his films (except the one or two never released in France; some of them I'd seen five, six, eight times), the first time he'd met someone who knew his films well and wanted to talk about them.'

They Live by Night, selected by the organizers of the Rendez-vous de Biarritz,[17] had marked the start of a dialogue with younger French critics which continued throughout Ray's Hollywood career, without interruption after *Johnny Guitar*. Up to *Rebel Without a Cause*, these critics recalled the revelation of his first film (seen by some at the Broadway, by others later at the Studio Parnasse). After 1955, Ray's films were awaited with prejudice in favour, and received with visionary understanding. Through the mediation of the *Cahiers* team writing in *Arts* (Truffaut, Rivette, Rohmer, Bitsch; later Claude de Givray, Jean Douchet), Bazin in *Le Parisien libéré*, Bazin and Doniol-Valcroze in *France-Observateur*, plus a few articles in *Radio-Cinéma-Télévision* (Daniel Kostoveski and Jean-Marie Straub in 1955, Claude Beylie in 1958),[18] Ray's films were watched and awaited by whatever France could boast in the way of an informed audience.

Arriving in Europe, Ray knew little of this dialogue, except that his films roused an echo that often surprised him. The attitude of *Cahiers du Cinéma* to his work left him perplexed. He wrote to Eric Rohmer after the latter reviewed *Rebel Without a Cause*: 'I had written that his heroes and heroines have a certain family resemblance,' Rohmer explains. 'He sent me a very short letter, saying thank you for your review, etc., but James Dean isn't like Sterling Hayden, nor is Natalie Wood like Joan Crawford. At the time I was very proud . . .' It is impossible to work in Hollywood and remain impervious to ideas which weld the entire profession together. Ray therefore had difficulty understanding an approach which attempted to trace a film-maker's impulses as one might a painter's (the comparison recurs frequently in Rohmer's reviews) with sympathetic understanding and a feeling for hidden kinships between films of which the film-maker himself is sometimes unaware. Ray joked about it to Sumner Williams: 'I'm beginning to believe my own write-up,' he said when he discovered the admiration in which *Johnny Guitar* was held, a film he still detested. French cinephiles attributed a film *a priori* to its director, and were interested in the film, not its box-office performance. Even the polemics with *Positif* (Ray, along with Fritz Lang, Cukor, Mankiewicz, Preminger, Hathaway and Hawks, featured in their collective

article of 1954, 'A Few Over-Admired Film-Makers') granted the director a status he was refused by American critics; while Roger Tailleur's
soundly documented criticisms of *Bigger Than Life*[19] were conceived on
an altogether more exacting level than those of American critics, who
never got beyond the obvious meanings, hamstrung by their fear of putting off 'the wider audience' whose interests they felt called upon to
defend.

French filmgoers shared a sense of Ray as a film-maker incarnating the
very idea of an *auteur*, in the meaning of the word developed during these
years. The Christmas 1955 issue of *Cahiers du Cinéma*, No. 54, was
devoted to 'The State of the American Cinema'. Jacques Rivette, in
'Notes on a Revolution', singled out four names, '*at present* the
undoubted spearheads' of what seemed to him to be ushering in 'the age
of the *auteur*'; Nicholas Ray, Richard Brooks, Anthony Mann, Robert
Aldrich. 'They are, in different ways, the *naïves*: Ray in the childlike
candour of his eye, the provocative humility of his narratives; Brooks and
Mann in the anachronistic intensity of their direction; Aldrich in the
frankness of his approach and childish delight in effects. For years the
cinema has been dying of intelligence and subtlety; Rossellini is breaking
down the doors, but take a breath, too, of this gust of fresh air blowing
from across the sea.'

This comparison with Rossellini (and similarly with Bresson) was not
uncommon. The reactions roused by Ray's films went far beyond the
respect and affection given to the three other American directors. There
was a sense of affiliation with his work, and after *Johnny Guitar* one
could see the symptoms of what Americans, in their resistance to their
native film-makers, later described as a cult. 'Nicholas Ray', Claude
Beylie wrote in retrospect, 'is one of the few American film-makers of his
generation about whom European critics were, and are, unanimous.'[20] In
1973, in a documentary about Ray, *I'm a Stranger Here Myself*, François
Truffaut essayed an explanation aimed at Americans:

A film like *Johnny Guitar* assumed greater importance in my life than
in Nicholas Ray's. It was a film I fell in love with as soon as I saw it
[. . .] I thought it very powerful, very profound about male-female
relationships, with a very interesting theme relating to a particular
stage in a love affair: the bitterness of people who have been in love
and meet up again. I don't think any other film handled this so well.
What attracted us was that there was something European about this
man from Hollywood. European in what way? Perhaps in the frailty,
the vulnerability of his leading characters. His male characters weren't

'macho'. There was this great sensitivity, especially in dealing with affairs of the heart, which lent a sense of great reality. At a time when Hollywood movies were rarely personal or autobiographical, you always had the feeling that the love stories in Nicholas Ray's films were true stories.[21]

The films are expressive of weakness or failure; they even display doubts about their own source material. Though not yet formulated, the idea was already taking shape (as witness Godard's review of *Bitter Victory*) of what Truffaut was to call 'the great crippled films'.

But French critics were also attracted by the power Ray managed to generate, by the liberties he took, by the example he gave of what could be done within an industry reputedly even more heavily policed than the French cinema. His essay on the genesis of *Rebel Without a Cause* was published in an issue of *Arts* devoted to scriptwriting problems. Critical writing remained vague about production circumstances in Hollywood, which tended to be distinctly idealized. 'You like these films,' Ray later told Barbet Schroeder, 'but you can't imagine how often they represent only fifty per cent of what I wanted to do. You have no idea how I had to fight to achieve even that fifty per cent.'[22] The real freedom represented by the director-producer status – achieved by Hitchcock and Hawks, but never by Ray – came to be understood only later. Paradoxically, however, this appreciation of freedom went hand-in-hand with an admiration for the way in which the strict rules of genre were handled. 'The element of constraint in his films,' Rohmer says, 'probably appealed more to my colleagues. I remember Rivette once saying, "I don't like *The Wrong Man*; I prefer Hitchcock's spy stories." Because there Hitchcock was under greater constraint. But what I liked about Ray was a certain spirit, a certain fervour, a sort of impulsiveness such as I have perhaps found only in Rossellini. There is this side to all his films, combined as you might expect with a certain naïvety, though not in any pejorative sense. And all of this is expressed not so much through the story as visually: not just *mise en scène*, but a *mise en scène* rather similar to the structural organization done by a painter. There is a painterly side to Ray, but not in the frame composition so much as in the image as an object complete in itself. It has to be seized in its movement through time, the sort of quintessence of gesture that I talked about in connection with *Bigger Than Life*.' If younger critics felt this kinship with Ray, it was also because an affinity was created by conceptions of *mise en scène*, and by the intimation of a return (unconscious on his part) to the fundamentals of classical style. 'There is good reason for comparing Nicholas Ray and

Robert Bresson', Kostoveski and Straub wrote in 1955, 'because each of these two young film-makers has a style similarly tending to abstraction. Nicholas Ray's style is also a distant heir to the work of the greatest of all film-makers, F. W. Murnau (who died in 1931), in the sense that in Ray's best films, the inventiveness of each shot is consistently astonishing. Each has its own inner autonomy, and the director plays on oppositions as they jostle each other.'[23] Philippe Demonsablon and Rohmer also mentioned Murnau; Louis Marcorelles cited Eisenstein. There was above all, as Rivette noted in writing about *The Lusty Men*, the intimation of a new kind of cinema emerging.

Cinema, first and foremost, as a form of personal expression: 'Each Ray film', Demonsablon wrote, 'is a moment from his life; the moment, I would say, of reflection, of recollection, of resolution.'[24] Unlike part of the cinephile faction, for whom an effacement of the first person singular was a virtue in itself,[25] the Nouvelle Vague felt drawn to Ray because of this element of subjectivity; even more so for his conception of improvisation, taken in the broadest sense, and his refusal to let the meaning and movement of a film be blocked at any stage whatsoever. ('It was all in the script, they always tell you. But if it was all in the script, why make the movie?') This idea was bound up with (and not opposed to) his conception of the cinema as a synthesis of the arts ('a cathedral' as he expressed it to Bitsch), which he hoped (in terminology that was extremely vague but did somehow relate to the Soviet avant-garde) might lead to something beyond cinema. (Godard was to talk about cinema and science in terms not unreminiscent of the links Ray saw between cinema and the unconscious.)

When the Bitsch interview finally appeared in *Cahiers du Cinéma* No. 89, in November 1958, the Nouvelle Vague had already been launched. The cover still was from *Les Amants*, the 'photograph of the month' showed *Le Beau Serge* being filmed. The issue signposted the transition from studio-dominated Hollywood to a new era of television and nostalgic reflection on the past: on page 2, an advertisement for *Twilight of the Gods*, a Universal film directed by Joseph Pevney, with a posed still of Cyd Charisse and Rock Hudson; on page 60, a review of Arthur Penn's *The Left-Handed Gun* — a new approach to cinema which, paradoxically, had less to do with the return to basics embodied by the Nouvelle Vague than with the films Ray made for the big studios. By that time, too, Ray's Hollywood career had come to an end. Since the interview, he had made three more films and 'seemed to have no thought of leaving Hollywood' – as Bitsch put it, with no way of knowing Ray would never work there again.

31

Wind Across the Everglades

The story for *Wind Across the Everglades* was an original written by Budd Schulberg, its producer and screenwriter. Son of one of the early Hollywood tycoons,[1] author of two novels about the film world, he found his style, for better or for worse, in his encounter with Kazan, whose desire for independence he shared, along with his decision, as a former Communist, to co-operate with the House Un-American Activities Committee and name fifteen of his former comrades. A vigorous, polemical writer, an anti-demagogical demagogue with a gutsy style derived from Hemingway, Schulberg had long been contemplating a script about the Everglades – the Florida swamplands – and the primitive savagery of the life there.[2] He teamed up on the project with his younger brother, Stuart, back from nine years in Europe, where he had produced documentaries for the Marshall Plan and a few fiction films.

As is well known, filming did not go entirely smoothly on *Wind Across the Everglades* for Ray, who – according to the official version – fell ill during production. In 1962 he refused to talk about the film to *Cahiers du Cinéma*, not having seen it since 'a preview following which I sent in five pages of notes'. Later, he waxed more violent about Budd Schulberg, whom he accused contradictorily of having wanted to direct the film himself and of having the script written from day to day by a ghost. The various articles and statements by the Schulberg brothers pointedly ignored the director. In his preface to the script, published the same month as the film was released, Budd Schulberg mentions 'the direction credited to Nick Ray' and the latter's fall into a river during shooting, and gives the generally accepted version of the facts: 'When Nick Ray was forced to withdraw because of illness, Maguire [the assistant director], Mr Brun [the cameraman] and I worked harmoniously to guide our vessel through tropical storms and safely into port.'

Yet *Wind Across the Everglades* is a film that bears Ray's stamp. Suffering from the conditions under which it was shot and completed, it draws its strengths from the clash of interests underlying it. Disparaged by those who worked on it, it has become one of the touchstones of Ray's work. It therefore had all the requirements to become a *cause célèbre* in the polemic between adherents of a literary cinema, in which the author, as in the theatre, is he who writes the words (a thesis defended and illustrated over the years by such as Nunnally Johnson, Schulberg or William Goldman), and the partisans of *mise en scène*: those who, in Europe in 1958, upheld the *politique des auteurs* (later Americanized as 'the *auteur* theory').

When I called Budd Schulberg in 1980, he became perturbed: 'Hiring Nick Ray was my worst professional mistake.' He told me that if the film had any qualities whatsoever, it was thanks to himself. Then he suggested that I see other people who had worked on the film before coming back to talk to him. A few days later, Roger Donoghue gave me a foretaste of what I was to hear: 'The whole thing was a disaster, and I could only say: "When I knew him, he was as sharp as a tack!" '

Charles Maguire, the assistant director, by then an associate producer at Paramount, gave me a run-down on his point of view: a director 'not functioning' who had to be removed for 'the last three or four weeks'. Sumner Williams spoke of three or four days. The Warner Brothers archives deposited at USC, and later in Paris the editor Georges Klotz, enabled me to establish a more accurate and less biased chronology. In New York, Barbara Schulberg, Stuart's widow, had a less categoric view both of Ray and of Manon, readily accused by the men of being responsible for her companion's personal problems. She well remembered the chaotic conditions under which the film was shot, but laid the blame on no one person. In my presence, Barbara Schulberg called the continuity girl, Roberta Hodes, who refused to see me (she wasn't the only one; others refused, hedged, failed to reply to repeated letters: Peter Falk, Burl Ives, Joseph Brun).

Two-and-a-half years after this first contact with Schulberg, he agreed to see me at his Long Island home, answered my questions, and went through an unedited transcript of our interview. Another visit to USC eventually brought to light the daily production sheets for the film, which I thought had vanished along with Schulberg Productions, enabling me to complete the chronology.

In March 1957 the trade papers and the gossip columnist Louella Parsons had announced a partnership between Budd and Stuart Schulberg to produce two projects, *In the Everglades* and *Eighth Avenue* (the Roger Donoghue story). On 1 April a production agreement was signed with Warner Brothers. On 10 April Hedda Hopper announced that Ray would direct both films. On 29 May Budd Schulberg finished the 100 pages of *Everglades*, 'original story and treatment'.

Early in August, Budd and Stuart Schulberg, with cameraman Joseph Brun, filmed egrets and herons during the nesting season, at the Duck Rock animal sanctuary off the southern tip of Florida. 'This is the only time of the year and the only place where so many of these birds congregate,' Budd Schulberg explained in the *New York Times*. Documentary shots by a second unit: adequate explanation for the absence of the official director?[3] Answering Ray's charge that Schulberg wanted to direct the film himself, which I brought to his attention, Schulberg said: 'It's just totally untrue that I wanted to direct it myself. I never wanted to direct it. If I had, I probably would have tried to do it, as at that time we had considerable power – since we were producing the picture. I really thought that Nick, that a director would bring to it an overall visual conception that I didn't think I . . . I've never really wanted to direct a picture.'

The starting date was set for mid-October, with interior scenes shot in New York. The final screenplay, comprising 141 pages, is dated 9 September. The unit took shape: mostly technicians who had worked with Kazan. On 20 September, Joseph Brun, production manager George Justin, and art director Richard Sylbert (who had worked on *Baby Doll* as a very young man) joined the producer and director in Florida to scout locations. During this trip and another a month later, Budd Schulberg made his 'final' changes, eliminating the opening sequence set in New York. Although the unity of the film gained by this cut, as he wrote to Jack Warner, the decision to film only in Florida was a false economy: everything had to be transported to a very remote spot. As Stuart Schulberg described it:

> We made our location headquarters in Everglades City. It is just off the Gulf of Mexico on Florida's southwest coast 78 miles from Miami and has about 700 inhabitants. Its unpaved streets and old frame houses made it ideal for shots of the Miami of fifty years ago [. . .] We built our plume hunters' village there [on Duck Rock] on stilts, and art director Richard Sylbert transferred plants and trees, widened and dredged existing canals and cut new ones to link the muddy village with the open waters of Chokoloskee Bay. We 'dressed' the fascinating old trading post on Chokoloskee Island to serve as an important Miami set. We also had to hack our way through swamps laying road beds for the trucks which carried our lights, cameras, sound equipment and props.
>
> We cast some of the fishermen and hunters of Collier County. These last wouldn't go to New York, where we had planned to shoot interiors in a studio. So we decided to do the interiors in Florida. While walking along the main street of Everglades City one day last October, Budd and I noticed a large stucco garage. Its dimension, façade and

door arrangements reminded us of the building on Mission Road in Los Angeles where our father and Louis B. Mayer produced silent pictures. We rented this garage and then learned it had been erected as a film studio in the first place! The late Barron Collier, the county's founder and chief developer, had once dreamed of making Everglades City a motion picture capital.[4]

The Schulbergs decided to create a bit of a stir round the production, and a great deal of publicity activity went on, starting with information about the cast. Then a number of journalists, not necessarily involved in writing about films, were invited on location. The Schulbergs welcomed their friends, during the initial weeks at least, and turned it into a family affair (Budd's children, David and Stephen, played small parts; while Stuart's daughter Sandra – now a producer – and the editor's son Nicolas Klotz – now a director – spent their holidays in Florida during filming). The film featured, in addition to the small-town citizens, a band of outlaws living deep in the heart of the Everglades, massacring birds to sell their plumage. A subject like this demanded an unusual cast. Some are obvious Ray choices: Burl Ives, Curt Conway, George Voskovec, old friends from the New York years. Others may equally well have been picked by Schulberg: the jockey Sammy Renick, the boxer 'Two-Ton' Tony Galento (ex-heavyweight challenger), the clown Emmett Kelly. A few days after filming started, the Pulitzer prizewinner MacKinlay Kantor,[5] who was living in Florida, was added to the cast, along with some of Schulberg's drinking companions and actresses from the local theatre in Sarasota. The prudish stripper-actress Gypsy Rose Lee, playing the madam of an establishment, was surprised to find filming frequently being interrupted for libations.[6]

The female lead, the young Jewish immigrant Naomi, was entrusted to an Israeli air hostess, Chana Messinger (renamed Chana Eden), who was studying singing and drama in New York; she was a Stuart Schulberg discovery. 'It was frankly a mistake we made in choosing her,' Budd Schulberg said, 'she was not experienced enough.' Ray later claimed to be responsible for casting Peter Falk. ('Nobody would give him a job because his eyes were crossed.') Ben Gazzara, originally set to play Walt Murdock, cried off at the last moment, and a few days later was replaced by Christopher Plummer ('who was always our top choice,' Budd Schulberg wrote to Jack Warner. Was Gazzara then Ray's choice?). This last-minute change and the unavailability of Burl Ives, who was finishing *The Big Country* under Wyler's direction, delayed the starting date. Filming began only on 7 November, and had to continue well beyond the end of the dry season.

But problems with the director had already been in the air for some time. According to Schulberg: 'I first met Nick with Gadg [Kazan], years before this. At that time he seemed a very sympathetic kind of person to me; I found him extremely appealing, he seemed artistic. And we talked about some day maybe doing a picture together, the way people so often do, I guess, everywhere.'

The Schulbergs had considered other directors: Robert Wise, Robert Aldrich. Kazan suggested Ray, an idea backed by Lew and Edie Wasserman, and which appealed to the brothers. 'We felt,' Budd Schulberg went on, 'that Nick would have that special feeling for primitive people, for the Glades, for the poetry of it, for the folk music, for Burl Ives, the whole thing . . . When we met Nick in New York at the Hotel Plaza, he had a girl with him from North Africa called Manon. She came out of the bedroom just in a bra and flopped in his lap during our first conversation about the picture. And that was the beginning of our trouble: in a sense, I think it was a symbol of something reflecting the problem that Nick was not the Nick that I had known three or four years before. He was under the influence, I didn't know of what.

'We talked to him about this girl. I said, "Nick, you're not seriously going to bring this girl to the Everglades?" Everglades City is not really a city, it's a tiny little fishing village, very provincial; they took a dim view of outsiders anyway, it was an extremely closed little community. We were concerned about maintaining good relations so that we could work with the people there, with the fishermen, and the last thing we thought would help was to bring this girl out. We worked out certain arrangements: that she could come as far as Naples, thirty miles north, but no further, and things like that. But of course, on the day before we started she was there in Everglades, in a sense breaking the agreement.

'I think it is the story of a really, obviously talented man – many of his films do show that – who had come back from Europe in very, very bad shape. It turned out he was . . . I thought it was just drinking; but a few days before principal photography, I realized that it was more than just drink.

'We took a trip down the Everglades with Bud Kirk, a guide and a marvellous man, on his fishing boat, just getting the feel of the Glades. Syd Solomon, the painter, was along. We thought we'd stay out for three days and just sop up the atmosphere. I think an earlier Nick, a healthier Nick, would have loved this. But as it was, being away from this girl, and maybe away from drugs, he'd go down in the cabin and stay there, holding his head in his hands. His attitude was, "When can we go back? When you've seen one Glade, you've seen them all." He was just not in a frame of mind to do this picture.

'The night before we started, we had a fiasco of a reading. We read the whole script through, with even bit players there, like the manager of the Everglades Hotel Rod and Gun Club. He shouldn't have been at such a reading anyway, but as he read his lines, Nick stopped him and said, "Now, do you understand your motivation for this?" Nick was talking Stanislavsky to this poor little man who was just thinking it would be fun to dress up and be in a movie! As this went on, Chris Plummer signalled to me. We went to the bathroom at this motel where we were staying, the Illinois Motel, and Chris said, "Budd, don't you realize that our director is mad?" I didn't know what to say. I didn't want to tell Plummer that our director was mad, but I thought so too.

'Shortly after this, Nick said to me: "I can't handle Chris. So what if I direct Burl, and I let you direct Chris?" I never heard of a picture being made that way. But in a sense that is what happened; he simply wouldn't communicate with Chris at all, and we just tried to work out together how to adjust to that situation.'

Why, in the circumstances, wasn't the director replaced from the start? Roberta Hodes, the continuity girl, felt that the mistake Budd and Stuart made was in not doing this after the first week of shooting.

Schulberg again: 'I wanted to fire him on the night before we started. This is what happened. MacKinlay Kantor was a very well-known writer, and a friend of mine until the picture started. He came over to see Nick. Nick and I had adjoining suites in the motel, and I thought we'd all get together more or less socially, as we were mutual friends. They were in there for hours, I think maybe two hours, as I was waiting for them. Finally Nick burst into my room with a script and said, "Budd, Mac and I have been working on the script, and I think we've made some marvellous improvements." And he had it all written down in the margins. I said, "Nick . . ." – I was shaking, I was so angry – "Nick, I want you to get away from me, just get away from me." He said, "But please, look at this . . ." He didn't seem to understand what he and Mac had done.

'After Nick finally left, I drove over to see my brother Stuart and said, "I really think we ought to fire Nick. I simply have to do it now. Because . . . he's crazy!" Stuart said, "If I call Jack Warner now and tell him we're firing Nick – after all, they approved him too – they will think we're so incompetent that they may call the whole production off. We've got a hundred people here, it will be a disaster. I just don't think we can do it." While I was over there telling my brother I thought we should fire

321

55 *Wind Across the Everglades*: Budd Schulberg and Nicholas Ray –
between them are Christopher Plummer, Curt Conway and Chana Eden

Nick, the owner of the hotel, who was also the only doctor in the area, called to say that Manon was in the bathroom, had taken sleeping pills, and claimed that she had committed suicide. So I came back, and this owner-doctor was all upset, of course. I said to him, "Doctor, I have a terrible feeling that she hasn't taken enough." And he looked at me . . . It was the first of three so-called attempts.

'So we kind of limped into beginning, the next day, in that sort of mood. As we started shooting, I guess almost every day I felt that Nick was out of control. He was in a way a distortion of the Nick that we had known, he was in a cloud, he just wasn't clear, he didn't know what the story was. It's true that our relationship flip-flopped almost overnight from one of being friends to being almost adversaries.

'A lot of sportswriters came down – Red Smith, Doris Lilly – because there were fighters and other sporting figures in the cast. Film reporters came too, and almost every one of them would take me aside, saying, "Budd, don't you realize . . . ?" or "What's the matter with Nick?" Doris Lilly was the first to say it: "He's flying." "Well, yeah," I said, "he's been drinking maybe too much." "Drinking?" she said, "He's on heroin. I know the eyes." Some mornings he was a little clearer than others. He would go back to the motel for lunch, and after that he was wiped out. Everybody could see that by the time he came back from lunch he was flying. And we just had to cope with that. He may have been on heroin, I don't know. But he was heavily drugged, plus drinking heavily.'

Filming started on Monday, 4 November, with the scene of the train arriving, using a 1904 Baldwin locomotive dispatched to Florida at great expense. According to Maguire, Ray was in good form for about the first week. There can be no doubt that he must have gone progressively to pieces as filming went on, whether because of the antagonism that set him against his scriptwriter-producer, or because of the exceptional tensions arising from an arduous, inadequately prepared production. The hostility between the two men was exacerbated by Budd Schulberg's conception of cinema, which held that the scriptwriter was the true *auteur* of a film. In December, a journalist from *Variety* summed it up after a trip to Florida: "He looks upon the role of the screenwriter as similar to that of the playwright. He insists on working closely with the director and being on hand to make script revisions as the need arises during production. That was his arrangement with Kazan during the filming of *Waterfront* and *Face in the Crowd*.'[7] In this instance, he seems to have invested every page of his script with undue importance, as witness his reaction to MacKinlay Kantor's intervention. The 29 October script still contained numerous pages comprising nothing but dialogue, with the writer trying to set down every aspect of his vision of the world in black and white. The preface to the published script gives some idea of this flowery prose – in the midst of which lurks some of the best dialogue in the film.

Schulberg and Maguire said nothing about the disproportion between the production and its logistics. George Voskovec (who summed the whole thing up by saying 'Everybody was drunk!') felt that: 'It was the whole organization of the picture that was very improvised, to say the least. And that was just as much the responsibility of the brothers Schulberg, mostly Budd Schulberg, because he was the drinking one.'[8] In the opinion of Georges Klotz, the editor, 'Filming it was an enormous task. Maybe with a skeleton crew they could have brought it off.'

As for Ray, he brought his defence mechanisms into play: calling for a good deal of histrionics, they were also strategic. Schulberg expressed indignation because Ray wouldn't let him tap his director on the shoulder during takes in order to make suggestions, which was his practice with Kazan.[9] 'I was really frustrated because, having been spoiled by Kazan, I had to stand back and watch things which I thought often were not right or could have been better; and I didn't have any rapport with him in order to be able to discuss things.'

In the circumstances, Ray probably didn't see that producer's hand on his shoulder as reflecting the same rapport as it did with Kazan. When Schulberg returned the transcript of our interview to me after reading it, Kazan was present. Schulberg brought the matter up again. Kazan smiled and said, 'He was just taking a pose': the dramatics and pretentious mannerisms were simply a way of resisting his writer-producer's aggressiveness. George Voskovec: 'I think that Nick was very unhappy personally. He had some sort of very tempestuous and unsuccessful love affair there – the French lady – and there were very big scenes at night . . .' The intimation that his companion must be kept at a certain distance, Schulberg's refusal to reconsider a single line in the script, and a series of pointless humiliations led Ray to comment: 'Schulberg refused to allow a range of respect among men.'

The conflict was aggravated by the hostility (confirmed by Sumner Williams, Voskovec and Klotz) of a crew used to other methods, or simply methods they could understand. 'The difference in style between Nick and Gadg affected the production,' according to Schulberg. 'For lunch, Gadg would just stand in line with everybody else, there was no such thing as being served special food, or being at the head of the line, or all these things Nick did that they didn't like. His relations with the crew were very, very bad.' Conveniently forgotten were the inadequately prepared production, the open house maintained for a coterie of sportswriters, everything that made Ray an intruder on the film.

Stuart Schulberg had engaged a French editor, Georges Klotz. He and Joe Zigman, the American editor who 'doubled' for him with the union and for the lab work, set up their cutting-room in Everglades City. The rushes were sent each day to California to be developed and printed; then they were coded, synchronized by the Warner sound department, viewed by Jack L. Warner and/or Rudi Fehr, head of the cutting department, and finally sent back to Florida. The unit viewed them at the local cinema (whose back rows were still set apart for Indians). And the editing was done in a cabin with a mesh door, which kept the mosquitoes out but let the dust in everywhere. Klotz and Ray were delighted to be working together. The editor appreciated the copious and varied material delivered to him ('more than forty set-ups for the arrival of the train'), but the director was no more given to discussion than he had been previously with Maurice Le Roux: 'You're the Frenchman, you should know.' His habit of using multiple set-ups in shooting a scene was, however, beginning to meet with criticism.

On 19 and 20 November, two telegrams arrived from Jack L. Warner, who was worried after watching the rushes: too much footage was being shot (Warner felt the same misgivings every time a director went on location). He could understand it at the start: establishing the atmosphere, filming backgrounds, the credit sequence – but where's the story? He remarked on the constant changes in camera set-up: 'Continuous changing angles slight but same action extremely costly and time consuming.' He worried about the budget, demanded 'action and speed', asked Nick to be careful about what he decided to shoot, and to hold off on doubtful takes until the rushes had been viewed. 'Am sure Nick knows what to do and what is really required.'

Schulberg agreed with Warner: 'Nick shot so many intermediary angles, varying the camera only a few feet. We felt he was just shooting somewhat aimlessly. There seemed to me to be too many angles that didn't make that much of a difference, and he seemed to be overshooting.' Barbara Schulberg recalled Ray sketching shots every night for the next day's filming. Was he shooting at random? We have seen the extent to which this fragmentation could, on films where he supervised the editing (*They Live by Night, Johnny Guitar*), be an integral factor in his method.

The Schulbergs and Ray telegraphed a joint reply to Jack Warner, announcing that cuts in the script had already been made amounting to twenty pages.[10]

Ray's work with the actors found equally little favour in the eyes of the producers and crew. Charles Maguire described his rehearsals as 'endless'. When he had been filming in a studio, they had rarely posed problems. A. I. Bezzerides, for example, sitting in on the filming of *On Dangerous Ground*, said of Ray: 'He was the most fumbling man I ever met. No insight at all, but everything was feeling. He directed by feeling.' This didn't bother Georges Klotz ('You must have the feeling in your fingers,' Ray told him), but it did bother the crew. One anecdote was particularly damning in the eyes of those who repeated it (the following is Maguire's version).

'There was one very important scene which was taken in a little garage we had made a covered set out of. This was the feather-robbers' place in the Glades, and Chris makes this long speech about birds and everything else, about ten minutes long, which is a terribly long time in motion picture-making. I said to Nick, "Where are you going to break it up?" He said, "No, I want to do it in one shot." OK, we set it up and rehearsed and were ready to go; it was getting to be warm because of the lights. Chris came up and said, "Nick, can I talk to you?" Nick said yeah. Chris is a very fine actor, very sensitive, used to direction. The two of them walked down the street, turned around and came back in like . . . I guess you've seen American football games where they pat each other on the ass? Nick patted Chris on the ass and said, "Go get 'em!" We went inside and did the scene, and being out of film had to reload for another take. Chris came outside and I asked, "What did Nick say to you?" He said, "He didn't open his mouth, for the two blocks up or for the two blocks down." Never said a word to him. Walked two blocks, turned and walked two blocks back, and only "Go get 'em!" So . . .'

Given an actor who thought he was mad, 'someone that Nick could never work with' (Schulberg), and whose loyalty he must have felt was to the producer, it isn't hard to imagine this example of 'the Nick Ray pause' as being a fairly effective form of direction. Until the final scenes, in fact, there are only rare moments when Plummer indulges his usual mannerisms, and there can be little doubt that this is one of his best performances. Later on, Ray had nothing but praise for him, noting his nervousness and insecurity in the film, and reflecting that Plummer may have underestimated his own abilities.[11] He considered working with him again on at least two occasions.

On 9 December, the *Hollywood Reporter* announced that a television crew from ABC's *Monitor* had left for Florida to shoot a 60-minute programme about the film. Burl Ives had just arrived, having finally completed his role for Wyler, and the TV unit was present for his first scene. This was a Ray invention: after their first kiss, Walt and Naomi hurry back to the house to make love. In the deserted street, they run into Cottonmouth, the outlaw leader, supporting his sick son: under cover of the Independence Day celebrations, he has ventured into town to seek help for the boy.

Filming of the town scenes was duly completed, more or less coinciding with the end of the hot season. ('The mosquitoes are still biting well, and we shall be happy to be at home,' production manager George Justin wrote on 30 November.) Leaving 'civilization' behind, work started on the scenes at Cottonmouth Key and in the swamps on 11 December. It was 'men only' in front of the camera now: Plummer, Ives and the motley cast of outlaws. A dismayed Budd Schulberg had invited Roger Donoghue down, but he was able to help only by contributing a fine piece of stage business: 'I choreographed the fight between Sammy Renick [Loser] and Tony Galento [Beef]. There was no way Renick could lick this 300-pound man. I said, "You need to give him a balance. Establish him as a jockey and give him a whip." That's what they did. While they were shooting, the felt came off the whip and he gave Galento a stroke on the cheek, so Galento lifted and threw him. That wasn't in the script!' The scene was shot on 18 December (with two cameras, plus a hand-held Eyemo).

On the 29th, a lengthy telegram signed only by the Schulbergs was sent to Jack Warner's right-hand man, Steve Trilling: 'Dear Steve, We are of course deeply concerned with overage and have been making maximum cuts in staff crew and script and every other effort to speed completion at the lowest cost without harming quality of picture. Script cuts to date total more than thirty pages and running time of film definitely will not exceed two hours provided by contract. Please remember we would be in full compliance with contract if picture came in for one million two sixty five. It is now our judgement that one hundred thirty five more will be necessary if final key scenes are to be of commensurate quality with rest of production. We have had difficult problems which you with your experience will understand. One, our revised schedule which was forced by Gazzara withdrawal and Ives delay includes Christmas and New Years in addition to Thanksgiving accounting for equivalent one week lost time and overtime. Two, miserable weather last two weeks has cost us several shooting hours almost every day. Three, methods of director unexpectedly intricate and expensive. We have pressed for simplification to maximum extent possible without destroying his effectiveness. Of course controlling him is our responsibility but as you know a difficult problem to be handled on the scene and on day-to-day basis. We have been taking as strenuous measures as possible to hold down costs under difficult location conditions. Re ending Budd has always respected Jack Warner's views but has reserved right revise script constantly as Walt-Cottonmouth relationship develops on film. He has now completed new ending which we are confident you will agree is a climax to be remembered. Copy ending being airmailed to you.'

These six pages, sent forty-eight hours later, do not introduce any radical changes. Cottonmouth has let himself be arrested by Walt, who tries to take him back to Miami, but gets lost in the swamps. The outlaw is bitten by a cottonmouth. The snake and the talk of 'natural causes' figured in the first version of the script (of 29 May); the only difference was that there Walt died too. The script ended on a burst of laughter from Cottonmouth as the camera moved away. The new text added Cottonmouth's final monologue as he refuses to make an incision to draw the poison, sends Walt away, preferring to die alone, and looks up at the birds: 'Guess I never had a good look at 'em before.' Cottonmouth dies. The birds.

This little game of great expectations played around the ending seems

56 *Wind Across the Everglades*: 'a Ray invention' – the meeting in town
between Naomi (Chana Eden), Walt (Christopher Plummer), Cottonmouth
(Burl Ives) and Slow Boy (Fred Grossinger)

to have been a smoke-screen hiding something else, which was not the
incapacity of the director: Ray, with his 'intricate methods', was still on
hand (otherwise there would have been no complaints about him). In
addition to their practical errors, the producers had miscalculated the
length of the script. That Sunday (29 December) the footage completed
ran just over two hours, and the forty-eighth day of filming – the last,
according to schedule – was coming up.

Bad weather was dogging the production. 'It was the coldest winter in
many, many years in the Florida area,' Charles Maguire recalled. 'A
lot of crops were damaged, and the hotels in Miami were strongly hit
financially. A lot of the picture was shot right in the Glades, and we were
working in chest-deep water. Somebody brought up the fact that it was
one degree warmer in Jacksonville, Florida, than it was in Everglades,
and Jacksonville was two degrees warmer than Anchorage, Alaska!
Maybe it compounded Nick's problem, I don't know . . . When we first
went there it was very warm, and the bad weather came later on, because
we had a tremendous problem in the beginning during the construction

57 *Wind Across the Everglades*: the last scene Ray directed

period with the mosquitoes and the heat. The only good thing that came out of the cold was that we had been worried about the snakes, but the cold kept them in hibernation. We had a New York crew, and they weren't used to doing Westerns like a California crew would have been. Most of them were New York City bred, and not used to this wilderness thing.'

The unit had been working on exteriors since 11 December.[12] On 2 January 1958 the action switched to an interior: Plummer and the outlaws in Cottonmouth's shack. Walt has arrived to arrest Cottonmouth, who – after promptly disarming him – invites him to share victuals and a jug.

Walt and Cottonmouth slowly proceed inside, followed by the rest of the outlaws, who form a circle round them. Sitting facing Walt, Cottonmouth plants a knife in the table and passes him a jug of liquor. The others see this as a last rite for the condemned man, but Cottonmouth insists on demonstrating his hospitality. The guitarist sings *Lostman's River*. Later, drunk, Walt insists on being called by his right name. The others burst out laughing, and come up one by one to shake his hand. In a dazed speech, Walt tries to make Cottonmouth understand about the balance of nature, but Cottonmouth recognizes only one commandment: 'Eat or be et.' Walt tucks in with relish to the roast alligator tail; Cottonmouth talks of the 'sweet-tastin' joys of this world', and tells Perfesser (Curt Conway) to say the word which resumes their way of life: 'Protest!' Walt approves: 'I've done a little bit of that myself, protesting.' All offer various protests, Cottonmouth last with 'I'm agin everythin', exceptin' the jug,' then announces, 'Boys, he's joinin' us!' Led by Walt, they go out into the storm and stagger around in the mud, brandishing their jugs.

This drunken confrontation was the last scene that the director, adjudged crazy by his unit, was to direct. 'The basis of the scene had to be there,' he said years later. 'I drink pretty good and so does Budd drink pretty good, but I know more about corn whiskey than he does. But we both learned how to handle the allegories.'

Between five and seven set-ups, representing three or four minutes of usable footage, were filmed each day. On the 10th, the Schulbergs sent word to Trilling that Plummer and Ives were both bedridden. Filming was impossible without them, since only the final scenes remained. Ambiguously, the telegram added, 'Nick also sick but still on his feet,' and concluded, 'Unless weather improves and actors recover immediately, fear new delays in winding up.'

The 15 January issue of *Variety* contained a short item about Ray: 'A hero to his colleagues on location scouting expeditions: always leads the party.' Ray was quoted as explaining, with his perverse sense of humour, 'Those rattlers never strike the first person in line, always the second or third!' Clearly friendly in intent, these lines were published two days after the director was personally proscribed from what Europeans – long contested by Schulberg on this point – see as *his* film.

It was on Monday the 13th, the fifty-eighth day of filming, with continuity girl Roberta Hodes recording 154 minutes 40 seconds of usable footage (34 minutes over the maximum stipulated in the Warner contract), that the final break between producer and director took place. Only the former's version is extant.

'I think it was about two-and-a-half weeks from the end when we finally decided. The Seminole chief Osceola was doing a scene when Nick told him to exit left, and Roberta said, "No, Nick, it won't match, he has to exit camera right." Nick said, "I want him to exit camera left." Roberta said, "Nick, I've got my notes, it just won't match." This went on for some time, and finally Charlie Maguire got into it. He was disciplined, knows his place as an assistant director, never talks back to directors, but he said, "Nick, Roberta's right, it won't match, it'll look as if instead of following up, he's going in the opposite direction." Nick said, "I will not have this. I will not have this kind of insubordination on my set." Then Joe Brun the cameraman spoke up – a gentle, artistic soul, he would never intervene, but finally he did – saying, "Nick, I really think that Roberta and Charlie are right, he has to go off . . ." Nick got more indignant, saying, "I will not have this kind of talk on my set," and started to direct it to go as he insisted it should. I guess that's when I finally cracked and said, "For God's sake, Nick, it's not a personal insult. I've seen Kazan, I've seen other people work, and if the script girl says . . . I mean, you can't keep every detail in your mind. If Roberta says right, if three knowledgeable people tell you it's right, why the hell don't you just say Thank you, Roberta, thank you for reminding me. For Christ's sake do what they suggest, they're just trying to help you!" It was an explosion, and he said, "I cannot and I will not work with this sort of interference" and so forth. So I said, "Well, maybe we had better stop right now." I went to see my brother, and Nick went back to the hotel. By this time he was in very bad shape; not really coherent, I would say.

'So everything stopped. I told Stuart that physically Nick couldn't go on any more, that he really was incapable of continuing to work. Stuart said, "What will we do? Who will direct it?" I said, "I guess I will. All I know is, it can only be better, it can't be worse. At least I'll know what the people should be doing, I'll know what they should be saying, I'll know what direction they should be going, I'll know the story. I'll get Joe and Charlie to help me, and somehow we'll get through it. It can only improve. At least the people won't be demoralized, the crew won't be laughing as they were at the whole thing . . ." And that is what happened.'

So Ray carried the can for the entire fiasco. Nobody, except possibly Burl Ives, cared whether his inability to continue was the result of obstacles set in his way, rather than the cause of those obstacles. Sumner Williams could testify only to 'I don't know what tensions built up inside him.' Schulberg and the technicians saw only the semblance of incoherence he presented, being incapable of assessing his coherence where the story and characters were concerned. Ray clearly felt that his editor was able to understand him, and Georges Klotz saw no incoherence in the results: 'He managed to give a tone to the film, quite unlike that tacky ending' (shot after Ray's departure).

Charles Maguire, the assistant director who 'knew his place', was specific: 'We finally just told Nick that he could stay in the motel and let us finish the picture, or they would fire him and tell everybody why.' This deal forced on Ray, with its faint tang of blackmail, was doubtless a practical solution for the producers, and for him just one more humiliation. The ruling established by the Directors' Guild stated that the director was the person whose name figured on the clapper-board. For an independent production in difficulties, on location far from the studio, sacking a director would have been a proof of weakness. The West Coast appears not to have been informed. No document makes any mention of the ban imposed on the director; and no press release (on a film busily courting publicity) was issued. One day Klotz saw 'Nicholas turn up where we were filming, lurking in the back of a car driven by Manon'. A few days later, he left for California.[13]

The film was finally finished at the end of January, in bad weather and low spirits.[14] 'Whether I could have directed the death of Burl better or not, I'll never know,' Schulberg said. 'I was just thinking to get through it, do it as well as we could. We had to finish the picture, that's all.' According to Burl Ives: 'After Nick Ray left, there was no director at all, everybody directed, you know . . . the first assistant directed, some of the writers directed, actors directed. It was . . . not a happy experience, no.' A month later, coming to California for *Cat on a Hot Tin Roof*, Ives offered his services – in vain – for refilming the final scenes.

The editors had already moved back to New York in January, where Klotz was 'getting to grips with the material' and completed a rough cut running almost three hours (when filming ended, the usable footage totalled 182 minutes 27 seconds, of which 27 minutes 46 seconds were added after Ray's departure). The studio then took strict measures to hasten the process. The negative was transferred to the West Coast. Jack Warner viewed a cut on 22 April, and wired Trilling: 'This about 100 per cent better than we thought it would be. It needs editing but doesn't need any retakes. Needs stock shots of animal life. Editing can be done between you me Rudi Fehr . . .' He put an end to the welter of publicity for the film. The Schulbergs and Klotz arrived in Burbank on 5 May.

'There,' Klotz said, 'I learned how the big studios worked. They said to me, "We have three weeks for the sound editing and mixing the sound effects." "Are you crazy?" I said, "How is that possible?" "It is," they said. "There will be several sound editors under your orders, and we'll give you a bicycle, so you can go from one cutting-room to another to supervise." And that's what happened: I co-ordinated the cutting-rooms on a bike. I didn't see Ray once at the studio; he was banned. Sumner served as a friendly go-between for us. I was struck by the bossiness of the head of the cutting department, Rudi Fehr.'

The film musicians of California were on strike, and at first there was some question of having a score recorded in Europe, in Munich. Then, at less expense, the studio delved into its music library, and a pot-pourri of pieces to which it owned the rights was recorded. As Klotz described it: 'I said, "This is awful, do something!" I was told, "Who cares?! The film cost less than two million dollars." That was when I got the message. Jack Warner moved very fast. He saw the film twice, and that was all. The old man was satisfied.'

In addition to this canned music (*Cat on a Hot Tin Roof* also suffered during the strike, and even *Party Girl* was affected), a travelogue-style commentary was tacked on over the opening sequence. A private screening took place on 9 July for about thirty people, guests of the Schulbergs and Warner Brothers – all couples with the exception of Nicholas Ray, pointedly invited alone. After this screening, two memos were despatched. One was from Jack Warner, indicating thirteen places where cuts should be made or the action 'speeded up'. The other, from Ray himself, is the film-maker's most detailed statement about *Wind Across the Everglades*:

> My dear Budd, I do not wish to go into any excursions which, because of my language or past experiences, might lead us into any further misunderstanding. Therefore, I wish to set down my reaction to the film.
>
> The story line is unclear. Therefore, to say that unity is lost is redundant. However, I do believe this: that, since you have deleted so much of the family story in Miami, the Voskovec [i.e. immigrant] theme emasculated, I would suggest forgetting it entirely and playing only the conflict between Chris and Burl. I believe it is necessary to be ruthless in this and ruthless to the extent of eliminating everything except the preparation for the love scene between Chana and Chris under the bandstand.
>
> I think it might be best to go directly from the plucking of the feather from Mrs Liggett's hat at the point where Chris says, 'How would you feel if this bird were wearing you?', to the posting of the sign of warning by the member of the Audubon Society [i.e. Walt Murdock]. If necessary to establish the Nathansons, take them there, but forget the arrest [of Walt, for plucking the feather from Mrs Liggett's hat], forget the judge and go directly, without any exposition, perhaps only one transition shot of Chris going into the Glades; intercut with another shot of wild birds flying, then to the posting of the warning on the tree and then to the entrance of Burl.

You might also consider the possibility of combining Walt's excursions; making two trips instead of three.

I severely miss the bedroom scene in the aforementioned preparation for Chana and Chris under the bandstand.

I would recommend for footage, that you lose much of Gypsy Rose Lee and the byplay between her and Mac Kantor.

I would get Chris back to Cottonmouth Key as quickly as possible, but not at the risk of losing a very important scene of conflict between Chris and Burl, when Cottonmouth is alone in town with Slow Boy and they have their encounter in the rain. The excision of this scene distresses me greatly because it was not only a scene of two people running away from a crowd toward a bed for the first time, but on their way, they run into a man who is showing a father-son tenderness which is almost embarrassing to Cottonmouth and it helps us to understand his final departure with Walt, which has always been terribly vague to me.

It seems to me that the most impressive scene in the film is the shack scene and the jug duel. Also Brad [Bradford] with the alligator, but even within these, which were largely improvisatory, I miss some of the moments of Emmett [Kelly], Curt [Conway] and Pete [Falk]. I find angles used differently than their intention. This was true in the final scene. I believe any moments of colour that spell conflict, whether pixie or bloody, deserve to remain in the film. The academics of repetition to make historic or folkloristic points, annoyed me and the audience because, no matter what our sentiments might be, the interference with entertainment is on film.

This is not creative cutting, but I am not in a position to do more than challenge it. As you invest your interest in each frame of the film, I suggest the provision of overlaps where you can, to increase tempo, negating repetition and omitting triteness.

And oh! I have forgotten something; another reason for replacing the scene between Burl and Slow Boy, Chris and Chana, is the almost ludicrous transition from beach to parade.

There was a point in the show where either Chris or Burl said the equivalent of 'something for the birds.'[15] I beg you to investigate that passage and delete it. There seemed to be some confusion at the point where Mary [Osceola] takes Walt away from the Manchinell tree and says, 'I take you to my people'. In the next scene he arrives at the Nathansons with Liggett. The audience reaction around me was, 'Funny lookin' Indians'. I would suggest using Mary's Seminole language at this point, rather than being specific.

The dubbing is atrocious and the canned score, of course, is impossible. But I'm certain you entertain no thoughts of releasing the film this
way.

I'm sure that my name means very little to the box-office revenue for
this film except in Europe. But unless the final scene shot after my
departure from Florida is reshot, I would be most acquiescent to
having my name removed from the film. I cannot allow it to be associated with the style of acting employed by Burl in the death scene.

The film has a potential of being interesting, but not in its present
state.

Good luck.

It goes almost without saying that no attention was paid to any of the
preceding remarks. The film was finished, apart from the cuts that were
made on Jack L. Warner's instructions after the screening.[16] And it was
released: in Florida in August, nationwide in September, adopting the
saturation technique preferred for minor films. Reviews and box-office
both poor.

In the three-hour version put together by Klotz, there were undoubtedly long dialogue passages which the published script, finalized between
the shooting and post-production stages, only partly recorded. There
were also many bits of scenes subsequently eliminated; these, too, contained a lot of Schulberg dialogue (visionary utterances by Cottonmouth's retarded son Slow Boy, for example). And there were certain
scenes which vanished entirely. According to Schulberg: 'We had to
make sacrifices, we had to cut scenes and shorten it just because things
weren't working very well.' Klotz described the cuts as 'enormous, murderous. The characters are mooted rather than revealed.' Since Ray was
not present during the editing, it was logical that the first things to be
eliminated (perhaps with a certain glee) should be those whose dramatic
significance appealed particularly to Ray.

A case in point is the meeting between Walt/Naomi and Cottonmouth/
Slow Boy, which Schulberg does not include in the published script. Ray
claimed to have improvised it: 'When the two men meet on the street,
silently, they appreciate each other's desire for aloneness and walk in
opposite directions. It was a beautiful scene, and why the hell they cut it
I'll never . . . Maybe because Budd hadn't written it.' Commenting on
Ray's remarks, Schulberg said: 'I do remember the scene, and watching it
being shot I thought it was quite nice. I thought it had some feeling such
as Nick describes. Have you looked at the picture recently? Isn't there
some of the scene still? It's not there at all? Again I don't remember

exactly why this was. When we put the picture together we had a terrible time trying to get any pace out of it. We may have been simply trying to *move* the picture more. I do remember watching the scene and thinking that it seemed to have a good feeling to it.' A two-minute scene: it could scarcely slow the film down. On the other hand, the absence now of any transition between the picnic on the beach (with the love scene under the bandstand) and the parade inaugurating Flagler Street, is one of the many aberrations for which the director cannot be held responsible. Ray also mentioned a prologue in which Murdock is arrested for drunkenness in Boston, but which was never shot.[17] It remains evident from the film that Ray did everything he could to stress the contradictions in the character (drinker, gambler, outsider, acknowledging that 'progress and I never got along very well' and becoming a staunch partisan of the birds), thus preventing the linear development that would let him become the mouthpiece for any sort of message.

The subplot involving the Nathansons, father and daughter, both firm believers in 'progress' and determined to better their status as immigrants by integrating, has been almost entirely removed, notably the two moments between Walt and Naomi which Ray set most store by. In one, showing Walt his room, she reveals herself: European, but trying to be modern (she smokes). In the other, when Walt arrives back drunk from Mrs Bradford's, she helps him remove his shoes, takes the initiative in kissing him, and leaves.[18] Schulberg ascribes the cutting of these scenes (and the immigrant theme) to Chana Eden's lack of talent and experience. There is room for disagreement here. In her handful of scenes, she displays a composure, a frankness of look and gesture that extends beyond the role as written. Only Jonathan Rosenbaum has commented on this 'highly original and unjustly neglected performance', noting that along with Gloria Grahame in *In a Lonely Place*, she is one of the few Ray heroines 'to have much identity apart from their relationship to men'.

It is difficult, then, to see the direction of actors here as erratic or fortuitous. Without expounding further on the cases of Plummer or Chana Eden, without stressing the excellence of George Voskovec, one might simply note the vitality and irony with which the minor characters are handled in the Miami scenes, Gypsy Rose Lee's manner as she welcomes her 'nieces' at the station or chides a couple for dancing too close ('Shame, shame, shame on you!'), the skilful touches sketching in the disreputable or merely amusing leading citizens. Ray has said that the scene under the bandstand had an autobiographical inspiration; one might say the same of his portrayal of a small town (very different, for example, from the Kazan-Schulberg collaboration in *A Face in the Crowd*), centred on the shipment of goods and the bordello, public celebrations and the business of getting drunk.

The presence of Burl Ives is one of the great strengths of the film. Ray, who had directed him only on radio, plays on the contrast between the soft, modulated timbre of his voice and his corpulence; a corpulence and nimbleness of foot reminiscent of the Thomas Gomez character in *High Green Wall*. His physical authority once established (right from his first appearance, seen upside-down through Walt's camera), Cottonmouth gradually monopolizes the film, but his is a triumph of ambivalence, and a far cry from Kazan's blustering fathers or villains: nuances, hints of tenderness abound (not to mention an aura of homosexuality unique in Ray's work – and Schulberg's too). The final scenes, when Ives adopts a purely external acting style – rolling his eyes and forcing his voice – leave the earlier subtleties forgotten.

Only in 1973 did Ray begin to talk a little about *Wind Across the Everglades*; at the time he was immersed in *We Can't Go Home Again*, a film on which the see-saw between control and frenzy, improvisation and illness, pressure to finish and the impossibility of doing so, repeated itself. He spoke then of what he liked about the film: 'The madness of casting Two-Ton Tony Galento, Sammy Renick and all the outcasts of the story. There is one man whom I just wanted to work with for a few moments before he died, Emmett Kelly. Everybody was fighting in the mud, and here is this wonderful clown of the American circus shadow-boxing. I'll always remember it as a moment of great joy and honour that I was able to work with him for those few minutes. The madness of choosing Chris Plummer . . . Ben Gazzara couldn't take it . . . and the script wasn't that good either. But Budd Schulberg had an idea of madness. And I have always had an affection for the outlaw. I prefer him to the banker, who's the more respectable outlaw. I prefer the outlaw to the sanctimonious and the righteous, and the indignant people who modify our architecture, our earth, our sex lives, and our desire to fly. I'll choose the alcohol any time.'

Schulberg, of course, had his hand in the 'great hallucinatory crescendo', the 'extreme harshness' (Claude Ollier)[19] of this second part. He laid claim, however, to sole responsibility for all of it: 'I get annoyed when I read things like the *Village Voice* saying, "These are the true outlaws that only a Nick Ray could create." It's absolute nonsense, he didn't create them. They were people we had seen, a life I had actually observed; those squatters in the Glades had been there for years and years, were still there, and to a large extent we got to use – backing up for the actors – the actual people in the Glades.' It is difficult, though, to imagine Wise or Aldrich, even at their best, managing to mould this incongruously random mixture of actors and non-actors into evoking quite the sense of haggard, spectre-haunted degeneracy, festering hatred, occupational viciousness and gleeful cruelty, simultaneously driven by a fervent, festive joy, that illuminates these scenes.

The Nick of the film 'was not the earlier, healthier Nick I had known,' Schulberg kept repeating. In which case (there would be others), it is the 'sickness' which gives this chaotic, contradictory film its power. Its own motive force carries one past the patched-up scenes that alternate with great moments. A picture postcard shot jostles next to – or illuminates – its exact opposite. The way in which the scenes are handled leaves no doubt as to their inspiration: a weft of relationships between characters, a musical rhythm on several occasions reinforced by blues or ballads (very cruelly mutilated in the editing) which play a dramatic role.[20]

It is the 'sickness', too, which quashes or ignores the solemn verbosity of Schulberg: instead of being defined by their vision, the characters are defined by their acts, their speeches reduced almost to the point of absurdity, or to the splendid laconicism of Naomi. The virtues of *A Face in the Crowd* (as enumerated by Roger Tailleur: 'a moral judgment diffidently incarnated by a lucid observer', 'bitterness', 'savage humour', 'uncontrollable dynamism', 'pace')[21] gave way here, as far as Schulberg was concerned, to a more grandiloquent, allegorical style of writing. These are characteristics to which Ray was no stranger, and he welcomed the biblical echoes, though stripping them of their emphasis. Jews, Indians, birds: the message towards which Schulberg was heading is evident. But the metaphor is never formulated, defused by a happy 'malfunction' in the director, who was fascinated purely by the germs of savagery and madness (he claimed to have filmed certain shots simply because of the colour contrasts). He retained only two pointers: Walt's speech about 'the dawn of creation', and Cottonmouth's profession of faith, the proclamation of the word 'protest', which becomes the high point of the film.[22] One is forced to conclude that Ray understood Schulberg better than the latter thought, that beyond the mutual hostility there lay a congeniality neither of them suspected. 'Nobody makes a film all alone,' Ray concluded, 'not even the madness.'

32

Party Girl

58 *Party Girl*: Robert Taylor at the death of Lee J. Cobb

Twelve days after the filming of *Wind Across the Everglades* was completed in his absence, Ray signed a contract with Euterpe, the Joe Pasternak company dependent on MGM, to direct *Party Girl*.[1] His contact with Metro had started, before the filming in Florida got under way, during a cocktail party at Edward G. Robinson's place. Ray has described how Benny Thau, then running the studio, had heard him tell Shelley Winters he had read a script that attracted him 'because at least it had a beginning, middle and end. That impressed Benny Thau, because I think people thought I must have liked to start from behind the 8-ball all the time without the benefit of a completed script.'

Finished the script of *Party Girl* certainly was, the end result of seven or eight versions of a bulky story by Leo Katcher, bought by the studio in 1956. Originally the producer was Charles Schnee – which perhaps explains the idea of engaging a director to whom he owed one of his earliest opportunities as a screenwriter. While Ray was filming in Florida, Schnee had passed the project on to Joe Pasternak, a Hungarian émigré who owed his success to Deanna Durbin comedies, and who was delighted to be changing genres and working with the man who made *Rebel Without a Cause*. It was, however, a routine venture, designed to justify the accumulated salaries of two expensive contract stars: Robert Taylor, winding down a career launched as Garbo's partner with roles as sleazy cop or psychopath, and Cyd Charisse, brilliant every year in one of the musicals that were steadily losing favour. Informed audiences may have seen them as at the height of their powers, but to their employers they were costly burdens not to be borne much longer. For both, *Party Girl* was to be their last film under contract to Metro.

The different versions (Katcher's 271-page story, treatments by William Ludwig in 1956, synopsis and various versions through 1957 by George Wells, a specialist in comedy) show that, even as the demand for MGM-style thrillers faded, this was what was being turned out through pure inertia. The *Party Girl* script had no more ambitions to revitalize or explore the genre than *Rogue Cop* (1954) or any of the ageing Robert Taylor's other vehicles: Thomas Farrell, a lawyer working for Chicago gangster Rico Angelo, and Vicki Gaye, dancer and party girl, lose their cynicism and regain their dignity through their love for each other. Farrell, who limps as a result of a childhood accident, undergoes a successful operation in Europe; he then decides to sever his ties with Angelo, who takes Vicki hostage. After a violent climax, the two lovers walk away into the future.

Without harbouring any illusions as to his margin of freedom, Ray was attracted by a setting he had known: Chicago during Prohibition. His salary: $3,750 a week, for a minimum of twenty weeks. His agent, Eric Weissman of MCA, tried in vain to have a morality clause removed from the contract which stipulated that, should any problem arise, Euterpe could not only remove his name from the credits, but also sue him for damages.

By the time Ray became involved, the art director Randall Duell had long since processed the sets, using the June 1957 script: all of them already standing, or built in the studio.[2] A music consultant had listed the songs from the 1920s and 1930s that could be used. Aside from this, Ray found the studio co-operative, which was a change from his recent experiences. Pasternak, with his European culture, had a certain respect for him, and was hoping to open new avenues for himself with the film. The only limitation imposed on Ray's work was that he had to adhere to the Metro view of the world. In the end, no period songs were used (the nostalgia mode was not yet considered box-office). Three days on location in Chicago were originally planned, but eliminated as soon as the film went over schedule. Ray's contribution to the script involved only the minor alterations usual when any contract director was preparing to shoot. They include cuts in the moments where the characters explain themselves, a few added medical details about both Farrell and Rico, and a meticulous, succinct description of the liquidation of Cookie La Motte (a young killer protected by Angelo, who subsequently turns against him) and his gang.

Time was at a premium. On 10 March 1958, Pasternak and Ray got down to casting the minor roles, considering Angie Dickinson (before *Rio Bravo*) or Doris Dowling for the part of Farrell's estranged wife (it finally went to an unknown, Claire Kelly). Ray chose Kent Smith (the District Attorney, Stewart), Rusty Lane in a tiny role as a judge, Corey Allen from *Rebel Without a Cause* as Cookie La Motte, and Carl Thayer (who had killed Jesse James) as another gangster. Also two intense New York actors: David Opatoshu (as a shyster lawyer) and Lee J. Cobb as Rico Angelo. And lastly – one of the dancers appearing with Cyd Charisse – Betty Utey, who had been very busy since their first encounter on *Androcles and the Lion*.[3]

On Monday, 24 March at 8.38 a.m., Ray joined cameraman Robert Bronner on a crane to set up the film's opening shot: customers and showgirls (65 extras) at the Golden Rooster night-club. At 11 o'clock, the first take was shot. Filming the 'book' – the non-musical scenes – continued until 9 May on the Culver City sound stages, with only one location exterior: the swing bridge, shot at San Pedro harbour. The production schedule, worked out in terms of sets and stages, began with scenes from the first part: the presentation of the girls on stage, Vicki's dressing-room, the discovery of her flatmate's suicide, Farrell's successful defence in court of the hood Louis Canetto (John Ireland), Farrell insulting Vicki.

The production was then disrupted, first by the leading lady's illness,[4] next by the musicians' strike, which delayed the filming of the two musical sequences (then called 'Bluesy' and 'Dixie'), initially set to follow on after the 'book'. To get round the difficulties caused by the strike, choreographer Robert Sidney left for Mexico, where he rehearsed the two numbers with doubles. They were finally shot without sound between 10 and 22 July, with fake trumpet players, a piano accompaniment, and bongo drummers; after which, once the strike was over, Andre Previn – uncredited – composed the score.[5] The musical sequences were directed, as was the rule, by the choreographer. Robert Sidney was a recruit from television, where he came to know Cyd Charisse's husband, Tony Martin, the crooner who can be heard over the credits, singing the title song. Anxious to fit in with the studio style, Sidney did not get on well with Ray. A natural alliance formed between producer, female lead, and what Ray described as this 'very efficient' but 'very dull' choreographer. Sidney felt that Ray's ideas, shaped by jazz and black music, were aberrant, and accused him (after the fact) of having tried to make Cyd Charisse wear break-shoes.

Not having much more to say, the director kept his distance. Cyd Charisse, talking to Jean-Claude Missiaen, spoke about his absences, but also about his vulnerability and his strangeness, what she saw as unfathomable direction like 'taking roses and inhaling deeply, as though you were smoking a joint'. Invited to be more specific when she appeared at the Deauville film festival in 1982, the dancer remained strictly professional, observing that erratic attendance by the director – if such was the case – would have no bearing on the end result.[6] With sacrosanct script, sets already built, second unit, choreography and special effects, a very high percentage of a major studio production could dispense with the director's presence altogether. This director was doubtless only too willing to have it so.

Filming took forty-two days, six over schedule. The accounts department dates Ray's services as terminating on 21 July: so he was not present during the editing. A little after this, the accumulating exhaustion of the preceding months caught up with him, and he was hospitalized in Boston. On 20 September, the cost of *Party Girl* was put at $1,695,491, plus an estimated $44,775 for post-production work; the budget had originally been set at $1,648,616. The film was released in October. Ray later declared himself satisfied with it, 'in the sense that I don't think I could have done much more with it'.[7] Corey Allen, who subsequently became a director himself, felt that: 'The picture was beneath him. It was an assignment. And now, as a director, I know how that feels. You do your best. And his best was very, very good. So all I can say about *Party Girl* is, I saw the man work like I do now. With a great investment in the quality of what he was doing, although what he was doing was not what he wished, really, to do. Casting where he could excitingly, or at least what he considered to be well. And very plastic. Very American plastic.'

The cast held some pleasant surprises in store for him. He was unable to break through Cyd Charisse's impassivity. To justify his belief in her as an actress, he tried in vain to persuade the front office to let him do a confrontation scene between her and Lee J. Cobb. Failing this, he invented images or bits of business for her: her red dress against a sofa of a different shade of red, droplets of water glistening on her face after she buries it in a bunch of roses, the moment when she drops her fur coat as she walks towards Taylor.

Robert Taylor – another stone face – is handled with sympathy, discreetly and intelligently directed so as to use both his strengths and his weaknesses. The signs of ageing (Taylor was born two days before Ray), an actor's vanity, his tiredness, are evident. 'My first image of Taylor,' Ray told Peter von Bagh, 'dates from the 1930s. I was working in a mining area in south-west Pennsylvania, where most people had been laid off recently, and nearly everyone lived in poverty. I went to a cinema in a town nearby, and first saw the favourite actor of the day, Paul Muni. My impression was that he was always playing in front of a mirror. Then came *Camille* and Robert Taylor, pale, handsome, remote. Two decades later, I saw Taylor working for me like a true Method actor.' Since childhood, Thomas Farrell has suffered from a crippled leg which he exploits theatrically. 'I wanted Taylor to feel the injury, so that he could be aware of what part of his body the pain was in at all times when he moved.' Ray took him to see an osteologist from whom he had once received treatment, and the actor won Ray's admiration by the professional thoroughness with which he examined X-rays and questioned the specialist. 'After that, he needed no kind of aid to create his limping. It is only very rarely that you find this kind of ambition, sensitivity and humbleness which Taylor stood for.'[8]

With Lee J. Cobb, Ray felt he was able 'to bring some of the Capone era to the film. Physically, Cobb had a resemblance to Capone, not so much facially, but Capone was a big man, a wrestler and a boxer.'[9] He also told Peter von Bagh that he had 'put in a few of my freaks'. At the banquet in honour of Frankie Gasto (Aaron Saxon), a bald-headed gangster, Rico's paean of praise turns into accusations of treachery and a violent assault on Gasto's skull with the solid silver miniature pool cue about to be presented to him. Ray cast a Zen Buddhist in the part, as being the only person with the necessary powers of concentration to sit still without blinking in anticipation of the blow.

The direction is negligent of the script's highlights. The idea of doing what is right and therefore lawful, so integral to MGM movies, here vanishes in the transfer (faithful to the letter rather than the spirit) of script to screen. The first kiss is handled with complete cynicism, the moral and physical regeneration is skimped, the decision to betray the gang totally unexplained. The accent is placed instead on the duplicitous relationships between the characters, on the maze of compromises within which they evolve. The parallels are stressed between the fetters, professional and personal, that keep both lawyer and dancer in a state of subjection. Right from the credit sequence, filmed that first day, the display of MGM opulence – the girlie parade – is tinged with ambiguity: these scantily clad bodies have a price, and immediately afterwards we see Louis Canetto make a list in his notebook of the names of those who are to be invited, for a hundred dollars apiece, to Rico Angelo's party. Throughout the film, human bodies are never far from becoming meat: a corpse drained of blood in a bathtub, a bald head split open by a metal club, Vicki's face menaced by the literal corruption of acid, with the stunning image of a bandage being slowly unwound to reveal the flesh as yet unscarred (this idea is taken up and transposed as a political anecdote in Godard's *La Chinoise*). *Party Girl* was not the first Ray film to deal with prostitution and self-awareness, showing how a man and a woman, hurt or benumbed, lose their cynicism and regain their self-respect through contact with each other. In the first stage of their encounter, Farrell adopts a hectoring moral stance with Vicki because she uses gangsters for her own profit; this just before he demonstrates, in her presence, his pride in the courtroom theatrics that make his position exactly the same as hers. The affair that develops between them is also a competition, right up to the dénouement, yet another compromise, this time with the forces of law that are doubtless equally corrupt: a compromise preferable solely from the couple's point of view.

In his contentious dealings with producers, Ray's relations with lawyers always played an important part. His own lawyers helped him on several occasions, starting with the letter sent to RKO by William Fitelson in 1944. He was also to accuse quite a few of them of having caused projects to break down. This obsession with the law, with Ray always convinced he held all the trumps but always destined to lose out, was to become even more pronounced in the years following the end of his Hollywood career. Ten years after *Party Girl*, back in Chicago once more, Ray hired a lawyer who had been Al Capone's legal advisor and mouthpiece (the latter called him 'Professor'); although neither the director nor the screenwriters realized it at the time, he had in fact served as the model for the Thomas Farrell character. Louis Kutner enjoyed Al Capone's confidence because he was cultivated and because he knew how to listen. He pictured for Ray a young hoodlum whose dream was to have his own shoeshine stand, and for whom the symbol of power remained a chair in which no one else could sit, its arms decorated with the heads of lions into whose mouths Capone liked to thrust his fingers and then snatch them quickly away, his strange way of tempting fate. Ray recorded several cassettes with the lawyer, he himself saying nothing, fascinated by stories which left the meagre fictional foundation MGM had supplied him with far behind.

From 'Chicago – early 1930s' (the film's opening title), Ray featured the bums and the apple-vendors in the windy streets, the speakeasies with their back exits. Echoes of other bridges – the one from which he used to dive into the Mississippi, another over the Chicago River – lend a note of intensity to the scene in which Farrell confides in Vicki, the only one shot outside the studio. 'I would like to have been able to get more of my own attitude to the Chicago of that period into the movie,' Ray said. 'The closest we came to it was in the montage and in the machine-gun bursts in the southern part of the state.' This was in fact the point at which the film took off, assuming more of the tone of a period chronicle. The sequence is introduced by two cars crossing paths (Rico's and Farrell's). Farrell goes to see Cookie and his men in their Indiana hideout; machine-gun fire mows them down before his eyes. Vicki hears the news on the radio. In a hotel corridor, Canetto fires point blank at a man coming in with a girl. As a gangster runs up the steps of an apartment house, the glass in the front door shatters and he is met by a hail of bullets. Someone else is gunned down at a billiard table, another man in a telephone booth, two more from the rear platform of a train they are running to catch. One shot was cut during editing (a man is killed in a barber's-shop). Three more were planned but never filmed: a car corners a gangster in a blind alley; a man is killed with an ice-pick; a body is thrown into the river. In their insistence on stereotypes, all these moments suggest an ironic intention. Each image is carefully conceived, dovetailed and combined into a single, fragmented sequence. Rather than a transition – normally entrusted to a second unit – this sequence becomes the last major articulation, the introduction to the final part. After the banal idyll of the European scenes, the horizons open out.

Party Girl, however, owes its homogeneity less to the director than to studio knowhow: the intervention in the narrative of simplified, sub-Eugene Loring/Hermes Pan choreography, the complete anonymity of several episodes (like the trip to Europe), certainly do not make this Ray's 'most balanced' film, nor yet a work of 'absolute mastery on the level of *mise en scène*'.[10] More showy than *Run for Cover* or *Hot Blood*, *Party Girl* is also more uneven. Sorely tried physically after two ventures that were exhilarating and traumatic in equal measure, Ray took refuge in the safety of formula (what Hitchcock in fact called a 'run for cover'):

traditional genre and packaging, at the most conservative, self-sufficient and stagnant of all the studios.

The gangster film, fallen out of fashion, survived only through parody (*Some Like It Hot*) or psychological introspection in the B movie (*Baby Face Nelson, Al Capone*). *Party Girl* met with a unanimously condescending critical reception in the United States. Ray made no attempt to modernize the genre, but treated it with manifest off-handedness, giving a skewed reality to gangsters no more 'realistic' than the ones in *Designing Woman* (scripted by the same George Wells). As Ray put it: 'When I couldn't contribute as much as I wanted to the script, I tried to do the next best thing in colour and performance, to give the kind of bizarre reality there was, which permitted people who lived that life to believe that theirs was the only reality.' MGM, like the gangsters, believed that their reality was the only one in the world, and their Chicago killers were installed in settings dripping with bad taste designed for society dramas. Effective enough as a secondary effect. But the context is not abstract here, it is completely empty. The *mise en scène* is reduced to flourishes, and Ray is lavish with his 'inventions', as Fereydoun Hoveyda described them in his effulgent review in *Cahiers du Cinéma*: 'In the dressing-room, a girl passing through steals some make-up remover; the money paid to the girls in powder-compacts, which are discarded on a table in the bedroom; the silhouette of a cop's head turning, indicating Farrell's arrival off-screen', etc.[11] *Mise en scène*, or simply rhetorical effects, tried and true bits of business. Their function is suggested by the byplay with the watch: Farrell uses it to win the sympathy of a panel of jurors by saying his father gave it to him, a sure-fire trick which he complacently confesses to Vicki, before using it again with Rico, this time to save *his own* skin.

Ray organizes a colour progression, using clashes and shadings, recurrent motifs and correspondences. Identifying Vicki with a red dress, using contrasting reds, then gradually introducing various splashes of blue (reflections on the bridge, a curtain in the dressing-room), and finally, macabre green lights towards the end. The link forged between the world of show business and the underworld makes *Party Girl* akin to the great musicals of the 1950s (*Singin' in the Rain* was among Ray's favourite films). Here he borrowed one of the characteristics of the genre: the overt display of its formal devices.

No photograph seems to be extant showing Ray on the set of *Party Girl*: but his presence during certain scenes, and likewise his absence (not necessarily physically) from others, is evident on the screen. 'A bread-and-butter job', 'shit film', was his own assessment. A film-maker's negative view of one of his films is of course no criterion for judgement (any more than his preference for another). But Ray stood at the crossroads between two types of film-maker: although usually required to work on assignments, he was further disadvantaged in being denied most of the privileges granted to a producer-director or a writer-director. More than any other Ray film for years, *Party Girl* reveals him in the position of employee: and its merits stem from the intervention of *mise en scène* in its strictest sense. It may be seen as a setback in his progress, or as an exercise in pure virtuosity. French critics, adopting an extremist stance within the *auteur* theory,[12] were of the opinion that Ray had here perfected his method in order to devote himself to essentials.

33

The Savage Innocents

On 13 October 1958 Nicholas Ray married Betty Utey at Grangley, in the woods of Maine. A reconciliation with Thoreau's America? This was, in a sense, to be the theme of his next film, although it was as yet far from his mind.

'When we married,' according to Betty, 'he was unsure about whether he ever wanted to make another film. I said: "I don't care if you never do another film. We'll stay in the woods and hunt and fish." We stayed in Maine for a few months; we were just there . . . he didn't want to return to Hollywood. Then he got a wire from MCA that Disney wanted him to do a film called *Hurricane*, something about a hurricane that rips through the world, which they had had in the works for a couple of years. He had mixed feelings about it, but it was enough to stir us out of the mountains, with some sauerkraut and his two Beagle puppies. We stopped in New York to check out the paintings in the Museum of Modern Art, and we drove across country.

'Got here [Los Angeles] and the deal fell through. He was literally broke then. I was doing some acting things and coasting along. And, through personal problems, he had a lot of people not wanting him to do another film. The story was – I don't know true fact from fiction – that he couldn't get insured because of his alcoholism. To prove that he wasn't drinking was the big thing. At that time of my life I thought vodka was men's cologne; I thought he'd stopped using whatever cologne he was using, so I was pretty innocent about what alcoholism was! So it was no big trip for me to appear sober at events. When we returned to LA, there were people in high places who believed in him, especially if he wasn't drinking. The Wassermans had been very close to Nick, and they came around, were very supportive of our marriage; and Al Bloomingdale actually set up a story development company for Nick. They gave us their blessing, so to speak.

'We were just here about two or three months when Ronnie Lubin, who was then his assigned agent at MCA, brought a project from Paramount. It was a book that Malenotti, an Italian producer, had the rights to. Nick liked the idea, and within a couple of weeks, he wrote a scenario. He had a secretary, and all of us who were close to him were running for research night and day. He put together a script that Para-

348

mount found acceptable, Tony Quinn signed to do it, and off we were into the Arctic.'

As usual, everything happened very quickly. Ray managed to establish that he would write the script himself. Hans Ruesch's novel, *Top of the World*, deals with the life of the polar Eskimo, as yet uncontaminated by civilization. Ray adapted the first half of it, incorporating the best of the dialogue. An English-speaking Swiss living in New York, Ruesch had not lived at the Pole, and Ray drew as much inspiration from his own reading, especially the Danish explorer Peter Freuchen. The first draft is dated 26 February 1959, but by then the production was well advanced: filming would start less than two months later. This first draft, signed by Ray alone, leaves little doubt as to the contribution made by the author of the novel and the Italian scriptwriter Franco Solinas; the inclusion of their names on the credit titles was merely a contractual formality.

Preparations had begun in Canada in January, under the direction of Baccio Bandini, associate to Maleno Malenotti and second unit director (on Italian prints he is credited as co-director). In March, Ray arrived in Ottawa, where he met his cameraman, Aldo Tonti; after a distinguished career that took in the early days of neo-realism and work with Rossellini and Fellini, he had recently become involved in big international productions. Ray sounded out members of the unit about the script, and seemed to share the misgivings of the Canadian assistant director, Jacques Giraldeau, as to the casting of Anthony Quinn. According to Giraldeau: 'The star of the film wasn't to be "Tony", but the frozen North: the cold, the ice, the wind, the snow, the sun that never sets. "What I want," Ray eventually told me, "is to deal with nature at its most raw, most hostile to man. Compared to a great star like this – nature in its prehistoric state, so to speak – the actors will seem like extras whom I shall keep well in hand." '

Ray, Tonti, Bandini and the technical adviser, Doug Wilkinson, spent ten days scouting locations, choosing exterior settings to the north of the town of Churchill (on Hudson Bay), and on Baffin Island, in Frobisher Bay. Ray, warned about Bandini by another director who had worked with him, had a clause inserted in his contract whereby 'the person in question was not to give instructions to me at any time'.[1] He thus established exactly what Bandini's position and responsibilities were (and subsequently had nothing but praise for his second unit). Location filming promised to be difficult. 'We worked up there with the help of the SAC [Strategic Air Command] based there,' Betty Utey said. 'We got a plane and went farther into the Arctic, shooting wild footage which was very hard to find. It was terrible, white hunters and Indians had pretty much knocked the wildlife; we couldn't find caribou. Tonti and a couple of English guys were up there with us, and every three hours the storms would come and everything would be demolished.' In his autobiography, Tonti wrote: 'It was in the month of April: 25–28 degrees below zero. When the wind blew, we felt our very souls freeze, despite all our ultra-scientifically organized equipment. The landscape, truth to tell, looked much the same all over, but the director went on rambling imperturbably around, as though strolling through summer meadows. He wanted to attend to everything; he took on the air of a real *condottiere*. He used to stride around on the ice as though he'd done it all his life. I would follow as best I could, but one morning, with the wind blowing in icy gusts, suddenly he was no longer by me. "That's it! He's fallen through a crack in the ice!" I began to run in all directions, calling out to him. I found him a bit further on, kneeling on the ground. He had one hand held to his brow, staring intently off into the infinite. Thinking he was praying, I was going to withdraw, but my modest shadow made him turn round. He looked at me with an air of inspiration. "I want the camera always to be this high!" he decreed, getting up and casting a shadow twice the length of mine. I remained puzzled. "The important thing is to get out of here alive," I stammered. And we went on.'

When Ray returned from the scouting trip, Giraldeau found him 'tired, gloomy and irritable. He had lost his enthusiasm. I've always felt that the discrepancy between the reality and what he had imagined from his desk in California was the cause of this change in attitude.' Shortly afterwards, an item in *The Times* described the project in terms strongly reminiscent of *Wind Across the Everglades*. It wouldn't be the only report to do so: 'Mr Doug Wilkinson, an old Arctic hand, will act as technical adviser and will lead one of the two outdoor camera units up north in a few weeks' time to shoot background and hunting material. Mr Wilkinson was at one time with the National Film Board here [in Canada], and was later a Northern Services Officer of the Federal Government in the Eastern Arctic. He will set up a camp at Coral Harbour on Southampton Island on the western side of the mouth of Hudson Bay. Mr Ray will direct a larger unit working out of Churchill in Northern Manitoba and from Frobisher Bay in Baffin Island. The outdoor scenes, complete with plastic igloos and Eskimo clothing, will be filmed in London in July with British facilities.'[2]

By then, Ray had already left for Europe: Rome, where he put the finishing touches to script and casting, for approval by Malenotti; London, where he prepared the studio interiors with Malenotti's associate, the British producer Joseph Janni – and where Betty learned that she was pregnant; Paris, where he saw Yoko Tani, a Japanese who had just completed her first major role in a British film, and was now appearing on the stage; persuaded – for the moment – by the theory that Eskimos were Asiatic in origin, he cast her in the role of Asiak, the hero's wife; East Berlin, with a visit to the Berliner Ensemble; Copenhagen for additional documentation, and to investigate the possibility of filming in Greenland (this seems to have led nowhere, although Greenland is mentioned in the credits); Quinn and Yoko Tani joined him in Denmark, to 'familiarize themselves with Eskimo customs and to listen to their music'.

Preparations were meanwhile continuing in Ottawa. At the end of April, Baccio Bandini started shooting second unit footage from the base in Churchill. Aldo Tonti: 'The equipment we had at our disposal was sometimes a bit rough and ready; for instance, the hulk of a plane in which I was supposed to get to the farthest locations for some of the bear-hunting shots. It was a patched-up old seaplane, with a couple of wheels hopefully tacked on. Arriving at a little air base, I would carry on to a trading post in a sled drawn by seven dogs. I camped in a wooden shack. The local inhabitants numbered about eighty in all. But there were two churches, one Roman Catholic and one Protestant. At Churchill, where Quinn, Tani and the other actors were to join us, our hotel, with its adjoining bar, was an alcoholic centre as inflammable as a box of matches.' Giraldeau had some problems over the stand-ins, no Eskimo having ever been as tall as Anthony Quinn (an Indian, with his own dog team, was finally chosen as Quinn's double), and with the dog teams, which obeyed only one master, and which were harnessed differently by Indians and Eskimos.

Three weeks later, Ray arrived in Churchill with his two leading actors. Bandini left to go farther north with the second unit. The main unit comprised some thirty technicians, mostly British, including Technicolor camera operators. During the following weeks, Ray shot the bulk of the exteriors, mostly – but not always – involving the actors. He told *Take One* that he 'went to a hibernation point to photograph polar bears as they came out of hibernation, when they're the most ferocious'. Cameras and crew suffered from the cold, and especially the wind. Tonti wrote of a night that would never fall, of a director 'ready to work twenty-four hours a day', of a wind at times reaching speeds of 100 mph. For Giraldeau, who felt he was beginning to understand Ray's attitude more clearly, 'Nick showed himself to be a sort of sensitive brute, preoccupied only with camera set-ups, camera movements, detailed instructions to the actors, who became objects in his hands. And this despite the material difficulties and day-to-day problems. Concentrating on detail, he would sometimes forget the continuity of the film. Visualizing it primarily in terms of individual shots, I don't think he had as yet formed a synthesis of his film. I remember one day when we spent nearly two hours working on a close-up of feet leaving tracks in the snow. We couldn't get the shot, and in the end he suddenly gave up because the quality of the light had changed. But he could have filmed this shot in the studio. The time allotted for location exteriors being limited for obvious reasons, it was important that we film only the remote places, things that couldn't be re-created in the studio . . . We had to be ready for anything; at the last moment, he'd reshuffle the daily shooting schedule fixed the night before. We were kept constantly in a state of alert. Sometimes he'd be very decent, and would reveal a certain naïvety that is, I think, a common American characteristic.'

After a month's filming, Ray flew back to London on 15 June. Catastrophe immediately descended on the film: a sizeable portion of the footage filmed was destroyed when the aircraft carrying it crashed (only some magnificent stills survive). Ray immediately left for Ireland to negotiate the hire of polar bears and other animals from the Chipperfield Circus. And filming started up again at Pinewood Studios, owned by Rank (the film's English distributor) and run by the much-detested John Davis. According to Simon Mizrahi, who was present on the set for three weeks, filming took place 'amid more or less general scorn and indifference' in studios 'renowned for the chauvinism of the management and the lack of co-operation extended to any foreign film-maker trying to do original work' (he cites the case of Joseph Losey and *The Gypsy and the Gentleman*). 'It was therefore amid the gravest difficulties – and on studio sets – that he was obliged to film snowstorms, fights with seals, polar bears and sled dogs. After each take, filming had to stop so that the vast set of igloos and icy wastes, tramped all over by actors and animals, could be resprayed with dry ice. The enthusiasm long gone, filming proceeded in the most listless manner imaginable.'[3] Yet, in the middle of the hottest summer London had known for thirteen years, Ray was working under normal conditions, and talked with optimism to reporters from both *Ciné-Revue* and *The Times*.[4] 'You know, I suppose I should be tired,' he said, 'but I don't feel at all tired; I always find working hard on a film which interests me has a tonic effect. Since we started location shooting, I've lost two stone and seldom felt better.'

He was pleased with his work with the actors, Yoko Tani in particular. Only with Quinn were relations strained, ever since the location work, when the latter expected to be given star treatment. 'I had terrible prob-

59   *The Savage Innocents*: Nicholas Ray with Marie Yang and Yoko Tani

lems with him,' Ray said a year later. 'On one or two occasions I even had to shoot scenes in two different ways: as Quinn saw it, and as I wanted it. When the rushes were screened in the evening, Quinn had to concede the logic of my point of view.'[5] Quinn told journalists that he 'had to revert to an unaffected, natural style of acting: in other words, I had to play him almost like an animal, instinctively. It's a wonderful lesson for an actor!'[6] But the tension ran high, and was resolved only years later on a personal level. For the role of the Canadian police trooper, Betty Utey discovered an Irish actor, Peter O'Toole, then attracting attention on the London stage in *The Long, the Short and the Tall*. Fascinated by the idea of acting under Ray's direction, O'Toole – whose second film this was – encountered difficulties: the studio lights made his eyes blink, and he was obliged to wear contact lenses. His nervousness led to several crises on set, but his performance fitted in well with Quinn's. 'The only thing that matters, in my opinion,' Ray said after the film was released, 'is a prior understanding between the actor and the director. This understanding can come only from a long and patient period of persuasion. This is why, when you are actually filming a scene,

353

it is impossible to direct an actor except from a straightforward dramatic viewpoint; by which I mean, purely in terms of the action. The real direction of actors, in other words the progressive, calculated possession of the (consenting) actor by the director, must take place away from the spotlights.' As in *Wind Across the Everglades*, Ray turned the disparity of experience in his actors to good advantage: 'The important part of Inuk's mother-in-law, for instance, is played by a Chinese woman who had never acted before; she is a housewife, and yet she is giving a wonderful performance. I often find that with non-professionals you can get a naturalness and spontaneity in front of the camera that a professional may have to work very hard for, and then not achieve. Most of the Eskimo characters are played by Orientals, who resemble the Eskimo very closely in physical type (and even in many customs), and who are more easily available in Europe and America, of course.'[7]

Filming, in other words, proceeded along much the same lines as in an American studio. But a technical decision was made that was to prove disastrous for the film's chances; this was, following the destruction of the location footage, to shoot a large number of exterior scenes using the sodium light matte process. This form of travelling matte was developed by Rank in Great Britain, and used by Walt Disney in the United States; it was apparently Disney who persuaded Ray of its quality. It was supposedly more direct, cheaper, and sharper in definition than the blue-backing screen generally used (the travelling matte was an older process than back-projection, its first patent dating from 1918). The sodium light process employs a special yellow screen and a three-strip Technicolor camera equipped with a beam-splitting prism. But it is far from successful in eliminating the blue fringe that surrounds people and objects in the foreground where the two images join. It was particularly noticeable in this case, with the film released in 70 mm, and its stark images dominated by the play of white on white.[8]

Filming was completed in October at the Cinecittà studios in Rome: this may have been an obligation occasioned by Italian legislation concerning co-productions, or it may have been to get Ray to re-shoot certain sequences with which Malenotti was dissatisfied. At the editing stage, it seems that Malenotti 'profited' by Ray's absence 'to do a little recutting in the Italian version', and – more seriously – to dub Peter O'Toole's voice in the English version (O'Toole promptly had his name removed from the English prints). But, Ray added in the same interview, 'for the first time since *Bigger Than Life*' he was able 'to supervise the editing throughout'.[9] It seems that the Italian version, at the time of release, was slightly *longer* than the international version (this is no longer true of the prints in circulation today). Which did not prevent a legend from springing up (and Ray was beginning to realize how damaging this could be) that *The Savage Innocents*, completed while the director had already embarked on a venture of a very different sort, had been tampered with like so many of his other films.

It was no mere chance that the initiative behind this Paramount film came from an Italian producer. For some time, lower production costs in Europe had encouraged the major companies to have European partners assume responsibility for technicians and studios; exporting the financial capital remained in line with their policy of market domination. The phenomenon of the 'runaway production', as they came to be called, emerged in the same year as *The Savage Innocents* was made, and was to take increasingly systematic forms, finally putting an end to 'Hollywood' and the old studio system, as well as to the careers of a number of film-makers. Ray's Canadian assistant, Giraldeau, described the aberrant circumstances of this sort of production: 'Italians, Americans, English, Eskimos, Indians, a Japanese, Canadians having to work together, mostly talking English (with assorted accents) but also using French (Tonti, Bianca Lattuada, Tani), Italian, Cree (the Indians among themselves), Eskimo (with the aid of an interpreter), sometimes two languages at once, not to mention the language of gesticulation (the Italians). Set this not exactly conventional unit down in a very specific setting, the cold and ice of the Arctic, add heavy Technirama equipment, taking care to put an international star with his whims and affectations right at the centre of things, and you get a pretty accurate idea of this sort of Tower of Babel.'

Yet, unlike other film-makers working in comparable conditions, Ray made *his* film, without the rhetorical overstatement of the exile, without the abdication of ambition or loss of control common to those temporarily uprooted. *The Savage Innocents* is the film he wanted to make, more faithful to his express intentions than anything since *Rebel Without a Cause*: less undermined, less errant than any of those films. Hence, perhaps, a misapprehension on the part of Ray's admirers, disconcerted by the narrative simplicity and little appreciative of his reflections on nature and civilization, as though these reflections were a negligible quantity and the only thing that mattered was the style. This attitude was *de rigueur* in dealing with *Party Girl*. Fereydoun Hoveyda, for instance, waxed indignant at the idea that script, performance or production method might merit consideration: 'While you're at it, why not also take the influence of the planets into account?' But the choice of material, the approach to the *mise en scène*, the factors that determine its elaboration, are all very personal to Ray. Increasingly, he was aligning himself with film-makers like Welles, Fuller and Mann, incapable of filming material that was alien to them, rather than with those like Cukor, Minnelli or Tourneur, for whom a denial of choice in their source material, and even the indiscriminate nature of that material, were almost a condition of *mise en scène*.

It is clear, given the nature of some important scenes filmed with travelling mattes, that all of these weren't lost in the Arctic, and that from the outset a large portion of the film was to be shot in the studio; Giraldeau's recollections confirm this. The unfortunate decision to use travelling mattes was not simply a matter of making good the lost footage. It was, in part, the consequence of a Hollywood attitude which Ray had not entirely shaken off: an indifference to the contrast between real and studio exteriors (in *The Lusty Men*, for example, an elaborate set is used for the grounds outside the arena). Part of it, too, stemmed from Ray's conception of the cinema as a synthetic art: since *Flying Leathernecks* he had known the exact degree of illusion he could obtain by combining footage from different sources; since *Johnny Guitar* (or indeed, since *They Live by Night*), structural editing within a shot had been an integral element in his *mise en scène*. Finally, too, there was Ray's lack of interest in simple photographic realism, and the prime importance he ascribed to dramatic effect (often cited by him in answering naïve questions about his intentions). This indifference hangs heavily over the film at moments where Ray's feeling for nature is more manifest than ever before, but it also indicates by implication what the film is not and should not be taken to be. Despite the documentation that went into it, *The Savage Innocents* has no documentary ambitions. This 'research of an anthropological nature' which, as always, Ray undertook, this 'complete and utter absorption in a context, a community and its customs' (Lomax), is the groundwork on which a fiction is built; in this case, a fiction having much in common with the fable or morality play.

Screened at the Cannes Festival in 1960, *The Savage Innocents* was greeted with condescension or contempt by critics who, instead of looking at the film, considered only the context: the memory of Flaherty's *Nanook of the North* (or Van Dyke's *Eskimo* for the more erudite); Ray's image as propounded by his admirers; the general exodus of American film-makers into Europe; the poor quality of the technical processing (paradoxically, the film did receive a special mention for effects,[10] the only prize ever awarded to a Ray film). Although it is not surprising that it should have gone unnoticed in the year of *L'Avventura* and *La Dolce Vita*, it is nevertheless a forceful film, as much a part of its time as the Antonioni and Fellini films. What was truly unusual about it simply went unnoticed.

A vast white landscape, sea and ice-floes, a bear swimming, suddenly struck by a harpoon and colouring the water with its blood. This violence which opens the film,[11] unlike the explosion in *Johnny Guitar* or the gunshots in *Wind Across the Everglades*, is not disruptive to the natural world, but rather part of it. Like the hero of *Hot Blood*, the hunter Inuk is a rebel against the traditions of his people. But he wants to change only his own customs, not those of others. At first, for a time, he succeeds: this is the story of his marriage. The second phase brings him face to face with the impossibility of his purpose: his encounter with the white man's civilization. The sequence at the trading post brings the spectator definitively round to the side of the Eskimo, who had hitherto seemed merely childish. Treated with humour, it blends the amazement of the Eskimo, witnessing behaviour which seems to him aberrant, with the spectator's amazement at finding himself forced to agree.

Curiously, Ray was accused of crude caricature in his portrayal of the missionary who rejects all the gifts (even his wife) offered by Inuk, and this by critics who had remained unembarrassed by the characterization of the parents in *Rebel Without a Cause*. Like *Rebel*, *The Savage Innocents* does hover on the verge of a somewhat monotonous Manichaeism. It is rescued by the joyous vitality which remains the keynote throughout the film: the feast shared with friends, the moments of 'laughing' or tussling. The birth of Asiak's child is filmed in a single shot (the script, rather tritely, intercut Asiak in labour with Inuk out hunting). Even the death of Asiak's mother is not seen as a rending moment. Death, its time calmly appointed by the old woman herself, is an inevitable term in life; and unlike the white man's civilization, here other people are excused from sharing its oppression. In a wonderful didactic moment, just before she is left alone in the icy wastes, the old woman gives the pregnant Asiak the benefit of her accumulated experience.

In the last part of the film, Inuk is arrested by two police troopers who have been hunting him down for the murder of the missionary (accidentally killed by Inuk, furious at the insult to his hospitality when the missionary refused the 'loan' of his wife). They try to take him back by sled; but on his own ground, Inuk's law — the law of harmony with nature — proves its validity over that of the white men. One of the troopers falls into the water, and instantly freezes to death; the other, although his hands are frozen, still insists that Inuk is his prisoner. Like Mokrane killing a camel to save Leith in *Bitter Victory*, Inuk plunges the trooper's hands into the bloody belly of a dog he guts. The trooper cries out in pain. 'Good,' says Inuk, 'Means life is coming back. Only death is painless.' He takes the trooper back to his igloo, describing him to Asiak (who assumes he has been hunting) as a 'miserable catch'. The couple's hospitality stands in contrast to the white man's (the other trooper had handcuffed Inuk for the night, and beaten him up when he resisted); and with the surviving trooper still baffled by Eskimo morality ('You don't lend your wife as if she were a sled'), Inuk laughingly explains: 'You lend your sled, it comes back cracked; you lend your knife, it comes back dull; you lend your dogs, they come back tired and crawling; but if you love your wife, no matter how often you lend her, she always comes back like new.' At last understanding, the trooper nevertheless insists that the law must be respected: if Inuk escorts him back to civilization, he will have to arrest him. Refusing to believe this of the man whose life he has saved, Inuk takes him back to within sight of the trading post, intending to accompany him there. The trooper has to insult him to make him leave with his wife and child, finally despairing of ever understanding the white man.

Among Ray's films, only this one and *Rebel Without a Cause* end for the protagonists with a 'going home': Inuk and Asiak are restored to the icy wastes. As well as *Bitter Victory*, there is a clear echo here of *Wind Across the Everglades*, of the ending Ray hadn't been able to film then and which he was determined to bring off successfully here. Ray had pondered (but never wrote) a 'third act' which would be the trial. He incorporated this aspect of the 'didactic play' (already very much present elsewhere) into the confrontation between Quinn and Peter O'Toole, aided in this by the understanding between the two actors. The scenes with O'Toole gain in force from the contrast between the two men; even the actor's nervous blinking (during his first days on set) becomes a sign of his disorientation. The same thing didn't happen with Quinn and Yoko Tani. Ray had tried to adapt the dialogue unchanged from Ruesch's book, where the Eskimos employ circumlocutions, avoiding the use of the first person. 'I had written all the Eskimo dialogue in beautiful, fluent, poetic language, and I thought that Yoko would be able to read it without accent. But when they began playing, Quinn found that he couldn't adjust to Yoko's rhythm without using pidgin English. I should have recast, or at least determined to dub. But I made concessions to the pidgin English.'[12]

Not for the first time in Ray's work, the man is a child who owes a lot to his wife's strength. It was to her that Ray gave the line (not used in the script, but attributed to the man in the novel): 'When you come to a strange land, you should bring your wives and not your laws.' As with many of his characters, their difficulties in expressing themselves entail a literal, childlike approach to the hazards of civilized language. Hence the rightness of these key lines one finds in his films.

The first draft of the script made reference to the fact that the Eskimos are now American citizens. The Canadian Eskimos had been citizens since the 1950s, but Alaska only became a State of the Union in the same month that the script was written. Press releases preferred to suggest that it was 'set in a period 40 or 50 years ago before the race came into general contact with white civilization'. Shorn in the end of all temporal references (except for the Twist enthusiastically danced by Asiak at the trading post), *The Savage Innocents* pursues Ray's reflections on America. Being American – sharing in that civilization, rather than that citizenship – assumed increasing importance for him now that he was going to live in Europe, and the comments of Alan Lomax (who had left earlier, during the Cold War years) are very much to the point here. This international film is an American film, the product of a time when a generation was rising which allied a rejection of society with a return to nature. Its leading light, Jack Kerouac, had his revelation of America through reading Thomas Wolfe.

The Savage Innocents did not reach the United States until 1961. Little seen, it nevertheless left its mark on the collective consciousness, if only by resurfacing in the song *The Mighty Quinn* (*Quinn the Eskimo*) by another of America's rebel poets, Bob Dylan; the album was called *Self Portrait*.[13]

34

Two Films in Spain: King of Kings and 55 Days at Peking

'Upon the hairy completion of *Savage Innocents*,' Betty Utey recalled, 'we were idling in Rome. The Israeli film people wanted to get their film industry going, so we went to Israel for a while, flirted with that. We had gone to the Arctic determined never to go back to America. Nick's plan at the time, his growing desire, was to film "a day in the life of . . ." very simple stories. He wasn't interested in documentary but in simple stories, in the idea of just setting out with a camera on his back. There was also the notion of creating an international film school in Switzerland. That was another aspect of his dream. We even had a sort of reception, with certain publishers from different parts of the world who were ready to finance this kind of school, where a film would be made every three years from international talents. We went back to Rome, and with the birth of my baby imminent, he told me he had signed with Bronston to do *King of Kings*. This wasn't what we had agreed between us, it wasn't what he wanted to do, and I was furious with him, because with the contract came a car, a mink coat, and all that crap. Anyway, we went to Spain and it was a hell of an experience.'

Aside from personal motives, there was a professional reason for Ray's exile: after the box-office failures of *Wind Across the Everglades* and *Party Girl*, it seemed unlikely that he would be able to direct another film in Hollywood. Besides, the era of the runaway production was just beginning.

Samuel Bronston held a peculiar position among American producers. Born in Bessarabia in 1909, he was said to have studied at the Sorbonne and to have had a brother who was a celebrated violinist. After one or two films in Hollywood, he went to Europe, where he produced a series of documentaries for the Vatican before establishing himself in Spain. Through the agency of one of his associates, Alan Brown, who knew Admiral Nimitz, he secured the backing of Pierre Du Pont III, head of one of the three great American families (Mellon and Rockefeller being the other two). The Du Ponts financed highly patriotic radio and television series, and the combination of Americanism, morality and grand spectacle proposed by Bronston appealed to them. Pierre Du Pont agreed to

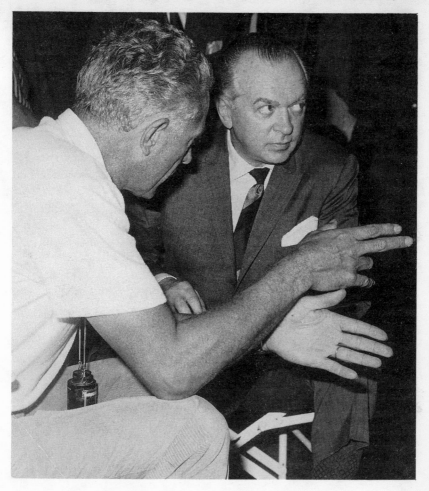

60   *King of Kings*: Samuel Bronston with Nicholas Ray

guarantee the financing of his films, initially with pesetas blocked in Spain: the result was *John Paul Jones*. The director, John Farrow, saw his opportunity to realize one of his dreams: a life of Christ, *Son of Man*, which he had been wanting to make since 1953. But, according to Alan Brown, 'his script was not really a script, it was the Four Gospels put down; and Sam called me and said, "I cannot even understand this, it's all Thee and Thou and everything else." ' Alan Brown, and then a veteran Hollywood screenwriter, Sonya Levien, rewrote the script; and finally, in November 1959, Nicholas Ray was signed as a replacement for Farrow. His contract to direct *The Sword and the Cross* (the new title) was negotiated by MCA London. His fee of $75,000 for 24 weeks

361

($3,125 per week, without compensation for eight additional weeks of post-production) was less than he had received for *Party Girl*, but he was to receive 2 per cent of the gross producer's share for the Western hemisphere. The contract also stipulated his supervision of the editing up to the first answer print (neither of the terms was ultimately honoured).[1]

According to the art director Georges Wakhévitch, who had been working with Farrow, when Ray arrived he 'found the film all prepared, and was pleased with the sets we showed him, merely asking for a few details to be added'.[2] Details of some consequence, because at the time not a word of the script had been written. Ray's first move was to turn to Philip Yordan, with whom he hadn't worked since *Johnny Guitar*. As Yordan described it: 'I got a call from Nick saying, "I'm on a project here, but I have no script. There *is* a script but it's hopeless. We can't get started." I didn't want to go to Spain, but he asked me to just come over there for the weekend. The picture was called *Son of Man*. Terrible title, and someone had taken chapters from the Bible and sort of tried to make it play, but it was awful. So what I did was, I told Sam, "Look, if you want me to do this project, if you'll cut me in, I'll get you a script, but not *Son of Man*, you can't sell that." It was my idea to call it *King of Kings*. So everybody says, "You can't call it *King of Kings*. DeMille made the picture [*The King of Kings*, 1927]." Well, *King of Kings* is in public domain, it's a title that goes way back ... I could show you books from the seventeenth century. They were talking about negotiating with the DeMille estate and giving them 10 per cent of the distributor's gross. So I said, "Register the title!" I remember it cost a six cent mail stamp. They sent it in to the MPAA and DeMille had never registered it. So for six cents we got the title!'

Ray claimed he had to make concessions to get Yordan, whose contract post-dated his own by only five days: 'I wanted a very tough constructionist and I knew he was the man, someone who could provide a connective tissue dramatically and keep the story going.' Yordan was to be the right man for similar jobs more than once in the years to come. Ray also brought in Franz Planer, whom he had tried to get for *Rebel Without a Cause*.[3] Planer, who had worked in Spain before, engaged a Spanish colleague, Manuel Berenguer.

Ray began the year 1960 in Rome, where his daughter Julie Christina was born on 10 January. He worked on the script, for which he assembled a mass of documentation. His relations with Bronston, very little older than himself and whose wife was also expecting a baby, were good. He was treated as an equal, and represented the production in London for discussions with Earl St John, the head of Rank.[4] Doubtless

Ray also felt a gambler's admiration for the master bluffer. Alan Brown commented: 'Sam was a real genius. He was a salesman, including using tears. Say he had $500,000. He'd have the contract of Loren, the promise of Pierre Du Pont, and he would build a magnificent set, which he would bring the distributors to see. He'd have no script. Sam took them in legitimately, those people who think they're geniuses. But the financing was always the worst, tense time for Sam. He would just have enough money to get through till Tuesday, and it was already Wednesday. I used to keep money on *King of Kings* in a Kleenex box – pesetas, with a Kleenex on top. Hidden for emergency, because Sam was in London or Zurich.'

The actual production, in other words, was left to its own devices, especially as Du Pont imposed no financial control and appointed no one to supervise his interests on the spot. Blind to this disorganization, Ray added to his team a character destined to play an important role in his career: Michael Waszynski. Born Michał Waszyński in Volhynia in 1904, he claimed to have been Murnau's assistant and, during the Second World War, to have fought (winning decorations) in the Second Corps of the 8th Polish Army. He was also to announce that he was a prince. One thing is certain, and that is that in Poland he was both prolific (more than thirty films in ten years) and commercially successful as a director (his big success was *Znachor*), whose only ambitious work was *The Dybbuk*. After the liberation, he made three films in Italy, then worked, in some-what nebulous capacities (co-director of *Othello*, his biographical particulars modestly suggest) on American productions in Europe. Ray hired him as casting director.

Meanwhile he continued working on the script with Yordan and a Catholic priest, the Rev. George Kilpatrick, an Oxford don, who remained on hand throughout filming. In February he wrote to Bronston to say that, thanks to Kilpatrick, he had solved the dramatic problem of how to treat the trial of Jesus. 'For the first time since I completed the script of *Savage Innocents* I feel like writing again.'[5] Simultaneously, he was scouring Europe for the actor who would play Christ: 'The greatest actor alive, or an unknown,' he told young interviewers. In London, he became interested – with no great conviction – in Keith Michell (the gentleman in Losey's *The Gypsy and the Gentleman*) and Tom Fleming, who had just played the role on television. Peter Cushing and Christopher Plummer were also considered. In Rome, he noticed a young actor in an Ingmar Bergman film. 'I remember Nick walking up to the screen,' Alan Brown said, '*this* close to the screen in the projection room, during a very dramatic moment, and saying, "Look at the eyes! And the ascetic look on the face!" ' This was Max von Sydow, who was to play the part, but two years later, under the direction of George Stevens. In the end, John Ford recommended a young actor from his 'family' to Brown and Ray: Jeffrey Hunter, the Frank James of *The True Story of Jesse James*, who had just finished his third film with 'Pappy', *Sergeant Rutledge*.[6]

Bronston obtained an audience with the Pope, and on 8 March, John XXIII approved a script credited to Yordan and the Italian Catholic writer, Diego Fabbri.[7] The production was in preparation at the Chamartin studios in Madrid. Bronston launched an extensive publicity campaign, making much of the fact that he had dispensed with any involvement from the major studios. On 27 April, three days after filming started, the *New York Times* published an article on the unconventionality of his financing.

But the shakiness of the structure could not be hidden much longer. The Directors' Guild alerted Ray to the irregular situation of Bronston Productions.[8] Stars sought or considered for roles – Richard Burton (as the Centurion, the role that had made him a star in *The Robe*), James Mason (Pilate) and John Gielgud – declined.[9] Only Robert Ryan, faithful to Ray, agreed to play John the Baptist. Internal dissension on the production side was flagrant from the outset. 'Bronston didn't really concern

61   *King of Kings*: the Baptism

himself with the day-to-day production,' according to Simon Mizrahi, who was present throughout filming, playing a small role. 'The Spanish and American production team he had gathered around him were a terrible lot of sharks from the first.' For the time being, apart from Alan Brown, this team comprised Jaime Prades, an Uruguayan producer who had influence with the Franco authorities, and (already) Philip Yordan. 'Very soon the money ran out,' Mizrahi went on, 'and crisis threatened the film. So a decision had to be made to turn to one of the American majors, and MGM was the one which made the most interesting offer.'[10] Yordan offered a picturesque account of the episode (possibly mythical but accepted as fact anyway):

'We had no money. Sol Siegel, who was head of production of Metro, and Vogel, who was president, were both coming over to make a deal on a picture that we're supposed to be shooting. "Nick," I says, "You're going to have to do something." So he says, "Well, let's take a scene like the 500 Jews praying in the courtyard, which we can do on a sandy floor. Then have Pompey riding with his troops through the gates" – there was a gate at the studio that we could use – "and they massacre the praying Jews." What happened was that Vogel and Siegel and five more arrive, they sit on chairs in the sun, there's a couple of *paesanos* to hold umbrellas over 'em, and they watch this scene. We get the extras for nothing. But we had no costumes. So Nick sent people out to buy every white sheet in every department store, and wrapped the extras in bed sheets. For Pompey we had a Spanish extra, one Spanish uniform, one horse. And from an old opera company they got about a hundred Roman legion costumes. We were out there, and the 500 Jews praying was very simple, just sitting and swaying – we said we'd add the chanting later. But Nick comes up to me, hysterical, saying, "Pompey looks terrific on the horse, but these 100 guys that come after him, these starving Spaniards – it's a mess." He sits there awhile, then says "I've got it! I'll have Pompey ride a little faster. I'll have them run!" So that's what we did: it would have taken months to teach them to march in step. The visitors were very impressed by this opening scene, and that night they sent a contract for a five-and-a-half million dollar pickup. So it was very successful.'

Ray approached the film with a seriousness and a fervour difficult to imagine in view of the completed artefact. According to Renée Lichtig, the original editor: 'He oversaw everything, sets, costumes . . . At home, he had two walls covered with books on the life of Jesus, in every language. I never saw such documentation in my whole life. It was extraordinary, absorbing knowledge of a subject to this extent.' Ray and

62 Nicholas Ray shooting *King of Kings*
(Sumner Williams in front of him)

Yordan conceived it as the story of a rebel, whose revolt, in contrast to
political or violent action (incarnated by Barabbas), was expressed
through moral or spiritual action. It was also to provide a context for this
revolt, describing the major forces confronting each other, and the central characters' relationship with these forces. Yordan's liberal ideology
(shared by Ray) can be glimpsed behind the many parallels between the
Roman occupation and Nazism. Ray's attitude also reveals his need to
filter everything through a personal investigation. But Yordan's script is
devoid of visual ideas; concerning the Last Supper, for instance, the script
simply notes that 'Here we have the semblance of the tableau that we are
so familiar with'. But it was in this area that Ray was at his best. For him,
all means were valid in pursuit of his ends: eliciting the 'dynamic' of
scenes petrified by visual tradition so as to rediscover their 'truth' (the
terms are his); lending actors' performances greater depth by giving them
a sense of delegated responsibility; experimenting with innovative optical
effects;[11] and, of course, all the tricks of the trade. Eye-witnesses confirm
the 'inspired' nature of the filming. 'What struck everybody on reading

63   *King of Kings*: the revolt

the script,' Simon Mizrahi said, 'was this extremely visceral rebellious dimension, which allied the film to Ray's other work. But I saw this aspect even more clearly when the rushes were screened; in particular, the whole Jewish background of the time, the revolt, the relations between Romans and Jews.' Renée Lichtig spoke of scenes showing corpses piled up, reminiscent of the concentration camps, in the episode dealing with the Roman conquest.

Betty Ray was responsible for the choreography, and had to arrange Salome's dance to music by Miklos Rosza. The part was played by the teenage Brigid Bazlen: 'A little girl who could not dance, who was not in touch with herself and who had claws for fingers, who was really like a spider-woman: hands in playing and dancing are very important. Nick had me imagining myself as Salome in those times, and kept asking questions about what feelings I'd have and how I would behave. We worked on who she was: a rebellious teenager was the focus. Then he got me on the stage, where we worked with the scenic designers and the composer. But what I worked out with Brigid at rehearsal wasn't playing

367

out on the set. So Nick started to work on camera settings and so on; then said, "We're going to construct a big bird cage, and she'll go to let all the birds out," and "Torches, lots of torches, we've got to *effect* her, rather than just take this actress . . ." That was the start of my knowing how he directed; how he would use every element and make a happening out of something that wasn't happening.'

Royal Dano had arrived in Madrid not knowing what part he was to play, having accepted out of confidence in Ray and Yordan: 'Once we had established the fact that I was going to play St Peter, I went to work on it; I had brought some research with me. Nick said, "I've got a number of amateurs. I won't have time to work with them. Why don't you see if you can get them into this thing?" So I embarked on a little thing of taking these guys playing the other Apostles to dinner every so often. One was a Brazilian, another Spanish, an American . . . plus a professional, Rip Torn, who was playing Judas. I also invited a monk, who spoke Portuguese and Spanish, and we needed an interpreter. At dinner – eleven, twelve, sometimes thirteen of us – we'd discuss the relationships; so even though you didn't have lines, with some idea of your background and what your attitude would be, you'd at least be paying attention to what was going on. At one point, Nick asked me to write a little sequence for them: they're standing up and being questioned by Christ. He needed a filler scene, so I wrote little questions and answers.' 'All our disciples except Peter are young,' Ray commented, 'as they were. Renaissance art made them old, giving them sainthood.'[12] He also noted that 'the more the actors can bring to their roles, the better it will be for the film as a whole. Unless the basic humanity of the Apostles is captured, they will be nothing more than wax figures.' Speaking of other episodes, Ray told *Film Ideal*: 'It seems to me that the historical reality was quite close to what we see in the film . . . I don't think there was a great deal of difference. Many attempts have been made to clear Pilate of any blame, all setting out from a simple exposition of the facts. We tried to show the facts as we believe they really happened.'

This attempt to root the film historically and to present events 'as though they were happening before us for the first time' (another of Ray's expressions) did not pass without incident. Alan Brown was constantly troubled to find no reference made to the divine nature of Christ – leaving Jesus as no more than one healer and miracle-worker among others – and the responsibility of the Jewish high priests played down. ('Caiaphas', Brown objected, 'was here out to get rid of a troublemaker who might cause thousands of his people to be crucified, he wasn't out to get Christ because he was Christian!') Yordan, Bronston and the MGM front office didn't pay too much attention to these arguments, thereby provoking acid gossip within an industry where Jewish involvement on one side and anti-Semitism on the other weighed heavily.[13]

It is impossible now to imagine, on the basis of individual scenes, with the editing probably distorted and a bland score added, what overall dramatic movement could conceivably have carried the film at the level which can just barely be glimpsed in certain scenes and roles. Yet in other equally mutilated films, it *is* possible. 'For the first time in my life,' Renée Lichtig asserted, 'I saw technicians weeping when silent rushes were screened of the moment where Christ reaches out his hand to John the Baptist in his prison cell.' This scene remains in the film, however, and it does not bring tears to the eyes. The reason: a systematic dismemberment of the film conceived by Ray. Could this film ever have existed, as several people who watched it being made affirm with total conviction? Or did the enormous ambition of the undertaking not carry within it the makings of a quite different balance sheet? Simon Mizrahi said: 'For me, it was a film of absolute purity and logic. But it probably harboured the germ of the disease that was hatching. The film grew bigger and bigger, and attracted all sorts of dross, cankers, enemies, spies. There was also the fact that Nicholas Ray was very weak, very unaware. A film-maker as tough and bloody-minded as Anthony Mann would never have allowed such a thing to happen. *El Cid*, good or bad, is a film under absolute control, from first shot to last. Made with the same Bronston, the same Prades, the same sharks who feathered their own nests in the same way . . . but not at Anthony Mann's expense.'

Guaranteeing an investment of several million dollars in June, MGM demanded that the production be expanded and the script reworked.[14] Bernard Smith, a businessman and tough negotiator embarking on a brief career as a producer, was assigned to the film. The rushes, developed by Technicolor in London, were sent to Culver City (to Sol Siegel) as well as to Madrid. According to Mizrahi, 'everyone who was present during filming retains an absolutely nightmarish memory of MGM's intervention.' Philip Yordan became spokesman for the Bronston side. After four days' work with Sol Siegel, he agreed to add a new character to the script, and to insert a big action sequence three-quarters of the way through. Richard Johnson, a British actor under contract to MGM, was to play the role of a Jewish Zealot, torn between Roman authority, resistance with Barabbas, and the teachings of Christ. Mizrahi again: 'MGM thought the film distinctly inadequate. "There's something missing, there's something missing!" Suddenly, "There's something missing" became "We've got it!" Along came this guy imposed by Metro, and he appeared in scenes totalling practically an hour of film.' Renée Lichtig: 'Every day we were given new pages in different colours, and Nick was obliged to assimilate this stuff.' The script, originally dated 2 April, does indeed contain revised pages on blue, yellow, pink and white paper, dated up to 6 September. The Richard Johnson character (David) didn't even make an appearance until this last date, and many of the scenes shot by Ray depart from the script, or don't figure in it at all.

Yordan's dilatoriness in writing, MGM's vacillation, and Ray's resistance to the situation turned the rest of the production into a chaotic business. 'There was no reason in the world for the [new] scenes to be put into the film,' Ray said later, 'and in the meantime they drew away strength from the other characters. You had to use stuff that belonged to Judas and Lucius, Barabbas and John the Baptist. Everybody seemed to suffer because of this, because they were draining off all the time.'[15] Any question of the film he wanted to make now had to take a back seat. Neither Yordan nor Smith had confidence in him, and from Culver City, Smith encouraged Yordan 'to strongly impose your will upon Nick instead of cajoling him'. Remarking on Ray's attitude, Smith added, 'Once again it is proved that directors practically never have any story sense'.[16]

In July, the unit left for Venta de Frascuelas, south-east of Madrid, to film the Sermon on the Mount, shot in five days after lengthy preparation, with five cameras and 5,400 extras. Ray saw it as the linchpin of his film: 'The Sermon on the Mount is always represented with the figure of Jesus standing there unmoving. But there were 7,500 people present, and the sermon probably lasted longer than is generally believed, because it seems illogical that people should have come from miles and miles

64   *King of Kings*: the Sermon on the Mount

around, 7,500 people flocking together for only a few minutes. More-over, the teaching method used in the synagogues at the time was a dialogue comprising question and answer, and all the indications were that this form of question and answer was used for the Sermon on the Mount. But if he was being asked questions, Jesus would have to move among the crowd in order to hear the questions and let his replies be heard. This decided, I asked for all the available track to be assembled, and if there wasn't enough, for more to be ordered; then we constructed what, according to my crew, was the longest track ever built, from the top of a hill to the bottom, with a track counterbalancing it on the opposite slope, the cables wound round a pair of olive trees, and we followed Jesus as he moved through the crowd, answering the questions he was asked. The Sermon thus takes a more dramatic turn: it probably required more effort from the actor playing Jesus, but I hope will also bring out the principal points of the Sermon more dramatically, making the audience pay closer attention to some of the greatest exhortations ever addressed to mankind.'[17]

Simon Mizrahi: 'It was a great moment, completely magical. This said, it was a difficult scene, because it hadn't really been properly prepared. Ray wasn't a film-maker who pre-planned his images; he had a poetic sense of the scene, he knew his characters, but what mattered was his feeling at the moment, in terms of the almost sensual sympathy or antipa-thy that might be aroused in him by an object, a set, a location. So he improvised his shots on the spot, and that posed problems, because he would often decide only at the last moment where he was going to put the camera, and whether he wanted a lot of extras or only a few. Some-times, with a couple of thousand extras on hand, he would change the camera position two or three times. So it took a long time, but since he would do all this with great courtesy, respect and amiability, there was never any real tension. This was probably the last big scene shot without outside interference. It was a few days later that things started to get bad.'

While the Sermon on the Mount was being filmed, Franz Planer was taken ill: officially the reason given was sunstroke, but in fact it was the first symptoms of the cancer from which he died two years later.[18] Manuel Berenguer, who had worked with him since the start, replaced him without friction. Soon, MGM sent out a contract cameraman, Milton Krasner. The latter had no problems in taking over (Planer was using his chief electrician; he was familiar, too, with the large screen format, which he had worked on for Fox in the early 1930s); he was accepted, and was later able to retain the impression of a production without interference or disagreements, and of a director who was pleasant, professional, and totally in control. The collaboration with Planer and Berenguer had been 'a dream' for Ray. Krasner's style was elegant, less contrasty, indifferent to deep focus effects, but he adapted it to Ray, as can be seen from the Last Supper sequence, which he shot. Berenguer went on working concurrently, often at a second camera (as he did for Salome's dance, shot during the summer at the Sevilla studios).

Another new arrival was more fraught with menace. Simply because she enjoyed Ray's confidence, Renée Lichtig was suspect. While waiting for a numbering machine, she had fallen behind. Irving Lerner was therefore called in to supervise the editing. The move was probably suggested by Yordan, for whom Lerner had just directed *Studs Lonigan*; accepted by the studio, since he had just served as second unit director and 'associate editor' on *Spartacus*; and supported by Ray, who had known Lerner since Frontier Film days, and who later claimed to have recommended him to Kubrick when the latter took over as director of *Spartacus* during filming. This pleasant unanimity soon turned to disillusionment. Mizrahi: 'Renée Lichtig had done a stunning editing job, which brought out the slightest nuances, the faintest undercurrents in certain scenes. Lerner amused himself by cynically experimenting with edgy, thriller-style cutting, hacking away at the film's expansive, lyrical style to show how modern he was.' The only Lerner contribution Lucie Lichtig liked was the documentary feeling and rhythmic sense he brought to the Massacre of the Innocents. An hour of film edited by Lerner was screened, and his intervention ended there. But after this, Ray felt that the film was no longer his in any way. 'The shock must have been very great to make him start drinking again,' Mizrahi said. 'It happened quite suddenly, as if he had decided to give up, to turn his back on the film, to reject it. A strange reaction: masochistic, suicidal.'

Gavin Lambert, who was in Rome, was asked by Ray to come and spend some time in Spain. 'We went out to visit this extraordinary open air set at the huge studio that Sam Bronston had bought – it was supposed to be the MGM of Spain – and it was a marvellous set, wonderful. The atmosphere was really evil: it was like two courts. By this time, Nick and Phil Yordan, who had been old friends, were not speaking. Yordan was executively above Nick, so he was there not only as a writer, but to see that Nick shot his script. And it was like an arena, these battlements, this enormous open air set. There was the court of Nick at one end, and the court of Yordan way over at the other, and they communicated only by walkie-talkie radio, they never spoke a word directly. "I wonder what they're up to down there," Nick would say, "I wonder what they're plotting . . . But I'm going to sneak in a few things . . .'"

With technicians being replaced, a character inserted, and the script under constant revision by both Yordan's people and MGM's, this battle for position – lost before it even started – was very hard on Ray. Around September he even had to be temporarily replaced by Charles Walters, a typical studio contract director who had fulfilled a similar function on Anthony Mann's *Cimarron*.[19] In a telegram to Bronston, Ray finally informed him that shooting had finished 'in good health and under budget, and your son sat up for breakfast', and that it would be a pleasure to film the pick-ups with Harry Guardino (playing Barabbas, he had been in a car crash).[20] But, he added, the situation as far as the editing and dubbing were concerned was far from clear. His feeling was that MGM was going back on the agreements assuring him control of post-production. 'What do you want me to do?' Bronston needed MGM money to start *El Cid*; and on 11 October, the Ray-Lichtig cut was handed over to the studio in exchange for a payment of six million dollars.[21] 'The film was taken out of Nick's hands,' as Renée Lichtig put it. 'He came to me one day and said, with tears in his eyes, "That's it, Renée, it's all over!" ' He left Spain and went home to Italy with his family.

A month later, however, Bronston asked him to go and finish the film in California.[22] At MGM's request, certain scenes were to be reshot and others added. As with all the studio's films, the editing of this one was supervised by Margaret Booth, the venerable head of the department, who no longer set foot in the cutting-rooms, but whose artistic judgements were law.[23] Faced with the film's three-and-a-half hour running time, unmoved by Ray's feeling that the length was necessary, Booth began by eliminating the Richard Johnson character, inserted at great cost by the studio themselves. The logic of a whole section of the film was thereby destroyed, and the task faced by the new editor, Harold F. Kress, was to cobble the whole thing together.[24] According to Ray, 'It had a very key scene in it which the Reverend Kilpatrick and I and Yordan were very unhappy to see go out. It was between the Richard Johnson character and Hurd Hatfield [Pilate], in which Johnson says: "Pagan, Jew or Christian, there is only one God and we are all involved." There was no other place to put that kind of statement into the film, since we had had to make room for the sequence.'[25]

Ray's stay in Culver City lasted only a fortnight, from 28 November to 13 December. Supported, it would seem, by Bronston, he tried to salvage what he could. 'A less than pleasant experience,' as he put it. Besides a little dubbing work with the actors on hand,[26] he tried to undo the havoc wrought on Jeffrey Hunter's diction by studio staff, taking him to Nina Moise (as he once had Natalie Wood). He was simultaneously working with Ray Bradbury on a new scene between Barabbas and Judas, in a cellar where Barabbas is forging arms which he means to use to storm a Roman fortress, taking advantage of Christ's arrival in Jerusalem for Easter. This paved the way for 'the big action sequence' in the second half: the attack on the fortress and the defeat of Barabbas. The scene had been conceived by Bernard Smith and Ray to replace one featuring Richard Johnson, and to formulate the opposition between Barabbas and Jesus (with Barabbas given one gem of a line: 'I am fire and he is water. How can we ever meet?' Moments before, the supremacy of water over fire had been demonstrated as a red-hot weapon withdrawn from the fire was plunged into water.) The cameraman this time was another studio veteran, George Folsey, and Ray remarked on 'the surprising lack of familiarity of the camera crew with the Technirama camera'.

The forge scene was shot in three days, and was followed, on 12 and 13 December, by what Ray saw as 'a test for a new scene which I had conceived for the ending of the picture . . . The need for an ending had been voiced both by Metro and me.' In the script, after Mary Magdalene learns of the Resurrection, Yordan cut to a montage of feet advancing through the ages, and to a statue of the Virgin Mary under a gigantic modern cross! In Ray's first ending, after the Resurrection, Jesus bids farewell to his disciples on a mountain in Galilee; another farewell scene, by the edge of a lake, had also been shot in Spain, and it was this idea he meant to film again. In the version finally used in the film, Christ takes leave of his disciples at the edge of a lake or sea, then his shadow lengthens, becoming immense and forming a cross with a line of fishing-nets lying on the shore. Not having scouted the location beforehand, Ray could not consider the 'test' he shot to be definitive: 'The surf was too high to have any boat anchored in the water (which seemed necessary for composition) and, most important, there was no way of making the kind of exit for the disciples, as I had conceived the sequence, without five of them on departing the scene giving the illusion that *they* were going to walk on water. Consequently the scene was shot regardless of performance values, etc., in order to test for light and for the effectiveness of the shadow cut out, and the potential effectiveness of the scene.' The version used in the film, static like a *tableau vivant*, was filmed after Ray's departure. 'I have seen neither the test footage I shot nor the final shooting,' Ray wrote[27] barely ten days before the first sneak preview: a further demonstration of the director's limited function as far as the major studios were concerned. Rumours once again went around that Ray had been sacked;[28] but whether MGM sacked him or whether the self-sufficient studio machine no longer needed him, makes little difference. Ray Bradbury wrote the commentary, Harold Kress completed the sound effects, and Margaret Booth supervised the finishing touches in London, where Orson Welles recorded the commentary on a very impersonal note.[29] The preview was a success, but the studio decided to add a scene between Mary (Siobhan McKenna) and Mary Magdalene (Carmen Sevilla). Siobhan McKenna was in Belfast, where she was appearing on stage every evening, Ray in Rome. They met for one day, 8 May 1961, at MGM's Boreham Wood studios, near London.[30] The scene, about which Ray knew nothing until the night before, was polished off in straightforward and effective reverse-angle shots.

Released in October, the film was greeted with contempt by the American press, and vigorously defended by Ray whenever he had the chance, showing himself more disposed than ever before in his career to expound at length on the motivations behind his work and its ambitions, while remaining silent about the mutilations. 'The thing we had to capture was an age of expectancy, a feeling that all this was happening for the first time. Our wording is close to the modern Bible, a kind of *Spoon River Anthology* English – mostly an avoidance of contractions.' Ray made this statement in December 1960, while he was filming in Culver City. It may be true of the first part of the film: the account of the conquest of Judea – almost a silent film, with music and commentary – the tersely sketched parameters of oppression, the reddening glow of blood and flames, the luminosity of the encounter between Lucius and Mary, the presence of water (with the baptism scene recapturing the tone of the one in *The True Story of Jesse James*), the intimist feeling of the first scenes with the disciples, the superb movement underpinning the Sermon on the Mount. The narrative gradually loses its power as it progresses. No doubt there was less to meddle with and mutilate in these early scenes. But one is forced to wonder whether, given ideal conditions, Ray would have known what to do with his liberty. Certainly, the tension between ambition and compromise is rarely more glaringly obvious than it is here. But a contradiction in Ray himself is also apparent: as a film-maker formed by the studio system, incapable (at this stage) of dispensing with it or opposing it, he could no longer resist its pressures and was unable to incorporate them. Hence the discrepancy, often evident in the same shot, between a powerful vision and conventionally pious imagery. The unifying idea, no doubt powerful, probably fell short of cinematic expression. Ray could display his *mise en scène*, now remarkable in its mastery, in the scenes set in Herod's palace – and expound on it – but it is only *mise en scène* not the dynamic impulse of a film. *King of Kings* is indeed 'the story of a moral crisis' (Jacques Rivette, years before), but the inspiration is now far from lying 'first and foremost in the pure pleasure of film-making, as a brush finds creative freedom on a canvas'.[31]

After his December stay in California, Ray returned to Italy, where he spent the major part of 1961, busying himself with domestic details. He moved into a house on the Via Appia Antica, on the outskirts of Rome. Betty was expecting another child. Reconciled with Yordan, Ray worked with him on various subjects, shuttling between Rome, London and Paris. 'He and Phil had a long alliance in this town [Hollywood]', Betty explained. 'In my opinion, he trusted Phil then. Nick was not high on trusting anybody. And even with Phil he would get paranoid. But they seemed to handle each other okay.' It was during one of these trips that he attended the first retrospective devoted to his work, at the Cinémathèque Française: at the rue d'Ulm auditorium, eleven of his films were screened between 9 and 14 March.[32]

For Yordan, he read and had an option taken on a biography of Cyrus the Great, and dreamed up a circus story. The idea, it seems, was simultaneously conceived and sold in the course of a brilliantly improvised recital: 'The script began to exist when he began to tell the story,' a witness reported. Not particularly interested himself, he tried to interest Robert Mitchum in *Circus World*, and let it be announced that he would direct the film. He showed little inclination to work with Bronston again. When he received a deferred payment from the latter, he invested it in projects he planned to produce himself. In Spain, he met the novelist William P. McGivern, Brigid Bazlen's uncle, and bought one of his novels, *The Road to the Snail*: not one of McGivern's thrillers, it is a simple story about a little village in southern Spain where an archaeological discovery is accidentally made. McGivern came to Rome to work with him during the summer.[33] He also wanted to make a film about the Children's Crusade, based on a 1959 novel by Henry Treece, the English writer of books for children. Treece also tried his hand at adapting his novel. With a naïvety which he took to be great strategy, Ray attempted to interest Charlton Heston (who, at the peak of his fame, was filming *El Cid* for Bronston) in both projects, inviting him to co-produce and co-direct(!) the second.[34] He was also working, this time with Yordan, on *The Tribe That Lost Its Head*, a Nicholas Monserrat novel set in Africa. And he vaguely considered adapting a novel by Yael Dayan, an Israeli writer he met through an American journalist in Rome, Curtis Bill Pepper.

During this year, 1961, the Italian capital briefly became the American movie capital: the whole place was pressed into active service for the filming of *Cleopatra*. But also passing through and working there were such directors as Richard Fleischer, Robert Aldrich, Jean Negulesco, André De Toth, Fritz Lang, Edgar G. Ulmer, Vincente Minnelli, Anthony Mann, Hugo Fregonese, Henry Levin, Rudolph Maté, Curtis Bernhardt, Melville Shavelson, Roy Baker, Guy Hamilton, Terence Young, Charles Frend, Frank Wisbar, Joseph Anthony; such producers as Sam Marx or Sam Spiegel, and such actors as Alan Ladd, Mel Ferrer, Jeanne Crain, Angie Dickinson, James Mason, David Niven, Ben Gazzara, Stewart Granger, Charlton Heston, Arthur Kennedy, Gene Kelly, Anthony Quinn, Ernest Borgnine, Guy Madison, Cyd Charisse, Edward G. Robinson, Kirk Douglas ... Absorbed in his life as a paterfamilias, Ray remained a little aloof from all the comings-and-goings centred on the Hotel Excelsior, but became friends with Van Heflin (whose career was then on a downward slide) and spent a weekend with John Houseman, there to produce a film featuring the Roman jet set, *Two Weeks in Another Town*. When he sensed, after the first preview in America, that *King of Kings* was going to be a success as far as the public and professional circles were concerned, he rejoined the social swim, associating with American expatriates in Rome: Bill Pepper and his artist wife, Beverly, and Claire Sterling, a specialist in scoops about the terrorist threat from Moscow, were his odd acquaintances at the time. Ray was invited to serve on the jury at the Berlin Festival, where he fought for *Une Femme est une femme* (and against *La Notte*). At Venice, courtesy of *King of Kings*, he chaired a symposium on 'Cinema and Civilization'. In all things he remained very American, never learning the language of the country in which he was living, seeing festivals as an opportunity to promote the film industry of his own country.

He was flirting with MGM. When Bernard Smith asked him to shoot the scene between Mary and Mary Magdalene, he replied: 'My only expression can be one of absolute joy – perhaps even a misunderstood exuberance – that this is the only thing such a critical group of people found lacking in the film.' The irony is rather heavy. This was no longer the case, however, when he wrote to Bronston to say he had 'every expectation of being in New York for the première. If you or Metro are apprehensive about my discussing the editing of the film, etc, please do not be.'[35] Between the birth of his daughter Nikka on 1 October, and his wedding anniversary on the 13th, he found the time to attend premières of the film on both coasts. In Hollywood, he anounced five or six films to be made in Europe, mentioning only three titles: two he intended to produce himself (*The Children's Crusade* and *The Road to the Snail*), and *The French Revolution* for Bronston. In private, though, he let it be known that, as far as he was concerned, the Bronston organization inspired increasingly diminishing confidence;[36] only enthusiasm for the subject led him to work on *The French Revolution* (passing through Paris, he took a look at Renoir's *La Marseillaise*). Only a few days after the Metro press lunch, however, Alan Brown wrote to say how delighted he was to be working again with him on *The Boxer Rebellion*. What could have interested Ray in this subject? With a certain hypocrisy, he wrote to Bronston: 'I have yet to encounter a single exception to the excitement about a story in which representatives of eleven nations are engaged in a mutual struggle for survival.'[37] (That it dealt with the survival of occupying forces, the equivalent of the Romans in *King of Kings*, occurred to no one except Ben Barzman a year later.)

Only Philip Yordan gave a concrete reason for interest in the subject: 'What interested me in *55 Days at Peking* was 400,000 dollars. That's what Bronston was paying me for the script. He pre-sold to the whole world. You could find a marvellous story for the United States, and they wouldn't buy it in England. So we had to have some idea that the whole world would buy in advance. Very difficult. I bought *Brave New World*, by Huxley. We had a meeting of all the distributors, and boy, there was almost a riot, they hated it, wouldn't touch it. I had to unload it and think up an idea they'd buy. The Boxer Rebellion, big sets, suspenseful, colourful . . . coming up with the title was kind of hard, but "55 Days" and "Peking", along with everything else . . . they bought it. So it was a commercial manufacture job.'[38]

Money wasn't Ray's motivation: 'I made the usual mistake of the journalist who says to his wife, "Darling, I've just had an offer from an advertising agency to become their chief writer for commercials. It'll bring me $200,000 a year, and that will give me the chance to move to Connecticut and write the Great American Novel." This gave me a lot more than $200,000, and I thought, "All right, for the last time I'll break my promise to myself never to do anything I don't want to do." ' (He was paid $400,000, or according to some sources, $1 million for three films, of which this would be the first.) This decision, which no one and nothing was forcing him to take, was none the less painful: 'I woke up one night and said to my wife: "Something has come to me in the night, and told me that if I do this film I will never make another." '[39] There was, of course, the pride in being (as he was to repeat often enough), 'the highest paid director in the American cinema' (which is doubtful), in achieving fashionable as well as more serious recognition, in becoming the darling of the trade papers. What he was forgetting was that it was impossible for him to shape his life, his habits and his cinema for very long in accordance with this aspiration, as Losey was to do successfully. (Losey, after ten years of political exile and mutilated films, had other reasons for wanting recognition, even from snobs and the wealthy). The psychological explanation – Ray being a manic depressive, an inherited family trait – is obvious, but not very helpful. At all events, the fear of moving from thought to action became increasingly marked in him. In 1961 he had never been closer to making the films he wanted to make: *The Road to the Snail* was budgeted at under three million dollars, had a subject considered to be commercial (Ted Richmond, at MGM, was interested), and enjoyed the backing of Al Bloomingdale, at a time when Ray's prestige had been restored by his most recent film.

But if no one had any intention of standing in his way, no one was there to force him to begin. So the scripts remained perpetually unsatisfactory, in need of polishing, etc. Talking to Buñuel, he did so in terms incompatible with his expressed desire to meet him. 'Finally,' Buñuel reported, 'he said to me: "Buñuel, I wanted to meet you to find out how you make such good films with so little money?" I said: "It's easy. You can do so much better in Hollywood. Instead of making a three-, five- or ten-million dollar film, make a film for 200,000 dollars." He was staggered! He told me, "If I did that in Hollywood, I'd be finished as a director!" He said it seriously. And I realized it was true. It's terrible.'[40]

It was Yordan who now coerced Ray into making the film. But Yordan was no more a producer than Bronston. Accounts of Ray during the making of *55 Days at Peking* portray, not a man who was drinking (the rationale often advanced), but a film-maker who couldn't make up his mind, seeking refuge in frenzied activity and loading himself with unnecessary burdens. 'It was my feeling from the very beginning,' scriptwriter Bernard Gordon said, 'that Nick was totally lost and frightened to death about the problems of making a large spectacle film. He had many exaggerated and non-real notions about bringing people from Hollywood, he spent hundreds of thousands of dollars trying to figure out ways to do things . . .' For Betty, *King of Kings* had marked the start of a self-betrayal; *55 Days at Peking* was to be the beginning of the end. The intrigues and plottings of the Bronston empire, then assuming extreme proportions, of course drove him to this attitude, while at the same time suiting his own inclinations. ('Even paranoiacs have enemies,' said the writer Delmore Schwartz.)

Bronston, after *El Cid*, wanted to work with Charlton Heston again.

When Heston turned down *The Fall of the Roman Empire*, he set Ray and Alan Brown on his trail, their mission being to persuade him to appear in *The Boxer Rebellion*, meanwhile setting about transforming the half-constructed Roman sets into Peking. Between Los Angeles, Washington, London and Madrid, Ray succeeded in persuading Heston (as the latter noted in his journal, published in 1978) 'that he may do what Tony [Mann] couldn't do last year: get an honest script out of Phil'. Such was not to be the case.

The first months of 1962 were devoted to preparation: to compiling the script, with Yordan and one of the many writers he had under contract, Bernard Gordon (Walsh's *The Lawless Breed* in 1952, then blacklisted; he had already worked for Yordan on *Studs Lonigan*); and to preparing the sets, with the Anglo-Italian team brought to the fore by *El Cid*, Veniero Colasanti and John Moore. As lighting cameraman, Ray's preference was for Aldo Tonti, with Claude Renoir as second choice (and Manuel Berenguer to assist in either case).

While Colasanti and Moore were preparing their sets, Ray brought in the Spanish painter Manuel Mampaso. His task was to provide not so much storyboards as dynamic images of the scenes. The painter drew on his own theatrical work, as well as on Eisenstein's drawings for *Alexander Nevsky*, which had just been published for the first time in Spain in *Cine Experimental*. He worked concurrently with the set designers and scriptwriters: sometimes he would conceive a scene before the set had been built, and his black-and-white gouaches were given to the writers with instructions to take their inspiration from them.[41] Ray planned to pursue the visual experiments he had envisaged for *Rebel Without a Cause*, and put into practice in a different form on *King of Kings*. James Leahy notes that he first wanted to use the multiple image 'to condense what he felt were rather prosaic sequences of narrative action: the unsuccessful expedition out of the city to try to raise help for the besieged community'. Bernard Gordon confirmed this in his own way: 'He was working the foreground and the background at the same time, and using the screen in a different way ... sort of ambitious and unrealistic and unrealized ideas.' But Ray was serious. Looking for technical means to achieve his ends, he had Linwood Dunn, one of Hollywood's great optical effects specialists, put under contract. Manuel Mampaso: 'Ray told me, for instance, that the eyes of the Empress would appear on one side of this huge screen, then you would begin to see what she was thinking about: the Boxers advancing. And at the other end of the screen, you would see the English ambassador, who was thinking about the same thing. Then the screen would be filled by the two heads, while simultaneously you would see flashes, a little in the manner of Mondrian, of the fighting.'[42]

Heston (Major Matt Lewis) being the only prescribed casting, Ray tried to push Ava Gardner as the tarnished romantic heroine: a cliché dear to Yordan. He ran up against opposition from Bronston, doubtless conforming to local sensitivities (Gardner had lived through some turbulent episodes in Spain), and from Heston. Bronston's preference was for Deborah Kerr, Heston's for a European actress: Melina Mercouri or Jeanne Moreau. But there was neither script nor role to show them; Ray, on the other hand, was able to persuade Gardner, whom Sumner Williams and his wife, Donna Anderson (who had just appeared with Gardner in *On the Beach*), were sent to Arizona to fetch. Yordan and Gordon dated their script 18 June; in other words, it was finished on the very eve of Heston's arrival. Immediately the latter, like David Niven later on, demanded that his part be rewritten. 'They were all a bunch of prima donnas,' Bernard Gordon commented.

Ray also selected three British actors to play Chinese dignitaries: Flora Robson as the Empress, Leo Genn as the General, and the dancer-choreographer Robert Helpmann, heavily made-up. The rest of the casting was entrusted to Maude Spector's London agency, which did an aberrant job: to please the distributors, there were stars of every nationality, but in every case the star failed to materialize and it was the third or fourth choice who turned up in Spain. Announced for the cast were Michel Simon, Moustache, O. E. Hasse, Peter McEnery, Tom Courtenay; what they got was Philippe Leroy, Jacques Sernas, Joseph Furst, Eric Pohlmann.

As the first day of filming approached, the film assumed less and less importance in the minds of its decision-makers. Among the higher echelons of the Bronston organization, the principal preoccupations were keeping the stars happy and earning the good graces of the Franco authorities. Jaime Prades had been shown the way out, and Michael Waszynski took over as vice-president, while remaining associate producer on the film. Yordan was already thinking about *The Fall of the Roman Empire* and his own productions in Europe. Work went ahead, as Ray put it, 'without my having a production manager, or anyone but myself and my twenty-one-year-old assistant director'. Theft was rife at every level of the organization: editing tables, typewriters, sets of stills disappeared. According to John Melson, 'Anyone at all could go to the concierge in the Hilton lobby and say, "Would you give me an airplane ticket to Paris, and charge it to the Bronston organization?" ' Whatever the number of extras used, half as many again would be accounted for.

Instead of using imitation silk, which showed up better on screen, real silk accessories were ordered. According to Alan Brown: 'Some of Sam's loyal lieutenants were departing for Zurich regularly with suitcases, and coming back without the suitcases the same day. Sam, apparently, didn't get any of that money.' 'It was very dramatic,' Ray commented. 'It's too bad; the show could have stood more of the drama that was going on off-stage. It wasn't unlike it in many ways. The intrigue of the court of the dowager monarch of China was not too much different from that of the dowager prince Michael Waszynski and Bronston.'

Peking had been constructed at the Marquis de Villabragima's *rancho grande* at Las Matas, 16 miles (25 km) from Madrid. The set was built in concrete, more to impress distinguished visitors than to meet any needs of filming. Bernard Gordon commented: 'Mike Waszynski thinking of his own person and interest, Colasanti and Moore trying to make a monument to themselves.' Charlton Heston noted that, 'Unhappily, we never turned a camera on two-thirds of this incredible city.' (He asked Bronston, without success, to let Orson Welles loose on this set with a camera and $100,000: 'Orson would have ad-libbed a marvellous spy story, shooting in the parts of the set we never got to.') Bernard Gordon recalled: 'When I first saw the mock-up of the set, I was appalled. I said, "Listen, Nick, I wrote the script and I have certain battle scenes described in detail, and I don't know where you're going to put the camera to get any of it." He said, "Don't worry, don't worry, Bernie, I know what I'm doing." As a matter of fact, they hired an Italian cameraman. He came and looked at the script and looked at the set, and he walked out! He just couldn't do it.'

Aldo Tonti did indeed cry off a month before filming and (after an attempt by Ray to get Michel Kelber) the British cameraman Jack Hild-yard (*The Bridge on the River Kwai*) took his place. The first evening, the entire Franco hierarchy, headed by the mayor of Madrid, was invited on to the set at Las Matas. 'The work itself was incidental tonight: all press and public, toasts in champagne, and so forth,' Heston noted. A scene intended to be shot at dusk, but delayed by the ceremonies (and by difficulties with Betty Ray's choreography for the Boxers), was eventually shot at dead of night and botched – because there was insufficient light – by Manuel Berenguer, who thereafter found himself relegated to second unit work.

After which the unit returned to the studios in Madrid where, for almost two months during the summer, Ray filmed – with a painstaking slowness aggravated by the problems surrounding him – the principal interiors: imperial palace, hotel, apothecary's shop, British Minister's

65 *55 Days at Peking*: the first night of shooting – Betty Ray
choreographs the dance

office, Taoist temple. Ray: 'The atmosphere could be good around the set
as long as we were not bothered by the assholes who were trying to
become vice-presidents of the Bronston corporation, enterprise, con-
game or what ever you want to call it. Even the new vice-presidents, like
[Paul] Lazarus, a long way from Columbia Pictures where he had enjoyed
the most part of his professional career, were well-meaning.' The scenes
filmed were often pretty to look at, and the director's hand could be seen
in the play of eyes, the splashes of colour, the subtle compositions, and
sometimes a striking dramatic surge. Ray particularly enjoyed directing
Ava Gardner, with whom he formed an alliance of outsiders. She was,
indeed, almost unanimously detested or considered impossible: her late-
ness and her outbursts on set were soon legendary. Ray clearly felt she
was worth waiting for, and soon fell behind schedule, even more so
because of the constant rewrites demanded – or even effected – by the
stars. Manuel Mampaso remembered Ray as 'a very placid man,
reserved, lofty in his dealings with people. I never saw him get angry.
The tensions were very great.' Others became anxious, however, sharing

Bernard Gordon's view: 'During the shooting, Nick was simply so insecure that he needed to have somebody to hold his hand every day before the shooting, and he actually had his wife rewriting dialogue on the set. And Nick was extremely dependent on Phil Yordan, who was very busy doing many other things, and interested in anything but writing. He thought of Phil Yordan as a very strong person, because he was simply frightened. Nick was thoroughly dominated by Yordan, and dependent on him to the point where he would come running during the shooting and say, "I've got to shoot this scene with Gardner in bed, and a doctor . . . I don't know how to get him to . . ." And Yordan would have to look at the screenplay: "Why don't you just have him take out his watch and take her pulse?" Anything to get over the frightened blocking that was going on in Nick's mind.'

In the eye of the storm, subject to all sorts of pressures having nothing to do with his job as a director, Ray sprinkled his text with personal but pointless nods. Among other things, the dialogue has its echoes of *Bitter Victory*: 'Your tight uniform will hold you together,' the Baroness (Gardner) tells Major Lewis; and later on, a sergeant (John Ireland) tells the same Major Lewis, who has to break the news to a little girl that her father has been killed, 'Tell her like you'd like someone to tell your own kid.'[43] Ray's sympathy for the character of the Baroness, a high-class prostitute, becomes apparent in her dialogue with the doctor (Paul Lukas): 'Don't you want to live?' – 'I have lived.' – 'Don't think back, don't think anything now, except of living. Give yourself a chance.' – 'A chance . . . a chance for what? A chance to do it all over again . . .' Early in August, the defection of one of the actors comprising Maude Spector's bizarre casting led Ray himself to take over the role of the American minister, Maxwell, the absentee who is reported to be suffering 'what might turn out to be a diplomatic illness'. He arrives to announce to his fellow ministers from the other nations that 'the United States has no territorial concession in China'.[44] In the end, the 55 Days at Madrid got the better of the director, too.

At the end of August, the unit returned to Las Matas and the Peking set, now filled with extras: the production office, having discovered that there were no more than 150 Chinese available in Spain, made a clean sweep of the Oriental restaurants in Europe. On the 55th day of filming, Thursday, 6 September, upset by the crowds, suffering agonies in front of the camera, Ava Gardner interrupted the filming of her scenes on several occasions. Meanwhile Heston, with whom Ray had been on very cool terms from the outset ('What Nick couldn't stand,' according to Lucie Lichtig, 'was that Chuck always had his son on the set, dressed like him:

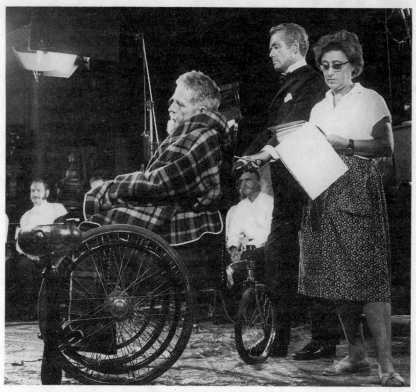

66   *55 Days at Peking*: Nicholas Ray as the American ambassador
(Lucie Lichtig at right)

he'd had all his costumes duplicated for the boy'), had pressed Yordan
and Bronston to bring in Ben Barzman, an excellent scriptwriter who
had been living in Europe since the blacklist, and who had collaborated
(anonymously) on *El Cid*. Barzman arrived on 10 September, and out of
deference to the director, started off by paying him a visit. 'It was in his
luxurious villa outside Madrid,' Barzman said. 'His wife, who was a
ballet dancer and had nothing to do with the film, apart from the fact
that she was married to the director, started off by telling me the story. It
was a scene right out of *Sunset Boulevard*.'

'He was a worn-out man,' Lucie Lichtig said. 'He couldn't take any
more. There were too many people he had to fight against, in addition to
being on set all day filming.' A young writer, Tom Weitzner, who was
then working with Ray on the script for *The Children's Crusade*, was a
witness to the situation: 'It was a combination of things. He was in an
impossible situation as far as the film was concerned. I think he and
Yordan were more or less rewriting the next day's scenes, and blocking

out the day after that. Then Nick would be on the set at 6 a.m. or so, he'd come home late, have supper with Phil . . . no sleep to speak of, maybe a few hours a night. He was always a man who experimented with all sorts of medications; he probably took every vitamin that came out, everything that would keep him awake, everything that would make him a better whatever. Of course his heart wouldn't take it. Plus the writing, directing, producing – it's a wonder to me he didn't collapse sooner.' On 10 September Heston noted in his journal that Ray was 'under too much pressure now'. The next day at 11 o'clock in the morning, as the first set-up was being prepared, Ray collapsed on the set at Las Matas.[45] 'The rumour was that he had a heart attack,' Yordan commented, 'but he had no heart attack. He just quit. One day he just quit on the set by 11 o'clock. An ambulance was called and took him to the hospital, and he never worked again.' Taken to the Anglo-American hospital, Ray was attended by Dr Pablo Azanares and English-speaking doctors. Most of his collaborators were no more credulous than Yordan of the heart attack story put out by the Bronston organization.[46] Betty Ray, however, confirmed that it was true: 'He had a tachycardia. It wasn't a major heart attack. There were not only Bronston doctors involved, there were English and American doctors too. But there was a lot of politics around it, true. As a result they used it so that he wouldn't have final cut. He was barred from going on the lot.'

The director being sidelined in fact suited the producers. Waszynski wanted to be done with Ava Gardner's costly proceedings and get on with *The Fall of the Roman Empire*. Bronston wanted to pay tribute to the Franco regime by making a half-hour film for them about the *Valle de los caídos*, a place of pilgrimage commemorating the Civil War.[47] In addition to the second unit director, Noël Howard, who had been working with Ray since the start (and had already given him valuable support on *King of Kings*), Bronston had called in Andrew Marton, one of the most highly-rated second unit directors (thanks to the chariot race in *Ben-Hur*), who had just a month earlier (28 July) finished the last battles for *Cleopatra* in Egypt. Marton was already at work in Madrid. Summoned by telephone to Las Matas, he managed to finish that day's filming during the afternoon. Marton confirmed that the director was indeed excluded after that day, during which he replaced him. 'The question was, do we call it off, or lay off and see what happens to Nick Ray? Then Bronston made the decision: "No, we don't stop, we go." So I jumped into this very important sequence [the ball] the next day. Then came the very embarrassing moment when the doctors said that Nick Ray could come back to work. About a week later, Bronston said, "I don't want him back." So I just kept on shooting and I finished the picture.'

Simultaneously, Ray's associates (like Mampaso) were fired. On 15 September, a telegram instructed Linwood Dunn to suspend all work on multiple image effects. Heston had Guy Green (who had just directed him in *Diamond Head*) asked to direct his last scenes with Ava Gardner. Green did it as a favour to him, refusing all publicity (or to have anything else to do with the film). Of the two scenes he shot, only one (lasting less than three minutes) was retained in the film: the one in the room where Major Lewis is living after his departure from the hotel, with Heston, Gardner and Kurt Kasznar (as the Baroness's brother-in-law), then the couple alone.

Meanwhile, Marton directed the battle scenes with his usual flair. He dreamed up a rocket-launching siege-tower and a makeshift cannon. He also directed a spirited prologue and epilogue: a cacophony of national anthems, accompanied by sweeping crane shots over the various bands and flags, and a final dialogue scene between Heston and Niven. 'I called these two scenes "book-ends",' Marton said. 'And they certainly gave the whole picture a different feeling, a different meaning. This is my contribution, and of this I'm very proud.' Ray liked the first scene, which

67 *55 Days at Peking*: Andrew Marton directs the arrival of the relief forces

he claimed to have written and prepared, apart from the brief dialogue exchange between two Chinese with which it ends.[48] If he persisted in the illusion that he could still talk of the film as though it was his, Ray nevertheless had nothing but praise for Marton, who (he told *Film Ideal* in 1963) 'did a truly heroic job, arriving totally without preparation. Noël Howard had had more time to prepare; I'm very pleased with the work they both did. Whenever Andy could, he came to my place to discuss things' Marton insisted, on the contrary, that 'there was very little rapport with Nicholas Ray'. With Waszynski's approval, Marton also took over supervision of the editing, judging the film as it stood to be very dated and repetitive. 'I threw out sequence after sequence that was shot. I said, we don't need this and we don't need that . . . now I'll shoot a new connecting bridge, and that's the way we go.' So it was, for instance, by Marton's own account, that he transformed 'the best scene Nick Ray had shot with Gardner' – a dialogue scene with Paul Lukas – into her death scene (eliminating the death scene Ray had laboured over on 4 and 5 September): he simply added a shot of Lukas changing expression, then drawing the sheet up over (the off-screen) Gardner.[49] Noël Howard, for his part, directed the foray through the sewers featuring David Niven, who had insisted that his character be given a little of the action.

Ray left the hospital on 24 September. 'I have another week at home, and then expect to be going full steam again,' he wrote in a letter on the 29th.[50] Heston, whom he had told of his intentions, became worried: 'I can't believe this is a good idea . . . either for him or for us. It's a horrifying thing to say, but maybe the best contribution he made to our enterprise was falling ill when he did. I recall now Bill Blowitz's wry estimate, when I asked him about Nick last spring: "He's talented, Chuck, but I've played poker with him for years. He's a loser." '

So filming continued without Ray, with two units working night and day so as to finish up as quickly as possible with the two male stars. The publicity drive was unaffected, since Marton was as marketable as Ray. The *Sunday Times* colour supplement even published a feature on the Bronston directorate, comprising interviews with the great man himself, his three vice-presidents (Lazarus, Waszynski, and ex-MGM publicist Ralph Wheelwright) and Yordan. Waszynski said: 'I look to the quality. I can't buy bad things. If it has to be Louis XIV, it has to be . . . Sometimes the actors find it easier to talk to me than to the director. I had two hours yesterday with Charlton Heston, I don't have to ask nobody.'[51]

On 22 October – Heston had completed his role the night before Ray attended a screening of footage for distributors. After which, the editor,

Robert Lawrence, denied him access to the film: 'Dear Nick, Mr Bronston has directed me not to project any more of the cut film. Would you please talk to him about it?'

Filming ended on 15 November. On the 17th, Ray was finally allowed to view the first twelve reels of cut film, and the next day he sent Waszynski some suggestions on matters of detail. He was still labouring under the illusion that he was in control of the film. 'I think,' he concluded, 'this version of the ending of the scene which Guy Green shot is preferable, by far, to the version which I originally saw, but I would still like a different reading from Heston before he crosses to Natalie [Gardner]. There are several other readings of Chuck's which annoy me, but we can go into those later. All in all, I am very pleased with the progress that you and Bob have made.'[52]

Ray was never to work for Bronston again, or for any other producer. The circus project was passed on to Frank Capra, who worked on it for nine months in Madrid in 1962 before he quit, disgusted with the Bronston organization, which had also undermined Anthony Mann's health.[53] It was a director with a thicker skin, Henry Hathaway, who finally made *Circus World (The Magnificent Showman)*. In 1964 Bronston's efforts were rewarded: the Spanish government awarded him the Grand Cross of Isabella the Catholic. A few weeks later, he announced the company's suspension of payments.[54] Michael Waszynski remained in Madrid. In February 1965, lunching with Hugo Fregonese, he collapsed at the table. 'He never got to *segundo plato*,' Alan Brown commented in Hispanglais. His obituary in *Variety* conferred upon him the title of prince to which – perhaps inspired by a character in *55 Days at Peking* – he had been so anxious to lay claim.

'At the time of *El Cid*,' Ben Barzman said, 'I suggested to Bronston that he should use his twenty million dollars to make twenty films with twenty young film-makers. His reply could stand as his epitaph: "Sam Bronston cannot allow himself to be involved with films costing less than ten million dollars."' In 1979, in his film-testament, Ray asked Wim Wenders: 'What is your budget?' – 'Ten million dollars.' – 'That's very unpretentious. For one per cent of that I could make . . . [long pause] lightning over water.'

35

In-Between Time

Early in 1963 Ray sold the house in Rome and moved to Madrid. It seems that, by way of compensation from the Bronston organization, he received payment in full of his million-dollar contract for three films, of which *55 Days at Peking* was slated to be only the first. With this money, he intended to further the setting up of his own productions. Most of it went into developing projects; John Melson, a writer from Yordan's stable, felt that most of these properties were 'non-workable', but they enabled him to go 'through that million in about a year'. For his part, Alan Brown wanted to use his experience with Bronston to produce more modest films in Spain, and wrote offering Ray a deal: 'I believe I have all the below the line money. Not luxury money, like Sam.' He started off with the *Road to the Snail* project, suggesting that Ray cast Peter O'Toole, Peter Ustinov or James Stewart. Nicholas Phipps, a veteran of British movies (*Doctor in the House*), worked with Ray on the script.[1] 'This was one of the many, many projects which always fall by the wayside in this business,' Alan Brown said. 'Nick had a lot of other ideas, I had some, we never got them off the ground . . . There was a story that Nick would have loved to have done on the Basque country, *A Flight of Wild Pigeons*, by Stewart Stern. It was a very personal story of a young Basque, his girl, his family, and a friend who goes to Idaho and dies there, and he brings him back . . . Nick could have done a beautiful job. Trouble was, Stewart Stern wanted to produce and direct, and he didn't have the skill. It was positive, it was beautiful. Maybe too lovely, too simple. Everybody liked it, including Walt Disney, but nobody could see spending that much money on a picture that might be a risk.'

Ray attended a gala performance of *55 Days at Peking* in London, the world première.[2] Prince Philip, Lord Mountbatten were there. Crisis with Betty: 'It was a really rough time for us. Because I had become very much confused, and defiant of that schism in him too. How can you go to meet the Queen on a film that you hate? That kind of thing. I couldn't go and hold his arm and be proper to meet the Queen. I don't mean that in any noble way. I just wasn't mature enough at that time to handle both sides of the thing.'

It was a chance for Ray, his last perhaps, to negotiate from what seemed to be a position of strength. 'Convinced', he wrote later, 'that we are living in the most savage century yet recorded and that women are at the lowest station in their history,' he prepared a treatment of Ibsen's *The Lady from the Sea*. This drama from Ibsen's maturity, in which social problems play second fiddle to psychology, may have been given him to read by Houseman, who had directed it for the stage in 1933. It is a play of atmosphere, revolving around an obsessive dream of escape from bourgeois life and its placidity. Ray planned to film the exteriors in Norway, and the interiors in London or Hollywood. He had reached an agreement with Ingrid Bergman, with whom he had wanted to work since at least 1957; and when the respected playwright John Whiting agreed to work on a contemporary transposition, Laurence Olivier also became interested. MGM (according to Ray, writing in 1968) was prepared to put up the $2,500,000 budget. In Paris, about to leave to go scouting locations with his actress and writer, Ray learned of the death of Whiting at the age of forty-five. He was to talk of the project again – thinking, in 1964, of Romy Schneider, whose age, while breaking with established tradition, would have been more faithful to Ibsen.[3]

Ray had also bought a Polish novel, *Nastepni do raju (Next Stop Paradise)* by Marek Hlasko, a tale of truck-drivers and the road which had been a controversial success in Poland. He went into partnership with the actor Stephen Boyd, who was in Spain for *The Fall of the Roman Empire*, and hoped to film it in Poland, or if that wasn't possible, in Alaska.[4] In Spain at the time, the *Bitter Victory* cameraman, Michel Kelber, used to visit Ray at home, and there met the novelist, who had promptly taken up residence: 'I became very friendly with Hlasko, an amazing roughneck type, with absolutely no moral sense but full of charm, a handsome young fellow who'd had trouble with the police in Germany because he'd fired off some shots in a dance hall, and whom Ray was very fond of.'[5] After a while, a quarrel came between writer and director; according to some accounts, Hlasko, during a nocturnal discussion about the script, drunkenly announced that he had already sold the rights to his book.[6]

There were other projects. Kelber mentioned a thriller called *Furax*, 'semi-humorous, a costume piece set in the Paris of 1900, in the style of *Fantômas*'. Still in 1963, Ray served on the jury at the *Semana del cine religioso y de valores humanos* at Valladolid. The 'Golden Banner' went to Bresson's *Procès de Jeanne d'Arc*, the 'Golden Sheaf' to *La Steppa* (Alberto Lattuada) and *Une aussi longue absence* (Henri Colpi). Meanwhile, he had embarked on a new profession: as a restaurateur. With a Spanish associate, he bought premises in Madrid which he turned into a restaurant/night-club, elegantly decorated with drawings. According to

Sumner Williams, 'Nick always wanted to have a place for theatre people and film people to hang out, and it opened as quite a nice restaurant and cocktail lounge, not chic but very well done, which he named after his daughter Nikka. And he did very well at first.' J. F. Aranda described a splendid-looking place, decorated all in red, with fine woodwork, log fires that barely lit the tables, a grand staircase . . . 'Like a Minnelli set,' Aranda exclaimed, to which Ray, no mean hand himself at red sets and staircases, laughingly retorted, 'Oh, much nicer!'[7] The first person to star at Nikka's was the black pianist and singer Hazel Scott, whom Ray knew from Café Society days. Everybody who was anybody in Madrid movie circles met there – the American movie circles of Bronston and *Dr Zhivago*, that is. Ray refused to let 'his friends' pay; and by the time Sumner Williams took over the management after a year, he had poured a quarter of a million dollars into the place.

Andrés Berenguer, son of the Spanish cameraman on *King of Kings*, himself a focus-puller on that film and often interpreter for his father, described this period: 'I used to go around to talk to Nick once in a while. He was in a very bad situation physically, sick. Drinking heavily, and I don't know what else. Sleeping very little, always saying, "I have to take some rest." ' With a friend, Andrés Berenguer came to ask for advice in adapting a book, *Luna y sol de Marisma*. Ray thought of a title, *Ritual Beneath the Sun*, and undertook to have the young man write a treatment. 'He was very tough with me, but I must say he taught me a lot. He taught me the American system of following a line, going through it to make the story move. So I'd come up with a terrific sequence, and he'd say, "Yes, Andrés, terrific. But what has this to do with the context?" – "I don't know yet, Nick, we're writing it." – "Yes-yes-yes. What's next?" That word, "next", drove me absolutely out of my mind. I'd be very mad with him, but at the same time I had the feeling he was right. He was right in a very despotic way. He was the boss of the project, not writing but controlling everything; he was just censoring. I'd be sitting there alone, writing in a corner at Nikka's, and he'd come up after an hour or two: "OK, what have you done, what's this?" Like in school, you know? "What's next?" I'd have no perspective on what was going to follow, and he always kept demanding what was next. He went around trying to sell this story, he even went to Greece. And never came up with the money.

'He also built Mari Trini out of nothing, a little girl of sixteen [later a singing star in Spain]. In those days she didn't even dare perform in public, she just wanted to be a singer. She got to Nick somehow, and Nick taught her, not how to sing but how to handle herself in public. He directed her on stage, taught her how to move in front of an audience. I used to see him talking to her: "You must do your entrance, climb up on a table like this, you should talk to people as you're singing." He gave her a lot of confidence. At this point in his life, he needed to create, to mould something positive and new. Because when she wasn't there, and I wasn't there, or someone like me – and there weren't many of us in those days – he'd just sit around alone with a bottle.'

In June 1964 Ray was once again invited to be a juror, this time at the San Sebastian festival. He fought for two films. First, *America, America*, being shown for the first time in Europe: he thought it was one of the few great American films of the decade ('whereas *On the Waterfront* is only operetta'), and was hoping until the last day for Kazan to put in an appearance. Secondly, he used all his influence to have the best actress prize awarded to Ava Gardner for John Huston's *The Night of the Iguana*. 'He called Ava Gardner', according to Berenguer, 'to tell her she had been given the award. He wanted to be the one; they were very close. He spoke to her on the telephone for an hour and a half. An hour and a half on a call to the States! A year after the San Sebastian festival, I went to Nikka's, and he was still sitting there in the same mood: very little sleep, a lot going on inside his head. I'd come to ask his advice. I had an opportunity to direct a film: should I do it, or should I prepare myself a little more? He said: "Do it, by all means. But be sure to give the proper introduction to the characters. In many of the Spanish films I've seen, they don't do this. Work with your actors, forget about everything else. No mechanics, somebody else will take care of that; just work with your actors." '

Nikka's was no longer a refuge. A separation from Betty became definitive in January 1964. They had moved house thirteen times during their life together. The years to follow were to comprise further wanderings through Europe. 'For eight years I had my suitcases packed,' Ray remarked later. Airports, friends' houses, meetings with backers who soon shied away, lots of brinkmanship in paying hotel bills. Meeting with Greek financiers, he upped the bidding for 'his' film, banking on Lew Wasserman's friendship, when his only trump card was a verbal agreement with Stanley Baker. He was insisting that it was he who wanted nothing more to do with the US film industry: 'All the talk I heard was about companies diversifying, conglomerates being created. Nothing about the creation of films.'

During the last months of 1963 he had come to Paris to work with James Jones on a script for a Western. Like so many other Americans, aping the 'lost generation' of the First World War, the author of *From Here to Eternity* had moved to Paris in the late 1950s. He was living on the Île Saint-Louis with his wife and their two children. Short on inspiration, he was working for the movies, developing and putting his name to scripts which stood little chance of being produced. Ray fell under the spell of the man – with his boxer's macho physique – and his wife Gloria, and literally invaded their life. In an ironical reply to a *Cahiers du Cinéma* questionnaire for their 150th issue (where he reiterated his mistrust of 'drawing-room anthropologists'), he stated concisely that he was himself going to produce and direct his three current projects, the Western being the first: 'So far, production conditions couldn't be better, given that both Jones and I are living ten minutes walk away from each other on the banks of the Seine.'

The idea for the Western came from Tom Weitzner: while working on *The Children's Crusade*, he had suggested Shakespeare's plays as a possible source, and Ray had asked him to prepare a treatment from *Hamlet*. James Jones's biographer gives a rather confused description of this *Under Western Skies*: a conflict between landowners in the American Southwest during the 1870s, with a 'bewildered and hesitant hero'. Jones 'spent a lot of time in conferring with Ray, who came to stay in his house'.[8] Was there ever any serious hope that the film might be made? After six months, in one of his periodic statements to the trade press, Ray let it be known that the project had been postponed until the following year after Jones suffered a skiing accident.[9]

Gradually, the chances of getting films into production dwindled, and Ray's health deteriorated. Jean Evans, who came to see him in Madrid in November 1963, was worried to find him insomniac and taking amphetamines. Then used in the treatment of alcoholism, amphetamines banish fatigue and stimulate mental activity, producing a sense of euphoria, being not dissimilar in this to cortisone; dependency can mean the onset of hallucinations, and ends in the vicious circle of tranquillizers and stimulants. Told of this, Joseph Losey put Ray in touch with a medical friend of his in London, Dr Barrington Cooper; the latter was the prime mover behind Ray's last important project in Europe, the one which came closest to fruition. Ray left Madrid for London. Soon, according to Dr Cooper, 'I had him stay with me. He rather took over my house and a certain proportion of my life. As an occupational therapy, I suggested that we do some script development. And in fact, we bought and sold a number of scripts which we edited and co-wrote. Nick was an extraordinary raconteur and an extraordinarily effective script editor. And we actually did rather well. We had a little company; the company was Nick, his public relations man, who was called Alan Tucker, and me. Out of that enterprise came two films that we were interested to do ourselves.'

The company was called Emerald Films. One of the two projects, *Only Lovers Left Alive*, was a science fiction novel by Dave Wallis – the author's only book – whose pre-hippie themes had given it cult status. The other, *The Doctor and the Devils*, was one of the scripts written by Dylan Thomas during the late 1940s (and the only one published in his lifetime: in 1953, the year, in fact, of his death). Closely linked to Thomas's work in poetry, the script revolves around notions of compromise, the morality of modern man, the price to be paid for seeking the truth. According to Dr Cooper, 'Nick was seized by Thomas's viewpoint. It was his flag for several years. It epitomized the point of view which he would like to have had, and persuaded himself that he had – in life, in general. Since I also had the misfortune to look after Dylan Thomas for a few months, while I was far too young for it, the temperamental similarities were fascinating. The deracinate nature of both men compare singularly.'

The Doctor and the Devils draws on the story of Dr Knox (renamed Rock by Dylan Thomas) and the Edinburgh body-snatchers, which had inspired a short story by Robert Louis Stevenson. Ray described his hero as 'a pioneer in medicine, very much ahead of this time, who defied prejudice and convention to achieve discoveries in anatomical and scientific research'. 'People practising his "profession" found themselves up against a strange difficulty: acquiring bodies to dissect. They were therefore forced to acquire them in devious ways. My anatomist has an assistant who absolutely worships him, but one day finds the body of his fiancée on the dissecting table. Another problem I tackled with feeling was that of women in those days, educated from A to Z by their husbands and completely dominated by them.'[10]

Dr Cooper: 'First of all, we decided to do *The Doctor and the Devils* in a very straight way. Very much trying to parallel the social, moral and physical levels of the society. I had set up a production with British Lion, to be done in Edinburgh, and it was agreed with Victor Saville. Nick by this time was travelling a little, making some money selling some scripts on which we had worked, and this became our capital fund. One day, in an airport in Paris, he met the directors of Avala Film of Yugoslavia. And he came back to London having signed an agreement which, as a director, was binding; our little company had agreed to do four major films a year, in or out of Yugoslavia, in partnership with Avala. At that time it seemed that it was going to be their development money, their resources of nature, our scripts, skills and sophistication. The film that had so extraordinarily been agreed to start with was *The Doctor and the Devils*. The script was transposed to fit the Austro-Hungarian Empire of that time, and Nick made his headquarters in the Intercontinental in Zagreb, lived very well, the Yugoslavs were very supportive and proud. I think there was nearly a year of script rewriting. And that was in itself fascinating, because Nick thought and spoke in English, the Yugoslavs thought and spoke in Serbo-Croat, and their Ministry of Culture thought and spoke in French. So the script meetings were just a little complicated.'

James Mason, to whom Ray had confided his excitement about the project, learned that Maximilian Schell had been cast in preference to himself: 'This was something I couldn't understand. He'd got a completely new slant on the whole picture, and evidently wanted to do it as a sort of Viennese medical picture, and that I suppose is why he had Schell. But he lost me there, because it seemed to me the only purpose in doing the subject was to take advantage of Dylan Thomas's script, because Dylan Thomas had written some marvellous words in there, and the story itself didn't seem to be of that much value. As a matter of fact, Nick didn't even want to follow the implications of the story, as I recall, that Dylan Thomas had written into it. Now, if you discard Dylan Thomas's idea and his dialogue, then I don't know what you have left.'[11]

Ray invited Howard Berk, one of Yordan's writers in Madrid and a visitor to Nikka's, to accompany him to Yugoslavia to rewrite the script and scout locations. He went to Prague to engage two technicians whose work on Oldrich Lipsky's film *Lemonade Joe* he had admired at San Sebastian: the cameraman Vladimir Novotny, and the art director Karel Skvor.[12] Novotny was keenly interested in technical matters and special effects; he had just devised a stereoscopic television system. 'Nick', he wrote, 'envisaged a multiscreen comparable to the *Laterna Magica* "polyscreen" presented by Czechoslovakia at the World Exposition in Brussels. With the difference that Nick envisaged having several parallel actions within the same frame, which wasn't at all easy. Since I love solving technical problems, I liked the idea, and suggested that it should be done without laboratory processing, filmed directly in the camera with the aid of mirrors that were partly two-way and polarization filters. At the Avala studios, I shot about 150 metres of test footage using this technique, and Nick was very pleased with it.'

Ray entrusted the costumes to Hanna Axmann: 'We lived in the Hotel Esplanade, a whole suite: Nick was treated very well, and he could do anything. All of Zagreb came to life. The façades of the houses, whole streets were completely changed. Everybody threw themselves body and soul into working with him. When he walked through the corridors of the hotel, with this beautiful white King Lear hair, he'd be surrounded by about fifty people. He made sketches of all the shots: he was a dynamo, a perpetual motion machine. He could drink a lot, take a sleeping pill and get a few hours sleep, then be on his feet again, working, working . . . At one end of the room, he'd be talking to the producer, at the other I'd be working with Vera Vrkljan [the associate producer], doing sketches or translating into German.'

In August 1965, *Variety* described Ray as living 'a great love affair with Yugoslavia', while noting that no role of any importance was being played by a Yugoslavian actor.[13] Besides Maximilian Schell (Rock), Susannah York (Jennie) and Geraldine Chaplin, among the actors considered at various stages were Peter Fonda, Roger Tréville, Michelo Gonzales, Tanya Lopert, George Segal, Jan Werich (Voskovec's partner, who had returned to Czechoslovakia) and Jean Vilar. In the article, which announced that filming would start on 1 September, Ray talked of a budget of $1,700,000: 'But, filmed anywhere else, it would be four million.' As always, he announced a number of projects: *The Leader, Only Lovers Left Alive, The Judge and His Hangman* (an adaptation by Robert Shaw), *Gun Hawks* (a Western), *End of the Line* (a Gavin Lambert short story), and films with and for Anthony Quinn, Geraldine Chaplin, and Omar Sharif (this last being about gambling).

Then, once again, a familiar reaction set in: he was seized by doubts about the script. It seems that Ray wanted to integrate elements extrinsic to the action; the historical coincidence, for example, which placed Dr Knox (the real-life model for Rock) and Burke (one of the two body-snatchers) on the same field of battle, at Waterloo. According to Lucie Lichtig, he was thinking of including such a scene, but hadn't yet made up his mind. In June, he had announced the engagement (which came to nothing) of a co-scriptwriter, Lionel Davidson. With the starting date being put off and then put off again, he embarked on another rewrite, this time with Gore Vidal (it is interesting to note that Dr Cooper was not informed of this development). The novelist was then dividing his time between Paris and Rome, and he lent highly-paid 'helping hands' to blockbusters like *Is Paris Burning?* or *The Night of the Generals*. It was the writer and bon vivant Harry Kurnitz, established in Europe since the blacklist, who put Ray and Gore Vidal in touch with each other (they had in fact met in 1955, at the Chateau Marmont).

As Gore Vidal described it: 'So Nick came to Rome and moved into the Parco de Principe hotel: he was in a sort of safari outfit, looked like a white hunter. I don't know why I got talked into that. I was a professional movie writer, you don't write anything for nothing; but he was a big con man, as all successful directors are. And I suppose we had enough past in common. Anyway, he didn't bore me, which most movie directors do. But he was quite crazy. The first sign when I realized that you could perhaps institutionalize him: he came to my flat in khaki trousers with one leg torn to shreds. I said, "What the hell did you do?" He said, "Well, I went to the zoo, where there's a new lion cub. I held it, then it fell and cut my trousers; but I want to own a lion cub and I'm going to buy it." I said, "Where are you going to keep it?" – "Oh, I have a little flat in Paris." I said, "But you're always away, how are you going to keep the lion?" – "Oh, it's not difficult, I'll find somebody to look after him." That was when I realized I was dealing with a madman. The script had a boy in it who gets killed and ends up on the slab, stolen by the two body-collectors. As I worked on the script, with the cast all hanging around waiting for it, Nick suddenly said, "Let's turn the boy into a girl." Now, here we are with a week to go before his money runs out. I said, "To do that, you've got to redo the entire script, and you have to forget Dylan Thomas." Anyway, I did the best I could; we didn't do anything mad like that. The next thing I hear, my agent receives word from Avala, or whatever it's called, saying the script had been turned down because of lack of quality! Imagine that from the Yugoslavs! Nick obviously had some trouble – a lot of trouble – and they just cancelled the thing.'

For what reason was the film never made? The most fantastic version is by no means the least probable, since it comes from Barrington Cooper, who was directly involved in the production: 'Ultimately the piece was rewritten, cast and fully ready to go – and on the first day of shooting there was no Nick and no Yugoslav producer. So far as I know, the Yugoslav producer has never been seen again; he was reputedly a Colonel of Secret Police, and reputedly the famous Yugoslav spy who stole the secret of striped toothpaste! But no one is quite sure about this. He was a very strange man, and he and I had a number of curious combats before he would accept me, one of which was to race by road from Belgrade to Zagreb in identical cars. The production fund vanished with the producer, and the film was closed down. The television aerials were re-erected, Zagreb's life resumed, but obviously there was an enormous contractual mess; most of which, happily for me, was Avala's. I discovered that the script had never been signed over as part of the agreement, and still belonged to us. Thus I was able, so to speak, to buy it back, and even get clearance from Avala. Getting a quit claim from them was a most fascinating undertaking.' (Twenty years later, thanks to Dr Cooper, the film was finally made, in a version superficially faithful to Dylan Thomas, but toned down by executive producer Mel Brooks and the bland direction of Freddie Francis.)

Renée Lichtig, who was to edit the film, arrived to join her sister Lucie, the script-girl. She was met by one of the actresses, Tanya Lopert. 'I got off the plane and she said, "Hello, I'm Tanya Lopert, the film's off." Nick had left the evening before, and heard about it in London. A week before filming was due to start.' According to Lucie Lichtig, 'The Yugoslavs were all ready to go. As far as they were concerned, it was their first major film made by an internationally-known film-maker. No one had any reservations that I saw, management or staff. Everyone was ready, everyone did what Nick wanted. The cameraman was as enthusiastic as a little boy. The only thing was, Nick demanded more every day.'

Ray's own explanations are inconsistent. Talking to Rui Nogueira (Christmas, 1966), he said: 'The day we were to start filming, the Yugoslav producers came to tell us they were very sorry, but the French producer-director Raoul Lévy had left them with so many debts on *Marco Polo* that they couldn't advance a penny for my film.'[14] Hanna Axmann, however, was told by Ray that the production collapsed because it proved impossible to find a co-producer in the West: 'I think Nick promised them a co-production, and they were counting on it. Then it didn't happen, mostly because he couldn't get anyone in Europe or America to put up the money after the disaster of *55 Days at Peking*. It was like Nick reaching into a basket and giving to everybody, and all of a sudden the basket was empty.' Ray had, in fact, between 7 and 20 October, tried without success to interest Eliot Hyman at Warners, hoping to bank on Gore Vidal's name.[15] Ray lingered on in Yugoslavia at least until 14 November. On that date, he wrote a falsely optimistic letter from Belgrade to the cameraman Novotny (who had, like the designer Skvor, been obliged to return to Prague): 'I am sorry not to have returned before you left Yugoslavia, but I have been fighting for the picture to go ahead until a few days ago. We were finally successful in getting the necessary concessions – I am happy to say – but by that time it had really become too late to be practical for this time of year, and I hope we can pick up in the spring.' After this lame excuse, he added: 'I resented every minute I had to spend away from the true efforts of film-making, but I hope to make up for it for both of us.' (Four years later, he did in fact try to get Novotny for another project.)[16]

Those close to Ray felt exactly the opposite: that he was now afraid to start filming.[17] Dr Cooper said: 'My own feeling was that Nick couldn't and wouldn't face up to making the film. He'd had a year or two of living as a great man in a small, unsophisticated community, and he liked that very much. He had done what came easily to him, which was story-telling and directing pre-production, when he could be a great man. But I think that he was terrified of fucking it up on the floor. And I think that was his motive. I think that the Yugoslav producer took most of the money. I think he properly deduced that Nick could easily be bought, and therefore bought him cheaply. Nick would respond impulsively to a perennial need. He was an extremely immature man, and immediacy and impulsiveness was the effervescent product of that: "I want it now!" In addition to the other things, the amount of mood swing was enormous and rapid. Some of the impetus to drinking lay in this rapidity of his mood change (I think one of the factors involved in his phobic response to shooting, from before 55 *Days at Peking*, was mood change), and there was certainly mood change exaggerated by alcohol. There would be shattering changes in a moment, in which everything that was possible became impossible, or in which everything that was impossible would become easily possible.'

What would Ray's film of *The Doctor and the Devils* have been like? According to Dr Cooper: 'First of all, it would have been set in Austro-Hungary, which means that it would have been grander and the people more extravagant at both extremes of society than in Dylan Thomas's script. Zagreb suited the story extraordinarily well, particularly since the old city has the same patterns of levels as Edinburgh, corresponding literally to the three social levels of the time. It would have been made with an explanation for Rock's eccentricity, achieved with scenes from the Napoleonic Wars, in which Rock would have been working as an unqualified army surgeon – as medical students did and do – while the grave robbers worked as medical orderlies. There would have been battle scenes, which would have shown how Rock came to have contempt for his own class, as represented by the officers of both sides in their con-tempt for human life and humanity. Which gave a founding of social conscience to the situation, and also a founding to his arrogance. Jennie [the prostitute involved with Rock's assistant] was more extensively writ-ten than in the film that was made, the number of murders was cut down, the piece more compressed; but the social factors were dealt with more extensively, using Dylan Thomas's language, and with much more sweeping visualization, more class contrast and detail. The music was intended to be relevant to the story; it was both comment and obser-vation. But I was by this time involved in a very cynical undertaking, because I enjoyed Nick as a talent, particularly editorially, and I loved hearing him con people because his stories were so delicious, but I no longer wanted to be one of those people.'

However, the other Emerald Films project, *Only Lovers Left Alive*, made progress during the months following the Yugoslavian débâcle. On 10 May 1966 Andrew Loog Oldham, manager of the Rolling Stones, announced that it would be (for a fee of a million dollars) the first of five films planned under their new contract with Decca. According to Barrington Cooper, 'A lot of work was done on it, and I think it was very viable then. The Stones wanted to do it, and did a lot of work with us on it.' Gillian Freeman's bulky (160pp) script depicts a contemporary city from which the adults gradually disappear, mostly by committing suicide. While the social structure collapses, the children and adolescents organize themselves into gangs (much later, Ray became interested in another 'urban guerrilla' science fiction story, J. G. Ballard's *High Rise*). The 'Lovers' are central to the plot: they fight other gangs to defend their territory, establish anti-authoritarian attitudes, and adumbrate a sort of primitive Utopian society. The Lovers' teacher is the only 'old person' not yet dead, but his suicide – a leap into the void of which we see only the start, repeated several times – remains uncertain until the closing images. The group breaks up, and the five survivors, one of them a pregnant girl, wander the countryside.

That the project came to nothing was no fault of Ray's, but rather because the Rolling Stones, taken in hand by their American manager, Allen Klein, whom they had adopted three days after meeting him, had come to a turning-point in their career. Dr Cooper: 'Allen Klein invited us to New York to discuss making *Only Lovers Left Alive*. We were lavishly accommodated, but the purpose of the meeting was really to abrogate our agreement with the Stones. They flew us to Los Angeles for another meeting, at which they offered Nick a very lucrative director's contract if he would forego his rights. He did, of course, and in the end the contract was not completed. It was quite clear that he was being conned, and on some level it was absolutely clear to himself, but it was a way of getting out of a difficult situation without too much stress; and if nothing else, it meant someone would keep him in hotels and spending money for a little while.'

The tension was noted by those close to Ray: both by Betty, whom he turned up to see in Los Angeles ('He was going to do a film with the Rolling Stones, going to work and running and playing with them, knowing the whole thing was a total fantasy . . .'), and by Jean Evans, who attributed his 'paranoid behaviour' to amphetamines, not realizing that in this case the behaviour was warranted by the facts. In correspondence with the Directors' Guild, Ray insisted that a starting date for filming with the Stones had been set for 1 October, then 15 October, 1966. He became fodder for the gossip columnists: Sheilah Graham – marketing memories of Scott Fitzgerald wasn't her only profession – announced that 'Susannah York may sue Nick Ray' over the Yugoslavian film, adding that 'the same thing happened with the Rolling Stones film'.[18] A few years later, it was Allen Klein whom the Stones took to court. The other films they were contracted for got no further than this one.

Ray left London and sought refuge in Munich with Hanna Axmann. She had worked on Volker Schlöndorff's first film, *Der junge Törless* (*Young Törless*), and introduced the two. For some months, Schlöndorff became an admiring disciple. When he completed his second film, *Mord und Totschlag* (*A Degree of Murder*), Ray handled its sale to Universal, keeping $50,000 as his percentage on the $173,000 deal, plus a further $10,000 for 'expenses'. 'He'd have been quite prepared to keep it all,' Schlöndorff said. 'He was highly paid in those days, and impressed people a lot.' At the end of 1966, he agreed to do a job (about which he remained very reticent) for Atlas Film, one of the main German distribution companies.[19] Rumour had it that what was involved was preparing an international version of Andrzej Wajda's *Popioly* (*Ashes*).[20] Whether it was this film or (more probably) another one, the mercenary nature of the task is in little doubt. 'It was a very difficult time then,' Hanna Axmann recalled. 'I think he was still thinking about *The Doctor and the Devils*; there were still negotiations with the Yugoslavs, back and forth. And he had projects, projects, projects, while I couldn't even find a brush to paint with any more. My apartment was not small, but I was squeezed into one little room, and everything else was Nick Ray, full of projects and telephoning . . . and my telephone bill! Nick didn't think like that, to him a thousand marks was nothing, but for me it was a lot. Nick knew me, he thought it was all right, but it wasn't any more. All other people drown, we are all in little boats, but Nick was a Titanic, an ocean liner, a sinking one.'

He discovered what for a time seemed to him an ideal place to live: the island of Sylt, off the northern coast of Germany. Sandy cliffs swept by winds, it was a summer resort for nudists and affluent Germans. As Stéphane Tchalgadjieff, who was to be involved in one of his projects, recalled, 'Nick's great idea was that Sylt was a sort of natural film set. He had grandiose plans. In a sense he was the King of Sylt, on a social level as well. He made tests, he started on an infrastructure of intended sets, with their own elements of built-in equipment: secondary roads which he'd persuaded the municipality to maintain, and which followed the main roads for miles, so that they could be used for tracking shots . . . He knew every hill, every dune on the island, whose possibilities he'd list. As a matter of fact, you got the tour of the island when you arrived, and he'd even show you how sequences, depending on the angle, could be taking place in a desert in the American Southwest, in Africa . . . a welter of totally different landscapes.'

As before in Spain, when he withdrew his son Tim from school, Ray summoned him again, now aged nineteen, this time from Cambridge, and talked with him for the first time. 'I wanted to become an oceanographer. He intimidated me into becoming a cameraman. He could be a very impressive man. To me, he wasn't a director, he was a father. He thought *Savage Innocents* was pretty important for me, because of "When you come to a strange land, you should bring your wives and not your laws." I didn't know anything about him, so, since he saw I was interested, he started doing this autobiography. He would do recordings every night, and I would transcribe them. That's the way I learned about him. Then he made money out of it, he got a publisher to give him an advance. He never finished the book.' Tim wrote three scripts with his father.

Sylt was not a retreat, Ray spent as much time at airports and in European capitals as he did on his island. On several occasions he changed 'nurses', like the one brought him by Hanna Axmann when she came to the end of her tether, or the one he introduced to Charles Bitsch at Stockholm airport; ten years earlier, at the time of their *Cahiers* interview, Ray had also introduced his 'nurse'.[21] Periodically he stopped drinking, switching to a diet of black coffee, going through stretches without sleep, then crashing for forty-eight hours at a time. He attended retrospectives of his work – Algiers, February 1968 – and the demonstrations in support of Henri Langlois that same month. In Paris, he lived by turns with James Jones and Barbet Schroeder, the young producer of two innovatory films, *Paris vu par . . . (Six in Paris)* and *La Collectionneuse*.

'At that stage,' Schroeder said, 'money would still arrive from Spain from time to time. He'd take modest options on films, he'd hustle a bit, he'd say: "I'll do the script and we'll do the film, give me ten thousand dollars," and the whole thing would eventually just go down the drain. It was really the beginning of the end. He was very disenchanted anyhow, never believed that anything was really going to come off. "You'll see," he'd say, "they'll try to screw me again." But each time he threw himself wholeheartedly into it, working twenty-four hours out of twenty-four until the crash came, then he'd start all over again, with a little money or with a little more bitterness, and so it went. Having said that, we've seen how someone like Sam Fuller, who isn't paranoid and who is perfectly capable of directing a film at the drop of a hat, went through the same torments in Europe. It isn't just the personality that does it.'

Barbet Schroeder's production company, les Films du Losange, tried for some time to cost and then find finance for a project called *The Scene*, the first version of a theme Ray returned to in various forms: it involved Sylt, his son Tim and the latter's boarding-school days, adolescent rebellion. 'He'd even done some tests, shooting little bits on 16mm, kids in a field seen from a distance, masturbating while looking at magazines. He used to say that adolescence is the most uncomfortable age in life. The script was well written, ultra-professional; at that stage things worked well, but later it became increasingly difficult . . . He always had his special little doctor's bag with him, everything just so. He even had books about amphetamines which showed how they destroy the brain, so he used to take vitamins at the same time to combat them. All according to plan; but every three hours he'd have his injection, in his backside, and that's terrible in the long run.'

It was in this state that Ray roamed through May 1968, filming – as per legend – amid all the violence. Traditionally anti-Gaullist, Americans in Paris welcomed the 'revolution' with enthusiasm and little understanding of what was going on; Ray was little better informed, but he wasn't surprised to find young people in revolt. On the first night of the barricades, he was attending a retrospective of his films in a Paris suburb, at the Antony students' hall of residence. According to a spectator, 'We were between *Johnny Guitar* and *They Live by Night* when someone came and told us things were happening in the Latin Quarter. So we watched *They Live by Night*, then headed off there with him in several cars.'[22] The opportunity for filming cropped up quite naturally, as it often did during those weeks. In Algiers, Ray had met a young film-maker, Jean-Pierre Bastid, who was working with Ben Barzman, then employed by ONCIC (Office National du Commerce et de l'Industrie Cinématographique d'Algérie). Back in Paris, the pair hatched the idea of making 'a film in the Nouvelle Vague manner, as he wanted' (Bastid). Joris Ivens was encouraging. During May, filming was improvised with 16mm, then 35mm cameras ('Everyone helped themselves; the deposits were rarely paid'), the footage being developed in Belgium. Bastid recalled having 'edited footage shot by Tim, using a 16mm projector and a little splicer in Switzerland. We did superimpositions by sticking one piece of film on to another, and managed to thread that through the projector!'

'Three twenty-minute episodes' were shot and edited under similar conditions: one on the barricades; one – with Tim on Sylt – about the father-son relationship; and lastly, one in London. 'Sixty minutes of film exposed,' Bastid remarked, 'sixty minutes of edited footage. We didn't have a foot of film more than we used.' The unit comprised Ray and Bastid (both behind the camera and in front of it), producer Henry

Lange, and cameraman Jean-Jacques Renon. Ray's companion, Brigida, had an acting role. Obsessed by the idea that someone was going to steal his film, Ray would periodically disappear for twenty-four hours, 'to put the footage in a safe place'. Actually, Bastid insists, he discovered that some of their footage of the demonstrations had been used in Belgian newsreels. When Ray prepared a synopsis of the film for Lange, giving it the title *Wha-a-at?*, he brought in a new character, a laboratory projectionist who was a police informer. Some shots from this footage appear in *We Can't Go Home Again*; through all the film's ups and downs, which continued after Lange withdrew, Ray managed to preserve at least one print. During the same period he wrote, also for Lange, a script (*Melody of Murder*) for which he had Brigitte Bardot in mind: the project came to nothing.[23]

He spent May in various Paris apartments: the Joneses helped him financially (James Jones wrote a mediocre novel, *The Merry Month of May*, about his feelings as an American rediscovering his youth during the 'events'; almost inevitably, one of the characters is a film-maker plagued by middle-aged love).[24] He used to visit a Pigalle night-club with whose owner he had become friendly, and who figured in his scripts and the footage he shot. Pressing for loans, he sent a 'despicable' telegram (Bastid's description) to Zanuck, who, barely remembering him, responded with a cheque. 'To him it was nothing, to us it was a lot.'

Wha-a-at?, like *The Scene* and, in the following year, *Inbetween Time*, marked the beginnings of an investigation into youth through the cinema. The characters running through the various versions are the father, 'a leonine white-haired man of fifty-seven, a professional artist who can sell his work'; Peter Kienzle, an obvious stand-in for Tim Ray (the latter was very conscious of the 'social pressures' his father had been subjected to, in particular what he felt had forced him to change his name); and the latter's friend Andrew Cromwell (recognizable as Harry Bromley-Davenport, Tim's school friend, also caught up on the merry-go-round of filming).

The opportunity to film a London segment for *Wha-a-at?* came with an offer from Eleni Collard, the producer of Godard's film with the Rolling Stones, *One Plus One*, and a grant of £12,000 from the British Film Institute.[25] Harry Bromley-Davenport described the filming: 'Mister Godard took it into his head at a particular juncture in the shooting of *One Plus One* to go back to Paris, leaving Eleni Collard sitting in London with the crew. So she rang Nick up in Germany, we left on a plane with loads of this appalling 16mm stuff, and during the flight, broached a sort of rough outline for a story which would use some of this 16mm footage, along with a sequence which could be shot in London. So, after about half-an-hour or so of pre-production, we were duly installed with a crew in a small projection room (now NFT3, I think) at the National Film Theatre. And this scene was shot, basically consisting of the reactions of about half-a-dozen actors looking at this 16mm stuff. Nothing came of the plot that had been wisped out of thin air. It cost about £10,000, though. Then the rough cut of the footage, which was about 800 feet long, was carted around Europe for years, along with other weird bits of film.'[26]

A few months later, Ray was working for a mainstream French producer, Michel Ardan. The latter pushed preparations for *L'Evadé (The Substitute)* through to a fairly advanced stage, including discussions with Terence Stamp. The strange script was described by a reader at 20th Century-Fox as, in his personal view, 'one of the most completely hopeless scripts I've ever seen'.[27] The action takes place on an island swept by the luminous beam of a lighthouse – both *idée fixe* and transition – between 9.30 at night and 6.30 the following morning. A police van suffers an accident. A convict escapes, changes clothes with an unconscious man, a mentally disturbed cop. During the night, the latter's path, and those of other escapees as well as various characters associated with them – accomplices, junkies – cross or interchange; recurring incidental characters, fluctuating identities (as in *The Janitor* later). In the end, convict and cop come face to face, and one is killed. We never discover which one is the survivor on whose wrist, in the last shot, the handcuffs close. 'So, like most of us, each is anonymous.' One doesn't have to read the report by George Byron Sage quoted above to realize that the schism is total here. On the one hand, an approach the least of whose concerns is consistency. On the other, a purely Hollywood mentality. Ray, however, now had no prospects within the industry, 'his' industry. In effect – whether by tacit agreement, decision taken at the top, or simply word-of-mouth awareness within the American community in Europe of his eccentric and hazardous life style – there was no longer any question of a major studio backing any project to which his name was attached; even though the themes in *The Substitute* – identity as an assumed social role, the drug culture, free sex – found 'fashionable' expression in a film made only slightly later which bears striking resemblances: Donald Cammell and Nicolas Roeg's *Performance*.

Opportunities for Ray could lie only with the younger independent producers: Barbet Schroeder, Henry Lange, Eleni Collard, Rob Houwer, Claude Chabrol, and shortly thereafter Stéphane Tchalgadjieff, were all prepared to take risks for him. But only if driven by necessity, as a last resort, would he resort to such collaborations. Very soon, mistrust would raise its head again, and he would hide negatives, play power games with friends, collaborators or producers. All these people found themselves embroiled in crazy enterprises – not so much the projects themselves as the proceedings – expected to play along with a lunatic logic that never achieved the visionary peaks of lunacy. Some tried to help or to work, swept along on the tide of his staggering bursts of energy, then left high and dry by the ebb, the suspicions, the retrenchment to a stance as 'a major film-maker'. Friends, unable to follow – since the road didn't lie through reality – could only look on, the best of them still fondly. Many such friends were attracted, then driven away. 'Everything came down to a trial of strength,' said Volker Schlöndorff, who started keeping his distance after *Mord und Totschlag*. 'At six o'clock in the morning, who's going to be the one to crack? He was very American in that way. I ended up in the role of the unworthy son. "I don't give a damn who cracks," I said.' It would have taken an exceptionally strong and understanding producer to bring a project to fruition in those years, and no John Houseman came to hand. Bert Kleiner, one of the financial backers approached, recalled: 'I heard a lot of talk about how he needed an extra $100,000 to finish, or $200,000 or whatever the number was, and it was always a new number, and a new amount of time before it would be finished. So it was very easy to say no to him.'

Stéphane Tchalgadjieff, a friend of Barbet Schroeder, had not yet become a producer: his first involvement was helping Ray to communicate with the producer of *The Substitute*, Michel Ardan, who was of Armenian origin like himself and who did not speak English. 'Nick and I found ourselves travelling together while the film was being prepared, going to Sylt, to London, seeing agents and actors. In London during one of these trips, I found Nick ashen-faced. Finally he showed me a telegram from Ardan, curtly informing him that the project was off. On the telephone, Ardan told me that all his dealings with the Americans had foundered on Nick as director. For Ardan, there had never been any question of making the film without American backing; a film in English, with stars who had some pull at the American box-office . . .'

Within twenty-four hours, Tchalgadjieff had raised half-a-million dollars from a private source, and took over the project: 'My plan was to make a million-dollar movie, which would allow Nick and me to retain control, having a majority interest. I wanted this for his sake. All I asked was that he observe one hard and fast rule: this was a film *we* were making, a family affair. With half-a-million in cash, you control a million-dollar film, and in those days this was amply sufficient for a film by European standards, a thriller with nothing very spectacular to it, some driving around on Sylt . . . We were counting on credit from the labs, and percentages for the cast: discussions were under way with Terence Stamp.

'I became a producer by putting my faith entirely in Nick, since he was the professional; all I saw myself as doing was managing the finance. We had a little team doing preparatory work between Sylt, Paris and London; Nick brought in an associate producer, Jud Kinberg [formerly an assistant to Houseman]. From that point on, certain things went on behind my back . . . I don't really know the details. As soon as his film was under way, it was like a whiff of oxygen encouraging Nick to raise the stakes in a game to which he was addicted almost like a drug. There were questions asked, pressure exerted to discover the source of the money and whether any pressure could be put on it. Since it was totally outside the usual channels, the film was going to go ahead. Then one day, Americans started arriving on Sylt – one of them was Bert Kleiner – and they were a very different species, movie bankers who talked in millions of dollars; for them, it was a business deal.

'In the space of about three weeks, full of comings and goings, I realized that, with revision after revision of both script and budget, Nick and Jud were adding $200,000 each time. Control of the budget was slipping out of my hands, and this was a sort of violation of our basic principle. Nick would say, "Don't worry, I guarantee you'll have control." He was openly lying. I let it go, because I wanted the film to be made . . . Until the day I happened to see a telegram telling Nick he should ditch me, that I was a millstone. I became aware of undercurrents I hadn't noticed before. I went to see Nick, and he didn't do the right thing. In short, he let me go.

'Obviously, he believed them. I had the feeling that he *wanted* to believe them, to believe that he had finally turned the corner, and was being brought back into the fold, coming home even if by a rather round-about route; that he had won his game and they had to re-accept him. Psychologically, he had adjusted himself completely to something that seemed to be going his way. He went with me to the little airport at Sylt, and we looked at each other – for the last time, because a chain of circumstances meant that I never saw him again. I said to him: "Nick, you won't make the film." There was a silence, he looked at me, and he didn't say anything.'28

While Kinberg was still trying to set up *The Substitute* or *Inbetween Time* – it isn't clear which – some young Americans came to visit Ray. Ellen Ray, aged twenty-nine, had worked for Preminger and for Seven

Arts. Bill Desloge, aged twenty-nine, and Bob Levis, aged twenty-eight, had produced a politico-erotic hippie Western, *Gold*, which Henri Langlois had liked at Cannes. They had a production company, Dome Films, and were looking for a director for a script written by Ellen Ray, *The Defendant*: 'A film about a young boy on trial, ostensibly for possession of marijuana, but in fact for having possessed freedom of the mind. Remember, it's 1968, this was the explosion of the drug culture and everything, but also a real breaking away from the 1960s, and a new feeling.'[29]

Ellen Ray had good contacts in Paris: Helen Scott (Truffaut's close associate), Henri Langlois. It was they who suggested Nicholas Ray; and on 4 October 1969, Ellen Ray and Bill Desloge took a train to Hamburg, then a boat for Westerland. 'He wasn't expecting us,' Ellen Ray said, 'we just came. We got to Sylt . . . I remember it was freezing cold . . . and I asked Nicholas Ray to direct this film and gave him a copy of the script.' Just another offer, but one which changed the course of things, bringing Ray back to America at an explosive time.[30]

36

Chicago

'He was in pretty bad shape,' according to Ellen Ray. 'He wasn't drinking, but he was shooting speed. That wasn't too shocking to me, because it was a drug era. But he was so intense – very, very intense – and *wanted* to come back to the United States, but was very nervous about it. So he read the script in the couple of days we spent with him, and I think he became excited – more, probably, about the idea of coming back to the United States than about my script, because I think it probably was very far away from anything he knew or imagined, he'd been away for so long. But in any case, he said he would come, and we went back to Washington to prepare.'

During his absence, Ray had in effect missed out on the escalation of the war in Vietnam, the rising tide of opposition to that war, the campus revolts, the assassinations of Martin Luther King and Robert Kennedy, the Democratic Convention in Chicago with its 'Festival of Life' and the police brutality, the rise of the Black Panthers, Woodstock, and organized judicial repression under the new Nixon Attorney General, John Mitchell. All this Ray soon soaked up, just as though he had been there. In fact, the script for *The Defendant* cut right across his own interests and obsessions, even echoing certain fashionable formal tics. Very soon, to Ellen Ray's shocked surprise, he was to feel that both subject and production belonged to him.

He arrived in Washington on 14 November 1969, on the eve of one of the biggest demonstrations against the war. Ellen Ray arranged for filming: 'We had eight camera crews of people with their own cameras and rigs, and we bought the film. We went out to the airport to meet Nick and brought him to Washington. It was very exciting, as you can imagine . . . half-a-million people, and it was the time of the Black Panthers, the Weathermen, and everything. So with his eight camera crews to work with, Nick went wild this weekend, running around Washington, filming here, there and everywhere. After the weekend, I brought a psychiatrist and a Chinese financier to meet him, and we raised some more money. We left the film with someone named Grady Watts to edit; and he produced a very nice, rather boring little film out of it, but we went on.'

So Ray had returned to America, as he put it, 'just in time to get

410

gassed'. If he is to be believed, he had been authorized to film the deliberations of the Revolutionary Contingent, the radical coalition whose marches on the South Vietnamese embassy and the Department of Justice triggered the clashes with the police and the extensive use of tear-gas. There is no sign of these debates in the totally anonymous film that emerged from what he shot: a street theatre performance in front of the obelisk in the Mall, white-painted faces bearing the anti-nuclear symbol. Young people talking to camera parrot *Rebel Without a Cause* ('[Our parents] don't give a shit about us here, in front of their TV sets'). One personality stands out: Abbie Hoffman, one of the defendants in the Chicago conspiracy trial which was then in progress, who harangues the crowd with a mixture of anarchist Utopianism and Jewish humour. For Ray, however, the idea was forming of a film encompassing everything he had experienced and filmed in recent years, much broader in scope than *The Defendant*, which Ellen Ray assumed he was still working on.

A week after the march, he told a journalist that this was indeed the project for which he had returned to the United States: 'When he arrived here on 14 November, however, Jane T. Silverman, a Washington woman who has been active in the civil rights and radical causes since the mid-1950s, broached the idea for the documentary. She, along with Dr Norman Termarkin, a psychiatrist with the National Institute of Health, Dr Larry Ng, editor of a book called *Alternatives to Violence*, and John Mudd, a member of a wealthy family from New York, put up the money, and Ray was persuaded.'[1] The film is then described as focusing on 'the young rebels of the 1960s', and the footage shot in Washington as an element within this overall view. 'He plans to travel to Chicago to film sequences dealing with the conspiracy trial of the Chicago Seven taking place there, and will combine these and the anti-war sequences with footage he has shot during youth uprisings in Europe, notably the Paris riots in May 1968. As yet, the forthcoming film has no name. Ray refers to it simply as "a documentary". He began the filming in Europe, where he has lived on and off for the last seven years, without any notion he would be working again in America. "I didn't care if it took five years," he said during an interview. "It's a film I was going to shoot. I was going to put it together and try to say this one thing: that there is nothing so important as an idea whose time has come. I'm going to try to make the spontaneity of the last eight years come alive." ' It was Jim Hormel, dean of the law school at the University of Chicago and one of the investors in Dome Films, who suggested that Ray should come and follow the trial. Ellen Ray thought this was for *The Defendant*, a fictional story about a trial: the misunderstanding could not but get worse.

Nicholas Ray

The Conspiracy Trial, or trial of the Chicago Eight (later Seven): eight organizers of the July 1968 demonstrations during the Democratic Convention were charged with conspiracy. The object was to prove their intention to incite violence, under a law which, if generally enforced, would allow protest leaders to be neutralized on a national scale. The defendants were Bobby Seale, of the Black Panther Party; Dave Dellinger, president of Mobe (National Mobilization Committee to End the War in Vietnam), and his associates Tom Hayden and Rennie Davis, founders of SDS (Students for a Democratic Society); Jerry Rubin and Abbie Hoffman, leaders of the Yippies (Youth International Party), very different from the aforementioned politically and personally (Hoffman gave his place of residence as 'Woodstock Nation'), John Froines and Lee Weiner, accused of 'teaching and demonstrating the use of incendiary devices'. Opening at the end of September, the trial soon became a violent confrontation between the defendants and their attorneys on the one hand, and on the other, the Attorney General and, especially, the seventy-four-year-old judge, Julius J. Hoffman. After having refused Bobby Seale the right to conduct his own defence, the judge ordered him to be gagged and chained in court. The Seale case was subsequently tried separately, and the Eight became the Chicago Seven. A trial of strength was under way between an increasingly repressive State and a movement – or more properly, a sense – of protest assuming extremely varied forms and ideologies. Susan Schwartz (later Susan Ray), for instance, then a student at the University of Chicago, said: 'I was into relationships but I wasn't into politics at all. I hated the Movement and I didn't identify with it; I thought they were all a bunch of frustrated rowdies with enormous pretensions. I was very much into the trial, yes, because I was into those three generations of Jews ... Judge Hoffman, Bill Kunstler and Abbie Hoffman. My thinking was very foggy and very rudimentary, very emotionally involved in these three generations of Jews, very curious about the defendants. These immigrants, these gifted immigrants, the different paths they chose, the different approaches, the enormous ambition ... and the relationships. Abbie used to say something about politics that turned me on a lot. It's in the film; he said, "What are politics? Fuck politics! Politics is living!" I really dug that. But I didn't notice, then, the rest of it.'

According to Ellen Ray: 'We arrived in Chicago just at the very end of the prosecution's case. And it was a real eye-opener for all of us, because it was really an armed camp; it was a very fascist, Mussolini-type courtroom in Chicago, and there were police everywhere. I mean it *felt* fascist, and Nick sensed that, I think, a lot.' This 'fascist, Mussolini-type' building was, as Judge Hoffman did not fail to point out, the work of Mies van der Rohe: one of the few architects to have found favour in the eyes of Frank Lloyd Wright . . . At the moment of Ray's return to this city after thirty-six years, the Attorney General had introduced 53 witnesses and 14 television films, and filled over 9,000 pages of courtroom transcript, in order to prove that eight radicals, and not the city of Chicago, were responsible for the riots of July 1968.

Ray was welcomed as an ally by the defendants. According to Abbie Hoffman, 'He asked us to make a documentary about the trial, and we were all . . . well, honoured, a little honoured. A lot of people had asked, and then on to the scene arrives somebody like Nicholas Ray, who in a sense was a rebel with a cause, an independent-minded, free spirit. Anybody who'd met Jimmy Dean, what the hell, gonna let him in the door! So we were all excited, and then he came, and there was this somewhat sad figure . . . He was a very desperate person when he came to Chicago. The ravages of drugs were certainly pretty evident, and it was quite evident that he didn't have too long to go, and that his confidence had been shaken. Ellen Ray and the others, they were babysitting for him; I don't think he could have survived alone at that period.'

The small crew set to work immediately upon arrival, but there wasn't much to film, since cameras were forbidden in court. Ray, fascinated by this 'political circus', decided to concentrate on the defendants from 3 December, the last day of the prosecution's presentation. Ellen Ray: 'We filmed the night the prosecution ended their case. It was a very strange sort of catharsis for most of the people who were on trial and for those around it. We had jugs of wine, and everyone got very drunk during the filming. There was no idea of what we were going to do. The young defendants, Tom Hayden, Abbie Hoffman, Jerry Rubin – all except Dellinger – saw themselves as potential James Deans, and they were all trying to capture Nick's attention. So we had this drunken four-hour party with everyone letting everything hang out, screaming fights in the middle of it – I remember someone poured a bottle of wine over a group of people. Tom Hayden got up on top of a ladder and played Judge Hoffman.' 'Which turned out to be very true,' Abbie Hoffman commented, alluding to Hayden's later activities. 'Life imitated art.'

As that night came to an end, while the crew were asleep in an apartment shared by Tom Hayden and the lawyer Leonard Weinglass, the Chicago police, on the pretext of a house search, gunned down the Black Panther leader Fred Hampton (aged twenty-one) in his sleep, along with another black militant, Mark Clark. Ellen Ray: 'In the middle of the night . . . I guess it must have been five or six in the morning . . . came the call that Fred Hampton had been murdered. We still had cameras and film, so we went there immediately and filmed Fred Hampton's bed and the blood dripping. We were there at, I think, six-thirty or seven o'clock in the morning, right after the bodies had been taken away.' A film crew under Mike Gray and Howard Alk had been working on a documentary about Fred Hampton and the Black Panther Party in Chicago since the beginning of the year. Gray, alerted a little later, first had to go and collect his equipment, and reached the apartment at 2337 Monroe Street only at 9.30 a.m.; he started shooting immediately (16mm black-and-white), with Francis 'Skip' Andrews, the Panthers' attorney, and various witnesses. In militant spirit, Ellen Ray later gave him a copy of the footage shot by Nick and his crew (16mm colour). Ray subsequently used shots of the bed and bloodbath in *We Can't Go Home Again*. Alk and Gray, however, used only their own footage in their film, *The Murder of Fred Hampton*, completed in 1971. This did not prevent Ray from accusing them of having stolen his material.

Ray's connection with Dome Films and Ellen Ray ended there. The latter attributes the parting to the trauma of that bullet-riddled apartment: the blood was no longer just red colour, as in *Party Girl*. Ray, to Ellen's way of thinking, took cover by reverting – or trying to revert – to a more traditional form of production. She also acknowledged that he must have been dismayed by the amateurism of Levis and Desloge: half of the Fred Hampton material, when looked at today, is out of focus or over-exposed (but then, he was to see worse with his students two years later). So Ray was preparing to negotiate on his own in order to go on with a film he genuinely thought of as his, and which no longer had anything to do with *The Defendant*. He set up a company, Leo Seven (the lion being his astrological sign), and his lawyer Lee Steiner got in touch with Michael Butler, the son of a millionaire, currently very 'hot' as the producer of the stage musical *Hair*, and tempted by film production.

During the 1969 Cannes Festival, an article by Vincent Canby in the *New York Times* had drawn American attention to Ray: *A fine director, Unemployed*. The article crystallized a mystique concerning the frustration and the belated discovery, by a younger generation of Americans, of film-makers whom they, or their predecessors, had failed to appreciate at the proper time. All this came under the heading of 'cult', with all the scorn and the limitations implied by the term. *Auteurist* excesses, and the irritated reactions of the discredited establishment, both escalated. Canby's article contained the seeds for everything likely to provoke irritation within the profession as well as among the American critical fraternity. (So much so that Canby himself, after Ray's death, never stopped repeating – among other banalities – that the film-maker had no worse enemies than his admirers.)

Among attentive readers of the article was Peter Bogdanovich, a critic turned film-maker, who wrote an enthusiastic letter to the *New York Times*,[2] and was to be of concrete assistance to Ray. There were also two movie enthusiasts whom Butler had engaged to develop his projects: Eric Sherman, a documentarist, and Stuart Byron, a journalist with *Variety* who had ambitions towards production. Both shared Canby's belated and irrational admiration for Ray, and had little difficulty in persuading Butler to take an interest in the film, then simply titled *Conspiracy*. 'I first went out to Chicago and met with Ray,' Stuart Byron recalled. 'He was staying in Jim Goode's apartment. Nick's first concern was apparently some debts which he had to repay immediately. I said, 'Well, how much money do you need?' And without blinking an eyelid, he named the exact amount: $15,200. Anyway, we advanced him that money (there was so much coming in from *Hair*), and we agreed to become the producers of the film. But it was Butler's position that we were not financiers of show business projects, that we did nothing more than develop and give the seed money. There would have to be investors for the actual production.' A position certainly not considered by Ray when he was making the sudden switch from militant cinema to the man responsible for the biggest hit on Broadway.

The idea which Ray then developed was a reconstruction of the trial in studio sets, with the defendants playing themselves. With the cameraman William Yale Wilson, he shot some 35mm tests on stage at the Coronet Film Company in Glenview, a suburb of Chicago. Abbie Hoffman said: 'I had a lot of disagreement with this very . . . let me say, avant-garde version of what was taking place. I thought he had been too influenced by Europeans. In America we want a good story, we want a movie, we don't want films. We don't believe in documentaries, we don't even believe in the truth.' Quite prepared to canvass stars, Ray considered and then contacted in turn – to play Judge Hoffman – Dustin Hoffman ('I was a bit confused,' Abbie commented, 'just why would he want to play the judge and not the other Hoffman, who was much handsomer!'), James Cagney, and Groucho Marx. Susan Schwartz, a little later on, noted the ambiguity of the relationship between the film-maker and the defendants: 'Nick's political reactions were always curious. His deepest predilection was just to be very curious. And in a way he was too curious to spend time deciding which side he was on. Certainly, his support was with the defendants, but it was a highly commercial brand of support. I remember a breakfast we had with Abbie, Jerry and Rennie, Nick and

68   *Conspiracy*: shooting in the studio

me. I had the feeling there were cameras all around. I'm sure there were; I saw a camera shining into the restaurant. We had a real sense that we were being followed and phones were tapped. It was heavy. Enjoyably heavy – I think everybody got off on it, in a weird way. Anyway, Abbie and Jerry were about to fly to New York, and I remember Nick peeling off $100 bills and handing them over. I mean, they did not *get* Nick at all, they just saw him as a means to get a film done.' In 1988, Susan commented on this: 'I do not now believe that Nick was politically naïve or insincere. He paid attention, watched, read, asked questions relentlessly. So his formulations were informed as well as intuited, although presented less in economic or sociological terms than in emotional ones. They were penetrating and fulfilling – although at times tinged with a brattiness and bitterness more psychological in origin than political: for example, his preoccupation with the betrayal of the younger generation by the older.'

A certain fetishism arose concerning the court transcripts of the hearings, then inaccessible. In return for a considerable sum, Ray had them passed on to him by one of the stenographers, planning to use them for his film. Even in 1986, having himself written a great deal about the trial, Abbie Hoffman could still say: 'I don't think anything can match the transcript itself. It's 28,000 pages long. There is a condensed version that is about 1,000 pages, and then there's a paperback. But what's really good is the full record, which was incredible because you hear the insanity and the blind obedience demanded by the judge, and his little peculiarities; he's a cartoon figure, a Mr Magoo, he's really old, he plays his role brilliantly. And then you hear all the different voices, the anger and the emotion, which are not things that you generally get in trials. Trials are very orderly, muted, polite affairs, even if they're gonna cut your head off. And we made it something very different.'

The four weeks during which Ray, officially working for Butler's company, Natoma, negotiated with the latter's representative while living in the Butler family home (complete with domestic staff and Butler aides, headed by Stuart Byron) were a time of misunderstandings and illusions. Byron discovered that 'Nick did not have the slightest idea of how much things cost, of anything that would be the pure producing side of a film-maker. He didn't say this, however. His claim was that he had really produced all his films; and he would make claims and boasts of how cheaply he could make films, because it was clear that this film could only be made at that time for $700,000–750,000. But someone like Mike Gray would come over – he was going to be the photographer – and Nick would start talking about what he wanted to do, the sets he wanted to make, the heavy Mitchells he wanted to use, the camera movements he had in mind. And Mike would say: 'If this is the kind of film you want to make, you're talking about a three or four million dollar movie.' Ray would be taken aback, but only momentarily, then he would come back with something like, 'Oh, I have ways of shooting that you don't even know about.' What became clear to us was that, really, the only way he knew how to film was in the Hollywood way. Yet he'd heard all of this talk, the hand-held revolution, Leacock and Drew and so on; and figuring correctly that a man in his position could only get the money to shoot in this way, he accepted it theoretically, but still did not understand the commitment one had to have to shoot in this way.'

On the other hand, the points over which Ray was insistent, without ever getting his own way, must have seemed crucial in his view. Butler's team of novices, flanked by lawyers, proved tougher and warier than professional producers during the discussions. Some of the matters under dispute can be gathered from a Stuart Byron memo: 'His artistic control always subject to *our* legal opinion. At *any* time during production we can object to the way a scene is being shot or characterization being done (or casting mistake) and he must alter it on *our* lawyer's say-so. We're not protected by final cut! What if we have to cut two-thirds of the film?' Or again: 'It must be clear that the producer has *all* the rights, and then these should be listed', etc. There was also the matter of compliance with union rules. Byron remarked that Ray 'never understood that in the

American system, either you had to make a completely union film, or a completely non-union film. If he hired even one actor who was a Screen Actors' Guild member, the whole thing would have to be, at least from the actor angle, a union film; and even the defendants, since they were acting at various times, would have to join SAG and get certain minimums.' A year later, Kazan was to ignore these rules in making *The Visitors*.

In point of fact, all Byron's grievances were determined by his personal opinion of Ray, put in a nutshell at the end of one of his memos: 'He just doesn't have the discipline.' Byron's disillusionment intensified when he found an explanation for this instability. 'His attitude so varied from listlessness to fantastic articulate rage, and I remember the day as if it was yesterday, when it just hit me like a thunderbolt. I suddenly got up and went to Randy [Hoey] and Bob [Peitscher], and said, "Speed freak!" All this circumstantial evidence suddenly just came together. I said, "Haven't you noticed that he's either practically falling asleep or screaming and yelling? Haven't you noticed that sometimes you can say anything to him and he's amenable, then he disappears and goes to the guest house, and when he comes back and you say the slightest thing against him, he goes into a rage? And that screening once for various members of the Chicago Seven – Tom Hayden, Rennie Davis and John Froines came with their attorneys, Leonard Weinglass and Kunstler? It was cold, and we were all sitting there huddled up, with Nick at the projector, pouring sweat all evening!" I knew that was a reaction to amphetamines too. As soon as I realized that, it was like . . . how can I put it? . . . I feel that my experience with Nick was an end to innocence of the film buff variety.'

Two arguments were decisive in favour of withdrawal, the only logical outcome as Byron saw it: uncertainty as to the fate of the defendants, and the impossibility of finding investors. 'I got on the phone with every investor in *Hair* and its various companies – for a while we had negotiations with Hugh Hefner and *Playboy*, with Barney Rosset at Grove Press, who was also involved with *Cahiers du Cinéma* [in English] – and it always came down to the same thing. At first they'd be very interested, and then when they realized what Ray had in mind, that the project depended on the availability of the defendants as actors after the trial, it was too great a risk. In the atmosphere of that time, with Judge Hoffman and so forth, it seemed that they would definitely go to jail. Now, given that vast uncertainty, the only thing that could have countered it would have been total certainty about everything else, like as complete a script as possible.' Pressed by Natoma, Ray eventually produced a script: according to Byron, this was 'a cut-and-paste job that could have been put together overnight; Allen Ginsberg's whole speech, for example, which took up ten pages, with just a little introduction . . .' (Ginsberg, in what was one of the trial's great moments, had been the first to reflect the life-style of the defendants in his dress and his attitude to the court, reciting his poems at the top of his voice and accompanying his 'Hare Krishnas' on a little harmonium.) 'Nothing that could convince any investor of what we needed this script for,' Byron concluded. 'At that moment, my heart sank. There was one last possibility, then we dropped out, and Tom Russell eventually took over.'

A few weeks later, Ray gave his version of the rift to journalist Roger Ebert: 'I never did meet Butler. Only talked to him on the phone. I dealt with his assistant. Butler said to go ahead. But then we began to get these horrible kinds of shame-faced indications from his assistants that the money wasn't being raised any more. Finally, too late, much too late, a telegram came saying they were 'unable' to raise the money. Hefner had some guy, connected with his film-making activities, who wanted to see the ending of the script before the trial was over, and so there went that opening . . . and then Grove Press, which had expressed an interest, pulled out. So we lost all three of our pornographers.'[3]

Ray persisted with filming, and when financing from Thomas Russell III dried up, he started investing his own money.[4] He had sent one of Butler's assistants, Bob Peitscher, to Paris and Sylt to try to sell some paintings, as he had during his time in Europe. After that he used an overdraft of $30,000 authorized by a bank.

Towards the end of January the last of the witnesses for the defence gave their testimony, among them several singers: Judy Collins, Arlo Guthrie, Pete Seeger, Country Joe. Ray was physically exhausted. One night, according to the story he repeated several times, 'At three o'clock in the morning, I found out that we had no backing, sent my staff home, and fell asleep at the editing table. I woke up and my eye was kind of heavy. It got worse. It took me six hours to find a doctor, and if I had made it twenty minutes sooner, they would have been able to inject nicotinic acid and save the eye.'[5] After a week's stay at the Wesley Memorial Hospital, from 28 January to 6 February, he started work again. Myron Meisel, a law student and film critic, came to collect him when he left the hospital: 'We didn't know it then, but that was the first time he had been treated for the cancer that would finally claim his life ten years later.'[6] The loss of sight in his right eye remained a mystery which he fostered, pretending he could see and – particularly in *The American Friend* – playing on ocular effects which bring to mind Cherkassov as directed by Eisenstein.

The filming continued: that is, Ray went on filming anything and everything, as best he could with whatever came to hand. Mike Gray and Howard Alk, whom he had hoped to take on as cameraman and editor, were increasingly preoccupied with their film about the Black Panthers, which was turning into an investigation into the murder of Fred Hampton. He assembled a new crew. David Turecamo described what happened: 'I was a student with Jim Leahy at Northwestern University and running a film society, when word came that Nick Ray was in town and that he was looking for money. We offered him $500, and his reaction was: "Wouldn't you also have cameras?" We had some equipment, so he used that. Then he asked me to work as a cameraman on the film. He didn't know anything about what I was able to do, but I suppose that's the way he liked to work: by instinct. The project was that there were seven defendants, and he would try to assign one documentary crew to each defendant. I think he got three crews together. I was working with John Lower, who did the sound. Mike Gray had another crew. John and I got on with Jerry Rubin and Abbie Hoffman, so Nick – who was quick in noticing these things – assigned us to them. To supply the defence with funds, they would go on speaking engagements at weekends, get a little money for that, then simply pass a hat round. Once, on a Sunday morning, Nick called us at 4 a.m. to go with Jerry Rubin to Salt Lake City: the plane was leaving at 6, and I had to go downtown to get the money. It was wild: the students came to meet us, all the TV crews were there for Jerry, and the students were a little worried because Salt Lake City is *not* a real hip town. They had rented the largest auditorium on the campus. The place was jammed, and Jerry was an amazing manipulator: we flew back the same evening with $20,000 in cash, champagne was flowing in the plane, we were all smoking dope . . .[7] Then, at one point, Nick ran out of 16mm, and he gave us 8mm cameras. That was the thing with him: we might have 16mm, 8mm, record things on cassette, *anything* to try to get it. That's when I started to trust Nick, even though there were many things I didn't like about him.'

One of the meetings Ray filmed, at Northwestern University, was chaired by his contemporary Studs Terkel, the Chicago writer and broadcaster. They became, for a brief period, friends and drinking companions. 'I enjoyed his company,' Terkel said, 'I admired his gallantry, his giftedness. He was more the shadow of a guy by then, but still trying to shoot something good. He'd smoke cigarette on cigarette, wear his eyepatch. Smoking and coughing and not feeling good. Nelson Algren was around at that time, and used to say, "Look at that guy's fingers!"

My feeling was that he was a very generous-hearted guy; he must have been taken advantage of pretty often.'

Judge Hoffman revoked Dave Dellinger's bail. Violent clashes ensued. During one of the last demonstrations, on 21 February 1970, outside the Cook County jail (it was the Cook County courthouse he had reconstructed for *Party Girl*), Ray met the son of one of his Hollywood friends: Marcel Ophuls, then filming, for German television, a personal pilgrimage, a return to America in the aftermath of the My Lai massacre, called *America Revisited*. 'The atmosphere was extremely violent,' Ophuls recalled, 'with the National Guard, a lot of tension. During the thirty seconds when the FBI agents crossed the sidewalk to pick up the ringleaders, shots were fired . . . We really did meet, Nick and I, while filming – me in 16mm with a small crew, Nick all alone using video. There was a moment when we happened quite by chance to film each other. We talked afterwards, and arranged to meet two evenings later, at a house where we recorded an interview for my film. He showed rushes on a 16mm projector – park benches overturned, the police charging, Abbie Hoffman and Rubin sitting at table – while he explained in voice-over. He ended with the story of his phone call to Groucho Marx, at Abbie Hoffman's request, to ask him to play Judge Hoffman; Groucho ducked out of it. In my film, I didn't use the fact that he had ducked out; instead, we cut to a clip from *The Big Store* of Groucho singing, then came back, using transparencies this time, to Nick Ray, ageing and already more or less over the hill, accompanied by the "Valse grise" since I was thinking of *Un Carnet de Bal*: the film was structured uniquely around people I had known in college, in the army, or in Nick's case, through my father.'

On 18 February the jury returned their verdict, acquitting the defendants on the charge of conspiracy, but finding five of them guilty of having crossed state lines with the intention of inciting a riot. On the 20th, Judge Hoffman imposed the maximum sentence of five years, plus costs and fines for contempt of court. On 28 February, the Court of Appeals quashed the sentence and overruled the government's argument that the defendants and their lawyers were 'a danger and a threat to the community'. They were released the following day. The seven had planned to perpetuate themselves as The Conspiracy. In fact, they parted as soon as they were freed. Only for Ray was the film still going on. He described it to Roger Ebert: the defendants playing their own roles, the courtroom reconstructed as a set, the transcript furnishing the dialogue. 'But the words in the courtroom will occasionally be illustrated by scenes from other places. Vietnam, possibly, or ancient Rome . . .' Ebert describes a few sequences: 'There was one long, Godardian sequence in the airplane, where Abbie and Rennie talked and kidded each other while a girl in the window seat pretended to be asleep. Every once in a while, the girl would open an eye. At the Washington rally, there was footage of Abbie lifting his shirt to expose his tummy in the L.B.J. gall bladder pose. Nick Ray chuckled. "No. 3's a born provocateur, like Mitchum," he said. Ray declared that he still had enough to go on shooting for two or three weeks: "I can promise you this film will be made. We'll get the money somewhere." '

Conspiracy was intended to combine material of three kinds: documentary footage, a dramatization of the trial, and multiple image techniques. Only the first element existed. In 16mm, video, Super–8, even 16mm with optical sound (in a montage of films and kinescopes about July 1968), the footage looks repetitive and unpromising: discussions between the defendants, speeches, demonstrations, comings and goings outside the courthouse . . . Without the intended intervention of *mise en scène*, the film had as yet no point; going on with the filming no longer had any. After the trial ended, 'Most people began to disappear. Which really made me wonder – where is everybody? So I thought I'd try to find them some place else.' Ray hadn't reached this conclusion yet: the words come from his opening commentary which sets the course for *We Can't Go Home Again*. The Chicago film thus found its meaning in its aftermath. In 1971, a Harpur student, Richie Bock, strung the material together in a rough cut, and it came to life: elements were incorporated in the film Ray was then shooting with his students. Richie Bock explained: 'The Conspiracy Trial was the period that we, of *We Can't Go Home Again*, sprung from. We were in a period of withdrawal in American history, and Nick was saying: This is what we're involved in, you people are involved in a period of withdrawal, we're going to dramatize that.'[8]

During the production's last days, Jason Epstein, vice-president of Random House, who wrote one of the first books about the trial, introduced Ray to Susan Schwartz, an eighteen-year-old first year student at the University of Chicago. At first she was in charge of the production office, but very soon there was no money left. 'This was in February,' she recalled, 'the day we went to La Crosse, to his lawyer Lou Kutner's office. Nick and I were going over the books, and sure enough he was overdrawn. It didn't sink in to me, because he'd been so free with money, but checks started bouncing and everything got so messy. It never really got better again.'

A few days after his discharge from hospital, Ray had been invited by Myron Meisel to introduce Fritz Lang at the University of Chicago's film society. Susan Ray: 'I remember how Nick was dressed. Pair of trousers that were blue and a sweater, a very far-out sweater with short sleeves and stripes and a white background. I remember being extemely thrown when I saw this sweater; I didn't think it was anything that any normal man would wear. We were just beginning our little dance together, and we sat in the back of this very small room at the University, necking through most of Lang's address. Then we went out to dinner. I was coming out of the ladies' room when Terry Fox, another of the people who ran that film society, said, "I gotta tell you something". I asked what. He said, "I was just coming out of the men's room with Lang, and he turned to me and asked who was this guy with the eyepatch." He didn't know who Nick was.'

At dinner, Meisel and Fox tried to draw the two film-makers into talking about films, hoping for a fresh slant on Gloria Grahame. But the conversation, at first a little constrained, remained very generalized. As Susan put it, 'They talked about directions, directions of film and directions of the world.' According to Myron Meisel: 'They started to discuss the future of the universe. Lang contended that God had predetermined everything, and that nothing we could do would change it. Ray thought that everything was random, that all was a matter of chance. Lang said that all sex would disappear, and there would only be test tube babies in the future. Then Ray said: "Maybe that will be the ultimate kick – breaking the test tube." '[9]

Invited to film societies by young admirers, short of money, Ray continued doing what he had been doing for years: trying to find the finance for a film in which nobody believed. He returned to New York, where he met friends, those from whom he had never become definitively estranged. Susan Ray: 'On this trip back, the first person he saw in New York that he knew was Max Gordon. It was a big thing for him, because thirty years before, it was a very similar scene. Something about Max being the first person once again.' Ray had seen Connie Bessie again *en route* to Chicago. This time he stayed in her Sullivan Street home in the Village, where she was living alone with her son. Nick Bessie was eighteen, going through a crisis, his mother was distraught, and Ray was able to get him to open up. Susan remained in Chicago: 'He went to New York in April, and he'd come back a couple of times to Chicago. He'd always say he was coming back, and then he'd keep getting delayed. I kept all the phone messages I'd get at my door; I still have them. I was trying to finish my first year at the University of Chicago, but I knew I was going to drop out. I went to New York in June, stayed with Nick at Alan Lomax's: he would commute between Alan's and Connie's, depending on how pissed off he was with me at the time or how pissed off with Connie. I was working with him then, shit work, running errands. On the way to my first nervous breakdown . . . He was hanging out at the jazz club, the Village Vanguard, he was hanging out with Connie and her salon, he was mucking around for money, he was editing in a room belonging to a guy by the name of Jerry Siegal, playing over the tapes and trying to cut some of the film. He was on speed, metamphetamine, intramuscular injections. He was on gin and beer, and hash and LSD and coke. And pot, and anything else he could get his hands on.'

Mike Myerberg, the unpredictable producer of *Lute Song*, offered him an office and the possibility of making a film: *Too Late the Phalarope*, based on the novel by the South African writer Alan Paton. It seems doubtful whether the project had any tangible actuality – was there even a script? – but the theme (Puritanism and sexual desire) seemed made for Ray. Susan Ray: 'Nick started casting, seeing actors, doing screen tests. He'd work around the clock at Mike's office, on the sixth floor of the Princess Theater, 47th Street and 7th Avenue. At night, he'd prowl around Times Square: he'd go to the Fascination bingo parlour and a couple of bars there, the Mayfair was one, just to hang out and watch the wild scene – wild whores and wild pimps, all dressing really hot. He used to wander round the sex shops, too. He really got into that scene. That's when he started to write *New York After Midnight*.'

As Alan Lomax saw it, this was Ray's last important project, drawing on everything he had once been. 'He wanted to do another typical piece of American life. He had streets full of loyal friends down there: he was crazy about them, they loved him. Because he went in not as an outsider; he always became an insider, everywhere he went.' *New York After Midnight* coalesced with other projects, with a return to the *Living Newspaper* formula, including among other things a variation for children. The script seems never to have been finished, and exists only in the form of notes and drafts for scenes, often repeated (with elements of science fiction), some of them dazzling (in particular a dramatization of the death of Ray's father).

The return to the metropolis, the ambience of political activism, and shortly the idea of teaching, all took Ray back to his early days with the Theatre of Action, some of whose members he re-encountered. Perry Bruskin said: 'One of the most emotionally dramatic moments in my life was seeing Nick again for the first time after all these years. He had called and was coming up to the house with this young woman. I opened the door, and there was . . . Nick, as though he had written a play about himself. With his eyepiece, standing there in all this enormous size.

69 Nicholas Ray: 'standing there in all this enormous size'

Standing in that doorway, we both of us almost began to cry, and we fell upon each other and embraced. The kind of sad note was saying hello to Susan . . . because here she is, young and pretty, and there's my memory of Jean. All my life, whenever I thought about Nick, there was Jean.' A meeting with two other veterans followed, Ben Berenberg and Will Lee: 'Nick was the instigator for a book. He wanted a book written, from a point of view that would reflect the '60s or '70s and bring together the similarity and the difference of our theatrical work. He felt that we could write it. He had just come from this defeat in Chicago, and he wanted some activity that . . . See, all of a sudden, Nick found himself very radical again. We didn't think we could do it, and invited Jay Williams, who was a very good writer, to take over and do the book.' *Stage Left*, a dispassionate survey, was published in 1974, disappointing Ray and his friends. Ray also thought about a history of the Café Society, and several patrons saw him filming in 16mm at the Village Vanguard. 'The music was a big part of that year in New York,' Susan Ray said. 'He was seeing Barney Josephson and Max [Gordon]. Mel Lewis and Thad Jones were at the Vanguard: he was really impressed with them, also with Keith Jarrett and Roland "Rahsaan" Kirk.'

He started recording an oral history with James Leahy, author of a book on Losey. The bars – Googie's – the poolrooms – with Robert Ryan, already suffering the effects of cancer – the theatre: rehearsals for *Cowboy Mouth*, with Sam Shepard and Patti Smith. 'He came to the rehearsals all the time,' Sam Shepard said, 'so he helped us out. He was probably sick at that point, but he was still functioning. I just liked his tenacity.'[10] A year of 'schemes, possibilities' (Susan Ray). Connie and Kazan wrote recommending him for a job at Brandeis College, Massachusetts. 'He didn't get it,' Susan Ray said. 'He was extremely, wildly depressed. His despair was like suction, quicksands. It was . . . wrenching.' Finally, in the spring of 1971, he left New York. Dennis Hopper, following the success of *Easy Rider*, had shot *The Last Movie* in Peru. 'To edit the film,' he bought the house in Taos, New Mexico, where the American heiress Mabel Dodge had lived with her fourth husband (Tony Luhan, an American Indian), trying – during the 1920s – to re-create her Italian salon and to provide a haven for artists (D. H. Lawrence, Robinson Jeffers and others). It was there that Ray arrived to spend a few months.

In the cutting-room, looking over Dennis Hopper's shoulder, he watched the film – initially four hours long – taking shape. Hopper said: 'He loved *The Last Movie*. Especially the scene – every time I see it, I think of him – where they're going to the whorehouse in a car. The whole cast is in there – Julie Adams, Donna Baccala, Roy Engel, Don Gordon and myself – and it's just a shot of all of us in this car at night, driving through the streets. Every time he saw it, he said, "God! I wish I could have shot that scene . . ." Exactly what it means, I don't know.'

'Some of the adventures at that time were not to be believed,' Susan Ray said. 'It was a very heavy macho trip. I mean, they were doing ounces of coke a day.' Susan rejoined Ray after a while. 'When Nick met me at the airport in Taos, I hadn't seen him for a month or so. He was just about to be sixty. He had grown a beard, and I remember hugging him and feeling that he had become an old man, that something had shifted. It remains very clear. We sat in the back part of a truck, Nick had his head up against a spare tyre, I think I was lying on his belly, and he didn't say anything, just let out these real deep sighs. I think he was glad to see me. It was like he could stop for a minute, he'd been on the run for a long time. He went through big changes in Taos. That's when I think he was on the way to being quite ill.'[11]

'With him living at the house and running up a $30,000 phone bill every month,' Dennis Hopper explained, 'I was finally forced to get him a job teaching school.' Ray had already been invited in May to give a lecture at Harpur College, Binghamton, in the north-west of New York State. The film department was founded around 1969 by two independent film-makers: Larry Gottheim and Ken Jacobs, the first a fervent admirer of *They Live by Night*.[12] The lecture was by way of a test for the job.

'Wearing a black eyepatch, black Levis, black turtleneck, black cowboy boots and a shock of white hair, he was a Hollywood legend who directed James Dean,' wrote one of the students, Tom Farrell. 'Nick arrived on campus immediately after the May Day demonstrations in Washington, DC, where some 7,000 students from across the country were arrested for civil disobedience. Invited to speak about his films, Nick staged a "scene" with the students, using all the cameras, tape-recorders and lights of the cinema department. Aware of the tumultuous events in the nation's capital, he called upon any student recently returning from Washington to tell what happened. I volunteered how I was clubbed and maced on my twenty-first birthday. Nick noted that sharing this experience was a lesson in acting. We stayed up all night talking with this man, who was keenly interested in political confrontation. Nick acted unusually young for someone his age.'[13]

On his return, Susan Ray said: 'He was very pleased with the job that he did, which meant that it was probably something special. Very pleased with his own performance, and very pleased with the response of the kids. He got the job. It was a real renewal for him, and he went out and bought himself a spat of new clothes. Really impossible clothes, like that bright red jacket . . .' The college offered him the post of visiting professor for two years (besides Hopper, Jean Stein and the Directors' Guild had intervened in his favour), and he left Taos. 'On the way back, Tony Quinn was in Albuquerque. We saw him in his hotel. I think it was the last time those two met. It was sort of like . . . old stuff being resolved there . . . not resolved.' By the end of August, Ray was at Harpur.

We Can't Go Home Again

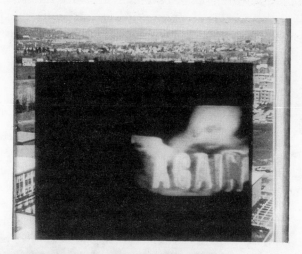

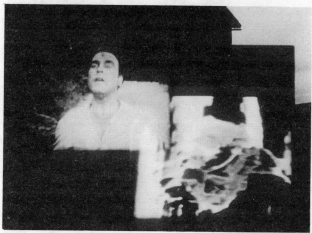

70a–b *We Can't Go Home Again*

'When one flies to Binghamton,' Vincent Canby wrote, 'whose Broome County Airport is like the flight deck of an aircraft carrier (actually it's the sawed-off top of a tame New York mountain), one is struck by the similarity between the rolling, wooded and laked countryside and the countryside surrounding La Crosse, Wis.[. . .] Binghamton is a city of big industry these days (IBM, Singer, etc.) and Ray describes it as a "hard-hat town", but the air last week was extraordinarily clear and the pace American rural.'[1]

Having borrowed money from Robert Wise to make the trip across the country, Ray wrote to the secretary of the Directors' Guild on 30 August 1971: 'I'm at the university now – preparing. At my own expense, of course, but it feels and looks like it might turn into a great show. We need equipment, material, raw stock (35 and 16 colour). Our budget between now and 30 April is 4 (FOUR) thousand dollars. We have one army surplus Mitchell, 6 varied 16mm cameras, and 1 16 moviola. If anybody on the board knows of anything that could be pried loose, a few hundred of us would be glad to know what we must do to get it.'

'You can only learn film-making by making films': the students would endlessly repeat their teacher's formula. Ray began by meeting them one by one. Richie Bock was twenty-one years old. Interested in experimental films, he transferred to Harpur to work with Ken Jacobs; during the long period of work with Ray, he was to take time off to direct a film himself. 'Nick said, "You're in my classes, aren't you? Good. I don't want to sit in the classroom and lecture to you people, that'd be a bore. We're going to make a film" – "Oh, really?" – "Yes." That was the first I'd heard of his idea. I think he wasn't sure of what he wanted or how he was going to go about it, but he mentioned that in our first meeting.' Richie, who needed to earn money, was put to work on the Chicago material, sorting it out.

The teacher combined his three classes into a single crew of forty-five students, who would learn from each other and train under his guidance as actors, camera operators, sound recordists, editors, script persons, electricians, assistant directors, props . . . Every two weeks, a rotation system allowed the students to change roles and pass on what they had learned. According to Tom Farrell, 'Nick emphasized the importance of getting involved by having everybody say hello to one another.' Camus's *Myth of Sisyphus* and Bergson's *Essay on Laughter* were required reading.[2] Over and above the teaching process and the collective enterprise, the idea for the film began to crystallize. Farrell quotes the preface to a preliminary script: 'It is intended that this film be a happening. The purpose in making the film is to give the students a wide variety of experience in the mechanics, techniques and art of film-making. It is also intended to tell an intimately personal story of a man harassed by one or more premonitions, and equally determined to overcome the negativism, even at the cost of his life, which is, of course, what the premonition is all about.' The premonition was the one that assailed Ray at the time of

55 Days at Peking: if I do this film, I will never make another. It was seconded by the memory of another premonition; the one described by the hero, George Webber, at the end of Thomas Wolfe's posthumous novel *You Can't Go Home Again*: 'Something has spoken to me in the night, burning the tapers of the waning year; something has spoken in the night, and told me I shall die, I know not where . . .' A film is nothing less than a life in the balance; in this, too, Ray was kin to the cinema's pioneers.

Susan, who was working in New York and spending four days a week at Harpur, sold Ray on this idea – a veritable flashpoint for fiction – principally because it meant that he would have to appear on screen himself: 'Nick wanted to know, like he asked in *Lightning Over Water*, "What shall I talk about, what shall I do?" Which is devil's advocacy: you know, making somebody enter a little dialogue, so he has something to work against. So I said, "Well, what you have to do is take the premonition and make it your story; and as you work with the premonition in the film, first of all you resolve the premonition, and second, you'll have a story." ' Ray thought up numerous scenes to introduce this premonition, but none of them was ever shot, and it remains the film's secret motif, providing the original title; *Gun Under My Pillow* (an echo of the gun under Plato's pillow in *Rebel Without a Cause*).

Susan Ray said, 'One night, when we were coming back from dinner in town to the infirmary [where Ray had an apartment in the basement], an ambulance drove up. Nick didn't see it at first. Then it parked, and somebody got out and left it. I looked at it and said, "There's a body in the back!" It set off shudders in both of us; it seemed charged. So the first scene to be shot was based on that.'

Different accounts of this sequence, by Tom Farrell and Richie Bock, give some idea of it as conceived and directed, as opposed to how it appears in the film, surviving only in two brief fragments. Farrell: 'Two men in white uniforms pound on the door of the infirmary. Nick opens it from inside, looking surprised and shirtless. He sees panic in their faces as they tell him someone's been hit by a car. Nick tells them to bang on the other door. They do. A nurse answers. They tell her what they told him. Perturbed, the nurse tells them the accident has been reported. She slams the door in their faces. The two men run away when a hearse speeds into the driveway. Nick peeks in the windows of the vehicle and walks back to the infirmary, shutting the door behind him.' For Richie Bock, this first scene established Ray as the pivotal character in the film: 'He looks into an ambulance and sees his own body inside it; he has a premonition of his own death. So right from the beginning he put himself into the film as the central figure: around him are these young kids. So he's a kind of catalyst.'

Ray's reluctance to appear in the film was genuine; right up to the end, he threatened to eliminate his character entirely. 'He did have trouble with his own image, and yet he wanted to use it,' Susan Ray explained. 'He wasn't liking himself very much then.' 'Nick is the most tormented character in all his films,' Tom Farrell wrote, 'a man "with a crucifixion in his face", as Melville described Ahab. He assumed the guilt for his whole generation, deeming it "more guilty of betrayal than any in history".' Richie Bock said: 'We didn't know what was going on; it was an odd sequence for us. First of all, it was our first bit of Hollywood film-making. We lit up a pretty big set there. As it turned out, the dailies had that underlying paranoia that you see so much in Nick's films. It was strange, out of this world, the events that took place . . . the nurse slams the door in the guy's face as if to say, "We're not listening", society is going to close the doors right in your face.' (In the film, the nurse's line echoes the title of *Knock on Any Door*: 'I know, it's already been reported. Don't come knocking on doors.')

The film grew out of the relationships between those involved in it, reflecting and shaping them. It extended and radicalized the recent tendencies in Ray's work, here closer to Jean Rouch and *La Pyramide humaine*[3] than to the American underground. Ray's energy was catching; it gave everyone a sense of the importance of what they were doing, inspiring Herculean efforts, with everyone working till they dropped, fuelled on Almaden, a cheap wine. 'It is difficult to distinguish the film from the conditions under which it was made,' Tom Farrell wrote. 'Nick expected a total commitment from everyone. Filming without a script, the crew worked mostly through the nights, since students had other classes during the day. We jokingly called ourselves creatures of the night.' Susan Ray: 'The necessity to make the film was felt by all, desperately. But what the film was, only Nick knew. I think I had an idea, because I was outside of it, but Nick knew the honesty of the film. He knew from the outside as well as from the inside. Look . . . the core group was with it for about four years, so that the intensity of their interactions fed the content . . . *was* the content . . . more than in any other film I've ever heard of.' To which Richie Bock added: 'We were kind of living in a mirror, living in our own history, and that's what the film was about. It was about our period of withdrawal, and we were able to dramatize that on screen. Nick was able to understand us, really understand us; and he understood himself too, as fucked up as he was.'

After the scene at the infirmary, Ray set up the production's headquarters in the basement of a classroom building. Richie Bock: 'Nick was a hard worker, like nothing we ever saw before, really. He converted a room down in the basement of that building, B–32, into a great cutting-room. This is what Nick was about, you see: he was about all of us. All of us were going to make this film, and all of us were going to make this into a cutting-room. And goddamn it, we did! The power, as he said at the end of the film, the power lay with us. So the first year was a lot of hard work and a lot of learning.'

The happiest period of Ray's life, as he told Susan, was the Depression. 'I understand this,' she said, 'both politically and emotionally, I think. Because the bottom was hit, you could only go up, on an emotional level, and Nick being a depressive, that was very comforting. Also, it was a grassroots thing, and that was very comforting for him, too; he was not at ease in the upper echelons, it was not his mould. So that his whole thing with the film was both a continuation and a return – as much as one can return. It was an attempt to return to a mode of working that he'd had forty years before.' Corresponding to the total commitment, was the idea of total cinema. 'What seemed to be very easy was the way the form came about,' Ray told Wim Wenders in 1979. No sooner had the first scenes been shot, than he was trying to screen them simul-taneously, using several projectors. 'We were experimenting with eight projectors in B–32,' Richie Bock said. 'We had all kinds of images going at the same time.' This was the logical outcome of an old struggle that can be traced back to *They Live by Night*, and which became more acute with the Berenguer process developed for *King of Kings*, the effects envisaged for *55 Days at Peking*, and the tests made with Novotny.

'I had dreamed for years of being able to destroy the rectangular frame. I couldn't stand the formality of it,' Ray said, echoing Frank Lloyd Wright ('The box is a Fascist symbol, and the architecture of freedom and democracy needed something basically better than the box').[4] 'I went through stages of giving the process a special name; I called it the Nimage. I had dreams of being able to tell all of Charles Dickens in one film, all of Dostoevsky in one film. I wondered if it was possible for one film to contain all the aspects of human personality, needs, desires, expressions, wants . . .'.[5] At Cannes in 1973, one of the students was more positive: 'The multiple screen broadens the horizon for seeing more [. . .] A film is like a dream. A visual image sparks off personal associ-ations that the director didn't intend. It creates more dimensions than a regular screen. Film is the only medium where time and space are forgot-ten. Everything is below the conscious level.'[6] What impact does the cinema have on the unconscious? The question obsessed Ray who, being little interested in film history, knew nothing of Abel Gance's researches. Along these lines, his classes also included experiments in colour, deriving from – and attempting to rationalize – his practice in his own films. He subjected the students to the Luscher test, designed to define the psychological impact of colours.

It took a year and a half to solve the problem of the fluid screens Ray dreamed of. In the meantime, the sequences were screened with a battery of carefully aligned projectors started at calculated intervals (a few weeks before Cannes, a screening at the Cinémathèque Française using this method resulted in various tragi-comic mishaps). Other technical problems arose, aggravated by the inexperience of the student-technicians and the rotation – every fortnight, as a rule – of their functions. While editing, Nick was in fact juxtaposing scenes, shot in direct sound, without worrying about synchronization. 'From the beginning, the sound was always fucked up,' Tom Farrell said. 'Nick didn't instruct us on how to take proper care of the soundtrack of synchro sound, because we were cutting workprints without having sound. We talked about that: we knew you can't really do that without disrupting the sound permanently. Then someone concluded, and we bought the idea, that when Nick was in Hollywood he had miracle men who could do those things!'

In September-October, Ray invited Dennis Hopper to present *The Last Movie* at Harpur. The film had just won the Golden Lion award at Venice, but in the wake of vituperative reviews from the New York press, Universal withdrew it from circulation. So Hopper arrived with Howard Alk, who showed *The Murder of Fred Hampton*. 'These people met us at the airport,' Hopper recalled. 'He had a crew with a band and everything. It was so funny, all these kids shooting . . . They'd just built a big crane, and when they went through the airport door, the crane fell over and fell apart. Nick was screaming and directing these kids, it was wonderful. I thought: "My God! What has he done here?" He had 'em all running around like a film company!'[7]

The presence on campus of the man who made *Easy Rider* roused wild excitement. Hopper and Ray talked about Hollywood before an enthusiastic audience. 'Afterwards,' Tom Farrell wrote, 'we shot a scene of Nick and Dennis embracing each other goodbye at the airport. Inspired by Hopper's visit, Nick directed a scene of his students brutally interrogating him: "What are you doing here?" and "Aren't you too old to teach us cinema?" Nick improvised with the group through provocations: "You are all guilty of conspiracy," and "Who will be my Judas?"' This scene appears in another form in the film. As Charles Bornstein put it: 'Nick always used stuff; he expanded on scenes and made them better. Even while filming, he changed and did them differently. There was a scene I never liked, where Nick, Richie, Jill and God knows who have a big fist-fight. That kind of antagonism was used in the scene, filmed much later [1972–3], where his students confront him aggressively: "Aren't you the guy that directed *Rebel Without a Cause?*" '

Tom Farrell was twenty-one, and a senior in his last year at the university. Very much into politics, he professed then to be an advocate of violent action; he had followed the trial of Father Berrigan, about which he wrote an article for the student newspaper. He sent Ray a long letter describing his departure from the seminary, his joining the Movement, his conflicts with his father. 'Nick responded, and right away he said, "I want to do a scene with this, let's start it right away." I was very shy and withdrawn; he gave me a chance to sort of stand in the limelight, and I liked that, I liked the attention. But he made all these promises right away, and at the beginning most of us believed that we were going to make a feature film, that it was going to make money, was going to be shown in college campuses and elsewhere, was going to be about our lives, and we were going to play ourselves . . .' This scene, according to Charles Bornstein, just showed 'Tom Farrell in B–32, with all these camera parts scutted up to the ceiling, kind of rummaging through the room. The camera was just on Tom talking about himself, "My name is Tom Farrell . . .", but it was sort of as if Nick was off-camera.' The line survived in one of two important moments 'cannibalized' from this scene, but used in different ways.

Richie Bock also took his turn in front of the camera: 'It was shot in the same room where he had directed Tom Farrell. Nick came up to me one day and said, "I want you to act in a scene." I said, "OK, Nick, just tell me what to do, I've never acted before." I'd seen other people do it, so I thought I could do it as well. Little did I know what Nick had up his sleeve . . . Believe me, I still think about that scene, I'm still dealing with it in my own development right now. It was about me, it was my character, it was Richie; and he knew what I was about, my problems, what was going on with me. He was able to incorporate my life into fiction. He had the ability to bring reality into a sharper focus, something that's beautiful and understandable, that purifies reality. And he was able to do this with my life in this scene.' Two masked figures, Richie and Jill, are making love, or rather pawing each other in increasing frenzy, until she cries, 'Take off your mask!' – 'No!' – 'It's unhealthy, it's no good!' The sensitive lovers of *They Live by Night* have become parodies of them-

435

selves, and the whole subplot involving Richie and Jill conveys an almost physical sense of suffocation.

One of the female roles was played by a student called Marcia Bronstein. After a quarrel with the group, she walked out of the film. An outsider not from the film department took her place, and her presence became vital to the history of the film and its development. Leslie Levinson was a dancer, marginally involved with the university. She was interested in the theatre, not the cinema. Brought along by a friend, at first reluctant, she appeared in one scene, then another, enriching both script and the filming through her personality. 'He never stopped putting me into new scenes,' Leslie Levinson recalled. 'The wonder was that there was always something to shoot. We did a scene, we edited it. We never stopped. That lasted three years, and it was twenty-four hours a day for those three years, except for a period when I went to Mexico to cool out, and another when Nick was in California cutting for about a month and a half. Mostly the experience was painful. The joyous times were when Nick and I were alone, and we sang and danced together; we had that in common, we liked the same kind of old songs . . . I was afraid at the time of technique, because I had so much natural stuff, and he made it easy for people not to worry about theory or technique, just to jump in and do it. He was not too discriminating in that way. In other words, he trusted most people. He expected people to dig where he was at, to love him and go with him, but most of the time they ended up by leaving him, informing on him, or undermining him . . . Which helped him to further his whole trip, his theme of betrayal that went throughout his life.'

Ray and Leslie Levinson established a mutual sense of solidarity, each recognizing in the other 'a certain quality of angst, a certain realm of experience and suffering', which forged material for the film. In 1979, during a discussion filmed for *Lightning Over Water*, Ray described how Leslie came one day to the basement, which he was busy repainting: 'She said, "Nick, I've got to talk to you in private." And she told me the story of a taxi driver/pimp and the wealthy national clothier who was going to offer her $2,000 for going to bed with him for two nights. She said, "Look, Nick, at least we'll get enough to finish our film." I said, "No, goddamnit, absolutely no!" She was going to have it her way, so I put I don't know how many students covering the area where this sonofabitch was going to meet her, and the rendezvous didn't take place. But the point is that, forty-five minutes after Leslie had told me the story, cameras were in place and lights were rigged and we were shooting. I had let her tell me only the barest outline of the story, and she told me the rest of it on film. That's the way quite a bit of this film was made.' ('We're

436

going to make this one differently,' the rather startled Wim Wenders commented.)

In another scene, Leslie is tearfully complaining that she can't see, that the 'teacher' won't help her. 'I have cramps. I took bad speed, I think.' Nick talks gently to her, calming her down while she continues her confession, describing her life in the East Village. 'I liked to be involved with scenes . . . I was dancing, and that was my cultural scene . . . but I also liked to feel raunchy . . . like real degenerate, you know . . . I met this guy who was wanted by the FBI, he was a dealer. I went over to him and said, "Listen, I know that you have the clap, will you give it to me?" And he did. And I felt so ugly. I'm always doing this to myself.' At which point, prompted by Nick, the students all bombard her with tomatoes. Flashes of 'Guernica' appear on two of the screens; a shot of Ben Cooper on his knees from *Johnny Guitar*. Then, in the cutting-room, Richie asks Leslie if 'that was real'. 'Yes, except for the tomatoes.' And the scene is repeated with variations. According to Leslie, it was shot three times, at two-weekly intervals; after which, exhausted, she left Binghamton. 'The biggest strain, after a while, was when is it going to end for everybody, when is this film going to be finished?'

Susan Ray: 'It got heavy fast enough. Nick could create a sucking vacuum, like a black hole: this enormous energy that was desperate and would just suck you up. It was also extremely creative. I mean, I'm sure none of these kids had ever been so close to the edge as they were with Nick. They were very turned on by the fact that it was a collective effort. From my point of view it wasn't at all; it was slave labour. I don't mean that the slaves didn't benefit – and I think it was the high point of their lives – but he was conscious and they were not. He knew what he was after, more or less; they just wanted it to work for them.'

At the end of the university year, on 29 and 30 April 1972, Harpur organized a symposium on independent cinema. Among the films shown was recent work by Stan Brakhage, Ernie Gehr, Lawrence Gottheim and Ken Jacobs, and *Don't Expect Too Much* – the new title of *Gun Under My Pillow* – 'directed by Nicholas Ray' and employing 'a unique film process'. Gottheim defended the unit's refusal to offer explanations: 'The film is evolving all the time. There is no shooting script. It's the not-knowing that characterizes a work-in-progress.'[8]

'This was to be the climax of the whole thing,' Tom Farrell said. 'We worked around the clock for a week, right up to the last moment, because we had everything on separate 16mm reels then. We were projecting five or six images at a time. We had a lot of film to show altogether, about an hour or so; and even while we began screening the film, there were still people working on the seventh reel. The sound was all fucked up, as usual, but in spite of that we knew then that we had something, something that reflected our own lives. Leslie's tomato scene, people were overwhelmed by that. Even though we knew we had a long way to go, we thought that we could finish it.'

At this stage, the film contained the following scenes: Nick and the students, blows exchanged – Tom in the cutting-room – Richie and Jill, the scene with the masks – 'Guernica' sequence (the scene with the tomatoes) – The unit doing physical exercises – All the scenes with Jill, and the scenes with a beggar disguised as Santa Claus, whom she asks, 'Can you light a fire on the water?' – 'The Fat Rap': a student tells Nick how he went to a camp to lose weight, talking about his experience of being fat – And scenes relating to events occurring during the year: beginning of term, demonstrations, etc. The one place where nothing was ever shot for the film was on the campus. Charles Bornstein, a student from the University of Syracuse, who joined the team early in the summer, thought that most of these scenes were subsequently developed or partially re-shot. 'It was a weird movie, but you knew that somehow it was exciting. Here was this incredible guy Nick, and all the kids vying for his attention: it was really like a lot of sibling rivalry. And you could see that there was a sense of energy and a lack of energy at the same time. That was the way Nick's style was, as I later found out.'

A few students, Bornstein among them, returned with Ray to New York, where he continued working on the editing with a professional cutter, Carol Lenoir. Tom Farrell had decided to attend the two presidential conventions, both taking place in Miami a month apart, the Democratic Party coming first. There he was surprised to encounter Ray, who had collected two cameramen on his way through Atlanta. Ray shot footage of students, of Allen Ginsberg, of Tom wandering amid the small-town carnival atmosphere. At the first ballot, Senator George McGovern won the nomination: a white hope for dissidents and left-wing Americans. A month later, Tom returned to Miami, hitchhiking again, for the Republican convention. Passing through South Carolina and Georgia with his heavy beard, he was beaten up. Unopposed, the retiring President, Richard Nixon, won the nomination. Tom returned to Binghamton: 'That was an impassioned time for me, shocking, full of disillusion. I was very fed up when I came back. I had grown that beard for about a year without trimming it at all. I finally decided I was going to shave it off, and told Nick I was sick of it, I wanted to change my image. He decided he wanted to film it. I said, "You're crazy, no one ever filmed somebody shaving a beard, I'm just going to shave." I didn't

realize anything was going to happen, but he made something happen
out there. That was the last day of August 1972.'

In this moment of psychodrama, Tom takes off his shirt and glasses,
and attacks his beard with scissors. 'I removed my mask, revealing a
naked face, shaking my fist at the stranger in the mirror,' he wrote later.
As he sobs and gasps, we see, as though in slow motion on another
screen, images of Nixon's victory. Images follow in counterpoint of still
waters, then of the Carmelite college where Tom had studied for the
priesthood. He starts to talk about his policeman father, at first in the
same terms he had used earlier in the film. He runs some water, lathers
his face, and continues shaving. Off-screen, Nick prompts him on some
of the lines which had seemed improvised before, then tells him to say it
again: 'Just talk to me, Tom. Tell me that again. Make me believe you.
Don't try to convince me, Tom, just tell me, "Don't you ever call him [my
father] a pig".' Tom repeats his lines more calmly.

When the new academic year started, relations with the cinema department deteriorated, with Jacobs and Gottheim accusing Ray of monopoli-
zing the equipment. The students were forced to pick one side or the
other. The unit diminished in numbers, and kept to itself during 1972-3.
In spite of this, the work went on through all these months. 'Thank
goodness for those guys,' Richie Bock said of Jacobs and Gottheim.
'They were very tolerant of what was going on. I think there was basically an understanding, and I think that even through the misunderstandings they kept their cool.' The nucleus now comprised Richie, back after
directing a film, as actor and editor; Danny Fisher, principal cameraman
with Bornstein after the departure of Stanley Liu (Tim Ray had shot a
few scenes during the summer); Doug Cohn, a cameraman during the
first year, was still there; also Phil Wiseman, Charles Levi and his girl
Hallie. The editing was shared by Richie Bock, Danny Fisher and Charlie
Bornstein. The division of labour was of course never as strict as this
listing suggests, even though the principle of rotation had long since
ceased to be applied. Of the actors, Leslie and Tom remained, both with
a vital stake in the film. And there was Susan, coming from New York to
spend a few days each week at Binghamton; her influence as an 'outside'
eye was indeterminate but real.

In September, Vincent Canby, the *New York Times* critic whose article
had revived interest in Ray in 1969, visited him at Binghamton just as the
students were coming back after the vacation. He described a screening
in a room with a ceiling that leaked, using four 16mm projectors and one
Super-8, breaking down every three or four minutes. 'The showing was
also meant to make use of a 35mm projector, but one of the young

technicians said that it certainly would blow a fuse.' The film, Canby reported, 'is technically more ambitious than anything Ray has tried before. If things work out, it will consist of a 35mm frame into which 16mm and super–8 images will be set, not optically in the lab, but via a videotape synthesizer. He calls it "an adventure in time and space".'

The synthesizer Ray had at his disposal belonged to the Korean artist-composer Nam June Paik, using from one to four video cameras. This made it possible to manipulate the images, to add highlights not in the original footage. Ray also discovered the instantaneity of the electronic image, which displays immediately what has been recorded, and can be wiped and re-recorded virtually ad infinitum. Excited after the first tests, he decided to use the synthesizer as one would an optical printer, to combine images on a single screen with the advantage of greater fluidity: images changing in form and contour, dissolving into each other.

'As I sat in the leaky screening-room,' Canby continued, 'the people in the movie sat there too, passing around a large bottle of beer and a large bottle of white wine [. . .] I was more aware of the time-space adventure than I'd thought would be possible, for the film, even though unfinished, breaking down, acted by non-pros, every now and then recalls the controlled, melodramatic density and sheer technique of *They Live By Night* and *Rebel Without a Cause*.'

Another visitor, Jeff Greenberg, arrived at Binghamton for the first Tuesday in November. *Tuesday in November*, Ray remembered, was the title of his first film, the day of the presidential election. Bolex in hand, he filmed Tom and Leslie casting their votes. 'The only time I ever voted was for McGovern,' Leslie recalled. 'We thought there was a chance, we all wanted it, and Nick thought that if Nixon won it would be . . .' 'We won't have a two-party system in a couple of years,' Ray said, according to Greenberg, 'we'll have a *ja, ja, nein*.'

Leslie's polling station was opposite the general store, Tom's in a garage. Jeff Greenberg: 'Nick sets up three lights but no attempt is made to balance them. He cleans a window through which light will shine with Windex and a dirty handkerchief. All the shooting is hand-held. Nick operates the camera quickly but he is sloppy about it, leaving an electric cord from one of the lights in the frame. The 100-foot load runs out before he gets all the footage he wants. The poll closes and the crew stays to watch this little bit of democracy in action. The backs of the voting machines are opened. Cheers go up on both sides as names are announced. Nixon wins this garage by 100 votes out of 400 cast. Nick says, "I want to vomit," and goes out to wait in the van.'

That night, Ray, Leslie and Jeff Greenberg watched the results on television: a landslide for Nixon. 'That night it was the beginning of the end,' Leslie recalled. 'Nick told me that one out of every ten people on the left were informers at one time or another.' Greenberg: 'Nick couldn't understand how Frank Mankiewicz, McGovern's campaign manager, could have miscalculated so badly. Nick said that Herman Mankiewicz, Frank's father, taught him everything he knew about screenwriting and that he was one of his dearest friends in Hollywood. Nick fell asleep on the floor, snoring and coughing. The next day it rained like hell.'

Other visitors have described this second year: the Finnish critic Peter von Bagh; a crew that arrived to shoot a documentary about Ray. This was headed by Myron Meisel, and the nominal directors were James C. Gutman and David Helpern Jr, who ran a cinema – the Orson Welles Theater – and a film school in Cambridge, Mass. Their film was initiated when they invited Ray to Cambridge. During that weekend, Meisel learned about his changeable personalities: 'In as dark a moment as I've ever witnessed, Nick put in a call to Mike Frankovich, a producer for whom Nick claimed he had made millions. Frankovich took the call, but he was in the middle of a bridge game, and wouldn't interrupt his play as he spoke. Nick hoped to persuade Frankovich to let some of the student film be processed with rushes from Frankovich's film then in production. Frankovich, between trumps, thanked Nick profusely for calling to his attention this sleazy student scam to drive up his lab bills. Nick's person-ality on the phone was quite different than I had become used to. With his kids, he affected the mannerisms of the counter-culture of the day. With Frankovich, he was bluff, cocky, transformed into a firmly remem-bered Hollywood persona. It was a humiliating conversation, and after Nick hung up, he sagged like a punctured paper bag, a gaunt, weary, naked man clad only in his purple jockey underwear.'[9]

The following weekend, in mid-February 1973, the documentary crew went to Binghamton to interview Ray and observe him at work. James Gutman: 'I don't think anybody slept for the four or five days that we were there. I know that Nick rarely slept, or if he slept, it was at very odd hours. He was constantly being followed, asked questions, and some-times he didn't have answers. The students idolized Nick, they thought he was wonderful; you could see that his talent with actors was still there. But at the same time I think that they also realized that he was having difficulties. It was quite clear, at the time, that the film was never going to be finished. He couldn't finish it; he kept changing it, re-editing it, re-shooting. I think he lost the focus of what he was trying to do, just trying new ways to get performances. What he was doing was manipulating them personally in certain ways to motivate their characters. He could be very warm and he could be very hostile, and he used emotions a lot to get people to do what he thought the character should be doing. I have the feeling that he used the same technique on *Rebel Without a Cause*: Natalie Wood spoke at some length about that in our film. So we tried hard to show that this guy was a great talent.'

Austin De Besche's camera recorded a long and exhausting slanging match between Ray and Leslie, with the same arguments repeatedly hurled back and forth. Described by everyone as typical, this was followed by the filming of a scene, accomplished astonishingly calmly and methodically, and the next day Ray commented: 'I try not to direct them until just before the scene, which was part of the hassle we had last night.'

But there was no longer any doubt that both film-maker and film were at the end of their tether. As his two-year contract with the university drew to its close, Ray bore the weight of months of toil on an object whose ins and outs no one, unless himself, could even pretend to understand. A time of physical attrition, it was also a time of turbulent college history. As Tom Farrell wrote: 'During Nick's two years at Harpur, the college was rocked by hysteria: Vietnam war protest, a memorial birthday party for Adolf Hitler, the Attica prison riot, an orgy the night Nixon was re-elected, rapes of female hitchhikers, drug raids, police harassment, suicides, and dozens of other insane episodes which determined the film we made. The environment was breeding a generation of Hamlets. We were at the mercy of fate, habitually indulging in sex, drugs, alcohol, and even violence. We lived by night, shooting and editing our bigger than life experiences in a lonely place on dangerous ground. Once, after drinking at a bar, Nick drove home on the back roads in darkness like he was James Dean, when he crashed into a ditch. Miraculously he was unharmed, but he could have been killed. Another time a crazed student on LSD challenged Nick to a fist fight, which had to be stopped . . .'

It was during this period, when he was at his lowest ebb, at times ready to give it all up, that Ray shot some of the best scenes in the film. The National Endowment for the Arts awarded the project a subsidy (hitherto it had been financed out of Ray's salary, loans, and – according to Tom Farrell – a grant from the State of New York). Although the university took a generous share, the money enabled Ray to hire a blimped Arriflex 35, with a small Nagra (which he used constantly, according to Charles Bornstein, concealing it on his person). It was with this camera, and not the Mitchell used earlier, that – some time around March – all the scenes were shot which remain full-screen in the film as it was presented at Cannes.

First comes a dialogue scene between Nick and Tom, both wearing red, wandering among the university buildings. (Tom has a false beard, since the scene is placed before the one in which he shaves.) Nick tells him the story of 'a wise man who travelled to every other man he knew throughout the world who had a reputation for wisdom. He said, "Tell me something that you have learned, that will help me pass on to other people something that will help them" [. . .] Until he got to the Sphinx in Egypt, and he said: "Hey, Sphinx! Would you open your mouth, tell me one single thing that I can tell man, that will help him and guide him through his life?" For the first time in 5,000 years, the Sphinx opened her mouth and said, "Don't expect too much" . . . Don't expect too much from a teacher,' Nick concludes. (In an early scripting of *Bitter Victory*, this was offered during a flashback as a key to the relationship between Leith and Jane.) Then Tom feints punches at Nick to discover whether they are both blind in the same eye. Tom describes how he lost his eye, then tells Nick about his problems with girls. Nick: 'Don't take anybody for granted.'

Then there was the first death of Nick which, in the continuity, takes place before the end of the university year (and therefore before the Miami convention). Nick, dressed as Santa Claus complete with eye-patch, is hitchhiking. The sound of an accident is heard. His props fly up into the air and come down again: wig, strips of film, boots. The students, to the accompaniment of the blues heard at the beginning of the film – *Lives the family that loves together* – pick the things up and close a large coffin, which they carry off. A hearse passes in the distance.

And finally, two scenes in a barn. Richie and Leslie, in their house, see Nick in a snowy landscape. Richie wakes Tom and tells him, as Nick heads towards the barn. 'Richie! He's going to the barn.' – 'Get the camera, then.' – 'Do you think he's going to kill himself?' Nick tests the noose; a trick of perspective makes it seem that he has already hanged himself. Richie and Leslie come and ask him to stay with them. He accepts. In the film as presented at Cannes, a scene between Jane, Stanley and another girl intervened before the second sequence in the barn (the end of the film, several times called in question). Nick is preparing to shoot. Tom refuses to be filmed and accuses him of never doing anything but point his camera into people's faces. Nick, troubled, lets him go. In a car, Leslie and Richie kiss. Tom sees them, runs into the barn, and starts crying. Nick enters the barn, afraid that Tom may hang himself with the rope Nick has prepared for himself. In a moment directly echoing the

443

deserted mansion sequence from *Rebel Without a Cause* – in its tranquillity and crepuscular lighting as much as in its content – Richie and Leslie come looking for Tom in the barn, where he has fallen asleep. Richie, thinking that Nick is going to hang himself, struggles with him. Trying to push him away, Nick does in fact hang himself, and pronounces his own epitaph: 'I have been. . . interrupted.' His voice is then heard: 'Let him sleep for a short time. Not too long a time, just long enough to get back his dream. The flood gates are opening and the water's rushing like the people against the dams . . . and the goddamns. But waken him in time. Take care of each other, it is your only chance for survival. All else is vanity. And let the rest of us swing.' In close-up, the two kids come together, and Leslie tucks a cover up over Tom as he sleeps in the straw. In the Cannes copy, the title with the blues from the beginning, continuing over black leader, ends the film.

Richie Bock: 'It was a frightening sequence to shoot, because we actually thought that Nick was going to kill himself. He was swinging on a rope and he didn't have anybody there underneath him . . . swinging up there trying to get that rope round his neck. You can see from the documentary what kind of state he was in at that time. But the scene was so accurate in illustrating what he says when that rope is swinging. He had it then, he knew he had it then.'

Ray conceived the idea of sending the film to the Cannes Festival. Of all the illusions he entertained about himself, the one about his European reputation was among those he clung to most tightly. The gambit came off, in part at least. What had to be reconciled here was a screening of the film in public, thus demonstrating that it was undeniably finished, with the fixed idea that if the film *wasn't* finished, it could be with a little more money, a little more work. Despite the film's obviously incomplete state, money *ought* to be available at Cannes (Ray's obsession with deals), and work *ought* to achieve the completion that had proved so elusive for months.

A lightning trip to Paris won over the Cannes selection committee, who declared that they were prepared to wait for the film until the very last moment. Ray had brought 35mm, 16mm and Super–8 reels which he screened at the Cinémathèque Française for some friends and acquaintances on the afternoon of 9 April.[10] The predominant reaction was puzzlement.

He had the cutting-room cleared out at Binghamton, where he never set foot again. Richie Bock, Charles Bornstein and Luke Oberley loaded all the material into a driveaway car (one they drove from coast to coast on behalf of the owner, who flew), crossing the country with the car scraping the ground under the weight. They met up again with Ray in the middle of a lecture he was giving at Cal-Arts for the American Film Institute on 26 April: a brilliant, rambling monologue in which he spoke (probably for the first time) about *Wind Across the Everglades*, recalled his encounter with Robinson Jeffers, talked by turns about improvisation, Herman Mankiewicz and Frank Lloyd Wright, revealed a surprising knowledge of Vakhtangov and Meyerhold, and ended with *We Can't Go Home Again* (now the definitive title of the film). 'The chances of our getting there [Cannes] are one tenth of 1 per cent.'

'Nick was always great at getting cutting-rooms and Steenbecks,' Charles Bornstein recalled. 'After Cal-Arts, we got a cutting-room at the AFI. We got thrown out of AFI after a few days, then Nick got another cutting-room, I think from a guy who cut TV commercials, then *he* threw us out. By the time we got to LA, I was so exhausted that I wound up getting shingles, and I spent half the time editing with Richie and Nick, half the time crashed out on the floor. Then we wound up at the Chateau Marmont, in the *Rebel Without a Cause* bungalow! The simple fact that this guy, who was completely indigent, could get an expensive bungalow at the Chateau Marmont, run up enormous bills – just the phone bills alone! – and never pay them, was a great experience. At the Chateau Marmont, he organized a big buffet lunch to which he invited all these "Hollywood people" to tap for money. And the saddest thing about it was that very few of them came. Natalie Wood and Robert Wagner were there, a scriptwriter and his wife whom he'd known at RKO, a former secretary to Howard Hughes. Very few people and we were starving, faced by all that food we couldn't touch! We ended up eating the leftovers. It ended as always with Nick getting out his address book, full of numbers that had probably been out-of-date since for ever.'

The main task now was to combine the various images (including those produced by the synthesizer, which had been transferred to 16mm) on the same piece of film. An optical process would have been too costly, and the results too inflexible. So the film had to be projected (using five projectors in all), and filmed in 35mm, on a transparent screen, sequence by sequence. Linwood Dunn, who was to have worked on *55 Days at Peking*, was approached first, but declined. The job was finally done not far from CFI, the RKO and Republic lab which had handled *Johnny Guitar*, and where Ray deposited all the material brought out from Binghamton. Richie Bock: 'We had to cut the best-achieved material together to make a negative, cut the negative, and get the print to France . . . We made it right under the wire. We never saw our cut; we just slam-banged the stuff together. To me, that film wasn't ready, and it's ridiculous to think that this was a finished film.'

To which Tom Farrell added: 'We worked for about four days straight, 24 hours a day. That's not an exaggeration; we stayed there for all that time, with just breaks. There were serious doubts then. Nick was ready to give up. He said "We're not going to make it," a few times, and I was almost in tears to have gone this far. We tried to patch up the sound by taking it to Glen Glenn Sound. That was very expensive, to have to dub from the picture. Even the engineer there said, "I can't do anything with this. It can't be done." That's where we recorded my narration.' At that stage, it was indeed Tom alone who spoke the commentary over the fine opening montage, starting with the Chicago Democratic Convention, then describing how he joined the SDS while some of his friends were joining the Peace Corps. (For Cannes, and therefore on all prints subsequently struck from this negative, a simultaneous translation into French of this opening passage was also recorded.)

Charles Bornstein: 'We all loved Nick so much and we were convinced he was going to die the next day, because he abused himself so much. We wound up drinking as much as he did, and doing as much drugs as he did. But somehow he was much better at it! Then when Nick left to go to Cannes, that was really the last time that I saw him as the Nick from Harpur College. Because any time after that, it was just like he was so much worse.'

The evening before departure, money for the tickets had still not been found (a cheque from Natalie Wood arrived too late). Susan had stayed in New York, where she was working for Viking Press. She finally laid her hands on $2,500 in cash, and alerted Leslie; and in the evening they both met Nick at the airport. As Susan Ray describes it: 'He was carrying the film under his arm, hadn't seen it yet since it got out of the lab. We arrived in Cannes the next afternoon, the film was put on the projector an hour later. Nick slept through the screening. I sat next to Sterling Hayden and smoked hash with him. He turned to me at one point and said, "Shit! Was Nick on psychedelics when he made this?" ' The film went unnoticed, even by the few people who might have been expected to acknowledge it. One single article, in *Le Monde*: it was written not by a film critic but by a jazz specialist, Claude Fléouter.[11]

It would be naïve to see *We Can't Go Home Again* as a deliberate destruction of Ray's image as a Hollywood director, and to find (as Jeff Greenberg did, for example) something heroic in the sabotage of technique without reason or purpose. Equally naïve to imagine that it was failing anything better – failing a return to the bosom of the industry –

that the film affected an avant-garde style. The decision to make the switch had been consciously taken, cost what it might and by whatever means. Both theme and manner of production dictated a form ('What seemed to be very easy was the way the form came about,' as Ray said) closer to Ray's dream than has been supposed. So *that's* what he wanted when he was making *They Live by Night, Johnny Guitar* . . . ? For many people, the hypothesis is difficult to accept.

Wim Wenders was genuinely upset by this during the filming of *Lightning Over Water*. He made no bones about having been shocked by 'the total negation of any sense of image'; but after seeing the film for the third time, he said, 'In a way there is an energy going on such as I was never able to put into any image I made.' [12] Wenders was probably also shocked by the frankness of Ray's self-portrait. A film in quest of his own image – as Ray wanted *Lightning Over Water* to be (it turned into something else) – *We Can't Go Home Again* was also a film about, in Susan's words, 'the flight from self, and the kind of distress caused in the mind by that flight'. The 'experimental' aspect was an attempt to plot mental tensions and mechanisms through a visual dimension whose freedom of form would reflect them.

It was also, of course, a film about the teaching process, instead of the straightforward account of the problems of youth it probably would have become but for the presence of the central character. The relationships, progressing from seduction to betrayal, are the very weft of the film. This was one of the aspects improved, after the Cannes screening, when Tom's commentary was replaced by Ray's own much longer one, a splendid piece of work (the beginning can be heard in *Lightning Over Water*). One of the few people to see both versions felt that 'the 1973 version was the students' film, whereas the 1976 one was really Nick's point of view'.

Glossing over the technical state of the 1973 version – the only one available for screening now – one should be able to recognize that the accent is placed on the same things, that Ray's work was unchanged in what made its power: the drive to spark a sort of 'truth', or a dramatic highlight, from a representational process encompassing everything from the architecture of the image to the interiority of the actors. One may perhaps feel that this work is weaker here than it had been in the past. It is certainly not carried over into the editing, which remains rough throughout. Perhaps, too, it is no longer marshalled by a dramatic structure, but this is something that may also be laid to Ray's credit: one might ask oneself whether he needed a dramatic structure, and whether his best films did not tend to do without one.

447

We Can't Go Home Again was Ray's last film (the short films he made later, *The Janitor* or *Marco*, can't be considered on the same level), the last profession of faith of a film-maker whose passionate involvement with his work was such that he could not part with it. A confession, too, which he invested with all his true strengths, as well as with his dreams and his limitations. One can see here the actuality of cinema as the 'Cathedral of the Arts', the work which aspires to embody everything by and in itself; the osmosis between the spirit of the times and the creative impulse; the element of work in progress, left open by default as much as by invading unexplored areas of cinema. That Ray had to make his voyage alone, despite the presence of several avant-garde film-makers on his doorstep (and arguably progressing very little further than they did), is only one more contradiction in his biography. Faced by this fragment, one must at least agree with the film-maker himself that it is an 'honest' film. One might go further: finished or not, in progress or interminable, *We Can't Go Home Again* was a staging-post for Ray, as important as the finest of his films.

After the Cannes Festival, all that was left of *We Can't Go Home Again* was the print. It was this print that Ray tirelessly pulled apart and put together again like Penelope's shroud, brooding over its possible completion right up to his death. He shot new scenes in July 1973 in Amsterdam; in January 1974 in New York, where the Gutman-Helpern unit lent him a camera and a cameraman while completing their documentary about him; in March the same year in San Francisco, while squatting in the cutting-room at Francis Ford Coppola's Zoetrope Studios. During the two years that followed, he edited, re-edited, recorded, re-recorded, eventually preparing, in 1976 – under pressure of a screening for a possible distributor – a version which was to remain the film's final state. It was this that was screened in Ray's loft, for Wim Wenders and his unit, on 2 April 1979. At the end of 1979, Pierre Cottrell negotiated a settlement of the debt owed to the CFI lab, and some prints could be struck from the negative edited in the spring of 1973. In this version, the film was screened in 1980 at the Rotterdam Film Festival and at the Action-République in Paris, and subsequently in various retrospectives.[13] Impressive as it is, it remains inferior in many respects to the version established in 1976, and which Susan Ray has not lost hope of restoring.

38

The Janitor (Wet Dreams)

Cannes 1973 ended in disaster for Ray. He lost or gambled away his money; seven reels of the *We Can't Go Home Again* print 'disappeared from the projection booth', stolen he supposed, but more likely mislaid. They reappeared between five and seven weeks later. In Paris without money or anywhere to stay, Ray and Susan wandered from brasserie to brasserie, saw friends: Dr Genon-Catelot, the photographer Tony Kent, Barbet Schroeder. Mary Meerson and François Truffaut lent them money, Françoise Sagan paid their bill at the Hotel Montalembert.[1] After Susan left, returning to New York and her job, Ray slept on Sterling Hayden's boat, moored at the Quai de Conti.

It was once again one of 'Langlois's children' who offered him the chance to work. Max Fischer had a studio in Amsterdam, Film Group One, where advertising films were made. Out of his profits, he produced and part-directed a portmanteau film satirizing, but also exploiting, the vogue for pornographic movies. The idea was to bring to the screen the erotic dreams of personalities like the writer Heathcote Williams, the painter Hans Kanters, the animation director Oscar Cigard, or the Yugoslav film-maker Dusan Makavejev (under the pseudonym of Sam Rotterdam). Langlois put Ray in touch with Fischer. 'One day I received a call from Paris. It was Nick Ray, who said: "I hear you're preparing a film called *Wet Dreams*. I'm very much interested." At first, being a devoted admirer of Nick Ray's, I thought someone was pulling my leg. He said: "I'm taking a plane, I'll be in Amsterdam this evening." I didn't know what to think, so I called Langlois, who confirmed that it was indeed him. So he turned up that evening, had to leave the next morning but one on a 7 a.m. flight, and we spent the whole night – he had incredible energy; no one could keep up with him – trying to settle on an idea, because he wanted to do the filming that very day. Afterwards he was leaving for Cannes, and after Cannes for the States. During the night he threw out dozens of ideas, including one which seemed quite absurd – I didn't see how it could be done.'

What he proposed to Fischer was the idea of strips of film ('One 35, one Super–8 and one 16mm') exploding together into the sky like an orgasm: an image in fact featured in *We Can't Go Home Again*, when the Santa Claus figure is run over by a car. At 7.30 a.m. Ray arrived at the studio and presented Fischer with another idea: the story of a preacher who simultaneously discovers oral sex and incest with his daughter. 'The most difficult thing,' Fischer said, 'was finding the little girl to play Nick's daughter, who was supposed to be thirteen years old and to suck him off. I said, "Nick, it's absolutely impossible . . ." On the other hand, he had to leave the following morning. I got all my people busy constructing what had to be constructed, we started rooting out props, time was passing, and we decided to start filming around one o'clock in the afternoon, except that we weren't ready at all and couldn't find a little girl. I started telephoning various people I knew, and then an absolutely incredible thing happened. I received a call from someone who said: "I hear you're making a porn movie" – "No, it's not a porn movie at all," etc. And he said, "Because you see, I have two daughters and we do that at home!" The kid turned up at three o'clock, and we started filming at around six in the evening. There was no script, it was all improvised. I was handling the main camera and we had a second cameraman, filming with two cameras to get the best out of the scene, because we could shoot it only once.' The second camera very soon broke down, and Fischer filmed the happening on his own, doing pretty much what Albert Maysles did for Godard on his *Montparnasse-Levallois* sketch in *Paris vu par . . . (Six in Paris).* Filming continued until Ray left for his plane at seven in the morning.

He in fact returned to the United States. A telephone call from his friend Arthur Withall, and finance provided by an Austin business-woman, Marilyn Maxwell, took him to Texas, where he filmed Willie Nelson's first 'Fourth of July Picnic'.[2] Annually at Dripping Springs, the singer brought together musicians and singers like Leon Russel and Kris Kristofferson at an open-air festivity.

Then he returned to Holland to finish the film. According to Max Fischer: 'We viewed the rushes, and it was then that Nick decided to do the beginning: Nick sweeping the studio, and the screen exploding, Nick's suicide, which also figures in *We Can't Go Home Again*.' Actually, in *The Janitor* – the title of the sketch, the twelfth 'dream' of the thirteen which make up *Wet Dreams* – Ray gave himself a dual role: the janitor in a film studio, an envious drudge, 'kills' the preacher on the screen, a tyrannical hypocrite. 'Nick is playing himself, several characters, all mixed into one,' Richie Bock commented. 'But in the end the screen burns up; he's destroyed and wants to start again. This is what *We Can't Go Home Again* is too: he kills himself to be reborn.'

This second filming session, just as improvised as the first, described as 'half a day' by Max Fischer, perhaps lasted a bit longer: a few hours or a few days in July, during which Ray, as usual, wore out his small crew. Enthusiastic about his collaborators from Film Group One, he wrote to Susan: 'The major talent of the company – editor, cameraman – fainted tonight from exhaustion when we were halfway thru a reel. His wife says he'll be ready to work at nine in the morning, so I shall sleep here on the floor to be here when he arrives; if he does, for tomorrow is our last chance to finish off one film, and will leave *We Can't Go* practically unaltered.' Fischer had, in fact, offered to help him finish the students' film.

Pornographic cinema fascinated Ray. Besides the plan to make a money-spinning porn movie during the second year at Binghamton (mentioned by Tom Farrell) – abortive, like all Ray's attempts to make easy money – the idea resurfaced three years later with his 'discovery' of the porn star Marilyn Chambers, and the project he announced which was to reveal the actress in her. He talked to David Turecamo at this time about a process that would stimulate ejaculation among the spectators at the same time as on screen! His fleeting enthusiasm for this unexampled version of Sensurround was not feigned, even if he was not entirely serious.[3] *The Janitor*, in short, is a perfectly legitimate reflection on porn movies as an extreme example of the medium, the one requiring maximum exposure.

It is a personal film from the word go. Not only does Ray, with rare complacency about his image, award himself both leading roles – complete with eyepatch, missing tooth, and socks tumbling about his ankles – but he mentions his psychoanalyst Dr Vanderhyde by name, he refers to his divorce, and he is playing the role of teacher-guru that he had filled for the past two years. The film is shot almost entirely in close-ups, giving an astonishing sense of brooding re-examination, or mirror effect, partly intentional and partly ineffective thanks to the lack of finish. The work print kept by Ray is in fact slightly different from the version released, edited by Max Fischer: at the beginning, a few video images match the preacher's glances off-screen, making the sequence easier to follow, although the editing is equally perfunctory.

The story is as follows: the janitor of a studio, whose broom serves him by turns as household implement, phallus, horse, gun and aspergillum, watches with exasperation as a puritanical preacher, his double, rejects the advances of his daughter. Before the worshippers who visit him, the preacher denounces Moses and the Ten Commandments, particularly those relating to theft and adultery. The religious ecstasy roused by his sermon degenerates into an orgy. The participants roll around on the floor, embracing and climbing on to each other. While the preacher

451

repeats that he 'still has something to say', he permits, with a brusque 'yes', the fellatio practised on him by a bespectacled woman with large teeth, a black woman, and finally his daughter. His sermon continues on screen. The janitor brandishes a gun and fires at the screen, which bursts into flames.[4]

'*Homo sapiens hipocritus*, says Ray at the end, wavering, like the paradoxical *mise en scène* of the sketch, between allegory, private joke, a sense of playfulness and a sense of the sanctity of pleasure. He is *caretaker* of these images and at the same time their transgressor, voyeur and exhibitionist, as if his image already incorporated his myth, offering both up to pornovision' (Joao Bénard da Costa).[5]

One probably has to be very involved with Ray's films (like the writer just quoted) or with his personal evolution (like Richie Bock) to appreciate *The Janitor* as anything more than a crude sketch. The frankness and compactness of the exhibitionism are probably preferable to the slack, affected licentiousness, desire become pose, of the later Losey. But frankness and a personal standpoint are no great merits in these days of flaunted sexual liberation (the film originated in a 'Wet Dreams Festival' sponsored by *Suck* magazine). Nevertheless, even in its self-complacency, it remains one of the few Ray films born, not of torment, but of an openly admitted pleasure. Max Fischer spoke of the film-maker's 'extraordinary sexual voracity': 'He had an erection the whole time! When the girls throw themselves at him, in the famous scene where I was wandering around, camera in hand, filming everything because it was all happening so quickly . . . I didn't show it in the edited version, but Nick had a hard-on all the time. He was like a fish in water in this situation, he loved it. The little black girl said to me, "My God, I never expected . . . he has such a big one!" '

Besides hypocrisy, the theme of incest looms large in this short film, underlined by an uncertainty (maintained until the closing shots) as to the relationship between the little girl and the man she calls 'Father'. Ray talked to Fischer about his childhood fantasies, crystallizing around his sisters. Together they discussed a scenario, at first sketched out on a paper napkin in a restaurant, later developed in New York. 'It was the story of a Hemingway-style writer (he wanted to play the part himself, of course) who lived in the American South, and there was incest between him and his daughter, and between the daughter and her brother. The day the townsfolk learn the truth, they burn the farm and try to lynch the trio. They flee and go to live in Amsterdam, where they go on as before, accepted by people, except that there is much more contact with the rest of the world. And the girl falls in love with a boy. From that moment on, danger lurks in the family. Father and son decide to put an end to the lover, not literally but in another way. They have him invited to dinner by the daughter. And half of the film was to be taken up with the dinner, with the lamb lured into the wolves' lair.'

A little later on, Ray was joined in Amsterdam by Leslie and two other students, in order to finish *We Can't Go Home Again*. Max Fischer photographed several new scenes: a new version of the suicide in the barn; a tranquil scene in a park, with Nick and Leslie walking round a pond, talking (also envisaged as an ending for the film). Leslie soon left for the States: 'How many endings do you want to shoot, Nick?' Ray mixed the film in Amsterdam, and Fischer felt it was finished. Returning to America after some months, Ray discovered that the negative had been impounded by the laboratory. All he had left was the Cannes copy, which had become his work print.

In January 1974, in New York, he met up again with the Gutman-Helpern documentary crew, who had in the meantime filmed interviews with Houseman, Truffaut and Natalie Wood. A double shooting session was arranged at the Anderson Theater, East 4th Street and Second Avenue, to complete the documentary and to film yet another version of the suicide in the barn, a scene with which neither Ray nor Susan was really satisfied. Gutman and Helpern provided the technical crew. In this new version, Tom cuts the rope with which Nick has hanged himself, the body falls, Tom covers up his face and says to Leslie, 'Let's make a scene of our own' – 'Anything but *Romeo and Juliet*' she replies. The camera pans over, discovering the theatre; Tom and Leslie climb from the apron to a balcony and walk away, leaving the empty auditorium. Towards the end of filming, Ray had an 18-foot fall, and arrived at the University of Minneapolis film society in a wheelchair with ice packs on his knee.[6]

There were some further screenings of *We Can't Go Home Again*: one at the Andy Warhol Factory; another, more fashionable (and mysteriously interrupted), attended by Houseman, Connie Bessie and Kazan, at the First Avenue Screening Room, in the autumn of 1974.[7] In the same screening room, on 7 January, 1975, Ray introduced the Meisel-Helpern-Gutman documentary, entitled *I'm a Stranger Here Myself*. The film, with narration delivered by Howard Da Silva, remains conventional and respectful, despite its efforts to take a different approach from the portraits of film-makers made fashionable by Richard Schickel (*The Men Who Made the Movies*) and Peter Bogdanovich (*Directed by John Ford*). It has the advantage over these films in that it shows its subject at work, in moving and revealing moments, above and beyond a straightforward reportage on the making of his film. The same critics who at around this time were sneering at Welles, the 'remnants' of his talent and his 'inability to finish a film', waxed even more indignant at the warm reception Ray met with at these screenings. The extreme devotion of younger spectators, and the natural tendency of the object of this adulation to play up to his admirers, seemed to them sufficient proof that there was nothing to admire. In an issue of *Take One* partly devoted to Ray, a certain Jay Cocks, future co-scriptwriter of *The Last Temptation of Christ*, offered a good illustration of this, presenting his opinion as being – naturally – that of an oppressed minority.[8] For Ray as for Welles, however, this sort of admiration represented their only concrete form of encouragement at certain times; they certainly couldn't expect any elsewhere. Peter von Bagh, well aware of the drama in Ray's situation, commented: 'It was such a cruel thing to live in the States surrounded by people who didn't know your work. He knew full well that the Museum of Modern Art would never show one of his films. It's a criminal thing, what MOMA did in regard to their own film-makers. In 1974 there was no question of showing Nick Ray there.' (The Museum of Modern Art did finally extend an invitation, a few weeks before his death.)

What museums didn't do, universities and local archives did. One of the liveliest of these, Tom Luddy's Pacific Film Archive, invited Ray to San Francisco for a retrospective in March 1974. Luddy, who was already thinking of turning producer, acted as Francis Ford Coppola's 'cultural conscience', and was able to help Ray for a time as the two worst years in his life got under way. A deal was made with Zoetrope Studios to shoot one or two new scenes there for *We Can't Go Home Again*, and Ray was allowed to squat, from midnight until eight in the morning, in the cutting-rooms where *The Conversation* was being edited.[9] It was then that, meeting up with Richie Bock in San Francisco, Ray shot the scene in which Richie hides hypodermics in Nick's drawer, so as to inform on him. The situation was uncomfortable, and with Luddy again acting as go-between, Ray moved to Cine Manifest, a group of independent film-makers (later the producers of *Northern Lights*). Then came a warehouse in Sausalito, part of a garment factory. On the whole, these were sterile months. Peter Buchanan, a lawyer introduced to Ray by Tom Luddy, fought for a while on behalf of *We Can't Go Home Again*, trying to sell it, with Ray hopeful of distribution on the then very active campus circuit. 'I had some friends in the distribution business in Los Angeles,' Peter Buchanan said, 'and I brought the film down to them to look at, with the idea that they were going to deal with it as a tax investment. The film looked really pretty good at that time, I thought. These people unfortunately didn't have all that much taste. It fell through, and after that Nick started to re-cut the film. I thought he just tore it apart, and it got worse and worse.' Peter von Bagh, who visited him in Sausalito, found him surrounded by a bunch of kids, totally different from the Harpur crew: 'It was even more obvious then that he wasn't going to finish it, that he wasn't meaning to either. To finish it would have been his death. It was tragic to see him surrounded by these kids, with this senseless feeling of community, but with no responsibility and no consequence.'

At Zoetrope, Jerry Jones, who directed films for *National Geographic*, offered to help Ray in exchange for help on a personal project. Jones advanced him some $20,000,[10] and brought about a productive encounter with a young woman of twenty-six, Sheri Nelson. 'Jerry Jones,' she explained, 'called me one morning and said, "I have a job for you." He came and picked me up, and took me over to American Zoetrope, where Nick was shooting another scene to insert in the film. There was no discussion at all between Nick and I about what I would do for him, whether I would work for him. He handed me a stack of script notes and said, "Here, darling, see what you can do with this." And that was sort of the beginning of our relationship.' Originally, Sheri Nelson was supposed to prepare a script for copyright purposes: Nick was obsessed by the legal threats that were hovering over the film. She had worked with independent film-makers in Austin, and her talent for organization was equal to the task, even though she arrived too late. Fascinated by Ray, receptive to his ideas, she became a dynamic assistant: 'I acted as production manager, script girl, a bit of everything. Within a month or two, I started taking more control of things, because Nick had great genius and very little discipline. Nick never budgeted anything. Neither time nor money. So by July I became financier as well, because we were out of money. We shouldn't have been: there was plenty of money in March to have completed the film, with enough left to try to market it. Jerry Jones had had an inheritance. But the mistake was that he handed it to Nick with no strings attached, no accountability, nothing, and then left the country.

'So in July I flew to Texas and talked to some investors. I set up a series of meetings in Austin, Houston and Dallas, then had Nick fly out. He was drinking so much that he couldn't pull it off. Then we went to Galveston Bay and spent a week, with him preparing to go to San Sebastian, trying to decide what to do with all the material in California, making phone calls to people for money. It was just a completely desperate situation. The whole thing ended basically in disaster. He left for

Spain. I flew back to California, packed up all the film at the studio in Sausalito, sent it to Los Angeles, to CFI.'

Ray had been invited to preside, in September 1974, over the San Sebastian jury on which he had served as a member ten years earlier. He was following in the footsteps of some distinguished film-makers, his elders: Sternberg, Lang, Vidor, Mamoulian, retrospectives of whose work on the occasion of their presidency had helped towards the redis-covery of these classics in Spain, still very isolated under Franco. Ray's presence, however, held a few surprises for his hosts. Friends came to see him: Harry Bromley-Davenport from London, Pierre Cottrell from Narbonne, where Jean Eustache had just finished filming *Mes petites amoureuses*. Cottrell remembered Ray as being in a dreadful state: 'The president of the jury had to take the floor at various award ceremonies and receptions. I went twice, and it was absolutely pathetic. He'd start a sentence, then ten minutes would go by before the next bit came . . . this in front of all these Spaniards dressed up in their Sunday best, watching and waiting.' The jury's award went to Terrence Malick's first feature, *Badlands*, a film which harks back to Ray with its tale of two kids on the run across America.

After this, he did not so much return to America as wander through it, a guest in turn of Susan and Arthur Withall in New York, Peter Buch-anan in Berkeley, Betty Ray (now Schwab) and Charles Bornstein in Los Angeles, Sheri Nelson in Austin. After marrying for the second time, Betty was working for ABC-TV. The first meeting between Nick and her daughters, aged fifteen and thirteen, was strained.

Betty found a cutting-room for Nick and Richie: 'It was very sad; it was like Gepetto with his puppets.' Another cutting-room followed, then another, in pursuit of this fantasy of finishing.[11] 'In his most emotional moments,' Susan said in an interview in 1980, 'he wanted to destroy the film, he didn't know what to do with it. He'd call me from all over, San Francisco, Los Angeles or Paris, and threaten to throw the whole lot into the sea. He'd be yelling on the phone, and I'd yell back that I'd strangle him with the film before it had time to sink. He was like Penelope: during the day, editors would assemble the film piece by piece, and at night Nick would tear everything they had done apart again.'[12] Philip Yordan attended a screening: 'It was just hopeless. It made no sense, it was something that somebody would do in a crazy-house. Bill Schiffrin was there, an agent, very insensitive, very uncultured man. When we got through looking at it, Nick says, "What do you think?" So Bill says, "Why, I think it's an insult to bring us here, Nick, to show us this. You're out of your marbles." They had a terrible row. I got hold of Schiffrin and threw him out, saying, "You're an idiot. So it doesn't make any sense. Do you have to tell him, for Chrissakes? Just tell him it's not for you and leave." Then Nick and I had dinner together; his wife [*sic*] was there, Betty. I couldn't help him: all I did was give him another couple of hundred bucks. Nick wasn't somebody you could do anything for. You couldn't help him. A very fine man, a beautiful Christian, he really was.'

Several detoxification cures followed one another, in Berkeley and then Los Angeles. 'Eventually,' according to Betty, 'he became too alcoholic and too full of drugs again to stay with me. So he lived in his editing-room. I got him out of the editing-room – he was dying – and back to the hospital. He had fucked up reels of film all by himself. Twenty-four hours a day with this film . . . it was really heavy.'

Finally, Nick's friend Arthur, whom Betty dubbed 'The Midnight Cowboy', came and took him back to New York. The film followed, and in April 1976 Ray turned his hand to *We Can't Go Home Again* one last time, with a view to screening it for the distributor Don Rugoff (Cinema 5). Susan Ray: 'I had a lot to do with that work print. For one thing, I outlined it, I established the order of the scenes. Nick was drinking very heavily at that point, and was almost useless on the last couple of days before the screening. I also did the music, because we didn't have double tracks, so we had to put it all on one track with the dialogue. Nick went home, and I did that with the editor, scouting around among my records for stuff we could fill in. If you listen carefully, there are some voice-overs, including mine to fill in for Jill, and somebody else filling in for Richie. But the order makes sense: that version is much more narrative. I think when you're dealing with very heavy and kind of crazed material, the more conservative the structure the better, and it was a fairly conservative structure.' The essential difference from the Cannes version is that this one pivoted on a fine commentary by Ray himself, which situates the action within a specific time span: the university year. 'I stayed to the end of the trial. Most people began to disappear. Which really made me wonder – where is everybody? So I thought I'd try to find them someplace else. Fortunately, I was offered a job in an upstate New York university. Hell, I decided I'd buy a crooked cane, grow a goatee, wear a crooked smile, and impress them with my rhetoric, rebellion, and ponderosity. Education is a very big business.'

This narration was recorded in San Francisco. Sheri Nelson: 'That, to me, was the most interesting part of the job. Nick did that kind of thing very well. It's kind of simple and it's kind of hammy, and if you get it, it's so beautiful. When I think about the opening of that film, I also think: he used to sing a lot. He would just wander around and sing: it was sort of corny and folksy and wonderful – it was so poignant and so poetic. He had a fabulous *joie de vivre*: he was a larger-than-life person.' The sequences shot after Cannes (some scenes from the 1973 version were missing, the laboratory not having granted access to the material at that time) provided further narrative milestones: the themes of betrayal, education, antagonism between the students and their teacher intersect in the scene with Richie (the one shot in San Francisco; it also figures in *Lightning Over Water*).

In the spring of 1976, in New York, Ray was offered a film. One may well wonder about the reasons which led Jan Welt (an associate of Norman Mailer's on the latter's first films) to seek him out, given his ruinous physical condition; it may well be that Ray was the victim – willing, as ever – of a manoeuvre that had more to do with money than cinema. The production was dependent on the tax shelter legislation, which enabled an investor to make a tax deduction, over a period of two to three years, of four times the amount invested. Once again Ray's name appeared in *Variety*, once again figures were cited, and once again the venture was doomed. Once again, too, only the force of his own conviction breathed life into it for a while.[13]

The film in question was a thriller featuring the most celebrated and highest paid star in porn movies, Marilyn Chambers (*Behind the Green Door, Insatiable* I & II). Ray claimed to have seen none of her films, and without making a test, compared her to Katharine Hepburn and Garbo. The first *Variety* article, in April, made no mention of technicians or other casting. Filming in Brooklyn, budget half a million dollars. Ray thought up a title, *City Blues*, and rewrote the script. He decided that David Turecamo, the Chicago student who had done some filming for him at the time of the conspiracy trial, should photograph the film, which was to be shot in Panavision. David Turecamo: 'By that time Nick had taken over a house at 285 Broadway at the corner of Canal Street (which is now a disco place) as offices and studio. A huge place, and typically, it became a commune. He started thinking of the set, and it was supposed to incorporate the offices, the cutting-room. He wanted it to be a living set: artists would live there as we were shooting, it was to be part of the background. We started painting the walls, etc. He had as his art director a great guy, Fred Mogubgub, who's a wonderful painter.[14] Fred would wander around with Nick and follow every look on his face. Nick was rambling – "it's gotta be like this . . ." – and Fred would turn to me, "What does he mean?" When Nick told him he was going to be the art director, Fred said, "Great, Nick! What's an art director?" But he could have done it. Nick had this ability to get everybody excited, to keep an energy going on.' Not surprisingly, the dialogue made reference to the opportunity the Depression had offered to artists. The protagonists were a prostitute and a seedy lawyer, and Ray invested both with personal overtones.

The setting for the film was a harbour town in New Jersey; but it was entirely a New York enterprise, attended with curiosity in the Village, many of whose characters were to feature in it. 'Everybody in New York wanted to work on it,' according to Turecamo. 'One guy gave up a month's work for three days with Nick.' In addition to Marilyn Chambers, Ray was banking on Rip Torn, his Judas in *King of Kings*, now one of the most important members of the Actors' Studio. Norman Mailer was also announced in a supporting role. Roger Donoghue (Mailer's novel *An American Dream* is dedicated to him) acted as go-between, and the writer lent a hand on the script.[15]

It was in July that Jan Welt's scaffolding collapsed. 'There was no money on the film,' David Turecamo explained. 'They had something like $10,000, which is a ridiculous sum – enough to pay the telephone bill – and we were about to start shooting. I went to the rental company, chose the equipment, came back to Nick, and told him that this was the time when we had to make a deposit. Then things started falling apart. I went to Jan, and this asshole told me: "I'm like a racing driver. When I see an accident ahead of me, I go full speed and I hope there's going to be a hole." Three days before we were supposed to shoot, the project fell apart. This was when I couldn't get to Nick. He split town and left me holding the bag.' According to Susan, there were several reasons: 'One was that the tax shelter laws fell through that summer. Another was that Nick was as drunk as a hoot. A third was that nobody knew what he was doing and what money he wanted. When it fell through, Nick hit it real hard.' Victor Perkins, one of the founders of the British magazine *Movie* and author of one of the best essays on Ray,[16] happened to be in New York. Together, he and Ray wrote a script for a thriller: Ray's copy bears two titles: *The Truth* and (added in his hand) *The Entertainment*. It was written at a time when, according to Susan, he was 'hallucinating 90 per cent of the time.'

The *City Blues* fiasco led to a crisis in the very strained relationship with Susan: 'I finally packed my bags and left. Nick evidently stayed around the outside world for another week or so, and then he went into detox. I was looking for a job at that point, came into the city for an interview, and went to see him. A social worker there took me aside and said: "I bet you think that if you leave him, he's going to kill himself." I said yes. She said, "Well, you're wrong about that. If you stay, he'll kill himself, because you make it easy for him to drink. You keep him from bottoming out." She explained this concept in alcoholism of the *enabler*, which is the wife or husband of the alcoholic, who keeps the house together, who lies for the drunk and makes it easy for him to stay drunk. "What you have to do," she said, "is tell him that you're not going to come back to him unless he stays sober for thirty days and goes through the Smithers Rehabilitation Center programme. If he can do that, then you'll take it from there. But stay away and get your own stuff together in the meantime." So he went through Smithers, and I used to go down and see him on Sundays. He came out and he was an AA. They didn't expect him to stay sober, but he did, pretty much.'

The decision to stop drinking was an unprecedented juncture in his life. Susan: 'At this point, Nick was no longer able to be a cool drunk, he looked like an asshole when drunk. Plus which he was constantly in and out of hospital with a series of ailments, from pneumonia to infected bruises, all of them the result of his alcoholism. Plus which he had worn out most of his friends now; he had no place to go, I had split, there was nobody to take care of him, he was really down and out, he had hit his bottom. That's really the issue in Alcoholics Anonymous; that nobody stays with it until they come to the understanding that their life depends on it. Because who wants to give up a pleasure, who wants to admit that there's a part of their life they can't control, who wants to go to meetings? You don't do it until you have to.'

When Ray was asked, a year later, to direct a film about the founder of Alcoholics Anonymous and rewrote the script, he depicted the obsessional nature of alcoholism, but found himself unable to dramatize the initiative taken by Bill W. A peculiarly American enterprise, AA treats alcoholism as a sickness and not as a stigma, concentrating its efforts on the pragmatism of the cure. The programme, with its meetings, serves to provide a stimulant greater than that offered by alcohol. Group therapy as much as individual treatment, it relies on the effectiveness of encounters and public confession. During his first ninety days of sobriety, the alcoholic goes to at least one meeting a day; Ray frequently went to two or three. He continued to do so as long as his health permitted.

The enormous energy expended on chaotic activities was now channelled into this task, the first of his ventures in fifteen years not to prove abortive, or not to be 'interrupted', to use the epitaph he had chosen for himself. It was the first step towards a restoration of his image, towards self-respect regained.

39

The Teacher

'I have been in a continuing black-out from around 1957 until now,' Ray noted.[1] 'When he stopped drinking, it was the most important act of his life,' his son Tim said. 'I think it was even more important than the movies, because he was able to accept himself.'

Towards the end of his ninety days of drying out, on 9 November 1976, Ray moved in again with Susan, in a first floor SoHo loft at 167 Spring Street. They were without work until the beginning of the following year. Among those who visited them was Pierre Cottrell, then production manager on a Patricia Highsmith adaptation being filmed in Hamburg, Paris and New York, directed by a thirty-one-year-old German film-maker, Wim Wenders.

According to Wenders: 'We had come to New York to film the sub-plot, the porn movie and Mafia business, with Dennis Hopper and Sam Fuller. We were to meet Sam in New York, and Sam simply didn't turn up. He was in Yugoslavia or Israel, no one was sure, preparing *The Big Red One*. There we were with a small crew, the hotel bill and wages had to be paid, and we couldn't shoot a thing. It was Cottrell, one of our first evenings there, who introduced me to Nick. I had never met Nicholas Ray before. I had tried once, on Sylt the previous year, because I had heard he was always there, but it was only a rumour. When we arrived, Nick and Susan had their coats on, ready to go to court. They were having trouble with their landlord, hadn't paid the rent or something like that. Later we had a drink, all except Nick. During that first dinner, he wouldn't even taste the zabaglione because there was a little drop of brandy in it. We played backgammon all night, Nick, Cottrell and I. Then Nick asked about the film, and I told him the plot. I also told him a bit about Ripley's history from the other two novels, and he got interested in the story of Derwatt, the painter/forger from the second book, whom we had more or less eliminated. I realized, as I talked to him, that we could equally well use this instead of the Mafia stuff to establish Ripley's past. As a matter of fact, it was even better. Two or three days later, I asked Nick how he felt about adding these scenes. Together, we wrote the three scenes between Ripley and the painter, and they were shot with Dennis and Nick.'

The New York filming for *Regel ohne Ausnahme* (which became *Der*

71   Nicholas Ray meets Sam Fuller

amerikanische Freund/The American Friend) took place between 3 and
11 March 1977. Derwatt's studio was one that belonged to a painter
living on West Broadway: 'It was the first time they had worked together
for twenty years, Dennis and Nick,' Wenders recalled. 'Dennis was very
moved. And Nick was nervous, because it was a long time since he had
been an actor. The funny thing was that he was teaching at the Actors'
Studio at the time, and on the first shot we did, after the very first take, he
stopped and said, "Listen, it's impossible. I'm making all the mistakes I
tell my students to avoid!" '

The character of Derwatt/Pogash, the painter who continues to produce paintings whose value increases because he is supposedly dead,
could hardly fail to fascinate Ray. 'Obviously the character meant something to Nick,' Susan said. 'When I think of lines like those in *Lightning
Over Water* about how much more entertaining it is to lie than to tell the
truth . . . that was a part of Nick, and an important part. I think there
was something about putting something over on people that made him
feel more in control.'[2]

The American Friend shows Ray now an old man, but sure of himself,
giving an expressive or indeed expressionist performance – eyes, hands,
body producing a sense of pent-up power. Although the editing is fragmented, Wenders shot the film in long, mobile takes. 'Each of Nick's
scenes,' according to Wenders, 'comprised only two or three shots, the

72 *Der amerikanische Freund*: Dennis Hopper and Nicholas Ray,
photographed by Wim Wenders

most elaborate one – the very first – maybe five or six. One very fine and
very lengthy scene was eliminated during the editing: a long, unbroken
dolly shot through Derwatt's studio. He was at the far end of the studio,
in front of a canvas painted blue all over, similar to others you see at the
beginning, canvases he doesn't sell but does for himself. The camera
moves towards Derwatt, he starts painting the whole thing black, softly
singing a Leadbelly tune to himself. By the time the camera comes up
quite close, he has finished blackening the whole canvas. Right at the end,
he turns his head towards the light – and the camera – and we see that he
has gone blind. This was to tie up with the first scene, in which he
complains of no longer seeing very well. It was meant to be the ending,
but we used a shot done on West Side Highway instead.

'One day right at the end of filming, Sam appeared. There's a photograph of Sam and Nick, who had never met before, didn't know each
other at all. It was a great moment. Those two who'd heard about each
other, and who in each other's presence came on a bit differently . . . like
two old lions, it was rather touching. They didn't talk cinema, they said
things like, "Do you know so-and-so?" People with whom they had both
worked. Actually, it only lasted ten minutes.'

At the time of filming, the role was important to Ray for many reasons:
working on a film which was going to be finished, facing up to the
problems of an actor under someone else's direction. The friendship with

Wenders mattered too. 'Wim was one of the few people who went after Nick who had something to offer,' Susan said. 'And Nick used Wim in a funny way. Nick was a user, anyhow. Of course Wim is as well, so it was a good contest.'

While acting for Wenders, Ray started taking a workshop at the Lee Strasberg Institute, the new organization which incorporated and developed the Actors' Studio, veritably canonizing Lee Strasberg in his lifetime, although his presence was more spiritual than actual.[3] There was nothing regressive about this teaching job, since it was a new experience, very different from Harpur: a chance to collate and formulate the methods and the results of his practice. His renewed contact with Strasberg, his elder by ten years, was occasion for an intellectual exchange in which he took pleasure. A chance, too, to measure teaching skills against those of the great man. He re-read Stanislavsky, and with Strasberg, discussed the 'third way' of Vakhtangov, less well known than Meyerhold and Stanislavsky, and whom he found a source of stimulating ideas, probably by way of Gorchakov's excellent book tracing the history of Vakhtangov's production of *Turandot*.[4]

Ray also went to talk wherever he was asked. That spring it was Bridgeport, then Wesleyan University, in Connecticut. A student, Dan Edelman, came to collect him for the two-hour drive from New York: 'In the car, right away, he asked me what the current controversies at Wesleyan were; he wanted to get a sense of what the students were, what was on their minds. Then we started talking about politics, that was when his interest really picked up. He was concerned about my role as a college student in this day when politics didn't seem to matter that much. In fact, it was the morning after Carter had given his "energy" speech, which shocked everybody, saying that this was a national emergency – a moral equivalent to war was the phrase he used, I think. Nick was very moved by Carter's speech, and I think sort of distressed to find that the speech, or even what Carter was talking about, meant much less on a college campus than it did to someone like him. That kind of reversal from his former contact with students in the Chicago riots, when the campuses were where that kind of idea really began, I think upset him. Then we started talking about the class he was going to teach.'

In the wake of the Strasberg Institute, the University of New York invited Ray to conduct a summer workshop on directing and acting. Dan Edelman went along, as did Robert La Cativa, one of the members of Newsreel, a politically active group of film-makers founded in 1967 (by Robert Kramer, among others). Disillusioned with militant film-making, La Cativa decided to start his film apprenticeship afresh. He was therefore one of the few non-students to seek admission to the summer school. At the first session, he recalled, 'Nick was very hard. He told people that if they wanted to take the course because of who he was, they should forget about it; and if they thought that directing films was a glamorous occupation, they should forget about it. "Making films in the industry is tough, and being a film director is the hardest thing of all." He minced no words about how hard it was going to be, and I think he scared away a lot of people.'

In 1977, Ray approached teaching from the same basic principle as at Harpur: do rather than explain. But the situation had changed. Rebellion against the Establishment was no longer a factor, the students were not concerned with politics but with their qualification to become professionals. And just as the decision to stop drinking had prompted a reassessment of his whole life, so the process of teaching could, for Ray, only be drawn from his own experience, constitute a reflection on that experience. 'I think he was developing his understanding as he went,' La Cativa said. 'I think he had used what he was teaching in his films, but really began to articulate it as he was teaching.' He elaborated neither a theory nor autobiography nor even a compendium of practical tricks. As in the past, he enjoyed Hollywood anecdotes – the sort that so exasperated people close to him. But now he used them not so much for effect as to point up working principles.[5]

La Cativa: 'He really liked teaching; it was clear that he didn't feel that this was something he was doing because he couldn't make films. I think it meant a lot to him; that formulating his ideas on the way he had made films into a teaching method, and passing this on to other people, was very important to him. He told us to read *The Vakhtangov School of Stage Art* and *Stanislavsky Directs*, and he also told us to read *Zen and the Art of Motorcycle Maintenance* [by Robert M. Pirsig], a very popular book at the time, a sort of pop-fiction about quality. People would say, "But this is a film course!" It was very typical of Nick.'

Students still recall his insistence on being concrete, being specific. The image of the film-maker as the great outsider was no longer the order of the day. He refused to screen his own films during the sessions. La Cativa: 'I took a second course at the Strasberg Institute, where he finally consented to show *They Live by Night*. But not in the first course, although from what he said I gathered it was one of his favourite films. I felt he didn't want to influence people too much. He made it clear that everybody had to find their own approach, and that he didn't want a lot of little Nick Rays trying to do Nick Ray scenes in his workshop. He always wanted to know what you thought, why you decided on something.

'He expanded a lot on his concept of action: that was something he stressed very much in class. "OK, what do you mean when you say *Action*? Most people just say that *action* means the scene begins. But no, *action* is a very specific word. Action is what you want to do. What does the character want to do in the scene? That's his action." Nick told us he would always get that clear with the actors: What's your action in this scene? What do you want to do? You can't play a scene without an action, it's formless, the actor doesn't have anywhere to go. He stressed constantly, to both student directors and student actors, that to do a given scene, the director has to know many different actions for each moment. Because there's no *one* right action. If you tell an actor, play this action, and it doesn't work, you have to have an alternative. Sometimes, play the opposite action and you'll get what you want, even though it seems crazy. So for every action, a director has to have three, four, five alternatives to suggest to the actors. And it's not the same as the objective. The "action" is really a "to do", it's an active verb; you always have to be able to phrase it in an active sense, and you can't play an emotion. You play an action, not an emotion, and the emotion will happen. Every actor has an action, but even the director has an action every day. We might not even be directing, but Nick would say, "What's your action today?" He'd keep us on our toes.'

In a workshop partly for directors and partly for actors, the accent was naturally placed on working with actors, although Ray would have preferred to call this work 'The Actor in Space'. 'He told us: "Find a common language with the actor. There's something in every actor – in their past or in their nature – you can find a bond with." Then, after all this about motivation and action and emotional memory, he said: "But sometimes you simply have to tell an actor . . . 'Pick up the newspaper, take three steps and go out the door.' Because it can get too much; and if they ask what the motivation is, you tell them they have to find the motivation!" He thought an actor shouldn't be comfortable, of course, and always threw something in to shake him up, make him think.

'He spoke about "bigger than life". He said that he wasn't interested in naturalistic performances. "How afraid are you of bigger than life?" Meaning, go for bigger than life performances. Which is something he got from Vakhtangov, I think, among other people. Maybe there were aspects of Vakhtangov that were very similar to Nick's work. Vakhtangov's notion of fantastic realism had something of the "bigger than life" question. And I see it in Nick's work, in the performances, especially if you compare him to Kazan and other directors of the 1950s. There is a difference.'

The students prepared a series of improvisations and scenes; they did some analysis of Sam Shepard's *Cowboy Mouth*. The work was recorded on half-inch black-and-white video, handled of course by the students themselves. The scenes were strung together in a very loose structure suggested by Ray, who was to give the final product its form. Soon the work was focusing around an idea injected into the collective by Ray: that of the Forger, obviously deriving from the character he played in *The American Friend*. La Cativa: 'He planted the idea that the Forger was among us, not just in the film: since he was a character in the film, he was among us, and who he was would emerge in the course of the six weeks we were together. The dividing line between the film, the workshop and people's real lives became blurred. The Forger became a mysterious figure who could even be Nick, but was probably one of us. The effect of that was to generate a lot of creativity outside the class, to have people involve themselves and their whole being in the creation of the project. For example, when we cast our scenes, we were always analysing people, thinking about them in ways that went far beyond how they were as actors, which I think was very good. Talking about casting, Nick said: "I don't believe in screen tests because I don't believe in actors doing a scene. You know how I cast? Take a walk around the block, go out for a drink, talk to them, see what they're really made of, what they're really like, then you'll know if you want to cast them." '

When the workshop ended, three of the students – Mike Rodgers, Dan Edelman and Robert La Cativa – worked with Ray on editing the material, under the enigmatic title of *Macho Gaspacho*, which was to comprise a dozen scenes illustrating the workshop and giving some idea of the 20–30 hours that had been recorded. But Ray soon became impatient with the frustrating limitations of editing video, and abandoned *Macho Gaspacho* in an unfinished state.

He saw a show by Gerry Bamman, an actor-director, who had worked with the avant-garde stage director André Gregory. 'But that's not how we met,' Bamman explained. 'We met in a poker game. He came home that night and told Susan he had just met somebody with a great voice.' The understanding between them was immediate, and Ray asked Bamman to be his assistant for his second class at the Strasberg Institute, starting in the autumn of 1977. Bamman said: 'He was interested in keeping up on any new theory of acting. Because he knew more about the nuts and bolts of acting than just about anybody I've ever met, but he didn't want to dwell in the past. He knew all of that Strasberg-Studio stuff very well, but he wanted to keep going forward; and André and Grotowski represented a whole new era of acting that he'd heard about but didn't know much about, and I think that intrigued him. I knew a lot of the Grotowski exercises, having worked with André; and many of them were sensory-oriented, which Nick knew a lot about, but he didn't know how to couple them with the physical exercises. So he asked me to teach these exercises to his class.' This was a surprise for the students, who found themselves – directors as well as actors – working on very precise physical movements which, combined, would permit non-verbal improvisations.

All this did not go unattended by certain differences with Lee Strasberg. The devotion to Ray shown by some of his students was something Strasberg expected for himself, with no wish to share it; and there was a divergence of opinion with Anna Strasberg as well as with Lee himself, concerning not so much the reference to Vakhtangov as to the techniques borrowed from the avant-garde. According to La Cativa: 'Anna was somewhat put out by the fact that Nick's class was the only one besides Lee's where people were fanatically devoted to the class and would put in a lot of extra time. She didn't like us staying there past midnight; she liked the course to go in the hours it was scheduled to. It wasn't as if the rooms were reserved for other classes, it was strictly a question of prestige.' Petty harassments – removal to a smaller room, the course ending two weeks early – testified to ill feelings on the part of the management.

Unlike the first class, this one led to a short film being made, directed by Ray, who chose the theme and the cast of students. Two scenes, the first being set in the reception area of a police station: various people picked up in Washington Square are brought in and booked by a police officer (Bamman) and a woman behind a desk. This is a classic improvisation for the student ensemble. The second scene takes place in a dark, cramped room. The last arrival, questioned by two detectives, is at first unable to speak, then confesses that he has killed his son. Removing them from their context, Ray used the first three pages of a novel called *Marco* by Bill Pepper, which dealt with the 'Thalidomide affair' in Italy. It was an Italian student, Claudio Mazzatenta, whom Ray chose to play the role of Marco. La Cativa: 'At the beginning of the workshop, he had told each of us, directors and actors, to pick a criminal character and to work on it. He never told us what it would be used for. He did do a couple of improvisations with us, where we were criminals caught in a round-up, brought together in this huge area for reasons we didn't know. He was working us up to the scene in the police station, big desk on a stairway, woman behind it booking everyone.'

73 The shooting of *Marco* at the Strasberg Institute: Nicholas Ray with
Claudio Mazzatenta

74 *Marco*: Nicholas Ray with Robert La Cativa

75 *Marco*: Nicholas Ray with Danny Fisher

According to Gerry Bamman: 'Nick's great strength was to be able to lead them to a performance without beating them over the head, just knowing which strings he had to pull to get them to work and encourage them to do the work themselves. He would start working with Claudio hours before they were going to shoot, and talk to him about how to prepare for the scene. Then he would leave him alone for an hour or two, come back and check in with him, then leave him alone, and maybe three, four hours later he was ready to go and Nick would shoot it. That was a very carefully orchestrated, step by step building of an emotional performance which I don't know that Claudio could ever really have done himself. I don't think he knew that he had it in him.'

La Cativa: 'I was cameraman on the scene in the upstairs room; we worked till four in the morning. There were only about five people at the shooting, and Nick was very perfectionist about it; he went for a number of takes, and really wanted something very specific. We all knew Claudio from the class, and we just never suspected that level of intensity was in him. Nick was able to draw out of him this incredible performance. And the way it's shot really feels like Nick's films, given all the limitations, totally non-professional crew, no money at all, cramped space. His style comes through.'

Ruthlessly subjected to retakes by Ray when he resorted to external effects, Claudio finally managed, during the three days of shooting, to match the results he had achieved the first day for the first part of the scene. 'With other teachers,' he commented, 'even Lee Strasberg, there's a basic preparation, you have to explore yourself; better understanding in body and mind is the main problem. But I learned much more from Nick. Nick was a film-maker. Lee was just a teacher; he could give a good explanation, but he was unable to follow up, as Nick did, to help you build a character.'

Bamman: 'As soon as he got the performance out of Claudio, as soon as it was on film, I remember very clearly how Nick went up to him and held him until he settled down. He knew exactly what he was about, how far he had to take Claudio, and then how to make sure that he wasn't just left out there on a limb. It was a very masterful and very caring orchestration, I thought. He didn't try to bludgeon it out of Claudio by making him hysterical, by slapping or insulting him, or any of those tricks. I don't know if Claudio remained an actor, but if he did, he would know more how to do it himself the next time, because of what he went through with Nick.'

While he was finding a new centre of interest in teaching, Ray also underwent a public renaissance, evident when he attended the screening of *The American Friend* at the New York Festival in September. During the summer of 1977 he was approached about two projects, but he was less eager than before to confirm rumours or press stories.[6] One of these was an adaptation of a two-character off-Broadway play, *The Sea Horse*, which came to him by way of the Coppola studios. The actors were to be the author, Edward J. Moore, and Susan Riskin (daughter of the actress Fay Wray), one of his students at the Strasberg Institute. Discussions went on all autumn, without getting far enough for a script to be written. The other, *The Story of Bill W.*, interested him more. About the founder of Alcoholics Anonymous, this was a costly project (the sum of eleven million dollars was mentioned). When he went to Wesleyan, Ray had told Dan Edelman about the two films he would still like to make: 'One was about energy, because he thought that was the most important future for young people to think about, and the other was about alcoholism.' According to Gerry Bamman, who worked with Ray on the script, 'The man who owned the property was Bill Borchert, and he had already put a lot of money into it. He was hoping that Nick was going to be able to come up with a script, and that he could get it capitalized and go on with it. We already had two versions of the script that Borchert owned. Nick had been thinking about it a little bit, and he asked me if I would help. We turned out a huge amount of material in a very short period of time. I would say that we ended up with, probably, 60 or 70 per cent new material, and 30 or 40 per cent from the old scripts.' The final draft comprised 143 densely packed pages. The problem, as summarized by Bamman, was that 'the first two-thirds of his life is very cinematic, because it's the conflict with the bottle and there's a real struggle, good and evil, and finally he wins. But once he wins, in the last thirty years of his life, it's the story of a saint, and that's not so dramatic. The earlier writers put in an affair, tried different things. We didn't solve it either.'

Ray, Bamman said, 'was juggling things constantly; he always had several things up in the air.' He sent various scripts to Wenders, in the hope that the latter could help him to set them up with German television: *City Blues, Mister Mister*, a Western set during the Civil War, on the frontier between North and South, about the adventures of sixty-five youths and 'a young Kansas cowboy, a muleskinner known only as Mister to the boys, who called him Mister Mister' (echoing a character from *The Cradle Will Rock*, one of the high-water marks of the Federal Theater).[7] A little later, he refused an invitation to direct *Junky*, a William Burroughs adaptation previously offered to Dennis Hopper. He had rarely been so circumspect, and continued to be so in December,

when interviewed by Bill Krohn for *Cahiers du Cinéma*. Perhaps directing a film had become too distant a goal; perhaps he realized that *We
Can't Go Home Again* was to be his last. 'My impression,' Bamman said,
'was that there were people beginning to nibble around like little fish to
see if he really was healthy again. If he had given them any indication
that he was not, that he was still drinking, they would have backed off,
but they were beginning to get interested. One of the major problems
with *The Story of Bill W.*, finally, was Nick's cancer.'[8]

Susan Ray: 'He was diagnosed as having lung cancer in November
1977, although he probably had it as much as two years before then,
from what I can tell. Nobody treated him, but the alcoholism was such a
heavy blanket and caused so many side illnesses. It was probably untreat-
able before then. They did one operation at that point; they opened him
up, thinking they could take out a compact tumour, and found it was too
close to the aorta, so they closed him up again, doing nothing. And began
a series of cobalt treatments, which from the X-rays seemed to have some
effect.'

Ray was admitted to the Roosevelt Hospital, 59th Street, a few days
after his class at the Strasberg Institute ended. He kept a journal, received
visitors, prepared for a role in a film: an adaptation of the musical *Hair*,
the stage version of which had 'made' Michael Butler a few years earlier.
The director, Milos Forman, who didn't know Ray, was looking for 'a
typical-looking General'; it was the scriptwriter Michael Weller, Ray's
companion in a weekly poker game, who recommended him. Forman, on
meeting Ray, felt his 'heart beating' and remembered the old saying that
a film director is a little like a general on a battlefield. In February 1978,
Ray was in Barstow, California, with a handsome contract.

'He was wonderful,' Forman recalled, 'totally professional. He said to
me: "I'm here as an actor, I'll do whatever you say, whether it seems silly
or brilliant." Of course I didn't know he had cancer, and we were blowing smoke at him from all sides: if you've seen the film, you'll know he
appears and disappears in the clouds being thrown at him. We shot a lot
more than we used in the film, and it horrifies me when I see it now.'
Ray's appearance in this hippie saga is very fleeting – he is listed four-
teenth in the cast credits – but Forman prolonged his stay to let him earn
a little more money, and he spent a pleasant time in the company of other
directors: Forman, Wenders, Dennis Hopper, Ivan Passer. A film-maker
(and novelist) himself, the Swedish critic Stig Björkman paid him a visit:
'Before retiring for a few hours of rest, Ray remarked that it was the first
time he had seen so many directors gathered together in such a small
room without blood being spilled.' The following day, Björkman saw

him on location: 'He took no hand in the business of filming. Most of the time he was to be seen sitting in the shade of a military hut, eternal Seven-Up in hand. He was not distant, but seemed concerned to maintain his solitude. In his long, sandy-coloured raincoat, he seemed almost to melt into the landscape.'[9]

A trip to Las Vegas, three hours by bus from Barstow, lost him the extra week's fee he had just earned. On 18 February, he visited John and Joan Houseman, 'the two dearest, most elegant people known to me', in Malibu. Tim came to collect him and take him to an AA meeting in Winter Canyon, where he met 'an old friend from the Garden of Allah and RKO days, Edith Sommers-Soderberg' (scriptwriter of *Born to Be Bad*). The meeting made him happy, but he was unable to hide several sharp attacks of pain.

Connie Bessie, who had twice suffered from cancer, represented a sort of 'miracle of survival' for Ray, and brought him comfort. She recommended a more modern establishment than Roosevelt, the Memorial Sloan-Kettering Cancer Center, one of the most advanced in the world, and a doctor, Dr William G. Cahan. The latter, after examining Ray, suggested surgical intervention, comprising the implantation of radioactive particles. This was an aggressive form of treatment which was physically weakening. Wenders, who was in San Francisco, signed up by Tom Luddy and Francis Ford Coppola to direct *Hammett*, went to see Ray in New York: 'I saw him just as he was going to have to make the decision. He wasn't sure. He asked me: "What do you think I should do? If I don't have the operation, the doctors have told me I won't last long, and if I do, I may die during the operation. No one is even sure it will be a success, because it's quite a new technique, but there's a chance." The doctors were very frank with him. Finally he said, "The more we talk, the more I realize that I'm going to try the operation, because even if it's pretty risky, that's how I've lived my whole life – taking risks.'

The lung operation and implantation of cells was carried out on 11 April 1978. Wenders: 'At that time, I came to New York several times from San Francisco; two or three times while he was in hospital, too. He stayed there a long time, or alternated between hospital and home. He had to be under medical supervision, to monitor the effects of this dose of radioactivity. Kazan came to see him several times. There were always quite a lot of people there at the hospital. To me, it was absolutely amazing the way this man, after two operations, seemed to be able to pull himself together again each time. He was always full of ideas, whether old scripts of his or new projects. He wrote quite a number of brief synopses. He really did want, very urgently, to work once more on a film.

I think it was during this period that he realized that perhaps *We Can't Go Home Again* would be his last film after all, which was something he hadn't wanted to accept before. I think his destructive attitude to the film stemmed partly from the fact that he didn't want it to be his last. Perhaps it was realizing this that made him begin seriously wanting to finish it.'

Susan Ray: 'Then began a series of problems from pain-killers, which his system could not process because his liver was shot. It was dangerous for him to have them: when he was out on the street he would fall. There were the problems of his losing too much weight, how to feed him, the smoking, all sorts of things. And depression. That was the worst part of all. Then he began to look really senile. It happened very quickly, and it was quite scary because he was no longer lucid at all. He couldn't be consulted about his own well-being, because he was so far out. One day – Wim was there and he was quite sweet – I was really terrified and trying to figure out how to get him into the hospital. I remember Wim sweeping the floor, and just sitting there holding Nick's hand. Anyway, I took him in; Bill [Pepper] informed me that they would be looking for a brain tumour, and they found one. So he had the brain operation and it worked, they got the tumour. That was the last major operation.' It took place on 26 May.

In July, the British critic David Thomson, familiar with the way Ray looked in *We Can't Go Home Again* and *The American Friend*, was shocked by his physical appearance when he saw him for the first time at a screening at Dartmouth College: 'I noticed a very thin, frail man proceeding down the aisle helped by a younger woman. He looked like Max Schreck's vampire in Murnau's *Nosferatu*, for he was utterly bald and the head was a glaring, eerie dome. It was Nicholas Ray, and it took him several minutes to make his way to the stage. He gave cryptic answers to polite questions, after immense hesitation and effort. There was no hint of indifference to the audience. It was just that the ordeal of speaking and reflecting was a great demand on his attenuated constitution.'[10]

A second summer workshop at NYU, delayed by a month, started in July. Fewer students; Ray was assisted by Gerry Bamman, his attention span having diminished although his mind remained as clear as ever. In the autumn, Laszlo Benedek had him engaged by the NYU School of the Arts to teach third-year film students. Despite his irregular attendance, Benedek recalled his teaching as 'absolutely brilliant. His function as a teacher was in a way limited by his physical weakness, and concentrating for two hours was very difficult for him. But certain people profited a great deal, and were inspired by him – mostly the kind of students who didn't keep asking, "What do you think will sell now in Hollywood?",

76a–b   Susan and Nicholas Ray, photographed by Wim Wenders

and the ones who didn't think they knew it all.'[11] Benedek suggested to one such student, discouraged by the school and on the point of leaving, that he should do his third year as Ray's assistant.

Jim Jarmusch: 'So I ended up going back to school temporarily. Nick was teaching for a while, but after about a month he refused even to go inside the school. He was too weak to go, but I also think he didn't really like the situation of teaching in that kind of rigid institution. He insisted that if anyone wanted to study with him, they had to come to his home. In a way, he was taking the school's money to live off rather than for really teaching there, which I can understand; I kind of did the same thing to make my film. So I ended up not finishing school, but independently studying with Nick, and then becoming a friend of his. At first there were about six people who'd come once a week or so; then after two months it was down to three, and a month later, there was no one coming.

'I feel I learned more from Nick's character than about the specifics of directing, or even anything to do with film. I think I learned a lot about what kind of backbone it takes to stand up to all the confusing problems in film production. It seemed odd that he wasn't receiving any royalties or anything for his films . . . Before I even met him, he was like a hero to me, for his films; and then meeting him and finding that films were just one aspect of the way he thought about things . . . I almost feel I learned more just talking to him about anything, books, music or baseball, anything besides the specifics of directing. He was always saying that the problem with film students was that they were only interested in learning aspects of film, and that they didn't look at paintings, weren't interested in music or other forms, and he couldn't understand that at all.

'There's a rock band, Television, whose first single Terry Ork produced. I remember going to see them – in 1975 or 1976, I hadn't met Nick yet – and outside the club where they were playing was a handwritten sign that said, "Four cats with a passion – Nick Ray". Really passionate . . . He was always investigating things, things happening in other forms.'

40

Lightning Over Water

After his last operation, Ray knew he no longer had the strength to make a film on his own. The idea took shape, vaguely, of a film around him, a film at the centre of which he would be and in which he would participate. The idea possibly originated in a conversation with his son Tim. 'When I realized that he had cancer,' Tim explained, 'I told him I wasn't interested in grieving for him at his funeral, and I came to New York and spent two weeks with him. That's when our father-and-son relationship really began. Then I left. He could die. It didn't mean that I wouldn't feel any pain, but he was free, it was his life, I wouldn't be clinging on to him and saying, "Daddy, don't die." We said, "Wouldn't it make a great movie?", and got the idea of making a documentary film about a father-and-son relationship. I went home and wrote a synopsis. But I didn't particularly care to be in it.'

The idea came to nothing, but did reverberate. Ray mentioned it to Wenders, and to others. In December, the actor Bob Glaudini, who had met Ray while directing Sam Shepard and Patti Smith in *Cowboy Mouth*, introduced him to the film-maker Jon Jost, who – just back from Europe and out of money – came to live in the loft. Glaudini was a sort of mascot presence in the work of Jost, an independent film-maker who turned out, on infinitesimal budgets – between $2,000 and $6,000 – ironic narrative movies comprising a structuralist dimension, like *Angel City* (a private eye yarn alternating with a political and economic critique of Los Angeles) or *Last Chants for a Slow Dance* (the odyssey of a trucker in Montana, long takes, Country & Western). Ray saw *Last Chants for a Slow Dance*, and doubtless appreciated Jost's originality and strong visual sense, even though there is no reason to suppose he felt particularly close to him. Jost had never seen a Ray film.

Ray and Susan asked Jost to help. Leaving for Hawaii, Jost informed Ray that he had $2,000, and received a promise of $3,000 more from Wenders. In March, he returned to stay at Spring Street, and tried to talk to Ray about the sort of film it would be possible to make, without feeling he was getting anywhere. Wenders then announced that he could lay his hands on $50,000, conditional upon having a treatment to show, and Ray concocted a story about a painter, which he would both act and direct. A few days later, Ray and Susan swept Jost aside. The reasons were probably much simpler than has been supposed: Jost felt that Ray's project was unrealistic, but offered no alternative, and his financial resources seemed inadequate. There were also 'negative vibrations': one of the charges levelled against him by Susan, according to Jost's account (published in 1981). Cottrell, who was present at a story conference with Ray, Jost and cameraman Ed Lachman, did not believe that the film with Jost was a possibility. According to Wenders: 'Nick had a story, but felt that with $2,000 and a 16mm camera, there was no chance of it being told. As far as I was concerned, there was no problem about working with Jost, since he was there and had offered to do it. It was Nick who said: "No, no, I'd rather work on something new, which the two of us can think up and develop." I told him he'd have to talk to Jost, because I didn't want him to feel that I was ditching him. Nick did that, I don't know how. I met Jost once afterwards, and he seemed to be mad at me. It was Nick himself to whom Jost should have said what he thought.'

To the project, Wenders brought German subvention fund money, and a crew with whom he had a close understanding, while Ray called on the services of those close to him: Susan, Tom Farrell, Gerry Bamman (who helped him to write), Pierre Cottrell, Jim Jarmusch (and, for a while, Kate Manheim, Larry Pine and Caroline Cox, who were to play friends). Most important, Wenders shared Ray's sense of urgency and started filming immediately: a tactic for which Jost took him to task, but which allowed the film to assume an objective reality, not least in Ray's eyes. Jost seemed to feel that Ray was once more grasping at the shadow rather than the substance, attracted by the lure of a bigger budget. This time, however, the impulse was the right one. Jost was also afraid that the bustling indifference of a crew of technicians was not at all what Ray needed; but in this he failed to understand him at all (quite apart from the fact that the crew were exceptionally considerate). 'For Nick, after all,' Cottrell said, 'his project was this: I want to die with a film crew around me. That was the important thing. He suffered a lot, that was obvious, and the pain stopped when he was filming. Strange things like that did happen.'

Wenders was, or made himself, available: 'Coincidentally, Coppola had at this point decided to change scriptwriters on *Hammett*, and we'd found Tom Pope. I'd done a bit of work with him, and he wanted to spend some weeks alone with the script. There wasn't much I could do in the meantime. Fred Roos [producer on *Hammett*] had a great respect for Nick, whom he had known for quite a while, and liked a lot: the three of us went together to see the Yankees playing baseball in New York. I asked him if I could take a leave of two or three weeks, and he agreed;

but it had to be very soon, because Tom Pope had already started work. I alerted Nick, telling him I could use German money to make a film in 35mm. He got very excited and said: "Get the first plane out. We can start tomorrow." I called Renée Gundelach, who was then managing my company Road Movies in Berlin, to tell her. It wasn't easy: the German authorities blocked the money since they had received no script, budget, etc. We didn't get it until much later. And that's where Cottrell proved absolutely brilliant at finding money from other sources, almost every day: a thousand dollars here, five thousand there, there was always a little.[1]

'After telephoning Nick, I started calling people for the crew. Robbie [Müller] couldn't do it, but his assistant Martin [Schäfer] was free, and there was also Eddie [Lachman], so we had a camera crew. On sound, Maryte [Kavaliauskas] was free, Martin Müller for two weeks only. That took care of the essentials, camera and sound: people I had worked with before on *The American Friend*.[2] They arrived the next day: Martin Müller from Brazil, Martin Schäfer from Paris. Eddie was in New York, and immediately started putting together a New Yorker team of electricians. Stephan [Czapsky] was terrific. And I was lucky enough to find Chris [Sievernich] as production manager. In other words, within two or three days, we had a crew. And the very day the crew turned up, saying, "Here we are, what do we do?" was the day of that session at Vassar, to which Nick had long been committed.'

The first day's filming at Vassar College (Poughkeepsie, New York) was strictly documentary. The limousine hired by the university was a luxury prop. Tom Farrell, to whom Ray was anxious to give a role, had a video camera: he filmed Ray in the car with Susan, and went on recording him throughout the discussion, thus defining his role in the film. (Off-screen, Tom also kept a journal of the making of the film.) Despite difficulties in speaking which threw some members of the crew, Ray led the discussion brilliantly, stressing the role of improvisation in *The Lusty Men* – not only by the actors but in the making of the film itself – and linking this method to the new film, which, he announced to both audience and camera, he was embarking on that very evening, 29 March 1979. He then introduced and summoned Wim Wenders, *directing* him while he was still off-screen.

Wenders: 'Up till then, he'd had several ideas, but come to no decision yet about the story. Nick's main idea was to return to the Derwatt character from *The American Friend* as a point of departure. He had written twenty or thirty pages. The painter knows he is dying of cancer; his closest friend is a Chinese laundryman who also has cancer. The

Chinese has heard tell of a fabled remedy that might exist in China, and they get the idea of sailing from New York to China. "The slow boat to China" means to die. The idea of going to China was a metaphor for dying with dignity. The remedy was really inner peace.' The outline comprised sequences (a hold-up in an art gallery, for instance) that it was physically impossible for Ray to enact, and Wenders (as we see in the finished film) tried to persuade him to play a film-maker rather than a painter, while retaining the fictional basis: 'Why make the detour of turning him into a painter? It's you, Nick. Why take the step away?' Ray also put forward the idea of an old man, about to die, who gathers his family round him, one of his sons being married to his former wife (an idea suggested by Tony's marriage to Gloria Grahame, which resurfaced in the *King Lear* scene). Wenders even considered the possibility of the old film-maker travelling by car across America (accompanied by a doctor) to see Hollywood one last time.[3]

After Vassar, the situation clarified itself. Wenders was thinking of a part-fiction and part-documentary film, one of whose themes could be the completion of *We Can't Go Home Again* (allowed for in the budget; Danny Fisher even proceeded to inventory the material). Filming at Vassar, according to Wenders, 'was already, of course, a step towards deciding to make the character a film-maker, which I really preferred. Also, one of the ideas behind the film from the outset had been to get him the money to finish *We Can't Go Home Again*. If the film became an integral part of our story, that would become much easier.

'Nick was pleased with the Vassar talk. He then accepted the idea of playing himself in the film, and was pleased that it had come out that way. He said to me, "My only condition is that if I'm in the film, you must be too." ' So filming that first week developed around Vassar and the two protagonists: Wim's arrival at the loft and Nick waking up, filmed in great detail; Vassar again, to incorporate Wim. 'And suddenly the whole crew was in the film. In other words, the film was about making a film. So as it happened, the film more or less took its own shape: it had found an anchorage. Then, in the days that followed, we devised and wrote scenes that would take us up to Vassar. We stopped for a day or two, then in three or four days we shot them. So after a week, we had the whole beginning of the film.'

The solution chosen by Wenders, or which forced itself on him and was accepted, inevitably roused different reactions. Cottrell, who had been brought in by Ray, was hoping the film could be a jointly directed Ray-Wenders venture: 'At Vassar, it was clearly so hard on Nick that Wim decided to take things in hand. I reproached him with this, saying:

"You could let Nick do things, but you're hogging all the limelight. You haven't the patience to let him be, to let him try to decide on camera placement, lighting, the actors' movements." Wim said: "But don't you realize that it's impossible to get that out of him?" I didn't agree, but . . . You can't say that any sequence in the film was Nick's, except perhaps the conversation between Wim and Nick, where Wim is lying on the bed in the little room in the middle. I still feel uncomfortable about it being presented as a Nicholas Ray and Wim Wenders film, but I don't think anyone was taken in.'

Susan, who had insisted that Wenders should be involved in the film as an actor along with Ray, saw that the fictional apparatus was leading to a confrontation between the two film-makers from which she would be excluded. At the time, she was irritated by Wenders's arrogance and his vagaries (occasioned by the *Hammett* production), and felt that he was opting out: 'Wim missed the bus. He wouldn't take up the challenge. To do so, he'd have had to let himself go. But he didn't want to, perhaps couldn't, let himself go' (1980).[4] She introduced a discordant note at a point where she was in a position to take Nick's distress upon herself, while Wim was distracted by the 'pressure of making a movie' that he talks about in his commentary. In 1983, Susan had a different opinion of the film itself: 'There are certain circumstances where, in a life or in a group of lives, when things go out of control, there is not one conscious human mind making decisions any more. In this film, nobody was in control: after the first days of shooting, things were out of control; so what happened then, happened through an intelligence that was not uniquely human. So I have to respect it. It had its own momentum: the film took on its own life.'

Using a crisis to trigger a fictional mechanism, which then assumes its own dynamism, was one of the mainsprings of *mise en scène* for Ray. In these exceptional circumstances, a little like the director of *Wind Across the Everglades* whom nobody saw at work, he is the Gepetto, the secret puppet-master. ('As if Nick's dying was his last directorial assertion,' Stephan Czapsky said.) For Susan, if this was typical, 'what *wasn't* typical of Nick was to leave it so ambiguous as to who was controlling. One of the tricks of Nick's illness, after the brain tumour especially, was that nobody could ever tell – not me, not anybody else – exactly how with it he was at any given moment. At one moment he'd look like poor doddering old Nick, and the next he'd wipe you all off. So that in the making of this film, it was not clear to me how much he understood what was going down, how much he was controlling. Because I saw flashes of incredible lucidity. I would say that he probably understood a lot more than Wim gave him credit for, and was probably controlling a lot more than Wim thought. I'm talking about a level of consciousness that very few get to: to be able to control without being seen, with nobody knowing that you're doing it. I suspect that's where he was at, because he covered a lot of ground during the last four years of his life.'

Wenders: 'Nick was very frail right from the outset, but didn't show it so much: he seemed to everyone to have a lot of energy during that first week, but it fell away very quickly. He told me later that, during that first week, he'd got hold of some cocaine. No one knew, but it had helped him. The doctor was very much in favour of the film. If I sometimes wasn't sure whether it was right to go on, because it was wearing him out so much, it was the doctor who said: "The most difficult thing in a case like this is the state of mind. The biggest problem facing our patients, at this stage in cancer, is mental rather than physical; and even if it does wear him out, that's better than lying worn out in hospital." While doing him harm physically, the film saved him from another kind of harm. But the question cropped up again every day, intimidating me: go on shooting, or stop? At each session, Nick pushed himself to the limits of his physical capacity. He also had a destructive attitude towards himself, and

77 *Lightning Over Water*: Wim Wenders and Nicholas Ray

I sometimes felt that he wanted the film to kill him. He drove himself so hard, physically, that the crew and I finally became terrified.'

When the first period of filming was interrupted on 9 April – Wenders having been summoned back to California – everyone had the feeling that a viable project was under way. Work began again on the 28th, when Wenders returned from Los Angeles with Ronee Blakley. Tim Ray, summoned from India, also arrived; he backed up Ed Lachman on camera. In the meantime, Ray had been hospitalized. 'I acted as liaison between the hospital and the outside world,' Cottrell said, 'taking him back there very late at night, coming to collect him in the mornings. It took quite a while to get him up, get him dressed and put him in a wheelchair, but there was a whole Marx Brothers side to the fact of making a film with someone in a state like that. He took enormous pleasure in it, he was the star turn of the hospital, and the cancer specialists thought it a very interesting experiment.'

Some visitors, on the other hand, were horrified by what they took to be the insensitivity of Wenders. In 1980, at the time having no intention of seeing the film, Elia Kazan said: 'The last time I went to see him in the hospital, his room was empty, so I went to the nurses' station on the floor and said, "Where's Mr Ray?" She said he was in the radiotherapy room. They showed me where it was, and I walked down there. Suddenly, coming up the aisle was a wheelchair, with a nurse pushing it, and this figure who looked like someone liberated from the German concentration camps. The hair on one side of his head was very thin and worn-looking, the hair on the other side was all gone, with a mark for the X-ray. I said hello, and we walked along together. He didn't talk much, that radiotherapy stuff erodes your energy. And by Christ, when we got to the room, there was Wenders waiting. They unpacked the camera and they started to shoot the goddamn picture, so I excused myself and left.'[5]

Gerry Bamman returned for two days from an engagement in Minneapolis, and acted out for the camera an adaptation of Kafka's *Report to the Academy*, which he had staged during one of the NYU workshops, and which had been recorded on video by Ned Motolo. ('Nick was very proud of that tape,' Bamman said. 'He showed it to Wim.')

Ray showed increasing dissatisfaction, though, on viewing the rushes. According to Wenders, 'He felt that it lacked a dramatic dimension, that there was no drama, no action, neither tension nor conflict. It was the lack of conflict that troubled him, and he had written a very fine scene between Susan and himself, a violent scene in which they ended up fighting. But it required physical action he was really no longer able to handle. In the *King Lear* scene with Ronee [Blakley], too, we wanted to do something different: he would hear her through the wall, and go looking for her on his knees. It distressed him deeply, his physical inability to follow through on the ideas he had. So he felt that the film was too descriptive, too measured, that something was lacking, something which he finally introduced in the last scene between him and me.'

Susan Ray: 'What I observed during the shooting of *Lightning Over Water* was really Nick in a nutshell. I think he wanted to quit all along, and I think he wanted to keep going all along. There was no way to tell which he felt most, both were very much a part of him. When you do something like this, it takes over pieces of your life and you watch yourself age fast. And in a film, where you're dealing with a momentum which is not only of your own mind but that of everybody else, it's a killer, it's a suicide trip. I think he felt that, and kept dancing on either side of the edge. What soured the film, oddly enough, was the most impersonal element introduced, which was Ronee. That's when things got weird all the way round.'

It was at the end of the second period of filming, handicapped by the presence of the singer-actress – everybody felt she was out of place in the context of the film – that Ray introduced the 'dimension of conflict' he felt was lacking. According to Wenders: 'We had envisaged a much longer scene, and the main idea was to reverse our roles in a nightmare sequence. It was a way to lead us into conflict. And we did it, but only superficially, because once again his strength wasn't up to it. In his last scene, which was totally improvised, he finally decided that he really couldn't go on. Once more he put all his sense of frustration into it. And it seems to me that you can see during the shot how he is losing the strength or the will to continue. I think he decided during the take that the film was over for him. He knew he would have to stay in the hospital: for a week already we'd been in the position of having to fetch him at two or three in the afternoon, and then take him back at seven o'clock.'

'Don't cut! Cut!': the last shot of Ray, taken in Ed Lachman's studio draped in parachute silk, in which he declares his nausea – 'I'm sick, and not with you and not because of you' – and orders the camera to cut and not to cut. ('I contradict myself, I always contradict myself.') Jon Jost commented, and others doubtless share his view, that 'One might admire Wenders's "honesty" in retaining this scene; one can hardly admire the callous manipulation it betrays.' Manipulation on the part of whom? A showman like Wenders; but a more seasoned campaigner, Ray undertook the venture with his eyes wide open. It was a reciprocal contract to make a film (behind and in front of the camera), and an equal partnership. All of which Wenders honoured by completing the film, and by making it a film, not a document.[6]

'The film was always lagging behind reality like this,' Wenders said. 'The cancer was always a little bit ahead of our preparations and our ideas. Although we moved really fast, our determination to treat the film as fiction, and not to make a documentary, always caught up too late.'

On 3 May filming stopped. Tom Farrell became twenty-nine years old that day. 'I don't know what the hell we're doing with this film any more,' he wrote. 'What Wim and Ronee say to each other in the final scene sounds phoney and smug. Don't they realize what they're doing? They're flying back to LA with Tim tonight. The film is about Nick dying of cancer and what happens to the people who are close to him while he is dying. I had this ideal that we could be a family, that we could take care of one another, but that is merely a dream. Goddamn it! This is a painful film to make and I feel absolutely dreadful on my birthday.'

Three days later, Ray agreed to go to the Museum of Modern Art on the occasion of a screening of two of his films. Cottrell had his talk recorded on video by Michel Auder. 'There was a total lack of collaboration between Ed and Michel Auder, who were jealous of each other,' Cottrell said, 'but I thought Nick's comments were extremely good. He had all his wits about him. He was suffering a lot while *They Live by Night* was being screened, but he rested in the office next to Adrienne Mancia's. He spoke between the two films, and again after the second one, *On Dangerous Ground*. It was incredible to see, close to death as he was, how clear his memory was, especially in his reminiscences of a dozen or so of the people who had worked with him on the films. Afterwards – it was the day I was leaving for Europe – he decided to take me to Kennedy in the limousine. He was in good spirits.'

Susan Ray: 'At the end of the shooting, he was already pretty close to shot. We went to the hospital, and there were swellings all over his body, around the groin and . . . he was very weak and real skinny, and his mental resistance was very low. It was clear that the cancer was all over the place. They gave him six weeks. I went to Chris and said: "It's very important to Nick that this film be finished. What I can suggest to you is that you film Nick's funeral on the junk." This blew Chris's mind at first. Nick had wanted to use the junk from the start, but they had expected Nick to be alive when the scene with it was filmed.'

Cottrell returned from Europe a month later: 'I arrived in New York on the eve of Nick's death. At the hospital I met a guy who'd been the sound engineer on *We Can't Go Home Again*. Nick was no longer in a private room, I think there were four or five others. There was a nurse he was giving the eye, having himself coddled a bit, with just a hint of salacity, and on the wall a poster saying "Give Your Blood". Nick'd had quite a lot of visitors, and he fell asleep. The other guy and I still wanted to spend a little time with him, but what can you find to do in a hospital? So we went to give blood for Nick.

'I had a notebook, and Nick said, "Have you something to write with? Write this down . . ." There was a long silence. I waited, and finally I said, "Listen, I'm off to California. I'll be back in three days." "Then you won't be seeing me again," he said. "Of course I will." That was our last conversation, and the next day, thirty hours later, I received a telephone call during the night from Susan to tell me he had died, peacefully.'

Susan Ray: 'He died way before anybody expected him to. Nick died, by the way, of heart failure. Which is what I figured he'd die of. The last week was very strange. I've learned that it's not uncommon with people who are dying this slowly to go through rituals. First of all, the divesting of belongings: Nick lost his wedding ring during that week, the ring I'd

78   The death of the old woman in *The Savage Innocents*:
'How Nick would do it'

given him. Also, our dear friend Tom went bombing into Nick's hospital room with news of John Wayne's death. There were several other things that happened; like me losing my wallet and having it returned the day after Nick died, and in it was the Kaddish . . . A lot of little coincidences. That everybody was gone on the day he died. Wim, Pierre, Bill, all my girlfriends, all my supporters. The night he died, when I was at the hospital, I couldn't reach anybody. One of the big puzzles for me was that I couldn't figure out why he would die without saying goodbye to me. I'd had a very clear image of how he would die; we'd be together. It was very disturbing to me that he had not allowed this to happen. Then a girlfriend of mine with whom Nick was close – she and I had been friends for almost the length of time I was with Nick – said: "Think of *Savage Innocents* and how the old lady went off by herself to die. That's how Nick would do it." And it made perfect sense.'

41

Trauerarbeit

The day after Ray's death, Jim Jarmusch began production on his first film, *Permanent Vacation*, which is 'unofficially dedicated' to Ray. He had discussed the script with Ray, doing the opposite of what the latter recommended, eliminating the tensions and stresses he suggested. While filming, too, he rebelled against his apprenticeship, trying to win the trust of the actors instead of manipulating them as he rather suspected Ray had done. It was only after his second feature (*Stranger Than Paradise*) that Jarmusch thought he understood the method better. 'He never said the same thing to two actors, even if they were playing a scene together. He never attacked from the front, he was very devious. Telling each of the protagonists something different, he could control the scene better. But he took enormous risks, too. He was on a tightrope, there was a grave danger of everything overbalancing, that it wouldn't work. That's why Ray's films are the finest in Hollywood, but also the most uneven.'[1]

Wenders' crew, dispersed when filming stopped, met again at a memorial service held in one of the auditoriums at Lincoln Center. Alan Lomax presided; Will Lee, Harry Bromley-Davenport, Tom Farrell, Michael Miller (dean of the NYU film school), Gerry Bamman, Luke McVay (a friend of Ray's from four or five years back), Nikka and Julie Ray, and Chris Sievernich all spoke. Gloria Grahame, Betty Utey, Elia Kazan and friends, some of them come from afar, then attended a screening of extracts from *We Can't Go Home Again* and the film henceforth to be known as *Lightning Over Water*. Then Susan and Tim, accompanied by Cottrell, took the ashes to the cemetery in La Crosse.

'We met again at this memorial service,' Wenders said. 'The whole crew was there, and they all felt this sense of frustration, the need to do something more, to do something which would write finish to the experience for them. None of them felt that the film was finished. So we did the shots with the helicopter and the funeral ceremony on the junk; then everybody got drunk to conclude this wake, and we filmed that, too.'

Village Voice, 9 July. An obituary appeared under the by-line of Terry Curtis Fox, who had worked with Ray, doubtless expressing more than

488

just a personal opinion. The title gave a foretaste of the tone: *Nicholas Ray, Without a Cause*.[2] Before asserting that none of the Hollywood rebels (he named Orson Welles, Samuel Fuller and Budd Boetticher) had proved 'capable of producing as sustained a body of work outside the system as they had managed within', and before accusing Ray (on the basis of a misreading of the scene in *We Can't Go Home Again* where Leslie announces her plan to prostitute herself) of the same kind of exploitation which Jon Jost was to attribute to Wenders on *Lightning Over Water*, Fox wrote: 'Nicholas Ray died two weeks ago of natural causes. He didn't die from finishing a movie he was proud of, as he had expected (. . .) It was not a satisfying ending. There was no final masterpiece, no return to greatness.' Fox evidently didn't know that Ray died making a film; coming from someone who knew him and whose malice hit close, the article made it clear how important *Lightning Over Water* was for Ray, whose very absence dictated its completion.

The film therefore came to be completed and, against the advice of many, shown (Myron Meisel: 'It was an act of witness for Nick's sake. It was made to be made, not made to be seen'). Wenders, once more caught up in the Coppola machine, had no time for his usual discussions with his editor, Peter Przygodda (himself a director: *Als Diesel geboren*). After having sorted the material in New York, he installed an editing table in his San Francisco apartment: 'We worked for three months; Peter edited by day while I worked on *Hammett*, at night I'd come home and look at what he'd done. But he couldn't do too much without me, so after three months we had only a rough cut. *Hammett* was becoming really pressing, and at that point Zoetrope moved from San Francisco to Los Angeles, me with them. We had to abandon this second cutting-room in San Francisco, Peter had to return to Germany, and when he came back, Chris [Sievernich] set up a cutting-room in Los Angeles. Just then, shooting started on *Hammett*. While the filming went on, I was only there at weekends, and this wasn't a good thing, because Peter spent so much time alone with the film that he became very close to it, whereas the material did, after all, deal with a very intimate relationship between Nick and myself. In other words, he was closer to the material than I was, and at the same time much more distanced from it. The further he progressed, the less I recognized what I saw. Decisions had to be made, however; every time I turned up, he'd show me something, and the fact of seeing Nick, seeing myself, but almost from a tourist viewpoint, made it increasingly difficult to express an opinion. It was a rather schizophrenic situation, and it was becoming too tough, coming from one job and trying to immerse myself in this other one, which was a very personal experience to boot.

'After a time, Peter said: "I can't go on like this, either. It's really your film, much more so than all the others which we edited before; you should be doing it but you're not here, and even though I know it's because of another film, I can't help feeling that's just an excuse to get out of it. Either you leave it to me and it's my responsibility, which I'm prepared to accept, or I'll pack my bags right now and you do it, as you should. If you can't do it, I will, but on my own terms." And he was right. I still had four weeks filming to do on *Hammett*. Peter was quite far advanced, and we didn't have the money to keep him much longer. "Do it your way," I told him. Peter didn't show me the film again, refused to, and I didn't come to see him. He went really crazy, never left the cutting-room, even slept there. He was so affected by this responsibility (which an editor doesn't normally have), not only towards the film but towards the characters, as well as by the fact that it wasn't his film and that he was doing what he called the *Trauerarbeit* (the Freudian term, "work of mourning") for someone else, that he went schizo, paranoid, insufferable – and I knew that this was the price of this sort of job. He finished the film. He showed it to me only after he had mixed it. When he left Los Angeles and the cutting-room, he was in a terrifying state, physically transformed. It had been hell for him, finishing it alone. It was really heroic. I don't know how he survived. It took him two weeks to recover from the job.

'I saw the film after the mixing was done in Los Angeles (I didn't even check the answer print). A few hours after this screening, Peter left Los Angeles. We talked for a couple of hours in a bar, and I told him I was pretty disappointed. Not disappointed by the film, because he'd done what was in itself a tremendous and thorough job, but because – which was absurd and appalling – I didn't recognize a single image. I thought it no longer reflected Nick's work and mine. It had become a documentary, whereas we had wanted to set up a fiction. I felt, nevertheless, that the film should be shown as it was, that I owed it to Peter and the efforts he had made, to accept that this was what the film was.

'So this version was shown at Cannes, and a few months later at Venice. At Cannes, I saw it for the second time. And the fact of seeing it with an audience . . . it had nothing to do with reactions, there weren't any, or there was just embarrassment, and I knew that any version whatsoever would still cause embarrassment . . . But I realized that if I left it like this, it would haunt me for ever that I hadn't finished it. We had gone so far, Nick and I, in our daily struggles, and I hadn't followed through to the bitter end. In a work as extreme as this, I hadn't gone to the same extremes in finishing it. I told Peter, and I told Chris we couldn't work on anything else until the problem of *Lightning Over Water* had been resolved, until a version existed that reflected what I had experienced.

'We rented another cutting-room in Hollywood from a soft-core porn producer, and ended up working on the same Steenbeck as Peter had used. In two months, we had done the picture editing. Then there was no longer any reason to stay there: *Hammett* was going to be interrupted for several months because Coppola was starting *One from the Heart*. So, since Chris lived in New York, we finished the film there, in a fourth cutting-room where we prepared the mixing. After that, one more week in a fifth room. Three months in all, during which we worked day and night, Chris and I. We hadn't the money to pay assistants, so we did it all ourselves. I had never physically edited before. Chris had training as an assistant editor. We finished, I think, in November 1980.

'We had often talked with Peter about using Nick's journal. Peter had the journal, but he said it was impossible for him to film it. So I did those inserts while we were preparing this final version; I also did the shots of the plane leaving New York and the landing at Los Angeles, so as to have a little space for the voice-over. The narration I did in *film noir* mood. That, of course, accentuated the fictional aspect; but also, this version

79 'Ahab'

was really a film told in the first person, and for that the voice-off suited pretty well.

'When I see it now, it seems to me that the film has become an entity. In the first version, it kept going off in all directions, and that was what hurt me the most, physically. The experience, or the memory of that experience with Nick, was after all a single occurrence, it wasn't all bits and pieces, despite the interruptions during filming. I think the film had to show that, and I think it does now. It's one block.'

Like others before him, Terry Fox compared Ray to Ahab: 'A true tragic figure, he rebelled against all restraints, and lived absolutely by the code he formulated. The only thing he lacked was an apotheosis.' In hospital after one of his last operations, thrust back into childhood, unable to tie his own shoelaces, the words that came to his lips in response to the doctor's questions were from *Moby Dick*: 'But even so, amid the tornadoed Atlantic of my being, do I myself still for ever centrally disport in mute calm; and while ponderous planets of unwaning woe revolve round me, deep down and deep inland there I still bathe me in eternal mildness of joy.'

Notes

1 Wisconsin Boy

Sources
Helen Hiegel, La Crosse (Wisc.), 15 April 1986; Gretchen Horner, Johnstown (Penn.), 5 April 1986; Alice and Sumner Williams, Laguna Hills (Calif.), 30 November 1980.

Manuscripts and memoranda by courtesy of Susan Ray (hereafter N. Ray Archives); autobiographical résumé and oral history by courtesy of Terry Ork (hereafter T. Ork Dossier).

Notes
1 Sources for the history of La Crosse: *Wisconsin: a Guide to the Badger State* (Federal Writers' Project American Guide Series), Duell, Sloan and Pierce, New York, 1941. Albert H. Sanford, H. J. Hirshheimer, *A History of La Crosse, Wisconsin, 1841–1900*, La Crosse County Historical Society, 1951.
2 Genealogical details relating to Jakob Kienzle, founder of the Kienzle watch factory, by courtesy of Alfred Reif, of Kienzle Uhrenfabriken GmbH, Villingen-Schwenningen.
3 Federal Bureau of Investigation, dossier 100–64818, Nicholas Ray.
4 Sinclair Lewis, 'Main Street's Been Paved!', *The Nation*, 10 September 1924, in Robert Sklar, ed., *The Plastic Age 1917–1930*, George Braziller, New York, 1970.
5 'Healthy Condition of Film Industry Pointed by Ray', *La Crosse Tribune*, 18 July 1954.
6 *La Crosse Central High School Booster*, photocopy by courtesy of Amy Groskopf, archivist, La Crosse Public Library.
7 Letter from Mary Losey Field, 14 November 1987; and further telephone conversation on 24 November 1987.
8 'Russell Huber, "Uncle Ken", Dies', *La Crosse Tribune*, after 18 November 1957. On Rusty Lane: production notes for *Bigger Than Life*.
9 'As soon as he got out of high school, Nick won an announcing scholarship – for one year – with station WKBH in La Crosse. He entered the La Crosse Teachers' College to learn the techniques of radio announcing' (CBS biographical note, 30 October 1940). 'He started out as a part-time announcer on a radio station in La Crosse. He won a Radio scholarship to any school in this country while in high school' (RKO biographical note, November 1947). 'A scholarship to any university in the world' (first mention in Charles Bitsch interview, 'Entretien avec Nicholas Ray', *Cahiers du Cinéma*, no. 89, November 1958. Original wire recording by courtesy of Charles Bitsch).

In March 1979, at Vassar, Ray said, 'I think that John Ford is one of the few fine poets of American cinema. He's also an enormous liar. And I may share that with him. It's very difficult to get a true statement out of John Ford. It's where his humour comes from.' However, like many people too readily taxed with 'lies' by interviewers who don't listen too closely, Ray – wherever verification proves possible – told the truth more often than not.

10 Connie Bessie, New York, 4 November 1980. Betty Schwab (Utey), Los Angeles, 27 November 1980. Lena Kienzle, born in 1873, died in La Crosse on 21 March 1959.

2   The Apprentice

Sources

Jean Evans, New York, 31 October 1980, 21 June 1981, 14 June 1982, 24 November 1987; Helen Hiegel; Henry Schubart Jr, letters of 22 October 1981 and 29 March 1982; Edgar Tafel, New York, 14 June 1982.

   N. Ray Archives; T. Ork Dossier.

Notes

1   Gilbert A. Harrison, *The Enthusiast, a Life of Thornton Wilder*, Ticknor and Fields, New Haven and New York, 1983. Robert Maynard Hutchins, author of *The Higher Learning in America* (1936), was president of the University of Chicago from 1929 to 1951.

2   Charles Bitsch, 'Entretien avec Nicholas Ray', *Cahiers du Cinéma*, no. 89, November 1958. Original wire recording by courtesy of Charles Bitsch.

3   Information by courtesy of the University of Chicago. Raymond Nicholas Kienzle enrolled on 28 September 1931; his matriculation number, 155853.

4   *Seminar: Nicholas Ray*. Center for Advanced Film Studies, American Film Institute, Louis B. Mayer Library, © 1975 (recorded in Los Angeles, 26 April 1973).

5   Claude Lévi-Strauss, 'New York post et préfiguratif', in *Paris-New York*, Centre Georges-Pompidou, 1977.

6   *New York City Guide* (Federal Writers' Project American Guide Series), Random House, New York, 1939.

7   Jean Abrams's family settled in California subsequent to her birth. Her elder brother, Morris R. Abrams (1911–89) was to make a career for himself in Hollywood, starting at the bottom of the ladder on *The Big Parade* (King Vidor, 1926), and becoming a senior official of the Screen Directors' Guild.

8   Max Gordon, *Live at the Village Vanguard*, St Martin's Press, New York, 1980, chapters 1 and 2.

9   Fatima Igraham, Kathryn Bigelow, 'Entretien avec Nicholas Ray', *Cinéma-tographe*, no. 49, July 1979.

10   Summer 1932, cited in Frank Lloyd Wright, *An Autobiography*, Horizon Press, New York, 1977, Book five.

11   Edgar Tafel, *Apprentice to Genius: Years With Frank Lloyd Wright*, McGraw-Hill, New York, 1979. Nicholas Ray figures (under that name) in the list of fifty-five 'fellows' in December 1933 (Frank Lloyd Wright, *Letters*

to Apprentices, selected and with commentaries by Bruce Brooks Pfeiffer, Press at California State University, Fresno, 1986).

12 Wright, *An Autobiography, op. cit.*, chapter, 'Our goodtime Playhouse out of the old gymnasium'.

13 Bitsch, 'Entretien avec Nicholas Ray', *op. cit.* In 1950, Ray told an interviewer he borrowed the idea of 'functionalism' from architecture. 'He tries, he says, to strip from the picture everything not essential to action and characterization, and to guard against overemphasis on sets and costumes which might distract attention from the drama' (J. D. Spiro, 'Hollywood's Bright Ray', *The Milwaukee Journal*, 2 July 1950).

14 Ray, interviewed in Ray Connolly's film, *James Dean, the First American Teenager* (1975).

15 Betty Schwab.

16 Jean Evans thought it was Henry Schubart who accompanied Ray to Mexico, which Schubart denied. It was Gore Vidal who supplied the name of Fred Dupee.

3 Theatre of Action

Sources
Perry Bruskin, New York, 31 October 1980, 25 November 1987; Jean Evans; Elia Kazan, Paris, 22 October 1980; Will Lee, New York, 30 October 1980; Norman Lloyd, Los Angeles, 24 June 1982; Martin Ritt, Los Angeles, 1 December 1980; Earl Robinson, Beverly Hills, 4 December 1980.

Jay Williams, *Stage Left*, Charles Scribner's Sons, New York 1974; *New Theater* magazine, 1934–6; Documentation on the Theatre of Action, Lincoln Center Library of the Performing Arts; Harold Clurman, *The Fervent Years: The Group Theater and the Thirties*, Harcourt Brace Jovanovich, New York, 1975; Morgan Y. Himelstein, *Drama Was a Weapon*, Rutgers University Press, New Brunswick, 1963.

Notes
1 V. J. Jerome was in charge of cultural affairs for the Communist Party. The poem appeared in *New Masses*.

2 Will Lee commented: 'For a time, use of lights was considered to be bourgeois. Then one day, to emphasize something, somebody said, "It's necessary". So lights were used, and we just went on using them. Who can say, "I cannot learn from this act or from this playwright?" Once we accepted this, we had the capacity to make things useful.'

3 *Workers' Laboratory Theatre Programme of Theatre of Action, 1933–4* etc.

4 Elia Kazan was not over-indulgent towards these practices: 'They had meetings all the time, they had something called socialist criticism. After a play opened, they would sit around and (*chuckle*) knock the shit out of each other. In other words, supposedly in the name of improving the production, they would really be pretty harsh with each other's performances. I never submitted to those sessions. But I heard about them, and I saw the result:

they changed the performances. They were very tough with each other, and they were very devoted.'

5 Quoted by Jay Williams, *Stage Left, op.cit.*

6 Lee Strasberg, on his return from his trip to the USSR in 1934, was enthusiastic in his praise of Meyerhold's work, but the name did not figure in his teachings. Visiting Moscow a year later, Losey came back somewhat disillusioned about Meyerhold.

7 The Communist Party campaigned against La Guardia during the municipal elections of 1933. The situation was to change two years later (cf. *Injunction Granted* in the next chapter).

8 In addition to Ray, these were Jean Harper, Greta Karnot, Ann Gold, Rhoda Rammelkamp, Harry Lessin, Perry Bruskin and Curt Conway.

9 Cited by Margaret Brenman-Gibbons, *Clifford Odets, American Playwright, The Years from 1906 to 1940*, Atheneum, New York, 1982.

10 These four final chapters summarize the Stanislavsky system, based on concepts of the unbroken line, of continuity (in play and character); the inner creative state (truth as opposed to convention); the super-objective (principal line of the play's action); and access to the subconscious. Stanislavsky's American followers – Boleslavsky, Clurman, Strasberg, Kazan – offered varying interpretations. Ray, writing early in 1977, inferred that *An Actor Prepares* had not been published in the United States until 1949; in fact, the first American edition dates from 1936.

11 According to his testimony before the House Un-American Activities Committee.

12 Kazan and Elman Koolish were the performers in *Pie in the Sky*, directed (Kazan: 'Nobody directed') by Ralph Steiner.

13 Seats cost less than a dollar with taxes.

14 For the circumstances in which *The Young Go First* was written, see Jay Williams, *Stage Left, op.cit.*, pp. 160–9. According to the programme, certain scenes were inspired by events that had occurred in various CCC camps across the country: Tennessee, Wyoming, Connecticut, Minnesota, New Jersey.

15 Quoted by Eric Sherman, *Directing the Film, Film Directors on Their Art*, AFI Series, Little, Brown, Boston, 1976, p. 192.

16 *The Young Go First*, by Peter Martin, George Scudder and Charles Friedman, staged by Alfred Saxe and Elia Kazan, settings designed by Mordecai Gorelik. Cast (in order of their appearance): Philip Robinson (Captain Hood), Stephen Karnot (Christy Stark), Paul Enders (Sergeant Thrush), Mitchell Grayson (Lieutenant Mullins), Jack Arnold (Orderly), Will Lee (Beebie Menucci), Edward Mann (Jeff Patten), Harry J. Lessin (Lempi Sawicki), Perry Bruskin (Giuseppe Calderone), Ben Ross (Hymie Kucher), Nik Ray [*sic*] (Glenn Campbell), Earl Robinson (Paul Crosby), David Kerman (Frank Clark), Curtis Conwaye [*sic*] (Edmund Burke O'Leary), Roslyn Harvey (Miss Ferris), Catherine Engels (Miss Ruth Kent Menzies), Roger Anderson (Clifford Stedman), Joan Madison (Florence Stedman), Jean Harper, (Robin Stedman), Greta Karnot (Polly), Rhoda Rammelkamp (Mrs Stedman), Joseph Lerner (Colonel Hager), George Parker/Bert Conwaye ('Dizzy' Scanlon).

17 *The Crime*, by Michael Blankfort, directed by Alfred Saxe and Elia Kazan.
Songs written by Earl Robinson and Ben Ross. Cast (in order of their
appearance): Curt Conway (Pete Brolyer), Martin Ritt (Al Edwards), David
Kerman (Charlie Long), Edward Mann (Bert Denton), Earl Robinson
(Gramps), Perry Bruskin (Jack Brolyer), Roslyn Harvey (Kate Brolyer), Ann
Gold (Tess Santley), Jean Harper (Amanda Edwards), Jane Kim (Mrs San-
tley), Eugene Pacht (Fred, Hal Shapiro, Harlan), Will Lee (Nicolai Norton),
Norman Lloyd (J. J. Donahue), Elizabeth Morison (Annie Olson), Kathleen
Hoyt (May Harris), Eda Reis (Edna Long), Yisrol Libman (Bob Ingersoll),
Leonard Asher (Perry Carson, Harris), Nicholas Ray (Larry Nelson), Ben
Ross (Barney Pratt), Margaret Craven (Sue Ingersoll), Alfred Saxe (Jim
Goddard), Bert Conway, Jess Kimmel (Pickets).

4   Federal Theater

Sources
Jean Evans; Norman Lloyd; Earl Robinson.
Documentation on the Federal Theater, Lincoln Center Library of the Performing
Arts; Library of Congress, Federal Theater Project Collection, Special Collections
and Archives, George Mason University Library, Fairfax, Virginia.

Notes
1   On the Federal Theater: Hallie Flanagan, *Arena*, Benjamin Blau, Inc., New
York, 1965; John O'Connor, Lorraine Brown, eds, *Free, Adult, Uncensored, the Living History of the Federal Theater Project*, New Republic
Books, Washington, DC, 1978; John Houseman, *Run-Through*, Simon and
Schuster, New York, 1972.
2   Françoise Kourilsky, Bernard Dort, Raphaël Nataf, 'Entretien avec Joseph
Losey', *Théâtre populaire*, no.53, 1964.
3   Case number U–2–753230.
4   FBI Dossier, report of 2 May 1942; on the Minneapolis Theater Project, see
Hallie Flanagan, *Arena*, op.cit.
5   Joseph Losey talking about himself and his work: *Losey on Losey*, edited
and introduced by Tom Milne, Secker and Warburg, London, 1967; Michel
Ciment, *Conversations with Losey*, Methuen, London, 1985.
6   *Injunction Granted*, presented by the *Living Newspaper* of the Federal
Theater Project, sponsored by the Newspaper Guild of New York, written
by the editorial staff of the *Living Newspaper* under the supervision of
Arthur Arent, managing editor, directed by Joe Losey, settings by Hjalmar
Hermanson, music by Virgil Thomson, entire production under the supervision of Morris Watson. Staff of the *Living Newspaper*: Managing Pro-
ducer, Morris Watson, Assistant Producer, Ned Glass, Managing Editor,
Arthur Arent, News Editor, Howard Cushman, City Editor, Jean Laurent,
Assistant Director, Brett Warren, Costume Director, Kathryn Wilson, Sound
Technician, Daniel Hoth, Theatre Manager, Sam Blair, General Stage Manager, Nicholas Ray, Technical Director, Leonard Barker. Cast of a hundred
includes Charles Dill (voice of the *Living Newspaper*), Norman Lloyd

(clown), Philip Clark, John Mack, H. H. McCollum, Frank McMunn, Charles T. Lewis, William Roselle, Raoul Henry, Joseph Allenton, Fuller Melish, Jack Fairbanks, Allan Tower, James Bradleigh, Jean Thomas, William J. Brady, Arthur Kaskl.

According to John Cage, the music for *Injunction Granted* 'was scored for piccolo, fife, trumpet, and the following battery (used to create noise rather than rhythmic lines): thunder drums, rattle machine gun, railroad train effect, ratchet machine effect, rumble cart, thunder sheet box, train bell, fire department bell, electric bell, factory whistle, locomotive whistle, ocean steamboat whistle, wind whistle, washtub for glass, and cuckoo call; also 16 snare drums, 16 bass drums, and 16 Bronx Cheers' (Kathleen Hoover and John Cage, *Virgil Thomson, His Life and Music*, Thomas Yoseloff, New York-London, 1959).

7 *New York Herald Tribune*, 25 July 1936.

5   Washington

Sources

Jean Evans; Max Gordon, New York, 18 November 1980; John Hammond, New York, 17 June 1981; Barney Josephson, 19 November 1980; Elia Kazan; Alan Lomax, 12 November 1980, 21 November 1987; Pete Seeger, Beacon (New York), 4 November 1980; Lenore Strauss-Thomas, letter of 18 August 1986; Charles Wagner, Washington, DC, 8 April 1986.

Library of Congress, Washington, DC, Archive of Folk Music, for Ray's recordings; Library of Congress, Sound Reference Room, for Ray's activities with the Resettlement Administration; National Archives and Records Administration, Washington, for Ray's activities with the WPA; N. Ray Archives.

Notes

1 Frederick Lewis Allen, *Since Yesterday*, New York, 1940.
2 'the ear of the common man': phrase used by Henry Wallace, US secretary of agriculture, 1933–40, progressive presidential candidate in 1948.
3 *The New Deal for Artists*, documentary by Wieland Schulz-Keil, 1979.
4 On the making of *People of the Cumberland*, see William Alexander, *Film on the Left, American Documentary Film from 1931 to 1942*, Princeton University Press, Princeton, 1981.
5 Helen Hiegel.
6 Information by courtesy of Robert Carneal, Library of Congress, Sound Reference Room.
7 Letter from Ray to Dr Harold Spivacke, director of the Music Division, Jefferson City, 30 October 1939.
8 The Washington Political Cabaret presents its first *Topical Revue*, entire production staged by Nicholas Ray, settings by Whitney Atchley, choreography by Sophia Delza. Production Manager: Cook Glassgold. Technical Director: Whitney Atchley. Stage Manager: Louis S. Hillman. Lighting: Joe Marsten. Costumes and Props: Diana Scott. Press Representative: Jean Evans. Sketches: *It's Later Than You Think* (mus. Freda Berla, lyrics

Bernard C. Schoenfeld), *Move Over Please* (written and directed by Cook Glassgold, mus. Freda Berla), *Message from a Refugee* (Jean Evans, mus. Ruth Crawford), *Civil Service Rating* (Berla-Schoenfeld), *Ask-Me-Another-True-Or-False-Question-Please* (written and directed by Cook Glassgold), *A Public Apology* (Derek Fox-Schoenfeld), *Counterpoint in Social Register* (mus. Goddard Lieberson, lyr. Sophia Delza), *Home Life of a Deputy Comptroller* (Donald Cameron), *Love on Relief* (Berla-Schoenfeld), *Castaways* (Nicholas Ray-Bernard C. Schoenfeld), *Girl Meets Boycott* (Berla-Schoenfeld), *Swing Into Action* (lyr. Sophia Delza, mus. Freda Berla). With Fulton Reichlin, Don Sisler, Ted Field, Blanche Mesitti, Ethel Davis, Frances Green, Helen Sinott, Eugene Kressin, Alexander Knowlton, Donald Cameron, Donald Kane, Sandy Tone, Don Acher, R. J. Porter, Mimi Norton, A. G. Cook, Charles Hohein, Sophia Delza, Lawrence Whisonant, Edward Sherman, Herbert Price, Carl Sutton, Derek Fox (master of ceremonies), Robert Callahan (at the piano).

9 William F. McDonald, *Federal Relief Administration and the Arts: the Origins and Administrative History of the Arts Projects of the Works Progress Administration*, Ohio State University Press, Columbus, 1969.
10 Joe Klein, *Woody Guthrie, A Life*, Alfred A. Knopf, New York, 1980.

6 New York 1940–1

Sources
Jean Evans; Max Gordon; John Hammond; Alan Lomax, 16 March 1983, 21 November 1987; Earl Robinson; Pete Seeger.
Programmes broadcast in the series *Back Where I Come From*, Library of Congress, Washington, DC, Sound Reference Room.

Notes
1 Burl Ives, *Wayfaring Stranger*, Whittlesey House, New York-Toronto, 1948; D. G. Bridson, *Prospero and Ariel*, Victor Gollancz, London, 1971.
2 According to Joe Klein (*Woody Guthrie, A Life*, Alfred A. Knopf, New York, 1980), who seems to have interviewed Ray.
3 Ibid.
4 Ibid. Based on recordings preserved by the Library of Congress and scripts in the possession of Alan Lomax, the following is an (incomplete) list of *Back Where I Come From* programmes: 19 August 1940, *The Weather* (pilot in the *Forecast* series) (Clifton Fadiman, Golden Gate Quartet [hereafter GGQ], Woody Guthrie, Josh White, Burl Ives, Len Doyle, Luther-Layman Singers). Then, after 30 October or thereabouts); 20 November, *Western Songs* (Leadbelly, Ives, Guthrie, Tony Kroeber and a contribution from Nick Ray); 22 November, *Points of View About Ol' Man Death* (Guthrie, Ives, Leadbelly, White); 25 November, *Jails* (Ives, Guthrie, Leadbelly); 27 November, *Animals* (Guthrie, GGQ); 29 November, *Love, True and Careless* (Ives, Willie Johnson, Guthrie); 2 December, *Children* (Ives, White, GGQ); 9 December, *Religion from the Point of View of the Negro* (GGQ, White); 11 December, *Work Songs, American Style* (Guthrie); 18 December, *13th*

Amendment (Guthrie, GGQ); 20 December, *Christmas* (Guthrie, Ives); 10 January 1941, *Gambling* (GGQ, Ives, White, Earl Robinson); 15 January, *Soldiers* (Robinson, GGQ, Ives, White); 20 January, *Railroad* (Robinson, GGQ, Ives, White); 22 January, *Money* (GGQ, Ives, White, Robinson, Pete Seeger; 27 January, *Food* (GGQ, Ives); ? and 3 February, *Women* (in two parts); 10 February, *On Sea* (GGQ, Ives); 14 February, *The Music of Leadbelly*; 17 February, *Time of the Gold Rush and 49ers* (GGQ); 19 February, *Women Pro and Con* (Seeger, White, Ives, Willie Johnson). Dates uncertain: *Courtin'* (Willie Johnson, GGQ, White, Sidney Bechet); *Nonsense Songs* (Ives, Guthrie, White, Willie Johnson, GGQ); *Work Songs of the City* (2 parts; in the first, GGQ, White, Ives); *Sailors* (2 parts; in the second, GGQ, Ives, Seeger, White).

5 FBI, dossier 100–64818, Nicholas Ray.
6 Max Gordon, *Live at the Village Vanguard*, St Martin's Press, New York, 1980.
7 Jon Bradshaw, *Dreams That Money Can Buy, the Tragic Life of Libby Holman*, William Morrow and Company, New York, 1985.

7   The Voice of America

Sources
John Houseman, Malibu, 29 November 1980; Connie Bessie, New York, 4 November 1980, 3 April 1983; George Voskovec, California, 30 June 1981; Norman Lloyd.
John Houseman, *Front and Center*, Simon and Schuster, New York, 1979.

Notes
1 John Houseman, *Run-Through*, Simon and Schuster, New York, 1972.
2 Quoted by John Houseman, *Front and Center*, op.cit., p. 67.
3 Between 31 July 1942 and 11 November 1944, no commercial recordings were made in the United States.
4 Josef Skvorecky, *All the Bright Young Men and Women*, Peter Martin Associates, Toronto, 1971.
5 According to Professor Howard Suber (UCLA, Los Angeles, June 1981), who has for twenty years been researching in depth the mechanisms of the blacklist in the cinema.
6 Cf. John Morton Blum, *V Was for Victory*, Harcourt Brace Jovanovich, New York-London, 1976, pp. 38–9.
7 'Probe Started of 22 Alleged Reds With OWI', *Washington Times-Herald*, 9 November 1943. *The Voice of America* had already hit the front page of the *World-Telegram* when Ray hired the Almanac Singers, 'the favourite ballad singers of American communists . . . to help present a picture of the American way of life to the world' (Joe Klein, *Woody Guthrie, A Life*, Knopf, New York, 1980, p. 245).
8 FBI dossier.
9 Mike Goodwin, Naomi Wise, 'Nicholas Ray: Rebel!' (interview), *Take One*,

vol. 5 no. 6, January 1977 (hereafter *Take One* interview); autobiographical texts by courtesy of Susan Ray.
10 Elia Kazan.

8   First Stay in Hollywood

Sources
Rodney Amateau, Burbank, 2 June 1981; John Houseman, Malibu, 29 November 1980; Elia Kazan; Gene Kelly, Los Angeles, 26 March 1986; Vladimir Pozner, Paris, 23 November 1981; Silvia Richards, Los Angeles, 10 June 1981.
20th Century-Fox Archives, Special Collections, University of Southern California, Los Angeles; 20th Century-Fox Archives, Special Collections, Theater Arts Library, University of California at Los Angeles; FBI dossier; annotated script of *A Tree Grows in Brooklyn*, N. Ray Archives; T. Ork Dossier.

Notes
1   Ray, interviewed by Derek Marlowe, San Francisco, March 1974.
2   Norman Lloyd, Will Lee, Perry Bruskin, Jean Evans, Susan Ray.
3   Nicholas Ray Dossier, RKO Archives. William Fitelson, New York, 7 April 1986. Fitelson remains renowned as the lawyer who advised Kazan, in 1952, just after he had informed on his former Party comrades, to publish a notoriously unfortunate full-page advertisement denouncing Communism.
4   Kazan in Michel Ciment, *Kazan par Kazan*, Stock, Paris, 1973. The 'temporary' script for *A Tree Grows in Brooklyn* is dated 16 February 1944; the final script, 'with contributions by Anita Loos', 5 April. In his preface to the published script of *A Face in the Crowd*, Kazan attributes the final shaping of the script to the producer, Louis D. Lighton.
5   Or so he told his students years later (1977).
6   Kazan told me he had no idea where this notebook might be.
7   Adriano Aprà, Barry Boys, Ian Cameron, José Luis Guarner, Paul Mayersberg, V. F. Perkins, 'Interview with Nicholas Ray', *Movie*, no. 9, May 1963 (hereafter *Movie* interview); *Kazan par Kazan*, *op. cit.*, pp. 80–1; Bitsch, 'Entretien avec Nicholas Ray', *Cahiers du Cinéma*, no. 89, November 1958.
8   FBI dossier.
9   One of his tasks was to direct tests with actors (J. D. Spiro, 'Hollywood's Bright Ray', *The Milwaukee Journal*, 2 July 1956).
10   Nancy Lynn Schwartz, *The Hollywood Writers' War*, Alfred A. Knopf, New York, 1982.
11   cf. a detailed analysis of this score in Kathleen Hoover and John Cage, *Virgil Thomson, His Life and Music*, Thomas Yoseloff, New York-London, 1959.
12   The performance took place under the dual aegis of the *Franklin Delano Roosevelt Memorial* and the *United Nations Rededication Program*. The programme lists thirteen writers: Maxwell Anderson, Alvah Bessie, Helen Deutsch, Milton Geiger, Ring Lardner Jr, Emmet Lavery, Mary McCall, Leon Meadows, Dudley Nichols, Vladimir Pozner, Maurice Rapf, Allen Rivkin, Barry Trivers. But according to Vladimir Pozner, three people did

the writing: 'Ring Lardner Jr, myself, and the Hollywood correspondent of the *New Yorker*, whom I saw there for the first and last time.' Pozner added that it was his participation in this tribute that led him to be blacklisted shortly afterwards. He was less surprised than others, whose activities for the Writers' Mobilization was to make them suspect of Communism in the eyes of the Attorney General a few years later.

13   The ceremony took place at Grauman's Chinese Theater on 15 March, with Bob Hope as Master of Ceremonies. Admissions for the second time only, was public: it was 'the biggest turnout for a film event since the war began' (*New York Times*, 16 March 1945). This was the year of triumph for Leo McCarey's *Going My Way*. Five minutes from the ceremony can be heard on the record *Academy Award Winners of the Air*, Star-Tone Records ST–215.

14   Judy Holliday was in Hollywood with the Revuers; they appeared in *Greenwich Village*, a Fox film.

15   This was the Villa Primavera, built in 1923 by Arthur and Nina Zwebell, at 1300–1308 North Harper.

16   Virginia Wright, *Los Angeles Daily News*, 25 April 1945.

9   New York Interlude

Sources
John Houseman; Alfred Drake, New York, 13 November 1980; Perry Bruskin.
John Houseman, *Front and Center*, Simon and Schuster, New York, 1979; Jon Bradshaw, *Dreams That Money Can Buy, the Tragic Life of Libby Holman*, William Morrow and Company, New York, 1985; *Scrapbook* (album of press-cuttings) for *Beggars' Holiday*, Lincoln Center Library of the Performing Arts.

Notes
1   The dramatic progression and mounting tension are similar to another radio play by Lucille Fletcher, *The Hitch-Hiker*, this one written for a man: Orson Welles directed and starred in it in 1942. A paradox in the cannibalization of sources: when *The Hitch-Hiker* was adapted for television in the *Twilight Zone* series, the protagonist became a woman.

2   Mary Martin's success in *South Pacific* (1949) was still to come.

3   *Front and Center*, op. cit., p. 166.

4   Gene Kelly, Los Angeles, 26 March 1986.

5   Michael Myerberg presents Mary Martin in a romantic musical play, *Lute Song* by Sidney Howard and Will Irwin. Adapted from the famous Chinese Play *Pi Pa Ki [Pipa ji]*. Music: Raymond Scott. Lyrics by Bernard Hanighen. Director: John Houseman. Choreography: Yeichi Nimura. Musical Director: Fritz Mahler (then Eugene Kusmiak). Scenery, costumes and lighting by Robert Edmond Jones. Miss Martin's costumes designed by Valentina. Cast: Mary Martin (Tchao-Ou-Niang, the Wife), McKay Norris (Prince Nieou, the Imperial Preceptor), Helen Craig (Princess Nieou-Chi, his daughter), Clarence Derwent (the Manager/the honourable Tschang), Augustin Duncan (Tsai, the Father), Mildred Dunnock (Madame Tsai, the Mother),

Rex O'Malley (Youen-Kong, the Steward), Ralph Clanton (the Imperial Chamberlain, the Genie), and Yul Brynner (Tsai Yong, the Husband). Nancy Davis (Si-Tchun), Pamela Wilde, Sydelle Sylovna, Blanche Zohar, Mary Anne Reeve (Women, Maiden, Children), Dianne De Brett (a Marriage Broker), Jack Amoroso (a Messenger), Gene Galvin (the Food Commissioner), Max Leavitt, Bob Turner (Clerks), Tom Emlyn Williams (an Applicant, Priest of Amida Buddha), Michael Blair (an Applicant, a Secretary), John Robert Lloyd, John High (Imperial Guards), Gordon Showalter, Ronald Fletcher (Imperial Attendants), Lisa Maslova (the White Tiger, Phoenix Bird), Lisan Kay (the Ape, Phoenix Bird), Gene Galvin (a Bonze), Joseph Camiolo, Leslie Rheinfeld (Two Lesser Bonzes), Bob Turner (a Rich Man), John High (a Merchant), Donald Rose (a Little Boy), Walter Stane, Alberto Vecchio (the Lion), Teddy Rose (Child).

Recordings: (78 rpm) *Lute Song*, Decca A–445; (33 rpm) *Lute Song/On the Town*, Decca DL–8030.

6   It could thus be announced that Ellington had composed seventy-eight songs or numbers, thirty-nine of which found their way into the show (programme for *Beggars' Holiday*, Lincoln Center Library). An appendix to Mercer Ellington's book, *Duke Ellington – an Intimate Portrait* (Houghton Mifflin Co., Boston, 1978), lists eighteen songs, probably coming closer to reality. To these should be added *How Happy Could I Be With Either*, 'quoted' from *The Beggar's Opera*. Some of these songs were revived over the years, by Lena Horne among others.

7   A last-minute announcement pleaded an 'ultimatum' from Libby Holman's doctor, Dr William H. Resnick. Libby Holman was to record only one song from *Beggars' Holiday*, and this 1965 recording was issued after her death: *In Between*. Despite the ageing of her voice, it is a very moving piece, both in its pure melodic line and in its lyrics, and Ray surely had not forgotten it when he gave one of his later projects the title *Inbetween Time*:

> Between the twilight and nightfall
> There's a time that's outside of time
> When you see yourself standing nowhere at all
> And watch the shadows leisurely climb
> Where there was once the Sun
> And now there is none.
> In between, neither happy or tearful,
> You're in between, neither confident or fearful,
> Half in a mist and half wide awake
> You wait for the moment when something will break . . .

(Libby Holman, *Something to Remember Her By*, Monmouth Evergreen, MES/7067.)

8   Letter from Jane Bowles to Paul Bowles, September 1947, in *Out in the World, Selected Letters of Jane Bowles 1935–1970*, ed. Millicent Dillon, Black Sparrow Press, Santa Barbara, 1985. For his part, Ray never replied, from Hollywood, to a letter from Oliver Smith trying to interest him in Jane Bowles's play, *In the Summer House*.

Jon Bradshaw (*Dreams That Money Can Buy*) offers a somewhat sordid version of the break between Ray and Libby Holman which might explain this antipathy, but the story remains unverifiable following the deaths not only of his sources but of Bradshaw himself. Houseman (*Front and Center, op. cit.*, p. 194) describes Ray at this same period as being ready to carry off the choreographer Valerie Bettis to Cuba to marry her. Houseman also mentions one of the chorus girls, Royce Wallace. And Ray's attachment to Marie Bryant, whom he called 'Madonna' and who makes a dazzling appearance in *They Live By Night*, remains in little doubt. *Take love easy*, says one of the songs in *Beggars' Holiday*.

9 *Scrapbook* for *Beggars' Holiday*, press cutting dated 23 December 1946. Houseman, *op. cit.*, p. 195.

10 Perry Watkins and John R. Sheppard Jr present Alfred Drake in *Beggars' Holiday*, suggested by John Gay's *The Beggar's Opera*, with score by Duke Ellington, book and lyrics by John Latouche. Book directed by Nicholas Ray. Production designed by Oliver Smith. Costumes designed by Walter Florell. Musical direction by Max Meth. Musical arrangements by Mr Ellington and Billy Strayhorn. Technical supervision, lighting: Peggy Clark. Choreography: Valerie Bettis. Cast: Alfred Drake (Macheath), Marie Bryant (the Cocoa Girl), Libby Holman, then Bernice Parks (Jenny), Jack Bittner (Highbinder), Gordon Nelson (O'Heister), Archie Savage (Gunsel), Stanley Carlson (Fingersmith), Walter Hoving (Strip), Perry Bruskin (Mooch), Albert Popwell (Slam), Douglas Henderson (the Caser), Lewis Charles (a Drunk), Herbert Ross (Bartender), Avon Long (Careless Love), Jet MacDonald (Polly Peachum), Dorothy Johnson (Mrs Peachum), Zero Mostel (Hamilton Peachum), Rollin Smith (Chief Lockit), Mildred Smith (Lucy Lockit), Pan Theodore (Blenkinson), Marjorie Belle [=Bell, later Marge Champion] (the Girl), Tommy Gomez (the Pursued, the Other Eye), Archie Savage (Cop), Herbert Ross, Lucas Hogin, Paul Godkin (Policemen), Lavina Nielsen (Dolly Trull), Leonne Hall (Betty Doxy), Tommie Moore (Rawdry Audrey), Doris Goodwin (Mrs Trapes), Royce Wallace (Annie Coaxer), Claire Hale (Baby Mildred), Nina Korda (Minute Lou), Malka Farber (Trixy Turner), Elmira Jones-Bey (Bessie Burns), Enid Williams (Flora, the Harpy), Bill Dillars (Deep Ellum), Lucas Hoving (Strip), Pan Theodore (the Eye), Paul Godkin (Wire Boy), Malka Farber, Doris Goodwin, Claire Hale, Elmira Jones-Bey, Lavina Nielsen, Royce Wallace, Enid Williams, Tommy Gomez, Walter Hoving, Albert Popwell, Herbert Ross, Archie Savage (Dancers).

11 '[Oliver Smith's settings] moved last night like clockwork on their intricate turntables, showing everything from sordid back alleys to shoddy fancy house, luxurious jail and striking hobo jungle' (*Boston Herald*, 5 December 1946; *Scrapbook* and extracts from the press quoted in the New York programme).

10   They Live by Night

Sources
Howard Da Silva, New York, 9 November 1980; Farley Granger, New York, 16
April 1986; John Houseman; Gene Palmer, Universal City, 7 July 1982.
RKO Archives; Directors' Guild of America West, Nicholas Ray dossier; N. Ray
Archives; Houseman, *Front and Center*, Simon and Schuster, New York, 1979.

Notes
1   Cf. Bernard Eisenschitz, 'Anderson – Ray – Altman' in Edward Anderson,
Tous des voleurs, Série B, Christian Bourgois Editeur, Paris, 1985.
2   His contract as scriptwriter having ended on 3 August, he then spent three
weeks completing his other job as assistant producer.
3   This was one of Leadbelly's most celebrated songs. Transcribed by Pete
Seeger, it features in B. A. Botkin's anthology, *A Treasury of American
Folklore*, preface by Carl Sandburg, Crown Publishers, New York, 1944.
4   On the censorship problems, see Eisenschitz, *op. cit.*
5   An ethnologist living in Hollywood that year (and who remained a lasting
target for Ray's sarcasm) noted that: 'The option contract, which binds the
employer to the studio for seven years and permits the studio to dismiss him
at the end of six months or one year, without having to show cause, smacks
more of medieval power relations between lord and serf, than of employer
and employee in the modern world of industry. It is interesting that the
guilds have never fought to change the option contract' (Hortense Powdermaker, *Hollywood, the Dream Factory*, Little, Brown and Co., Boston,
1950).
6   Dore Schary, *Heyday, an Autobiography*, Little, Brown and Co., Boston-
Toronto, 1979; Michel Ciment, *Conversations with Losey*, Methuen,
London, 1985; Richard B. Jewell and Vernon Harbin, *The RKO Story*,
Arlington House, New York, 1982. In his autobiography, Schary claims
credit for the following titles (*films noirs* only): *Crossfire* (Dmytryk), *The
Window* (Tetzlaff), *They Live by Night*, *The Set-Up* (Wise), *Berlin Express*
(Tourneur), *Nocturne* (Edwin L. Marin), *The Locket* (John Brahm), *They
Won't Believe Me* (Irving Pichel), *Desperate* (Anthony Mann), *Riff Raff*
(Tetzlaff), *The Clay Pigeon* (Richard Fleischer), *Out of the Past* (Jacques
Tourneur).
7   'I'm a stranger here myself': a phrase dear to Ogden Nash, who used it as a
title for a collection of his poems (1938) and for the first song in the musical
comedy *One Touch of Venus* (1943), staged by Elia Kazan.
8   *Thieves Like Us* (1974), directed by Robert Altman, based on the novel by
Edward Anderson.
9   Robert Mitchum, interviewed by Philippe Garnier for the French TV programme, *Cinéma Cinémas*, June 1982.
10   cf. Houseman, *Run-Through*, Simon and Schuster, New York, 1972.
11   Pete Seeger, 4 November, 1980.
12   'Heading Toward Los Angeles', 1937. This photograph is 'reconstructed' in
at least two films: *Dust Be My Destiny* (Lewis Seiler, 1939) and *Of Mice and
Men* (Lewis Milestone, 1939).

13 George Diskant (1907–65) had worked with Burnett Guffey as second assistant at RKO before the 1933 strike. He had become a director of photography the preceding year: *Dick Tracy Versus Cueball* (Gordon Douglas, 1946), *Banjo* (Fleischer, 1947), *Desperate* (Mann), *Riff Raff* (Tetzlaff). He was thus not quite a beginner. His penchant for taking risks was equally striking, a little later on, in *The Narrow Margin* (Fleischer, 1952).

14 *Take One* interview.

15 Bill Krohn, 'Rencontre avec Nicholas Ray', *Cahiers du Cinéma*, no. 288, May 1978. Sherman Todd was born in 1904; he had worked not only as an editor, but also as associate producer on a few films. No trace of him is apparent after 1951.

16 Leigh Harline (1907–69) had received an Oscar for the song *When You Wish Upon a Star* in *Pinocchio*, and left the Disney Studios for RKO a few years later.

17 Original themes for the film: the credit sequence, *Boy Gets Girl* and *Dreams*. Some direct illustrations: the wedding march from *Lohengrin* during the second visit to Hawkins, the marriage office registrar (irony as well as illustration); *Adestes Fideles* and *Jingle Bells* on the radio when the quarrel erupts just before Christmas; etc.

18 *Take One* interview.

19 Letter from David O. Selznick to Ned Depinet, 26 November 1948.

20 Rodney Amateau, Burbank, 2 June 1981.

21 Thomas Wolfe, *The Story of a Novel*, 1936.

22 Gavin Lambert, Santa Monica, 29 November 1980. Gavin Lambert, 'They Live by Night and The Window', *Sequence*, no. 7, Spring 1950. Richard Winnington, *News Chronicle*, 14 March, 4 and 6 June, 1949. cf. also William Whitebait, *New Statesman*, 11 June 1949, and Virginia Graham, *Spectator*, 10 June 1949.

23 The 'Rendez-vous de Biarritz' succeeded the 'Festival du Film Maudit' of the preceding year. The organizers (Denise Tual, Jacques Doniol-Valcroze, Jacques Bourgeois and Grisha Dabat) had sought the participation of American companies, which explains the presence of *They Live by Night*. Also screened were Michelangelo Antonioni's *Cronaca di un amore* and Edward Dmytryk's *Give Us This Day* (Jacques Doniol-Valcroze, 1 December 1988).

24 André Bazin, 'A l'ombre des potences', *France-Observateur*, 6 October 1955.

25 Jacques Doniol-Valcroze, 'Paul et Virginie se sont mariés la nuit', *Cahiers du Cinéma*, no.5, September 1951; François Truffaut, 'Les extrêmes me touchent', *Cahiers du Cinéma*, no.21, March 1953.

26 Jean Douchet, 6 October 1988.

11 A Woman's Secret

Sources
Rodney Amateau.
RKO Archives; T. Ork Dossier; Charles Bitsch, 'Entretien avec Nicholas Ray',

Cahiers du Cinéma, no. 89, November 1958. Original wire recording by courtesy of Charles Bitsch.

Notes

1 Press release, 7 October 1947.
2 John Houseman, *Front and Center*, Simon and Schuster, New York, 1979.
3 *Man in the Zoo* was eventually adapted by Howard Koch for Charles Chaplin, and much later became a pet project for another film-maker admired by the British magazine *Movie*, which championed Ray during the 1960s: Seth Holt.
4 'Actress Plans to Wed Again Five Hours After Divorce', unidentified press cutting of 1 June 1948 (USC, Special Collections).
5 Philippe Garnier, 'La femme à battre', *Libération*, 7–8 November 1981.
6 Ray's finances at Las Vegas: on 9 April he had received a bonus of $5,000 for *A Woman's Secret*. On 28 April the studio wired him an advance of $2,000 (two weeks' salary) in Las Vegas, c/o Western Union. On 5 May his agents Berg and Allenberg announced that for their part they had advanced him $3,000.
7 Louella O. Parsons, 'Miss Grahame Mother of Boy', 13 November 1948.
8 Alice Williams; Gretchen Horner; Sumner Williams.

12   Knock on Any Door

Sources
Rodney Amateau; Burnett Guffey, Goleta, 5 June 1981; Daniel Taradash, Los Angeles, 28 November 1980.
N. Ray Archives; T. Ork Dossier.

Notes

1 Jim Bishop, *The Mark Hellinger Story*, Appleton-Century-Crofts, Inc., New York, 1952. 1947 was the time of that liberal flash in the pan, the Committee for the First Amendment.
2 Robert Lord (1902–76) served, as screenwriter or producer, on such films as *Five Star Final* (1931), *20,000 Years in Sing Sing* (1933), *Heroes for Sale* (1933), *Black Legion* (1937), *Confessions of a Nazi Spy* (1939).
3 The beginning of the film – a rapid description of the milieu, crime, police investigation and arrest of the youthful suspect, leading to the introduction of the attorney hero, at first sceptical but becoming convinced – was repeated unaltered by John Monks in *The People Against O'Hara* (John Sturges, 1951), on which he was sole scriptwriter.
4 In the book, Andrew Morton (Bogart) does not appear until page 352, and the script invests him with some aspects of another character, Grant Holloway. The cinema in the post-war period could never have tolerated Nick Romano's bisexuality and occasional cruising, or the description of police and prison methods: the cop killed by Nick was a sadist, proud of the three notches on his gun tallying his three victims. Morton enters a plea of not guilty, knowing Nick to be guilty; he accepts phony alibis, using tactics

comparable to those of his adversary on the prosecution side. He does not seek to plead guilty after Nick confesses, and it is the jury which condemns him. In the film, Nick is a ladies' man; no details are offered about the cop he kills; only one period in a reformatory is shown (but the sadism of the warders is stressed); Morton learns of Nick's guilt only when he confesses; he then asks to change the plea to guilty, and it is up to the judge to pronounce sentence, without the jury being involved.

5 In *Bigger Than Life*, too, a crucial scene, shot in a single nine-minute take, was to be segmented during the editing.
6 Jean Evans, *Three Men*, Random House, New York, 1950.

13   Howard Hughes

Sources
William Fadiman, Bel Air, 10 July 1982; Farley Granger; Vernon Harbin, Los Angeles, 29 June 1982.
RKO Archives; Directors' Guild of America West, Nicholas Ray Dossier; T. Ork Dossier; Richard B. Jewell and Vernon Harbin, *The RKO Story*, Arlington House, New York, 1982; Donald L. Barlett, James B. Steele, *Empire, the Life, Legend and Madness of Howard Hughes*, W. W. Norton and Co., New York, 1979.

Notes
1 Ned Depinet, quoted by David Bellfort, *Histoire de la RKO*, IDHEC [film school] dissertation, 1966.
2 Barlett and Steele, *Empire*, op. cit., p. 164.
3 10 May, according to *Empire*, p. 165.
4 Dore Schary, *Heyday, an Autobiography*, Little, Brown and Co., Boston-Toronto, 1979, pp. 171–2.
5 According to Jewell and Harbin, *The RKO Story*, op. cit., 75 per cent of the total staff; 700 employees, or 50 to 75 per cent, according to Bellfort; 33 per cent according to Barlett and Steele.
6 Jewell and Harbin, op. cit., p. 243.
7 Tom Milne, *Losey on Losey*, Secker and Warburg, London, 1967, pp. 73–6.
8 Susan Dalton and John Davis, 'An Interview with John Cromwell', *The Velvet Light Trap*, no. 10, Autumn 1973.
9 Michel Ciment, *Conversations with Losey*, Methuen, London, 1985.
10 *Take One* interview.
11 T. Ork Dossier.
12 Professor Suber negotiated the acquisition of the RKO archives by UCLA.
13 John Houseman, *Front and Center*, Simon and Schuster, New York, 1979, pp. 416–17.
14 Jean Evans, New York, 21 June 1981, 14 June 1982. '*Naming Names* spoke of how you could arrange, off the record, to go before the Committee and not have any publicity. I think that's what Nick did.' Victor Navasky's book *Naming Names* (Viking Press, New York, 1980) relaunched the controversy

about HUAC and the blacklist; I was to hear it mentioned frequently when I started my researches, either directly, or by allusion, as in Kazan's case.

15 Ben Barzman, Los Angeles, 14 June 1981.

16 Pete Seeger, 4 November 1980.

17 Cf. Robert Parrish, *Growing Up in Hollywood*, Harcourt Brace Jovanovich, New York-London, 1977. The other RKO employees who signed the petition – Mark Robson, Robert Wise, Richard Fleischer and John Farrow – had already left the studio. Ray, although he signed the petition demanding the meeting, seems not to have attended; he delegated his vote to 'Stanley Donen or Don Hartman'. A week later, he sent a message of thanks to Joseph L. Mankiewicz. Later on, in 1954–5, he sat on the board of the Screen Directors' Guild as a deputy member.

18 Perry Bruskin, 31 October 1980.

19 The actors were Laraine Day, Robert Ryan (a test for him, too, since excessive liberalism was suspect), John Agar and Thomas Gomez. The script is credited to Charles Grayson and Robert Hardy Andrews, from a story by George W. George and George F. Slavin. Following previews, the title – one of the most notorious in film history – was changed to *The Woman on Pier 13*.

20 Mindret Lord had written a wildly fanciful script for an Anthony Mann B movie, *Strange Impersonation*, in 1946. Her name turns up in various mystery magazines of the 1950s (I have been unable to ascertain whether she was related to Robert Lord).

21 cf. also Carol Easton, *The Search for Sam Goldwyn*, William Morrow and Co., New York, 1976, which mentions Ben Hecht as having worked on the script. A. Scott Berg's authorized biography, *Goldwyn* (Alfred A. Knopf, New York, 1989) makes no mention of Ray's contribution to *Roseanna McCoy*.

22 Charles Higham, *Hollywood Cameramen*, Thames and Hudson, London, 1970, pp. 50–1.

14   Born to Be Bad

Sources
Rodney Amateau.
RKO Archives; T. Ork Dossier; Joan Fontaine, *No Bed of Roses*, William Morrow and Co., New York, 1978; John Houseman, *Front and Center*, Simon and Schuster, New York, 1979.

Notes
1 Ray and Sparks viewed *The Saxon Charm*, a Universal film in which Robert Montgomery plays a megalomaniac (theatre) producer, and *Odd Man Out*, the film which brought James Mason to American attention.

2 Ferrer had taken over from Max Ophüls and Preston Sturges to complete a disastrous Hughes production, *Vendetta*.

3 Houseman, *op. cit.*, p. 437.

4 'Nick and the cast agreed to work beyond normal shooting hours, for

several days, in order to finish quickly,' Sparks wrote to Sid Rogell on 27 July.

5 Three versions survive: the shortest, as described here; an intermediate version, with the scene at the lawyer's office, and a repeat of the brief scene with Ferrer alone (in the first, he changes the price tag on his painting of Christabel from $250 to $500; in the second, to $1,000); and a complete version, comprising the departure from the house, Christabel's car accident, the hospital, the scene at the airfield (coming much later than in the short version), Christabel's seduction of the doctor, and the two scenes with Ferrer framing the one in the lawyer's office.

6 An image that recurs in *Bigger Than Life* on another social occasion.

7 Nicholas Musuraca (1892–1975) shot (among other films) *Cat People* (Jacques Tourneur, 1942), *The Spiral Staircase* (Robert Siodmak, 1946), *Deadline at Dawn* (Harold Clurman, 1946), *Out of the Past* (Jacques Tourneur, 1947), *The Blue Gardenia* (Fritz Lang, 1953).

15 In a Lonely Place

Sources
Rodney Amateau; Burnett Guffey; Andrew Solt, Los Angeles, 28 November 1980.
T. Ork Dossier; N. Ray Archives (including annotated script); Mike Wilmington, 'Nicholas Ray on the Years at RKO', *The Velvet Light Trap*, no. 10, Autumn 1973.

Notes
1 'It's in a lonesome place you do have to be talking with someone, and looking for someone, in the evening of the day.'
     Andrew Solt thought that Santana had bought the novel for John Derek. Set in Los Angeles, but not in film circles, it's the story of a young killer.

2 In the titles, the adaptation is credited to Edmund H. North. This must relate to an earlier version: his name does not appear on the final shooting script. Solt, naturally, claimed never to have heard of North's contribution.

3 Andrew Solt, subsequently confirmed by him: *Programme Notes*, AFI (n.d., 1982?), and A.S., 'The Star and the Screenwriter', in duplicated programme for the Los Angeles County Museum of Art, 20 October 1984.

4 Wilmington, *op. cit.*

5 Ginger Rogers was in fact desperately looking for a part at this stage in her career, making Ray's story quite plausible. It is true that Hughes and Cohn had not been on speaking terms for at least a year, if not five: Hughes had asked Cohn to take charge of RKO for him, and Cohn refused.

6 Rodney Amateau is listed on the credits as 'technical adviser', meaning nothing. A friend of Ray's, he worked, officially or unofficially, in various capacities (dialogue director, second unit director, etc.) on several of his films at this time. He was soon to become a director himself.

7 In the two films which won Gloria Grahame official recognition (Oscar nominations), the circumstances attending her are very different. In

Crossfire, her characteristics as an actress are already evident: very mobile eyes, sometimes pursed smilingly or in interrogation, movements of the head, imperceptible nods. The character is constructed in the editing, and the actress's performance, already very distinctive, remains a secondary element. In *The Bad and the Beautiful*, Grahame owed her Oscar to less than thirteen minutes on screen, almost always in medium or two-shot, except for two very sensual kisses. Cameraman Robert Surtees makes little attempt to sculpt her face, lit in soft shadows, by comparison with the impressive job he does on Lana Turner. Everything about her heralds the performance, she is 'putting on an act': Southern accent, simpering, effervescently silly (a nod to her favourite role, Sabina in Thornton Wilder's *The Skin of Our Teeth*?). Minnelli makes her a moving figure through the contrast between her foolishness and her death; further to this, Grahame adds an engaging quality through the simplicity of her performance, playing a character held up for contempt while feeling no contempt herself.

8   Don Ray, 'Singer Hadda Brooks Recalls *Lonely Place* Role', Ray retrospective at USC, October 1983.

9   cf. J. A. Place and L. S. Peterson, 'Some Visual Motifs of Film Noir', in Bill Nichols, ed., *Movies and Methods*, University of California Press, Berkeley-Los Angeles-London, 1976.

10   Edwin Schallert, 'Special Agreement Keeps Grahame-Lord Team Going', *L.A. Times*, 4 December 1949. *In a Lonely Place* had provisionally been retitled *Behind This Mask*.

11   The break was only made public, to both friends and press, a month later (Robert Sparks sent Ray a message of sympathy on December 28).

12   *Movie* interview.

16   On Dangerous Ground

Sources
A. I. Bezzerides, Los Angeles, 1 December 1980; William Fadiman, Bel Air, 10 July 1982; Roland Gross, Los Angeles, 1 December 1980; John Houseman; Ida Lupino, Pacific Palisades, 11 April 1983; Sumner Williams, Laguna Hills, 30 November 1980, Los Angeles, 12 April 1983.
John Houseman, *Front and Center*, Simon and Schuster, New York, 1979; RKO Archives; Rui Nogueira and Nicoletta Zalaffi, 'Rencontre avec Robert Ryan', *Cinéma 70*, no. 145, April 1970.

Notes
1   Raymond Chandler wrote to Houseman about it: 'It has no humour at all [. . .] The cop is a ridiculous character [. . .] There's hardly a line of dialogue which would not be pure slop on the screen' (Houseman, *op. cit*, p. 318).

2   The rights to *Mad With Much Heart* cost $7,500 (negotiated by Berg and Allenberg). Gerald Butler asked to be paid in dollars and not in sterling.

3   Philippe Garnier remarked that Bezzerides's script for *Kiss Me Deadly* comprised an unusual wealth of detail, and that the detail found its way to the screen.

4   *Mad With Much Heart*, Treatment, pp. 32–4.
5   Charles Schnee had adapted an article by John Bartlow Martin for MGM (*Scene of the Crime*, directed by Roy Rowland). Martin was to work with Houseman, served as an American ambassador, and wrote Adlai Stevenson's biography.
6   William Wyler was just getting an adaptation of this play under way. Shot a year after Ray's film, from a script by Philip Yordan and Robert Wyler, *Detective Story* was released a few months before *On Dangerous Ground*.
7   Thanking Commissioner Thomas Sullivan of the Special Service Division, Sid Rogell wrote (19 January) that Ray 'was especially impressed with the methods of work and operations of the Special Service Division and with the character, courage and know-how of detectives Tom Reilly, John Preston and Frank Mulvey from whose point of view he was able to gather valuable first-hand, on-the-spot information which could only reflect credit upon your organization.'
8   *Movie* interview.
9   *First draft continuity*, 14 February, 150 pages; 26 February, 122 pages. The treatment comprised 116 pages.
10   Margaret Phillips made no more films.
11   Nogueira and Zalaffi, *op. cit.*
12   *L. A. Daily News*, 5 April 1950.
13   Diskant subsequently shot several films for Ida Lupino: *Beware My Lovely*, *The Bigamist*. He was also involved in her television work.
14   Roland Gross (twenty-five years at RKO) reckoned that he had mostly worked on Rosalind Russell comedies; but he was especially proud of having edited *Woman on the Beach* (Jean Renoir, 1946), *The Set-Up* (Robert Wise, 1948), and *The Thing from Another World* (Christian Nyby/ Howard Hawks, 1951).
15   Bernard Herrmann, letter of 21 November 1950.
16   The viola d'amore is an instrument which usually has seven playing strings (gut) and seven sympathetic or resonating strings (wire). Its tone is soft, sweet and metallic. Cf. also Christopher Palmer's notes for the record *Bernard Herrmann, Citizen Kane and Other Classic Film Scores*, RCA Red Seal ARL 1–0707.
17   Cuts: 'Chasing boy up the rocks, carrying the dead boy to the house, girl overhearing yokels, girl in chair, and dialogue between Lupino and Ryan' (Memo of 27 April).
18   Cuts: 'The chase-trek from Bond's house to Lupino's house; trek of Bond and Ryan after the car-wreck; chase of Bond and Ryan up the rocks to where the boy is killed' (Jim Wilkinson memo of 6 June).
19   Wald-Krasna memo to C. J. Tevlin, 11 July 1952.
20   A double for Anthony Ross (playing Santos, a cop) was also used to shoot a night street exterior.
21   Richard B. Jewell and Vernon Harbin, *The RKO Story*, Arlington House, New York, 1982.

17 Flying Leathernecks

Sources
Rodney Amateau.
Nicholas Ray Deposit, Cinémathèque Française; Rui Nogueira and Nicoletta Zalaffi, 'Rencontre avec Robert Ryan', *Cinéma 70* no. 145, April 1970; RKO Archives

Notes
1   Edmund Grainger, son of Republic's sales director, had spent the war producing films for the Army's photographic section. Kenneth Gamet, author of the first screenplay, hadn't done any fighting either, but had written war movies – for Grainger – including *Flying Tigers* (David Miller, 1942).
2   As he confirmed to James Leahy.
3   Nogueira and Zalaffi, *op. cit.*
4   'I used 16mm all during my Hollywood career,' Ray told Jeff Greenberg in November 1972 while working on *We Can't Go Home Again*, but mentioned only two films: this one and *The Lusty Men*. 'In *Flying Leathernecks*, I used two wing cameras for my process work in Technicolor. No technical expert in Hollywood believed it could be done. I did it over the protests of every lab in Hollywood' (Jeff Greenberg, 'Nicholas Ray Today', *Filmmakers Newsletter*, vol. 6, no. 3, January 1973).
5   Gretchen Horner.

18 The Racket and Macao

Sources
William Fadiman; Roland Gross; Vernon Harbin; Gene Palmer; Jane Russell, Sedona (Arizona), 27 June 1981; Sumner Williams.
RKO Archives; Directors' Guild of America, Nicholas Ray Dossier.

Notes
1   Jane Russell: 'I'd have loved to see *The Outlaw* if Hawks had done it; now today you look at it, and it's slow and ponderous. Jack [Buetel] and I look like a pair of idiots, because they made us do it over and over and over until we were just . . . It would have been quite a different film if Hawks had made it.'
2   In the film in question (Robert Stevenson's *Walk Softly, Stranger*), Palmer added, 'we found out later that when the actors parted their lips . . . (*smacking noise*) . . . that's what Hughes was hearing.'
3   Quoted by Noah Dietrich, *Howard, the Amazing Mr Hughes*, Fawcett, New York, 1972.
4   *Take One* interview. The film in question was *I Married a Communist*. Ray places this encounter on Christmas Eve (Hughes's birthday), and says that the tycoon was viewing Max Ophüls's *Caught* (in which some aspects of the Robert Ryan character are borrowed from Hughes). *Caught* was released in February 1949. The date suggested by this, Christmas 1948, is hardly

compatible with the telegram Ray sent Hughes on 31 December that year (see Chapter 13). 'A year later' might refer to the period early in 1951 when *Jet Pilot*, *His Kind of Woman* and *Macao* were directorless and unfinished.

Hughes's round-the-world flight: 10–14 July 1938; the XF-II he was piloting crashed in Beverly Hills on 8 July 1947. Hughes did continue working on the plane, but didn't destroy it; late in 1947, he delivered it to the US Air Force, who discarded it less than two years later.

5 Sumner Williams, Laguna Hills, 1980.

6 Years later, this same Senate Committee investigating organized crime was to reveal links between the Hughes empire and gangsterism (Michael Drosnin, *Citizen Hughes*, Holt, Rinehart and Winston, New York, 1984).

7 Fuller's version shows the cop, McQuigg, as rivalling gangster Nick Scarsi in his unscrupulousness and egocentricity, redeeming himself only through his heroic death. This was a genuinely original script, identifiable – if need be – through the names given to the cops as well as its view of the underworld, including an elderly informer who talks and gets herself killed *because that is her role*, and an obese blind man who *dies of fear*.

8 Actors appearing only in this scene (along with Les Tremayne): Howard Petrie, William Forrest, Tom Martin, Franklin Parker, Frank Marlowe.

9 W. R. Burnett had written three other scenes in the bludgeoning style Hughes liked: the cops casually bestriding Nick Scanlon's body, etc. They were not shot. Robert Ryan, who could not recall having been directed by Ray (Nogueira and Zalaffi, *op. cit.*) was in at least one scene, described above, and possibly in some pick-up shots (call sheets, 18 and 22 June).

10 Tay Garnett directed one scene in the precinct house involving the actors Ray Collins and William Conrad.

11 André Bazin, 'Peut-on être policier?', *l'Observateur*, 26 June 1942.

12 Josef von Sternberg, *Fun in a Chinese Laundry*, Macmillan, New York, Secker and Warburg, London, 1965.

13 Sternberg made many changes to Bernard Schoenfeld's script. Meanwhile (July 1950), Edward Chodorov was finishing another version, not used. Stanley Rubin, credited along with Schoenfeld, was responsible for an earlier version.

14 Robert Mitchum, *Guardian Lecture* at the National Film Theatre, London, 24 June 1984 (in Andrew Britton, ed., *Talking Films*, Fourth Estate, London, 1991).

15 Jorge Luis Borges, *Two Films* (*Crime and Punishment*, *The Thirty-Nine Steps*) collected and translated in Edgardo Cozarinsky, *Borges in/and/on Film*, Lumen Books, New York, 1988.

16 The unpublished Granados piece threw RKO's legal and musical departments into agonies of perplexity: how did the actor Don Zelayo (the nightclub pianist) come to know this piece?

17 'I wish you well,' the police lieutenant (Thomas Gomez) says to Mitchum. 'It is our fond hope that all visitors to Macao should feel as untroubled here as Adam in the Garden of Eden.' 'Untroubled?' says Mitchum. 'That ain't the way I heard it.' This exchange is retained in the film, but the last line in Sternberg's version (Mitchum: 'I can't keep Eve waiting') is not.

18 Andrew Velez, ed., *Josef von Sternberg's Macao*, Frederick Ungar Publishing Co., New York, 1980

19 Stevenson shot the last scene in the hotel, where Mitchum tells Russell that Trumble (Bendix) is dead, and the last shot of the final sequence: on the yacht, Mitchum tells Russell, who complains that he is all wet, 'You'd better start getting used to me fresh out of a shower,' and kisses her. The Hughes touch, unmistakably. The scenes were written by George Bricker and Frank Moss. The crew remained unchanged, with Sam Bischoff producing and Harry Wild on camera.

20 Letter from Ray to the Directors' Guild, 2 July 1951.

21 *Take One* interview.

22 Herman G. Weinberg, *Josef von Sternberg*, E. P. Dutton and Co., Inc., New York, 1967, p. 244.

23 The Howard Hughes aesthetic: the examples that come to mind are *Flying Leathernecks, Two Tickets to Broadway, His Kind of Woman*, the worst bits of *Jet Pilot*.

24 Rui Nogueira, 'Writing for the Movies: Walter Newman', *Focus on Film*, no. 11, Autumn 1972.

25 In interviews over the years, Ray also spoke of working on two films during the course of which Hughes's freakish whims assumed crazy dimensions: *Jet Pilot* and *His Kind of Woman*. I have been unable to find any trace of his involvement with either film. It may be that he was consulted at the editing stage; but if he had shot scenes, his name would certainly have figured on the daily call sheets, and the accounts department would have noted any such work among the services rendered under the terms of his contract.

   The film-makers attested as having worked on *Jet Pilot*, after Sternberg had been directing for 56 days between December 1949 and February 1950, were principally the film's writer-producer, Jules Furthman, the second unit director Phil Cochran, the assistant Ed Killy (a former B-movie director), Byron Haskin (for the model work), Don Siegel (one scene, not used). The final day's shooting took place on 7 May 1953, and the film was released in October 1957.

   His Kind of Woman, directed by John Farrow, underwent some tinkering by Robert Stevenson, then was almost entirely re-shot and completed (in three separate attempts and with cast changes) by Richard Fleischer. Jane Russell had a vague recollection of Ray as having directed one of the final scenes (on his yacht, Raymond Burr tries to inject Mitchum with a drug), but she was probably mixing him up with Fleischer (as Fleischer himself, Vernon Harbin, Gene Palmer and the production sheets attest).

The Two Versions of *Macao*

The Sternberg version, running for 84 minutes 36 seconds, starts with a pre-credits sequence in which the three principal characters, outcasts from America, meet on board the ferry from Hong Kong to Macao. Credits over shots of the harbour. Stabbed in the back, a coolie falls into the sea; Nick (Mitchum) dives into the water and fishes him out, dead. Which does not prevent the captain from hassling him because he has no ticket.

The trio go ashore and pass through the customs shed, watched by the police lieutenant, Sebastian (Thomas Gomez); their photographs are taken by an old Chinaman, who hands the pictures to Sebastian.

Then they leave, Julie (Jane Russell) by rickshaw, Nick and Trumble (William Bendix) by bus.

Outside the gaming-house, The Quick Reward: a Chinaman is violently ejected, curses the Russian doorman. Inside, Marge (Gloria Grahame) is fascinated by some diamonds; Sebastian arrives to show the owner, Halloran (Brad Dexter), the photographs of the new arrivals. One of them is a New York cop: Sebastian indicates Nick.

At the hotel, bare-chested, Nick tries to find someone to do his laundry. He meets Julie, who is leaving her room, then Trumble, who goes down for a shave at the hands of a waggish Eurasian woman. Nick and Julie are arguing in her room when Sebastian arrives to talk to Julie. He sends Julie off to see Halloran about a job. Leaving, he casts an eye over Nick's room through the shutters.

Dissolve to a blind beggar outside the Quick Reward. The traffic is being directed by a bearded Sikh (an echo of *The Shanghai Gesture*). Julie arrives, argues over money with the rickshaw man, and enters the club. She meets Marge, then Halloran. The latter hires her, introduces her to his pianist. Nick also arrives looking for a job, but Halloran advises him to leave Macao.

Going out, Nick prevents the Russian doorman from breaking the blind beggar's stick. He is nearly run over by Sebastian, and meets Trumble. From this street scene (for which Sternberg had ordered a dozen ducks, two goats, a bus and a honeywagon), dissolve to:

Interior of the Quick Reward, bustling with activity. In the gaming-room, the croupiers are female. Baskets soar up to the first floor, carrying jewels or other pledges. In the first-floor café, Julie sings *You Kill Me*. Marge is handling the dice. Watched by Halloran and Trumble, Nick wins handsomely, then loses. Halloran offers him $6,000 to leave Macao. A scene follows between Nick and Julie in the gaming-room.

They leave the place and take a rickshaw, watched by Halloran. Scene with the two of them in a sampan.

At the hotel, next morning, Trumble proposes that Nick should sell some diamonds for him. Nick accepts.

Nick goes to the Quick Reward and shows one stone to Marge, then Halloran, offering them the complete necklace, which is in Hong Kong. Halloran recognizes it as a piece he had himself stolen.

Nick returns to the hotel; he tells Trumble why he left America (an accidental homicide). Nick tells Julie he is going to Hong Kong.

Trumble pretends to be going fishing. Just outside territorial waters, he boards an Interpol boat; he is the cop charged with putting Halloran under lock and key.

On the wharves, night. Nick is overpowered by Halloran's men.

The police boat waits for him in vain.

Trumble, unaware of what has happened to Nick, sneaks aboard Halloran's boat, and telegraphs a message to Interpol.

On the wharves, Trumble questions a blind beggar, who heard sounds of a struggle.

Halloran tells Julie that Nick is a cop. She repeats this to Trumble, who informs Halloran that Interpol knows all about Nick's disappearance.

The Quick Reward: Julie sings *One for My Baby*.

Imprisoned, Nick argues with Marge, left to watch him.

Guided by the blind man, Julie finds Nick, who – under threat from a gun – persuades her that Marge is the only reason he is there.

Sebastian and Halloran are worried about what Trumble is up to, and Halloran decides to go to Hong Kong himself.

Nick has a chance to escape (his captors hope he will lead them to his colleagues); although Marge assures him that he will be safer with her, he escapes into the night.

The chase that follows, through the streets, across roofs, and finally through the wharves, with the tin can rattling off the roof, the mysterious black cat (Sternberg's signature), the pole snapping as a body falls on an awning, the planks dipping into the water when run across, the fishing-net ripped open by a killer's knife, and the eventual death of Trumble, mistaken for Nick but in fact the man they really want to eliminate, remains the best sequence in the film as it has come down to us (and was the one most liked by the original preview audience on 4 April 1951).

Without transition, Marge is on the wharf, talking to one of the Chinese killers, Itzumi, distracting his attention and helping Nick to sneak aboard Halloran's boat.

Nick has taken the captain's place at the tiller. Outside territorial waters, where Halloran was safe, the latter comes up from below to find Nick there. They fight.

Halloran is handed over to Interpol, who arrive by launch. Nick says he has a job to finish: 'I can't keep Eve waiting.' The film ends at the bar of the ferryboat as it leaves Macao. Sebastian is there in civilian clothes. We see Julie's legs pass, joined by Nick.

Attribution of scenes in the definitive version, running for exactly 80 minutes: After the credits and opening commentary (over documentary shots) come two studio scenes directed by Ray: a man keeping the Quick Reward under surveillance is pursued, then killed on the wharves by Halloran and his two Chinese killers; at Interpol, we learn that the dead man was a policeman.

The ferry enters the harbour (documentary). Brief scene (Sternberg) in the wheelhouse, at the helm. Nick rescues Julie from the attentions of a passenger (censorship prevented it from being the captain), and kisses her; she then gets into conversation with Trumble; Nick discovers that his wallet has gone (scenes shot by Ray).

The scene in the customs shed was partially re-shot by Ray; it ends with the reference, now shorn of context, to Adam in the Garden of Eden.

Trumble and Nick cross Macao by bus (Ray).

Brief dolly (no characters) up to the façade of the Quick Reward (Sternberg, but the Russian doorman has gone), then the scenes with Marge, Halloran and Sebastian in the gaming-house; all the scenes in this setting are Sternberg's.

At the hotel, a bellboy brings Nick a dollar bill, which he recognizes as his, stolen by Julie. He hears a voice singing *Ocean Breeze*, enters Julie's room: it's a gramophone playing. Julie comes in as he is retrieving his money from her bag. Up to this point, the sequence was re-shot by Ray in the interests of plot coherence (and to put a shirt on Mitchum, who proved to be a little overweight). The rest of the sequence was Sternberg's, probably re-edited (Mitchum on Sternberg's version: 'There was no way they could glue it together, I kept meeting myself'): Sebastian telling Julie he has found her a job. Also Sternberg's is the little comedy scene with the female barber (probably shortened).

After further stock shots, a group of scenes directed by Sternberg, with 'irrelevant' details excised or curtailed: Julie arrives in a rickshaw at the Quick Reward. Scene with Julie and Marge, then with Halloran and the pianist, then Nick and Halloran. Then the gaming-room, *You Kill Me*, Marge sees to it that Nick wins, then loses.

The following scene between Nick and Halloran in the office was re-shot by Ray: Nick's numerous cigarettes in the Sternberg version were eliminated (at the preview, a 12-year-old girl had complained that he smoked too much!).

Outside the gaming-house, Nick meets up again with Julie (Ray); Halloran watches them leave (Sternberg). The two long dialogue scenes that follow, first in a rickshaw, then in a sampan, were shot by Ray, very economically. Walter Newman recalled having written the second scene: 'I wrote about three scenes after discussion with Nick, it didn't take more than a day or two. I seem to remember some sort of little love scene in a Chinese junk that tied the story together a bit.'

Trumble's proposition to Nick, Nick's visit to the Quick Reward with the sample stone, and the second scene between Nick and Trumble, are by Sternberg. The scene between Nick and Julie on the hotel stairs was re-shot by Ray to accommodate the plot changes. The scene outside the hotel with the blind beggar (Ray?).

Also by Sternberg: Trumble on the Interpol boat; Nick attacked on the wharves by Halloran and one of his killers; Halloran jealously talking to Julie about Nick. The ensuing sequence is Sternberg's, although re-edited: Trumble learns from the blind man what happened to Nick, *then* sneaks aboard Halloran's boat to telegraph a message to Interpol. The scene between Halloran and Sebastian, very poorly conceived and played out on a note of caricature, appears to have been Sternberg's work. After another stock shot, Nick opens a window behind bars, whistles to the blind man in the street below, discovers who his jailer is when Marge comes in (Sternberg scenes). At the hotel, Julie questions the receptionist. She leaves, is approached by the blind man, who leads her on foot to Marge's house (Sternberg scenes). Julie enters, finds Marge and Nick, who has to feign an involvement with Marge (Sternberg and Mel Ferrer). Julie leaves with the blind man (Sternberg or Ray).

The third song, *One for My Baby*, is retained from the Sternberg version (though relocated); also the last scene between Halloran and Sebastian. Marge's house: shot of a door mysteriously swinging open, the camera dollying behind mosquito-netting up to Mitchum (Sternberg). The rest of the sequence was directed by Mel Ferrer: Marge arriving, helping Nick to escape without alerting the killers. The great nocturnal chase and murder of Trumble are by Sternberg (with Ray adding the close-up of the dying Trumble). Nick walks along a neon-lit arcade (Sternberg, but used out of context). Nick enters the hotel by a side door (Robert Stevenson). The scene between Nick and Julie, she threatening him with an electric fan that rips up a pillow, was directed by Ray (incorporating a few shots done by Stevenson): 'All the scenes between Nick and me that work, Nick Ray shot,' Jane Russell commented. Halloran and Julie boarding his boat, Marge helping Nick to eliminate a killer, and all the action on board were directed by Sternberg (with some cuts, with Ray adding a close-up of Mitchum strangling the killer, and with at least one Stevenson contribution: the final shot and line).

19   The Lusty Men

Sources

David Dortort, letter of 30 December 1980; William Fadiman; Robert Parrish, New York, 16 June 1982.

RKO Archives; Robert Mitchum, interviewed by Philippe Garnier for the French TV programme, *Cinéma Cinémas*, June 1982.

Notes

1   cf. Wim Wenders, 'Die Männer in der Rodeo-Arena: gierig', *Tip*, 3/83; reprinted and translated in Wim Wenders, *Emotion Pictures*, Faber and Faber, London, 1989.

2   It was Stanush he meant. Questioned on the telephone (El Paso, 21 June 1982), Tom Lea confirmed that he'd had nothing to do either with this film or with rodeo.

3   'Laconically, Mitchum declared that his favourite director was Ed Kelly. But Ed Kelly doesn't exist, any more than the films he cites. He admits this, though cherishing the hope that "Ed Kelly" may some day become real' (Jacques Siclier, 'L'Humour de Robert Mitchum', *Le Monde*, 16 May 1978). Edward Killy (wrongly transcribed here as Kelly), was indeed an RKO B-movie director who, after *Nevada* and *West of the Pecos* (the last two Poverty Row Westerns in which Mitchum appeared), became an assistant and second unit director.

4   Lewis MacAdams, 'Robert Mitchum: Lemme tell you how films are made', *L.A. Weekly*, 16–22 April 1982. Robert Mitchum interviewed by Philippe Garnier, *op. cit.*

5   Information by courtesy of Philippe Garnier. In July-August, McCoy also completed the final script for Universal's film about the rodeo, *Bronco Buster*, directed by an off-form Budd Boetticher.

6   Letter from Claude Stanush, 30 January 1952.

7   Letter from Jerry Wald to Claude Stanush, 22 December 1951.

8   Ray at Vassar, 1979. Lee Garmes was born in 1898, and died in 1978. Jerry Wald was thinking of using an RKO contract cameraman: Nick Musuraca or Harry Wild.

9   Ben Hecht, *A Child of the Century*, Simon and Schuster, New York, 1954.

10   Robert La Cativa, New York, 24 June 1982.

11   Andrew Solt.

12   Lee Garmes in Charles Higham, *Hollywood Cameramen*, Thames and Hudson, London, 1970: 'We used a white overhead light and for the close-ups I used the north-light effect which gave the illusion they were under

the sun. It was all totally artificial, but I don't think anybody knew the difference.'

13 The incident is recalled by the stuntman in his autobiography: 'Bad Chuck' Roberson with Boedie Thoene, *The Fall Guy, 30 Years as the Duke's Double*, Hancock House, North Vancouver, 1980, pp. 37–9.

14 According to the production records. Robert Parrish ('De Chaplin à Fuller', *Cahiers du Cinéma*, no. 142, April 1963) mentions 'the scene where Mitchum goes to get his money after the rodeo'; but there is no such scene in the film.

15 Even while Ray was working on *Androcles and the Lion*, in August.

16 These were shot by Harold Wellman, Nick Musuraca and Harry Wild.

17 Jacques Rivette, 'De l'invention', *Cahiers du Cinéma*, no. 27, October 1953, translated as 'On Imagination,' in Jim Hillier (ed.), *Cahiers du Cinéma*, Harvard University Press, Cambridge, Mass., 1985, pp. 104–5.

20   Last Year at RKO

Sources
Hanna Axmann, Saint-Firmin-sur-Loire, 27 March 1985; Jean Evans; William Fadiman; Betty Schwab (Utey), Los Angeles, 27 November 1980, 11 June 1981; Harry Tatelman, Universal City, 7 July 1982.
N. Ray Archives; RKO Archives.

Notes
1 At this time, Walter Newman had co-scripted *Ace in the Hole* (Billy Wilder, 1951).

2 Quoted in a memo of 27 August 1951. The last opinion cited came from Ardel Wray, young co-writer of *I Walked With a Zombie* (Jacques Tourneur, 1943).

3 The writer Paul Jarrico had been an 'unfriendly' witness, and Hughes had removed his name from the credits of *The Las Vegas Story*. The Screen Writers' Guild ruled in favour of Jarrico, and were then attacked by Hughes.

4 This was one of the final disappointments in Herman J. Mankiewicz's career, hired by Pascal to write the script and then promptly fired. After a court case, which he won, he was at least well compensated.

5 The actors in this scene: Robert Newton, Fred Sarver, Charmienne Harker, John Dodsworth, Dayton Lummis.

6 Ray at Vassar, 1979.

7 Rui Nogueira, 'Writing for the Movies: Walter Newman', *Focus on Film*, no. 11, Autumn 1972. Pascal was already suffering from the illness that was to prove fatal two years later. Harry Horner, the film's production designer and originally slated as the director, recalled that he had to fly to the East Coast to hold production meetings at Rochester, in Pascal's room at the Mayo Clinic, which specialized in the treatment of cancer (Harry Horner, Pacific Palisades, 6 June 1981).

8 A few days after the *Wall Street Journal* revelations, the syndicate bowed out, and shortly after that Hughes resumed control of RKO, keeping the

advance payment of $1,500,000. Barlett and Steele (*Empire, the Life, Legend and Madness of Howard Hughes*, W. W. Norton and Company, New York, 1979) reckoned that this 'was small consolation for the problem the syndicate imbroglio had caused', and that 'Hughes was still stuck with RKO'. Others suggest that he knew exactly what he was doing, and arranged himself for the story to be 'leaked' to the press at the right time (Dan E. Moldea, *Dark Victory, Ronald Reagan, MCA and the Mob*, Viking, New York, 1986, p. 105).

9 King Vidor, *A Tree Is a Tree*, Harcourt, Brace and Co., New York, 1953, pp. 288–90.

10 N. Ray Archives.

11 Louella Parsons, 10 December 1952.

12 Rui Nogueira and Nicoletta Zalaffi, 'Encontro com Nicholas Ray,' *O Tempo e o Modo*, no. 62–3, July–August, 1968, reprinted in *Nicholas Ray*, Cinemateca Portuguesa, Lisbon, 1985.

13 *Los Angeles Examiner*, 15 August 1952.

14 Charles Bitsch, 'Entretien avec Nicholas Ray', *Cahiers du Cinéma*, no. 89, November 1958.

15 Howard Koch, *As Time Goes By*, Harcourt Brace Jovanovich, New York–London, 1979, pp. 182, 186.

21 MCA

Sources
John Houseman; Andrew Solt; Harry Tatelman; Philip Yordan, La Jolla, 12 June 1981.
Margaret Herrick Library, Academy of Motion Picture Arts and Sciences, Beverly Hills.

Notes
1 'Who's Who in Hollywood', *Film Daily*, no. 104, 16 December 1953; press release, 19 January 1954; *Daily Variety*, 2 April 1954; etc.

2 Leo Rosten, *Hollywood, the Movie Colony, the Movie Makers*, Harcourt, Brace and Co., New York, 1941, p. 94.

3 John Gregory Dunne, *The Studio*, Farrar, Straus and Giroux, 1969.

4 cf. the autobiographies of Curtis Bernhardt, Joshua Logan, Otto Preminger, Dore Schary, Hal Wallis, Raoul Walsh, and biographies of Montgomery Clift, John Garfield, Alfred Hitchcock, etc.

5 The most recent being a reportage of 24 September 1964.

6 Letters from Melody M. Sherwood, secretary to Lew Wasserman, 7 June 1982, 27 January 1984.

7 Dore Schary, *Heyday, an Autobiography*, Little, Brown and Co., Boston-Toronto, 1979, pp. 174–5.

8 Hortense Powdermaker, *Hollywood, the Dream Factory*, Little, Brown and Co., Boston, 1950.

9 Bosley Crowther, *Hollywood Rajah, the Life and Times of Louis B. Mayer*, Holt, Rinehart and Winston, New York, 1960.

10   Dan E. Moldea, *Dark Victory, Ronald Reagan, MCA and the Mob*, Viking, New York, 1986.

11   *Additional Dialogue, Letters of Dalton Trumbo 1942–1962*, M. Evans and Co., Inc., New York, 1970, p. 484. cf. also Clive Hirschhorn, *The Universal Story*, Octopus Books, London, 1983.

22   Johnny Guitar

Sources
Royal Dano, Santa Monica, 26 June 1982; Mercedes McCambridge, 19 June 1981; Sidney Solow, Los Angeles, 22 June 1982; Summer Williams; Philip Yordan.
N. Ray Deposit, Cinémathèque Française; Theater Arts Library, UCLA; N. Ray Archives; Roy Chanslor script, courtesy of Robert Carringer, Library, University of Illinois, Urbana Champaign.

Notes
1   Simon and Schuster, New York.

2   Gavin Lambert, *The Slide Area, Scenes of Hollywood Life*, Hamish Hamilton, London, 1959.

3   Production no. 1964. *Johnny Guitar. Screenplay De Luxe by Roy Chanslor, First Draft*, 10 June 1953.

4   Ben Barzman, Los Angeles, 14 June 1981; Bernard Gordon, Los Angeles, 9 April 1983; John Melson, Paris, 19 March 1981. cf. Richard Corliss, ed., *The Hollywood Screenwriters*, Avon Books, New York, 1972, p. 326.

5   cf. *Corliss, op. cit.*, p. 274.

6   Information furnished independently by Pierre Rissient and Bob Carringer. cf. also *Film Dope*, no. 38, December 1987, citing an interview with Maddow by Bertrand Tavernier; also, Patrick McGilligan, 'Ben Maddow: The Invisible Man', *Sight and Sound*, Summer 1989 (reprinted in *Backstory* 2, University of California Press, 1991).

7   'After I hired Phil Yordan I moved into the house next to him, because he had a reputation at that time for farming his scripts out. He was a road company Ben Hecht' (N. Ray Archives).

8   Blaine Allan, *Nicholas Ray, a Guide to References and Resources*, G. K. Hall and Co., Boston, 1984, mentions (p. 228) the existence of a copy of the script in the UCLA Library. In 1985, this copy seemed to have disappeared.

9   By way of Jules Furthman, scriptwriter for both Sternberg and Hawks. In *To Have and Have Not*, Bacall says to Bogart: 'Who was the girl, Steve? The one who left you with such a high opinion of women. She must have been quite a gal.' Johnny Guitar's last line here echoes another line of Bacall's: 'I'm hard to get, Steve. All you have to do is ask me.'

10   Sterling Hayden, interviewed by Philippe Garnier for the French TV programme, *Cinéma Cinémas*, 1983.

11   Mercedes McCambridge, *The Quality of Mercy*, Times Books, New York, 1981.

12   *Take One* interview.

13 Bob Thomas, *Joan Crawford*, Simon and Schuster, New York, 1978, p. 189.

14 Joan Crawford with Jane Kesner Ardmore, *A Portrait of Joan*, Doubleday and Co., New York, 1962.

15 Roy Newquist, *Conversations with Joan Crawford*, Citadel Press, Secaucus (N. J.), 1980. It is all the more surprising that, at the time when she was giving these interviews, Crawford agreed to pay tribute to Ray by appearing in the documentary *I'm a Stranger Here Myself*: the producers were unable to raise enough money for the shooting (Myron Meisel, Los Angeles, 9 June 1981). Ray seems to have had a contract for two films with Crawford; Bob Thomas mentions another mutual project for Paramount, *Lisbon*: Crawford's dresser, Sheila O'Brien, even claimed tests were made (according to David Chierichetti).

16 John Ford's *Rio Grande* was shot in 39 days, Fritz Lang's *House by the River* in 33, Edward Ludwig's *The Wake of the Red Witch* in 39 (Todd McCarthy, Charles Flynn, eds, *Kings of the Bs*, E. P. Dutton and Co., New York, 1975, pp. 29–30).

17 On 19 January 1954, a press handout announced that Ray finished his job with Republic 'last Saturday'. Joao Bénard Da Costa (*Nicholas Ray*, Cinemateca Portuguesa, Lisbon, 1985, p. 83) gives 7 February as the date on which the editing was completed.

18 The *Cahiers du Cinéma* review ('L'admirable certitude', no. 46, 1955, by François Truffaut writing under the name Robert Lachenay) noted for the first time that all Ray's films 'are full of bad matches, but it is clear that Ray is less interested in the traditional overall success of a film than in investing his shots with a certain emotional quality. *Johnny Guitar* is rather hurriedly "done" in very long shots chopped into pieces, the editing is deplorable. But the interest lies elsewhere . . .'

19 *Daily Variety*, 2 April 1954. In Los Angeles, the film was shown in a double bill with John Ford's *The Sun Shines Bright*.

20 *Monthly Film Bulletin*, July 1954; *Arts*, 23 February 1955.

21 Creating dissolves in the laboratory, of course, whatever the colour process used, involved the duping of both shots. Ray boldly opted for another formal solution, more or less eliminating dissolves, a mandatory narrative device at the time. The film contains only four, as against twenty in *The Lusty Men* and ten in *Rebel Without a Cause*, for example. Three of these dissolves denote brief temporal ellipses, only one having any rhetorical function: the Kid, outside the cabin, is meditating before a mountain landscape, dissolve to Vienna, in crimson *déshabillé*, coming down the stairs into the saloon (the start of her long scene with Johnny).

22 According to Sidney Solow (Technical Oscar in 1964), who was in charge of the CFI laboratory for several decades and enjoyed friendly relations with Ray at the time of both *Johnny Guitar* and *We Can't Go Home Again*: 'Trucolor went through three phases. First, it was a two-colour process, which had one colour on one side of the positive, and the other colour on the other side, and which one printed sequentially. Then it was a three-colour process printed sequentially, which used a special Du Pont positive film, which had two colours on one side, and another colour on the other side. And then it was simply the Eastmancolor process. But we continued the

name Trucolor: that was the favourite invention of Mr Yates, the president of the company.'

Marketed in 1949, the Eastmancolor monopack had in four years buried such marginal processes as the second phase Trucolor, Cinecolor and Magnacolor, as well as the then dominant process, three-strip Technicolor. The various names that subsequently appeared on credits (WarnerColor, Metro-Color, De Luxe Color, etc.) merely refer to the studio and/or laboratory.

23 Harry Stradling (1902–70).

24 David O. Selznick sketched a portrait of Victor Young: 'He is an extremely practical and successful man in doing scores without chichi, and without tricks and without nonsense, and within economic boundaries. He operates to budget, and can do an impressive score very effectively' (*Memo From David O. Selznick*, Grove Press, New York, 1972).

25 Apart from this scene, filming had been very economical; on 11 December 119 minutes 36 seconds of usable footage had been shot, as against the film's running time of 110 minutes.

26 *Take One* interview.

27 Michael Wilmington, 'Nicholas Ray's *Johnny Guitar*', *The Velvet Light Trap*, no. 12, Spring 1974.

28 Bertrand Tavernier, 'Rencontre avec Philip Yordan', *Cahiers du Cinéma*, no. 128, February 1962.

29 Ann Laemmle, 'Program Notes', University of Texas, Austin, 1979.

30 Neither José Luis Guarner (Madrid, September 1983), nor Jos Oliver and Victor Erice (*Nicholas Ray y su tiempo*, Filmoteca Española, Madrid, 1986) know what Ray was referring to. In 1960, he attended the 'Semana de Cine en Color' in Barcelona, where *The Savage Innocents* was awarded an honorary mention. '*Johnny Guitar*, released in 1954, had of course provoked no political reaction' (Oliver-Erice, p. 150).

31 'What she did was, she didn't mention any names, but if the names were mentioned she would say, "Yes, he was", because they'd already been mentioned. To this day she's been very upset about that' (scriptwriter talking about his wife, also a scriptwriter).

23 Run for Cover

Sources
Henry Bumstead, Astoria, Long Island, 25 June 1981; Daniel L. Fapp, Los Angeles, 8 June 1981; Viveca Lindfors, New York, 10 November 1980.
N. Ray Archives (including script annotated with storyboards).

Notes
1 Press release, 19 January 1954, RKO Archives.
2 Penelope Houston and John Gillett, 'Conversations with Nicholas Ray and Joseph Losey', *Sight and Sound*, Autumn 1961.
3 Winston Miller's sole claim to glory: his share in the script for John Ford's *My Darling Clementine*.

4   In a superb brass-finished leather binding, presented 'in appreciation by the *Johnny Guitar* Posse-Kids Gang'.

5   James Cagney, *Cagney by Cagney*, Doubleday, New York, 1976.

6   André Bazin, 'A l'ombre des potences', *France-Observateur*, 6 October 1955.

7   *Movie* interview.

8   Viveca Lindfors had met Ray at a screening of *The Boy With Green Hair*: 'I worked with him at a time when I was so unaware of so much. I was so young, so dumb. I remember so little. So much nonsense going on about the hair, the clothes [. . .] He was a seductive director, he would come up and whisper in your ear, there was great warmth, something going on [. . .] He really trusted only the murky corners. Nothing happened in sunshine. He was very Swedish, I suppose.'

9   In France, *Run for Cover* was released in the same month as *Les Mauvaises Rencontres*, directed by Alexandre Astruc, a forerunner of the Nouvelle Vague.

10   cf. Norbert Jochum, 'Vertrauen, und dass es enttäuscht werden kann', *Filme* (Berlin) no. 2, 1980.

11   Philippe Demonsablon, 'Le bouquet d'Helga', *Cahiers du Cinéma*, no. 52, November 1955.

12   Daniel Fapp on VistaVision: 'The camera we used we got from Fox; it was a 70 mm camera [used for the Fox Grandeur process in the early 1930s] and they turned it over on the side. It had to be redone for the blimp, of course, but these were Fox cameras. Then VistaVision built their own cameras at Paramount.'

24   High Green Wall

Sources
Joseph Cotten, Los Angeles, 2 June 1981; Jennings Lang, Los Angeles, 4 April 1981; Sumner Williams.
Script by courtesy of Sumner Williams; script (another version) by courtesy of Patrick Brion; N. Ray Archives.

Notes

1   *G. E. Theater* was presented by Ronald Reagan, whose public image MCA was trying to revive, cf. Dan E. Moldea, *Dark Victory, Ronald Reagan, MCA and the Mob*, Viking, New York, 1986.

2   Charles Jackson (1903–68, author of *The Lost Weekend, The Fall of Valor, A Second-Hand Life*, etc.), was employed by CBS until 1939, and subsequently wrote a number of teleplays.

3   Antonio-Pedro Vasconcelos, 'Nick Ray na TV', *Jornal de Letras e Artes*, March-April (or June?) 1969 (occasioned by a screening on Purtuguese TV, 28 April 1968). Blaine Allan (*Nicholas Ray, a Guide to References and Resources*, G. K. Hall and Co., Boston, 1984) had doubts as to the paternity of the film: the CBS files attribute production and direction of this episode,

respectively, to Mort Abrahams and Don Medford! It was screened on French TV, 30 December 1984.

25 Rebel without a Cause

Sources
Corey Allen, Los Angeles, 2 December 1980; Connie Bessie; Roger Donoghue, New York, 12 November 1980; Dennis Hopper, Venice, 28 March 1986; Silvia Richards; Sumner Williams.
Warner Brothers Archive, Special Collections, University of Southern California; N. Ray Deposit, Cinémathèque Française (including annotated shooting script); N. Ray Archives; N. Ray, 'Story Into Script', *Sight and Sound*, Autumn, 1956; N. Ray, 'Rebel – the Life Story of a Film', *Daily Variety*, 31 October 1956, T. Ork Dossier.

Notes
1 Undated notes by Ray.
2 Albert Camus, *The Rebel: An Essay on Man in Revolt*, Alfred A. Knopf, New York, 1952.
3 Derek Marlowe, interview with Ray, San Francisco, 1974 (transcription in N. Ray Archives).
4 'He [Brooks] had already directed two or three pics by that time but in my opinion he had shown no talent as a film-maker and I think he knew it and that's why he wrote the book [his novel, *The Producer*]. It was a very cool con and I'm glad he wrote it because then he had a chance to make *Blackboard Jungle* and the talent began to show. After Richard directed his first film I was always embarrassed to meet up with him and meeting up with him was inevitable because he was singing for his ego at Bogart's most of the time. He didn't disgust me artistically like Mervyn LeRoy and a thousand others. One day at the racetrack I got a vicious pleasure out of returning his pleasant greeting by yelling from the box: "Hi! WRITER!" ' (Notes by Ray.)
5 Memos from Ray to Weisbart, 7 and 18 October 1954; Azteca Films invoice, 14 October. Ray also viewed *Successful Scholarship*, an American documentary in 16mm (production/distribution: McGraw-Hill Textfilms, 1954).
6 Uris dictated beginnings for a script: *Rebel Without a Cause*, five pages, 13 October; *Juvenile Story*, twenty-four pages, 20 October, sixteen on 1 November, twelve on 2 November.
7 Elia Kazan, 22 October 1980.
8 On the night of 28 January 1952, the premises of the Clover Club, a celebrated casino during the 1930s at 8477 Sunset Strip, were destroyed by fire. 'The director Nick Ray, who lives in a four-room bungalow adjoining the club, cut his foot on a piece of glass while running down an alley to the street to escape the flames. The bungalow was untouched' (unidentified press cutting, 29 January 1952).
9 Andrew Solt was put to the test, summoned by Ray to the Chateau Marmont on some pretext: 'There sat in the corner a little boy, emaciated, the

whole thing could have been 125 pounds, a little effeminate, dark, the only thing that made him a little interesting was that he had a cat on his shoulder. Then Nick came out, positive and beaming, and he said, "Bundy, hi, I want you to meet my new star, Jimmy Dean." We talked, I forget what about, and he said, "What do you think of him?" I couldn't lie. I said, "This, a star?" He said, "He'll be the biggest star." I said, "Well, I wish you lots of luck," but I couldn't see it. And of course he saw exactly what this boy would look and act like on the screen' (28 November 1980).

10   Irving Shulman, *Juvenile Story*, beginning of treatment, 25 pages, 15 November 1954; then 77 pages. *Juvenile Story, Progression*, 17 pages, 12 January 1955. Treatment, 40 pages, 13–18 December; *Juvenile Story, Screenplay*, 4 December – 26 January.

11   Irving Shulman, letter to Jack L. Warner, 3 March 1956.

12   Ray, *Jim at home*, 6 pages, 2 December.

13   Irving Shulman, *Children of the Dark* (Holt, Rinehart and Winston, New York). Published in January 1956, it is dedicated to Finlay McDermid, head of the Warner literary department, and to David Weisbart, 'under whose direction and suggestion I developed the treatment and screenplay'. The introduction, which thanks everybody down to the secretary, pointedly omits Ray's name. The novel is set in a small town in eastern Mississippi, and includes rough approximations of the first scene in the Planetarium and of the chicken run (although the hero does not take part in it), but differs from the film more than the various versions of the script on which Shulman worked. A novelization of dubious authenticity appeared in Belgium under Ray's name (*La Fureur de vivre*, translated by Annie Mesritz, Editions Gérard, then Collection Marabout, Verviers, 1956), but was never published in English.

14   Tony was waiting for his father in New York. His disappointment at finding the latter paying more attention to Dean led him, in a spirit of emulation, into a brief acting career in films: *The True Story of Jesse James, Men in War* (Anthony Mann, 1957), and most notably, *Shadows* (John Cassavetes, 1958–61).

15   Ray thought Cassavetes too old; Lee Remick wrong for the part; only Carroll Baker, a fellow-student of Dean's at the Actors' Studio, interested him very much.

16   *Thunder of Silence* was shown on TV (Thanksgiving, 1954) while preparations for *Rebel Without a Cause* were under way; Ray certainly saw it.

17   Stewart Stern in Mike Steen, *Hollywood Speaks*, G. P. Puttnam's Sons, New York, 1974.

18   Uris had been hired at $750 a week, Shulman at $650; Stern was paid $1,000 a week.

19   Stewart Stern, *Rebel Without a Cause*, 11 pages, 21 January 1955; 120 pages, 31 January.
     The opening scene of the passer-by being beaten up survived into the 'final' script (and figures in the script published in 1989 in *Best Screenplays*, Crown Publishers, New York). It was never shot, but it was from the victim that Jim acquired the mechanical monkey seen in the credit sequence.

20   Scene no. 242 in the 'final'. The second scene is described by Stewart Stern in

David Dalton, *James Dean, the Mutant King*, Straight Arrow Books, San Francisco, 1974, p. 239.

21   Quoted by Victor Navasky, *Naming Names*, The Viking Press, New York, 1980.

22   'Dialogue on Film: Stewart Stern', *American Film*, October 1983.

23   With characteristically perverse humour, Ray later said he had chosen Haller (active since 1920, at Warners since 1929) among the contract cameramen because he had once been fired from a Joan Crawford film.

24   Sal Mineo in the film *James Dean, First American Teenager*. Plato was the last of the juvenile roles to be filled; Mineo was tested on 23 March, along with Richard Beymer (later to partner Natalie Wood in *West Side Story*).

25   James Leahy, letter to Gavin Millar, 19 December 1979.

26   Ray may have come across Jim Backus on *Androcles and the Lion*. On 2 March he was not even mentioned among the candidates for the part: Walter Matthau, Raymond Burr, Hume Cronyn, Royal Dano and John Dehner.

27   Marsha Hunt was on the blacklist and made no films between 1952 and 1956, but in this case she seems to have elected to accept a stage role, as *Daily Variety* announced (5 April 1955). cf. John Cogley, *Report on Blacklisting. 1. Movies*, The Fund for the Republic, Inc., 1956, pp. 154–5. Rochelle Hudson, cast as Judy's mother, was a former ingénue whom Ray brought out of retirement ('nervous as a puppy,' he told Derek Marlowe).

28   *New York Times*, 5 April 1955. An MGM film, *Trial*, faced the same problem and was switched to standard ratio.

29   Jack L. Warner, note to Weisbart, 2 April.

30   Characteristically, the synopsis for the projected book ends with these words. Elsewhere, Ray has pointed out that his proposal had a precedent, George Stevens having offered to buy *Shane* back from Paramount (Nogueira-Zalaffi interview in *O Tempo e o Modo*).

31   The house belonged to the Getty family, and had already featured in *Sunset Boulevard*.

32   Natalie Wood in *I'm a Stranger Here Myself*.

33   Dalton, *op. cit*, p. 236. The format of Manet's *Le Torero mort* (1864) is 1.53 × 0.75 metres (5ft × 2½ft).

34   In the script, Jim sees Judy rub Buzz's hands with dirt as he prepares to grip the wheel, and picks some up himself. It was Ray who had Jim, instead of picking up the earth as he watches Judy kiss Buzz after attending to his hands, say to her, 'Me too?', thus extending the desire to be 'with it' in this duel of aggression into its echo that is apparent between Jim and Judy.

35   Stewart Stern, letter to Steve Trilling, 5 May 1955.

36   Expression used by Leonard Rosenman in the film *James Dean, First American Teenager*; reportage by Harrison Carroll, unidentified cutting, 21 May 1955.

37   Memo of 23 May.

38   During the last days of shooting, the crew sometimes split up, and assistant director Don Page filmed pick-ups and second unit shots, as did the special effects cameraman, Koenenkamp. For the chicken run (cars only), Haller was joined by Ted McCord (cameraman on *East of Eden*) and Philip

Lathrop on second unit. On some retakes, Lathrop was also backed up on camera by Lynch and Harold Wellman. On 23 June, Don Page did one more day of pick-ups with McCord.

39   Ray noted that there was a hole at this point, and that music might help ('Cutting notes'). In Dalton *op. cit.*, Ray says that Rosenman couldn't get the rhythm he was after, and that he eliminated the scene for that reason.

40   'Written and acted so ineptly, directed so sluggishly, that all names but one (James Dean's) will be omitted here' (William K. Zinsser, *New York Herald Tribune*, 27 October). Bosley Crowther (*New York Times*) and the weeklies declared themselves appalled, numbed or bored. The critic of *The Nation* (3 December) recorded his impression that the youth gangs of the West Coast had been organized by Jean Cocteau.

In 1962, in *Variety*'s list of all-time box-office winners (United States and Canada), *Rebel Without a Cause* figured in 173rd place with $4.5 million – far behind *King of Kings*, 41st with its $8 million.

41   Harrison Carroll, unidentified cutting, 21 May 1955.

42   In a television film written by William Inge, *Glory in the Flower* (1953), this cliché line is given to a secondary character played by James Dean, who also complains that 'everybody blames me'.

43   Stewart Stern in Mike Steen, *op. cit.*

26   Hot Blood

Sources

Roger Donoghue; Jean Evans; Jesse Lasky Jr, Paris, 23 October 1982; Jane Russell; Harry Tatelman; Cornel Wilde, Los Angeles, 11 June 1982.
T. Ork Dossier; N. Ray Deposit, Cinémathèque Française; script, by courtesy of Sumner Williams.

Notes

1   Rui Nogueira, 'Writing for the Movies: Walter Newman', *Focus on Film*, no. 11, Autumn 1972.

2   Jesse Lasky Jr (1908–88) had worked mainly on DeMille productions. He retailed some anecdotes about *Hot Blood*, in a slightly disguised form, in his book of memoirs, *Whatever Happened to Hollywood?*, Funk, Wagnalls, New York, 1975.

3   'Outside of a section of a book called *McSorley's Saloon*' (Ray, T. Ork Dossier).

4   Ross Bagdasarian was best known for the song *Come Up to My House*, lyrics by William Saroyan, which was made famous by Eartha Kitt, among others.

5   Mickey Katz was the father of Joel Grey, Oscar-winner for his role in *Cabaret*.

6   Ray June (1898–1958), who made his debut in the 1920s, had only one more chance to display his talent: *Funny Face* (Stanley Donen, 1957).

7   Luc Moullet, 'Filmographie de Nicholas Ray', *Cahiers du Cinéma*, no. 89,

November 1958. cf. also François Truffaut, 'La joie de vivre', *Arts*, no. 602, 16 January 1957.

8   Mikhail Rasumny died on 17 February 1956, aged sixty-two.

9   T. Ork Dossier.

10 Marco is still called Mike in the script (final draft of 17 June 1955).

11 Jean-Luc Godard, 'Rien que le cinéma', *Cahiers du Cinéma*, no. 68, February 1957.

12 What Truffaut wrote was 'Après *la Fureur de vivre*, Ray nous donne sa joie de vivre avec ce film endiablé . . .' The words 'joie de vivre' cause no problems in English; but '*la Fureur de vivre*' is the French release title of *Rebel Without a Cause*, and the translation has to make the connection.

27   European Parenthesis, 1955

Sources
Hanna Axmann; Connie Bessie; Roger Donoghue; Gavin Lambert, Santa Monica, 29 November 1980, Los Angeles, 10 April 1983.
Warner Archives, USC; N. Ray Archives.

Notes
1   *Take One* interview.
2   Later synopsis (c. 1974).
3   Postcard to Steve Trilling, 14 October 1955.

28   Bigger Than Life

Sources
Gavin Lambert; James Mason, Paris, 11 February 1983; Walter Matthau, letter of 1 July 1982.
Gavin Lambert, 'Good-Bye to Some of All That', *Film Quarterly*, no. 12, Autumn 1958; James Mason, *Before I Forget*, Hamish Hamilton, London, 1981; 20th Century-Fox Archives, Special Collections, Theater Arts Library, UCLA; 20th Century-Fox Archives, Special Collections, USC; N. Ray Deposit, Cinémathèque Française; T. Ork Dossier.

Notes
1   Lillian Ross, 'Bons reporters', *Vogue* (John Huston number), December-January, 1981–2.
2   In the first announcements, Charles K. Feldman was listed as co-producer of *In a Lonely Place* (*Hollywood Reporter*, 28 October 1949, cited by Blaine Allan).
3   It was at this time, too, that Clifford Odets wrote one of his best scripts, for *Sweet Smell of Success* (Alexander Mackendrick, 1957).
4   Only page preserved by Ray (N. Ray Deposit, Cinémathèque Française).
5   Letter from Mason to Sid Rogell, 9 May 1956.
6   Letter from Mason to Buddy Adler, 22 June 1956.

7   Richard Maibaum *in* Pat McGilligan, *Backstory*, University of California Press, Berkeley-Los Angeles-London, 1986.

8   In his journal for 1940, Odets recounts a dream in which he walked not with Lincoln, but in the company of the Roosevelts (*The Time Is Ripe*, Grove Press, New York, 1988, p. 90). The line about the sun appears to be a reference to Ibsen's *Ghosts*.

9   Roger Donoghue; autobiographical notes by Ray. Marilyn Monroe was already making 'appearances' at Ray's home in Malibu while he was married to Gloria Grahame (Gretchen Horner). Shelley Winters claimed to have known Ray, and to have introduced him to Marilyn, *before* this marriage; but her book is rather muddled over dates (*Shelley II: the Middle of My Century*, Simon and Schuster, New York, 1989).

10 Ray saw Charles Laughton's film while looking for a young actor to play James Mason's son.

11 Quoted in David Dalton, *James Dean, the Mutant King*, Straight Arrow Books, San Francisco, 1974, p. 225.

12 François Truffaut, reprinted in *The Films in My Life*, Allen Lane, London, 1980. Robert Benayoun, 'La cortisone à l'estomac', reprinted in *Cinéma américain 1, la Méthode*, no. 8, March 1962.

13 Eric Rohmer, 'Ou bien . . . ou bien', *Cahiers du Cinéma*, no. 69, March 1957, reprinted and translated in Eric Rohmer, *The Taste for Beauty*, Cambridge University Press, New York, 1989.

14 *New York Times*, 3 August 1956.

29   The True Story of Jesse James

Sources
Gavin Lambert; Walter M. Scott, Century City, 24 June 1982; Sumner Williams. Gavin Lambert, 'Good-Bye to Some of All That', *Film Quarterly*, no. 12, Autumn 1958; Rui Nogueira, 'Writing for the Movies: Walter Newman', *Focus on Film*, no. 11, Autumn 1972; 20th Century-Fox Archives, USC; 20th Century-Fox Archives, UCLA; T. Ork Dossier; script, by courtesy of Sumner Williams.

Notes

1   Rogers and Cowan, 'News Release' (press release), 25 June 1956; Bill Barton, 'Ray Ready to Back His Own Judgment', *Film Daily*, 9 July 1956.

2   Temporary script of 4 September. The dandyism and elegant affectation of the Quantrill character were historically attested, but not his feminine delicacy.

3   Temporary script of 4 September. This version differs slightly from the blue page in the final script, dated 28 September, which indicates 'Already shot' for this scene.

4   In the new version of the scene, only one neighbour accuses the James family, not two; and Zee is not present.

5   Jean-Luc Godard wrote of 'a sensitivity to décor, which no other American director since Griffith has been able to use so vividly and powerfully' ('Le cinéaste bien-aimé', *Cahiers du Cinéma*, no. 74, August-September 1957,

reprinted and translated in Jean Narboni and Tom Milne, eds, *Godard on Godard*, Secker & Warburg, London, 1972.

6 Paul I. Wellman, *A Dynasty of Western Outlaws*, Doubleday, New York, 1961.

7 'The film-maker [. . .] saw the legend already taking shape behind the true facts, and behind the existence, the essence' (Jean-Luc Godard, *op. cit.*).

8 Ray was unable to undertake the preliminary researches which always stimulated him (and blames Walter Newman who, in his view at least, seemed to side with the producer early on). The credits list the two historical advisers from King's film, completely inaccurate in this area; from every point of view Ray's version is a departure from it.

9 *A Treasury of American Folklore*, edited by B. A. Botkin, *op. cit.*

10 Evidently a slip by the singer for '*he was born . . .*' Jesse James was born in Clay County, and died at St Joseph.

30 Bitter Victory

Sources
Charles Bitsch, Paris, 13 January 1986; Michel Kelber, Boulogne, 26 November 1981; Gavin Lambert; Maurice Le Roux, Paris, 8 December 1981; Renée and Lucie Lichtig, Paris, 10 February 1987; Edouard Luntz, Paris, 2 December 1981; Vladimir Pozner, Paris, 23 November 1981; Eric Rohmer, Paris, 28 November 1988; Sumner Williams.
N. Ray and Lucie Lichtig Deposits, Cinémathèque Française; N. Ray Archives; T. Ork Dossier; Temporary Revised script, by courtesy of Sumner Williams; Gavin Lambert, 'Good-bye to Some of All That', *Film Quarterly*, no. 12, Autumn 1958.

Notes
1 Charles Bitsch, 'Entretien avec Nicholas Ray', *Cahiers du Cinéma*, no. 89, November 1958.

2 Ray assured both Terry Ork and James Leahy that black-and-white was Graetz's choice, not his.

3 Ray talked to Peter von Bagh (and others) about a collaboration with Abraham Polonsky, clearly getting his name mixed up with Pozner's (he mentioned working in Paris, whereas in 1956 Polonsky had long been gone from Paris).

4 Lambert went on: 'Nick and I weren't alone in this feeling. When I mentioned Graetz to René Clément, he hit the roof.' The conflict that was to erupt is not unlike the one experienced by Claude Autant-Lara and his crew when they made *Le Diable au corps* against, rather than for, their producer Paul Graetz.

5 Curd Jürgens, *. . . und kein bisschen weise*, Droemer Knaur Verlag, Munich, 1976.

6 'In the evenings, Nick used to say, "Manon, let's go", so for us she became Manon Lescaut' (Michel Kelber). Described as 'Not very intelligent, nor very cultivated nor very pretty', Manon played an important role in the year that followed. Men tend to blame her for all Ray's sins, accusing her of

having led him to drugs, of being largely responsible for his physical ruination and the disasters of *Wind Across the Everglades*. The truth, as Barbara Schulberg (among others) suggested, is certainly more complex.

7   Ray gave Peter von Bagh a colourful, if implausible, reason for this episode. His salary, he explained, went in paying Pozner and in gambling. 'He discovered that there was only one thing in the world the producer had respect for: gambling. Ray had never played chemin de fer, but after this he went every evening to the casino in Nice. In this way, he could spend four or five hours in peace, relaxing and thinking about the film. The price to be paid was $60,000. "I didn't make a penny on the film, but I could think in peace" ' (Peter von Bagh, 'Nicholas Ray, Rebell', *Chaplin*, no. 126, November 1973).

8   Lambert was to leave for Hollywood and write scripts for television, before making a name as a novelist (*Inside Daisy Clover, Running Time*) and scriptwriter (*Sons and Lovers, The Roman Spring of Mrs Stone, I Never Promised You a Rose Garden*).

9   Eric Rohmer, 'Venise 1957', *Cahiers du Cinéma*, no. 75, October 1957.

10 James Leahy, London, April 1981.

11 On the strength of this score, Jean-Luc Godard hired Le Roux to do the music for *Le Petit Soldat* (1960).

12 In Algeria, military censorship required the shot of Wilkins killing the two Berber horsemen to be excised (Jean Narboni).

13 *Arts*, 18 September 1957; Jean Domarchi, 'Nicholas Ray à Venise', *Cahiers du Cinéma*, no. 75, October 1957; Gene Moscowitz, 'Paris Shooting Carries a "Strain", But Now Nick Ray Seeks Encore', *Variety*, 10 July 1957.

14 Eric Rohmer, '*Amère victoire*, seul film intelligent présenté au Festival', *Arts*, no. 634, 4 September 1957. In the list of 'Ten Best Films of 1957' published by *Cahiers du Cinéma*, featuring twenty-four selections, *Bitter Victory* was cited seven times; in all, Ray received fourteen votes, covering four different films (no. 79, January 1958).

15 Jean Domarchi, *op. cit.*

16 Jean-Luc Godard, 'Au-delà des étoiles', *Cahiers du Cinéma*, no. 79, January 1958, translated into English in Jim Hillier (ed.), *Cahiers du Cinéma*, Harvard University Press, Cambridge, Mass., 1985, pp. 118–9.

17 The Rendez-vous de Biarritz: cf. Chapter 10, note 23.

18 Fereydoun Hoveyda should also be mentioned for his laudatory review of *Hot Blood*, in *Positif* (writing as F. Hoda, no. 21, February 1957), and later panegyric on *Party Girl* (eleven pages in *Cahiers*). In New York, Hoveyda was to be a loyal friend to Ray in the latter's last years.

19 Roger Tailleur, '*Derrière le miroir*: les adolescents', *Positif*, no. 22, March 1957.

20 Claude Beylie, *Pour une cinémathèque idéale*, Henri Veyrier, Paris, 1982.

21 Truffaut wrote about *Johnny Guitar* in *Arts* and in *Cahiers du Cinéma*. The theme of his own penultimate film, *La Femme d'à côté*, was precisely the 'loving disenchantment' he found in Ray's film.

22 Barbet Schroeder, interviewed by Joëlle Naïm, in *Nicholas Ray y su tiempo*, Filmoteca Española, Madrid, 1986.

23 Daniel Kostoveski and Jean-Marie Straub, 'Qui est Nicholas Ray?', *Radio Cinéma*, no. 269, 13 March 1955.

24 Philippe Demonsablon, 'Le bouquet d'Helga', *Cahiers du Cinéma*, no. 52, November 1955.

25 Jean-Pierre Melville, a great connoisseur of American cinema and admirer of brilliantly contrived mechanisms like *Odds Against Tomorrow* (Robert Wise, 1959), was one of the few devotees of American movies at the time to detest Ray's films. Nothing, he explained to Claude Beylie, excused their slapdash quality (*Pour une cinémathéque idéale, op. cit.*).

31   Wind Across the Everglades

Sources
Roger Donoghue; Burl Ives, Santa Barbara, 15 June 1981; Georges Klotz, Boulogne, 14 April 1981; Charles Maguire, Hollywood, 3 December 1980; Budd Schulberg, Quoge, Long Island, 17 June 1982; George Voskovec, California, 30 June 1981; Sumner Williams. Conversations with Barbara Schulberg, New York, 23 June 1981; with Joseph Brun (Pierre Cottrell), Fort Lauderdale, 14 October 1985.
Budd Schulberg, *Across the Everglades, a Play for the Screen*, Random House, New York, 1958; Warner Brothers Archive, Special Collections, University of Southern California, Los Angeles; *Seminar: Nicholas Ray* (26 April 1973), American Film Institute, Louis B. Mayer Library.

Notes
1   B. P. Schulberg, who was to come out of retirement to serve as adviser to his two sons, died on 25 February 1957.

2   Jack L. Warner noted, in October 1955, that Schulberg had received an advance of $2,500 and was making 'good progress on screenplay in Florida'.

3   According to Roger Donoghue, Ray vanished for a while between Europe and America, but probably later on (cf. Chapter 30, note 13). At all events, he attended the Venice Festival, where *Bitter Victory* was shown.

4   Letter from Stuart Schulberg to *Films in Review*, vol. IX, no. 6, June 1958. cf. also Stuart Schulberg, 'Florida Screen Safari', *New York Times*, 19 January 1958.

5   MacKinlay Kantor, particularly noted for his novels about the American Civil War, was also a folk music enthusiast (cf. for example, the end of Burl Ives's book *Wayfaring Stranger*).

6   Erik Lee Preminger, *Gypsy and Me*, Little, Brown and Co., Boston-Toronto, 1984.

7   Hy Hollinger, 'Schulberg Freres in Swampland', *Variety*, 4 December 1957.

8   It seems, for instance, to judge by a sweet-and-sour correspondence, that the studio never managed to get hold of a copy of the shooting script listing numbered scenes.

9   Donald Chase, ed., *Filmmaking – The Collaborative Art* (AFI Series), Little, Brown and Co., Boston-Toronto, 1975, p. 64.

10 Scenes eliminated from the script: '1. Interior Miami Jail pp. 6–7. 2. Interior

Nathanson Store pp. 21–22–23. 3. Med. Close Hammock – Day, p. 27, from line 10 to dissolve p. 28. 4. Med. Close Walt and Billy pp. 72–3. 5. Sloop and Pelican Key Dock p. 104.' The Fourth of July Picnic scene was shortened and reduced: instead of 200 extras, about twenty, plus the principals, remain on the beach after the parade.

11 Ray on Plummer: 'He was daily full of nice surprises. At that point, how flexible he was, but not flexible about himself. He couldn't conceive of it when, just a year or two later, I seriously asked him to do O'Neill's *A Touch of the Poet*' (T. Ork Dossier). Plummer was also one of a number of actors considered for the role of Christ in *King of Kings*; Ray ruled him out, judging him to be 'a superior actor' but 'reliant upon external tricks': 'I am hesitant to accept the truth of his warmth under the microscopic eye of the camera' (letter to Samuel Bronston, 6 February 1960). The story about the silent stroll has also been told about David Niven on *55 Days at Peking*.

12 At 'Buzzard Key Bay', the muddy shore where Mary Melon's barge is moored and the romance is adumbrated between Mary's daughter and the mute boy played by Sumner Williams; then at 'Cottonmouth Key', for exteriors with the same group of actors, Cottonmouth's gang, with the addition of Plummer, from the 13th to the 30th. On the last day of 1957: exteriors involving the Manchinell tree and the mosquito net camp.

13 The liaison was to end shortly afterwards. Roger Donoghue and a friend put Manon on a plane to Paris, believing they were saving Ray's life.

14 The exteriors at the gang's hideout were wrapped up on 14–15 January: the very first scene, before the arrival of the two escaped convicts: four pages of script, 7 minutes 20 seconds of usable footage, barely more than a minute used in the completed film. All the actors were finished with, except the two principals and the two Indians. For a week, the weather prevented filming, except for pick-ups. 'Only day and a half left to finish dialogue scenes', Stuart Schulberg cabled Trilling on the 21st. 'End requires vast expanse and water, both impossible with local improvised [studio] facilities.' The ending was shot on 24, 25, 26 (Sunday), 27, 28, and 29 January (pick-ups of Plummer alone).

15 Although the line was not used in the film, critics (cf. *Evening News, Time*) couldn't resist the joke.

16 Five further minutes were cut between August and September. Vincent Canby saw the film at Warners' New York screening-room, and recorded a running time of 98 minutes (*Motion Picture Herald*, 23 August); the definitive version ran for 93 minutes.

17 'That scene was always very important to me' (Ray, *Take One* interview). It had been cut before shooting started. A scene in the Miami prison was eliminated during shooting (memo from Schulberg to Jack L. Warner, 20 November 1957): the following scene (Walt appearing before the judge, and subsequently being hired by Morgan as an Audubon Society warden) was in fact shot. In these three scenes, Walt clashes with the law less in protest than because of his impulsive, even fiery, nature.

18 Another cut: accused by Walt of trading in plumage, Liggett responds by blaming the Nathansons, who – worried about a possible resurgence of the racism they had fled in Europe – ask Walt to withdraw his charge. The two

scenes before the judge were thus reduced to one, and nine scenes that had been shot became six: 1. The Fourth of July picnic (shortened before filming); 2. Love scene under the bandstand (shortened on the instructions of Jack L. Warner); 3. Meeting with Cottonmouth and his son (scene cut); 4. Inauguration of Flagler Street; 5. Walt discovers the plumage being smuggled in a mattress; 6. He denounces Liggett before the judge and the Urban Improvement commissioners (shortened and amalgamated with 8); 7. The Nathansons ask him to withdraw his charge (scene cut); 8. He withdraws the charge and the judge issues a warrant against Cottonmouth, to be delivered by Walt personally (shortened and amalgamated with 6); 9. The furious Morgan proposes to fire Walt (different dialogue dubbed in; Morgan now says, 'I can't urge you to go. But sooner or later I know we've got to stand up and fight the Liggetts and the Cottonmouths to a finish').

19 Claude Ollier, *Fables sous rêves*, Flammarion, Paris, 1985.

20 Only fragments remain of the four songs that should have provided the film's musical core: *Her lily-white hands held the dagger/As she gave him a kiss*; the blues *I Drink Whiskey Like Water; Lostman's River* (the outlaws' song); and the one sung by the drunken Walt. In all, three ballads to guitar accompaniment, two of them specially written and one traditional, and a blues.

21 Roger Tailleur, 'Le Chiffre 13', in *L'Avant-Scène Cinéma*, no. 40, 1 September 1964.

22 In Britain, the film was shorn of 8 minutes, in particular removing the whole drunken celebration of the word 'protest'. That year, an anthology-manifesto of the American Beat Generation and the British Angry Young Men was published under that title (*Protest*, ed. Gene Feldman and Max Gartenberg, Citadel Press, Secaucus, N. J., 1958 / Souvenir Press, London, 1959).

32 Party Girl

Sources

Corey Allen; Betty Schwab (Utey), Los Angeles, 27 November 1980, 11 June 1981.
Joe Pasternak Archives, Special Collections, University of Southern California; N. Ray Archives; T. Ork Dossier.

Notes

1 10 February 1958.

2 cf. 'Rebuilding Chicago of 1930s Big Job for Set Designers', *L.A. Mirror-News*, 2 September 1958, interview with Randall Duell. The cars came from vintage automobile museums and clubs. 'We used the newspaper files of the Leopold-Loeb case as our guide. Newspaper descriptions and several photographs of the trial in progress provided valuable information [. . .] Neon was just beginning to make its appearance in the early 1930s. What neon signs existed were very small because they were very expensive. The popular type of street sign during the time was composed of single electric

lamps arranged in a pattern or in letters and designed to blink on and off.'
The Hollywood Reporter (20 October 1958) noted the accuracy with which
the Cook County courthouse was reproduced.

3 Just before *Party Girl*, Betty Utey had appeared as a dancer in *Tarnished
Angels* and *Silk Stockings*.

4 Document of 6 July 1958: proof of loss, $26,861.

5 Information by courtesy of Jean-Claude Missiaen. cf. the latter's book, *Cyd
Charisse, du ballet classique à la comédie musicale*, Editions Veyrier, Paris,
1978.

6 cf. Louella Intérim, 'Voir Cyd et mourir', *Libération*, 8 September 1982;
Pierre Murat, 'Cyd Charisse, ses robes avaient du talent', *Télérama*, no.
1707, 29 September 1982.

7 Interviewed in 1961, Ray complained mildly about the editing and the
botched music, without specifying that he wasn't on hand to protect his
work (Jean Douchet and Jacques Joly, 'Nouvel entretien avec Nicholas
Ray', *Cahiers du Cinéma*, no. 127, January 1962).

8 Peter von Bagh, 'Nicholas Ray, Rebell', *Chaplin*, no. 126, November 1973.

9 T. Ork Dossier.

10 Tristan Renaud, 'Traquenard', in *Dossiers du Cinéma: Films II*, Casterman,
1972.

11 Fereydoun Hoveyda, 'La réponse de Nicholas Ray', *Cahiers du Cinéma*, no.
107, May 1960.

12 Jean Douchet, 'L'or et la poutre', *Arts*, no. 765, 9 March 1960; Christian
Ledieu, 'Aux grilles d'or de la beauté', *Études Cinématographiques*, no.
8–9, 1961; François Truchaud, *Nicholas Ray*, Editions Universitaires, Paris,
1965, pp. 136–45; Noël Simsolo, 'Nicholas Ray', *la Revue du Cinéma-
Image et Son*, no. 240, June-July, 1970; etc.

33 The Savage Innocents

Sources
Betty Schwab (Utey); Simon Mizrahi, Paris, 29 July 1986, 13 January 1988.
Jacques Giraldeau, 'Nicholas Ray chez les Esquimaux', *Objectif*, no. 2, November 1960; Aldo Tonti, *Odore di cinema*, Vallecchi Editore, Florence, 1964; N.
Ray Archives (script, first draft); T. Ork Dossier; 'The Savage Innocents' in
*Values in Conflict, Print Versions of High Noon, The Hustler, The Savage Inno-
cents*, edited by Richard A. Maynard, Scholastic Literature of the Screen, Scholastic Book Services, New York 1974 (rather inaccurate description of a cut version
of the film).

Notes
1 Letter to Morris Abrams (brother of Jean Evans) and Joe Youngerman of the
Screen Directors' Guild, 13 July 1959.

2 'Italian Film About Eskimos', *The Times*, 6 April 1959.

3 Simon Mizrahi, 'La photo du mois', *Cahiers du Cinéma*, no. 103, January
1960.

4 Jean Vietti and Jacques Guittet, 'Yoko Tani, ravissante Esquimaude,

apprend à fuir la civilisation', *Ciné-Télé-Revue*, September 1959; 'Nanook 1960: Making a Film of Eskimo Life To-day', *The Times*, 5 August 1959.

5   Jean Douchet, 'Nicholas Ray: *les Dents du Diable* sont mon meilleur film', *Arts*, no. 773, 4 May 1960.

6   Vietti and Guittet, *op. cit.*

7   'Nanook, 1960', *The Times, op. cit.*

8   'Traveling Matte Systems', *American Cinematographer*, September 1962. Similar disastrous effects from traveling mattes, doubtless using the sodium light process, can be seen in other American films made in Britain: '*The Sheriff of Fractured Jaw, Satan Never Sleeps*, etc.

9   Jean Douchet, op. cit.

10 'Special mention by the Commission supérieure technique to *Ombre Bianche* (Italy) for the harmonious rendering of colours in the Arctic landscapes, and the definition achieved by the photographic processes and projection.' The film also received a special mention at the Semana de Cine en Color at Barcelona the same year.

11 This pre-credits sequence is missing in some prints, including the one shown on BBC TV in 1991.

12 *Take One* interview.

13 Ray and Bob Dylan met much later, when the latter was living in the East Village, opposite Connie Bessie. The three of them went together to attend a screening of rushes for *The Last Movie*. There wasn't much talk on the way there: 'The pair barely met, just grazed each other,' Connie Bessie said. *The Mighty Quinn* wasn't mentioned, only – briefly – Woody Guthrie. Connie asked Dylan why he admired Guthrie. 'Because he didn't belong to a group, because he was alone.'

34   Two Films in Spain: *King of Kings* and *55 Days at Peking*

Sources
Ben Barzman, Los Angeles, 14 June 1981; Manuel Berenguer, Benidorm, 21 September 1983; Janet Brandt (Mrs Lou Brandt), Los Angeles, 10 April 1983; Alan Brown, Madrid, 24 September 1983; Royal Dano, Santa Monica, 26 June 1982; Bernard Gordon, Los Angeles, 9 April 1983; Guy Green, letter of 30 January 1984; Milton Krasner, Los Angeles, 9 June 1981; Gavin Lambert; Lucie and Renée Lichtig; Viveca Lindfors, New York, 10 November 1980; John Melson, Paris, 19 March 1981; Simon Mizrahi; Betty Schwab (Utey); Tom Weitzner, New York, 18 March 1983; Sumner Williams; Philip Yordan.
Charlton Heston, *The Actor's Life: Journals 1956–1976*, E. P. Dutton, New York, 1978; *Bundy: An Oral History of Andrew Marton*, interviewed by Joanne d'Antonio, Directors' Guild of America, 1980; Collection of *The Star*, Lincoln Center Library of the Performing Arts; Deposits L. and R. Lichtig, N. Ray, Cinémathèque Française; Dimitri Tiomkin Archives, Special Collections, USC; script of *King of Kings* by courtesy of Renée Lichtig; correspondence from Nicholas Ray, by courtesy of Pierre Cottrell; T. Ork Dossier.

Notes

1   *Variety*, 2 December 1959; Ray, letter to Harry Friedman (MCA, London), 17 November 1959; contract of 18 November 1959.

2   Georges Wakhévitch, *L'Envers des décors*, Robert Laffont, Paris, 1977.

3   Philip K. Scheuer, 'Ray Tells Directing of *King of Kings*', *Los Angeles Times*, 21 December 1960. Contract between Security Pictures (Yordan) and Samuel Bronston Productions, 30 November 1959. Planer was in Spain for the film from 3 December or before.

4   Letter from Ray to Bronston, 6 February 1960.

5   Letter to Bronston, 6 February 1960.

6   Alan Brown. cf. also Dick Williams, quoting Robert Ryan, *L.A. Mirror News*, 20 June 1960.

7   'Pope's Direct OK Simplifies King's Coin Problem', *Variety*, 8 March 1960; *The Star*, no. 1, 11 May 1960. Diego Fabbri had written a play, *Processo a Gesù*, on which the script drew for the character of Judas. He worked on *El Cid*. *The Star*, a bulletin devoted exclusively to the *King of Kings* production, ran to four issues (11 May, 18 May, 1 June, 18 June); once the film was taken over by a major, it no longer served any purpose.

8   Letter from Joseph C. Youngerman (Directors' Guild of America) to Lou Brandt, 26 April 1960.

9   The rumour that filming actually began with Mason and Burton is without foundation.

10 Press release of 28 April 1960. Simon Mizrahi, in Noël Simsolo's radio programme, *Metro-Goldwyn-Mayer, la firme au lion*, France Culture, 19 December 1986.

11 'The polyfocal system invented by Franz Planer and Manuel Berenguer consisted of a triple lens placed in front of the normal lens; the lenses are graduated so as to keep each zone of the image in focus' (interview with Berenguer in *Documentos Cinematográficos*, no. 6, November 1960, quoted in *Nicholas Ray y su tiempo*, Filmoteca Española).

12 Ray quoted by Scheuer, *op. cit.* cf. also, '12 Apostles Give Roles Deep Study', *L.A. Mirror-News*, 25 July 1960.

13 Scheuer; letter from Alan Brown to Ray, 14 July 1960; Alan Brown, passim.

14 Press release, 8 June 1960.

15 *Movie* interview.

16 Letter from Bernard Smith to Philip Yordan, 5 August 1960.

17 Jean Douchet and Jacques Joly, 'Nouvel entretien avec Nicholas Ray', *Cahiers du Cinéma*, no. 127, January 1962. This account gave birth to the legend whereby Ray's intention was to film the Sermon on the Mount in a single shot-sequence. Had that been so, what purpose would the five cameras have served, and why would an editor have been on hand? To edit the sequence, Renée Lichtig said, 'I shut myself away. I had thirteen-and-a-half reels of rushes to get down to a reel and a half. I showed it to Nick, and he said just one thing: "Tremendous job." Not much of that survived.' In the completed film, the sequence runs for 14 minutes, the Sermon itself for 11.

18 Press release, 19 August 1960. Before his death in 1963, Planer was to photograph *Breakfast at Tiffany's* (where discreet use of the Planer-Berenguer process may be noted) and *The Children's Hour*.

19 Simon Mizrahi in Noël Simsolo's programme, *op. cit.*

20 Undated telegram from Ray to Bronston. When the accident happened, Guardino was in a car with Simon Mizrahi and the stuntman Art Reese, who was killed.

21 Press release, 11 October; *Variety*, 12 October 1960 (the two accounts differ as to the respective percentages of MGM, Du Pont, Bronston and the banks).

22 Letter from Bronston to Ray, 19 November 1960.

23 Margaret Booth started as a film splicer for D. W. Griffith, and hadn't set foot in a cutting-room since 1937. She was editor-in-chief at MGM from 1939 to 1968. According to Andrew Marton, her verdict on rushes could result in a director being fired or a film remade.

24 Ray managed to have Renée Lichtig credited as editor along with Harold Kress, except on American prints.

25 *Movie* interview.

26 A good deal of the post-synchronization had been done in Hollywood (Sumner Williams did a little in Madrid during the shooting). Ray re-did as much of it as possible with the few actors available. Viveca Lindfors described his mood as very different from what it had been during shooting.

27 Letter from Ray to Bronston, 8 April 1961.

28 This was what Charles Wagner, a friend of Ray's from the 1930s, was told when he happened to be in Hollywood and asked for him at the studio (Charles Wagner, 8 April 1981).

29 Letters from Ralph Wheelwright and Stanley E. Goldsmith, MGM, to Bronston, 7 March 1961. The film then comprised twenty-one reels. Welles 'asked for credit equal to that of Jeffrey Hunter or no credit at all, which made it very easy for the executives of Metro-Goldwyn-Mayer.' This explanation comes from Ray (*Movie*); it is the only one extant explaining the absence of Welles's name from the credits.

Ray evidently did not on this occasion meet Welles, whom he held in very high esteem. The admiration he expressed to Peter Noble in 1955 was no commonplace in those days, when the exiled Welles was held in almost unanimous contempt by his compatriots. 'A great director, perhaps one of the greatest in the whole history of the cinema. We beginners can never be grateful enough to him for having explored so many new avenues' (Peter Noble, *The Fabulous Orson Welles*, Hutchinson, London, 1956).

30 Letter from Ray to Bernard Smith, 4 May 1961; letter from Cecil R. Foster Kemp to Ray, 5 May 1961.

31 Jacques Rivette, 'De l'invention', *Cahiers du Cinéma*, no. 27, October 1953.

32 *In a Lonely Place, The Lusty Men, Johnny Guitar, Run for Cover, Rebel Without a Cause, Hot Blood, Bigger Than Life, The True Story of Jesse James, Bitter Victory, Wind Across the Everglades* and *Party Girl*. Despite a sizeable number of dubbed versions, people were able to catch up with the whole second stage of his career (*The Savage Innocents* had just been released). On 26 November Ray gave a Celebrity Lecture at the National Film Theatre in London, which was followed by a retrospective of ten films, coinciding with the British première of *King of Kings*. Ray gave long interviews to *Cahiers du Cinéma*, to Adriano Aprà (*Filmcritica*), to José Luis

Guarner and his colleagues on *Film Ideal*, and to the new British magazine *Movie*.

33 'Entretien avec William Peter McGivern', *Hard-Boiled Dicks* (Paris), No. 5, February 1983.

34 Charlton Heston, *op. cit.* (20–21 April 1961 entry).

35 Letter to Bernard Smith, 4 May 1961; to Bronston, 9 September 1961.

36 Letter to Stanley Goldsmith, 18 September 1961.

37 Letter to Bronston, 20 December 1961 (misdated 20 November by Ray).

38 When the film was announced, Jerry Wald claimed that in 1957 he had discussed his project about the Boxer Rebellion, *Hell Raisers*, with Yordan, and protested against the 'plagiarism' ('Jerry Wald Raises Hell', *Daily Variety*, 14 September 1961). Samuel Fuller later recalled that Harry Cohn and Jerry Wald had shown him a project 'about the siege of Peking in the Quirt and Flagg manner [the brawling military rivals of *What Price Glory*], in other words, the dumbest idea kicked around in fifty years. "Who's going to play the Dowager Empress?" I asked. "Er . . . who do you see?" I suggested Flora Robson or Wendy Hiller, aged up: "The best thing would be a Chinese woman, but you won't have the balls." ' (Fuller, on the set of *White Dog*.) Bernard Gordon, finally, said he had talked to Yordan about a play dealing with the Siege of Peking which he had read at Paramount. 'Yordan came back a few weeks later and said that his wife had seen a book on the shelves in London about the 55 days at Peking, and that it was his idea!'

39 *Take One* interview.

40 Luis Buñuel, in Jean-Claude Carrière's film, *Petite Confession*.

41 Manuel Mampaso, in *Nicholas Ray y su tiempo*, Filmoteca Española, pp. 215–16; sixteen of his sketches are reproduced.

42 Ray, of course, had wanted to use split screen from the time of *Rebel Without a Cause*. Three split-screen methods were considered: directly in the camera, using the original negative with foreground mattes; a system of supplementary lenses suggested by Berenguer, which also permitted use of the original negative; and in the laboratory, which required the use of a dupe negative. It was this last method, in which Linwood Dunn was one of the great specialists, that was chosen.

43 In the script, the two lines are respectively dated 11 July and 22 May.

44 Maxwell-Ray went on to say: 'China is a giant factory with no machinery. We're willing to supply the machines. But if she wants to burn the factory down, that's her privilege.' The scene was shot on 7 August, but these lines were cut during editing. Ray quoted them exactly a year later (to Juan Cobos, 'Nueva entrevista con Nicholas Ray', *Film Ideal* no. 136, 15 January 1964).

45 Letter from Ray to Abe Glazer (Bronston Productions), 15 October 1962; Charlton Heston, *op. cit.*; Yordan.

46 On 14 September *Daily Variety* announced a gastrointestinal attack. In the *Sunday Express* of 30 September Roderick Mann, in Spain at the invitation of the Bronston organization, confirmed the heart attack.

47 *Valley of the Fallen* (1963), written by Jim Bishop, directed by Andrew Marton, photographed by Jack Hildyard.

48 Juan Cobos, *op. cit.*; letter from Ray to Waszynski, 18 December. Although

Ray stated that he didn't shoot it, this scene with the national anthems is among the clips used in the film devoted to him, *I'm a Stranger Here Myself.*

49 The close-up of Paul Lukas was shot on 10 October. Ben Barzman was involved in this task of pruning the Gardner scenes.

50 Letter from Ray to Leon Patlach.

51 Trevor Philpott, *Sunday Times Mazagine*, 21 April 1963. Philip Yordan is quoted as saying: 'After all, we ain't playing games. We ain't struggling to be artists, not any one of us. We're making pictures that go up all the way to 11 million dollars, we've got to satisfy the distributors and they're business people. We have to satisfy the public and the public's an animal.'

52 Letter to Waszynski, 18 December 1962.

Marton claimed to have directed 64 per cent of the completed film. A breakdown, checking Lucie Lichtig's continuity notes against a video recording of the film, yielded (after correction for projection speeds) more likely, though still approximate, proportions: 62 minutes directed by Ray, 65 by Marton (as second unit director and director), less than 3 minutes by Guy Green, the rest (about 10 minutes) by Noel Howard.

53 Frank Capra, *The Name Above the Title*, Macmillan Company, New York, 1971, pp. 489–90.

54 On 17 July 1964, the bankrupt Bronston told *The Hollywood Reporter* that *55 Days at Peking* had beaten all records in guarantees, taking in $7.2 million in a little over a year, against a production cost of $9 million.

35   In-Between Time

Sources
Hanna Axmann; Jean-Pierre Bastid, Paris, 8 June 1988; Andrés Berenguer, Madrid, 24 September, 1983; Howard Berk, Los Angeles, 11 April 1983; Harry Bromley-Davenport, London, 20 December 1983; Alan Brown; Dr Barrington Cooper, London, 1 December 1985; Tony Kent, Santa Monica, 27 March 1986; Bert Kleiner, Los Angeles, 29 March 1986; Renée and Lucie Lichtig; John Melson; Vladimir Novotny, letter of 21 October 1986 (translated by Ivo Palec); Tim Ray, Los Angeles, April 1983; Volker Schlöndorff, Paris, August 1981; Barbet Schroeder, Paris, 11 December 1980; Betty Schwab (Utey); Stéphane Tchalgadjieff, Paris, 10 September 1981; Ethel Tyne, California, 12 April 1983; Gore Vidal (interviewed by Robert Louit), Paris, 1985; Tom Weitzner; Sumner Williams.

Script of *Only Lovers Left Alive*, by courtesy of the Cinémathèque Royale de Belgique; script of *Inbetween Time* by courtesy of Stéphane Tchalgadjieff; N. Ray Archives; N. Ray correspondence; T. Ork Dossier.

Notes
1 Letters from Alan Brown to Ray, 26 December 1962 and 21 January 1963 (Nicholas Phipps was hired subsequent to the second letter).

2 6 May 1963.

3 J. F. Aranda, 'Nicholas Ray habla de España', *Arte Fotografico*, n.d., 1964 by courtesy of the San Sebastian Festival.

4 *Ita*, Rome, no. 7–8, 15 August 1963.

5 Michel Kelber, 26 November 1981.

6 *Baza Ludzi Umarłych* (The Base of Dead Men), a Polish film of 1959, was in fact an adaptation of the novel *Next Stop Paradise*, although Hłasko was not credited (perhaps because he had already emigrated). It was written and directed by Czesław Petelski, and produced by the Ensemble Studio (information by courtesy of Philippe Haudiquet).

7 J. F. Aranda, *op. cit.*

8 Frank McShane, *Into Eternity, the Life of James Jones, American Writer*, Houghton-Mifflin, Boston, 1985.

9 Philip K. Scheuer, 'Ibsen's *Sea Lady* New Ray Prospect', *Los Angeles Times*, 28 July 1964.

10 Marie-Gisèle Landes, 'Nicholas Ray à Paris cherche des cadavres', *Arts*, no. 999, 31 March 1965. Marie-Gisèle Landes covered the preparation period, accompanying Ray to Yugoslavia.

11 Rui Nogueira, 'James Mason Talks About His Career in the Cinema', *Focus on Film*, no. 2, March-April 1970.

12 'Nicholas Ray v Praže', *Kino*, no. 10, 20 May 1965.

13 'Nicholas Ray's $14,000,000 Film Agenda', *Variety*, 4 August 1965.

14 Rui Nogueira and Nicoletta Zalaffi, 'Encontro com Nicholas Ray', *O Tempo e o modo*, no. 62–63, July-August, 1968, reprinted in *Nicholas Ray*, Cinemateca Portuguesa, Lisbon, 1985. Contrary to what various biographies suggest, *The Doctor and the Devils* was not taken over, after Ray's departure, by an Italian director named Baldi (whether Gian Vittorio, Ferdinando or Marcello).

15 Warner Brothers Archive of Historical Papers, Princeton University. This correspondence (about 20 pages) was not currently accessible.

16 Letter of 14 November 1965, by courtesy of Vladimir Novotny. Ray gave as his address: Milutina Bojica 4, Belgrade. Letter from Jud Kinberg to Novotny, September 2 1969 (by courtesy of Vladimir Novotny).

17 Renée and Lucie Lichtig, Volker Schlöndorff, Janet Brandt (widow of Lou Brandt, production manager on *King of Kings* and *The Doctor and the Devils*).

18 Letter to Jo Youngerman, Directors' Guild of America, 3 April 1967. Sheilah Graham, 'Susannah York May Sue Nick Ray', *New York Post*, 6 January 1967.

19 cf., for example, Jean-Marie Straub in *Cahiers du Cinéma*, no. 185, Christmas 1965.

20 After its screening at Cannes, running 233 minutes, Wajda himself seems to have prepared a shorter version (169 minutes) of his film in Hamburg. cf. *Andrzej Wajda*, Reihe Film, no. 23, Carl Hanser Verlag, Munich-Vienna, 1980.

21 Charles Bitsch, 13 January 1986.

22 According to Jean-Pierre Sarrazac, Jean Douchet, etc.

23 cf. synopsis of *Wha-a-at?* and interview with Jean-Pierre Bastid and Henry Lange by Joëlle Naïm in *Nicholas Ray y su tiempo*, Filmoteca Española, Madrid, 1986.

24 James Jones, *The Merry Month of May*, William Collins Sons and Co., London, 1971.

25 *Hollywood Reporter*, 19 August 1966; Allen Eyles, ed., *Nicholas Ray – Writer, Director*, National Film Theatre, London, 1969 (brochure published on the occasion of a John Player Lecture by Ray, 19 January 1969).
26 The director of photography, as for *One Plus One*, was Tony Richmond.
27 Quoted by Tom Stempel, 'George Byron Who?', *Sight and Sound*, Summer, 1965.
28 The money raised by Stéphan Tchalgadjieff was eventually used to produce Jacques Rivette's *Out 1* (1971).
29 Ellen Ray, New York, 24 November, 1987.
30 It is impossible to list all the projects and proposals from these European years. Myron Meisel, visiting Ray in 1973, noted a whole shelf full of unrealized scripts (three adaptations from Victor Hugo alone, including his *Toilers of the Sea*!). This activity was not limited to his own films: as he had done earlier with Andrés Berenguer, Ray helped his friend Tony Kent, the photographer, to write a script in which he was to appear as himself. He also wrote the text for the voice-off in Barbet Schroeder's *More* (1969).

To the projects mentioned in this chapter, however, one might add: – an updated version of *La Bohème*, written with Ethel Tyne (*c.* 1963); – a script commissioned from David Mercer, who had just attracted attention with his television play *A Suitable Case for Treatment* (August 1963); – *Before Dawn*, a Western with Anthony Quinn, about a young boy in love with an older woman (announced in March 1965); – *The Chinese Executioner*, an adaptation of Pierre Boulle's first novel, written by Ray and John McNab, and submitted to Warner Brothers (before June 1967); – an adaptation of Selma Lagerlöf's *The Saga of Gösta Berling*, on which he worked with Maurice Pons (Christmas 1966); – *Girl of the Dunes*, written with his son Tim on Sylt.

He was approached to direct various films: an episode for *Histoires extraordinaires* (around 1967; eventually directed by Roger Vadim, Louis Malle, and Federico Fellini); *Le Désert des Tartares* (around 1968, producer Jacques Perrin, directed by Valerio Zurlini in 1976); *The Light at the Edge of the World* (same period, producers Alexandre Salkind and Claude Jaeger, directed by Kevin Billington in 1971).

As for the plan to film a life of Rimbaud, frequently attributed to him by French sources, this was probably more a reflection of the image Europeans had of Ray than an 'old project and long-cherished wish'.

36 Chicago

Sources
Connie Bessie; Perry Bruskin; Stuart Byron, New York, 29 June 1981; Mike Gray, Paris, 15 September 1971; Abbie Hoffman, New York, 18 April 1986; Dennis Hopper; Alan Lomax; Myron Meisel, Los Angeles, 9 June 1981; Marcel Ophuls, Billancourt, 20 January 1988; Ellen Ray, New York, 24 November 1987; Susan Schwartz Ray, New York, 15 November 1980, 14 June 1982, 28 March 1983; Studs Terkel, Chicago, 11 June 1981; David Turecamo, New York, 25 June 1981. N. Ray Archives; Vincent Canby, 'A Fine Director, Unemployed', *New York*

Times, 8 June 1969; correspondence and notes by courtesy of Stuart Byron; Susan Ray Deposit, Cinémathèque Française; Jason Epstein, *The Great Conspiracy Trial*, Random House, New York, 1970; script for *New York After Midnight* by courtesy of Wim Wenders.

Notes
1 'Director, 58, Returns to U.S. to Film '60s Young Rebels', *The Sunday Star*, Washington, 23 November 1969.
2 *New York Times*, 22 June 1969.
3 Roger Ebert, 'Nick Ray Promises a Movie on "Chicago Seven" ', *Los Angeles Times*, 8 March 1970.
4 The cameraman William Yale Wilson said he shot 60,000 feet of film on 16mm, plus studio tests (in 35mm) and a little Super-8 (letter from Jonathan Rosenbaum, 17 May 1989). Todd McCarthy, in his Ray obituary for *Variety*, mentioned a grant from the Swedish Film Institute.
5 *Take One* interview.
6 Myron Meisel, 'Portrait of the Artist Buried in Film', *L. A. Reader*, 16 November 1979.
7 This was characteristic of what was being filmed towards the end of the trial: Bill Kunstler at George Williams College, Rubin at the Highland Park girls' school, Rennie Davis and Abbie Hoffman in Baltimore, lunches, taxi rides, plane trips . . .
8 Richard L. Bock, Los Angeles, 25 June 1982.
9 cf. also Terry Curtis Fox, 'Nicholas Ray, Without a Cause', *Village Voice*, no. 24, 9 July 1979.
10 Sam Shepard, Santa Fé, 15 April 1984.
11 Susan Ray returned to this in a letter of 22 October 1988: 'Re: Nick "losing it" during *We Can't Go Home Again*. Yes, he probably did, but not in a sudden snap. There was a dramatic change in him during his stay in Taos, most likely attributable to the illegalization and unavailability at that time of metamphetamine. Although he found other sources of crystalline speed during his time at Harpur, I believe the drugs and booze had by then taken an irreparable toll.'
12 Ken Jacobs (born 1933); *Blonde Cobra* (1959–63), *Tom, Tom, the Piper's Son* (1969). Larry Gottheim: *Horizons* (1971–3).
13 Tom Farrell, 'We Can't Go Home Again', *Sight and Sound*, vol. 50, no. 2, Spring 1981.

37   We Can't Go Home Again

Sources
Richard L. Bock, Los Angeles, 25 June 1982; Charles and Judy Bornstein, Los Angeles, 15 June 1981; Tom Farrell, New York, 21 March 1983; James C. Gutman, New York, 24 March 1983; Leslie Levinson, New York, 13 November 1980; Susan Ray.
N. Ray Archives; Susan Ray Deposit, Cinémathèque Française; Tom Farrell, 'We Can't Go Home Again', *Sight and Sound*, vol. 50, no. 2, Spring 1981; Working

notes, by courtesy of Tom Farrell; Jeff Greenberg, 'Nicholas Ray Today', *Filmmakers Newsletter*, vol. 6, no. 3, January 1973; Ray lecture at the American Film Institute, 26 April 1973; Directors' Guild of America, Ray Dossier.

Notes
1 Vincent Canby, 'Nicholas Ray: Still a Rebel With a Cause', *New York Times*, 24 September 1972.
2 In Bergson's *Essay on Laughter* (1900), Ray found (as he told Peter von Bagh), 'unity of comedy and tragedy'. To these two texts, Ray sometimes added Theodor Reik's *Listening With the Third Ear* (Grove Press, New York, 1948). In this book, subtitled *The inner experience of a psychoanalyst*, Reik – a friend of Freud's who emigrated to America – set out to widen the field of investigation for psychoanalysis, through a method whose parallels with Ray's approach are interesting; the first two sections of the book are entitled 'I'm a stranger here myself' and 'The Workshop'.
3 *La Pyramide humaine* (1961): Rouch's film was a sort of ethnological psycho-drama. He took a group of sixth-form students from a school in Abidjan – black and white, who never mixed socially – had them play an integrated group of friends in a fictional story, and filmed what happened as they improvised to meet given situations.
4 Frank Lloyd Wright, *The Future of Architecture*, Horizon Press, New York, 1953.
5 During the filming of *Lightning Over Water*, 2 April 1979.
6 Betty Jeffries Demby, 'Highlights From Cannes', *Filmmakers Newsletter*, November 1973.
7 Dennis Hopper, 28 March 1986. An episode in *The Last Movie* is not without its parallels to this story.
8 Robert Lowe, 'Cinema Department – Rebels With a Cause', *Pipe Dream* (Binghamton), 25 April 1972.
9 Myron Meisel, 'Portrait of the Artist Buried in Film', *L. A. Reader*, 16 November 1979.
10 Mary Meerson, Lucie and José Lichtig, André Rieupeyrout, Pierre Cottrell, Jonathan Rosenbaum, Bernard Eisenschitz, etc.
11 Claude Fléouter, 'Nicholas Ray et les étudiants', *Le Monde*, 26 May 1973.
12 Wim Wenders, 2 April 1979.
13 Rotterdam Film Festival, January 1980; Action-République, Paris, February 21–6, 1980; Action-Christine, Paris, December 1984; Cinemateca Portuguesa, Lisbon, 10 and 31 July 1985; National Film Theatre, London, 30 August, 1986, etc.

38 The Janitor

Sources
Richard L. Bock; Charles and Judy Bornstein; Harry Bromley-Davenport; Peter Buchanan (interviewed by Pierre Cottrell), San Francisco, 24 February 1984; Pierre Cottrell, 29 September 1983; Tom Farrell; Max Fischer, Montreal, 31 August 1988; Leslie Levinson; Sheri Nelson McLean, Paris, 27 September 1987,

letter of 14 September 1988; Susan Ray; Betty Schwab (Utey); David Turecamo; Peter von Bagh; Philip Yordan.

Script for *City Blues*, by courtesy of David Turecamo.

Notes

1   Susan Ray; notes on the budget for *We Can't Go Home Again* (Truffaut $2,000; Françoise Sagan $5,000; Cinémathèque Française $3,500).

2   Sheri Nelson McLean.

3   Sensurround, a sound system developed at this time (*Earthquake*, 1974) involved high-frequency sound and modulation control to provoke a sensation of vibration in cinema seats.

4   The most complete description of *The Janitor* was given during the West Berlin court proceedings, 28 August 1975; quoted by Karlheinz Oplustil in Norbert Grob, Manuela Reichart, eds, *Nicholas Ray*, Edition Filme im Wissenschaftsverlag Volker Spiess, West Berlin, 1989. In France, Italy and Britain, too, *Wet Dreams* (in toto) ran into trouble with the censors.

5   *Nicholas Ray*, Cinemateca Portuguesa, Lisbon, 1985, p. 161.

6   'Nick Ray's Mishap, Limps to Workshop', *Variety*, 6 February 1974.

7   About the interrupted screening: Connie Bessie; Bill Krohn, 'Rencontre avec Nicholas Ray', *Cahiers du Cinéma*, no. 288, May 1978. Fabiano Canosa, who met Ray on the occasion of this screening, accompanied him to the Brazilian consulate to discuss the possibility of adapting a novel by Machado de Assis, *Epitaph for a Small Man*.

8   Jay Cocks, 'Director in Aspic', *Take One*, vol. 5, no. 6, January 1977.

9   Tom Luddy, quoted by Jonathan Rosenbaum, 'Looking for Nicholas Ray', *American Film*, vol. vii, no. 3, December 1981.

10 In his notes, Ray mentions two figures: $15,000 and $18,000.

11 F and B/Ceco Center, possibly the Warner studios at Burbank.

12 Patrick Bensard, 'Entretien avec Susan Ray', *Caméra/Stylo*, no. 1, January 1981.

13 Addison Verrill, 'Nick Ray's Back; Lead Is Porno Queen', *Variety*, 21 April, 1976; 'Ray Cites Need for Instruction in Scientific Films', *Hollywood Reporter*, 2 July 1976; 'Tax Shelter Wobbles Delays Filming of Nick Ray's City Blues', *Variety*, 4 August 1976; 'Nick Ray *Blues*', *Variety*, 11 August, 1976; 'Latest Flash' and 'Marilyn's Story', *Take One*, January 1977.

14 Fred Mogubgub had made a number of short films, including the animated *Enter Hamlet* (1965), and *The Great Society* (1967).

15 According to Roger Donoghue, Mailer's contribution was minimal. The title-page of the script (last version) reads: *City Blues* by William Maidment, Additional scenes and dialogue by Nicholas Ray and Norman Mailer.' Marilyn Chambers proved she was the actress Ray trusted her to be in *Rabid* (directed by David Cronenberg, Canada, 1976).

16 V. F. Perkins, 'The Cinema of Nicholas Ray', *Movie*, no. 9, May 1963. It was Perkins who inscribed his book *Film as Film: Understanding and Judging Movies* (Penguin, London, 1972) to Ray with the words, 'To Nick, who will never really know how much we owe him'.

39   The Teacher

Sources
Gerry Bamman, New York, 7 April 1986; Pierre Cottrell, Paris; Dan Edelman, New York, 30 June 1981; Milos Forman, Paris, 30 October 1984; Samuel Fuller, on the set of *White Dog*, 9 June 1981; Robert Herman, New York, 21 June 1982; Jim Jarmusch, Paris, 4 August, 1982; Robert La Cativa, New York, 24 June 1981; Claudio Mazzatenta, New York, 29 June 1981; Susan Ray; Wim Wenders, New York, 25 March 1983.
N. Ray Archives; Claudio Mazzatenta, 'Un allievo descrive il suo metodo', *L'Ora* (Palermo), 15 September 1979; notes by courtesy of Robert La Cativa and Tom Farrell.

Notes
1   Manuscript notes, N. Ray Archives.
2   In 1988, Susan Ray commented: 'I don't now believe, if ever I truly did, that Nick lied merely for the pleasure of deceiving people. He did lie, and he did derive some pleasure from lying, although he didn't often lie well. Lying for him was pragmatic, a way toward the functioning and realization of his imaginations.'
3   The first audio tape relating to the workshop at the Strasberg Institute is dated 30 March 1977.
4   Nicolai Gorchakov, *The Vakhtangov School of Stage Art*, Foreign Language Publishing House, Moscow, n.d.
5   The summer school ran from 13 June to 22 July (Ray was absent for four days in July, invited to San Francisco by the Pacific Film Archive). Ray's elder daughter, Julie, attended.
6   'Nick Ray Awaits', *Variety*, 20 August 1977; 'Nick Ray to Direct', *Variety*, 31 August 1977.
7   The beginning of *Mister Mister*, with introduction by Wim Wenders, was published in *Cahiers du Cinéma*, no. 400, October 1987.
8   William G. Borchert was sole credited author of the script that was finally produced in 1989, as *My Name Is Bill W.*, by Warner Bros. Television, produced and directed by Daniel Petrie, with James Woods, JoBeth Williams and James Garner.
9   Stig Björkman, 'I'm a Stranger Here Myself', *Chaplin*, no. 165, December 1979.
10 David Thomson, 'In a Lonely Place', *Sight and Sound*, vol. 48, no. 4, Autumn 1979.
11 Laslo Benedek, quoted by Jonathan Rosenbaum, 'Looking for Nicholas Ray', *American Film*, vol. vii, no. 3, December 1981.

40   Lightning Over Water

Sources
Gerry Bamman; Pierre Cottrell; Tom Farrell; Jim Jarmusch; Elia Kazan; Susan Ray; Tim Ray; Wim Wenders.

Wim Wenders and Chris Sievernich, *Nick's Film/Lightning Over Water*, Zweitausendeins, Frankfurt, 1981 (in German and English); Tom Farrell, 'Journal of a Film', manuscript, available only in French: 'Journal d'un tournage', *Cahiers du Cinéma*, no. 318, December 1980; Jon Jost, 'Wrong Move', *Sight and Sound*, vol. 50, no. 2, Spring 1981; Videotape recording of Nicholas Ray's presentation, Museum of Modern Art, New York, by courtesy of Chris and Lilyan Sievernich, Gray City, Inc., New York.

Notes
1   The money was lent by the documentarists Albert and David Maysles; the journalist and scriptwriter Laurie Frank; Jonathan Becker, Janus Films. Pascale Dauman (Pari Films) contributed to the financing with a prepayment for French distribution.
2   Since his first commercial feature, *Die Angst des Tormanns beim Elfmeter (The Goalkeeper's Fear of the Penalty)*, Wenders had worked with the same crew (*Hammett* was to be the first exception): Robby Müller, assisted by Martin Schäfer, on camera; Martin Müller, sound; Peter Przygodda, editor. Pierre Cottrell, Ed Lachman and Maryte Kavaliauskas had worked on the New York sequences of *The American Friend*. Chris Sievernich here began an association with Wenders that was to continue until 1987.
3   cf. also Jochen Brunow, 'Wenders in den Städten – Verhältnisse in Amerika', *Tip*, no. 2, 7 September 1979.
4   Patrick Bensard, 'Entretien avec Susan Ray', *Caméra/Stylo*, no. 1, January 1981.
5   A few years later, Kazan gave a slightly different account of this visit in his autobiography, *A Life*, Alfred A. Knopf, New York, 1988.
6   On this question, cf. Serge Daney, 'Wim's Movie', *Cahiers du Cinéma*, no. 318, December 1980 (reprinted in Serge Daney, *La Rampe*, Cahiers du Cinéma-Gallimard, Paris, 1983); Bernardo Bertolucci, preface to Wenders and Sievernich, *op. cit.*; Timothy Corrigan, 'Cinematic Snuff: German Friends and Narrative Murders', *Cinema Journal* 24, no. 2, Winter 1984–5; James Naremore, 'Film and the Performance Frame', *Film Quarterly*, vol. xxxviii, no. 2, Winter 1984–5.

41   Trauerarbeit

Sources
Pierre Cottrell; Jim Jarmusch; Susan Ray; Wim Wenders.
Wim Wenders and Chris Sievernich, *Nicks Film/Lightning Over Water*, Zweitausendeins, Frankfurt, 1981; recording of Memorial Service, by courtesy of Chris and Lilyan Sievernich, Gray City, Inc., New York.

Notes
1   Louis Skorecki, 'Introduction à Jarmusch', *Libération*, 2 May 1984.
2   Terry Curtis Fox, 'Nicholas Ray, Without a Cause', *Village Voice*, no. 24, 9 July 1979.

Filmography

Titles are listed chronologically as Ray worked on them. The date given at the start of each entry is the release date, or the date of completion if release was delayed.

1   *Films directed by Ray, and those to which he contributed as writer, director or on the production side*

1945   A Tree Grows in Brooklyn

20th Century-Fox. Director: Elia Kazan. Screenplay: Tess Slesinger, Frank Davis (with contributions by Anita Loos). From the novel *A Tree Grows in Brooklyn* by Betty Smith. Director of photography: Leon Shamroy. Music: Alfred Newman. Art director: Lyle R. Wheeler. Set decorator: Thomas Little. Editor: Dorothy Spencer. Special effects: Fred Sersen. Costumes: Bonnie Cassin. *Second assistant director*: Nicholas Ray. Producer: Louis D. Lighton.

Cast: Dorothy McGuire, Joan Blondell, James Dunn, Lloyd Nolan, Peggy Ann Garner, Ted Donaldson, James Gleason, Ruth Nelson, John Alexander, J. Farrell McDonald, B. S. Pully, Charles Halton, Art Smith, Ferike Bozos, Lillian Bronson, Peter Cusanelli, Adeline de Walt Reynolds, George Melford, Mae Marsh, Edna Jackson, Vincent Graeff, Susan Lester, Johnnie Barnes, Alec Craig, Al Bridge, Joseph J. Greene, Virginia Brissac, Harry Harvey Jr, Robert Andersen, Erskine Sanford, Martha Wentworth, Francis Pierlot.

Start of filming: April 1944. Release: February 1945. Running time: 128 min.

1945   Caribbean Mystery

20th Century-Fox. Director: Robert D. Webb. Screenplay: Jack Andrews, Leonard Praskins (*dialogue revisions* by Nicholas Ray). Adaptation by W. Scott Darling, from the novel *Murder in Trinidad* by John Vandercook. Director of photography: Clyde De Vinna. Editor: John McCafferty. Assistant director: Eli Dunn. *Dialogue director*: Nicholas Ray. Producer: William Girard.

Cast: James Dunn, Sheila Ryan, Edward Ryan, Jackie Paley, Reed Hadley, Roy Roberts, Richard Shaw, Daral Hudson, William Forrest, Roy Gordon, Virginia Walker, Lal Chand Mehra, Katherine Connors, Robert Filmer, Lucien Littlefield, Selmer Jackson, Eddie Borden, Charles Miller.

Start of filming: 17 January 1945. Release: June 1945. Running time: 65 min.

1945   Tuesday in November

Office of War Information Overseas Branch. *The American Scene* series no.
13. Director (staged scenes): John Berry. Screenplay: Howard Koch, for The
Hollywood Mobilization. Animation: United Films, Inc. (John Hubley). Director
of photography (staged scenes): Ernest Laszlo. Editor: Harvey Johnston. Music:
Virgil Thomson. Musical director: Irving Talbot. Commentary spoken by: Gene
Kern. Production manager: Irving Lerner. *Associate producer*: Nicholas Ray.
Producer: John Houseman.
  Running time: 18 min.

1946   Swing Parade of 1946

Monogram. Director: Phil Karlson. Screenplay: Tim Ryan. From an original
story by Edmund Kelso (*in collaboration with* Nicholas Ray). Choreography:
Jack Boyle. Producers: Lindley Parsons, Harry A. Romm.
  Cast: Gale Storm, Connee Boswell, The Three Stooges, Ed Brophy, Russell
Hicks, John Eldredge.
  Release: 28 January 1946. Running time: 74 min.

1948   They Live by Night

RKO Radio. *Director*: Nicholas Ray. Screenplay: Charles Schnee. *Adaptation by*
Nicholas Ray, from the novel *Thieves Like Us* by Edward Anderson. Director
of photography: George E. Diskant. Camera operator: Edward Bergholz. Art
directors: Albert S. D'Agostino, Al Herman. Set decorators: Darrell Silvera, Maurice Yates. Special effects: Russell A. Cully. Editor: Sherman Todd, assisted by
Gene Palmer. Assistant director: James Lane. Costumes: Adele Balkan. Conti-
nuity: Mercy Weireter. Make-up: Gordon Bau. Sound: John Cass, Clem Port-
man. Music: Leigh Harline. Musical director: C. Bakaleinikoff. Song: 'Your Red
Wagon' (Don Raye, Gene De Paul). Producer: John Houseman.
  Cast: Cathy O'Donnell (Keechie), Farley Granger (Bowie), Howard Da Silva
(Chickamaw), Jay C. Flippen (T-Dub), Helen Craig (Mattie), Will Wright
(Mobley), Marie Bryant (Singer), Ian Wolfe (Hawkins), William Phipps (Young
Farmer), Harry Harvey (Hagenheimer), Will Lee (Jeweller), Jim Nolan (Schrei-
ber), Charles Meredith (Commissioner Hubbell), Frank Marlowe (Mattie's Hus-
band), Teddy Infuhr (Alvin), Byron Foulger (Lambert), Guy L. Beach (Plumber),
Curt Conway (Man in Tuxedo), Regan Callais (Young Wife), J. Louis Johnson
(Porter), Myra Marsh (Mrs Schaeffer), Tom Kennedy (Cop-Bumper Gag), Stan-
ley Prager (Short Order Man), Suzi Crandall (Lula), Fred Graham (Motorcycle
Cop), Lewis Charles (Parking Lot Attendant), Dan Fister (Groom), Marilyn
Mercer (Bride), Jimmy Dobson (Boy at Parking Lot), Lynn Whitney (Waitress),
N. L. Hitch (Bus Driver), Carmen Morales (Mother), Ralph Dunn (Policeman),
Paul Bakanas and Mickey Simpson (Shadows), Boyd Davis (Herman), Kate
Lawson (Tillie), Gail Davis (Girl at Parking Lot), Chester Jones (Waiter in Night-
club), Douglas Williams (Drunk), Helen Crozier (Nurse), Jimmy Moss (Boy),

Eula Guy (Mrs Haviland), Russ Whitman and Jane Allen (People). [In deleted scenes: Erskine Sanford (Doctor), Frank Ferguson (Bum)]

Start of filming: 23 June 1947. Release: Spring 1949 (London). Running time: 96 min.

1949   A Woman's Secret

RKO Radio. A Dore Schary Presentation. *Director*: Nicholas Ray. Screenplay: Herman J. Mankiewicz. From the novel *Mortgage on Life* by Vicki Baum. Director of photography: George E. Diskant (additional scene: Harry J. Wild). Camera operator: Charles Burke. Art directors: Albert S. D'Agostino, Clark Burke. Set decorators: Darrell Silvera, Harley Miller. Special effects: Russell A. Cully. Editor: Sherman Todd. Assistant director: Doran Cox. Gowns: Edward Stevenson. Continuity: Mercy Weireter. Make-up: Gordon Bau. Sound: Frank Sarver, Clem Portman (additional scene: Earl Wolcott). Music: Frederick Hollander. Musical director: C. Bakaleinikoff. Producer: Herman J. Mankiewicz.

Cast: Maureen O'Hara (Marian Washburn), Melvyn Douglas (Luke Jordan), Gloria Grahame (Susan Caldwell), Bill Williams (Lee), Victor Jory (Brook Matthews), Mary Philips (Mrs Fowler), Jay C. Flippen (Fowler), Robert Warwick (Roberts), Curt Conway (Doctor), Ann Shoemaker (Mrs Matthews), Virginia Farmer (Mollie), Ellen Corby (Nurse), Emory Parnell (Desk Sergeant), Dan Foster (Stage Manager), Alphonse Martel (Waiter), Charles Wagenheim (Piano Player), Marcelle De La Brosse (Baker), Lynne Whitney (Actress), Rory Mallinson (Benson), George Douglas (Policeman), Raymond Bond (Dr Ferris), Bill Purington (Intern), Guy L. Beach (Policeman), Bernice Young (Nurse), Loreli Vitek (Waitress), Lee Phelps (Policeman), John Laing (Radio Announcer), Bert Davidson (Radio Director), Alvin Hammer (Fred), Frank Marlowe (Whitey), Mickey Simpson (Policeman), Ralph Montgomery (Photographer), Tom Coleman (Policeman), John Goldsworthy (Harold), Frederick Nay (Master of Ceremonies), Forbes Murray (Mr Emory), Donna Gibson (Girl), Evelyn Underwood (Girl), Eddie Borden (Waiter), John Parrish (Professor Camelli), Oliver Blake (Mr Pierson), Paul Guilfoyle (Moderator), Norman Nesbitt and Jack Rourke (Announcers), Conrad Binyon (Messenger Boy), Ralph Stein (Mr Harris), Robert Malcolm (Bit).

Start of filming: 16 February 1948. Release: 5 March 1949. Running time: 84 min.

1949   Knock on Any Door

Columbia Pictures. A Santana Production. *Director*: Nicholas Ray. Screenplay: Daniel Taradash, John Monks Jr. From the novel *Knock on Any Door* by Willard Motley, Director of photography: Burnett Guffey. Art Director: Robert Peterson. Set decorator: William Kiernan. Editor: Viola Lawrence. Assistant director: Arthur S. Black. Continuity: Frances McDowell. Stills photographer: Joe Walters. Gowns: Jean Louis. Make-up: Clay Campbell. Hair stylist: Helen Hunt. Sound: Frank Goodwin. Technical adviser: National Probation and Parole

Association. Music: George Antheil. Musical director: Morris W. Stoloff. Associate producer: Henry S. Kesler. Producer: Robert Lord.

Cast: Humphrey Bogart (Andrew Morton), John Derek (Nick Romano), George Macready (District Attorney Kerman), Arlene Roberts (Emma), Susan Perry (Adele), Mickey Knox (Vito), Barry Kelley (Judge Drake), Dooley Wilson (Piano Player), Cara Williams (Nelly), Jimmy Conlin (Kid Fingers), Sumner Williams (Jimmy), Sid Melton (Squint), Pepe Hern (Juan), Dewey Martin (Butch), Robert A. Davis (Sunshine), Houseley Stevenson (Junior), Vince Barnett (Bartender), Thomas Sully (Officer Hawkins), Florence Auer (Aunt Lena), Pierre Watkin (Purcell), Gordon Nelson (Corey), Argentina Brunetti (Ma Romano), Dick Sinatra (Julian Romano), Carol Coombs (Ang Romano), Joan Baxter (Maria Romano), Evelyn Underwood, Mary Emery, Franz Roehn, Betty Hall, Jack Jahries, Rose Plumer, Mabel Smaney, Joy Hallward, John Mitchum, Sidney Dubin, Homer Dickinson and Netta Packer (Jury Members), Ann Duncan and Lorraine Comerford (Teenagers), Chuck Hamilton, Ralph Volkie and Frank Marlo (Bailiffs), Joe Palma, Dick Bartell, Eddie Randolph, Eda Reiss Merin and Joan Danton (Reporters), Donald Kerr (Court Clerk), Myron Healey (Assistant District Attorney), Jane Lee and Dorothy Vernon (Women), John Indrisano, Blackie Whiteford, Charles Sullivan, Ray Johnson, Jack Perry, Joe Brockman, Franklin Farnum, Dudley Dickerson, Tex Swan, Harry Wilson, Joe Dougherty, George Hickman, Eddie Borden, Cliff Heard, Jeff York, Paul Kreibich, Charles Camp and Charles Colean (Men), Connie Conrad, Ann Cornwall, Beulah Parkington, Betty Taylor, Hazel Boyne and Roberta Haynes (Women), Jack Clisby, Glen Thompson, Paul Baxley and Lee Phelps (Policemen), Gary Owen (Larry), Chester Conklin (Barber), George Chandler (Cashier), Theda Barr (Girl), Wesley Hopper (Boss), Sid Tomack (Duke), Frank Hagney and Peter Virgo (Suspects), George Hickman, Saul Gorss, Al Hill and Phillip Morris (Detectives), Helen Mowery (Miss Holiday), Jody Gilbert (Gussie), Curt Conway (Elkins), Edwin Parker and Al Ferguson (Guards).

Start of filming: August 1948. Release: 22 February, 1949. Running time: 100 min.

1949   Roseanna McCoy

A Samuel Goldwyn production distributed by RKO Radio. *Director*: Irving Reis (and Nicholas Ray). Screenplay: John Collier (and Ben Hecht). From the novel by Alberta Hannum. Director of photgraphy: Lee Garmes. Producer: Samuel Goldwyn.

Cast: Farley Granger, Joan Evans, Charles Bickford, Raymond Massey, Richard Basehart, Gigi Perreau, Aline MacMahon, Marshall Thompson, Lloyd Gough, Peter Miles, Arthur Franz, Frank Ferguson, Elizabeth Fraser, Hope Emerson, Dan White, Mabel Paige, Almira Sessions, William Mauch.

Release: 12 October 1949. Running time: 100 min.

Nicholas Ray

1950   Born to Be Bad

RKO Radio. *Director*: Nicholas Ray. Screenplay: Edith Sommers. Adaptation by Charles Schnee, from the novel *All Kneeling* by Ann Parrish. Additional dialogue by Robert Soderberg, George Oppenheimer. Director of photography: Nicholas Musuraca (additional scenes: Cliff Stine, Harry J. Wild, Sam De Grasse). Camera operator: Fred Bentley. Art directors: Albert S. D'Agostino, Jack Okey. Set decorators: Darrell Silvera, Harley Miller. Editor: Frederick Knudtson. Assistant director: Fred Fleck. Joan Fontaine's wardrobe: Hattie Carnegie. Joan Leslie's wardrobe: Michael Woulfe. Continuity: Mercy Weireter. Make-up: Gordon Bau. Sound: Phil Brigandi, Clem Portman (additional scene: Earl Mounds). Dialogue director: Rodney Amateau. Portrait: Ernst van Leyden. Music: Frederick Hollander. Musical director: C. Bakaleinikoff. Executive producer: Sid Rogell. Producer: Robert Sparks.

Cast: Joan Fontaine (Christabel Caine), Robert Ryan (Nick), Zachary Scott (Curtis), Joan Leslie (Donna), Mel Ferrer (Gobby), Harold Vermilyea (John Caine), Virginia Farmer (Aunt Clara), Kathleen Howard (Mrs Bolton), Dick Ryan (Arthur), Bess Flowers (Mrs Worthington), Joy Hallward (Mrs Porter), Hazel Boyne (Committee Woman), Irving Bacon (Jewellery Salesman), Gordon Oliver (The Lawyer), Sam Lufkin (Taxi Driver), Helen Crozier (Ann), Bobby Johnson (Kenneth), Tim Taylor (Messenger Boy), Peggy Leon (Caine's Secretary), Ray Johnson, John Mitchum and Evelyn Underwood (Guests), Jack Chefe, Barry Brooks and Al Murphy (Men), Homer Dickinson (Art Gallery Attendant), Georgiana Wulff and Ann Burr (Schoolgirls), Frank Arnold (Man at Art Gallery), Don Dillaway (Photographer), Avery Graves (Curtis's Friend), Jane Hedges (Lawyer's Secretary), Sam Harris (Old Man at Ball). In scene shot by Stevenson: J. Park, M. Russell, J. Holland. In Fleischer scene: Russell Fillman, Percy Launders, Stan Hollbrook, Ted Cooper.

Start of filming: 20 June 1949. Release: 27 August 1950. Running time: 94 min.

1950   In a Lonely Place

Columbia Pictures. A Santana Production. *Director*: Nicholas Ray. Screenplay: Andrew Solt. Adaptation by Edmund H. North, from the novel *In a Lonely Place* by Dorothy B. Hughes. Director of photography: Burnett Guffey. Camera operator: Gert Anderson. Art director: Robert Peterson. Set decorator: William Kiernan. Editor: Viola Lawrence. Assistant director: Earl Bellamy. Continuity: Charlie Bryant. Stills photographer: Lippman. Gowns: Jean Louis. Make-up: Clay Campbell. Hair stylist: Helen Hunt. Sound: Howard Fogetti. Technical adviser: Rodney Amateau. Music: George Antheil. Musical director: Morris W. Stoloff. Song: 'I Hadn't Anyone Till You'. Associate producer: Henry S. Kesler. Producer: Robert Lord.

Cast: Humphrey Bogart (Dixon Steele), Gloria Grahame (Laurel Gray), Frank Lovejoy (Brub Nicolai), Carl Benton Reid (Captain Lochner), Art Smith (Mel Lippman), Jeff Donnell (Sylvia Nicolai), Martha Stewart (Mildred Atkinson), Robert Warwick (Charlie Waterman), Morris Ankrum (Lloyd Barnes), William

Ching (Ted Barton), Steven Geray (Paul), Hadda Brooks (Singer), Alice Talton (Frances Randolph), Jack Reynolds (Henry Kesler), Ruth Warren (Effie), Ruth Gillette (Martha), Guy L. Beach (Mr Swan), Lewis Howard (Junior), Mike Romanoff (Himself), Arno Frey (Joe), Pat Barton (Second Hatcheck Girl), Cosmo Sardo (Bartender), Don Hamin (Young Driver), George Davis (Waiter), Billy Gray (Young Boy), Melinda Erickson (Tough Girl), Jack Jahries (Officer), David Bond (Dr Richards), Myron Healey (Post Office Clerk), Robert Lowell (Airline Clerk), Tony Laing, Robert Davis, Laura K. Brooks, Jack Santoro, Frank Marlowe, Evelyn Underwood, Hazel Boyne, Mike Lally, John Mitchum, Joy Hallward, Allen Pinson, Oliver Cross, June Vincent, Charles Cane.

Start of filming: 25 October 1949. Release: 17 May 1950. Running time: 94 min.

1951   On Dangerous Ground

RKO Radio. *Director*: Nicholas Ray. Screenplay: A. I. Bezzerides. Adaptation by A. I. Bezzerides and Nicholas Ray, from the novel *Mad With Much Heart* by Gerald Butler. Director of photography: George E. Diskant. Art directors: Albert S. D'Agostino, Ralph Berger. Set decorators: Darrell Silvera, Harley Miller. Special effects: Harold Stine. Editor: Roland Gross. Assistant directors: William Dorfman, Lloyd Richards. Sound editor: George Marsh. Make-up: Mel Berns. Hair stylist: Larry Germain. Sound: Phil Brigandi, Clem Portman. Music: Bernard Herrmann, conducted by the composer. Viola d'amore played by: Virginia Majewski. Musical director: C. Bakaleinikoff. Executive producer: Sid Rogell. Producer: John Houseman.

Cast: Robert Ryan (Jim Wilson), Ida Lupino (Mary Malden), Ward Bond (Walter Brent), Charles Kemper (Bill Daly), Anthony Ross (Pete Santos), Ed Begley (Captain Brawley) Ian Wolfe (Carrey), Sumner Williams (Danny Malden), Gus Schilling (Lucky), Frank Ferguson (Willows), Cleo Moore (Myrna), Olive Carey (Mrs Brent), Richard Irving (Bernie), Pat Prest (Julie), Bill Hammond (Fred), Gene Persson (2nd Boy), Tommy Gosser (Crying Boy), Ruth Lee (Helen Daly), Ronnie Garner (Boy), Dee Garner (Boy), Kate Lawson (Woman), William Challee (Thug), Eddie Borden (Old Man), Ken Terrell (Crook), W. J. O'Brien (Hotel Clerk), Jim Drum (Stretcher Bearer), Joe Devlin (Bartender), Nita Talbot (B-Girl), A. I. Bezzerides (Gatos), Esther Zeitlin (Woman), Tracy Roberts (Peggy Santos), Vera Stokes (Mother), Harry Joel Weiss (Boy), Steve Roberts (Running Man), Nestor Paiva (Gabbanierri), Leslie Bennett (Newsboy), G. Pat Collins (Sgt. Wendell), Vince Barnett (Waiter), Jimmy Conlin (Doc Hyman), Joan Taylor (Hazel), Budd Fine, Mike Lally, Don Dillaway, Al Murphy, Art Dupuis, Frank Arnold, Homer Dickinson, and inhabitants of Granby, Colorado: Birdsill, Davis, Thompson, Heckert, Knight, Hodgson, Yager (Men), Weiss, Spencer (Women).

Start of filming: 30 March 1950. Release: 12 February 1952. Running time: 82 min.

Nicholas Ray

1951 Flying Leathernecks

RKO Radio. Howard Hughes presents an Edmund Grainger production. *Director*: Nicholas Ray. Screenplay: James Edward Grant (and Beirne Lay Jr, Kenneth Gamet). From a story by Kenneth Gamet. Director of photography: William E. Snyder. Technicolor. Technicolor colour consultant: Morgan Padelford. Art directors: Albert S. D'Agostino, James W. Sullivan. Set decorators: Darrell Silvera, John Sturtevant. Editor: Sherman Todd, assisted by Bob Belcher (and A. Soria, Chan House, Roland Gross). Assistant director: Sam Ruman. Stills photographer: Alex Kahle. Make-up: Mel Berns. Hair stylist: Larry Germain. Costumes: Robert Martine. Sound: Frank McWhorter, Clem Portman, Jimmy Thompson (boom man), Kenny Wesson (recorder). Technical adviser: Col. Richard Hughes, USMC. Music: Roy Webb. Musical director: C. Bakaleinikoff. Production supervisor: Cliff P. Broughton. Producer: Edmund Grainger.

Cast: John Wayne (Major Dan Kirby), Robert Ryan (Capt. Carl 'Griff' Griffith), Don Taylor (Lieut. Vern 'Cowboy' Blythe), Janis Carter (Joan Kirby), Jay C. Flippen (Master Sgt Clancy), William Harrigan (Dr Curan), James Bell (Colonel), Barry Kelley (General), Maurice Jara (Lieut. Shorty Vegay), Adam Williams (Lieut. Malotke), James Dobson (Lieut. Pudge McCabe), Carleton Young (Capt. McAllister), Steve Flagg (Lieut. Jorgenson), Brett King (Lieut. Ernie Stark), Gordon Gebert (Tommy Kirby), Lynn Stalmaster (Lieut. Castle), Brit Norton (Lieut. Tanner), John Mallory (Lieut. Black), Douglas Henderson (Lieut. Foster), Ralph Cook (Lieut. Kelvin), Frank Fuimara (Lieut. Hawkins), Michael Devry (Lieut. Hoagland), Adam York (Lieut. Simmons), Don Rockland (Lieut. Stuart), Hal Bokar (Lieut. Deal), Tony Laing (Lieut. Woods), Hugh Sanders (General), Mack Williams (Colonel), Leslie O'Pace (Peter), Milton Kibbee (Clerk), Bernard Szold (Papa Malotke), Eda Reis Merin (Mama Malotke), Pat Prest (Greta Malotke), Shela Fritz (Old Indian), Charles Bruner (Old Indian), Jimmy Ogg (Messenger), Al Murphy (Grease Monkey), Richard Wessel (M.P.), Fred Graham (Marine), Robert Condon (1st Pilot Replacement), Victor Cutrer (2nd Pilot Replacement), Charles Courtney (3rd Pilot Replacement), Grady Galloway (4th Pilot Replacement), Mort Thompson (5th Pilot Replacement), Eugene Marshall (6th Pilot Replacement), Barry Brooks (Squadron Commander), James Hickman (Hicks), Noel Reyburn (Madden), Mavis Russell (Mrs Jorgenson), Gail Davis (Virginia), Elaine Robert (Jill), Melville Robert (Jack), Paul McGuire (Major Benson), Mona Knox (Annabelle), Jane Easton (Girl), Inez Cooper (Nurse), Jayn Lee Dockstader (Infant), Chuck Hamilton (Intelligence Officer), Peter Ortiz (Captain), Frank Marlowe (Taxi Driver), Richard Ullman (Jeep Driver), Chris Drake (Lieutenant), Mickey McCardle (Marine), Frank Iwanaga (Jap Pilot), Rollib Moriyama (Jap Pilot), Milburn Stone (Ground Control Officer), Keith Larsen.

Start of filming: 20 November 1950. Release: 19 September 1951. Running time: 102 min.

1951 The Racket

RKO Radio. *Director*: John Cromwell (and Nicholas Ray). Screenplay: William Wister Haines, W. R. Burnett. From the play by Bartlett Cormack. Director of photography: George E. Diskant. Editor: Sherman Todd. Sound: Frank McWhorter, Clem Portman. Producer: Edmund Grainger.

Cast (actors directed by Ray italicized): *Robert Mitchum* (Captain McQuigg), *Lizabeth Scott* (Irene), *Robert Ryan* (Nick Scanlon), *William Talman* (Johnson), *Ray Collins* (Welch), Joyce MacKenzie (Mary McQuigg), *Robert Hutton* (Ames), Virginia Huston (Lucy Johnson), William Conrad (Turck), *Walter Sande* (Delaney), *Les Tremayne* (Chief Craig), *Don Porter* (Connolly), Walter Baldwin (Sullivan), Brett King (Joe Scanlon), Richard Karlan (Enright), Tito Vuolo (Tony), Howard Chamberlin (Higgins), *Ralph Peters* (Davis), Iris Adrian (Sadie), Jane Hazzard and Claudia Constant (Girls), Jack Shea, Eric Alden and Mike Lally (Sergeants), *Howard Joslyn* (Sgt Werker), Bret Hamilton and Joey Ray (Reporters), Duke Taylor and Miles Shepard (Policemen), Dulcie Day and Hazel Keener (Secretaries), *Steve Roberts* (Schmidt), *Pat Flaherty* (Clerk), Milburn Stone (Foster), Max Wagner (Durco), Richard Reeves (Leo), *Johnny Day* (Menig), Don Beddoe (Mitchell), Matthew Boulton (Simpson), Don Dillaway (Harris), Barry Brooks (Cameron), George Sherwood (Douglas), Jack Gargan (Lewis), Herb Vigran (Headwaiter), Bud Wolfe (Detective), Ronald Lee (Elevator Boy), Dick Gordon, Allen Mathews and Ralph Montgomery (Men), Al Murphy (Newsboy), Bob Bice, Sally Yarnell, Jane Easton and Kate Belmont (Operators), Harriet Matthews (Librarian), Curtis Jarrett, *Art Dupuis* and *Harry Lauter* (Policemen), *Ed Parker* (Thug), *Howard Petrie, William Forrest, Tom Martin, Franklin Parker* and *Frank Marlowe* (People in Governor's Office), *Walter Reed, Paul Stader, Rory Mallinson, Greg Barton, John McGuire, Herbert Lytton*.

Release: 12 December 1951. Running time: 88 min.

1952 Macao

RKO Radio. *Director*: Josef von Sternberg (and Nicholas Ray; additional scenes by Robert Stevenson, Mel Ferrer). Screenplay: Bernard C. Schoenfeld, Stanley Rubin (and Norman Katkov, George Bricker, Frank Moss, Walter Newman). From a story by Bob Williams. Director of photography: Harry J. Wild. Editors: Samuel Beetley, Robert Golden. Sound: Earl Wolcott, Clem Portman. Assistant director: Lowell Farrell. Executive producer: Samuel Bischoff (and Jerry Wald). Producer: Alex Gottlieb.

Cast (actors directed by Ray italicized): *Robert Mitchum* (Nick Cochran), *Jane Russell* (Julie Benson), *William Bendix* (Lawrence Trumble), *Thomas Gomez* (Lieut. Sebastian), Gloria Grahame (Margie), *Brad Dexter* (Halloran), *Edward Ashley* (Martin Stewart), *Philip Ahn* (Itzumi), *Vladimir Sokoloff* (Kwan Sum Tang), Don Zelayo (Gimpy), Emory Parnell (Ship Captain), Nacho Galindo (Bus Driver), *Philip Van Zandt* (Customs Official), *George Chan* (Chinese Photographer), Sheldon Jett (Dutch Tourist), Genevieve Bell (Woman Passenger), Tommy Lee (Chinese Knifed in Water), Alex Montoya and Manuel Paris (Bartenders), Spencer Chan, *James B. Leong* and Alfredo Santos (Hoodlums), Marc

Nicholas Ray

Krah (Desk Clerk), May Takasugi (Barber), Lee Tung Foo (Merchant), Maria Sen Young and Iris Wong (Croupiers), Abdullah Abbas (Arabian), Everett Glass (Garcia), Walter Ng (Fisherman), Rico Alaniz (Bus Driver), Trevor Bardette (Alvaris), Weaver Levy (Chang), W. T. Chang (Old Fisherman), Michael Visaroff (Russian Doorman), Phil Harron (Sikh), William Yip (Rickshaw Driver), Art Dupuis (Portuguese Pilot), Helen Thurston, *John Daheim* and *Dick Coe* (Stunt Doubles), *Robert Wah Lee* (Bellhop), *Clarence Lung* (Clerk), *Harold J. Kennedy* (Passenger).

Release: 30 April 1952. Running time: 80 min.

1952 The Lusty Men

RKO Radio. A Wald-Krasna Production. *Director*: Nicholas Ray (and Robert Parrish on a few scenes). Screenplay: Horace McCoy, David Dortort (collaboration on dialogue: Ray, Robert Mitchum, Alfred Hayes, Andrew Solt). Suggested by a story by Claude Stanush. Director of photography: Lee Garmes. Art directors: Albert S. D'Agostino, Alfred Herman. Set decorators: Darrell Silvera, Jack Mills. Editor: Ralph Dawson. Assistant director: Ed Killy. 2nd Unit camera operator: Harold Wellman. Wardrobe: Michael Woulfe. Make-up: Mel Berns. Hair stylist: Larry Germain. Sound: Phil Brigandi, Clem Portman. Music: Roy Webb. Musical Director: C. Bakaleinikoff. Associate producer: Thomas S. Gries. Producers: Jerry Wald, Norman Krasna.

Cast: Susan Hayward (Louise Merritt), Robert Mitchum (Jeff McCloud), Arthur Kennedy (Wes Merritt), Arthur Hunnicutt (Booker Davis), Frank Faylen (Al Dawson), Walter Coy (Buster Burgess), Carol Nugent (Rusty), Maria Hart (Rosemary Maddox), Lorna Thayer (Grace Burgess), Burt Mustin (Jeremiah Watrous), Karen King (Ginny Logan), Jimmy Dodd (Red Logan), Eleanor Todd (Babs), Riley Hill (Hoag), Bob Fray (Fritz), Sheb Wooley (Slim), Wayne Burson, Dick Farnsworth and Rocky Shahan (Cowboys), Marshall Reed (Jim Bob), Paul E. Burns (Travis Waite), Sally Yarnell, Jean Stratton, Nancy Moore, Louise Saraydar, Mary Jane Carey and Alice Kirby (Girls), Benny Burt and Joey Ray (Slickers), Dennis Moore and George Wallace (Committee Men), Chuck Roberson (Tall Cowboy), John McKee (Cowboy), Mike Ragan (Karl Inman), Edward McNally (Wise Guy), Bob Burrows, George Ross, Carol Henry and Jim Van Horn (Cowboys), Mike Lally (Slicker), Dick Crockett (Slicker), Les Sanborn (Jim Bob Tyler), Barbara Blaine and Hazel Boyne (Women), Ralph Stein (Man), Sam Flint (Doctor), Chili Williams (Woman), Richard Reeves (Emmett Vaughn), Roy Glenn (Cook), Glenn Strange (Rig Ferris), George Sherwood (Vet), Denver Pyle (Niko), Frank Matts (Lansing), John Mallory (Nemo), Jack Braddock (Slim), Sam Reynoso (Barrel Clown), William Holmes and Charles Parkinson (Rodeo Announcers), Ralph Volkie (Slicker), William Bailey (Man), Steve Raines (Second Cowboy), Le Roy Johnson and Wally Russell (Cowboys), Paul Kreibich (Man), Dan White and Jack Rourke (Announcers). Rodeo rider: Casey Tibbs. Doubles: Dan Poore (for Mitchum), Don McGuire (for Kennedy), Eddie Jauregui, Don Happy.

Start of filming: 27 December 1951. Release: October 1952. Running time: 113 min.

1953   Androcles and the Lion

RKO Radio. G. P. Productions. *Director*: Chester Erskine (additional scenes: Nicholas Ray). Screen adaptation: Chester Erskine, Noel Langley, Ken Englund, from the play *Androcles and the Lion* by George Bernard Shaw. Director of photography: Harry Stradling. Production designer: Harry Horner. Art director: Albert S. D'Agostino. Set decorator: Darrell Silvera. Special effects: Linwood Dunn. Editor: Roland Gross. Music: Frederick Hollander. Associate producer: Lewis Rachmil. Producer: Gabriel Pascal.

Cast (actors directed by Ray italicized): Jean Simmons (Lavinia), Alan Young (Androcles), Victor Mature (Captain), *Robert Newton* (Ferrovius), Maurice Evans (Caesar), Elsa Lanchester (Megaera), Reginald Gardiner (Lentulus), Gene Lockhart (Menagerie Keeper), Alan Mowbray (Editor), Noel Willman (Spintho), John Hoyt (Cato), Jim Backus (Centurion), Lowell Gilmore (Metellus), Don Garrett, Alex Sharp, John Merton and Dennis Dengate (Officers), Jack Shea and Clark Howatt (Officers), Robert Counsell (Bucinator), Harry Lauter (Officer), Lillian Clayes (Christian Woman), Midge Ware (Christian Woman), Bob Foulk, John Pickard, Harry Cording and Gaylord Pendleton (Soldiers), Bobby Rose (Slave), George Sherwood and William Slack (Guards), Larry Johns (Old Christian), Strother Martin, Ray Hyke and Jackson Halliday (Soldiers), John McGuire (Stricken Soldier), Sara Taft (Old Christian), Woody W. Strode (The Lion), Chet Marshall (Call Boy), Richard Reeves (Secutor), Michael Road (Retiarius), Dick Elliott (Ox Cart Driver), Mary MacLaren, Frank O'Connor and Millard Sherwood (Christians), Charles Hall (Town Crier), Larry McGrath (Vendor), *Clint Dorrington* and *Stubby Krueger* (Officers in Forest), *Fred Sarver, Charmienne Harker, John Dodsworth, Dayton Lummis*. Scene shot, but deleted: *The Carmelita Maracci Corps de Ballet, Shirley Lewis* and *Betty Utey* (Vestal Virgins).

Release: 3 January 1953. Running time: 95 min.

1954   Johnny Guitar

Republic Pictures. *Director*: Nicholas Ray. Screenplay: Philip Yordan. From the novel *Johnny Guitar* by Roy Chanslor. Director of photography: Harry Stradling. Trucolor. Art director: James Sullivan. Set decorators: John McCarthy Jr, Edward G. Boyle. Special effects: Howard Lydecker, Theodore Lydecker. Editor: Richard L. Van Enger. Assistant directors: Herb Mendelson, Judd Cox. Production manager: Johnny Guibbs. Costumes: Sheila O'Brien. Make-up: Bob Mara. Hair stylist: Peggy Gray. Sound: T. A. Carman, Howard Wilson. Music: Victor Young. Song: 'Johnny Guitar' (Victor Young, Peggy Lee) sung by Peggy Lee. *Associate producer*: (uncredited) Nicholas Ray. Producer: Herbert J. Yates.

Cast: Joan Crawford (Vienna), Sterling Hayden (Johnny Guitar), Mercedes McCambridge (Emma Small), Scott Brady (Dancing Kid), Ward Bond (John McIvers), Ben Cooper (Turkey Ralston), Ernest Borgnine (Bart Lonergan), John Carradine (Old Tom), Royal Dano (Corey), Frank Ferguson (Marshal Williams), Paul Fix (Eddie), Rhys Williams (Mr Andrews), Ian MacDonald (Pete), Will Wright (Ned), John Maxwell (Jake), Robert Osterloh (Sam), Frank Marlowe (Frank), Trevor Bardette (Jenks), Sumner Williams, Sheb Wooley, Denver Pyle,

Nicholas Ray

Clem Harvey and Jack Ingram (Men of the Posse). Stunt doubles: Helen Griffith (for McCambridge), Bob Folkerson (for Brady), Pete Kellett, Forest Burns (for Hayden and Borgnine), Rocky Shahan (for Bond), Phil Shoomaker.

Start of filming: 19 October 1953. Release: 27 May 1954. Running time: 110 min.

1955   Run for Cover

Paramount. *Director*: Nicholas Ray. Screenplay: Winston Miller. From a story by Harriet Frank Jr and Irving Ravetch. Director of photography: Daniel Fapp. VistaVision. Technicolor. Technicolor colour consultant: Richard Mueller. Art directors: Hal Pereira, Henry Bumstead. Set decorators: Sam Comer, Frank McKelvy. Special photographic effects: John P. Fulton. Special effects: Farciot Edouard. Editor: Howard Smith. Assistant director: Francisco Day. Costumes: Edith Head. Make-up: Wally Westmore. Sound: Gene Merritt, John Cobe. Music: Howard Jackson. Song: 'Run for Cover' (Howard Jackson, Jack Brooks). Producers: William H. Pine, William C. Thomas.

Cast: James Cagney (Matt Dow), Viveca Lindfors (Helga Swenson), John Derek (Davey Bishop), Jean Hersholt (Mr Swenson), Grant Withers (Gentry), Jack Lambert (Larsen), Ernest Borgnine (Morgan), Ray Teal (Sheriff), Irving Bacon (Scotty), Trevor Bardette (Paulsen), John Miljan (Mayor Walsh), Gus Schilling (Doc Ridgeway), Emerson Treacy (Bank Clerk), Denver Pyle (Harvey), Henry Wills (Citizen), Phil Chambers, Harold Kennedy, Joe Haworth.

Start of filming: 25 May 1954. Release: 29 April 1955. Running time: 93 min.

1954   High Green Wall

Revue Productions. *General Electric Theater* series. *Director*: Nicholas Ray. Teleplay: Charles Jackson. From a short story, 'The Man Who Liked Dickens', by Evelyn Waugh. Director of photography: Franz Planer. Art Director: Martin Obzina. Set decorator: James S. Redd. Editor: Michael R. McAdam. Assistant director: Robert Shannon. Wardrobe: Vincent Dee. Sound: Roy Meadows. Producer: Leon Gordon.

Cast: Joseph Cotten (Henty), Thomas Gomez (McMaster), Maurice Marsac (Aubert), Marshall Bradford, Ward Wood (Search Party).

Start of filming: August 1954. Broadcast: 3 October 1954, CBS. Running time: 26 min.

1955   Rebel Without a Cause

Warner Brothers. *Director*: Nicholas Ray. *Screenplay*: Stewart Stern (with contributions by Ray and David Weisbart). Adaptation by Irving Shulman (first version by Leon Uris) from a story by Nicholas Ray. Director of photography: Ernest Haller. CinemaScope. WarnerColor. Art director: Malcolm Bert. Set decorator: William Wallace. Editor: William Ziegler. Assistant directors: Don Page, Robert

Farfan. Stills photographer: Floyd McCarty. Costumes: Moss Mabry. Make-up: Gordon Bau. Sound: Stanley Jones. Technical adviser: Frank Mazzola. Dialogue supervisor: Dennis Stock. Music: Leonard Rosenman. Producer: David Weisbart.

Cast: James Dean (Jim Stark), Natalie Wood (Judy), Sal Mineo (Plato), Jim Backus (Jim's Father), Ann Doran (Jim's Mother), Corey Allen (Buzz Gunderson), William Hopper (Judy's Father), Rochelle Hudson (Judy's Mother), Dennis Hopper (Goon), Edward Platt (Ray), Steffi Sidney (Mil), Marietta Canty (Plato's Nurse), Virginia Brissac (Jim's Grandmother), Beverly Long (Helen), Ian Wolfe (Professor), Frank Mazzola (Crunch), Robert Foulk (Gene), Jack Simmons (Cookie), Tom Bernard (Harry), Nick Adams (Moose), Jack Grinnage (Chick), Clifford Morris (Cliff), Robert B. Williams (Ed, Moose's Father), Louise Lane (Policewoman), Jimmy Baird (Beau), Dick Wessel (Guide), Nelson Leigh (Sergeant), Dorothy Abbott (Nurse), House Peters (Officer), Gus Schilling (Attendant), Bruce Noonan (Monitor), Almira Sessions (Old Lady Teacher), Peter Miller (Hoodlum), Paul Bryar (Desk Sergeant), Paul Birch (Police Chief), David McMahon (Crunch's Father), Nicholas Ray (Man in last shot).

Start of filming: 30 March 1955. Release: 27 October 1955. Running time: 111 min.

1956   Hot Blood

Columbia Pictures. A Howard Welsch Production. *Director*: Nicholas Ray. Screenplay: Jesse Lasky Jr. From a story by Jean Evans (and an earlier script by Walter Newman). Director of photography: Ray June. CinemaScope. Technicolor. Technicolor colour consultant: Henri Jaffe. Art director: Robert Peterson. Set decorator: Frank Tuttle. Editor: Otto Ludwig. Assistant director: Milton Feldman. Sound: Lambert Day, John Livadary. Jane Russell's make-up: Layne Britton. Jane Russell's hair stylist: Stephanie McGraw. Music: Les Baxter. Songs: Ross Bagdasarian. Choreography: Matt Mattox, Sylvia Lewis. Producer: Harry Tatelman.

Cast: Jane Russell (Annie Caldash), Cornel Wilde (Stephan Torino), Luther Adler (Marco Torino), Joseph Calleia (Papa Theodore), Mikhail Rasumny (Old Johnny), Nina Koshetz (Nita Johnny), Helen Westcott (Velma), Jamie Russell (Xano), Wally Russell (Bimbo), Nick Dennis (Korka), Richard Deacon (Mr Swift), Robert Foulk (Sergeant McGrossin), John Raven (Joe Randy), Joe Merritt (Skinny Gypsy), Faye Nuell (Gypsy Woman), Peter Brocco (Doctor), Joan Reynolds (Girl), Ethan Laidlace (Bit), Les Baxter and Ross Bagdasarian (Gas Station Attendants), Manuel Paris (Elder).

Start of filming: 18 July 1955. Release 23 March 1956. Running time: 85 min.

1956   Bigger Than Life

20th Century-Fox. *Director*: Nicholas Ray. *Screenplay*: Cyril Hume, Richard Maibaum (with contributions by Ray, James Mason, Gavin Lambert, Clifford Odets). Based on an article, *Ten Feet Tall*, by Berton Roueché. Director of photography: Joe MacDonald. CinemaScope. De Luxe. Colour consultant:

Leonard Doss. Art directors: Lyle R. Wheeler, Jack Martin Smith. Set decorators: Walter M. Scott, Stuart A. Reiss. Special photographic effects: Ray Kellogg. Editor: Louis Loeffler. Assistant director: Eli Dunn. Costumes: Charles LeMaire, Mary Wills. Sound: W. D. Flick, Harry M. Leonard. Make-up: Ben Nye. Hair stylist: Helen Turpin. Music: David Raksin, conducted by Lionel Newman. Orchestrations: Edward B. Powell. Producer: James Mason.

Cast: James Mason (Ed Avery), Barbara Rush (Lou), Walter Matthau (Wally), Robert Simon (Dr Norton), Christopher Olsen (Richie Avery), Roland Winters (Dr Ruric), Rusty Lane (La Porte), Rachel Stephens (Nurse), Kipp Hamilton (Pat Wade), Betty Caulfield (Mrs La Porte), Virginia Carroll (Mrs Jones), Renny McEvoy (Mr Jones), Bill Jones (Mr Byron), Lee Aaker (Joe), Jerry Mather (Freddie), Portland Mason (Nancy), Natalie Masters (Mrs Tyndal), Richard Collier (Milkman), Lewis Charles (Dr MacLennan), William Schallert (Pharmacist), John Monaghan (Cabby), Gus Schilling (Druggist), Alex Frazier (Clergyman), Mary McAdoo (Mrs Edwards), Mary Carver and Eugenia Paul (Salesladies), Gladys Richards (Lab Nurse), David Bedell (X-Ray Doctor), Ann Spencer (Nurse), Nan Dolan (Dr Norton's Nurse).

Start of filming: 26 March 1956. Première: 2 August 1956. Running time: 95 min.

1957   The True Story of Jesse James (British title: *The James Brothers*)

20th Century-Fox. *Director*: Nicholas Ray. Screenplay: Walter Newman (with contributions by Gavin Lambert, Arthur Kramer). Based on the screenplay by Nunnally Johnson for the film *Jesse James* (director Henry King, 1938). Director of photography: Joe MacDonald. CinemaScope. De Luxe. Colour consultant: Leonard Doss. Art directors: Lyle R. Wheeler, Addison Hehr (and Mark Lee Kirk). Set decorators: Walter M. Scott, Stuart A. Reiss. Special photographic effects: Ray Kellogg. Editor: Robert Simpson. Assistant directors: Al Herman, Joseph E. Rickards. Costumes: Charles LeMaire, Mary Wills. Sound: Eugene Grossman, Harry M. Leonard. Make-up: Ben Nye. Hair stylist: Helen Turpin. Historical data: Rosalind Shaffer, Jo Frances James (this in fact relates to the 1938 film). Music: Leigh Harline, conducted by Lionel Newman. Orchestrations: Edward B. Powell. Producer: Herbert B. Swope Jr.

Cast: Robert Wagner (Jesse James), Jeffrey Hunter (Frank James), Hope Lange (Zee), Agnes Moorehead (Mrs Samuel), Alan Hale (Cole Younger), Alan Baxter (Remington), John Carradine (Reverend Jethro Bailey), Rachel Stephens (Anne James), Barney Phillips (Dr Samuel), Biff Elliot (Jim Younger), John Doucette (Sheriff Hillstrom), Frank Overton (Major Rufus Cobb), Barry Atwater (Attorney Walker), Marian Seldes (Rowena Cobb), Chubby Johnson (Askew), Frank Gorshin (Charley Ford), Carl Thayer (Bob Ford), Robert Adler (Sheriff Trump), Clancy Cooper (Sheriff Joe), Sumner Williams (Sam Wells), Tom Greenway (Deputy Leo), Mike Steen (Deputy Ed), Aaron Saxon (Wiley), Anthony Ray (Bob Younger), Tom Pittman (Hughie), Jason Wingreen (Tucker Bassham), Louis Zito (Clell Miller), Mark Hickman (Bill Stiles), Adam Marshall (Dick Liddell), Joseph Di Reda (Bill Ryan), J. Frederick Albeck (Jorgensen), Kellog Junge Jr (Archie, age 4), Ken Clark (Sergeant), Kendall Scott (Man), Kay Kuter (Fleming),

Bing Russell (Jayhawker Sergeant), James F. Stone (Flower), Edmund Cobb (Bartock), Howard Negley (Burnside), Paul Webber (Telegraph Operator), Jeane Wood (Mrs Younger), Mike Ross (Mr Younger), Sally Corner (Widow Keevey), Fay Roope (Tom Trope), Gene Roth (Engineer), Jason Johnson (Engineer), George Comfort Sr (Singer), Ruth Robinson (Mary, age 5), Ray Ferrell (Tim, age 6), Alex Campbell (Judge).

Start of filming: 6 September 1956. Release: 22 March 1957. Running time: 93 min.

1957   Bitter Victory (French title: *Amère Victoire*)

Transcontinental Films S.A./Robert Laffont Productions/Columbia. *Director*: Nicholas Ray. *Screenplay*: René Hardy, Nicholas Ray, Gavin Lambert (and Vladimir Pozner). From the novel *Amère Victoire* by René Hardy. Additional dialogue: Paul Gallico. Director of photography: Michel Kelber. CinemaScope. Camera operator: Wladimir Ivanoff. Camera assistants: Roger Tellier, André Domage. Art director: Jean d'Eaubonne, assisted by Marc Frederix, G. Petitot. Editor: Léonide Azar, assisted by Denise Charvein. Assistant directors: Christian Ferry, Edouard Luntz. Sound editor: Renée Lichtig, assisted by Suzanne Cabon, Suzanne Rondeau, Kenout Peltier. Continuity: Lucie Lichtig. Stills photographer: Jacques Boutinot. Costumes: Jean Zay. Make-up: René Daudin. Sound: Joseph de Bretagne. Military adviser: Major General C. M. F. White. Music: Maurice Le Roux, conducted by the composer (Orchestre de la Radiodiffusion française). Production managers: Paul Joly, Giorgio Riganti, Mario Del Papa. Executive producer on location: Janine Graetz. Producer: Paul Graetz.

Cast: Richard Burton (Captain Leith), Curd Jürgens (Major Brand), Ruth Roman (Jane Brand), Raymond Pellegrin (Mokrane), Sean Kelly (Lt Barton), Anthony Bushell (General Paterson), Alfred Burke (Lt-Col Callander), Andrew Crawford (Pte Roberts), Nigel Green (Pte Wilkins), Ronan O'Casey (Sgt Dunnigan), Christopher Lee (Sgt Barney), Fred Matter (Oberst Lutze), Raoul Delfosse (Lt Kassel), Harry Landis (Pte Browning), Ramon de Larrocha (Lt Sanders), Christian Melsen (Pte Abbot), Sumner Williams (Pte Anderson), Joe Davray (Pte Spicer), Lt Harris (Evans).

Start of filming: 15 February 1957. Première: September 1957 (Venice Festival). Running time: 103 min. In the US: release, March 1958; running time: 82 min.

1958   Wind Across the Everglades

Warner Brothers. A Schulberg Production. *Director*: Nicholas Ray (and Budd Schulberg). Screenplay: Budd Schulberg. Director of photography: Joseph Brun. Technicolor. Camera operator: Saul Midwall. Art director: Richard Sylbert. Editors: George Klotz, Joseph Zigman. Assistant director: Charles Maguire Jr. Continuity: Roberta Hodes. Stills photographer: Muky. Costumes: Frank L. Thompson. Make-up: Robert Jiras. Hair Stylist: Willis Hanchett. Sound: Ernest Zatorsky. Dialogue supervisor: Sumner Williams. Technical adviser: Bud Kirk.

Nicholas Ray

Research supervisor: Earl Mohn. Music: Warners' Music Library. Production manager: George Justin. Producer: Stuart Schulberg.

Cast: Burl Ives (Cottonmouth), Christopher Plummer (Walt Murdock), Gypsy Rose Lee (Mrs Bradford), George Voskovec (Aaron Nathanson), Tony Galento (Beef), Howard I. Smith (George), Emmet Kelly (Bigamy Bob), Pat Henning (Sawdust), Chana Eden (Naomi), MacKinlay Kantor (Judge Harris), Curt Conway (Perfesser), Peter Falk (Writer), Fred Grossinger (Slow Boy), Sammy Renick (Loser), Toch Brown (One-Note), Frank Rothe (Howard Ross Morgan), Cory Osceola (Billy One-Arm), Mary Osceola (Suzy Billy), Sumner Williams (Windy), Toby Bruce (Joe Bottles), Mary Pennington (Mrs George Leggett), Hugh Parker (Lord Harry), Brad Bradford (Thumbs), Dorothy Rogers (Mary Melon), Cynthia Betout (Memory), Owen Pavitt (Sheriff), Rufus Beecham (Pianist), David Schulberg, Stephen Schulberg, Sandra Schulberg, Sally Marlowe, Minella Jiras. Inhabitants of Everglades City: Thelma Smallwood, Constable Joe Hunter, Ray Osmer. Narration spoken by Hank Simms.

Start of filming: 4 November 1957. Release: 20 August 1958 (Florida). Running time: 93 min.

1958   Party Girl

Metro-Goldwyn-Mayer. A Euterpe Production. *Director*: Nicholas Ray. Screenplay: George Wells. From a story by Leo Katcher. Director of photography: Robert Bronner. CinemaScope. Metrocolor. Colour consultant: Charles K. Hagedorn. Art Directors: William A. Horning, Randall Duell. Set decorators: Henry Grove, Richard Pefferle. Special effects: Lee Le Blanc. Editor: John McSweeney Jr. Assistant director: Erich von Stroheim Jr. Continuity: Grace Dubray. Costumes: Helen Rose. Make-up: William Tuttle. Hair Stylist: Sydney Guilaroff. Sound: Dr Wesley C. Miller. Music: Jeff Alexander (and André Previn). Song: 'Party Girl' (Nicholas Brodszky, Sammy Cahn) sung by Tony Martin. Choreographer: Robert Sidney. Producer: Joe Pasternak.

Cast: Robert Taylor (Thomas Farrell), Cyd Charisse (Vicki Gaye), Lee J. Cobb (Rico Angelo), John Ireland (Louis Canetto), Kent Smith (Jeffrey Stewart), Claire Kelly (Genevieve), Corey Allen (Cookie La Motte), Lewis Charles (Danny Rimett), David Opatoshu (Lou Forbes), Ken Dibbs (Joey Vulner), Patrick McVey (O'Malley), Barbara Lang (Tall Blonde Party Girl), Myrna Hansen (Joy Hampton), Betty Utey (Party Girl), Jack Lambert (Nick), Sam McDaniel (Jesse), Floyd Simmons (Assistant Prosecutor), Sydney Smith (Judge Bookwell), Rusty Lane (Judge John A. Davis), Michael Dugan (Jenks), Irving Greenberg, Richard Devine and George Saurel (Rico's Hoods), Carl Thayer, Mike Pierce, John Franco and Ken Perry (Cookie's Henchmen), Barrie Chase (?), Sanita Pelkey and Sandy Warner (Showgirls), Burt Douglas (P.A. Voice), Harry Tom McKenna (Politician), Erich von Stroheim Jr (Police Lieutenant), Herbert Armstrong (Intern), Carmen Phillips (Rico's Girlfriend), Pat Cawley (Farrell's Secretary), Marshall Bradford (District Attorney), Tom Hernandez (Sketch Artist), David McMahon (Guard), Andrew Buck (Chauffeur), Aaron Saxon (Frankie Gasto), Vaughn Taylor (Dr Caderman), Peter Bourne (Cab Driver), Vito Scotti (Hotel Clerk), Ralph Smiley (Hotel Proprietor), Herbert Lytton (Judge Alfino), Benny

Rubin (Mr Field), Paul Keast (Judge Davers), Jerry Schumacher (Newsboy), John Damler (Detective), Geraldine Wall (Day Matron), Robert B. Williams (Guard), Dolores Reed (Woman), David Garcia (Newsman), Harry Hines (Newsboy), Jack Gargan (Officer), Margaret Bert (Wardrobe Woman), Hy Anzel (Man), Maggie O'Byrne (Woman), Stuart Holmes and J. Lewis Smith (Jurors), Bob Calder, Herman Bode, Marc Wilder and Jack Dodd (Speciality Dancers).

Start of filming: 24 March 1958. Release: 28 October 1958. Running time: 99 min.

1960   The Savage Innocents (Italian title: *Ombre Bianche*; French title: *Les Dents du diable*)

An Italian/British/French co-production: Magic Film (Rome)/Joseph Janni, Appia Films (London)/Gray Film-Pathé (Paris). Released by Rank (UK), Paramount (US). *Director*: Nicholas Ray. *Screenplay*: Nicholas Ray. Adaptation by Hans Ruesch and Franco Solinas, from the novel *Top of the World* by Hans Ruesch. Director of photography: Aldo Tonti, Peter Hennessy. Super-Technirama 70. Technicolor. Camera operator: Jack Atcheler. Art directors: Don Ashton, Dario Cecchi. Set decorator: Edward Clements. Editor: Ralph Kemplen, Eraldo Da Roma. Assistant director: Tom Pevsner. 2nd unit director: Baccio Bandini. 2nd unit cameramen: Paddy Carey, Riccardo Pallottini. 2nd unit camera operator: Allan Bryce. 2nd unit assistant director: Jacques Giraldeau. Continuity: Penny Daniels. Stills photographers: Harry Gillard, Albert Clarke. Costumes: Vittorio Nino Novarese. Make-up: Geoffrey Rodway. Hair stylist: Stella Rivers. Sound: Geoffrey Daniels. Arctic consultant: Doug Wilkinson. Music: Angelo Francesco Lavagnino, conducted by Muir Mathieson. Songs: 'Iceberg' composed and sung by The Four Saints, 'Sexy Rock' (Lavagnino, Panzeri) sung by Colin Hicks. Production managers: Douglas Pierce, Bianca Lattuada. Producer: Maleno Malenotti.

Cast: Anthony Quinn (Inuk), Yoko Tani (Asiak), Peter O'Toole (1st Trooper), Carlo Giustini (2nd Trooper), Marie Yang (Powtee), Andy Ho (Anarvik), Kaida Horiuchi (Imina), Yvonne Shima (Lulik), Lee Montague (Ittimangnerk), Francis De Wolff (Proprietor of Trading Post), Marco Guglielmi (Missionary), Anthony Chin (Kidok), Anna May Wong (Hiko), Michael Chow (Undik), Ed Devereau (Pilot). Narration spoken by Nicholas Stuart.

NB – 1. Several of these technical credits are dubious, given the co-production practice (in Britain as well as Italy) of doubling up on technicians to satisfy union requirements. This is why Baccio Bandini, for example, is credited as co-director in Italian sources.

– 2. In the English language version, Peter O'Toole is dubbed by Robert Rietty. Evidently this was why O'Toole had his name removed from the credits before the film's British release (David Robinson, *The Times*, 27 June 1960). He *is* credited, third in the cast list, on American, French and Italian versions.

– 3. The Anna May Wong who figures in the cast bears no relation to the well-known Chinese-American actress of the same name.

Start of filming: end of April 1959. Release: March 1960 (Rome). Running time: 107 min. In the US, release: 24 May 1961; running time: 89 min.

Nicholas Ray

1961 King of Kings

Metro-Goldwyn-Mayer. A Samuel Bronston Production. *Director*: Nicholas Ray (and Charles Walters on a few scenes). Screenplay: Philip Jordan. Directors of photography: Franz F. Planer, Milton Krasner, Manuel Berenguer. Super-Technirama 70. Technicolor. Camera operator: Enzo Barboni. Art director/costumes: Georges Wakhévitch. Set decorator: Enrique Alarcon. Special effects: Alex Weldon. Special photographic effects: Lee LeBlanc. Editors: Harold F. Kress, Renée Lichtig. Assistant directors: Carlo Lastricati, José Maria Ochoa, José Lopez Rodero, Pedro Vidal. 2nd unit directors: Noel Howard, Sumner Williams. Continuity: Winifred Elsie Alice Clarke. Master of properties: Stanley Detlie. Stills photographers: Claudio Gomez Grau, Antonio Luengo. Supervisor of costuming: Eric Seelig. Make-up: Mario Van Riel, Charles Parker. Hair stylist: Anna Cristofani. Casting: Michael Waszynski. Sound: Basil Fenton Smith. Recording supervisor: Franklin Milton. Murals: Maciek Piotrowski. Music: Miklos Rosza. Choreography for Salome's dance: Betty Utey. General production manager: Stanley Goldsmith. Production manager: Lou Brandt. Associate producers: Alan Brown, Jaime Prades. Producer: Samuel Bronston.

Cast: Jeffrey Hunter (Jesus Christ), Robert Ryan (John the Baptist), Siobhan McKenna (Mary, Mother of Jesus), Hurd Hatfield (Pontius Pilate), Ron Randell (Lucius, the Centurion), Viveca Lindfors (Claudia), Rita Gam (Herodias), Carmen Sevilla (Mary Magdalene), Brigid Bazlen (Salome), Harry Guardino (Barabbas), Rip Torn (Judas), Frank Thring (Herod Antipas), Guy Rolfe (Caiaphas), Maurice Marsac (Nicodemus), Grégoire Aslan (Herod), Royal Dano (Peter), Edric Connor (Balthazar), George Coulouris (The Camel Driver), Conrado San Martin (General Pompey), Gerard Tichy (Joseph), José Antonio (Young John), Luis Prendes (The Good Thief), David Davies (The Burly Man), José Nieto (Caspar), Ruben Rojo (Matthew), Fernando Sancho (The Madman), Michael Wager (Thomas), Felix de Pomes (Joseph of Arimathea), Adriano Rimoldi (Melchior), Barry Keegan (The Bad Thief), Rafael Luis Calvo (Simon of Cyrene), Tino Barrero (Andrew), Francisco Moran (The Blind Man), Barry Roomans (James), Simon Mizrahi (James the Younger), Jean Moraes (Nathaniel), David Moss (Philip), Milo Quesada (Simon), Bud Straight (Thaddeus), Juan Manuel Maeztu (Executioner), Randy Paar. Uncredited: narration spoken by Orson Welles. Stuntmen: Art Reese, Manolo Gonzalez. Featured in scenes shot but deleted: Richard Johnson (David), Abraham Sofaer (Rabbi Eli), Anthony Bevin (Astrologer), Barta Barri (Scholar), Fernando Rey (Abdul).

Start of filming: 24 April 1960. Release: 30 October 1961. Running time: 168 min.

1963 55 Days at Peking

Samuel Bronston Productions. Released by Rank (UK), Allied Artists (US). *Director*: Nicholas Ray (and Andrew Marton, Guy Green). Screenplay: Philip Yordan, Bernard Gordon (with contributions by Betty Utey, Ben Barzman, etc.). Additional dialogue: Robert Hamer. Director of photography: Jack Hildyard. Super-Technirama 70. Technicolor. Production design/costumes: Veniero Colasanti, John Moore. Special effects: Alex Weldon. Editor: Robert Lawrence. Assistant director: José Lopez Rodero. Director 2nd unit operations: Andrew Marton. 2nd unit director: Noel Howard. 2nd unit cameraman: Manuel Berenguer. 2nd unit assistant director: José Maria Ochoa. Sound mixer: David Hildyard. Sound re-recordist: Gordon K. McCallum. Sound effects editor: Milton Burrow. Continuity: Lucie Lichtig. Master of properties: Stanley Detlie. Stills photographers: Gomez Grau, Antonio Luengo. Make-up: Mario Van Riel. Hair stylist: Grazia Di Rossi, Alexandre de Paris (for Ava Gardner). Casting: Maude Spector. Technical adviser: Col. J. R. Johnson. Paintings for credit sequence: Don Kingman. Music: Dimitri Tiomkin, conducted by the composer. Song: 'So Little Time' (Paul Francis Webster) sung by Andy Williams. Executive production manager: C. O. Erickson. Associate producer: Alan Brown. Executive associate producer: Michael Waszynski. Producer: Samuel Bronston.

Cast: Charlton Heston (Major Matt Lewis), Ava Gardner (Baroness Natalie Ivanoff), David Niven (Sir Arthur Robertson), Flora Robson (Dowager Empress Tzu-Hsi), John Ireland (Sergeant Harry), Harry Andrews (Father de Bearn), Leo Genn (General Jung-Lu), Robert Helpmann (Prince Tuan), Ichizo Itami [= Juzo Itami] (Colonel Shiba), Kurt Kasznar (Baron Sergei Ivanoff), Philippe Leroy (Julliard), Paul Lukas (Dr Steinfeldt), Lynne Sue Moon (Teresa), Elizabeth Sellars (Lady Sarah Robertson), Massimo Serato (Garibaldi), Jacques Sernas (Major Bobrinski), Jerome Thor (Capt. Andy Marshall), Geoffrey Bayldon (Smythe), Joseph Furst (Capt. Hanselman), Walter Gotell (Capt. Hoffman), Alfred Lynch (Gerald), Alfredo Mayo (Spanish Minister), Martin Miller (Hugo Bergmann), Conchita Montes (Mme Gaumaire), José Nieto (Italian Minister), Eric Pohlmann (Baron von Meck), Aram Stephan (Gaumaire), Robert Urquhart (Capt. Hanley), Ex-RSM Brittain (Sergeant Brittain), Felix Defauce (Dutch Minister), Andre Esterhazy (Austrian Minister), Carlos Casaravilla (Japanese Minister), Fernando Sancho (Belgian Minister), Michael Chow (Chiang), Mitchell Kowal (US Marine), George Wang (Boxer Chief), Nicholas Ray (US Minister). Credited, but not in the film: Mervyn Johns (Clergyman).

Start of filming: 2 July 1962. Première 6 May 1963 (London). Running time: 154 min.

1964   Circus World (British title: *The Magnificent Showman*)

Samuel Bronston Productions. Director: Henry Hathaway. Screenplay: Ben Hecht, Julian Halevy, James Edward Grant. From a story by Philip Yordan, Nicholas Ray. Director of photography: Jack Hildyard. Super-Technirama 70. Technicolor. Producer: Samuel Bronston.

Cast: John Wayne, Claudia Cardinale, Rita Hayworth, Lloyd Nolan, Richard Conte, John Smith, Henri Dantes, Wanda Rotha, Katharyna, Miles Malleson, Katharine Kath, Kay Walsh, Margaret MacGrath, Kate Ellison, Moustache, Franz Althoff and his Circus.

Release: 25 June 1964 (New York). Running time: 137 min.

Nicholas Ray

1970   March on Washington. Nov. 15, 1969

Dome Films, Inc. A film by Grady Watts [editing], and Claudia (Weill) [camera], Bill (Desloge) [camera], Bob (Levis) [sound], François (de Ménil), Sarah, Jim, Eli, Marty, Ellen (Ray), Nick (Ray) [*direction*], Tom, Mike. Thanks to Pacifica Radio and Richie Havens (song 'Freedom'). 16 mm, colour.

Filmed: 15–16 November 1969. Running time: 18 min.

1973–6   We Can't Go Home Again

'A film By Us'. *Producer/director/screenplay*: Nicholas Ray. Collaboration on screenplay: Susan Schwartz. Film crew: students from Harpur College, Bingham-ton (N.Y.). Among the successive technicians: Camera: Doug Cohn (35 mm), Stanley Liu (1st year), Danny Fisher (2nd year), Tim Ray (35 mm, summer 1972), Charles Bornstein (35 mm, 1973), Jerry Jones (San Francisco, 1974). Music: 'Bless the Family' by Norman and Suzy Zamchek. Sound: Ken Ross, Helen Kaplan, Barbara Di Benedetto. Editing: Carol Lenoir (New York, summer 1972), Richie Bock (1973 version, then San Francisco, 1974), Charles Bornstein, Danny Fisher, Max Fischer (Amsterdam, summer 1973), Frank Ceverich (Sausalito, 1974), Tony Margo (Burbank, 1975). Production associates: Arthur Withall, Susan Schwartz.

Cast (all the leading characters play themselves): Nicholas Ray, Tom Farrell, Leslie Levinson, Richie Bock, Danny Fisher, Jane Heymann, Jim North (Bum/ Santa Claus), Steve Maurer, Stanley Liu, Jill, Hallie, Phil Wiseman, Steve Anker, etc. Brief glimpses of: Jane Fonda, Tom Hayden, Rennie Davis, Bill Kunstler, Abbie Hoffman, Allen Ginsberg, Jon Voight.

Start of filming: September 1971. Première screening: May 1973 (Cannes Festival). Running time: (Cannes) 90 min.

1974   The Janitor
(Episode no. 12 of *Wet Dreams*)

Film Group One, Amsterdam, with Cinereal Film, West Berlin. *A dream by* Nicholas Ray. Director of photography: Max Fischer. 16mm colour, blown up to 35mm. Music: none. Editor: Max Fischer. Production co-ordinators: Max Fischer, Jim Haynes.

Cast: Nicholas Ray (The Preacher/The Janitor), Melvin Miracle, Anneke Spier-enburg, Dawn Cumming, Marvelle Williams, Mary Moore, Kees Koedood, Falcon Stuart, Barbara, Burnie Taylor.

Start of filming (Ray's episode): May 1973. Other episodes directed by Jens Joergen Thorsen, Sam Rotterdam [Dusan Makavejev], Oscar Cigard, Falcon Stuart, Max Fischer, Heathcote Williams, Lee Kraft, Geert Koolman, Hans Kanters. Release: 25 January 1974. Running time of episode: 14 min.

1978 Marco

Direction: Nicholas Ray. Based on the first chapter of the novel *Marco, A Novel of Love* by Curtis Bill Pepper. Directors of photography: Robert La Cativa, Danny Fisher. 16 mm colour.

Cast: Claudio Mazzatenta (Dario), Jim Ballagh and Ned Motolo (Cops), Gerry Bamman (Booking Officer), Connie (Woman at Desk), Charles W., Joaquin.

Start of filming: 2 December 1977. Running time: 11 min.

1980 Lightning Over Water (German title: *Nicks Movie*)

Road Movies Filmproduktion GmbH, Berlin, Wim Wenders Produktion, Berlin, in association with Viking Film, Stockholm. *Directors/screenplay*: Nicholas Ray, Wim Wenders. Director of photography: Ed Lachman. In colour. Camera operator: Martin Schäfer. Camera assistants: Mitch Dubin, Timothy Ray. Gaffer: Stephan Czapsky. Video: Tom Farrell. Editor: Peter Przygodda, assisted by Barbara von Weitershausen (first version); Wim Wenders, assisted by Chris Sievernich (definitive version). Assistant director: Pat Kirck. Re-recording mixer: Hiroaki 'Zom' Yamamoto (first version); Jack Higgins (definitive version). Sound: Martin Müller, Maryte Kavaliauskas, Gary Steele. Music: Ronee Blakley. Associate producers: Laurie Frank, Jonathan Becker. Executive producer: Renée Gundelach. Producers: Chris Sievernich, Pierre Cottrell.

Cast (all playing themselves): Gerry Bamman, Ronee Blakley, Pierre Cottrell, Stephan Czapsky, Mitch Dubin, Tom Farrell, Becky Johnston, Tom Kaufman, Maryte Kavaliauskas, Pat Kirck, Edward Lachman, Martin Müller, Craig Nelson, Timothy Ray, Susan Ray, Nicholas Ray, Martin Schäfer, Chris Sievernich, Wim Wenders.

Start of filming: 29 March 1979. Première (first version): May 1980 (Cannes Festival); definitive version, 1 November 1980 (Internationale Filmtage, Hof). Running time: 116 min. (first version), 91 min. (definitive version).

2 *Acting roles*

1977 Der amerikanische Freund (*The American Friend*)

Road Movies Filmproduktion GmbH, Berlin/Wim Wenders Produktion, Munich/Les Films du Losange, Paris. Director: Wim Wenders. Screenplay: Wim Wenders. From the novel *Ripley's Game* by Patricia Highsmith. Director of photography: Robby Müller. Music: Jürgen Knieper. Producer: Wim Wenders.

Cast: Bruno Ganz, Dennis Hopper, Lisa Kreuzer, Gérard Blain. As guests, the directors Nicholas Ray (Derwatt/Pogash), Samuel Fuller, Peter Lilienthal, Daniel Schmid, Sandy Whitelaw, Jean Eustache.

Start of New York filming: 3 March 1977. Première: 26 May 1977 (Cannes Festival). Running time: 126 min.

Nicholas Ray

1979   Hair

A Lester Persky and Michael Butler Production. Director: Milos Forman. Screenplay: Michael Weller. From the stage musical *Hair* by Gerome Ragni and James Rado (book and lyrics) and Galt MacDermot (music). Director of photography: Miroslav Ondricek. Vocal arrangements/musical director: Tom Pierson. Choreography: Twyla Tharp. Producers: Lester Persky, Michael Butler.

Cast: John Savage, Treat Williams, Beverly D'Angelo, Annie Golden, Dorsey Wright, Don Dacus, Cheryl Barnes, Melba Moore, Ronnie Dyson, Richard Bright, Charlotte Rae, Nicholas Ray (The General).

Filming at Barstow, California: January-February 1978. Running time: 122 min.

3   *Appearances in, or contributions to, documentary films*

1957   The James Dean Story

Warner Brothers. Directors: George W. George, Robert Altman. Commentary: Stewart Stern, spoken by Martin Gabel. Running time: 82 min. Incorporates documentary footage (black-and-white) of the filming of *Rebel Without a Cause*.

1963   Peking in Madrid

ABC Television. Commentary spoken by Charlton Heston. In colour. Broadcast on 9 June 1963. Running time: 30 min. (*Film Daily*, 11 March and 29 April 1963).

Documentary about the filming of *55 Days at Peking*

1970   Auf der Suche nach meinen Amerika – Eine Reise nach 20 Jahren (*America Revisited*)

NDR (Norddeutscher Rundfunk, Hamburg).
Director/Screenplay: Marcel Ophuls. Directors of photography: Nils-Peter Mahlau, Udo Franz. 16 mm colour. Sound: Christian Schmidt. Editor: Karin Baumhofner, Marguerite Oboussier. Broadcast on 20 and 23 October 1970.

Ray appears in the second part (cf. chapter 36).

1974   I'm a Stranger Here Myself

October Films, Cambridge (Massachusetts). Directors: David Helpern Jr, James C. Gutman. Screenplay/commentary: Myron Meisel. Director of photography: Austin De Besche. 16 mm colour. Editors: Richie Bock, Frank Galvin. Sound:

Richie Bock. Commentary spoken by Howard Da Silva. *Contributions by* Nicholas Ray, John Houseman, François Truffaut, Natalie Wood, Tom Farrell, Leslie Levinson and the group from *We Can't Go Home Again*. Running time: 58 min. Première: 7 January 1975.

Documentary about Ray (cf. chapters 37 and 38).

1975   James Dean: The First American Teenager

Visual Programme Systems. Director: Ray Connolly. Producers: David Puttnam, Sandy Lieberson. Directors of photography: Mike Mallory, Robert Gersicoff. In colour. *Contributions by* Corey Allen, Carroll Baker, Leslie Caron, Sammy Davis Jr, Dennis Hopper, Kenneth Kendall, Jack Larson, Sal Mineo, Maila Nurmi, Gene and Hal Owen, Nicholas Ray, Leonard Rosenman, Christine White, Peter Witt, Natalie Wood. Running time: 80 min.

The interview with Ray (only fragments of which are included in the film) was recorded in a cutting room, *c.* 1974.

1979   Garlic Is as Good as Ten Mothers

Flower Films. Director/screenplay: Les Blank. Director of photography: Les Blank. 16 mm colour. Sound/assistant director: Maureen Gosling. Running time: 51 min.

A documentary about garlic, shot over a period of five years. Ray appears in a single shot, filmed at the Chez Panisse restaurant in Berkeley, during the annual garlic festival in July 1977.

4   Television

1945 *Climax* series, CBS: *Sorry, Wrong Number*. Production: John Houseman. *Direction*: Nicholas Ray. *Teleplay*: John Houseman, Nicholas Ray. From the radio play by Lucille Fletcher. Cast: Mildred Natwick. Broadcast: Summer 1945. Running time: 30 min.

1957 *Monitor* programme, ABC: a 60-minute feature on the filming of *Wind Across the Everglades*. Filmed in December 1957 (*Hollywood Reporter*, 9 December).

1977 *Camera Three* programme, CBS: a portrait of Ray, who talks about his career with critic Cliff Jahr. Production: John Musilli. Broadcast: 17 April 1977 (Blaine Allan, *Nicholas Ray: a Guide to References and Resources*, no. 629).

Index

Figures in italics refer to captions.

Index

IMPORTANT:

HERE IS YOUR REGISTRATION CODE TO ACCESS
YOUR PREMIUM McGRAW-HILL ONLINE RESOURCES.

For key premium online resources you need THIS CODE to gain access. Once the code is entered, you will be able to use the Web resources for the length of your course.

If your course is using **WebCT** or **Blackboard**, you'll be able to use this code to access the McGraw-Hill content within your instructor's online course.

Access is provided if you have purchased a new book. If the registration code is missing from this book, the registration screen on our Website, and within your WebCT or Blackboard course, will tell you how to obtain your new code.

Registering for McGraw-Hill Online Resources

To gain access to your McGraw-Hill web resources simply follow the steps below:

(1) USE YOUR WEB BROWSER TO GO TO: **http://www.mhhe.com/dugopolski**

(2) CLICK ON **FIRST TIME USER**.

(3) ENTER THE REGISTRATION CODE* PRINTED ON THE TEAR-OFF BOOKMARK ON THE RIGHT.

(4) AFTER YOU HAVE ENTERED YOUR REGISTRATION CODE, CLICK **REGISTER**.

(5) FOLLOW THE INSTRUCTIONS TO SET-UP YOUR PERSONAL UserID AND PASSWORD.

(6) WRITE YOUR UserID AND PASSWORD DOWN FOR FUTURE REFERENCE.
KEEP IT IN A SAFE PLACE.

TO GAIN ACCESS to the McGraw-Hill content in your instructor's **WebCT** or **Blackboard** course simply log in to the course with the UserID and Password provided by your instructor. Enter the registration code exactly as it appears in the box to the right when prompted by the system. You will only need to use the code the first time you click on McGraw-Hill content.

Thank you, and welcome to your McGraw-Hill online resources!

* YOUR REGISTRATION CODE CAN BE USED ONLY ONCE TO ESTABLISH ACCESS. IT IS NOT TRANSFERABLE.

0-07-244392-8 DUGOPOLSKI: ALGEBRA FOR COLLEGE STUDENTS, 3E

MCGRAW-HILL
ONLINE RESOURCES

REGISTRATION CODE

physiology-80175170

Algebra for College Students

EDITION 3

Algebra for College Students

EDITION 3

Mark Dugopolski

Southeastern Louisiana University

 Higher Education

Boston   Burr Ridge, IL   Dubuque, IA   Madison, WI
New York   San Francisco   St. Louis   Bangkok
Bogotá   Caracas   Kuala Lumpur   Lisbon   London   Madrid
Mexico City   Milan   Montreal   New Delhi   Santiago
Seoul   Singapore   Sydney   Taipei   Toronto

ALGEBRA FOR COLLEGE STUDENTS, THIRD EDITION

Published by McGraw-Hill, a business unit of The McGraw-Hill Companies, Inc., 1221 Avenue of the Americas, New York, NY 10020. Copyright © 2004, 2000 by The McGraw-Hill Companies, Inc. All rights reserved. Previous editions © 1996 by Addison-Wesley Publishing Company, Inc. All rights reserved. No part of this publication may be reproduced or distributed in any form or by any means, or stored in a database or retrieval system, without the prior written consent of The McGraw-Hill Companies, Inc., including, but not limited to, in any network or other electronic storage or transmission, or broadcast for distance learning.

Some ancillaries, including electronic and print components, may not be available to customers outside the United States.

This book is printed on acid-free paper.

1 2 3 4 5 6 7 8 9 0 VNH/VNH 0 9 8 7 6 5 4 3

ISBN 0–07–244392–8

Publisher: *William K. Barter*
Senior sponsoring editor: *David Dietz*
Developmental editor: *Erin Brown*
Executive marketing manager: *Marianne C. P. Rutter*
Senior marketing manager: *Mary K. Kittell*
Senior project manager: *Vicki Krug*
Lead production supervisor: *Sandy Ludovissy*
Lead media project manager: *Audrey A. Reiter*
Media technology producer: *Jeff Huettman*
Coordinator of freelance design: *Rick D. Noel*
Cover designer: *Todd Damotte/Rokusek Design*
Cover image: *@Corbis, Volume 622, Architectural Details, No.5*
Lead photo research coordinator: *Carrie K. Burger*
Supplement producer: *Brenda A. Ernzen*
Compositor: *Interactive Composition Corporation*
Typeface: *10.5/12 Times Roman*
Printer: *Von Hoffmann Corporation*

Photo Credits
Page 1: © Robert Brenner/PhotoEdit; p. 30, p. 57: U.S. Army Corps of Engineers; p. 54: © Digital Vision/Volume 185; p. 78, p. 204, p. 399, p. 717: © Susan Van Etten; p. 125, 659: © Reuters NewMedia Inc./CORBIS; p. 168 (bottom), p. 310, p. 374, p. 467, p. 545, p. 721: © The McGraw-Hill Companies, Inc.; p. 255: © Paul Conklin/PhotoEdit; p. 327: © Digital Vision/Volume 285; p. 393: © Herb Snitzer/Stock Boston; p. 623: Courtesy Molly McCallister; p. 682: Courtesy Friedrich von Huene Workshop. All other photos © PhotoDisc, Inc.

Library of Congress Cataloging-in-Publication Data

Dugopolski, Mark.
  Algebra for college students / Mark Dugopolski. — 3rd ed.
      p.   cm.
  Includes index.
  ISBN 0–07–244392–8 (hard copy : alk. paper)
  1. Algebra. I. Title.

QA152.3 .D837   2004
512.9—dc21   2002153999
                                              CIP

www.mhhe.com

*To my wife and daughters,
Cheryl, Sarah, and Alisha*

CONTENTS

Appendix   A-1

Answers   A-7

Index   I-1

A lgebra for College Students, Third Edition, is designed to provide students with the algebra background needed for further college-level mathematics courses. The unifying theme of this text is the development of the skills necessary for solving equations and inequalities, followed by the application of those skills to solving applied problems. My primary goal in writing the third edition of *Algebra for College Students,* has been to retain the features that made the second edition so successful, while incorporating the comments and suggestions of second-edition users. As always, I endeavor to write texts that students can read, understand, and enjoy, while gaining confidence in their ability to use mathematics. Although a complete development of each topic is provided in *Algebra for College Students,* Third Edition, the text *Elementary Algebra,* Fourth Edition, in this series would be more appropriate for students with no prior experience in algebra.

Content Changes

While the essence of previous editions remains, the topics have been rearranged to reflect the current needs of instructors.

- Functions are introduced in Section 3.5. After that, function topics are revisited where appropriate. For example, polynomial functions appear in Section 5.3, the domain of rational expressions and functions is covered in Section 6.1, and the domain of radical functions is covered in Section 7.1. Functions also appear in Chapter 8, with quadratic equations, and again in Chapters 9, 10, and 11.

- Section 3.5 on functions and relations has been revised with expanded coverage of the concepts of domain and range and the different forms of a function. *Graphs of Functions*, previously Section 3.6, which included graphs of constant functions, quadratic functions, absolute value functions, and square-root functions has been moved to Chapter 9, Section 1.

- The distance and midpoint formulas now appear in Section 3.1, where graphing lines is introduced. The distance formula also appears in Section 12.2, where it is used to develop the equation of a parabola from the geometric definition.

- In Chapter 4, the two sections on determinants and Cramer's rule have been condensed into one, Section 4.5.

- To streamline Chapter 5, the section covering division of polynomials has been moved to Chapter 6 on rational expressions.

- Sections 7.1 and 7.2 have been swapped from the second edition so that radicals now appears as the first topic in Chapter 7, Section 1, and rational exponents now appears in Section 7.2.

- **NEW!** Transformations of graphs has been added to Chapter 9 and appears in Section 9.2.

- **NEW!** The factor theorem has been added to Chapter 10 and appears in Section 10.1.

with Chapter 2. Making Connections are cumulative sets of exercises that help students to continually practice what they learn. Also, functions are introduced in Section 3.5 and revisited where appropriate throughout the text. This constant reinforcement helps students retain and strengthen their understanding of this important concept. The distance formula is covered in Section 3.1 and reviewed in Section 12.2 where it is used to develop the equations of the conic sections. In Chapter 9, solving quadratics by factoring and the square root property are reviewed prior to the new ideas of completing the square and the quadratic formula. Through these, and similar methods, students retain what they learn and apply what they learn to new concepts.

Supplements for the Instructor

ANNOTATED INSTRUCTOR'S EDITION

This ancillary includes answers to all section ending exercises, review exercises, Making Connections exercises, and chapter tests. Each answer is printed next to each problem on the page where the problem appears. The answers are printed in a second color for ease of use by instructors.

INSTRUCTOR'S TESTING AND RESOURCE CD-ROM

This CD-ROM contains a computerized test bank that utilizes Brownstone Diploma® testing software. The computerized test bank enables instructors to create well-formatted quizzes or tests using a large bank of algorithmically generated and static questions. When creating a quiz or test, the user can manually choose individual questions or have the software randomly select questions based on section, question type, difficulty level, and other criteria. Instructors also have the ability to add or edit test bank questions to create their own customized test bank. In addition to printed tests, the test generator can deliver tests over a local area network or the World Wide Web, with automatic grading.

Also available on the CD-ROM are pre-formatted tests that appear in two forms: Adobe Acrobat (pdf) and Microsoft Word files. These files are provided for convenient access to "ready to use" tests. The tests can also be downloaded as a Word (.doc) file or can be viewed and printed as a (.pdf) file at www.mhhe.com/dugopolski.

INSTRUCTOR'S SOLUTIONS MANUAL

Prepared by Mark Dugopolski, this supplement contains detailed worked solutions to all of the exercises in the text. The solutions are based on by the techniques used in the text. Instructions and suggestions for using the Collaborative Activities feature in the text are also included in the Instructor's Solutions Manual.

PageOut

PageOut is McGraw-Hill's unique point-and-click course website tool, enabling instructors to create a full-featured, professional quality course Website without knowing HTML coding. With PageOut instructors can post a syllabus online, assign McGraw-Hill Online Learning Center content, add links to important off-site resources, and maintain student results in the online grade book. Instructors can also send class announcements, copy a course site to share with colleagues, and upload original files. PageOut is free for every McGraw-Hill user. For those instructors who are short on time, there is a team on hand, ready to help build a site!

Learn more about PageOut and other McGraw-Hill digital solutions at www.mhhe.com/solutions.

Supplements for the Student

STUDENT'S SOLUTIONS MANUAL

Prepared by Mark Dugopolski, the *Student's Solutions Manual* contains complete worked-out solutions to all of the odd-numbered exercises in the text. It also contains solutions for all exercises in the Chapter Tests. It may be purchased from McGraw-Hill.

DUGOPOLSKI VIDEO SERIES (Videotapes or CD-ROMs)

The videos are text-specific and cover all chapters of the text. The videos feature an instructor who introduces topics and works through selected problems from the exercise sets. Students are encouraged to work the problems on their own and to check their results with those provided.

DUGOPOLSKI TUTORIAL CD-ROM

This interactive CD-ROM is a self-paced tutorial specifically linked to the text that reinforces topics through unlimited opportunities to review concepts and practice problem solving. The CD-ROM contains algorithmically generated chapter-, and section-specific questions. It requires virtually no computer training on the part of students and supports Windows and Macintosh computers.

ONLINE LEARNING CENTER

The Online Learning Center (OLC), located at www.mhhe.com/dugopolski, contains resources for students and instructors.

Through the Instructor Resource Site, instructors can access links to professional resources, a PowerPoint presentation (transparencies), printable tests, group projects, and a link to PageOut.

To access the Instructor Resource Site, instructors must have a passcode that can be obtained by contacting a McGraw-Hill Higher Education representative.

The Student Learning Site is also passcode-protected. Passcodes for students can be found at the front of their texts when newly purchased. *Passcodes are available free to students when they purchase a new text.* Students also have access to algorithmically generated "bookmarkable" practice exercises (including hints), section- and chapter-level testing, audiovisual tutorials, interactive applications, and links to NetTutor™ and other interesting websites.

The Information Center can be accessed by students and instructors without a passcode. Through the Information Center, users can access general information about the text and its supplements.

ALEKS®

ALEKS® (**A**ssessment and **LE**arning in **K**nowledge **S**paces) is an artificial intelligence-based system for individualized math learning, available over the World Wide Web. ALEKS® delivers precise, qualitative diagnostic assessments of students' math knowledge, guides them in the selection of appropriate new study material, and records their progress toward mastery of curricular goals in a robust classroom management system. It interacts with the student much as a skilled human tutor would, moving between explanation and practice as needed, correcting and analyzing errors, defining terms, and changing topics on request. By sophisticated modeling of a student's "knowledge state" for a given subject matter, ALEKS® can focus clearly on what the student is most ready to learn next, building a learning momentum that fuels success.

To learn more about ALEKS® including purchasing information, visit the ALEKS® website at www.highedmath.aleks.com.

NetTutor

NetTutor is a revolutionary system that enables students to interact with a live tutor over the World Wide Web by using NetTutor's Web-based, graphical chat capabilities. Students can also submit questions and receive answers, browse previously answered questions, and view previous live chat sessions.

NetTutor can be accessed on the Online Learning Center through the Student Learning Site.

Acknowledgments

First of all I thank all of the students and professors who used the previous editions of this text, for without their support there would not be a third edition. I sincerely appreciate the efforts of the reviewers who made many helpful suggestions for improving the second edition:

Henry C. Bailey, *Cuyahoga Community College*
Carole Bergen, *Mercy College*
Adrian M. DeWindt-King, *Cumberland County College*
Suzanne Doviak, *Old Dominion University*
Paul C. Rokicky, *Cuyahoga Community College*
Alexis Thurman, *County College of Morris*

In addition, I would also like to thank the following reviewers of *Intermediate Algebra*, Third Edition. Their suggestions were also helpful in improving this volume.

Corinna Goehring, *Jackson State Community College*
Domingo Javier-Litong, *Houston Community College*
Joselle D. Kehoe, *DeVry Institute of Technology*
Susann Kyriazopoulos, *DeVry University–Chicago Campus*
Mitchel Levy, *Broward Community College*
Margaret Michener, *University of Nebraska–Kearney*
Joyce Nemeth, *Broward Community College–South Campus*
Charles Odion, *Houston Community College*
Avis Proctor, *Broward Community College*
Togba Sapolucia, *Houston Community College*
Donald W. Solomon, *University of Wisconsin–Milwaukee*
Burnette Thompson, *Houston Community College–Northwest*
Emmanuel Ekwere Usen, *Houston Community College*
Pam Wahl, *Middlesex Community College*
Joel D. Williams, *Houston Community College System*
Walter Wooden, *Broward Community College*

I also want to express my sincere appreciation to my wife, Cheryl, for her invaluable patience and support.

Hammond, Louisiana   M.D.

CHAPTER **1**

The Real Numbers

E verywhere you look people are running, riding, dancing, and exercising their way to fitness. In the past year more than $25 billion has been spent on sports equipment alone, and this amount is growing steadily.

Proponents of exercise claim that it can increase longevity, improve body image, decrease appetite, and generally enhance a person's health. While many sports activities can help you to stay fit, experts have found that aerobic, or dynamic, workouts provide the most fitness benefit. Some of the best aerobic exercises include cycling, running, and even jumping rope. Whatever athletic activity you choose, trainers recommend that you set realistic goals and work your way toward them consistently and slowly. To achieve maximum health benefits, experts suggest that you exercise three to five times a week for 15 to 60 minutes at a time.

There are many different ways to measure exercise. One is to measure the energy used, or the rate of oxygen consumption. Since heart rate rises as a function of increased oxygen, another easier measure of intensity of exercise is your heart rate during exercise. The desired heart rate, or target heart rate, for beneficial exercise varies for each individual depending on conditioning, age, and gender. In Exercises 101 and 102 of Section 1.4 you will see how an algebraic expression can determine your target heart rate for beneficial exercise.

Chapter Opener

Each **chapter opener** features a real-world situation that can be modeled using mathematics. Each chapter contains exercises that relate back to the chapter opener.

Evaluate each expression for $a = -1$, $b = 3$, and $c = -4$. See Example 7.

57. $b^2 - 4ac$

58. $\sqrt{a^2 - 4bc}$

59. $\dfrac{a - b}{a - c}$

60. $\dfrac{b - c}{b - a}$

61. $(a - b)(a + b)$

62. $(a - c)(a + c)$

63. $\sqrt{c^2 - 2c + 1}$

64. $b^2 - 2b - 3$

65. $\dfrac{2}{a} + \dfrac{b}{c} - \dfrac{1}{c}$

66. $\dfrac{c}{a} + \dfrac{c}{b} - \dfrac{a}{b}$

67. $|a - b|$

68. $|b + c|$

Find the value of $\dfrac{y_2 - y_1}{x_2 - x_1}$ for each choice of y_1, y_2, x_1, and x_2. See Example 8.

69. $y_1 = 4$, $y_2 = -6$, $x_1 = 2$, $x_2 = -7$

70. $y_1 = -3$, $y_2 = -3$, $x_1 = 4$, $x_2 = -5$

71. $y_1 = -1$, $y_2 = 2$, $x_1 = -3$, $x_2 = 1$

72. $y_1 = -2$, $y_2 = 5$, $x_1 = 2$, $x_2 = 6$

73. $y_1 = 2.4$, $y_2 = 5.6$, $x_1 = 5.9$, $x_2 = 4.7$

74. $y_1 = -5.7$, $y_2 = 6.9$, $x_1 = 3.5$, $x_2 = 4.2$

Evaluate each expression without a calculator. Use a calculator to check.

75. $-2^2 + 5(3)^2$

76. $-3^2 + 3(6)^2$

77. $(-2 + 5)3^2$

78. $(-3 + 3)6^2$

79. $\sqrt{5^2 - 4(1)(6)}$

80. $\sqrt{6^2 - 4(2)(4)}$

81. $[13 + 2(-5)]^2$

82. $[6 + 2(-4)]^2$

83. $\dfrac{4 - (-1)}{-3 - 2}$

84. $\dfrac{2 - (-3)}{3 - 5}$

85. $3(-2)^2 - 5(-2) + 4$

86. $3(-1)^2 + 5(-1) - 6$

87. $-4\left(\dfrac{1}{2}\right)^2 + 3\left(\dfrac{1}{2}\right) - 2$

88. $8\left(\dfrac{1}{2}\right)^2 - 6\left(\dfrac{1}{2}\right) + 1$

89. $-\dfrac{1}{2}|6 - 2|$

90. $-\dfrac{1}{3}|9 - 6|$

91. $\dfrac{1}{2} - \dfrac{1}{3}\left|\dfrac{1}{4} - \dfrac{1}{2}\right|$

92. $\dfrac{1}{3} - \dfrac{1}{2}\left|\dfrac{1}{3} - \dfrac{1}{2}\right|$

93. $|6 - 3 \cdot 7| + |7 - 5|$

94. $|12 - 4| - |3 - 4 \cdot 5|$

95. $3 - 7[4 - (2 - 5)]$

96. $9 - 2[3 - (4 + 6)]$

97. $3 - 4[2 - |4 - 6|]$

98. $3 - (|-4| - |-5|)$

99. $4[2 - (5 - |-3|)^2]$

100. $[5 - (-3)]^2 + [4 - (-2)]^2$

Solve each problem. See Example 9.

101. *Female target heart rate.* The algebraic expression $0.65(220 - A)$ gives the target heart rate for beneficial exercise for women, where A is the age of the woman. How much larger is the target heart rate of a 25-year-old woman than that of a 65-year-old woman? Use the accompanying graph to estimate the age at which a woman's target heart rate is 115.

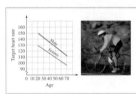

FIGURE FOR EXERCISES 101 AND 102

102. *Male target heart rate.* The algebraic expression $0.75(220 - A)$ gives the target heart rate for beneficial exercise for men, where A is the age of the man. Use the algebraic expression to find the target heart rate for a 20-year-old and a 50-year-old man. Use the accompanying graph to estimate the age at which a man's target heart rate is 115.

Solve each problem.

103. *Perimeter of a pool.* The algebraic expression $2L + 2W$ gives the perimeter of a rectangle with length L and width W. Find the perimeter of a rectangular swimming pool that has length 34 feet and width 18 feet.

104. *Area of a lot.* The algebraic expression for the area of a trapezoid, $0.5h(b_1 + b_2)$, gives the area of the property shown in the figure. Find the area if $h = 150$ feet, $b_1 = 260$ feet, and $b_2 = 220$ feet.

220 ft

150 ft

260 ft

FIGURE FOR EXERCISE 104

105. *Saving for retirement.* The expression $P(1 + r)^n$ gives the amount of an investment of P dollars invested for n years at interest rate r compounded

Margin Notes

Margin notes include **helpful hints, study tips,** and **calculator close-ups.** The **helpful hints** point out common errors or reminders. The **study tips** provide practical suggestions for improving study habits. The optional **calculator close-ups** provide tips on using a graphing calculator to aid in your understanding of the material. They also include insightful suggestions for increasing calculator proficiency.

The solution set is $(-\infty, 4]$, and its graph is shown in Fig. 2.13.

$$\xleftarrow{\hspace{1em}}\!{\overset{\bullet}{\underset{-5\;-4\;-3\;-2\;-1\;\;0\;\;1\;\;2\;\;3\;\;4\;\;5}{\rule{6cm}{0.4pt}}}}$$

FIGURE 2.13   ■

E X A M P L E   5   **An inequality with fractions**

Solve $\frac{1}{2}x - \frac{2}{3} \le x + \frac{4}{3}$. State and graph the solution set.

Helpful Hint

Notice that we use the same strategy for solving inequalities as we do for solving equations. But we must remember to reverse the inequality symbol when we multiply or divide by a negative number. For inequalities it is usually best to isolate the variable on the left-hand side.

Solution

First multiply each side of the inequality by 6, the LCD:

$$\frac{1}{2}x - \frac{2}{3} \le x + \frac{4}{3} \qquad \text{Original inequality}$$
$$6\left(\frac{1}{2}x - \frac{2}{3}\right) \le 6\left(x + \frac{4}{3}\right) \quad \text{Multiplying by positive 6 does not reverse the inequality.}$$
$$3x - 4 \le 6x + 8 \qquad \text{Distributive property}$$
$$3x \le 6x + 12 \qquad \text{Add 4 to each side.}$$
$$-3x \le 12 \qquad \text{Subtract 6x from each side.}$$
$$x \ge -4 \qquad \text{Divide each side by } -3 \text{ and reverse the inequality.}$$

The solution set is the interval $[-4, \infty)$. Its graph is shown in Fig. 2.14.

$$\xleftarrow{\hspace{1em}}\!{\overset{\bullet}{\underset{-5\;-4\;-3\;-2\;-1\;\;0\;\;1\;\;2\;\;3\;\;4\;\;5}{\rule{6cm}{0.4pt}}}}$$

FIGURE 2.14   ■

In Example 6 we see an inequality that is satisfied by all real numbers and one that has no solution.

E X A M P L E   6   **All or nothing**

Solve each inequality and graph the solution set.

a) $6 - 4x < -4x + 7$ **b)** $2(4x - 5) \ge 4(2x - 1)$

$$\xleftarrow{\hspace{1em}}\!{\underset{-2\;-1\;\;0\;\;1\;\;2}{\rule{3cm}{0.4pt}}}\!\xrightarrow{\hspace{1em}}$$

FIGURE 2.15

Solution

a) Adding $4x$ to each side will greatly simplify the inequality:

$$6 - 4x < -4x + 7 \qquad \text{Original inequality}$$
$$6 < 7 \qquad \text{Add 4x to each side.}$$

Since $6 < 7$ is correct no matter what real number is used in place of x, the solution set is the set of all real numbers $(-\infty, \infty)$. Its graph is shown in Fig. 2.15.

b) Start by simplifying each side of the inequality.

$$2(4x - 5) \ge 4(2x - 1) \qquad \text{Original inequality}$$
$$8x - 10 \ge 8x - 4 \qquad \text{Distributive property}$$
$$-10 \ge -4 \qquad \text{Subtract 8x from each side.}$$

Since $-10 \ge -4$ is false no matter what real number is used in place of x, the solution set is the empty set $\varnothing$ and there is no graph to draw.   ■

Study Tip

When you get a test back, don't simply file it in your notebook or the waste basket. While the material is fresh in your mind, rework all the problems that you missed. Ask questions about anything that you don't understand and save your test for future reference.

Linear Equation in One Variable

A **linear equation in one variable** x is an equation of the form $ax + b = 0$, where a and b are real numbers, with $a \ne 0$.

The equations in Examples 2 through 5 are called linear equations in one variable, or simply linear equations, because they could all be rewritten in the form $ax + b = 0$. At first glance the equations in Example 6 appear to be linear equations. However, they cannot be written in the form $ax + b = 0$, with $a \ne 0$, so they are not linear equations. A linear equation has exactly one solution. The strategy that we use for solving linear equations is summarized in the following box.

Strategy for Solving a Linear Equation

1. If fractions are present, multiply each side by the LCD to eliminate them.
2. Use the distributive property to remove parentheses.
3. Combine any like terms.
4. Use the addition property of equality to get all variables on one side and numbers on the other side.
5. Use the multiplication property of equality to get a single variable on one side.
6. Check by replacing the variable in the original equation with your solution.

Note that not all equations require all of the steps.

E X A M P L E   7   **Using the equation-solving strategy**

Solve the equation $\frac{y}{2} - \frac{y - 4}{5} = \frac{23}{10}$

Calculator Close-Up

You can use the fraction feature of a graphing calculator to check that 5 satisfies the equation. If you make a mistake entering an expression, you can recall the expression by pressing the ENTRY key and modify the expression.

```
5/2-(5-4)/5►Frac
              23/10
```

Solution

We first multiply each side of the equation by 10, the LCD for 2, 5, and 10. However, we do not have to write down that step. We can simply use the distributive property to multiply each term of the equation by 10.

$$\frac{y}{2} - \frac{y - 4}{5} = \frac{23}{10}$$
$$10\left(\frac{y}{2}\right) - 10\left(\frac{y - 4}{5}\right) = 10\left(\frac{23}{10}\right) \quad \text{Multiply each side by 10.}$$
$$5y - 2(y - 4) = 23 \qquad \text{Divide each denominator into 10 to eliminate fractions.}$$
$$5y - 2y + 8 = 23 \qquad \text{Be careful to change all signs: } -2(y - 4) = -2y + 8$$
$$3y + 8 = 23 \qquad \text{Combine like terms.}$$
$$3y + 8 - 8 = 23 - 8 \qquad \text{Subtract 8 from each side.}$$
$$3y = 15 \qquad \text{Simplify.}$$
$$\frac{3y}{3} = \frac{15}{3} \qquad \text{Divide each side by 3.}$$
$$y = 5$$

Check that 5 satisfies the original equation. The solution set is $\{5\}$.   ■

80 (2-24)   Chapter 2   Linear Equations and Inequalities in One Variable

Helpful Hint

Making a guess can be a good way to become familiar with the problem. For example, let's guess that the answers to Example 2 are 50, 51, and 52. Since $50 + 51 + 52 = 153$, these are not the correct numbers. But now we realize that we should use x, $x + 1$, and $x + 2$ and that the equation should be

$$x + x + 1 + x + 2 = 228.$$

Since the sum of these three expressions for the consecutive integers is 228, we can write the following equation and solve it:

$$x + (x + 1) + (x + 2) = 228 \qquad \text{The sum of the integers is 228.}$$
$$3x + 3 = 228$$
$$3x = 225$$
$$x = 75$$
$$x + 1 = 76 \qquad \text{Identify the other unknown quantities.}$$
$$x + 2 = 77$$

To verify that these values are the correct integers, we compute

$$75 + 76 + 77 = 228.$$

The three consecutive integers that have a sum of 228 are 75, 76, and 77. ■

General Strategy for Problem Solving

The steps to follow in providing a complete solution to a verbal problem can be stated as follows.

Study Tip

Don't simply work exercises to get answers. Keep reminding yourself of what you are actually doing. Keep trying to obtain the big picture. How does this section relate to what we did in the previous section? Where are we going next? When is the picture complete?

> **Strategy for Solving Word Problems**
>
> 1. Read the problem until you understand the problem. Making a guess and checking it will help you to understand the problem.
> 2. If possible, draw a diagram to illustrate the problem.
> 3. Choose a variable and write down what it represents.
> 4. Represent any other unknowns in terms of that variable.
> 5. Write an equation that models the situation.
> 6. Solve the equation.
> 7. Be sure that your solution answers the question posed in the original problem.
> 8. Check your answer by using it to solve the original problem (not the equation).

We will now see how this strategy can be applied to various types of problems.

Geometric Problems

Any problem that involves a geometric figure may be referred to as a **geometric problem.** For geometric problems the equation is often a geometric formula.

EXAMPLE 3   **Finding the length and width of a rectangle**
The length of a rectangular piece of property is 1 foot more than twice the width. If the perimeter is 302 feet, find the length and width.

Solution
First draw a diagram as in Fig. 2.4. Because the length is 1 foot more than twice the width, we let

$$x = \text{the width}$$

and

$$2x + 1 = \text{the length.}$$

$2x + 1$
FIGURE 2.4

Strategy Boxes

The **strategy boxes** provide a numbered list of concepts from a section or a set of steps to follow in problem solving. They can be used by students who prefer a more structured approach to problem solving or they can be used as a study tool to review important points within sections.

---

168 (3-44)   Chapter 3   Linear Equations and Inequalities in Two Variables

Solution
If x represents the number of AM ads and y represents the number of FM ads, then x and y must satisfy the inequality $50x + 75y \leq 3000$. Because the number of ads cannot be negative, we also have $x \geq 0$ and $y \geq 0$. So we graph only points in the first quadrant that satisfy $50x + 75y \leq 3000$. The line $50x + 75y = 3000$ goes

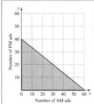

FIGURE 3.35

> **MATH AT WORK**
>
> "We will return after these messages." We often hear these words on television and radio just before several minutes of commercials. Carolanne Johnson, Account Executive and Media Salesperson for WBOQ, a classical radio station, is involved in every step of creating such advertisements.
> The first step is finding clients that are consistent with the station's image. Ms. Johnson generates her own leads from a number of sources, such as print ads and billboards. The next steps are sitting down with the client, gathering information about the product or service, assessing the competition, and finally determining how much of the client's advertising budget should be spent on radio. Typically, this can be 2% to 4% of the total budget.
> Radio ads usually run for 60 seconds, but reminder ads can be as short as 30 seconds. Some of the radio spots are time-sensitive and run 40 to 60 times a month for a specific month. Other clients are concerned with image building and may sponsor one particular broadcast every day for the whole year.
> Ms. Johnson is concerned that the clients receive an adequate return on their investment. She is constantly reviewing the budget and making sure that the commercials present what the client wishes to project.
> Example 7 and Exercise 77 of this section give problems that involve allocation of advertising dollars.
>
> **MEDIA SALESPERSON**

Math at Work

The **Math at Work** feature that appears in each chapter explores the careers of individuals who use the mathematics presented in the chapter in their work. Students are referred to exercises that directly relate to the occupation highlighted in **Math at Work.**

Warm-ups

Warm-ups appear before each set of exercises at the end of every section. They are true or false statements that can be used to check conceptual understanding of material within each section.

Helpful Hint

A problem involving two unknowns can often be solved with one variable as in Chapter 2. Likewise, you can often solve a problem with three unknowns using only two variables. Solve Example 5 by letting a, b, and $2a$ be the rent for a one-bedroom, two-bedroom, and a three-bedroom condo.

equation for the total repairs, and a third equation expressing the fact that the rent for the three-bedroom condo is twice that for the one-bedroom condo:

$$x + y + z = 1240$$
$$0.1x + 0.2y + 0.3z = 276$$
$$z = 2x$$

Substitute $z = 2x$ into both of the other equations to eliminate z:

$$x + y + 2x = 1240$$
$$0.1x + 0.2y + 0.3(2x) = 276$$

$$3x + y = 1240$$
$$0.7x + 0.2y = 276$$

$$-2(3x + y) = -2(1240) \quad \text{Multiply each side by } -2.$$
$$10(0.7x + 0.2y) = 10(276) \quad \text{Multiply each side by 10.}$$

$$-6x - 2y = -2480$$
$$\underline{7x + 2y = 2760} \quad \text{Add.}$$
$$x = 280$$

$$z = 2(280) = 560 \quad \text{Because } z = 2x$$
$$280 + y + 560 = 1240 \quad \text{Because } x + y + z = 1240$$
$$y = 400$$

Check that (280, 400, 560) satisfies all three of the original equations. The condos rent for $280, $400, and $560 per week. ■

WARM-UPS

True or false? Explain your answer.

1. The point $(1, -2, 3)$ is in the solution set to the equation $x + y - z = 4$.

2. The point $(4, 1, 1)$ is the only solution to the equation $x + y - z = 4$.

3. The ordered triple $(1, -1, 2)$ satisfies $x + y + z = 2$, $x - y - z = 0$, and $2x + y - z = -1$.

4. Substitution cannot be used on three equations in three variables.

5. Two distinct planes are either parallel or intersect in a single point.

6. The equations $x - y + 2z = 6$ and $x - y + 2z = 4$ are inconsistent.

7. The equations $3x + 2y - 6z = 4$ and $-6x - 4y + 12z = -8$ are dependent.

8. The graph of $y = 2x - 3z + 4$ is a straight line.

9. The value of x nickels, y dimes, and z quarters is $0.05x + 0.10y + 0.25z$ cents.

10. If $x = -2$, $z = 3$, and $x + y + z = 6$, then $y = 7$.

---

32. *Buying texts.* Melissa purchased an English text, a math text, and a chemistry text for a total of $276. The English text was $20 more than the math text and the chemistry text was twice the price of the math text. What was the price of each text?

33. *Three-day drive.* In three days, Carter drove 2196 miles in 36 hours behind the wheel. The first day he averaged 64 mph, the second day 62 mph, and the third day 58 mph. If he drove 4 more hours on the third day than on the first day, then how many hours did he drive each day?

34. *Three-day trip.* In three days, Katy traveled 146 miles down the Mississippi River in her kayak with 30 hours of paddling. The first day she averaged 6 mph, the second day 5 mph, and the third day 4 mph. If her distance on the third day was equal to her distance on the first day, then for how many hours did she paddle each day?

35. *Diversification.* Ann invested a total of $12,000 in stocks, bonds, and a mutual fund. She received a 10% return on her stock investment, an 8% return on her bond investment, and a 12% return on her mutual fund. Her total return was $1,230. If the total investment in stocks and bonds equaled her mutual fund investment, then how much did she invest in each?

36. *Paranoia.* Fearful of a bank failure, Norman split his life savings of $60,000 among three banks. He received 5%, 6%, and 7% on the three deposits. In the account earning 7% interest, he deposited twice as much as in the account earning 5% interest. If his total earnings were $3,760, then how much did he deposit in each account?

37. *Weighing in.* Anna, Bob, and Chris will not disclose their weights but agree to be weighed in pairs. Anna and Bob together weigh 226 pounds. Bob and Chris together weigh 210 pounds. Anna and Chris together weigh 200 pounds. How much does each student weigh?

Anna & Bob   Bob & Chris   Anna & Chris
FIGURE FOR EXERCISE 37

38. *Big tipper.* On Monday Headley paid $1.70 for two cups of coffee and one doughnut, including the tip. On Tuesday he paid $1.65 for two doughnuts and a cup of

coffee, including the tip. On Wednesday he paid $1.30 for one coffee and one doughnut, including the tip. If he always tips the same amount, then what is the amount of each item?

39. *Three coins.* Nelson paid $1.75 for his lunch with 13 coins, consisting of nickels, dimes, and quarters. If the number of dimes was twice the number of nickels, then how many of each type of coin did he use?

40. *Pocket change.* Harry has $2.25 in nickels, dimes, and quarters. If he had twice as many nickels, half as many dimes, and the same number of quarters, he would have $2.50. If he has 27 coins altogether, then how many of each does he have?

41. *Working overtime.* To make ends meet, Ms. Farnsby works three jobs. Her total income last year was $48,000. Her income from teaching was just $6,000 more than her income from house painting. Royalties from her textbook sales were one-seventh of the total money she received from teaching and house painting. How much did she make from each source last year?

42. *Lunch-box special.* Salvador's Fruit Mart sells variety packs. The small pack contains three bananas, two apples, and one orange for $1.80. The medium pack contains four bananas, three apples, and three oranges for $3.05. The family size contains six bananas, five apples, and four oranges for $4.65. What price should Salvador charge for his lunch-box special that consists of one banana, one apple, and one orange?

43. *Three generations.* Edwin, his father, and his grandfather have an average age of 53. One-half of his grandfather's age, plus one-third of his father's age, plus one-fourth of Edwin's age is 65. If 4 years ago, Edwin's grandfather was four times as old as Edwin, then how old are they all now?

44. *Three-digit number.* The sum of the digits of a three-digit number is 11. If the digits are reversed, the new number is 46 more than five times the old number. If the hundreds digit plus twice the tens digit is equal to the units digit, then what is the number?

GETTING MORE INVOLVED

45. *Exploration.* Draw diagrams showing the possible ways to position three planes in three-dimensional space.

46. *Discussion.* Make up a system of three linear equations in three variables for which the solution set is $\{(0, 0, 0)\}$. A system with this solution set is called a *homogeneous* system. Why do you think it is given that name?

Exercises

The theme of mathematics in everyday situations is carried over to the exercise sets. Applications based on real-world data are included in each set. The **Index of Selected Applications** can help students to quickly identify exercises that associate the mathematics that may be used in their areas of interest.

148 (3-24) Chapter 3 Linear Equations and Inequalities in Two Variables

MISCELLANEOUS

55. The points (3,) and (, −7) are on the line that passes through (2, 1) and has slope 4. Find the missing coordinates of the points.

56. If a line passes through (5, 2) and has slope $\frac{2}{3}$, then what is the value of y on this line when $x = 8$, $x = 11$, and $x = 12$?

57. Find k so that the line through $(2, k)$ and $(−3, −5)$ has slope $\frac{1}{2}$.

58. Find k so that the line through $(k, 3)$ and $(−2, 0)$ has slope 3.

59. What is the slope of a line that is perpendicular to a line with slope 0.247?

60. What is the slope of a line that is perpendicular to the line through $(3.27, −1.46)$ and $(−5.48, 3.61)$?

GETTING MORE INVOLVED

61. *Writing.* What is the difference between zero slope and undefined slope?

62. *Writing.* Is it possible for a line to be in only one quadrant? Two quadrants? Write a rule for determining whether a line has positive, negative, zero, or undefined slope from knowing in which quadrants the line is found.

63. *Exploration.* A rhombus is a quadrilateral with four equal sides. Draw a rhombus with vertices $(−3, −1)$, $(0, 3)$, $(2, −1)$, and $(5, 3)$. Find the slopes of the diagonals of the rhombus. What can you conclude about the diagonals of this rhombus?

64. *Exploration.* Draw a square with vertices $(−5, 3)$, $(−3, −3)$, $(1, 5)$, and $(3, −1)$. Find the slopes of the diagonals of the square. What can you conclude about the diagonals of this square?

GRAPHING CALCULATOR EXERCISES

65. Graph $y = 1x$, $y = 2x$, $y = 3x$, and $y = 4x$ together in the standard viewing window. These equations are all of the form $y = mx$. What effect does increasing m have on the graph of the equation? What are the slopes of these four lines?

66. Graph $y = −1x$, $y = −2x$, $y = −3x$, and $y = −4x$ together in the standard viewing window. These equations are all of the form $y = mx$. What effect does decreasing m have on the graph of the equation? What are the slopes of these four lines?

In This Section
- Point-Slope Form
- Slope-Intercept Form
- Standard Form
- Using Slope-Intercept Form for Graphing
- Applications

3.3 THREE FORMS FOR THE EQUATION OF A LINE

In Section 3.1 you learned how to graph a straight line corresponding to a linear equation. The line contains all of the points that satisfy the equation. In this section we start with a line or a description of a line and write an equation corresponding to the line.

Point-Slope Form

Figure 3.20 shows the line that has slope $\frac{2}{3}$ and contains the point $(3, 5)$. In Section 3.2 you learned that the slope is the same no matter which two points of the line are used to calculate it. So if we find the slope m for this line using an arbitrary point of the line, say (x, y), and the specific point $(3, 5)$, we get

$$m = \frac{y - 5}{x - 3}.$$

Getting More Involved appears within selected exercise sets. This feature may contain

 Writing,

 Cooperative Learning,

Exploration, and/or

Discussion exercises. Each of these components is designed to give students an opportunity to improve and develop the ways in which they express mathematical ideas.

The exercise sets contain exercises that are keyed to examples, as well as exercises that are not keyed to examples.

3.4 Linear Inequalities and Their Graphs (3-37) **161**

c) Write the equation of the line through $(0, 3)$ and $(−5, 0)$ in intercept form.

d) Which lines cannot be written in intercept form?

GRAPHING CALCULATOR EXERCISES

98. Graph the equation $y = 0.5x − 1$ using the standard viewing window. Adjust the range of y-values so that the line goes from the lower left corner of your viewing window to the upper right corner.

99. Graph $y = x − 3000$, using a viewing window that shows both the x-intercept and the y-intercept.

100. Graph $y = 2x − 400$ and $y = −0.5x + 1$ on the same screen, using the viewing window $−500 \leq x \leq 500$ and $−1000 \leq y \leq 1000$. Should these lines be perpendicular? Explain.

101. The lines $y = 2x − 3$ and $y = 1.9x + 2$ are not parallel. Find a viewing window in which the lines intersect. Estimate the point of intersection.

In This Section
- Definition
- Graphing Linear Inequalities
- The Test Point Method
- Graphing Compound Inequalities
- Applications

3.4 LINEAR INEQUALITIES AND THEIR GRAPHS

In the first three sections of this chapter you studied linear equations. We now turn our attention to linear inequalities.

Definition

A linear inequality is a linear equation with the equal sign replaced by an inequality symbol.

> **Linear Inequality**
>
> If A, B, and C are real numbers with A and B not both zero, then
>
> $$Ax + By \leq C$$
>
> is called a **linear inequality.** In place of $\leq$, we can also use $\geq$, $<$, or $>$.

Graphing Linear Inequalities

Consider the inequality $−x + y > 1$. If we solve the inequality for y, we get

$$y > x + 1.$$

Study Tip

Working problems one hour per day every day of the week is better than working problems for 7 hours on one day of the week. It is usually better to spread out your study time than to try and learn everything in one big session.

Which points in the xy-plane satisfy this inequality? We want the points where the y-coordinate is larger than the x-coordinate plus 1. If we locate a point on the line $y = x + 1$, say $(2, 3)$, then the y-coordinate is equal to the x-coordinate plus 1. If we move upward from that point, to say $(2, 4)$, the y-coordinate is larger than the x-coordinate plus 1. Because this argument can be made at every point on the line, all points above the line satisfy $y > x + 1$. Likewise, points below the line satisfy $y < x + 1$. The solution sets, or graphs, for the inequality $y > x + 1$ and the inequality $y < x + 1$ are the shaded regions shown in Figs. 3.24(a) and 3.24(b) on the next page. In each case the line $y = x + 1$ is dashed to indicate that points on the line do not satisfy the inequality and so are not in the solution set. If the inequality symbol is $\leq$ or $\geq$, then points on the boundary line also satisfy the inequality, and the line is drawn solid.

Calculator Exercises

Calculator Exercises are optional. They provide an opportunity for students to learn how a scientific or graphing calculator might be useful in solving various problems.

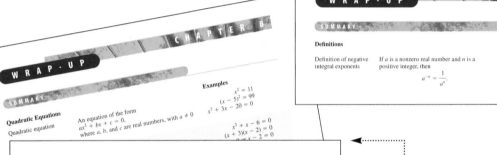

318 (5-64) Chapter 5 Exponents and Polynomials

you get $x^2 - x = 0$, which has two solutions. Which method is correct? Explain.

96. *Cooperative learning.* Work with a group to examine the following solution to $x^2 - 2x = -1$:

$$x(x - 2) = -1$$
$$x = -1 \quad \text{or} \quad x - 2 = -1$$
$$x = -1 \quad \text{or} \quad x = 1$$

Is this method correct? Explain.

97. *Cooperative learning.* Work with a group to examine the following steps in the solution to $5x^2 - 5 = 0$

$$5(x^2 - 1) = 0$$
$$5(x - 1)(x + 1) = 0$$
$$x - 1 = 0 \quad \text{or} \quad x + 1 = 0$$
$$x = 1 \quad \text{or} \quad x = -1$$

What happened to the 5? Explain.

COLLABORATIVE ACTIVITIES

Magic Tricks

Jim and Sadar are talking one day after class.

Sadar: Jim, I have a trick for you. Think of a number between 1 and 10. I will ask you to do some things to this number. Then at the end tell me your result, and I will tell you your number.

Jim: Oh, yeah you probably rig it so the result is my number.

Sadar: Come on Jim, give it a try and see.

Jim: Okay, okay, I thought of a number.

Sadar: Good, now write it down, and don't let me see your paper. Now add x. Got that? Now multiply everything by 2.

Jim: Hey, I didn't know you were going to make me think! This is algebra!

Sadar: I know, now just do it. Okay, now square the polynomial. Got that? Now subtract $4x^2$.

Jim: How did you know I had a $4x^2$? I told you this was rigged!

Sadar: Of course it's rigged, or it wouldn't work. Do you want to finish or not?

Jim: Yeah, I guess so. Go ahead, what do I do next?

Sadar: Divide by 4. Okay, now subtract the x-term.

Grouping: Two students per group
Topic: Practice with exponent rules, multiplying polynomials

Jim: Just any old x-term? Got any particular coefficient in mind?

Sadar: Now stop teasing me. I know you only have one x-term left, so subtract it.

Jim: Ha, ha, I *could* give you a hint about the coefficient, but that wouldn't be fair, would it?

Sadar: Well you could, and then I could tell you your number, or you could just tell me the number you have left after subtracting.

Jim: Okay, the number I had left at the end was 25. Let's see if you can tell me what the coefficient of the x-term I subtracted is.

Sadar: Aha, then the number you chose at the beginning was 5, and the coefficient was 10!

Jim: Hey, you're right! How did you do that?

In your group, follow Sadar's instructions and determine why she knew Jim's number. Make up another set of instructions to use as a magic trick. Be sure to use variables and some of the exponent rules or rules for multiplying polynomials that you learned in this chapter. Exchange instructions with another group and see whether you can figure out how their trick works.

WRAP-UP CHAPTER 5

SUMMARY

Definitions		Examples
Definition of negative integral exponents	If a is a nonzero real number and n is a positive integer, then $$a^{-n} = \frac{1}{a^n}.$$	$2^{-3} = \frac{1}{2^3} = \frac{1}{8}$

Collaborative Activities

Collaborative Activities appear at the end of each chapter. The activities are designed to encourage interaction and learning in a group setting.

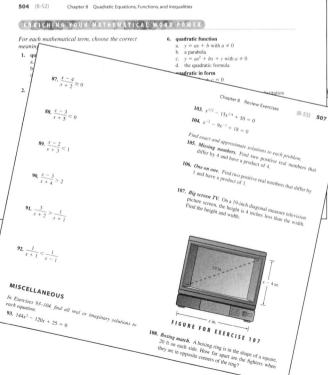

WRAP-UP CHAPTER 8

SUMMARY

Quadratic Equations		Examples
Quadratic equation	An equation of the form $ax^2 + bx + c = 0$, where a, b, and c are real numbers, with $a \neq 0$	$x^2 = 11$ $(x - 5)^2 = 99$ $x^2 + 3x - 20 = 0$
		$x^2 + x - 6 = 0$ $(x + 3)(x - 2) = 0$

504 (8-52) Chapter 8 Quadratic Equations, Functions, and Inequalities

ENRICHING YOUR MATHEMATICAL WORD POWER

For each mathematical term, choose the correct meaning

1. qu

6. quadratic function
a. $y = ax + b$ with $a \neq 0$
b. a parabola
c. $y = ax^2 + bx + c$ with $a \neq 0$
d. the quadratic formula

87. $\frac{x - 4}{x + 2} \geq 0$

88. $\frac{x - 3}{x + 5} < 0$

89. $\frac{x - 2}{x + 3} < 1$

90. $\frac{x - 3}{x + 4} > 2$

91. $\frac{3}{x + 2} > \frac{1}{x + 1}$

92. $\frac{1}{x + 1} < \frac{1}{x - 1}$

MISCELLANEOUS

In Exercises 93–104, find all real or imaginary solutions to each equation.

93. $144x^2 - 120x + 25 = 0$

Chapter 8 Review Exercises (8-55) 507

103. $x^{1/2} - 15x^{1/4} + 50 = 0$

104. $x^{-2} - 9x^{-1} + 18 = 0$

Find exact and approximate solutions to each problem.

105. *Missing numbers.* Find two positive real numbers that differ by 4 and have a product of 4.

106. *One on one.* Find two positive real numbers that differ by 1 and have a product of 1.

107. *Big screen TV.* On a 19-inch diagonal measure television picture screen, the height is 4 inches less than the width. Find the height and width.

19 in. $x - 4$ in. x in.

FIGURE FOR EXERCISE 107

108. *Boxing match.* A boxing ring is in the shape of a square, 20 ft on each side. How far apart are the fighters when they are in opposite corners of the ring?

Wrap-up

Every chapter ends with a four-part **Wrap-up:**

The **Summary** lists important concepts along with brief illustrative examples.

Enriching Your Mathematical Word Power enables students to review terms introduced in each chapter. It is intended to help reinforce students' command of mathematical terminology.

Review Exercises contain problems that are keyed to each section of the chapter as well as **miscellaneous exercises,** which are not keyed to the sections. The *miscellaneous exercises* are designed to test the student's ability to synthesize various concepts.

CHAPTER 8 TEST

Calculate the value of $b^2 - 4ac$, and state how many real solutions each equation has.

1. $2x^2 - 3x + 2 = 0$

2. $-3x^2 + 5x - 1 = 0$

3. $4x^2 - 4x + 1 = 0$

Solve by using the quadratic formula.

4. $2x^2 + 5x - 3 = 0$

5. $x^2 + 6x + 6 = 0$

Solve by completing the square.

6. $x^2 + 10x + 25 = 0$

7. $2x^2 + x - 6 = 0$

Solve by any method.

8. $x(x + 1) = 12$

9. $a^4 - 5a^2 + 4 = 0$

10. $x - 2 - 8\sqrt{x - 2} + 15 = 0$

Find the complex solutions to the quadratic equations.

11. $x^2 + 36 = 0$

12. $x^2 + 6x + 10 = 0$

13. $3x^2 - x + 1 = 0$

Graph each quadratic function. State the domain and range.

14. $f(x) = 16 - x^2$

15. $g(x) = x^2 - 3x$

Write a quadratic equation that has each given pair of solutions.

16. $-4, 6$

17. $-5i, 5i$

Solve each inequality. State and graph the solution set.

18. $w^2 + 3w < 18$

19. $\dfrac{2}{x - 2} < \dfrac{3}{x + 1}$

Find the exact solution to each problem.

20. The length of a rectangle is 2 ft longer than the width. If the area is 16 ft², then what are the length and width?

21. A new computer can process a company's monthly payroll in 1 hour less time than the old computer. To really save time, the manager used both computers and finished the payroll in 3 hours. How long would it take the new computer to do the payroll by itself?

Solve each problem.

22. Find the x-intercepts for the parabola $y = x^2 - 6x + 5$.

23. The height in feet for a ball thrown upward at 48 feet per second is given by $s(t) = -16t^2 + 48t$, where t is the time in seconds after the ball is tossed. What is the maximum height that the ball will reach?

Chapter Test

This is designed to help the student assess his or her readiness for a test. The **Chapter Test** has no keyed exercises, which affords students an opportunity to synthesize concepts found within the chapter.

Making Connections

These nonkeyed exercises are designed to help students synthesize new material with ideas from previous chapters and, in some cases, review material necessary for success in the upcoming chapter. They may serve as a cumulative review.

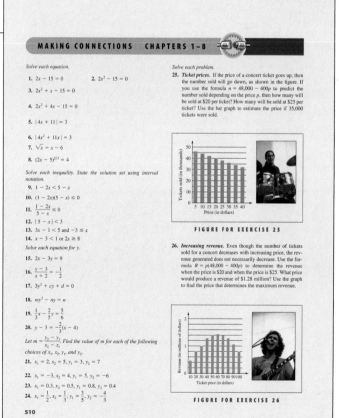

MAKING CONNECTIONS   CHAPTERS 1–8

Solve each equation.

1. $2x - 15 = 0$

2. $2x^2 - 15 = 0$

3. $2x^2 + x - 15 = 0$

4. $2x^2 + 4x - 15 = 0$

5. $|4x + 11| = 3$

6. $|4x^2 + 11x| = 3$

7. $\sqrt{x} = x - 6$

8. $(2x - 5)^{2/3} = 4$

Solve each inequality. State the solution set using interval notation.

9. $1 - 2x < 5 - x$

10. $(1 - 2x)(5 - x) \le 0$

11. $\dfrac{1 - 2x}{5 - x} \le 0$

12. $|5 - x| < 3$

13. $3x - 1 < 5$ and $-3 \le x$

14. $x - 3 < 1$ or $2x \ge 8$

Solve each equation for y.

15. $2x - 3y = 9$

16. $\dfrac{y - 3}{x + 2} = \dfrac{1}{2}$

17. $3y^2 + cy + d = 0$

18. $my^2 - ny = w$

19. $\dfrac{1}{3}x - \dfrac{2}{5}y = \dfrac{5}{6}$

20. $y - 3 = -\dfrac{2}{3}(x - 4)$

Let $m = \dfrac{y_2 - y_1}{x_2 - x_1}$. Find the value of m for each of the following choices of x_1, x_2, y_1, and y_2.

21. $x_1 = 2, x_2 = 5, y_1 = 3, y_2 = 7$

22. $x_1 = -3, x_2 = 4, y_1 = 5, y_2 = -6$

23. $x_1 = 0.3, x_2 = 0.5, y_1 = 0.8, y_2 = 0.4$

24. $x_1 = \dfrac{1}{2}, x_2 = \dfrac{1}{3}, y_1 = \dfrac{3}{5}, y_2 = -\dfrac{4}{3}$

Solve each problem.

25. *Ticket prices.* If the price of a concert ticket goes up, then the number sold will go down, as shown in the figure. If you use the formula $n = 48,000 - 400p$ to predict the number sold depending on the price p, then how many will be sold at $20 per ticket? How many will be sold at $25 per ticket? Use the bar graph to estimate the price if 35,000 tickets were sold.

FIGURE FOR EXERCISE 25

26. *Increasing revenue.* Even though the number of tickets sold for a concert decreases with increasing price, the revenue generated does not necessarily decrease. Use the formula $R = p(48,000 - 400p)$ to determine the revenue when the price is $20 and when the price is $25. What price would produce a revenue of $1.28 million? Use the graph to find the price that determines the maximum revenue.

FIGURE FOR EXERCISE 26

The Real Numbers

Everywhere you look people are running, riding, dancing, and exercising their way to fitness. In the past year more than $25 billion has been spent on sports equipment alone, and this amount is growing steadily.

Proponents of exercise claim that it can increase longevity, improve body image, decrease appetite, and generally enhance a person's health. While many sports activities can help you to stay fit, experts have found that aerobic, or dynamic, workouts provide the most fitness benefit. Some of the best aerobic exercises include cycling, running, and even jumping rope. Whatever athletic activity you choose, trainers recommend that you set realistic goals and work your way toward them consistently and slowly. To achieve maximum health benefits, experts suggest that you exercise three to five times a week for 15 to 60 minutes at a time.

There are many different ways to measure exercise. One is to measure the energy used, or the rate of oxygen consumption. Since heart rate rises as a function of increased oxygen, another easier measure of intensity of exercise is your heart rate during exercise. The desired heart rate, or target heart rate, for beneficial exercise varies for each individual depending on conditioning, age, and gender. In Exercises 101 and 102 of Section 1.4 you will see how an algebraic expression can determine your target heart rate for beneficial exercise.

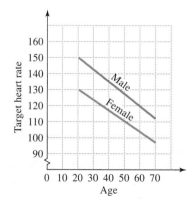

1.1   S E T S

Every subject has its own terminology, and **algebra** is no different. In this section we will learn the basic terms and facts about sets.

Set Notation

A **set** is a collection of objects. At home you may have a set of dishes and a set of steak knives. In algebra we generally discuss sets of numbers. For example, we refer to the numbers 1, 2, 3, 4, 5, and so on as the set of **counting numbers** or **natural numbers.** Of course, these are the numbers that we use for counting.

The objects or numbers in a set are called the **elements** or **members** of the set. To describe sets with a convenient notation, we use braces, { }, and name the sets with capital letters. For example,

$$A = \{1, 2, 3\}$$

means that set A is the set whose members are the natural numbers 1, 2, and 3. The letter N is used to represent the entire set of natural numbers.

A set that has a fixed number of elements such as $\{1, 2, 3\}$ is a **finite** set, whereas a set without a fixed number of elements such as the natural numbers is an **infinite** set. When listing the elements of a set, we use a series of three dots to indicate a continuing pattern. For example, the set of natural numbers is written as

$$N = \{1, 2, 3, \ldots\}.$$

The set of natural numbers *between* 4 and 40 can be written

$$\{5, 6, 7, 8, \ldots, 39\}.$$

Note that since the members of this set are *between* 4 and 40, it does not include 4 or 40.

Set-builder notation is another method of describing sets. In this notation we use a variable to represent the numbers in the set. A **variable** is a letter that is used to stand for some numbers. The set is then built from the variable and a description of the numbers that the variable represents. For example, the set

$$B = \{1, 2, 3, \ldots, 49\}$$

is written in set-builder notation as

$$B = \{x \mid x \text{ is a natural number less than } 50\}.$$

↑ ↑   ↑

The set of numbers   such that   condition for membership

This notation is read as "B is the set of numbers x such that x is a natural number less than 50." Notice that the number 50 is not a member of set B.

The symbol $\in$ is used to indicate that a specific number is a member of a set, and $\notin$ indicates that a specific number is not a member of a set. For example, the statement $1 \in B$ is read as "1 is a member of B," "1 belongs to B," "1 is in B," or "1 is an element of B." The statement $0 \notin B$ is read as "0 is not a member of B," "0 does not belong to B," "0 is not in B," or "0 is not an element of B."

Two sets are **equal** if they contain exactly the same members. Otherwise, they are said to be not equal. To indicate equal sets, we use the symbol $=$. For sets that are not equal we use the symbol $\neq$. The elements in two equal sets do not need to be written in the same order. For example, $\{3, 4, 7\} = \{3, 4, 7\}$ and $\{2, 4, 1\} = \{1, 2, 4\}$, but $\{3, 5, 6\} \neq \{3, 5, 7\}$.

E X A M P L E 1

Set notation

Let $A = \{1, 2, 3, 5\}$ and $B = \{x \mid x$ is an even natural number less than 10$\}$. Determine whether each statement is true or false.

a) $3 \in A$ **b)** $5 \in B$ **c)** $4 \notin A$ **d)** $A = N$
e) $A = \{x \mid x$ is a natural number less than 6$\}$ **f)** $B = \{2, 4, 6, 8\}$

Solution

a) True, because 3 is a member of set A.

b) False, because 5 is not an even natural number.

c) True, because 4 is not a member of set A.

d) False, because A does not contain all of the natural numbers.

e) False, because 4 is a natural number less than 6, and $4 \notin A$.

f) True, because the even counting numbers less than 10 are 2, 4, 6, and 8.   ■

Union of Sets

Any two sets A and B can be combined to form a new set called their union that consists of all elements of A together with all elements of B.

> ### Union of Sets
>
> If A and B are sets, the **union** of A and B, denoted $A \cup B$, is the set of all elements that are either in A, in B, or in both. In symbols,
>
> $$A \cup B = \{x \mid x \in A \text{ or } x \in B\}.$$

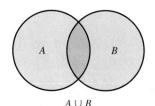

$A \cup B$

FIGURE 1.1

In mathematics the word "or" is always used in an inclusive manner (allowing the possibility of both alternatives). The diagram in Fig. 1.1 can be used to illustrate $A \cup B$. Any point that lies within circle A, circle B, or both is in $A \cup B$. Diagrams (like Fig. 1.1) that are used to illustrate sets are called **Venn diagrams.**

E X A M P L E 2

Union of sets

Let $A = \{0, 2, 3\}$, $B = \{2, 3, 7\}$, and $C = \{7, 8\}$. List the elements in each of these sets.

a) $A \cup B$ **b)** $A \cup C$

Helpful Hint

To remember what "union" means think of a labor union, which is a group formed by joining together many individuals.

Solution

a) $A \cup B$ is the set of numbers that are in A, in B, or in both A and B.

$$A \cup B = \{0, 2, 3, 7\}$$

b) $A \cup C = \{0, 2, 3, 7, 8\}$ ■

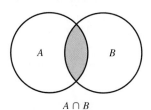

$A \cap B$

FIGURE 1.2

Intersection of Sets

Another way to form a new set from two known sets is by considering only those elements that the two sets have in common. The diagram shown in Fig. 1.2 illustrates the intersection of two sets A and B.

Helpful Hint

To remember the meaning of "intersection," think of the intersection of two roads. At the intersection you are on both roads.

Intersection of Sets

If A and B are sets, the **intersection** of A and B, denoted $A \cap B$, is the set of all elements that are in both A and B. In symbols,

$$A \cap B = \{x \mid x \in A \text{ and } x \in B\}.$$

It is possible for two sets to have no elements in common. A set with no members is called the **empty set** and is denoted by the symbol $\varnothing$. Note that $A \cup \varnothing = A$ and $A \cap \varnothing = \varnothing$ for any set A.

CAUTION   The set $\{0\}$ is not the empty set. The set $\{0\}$ has one member, the number 0. Do not use the number 0 to represent the empty set.

E X A M P L E   3

Intersection of sets

Let $A = \{0, 2, 3\}$, $B = \{2, 3, 7\}$, and $C = \{7, 8\}$. List the elements in each of these sets.

a) $A \cap B$ **b)** $B \cap C$ **c)** $A \cap C$

Solution

a) $A \cap B$ is the set of all numbers that are in both A and B. So $A \cap B = \{2, 3\}$.

b) $B \cap C = \{7\}$ **c)** $A \cap C = \varnothing$ ■

E X A M P L E   4

Membership and equality

Let $A = \{1, 2, 3, 5\}$, $B = \{2, 3, 7, 8\}$, and $C = \{6, 7, 8, 9\}$. Place one of the symbols $=$, $\neq$, $\in$, or $\notin$ in the blank to make each statement correct.

a) $5 \underline{\hspace{1cm}} A \cup B$ **b)** $5 \underline{\hspace{1cm}} A \cap B$

c) $A \cup B \underline{\hspace{1cm}} \{1, 2, 3, 5, 7, 8\}$ **d)** $A \cap B \underline{\hspace{1cm}} \{2\}$

Solution

a) $5 \in A \cup B$ because 5 is a member of A.

b) $5 \notin A \cap B$ because 5 must belong to *both* A and B to be a member of $A \cap B$.

c) $A \cup B = \{1, 2, 3, 5, 7, 8\}$ because the elements of A together with those of B are listed. Note that 2 and 3 are members of both sets but are listed only once.

d) $A \cap B \neq \{2\}$ because $A \cap B = \{2, 3\}$.   ■

Subsets

If every member of set A is also a member of set B, then we write $A \subseteq B$ and say that A is a **subset** of B. See Fig. 1.3. For example,

$$\{2, 3\} \subseteq \{2, 3, 4\}$$

because $2 \in \{2, 3, 4\}$ and $3 \in \{2, 3, 4\}$. Note that the symbol for membership ($\in$) is used between a single element and a set, whereas the symbol for subset ($\subseteq$) is used between two sets. If A is not a subset of B, we write $A \nsubseteq B$.

$A \subseteq B$

F I G U R E   1 . 3

CAUTION   To claim that $A \nsubseteq B$, there *must* be an element of A that does *not* belong to B. For example,

$$\{1, 2\} \nsubseteq \{2, 3, 4\}$$

because 1 is a member of the first set but not of the second.

Is the empty set $\varnothing$ a subset of $\{2, 3, 4\}$? If we say that $\varnothing$ is *not* a subset of $\{2, 3, 4\}$, then there must be an element of $\varnothing$ that does not belong to $\{2, 3, 4\}$. But that cannot happen because $\varnothing$ is empty. So $\varnothing$ is a subset of $\{2, 3, 4\}$. In fact, by the same reasoning, *the empty set is a subset of every set.*

E X A M P L E   5

Subsets

Determine whether each statement is true or false.

a) $\{1, 2, 3\}$ is a subset of the set of natural numbers.

b) The set of natural numbers is not a subset of $\{1, 2, 3\}$.

c) $\{1, 2, 3\} \not\subseteq \{2, 4, 6, 8\}$

d) $\{2, 6\} \subseteq \{1, 2, 3, 4, 5\}$

e) $\varnothing \subseteq \{2, 4, 6\}$

Helpful Hint

The symbols $\subseteq$ and $\subset$ are often used interchangeably. The symbol $\subseteq$ combines the subset symbol $\subset$ and the equal symbol $=$. We use it when sets are equal, $\{1, 2\} \subseteq \{1, 2\}$, and when they are not, $\{1\} \subseteq \{1, 2\}$. When sets are not equal, we could simply use $\subset$, as in $\{1\} \subset \{1, 2\}$.

Solution

a) True, because 1, 2, and 3 are natural numbers.

b) True, because 5, for example, is a natural number and $5 \notin \{1, 2, 3\}$.

c) True, because 1 is in the first set but not in the second.

d) False, because 6 is in the first set but not in the second.

e) True, because we cannot find anything in $\varnothing$ that fails to be in $\{2, 4, 6\}$. ∎

Combining Three or More Sets

We know how to find the union and intersection of two sets. For three or more sets we use parentheses to indicate which pair of sets to combine first. In Example 6, notice that different results are obtained from different placements of the parentheses.

E X A M P L E   6

Operations with three sets

Let $A = \{1, 2, 3, 4\}$, $B = \{2, 5, 6, 8\}$, and $C = \{4, 5, 7\}$. List the elements of each of these sets.

a) $(A \cup B) \cap C$ **b)** $A \cup (B \cap C)$

Study Tip

Exercise sets are designed to increase gradually in difficulty. So start from the beginning and work lots of exercises. If you get stuck, go back and study the corresponding examples. If you are still stuck, move ahead to a new type of exercise.

Solution

a) The parentheses indicate that the union of A and B is to be found first and then the result, $A \cup B$, is to be intersected with C.

$$A \cup B = \{1, 2, 3, 4, 5, 6, 8\}$$

Now examine $A \cup B$ and C to find the elements that belong to both sets:

$$A \cup B = \{1, 2, 3, 4, 5, 6, 8\}$$
$$C = \{4, 5, 7\}$$

The only numbers that are members of $A \cup B$ and C are 4 and 5. Thus

$$(A \cup B) \cap C = \{4, 5\}.$$

b) In $A \cup (B \cap C)$, first find $B \cap C$:

$$B \cap C = \{5\}$$

Now $A \cup (B \cap C)$ consist of all members of A together with 5 from $B \cap C$:

$$A \cup (B \cap C) = \{1, 2, 3, 4, 5\}$$ ∎

WARM-UPS

True or false? Explain your answer.

Let $A = \{1, 2, 3, 4\}$, $B = \{3, 4, 5\}$, and $C = \{3, 4\}$.

1. $A = \{x \mid x$ is a counting number$\}$

2. The set B has an infinite number of elements.

3. The set of counting numbers less than 50 million is an infinite set.

4. $1 \in A \cap B$ **5.** $3 \in A \cup B$ **6.** $A \cap B = C$

7. $C \subseteq B$ **8.** $A \subseteq B$ **9.** $\varnothing \subseteq C$

10. $A \nsubseteq C$

1.1 EXERCISES

Reading and Writing   *After reading this section, write out the answers to these questions. Use complete sentences.*

1. What is a set?

2. What is the difference between a finite set and an infinite set?

3. What is a Venn diagram used for?

4. What is the difference between the intersection and the union of two sets?

5. What does it mean to say that set A is a subset of set B?

6. Which set is a subset of every set?

For Exercises 7–52 let N represent the natural numbers, $A = \{x \mid x$ is an odd counting number smaller than 10$\}$, $B = \{2, 4, 6, 8\}$, and $C = \{1, 2, 3, 4, 5\}$.

Determine whether each statement is true or false. Explain your answer. See Example 1.

7. $6 \in A$ **8.** $8 \in A$

9. $A \neq B$ **10.** $A = \{1, 3, 5, 7, \ldots\}$

11. $3 \in C$ **12.** $4 \notin B$

13. $A = \{1, 3, 7, 9\}$ **14.** $B \neq C$

15. $0 \in N$ **16.** $2.5 \in N$

17. $C = N$ **18.** $N = A$

List the elements in each set. If the set is empty, write $\varnothing$. See Examples 2 and 3.

19. $A \cap B$ **20.** $A \cup B$

21. $A \cap C$ **22.** $A \cup C$

23. $B \cup C$ **24.** $B \cap C$

25. $A \cup \varnothing$ **26.** $B \cup \varnothing$ **27.** $A \cap \varnothing$

28. $B \cap \varnothing$ **29.** $A \cap N$ **30.** $A \cup N$

Use one of the symbols $\in$, $\notin$, $=$, $\neq$, $\cup$, or $\cap$ in the blank of each statement to make it correct. See Example 4.

31. $A \cap B$ _____ $\varnothing$ **32.** $A \cap C$ _____ $\varnothing$

33. A _____ $B = \{1, 2, 3, 4, 5, 6, 7, 8, 9\}$

34. A _____ $B = \varnothing$ **35.** B _____ $C = \{2, 4\}$

36. B _____ $C = \{1, 2, 3, 4, 5, 6, 8\}$

37. 3 _____ $A \cap B$ **38.** 3 _____ $A \cap C$

39. 4 _____ $B \cap C$ **40.** 8 _____ $B \cup C$

Determine whether each statement is true or false. Explain your answer. See Example 5.

41. $A \subseteq N$ **42.** $B \subseteq N$

43. $\{2, 3\} \subseteq C$ **44.** $C \subseteq A$

45. $B \nsubseteq C$ **46.** $C \nsubseteq A$

47. $\varnothing \subseteq B$ **48.** $\varnothing \subseteq C$

49. $A \subseteq \varnothing$ **50.** $B \subseteq \varnothing$

51. $A \cap B \subseteq C$ **52.** $B \cap C \subseteq \{2, 4, 6, 8\}$

For Exercises 53–78, let $D = \{3, 5, 7\}$, $E = \{2, 4, 6, 8\}$, and $F = \{1, 2, 3, 4, 5\}$.

List the elements in each set. If the set is empty, write $\varnothing$. See Example 6.

53. $D \cup E$ **54.** $D \cap E$

55. $D \cap F$ **56.** $D \cup F$

57. $E \cup F$

58. $E \cap F$

59. $(D \cup E) \cap F$

60. $(D \cup F) \cap E$

61. $D \cup (E \cap F)$

62. $D \cup (F \cap E)$

63. $(D \cap F) \cup (E \cap F)$

64. $(D \cap E) \cup (F \cap E)$

65. $(D \cup E) \cap (D \cup F)$

66. $(D \cup F) \cap (D \cup E)$

Use one of the symbols $\in$, $\subseteq$, $=$, $\cup$, or $\cap$ in the blank of each statement to make it correct.

67. D _____ $\{x \mid x$ is an odd natural number$\}$

68. E _____ $\{x \mid x$ is an even natural number smaller than 9$\}$

69. 3 _____ D

70. $\{3\}$ _____ D

71. D _____ $E = \varnothing$

72. $D \cap E$ _____ D

73. $D \cap F$ _____ F

74. $3 \notin E$ _____ F

75. $E \not\subseteq E$ _____ F

76. $E \subseteq E$ _____ F

77. D _____ $F = F \cup D$

78. E _____ $F = F \cap E$

List the elements in each set.

79. $\{x \mid x$ is an even natural number less than 20$\}$

80. $\{x \mid x$ is a natural number greater than 6$\}$

81. $\{x \mid x$ is an odd natural number greater than 11$\}$

82. $\{x \mid x$ is an odd natural number less than 14$\}$

83. $\{x \mid x$ is an even natural number between 4 and 79$\}$

84. $\{x \mid x$ is an odd natural number between 12 and 57$\}$

Write each set using set-builder notation. Answers may vary.

85. $\{3, 4, 5, 6\}$

86. $\{1, 3, 5, 7\}$

87. $\{5, 7, 9, 11, \ldots\}$

88. $\{4, 5, 6, 7, \ldots\}$

89. $\{6, 8, 10, 12, \ldots, 82\}$

90. $\{9, 11, 13, 15, \ldots, 51\}$

GETTING MORE INVOLVED

91. *Discussion.* If A and B are finite sets, could $A \cup B$ be infinite? Explain.

92. *Cooperative learning.* Work with a small group to answer the following questions. If $A \subseteq B$ and $B \subseteq A$, then what can you conclude about A and B? If $(A \cup B) \subseteq (A \cap B)$, then what can you conclude about A and B?

93. *Discussion.* What is wrong with each statement? Explain.
a) $3 \subseteq \{1, 2, 3\}$
b) $\{3\} \in \{1, 2, 3\}$
c) $\varnothing = \{\varnothing\}$

94. *Exploration.* There are only two possible subsets of $\{1\}$, namely, $\varnothing$ and $\{1\}$.
a) List all possible subsets of $\{1, 2\}$. How many are there?
b) List all possible subsets of $\{1, 2, 3\}$. How many are there?
c) Guess how many subsets there are of $\{1, 2, 3, 4\}$. Verify your guess by listing all the possible subsets.
d) How many subsets are there for $\{1, 2, 3, \ldots, n\}$?

In This Section

- The Rational Numbers
- Graphing on the Number Line
- The Irrational Numbers
- Intervals of Real Numbers

1.2   # THE REAL NUMBERS

The set of real numbers is the basic set of numbers used in algebra. There are many different types of real numbers. To understand better the set of real numbers, we will study some of the subsets of numbers that make up this set.

The Rational Numbers

We have already discussed the set of counting or natural numbers. The set of natural numbers together with the number 0 is called the set of **whole numbers.** The whole numbers together with the negatives of the counting numbers form the set of

Helpful Hint

A negative number can be used to represent a loss or a debt. The number −10 could represent a debt of $10, a temperature of 10° below zero, or an altitude of 10 feet below sea level.

integers. We use the letters N, W, and J to name these sets:

$$N = \{1, 2, 3, \ldots\} \qquad \text{The natural numbers}$$
$$W = \{0, 1, 2, 3, \ldots\} \qquad \text{The whole numbers}$$
$$J = \{\ldots, -3, -2, -1, 0, 1, 2, 3, \ldots\} \qquad \text{The integers}$$

Rational numbers are numbers that are written as ratios or as quotients of integers. We use the letter Q (for quotient) to name the set of rational numbers and write the set in set-builder notation as follows:

$$Q = \left\{ \frac{a}{b} \,\middle|\, a \text{ and } b \text{ are integers, with } b \neq 0 \right\} \qquad \text{The rational numbers}$$

Examples of rational numbers are

$$7, \quad \frac{9}{4}, \quad -\frac{17}{10}, \quad 0, \quad \frac{0}{4}, \quad \frac{3}{1}, \quad -\frac{47}{3}, \quad \text{and} \quad \frac{-2}{-6}.$$

Note that the rational numbers are the numbers that can be expressed as a ratio (or quotient) of integers. The integer 7 is rational because we can write it as $\frac{7}{1}$.

Another way to describe rational numbers is by using their decimal form. To obtain the decimal form, we divide the denominator into the numerator. For some rational numbers the division terminates, and for others it continues indefinitely. These examples show some rational numbers and their equivalent decimal forms:

Calculator Close-Up

Display a fraction on a graphing calculator, then press ENTER to convert to a decimal. The fraction feature converts a repeating decimal into a fraction. Try this with your calculator.

```
4177/990
         4.219191919
4.21919191919►Fr
ac
          4177/990
```

$$\frac{26}{100} = 0.26 \qquad \text{Terminating decimal}$$

$$\frac{4}{1} = 4.0 \qquad \text{Terminating decimal}$$

$$\frac{1}{4} = 0.25 \qquad \text{Terminating decimal}$$

$$\frac{2}{3} = 0.6666\ldots \qquad \text{The single digit 6 repeats.}$$

$$\frac{25}{99} = 0.252525\ldots \qquad \text{The pair of digits 25 repeats.}$$

$$\frac{4177}{990} = 4.2191919\ldots \qquad \text{The pair of digits 19 repeats.}$$

Rational numbers are defined as ratios of integers, but they can be described also by their decimal form. *The rational numbers are those decimal numbers whose digits either repeat or terminate.*

E X A M P L E 1   **Subsets of the rational numbers**

Determine whether each statement is true or false.

a) $0 \in W$ **b)** $N \subseteq J$ **c)** $0.75 \in J$ **d)** $J \subseteq Q$

Solution

a) True, because 0 is a whole number.

b) True, because every natural number is also a member of the set of integers.

c) False, because the rational number 0.75 is not an integer.

d) True, because the rational numbers include the integers.

Graphing on the Number Line

To construct a number line, we draw a straight line and label any convenient point with the number 0. Now we choose any convenient length and use it to locate points to the right of 0 as points corresponding to the positive integers and points to the left of 0 as points corresponding to the negative integers. See Fig. 1.4. The numbers corresponding to the points on the line are called the **coordinates** of the points. The distance between two consecutive integers is called a **unit,** and it is the same for any two consecutive integers. The point with coordinate 0 is called the **origin.** The numbers on the number line increase in size from left to right. When we compare the size of any two numbers, the larger number lies to the right of the smaller one on the number line.

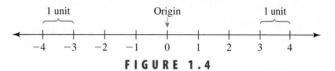

FIGURE 1.4

It is often convenient to illustrate sets of numbers on a number line. The set of integers, *J*, is illustrated or **graphed** as in Fig. 1.5. The three dots to the right and left on the number line indicate that the integers go on indefinitely in both directions.

FIGURE 1.5

E X A M P L E   2

Graphing on the number line

List the elements of each set and graph each set on a number line.

a) $\{x \mid x$ is a whole number less than $4\}$

b) $\{a \mid a$ is an integer between 3 and $9\}$

c) $\{y \mid y$ is an integer greater than $-3\}$

Solution

a) The whole numbers less than 4 are 0, 1, 2, and 3. Figure 1.6 shows the graph of this set.

FIGURE 1.6

b) The integers between 3 and 9 are 4, 5, 6, 7, and 8. The graph is shown in Fig. 1.7.

FIGURE 1.7

c) The integers greater than -3 are -2, -1, 0, 1, and so on. To indicate the continuing pattern, we use a series of dots on the graph in Fig. 1.8.

FIGURE 1.8

The Irrational Numbers

Some numbers can be expressed as ratios of integers and some cannot. Numbers that cannot be expressed as a ratio of integers are called **irrational numbers.** To better understand irrational numbers consider the positive square root of 2 (in symbols $\sqrt{2}$). The square root of 2 is a number that you can multiply by itself to get 2. So we can write (using a raised dot for times)

$$\sqrt{2} \cdot \sqrt{2} = 2.$$

If we look for $\sqrt{2}$ on a calculator or in Appendix B, we find 1.414. But if we multiply 1.414 by itself, we get

$$(1.414)(1.414) = 1.999396.$$

So $\sqrt{2}$ is not equal to 1.414 (in symbols, $\sqrt{2} \neq 1.414$). The square root of 2 is approximately 1.414 (in symbols, $\sqrt{2} \approx 1.414$). There is no terminating or repeating decimal that will give exactly 2 when multiplied by itself. So $\sqrt{2}$ is an irrational number. It can be shown that other square roots such as $\sqrt{3}$, $\sqrt{5}$, and $\sqrt{7}$ are also irrational numbers.

In decimal form the rational numbers either repeat or terminate. The irrational numbers neither repeat nor terminate. Examine each of these numbers to see that it has a continuing pattern that guarantees that its digits will neither repeat nor terminate:

$$0.606000600000600000006\ldots$$
$$0.15115111511115\ldots$$
$$3.12345678910111213\ldots$$

So each of these numbers is an irrational number.

Since we generally work with rational numbers, the irrational numbers may seem to be unnecessary. However, irrational numbers occur in some very real situations. Over 2000 years ago people in the Orient and Egypt observed that the ratio of the circumference and diameter is the same for any circle. This constant value was proven to be an irrational number by Johann Heinrich Lambert in 1767. Like other irrational numbers, it does not have any convenient representation as a decimal number. This number has been given the name π (Greek letter pi). See Fig. 1.9. The value of π rounded to nine decimal places is 3.141592654. When using π in computations, we frequently use the rational number 3.14 as an approximate value for π.

The set of irrational numbers I and the set of rational numbers Q have no numbers in common and together form the set of **real numbers** R. The set of real numbers can be visualized as the set of all points on the number line. Two real numbers are **equal** if they correspond to the same point on the number line. See Fig. 1.10.

Calculator Close-Up

A calculator gives a 10-digit rational approximation for $\sqrt{2}$. Note that if the approximate value is squared, you do not get 2.

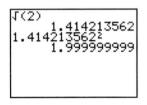

The screen shot that appears on this page and in succeeding pages may differ from the display on your calculator. You may have to consult your manual to get the desired results.

$$\pi = \frac{\text{Circumference}}{\text{Diameter}} \qquad \pi = \frac{C}{D}$$

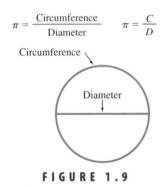

FIGURE 1.9

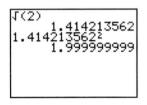

FIGURE 1.10

Figure 1.11 illustrates the relationship between the set of real numbers and the various subsets that we have been discussing.

Study Tip

Start a personal library. This book as well as other books from which you study should be the basis for your library. You can also add books to your library at garage sale prices when your bookstore sells its old texts. If you need to reference some material in the future, it is much easier to use a book with which you are familiar.

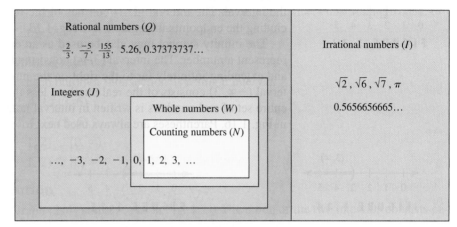

FIGURE 1.11

E X A M P L E   3

Classifying real numbers

Determine which elements of the set

$$\left\{-\sqrt{7}, -\frac{1}{4}, 0, \sqrt{5}, \pi, 4.16, 12\right\}$$

are members of each of these sets.

a) Real numbers   **b)** Rational numbers   **c)** Integers

Solution

a) All of the numbers are real numbers.

b) The numbers $-\frac{1}{4}$, 0, 4.16, and 12 are rational numbers.

c) The only integers in this set are 0 and 12.   ■

E X A M P L E   4

Subsets of the real numbers

Determine whether each of these statements is true or false.

a) $\sqrt{7} \in Q$ **b)** $J \subseteq W$ **c)** $I \cap Q = \varnothing$ **d)** $-3 \in N$
e) $J \cap I = \varnothing$ **f)** $Q \subseteq R$ **g)** $R \subseteq N$ **h)** $\pi \in R$

Solution

a) False   **b)** False   **c)** True   **d)** False
e) True   **f)** True   **g)** False   **h)** True   ■

Intervals of Real Numbers

An **interval of real numbers** is the set of real numbers that lie between two real numbers, which are called the **endpoints** of the interval. **Interval notation** is used to represent intervals. For example, the interval notation (2, 3) is used to represent the real numbers that lie between 2 and 3 on the number line. The graph of (2, 3) is shown in Fig. 1.12. Parentheses are used to indicate that the endpoints do not belong

FIGURE 1.12

1.2   EXERCISES

Reading and Writing   *After reading this section, write out the answers to these questions. Use complete sentences.*

1. What are the integers?

2. What are the rational numbers?

3. What kinds of decimal numbers are rational numbers?

4. What kinds of decimal numbers are irrational?

5. What are the real numbers?

6. What is the ratio of the circumference and diameter of any circle?

Determine whether each statement is true or false. Explain your answer. See Example 1.

7. $-6 \in Q$ **8.** $\dfrac{2}{7} \in Q$

9. $0 \notin Q$ **10.** $0 \notin N$

11. $0.6666\ldots \in Q$ **12.** $0.00976 \notin Q$

13. $N \subseteq Q$ **14.** $Q \subseteq J$

List the elements in each set and graph each set on a number line. See Example 2.

15. $\{x \mid x \text{ is a whole number smaller than 6}\}$

16. $\{x \mid x \text{ is a natural number less than 7}\}$

17. $\{a \mid a \text{ is an integer greater than } -5\}$

18. $\{z \mid z \text{ is an integer between 2 and 12}\}$

19. $\{w \mid w \text{ is a natural number between 0 and 5}\}$

20. $\{y \mid y \text{ is a whole number greater than 0}\}$

21. $\{x \mid x \text{ is an integer between } -3 \text{ and 5}\}$

22. $\{y \mid y \text{ is an integer between } -4 \text{ and 7}\}$

Determine which elements of the set

$$A = \left\{ -\sqrt{10},\ -3,\ -\frac{5}{2},\ -0.025,\ 0,\ \sqrt{2},\ 3\frac{1}{2},\ \frac{8}{2} \right\}$$

are members of these sets. See Example 3.

23. Real numbers

24. Natural numbers

25. Whole numbers

26. Integers

27. Rational numbers

28. Irrational numbers

Determine whether each statement is true or false. Explain. See Example 4.

29. $Q \subseteq R$ **30.** $I \subseteq Q$

31. $I \cap Q = \{0\}$ **32.** $J \subseteq Q$

33. $I \cup Q = R$ **34.** $J \cap Q = \varnothing$

35. $0.2121121112\ldots \in Q$ **36.** $0.3333\ldots \in Q$

37. $3.252525\ldots \in I$ **38.** $3.1010010001\ldots \in I$

39. $0.999\ldots \in I$ **40.** $0.666\ldots \in Q$

41. $\pi \in I$ **42.** $\pi \in Q$

Place one of the symbols $\subseteq$, $\not\subseteq$, $\in$, or $\notin$ in each blank so that each statement is true.

43. N ___ W **44.** J ___ Q

45. J ___ N **46.** Q ___ W

47. Q ___ R **48.** I ___ R

49. $\varnothing$ ___ I **50.** $\varnothing$ ___ Q

51. N ___ R **52.** W ___ R

53. 5 ___ J **54.** -6 ___ J

55. 7 ___ Q

56. 8 ___ Q

57. $\sqrt{2}$ ___ R

58. $\sqrt{2}$ ___ I

59. 0 ___ I

60. 0 ___ Q

61. $\{2, 3\}$ ___ Q

62. $\{0, 1\}$ ___ N

63. $\{3, \sqrt{2}\}$ ___ R

64. $\{3, \sqrt{2}\}$ ___ Q

Write each interval of real numbers in interval notation and graph it. See Example 5.

65. The set of real numbers greater than 1

66. The set of real numbers greater than -2

67. The set of real numbers less than -1

68. The set of real numbers less than 5

69. The set of real numbers between 3 and 4

70. The set of real numbers between -1 and 3

71. The set of real numbers between 0 and 2 inclusive

72. The set of real numbers between -1 and 1 inclusive

73. The set of real numbers greater than or equal to 1 and less than 3

74. The set of real numbers greater than 2 and less than or equal to 5.

Write the interval notation for the interval of real numbers shown in each graph.

75.

76.

77.

78.

79.

80.

81.

82.

Write each union or intersection as a single interval. See Example 6.

83. $(1, 5) \cup (4, 9)$

84. $(-1, 2) \cup (0, 8)$

85. $(0, 3) \cap (2, 8)$

86. $(1, 8) \cap (2, 10)$

87. $(-2, 4) \cup (0, \infty)$

88. $(-\infty, 4) \cup (1, 5)$

89. $(-\infty, 2) \cap (0, 6)$

90. $(3, 6) \cap (0, \infty)$

91. $[2, 5) \cup (4, 9]$

92. $[-2, 2] \cup [2, 6)$

93. $[2, 6) \cap [2, 8)$

94. $[1, 5] \cap [2, 9]$

GETTING MORE INVOLVED

 95. *Writing.* What is the difference between a rational and an irrational number? Why is $\sqrt{9}$ rational and $\sqrt{3}$ irrational?

 96. *Cooperative learning.* Work in a small group to make a list of the real numbers of the form $\sqrt{n}$, where n is a natural number between 1 and 100 inclusive. Decide on a method for determining which of these numbers are rational and find them. Compare your group's method and results with other groups' work.

97. *Exploration.* Find the decimal representations of

$$\frac{2}{9}, \quad \frac{2}{99}, \quad \frac{23}{99}, \quad \frac{23}{999}, \quad \frac{234}{999}, \quad \frac{23}{9999}, \quad \text{and} \quad \frac{1234}{9999}.$$

a) What do these decimals have in common?

b) What is the relationship between each fraction and its decimal representation?

Additive Inverse Property

For any real number a, there is a unique number $-a$ such that

$$a + (-a) = -a + a = 0.$$

To understand the sum of a positive and a negative number, consider this situation. If you have a debt of $7 and $10 in cash, you may have $10 in hand, but your net worth is only $3. Your assets exceed your debts (in absolute value), and you have a positive net worth. In symbols,

$$-7 + 10 = 3.$$

Note that to get 3, we actually subtract 7 from 10. If you have a debt of $8 but have only $5 in cash, then your debts exceed your assets (in absolute value). You have a net worth of $-$$3. In symbols,

$$-8 + 5 = -3.$$

Note that to get the 3 in the answer, we subtract 5 from 8.

As you can see from these examples, the sum of a positive number and a negative number (with different absolute values) may be either positive or negative. These examples illustrate the rule for adding numbers with unlike signs and different absolute values.

Helpful Hint

The sum of two numbers with unlike signs and the same absolute value is zero because of the additive inverse property.

Sum of Two Numbers with Unlike Signs (and Different Absolute Values)

To find the sum of two numbers with unlike signs, subtract their absolute values.

The sum is positive if the number with the larger absolute value is positive.
The sum is negative if the number with the larger absolute value is negative.

E X A M P L E   3

Calculator Close-Up

A graphing calculator can add signed numbers in any form. If you use the fraction feature, the answer is given as a fraction.

```
-9+ -7
              -16
-35.4+2.51
           -32.89
1/5+ -3/4▸Frac
           -11/20
```

No one knows what calculators will be like in 10 or 20 years. So concentrate on understanding the mathematics and you will have no trouble with changing technology.

Adding signed numbers

Find each sum.

a) $-6 + 13$ **b)** $-9 + (-7)$ **c)** $2 + (-2)$

d) $-35.4 + 2.51$ **e)** $-7 + 0.05$ **f)** $\dfrac{1}{5} + \left(-\dfrac{3}{4}\right)$

Solution

a) The absolute values of -6 and 13 are 6 and 13. Subtract 6 from 13 to get 7. Because the number with the larger absolute value is 13 and it is positive, the result is 7.

b) $-9 + (-7) = -16$

c) $2 + (-2) = 0$

d) Line up the decimal points and subtract 2.51 from 35.40 to get 32.89. Because 35.4 is larger than 2.51 and 35.4 has a negative sign, the answer is negative.

$$-35.4 + 2.51 = -32.89$$

e) Line up the decimal points and subtract 0.05 from 7.00 to get 6.95. Because 7.00 is larger than 0.05 and 7.00 has a negative sign, the answer is negative.

$$-7 + 0.05 = -6.95$$

f) $\dfrac{1}{5} + \left(-\dfrac{3}{4}\right) = \dfrac{4}{20} + \left(-\dfrac{15}{20}\right)$ The LCD for 5 and 4 is 20.

$= -\dfrac{11}{20}$ Add.   ∎

Subtraction

Think of subtraction as removing debts or assets, and think of addition as receiving debts or assets. For example, if you have $10 in cash and $4 is taken from you, your resulting net worth is the same as if you have $10 and a water bill for $4 arrives in the mail. In symbols,

$$10 \quad - \quad 4 \quad = \quad 10 \quad + \quad (-4).$$

↑ Remove   ↑ Cash   ↑ Receive   ↑ Debt

Removing cash is equivalent to receiving a debt.

Suppose that you have $17 in cash but owe $7 in library fines. Your net worth is $10. If the debt of $7 is canceled or forgiven, your net worth will increase to $17, the same as if you received $7 in cash. In symbols,

$$10 \quad - \quad (-7) \quad = \quad 10 \quad + \quad 7.$$

↑ Remove   ↑ Debt   ↑ Receive   ↑ Cash

Removing a debt is equivalent to receiving cash.

Notice that each preceding subtraction problem is equivalent to an addition problem in which we add the opposite of what we were going to subtract. These examples illustrate the definition of subtraction.

> **Subtraction of Real Numbers**
>
> For any real numbers a and b,
>
> $$a - b = a + (-b).$$

EXAMPLE 4

Subtracting signed numbers

Find each difference.

a) $-7 - 3$ **b)** $7 - (-3)$ **c)** $48 - 99$

d) $-3.6 - (-7)$ **e)** $0.02 - 7$ **f)** $\dfrac{1}{3} - \left(-\dfrac{1}{6}\right)$

Solution

a) To subtract 3 from -7, add the opposite of 3 and -7:

$$-7 - 3 = -7 + (-3) \quad a - b = a + (-b)$$
$$= -10 \quad \text{Add.}$$

b) To subtract -3 from 7, add the opposite of -3 and 7. The opposite of -3 is 3:

$$7 - (-3) = 7 + (3) \quad a - b = a + (-b)$$
$$= 10 \quad \text{Add.}$$

c) To subtract 99 from 48, add -99 and 48:

$$48 - 99 = 48 + (-99) \qquad a - b = a + (-b)$$
$$= -51 \qquad \text{Add.}$$

d) $-3.6 - (-7) = -3.6 + 7 \qquad a - b = a + (-b)$
$$= 3.4 \qquad \text{Add.}$$

e) $0.02 - 7 = 0.02 + (-7) \qquad a - b = a + (-b)$
$$= -6.98 \qquad \text{Add.}$$

f) $\dfrac{1}{3} - \left(-\dfrac{1}{6}\right) = \dfrac{1}{3} + \left(\dfrac{1}{6}\right) \qquad a - b = a + (-b)$

$$= \frac{2}{6} + \frac{1}{6} \qquad \text{Get common denominators.}$$

$$= \frac{3}{6} \qquad \text{Add.}$$

$$= \frac{1}{2} \qquad \text{Reduce.} \qquad\blacksquare$$

Multiplication

Study Tip

Exchange phone numbers, cellular phone numbers, pager numbers, and e-mail addresses with several students in your class. If you miss class and you can't reach your instructor, then you will have someone who can tell you the assignments. If you are stuck on a problem, you can contact a classmate for help.

The result of multiplying two numbers is called the **product** of the numbers. The numbers multiplied are **factors**. In algebra we use a raised dot to indicate multiplication, or we place symbols next to one another. For example, the product of a and b is written as $a \cdot b$ or ab. The product of 4 and x is $4x$. We also use parentheses to indicate multiplication. For example, the product of 4 and 3 is written as $4 \cdot 3$, $4(3)$, $(4)3$, or $(4)(3)$.

Multiplication is just a short way to do repeated additions. Adding five 2's gives

$$2 + 2 + 2 + 2 + 2 = 10.$$

So we have the multiplication fact $5 \cdot 2 = 10$. Adding together five negative 2's gives

$$(-2) + (-2) + (-2) + (-2) + (-2) = -10.$$

So we must have $5(-2) = -10$. We can think of $5(-2) = -10$ as saying that taking on five debts of \$2 each is equivalent to a debt of \$10. Losing five debts of \$2 each is equivalent to gaining \$10, so we must have $-5(-2) = 10$.

The rules for multiplying signed numbers are easy to state and remember.

Product of Signed Numbers

To find the product of two nonzero real numbers, multiply their absolute values.
    The product is *positive* if the numbers have the *same* sign.
    The product is *negative* if the numbers have *unlike* signs.

For example, to multiply -4 and -5, we multiply their absolute values $(4 \cdot 5 = 20)$. Since -4 and -5 have the same sign, $(-4)(-5) = 20$. To multiply -6 and 3, we multiply their absolute values $(6 \cdot 3 = 18)$. Since -6 and 3 have unlike signs, $-6 \cdot 3 = -18$.

EXAMPLE 5

Multiplying signed numbers

Find each product.

a) $(-3)(-6)$ b) $-4(10)$ c) $(-0.01)(0.02)$ d) $\dfrac{4}{9} \cdot \left(-\dfrac{1}{5}\right)$

Solution

a) First multiply the absolute values $(3 \cdot 6 = 18)$. Because -3 and -6 have the same sign, we get $(-3)(-6) = 18$.

b) $-4(10) = -40$ Opposite signs, negative result

c) When multiplying decimals, we total the number of decimal places used in the numbers multiplied to get the number of decimal places in the answer. Thus $(-0.01)(0.02) = -0.0002$.

d) $\dfrac{4}{9} \cdot \left(-\dfrac{1}{5}\right) = -\dfrac{4}{45}$ Opposite signs, negative result   ■

Division

Just as every real number has an additive inverse or opposite, every nonzero real number a has a **multiplicative inverse** or **reciprocal** $\dfrac{1}{a}$. The reciprocal of 3 is $\dfrac{1}{3}$, and

$$3 \cdot \dfrac{1}{3} = 1.$$

> **Multiplicative Inverse Property**
>
> For any nonzero real number a, there is a unique number $\dfrac{1}{a}$ such that
>
> $$a \cdot \dfrac{1}{a} = \dfrac{1}{a} \cdot a = 1.$$

EXAMPLE 6

Finding multiplicative inverses

Find the multiplicative inverse (reciprocal) of each number.

a) -2 b) $\dfrac{3}{8}$ c) -0.2

Helpful Hint

A doctor told a nurse to give a patient half the usual dose of a certain medicine. The nurse figured, "dividing in half means dividing by $\frac{1}{2}$, which means multiplying by 2." So the patient got four times the prescribed amount and died (true story). There is a big difference between dividing a quantity in half and dividing by one-half.

Solution

a) The multiplicative inverse (reciprocal) of -2 is $-\dfrac{1}{2}$ because

$$-2\left(-\dfrac{1}{2}\right) = 1.$$

b) The reciprocal of $\dfrac{3}{8}$ is $\dfrac{8}{3}$ because

$$\dfrac{3}{8} \cdot \dfrac{8}{3} = 1.$$

c) First convert the decimal number -0.2 to a fraction:

$$-0.2 = -\dfrac{2}{10}$$

$$= -\dfrac{1}{5}$$

So the reciprocal of -0.2 is -5 and $-0.2(-5) = 1$.   ■

Note that the reciprocal of any negative number is negative.

Earlier we defined subtraction for real numbers as addition of the additive inverse. We now define division for real numbers as multiplication by the multiplicative inverse (reciprocal).

Division of Real Numbers

For any real numbers a and b with $b \neq 0$,

$$a \div b = a \cdot \frac{1}{b}.$$

If $a \div b = c$, then a is called the **dividend,** b the **divisor,** and c the **quotient.** We also refer to $a \div b$ and $\frac{a}{b}$ as the quotient of a and b.

E X A M P L E   7

Dividing signed numbers

Find each quotient.

a) $-60 \div (-2)$ **b)** $-24 \div \dfrac{3}{8}$ **c)** $6 \div (-0.2)$

Calculator Close-Up

A graphing calculator uses a forward slash to indicate division. Note that to divide by the fraction $\frac{3}{8}$ you must use parentheses around the fraction.

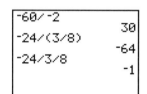

```
-60/-2
                    30
-24/(3/8)
                   -64
-24/3/8
                    -1
```

Solution

a) $-60 \div (-2) = -60 \cdot \left(-\dfrac{1}{2}\right)$ Multiply by $-\frac{1}{2}$, the reciprocal of -2.

$\qquad\qquad\quad = 30$ Same sign, positive product

b) $-24 \div \dfrac{3}{8} = -24 \cdot \dfrac{8}{3}$ Multiply by $\frac{8}{3}$, the reciprocal of $\frac{3}{8}$.

$\qquad\qquad\quad = -64$ Opposite signs, negative product

c) $6 \div (-0.2) = 6(-5)$ Multiply by -5, the reciprocal of -0.2.

$\qquad\qquad\quad = -30$ Opposite signs, negative product   ■

You can see from Examples 6 and 7 that a product or quotient is positive when the signs are the same and is negative when the signs are opposite:

$$\text{same signs} \leftrightarrow \text{positive result,}$$

$$\text{opposite signs} \leftrightarrow \text{negative result.}$$

Even though all division can be done as multiplication by a reciprocal, we generally use reciprocals only when dividing fractions. Instead, we find quotients using our knowledge of multiplication and the fact that

$$a \div b = c \qquad \text{if and only if} \qquad c \cdot b = a.$$

Helpful Hint

Some people remember that "two positives make a positive, a negative and a positive make a negative, and two negatives make a positive." Of course, that is true only for multiplication, division, and cute stories like this: If a good person comes to town, that's good. If a bad person comes to town, that's bad. If a good person leaves town, that's bad. If a bad person leaves town, that's good.

For example, $-72 \div 9 = -8$ because $-8 \cdot 9 = -72$. Using long division or a calculator, you can get

$$-43.74 \div 1.8 = -24.3$$

and check that you have it correct by finding $-24.3 \cdot 1.8 = -43.74$.

We use the same rules for division when division is indicated by a fraction bar. For example,

$$\frac{-6}{3} = -2, \qquad \frac{6}{-3} = -2, \qquad \frac{-1}{3} = \frac{1}{-3} = -\frac{1}{3}, \qquad \text{and} \qquad \frac{-6}{-3} = 2.$$

Note that if one negative sign appears in a fraction, the fraction has the same value whether the negative sign is in the numerator, in the denominator, or in front of the fraction. If the numerator and denominator of a fraction are both negative, then the fraction has a positive value.

Division by Zero

Why do we omit division by zero from the definition of division? If we write $10 \div 0 = c$, we need to find c such that $c \cdot 0 = 10$. But there is no such number. If we write $0 \div 0 = c$, we need to find c such that $c \cdot 0 = 0$. But $c \cdot 0 = 0$ is true for any number c. Having $0 \div 0$ equal to any number would be confusing. Thus $a \div b$ is defined only for $b \neq 0$. Quotients such as

$$5 \div 0, \qquad 0 \div 0, \qquad \frac{7}{0}, \qquad \text{and} \qquad \frac{0}{0}$$

are said to be *undefined*.

WARM-UPS

True or false? Explain your answer.

1. The additive inverse of -6 is 6.

2. The opposite of negative 5 is positive 5.

3. The absolute value of 6 is -6.

4. The result of a subtracted from b is the same as $b + (-a)$.

5. If a is positive and b is negative, then ab is negative.

6. If a is positive and b is negative, then $a + b$ is negative.

7. $(-3) - (-6) = -9$ **8.** $6 \div \left(-\dfrac{1}{2}\right) = -3$

9. $-3 \div 0 = 0$ **10.** $0 \div (-7) = 0$

1.3   EXERCISES

Reading and Writing   *After reading this section, write out the answers to these questions. Use complete sentences.*

1. What is absolute value?

2. How do you add two numbers with the same sign?

3. How do you add two numbers with unlike signs and different absolute values?

4. What is the relationship between subtraction and addition?

5. How do you multiply signed numbers?

6. What is the relationship between division and multiplication?

Evaluate. See Examples 1 and 2.

7. $\lvert -34 \rvert$	**8.** $\lvert 17 \rvert$
9. $\lvert 0 \rvert$	**10.** $\lvert -15 \rvert$
11. $\lvert -6 \rvert - \lvert -6 \rvert$	**12.** $\lvert 8 \rvert - \lvert -8 \rvert$
13. $-\lvert -9 \rvert$	**14.** $-\lvert -3 \rvert$
15. $-(-9)$	**16.** $-(-(8))$
17. $-(-(-3))$	**18.** $-(-(-2))$

Find each sum. See Example 3.

19. $(-5) + 9$

20. $(-3) + 10$

21. $(-4) + (-3)$

22. $(-15) + (-11)$

23. $-6 + 4$

24. $5 + (-15)$

25. $7 + (-17)$

26. $-8 + 13$

27. $(-11) + (-15)$

28. $-18 + 18$

29. $18 + (-20)$

30. $7 + (-19)$

31. $-14 + 9$

32. $-6 + (-7)$

33. $-4 + 4$

34. $-7 + 9$

35. $-\dfrac{1}{10} + \dfrac{1}{5}$

36. $-\dfrac{1}{8} + \left(-\dfrac{1}{8}\right)$

37. $\dfrac{1}{2} + \left(-\dfrac{2}{3}\right)$

38. $\dfrac{3}{4} + \dfrac{1}{2}$

39. $-15 + 0.02$

40. $0.45 + (-1.3)$

41. $-2.7 + (-0.01)$

42. $0.8 + (-1)$

43. $47.39 + (-44.587)$

44. $0.65357 + (-2.375)$

45. $0.2351 + (-0.5)$

46. $-1.234 + (-4.756)$

Find each difference. See Example 4.

47. $7 - 10$

48. $8 - 19$

49. $-4 - 7$

50. $-5 - 12$

51. $7 - (-6)$

52. $3 - (-9)$

53. $-1 - 5$

54. $-4 - 6$

55. $-12 - (-3)$

56. $-15 - (-6)$

57. $20 - (-3)$

58. $50 - (-70)$

59. $\dfrac{9}{10} - \left(-\dfrac{1}{10}\right)$

60. $\dfrac{1}{8} - \dfrac{1}{4}$

61. $1 - \dfrac{3}{2}$

62. $-\dfrac{1}{2} - \left(-\dfrac{1}{3}\right)$

63. $2 - 0.03$

64. $-0.02 - 3$

65. $5.3 - (-2)$

66. $-4.1 - 0.13$

67. $-2.44 - 48.29$

68. $-8.8 - 9.164$

69. $-3.89 - (-5.16)$

70. $0 - (-3.5)$

Find each product. See Example 5.

71. $(25)(-3)$

72. $(5)(-7)$

73. $\left(-\dfrac{1}{3}\right)\left(-\dfrac{1}{2}\right)$

74. $\left(-\dfrac{1}{2}\right)\left(-\dfrac{6}{7}\right)$

75. $(0.3)(-0.3)$

76. $(-0.1)(-0.5)$

77. $(-0.02)(-10)$

78. $(0.05)(-2.5)$

Find the multiplicative inverse of each number. See Example 6.

79. 20

80. -5

81. $-\dfrac{6}{5}$

82. $-\dfrac{1}{8}$

83. -0.3

84. 0.125

Evaluate. See Example 7.

85. $-6 \div 3$

86. $84 \div (-2)$

87. $30 \div (-0.8)$

88. $(-9)(-6)$

89. $(-0.8)(0.1)$

90. $7 \div (-0.5)$

91. $(-0.1) \div (-0.4)$

92. $(-18) \div (-0.9)$

93. $9 \div \left(-\dfrac{3}{4}\right)$

94. $-\dfrac{1}{3} \div \left(-\dfrac{5}{8}\right)$

95. $-\dfrac{2}{3}\left(-\dfrac{9}{10}\right)$

96. $\dfrac{1}{2}\left(-\dfrac{2}{5}\right)$

97. $(0.25)(-365)$

98. $7.5 \div (-0.15)$

99. $(-51) \div (-0.003)$

100. $(-2.8)(5.9)$

Perform these computations.

101. $-62 + 13$

102. $-88 + 39$

103. $-32 - (-25)$

104. $-71 - (-19)$

105. $|-15|$

106. $-|-75|$

107. $\dfrac{1}{2}(-684)$

108. $\dfrac{1}{3}(-123)$

109. $\dfrac{1}{2} - \left(-\dfrac{1}{4}\right)$

110. $\dfrac{1}{8} - \left(-\dfrac{1}{4}\right)$

111. $-57 \div 19$

112. $0 \div (-36)$

113. $|-17| + |-3|$

114. $64 - |-12|$

115. $0 \div (-0.15)$

116. $-20 \div \left(-\dfrac{8}{3}\right)$

117. $27 \div (-0.15)$

118. $33 \div (-0.2)$

119. $-\dfrac{1}{3} + \dfrac{1}{6}$

120. $-\dfrac{2}{3} + \dfrac{1}{6}$

121. $-63 + |8|$

122. $|-34| - 27$

123. $-\dfrac{1}{2} + \left(-\dfrac{1}{2}\right)$

124. $-\dfrac{2}{3} + \left(-\dfrac{2}{3}\right)$

125. $-\dfrac{1}{2} - 19$

126. $-\dfrac{1}{3} - 22$

127. $28 - 0.01$

128. $55 - 0.1$

129. $-29 - 0.3$

130. $-0.241 - 0.3$

131. $(-2)(0.35)$

132. $(-3)(0.19)$

133. $(-10)(-0.2)$

134. $\left(-\dfrac{1}{2}\right)(-50)$

Use an operation with signed numbers to solve each problem.

135. *Net worth of a family.* The average American family has an $85,000 house, a $45,000 mortgage, $2,300 in credit card debt, $1,500 in other debts, $1,200 in savings, and two cars worth $3,500 each. What is the net worth of the average American family?

136. *Net worth of a bank.* Just before the recession, First Federal Homestead had $15.6 million in mortgage loans, had $23.3 million on deposit, and owned $8.5 million worth of real estate. After the recession started, the value of the real estate decreased to $4.8 million. What was the net worth of First Federal before the recession and after the recession started? (To a financial institution a loan is an asset and a deposit is a liability.)

137. *Warming up.* On January 11 the temperature at noon was 14°F in St. Louis and −6°F in Duluth. How much warmer was it in St. Louis?

138. *Bitter cold.* On January 16 the temperature at midnight was −31°C in Calgary and −20°C in Toronto. How much warmer was it in Toronto?

139. *Below sea level.* The altitude of the floor of Death Valley is −282 feet (282 feet below sea level); the altitude of the shore of the Dead Sea is −1,296 feet (*Rand McNally World Atlas*). How many feet above the shore of the Dead Sea is the floor of Death Valley?

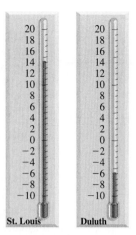

FIGURE FOR EXERCISE 137

140. *Highs and lows.* The altitude of the peak of Mt. Everest, the highest point on earth, is 29,028 feet. The world's greatest known ocean depth of −36,201 feet was recorded in the Marianas Trench (*Rand McNally World Atlas*). How many feet above the bottom of the Marianas Trench is a climber who has reached the top of Mt. Everest?

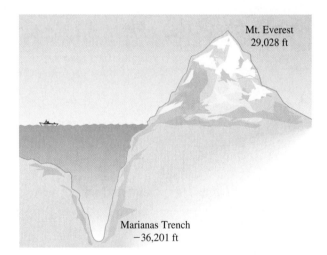

FIGURE FOR EXERCISE 140

GETTING MORE INVOLVED

141. *Discussion.* Why is it necessary to learn addition of signed numbers before learning subtraction of signed numbers and to learn multiplication of signed numbers before division of signed numbers?

142. *Writing.* Explain why 0 is the only real number that does not have a multiplicative inverse.

1.4 EVALUATING EXPRESSIONS

In algebra you will learn to work with variables. However, there is often nothing more important than finding a numerical answer to a question. This section is concerned with computation.

Arithmetic Expressions

The result of writing numbers in a meaningful combination with the ordinary operations of arithmetic is called an **arithmetic expression** or simply an **expression.** An expression that involves more than one operation is called a **sum, difference, product,** or **quotient** if the last operation to be performed is addition, subtraction, multiplication, or division, respectively. Parentheses are used as **grouping symbols** to indicate which operations are performed first. The expression

$$5 + (2 \cdot 3)$$

is a sum because the parentheses indicate that the product of 2 and 3 is to be found before the addition is performed. So we evaluate this expression as follows:

$$5 + (2 \cdot 3) = 5 + 6 = 11$$

If we write $(5 + 2)3$, the expression is a product and it has a different value.

$$(5 + 2)3 = 7 \cdot 3 = 21$$

Brackets [ ] are also used to indicate grouping. If an expression occurs within absolute value bars | |, it is evaluated before the absolute value is found. So absolute value bars also act as grouping symbols. We perform first the operations within the innermost grouping symbols.

E X A M P L E   1

Grouping symbols

Evaluate each expression.

a) $5[(2 \cdot 3) - 8]$ **b)** $2[(4 \cdot 5) - |\, 3 - 6 \,|]$

Solution

a) $5[(2 \cdot 3) - 8] = 5[6 - 8]$ Innermost grouping first

$$= 5[-2]$$
$$= -10$$

b) $2[(4 \cdot 5) - |\, 3 - 6 \,|] = 2[20 - |\, -3 \,|]$ Innermost grouping first

$$= 2[20 - 3]$$
$$= 2[17]$$
$$= 34$$

Calculator Close-Up

You can use parentheses to control the order in which your calculator performs the operations in an expression.

```
5((2*3)-8)
               -10
2((4*5)-abs(3-6)
)
               34
```

Exponential Expressions

We use the notation of exponents to simplify the writing of repeated multiplication. The product $5 \cdot 5 \cdot 5 \cdot 5$ is written as 5^4. The number 4 in 5^4 is called the exponent, and it indicates the number of times that the factor 5 occurs in the product.

Exponential Expression

For any natural number n and real number a,
$$a^n = \underbrace{a \cdot a \cdot a \cdot \ldots \cdot a}_{n \text{ factors of } a}.$$

We call a the **base,** n the **exponent,** and a^n an **exponential expression.**

We read a^n as "the nth power of a" or "a to the nth power." The exponential expressions 3^5 and 10^6 are read as "3 to the fifth power" and "10 to the sixth power." We can also use the words "squared" and "cubed" for the second and third powers, respectively. For example, 5^2 and 2^3 are read as "5 squared" and "2 cubed," respectively.

EXAMPLE 2

Exponential expressions

Evaluate.

a) 2^3 b) $(-3)^4$ c) $\left(-\dfrac{1}{2}\right)^5$

Calculator Close-Up

Powers are indicated on a graphing calculator using a caret (^). Most calculators also have an x^2-key for squaring. Note that parentheses are necessary in $(-3)^4$. Without parentheses, your calculator should get $-3^4 = -81$. Try it.

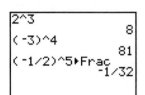

Solution

a) $2^3 = 2 \cdot 2 \cdot 2$ The factor 2 is used three times.
   $= 8$

b) $(-3)^4 = (-3)(-3)(-3)(-3)$ The factor -3 is used four times.
   $= 81$ Even number of negative signs, positive product

c) $\left(-\dfrac{1}{2}\right)^5 = \left(-\dfrac{1}{2}\right)\left(-\dfrac{1}{2}\right)\left(-\dfrac{1}{2}\right)\left(-\dfrac{1}{2}\right)\left(-\dfrac{1}{2}\right)$ The factor $-\dfrac{1}{2}$ is used five times.
   $= -\dfrac{1}{32}$ Odd number of negative signs, negative product ■

Square Roots

Because $3^2 = 9$ and $(-3)^2 = 9$, both 3 and -3 are square roots of 9. We use the **radical symbol** $\sqrt{}$ to indicate the nonnegative or principal square root of 9. We write $\sqrt{9} = 3$.

Square Roots

If $a^2 = b$, then a is called a **square root** of b. If $a \geq 0$, then a is called the **principal square root** of b and we write $\sqrt{b} = a$.

The radical symbol is a grouping symbol. We perform all operations within the radical symbol before the square root is found.

EXAMPLE 3

Evaluating square roots

Evaluate.

a) $\sqrt{64}$ b) $\sqrt{9 + 16}$ c) $\sqrt{3(17 - 5)}$

Solution

a) Because $8^2 = 64$, we have $\sqrt{64} = 8$.

b) Because the radical symbol is a grouping symbol, add 9 and 16 before finding the square root:
$$\sqrt{9 + 16} = \sqrt{25} \quad \text{Add first.}$$
$$= 5 \quad \text{Find square root.}$$

Note that $\sqrt{9} + \sqrt{16} = 3 + 4 = 7$. So $\sqrt{9 + 16} \neq \sqrt{9} + \sqrt{16}$.

c) $\sqrt{3(17 - 5)} = \sqrt{3(12)} = \sqrt{36} = 6$ ■

Calculator Close-Up

Because the radical symbol on most calculators cannot be extended, parentheses are used to group the expression that is inside the radical.

```
√(64)
              8
√(9+16)
              5
√(3(17-5))
              6
```

Order of Operations

To simplify the writing of expressions, we often omit some grouping symbols. If we saw the expression

$$5 + 2 \cdot 3$$

written without parentheses, we would not know how to evaluate it unless we had a rule for which operations to perform first. Expressions in which some or all grouping symbols are omitted, are evaluated consistently by using a rule called the **order of operations.**

Order of Operations

Evaluate inside any grouping symbols first. Where grouping symbols are missing use this order.
   1. Evaluate each exponential expression (in order from left to right).
   2. Perform multiplication and division (in order from left to right).
   3. Perform addition and subtraction (in order from left to right).

"In order from left to right" means that we evaluate the operations in the order in which they are written. For example,

$$20 \cdot 3 \div 6 = 60 \div 6 = 10 \qquad \text{and} \qquad 10 - 3 + 6 = 7 + 6 = 13.$$

If an expression contains grouping symbols, we evaluate within the grouping symbols using the order of operations.

EXAMPLE 4

Order of operations

Evaluate each expression.

a) $5 + 2 \cdot 3$ **b)** $9 \cdot 2^3$ **c)** $(6 - 4^2)^2$ **d)** $40 \div 8 \cdot 2 \div 5 \cdot 3$

Calculator Close-Up

When parentheses are omitted, most (but not all) calculators follow the same order of operations that we use in this text. Try these computations on your calculator. To use a calculator effectively, you must practice with it.

```
5+2*3
              11
(6-4²)²
              100
40/8*2/5*3
              6
```

Solution

a) $5 + 2 \cdot 3 = 5 + 6$ Multiply first.

         $= 11$ Then add.

b) $9 \cdot 2^3 = 9 \cdot 8$ Evaluate the exponential expression first.

       $= 72$ Then multiply.

c) $(6 - 4^2)^2 = (6 - 16)^2$ Evaluate 4^2 within the parentheses first.

          $= (-10)^2$ Then subtract.

          $= 100$ $(-10)(-10) = 100$

d) Multiplication and division are done from left to right.

$$40 \div 8 \cdot 2 \div 5 \cdot 3 = 5 \cdot 2 \div 5 \cdot 3$$
$$= 10 \div 5 \cdot 3$$
$$= 2 \cdot 3$$
$$= 6$$
■

CAUTION Don't confuse -3^2 and $(-3)^2$. We interpret -3^2 as the opposite of 3^2. So $-3^2 = -(3^2) = -9$, whereas $(-3)^2 = (-3)(-3) = 9$.

EXAMPLE 5

The order of negative signs

Evaluate each expression.

a) -2^4 **b)** -5^2 **c)** $(3 - 5)^2$ **d)** $-(5^2 - 4 \cdot 7)^2$

Helpful Hint

"Everybody Loves My Dear Aunt Sally" is often used as a memory aid for the order of operations. Do **E**xponents and **L**ogarithms, **M**ultiplication and **D**ivision, and then **A**ddition and **S**ubtraction. Logarithms are discussed later in this text.

Solution

a) To evaluate -2^4, find 2^4 first and then take the opposite. So $-2^4 = -16$.

b) $-5^2 = -(5^2)$ The exponent applies to 5 only.

     $= -25$

c) Evaluate within the parentheses first, then square that result.

$$(3 - 5)^2 = (-2)^2 \quad \text{Evaluate within parentheses first.}$$
$$= 4 \quad \text{Square } -2 \text{ to get 4.}$$

d) $-(5^2 - 4 \cdot 7)^2 = -(25 - 28)^2$ Evaluate 5^2 within the parentheses first.

        $= -(-3)^2$ Then subtract.

        $= -9$ Square -3 to get 9, then take the opposite of 9 to get -9.

When an expression involves a fraction bar, the numerator and denominator are each treated as if they are in parentheses. Example 6 illustrates how the fraction bar groups the numerator and denominator.

EXAMPLE 6

Order of operations in fractions

Evaluate each quotient.

a) $\dfrac{10 - 8}{6 - 8}$ **b)** $\dfrac{-6^2 + 2 \cdot 7}{4 - 3 \cdot 2}$

Calculator Close-Up

Some calculators use the built-up form for fractions $\left(\frac{1}{2}\right)$, but some do not $(1/2)$. If your calculator does not use the built-up form, then you must enclose numerators and denominators (that contain operations) in parentheses as shown here.

```
(10-8)/(6-8)
                -1
(-6²+2*7)/(4-3*2)
                11
```

Solution

a) $\dfrac{10 - 8}{6 - 8} = \dfrac{2}{-2}$ Evaluate the numerator and denominator separately.

        $= -1$ Then divide.

b) $\dfrac{-6^2 + 2 \cdot 7}{4 - 3 \cdot 2} = \dfrac{-36 + 14}{4 - 6}$

        $= \dfrac{-22}{-2}$ Evaluate the numerator and denominator separately.

        $= 11$ Then divide.

Algebraic Expressions

The result of combining numbers and variables with the ordinary operations of arithmetic (in some meaningful way) is called an **algebraic expression.** For example,

$$2x - 5y, \quad 5x^2, \quad (x - 3)(x + 2), \quad b^2 - 4ac, \quad 5, \quad \text{and} \quad \frac{x}{2}$$

are algebraic expressions, or simply **expressions.** An expression such as $2x - 5y$ has no definite value unless we assign values to x and y. For example, if $x = 3$ and $y = 4$, then the value of $2x - 5y$ is found by replacing x with 3 and y with 4 and evaluating:

$$2x - 5y = 2(3) - 5(4) = 6 - 20 = -14$$

Nancy Gittins, Assistant Director of Financial Aid at Babson College, helps graduate and undergraduate students to achieve their goal of financing their educations. Because recent tuition and fees can be as high as $20,000 a year, many students need financial aid to help defray these expenses. Federal loans and state loans, as well as grants from the federal and state levels, can be given to students who qualify. Ms. Gittins administers many of these loans and grants and helps students to understand the different options that are available. The interest rate for these loans is now a variable rate that is tied to treasury bills. The rate can be as high as 9.0% and as low as 7.3%. In Exercise 107 of this section you will work with interest rates compounded annually.

FINANCIAL AID DIRECTOR

Note the importance of the order of operations in evaluating an algebraic expression.

To find the value of the difference $2x - 5y$ when $x = -2$ and $y = -3$, replace x and y by -2 and -3, respectively, and then evaluate.

$$2x - 5y = 2(-2) - 5(-3) = -4 - (-15) = -4 + 15 = 11$$

E X A M P L E   7

Value of an algebraic expression

Evaluate each expression for $a = 2$, $b = -3$, and $c = 4$.

a) $a - c^2$ b) $a - b^2$ c) $b^2 - 4ac$ d) $\dfrac{a - b}{c - b}$

Calculator Close-Up

To evaluate $a - c^2$, first store the values for a and c using the STO key. Then enter the expression.

```
2→A
             2
4→C
             4
A-C²
           -14
```

Solution

a) Replace a by 2 and c by 4 in the expression $a - c^2$.

$$a - c^2 = 2 - 4^2 = 2 - 16 = -14$$

b) $a - b^2 = 2 - (-3)^2$ Let $a = 2$ and $b = -3$.

$\qquad\quad\;\; = 2 - 9$ Evaluate the exponential expression first.

$\qquad\quad\;\; = -7$ Then subtract.

c) $b^2 - 4ac = (-3)^2 - 4(2)(4)$ Let $a = 2$, $b = -3$, and $c = 4$.

$\qquad\qquad\;\; = 9 - 32$ Evaluate the exponential expression and product.

$\qquad\qquad\;\; = -23$ Subtract last.

d) $\dfrac{a - b}{c - b} = \dfrac{2 - (-3)}{4 - (-3)}$ Let $a = 2$, $b = -3$, and $c = 4$.

$\qquad\quad\;\; = \dfrac{5}{7}$ Evaluate the numerator and denominator.   ■

CAUTION When you replace a variable by a negative number, be sure to use parentheses around the negative number. If we were to omit the parentheses in Example 7(c), we would get $-3^2 - 4(2)(4) = -41$ instead of -23.

A symbol such as y_1 is treated like any other variable. We read y_1 as "y one" or "y sub one." The 1 is called a **subscript.** We can think of y_1 as the "first y" and y_2 as the "second y." We use the subscript notation in Example 8.

EXAMPLE 8

An algebraic expression with subscripts

Let $y_1 = -12$, $y_2 = -5$, $x_1 = -3$, and $x_2 = 4$. Find the value of $\dfrac{y_2 - y_1}{x_2 - x_1}$.

Helpful Hint

Many of the expressions that we evaluate in this section are expressions that we will study later in this text. We use the expression in Example 8 to find the slope of a line in Chapter 3.

Solution

Substitute the appropriate values into the expression:

$$\frac{y_2 - y_1}{x_2 - x_1} = \frac{-5 - (-12)}{4 - (-3)} \quad \text{Let } y_1 = -12, y_2 = -5,\ x_1 = -3, \text{ and } x_2 = 4.$$

$$= \frac{7}{7} = 1 \quad \text{Evaluate.} \qquad \blacksquare$$

When we evaluate an algebraic expression involving only one variable for many values of that variable, we get a collection of data. A graph (picture) of these data can give us useful information.

EXAMPLE 9

Study Tip

If you don't know how to get started on the exercises, go back to the examples. Cover the solution in the text with a piece of paper and see if you can solve the example. After mastering the examples, then try the exercises again.

Reading a graph

The expression $0.85(220 - A)$ gives the target heart rate for beneficial exercise for an athlete who is A years old. Use the graph in Fig. 1.24 to estimate the target heart rate for a 40-year-old athlete. Use the graph to estimate the age of an athlete with a target heart rate of 170.

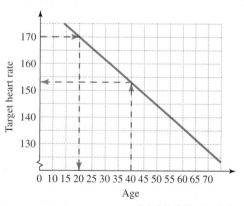

FIGURE 1.24

Solution

To find the target heart rate for a 40-year-old athlete, first draw a vertical line from age 40 up to the graph as shown in Fig. 1.24. From the point of intersection, draw a horizontal line to the heart rate scale. So the target heart rate for a 40-year-old athlete is about 153. To find the age corresponding to a heart rate of 170, first draw a horizontal line from heart rate 170 to the graph as shown in the figure. From the point of intersection, draw a vertical line down to the age scale. The heart rate of 170 corresponds to an age of about 20. $\qquad \blacksquare$

True or false? Explain your answer.

1. $2^3 = 6$

2. $-1 \cdot 2^2 = -4$

3. $-2^2 = -4$

4. $6 + 3 \cdot 2 = 18$

5. $(6 + 3) \cdot 2 = 81$

6. $(6 + 3)^2 = 18$

7. $6 + 3^2 = 15$

8. $(-3)^3 = -3^3$

9. $|-3 - (-2)| = 5$

10. $|7 - 8| = |7| - |8|$

1.4 EXERCISES

Reading and Writing   *After reading this section, write out the answers to these questions. Use complete sentences.*

1. What is an arithmetic expression?

2. How do you know whether to call an expression a sum, a difference, a product, or a quotient?

3. Why are grouping symbols used?

4. What is an exponential expression?

5. What is the purpose of the order of operations?

6. What is the difference between -3^2 and $(-3)^2$?

Evaluate each expression. See Example 1.

7. $(-3 \cdot 4) - (2 \cdot 5)$

8. $|-3 - 2| - |2 - 6|$

9. $4[5 - |3 - (2 \cdot 5)|]$

10. $-2|(-3 \cdot 4) - 6|$

11. $(6 - 8)(|2 - 3| + 6)$

12. $-5(6 + [(5 - 7) - 4])$

Evaluate each exponential expression. See Example 2.

13. 2^5

14. 3^4

15. $(-1)^4$

16. $(-1)^5$

17. $\left(-\dfrac{1}{3}\right)^2$

18. $\left(-\dfrac{1}{2}\right)^6$

Evaluate each radical. See Example 3.

19. $\sqrt{49}$

20. $\sqrt{100}$

21. $\sqrt{36 + 64}$

22. $\sqrt{25 - 9}$

23. $\sqrt{4(7 + 9)}$

24. $\sqrt{(11 + 2)(18 - 5)}$

Evaluate each expression. See Examples 4 and 5.

25. $4 - 6 \cdot 2$

26. $8 - 3 \cdot 9$

27. $5 - 6(3 - 5)$

28. $8 - 3(4 - 6)$

29. $\left(\dfrac{1}{3} - \dfrac{1}{2}\right)\left(\dfrac{1}{4} - \dfrac{1}{2}\right)$

30. $\left(\dfrac{1}{2} - \dfrac{1}{4}\right)\left(\dfrac{1}{2} - \dfrac{3}{4}\right)$

31. $-3^2 + (-8)^2 + 3$

32. $-6^2 + (-3)^3$

33. $-(2 - 7)^2$

34. $-(1 - 3 \cdot 2)^3$

35. $-5^2 \cdot 2^3$

36. $2^4 - 4^2$

37. $(-5)(-2)^3$

38. $(-1)(2 - 8)^3$

39. $-(3^2 - 4)^2$

40. $-(6 - 2^3)^4$

41. $-60 \div 10 \cdot 3 \div 2 \cdot 5 \div 6$

42. $75 \div (-5)(-3) \div \dfrac{1}{2} \cdot 6$

43. $5.5 - 2.3^4$

44. $5.3^2 - 4 \cdot 6.1$

45. $(1.3 - 0.31)(2.9 - 4.88)$

46. $(6.7 - 9.88)^3$

47. $-388.8 \div (13.5)(9.6)$

48. $(-4.3)(5.5) \div (3.2)(-1.2)$

Evaluate each expression. See Example 6.

49. $\dfrac{2 - 6}{9 - 7}$

50. $\dfrac{9 - 12}{4 - 5}$

51. $\dfrac{-3 - 5}{6 - (-2)}$

52. $\dfrac{-14 - (-2)}{-3 - 3}$

53. $\dfrac{4 + 2 \cdot 7}{3 \cdot 2 - 9}$

54. $\dfrac{-6 - 2(-3)}{8 - 3(-3)}$

55. $\dfrac{-3^2 - (-9)}{2 - 3^2}$

56. $\dfrac{-2^4 - 5}{3^2 - 2^4}$

Evaluate each expression for $a = -1$, $b = 3$, and $c = -4$. See Example 7.

57. $b^2 - 4ac$

58. $\sqrt{a^2 - 4bc}$

59. $\dfrac{a - b}{a - c}$

60. $\dfrac{b - c}{b - a}$

61. $(a - b)(a + b)$

62. $(a - c)(a + c)$

63. $\sqrt{c^2 - 2c + 1}$

64. $b^2 - 2b - 3$

65. $\dfrac{2}{a} + \dfrac{b}{c} - \dfrac{1}{c}$

66. $\dfrac{c}{a} + \dfrac{c}{b} - \dfrac{a}{b}$

67. $|a - b|$

68. $|b + c|$

Find the value of $\dfrac{y_2 - y_1}{x_2 - x_1}$ for each choice of y_1, y_2, x_1, and x_2. See Example 8.

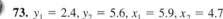

69. $y_1 = 4$, $y_2 = -6$, $x_1 = 2$, $x_2 = -7$

70. $y_1 = -3$, $y_2 = -3$, $x_1 = 4$, $x_2 = -5$

71. $y_1 = -1$, $y_2 = 2$, $x_1 = -3$, $x_2 = 1$

72. $y_1 = -2$, $y_2 = 5$, $x_1 = 2$, $x_2 = 6$

73. $y_1 = 2.4$, $y_2 = 5.6$, $x_1 = 5.9$, $x_2 = 4.7$

74. $y_1 = -5.7$, $y_2 = 6.9$, $x_1 = 3.5$, $x_2 = 4.2$

Evaluate each expression without a calculator. Use a calculator to check.

75. $-2^2 + 5(3)^2$

76. $-3^2 + 3(6)^2$

77. $(-2 + 5)3^2$

78. $(-3 + 3)6^2$

79. $\sqrt{5^2 - 4(1)(6)}$

80. $\sqrt{6^2 - 4(2)(4)}$

81. $[13 + 2(-5)]^2$

82. $[6 + 2(-4)]^2$

83. $\dfrac{4 - (-1)}{-3 - 2}$

84. $\dfrac{2 - (-3)}{3 - 5}$

85. $3(-2)^2 - 5(-2) + 4$

86. $3(-1)^2 + 5(-1) - 6$

87. $-4\left(\dfrac{1}{2}\right)^2 + 3\left(\dfrac{1}{2}\right) - 2$

88. $8\left(\dfrac{1}{2}\right)^2 - 6\left(\dfrac{1}{2}\right) + 1$

89. $-\dfrac{1}{2}|6 - 2|$

90. $-\dfrac{1}{3}|9 - 6|$

91. $\dfrac{1}{2} - \dfrac{1}{3}\left|\dfrac{1}{4} - \dfrac{1}{2}\right|$

92. $\dfrac{1}{3} - \dfrac{1}{2}\left|\dfrac{1}{3} - \dfrac{1}{2}\right|$

93. $|6 - 3 \cdot 7| + |7 - 5|$

94. $|12 - 4| - |3 - 4 \cdot 5|$

95. $3 - 7[4 - (2 - 5)]$

96. $9 - 2[3 - (4 + 6)]$

97. $3 - 4(2 - |4 - 6|)$

98. $3 - (|-4| - |-5|)$

99. $4[2 - (5 - |-3|)^2]$

100. $[5 - (-3)]^2 + [4 - (-2)]^2$

Solve each problem. See Example 9.

101. Female target heart rate. The algebraic expression $0.65(220 - A)$ gives the target heart rate for beneficial exercise for women, where A is the age of the woman. How much larger is the target heart rate of a 25-year-old woman than that of a 65-year-old woman? Use the accompanying graph to estimate the age at which a woman's target heart rate is 115.

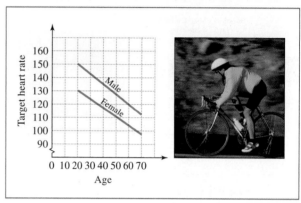

FIGURE FOR EXERCISES 101 AND 102

102. Male target heart rate. The algebraic expression $0.75(220 - A)$ gives the target heart rate for beneficial exercise for men, where A is the age of the man. Use the algebraic expression to find the target heart rate for a 20-year-old and a 50-year-old man. Use the accompanying graph to estimate the age at which a man's target heart rate is 115.

Solve each problem.

103. Perimeter of a pool. The algebraic expression $2L + 2W$ gives the perimeter of a rectangle with length L and width W. Find the perimeter of a rectangular swimming pool that has length 34 feet and width 18 feet.

104. Area of a lot. The algebraic expression for the area of a trapezoid, $0.5h(b_1 + b_2)$, gives the area of the property shown in the figure. Find the area if $h = 150$ feet, $b_1 = 260$ feet, and $b_2 = 220$ feet.

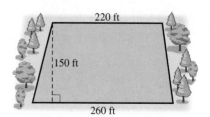

FIGURE FOR EXERCISE 104

105. Saving for retirement. The expression $P(1 + r)^n$ gives the amount of an investment of P dollars invested for n years at interest rate r compounded annually. Long-term corporate bonds have had an average yield of 6.2% annually over the last 40 years (Fidelity Investments, www.fidelity.com).

a) Use the accompanying graph to estimate the amount of a $10,000 investment in corporate bonds after 30 years.

b) Use the given expression to calculate the value of a $10,000 investment after 30 years of growth at 6.2% compounded annually.

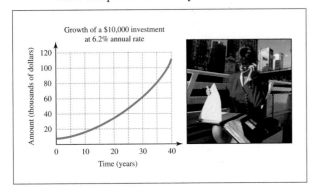

Growth of a $10,000 investment at 6.2% annual rate

FIGURE FOR EXERCISE 105

106. *Saving for college.* The average cost of a B.A. at a private college in 2021 will be $100,000 (U.S. Department of Education, www.ed.gov). The principal that must be invested at interest rate r compounded annually to have A dollars in n years is given by the algebraic expression

$$\frac{A}{(1 + r)^n}.$$

What amount must Melanie's generous grandfather invest in 2003 at 7% compounded annually so that Melanie will have $100,000 for her college education in 2021?

107. *Student loan.* A college student borrowed $4000 at 8% compounded annually in her freshman year and did not have to make payments until four years later.

Use the accompanying graph to estimate the amount that she owes at the time the payments start. Use the expression $P(1 + r)^n$ to find the actual amount of the debt at the time the payments start.

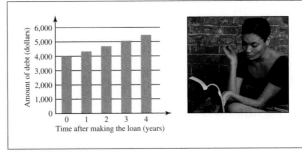

Time after making the loan (years)

FIGURE FOR EXERCISE 107

108. *Nursing home costs.* The average cost of a one-year stay in a nursing home in 2002 was $45,600 (www.medicare.gov). In n years from 2002 the average cost will be $45,600(1.05)^n$ dollars. Find the projected cost for a one-year stay in 2012.

109. *Higher nursing home costs.* Some economists project that the average cost of a one-year stay in a nursing home n years from 2002 will be $45,600(1.08)^n$ dollars. How much more would you pay for a one-year stay in 2012 using this expression rather than the expression in the last exercise?

GETTING MORE INVOLVED

110. *Discussion.* Evaluate $5(5(5 \cdot 3 + 6) + 4) + 7$ and $3 \cdot 5^3 + 6 \cdot 5^2 + 4 \cdot 5 + 7$. Explain why these two expressions must have the same value.

111. *Cooperative learning.* Find some examples of algebraic expressions that are not mentioned in this text and explain to your class what they are used for.

In This Section

- Commutative Properties
- Associative Properties
- Distributive Property
- Identity Properties
- Inverse Properties
- Multiplication Property of Zero

1.5 PROPERTIES OF THE REAL NUMBERS

You know that the price of a hamburger plus the price of a Coke is the same as the price of a Coke plus the price of a hamburger. But, do you know which property of the real numbers is at work in this situation? In arithmetic we may be unaware when to use properties of the real numbers, but in algebra we need a better understanding of those properties. In this section we will study the properties of the basic operations on the set of real numbers.

Commutative Properties

We get the same result whether we evaluate $3 + 7$ or $7 + 3$. With multiplication, we have $4 \cdot 5 = 5 \cdot 4$. These examples illustrate the commutative properties.

Commutative Property of Addition

For any real numbers a and b,
$$a + b = b + a.$$

Commutative Property of Multiplication

For any real numbers a and b,
$$ab = ba.$$

In writing the product of a number and a variable, it is customary to write the number first. We write $3x$ rather than $x3$. In writing the product of two variables, it is customary to write them in alphabetical order. We write cd rather than dc.

Addition and multiplication are commutative operations, but what about subtraction and division? Because $7 - 3 = 4$ and $3 - 7 = -4$, subtraction is not commutative. To see that division is not commutative, consider the amount each person gets when a \$1 million lottery prize is divided between two people and when a \$2 prize is divided among 1 million people.

Associative Properties

Consider the expression $2 + 3 + 7$. Using the order of operations, we add from left to right to get 12. If we first add 3 and 7 to get 10 and then add 2 and 10, we also get 12. So

$$(2 + 3) + 7 = 2 + (3 + 7).$$

Now consider the expression $2 \cdot 3 \cdot 5$. Using the order of operations, we multiply from left to right to get 30. However, we can first multiply 3 and 5 to get 15 and then multiply by 2 to get 30. So

$$(2 \cdot 3) \cdot 5 = 2 \cdot (3 \cdot 5).$$

These examples illustrate the associative properties.

Associative Property of Addition

For any real numbers a, b, and c,
$$(a + b) + c = a + (b + c).$$

Associative Property of Multiplication

For any real numbers a, b, and c,
$$(ab)c = a(bc).$$

Consider the expression

$$4 - 9 + 8 - 5 - 8 + 6 - 13.$$

According to the accepted order of operations, we could evaluate this expression by computing from left to right. However, if we use the definition of subtraction, we can rewrite this expression as

$$4 + (-9) + 8 + (-5) + (-8) + 6 + (-13).$$

The commutative and associative properties of addition allow us to add these numbers in any order we choose. A good way to add them is to add the positive numbers, add the negative numbers, and then combine the two totals:

$$4 + 8 + 6 + (-9) + (-5) + (-8) + (-13) = 18 + (-35)$$
$$= -17$$

For speed we usually do not rewrite the expression. We just sum the positive numbers and sum the negative numbers, and then combine their totals.

E X A M P L E   1

Using commutative and associative properties

Evaluate.

a) $4 - 7 + 10 - 5$

b) $6 - 5 - 9 + 7 - 2 + 5 - 8$

Solution

a) $4 - 7 + 10 - 5 = 14 + (-12) = 2$

                  ↑   ↑

      Sum of the positive   Sum of the negative
          numbers   numbers

b) $6 - 5 - 9 + 7 - 2 + 5 - 8 = 18 + (-24)$ Add positive numbers;
                             $= -6$ add negative numbers.

Not all operations are associative. Using subtraction, for example, we have

$$(8 - 4) - 1 \neq 8 - (4 - 1)$$

because $(8 - 4) - 1 = 3$ and $8 - (4 - 1) = 5$. For division we have

$$(8 \div 4) \div 2 \neq 8 \div (4 \div 2)$$

because $(8 \div 4) \div 2 = 1$ and $8 \div (4 \div 2) = 4$. So subtraction and division are not associative.

Helpful Hint

Imagine a parade in which 6 rows of horses are followed by 4 rows of horses with 3 horses in each row.

+ + + + + +   + + + +
+ + + + + +   + + + +
+ + + + + +   + + + +

There are 10 rows of 3 horses or 30 horses, or there are 18 horses followed by 12 horses for a total of 30 horses.

Distributive Property

Using the order of operations, we evaluate the product $3(6 + 4)$ first by adding 6 and 4 and then multiplying by 3:

$$3(6 + 4) = 3 \cdot 10 = 30$$

Note that we also have

$$3 \cdot 6 + 3 \cdot 4 = 18 + 12 = 30.$$

Therefore

$$3(6 + 4) = 3 \cdot 6 + 3 \cdot 4.$$

Note that multiplication by 3 from outside the parentheses is *distributed* over each term inside the parentheses. This example illustrates the distributive property.

Distributive Property

For any real numbers a, b, and c,

$$a(b + c) = ab + ac.$$

Because subtraction is defined in terms of addition, multiplication distributes over subtraction as well as over addition. For example,

$$3(x - 2) = 3(x + (-2))$$
$$= 3x + (-6)$$
$$= 3x - 6.$$

Because multiplication is commutative, we can write the multiplication before or after the parentheses. For example,

$$(y + 6)3 = 3(y + 6)$$
$$= 3y + 18.$$

The distributive property is used in two ways. If we start with the product $5(x + 4)$ and write

$$5(x + 4) = 5x + 20,$$

we are writing a product as a sum. We are removing the parentheses. If we start with the difference $6x - 18$ and write

$$6x - 18 = 6(x - 3),$$

we are using the distributive property to write a difference as a product.

E X A M P L E   2

Using the distributive property

Use the distributive property to rewrite each sum or difference as a product and each product as a sum or difference.

a) $9x - 9$ **b)** $b(2 - a)$ **c)** $3a + ac$ **d)** $-2(x - 3)$

Solution

a) $9x - 9 = 9(x - 1)$

b) $b(2 - a) = 2b - ab$ Note that $b \cdot 2 = 2b$ by the commutative property.

c) $3a + ac = a(3 + c)$

d) $-2(x - 3) = -2x - (-2)(3)$ Distributive property
$$= -2x - (-6)$$ Multiply.
$$= -2x + 6$$ $a - (-b) = a + b$ ■

Identity Properties

The numbers 0 and 1 have special properties. Addition of 0 to a number does not change the number, and multiplication of a number by 1 does not change the number. For this reason, 0 is called the **additive identity** and 1 is called the **multiplicative identity.**

Additive Identity Property

For any real number a,

$$a + 0 = 0 + a = a.$$

Multiplicative Identity Property

For any real number a,

$$a \cdot 1 = 1 \cdot a = a.$$

Inverse Properties

The ideas of *additive inverses* and *multiplicative inverses* were introduced in Section 1.3. Every real number a has a unique additive inverse or opposite, $-a$, such that $a + (-a) = 0$. Every nonzero real number a also has a unique multiplicative inverse (reciprocal), written $\frac{1}{a}$, such that $a\left(\frac{1}{a}\right) = 1$. For rational numbers the multiplicative inverse is easy to find. For example, the multiplicative inverse of $\frac{2}{5}$ is $\frac{5}{2}$ because

$$\frac{2}{5} \cdot \frac{5}{2} = \frac{10}{10} = 1.$$

Calculator Close-Up

Most scientific calculators have a key labeled 1/x, which gives the reciprocal of the number on the display. Graphing calculators do not have a reciprocal key, but you can find reciprocals as shown here.

```
1/0.002+1/0.0012
5
            1300
```

Additive Inverse Property

For any real number a, there is a unique number $-a$ such that

$$a + (-a) = -a + a = 0.$$

Multiplicative Inverse Property

For any nonzero real number a, there is a unique number $\frac{1}{a}$ such that

$$a \cdot \frac{1}{a} = \frac{1}{a} \cdot a = 1.$$

Reciprocals are used in problems involving rates. For example, if Brandon washes one car in $\frac{1}{3}$ of an hour, then he is washing cars at the rate of $1/\left(\frac{1}{3}\right)$ or 3 cars/hour (3 cars per hour). If Gilda washes one car in $\frac{1}{4}$ of an hour, then she is washing at the rate of $1/\left(\frac{1}{4}\right)$ or 4 cars/hour. In general, if one task is completed in x hours, then the rate is $\frac{1}{x}$ tasks/hour. If Brandon and Gilda maintain the same rates when working together, then their rate together is the sum of their individual rates, or 7 cars/hour.

EXAMPLE 3

Work rates

An old computer system can process one water bill in 0.002 hour. A new computer system can process one water bill in 0.00125 hour. If the old system is used simultaneously with the new one, then at what rate will the processing of the water bills be accomplished?

Solution

Since the old system does one bill in 0.002 hour, its rate is $\frac{1}{0.002}$ bills per hour. Since the new system does one bill in 0.00125 hour, its rate is $\frac{1}{0.00125}$ bills per hour. Their rate when working together is the sum of their individual rates:

$$\frac{1}{0.002} + \frac{1}{0.00125} = 1300$$

They are working together at the rate of 1300 bills per hour. ∎

Multiplication Property of Zero

Zero has a property that no other number has. Multiplication involving zero always results in zero. It is the multiplication property of zero that prevents 0 from having a reciprocal.

Multiplication Property of Zero

For any real number a,

$$0 \cdot a = a \cdot 0 = 0.$$

E X A M P L E 4   **Recognizing properties**

Identify the property that is illustrated in each case.

a) $5 \cdot 9 = 9 \cdot 5$

b) $3 \cdot \dfrac{1}{3} = 1$

c) $1 \cdot 865 = 865$

d) $3 + (5 + a) = (3 + 5) + a$

e) $4x + 6x = (4 + 6)x$

f) $7 + (x + 3) = 7 + (3 + x)$

g) $4567 \cdot 0 = 0$

h) $239 + 0 = 239$

i) $-8 + 8 = 0$

j) $-4(x - 5) = -4x + 20$

Solution

a) Commutative property of multiplication

b) Multiplicative inverse property

c) Multiplicative identity property

d) Associative property of addition

e) Distributive property

f) Commutative property of addition

g) Multiplication property of zero

h) Additive identity property

i) Additive inverse property

j) Distributive property   ■

WARM-UPS

True or false? Explain your answer.

1. Addition is a commutative operation.
2. $8 \div (4 \div 2) = (8 \div 4) \div 2$
3. $10 \div 2 = 2 \div 10$
4. $5 - 3 = 3 - 5$
5. $10 - (7 - 3) = (10 - 7) - 3$
6. $4(6 \div 2) = (4 \cdot 6) \div (4 \cdot 2)$
7. The multiplicative inverse of 0.02 is 50.
8. Division is not an associative operation.
9. $3 + 2x = 5x$ for any value of x.
10. A machine that washes one car in 0.04 hour is washing at the rate of 25 cars per hour.

1.5   **EXERCISES**

Reading and Writing   *After reading this section, write out the answers to these questions. Use complete sentences.*

1. What are the commutative properties?

2. What are the associative properties?

3. What is the difference between the commutative property of addition and the associative property of addition?

4. What is the distributive property?

5. Why is 0 called the additive identity?

6. Why is 1 called the multiplicative identity?

Evaluate. See Example 1.

7. $9 - 4 + 6 - 10$

8. $-3 + 4 - 12 + 9$

9. $6 - 10 + 5 - 8 - 7$

10. $5 - 11 + 6 - 9 + 12 - 2$

11. $-4 - 11 + 6 - 8 + 13 - 20$

12. $-8 + 12 - 9 - 15 + 6 - 22 + 3$

13. $-3.2 + 1.4 - 2.8 + 4.5 - 1.6$

14. $4.4 - 5.1 + 3.6 - 2.3 + 8.1$

15. $3.27 - 11.41 + 5.7 - 12.36 - 5$

16. $4.89 - 2.1 + 7.58 - 9.06 - 5.34$

Use the distributive property to rewrite each sum or difference as a product and each product as a sum or difference. See Example 2.

17. $4(x - 6)$ **18.** $5(a - 1)$

19. $2m + 10$ **20.** $3y + 9$

21. $a(3 + t)$ **22.** $b(y + w)$

23. $-2(w - 5)$ **24.** $-4(m - 7)$

25. $-2(3 - y)$ **26.** $-5(4 - p)$

27. $5x - 5$ **28.** $3y + 3$

29. $-1(-2x - y)$ **30.** $-1(-4y - w)$

31. $-3(-2w - 3y)$

32. $-4(-x - 6)$

33. $3y - 15$ **34.** $5x + 10$

35. $3a + 9$ **36.** $7b - 49$

37. $\dfrac{1}{2}(4x + 8)$ **38.** $\dfrac{1}{3}(3x + 6)$

39. $-\dfrac{1}{2}(2x - 4)$ **40.** $-\dfrac{1}{3}(9x - 3)$

Find the multiplicative inverse (reciprocal) of each number.

41. $\dfrac{1}{2}$ **42.** $\dfrac{1}{3}$ **43.** 1

44. -1 **45.** 6 **46.** 8

47. 0.25 **48.** 0.75 **49.** -0.7

50. -0.9 **51.** -1.8 **52.** -2.6

 Use a calculator to evaluate each expression. Round answers to four decimal places.

53. $\dfrac{1}{2.3} + \dfrac{1}{5.4}$ **54.** $\dfrac{1}{13.5} - \dfrac{1}{4.6}$

55. $\dfrac{\dfrac{1}{4.3}}{\dfrac{1}{5.6} + \dfrac{1}{7.2}}$ **56.** $\dfrac{\dfrac{1}{4.5} - \dfrac{1}{5.6}}{\dfrac{1}{3.2} + \dfrac{1}{2.7}}$

 Solve each problem. See Example 3.

57. *Fastest airliner.* The Concorde travels 1 mile in 0.0006897 hour and carries 128 passengers (www.british-airways.com/concorde). Find its rate in miles per hour.

58. *Fastest jet plane.* On March 6, 1990, the SR-71 Blackbird set a record by flying coast to coast in 68 minutes (National Air and Space Museum, www.nasm.si.edu). The Blackbird averaged one mile every 0.000471 hour. Find the rate in miles per hour.

59. *Who's got the button.* A small clothing factory has three workers who attach buttons. Rita, Mary, and Sam can attach a single button in 0.01 hour, 0.02 hour, and 0.015 hour, respectively. At what hourly rate are they attaching buttons when working simultaneously?

60. *Modern art.* Emilio can paint the exterior of a certain house in 36.5 hours. Alex can paint the same house in 30 hours. If they work together without interfering with each other, then at what hourly rate will the house be painted?

Name the property that is illustrated in each case. See Example 4.

61. $3 + x = x + 3$
62. $x \cdot 5 = 5x$
63. $5(x - 7) = 5x - 35$
64. $a(3b) = (a \cdot 3)b$
65. $3(xy) = (3x)y$
66. $3(x - 1) = 3x - 3$
67. $4(0.25) = 1$
68. $0.3 + 9 = 9 + 0.3$
69. $y^3x = xy^3$
70. $0 \cdot 52 = 0$
71. $1 \cdot x = x$
72. $(0.1)(10) = 1$
73. $2x + 3x = (2 + 3)x$
74. $8 + 0 = 8$
75. $7 + (-7) = 0$
76. $1 \cdot y = y$
77. $(36 + 79)0 = 0$
78. $5x + 5 = 5(x + 1)$
79. $xy + x = x(y + 1)$
80. $ab + 3ac = a(b + 3c)$

Complete each statement using the property named.

81. $5 + w = $ _____, commutative property of addition

82. $2x + 2 = $ _____, distributive property

83. $5(xy) = $ ____, associative property of multiplication

84. $x + \dfrac{1}{2} = $ _____, commutative property of addition

85. $\dfrac{1}{2}x - \dfrac{1}{2} = $ _____, distributive property

86. $3(x - 7) = $ _____, distributive property
87. $6x + 9 = $ _____, distributive property
88. $(x + 7) + 3 = $ _____, associative property of addition

89. $8(0.125) = $ _____, multiplicative inverse property
90. $-1(a - 3) = $ _____, distributive property
91. $0 = 5($_____$)$, multiplication property of zero
92. $8 \cdot ($_____$) = 8$, multiplicative identity property
93. $0.25 ($_____$) = 1$, multiplicative inverse property
94. $45(1) = $ _____, multiplicative identity property

GETTING MORE INVOLVED

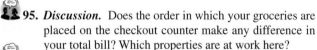

95. *Discussion.* Does the order in which your groceries are placed on the checkout counter make any difference in your total bill? Which properties are at work here?

96. *Discussion.* Suppose that you just bought 10 grocery items and paid a total bill that included 6% sales tax. Would there be any difference in your total bill if you purchased the items one at a time? Which property is at work here?

In This Section

- Using the Properties in Computation
- Like Terms
- Combining Like Terms
- Products and Quotients
- Removing Parentheses

1.6   **USING THE PROPERTIES**

The properties of the real numbers can be helpful when we are doing computations. In this section we will see how the properties can be applied in arithmetic and algebra.

Using the Properties in Computation

Consider the product of 36 and 200. Using the associative property of multiplication, we can write

$$(36)(200) = (36)(2 \cdot 100) = (36 \cdot 2)(100).$$

To find this product mentally, first multiply 36 by 2 to get 72, then multiply 72 by 100 to get 7200.

EXAMPLE 1   **Using properties in computation**

Evaluate each expression mentally by using an appropriate property.

a) $536 + 25 + 75$ **b)** $5 \cdot 426 \cdot \dfrac{1}{5}$ **c)** $7 \cdot 45 + 3 \cdot 45$

Solution

a) To perform this addition mentally, the associative property of addition can be applied as follows:

$$536 + (25 + 75) = 536 + 100 = 636$$

b) Use the commutative and associative properties of multiplication to rearrange mentally this product.

$$5 \cdot 426 \cdot \frac{1}{5} = 426 \cdot 5 \cdot \frac{1}{5} \qquad \text{Commutative property of multiplication}$$

$$= 426\left(5 \cdot \frac{1}{5}\right) \qquad \text{Associative property of multiplication}$$

$$= 426 \cdot 1 \qquad \text{Multiplicative inverse property}$$

$$= 426$$

c) Use the distributive property to rewrite the expression, then evaluate it.

$$7 \cdot 45 + 3 \cdot 45 = (7 + 3)45 = 10 \cdot 45 = 450 \qquad ■$$

Like Terms

The properties of the real numbers are used also with algebraic expressions. Simple algebraic expressions such as

$$-2, \qquad 4x, \qquad -5x^2y, \qquad b, \qquad \text{and} \qquad -abc$$

are called terms. A **term** is a single number or the product of a number and one or more variables raised to powers. The number preceding the variables in a term is called the **coefficient.** In the term $4x$ the coefficient of x is 4. In the term $-5x^2y$ the coefficient of x^2y is -5. In the term b the coefficient of b is 1, and in the term $-abc$ the coefficient of abc is -1. If two terms contain the same variables with the same powers, they are called **like terms.** For example, $3x^2$ and $-5x^2$ are like terms, whereas $3x^2$ and $-2x^3$ are not like terms.

Combining Like Terms

We can combine any two like terms involved in a sum by using the distributive property. For example,

$$2x + 5x = (2 + 5)x \qquad \text{Distributive property}$$

$$= 7x \qquad \text{Add 2 and 5.}$$

Because the distributive property is valid for any real numbers, we have $2x + 5x = 7x$ for any real number x.

We can also use the distributive property to combine any two like terms involved in a difference. For example,

$$-3xy - (-2xy) = [-3 - (-2)]xy \qquad \text{Distributive property}$$

$$= -1xy \qquad \text{Subtract.}$$

$$= -xy \qquad \text{Multiplying by } -1 \text{ is the same as taking the opposite.}$$

Of course, we do not want to write out these steps every time we combine like terms. We can combine like terms as easily as we can add or subtract their coefficients.

E X A M P L E   2

Combining like terms

Perform the indicated operation.

a) $b + 3b$ b) $5x^2 - 7x^2$

c) $5xy - (-13xy)$ d) $-2a + (-9a)$

Solution

a) $b + 3b = 1b + 3b = 4b$ b) $5x^2 - 7x^2 = -2x^2$

c) $5xy - (-13xy) = 18xy$ d) $-2a + (-9a) = -11a$ ■

C A U T I O N   The distributive property allows us to combine only *like* terms. Expressions such as

$$3xw + 5, \qquad 7xy + 9t, \qquad 5b + 6a, \qquad \text{and} \qquad 6x^2 + 7x$$

do not contain like terms, so their terms cannot be combined.

Products and Quotients

We can use the associative property of multiplication to simplify the product of two terms. For example,

$$4(7x) = (4 \cdot 7)x \qquad \text{Associative property of multiplication}$$
$$= (28)x$$
$$= 28x. \qquad \text{Remove unnecessary parentheses.}$$

C A U T I O N   Multiplication does not distribute over multiplication. For example, $2(3 \cdot 4) \neq 6 \cdot 8$ because $2(3 \cdot 4) = 2(12) = 24$.

In the next example we use the fact that dividing by 3 is equivalent to multiplying by $\frac{1}{3}$, the reciprocal of 3:

$$3\left(\frac{x}{3}\right) = 3\left(x \cdot \frac{1}{3}\right) \qquad \text{Definition of division}$$

$$= 3\left(\frac{1}{3} \cdot x\right) \qquad \text{Commutative property of multiplication}$$

$$= \left(3 \cdot \frac{1}{3}\right)x \qquad \text{Associative property of multiplication}$$

$$= 1 \cdot x \qquad 3 \cdot \frac{1}{3} = 1 \text{ (Multiplicative inverse property)}$$

$$= x \qquad \text{Multiplicative identity property}$$

To find the product $(3x)(5x)$, we use both the commutative and associative properties of multiplication:

$$(3x)(5x) = (3x \cdot 5)x \qquad \text{Associative property of multiplication}$$
$$= (3 \cdot 5x)x \qquad \text{Commutative property of multiplication}$$
$$= (3 \cdot 5)(x \cdot x) \qquad \text{Associative property of multiplication}$$
$$= (15)(x^2) \qquad \text{Simplify.}$$
$$= 15x^2 \qquad \text{Remove unnecessary parentheses.}$$

All of the steps in finding the product $(3x)(5x)$ are shown here to illustrate that every step is justified by a property. However, you should write $(3x)(5x) = 15x^2$ without doing any intermediate steps.

E X A M P L E   3

Multiplying terms

Find each product.

a) $(-5)(6x)$　　**b)** $(-3a)(-8a)$　　**c)** $(-4y)(-6)$　　**d)** $(-5a)\left(\dfrac{b}{5}\right)$

Solution

a) $-30x$　　**b)** $24a^2$　　**c)** $24y$　　**d)** $-ab$　■

In Example 4 we use the properties to find quotients. Try to identify the property that is used at each step.

E X A M P L E   4

Dividing terms

Find each quotient.

a) $\dfrac{5x}{5}$　　　　　　　　　　　　**b)** $\dfrac{4x + 8}{2}$

Solution

a) First use the definition of division to change the division by 5 to multiplication by $\frac{1}{5}$.

$$\frac{5x}{5} = 5x \cdot \frac{1}{5} = \left(\frac{1}{5} \cdot 5\right)x = 1 \cdot x = x$$

b) First use the definition of division to change division by 2 to multiplication by $\frac{1}{2}$.

$$\frac{4x + 8}{2} = (4x + 8) \cdot \frac{1}{2} = \frac{1}{2} \cdot (4x + 8) = 2x + 4$$

Since both $4x$ and 8 are divided by 2, we could have written

$$\frac{4x + 8}{2} = \frac{4x}{2} + \frac{8}{2} = 2x + 4.$$　■

C A U T I O N　　Do not divide a number into just one term of a sum. For example,

$$\frac{2 + 7}{2} \neq 1 + 7$$

because

$$\frac{2 + 7}{2} = \frac{9}{2} \quad \text{and} \quad 1 + 7 = 8.$$

Removing Parentheses

Multiplying a number by -1 merely changes the sign of the number. For example,

$$(-1)(6) = -6 \quad \text{and} \quad (-1)(-15) = 15.$$

Thus -1 times a number is the same as the *opposite* of the number. Using variables, we have

$$(-1)x = -x \quad \text{or} \quad -1(a + 2) = -(a + 2).$$

When a minus sign appears in front of a sum, we can think of it as multiplication by -1 and use the distributive property. For example,

$$
\begin{aligned}
-(a + 2) &= -1(a + 2) \\
&= (-1)a + (-1)2 \quad \text{Distributive property} \\
&= -a + (-2) \\
&= -a - 2.
\end{aligned}
$$

If a minus sign occurs in front of a difference, we can rewrite the expression as a sum. For example,

$$
\begin{aligned}
-(x - 5) &= -1(x - 5) \quad\quad\quad -a = -1 \cdot a \\
&= (-1)x - (-1)5 \quad \text{Distributive property} \\
&= -x + 5. \quad\quad\quad\quad \text{Simplify.}
\end{aligned}
$$

Note that a minus sign in front of a set of parentheses affects each term in the parentheses, changing the sign of each term.

E X A M P L E   5

Removing parentheses

Simplify each expression.

a) $6 - (x + 8)$ **b)** $4x - 6 - (7x - 4)$ **c)** $3x - (-x + 7)$

Solution

a)
$$
\begin{aligned}
6 - (x + 8) &= 6 - x - 8 \quad \text{Change the sign of each term in parentheses.} \\
&= 6 - 8 - x \quad \text{Rearrange the terms.} \\
&= -2 - x \quad\quad\; \text{Combine like terms.}
\end{aligned}
$$

b)
$$
\begin{aligned}
4x - 6 - (7x - 4) &= 4x - 6 - 7x + 4 \quad \text{Remove parentheses.} \\
&= 4x - 7x - 6 + 4 \quad \text{Rearrange the terms.} \\
&= -3x - 2 \quad\quad\quad\quad\;\; \text{Combine like terms.}
\end{aligned}
$$

c)
$$
\begin{aligned}
3x - (-x + 7) &= 3x + x - 7 \quad \text{Remove parentheses.} \\
&= 4x - 7 \quad\quad\quad\; \text{Combine like terms.} \quad\blacksquare
\end{aligned}
$$

The commutative and associative properties of addition allow us to rearrange the terms so that we may combine like terms. However, it is not necessary actually to write down the rearrangement. We can identify like terms and combine them without rearranging.

E X A M P L E   6

More parentheses and like terms

Simplify each expression.

a) $(-5x + 7) + (2x - 9)$ **b)** $-4x + 7x + 3(2 - 5x)$

c) $-3x(4x - 9) - (x - 5)$ **d)** $x - 0.03(x + 300)$

Solution

a) $(-5x + 7) + (2x - 9) = -3x - 2$ Combine like terms.

b) $-4x + 7x + 3(2 - 5x) = -4x + 7x + 6 - 15x$ Distributive property

$$= -12x + 6 \qquad \text{Combine like terms.}$$

c) $-3x(4x - 9) - (x - 5) = -12x^2 + 27x - x + 5$ Remove parentheses.

$$= -12x^2 + 26x + 5 \qquad \text{Combine like terms.}$$

d) $x - 0.03(x + 300) = 1x - 0.03x - 9$ Distributive property; $(-0.03)(300) = -9$

$$= 0.97x - 9 \qquad \text{Combine like terms: } 1.00 - 0.03 = 0.97$$

WARM-UPS

True or false? Explain your answer.

A statement involving variables should be marked true only if it is true for all values of the variable.

1. $5(x + 7) = 5x + 35$

2. $-4x + 8 = -4(x + 8)$

3. $-1(a - 3) = -(a - 3)$

4. $5y + 4y = 9y$

5. $(2x)(5x) = 10x$

6. $-2t(5t - 3) = -10t^2 + 6t$

7. $a + a = a^2$

8. $b \cdot b = 2b$

9. $1 + 7x = 8x$

10. $(3x - 4) - (8x - 1) = -5x - 3$

1.6   EXERCISES

Reading and Writing *After reading this section, write out the answers to these questions. Use complete sentences.*

1. What is a term?

2. What are like terms?

3. What is the coefficient of a term?

4. Which property is used to combine like terms?

5. What operations can you perform with unlike terms?

6. How do you remove parentheses that are preceded by a negative sign?

Perform each computation. Make use of appropriate rules to simplify each problem. See Example 1.

7. $45(200)$

8. $25(300)$

9. $\dfrac{4}{3}(0.75)$

10. $5(0.2)$

11. $(427 + 68) + 32$

12. $(194 + 78) + 22$

13. $47 \cdot 4 + 47 \cdot 6$

14. $53 \cdot 3 + 53 \cdot 7$

15. $19 \cdot 5 \cdot 2 \cdot \dfrac{1}{5}$

16. $17 \cdot 4 \cdot 2 \cdot \dfrac{1}{4}$

17. $(120)(400)$

18. $150 \cdot 300$

19. $13 \cdot 377(-5 + 5)$

20. $(456 \cdot 8)\dfrac{1}{8}$

21. $(348 + 5) + 45$

22. $(135 + 38) + 12$

23. $\dfrac{2}{3}(1.5)$

24. $(1.25)(0.8)$

25. $17 \cdot 101 - 17 \cdot 1$

26. $33 \cdot 2 - 12 \cdot 33$

27. $354 + 7 + 8 + 3 + 2$

28. $564 + 35 + 65 + 72 + 28$

29. $(567 + 874)(-2 \cdot 4 + 8)$

30. $(567^2 + 48)[3(-5) + 15]$

Combine like terms where possible. See Example 2.

31. $-4n + 6n$

32. $-3a + 15a$

33. $3w - (-4w)$

34. $3b - (-7b)$

35. $4mw^2 - 15mw^2$

36. $2b^2x - 16b^2x$

37. $-5x - (-2x)$

38. $-11 - 7t$

39. $-4 - 7z$

40. $-19m - (-3m)$

41. $4t^2 + 5t^2$

42. $5a + 4a^2$

43. $-4ab + 3a^2b$

44. $-7x^2y + 5x^2y$

45. $9mn - mn$

46. $3cm - cm$

47. $x^3y - 3x^3y$

48. $s^4t - 5s^4t$

49. $-kz^6 - kz^6$

50. $m^7w - m^7w$

Find each product or quotient. See Examples 3 and 4.

51. $4(7t)$ **52.** $-3(4r)$ **53.** $(-2x)(-5x)$

54. $(-3h)(-7h)$ **55.** $(-h)(-h)$ **56.** $x(-x)$

57. $7w(-4)$ **58.** $-5t(-1)$ **59.** $-x(1 - x)$

60. $-p(p - 1)$ **61.** $(5k)(5k)$ **62.** $(-4y)(-4y)$

63. $3\left(\dfrac{y}{3}\right)$ **64.** $5z\left(\dfrac{z}{5}\right)$ **65.** $9\left(\dfrac{2y}{9}\right)$

66. $8\left(\dfrac{y}{8}\right)$ **67.** $\dfrac{6x^3}{2}$ **68.** $\dfrac{-8x^2}{4}$

69. $\dfrac{3x^2y + 15x}{3}$ **70.** $\dfrac{6xy^2 - 8w}{2}$ **71.** $\dfrac{2x - 4}{-2}$

72. $\dfrac{-6x - 9}{-3}$ **73.** $\dfrac{-xt + 10}{-2}$ **74.** $\dfrac{-2xt^2 + 8}{-4}$

Simplify each expression. See Example 5.

75. $a - (4a - 1)$

76. $5x - (2x - 7)$

77. $6 - (x - 4)$

78. $9 - (w - 5)$

79. $4m + 6 - (m + 5)$

80. $5 - 6t - (3t + 4)$

81. $-5b - (-at + 7b)$

82. $-4x^2 - (-7x^2 + 2y)$

83. $t^2 - 5w - (-2w - t^2)$

84. $n^2 - 6m - (-n^2 - 2m)$

85. $x^2 - (x^2 - y^2 - z)$

86. $5w - (6w - 3xy - zy)$

Simplify each expression. See Example 6.

87. $(2x + 7x) + (3 + 5)$

88. $(3x + 4x) + (5 + 12)$

89. $(-3x + 4) + (5x - 6)$

90. $(-4x + 11) + (6x - 8)$

91. $4a^2 - 5c - (6a^2 - 7c)$

92. $3x^2 - 4 - (x^2 - 5)$

93. $5(t^2 - 3w) - 2(-3w - t^2)$

94. $6(xy^2 + 2) - 5(-xy^2 - 1)$

95. $-7m + 3(m - 4) + 5m$

96. $-6m + 4(m - 3) + 7m$

97. $8 - 7(k^3 + 3) - 4$

98. $6 + 5(k^3 - 2) - k^3 + 5$

99. $x - 0.04(x + 50)$

100. $x - 0.03(x + 500)$

101. $0.1(x + 5) - 0.04(x + 50)$

102. $0.06x + 0.14(x + 200)$

103. $3k + 5 - 2(3k - 4) - k + 3$

104. $5w - 2 + 4(w - 3) - 6(w - 1)$

105. $5.7 - 4.5(x - 3.9) - 5.42$

106. $0.04(5.6x - 4.9) + 0.07(7.3x - 34)$

Simplify.

107. $3(1 - xy) - 2(xy - 5) - (35 - xy)$

108. $2(x^2 - 3) - (6x^2 - 2) + 2(-7x^2 - 4)$

109. $w \cdot 3w + 5w (-6w) - w(2w)$

110. $3w^3 + 5w^3 - 4w^3 + 12w^3 - 2w^2$

111. $3a^2w^2 - 5w^2 \cdot a^2 - 2aw \cdot 2aw$

112. $-3(aw^2 + 5a^2w) - 2(-a^2w - a^2w)$

113. $\dfrac{1}{6} - \dfrac{1}{3}\left(-6x^2y - \dfrac{1}{2}\right)$

114. $-\dfrac{1}{2}bc - \dfrac{1}{2}bc(3 - a)$

115. $-\dfrac{1}{2}m\left(-\dfrac{1}{2}m\right) - \dfrac{1}{2}m - \dfrac{1}{2}m$

116. $\dfrac{4wyt}{4} + \dfrac{-8wyt}{2} - \dfrac{-2wy}{2}$

117. $\dfrac{-8t^3 - 6t^2 + 2}{-2}$

118. $\dfrac{7x^3 - 5x^3 - 4}{-2}$

119. $\dfrac{-6xyz - 3xy + 9z}{-3}$

120. $\dfrac{20a^2b^4 - 10a^2b^4 + 5}{-5}$

Write an algebraic expression for each problem.

121. *Triangle.* The lengths of the sides of a triangular flower bed are s feet, $s + 2$ feet, and $s + 4$ feet. What is its perimeter?

122. *Parallelogram.* The lengths of the sides of a lot in the shape of a parallelogram are w feet and $w + 50$ feet. What is its perimeter? Is it possible to find the area from this information?

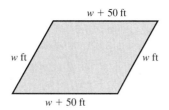

FIGURE FOR EXERCISE 122

123. *Parthenon.* To obtain a pleasing rectangular shape, the ancient Greeks constructed buildings with a length that was about $\frac{1}{6}$ longer than the width. If the width of the Parthenon is x meters and its length is $x + \frac{1}{6}x$ meters, then what is the perimeter? What is the area?

124. *Square.* If the length of each side of a square sign is x inches, then what are the perimeter and area of the square?

FIGURE FOR EXERCISE 124

COLLABORATIVE ACTIVITIES

OOOP! Order of Operations Game

This game reviews the established order of operations for real numbers.

1. Before Play Begins

You will need three to five players on a team. Assign each player one of the roles or operations listed in part (3). Write one of these expressions on a sheet of paper.

a) $\dfrac{5^2 - 2(-3)}{-2^3 - 6}$ **b)** $\dfrac{(-2)^2 + 3(-5)}{4 \cdot 5 + 2}$

c) $75 \div 3(2 + 6) - (4^2 \div 2)$

d) $[13 - 5 + 4 \div (-2^2)(7 + 8)] + (-4)$

2. Determining a Player's Turn at Play

All players working together analyze the expression and decide which part to complete. If there are parentheses, then the players decide whether what is inside the parentheses needs simplification. **E** *performs his or her operation before* **M**, *and* **M** *performs his or her operation before* **A**. Each player's turn ends when he or she encounters an operation that precedes his or hers or when he or she reaches the end of the expression.

Grouping: Three to five students per group
Topic: Order of operations, learning to work in groups

3. Each Player's Task

E—Exponents: Working left to right, **E** evaluates exponential expressions in order.

M—Multiply/Divide: Working left to right, **M** performs multiplications and divisions in order. Multiplication and division may be done by two players working as a team. If these tasks are split, then the two players perform their assigned operations in order, taking turns as needed.

A—Add/Subtract: Working left to right, **A** performs additions and subtractions in order. Addition and subtraction may be done by two players working as a team. If these tasks are split, then the two players perform their assigned operations in order, taking turns as needed.

4. Recording Results

Results are recorded on one sheet of paper. As each player finishes his or her operation, she or he passes the paper to the player with the next task. Each player rewrites the new form of the expression on the next line of the page and initials his or her work with **E**, **M**, or **A**.

WRAP-UP

SUMMARY

Sets		Examples
Set-builder notation	Notation for describing a set using variables.	$C = \{x \mid x$ is a natural number smaller than 4$\}$ $D = \{3, 4\}$
Membership	The symbol $\in$ means "is an element of."	$1 \in C, 4 \notin C$
Union	$A \cup B = \{x \mid x \in A \text{ or } x \in B\}$	$C \cup D = \{1, 2, 3, 4\}$
Intersection	$A \cap B = \{x \mid x \in A \text{ and } x \in B\}$	$C \cap D = \{3\}$
Subset	A is a subset of B if every element of A is also an element of B. $\varnothing \subseteq A$ for any set A.	$\{1, 2\} \subseteq C$ $\varnothing \subseteq C, \varnothing \subseteq D$

Real Numbers		Examples
Rational numbers	$Q = \left\{ \dfrac{a}{b} \mid a \text{ and } b \text{ are integers with } b \neq 0 \right\}$	$\dfrac{3}{2}, 5, -6, 0, 0.25252525\ldots$
Irrational numbers	$I = \{x \mid x \text{ is a real number that is not rational}\}$	$\sqrt{2}, \sqrt{3}, \pi, 0.1515515551\ldots$
Real numbers	$R = \{x \mid x \text{ is the coordinate of a point on the number line}\}$	$R = Q \cup I$
Intervals of real numbers	An interval of real numbers is the set of real numbers that lie between two real numbers, which are called the endpoints of the interval. We may use $-\infty$ or ∞ as endpoints.	The real numbers between 3 and 4: $(3, 4)$ The real numbers greater than or equal to 6: $[6, \infty)$

Operations with Real Numbers		Examples
Absolute value	$|a| = \begin{cases} a & \text{if } a \text{ is positive or zero} \\ -a & \text{if } a \text{ is negative} \end{cases}$	$|6| = 6, |0| = 0$ $|-6| = 6$
Addition and subtraction	To find the sum of two numbers with the same sign, add their absolute values. The sum has the same sign as the original numbers.	$-2 + (-7) = -9$
	To find the sum of two numbers with unlike signs, subtract their absolute values. The sum is positive if the number with the larger absolute value is positive. The sum is negative if the number with the larger absolute value is negative.	$-6 + 9 = 3$ $-9 + 6 = -3$

Subtraction: $a - b = a + (-b)$
(Change the sign and add.)

$4 - 7 = 4 + (-7) = -3$
$5 - (-3) = 5 + 3 = 8$

Multiplication and division

To find the product or quotient of two numbers, multiply or divide their absolute values:
Same signs $\leftrightarrow$ positive result
Opposite signs $\leftrightarrow$ negative result

$(-4)(-2) = 8, (-4)(2) = -8$

$-8 \div (-2) = 4, -8 \div 2 = -4$

Exponential expressions

In the expression a^n, a is the base and n is the exponent.

$2^3 = 2 \cdot 2 \cdot 2 = 8$

Square roots

If $a^2 = b$, then a is a square root of b.
If $a \geq 0$ and $a^2 = b$, then $\sqrt{b} = a$.

Both 3 and -3 are square roots of 9.
Because $3 \geq 0$, $\sqrt{9} = 3$.

Order of operations

In an expression without parentheses or absolute value:
1. Evaluate exponential expressions.
2. Perform multiplication and division.
3. Perform addition and subtraction.
With parentheses or absolute value:
First evaluate within each set of parentheses or absolute value, using the above order.

$7 + 2^3 = 15$
$3 + 4 \cdot 6 = 27$
$5 + 4 \cdot 3^2 = 41$

$(2 + 4)(5 - 9) = -24$
$3 + 4 |2 - 3| = 7$

Properties of the Real Numbers   Examples

For any real numbers a, b, and c:

Commutative property of
   addition $a + b = b + a$ $3 + 7 = 7 + 3$
   multiplication $ab = ba$ $4 \cdot 3 = 3 \cdot 4$

Associative property of
   addition $(a + b) + c = a + (b + c)$ $(1 + 3) + 5 = 1 + (3 + 5)$
   multiplication $(ab)c = a(bc)$ $(3 \cdot 5)7 = 3(5 \cdot 7)$

Distributive property $a(b + c) = ab + ac$ $3(4 + x) = 12 + 3x$
                                                               $5x - 10 = 5(x - 2)$

Additive identity property $a + 0 = 0 + a = a$ $6 + 0 = 0 + 6 = 6$

Multiplicative identity property $1 \cdot a = a \cdot 1 = a$ $1 \cdot 6 = 6 \cdot 1 = 6$

Additive inverse property $a + (-a) = -a + a = 0$ $8 + (-8) = 0, -8 + 8 = 0$

Multiplicative inverse property $a \cdot \dfrac{1}{a} = \dfrac{1}{a} \cdot a = 1$ for $a \neq 0$ $8 \cdot \dfrac{1}{8} = 1, -2\left(-\dfrac{1}{2}\right) = 1$

| Multiplication property of zero | $0 \cdot a = a \cdot 0 = 0$ | $9 \cdot 0 = 0$ |
| | | $(0)(-4) = 0$ |

Algebraic Concepts

		Examples
Algebraic expressions	Any meaningful combination of numbers, variables, and operations	$x^2 + y^2, \ -5abc$
Term	An expression containing a number or the product of a number and one or more variables raised to powers	$3x^2, \ -7x^2y, \ 8$
Like terms	Terms with identical variable parts	$4bc - 8bc = -4bc$

ENRICHING YOUR MATHEMATICAL WORD POWER

For each mathematical term, choose the correct meaning.

1. **term**
   a. an expression containing a number or the product of a number and one or more variables raised to powers
   b. the amount of time spent in this course
   c. a word that describes a number
   d. a variable

2. **like terms**
   a. terms that are identical
   b. the terms of a sum
   c. terms that have the same variables with the same exponents
   d. terms with the same variables

3. **variable**
   a. a letter that is used to represent some numbers
   b. the letter x
   c. an equation with a letter in it
   d. not the same

4. **additive inverse**
   a. the number -1
   b. the number 0
   c. the opposite of addition
   d. opposite

5. **order of operations**
   a. the order in which operations are to be performed in the absence of grouping symbols
   b. the order in which the operations were invented
   c. the order in which operations are written
   d. a list of operations in alphabetical order

6. **absolute value**
   a. a definite value
   b. a positive number
   c. the distance from 0 on the number line
   d. the opposite of a number

7. **natural numbers**
   a. the counting numbers
   b. numbers that are not irrational
   c. the nonnegative numbers
   d. numbers that we find in nature

8. **rational numbers**
   a. the numbers 1, 2, 3, and so on
   b. the integers
   c. numbers that make sense
   d. numbers of the form $\frac{a}{b}$ where a and b are integers with $b \neq 0$

9. **irrational numbers**
   a. cube roots
   b. numbers that cannot be expressed as a ratio of integers
   c. numbers that do not make sense
   d. integers

10. **additive identity**
    a. the number 0
    b. the number 1
    c. the opposite of a number
    d. when two sums are identical

11. **multiplicative identity**
    a. the number 0
    b. the number 1
    c. the reciprocal
    d. when two products are identical

12. **dividend**
    a. a in $\frac{a}{b}$ b. b in $\frac{a}{b}$
    c. the result of $\frac{a}{b}$ d. what a bank pays on deposits

13. divisor

    a: a in $\dfrac{a}{b}$ b: b in $\dfrac{a}{b}$

    c: the result of $\dfrac{a}{b}$ d: two visors

14. quotient

    a: a in $\dfrac{a}{b}$ b: b in $\dfrac{a}{b}$

    c: $\dfrac{a}{b}$ d: the divisor plus the remainder

REVIEW EXERCISES

1.1 *Let $A = \{1, 2, 3\}$, $B = \{3, 4, 5\}$, $C = \{1, 2, 3, 4, 5\}$, $D = \{3\}$, and $E = \{4, 5\}$. Determine whether each statement is true or false.*

1. $A \cap B = D$

2. $A \cap B = E$

3. $A \cup B = E$

4. $A \cup B = C$

5. $B \cup C = C$

6. $A \cap C = B$

7. $A \cap \varnothing = A$

8. $A \cup \varnothing = \varnothing$

9. $(A \cap B) \cup E = B$

10. $(C \cap B) \cap A = D$

11. $B \subseteq C$

12. $A \subseteq E$

13. $A = B$

14. $B = C$

15. $3 \in D$

16. $5 \notin A$

17. $0 \in E$

18. $D \subseteq \varnothing$

19. $\varnothing \subseteq E$

20. $1 \in A$

Study Tip

Note how the review exercises are arranged according to the sections in this chapter. If you are having trouble with a certain type of problem, refer back to the appropriate section for examples and explanations.

1.2 *Which elements of the set*

$$\left\{-\sqrt{2}, -1, 0, 1, 1.732, \sqrt{3}, \pi, \frac{22}{7}, 31\right\}$$

are members of these sets?

21. Whole numbers

22. Natural numbers

23. Integers

24. Rational numbers

25. Irrational numbers

26. Real numbers

Write each interval of real numbers in interval notation and graph it.

27. The set of real numbers greater than 0

28. The set of real numbers less than 4

29. The set of real numbers between 5 and 6

30. The set of real numbers between 5 and 6 inclusive

31. The set of real numbers greater than or equal to -1 and less than 2

32. The set of real numbers greater than 3 and less than or equal to 6

Write each union or intersection as a single interval.

33. $(0, 2) \cup (1, 5)$

34. $(0, 2) \cap (1, 5)$

35. $(2, 4) \cap (3, \infty)$

36. $(-\infty, 3) \cup (1, 6)$

37. $[2, 6) \cup (4, 8)$

38. $[-2, 1] \cap [0, 5)$

1.3 *Evaluate.*

39. $-4 + 9$

40. $-3 + (-5)$

41. $25 - 37$

42. $-6 - 10$

43. $(-4)(6)$

44. $(-7)(-6)$

45. $(-8) \div (-4)$

160. *Lots of water.* The volume of water in a round swimming pool with radius r feet and depth h feet is $7.5\pi r^2 h$ gallons. Find the volume of water in a pool that has diameter 24 feet and depth 3 feet.

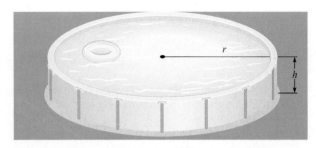

FIGURE FOR EXERCISE 160

CHAPTER 1 TEST

Let $A = \{2, 4, 6, 8, 10\}$, $B = \{3, 4, 5, 6, 7\}$, and $C = \{6, 7, 8, 9, 10\}$. List the elements in each of these sets.

1. $A \cup B$

2. $B \cap C$

3. $A \cap (B \cup C)$

Study Tip

Before you take an in-class exam on this chapter, work the sample test given here. Set aside one hour to work this test and use the answers in the back of this book to grade yourself. Even though your instructor might not ask exactly the same questions, you will get a good idea of your test readiness.

Which elements of $\left\{-4, -\sqrt{3}, -\dfrac{1}{2}, 0, 1.65, \sqrt{5}, \pi, 8\right\}$ are members of these sets?

4. Whole numbers

5. Integers

6. Rational numbers

7. Irrational numbers

Graph each of these sets.

8. The integers between -3 and 5

9. The interval $(-3, 5]$

Write each union or intersection as a single interval.

10. $(-\infty, 2) \cup (1, 4)$

11. $(2, 8) \cap [4, 9)$

Evaluate each expression.

12. $6 + 3(-5)$

13. $\sqrt{(-2)^2 - 4(3)(-5)}$

14. $-5 + 6 - 12$

15. $0.02 - 2$

16. $\dfrac{-3 - (-7)}{3 - 5}$

17. $\dfrac{-6 - 2}{4 - 2}$

18. $\left(\dfrac{2}{3} - 1\right)\left(\dfrac{1}{3} - \dfrac{1}{2}\right)$

19. $-\dfrac{4}{7} - \dfrac{1}{2}\left(24 - \dfrac{8}{7}\right)$

20. $|3 - 5(2)|$

21. $5 - 2|6 - 10|$

22. $(452 + 695)[2(-4) + 8]$

23. $478(8) + 478(2)$

24. $-8 \cdot 3 - 4(6 - 9 \cdot 2^3)$

Evaluate each expression for $a = -3$, $b = -4$, and $c = 2$.

25. $b^2 - 4ac$

26. $\dfrac{a^2 - b^2}{b - a}$

27. $\dfrac{ab - 6c}{b^2 - c^2}$

Identify the property that justifies each equation.

28. $2(5 + 7) = 10 + 14$

29. $57 \cdot 4 = 4 \cdot 57$

30. $2 + (6 + x) = (2 + 6) + x$

31. $-6 + 6 = 0$

32. $1 \cdot (-6) = (-6) \cdot 1$

Simplify each expression.

33. $3(m - 5) - 4(-2m - 3)$

34. $x + 3 - 0.05(x + 2)$

35. $\dfrac{1}{2}(x - 4) + \dfrac{1}{4}(x + 3)$

36. $-3(x^2 - 2y) - 2(3y - 4x^2)$

37. $\dfrac{-6x^2 - 4x + 2}{-2}$

Use the distributive property to rewrite each expression as a product.

38. $5x - 40$

39. $7t - 7$

Solve each problem.

40. If Celeste and her crew of loggers can cut and load one tree in 0.0625 hour, then how many trees per hour can they cut and load?

41. The rectangular table for table tennis is x feet long and $x - 4$ feet wide. Write algebraic expressions for the perimeter and the area of the table. Find the actual perimeter and area using $x = 9$.

 42. If the population of the earth grows at 3% annually, then in n years the present population P will grow to $P(1.03)^n$. Assuming an annual growth rate of 3% and a present population of 6 billion people, what will the population be in 25 years?

C H A P T E R 2

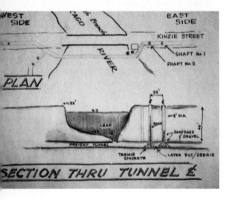

SECTION THRU TUNNEL É

Linear Equations and Inequalities in One Variable

O n April 13, 1992, the headline of *The Chicago Tribune* read, "Flood Cripples Loop Businesses." Workers driving pilings around a bridge had ruptured an abandoned freight tunnel under the Chicago River. Water was gushing into the 40 miles of open tunnels below the 12 square blocks of Chicago's downtown area called the Loop. The rapidly rising water entered basements, saturated foundations, and quickly forced the shutdown of most utilities. Some subway lines were closed, and eventually thousands of workers were evacuated. While divers were used to survey the problem, the Army Corps of Engineers was called in. Their solution was to seal off the portion of the tunnel that was ruptured, using a steel-reinforced concrete plug. Once the plug was in place, the engineers worked on reversing the flow of the water. For over a month, millions of gallons of water were drained off to a water reclamation plant, and the Loop slowly returned to normal.

In this chapter we will study algebraic equations and formulas. In Exercises 89 and 90 of Section 2.2 you will see how the engineers used very simple algebraic formulas to calculate the amount of force the water would have on the plug and how much force the concrete plug would withstand. The story of the Chicago flood is just one example of how algebraic formulas are used daily in practical situations.

2.1 LINEAR EQUATIONS IN ONE VARIABLE

The applications of algebra often lead to equations. The skills that you learned in Chapter 1, such as combining like terms and performing operations with algebraic expressions, will now be used to solve equations.

Basic Ideas and Definitions

An **equation** is a sentence that expresses the equality of two algebraic expressions. Consider the equation

$$2x + 1 = 7.$$

Because $2(3) + 1 = 7$ is true, we say that 3 **satisfies** the equation. No other number in place of x will make the statement $2x + 1 = 7$ true. However, an equation might be satisfied by more than one number. For example, both 3 and -3 satisfy $x^2 = 9$. Any number that satisfies an equation is called a **solution** or **root** to the equation.

> ### Solution Set
>
> The set of all solutions to an equation is called the **solution set** to the equation.

The solution set to $2x + 1 = 7$ is $\{3\}$. To determine whether a number is in the solution set to an equation, we simply replace the variable by the number and see whether the equation is correct.

E X A M P L E   1

Satisfying an equation

Determine whether each equation is satisfied by the number following the equation.

a) $3x + 7 = -8$, -5 　　　　　　　　**b)** $2(x - 1) = 2x + 3$, 4

Solution

a) Replace x by -5 and evaluate each side of the equation.

$$3x + 7 = -8$$
$$3(-5) + 7 = -8$$
$$-15 + 7 = -8$$
$$-8 = -8 \quad \text{Correct}$$

Because -5 satisfies the equation, -5 is in the solution set to the equation.

b) Replace x by 4 and evaluate each side of the equation.

$$2(x - 1) = 2x + 3$$
$$2(4 - 1) = 2(4) + 3 \quad \text{Replace } x \text{ by 4.}$$
$$2(3) = 8 + 3$$
$$6 = 11 \quad \text{Incorrect}$$

The two sides of the equation have different values when $x = 4$. So 4 is *not* in the solution set to the equation. ∎

Solving Equations

To **solve** an equation means to find its solution set. It is easy to determine whether a given number is in the solution set of an equation as in Example 1, but that example does not provide a method for *solving* equations. The most basic method for solving equations involves the **properties of equality.**

Properties of Equality

Addition Property of Equality
Adding the same number to both sides of an equation does not change the solution set to the equation. In symbols, if $a = b$, then $a + c = b + c$.

Multiplication Property of Equality
Multiplying both sides of an equation by the same nonzero number does not change the solution set to the equation. In symbols, if $a = b$ and $c \neq 0$, then $ca = cb$.

Because subtraction is defined in terms of addition, the addition property of equality also allows us to subtract the same number from both sides. For example, subtracting 3 from both sides is equivalent to adding -3 to both sides. Because division is defined in terms of multiplication, the multiplication property of equality also allows us to divide both sides by the same nonzero number. For example, dividing both sides by 2 is equivalent to multiplying both sides by $\frac{1}{2}$.

Equations that have the same solution set are called **equivalent equations.** In Example 2 we use the properties of equality to solve an equation by writing an equivalent equation with x isolated on one side of the equation.

E X A M P L E   2

Using the properties of equality
Solve the equation $6 - 3x = 8 - 2x$.

Solution
We want to obtain an equivalent equation with only a single x on the left-hand side and a number on the other side.

$$6 - 3x = 8 - 2x$$
$$6 - 3x - 6 = 8 - 2x - 6 \quad \text{Subtract 6 from each side.}$$
$$-3x = 2 - 2x \quad \text{Simplify.}$$
$$-3x + 2x = 2 - 2x + 2x \quad \text{Add } 2x \text{ to each side.}$$
$$-x = 2 \quad \text{Combine like terms.}$$
$$-1 \cdot (-x) = -1 \cdot 2 \quad \text{Multiply each side by } -1.$$
$$x = -2$$

Replacing x by -2 in the original equation gives us

$$6 - 3(-2) = 8 - 2(-2),$$

which is correct. So the solution set to the original equation is $\{-2\}$. ■

The addition property of equality allows us to add $2x$ to each side of the equation in Example 2 because $2x$ represents a real number.

CAUTION If you add an expression to each side that does not always represent a real number, then the equations might not be equivalent. For example,

$$x = 0 \qquad \text{and} \qquad x + \frac{1}{x} = 0 + \frac{1}{x}$$

are *not* equivalent because 0 satisfies the first equation but not the second one. (The expression $\frac{1}{x}$ is not defined if x is 0.)

To solve some equations, we must simplify the equation before using the properties of equality.

E X A M P L E   3

Simplifying the equation first

Solve the equation $2(x - 4) + 5x = 34$.

Solution

Before using the properties of equality, we simplify the expression on the left-hand side of the equation:

$$
\begin{aligned}
2(x - 4) + 5x &= 34 \\
2x - 8 + 5x &= 34 && \text{Distributive property} \\
7x - 8 &= 34 && \text{Combine like terms.} \\
7x - 8 + 8 &= 34 + 8 && \text{Add 8 to each side.} \\
7x &= 42 && \text{Simplify.} \\
\frac{7x}{7} &= \frac{42}{7} && \text{Divide each side by 7 to get} \\
& && \text{a single } x \text{ on the left side.} \\
x &= 6
\end{aligned}
$$

To check, we replace x by 6 in the original equation and simplify:

$$
\begin{aligned}
2(6 - 4) + 5 \cdot 6 &= 34 \\
2(2) + 30 &= 34 \\
34 &= 34
\end{aligned}
$$

The solution set to the equation is $\{6\}$.   ■

When an equation involves fractions, we can simplify it by multiplying each side by a number that is evenly divisible by all of the denominators. The smallest such number is called the **least common denominator (LCD).** Multiplying each side of the equation by the LCD will eliminate all of the fractions.

E X A M P L E   4

An equation with fractions

Find the solution set for the equation

$$\frac{x}{2} - \frac{1}{3} = \frac{x}{3} + \frac{5}{6}.$$

Solution

To solve this equation, we multiply each side by 6, the LCD for 2, 3, and 6:

$$6\left(\frac{x}{2} - \frac{1}{3}\right) = 6\left(\frac{x}{3} + \frac{5}{6}\right) \qquad \text{Multiply each side by 6.}$$

$$6 \cdot \frac{x}{2} - 6 \cdot \frac{1}{3} = 6 \cdot \frac{x}{3} + 6 \cdot \frac{5}{6} \qquad \text{Distributive property}$$

$$3x - 2 = 2x + 5 \qquad \text{Simplify.}$$

$$3x - 2 - 2x = 2x + 5 - 2x \qquad \text{Subtract } 2x \text{ from each side.}$$

$$x - 2 = 5 \qquad \text{Combine like terms.}$$

$$x - 2 + 2 = 5 + 2 \qquad \text{Add 2 to each side.}$$

$$x = 7 \qquad \text{Combine like terms.}$$

Check 7 in the original equation. The solution set is $\{7\}$. ∎

Equations that involve decimal numbers can be solved like equations involving fractions. If we multiply a decimal number by 10, 100, or 1000, the decimal point is moved one, two, or three places to the right, respectively. If the decimal points are all moved far enough to the right, the decimal numbers will be replaced by whole numbers. Example 5 shows how to use the multiplication property of equality to eliminate decimal numbers in an equation.

EXAMPLE 5

An equation with decimals

Solve the equation $x - 0.1x = 0.75x + 4.5$.

Solution

Because the number with the most decimal places in this equation is 0.75 (75 hundredths), multiplying each side by 100 will eliminate all decimals.

$$100(x - 0.1x) = 100(0.75x + 4.5) \qquad \text{Multiply each side by 100.}$$

$$100x - 10x = 75x + 450 \qquad \text{Distributive property}$$

$$90x = 75x + 450 \qquad \text{Combine like terms.}$$

$$90x - 75x = 75x + 450 - 75x \qquad \text{Subtract } 75x \text{ from each side.}$$

$$15x = 450 \qquad \text{Combine like terms.}$$

$$\frac{15x}{15} = \frac{450}{15} \qquad \text{Divide each side by 15.}$$

$$x = 30$$

Check that 30 satisfies the original equation. The solution set is $\{30\}$. ∎

Types of Equations

We often think of an equation such as $3x + 4x = 7x$ as an "addition fact" because the equation is satisfied by all real numbers. However, some equations that we think of as facts are not satisfied by all real numbers. For example, $\frac{x}{x} = 1$ is satisfied by every real number except 0 because $\frac{0}{0}$ is undefined. The equation $x + 1 = x + 1$ is satisfied by all real numbers because both sides are identical. All of these equations are called *identities*.

The equation $2x + 1 = 7$ is true only on condition that we choose $x = 3$. For this reason, it is called a *conditional equation*. The equations in Examples 2 through 5 are conditional equations.

Some equations are false no matter what value is used to replace the variable. For example, no number satisfies $x = x + 1$. The solution set to this *inconsistent* equation is the empty set, $\varnothing$.

Identity, Conditional Equation, Inconsistent Equation

An **identity** is an equation that is satisfied by every number for which both sides are defined.

A **conditional equation** is an equation that is satisfied by at least one number but is not an identity.

An **inconsistent equation** is an equation whose solution set is the empty set.

It is easy to classify $2x = 2x$ as an identity and $x = x + 2$ as an inconsistent equation, but some equations must be simplified before they can be classified.

E X A M P L E   6

An inconsistent equation and an identity

Solve each equation.

a) $8 - 3(x - 5) + 7 = 3 - (x - 5) - 2(x - 11)$

b) $5 - 3(x - 6) = 4(x - 9) - 7x$

Helpful Hint

Removing parentheses with the distributive property and combining like terms was discussed in Chapter 1. If you are having trouble with these equations, your problem might be in the preceding chapter.

Solution

a) First simplify each side of the equation:

$$8 - 3(x - 5) + 7 = 3 - (x - 5) - 2(x - 11)$$
$$8 - 3x + 15 + 7 = 3 - x + 5 - 2x + 22 \qquad \text{Distributive property}$$
$$30 - 3x = 30 - 3x \qquad\qquad \text{Combine like terms.}$$

This last equation is satisfied by any value of x because the two sides are identical. Because the last equation is equivalent to the original equation, the original equation is satisfied by any value of x and is an identity. The solution set is R, the set of all real numbers.

b) First simplify each side of the equation.

$$5 - 3(x - 6) = 4(x - 9) - 7x$$
$$5 - 3x + 18 = 4x - 36 - 7x \qquad \text{Distributive property}$$
$$23 - 3x = -36 - 3x \qquad\qquad \text{Combine like terms.}$$
$$23 - 3x + 3x = -36 - 3x + 3x \qquad \text{Add } 3x \text{ to each side.}$$
$$23 = -36 \qquad\qquad\qquad \text{Combine like terms.}$$

The equation $23 = -36$ is false for any choice of x. Because these equations are all equivalent, the original equation is also false for any choice of x. The solution set to this inconsistent equation is the empty set, $\varnothing$. ∎

Strategy for Solving Linear Equations

The most basic equations of algebra are linear equations. In Chapter 3 we will see a connection between linear equations in one variable and straight lines.

Linear Equation in One Variable

A **linear equation in one variable** x is an equation of the form $ax + b = 0$, where a and b are real numbers, with $a \neq 0$.

The equations in Examples 2 through 5 are called linear equations in one variable, or simply linear equations, because they could all be rewritten in the form $ax + b = 0$. At first glance the equations in Example 6 appear to be linear equations. However, they cannot be written in the form $ax + b = 0$, with $a \neq 0$, so they are not linear equations. A linear equation has exactly one solution. The strategy that we use for solving linear equations is summarized in the following box.

Strategy for Solving a Linear Equation

1. If fractions are present, multiply each side by the LCD to eliminate them.
2. Use the distributive property to remove parentheses.
3. Combine any like terms.
4. Use the addition property of equality to get all variables on one side and numbers on the other side.
5. Use the multiplication property of equality to get a single variable on one side.
6. Check by replacing the variable in the original equation with your solution.

Note that not all equations require all of the steps.

E X A M P L E   7

Using the equation-solving strategy

Solve the equation $\frac{y}{2} - \frac{y-4}{5} = \frac{23}{10}$.

Solution

We first multiply each side of the equation by 10, the LCD for 2, 5, and 10. However, we do not have to write down that step. We can simply use the distributive property to multiply each term of the equation by 10.

$$\frac{y}{2} - \frac{y-4}{5} = \frac{23}{10}$$

$$\overset{5}{\cancel{10}} \left(\frac{y}{2}\right) - \overset{2}{\cancel{10}} \left(\frac{y-4}{5}\right) = \cancel{10} \left(\frac{23}{10}\right) \qquad \text{Multiply each side by 10.}$$

$$5y - 2(y-4) = 23 \qquad \text{Divide each denominator into 10 to eliminate fractions.}$$

$$5y - 2y + 8 = 23 \qquad \text{Be careful to change all signs:} \; -2(y-4) = -2y + 8$$

$$3y + 8 = 23 \qquad \text{Combine like terms.}$$

$$3y + 8 - 8 = 23 - 8 \qquad \text{Subtract 8 from each side.}$$

$$3y = 15 \qquad \text{Simplify.}$$

$$\frac{3y}{3} = \frac{15}{3} \qquad \text{Divide each side by 3.}$$

$$y = 5$$

Check that 5 satisfies the original equation. The solution set is $\{5\}$. ∎

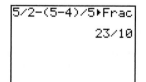

Techniques

Writing down every step when solving an equation is not always necessary. Solving an equation is often part of a larger problem, and anything that we can do to make the process more efficient will make solving the entire problem faster and easier. For example, we can combine some steps.

<table>
<tr><td align="center">***Combining Steps***</td><td align="center">***Writing Every Step***</td></tr>
</table>

Combining Steps		Writing Every Step
$4x - 5 = 23$		$4x - 5 = 23$
$4x = 28$ — Add 5 to each side.		$4x - 5 + 5 = 23 + 5$
$x = 7$ — Divide each side by 4.		$4x = 28$
		$\dfrac{4x}{4} = \dfrac{28}{4}$
		$x = 7$

The same steps are used in each of the solutions. However, when 5 is added to each side in the solution on the left, only the result is written. When each side is divided by 4, only the result is written.

The equation $-x = -5$ says that the additive inverse of x is -5. Since the additive inverse of 5 is -5, we conclude that x is 5. So instead of multiplying each side of $-x = -5$ by -1, we solve the equation as follows:

$$-x = -5$$
$$x = 5 \quad \text{Additive inverse property}$$

Sometimes it is simpler to isolate x on the right-hand side of the equation:

$$3x + 1 = 4x - 5$$
$$6 = x \qquad \text{Subtract } 3x \text{ from each side and add 5 to each side.}$$

You can rewrite $6 = x$ as $x = 6$ or leave it as is. Either way, 6 is the solution.

For some equations with fractions it is more efficient to multiply by a multiplicative inverse instead of multiplying by the LCD:

$$-\frac{2}{3}x = \frac{1}{2}$$
$$-\frac{3}{2}\left(-\frac{2}{3}x\right) = -\frac{3}{2}\left(\frac{1}{2}\right) \qquad \text{Multiply each side by } -\frac{3}{2}\text{, the reciprocal of } -\frac{2}{3}.$$
$$x = -\frac{3}{4}$$

The techniques shown here should not be attempted until you have become proficient at solving equations by writing out every step. The more efficient techniques shown here are not a requirement of algebra, but they can be a labor-saving tool that will be useful when we solve more complicated problems.

E X A M P L E 8   Efficient solutions

Solve each equation.

a) $3x + 4 = 0$

b) $2 - (x + 5) = -2(3x - 1) + 6x$

Solution

a) Combine steps to solve the equation efficiently.

$$3x + 4 = 0$$

$$3x = -4 \qquad \text{Subtract 4 from each side.}$$

$$x = -\frac{4}{3} \qquad \text{Divide each side by 3.}$$

Check $-\frac{4}{3}$ in the original equation:

$$3\left(-\frac{4}{3}\right) + 4 = -4 + 4 = 0$$

The solution set is $\left\{-\frac{4}{3}\right\}$.

b) $2 - (x + 5) = -2(3x - 1) + 6x$

$$-x - 3 = 2 \qquad \text{Simplify each side.}$$

$$-x = 5 \qquad \text{Add 3 to each side.}$$

$$x = -5 \qquad \text{Additive inverse property}$$

Check that -5 satisfies the original equation. The solution set is $\{-5\}$.   ■

Applications

In Example 9 we show how a linear equation can occur in an application.

E X A M P L E   9   **Completing high school**

The percentage of persons 25 years and over who had completed 4 years of high school was only 25% in 1940 (Census Bureau, www.census.gov). See Fig. 2.1. The expression $0.96n + 25$ gives the percentage of persons 25 and over who have completed 4 years of high school in the year $1940 + n$.

a) What was the percentage in 1990?

b) When will the percentage reach 95%?

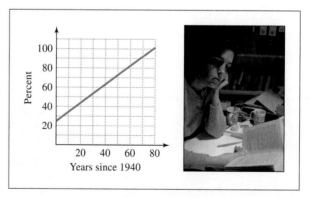

F I G U R E   2 . 1

Solution

a) Since 1990 is 50 years after 1940, $n = 50$ and

$$0.96(50) + 25 = 73.$$

So in 1990 approximately 73% of persons 25 and over had completed 4 years of high school.

b) To find when the percentage will reach 95%, solve this equation:

$$0.96n + 25 = 95$$
$$0.96n = 70$$
$$n = \frac{70}{0.96} \approx 73$$

So 73 years after 1940 or in 2013 the percentage will reach 95%. ■

WARM-UPS

True or false? Explain your answer.

1. The equation $-2x + 3 = 8$ is equivalent to $-2x = 11$.
2. The equation $x - (x - 3) = 5x$ is equivalent to $3 = 5x$.
3. To solve $\frac{3}{4}x = 12$, we should multiply each side by $\frac{3}{4}$.
4. The equation $-x = -6$ is equivalent to $x = 6$.
5. To eliminate fractions, we multiply each side of an equation by the LCD.

6. The solution set to $3x + 5 = 7$ is $\left\{\frac{2}{3}\right\}$.
7. The equation $2(3x + 4) = 6x + 12$ is an inconsistent equation.
8. The equation $4(x + 3) = x + 3$ is a conditional equation.
9. The equation $x - 0.2x = 0.8x$ is an identity.
10. The equation $3x - 5 = 7$ is a linear equation.

2.1 EXERCISES

Reading and Writing   *After reading this section, write out the answers to these questions. Use complete sentences.*

1. What is an equation?

2. How do you know if a number satisfies an equation?

3. What are equivalent equations?

4. What is a linear equation in one variable?

5. What is the usual first step in solving an equation that involves fractions?

6. What is an identity?

7. What is a conditional equation?

8. What is an inconsistent equation?

Determine whether each equation is satisfied by the given number. See Example 1.

9. $3x + 7 = -5$, -4
10. $-3x - 5 = 13$, -6
11. $\frac{1}{2}x - 4 = \frac{1}{3}x - 2$, 12
12. $\frac{y - 7}{2} - \frac{1}{3} = \frac{y - 7}{3}$, 9

13. $0.2(x - 50) = 20 - 0.05x$,   200
14. $0.12x - (4 - x) = 1.02x + 1$,   50
15. $0.1x - 30 = 16 - 0.06x$,   80
16. $0.08x + 3.2 = 0.1x + 2.8$,   20

Solve each linear equation. Show your work and check your answer. See Examples 2 and 3.

17. $-72 - x = 15$ **18.** $51 - x = -9$

19. $-3x - 19 = 5 - 2x$ **20.** $-5x + 4 = -9 - 4x$

21. $2x - 3 = 0$ **22.** $5x + 7 = 0$

23. $-2x + 5 = 7$ **24.** $-3x - 4 = 11$

25. $-12x - 15 = 21$ **26.** $-13x + 7 = -19$

27. $26 = 4x + 16$ **28.** $14 = -5x - 21$

29. $-3(x - 16) = 12 - x$ **30.** $-2(x + 17) = 13 - x$

31. $2(x + 9) - x = 36$ **32.** $3(x - 13) - x = 9$

33. $2 + 3(x - 1) = x - 1$ **34.** $x + 9 = 1 - 4(x - 2)$

Solve each equation. See Example 4.

35. $-\dfrac{3}{7}x = 4$ **36.** $\dfrac{5}{6}x = -2$

37. $-\dfrac{5}{7}x - 1 = 3$ **38.** $4 - \dfrac{3}{5}x = -6$

39. $\dfrac{x}{3} + \dfrac{1}{2} = \dfrac{7}{6}$ **40.** $\dfrac{1}{4} + \dfrac{1}{5} = \dfrac{x}{2}$

41. $\dfrac{2}{3}x + 5 = -\dfrac{1}{3}x + 17$ **42.** $\dfrac{1}{4}x - 6 = -\dfrac{3}{4}x + 14$

43. $\dfrac{1}{2}x + \dfrac{1}{4} = \dfrac{1}{4}(x - 6)$ **44.** $\dfrac{1}{3}(x - 2) = \dfrac{2}{3}x - \dfrac{13}{3}$

45. $8 - \dfrac{x - 2}{2} = \dfrac{x}{4}$ **46.** $\dfrac{x}{3} - \dfrac{x - 5}{5} = 3$

47. $\dfrac{y - 3}{3} - \dfrac{y - 2}{2} = -1$ **48.** $\dfrac{x - 2}{2} - \dfrac{x - 3}{4} = \dfrac{7}{4}$

Solve each equation. See Example 5.

49. $x - 0.2x = 72$
50. $x - 0.1x = 63$
51. $0.03(x + 200) + 0.05x = 86$
52. $0.02(x - 100) + 0.06x = 62$
53. $0.1x + 0.05(x - 300) = 105$
54. $0.2x - 0.05(x - 100) = 35$

Solve each equation. Identify each as a conditional equation, an inconsistent equation, or an identity. See Example 6.

55. $2(x + 1) = 2(x + 3)$
56. $2x + 3x = 6x$
57. $x + x = 2x$
58. $4x - 3x = x$
59. $x + x = 2$
60. $4x - 3x = 5$
61. $\dfrac{4x}{4} = x$
62. $5x \div 5 = x$
63. $x \cdot x = x^2$
64. $\dfrac{2x}{2x} = 1$
65. $2(x + 3) - 7 = 5(5 - x) + 7(x + 1)$

66. $2(x + 4) - 8 = 2x + 1$
67. $2\left(\dfrac{1}{2}x + \dfrac{3}{2}\right) - \dfrac{7}{2} = \dfrac{3}{2}(x + 1) - \left(\dfrac{1}{2}x + 2\right)$
68. $2\left(\dfrac{1}{4}x + 1\right) - 2 = \dfrac{1}{2}x$
69. $2(0.5x + 1.5) - 3.5 = 3(0.5x + 0.5)$

70. $2(0.25x + 1) - 2 = 0.75x - 1.75$

Solve each equation. See Example 7.
71. $4 - 6(2x - 3) + 1 = 3 + 2(5 - x)$

72. $3x - 5(6 - 2x) = 4(x - 8) + 3$

73. $\dfrac{1}{2}\left(y - \dfrac{1}{6}\right) + \dfrac{2}{3} = \dfrac{5}{6} + \dfrac{1}{3}\left(\dfrac{1}{2} - 3y\right)$

74. $\dfrac{3}{4} - \dfrac{1}{3}\left(\dfrac{1}{2}y - 2\right) = 3\left(y - \dfrac{1}{4}\right)$

75. $8 - \dfrac{2}{3}(60x - 900) = \dfrac{1}{2}(400x + 6)$

76. $\dfrac{40x - 5}{2} + \dfrac{5}{2} = \dfrac{33 - 2x}{3} - 11$

77. $\dfrac{a - 3}{4} - \dfrac{2a - 5}{2} = \dfrac{a + 1}{3} - \dfrac{1}{6}$

78. $\dfrac{1}{2}\left(\dfrac{b}{3} - \dfrac{4b}{5}\right) + \dfrac{1}{6} = \dfrac{1}{3} - \dfrac{b - 1}{2}$

79. $1.3 - 0.2(6 - 3x) = 0.1(0.2x + 3)$

80. $0.01(500 - 30x) = 5.4x + 200$

Solve each equation. Practice combining some steps. Look for more efficient ways to solve each equation. See Example 8.

81. $3x - 9 = 0$

82. $5x + 1 = 0$

83. $7 - z = -9$

84. $-3 - z = 3$

85. $\dfrac{2}{3}x = \dfrac{1}{2}$

86. $\dfrac{3}{2}x = -\dfrac{9}{5}$

87. $-\dfrac{3}{5}y = 9$

88. $-\dfrac{2}{7}w = 4$

89. $3y + 5 = 4y - 1$

90. $2y - 7 = 3y + 1$

91. $5x + 10(x + 2) = 110$

92. $1 - 3(x - 2) = 4(x - 1) - 3$

Solve each equation.

93. $\dfrac{P + 7}{3} - \dfrac{P - 2}{5} = \dfrac{7}{3} - \dfrac{P}{15}$

94. $\dfrac{w - 3}{8} - \dfrac{5 - w}{4} = \dfrac{4w - 1}{8} - 1$

 95. $x - 0.06x = 50,000$

96. $x - 0.05x = 800$

97. $2.365x + 3.694 = 14.8095$

98. $-3.48x + 6.981 = 4.329x - 6.851$

Solve each problem. See Example 9.

99. *Public school enrollment.* The expression

$$0.45x + 39.05$$

can be used to approximate in millions the total enrollment in public elementary and secondary schools in the

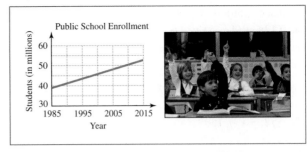

FIGURE FOR EXERCISE 99

year $1985 + x$ (National Center for Education Statistics, www.nces.ed.gov).

a) What was the public school enrollment in 1992?

b) In which year will enrollment reach 50 million students?

c) Judging from the accompanying graph, is enrollment increasing or decreasing?

100. *Teacher's average salary.* The expression

$$553.7x + 27,966$$

can be used to approximate the average annual salary in dollars of public school teachers in the year $1985 + x$ (National Center for Education Statistics, www.nces.ed.gov).

a) What was the average teacher's salary in 1993?

b) In which year will the average salary reach $45,000?

GETTING MORE INVOLVED

101. *Writing.* Explain how to eliminate the decimals in an equation that involves numbers with decimal points. Would you use the same technique when using a calculator?

102. *Discussion.* Explain why the multiplication property of equality does not allow us to multiply each side of an equation by zero.

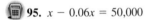
In This Section

- Solving for a Variable
- Finding the Value of a Variable
- Geometric Formulas

2.2   FORMULAS

A real-life problem may involve many variable quantities that are related to each other. The relationship between these variables may be expressed by a formula. In this section we will combine our knowledge of evaluating expressions from Chapter 1 with the equation-solving skills of Section 2.1 to work with formulas.

Solving for a Variable

A **formula** or **literal equation** is an equation involving two or more variables. For example, the formula

$$A = LW$$

expresses the known relationship among the length L, width W, and area A of a rectangle. The formula

$$C = \frac{5}{9}(F - 32)$$

expresses the relationship between the Fahrenheit and Celsius measurements of temperature. The Celsius temperature is determined by the Fahrenheit temperature. For example, if the Fahrenheit temperature F is 95°, we can use the formula to find the Celsius temperature C as follows:

$$C = \frac{5}{9}(95 - 32) = \frac{5}{9}(63) = 35$$

A temperature of 95°F is equivalent to 35°C.

Sometimes it is necessary to solve a formula for one variable in terms of the others without substituting numbers for the variables. We will use the same steps in solving for a particular variable as we did in solving linear equations.

E X A M P L E   1

Solving for a variable

Solve the formula $C = \frac{5}{9}(F - 32)$ for F.

Solution

To solve the formula for F, we isolate F on one side of the equation. We can eliminate both the 9 and the 5 from the right-hand side of the equation by multiplying by $\frac{9}{5}$, the reciprocal of $\frac{5}{9}$:

$$C = \frac{5}{9}(F - 32)$$

$$\frac{9}{5}C = \frac{9}{5} \cdot \frac{5}{9}(F - 32) \quad \text{Multiply each side by } \frac{9}{5}.$$

$$\frac{9}{5}C = F - 32 \qquad \frac{9}{5} \cdot \frac{5}{9} = 1$$

$$\frac{9}{5}C + 32 = F \qquad \text{Add 32 to each side.}$$

So the formula $F = \frac{9}{5}C + 32$ expresses F in terms of C. With this formula, we can use the value of C to determine the corresponding value of F. ■

Note that both $F = \frac{9}{5}C + 32$ and $C = \frac{5}{9}(F - 32)$ express the relationship between C and F. The formula $F = \frac{9}{5}C + 32$ gives F in terms of C and $C = \frac{5}{9}(F - 32)$ gives C in terms of F. If we substitute 35 for C in $F = \frac{9}{5}C + 32$, we get

$$F = \frac{9}{5}(35) + 32 = 63 + 32 = 95.$$

In Chapter 3 we will study linear equations involving x and y. We often need to solve such equations for one of the variables.

E X A M P L E   2

Equations involving x and y

Write y in terms of x, if $3x - 2y = 6$.

Helpful Hint

There may be more than one correct answer when solving for a variable. For example,

$$y = \frac{3x - 6}{2}$$

also expresses y in terms of x. The main thing is to isolate y.

Solution

We can isolate y on the left-hand side:

$$3x - 2y = 6$$

$$-2y = -3x + 6 \qquad \text{Subtract } 3x \text{ from each side.}$$

$$\frac{-2y}{-2} = \frac{-3x + 6}{-2} \qquad \text{Divide each side by } -2.$$

$$y = \frac{3}{2}x - 3 \qquad \text{This equation expresses } y \text{ in terms of } x. \qquad \blacksquare$$

The formula $A = P + Prt$ is used to find the amount A after t years for an investment of P dollars at simple interest rate r. Note that the variable P occurs twice in the formula. To solve the formula for P, we use the distributive property as shown in the next example.

EXAMPLE 3

Helpful Hint

The key step in Example 3 is the distributive property. We cannot make P occur only once without it.

Specified variable occurring twice

Solve $A = P + Prt$ for P.

Solution

We can use the distributive property to write the sum $P + Prt$ as a product of P and $1 + rt$:

$$A = P + Prt$$

$$A = P(1 + rt) \qquad \text{Distributive property}$$

$$\frac{A}{1 + rt} = \frac{P(1 + rt)}{1 + rt} \qquad \text{Divide each side by } 1 + rt.$$

$$\frac{A}{1 + rt} = P$$

The formula $P = \dfrac{A}{1 + rt}$ expresses P in terms of A, r, and t. Note that parentheses are not needed around the expression $1 + rt$ in the denominator because the fraction bar acts as a grouping symbol. $\blacksquare$

CAUTION If you write $A = P + Prt$ as $P = A - Prt$, then you have not solved the formula for P. When a formula is solved for a specified variable, that variable must be isolated on one side, and it must not occur on the other side.

When the variable for which we are solving occurs on opposite sides of the equation, we must move all terms involving that variable to the same side and then use the distributive property to write the expression as a product.

EXAMPLE 4

Specified variable occurring on both sides

Suppose $3a + 7 = -5ab + b$. Solve for a.

Solution

Get all terms involving a onto one side and all other terms onto the other side:

$$3a + 7 = -5ab + b$$

$$3a + 5ab + 7 = b \qquad \text{Add } 5ab \text{ to each side.}$$

$$3a + 5ab = b - 7 \qquad \text{Subtract } 7 \text{ from each side.}$$

$$a(3 + 5b) = b - 7 \qquad \text{Use the distributive property to write the left-hand side as a product.}$$

If you do the steps in Example 4 in a different way, you might end up with

$$a = \frac{7 - b}{-3 - 5b}.$$

This answer is correct because a is isolated. However, we usually prefer to see fewer negative signs. So we multiply this numerator and denominator by -1 and get the answer in Example 4.

$$\frac{a(3 + 5b)}{3 + 5b} = \frac{b - 7}{3 + 5b} \qquad \text{Divide each side by } 3 + 5b.$$

$$a = \frac{b - 7}{3 + 5b} \qquad \blacksquare$$

When solving an equation in one variable that contains many decimal numbers, we usually use a calculator for the arithmetic. However, if you use a calculator at every step and round off the result of every computation, the final answer can differ greatly from the correct answer. Example 5 shows how to avoid this problem. The numbers are treated as if they were variables and no arithmetic is performed until all of the numbers are on one side of the equation. This technique is similar to solving an equation for a specified variable.

E X A M P L E 5

Calculator Close-Up

A graphing calculator allows you to enter the entire expression in Example 5 and to evaluate it in one step. The ANS key holds the last value calculated. If we use ANS for x in the original equation, the calculator returns a 1, indicating that the equation is satisfied.

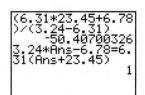

```
(6.31*23.45+6.78
)/(3.24-6.31)
       -50.40700326
3.24*Ans-6.78=6.
31(Ans+23.45)
                  1
```

Doing computations last

Solve $3.24x - 6.78 = 6.31(x + 23.45)$.

Solution

Use the distributive property on the right-hand side, but simply write $(6.31)(23.45)$ rather than the result obtained on a calculator.

$$3.24x - 6.78 = 6.31x + (6.31)(23.45) \qquad \text{Distributive property}$$

$$3.24x - 6.31x = (6.31)(23.45) + 6.78 \qquad \text{Get all } x\text{-terms on the left.}$$

$$(3.24 - 6.31)x = (6.31)(23.45) + 6.78 \qquad \text{Distributive property}$$

$$x = \frac{(6.31)(23.45) + 6.78}{3.24 - 6.31} \qquad \text{Divide each side by } (3.24 - 6.31).$$

$$\approx -50.407 \qquad \text{Round to three decimal places.}$$

Check -50.407 in the original equation. When you check an approximate answer, you will get approximately the same value for each side of the equation. The solution set is $\{-50.407\}$. $\blacksquare$

Finding the Value of a Variable

In many situations we know the values of all of the variables in a formula except one. We can use the formula to determine the unknown value. A list of common formulas and their meanings is given at the back of the text. This list may be helpful for doing the exercises at the end of this section.

E X A M P L E 6

Helpful Hint

It doesn't matter what form to use when solving for y here. If you use

$$y = \frac{2x + 9}{3}$$

and let $x = -3$, you get $y = 1$.

Finding the value of a variable

Use the formula $-2x + 3y = 9$ to find y given that $x = -3$.

Solution

To find y, we first write y in terms of x:

$$-2x + 3y = 9 \qquad \text{Original equation}$$

$$3y = 2x + 9 \qquad \text{Add } 2x \text{ to each side.}$$

$$y = \frac{2}{3}x + 3 \qquad \text{Divide each side by 3.}$$

Now replace x by -3:

$$y = \frac{2}{3}(-3) + 3$$

$$y = 1 \qquad \blacksquare$$

E X A M P L E   7

Finding the interest rate

The simple interest on a loan is $50, the principal is $500, and the time is 2 years. What is the simple interest rate?

Solution

The formula $I = Prt$ expresses the interest I in terms of the principal P, rate r, and time t. To find the rate, we first solve the formula for r, then insert the values of P, I, and t:

$$Prt = I$$

$$\frac{Prt}{Pt} = \frac{I}{Pt} \qquad \text{Divide each side by } Pt.$$

$$r = \frac{I}{Pt} \qquad \text{This formula expresses the rate in terms of } I, P, \text{ and } t.$$

$$r = \frac{50}{500(2)} \qquad \text{Substitute values for } I, P, \text{ and } t.$$

$$r = 0.05 = 5\% \qquad \text{A rate is usually written as a percent.} \qquad \blacksquare$$

In Example 7 we solved the formula for r and then inserted the values of the other variables. If we had to find the interest rate for many different loans, this method would be the most direct. But we could also have inserted the values of I, P, and t into the original formula and then solved for r. Examples 8 and 9 illustrate this second approach.

Geometric Formulas

Appendix A contains some geometric formulas that will be useful in problems that involve geometric shapes. In geometry it is common to use variables with subscripts. A subscript is a slightly lowered number following the variable. For example, the areas of two triangles might be referred to as A_1 and A_2. (We read A_1 as "A sub one" or simply "A one.") You will see subscripts in the next example.

E X A M P L E   8

Area of a trapezoid

The wildlife sanctuary shown in Fig. 2.2 on the next page has a trapezoidal shape with an area of 30 square kilometers. If one base, b_1, of the trapezoid is 10 kilometers and its height is 5 kilometers, find the length of the other base, b_2.

Solution

In any geometric problem it is helpful to have a diagram, as in Fig. 2.2. Substitute the given values into the formula for the area of a trapezoid, found in Appendix A, and then solve for b_2:

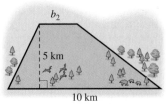

FIGURE 2.2

$$A = \frac{1}{2}h(b_1 + b_2) \qquad \text{The area depends on } h, b_1, \text{ and } b_2.$$

$$30 = \frac{1}{2} \cdot 5(10 + b_2) \qquad \text{Substitute given values into the formula for the area of a trapezoid.}$$

$$60 = 5(10 + b_2) \qquad \text{Multiply each side by 2.}$$

$$12 = 10 + b_2 \qquad \text{Divide each side by 5.}$$

$$2 = b_2 \qquad \text{Subtract 10 from each side.}$$

The length of the base b_2 is 2 kilometers. $\qquad \blacksquare$

EXAMPLE 9

Volume of a rectangular solid

Millie has just completed pouring 14 cubic yards of concrete to construct a rectangular driveway. If the concrete is 4 inches thick and the driveway is 18 feet wide, then how long is her driveway?

Solution

First draw a diagram as in Fig. 2.3. The driveway is a rectangular solid. The formula for the volume of a rectangular solid is $V = LWH$ (from Appendix A). Before we insert the values of the variables into the formula, we must convert all of them to the same unit of measurement. We will convert feet and inches to yards:

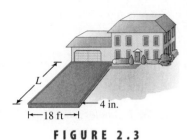

FIGURE 2.3

$$4 \text{ inches} = 4 \text{ in.} \cdot \frac{1 \text{ yd}}{36 \text{ in.}} = \frac{1}{9} \text{ yard}$$

$$18 \text{ feet} = 18 \text{ ft} \cdot \frac{1 \text{ yd}}{3 \text{ ft}} = 6 \text{ yards}$$

Now replace W, H, and V by the appropriate values:

$$V = LWH \qquad \text{The volume is determined by the length, width, and height.}$$

$$14 = L \cdot 6 \cdot \frac{1}{9}$$

$$\frac{9}{6} \cdot 14 = L \qquad \text{Multiply each side by } \frac{9}{6}.$$

$$21 = L$$

The length of the driveway is 21 yards, or 63 feet. ∎

WARM-UPS

True or false? Explain your answer.

1. The formula $A = P + Prt$ solved for P is $P = A - Prt$.
2. In solving $A = P + Prt$ for P, we do not need the distributive property.
3. Solving $I = Prt$ for t gives us $t = I - Pr$.
4. If $a = \dfrac{bh}{2}$, $b = 5$, and $h = 6$, then $a = 15$.
5. The perimeter of a rectangle is found by multiplying its length and width.
6. The volume of a rectangular box is the product of its length, width, and height.
7. The area of a trapezoid with parallel sides b_1 and b_2 is $\frac{1}{2}(b_1 + b_2)$.
8. If $x - y = 5$, then $y = x - 5$ expresses y in terms of x.
9. If $x = -3$ and $y = -2x - 4$, then $y = 2$.
10. The area of a rectangle is the total distance around the outside edge.

2.2 EXERCISES

Reading and Writing *After reading this section, write out the answers to these questions. Use complete sentences.*

1. What is a formula?

2. What is a formula used for?

3. What does it mean to solve a formula for a particular variable?

4. How do you solve for a variable that occurs twice in a formula?

5. How do you find the value of a variable in a formula?

6. What formula expresses the volume of a rectangular solid in terms of its length, width, and height?

Solve each formula for the specified variable. See Example 1.

7. $I = Prt$ for t

8. $d = rt$ for r

9. $F = \dfrac{9}{5}C + 32$ for C

10. $A = \dfrac{1}{2}bh$ for h

11. $A = LW$ for W

12. $C = 2\pi r$ for r

13. $A = \dfrac{1}{2}(b_1 + b_2)$ for b_1

14. $A = \dfrac{1}{2}(b_1 + b_2)$ for b_2

15. $P = 2L + 2W$ for L

16. $P = 2L + 2W$ for W

17. $V = \pi r^2 h$ for h

18. $V = \dfrac{1}{3}\pi r^2 h$ for h

Write y in terms of x. See Example 2.

19. $2x + 3y = 9$

20. $4y + 5x = 8$

21. $x - y = 4$

22. $y - x = 6$

23. $\dfrac{1}{2}x - \dfrac{1}{3}y = 2$

24. $\dfrac{1}{3}x - \dfrac{1}{4}y = 1$

25. $y - 2 = \dfrac{1}{2}(x - 3)$

26. $y - 3 = \dfrac{1}{3}(x - 4)$

Solve for the specified variable. See Examples 3 and 4.

27. $A = P + Prt$ for t

28. $A = P + Prt$ for r

29. $ab + a = 1$ for a

30. $y - wy = m$ for y

31. $xy + 5 = y - 7$ for y

32. $xy + 5 = x + 7$ for x

33. $xy^2 + xz^2 = xw^2 - 6$ for x

34. $xz^2 + xw^2 = xy^2 + 5$ for x

35. $\dfrac{1}{R} = \dfrac{1}{R_1} + \dfrac{1}{R_2}$ for R_1

36. $\dfrac{1}{a} + \dfrac{1}{b} = \dfrac{1}{2}$ for a

 Solve each equation. Use a calculator only on the last step. Round answers to three decimal places and use your calculator to check your answer. See Example 5.

37. $3.35x - 54.6 = 44.3 - 4.58x$

38. $-4.487x - 33.41 = 55.83 - 22.49x$

39. $4.59x - 66.7 = 3.2(x - 5.67)$

40. $457(36x - 99) = 34(28x - 239)$

41. $\dfrac{x}{19} - \dfrac{3}{23} = \dfrac{4}{31} - \dfrac{3x}{7}$

42. $\dfrac{1}{8} - \dfrac{5}{7}\left(x - \dfrac{5}{22}\right) = \dfrac{4x}{9} + \dfrac{1}{12}$

Find y given that x = 3. See Example 6.

43. $2x - 3y = 5$

44. $-3x - 4y = 4$

45. $-4x + 2y = 1$

46. $x - y = 7$

47. $y = -2x + 5$ **48.** $y = -3x - 6$

49. $-x + 2y = 5$ **50.** $-x - 3y = 6$

51. $y - 1.046 = 2.63(x - 5.09)$

52. $y - 2.895 = -1.07(x - 2.89)$

Find x *in each formula given that* $y = 2$, $z = -3$, *and* $w = 4$. *See Example 6.*

53. $wxy = 5$ **54.** $wxz = 4$

55. $x + xz = 7$ **56.** $xw - x = 3$

57. $w(x - z) = y(x - 4)$

58. $z(x - y) = y(x + 5)$

59. $w = \dfrac{1}{2}xz$ **60.** $y = \dfrac{1}{2}wx$

61. $\dfrac{1}{w} + \dfrac{1}{x} = \dfrac{1}{y}$ **62.** $\dfrac{1}{w} + \dfrac{1}{y} = \dfrac{1}{x}$

Find the geometric formula in each case.

63. The area of a circle in terms of its radius

64. The circumference of a circle in terms of its diameter

65. The radius of a circle in terms of its circumference

66. The diameter of a circle in terms of its circumference

67. The width of a rectangle in terms of its length and perimeter

68. The length of a rectangle in terms of its width and area

Solve each problem. Draw a diagram for each geometric problem. See Examples 7–9.

69. *Simple interest.* If the simple interest on $1000 for 2 years is $300, then what is the rate?

70. *Finding time.* If the simple interest on $2000 at 18% is $180, then what is the time?

71. *Rectangular floor.* The area of a rectangular floor is 23 square yards. The width is 4 yards. Find the length.

72. *Rectangular garden.* The area of a rectangular garden is 55 square meters. The length is 7 meters. Find the width.

73. *Ice sculpture.* The volume of a rectangular block of ice is 36 cubic feet. The bottom is 2 feet by 2.5 feet. Find the height of the block.

74. *Cardboard box.* A shipping box has a volume of 2.5 cubic meters. The box measures 1 meter high by 1.25 meters wide. How long is the box?

75. *Fish tank.* The volume of a rectangular aquarium is 900 gallons. The bottom is 4 feet by 6 feet. Find the height of the tank. (*Hint:* There are 7.5 gallons per cubic foot.)

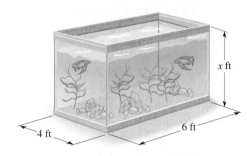

FIGURE FOR EXERCISE 75

76. *Reflecting pool.* A rectangular reflecting pool with a horizontal bottom holds 60,000 gallons of water. If the pool is 40 feet by 100 feet, how deep is the water?

77. *Area of a triangle.* The area of a triangle is 30 square feet. If the base is 4 feet, then what is the height?

78. *Larger triangle.* The area of a triangle is 40 square meters. If the height is 10 meters, then what is the length of the base?

79. *Second base.* The area of a trapezoid is 300 square inches. If the height is 20 inches and the lower base is 16 inches, then what is the length of the upper base?

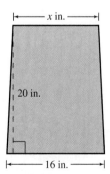

FIGURE FOR EXERCISE 79

80. *Height of a trapezoid.* The area of a trapezoid is 200 square centimeters. The bases are 16 centimeters and 24 centimeters. Find the height.

81. *Fencing.* If it takes 600 feet of fence to enclose a rectangular lot that is 132 feet wide, then how deep is the lot?

82. *Football.* The perimeter of a football field in the NFL, excluding the end zones, is $306 \frac{2}{3}$ yards. How wide is the field?

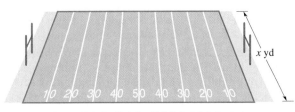

FIGURE FOR EXERCISE 82

83. *Radius of a circle.* If the circumference of a circle is 3π meters, then what is the radius?

84. *Diameter of a circle.* If the circumference of a circle is 12π inches, then what is the diameter?

85. *Radius of the earth.* If the circumference of the earth is 25,000 miles, then what is the radius?

86. *Altitude of a satellite.* If a satellite travels 26,000 miles in each circular orbit of the earth, then how high above the earth is the satellite orbiting? See Exercise 85.

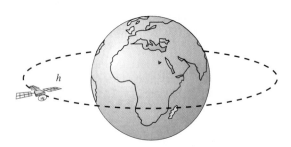

FIGURE FOR EXERCISE 86

87. *Height of a can.* If the volume of a can is 30 cubic inches and the diameter of the top is 3 inches, then what is the height of the can?

FIGURE FOR EXERCISE 87

88. *Height of a cylinder.* If the volume of a cylinder is 6.3 cubic meters and the diameter of the lid is 1.2 meters, then what is the height of the cylinder?

89. *Great Chicago flood.* The great Chicago flood of April 1992 occurred when an old freight tunnel connecting buildings in the Loop ruptured. As shown in the figure, engineers plugged the tunnel with concrete on each side of the hole. They used the formula $F = WDA$ to find the force F of the water on the plug. In this formula the weight of water W is 62 pounds per cubic foot (lb/ft^3), the average depth D of the tunnel below the surface of the river is 32 ft, and the cross-sectional area A of the tunnel is 48 ft^2. Find the force on the plug.

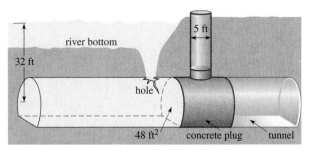

FIGURE FOR EXERCISE 89

90. *Will it hold?* To plug the tunnel described in the previous exercise, engineers drilled a 5-foot-diameter shaft down to the tunnel. The concrete plug was made so that it extended up into the shaft. For the plug to remain in place, the shear strength of the concrete in the shaft would have to be greater than the force of the water. The amount of force F that it would take for the water to shear the concrete in the shaft is given by $F = s\pi r^2$, where s is the shear strength of concrete and r is the radius of the shaft in inches. If the shear strength of concrete is 38 lb/in.^{2}, then what force of water would shear the concrete in the shaft? Use the result from Exercise 89 to determine whether the concrete would be strong enough to hold back the water.

91. *Estimating armaments.* During World War II the Allies captured some German tanks on which the smallest serial number was S and the biggest was B. Assuming the entire production of tanks was numbered 1 through N, the Allies used the formula $N = B + S - 1$ to estimate the number of tanks in the German army (*New Scientist*, May 1998).
   a) Find N if $B = 2003$ and $S = 455$.
   b) If this formula was used to estimate $N = 1452$ and the largest serial number was 1033, what was the smallest serial number?

92. *Cigarette usage.* The percentage of Americans 18 to 25 who use cigarettes has been decreasing at an approximately constant rate since 1974 (National Institute on Drug Abuse, www.nida.nih.gov). The formula

$$P = 47.9 - 0.94n$$

can be used to estimate the percentage of smokers in this age group n years after 1974.
   a) Use the formula to find the percentage of smokers in this age group in 2004.

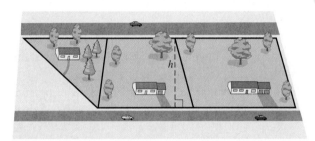

$P = 47.9 - 0.94n$

Years since 1974

FIGURE FOR EXERCISE 92

b) Use the accompanying graph to estimate the year in which smoking will be eliminated from this age group.
c) Use the formula to find the year in which smoking will be eliminated from this age group.
93. *Distance between streets.* Harold Johnson lives on a four-sided, 50,000-square-foot lot that is bounded on two sides by parallel streets. The city has assessed him

FIGURE FOR EXERCISES 93–95

$1,000 for curb repair, $2 for each foot of property bordering on these two streets. How far apart are the streets?

94. *Assessed for repairs.* Harold's sister, Maude, lives next door on a triangular lot of 25,000 square feet that also extends from street to street but has frontage only on one street. What will her assessment be? (See Exercise 93.)

95. *Juniper's lot.* Harold's other sister, Juniper, lives on the other side of him on a lot of 60,000 square feet in the shape of a parallelogram. What will her assessment be? (See Exercise 93.)

96. *Mother's driveway.* Harold's mother, who lives across the street, is pouring a concrete driveway, 12 feet wide and 4 inches thick, from the street straight to her house. This is too much work for Harold to do in one day, so his mother has agreed to buy 4 cubic yards of concrete each Saturday for three consecutive Saturdays. How far is it from the street to her house?

GETTING MORE INVOLVED

97. *Exploration.* Electric companies often point out the low cost of electricity in performing common household tasks.
  a) Find the cost of a kilowatt-hour of electricity in your area.
  b) Write a formula for finding the cost of electricity for a household appliance to perform a certain task and to explain what each variable represents.
  c) Use your formula to find the cost in your area for baking a $1\frac{1}{2}$-pound loaf of bread for 5 hours in a 750-watt Welbilt breadmaker.

In This Section

- Writing Algebraic Expressions
- Solving Problems
- General Strategy for Problem Solving
- Geometric Problems
- Investment Problems
- Mixture Problems
- Uniform Motion Problems
- Commission Problems

2.3   APPLICATIONS

We often use algebra to solve problems by translating them into algebraic equations. Sometimes we can use formulas such as those in Appendix A. More often we have to set up a new equation that represents or **models** the problem. We begin with translating verbal expressions into algebraic expressions.

Writing Algebraic Expressions

Consider the three consecutive integers 5, 6, and 7. Note that each integer is 1 larger than the previous integer. To represent three *unknown* consecutive integers, we let

$$x = \text{the first integer,}$$
$$x + 1 = \text{the second integer,}$$
and
$$x + 2 = \text{the third integer.}$$

Consider the three consecutive odd integers 7, 9, and 11. Note that each odd integer is 2 larger than the previous odd integer. To represent three *unknown*

consecutive odd integers, we let

$$x = \text{the first odd integer},$$
$$x + 2 = \text{the second odd integer},$$

and
$$x + 4 = \text{the third odd integer}.$$

Note that consecutive even integers as well as consecutive odd integers differ by 2. So the same expressions are used in either case.

How would we represent two numbers that have a sum of 8? If one of the numbers is 2, the other is certainly 6, or $8 - 2$. So if x is one of the numbers, then $8 - x$ is the other number. The expressions x and $8 - x$ have a sum of 8 for any value of x.

E X A M P L E   1

Writing algebraic expressions

Write algebraic expressions to represent each verbal expression.

a) Two numbers that differ by 12

b) Two consecutive even integers

c) Two investments that total $5000

d) The length of a rectangle if the width is x meters and the perimeter is 10 meters

Solution

a) The expressions x and $x + 12$ differ by 12. Note that we could also use x and $x - 12$ for two numbers that differ by 12.

b) The expressions x and $x + 2$ represent two consecutive even integers.

c) If x represents the amount of one investment, then $5000 - x$ represents the amount of the other investment.

d) Because the perimeter is 10 meters and $P = 2L + 2W = 2(L + W)$, the sum of the length and width is 5 meters. Because the width is x, the length is $5 - x$. ∎

M A T H   A T   W O R K

Mark Cromett, General Manager of the Charles Street Starbucks Coffee Store, arrives at work early in the morning to make sure each customer receives a perfect cup of coffee. Coffee beans from Central and South America, East Africa, and the Pacific are ground daily. Careful calibrations for the grinding are done by weighing each specific type of coffee. Even humidity frequently becomes part of the equation on how coffee is prepared. Besides the geographical area where

**COFFEE STORE
MANAGER**

the beans originate, customers have many choices for coffee. Selections are made among full city, espresso, Italian, and French roasts. Even seven decaffeinated coffees are available. But even with all of the choices, customers sometimes prefer their own special blend, requesting a mixture of different types of beans. Mr. Cromett is glad to brew or grind any special blend for a customer, and his charge depends on the different prices of the coffees mixed together. In Exercise 49 of this section you will determine the price of a specially blended coffee.

Many verbal phrases occur repeatedly in applications. This list of some frequently occurring verbal phrases and their translations into algebraic expressions will help you to translate words into algebra.

Translating Words into Algebra		
	Verbal Phrase	**Algebraic Expression**
Addition:	The sum of a number and 8	$x + 8$
	Five is added to a number	$x + 5$
	Two more than a number	$x + 2$
	A number increased by 3	$x + 3$
Subtraction:	Four is subtracted from a number	$x - 4$
	Three less than a number	$x - 3$
	The difference between 7 and a number	$7 - x$
	Some number decreased by 2	$x - 2$
	A number less 5	$x - 5$
Multiplication:	The product of 5 and a number	$5x$
	Seven times a number	$7x$
	Twice a number	$2x$
	One-half of a number	$\frac{1}{2}x \left(\text{or } \frac{x}{2}\right)$
Division:	The ratio of a number to 6	$\frac{x}{6}$
	The quotient of 5 and a number	$\frac{5}{x}$
	Three divided by some number	$\frac{3}{x}$

More than one operation can be combined in a single expression. For example, 7 less than twice a number is written as $2x - 7$.

Solving Problems

We will now see how algebraic expressions can be used to form an equation. If the equation correctly models a problem, then we may be able to solve the equation to get the solution to the problem. Some problems in this section could be solved without using algebra. However, the purpose of this section is to gain experience in setting up equations and using algebra to solve problems. We will show a complete solution to each problem so that you can gain the experience needed to solve more complex problems. We begin with a simple number problem.

E X A M P L E   2   **A number problem**

The sum of three consecutive integers is 228. Find the integers.

Solution

We first represent the unknown quantities with variables. The unknown quantities are the three consecutive integers. Let

$$x = \text{the first integer,}$$
$$x + 1 = \text{the second integer,}$$

and $$x + 2 = \text{the third integer.}$$

Since the sum of these three expressions for the consecutive integers is 228, we can write the following equation and solve it:

$$x + (x + 1) + (x + 2) = 228 \quad \text{The sum of the integers is 228.}$$
$$3x + 3 = 228$$
$$3x = 225$$
$$x = 75$$
$$x + 1 = 76 \quad \text{Identify the other unknown quantities.}$$
$$x + 2 = 77$$

To verify that these values are the correct integers, we compute

$$75 + 76 + 77 = 228.$$

The three consecutive integers that have a sum of 228 are 75, 76, and 77. ■

General Strategy for Problem Solving

The steps to follow in providing a complete solution to a verbal problem can be stated as follows.

Strategy for Solving Word Problems

1. Read the problem until you understand the problem. Making a guess and checking it will help you to understand the problem.
2. If possible, draw a diagram to illustrate the problem.
3. Choose a variable and write down what it represents.
4. Represent any other unknowns in terms of that variable.
5. Write an equation that models the situation.
6. Solve the equation.
7. Be sure that your solution answers the question posed in the original problem.
8. Check your answer by using it to solve the original problem (not the equation).

We will now see how this strategy can be applied to various types of problems.

Geometric Problems

Any problem that involves a geometric figure may be referred to as a **geometric problem.** For geometric problems the equation is often a geometric formula.

E X A M P L E   3

Finding the length and width of a rectangle

The length of a rectangular piece of property is 1 foot more than twice the width. If the perimeter is 302 feet, find the length and width.

Solution

First draw a diagram as in Fig. 2.4. Because the length is 1 foot more than twice the width, we let

$$x = \text{the width}$$

and

$$2x + 1 = \text{the length.}$$

$2x + 1$

FIGURE 2.4

Helpful Hint

To become familiar with the problem, let's guess that the width is 20 feet. The length would be 41 feet (1 foot more than twice the width). The perimeter of a 20 foot by 41 foot rectangle is 2(20) + 2(41) or 122 feet, which is not correct, but now we understand the problem.

The perimeter of a rectangle is modeled by the equation $2L + 2W = P$:

$$2L + 2W = P$$
$$2(2x + 1) + 2(x) = 302 \quad \text{Replace } L \text{ by } 2x + 1 \text{ and } W \text{ by } x.$$
$$4x + 2 + 2x = 302 \quad \text{Remove the parentheses.}$$
$$6x = 300$$
$$x = 50$$
$$2x + 1 = 101 \quad \text{Because } 2(50) + 1 = 101$$

Because $P = 2(101) + 2(50) = 302$ and 101 is 1 more than twice 50, we can be sure that the answer is correct. So the length is 101 feet, and the width is 50 feet. ■

Investment Problems

Investment problems involve sums of money invested at various interest rates. In this chapter we consider simple interest only.

E X A M P L E   4

Investing at two rates

Greg Smith invested some money in a certificate of deposit (CD) with an annual yield of 9%. He invested twice as much money in a mutual fund with an annual yield of 12%. His interest from the two investments at the end of the year was $396. How much money was invested at each rate?

Helpful Hint

To become familiar with the problem, let's guess that he invested $400 in a CD at 9% and $800 (twice as much) in a mutual fund at 12%. His total interest is

$$0.09(400) + 0.12(800)$$

or $132, which is not correct, but now we understand the problem.

Solution

Recall the formula $I = Prt$. In this problem the time t is 1 year, so $I = Pr$. If we let x represent the amount invested at the 9% rate, then $2x$ is the amount invested at 12%. The interest on these investments is the principal times the rate, or $0.09x$ and $0.12(2x)$. It is often helpful to make a table for the unknown quantities.

	Principal	Rate	Interest
Certificate of deposit	x dollars	9%	$0.09x$ dollars
Mutual fund	$2x$ dollars	12%	$0.12(2x)$ dollars

The fact that the total interest from the investments was $396 is expressed in this equation:

$$0.09x + 0.12(2x) = 396$$
$$0.09x + 0.24x = 396 \quad \text{We could multiply each side by 100}$$
$$0.33x = 396 \quad \text{to eliminate the decimals.}$$
$$x = \frac{396}{0.33}$$
$$x = 1200$$
$$2x = 2400$$

To check this answer, we find that $0.09(\$1200) = \$108$ and $0.12(\$2400) = \$288$. Now $\$108 + \$288 = \$396$. So Greg invested $1200 at 9% and $2400 at 12%. ■

Mixture Problems

Mixture problems involve solutions containing various percentages of a particular ingredient.

E X A M P L E 5

Mixing milk

How many gallons of milk containing 5% butterfat must be mixed with 90 gallons of 1% milk to obtain 2% milk?

Solution

If x represents the number of gallons of 5% milk, then $0.05x$ represents the amount of fat in that milk. If we mix x gallons of 5% milk with 90 gallons of 1% milk, we will have $x + 90$ gallons of 2% milk. See Fig. 2.5. We can make a table to classify all of the unknown amounts.

	Amount of milk	% fat	Amount of fat
5% milk	x gal	5	$0.05x$ gal
1% milk	90 gal	1	$0.01(90)$ gal
2% milk	$x + 90$ gal	2	$0.02(x + 90)$ gal

In mixture problems we always write an equation that accounts for one of the ingredients in the process. In this case we write an equation to express the fact that the total amount of fat from the first two types of milk is the same as the amount of fat in the mixture.

$$0.05x + 0.01(90) = 0.02(x + 90)$$
$$0.05x + 0.9 = 0.02x + 1.8 \quad \text{Remove parentheses.}$$
$$0.03x = 0.9 \quad \text{Note that we chose to work with the decimals}$$
$$x = 30 \quad \text{rather than eliminate them.}$$

We should use 30 gallons of 5% milk. There are 1.5 gallons of fat in the 30 gallons of 5% milk. The 1% milk will contribute 0.9 gallon of fat, and there will be 2.4 gallons of fat in 120 gallons of 2% milk. Because $1.5 + 0.9 = 2.4$, we have the correct solution. ∎

Helpful Hint

To become familiar with the problem, let's guess that 100 gallons of 5% milk should be mixed with 90 gallons of 1% milk. The total amount of fat would be 0.05(100) + 0.01(90) or 5.9 gallons of fat. But 2% of 190 is 3.8 gallons of fat. Since the amounts of fat should be equal, our guess is incorrect.

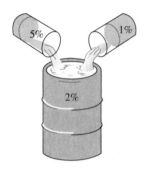

FIGURE 2.5

E X A M P L E 6

Blending gasoline

A dealer has 10,000 gallons of unleaded gasoline. He wants to add just enough ethanol to make the fuel a 10% ethanol mixture. How many gallons of ethanol should be added?

Solution

Let x represent the number of gallons of 100% pure ethanol that should be added. (The original gasoline has no ethanol in it.) We can classify all of this information in a table.

	Amount of gasoline	% ethanol	Amount of ethanol
Gasoline	10,000 gal	0	0 gal
Ethanol	x gal	100	x gal
Mixture	$x + 10,000$ gal	10	$0.1(x + 10,000)$ gal

Calculator Close-Up

If you replace *x* in the original equation by ANS, you can check without rounding. The calculator returns a 1 to indicate that the equation is satisfied. Try checking 1,111.1 with your calculator.

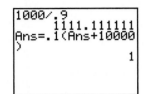

```
1000/.9
        1111.111111
Ans=.1(Ans+10000
)
                  1
```

We can write $0 + x = 0.1(x + 10,000)$ to express the fact that the amount of ethanol in the gasoline plus the amount of ethanol added is equal to the amount of ethanol in the final mixture. This model accounts for all of the ethanol in the process.

$$0 + x = 0.1(x + 10,000)$$

$$x = 0.1x + 1000 \quad \text{Remove parentheses.}$$

$$0.9x = 1000 \quad \text{Subtract } 0.1x \text{ from each side of the equation.}$$

$$x = \frac{1000}{0.9} \quad \text{Divide each side by 0.9.}$$

$$x \approx 1,111.1 \text{ gallons}$$

The amount of ethanol has been rounded to the nearest tenth of a gallon, so we cannot expect checking to be exact. If we combine 10,000 gallons of gasoline with 1,111.1 gallons of ethanol, we obtain 11,111.1 gallons of fuel. Notice that the amount of ethanol is 10% of the total mixture, 10% of $(10,000 + x)$. ∎

Uniform Motion Problems

Problems that involve motion at a constant rate are referred to as **uniform motion problems.**

EXAMPLE 7

Driving Miss Jennifer

Jennifer drove her car for 3 hours in a dust storm. When the skies cleared, she increased her speed by 30 miles per hour and drove for 4 more hours, completing her 295-mile trip. How fast did she travel during the dust storm?

Study Tip

As you leave class, talk to a classmate about what happened in class. What was the class about? What new terms were mentioned and what do they mean? How does this lesson fit in with the last lesson?

Solution

If x was Jennifer's speed during the dust storm, then her speed under clear skies was $x + 30$. For problems involving motion we use the formula $D = RT$ (distance equals rate times time). It is again helpful to make a table to classify the given information.

	Rate	Time	Distance
Dust storm	x mph	3 hr	$3x$ mi
Clear skies	$x + 30$ mph	4 hr	$4(x + 30)$ mi

This equation indicates that the total distance traveled was 295 miles:

$$3x + 4(x + 30) = 295$$

$$3x + 4x + 120 = 295 \quad \text{Remove parentheses.}$$

$$7x = 175$$

$$x = 25 \text{ miles per hour}$$

Check this answer in the original problem. Jennifer traveled 25 miles per hour (mph) during the storm. ∎

Commission Problems

When property is sold, the percentage of the selling price that the selling agent receives is the **commission.**

E X A M P L E   8

Selling price of a house

Sonia is selling her house through a real estate agent whose commission is 6% of the selling price. What should be the selling price so that Sonia can get $84,600?

Helpful Hint

To become familiar with the problem, let's guess that the selling price is $100,000. The commission is 6% of the selling price: 0.06(100,000) or $6,000. So Sonia receives $94,000, which is incorrect.

Solution

Let x be the selling price. The commission is 6% of x (not 6% of $84,600). Sonia receives the selling price less the sales commission.

$$\text{Selling price} - \text{commission} = \text{Sonia's share}$$
$$x - 0.06x = 84{,}600$$
$$0.94x = 84{,}600$$
$$x = \frac{84{,}600}{0.94}$$
$$= \$90{,}000$$

The commission is 0.06($90,000), or $5,400. Sonia's share is $90,000 − $5,400, or $84,600. The house should sell for $90,000. ∎

WARM-UPS

True or false? Explain your answer.

1. The recommended first step in solving a word problem is to write the equation.
2. When solving word problems, always write what the variable stands for.
3. Any solution to your equation must solve the word problem.
4. To represent two consecutive odd integers, we use x and $x + 1$.
5. We can represent two numbers that have a sum of 6 by x and $6 - x$.
6. Two numbers that differ by 7 can be represented by x and $x + 7$.
7. If $5x$ feet is 2 feet more than $3(x + 20)$ feet, then $5x + 2 = 3(x + 20)$.
8. If x is the selling price and the commission is 8% of the selling price, then the commission is $0.08x$.
9. If you need $80,000 for your house and the agent gets 10% of the selling price, then the agent gets $8,000, and the house sells for $88,000.
10. When we mix a 10% acid solution with a 14% acid solution, we can obtain a solution that is 24% acid.

2.3   EXERCISES

Reading and Writing *After reading this section, write out the answers to these questions. Use complete sentences.*

1. How do you algebraically represent three unknown consecutive integers?

2. What is the difference between representing three unknown consecutive even or odd integers?

3. What formula expresses the perimeter of a rectangle in terms of length and width?

4. What verbal phrases are used to indicate the operation of addition?

5. What is the commission when a real estate agent sells property?

6. What is uniform motion?

Find algebraic expressions for each of these verbal expressions. See Example 1.

7. Two consecutive even integers

8. Two consecutive odd integers

9. Two numbers with a sum of 10

10. Two numbers with a difference of 3

11. Eighty-five percent of the selling price

12. The product of a number and 3

13. The distance traveled in 3 hours at x miles per hour

14. The time it takes to travel 100 miles at $x + 5$ miles per hour

15. The perimeter of a rectangle if the width is x feet and the length is 5 feet longer than the width

16. The width of a rectangle if the length is x meters and the perimeter is 20 meters

Show a complete solution for each number problem. See Example 2.

17. The sum of three consecutive integers is 84. Find the integers.

18. Find three consecutive integers whose sum is 171.

19. Find three consecutive even integers whose sum is 252.

20. Find three consecutive even integers whose sum is 84.

21. Two consecutive odd integers have a sum of 128. What are the integers?

22. Four consecutive odd integers have a sum of 56. What are the integers?

Show a complete solution to each geometric problem. See Example 3.

23. **Length and width.** If the perimeter of a rectangle is 278 meters and the length is 1 meter longer than twice the width, then what are the length and width?

24. **Dimensions of a frame.** A frame maker made a large picture frame using 10 feet of frame molding. If the length of the finished frame was 2 feet more than the width, then what were the dimensions of the frame?

25. **Perimeter of a lot.** Having finished fencing the perimeter of a triangular piece of land, Lance observed that the second side was just 10 feet short of being twice as long as the first side, and the third side was exactly 50 feet longer than the first side. If he used 684 feet of fencing, what are the lengths of the three sides?

26. **Isosceles triangle.** A flag in the shape of an isosceles triangle has a base that is 3.5 inches shorter than either of the equal sides. If the perimeter of the triangle is 49 inches, what is the length of the equal sides?

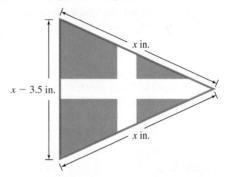

FIGURE FOR EXERCISE 26

27. **Hog heaven.** Farmer Hodges has 50 feet of fencing to make a rectangular hog pen beside a very large barn. He needs to fence only three sides because the barn will form the fourth side. Studies have shown that under those conditions the side parallel to the barn should be 5 feet longer than twice the width. If Farmer Hodges uses all of the fencing, what should the dimensions be?

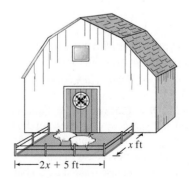

FIGURE FOR EXERCISE 27

28. **Doorway dimensions.** A carpenter made a doorway that is 1 foot taller than twice the width. If she used three pieces of door edge molding with a total length of 17 feet, then what are the approximate dimensions of the doorway?

Show a complete solution to each investment problem. See Example 4.

29. Investing money. Mr. and Mrs. Jackson invested some money at 6% simple interest and some money at 10% simple interest. In the second investment they put $1000 more than they put in the first. If the income from both investments for one year was $340, then how much did they invest at each rate?

30. Sibling rivalry. Samantha lent her brother some money at 9% simple interest and her sister one-half as much money at 16% simple interest. If she received a total of 34 cents in interest, then how much did she lend to each one?

31. Investing inheritance. Norman invested one-half of his inheritance in a CD that had a 10% annual yield. He lent one-quarter of his inheritance to his brother-in-law at 12% simple interest. His income from these two investments was $6400 for one year. How much was the inheritance?

32. Insurance settlement. Gary invested one-third of his insurance settlement in a CD that yielded 12%. He also invested one-third in Tara's computer business. Tara paid Gary 15% on this investment. If Gary's total income from these investments was $10,800 for one year, then what was the amount of his insurance settlement?

Show a complete solution to each mixture problem. See Examples 5 and 6.

33. Acid solutions. How many gallons of 5% acid solution should be mixed with 20 gallons of a 10% acid solution to obtain an 8% acid solution?

34. Alcohol solutions. How many liters of a 10% alcohol solution should be mixed with 12 liters of a 20% alcohol solution to obtain a 14% alcohol solution?

35. Increasing acidity. A gallon of Del Monte White Vinegar is labeled 5% acidity. How many fluid ounces of pure acid must be added to get 6% acidity?

36. Chlorine bleach. A gallon of Clorox bleach is labeled "5.25% sodium hypochlorite by weight." If a gallon of bleach weighs 8.3 pounds, then how many ounces of sodium hypochlorite must be added so that the bleach will be 6% sodium hypochlorite?

Show a complete solution to each uniform motion problem. See Example 7.

37. Driving in a fog. Carlo drove for 3 hours in a fog, then increased his speed by 30 miles per hour (mph) and drove 6 more hours. If his total trip was 540 miles, then what was his speed in the fog?

38. Walk, don't run. Louise walked for 2 hours then ran for $1\frac{1}{2}$ hours. If she runs twice as fast as she walks and the total trip was 20 miles, then how fast does she run?

39. Commuting to work. A commuter bus takes 2 hours to get downtown; an express bus, averaging 25 mph faster, takes 45 minutes to cover the same route. What is the average speed for the commuter bus?

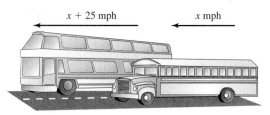

x + 25 mph   *x* mph

FIGURE FOR EXERCISE 39

40. Passengers versus freight. A freight train takes $1\frac{1}{4}$ hours to get to the city; a passenger train averaging 40 mph faster takes only 45 minutes to cover the same distance. What is the average speed of the passenger train?

Show a complete solution to each problem. See Example 8.

41. Listing a house. Karl wants to get $80,000 for his house. The real estate agent charges 8% of the selling price for selling the house. What should the selling price be?

42. Hot tamales. Martha sells hot tamales at a sidewalk stand. Her total receipts including the 5% sales tax were $915.60. What amount of sales tax did she collect?

43. Mustang Sally. Sally bought a used Mustang. The selling price plus the 7% state sales tax was $9041.50. What was the selling price?

44. Choosing a selling price. Roy is selling his car through a broker. Roy wants to get $3000 for himself, but the broker gets a commission of 10% of the selling price. What should the selling price be?

Show a complete solution to each problem.

45. Tennis. The distance from the baseline to the service line on a tennis court is 3 feet longer than the distance from the service line to the net. If the distance from the

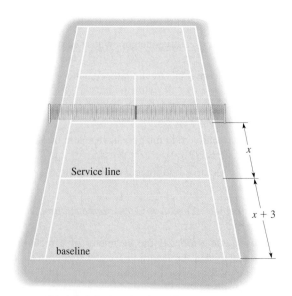

Service line

baseline

x

x + 3

FIGURE FOR EXERCISE 45

baseline to the net is 39 feet, then what is the distance from the service line to the net?

46. Mixed doubles. The doubles court in tennis is one-third wider than the singles court. If the doubles court is 36 feet wide, then what is the width of the singles court?

47. First Super Bowl. In the first Super Bowl game in the Los Angeles Coliseum in 1967, the Green Bay Packers out-scored the Kansas City Chiefs by 25 points. If 45 points were scored in that game, then what was the final score?

48. Toy sales. In 1998 Toys "R" Us and Wal-Mart together held 36% of the toy market share (*Fortune*, June 1, 1998, www.fortune.com). If the market share for Toys "R" Us was 4 percentage points higher than the market share for Wal-Mart, then what was the market share for each company?

49. Blending coffee. Mark blends $\frac{3}{4}$ of a pound of premium Brazilian coffee with $1\frac{1}{2}$ pounds of standard Colombian coffee. If the Brazilian coffee sells for $10 per pound and the Colombian coffee sells for $8 per pound, then what should the price per pound be for the blended coffee?

FIGURE FOR EXERCISE 49

50. 'Tis the seasoning. Cheryl's Famous Pumpkin Pie Seasoning consists of a blend of cinnamon, nutmeg, and cloves. When Cheryl mixes up a batch, she uses 200 ounces of cinnamon, 100 ounces of nutmeg, and 100 ounces of cloves. If cinnamon sells for $1.80 per ounce, nutmeg sells for $1.60 per ounce, and cloves sell for $1.40 per ounce, what should be the price per ounce of the mixture?

51. Health food mix. Dried bananas sell for $0.80 per quarter-pound, and dried apricots sell for $1.00 per quarter-pound. How many pounds of apricots should be mixed with 10 pounds of bananas to get a mixture that sells for $0.95 per quarter-pound?

52. Mixed nuts. Cashews sell for $1.20 per quarter-pound, and Brazil nuts sell for $1.50 per quarter-pound. How many pounds of cashews should be mixed with 20 pounds of Brazil nuts to get a mix that sells for $1.30 per quarter-pound?

53. Antifreeze mixture. A mechanic finds that a car with a 20-quart radiator has a mixture containing 30% antifreeze in it. How much of this mixture would he have to drain out and replace with pure antifreeze to get a 50% antifreeze mixture?

54. Increasing the percentage. A mechanic has found that a car with a 16-quart radiator has a 40% antifreeze mixture in the radiator. She has on hand a 70% antifreeze solution. How much of the 40% solution would she have to replace with the 70% solution to get the solution in the radiator up to 50%?

55. Profit. The profit for General Electric was $12,735 million in 2001 (www.forbes.com). This figure represents an increase of 18.8% from the previous year. What was the profit in 2000?

56. Market Value. The market value for General Electric was $406,525 million in 2001 (www.forbes.com). This figure represents a 6.3% decrease from the previous year. What was the market value in 2000?

57. Dividing the estate. Uncle Albert's estate is to be divided among his three nephews. The will specifies that Daniel receive one-half of the amount that Brian receives and that Raymond receive $1000 less than one-third of the amount that Brian receives. If the estate amounts to $25,400, then how much does each inherit?

58. Mary's assets. Mary Hall's will specifies that her lawyer is to liquidate her assets and divide the proceeds among her three sisters. Lena's share is to be one-half of Lisa's, and Lisa's share is to be one-half of Lauren's. If the lawyer has agreed to a fee that is equal to 10% of the largest share and the proceeds amount to $164,428, then how much does each person get?

59. Missing integers. If the larger of two consecutive integers is subtracted from twice the smaller integer, then the result is 21. Find the integers.

60. Really odd integers. If the smaller of two consecutive odd integers is subtracted from twice the larger one, then the result is 13. Find the integers.

61. Highway miles. Berenice and Jarrett drive a rig for Continental Freightways. In one day Berenice averaged 50 mph and Jarrett averaged 56 mph, but Berenice drove for two more hours than Jarrett. If together they covered 683 miles, then for how many hours did Berenice drive?

62. Spring break. Fernell and Dabney shared the driving to Florida for spring break. Fernell averaged 50 mph, and Dabney averaged 64 mph. If Fernell drove for 3 hours longer than Dabney but covered 18 miles less than Dabney, then for how many hours did Fernell drive?

63. Stacy's square. Stacy has 70 meters of fencing and plans to make a square pen. In one side she is going to leave an opening that is one-half the length of the side. If she uses all 70 meters of fencing, how large can the square be?

64. *Shawn's shed.* Shawn is building a tool shed with a square foundation and has enough siding to cover 32 linear feet of walls. If he leaves a 4-foot space for a door, then what size foundation would use up all of his siding?

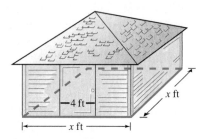

FIGURE FOR EXERCISE 64

65. *Splitting investments.* Joan had $3000 to invest. She invested part of it in an investment paying 8% and the remainder in an investment paying 10%. If the total income on these investments was $290, then how much did she invest at each rate?

66. *Financial independence.* Dorothy had $8000 to invest. She invested part of it in an investment paying 6% and the rest in an investment paying 9%. If the total income from these investments was $690, then how much did she invest at each rate?

67. *Alcohol solutions.* Amy has two solutions available in the laboratory, one with 5% alcohol and the other with 10% alcohol. How much of each should she mix together to obtain 5 gallons of an 8% solution?

68. *Alcohol and water.* Joy has a solution containing 12% alcohol. How much of this solution and how much water must she use to get 6 liters of a solution containing 10% alcohol?

69. *Chance meeting.* In 6 years Todd will be twice as old as Darla was when they met 6 years ago. If their ages total 78 years, then how old are they now?

70. *Centennial Plumbing Company.* The three Hoffman brothers advertise that together they have a century of plumbing experience. Bart has twice the experience of Al, and in 3 years Carl will have twice the experience that Al had a year ago. How many years of experience does each of them have?

In This Section

- Inequality Symbols
- Interval Notation and Graphs
- Solving Linear Inequalities
- Applications

2.4   **INEQUALITIES**

An equation is a statement that indicates that two algebraic expressions are equal. An **inequality** is a statement that indicates that two algebraic expressions are not equal in a specific way, one expression being greater than or less than the other.

Inequality Symbols

The inequality symbols that we will be using are listed along with their meanings in the box.

Inequality Symbols

Symbol	Meaning
<	Is less than
≤	Is less than or equal to
>	Is greater than
≥	Is greater than or equal to

It is clear that 5 is less than 10, but how do we compare -5 and -10? If we think of negative numbers as debts, we would say that -10 is the larger debt. However,

Helpful Hint

A good way to learn inequality symbols is to notice that the inequality symbol always points at the smaller number. An inequality symbol can be read in either direction. For example, we can read $-4 < x$ as "-4 is less than x" or as "x is greater than -4." It is usually easier to understand an inequality if you read the variable first.

in algebra the size of a number is determined only by its position on the number line. For two numbers a and b we say that a *is less than b* if and only if a is to the *left* of b on the number line. To compare -5 and -10, we locate each point on the number line in Fig. 2.6. Because -10 is to the left of -5 on the number line, we say that -10 is less than -5. In symbols,

$$-10 < -5.$$

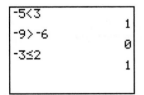

FIGURE 2.6

We say that a is greater than b if and only if a is to the *right* of b on the number line. Thus we can also write

$$-5 > -10.$$

The statement $a \leq b$ is true if a is less than b or if a is equal to b. The statement $a \geq b$ is true if a is greater than b or if a equals b. For example, the statement $3 \leq 5$ is true, and so is the statement $5 \leq 5$.

EXAMPLE 1

Inequalities

Determine whether each statement is true or false.

a) $-5 < 3$ b) $-9 > -6$

c) $-3 \leq 2$ d) $4 \geq 4$

Calculator Close-Up

We can use a calculator to check whether an inequality is satisfied in the same manner that we check equations. The calculator returns a 1 if the inequality is correct or a 0 if it is not correct.

```
-5<3
              1
-9>-6
              0
-3≤2
              1
```

Solution

a) The statement $-5 < 3$ is true because -5 is to the left of 3 on the number line. In fact, any negative number is less than any positive number.

b) The statement $-9 > -6$ is false because -9 lies to the left of -6.

c) The statement $-3 \leq 2$ is true because -3 is less than 2.

d) The statement $4 \geq 4$ is true because $4 = 4$ is true.   ■

Interval Notation and Graphs

If an inequality involves a variable, then which real numbers can be used in place of the variable to obtain a correct statement? The set of all such numbers is the **solution set** to the inequality. For example, $x < 3$ is correct if x is replaced by any number that lies to the left of 3 on the number line:

$$1.5 < 3, \qquad 0 < 3, \qquad \text{and} \qquad -2 < 3$$

Using interval notation from Section 1.2, the solution set to $x < 3$ is the interval of real numbers $(-\infty, 3)$. The graph of the solution set or the graph of $x < 3$ is shown in Fig. 2.7.

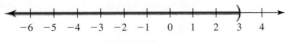

FIGURE 2.7

An inequality such as $x \geq 1$ is satisfied by 1 and any real number that lies to the right of 1 on the number line. So the solution set to $x \geq 1$ is the interval $[1, \infty)$. Its graph is shown in Fig. 2.8.

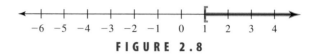

FIGURE 2.8

The solution set and graph for each of the four basic inequalities are given in the box. Note that a bracket indicates that a number is included in the solution set and a parenthesis indicates that a number is not included.

Basic Interval Notation (k any real number)

Inequality	Solution Set with Interval Notation	Graph
$x > k$	(k, ∞)	
$x \geq k$	$[k, \infty)$	
$x < k$	$(-\infty, k)$	
$x \leq k$	$(-\infty, k]$	

E X A M P L E 2

Interval notation and graphs

Write the solution set to each inequality in interval notation and graph it.

a) $x > -5$　　　　　　　　　　**b)** $x \leq 2$

Solution

a) Every real number to the right of -5 satisfies $x > -5$. So the solution set is the interval $(-5, \infty)$. The graph is shown in Fig. 2.9.

FIGURE 2.9

b) The inequality $x \leq 2$ is satisfied by 2 and every real number to the left of 2. So the solution set is $(-\infty, 2]$. The graph is in Fig. 2.10.

FIGURE 2.10　　■

Solving Linear Inequalities

In Section 2.1 we defined a linear equation as an equation of the form $ax + b = 0$. If we replace the equality symbol in a linear equation with an inequality symbol, we have a linear inequality.

Linear Inequality

A **linear inequality** in one variable x is any inequality of the form $ax + b < 0$, where a and b are real numbers, with $a \neq 0$. In place of $<$ we may also use $\leq$, $>$, or $\geq$.

Inequalities that can be *rewritten* in the form of a linear inequality are also called linear inequalities.

Before we solve linear inequalities, let's examine the results of performing various operations on each side of an inequality. If we start with the inequality $2 < 6$ and add 2 to each side, we get the true statement $4 < 8$. Examine the results in the table shown here.

Perform these operations on each side of $2 < 6$:

	Add 2	**Subtract 2**	**Multiply by 2**	**Divide by 2**
Resulting inequality	$4 < 8$	$0 < 4$	$4 < 12$	$1 < 3$

All of the resulting inequalities are correct. However, if we perform operations on each side of $2 < 6$ using -2, the situation is not as simple. For example, $-2 \cdot 2 = -4$ and $-2 \cdot 6 = -12$, but -4 is greater than -12. To get a correct inequality when each side is multiplied or divided by -2, we must reverse the inequality symbol, as shown in this table.

Perform these operations on each side of $2 < 6$:

	Add −2	**Subtract −2**	**Multiply by −2**	**Divide by −2**
Resulting inequality	$0 < 4$	$4 < 8$	$-4 > -12$	$-1 > -3$

Inequality reverses

These examples illustrate the properties that we use for solving inequalities.

Properties of Inequality

Addition Property of Inequality
If the same number is added to both sides of an inequality, then the solution set to the inequality is unchanged.

Multiplication Property of Inequality
If both sides of an inequality are multiplied by the same *positive number*, then the solution set to the inequality is unchanged.
If both sides of an inequality are multiplied by the same *negative number* and *the inequality symbol is reversed*, then the solution set to the inequality is unchanged.

Because subtraction is defined in terms of addition, the addition property of inequality also allows us to subtract the same number from both sides. Because division is defined in terms of multiplication, the multiplication property of inequality also allows us to divide both sides by the same nonzero number *as long as we reverse the inequality symbol when dividing by a negative number*.

Equivalent inequalities are inequalities with the same solution set. We find the solution to a linear inequality by using the properties to convert it into an equivalent inequality with an obvious solution set, just as we do when solving equations.

EXAMPLE 3

Solving inequalities

Solve each inequality. State the solution set in interval notation and graph it.

a) $2x - 7 < -1$ **b)** $5 - 3x < 11$

Solution

a) We proceed exactly as we do when solving equations:

$$2x - 7 < -1 \quad \text{Original inequality}$$
$$2x < 6 \quad \text{Add 7 to each side.}$$
$$x < 3 \quad \text{Divide each side by 2.}$$

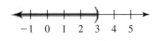

FIGURE 2.11

The solution set is the interval $(-\infty, 3)$. The graph is shown in Fig. 2.11.

b) We divide by a negative number to solve this inequality.

$$5 - 3x < 11 \quad \text{Original inequality}$$
$$-3x < 6 \quad \text{Subtract 5 from each side.}$$
$$x > -2 \quad \text{Divide each side by } -3 \text{ and reverse the inequality symbol.}$$

FIGURE 2.12

The solution set is the interval $(-2, \infty)$. The graph is shown in Fig. 2.12. ∎

Calculator Close-Up

To check the solution to Example 3, press the Y = key and let $y_1 = 5 - 3x$.

Press TBLSET to set the starting point for x and the distance between the x-values.

Now press TABLE and scroll through values of x until y_1 gets smaller than 11.

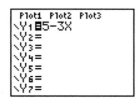

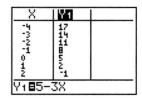

This table supports the conclusion that if $x > -2$, then $5 - 3x < 11$.

EXAMPLE 4

Solving inequalities

Solve $\dfrac{8 + 3x}{-5} \geq -4$. State and graph the solution set.

Solution

$$\frac{8 + 3x}{-5} \geq -4 \quad \text{Original inequality}$$

$$-5\left(\frac{8 + 3x}{-5}\right) \leq -5(-4) \quad \text{Multiply each side by } -5 \text{ and reverse the inequality symbol.}$$

$$8 + 3x \leq 20 \quad \text{Simplify.}$$

$$3x \leq 12 \quad \text{Subtract 8 from each side.}$$

$$x \leq 4 \quad \text{Divide each side by 3.}$$

The solution set is $(-\infty, 4]$, and its graph is shown in Fig. 2.13.

FIGURE 2.13 ■

EXAMPLE 5

An inequality with fractions

Solve $\frac{1}{2}x - \frac{2}{3} \le x + \frac{4}{3}$. State and graph the solution set.

Helpful Hint

Notice that we use the same strategy for solving inequalities as we do for solving equations. But we must remember to reverse the inequality symbol when we multiply or divide by a negative number. For inequalities it is usually best to isolate the variable on the left-hand side.

Solution

First multiply each side of the inequality by 6, the LCD:

$$\frac{1}{2}x - \frac{2}{3} \le x + \frac{4}{3} \quad \text{Original inequality}$$

$$6\left(\frac{1}{2}x - \frac{2}{3}\right) \le 6\left(x + \frac{4}{3}\right) \quad \text{Multiplying by positive 6 does not reverse the inequality.}$$

$$3x - 4 \le 6x + 8 \quad \text{Distributive property}$$

$$3x \le 6x + 12 \quad \text{Add 4 to each side.}$$

$$-3x \le 12 \quad \text{Subtract } 6x \text{ from each side.}$$

$$x \ge -4 \quad \text{Divide each side by } -3 \text{ and reverse the inequality.}$$

The solution set is the interval $[-4, \infty)$. Its graph is shown in Fig. 2.14.

FIGURE 2.14 ■

In Example 6 we see an inequality that is satisfied by all real numbers and one that has no solution.

EXAMPLE 6

All or nothing

Solve each inequality and graph the solution set.

a) $6 - 4x < -4x + 7$ **b)** $2(4x - 5) \ge 4(2x - 1)$

Solution

a) Adding $4x$ to each side will greatly simplify the inequality:

$$6 - 4x < -4x + 7 \quad \text{Original inequality}$$

$$6 < 7 \quad \text{Add } 4x \text{ to each side.}$$

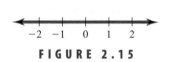

FIGURE 2.15

Since $6 < 7$ is correct no matter what real number is used in place of x, the solution set is the set of all real numbers $(-\infty, \infty)$. Its graph is shown in Fig. 2.15.

b) Start by simplifying each side of the inequality.

$$2(4x - 5) \ge 4(2x - 1) \quad \text{Original inequality}$$

$$8x - 10 \ge 8x - 4 \quad \text{Distributive property}$$

$$-10 \ge -4 \quad \text{Subtract } 8x \text{ from each side.}$$

Since $-10 \ge -4$ is false no matter what real number is used in place of x, the solution set is the empty set $\varnothing$ and there is no graph to draw. ■

Applications

There are a variety of ways to express inequalities verbally. Some of the most common are illustrated in this table.

Verbal Sentence	Inequality
x is greater than 6; x is more than 6	$x > 6$
y is smaller than 0; y is less than 0	$y < 0$
w is at least 9; w is not less than 9	$w \geq 9$
m is at most 7; m is not greater than 7	$m \leq 7$

E X A M P L E 7 **Writing inequalities**

Identify the variable and write an inequality that describes the situation.

a) Chris paid more than $200 for a suit.

b) A candidate for president must be at least 35 years old.

c) The capacity of an elevator is at most 1500 pounds.

d) The company must hire no fewer than 10 programmers.

Solution

a) If c is the cost of the suit in dollars, then $c > 200$.

b) If a is the age of the candidate in years, then $a \geq 35$.

c) If x is the capacity of the elevator in pounds, then $x \leq 1500$.

d) If n represents the number of programmers and n is not less than 10, then $n \geq 10$. ■

In Example 7(d) we knew that n was not less than 10. So there were exactly two other possibilities: n was greater than 10 or equal to 10. The fact that there are only three possible ways to position two real numbers on a number line is called the **trichotomy property.**

> **Trichotomy Property**
>
> For any two real numbers a and b, exactly one of these is true:
>
> $$a < b, \quad a = b, \quad \text{or} \quad a > b$$

We follow the same steps to solve problems involving inequalities as we do to solve problems involving equations.

E X A M P L E 8 **Price range**

Lois plans to spend less than $500 on an electric dryer, including the 9% sales tax and a $64 setup charge. In what range is the selling price of the dryer that she can afford?

Solution

If we let x represent the selling price in dollars for the dryer, then the amount of sales tax is $0.09x$. Because her total cost must be less than $500, we can write the following inequality:

$$x + 0.09x + 64 < 500$$
$$1.09x < 436 \quad \text{Subtract 64 from each side.}$$
$$x < \frac{436}{1.09} \quad \text{Divide each side by 1.09.}$$
$$x < 400$$

The selling price of the dryer must be less than \$400. ■

Note that if we had written the equation $x + 0.09x + 64 = 500$ for the last example, we would have gotten $x = 400$. We could then have concluded that the selling price must be less than \$400. This would certainly solve the problem, but it would not illustrate the use of inequalities. The original problem describes an inequality, and we should solve it as an inequality.

E X A M P L E   9

Paying off the mortgage

Tessie owns a piece of land on which she owes \$12,760 to a bank. She wants to sell the land for enough money to at least pay off the mortgage. The real estate agent gets 6% of the selling price, and her city has a \$400 real estate transfer tax paid by the seller. What should the range of the selling price be for Tessie to get at least enough money to pay off her mortgage?

Solution

If x is the selling price in dollars, then the commission is $0.06x$. We can write an inequality expressing the fact that the selling price minus the real estate commission minus the \$400 tax must be at least \$12,760:

$$x - 0.06x - 400 \geq 12,760$$
$$0.94x - 400 \geq 12,760 \quad 1 - 0.06 = 0.94$$
$$0.94x \geq 13,160 \quad \text{Add 400 to each side.}$$
$$x \geq \frac{13,160}{0.94} \quad \text{Divide each side by 0.94.}$$
$$x \geq 14,000$$

The selling price must be at least \$14,000 for Tessie to pay off the mortgage. ■

WARM-UPS

True or false? Explain your answer.

1. $0 < 0$ 2. $-300 > -2$ 3. $-60 \leq -60$
4. The inequality $6 < x$ is equivalent to $x < 6$.
5. The inequality $-2x < 10$ is equivalent to $x < -5$.
6. The solution set to $3x \geq -12$ is $(-\infty, -4]$.
7. The solution set to $-x > 4$ is $(-\infty, -4)$.
8. If x is no larger than 8, then $x \leq 8$.
9. If m is any real number, then exactly one of these is true: $m < 0$, $m = 0$, or $m > 0$.
10. The number -2 is a member of the solution set to the inequality $3 - 4x \leq 11$.

2.4 EXERCISES

Reading and Writing *After reading this section, write out the answers to these questions. Use complete sentences.*

1. What is an inequality?

2. What symbols are used to express inequality?

3. What does it mean when we say that *a* is less than *b*?

4. What is a linear inequality?

5. How does solving linear inequalities differ from solving linear equations?

6. What verbal phrases are used to indicate an inequality?

Determine whether each inequality is true or false. See Example 1.

7. $-3 < -9$ **8.** $-8 > -7$

9. $0 \le 8$ **10.** $-6 \ge -8$

11. $(-3)20 > (-3)40$ **12.** $(-1)(-3) < (-1)(5)$

13. $9 - (-3) \le 12$ **14.** $(-4)(-5) + 2 \ge 21$

Determine whether each inequality is satisfied by the given number.

15. $2x - 4 < 8, -3$ **16.** $5 - 3x > -1, 6$

17. $2x - 3 \le 3x - 9, 5$ **18.** $6 - 3x \ge 10 - 2x, -4$

19. $5 - x < 4 - 2x, -1$ **20.** $3x - 7 \ge 3x - 10, 9$

Write the solution set in interval notation and graph it. See Example 2.

21. $x \le -1$

22. $x \ge -7$

23. $x > 20$

24. $x < 30$

25. $3 \le x$

26. $-2 > x$

27. $x < 2.3$

28. $x \le 4.5$

Fill in the blank with an inequality symbol so that the two statements are equivalent.

29. $x + 5 > 12$ **30.** $2x - 3 \le -4$ **31.** $-x < 6$
  x ___ 7 $2x$ ___ -1 x ___ -6

32. $-5 \ge -x$ **33.** $-2x \ge 8$ **34.** $-5x > -10$
  5 ___ x x ___ -4 x ___ 2

35. $4 < x$ **36.** $-9 \le -x$
  x ___ 4 x ___ 9

Solve each of these inequalities. Express the solution set in interval notation and graph it. See Examples 3–5.

37. $7x > -14$

38. $4x \le -8$

39. $-3x \le 12$

40. $-2x > -6$

41. $2x - 3 > 7$

42. $3x - 2 < 6$

43. $18 \ge 3 - 5x$

44. $19 \le 5 - 4x$

45. $\dfrac{x - 3}{-5} < -2$

46. $\dfrac{2x - 3}{4} > 6$

47. $2 \geq \dfrac{5 - 3x}{4}$

48. $-1 \leq \dfrac{7 - 5x}{-2}$

49. $3 - \dfrac{1}{4}x \geq 2$

50. $5 - \dfrac{1}{3}x > 2$

51. $\dfrac{1}{4}x - \dfrac{1}{2} < \dfrac{1}{2}x - \dfrac{2}{3}$

52. $\dfrac{1}{3}x - \dfrac{1}{6} < \dfrac{1}{6}x - \dfrac{1}{2}$

53. $\dfrac{y - 3}{2} > \dfrac{1}{2} - \dfrac{y - 5}{4}$

54. $\dfrac{y - 1}{3} - \dfrac{y + 1}{5} > 1$

Solve each inequality and graph the solution set. See Example 6.

55. $3(x + 2) \leq 9 + 3x$

56. $2x + 3 > 2(x - 4)$

57. $-2(5x - 1) \leq -5(5 + 2x)$
58. $-4(2x - 5) \leq 2(6 - 4x)$
59. $3x - (4 - 2x) < 5 - (2 - 5x)$

60. $6 - (5 - 3x) > 7x - (3 + 4x)$

61. $\dfrac{1}{2}x + \dfrac{1}{4}x < \dfrac{1}{8}(6x - 4)$

62. $\dfrac{3}{8}x - \dfrac{1}{4}x < \dfrac{1}{6}\left(\dfrac{3}{4}x - 6\right)$

Identify the variable and write an inequality that describes each situation. See Example 7.

63. Tony is taller than 6 feet.

64. Glenda is under 60 years old.

65. Wilma makes less than $80,000 per year.

66. Bubba weighs over 80 pounds.

67. The maximum speed for the Concorde is 1450 miles per hour (mph).

68. The minimum speed on the freeway is 45 mph.

69. Julie can afford at most $400 per month.

70. Fred must have at least a 3.2 grade point average.

71. Burt is no taller than 5 feet.

72. Ernie cannot run faster than 10 mph.

73. Tina makes no more than $8.20 per hour.

74. Rita will not take less than $12,000 for the car.

Solve each problem by using an inequality. See Examples 8 and 9.

75. *Car shopping.* Jennifer is shopping for a new car. In addition to the price of the car, there is an 8% sales tax and a $172 title and license fee. If Jennifer decides that she will spend less than $10,000 total, then what is the price range for the car?

76. *Sewing machines.* Charles wants to buy a sewing machine in a city with a 10% sales tax. He has at most $700 to spend. In what price range should he look?

77. *Truck shopping.* Linda and Bob are shopping for a new truck in a city with a 9% sales tax. There is also an $80 title and license fee to pay. They want to get a good truck and plan to spend at least $10,000. What is the price range for the truck?

78. *DVD rental.* For $19.95 per month you can rent an unlimited number of DVD movies through an Internet rental service. You can rent the same DVDs at a local store for $3.98 each. How many movies would you have to rent per month for the Internet service to be the better deal?

79. *Declining birth rate.* The graph on the next page shows the number of births per 1000 women per year since 1980 in the United States (www.census.gov).
a) Has the number of births per 1000 women been increasing or decreasing since 1980?
b) The formula $B = -0.52n + 71.1$ can be used to approximate the number of births per 1000 women,

Births (vertical axis)

80
60
40
20

10 20 30 40
Years since 1980

FIGURE FOR EXERCISE 79

Grading	Scale
90–100	A
80–89	B
70–79	C
60–69	D

TABLE FOR EXERCISES 81 AND 82

where n is the number of years since 1980. What is the first year in which the number of births will be less than 55?

80. **Bachelor's degrees.** The number of bachelor's degrees in thousands awarded in the United States can be approximated using the formula

$$B = 16.45n + 980.2,$$

where n is the number of years since 1985 (National Center for Education Statistics, www.nces.ed.gov). What is the first year in which the number of bachelor's degrees will exceed 1.5 million?

81. **Weighted average.** Professor Jorgenson gives only a midterm exam and a final exam. The semester average is computed by taking $\frac{1}{3}$ of the midterm exam score plus $\frac{2}{3}$ of the final exam score. The grade is determined from the semester average by using the grading scale given in the table. If Stanley scored only 56 on the midterm, then for what range of scores on the final exam would he get a C or better in the course?

82. **C or better.** Professor Brown counts her midterm as $\frac{2}{3}$ of the grade and her final as $\frac{1}{3}$ of the grade. Wilbert scored only 56 on the midterm. If Professor Brown also uses the grading scale given in the table, then what range of scores on the final exam would give Wilbert a C or better in the course?

83. **Designer jeans.** A pair of ordinary jeans at A-Mart costs $50 less than a pair of designer jeans at Enrico's. In fact, you can buy four pairs of A-Mart jeans for less than one pair of Enrico's jeans. What is the price range for a pair of A-Mart jeans?

84. **United Express.** Al and Rita both drive parcel delivery trucks for United Express. Al averages 20 mph less than Rita. In fact, Al is so slow that in 5 hours he covered fewer miles than Rita did in 3 hours. What are the possible values for Al's rate of speed?

GETTING MORE INVOLVED

85. **Discussion.** If 3 is added to every number in $(4, \infty)$, the resulting set is $(7, \infty)$. In each of the following cases, write the resulting set of numbers in interval notation. Explain your results.
a) The number -6 is subtracted from every number in $[2, \infty)$.
b) Every number in $(-\infty, -3)$ is multiplied by 2.
c) Every number in $(8, \infty)$ is divided by 4.
d) Every number in $(6, \infty)$ is multiplied by -2.
e) Every number in $(-\infty, -10)$ is divided by -5.

86. **Writing.** Explain why saying that x is *at least* 9 is equivalent to saying that x is *greater than or equal to* 9. Explain why saying that x is *at most* 5 is equivalent to saying that x is *less than or equal to* 5.

In This Section

- Basics
- Graphing the Solution Set
- Applications

2.5 COMPOUND INEQUALITIES

In this section we will use the ideas of union and intersection from Chapter 1 along with our knowledge of inequalities from Section 2.4 to work with compound inequalities.

Basics

The inequalities that we studied in Section 2.4 are referred to as **simple inequalities.** If we join two simple inequalities with the connective "and" or the connective "or," we get a **compound inequality.** A compound inequality using the connective "and" is true if and only if *both* simple inequalities are true.

E X A M P L E   1

Compound inequalities using the connective "and"

Determine whether each compound inequality is true.

a) $3 > 2$ and $3 < 5$

b) $6 > 2$ and $6 < 5$

Solution

a) The compound inequality is true because $3 > 2$ is true and $3 < 5$ is true.

b) The compound inequality is false because $6 < 5$ is false.   ■

A compound inequality using the connective "or" is true if one or the other or both of the simple inequalities are true. It is false only if both simple inequalities are false.

E X A M P L E   2

Compound inequalities using the connective "or"

Determine whether each compound inequality is true.

a) $2 < 3$ or $2 > 7$

b) $4 < 3$ or $4 \geq 7$

Helpful Hint

There is a big difference between "and" and "or." To get money from an automatic teller you must have a bank card *and* know a secret number (PIN). There would be a lot of problems if you could get money by having a bank card *or* knowing a PIN.

Solution

a) The compound inequality is true because $2 < 3$ is true.

b) The compound inequality is false because both $4 < 3$ and $4 \geq 7$ are false.   ■

If a compound inequality involves a variable, then we are interested in the solution set to the inequality. The solution set to an "and" inequality consists of all numbers that satisfy both simple inequalities, whereas the solution set to an "or" inequality consists of all numbers that satisfy at least one of the simple inequalities.

E X A M P L E   3

Solutions of compound inequalities

Determine whether 5 satisfies each compound inequality.

a) $x < 6$ and $x < 9$

b) $2x - 9 \leq 5$ or $-4x \geq -12$

Solution

a) Because $5 < 6$ and $5 < 9$ are both true, 5 satisfies the compound inequality.

b) Because $2 \cdot 5 - 9 \leq 5$ is true, it does not matter that $-4 \cdot 5 \geq -12$ is false. So 5 satisfies the compound inequality.   ■

Graphing the Solution Set

The solution set to a compound inequality using the connective "and" is the intersection of the two solutions sets, because it consists of all real numbers that satisfy both simple inequalities.

E X A M P L E   4

Graphing compound inequalities

Graph the solution set to the compound inequality $x > 2$ and $x < 5$.

Solution

First sketch the graph of $x > 2$ and then the graph of $x < 5$, as shown in the top two number lines in Fig. 2.16. The intersection of these two solution sets is the portion of the number line that is shaded on both graphs, just the part between 2 and 5, not including the endpoints. So the solution set is the interval (2, 5) and its graph is shown at the bottom of Fig. 2.16.

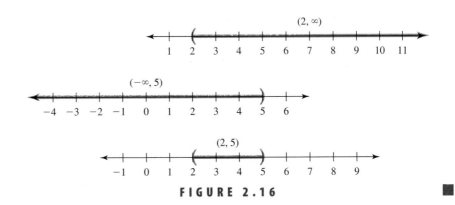

FIGURE 2.16

The solution set to a compound inequality using the connective "or" is the union of the two solution sets, because it consists of all real numbers that satisfy one or the other or both simple inequalities.

E X A M P L E   5

Graphing compound inequalities

Graph the solution set to the compound inequality $x > 4$ or $x < -1$.

Solution

First graph the solution sets to the simple inequalities as shown in Fig. 2.17. The union of these two intervals is shown at the bottom of Fig. 2.17. Since the union does not simplify to a single interval, the solution set is written using the symbol for union as $(-\infty, -1) \cup (4, \infty)$.

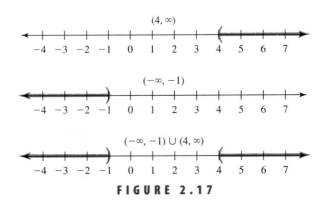

FIGURE 2.17

CAUTION   When graphing the intersection of two simple inequalities, do not draw too much. For the intersection, graph only numbers that satisfy *both* inequalities. Omit numbers that satisfy one but not the other inequality. Graphing a union is usually easier because we can simply draw both solution sets on the same number line.

It is not always necessary to graph the solution set to each simple inequality before graphing the solution set to the compound inequality. We can save time and work if we learn to think of the two preliminary graphs but draw only the final one.

E X A M P L E   6

Overlapping intervals

Sketch the graph and write the solution set in interval notation to each compound inequality.

a) $x < 3$ and $x < 5$ **b)** $x > 4$ or $x > 0$

Solution

a) To graph $x < 3$ and $x < 5$, we shade only the numbers that are both less than 3 and less than 5. So numbers between 3 and 5 are not shaded in Fig. 2.18. The compound inequality $x < 3$ and $x < 5$ is equivalent to the simple inequality $x < 3$. The solution set can be written as $(-\infty, 3)$.

FIGURE 2.18

b) To graph $x > 4$ or $x > 0$, we shade both regions on the same number line as shown in Fig. 2.19. The compound inequality $x > 4$ or $x > 0$ is equivalent to the simple inequality $x > 0$. The solution set is $(0, \infty)$.

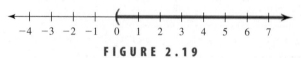

FIGURE 2.19   ■

Example 7 shows a compound inequality that has no solution and one that is satisfied by every real number.

E X A M P L E   7

All or nothing

Sketch the graph and write the solution set in interval notation to each compound inequality.

a) $x < 2$ and $x > 6$ **b)** $x < 3$ or $x > 1$

Solution

a) A number satisfies $x < 2$ and $x > 6$ if it is both less than 2 *and* greater than 6. There are no such numbers. The solution set is the empty set, $\varnothing$.

b) To graph $x < 3$ or $x > 1$, we shade both regions on the same number line as shown in Fig. 2.20. Since the two regions cover the entire line, the solution set is the set of all real numbers $(-\infty, \infty)$.

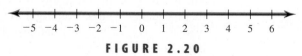

FIGURE 2.20   ■

If we start with a more complicated compound inequality, we first simplify each part of the compound inequality and then find the union or intersection.

EXAMPLE 8

Calculator Close-Up

To check Example 8, press Y= and let $y_1 = x + 2$ and $y_2 = x - 6$. Now scroll through a table of values for y_1 and y_2. From the table you can see that y_1 is greater than 3 and y_2 is less than 7 precisely when x is between 1 and 13.

Intersection

Solve $x + 2 > 3$ and $x - 6 < 7$. Graph the solution set.

Solution

First simplify each simple inequality:

$$x + 2 - 2 > 3 - 2 \quad \text{and} \quad x - 6 + 6 < 7 + 6$$
$$x > 1 \quad \text{and} \quad x < 13$$

The intersection of these two solution sets is the set of numbers between (but not including) 1 and 13. Its graph is shown in Fig. 2.21. The solution set is written in interval notation as (1, 13).

$$\text{FIGURE 2.21}$$

EXAMPLE 9

Calculator Close-Up

To check Example 9, press Y= and let $y_1 = 5 - 7x$ and $y_2 = 3x - 2$. Now scroll through a table of values for y_1 and y_2. From the table you can see that either $y_1 \geq 12$ or $y_2 < 7$ is true for $x < 3$. Note also that for $x \geq 3$ both $y_1 \geq 12$ and $y_2 < 7$ are incorrect. The table supports the conclusion of Example 9.

Union

Graph the solution set to the inequality

$$5 - 7x \geq 12 \quad \text{or} \quad 3x - 2 < 7.$$

Solution

First solve each of the simple inequalities:

$$5 - 7x - 5 \geq 12 - 5 \quad \text{or} \quad 3x - 2 + 2 < 7 + 2$$
$$-7x \geq 7 \quad \text{or} \quad 3x < 9$$
$$x \leq -1 \quad \text{or} \quad x < 3$$

The union of the two solution intervals is $(-\infty, 3)$. The graph is shown in Fig. 2.22.

$$\text{FIGURE 2.22}$$

An inequality may be read from left to right or from right to left. Consider the inequality $1 < x$. If we read it in the usual way, we say, "1 is less than x." The meaning is clearer if we read the variable first. Reading from right to left, we say, "x is greater than 1."

Another notation is commonly used for the compound inequality

$$x > 1 \quad \text{and} \quad x < 13.$$

This compound inequality can also be written as

$$1 < x < 13.$$

Reading from left to right, we read $1 < x < 13$ as "1 is less than x is less than 13." The meaning of this inequality is clearer if we read the variable first and read the first inequality symbol from right to left. Reading the variable first, $1 < x < 13$ is read as "x is greater than 1 and less than 13." So x is between 1 and 13, and reading x first makes it clear.

CAUTION   We write $a < x < b$ only if $a < b$, and we write $a > x > b$ only if $a > b$. Similar rules hold for $\leq$ and $\geq$. So $4 < x < 9$ and $-6 \geq x \geq -8$ are correct uses of this notation, but $5 < x < 2$ is not correct. Also, the inequalities should *not* point in opposite directions as in $5 < x > 7$.

EXAMPLE 10

Another notation

Solve the inequality and graph the solution set:

$$-2 \leq 2x - 3 < 7$$

Calculator Close-Up

Do not use a table on your calculator as a method for solving an inequality. Use a table to check your algebraic solution and you will get a better understanding of inequalities.

Solution

This inequality could be written as the compound inequality

$$2x - 3 \geq -2 \qquad \text{and} \qquad 2x - 3 < 7.$$

However, there is no need to rewrite the inequality because we can solve it in its original form.

$$-2 + 3 \leq 2x - 3 + 3 < 7 + 3 \qquad \text{Add 3 to each part.}$$

$$1 \leq 2x < 10$$

$$\frac{1}{2} \leq \frac{2x}{2} < \frac{10}{2} \qquad \text{Divide each part by 2.}$$

$$\frac{1}{2} \leq x < 5$$

The solution set is $\left[\frac{1}{2}, 5\right)$, and its graph is shown in Fig. 2.23.

FIGURE 2.23   ■

EXAMPLE 11

Solving a compound inequality

Solve the inequality $-1 < 3 - 2x < 9$ and graph the solution set.

Calculator Close-Up

Let $y_1 = 3 - 2x$ and make a table. Scroll through the table to see that y_1 is between -1 and 9 when x is between -3 and 2. The table supports the conclusion of Example 11.

Solution

$$-1 - 3 < 3 - 2x - 3 < 9 - 3 \qquad \text{Subtract 3 from each part of the inequality.}$$

$$-4 < -2x < 6$$

$$2 > x > -3 \qquad \text{Divide each part by } -2 \text{ and reverse both inequality symbols.}$$

$$-3 < x < 2 \qquad \text{Rewrite the inequality with the smallest number on the left.}$$

The solution set is $(-3, 2)$, and its graph is shown in Fig. 2.24.

FIGURE 2.24   ■

Applications

When final exams are approaching, students are often interested in finding the final exam score that would give them a certain grade for a course.

E X A M P L E   1 2   Final exam scores

Fiana made a score of 76 on her midterm exam. For her to get a B in the course, the average of her midterm exam and final exam must be between 80 and 89 inclusive. What possible scores on the final exam would give Fiana a B in the course?

Helpful Hint

When you use two inequality symbols as in Example 12, they must both point in the same direction. In fact, we usually have them both point to the left so that the numbers increase in size from left to right.

Solution

Let x represent her final exam score. Between 80 and 89 inclusive means that an average between 80 and 89 as well as an average of exactly 80 or 89 will get a B. So the average of the two scores must be greater than or equal to 80 and less than or equal to 89.

$$80 \le \frac{x + 76}{2} \le 89$$

$$160 \le x + 76 \le 178 \quad \text{Multiply by 2.}$$

$$160 - 76 \le x \le 178 - 76 \quad \text{Subtract 76.}$$

$$84 \le x \le 102$$

If Fiana scores between 84 and 102 inclusive, she will get a B in the course.   ■

WARM-UPS

True or false? Explain your answer.

1. $3 < 5$ and $3 \le 10$
2. $3 < 5$ or $3 < 10$
3. $3 > 5$ and $3 < 10$
4. $3 \ge 5$ or $3 \le 10$
5. $4 < 8$ and $4 > 2$
6. $4 < 8$ or $4 > 2$
7. $-3 < 0 < -2$
8. $(3, \infty) \cap (8, \infty) = (8, \infty)$
9. $(3, \infty) \cup [8, \infty) = [8, \infty)$
10. $(-2, \infty) \cap (-\infty, 9) = (-2, 9)$

2.5   EXERCISES

Reading and Writing   After reading this section, write out the answers to these questions. Use complete sentences.

1. What is a compound inequality?

2. When is a compound inequality using "and" true?

3. When is a compound inequality using "or" true?

4. How do we solve compound inequalities?

5. What is the meaning of $a < b < c$?

6. What is the meaning of $5 < x > 7$?

Determine whether each compound inequality is true. See Examples 1 and 2.

7. $-6 < 5$ and $-6 > -3$
8. $3 < 5$ or $0 < -3$
9. $4 \le 4$ and $-4 \le 0$
10. $1 < 5$ and $1 > -3$
11. $6 < 5$ or $-4 > -3$
12. $4 \le -4$ or $0 \le 0$

Determine whether -4 satisfies each compound inequality. See Example 3.

13. $x < 5$ and $x > -3$
14. $x < 5$ or $x > -3$

15. $x - 3 \geq -7$ or $x + 1 > 1$

16. $2x \leq -8$ and $5x \leq 0$

17. $2x - 1 < -7$ or $-2x > 18$

18. $-3x > 0$ and $3x - 4 < 11$

Graph the solution set to each compound inequality. See Examples 4–7.

19. $x > -1$ and $x < 4$

20. $x \leq 3$ and $x \leq 0$

21. $x \geq 2$ or $x \geq 5$

22. $x < -1$ or $x < 3$

23. $x \leq 6$ or $x > -2$

24. $x > -2$ and $x \leq 4$

25. $x \leq 6$ and $x > 9$

26. $x < 7$ or $x > 0$

27. $x \leq 6$ or $x > 9$

28. $x \geq 4$ and $x \leq -4$

29. $x \geq 6$ and $x \leq 1$

30. $x > 3$ or $x < -3$

Solve each compound inequality. Write the solution set using interval notation and graph it. See Examples 8 and 9.

31. $x - 3 > 7$ or $3 - x > 2$

32. $x - 5 > 6$ or $2 - x > 4$

33. $3 < x$ and $1 + x > 10$

34. $-0.3x < 9$ and $0.2x > 2$

35. $\frac{1}{2}x > 5$ or $-\frac{1}{3}x < 2$

36. $5 < x$ or $3 - \frac{1}{2}x < 7$

37. $2x - 3 \leq 5$ and $x - 1 > 0$

38. $\frac{3}{4}x < 9$ and $-\frac{1}{3}x \leq -15$

39. $\frac{1}{2}x - \frac{1}{3} \geq -\frac{1}{6}$ or $\frac{2}{7}x \leq \frac{1}{10}$

40. $\frac{1}{4}x - \frac{1}{3} > -\frac{1}{5}$ and $\frac{1}{2}x < 2$

41. $0.5x < 2$ and $-0.6x < -3$

42. $0.3x < 0.6$ or $0.05x > -4$

Solve each compound inequality. Write the solution set in interval notation and graph it. See Examples 10 and 11.

43. $5 < 2x - 3 < 11$

44. $-2 < 3x + 1 < 10$

45. $-1 < 5 - 3x \leq 14$

46. $-1 \leq 3 - 2x < 11$

47. $-3 < \dfrac{3m + 1}{2} \leq 5$

48. $0 \leq \dfrac{3 - 2x}{2} < 5$

49. $-2 < \dfrac{1 - 3x}{-2} < 7$

50. $-3 < \dfrac{2x - 1}{3} < 7$

51. $3 \leq 3 - 5(x - 3) \leq 8$

52. $2 \leq 4 - \dfrac{1}{2}(x - 8) \leq 10$

Write each union or intersection of intervals as a single interval if possible.

53. $(2, \infty) \cup (4, \infty)$ **54.** $(-3, \infty) \cup (-6, \infty)$

55. $(-\infty, 5) \cap (-\infty, 9)$

56. $(-\infty, -2) \cap (-\infty, 1)$

57. $(-\infty, 4] \cap [2, \infty)$

58. $(-\infty, 8) \cap [3, \infty)$

59. $(-\infty, 5) \cup [-3, \infty)$

60. $(-\infty, -2] \cup (2, \infty)$

61. $(3, \infty) \cap (-\infty, 3]$

62. $[-4, \infty) \cap (-\infty, -6]$

63. $(3, 5) \cap [4, 8)$

64. $[-2, 4] \cap (0, 9]$

65. $[1, 4) \cup (2, 6]$

66. $[1, 3) \cup (0, 5)$

Write either a simple or a compound inequality that has the given graph as its solution set.

67.

68.

69.

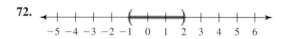

70.

71.

72.

73.

74.

75.

76.

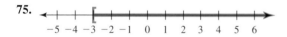

Solve each problem by using a compound inequality. See Example 12.

77. Aiming for a C. Professor Johnson gives only a midterm exam and a final exam. The semester average is computed by taking $\frac{1}{3}$ of the midterm exam score plus $\frac{2}{3}$ of the final exam score. To get a C, Beth must have a semester average between 70 and 79 inclusive. If Beth scored only 64 on the midterm, then for what range of scores on the final exam would Beth get a C?

78. Two tests only. Professor Davis counts his midterm as $\frac{2}{3}$ of the grade, and his final as $\frac{1}{3}$ of the grade. Jason scored only 64 on the midterm. What range of scores on the final exam would put Jason's average between 70 and 79 inclusive?

79. Keep on truckin'. Abdul is shopping for a new truck in a city with an 8% sales tax. There is also an $84 title and license fee to pay. He wants to get a good truck and plans to spend at least $12,000 but no more than $15,000. What is the price range for the truck?

80. Selling-price range. Renee wants to sell her car through a broker who charges a commission of 10% of the selling price. The book value of the car is $14,900, but Renee still owes $13,104 on it. Although the car is in only fair condition and will not sell for more than the book value, Renee must get enough to at least pay off the loan. What is the range of the selling price?

81. Hazardous to her health. Trying to break her smoking habit, Jane calculates that she smokes only three full cigarettes a day, one after each meal. The rest of the time she smokes on the run and smokes only half of the cigarette. She estimates that she smokes the equivalent of 5 to 12 cigarettes per day. How many times a day does she light up on the run?

82. Possible width. The length of a rectangle is 20 meters longer than the width. The perimeter must be between 80 and 100 meters. What are the possible values for the width of the rectangle?

83. Higher education. The formulas

$$B = 16.45n + 1062.45$$

and

$$M = 7.79n + 326.82$$

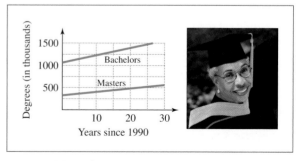

FIGURE FOR EXERCISE 83

can be used to approximate the number of bachelor's and master's degrees in thousands, respectively, awarded per year, *n* years after 1990 (National Center for Educational Statistics, www.nces.ed.gov).

a) How many bachelor's degrees were awarded in 2000?

b) In what year will the number of bachelor's degrees that are awarded reach 1.4 million?

c) What is the first year in which both *B* is greater than 1.4 million and *M* is greater than 0.55 million?

d) What is the first year in which either *B* is greater than 1.4 million or *M* is greater than 0.55 million?

84. **Senior citizens.** The number of senior citizens (65 and over) in the United States in millions *n* years after 1990 can be estimated by using the formula

$$s = 0.38n + 31.2$$

(U.S. Bureau of the Census, www.census.gov). The percentage of senior citizens living below the poverty level

n years after 1990 can be estimated by using the formula

$$p = -0.25n + 12.2.$$

a) How many senior citizens were there in 2000?

b) In what year will the percentage of seniors living below the poverty level reach 7%?

c) What is the first year in which we can expect both the number of seniors to be greater than 40 million and fewer than 7% living below the poverty level?

GETTING MORE INVOLVED

85. **Discussion.** If −*x* is between *a* and *b*, then what can you say about *x*?

86. **Discussion.** For which of the inequalities is the notation used correctly?
a) $-2 \le x < 3$ **b)** $-4 \ge x < 7$ **c)** $-1 \le x > 0$
d) $6 < x \le -8$ **e)** $5 \ge x \ge -9$

87. **Discussion.** In each case, write the resulting set of numbers in interval notation. Explain your answers.
a) Every number in (3, 8) is multiplied by 4.
b) Every number in [−2, 4) is multiplied by −5.

c) Three is added to every number in (−3, 6).
d) Every number in [3, 9] is divided by −3.

88. **Discussion.** Write the solution set using interval notation for each of these inequalities in terms of *s* and *t*. State any restrictions on *s* and *t*. For what values of *s* and *t* is the solution set empty?
a) $x > s$ and $x < t$
b) $x > s$ and $x > t$

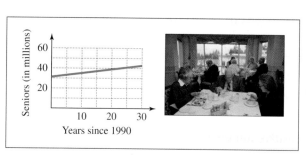

FIGURE FOR EXERCISE 84

2.6

ABSOLUTE VALUE EQUATIONS AND INEQUALITIES

In Chapter 1 we learned that absolute value measures the distance of a number from 0 on the number line. In this section we will learn to solve equations and inequalities involving absolute value.

Absolute Value Equations

Solving equations involving absolute value requires some techniques that are different from those studied in previous sections. For example, the solution set to the equation

$$|x| = 5$$

40. *Motor city.* Delmas flew to Detroit in 90 minutes and drove his new car back home in 6 hours. If he drove 150 mph slower than he flew, then how fast did he fly?

Speed to Detroit = x mph

Speed from Detroit = $x - 150$ mph

FIGURE FOR EXERCISE 40

2.4 *Solve each inequality. State the solution set using interval notation and graph it.*

41. $3 - 4x < 15$

42. $5 - 6x > 35$

43. $2(x - 3) > -6$

44. $4(5 - x) < 20$

45. $-\dfrac{3}{4}x \geq 6$

46. $-\dfrac{2}{3}x \leq 4$

47. $3(x + 2) > 5(x - 1)$

48. $4 - 2(x - 3) < 0$

49. $\dfrac{1}{2}x + 7 \leq \dfrac{3}{4}x - 5$

50. $\dfrac{5}{6}x - 3 \geq \dfrac{2}{3}x + 7$

2.5 *Solve each compound inequality. State the solution set using interval notation and graph it.*

51. $x + 2 > 3$ or $x - 6 < -10$

52. $x - 2 > 5$ or $x - 2 < -1$

53. $x > 0$ and $x - 6 < 3$

54. $x \leq 0$ and $x + 6 > 3$

55. $6 - x < 3$ or $-x < 0$

56. $-x > 0$ or $x + 2 < 7$

57. $2x < 8$ and $2(x - 3) < 6$

58. $\dfrac{1}{3}x > 2$ and $\dfrac{1}{4}x > 2$

59. $x - 6 > 2$ and $6 - x > 0$

60. $-\dfrac{1}{2}x < 6$ or $\dfrac{2}{3}x < 4$

61. $0.5x > 10$ or $0.1x < 3$

62. $0.02x > 4$ and $0.2x < 3$

63. $-2 \leq \dfrac{2x - 3}{10} \leq 1$

64. $-3 < \dfrac{4 - 3x}{5} < 2$

Write each union or intersection of intervals as a single interval.

65. $[1, 4) \cup (2, \infty)$

66. $(2, 5) \cup (-1, \infty)$

67. $(3, 6) \cap [2, 8]$

68. $[-1, 3] \cap [0, 8]$

69. $(-\infty, 5) \cup [5, \infty)$

70. $(-\infty, 1) \cup (0, \infty)$

71. $(-3, -1] \cap [-2, 5]$

72. $[-2, 4] \cap (4, 7]$

2.6 *Solve each absolute value equation and graph the solution set.*

73. $|x| + 2 = 16$

74. $\left|\dfrac{x}{2}\right| - 5 = -1$

75. $|4x - 12| = 0$

76. $|2x - 8| = 0$

77. $|x| = -5$

78. $\left|\dfrac{x}{2} - 5\right| = -1$

79. $|2x - 1| - 3 = 0$

80. $|5 - x| - 2 = 0$

Solve each absolute value inequality and graph the solution set.

81. $|2x| \geq 8$

82. $|5x - 1| \leq 14$

83. $\left|1 - \dfrac{x}{5}\right| > \dfrac{9}{5}$

84. $\left|1 - \dfrac{1}{6}x\right| < \dfrac{1}{2}$

85. $|x - 3| < -3$ **86.** $|x - 7| \leq -4$

87. $|x + 4| \geq -1$

88. $|6x - 1| \geq 0$

89. $1 - \dfrac{3}{2}|x - 2| < -\dfrac{1}{2}$

90. $1 > \dfrac{1}{2}|6 - x| - \dfrac{3}{4}$

MISCELLANEOUS

Solve each problem by using equations or inequalities.

91. *Rockbuster video.* Stephen plans to open a video rental store in Edmonton. Industry statistics show that 45% of the rental price goes for overhead. If the maximum that anyone will pay to rent a tape is $5 and Stephen wants a profit of at least $1.65 per tape, then in what range should the rental price be?

92. *Working girl.* Regina makes $6.80 per hour working in the snack bar. To keep her grant, she may not earn more

than $51 per week. What is the range of the number of hours per week that she may work?

93. *Skeletal remains.* Forensic scientists use the formula $h = 60.089 + 2.238F$ to predict the height h (in centimeters) for a male whose femur measures F centimeters. (See the accompanying figure.) In what range is the length of the femur for males between 150 centimeters and 180 centimeters in height? Round to the nearest tenth of a centimeter.

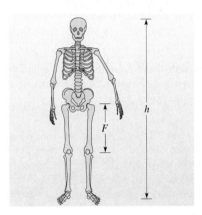

FIGURE FOR EXERCISE 93

94. *Female femurs.* Forensic scientists use the formula $h = 61.412 + 2.317F$ to predict the height h in centimeters for a female whose femur measures F centimeters.

a) Use the accompanying graph to estimate the femur length for a female with height of 160 centimeters.

b) In what range is the length of the femur for females who are over 170 centimeters tall?

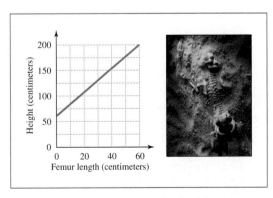

FIGURE FOR EXERCISE 94

95. *Car trouble.* Dane's car was found abandoned at mile marker 86 on the interstate. If Dane was picked up by the police on the interstate exactly 5 miles away, then at what mile marker was he picked up?

96. *Comparing scores.* Scott scored 72 points on the midterm, and Katie's score was more than 16 points away from Scott's. What was Katie's score?

97. *Year-end bonus.* A law firm has agreed to distribute 20% of its profits to its employees as a year-end bonus. To the firm's accountant, the bonus is an expense that must be used to determine the profit. That is, bonus = 20% × (profit before bonus − bonus). Given that the profit before the bonus is $300,000, find the amount of the bonus using the accountant's method. How does this answer compare to 20% of $300,000, which is what the employees want?

98. *Higher rate.* Suppose that the employees in Exercise 97 got the bonus that they wanted. To the accountant, what percent of the profits was given in bonuses?

99. *Dairy cattle.* Thirty percent of the dairy cattle in Washington County are Holsteins, whereas 60% of the dairy cattle in neighboring Cade County are Holsteins. In the combined two-county area, 50% of the 3600 dairy cattle are Holsteins. How many dairy cattle are in each county?

100. *Profitable business.* United Home Improvement (UHI) makes 20% profit on its good grade of vinyl siding, 30% profit on its better grade, and 60% profit on its best grade. So far this year, UHI has $40,000 in sales of good siding and $50,000 in sales of better siding. The company goal is to have at least an overall profit of 50% of total sales. What would the sales figures for the best grade of siding have to be to reach this goal?

For each graph in Exercises 101–118, write an equation or inequality that has the solution set shown by the graph. Use absolute value when possible.

101.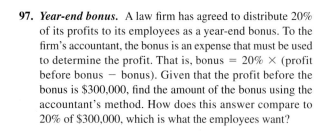

102.

103.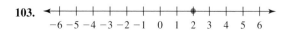

104.

105.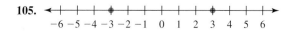

106.

107.

108.

109.

110.

111.

112.

113.

114.

115.

116.

117.

118.

CHAPTER 2 TEST

Solve each equation.

1. $-10x - 5 + 4x = -4x + 3$

2. $\dfrac{y}{2} - \dfrac{y-3}{3} = \dfrac{y+6}{6}$

3. $|w| + 3 = 9$

4. $|3 - 2(5 - x)| = 3$

Write y in terms of x.

5. $2x - 5y = 20$ **6.** $y = 3xy + 5$

Solve each inequality. State the solution set using interval notation and graph the solution set.

7. $|m - 6| \le 2$

8. $2|x - 3| - 5 > 15$

9. $2 - 3(w - 1) < -2w$

10. $2 < \dfrac{5 - 2x}{3} < 7$

11. $3x - 2 < 7$ and $-3x \le 15$

12. $\dfrac{2}{3}y < 4$ or $y - 3 < 12$

Solve each equation or inequality.

13. $|2x - 7| = -3$

14. $x - 4 > 1$ or $x < 12$ **15.** $3x < 0$ and $x - 5 > 2$

16. $|2x - 5| \le 0$ **17.** $|x - 3| < 0$

18. $x + 3x = 4x$ **19.** $2(x + 7) = 2x + 9$

20. $|x - 6| > -6$ **21.** $x - 0.04(x - 10) = 96.4$

Write a complete solution to each problem.

22. The perimeter of a rectangle is 84 meters. If the width is 16 meters less than the length, then what is the width of the rectangle?

23. If the area of a triangle is 21 square inches and the base is 3 inches, then what is the height?

24. Joan bought a gold chain marked 30% off. If she paid $210, then what was the original price?

25. How many liters of an 11% alcohol solution should be mixed with 60 liters of a 5% alcohol solution to obtain a mixture that is 7% alcohol?

26. Al and Brenda do the same job, but their annual salaries differ by more than $3,000. Assume, Al makes $28,000 per year and write an absolute value inequality to describe this situation. What are the possibilities for Brenda's salary?

Study Tip

Before you take an in-class exam on this chapter, work the sample test given here. Set aside one hour to work this test and use the answers in the back of this book to grade yourself. Even though your instructor might not ask exactly the same questions, you will get a good idea of your test readiness.

Simplify each expression.

1. $5x + 6x$

2. $5x \cdot 6x$

3. $\dfrac{6x + 2}{2}$

4. $5 - 4(2 - x)$

5. $(30 - 1)(30 + 1)$

6. $(30 + 1)^2$

7. $(30 - 1)^2$

8. $(2 + 3)^2$

9. $2^2 + 3^2$

10. $(8 - 3)(3 - 8)$

11. $(-1)(3 - 8)$

12. -2^2

13. $3x + 8 - 5(x - 1)$

14. $(-6)^2 - 4(-3)2$

15. $3^2 \cdot 2^3$

16. $4(-6) - (-5)(3)$

17. $-3x \cdot x \cdot x$

18. $(-1)(-1)(-1)(-1)(-1)(-1)$

Solve each equation.

19. $5x + 6x = 8x$

20. $5x + 6x = 11x$

21. $5x + 6x = 0$

22. $5x + 6 = 11x$

23. $3x + 1 = 0$

24. $5 - 4(2 - x) = 1$

25. $3x + 6 = 3(x + 2)$

26. $x - 0.01x = 990$

27. $|5x + 6| = 11$

Solve the problem.

28. *Cost analysis.* Diller Electronics can rent a copy machine for 5 years from American Business Supply for $75 per month plus 6 cents per copy. The same copier can be purchased for $8000, but then it costs only 2 cents per copy for supplies and maintenance. The purchased copier has no value after 5 years.

a) Use the accompanying graph to estimate the number of copies for 5 years for which the cost of renting would equal the cost of buying.

b) Write a formula for the 5-year cost under each plan.

c) Algebraically find the number of copies for which the 5-year costs would be equal.

d) If Diller makes 120,000 copies in 5 years, which plan is cheaper and by how much?

e) For what range of copies do the two plans differ by less than $500?

Study Tip

Don't wait until the final exam to review material. Do some review on a regular basis. The Making Connections exercises on this page can be used to review, compare, and contrast different concepts that you have studied. A good time to work these exercises is between a test and the start of new material.

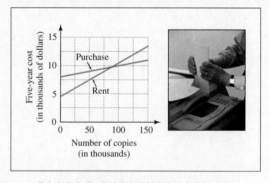

FIGURE FOR EXERCISE 28

Linear Equations and Inequalities in Two Variables

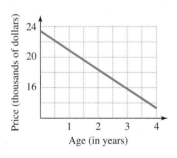

The first self-propelled automobile to carry passengers was built in 1801 by the British inventor Richard Trevithick. By 1911 about 600,000 automobiles were operated in the United States alone. Some were powered by steam and some by electricity, but most were powered by gasoline. In 1913, to meet the ever growing demand, Henry Ford increased production by introducing a moving assembly line to carry automobile parts. Today the United States is a nation of cars. Over 11 million automobiles are produced here annually, and total car registrations number over 114 million.

Prices for new cars rise every year. Today the most basic Ford Focus sells for $13,000 to $15,000, whereas Henry Ford's early model T sold for $850. Unfortunately, the moment you buy your new car its value begins to decrease. Much of the behavior of automobile prices can be modeled with linear equations. In Exercises 81 and 82 of Section 3.1 you will use linear equations to find increasing new car prices and depreciating used car prices.

3.1 GRAPHING LINES IN THE COORDINATE PLANE

In Chapter 2 we used the number line to illustrate the solution sets to equations and inequalities in one variable. In this chapter we will use a new coordinate system made from a pair of number lines to illustrate the solution sets to equations and inequalities in two variables.

Graphing Ordered Pairs

The **rectangular** or **Cartesian coordinate system** consists of a horizontal number line, the **x-axis,** and a vertical number line, the **y-axis,** as shown in Fig. 3.1. The intersection of the axes is the **origin.** The axes divide the coordinate plane, or the **xy-plane,** into four regions called **quadrants.** The quadrants are numbered as shown in Fig. 3.1, and they do not include any points on the axes.

Helpful Hint

In this chapter you will be doing a lot of graphing. Using graph paper will help you to understand the concepts and to recognize errors. For your convenience, a page of graph paper can be found at the end of this chapter. Make as many copies of it as you wish.

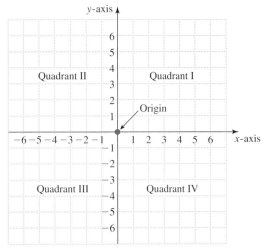

FIGURE 3.1

Just as every real number corrresponds to a point on the number line, every pair of real numbers corresponds to a point in the rectangular coordinate system. Locating a point in the rectangular coordinate system that corresponds to a pair of real numbers is referred to as **plotting** or **graphing** the point.

EXAMPLE 1

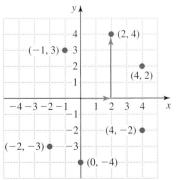

FIGURE 3.2

Plotting points

Graph the points corresponding to the pairs (2, 4), (4, 2), (−2, −3), (−1, 3), (0, −4), and (4, −2).

Solution

To plot (2, 4), start at the origin, move two units to the right, then up four units as shown in Fig. 3.2. To plot (4, 2), start at the origin, move four units to the right, then two units up as shown in Fig. 3.2. To plot (−2, −3), start at the origin, move two units to the left, then down three units. All six points are shown in Fig. 3.2. ∎

A pair of numbers, such as (2, 4), is called an **ordered pair** because the order of the numbers is important. The pairs (4, 2) and (2, 4) correspond to different points in Fig. 3.2. The first number in an ordered pair is the **x-coordinate** and the second number is the **y-coordinate.**

Note that we use the same notation for ordered pairs that we use for intervals of real numbers, but the meaning should always be clear from the context. The ordered pair (2, 4) represents a single pair of real numbers and a single point in the xy-plane, whereas the interval (2, 4) represents all real numbers between 2 and 4. Since ordered pairs correspond to points, we often refer to them as points.

The Midpoint and Distance Formulas

The **midpoint** of a line segment is a point that is on the line segment and equidistant from the end points. We use the notation $(\bar{x}, \bar{y})$ (read "x bar, y bar") for the midpoint of a line segment. The midpoint is found by "averaging" the x-coordinates and y-coordinates of the endpoints, in the same manner that you would average two test scores:

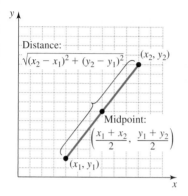

FIGURE 3.3

Midpoint Formula

The midpoint of the line segment with endpoints (x_1, y_1) and (x_2, y_2) is given by

$$(\bar{x}, \bar{y}) = \left(\frac{x_1 + x_2}{2}, \frac{y_1 + y_2}{2} \right).$$

The length of a line segment or the distance between the endpoints is given by the **distance formula.** See Fig. 3.3.

Distance Formula

The distance between the points (x_1, y_1) and (x_2, y_2) is

$$\sqrt{(x_2 - x_1)^2 + (y_2 - y_1)^2}.$$

We will see a proof of the distance formula later in this text.

E X A M P L E   2

Finding the midpoint and length of a line segment

Find the midpoint and length of the line segment with endpoints (1, 7) and (5, 4).

Solution

Use the midpoint formula with $(x_1, y_1) = (1, 7)$ and $(x_2, y_2) = (5, 4)$:

$$(\bar{x}, \bar{y}) = \left(\frac{1 + 5}{2}, \frac{7 + 4}{2} \right) = \left(3, \frac{11}{2} \right)$$

Use the distance formula to find the length of the line segment:

$$\sqrt{(x_2 - x_1)^2 + (y_2 - y_1)^2} = \sqrt{(5 - 1)^2 + (4 - 7)^2}$$
$$= \sqrt{16 + 9}$$
$$= \sqrt{25} = 5$$

Note that $(x_1, y_1) = (5, 4)$ and $(x_2, y_2) = (1, 7)$ gives the same midpoint and length. Try it. ∎

Graphing a Linear Equation

An equation in two variables, such as $y = 2x + 3$, is satisfied only if we find a number for x and a number for y that make it true. For example, if $x = 4$ and $y = 11$, then the equation becomes $11 = 2 \cdot 4 + 3$, which is a true statement. So the ordered pair (4, 11) satisfies the equation. The solution set to this equation consists of all ordered pairs that satisfy the equation. In set notation it is written as $\{(x, y) \mid y = 2x + 3\}$. However, this set notation does not shed any light on the solution set to $y = 2x + 3$. We can get a better understanding of the solution set if we graph all of the points in the solution set.

E X A M P L E   3

Graphing a linear equation

Graph the solution set to $y = 2x + 3$.

Solution

We arbitrarily choose some values for x and find corresponding y-values:

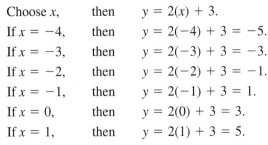

Choose x,	then	$y = 2(x) + 3$.
If $x = -4$,	then	$y = 2(-4) + 3 = -5$.
If $x = -3$,	then	$y = 2(-3) + 3 = -3$.
If $x = -2$,	then	$y = 2(-2) + 3 = -1$.
If $x = -1$,	then	$y = 2(-1) + 3 = 1$.
If $x = 0$,	then	$y = 2(0) + 3 = 3$.
If $x = 1$,	then	$y = 2(1) + 3 = 5$.

We can display the corresponding x- and y-values in this table:

x	-4	-3	-2	-1	0	1
$y = 2x + 3$	-5	-3	-1	1	3	5

FIGURE 3.4

Now plot the points $(-4, -5)$, $(-3, -3)$, $(-2, -1)$, $(-1, 1)$, $(0, 3)$, and $(1, 5)$, as shown in Fig. 3.4, and draw a line through them. There are infinitely many ordered pairs that satisfy $y = 2x + 3$, but they all lie on this line. The arrows on the ends of the line indicate that it extends without bound in both directions. The line in Fig. 3.4 is the graph of the solution set to $y = 2x + 3$ or simply the graph of $y = 2x + 3$. ■

Since the value of y in $y = 2x + 3$ is determined from the value of x, y is the **dependent variable** and x is the **independent variable.** Because the graph of $y = 2x + 3$ is a line, the equation is a **linear equation.**

When we draw any graph, we are attempting to put on paper an image that exists in our minds. The line for $y = 2x + 3$ that we have in mind has no thickness, is perfectly straight, and extends infinitely. All attempts to draw it on paper fall short. The best we can do is to use a sharp pencil to keep it as thin as possible, a ruler to make it as straight as possible, and arrows to indicate that it does not end.

Study Tip

It is a good idea to work with others, but don't be misled. Working a problem with help is not the same as working a problem on your own. In the end, mathematics is personal. Make sure that you can do it.

E X A M P L E   4

Graphing a linear equation

Graph $y + 2x = 1$. Plot at least four points.

Solution

First rewrite $y + 2x = 1$ as $y = -2x + 1$. Now arbitrarily select some values for x and find the corresponding y-values:

If $x = -1$,	then	$y = -2(-1) + 1 = 3$.
If $x = 0$,	then	$y = -2(0) + 1 = 1$.
If $x = 1$,	then	$y = -2(1) + 1 = -1$.
If $x = 2$,	then	$y = -2(2) + 1 = -3$.

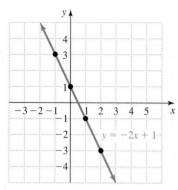

FIGURE 3.5

We can display the corresponding x- and y-coordinates in a table:

x	-1	0	1	2
$y = -2x + 1$	3	1	-1	-3

Plot the points $(-1, 3)$, $(0, 1)$, $(1, -1)$, and $(2, -3)$ and draw a line through them, as shown in Fig. 3.5. ■

Calculator Close-Up

To graph $y + 2x = 1$ with a graphing calculator, first press Y= and enter $y_1 = -2x + 1$.

Xmin = -10, X max = 10, Xscl = 1, Ymin = -10, Ymax = 10, Yscl = 1 These settings are referred to as the standard window.

Press GRAPH to draw the graph. Even though the calculator does not draw a very good straight line, it supports our conclusion that Fig. 3.5 is the graph of $y + 2x = 1$.

Next press WINDOW to set the viewing window as follows:

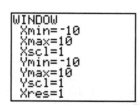

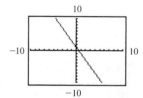

If the coefficient of a variable in a linear equation is 0, then that variable is usually omitted from the equation. For example, the equation $y = 0 \cdot x + 2$ is written as $y = 2$. Because x is multiplied by 0, any value of x can be used as long as y is 2. Because the y-coordinates are all the same, the graph is a horizontal line.

EXAMPLE 5

Graphing a horizontal line

Graph $y = 2$. Plot at least four points.

Solution

This table gives four points that satisfy $y = 2$, or $y = 0 \cdot x + 2$. Note that it is easy to determine y in this case because y is always 2.

x	-2	-1	0	1
$y = 0 \cdot x + 2$	2	2	2	2

The horizontal line through these points is shown in Fig. 3.6. ■

FIGURE 3.6

If the coefficient of y is 0 in a linear equation, then the graph is a vertical line.

E X A M P L E   6

Graphing a vertical line

Graph $x = 4$. Plot at least four points.

Solution

We can think of the equation $x = 4$ as $x = 4 + 0 \cdot y$. Now arbitrarily select some y-values and find the corresponding x-values:

$$
\begin{aligned}
&\text{If } y = -2, &&\text{then} &&x = 4 + 0(-2) = 4. \\
&\text{If } y = -1, &&\text{then} &&x = 4 + 0(-1) = 4. \\
&\text{If } y = 0, &&\text{then} &&x = 4 + 0(0) = 4.
\end{aligned}
$$

Because y is multiplied by 0, the equation is satisfied by every ordered pair with an x-coordinate of 4:

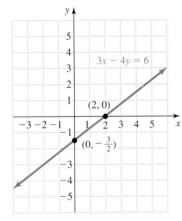

FIGURE 3.7

x	4	4	4	4	4	4
y	-2	-1	0	1	2	3

Graphing these points produces the vertical line shown in Fig. 3.7. ∎

Using Intercepts for Graphing

The **x-intercept** is the point where the line crosses the x-axis. The x-intercept has a y-coordinate of 0. Similarly, the **y-intercept** is the point where the line crosses the y-axis. The y-intercept has an x-coordinate of 0. If a line has distinct x- and y-intercepts, then they can be used as two points that determine the location of the line. Since horizontal lines, vertical lines, and lines through the origin do not have two distinct intercepts, they cannot be graphed using only the intercepts.

E X A M P L E   7

Using intercepts to graph

Use the intercepts to graph the line $3x - 4y = 6$.

Solution

Let $x = 0$ in $3x - 4y = 6$ to find the y-intercept:

$$
\begin{aligned}
3(0) - 4y &= 6 \\
-4y &= 6 \\
y &= -\frac{3}{2}
\end{aligned}
$$

Let $y = 0$ in $3x - 4y = 6$ to find the x-intercept:

$$
\begin{aligned}
3x - 4(0) &= 6 \\
3x &= 6 \\
x &= 2
\end{aligned}
$$

FIGURE 3.8

The y-intercept is $\left(0, -\frac{3}{2}\right)$, and the x-intercept is $(2, 0)$. The line through the intercepts is shown in Fig. 3.8. To check, find another point that satisfies the equation. The point $(-2, -3)$ satisfies the equation and is on the line in Fig. 3.8. ∎

C A U T I O N   Even though two points determine the location of a line, finding at least three points will help you to avoid errors.

Applications

When we graph equations involving the variables x and y we always put the independent variable x on the horizontal axis and the dependent variable y on the vertical axis. When we use variables such as C for cost, n for the number of items, r for radius, and A for area, we usually have one variable (the dependent variable) written in terms of the other (the independent variable). For example, in $C = 2n + 9$ and $A = \pi r^2$, C and A are the dependent variables, whereas n and r are the independent variables. When we graph these equations, we always put the independent variable on the horizontal axis and the dependent variable on the vertical axis.

E X A M P L E   8

Graphing a linear equation in an application

The cost per week C (in dollars) of producing n pairs of shoes for the Reebop Shoe Company is given by the linear equation $C = 2n + 8000$. Graph the equation for n between 0 and 800 inclusive ($0 \leq n \leq 800$).

Solution

Make a table of values for n and C as follows:

n	0	200	400	600	800
$C = 2n + 8000$	8000	8400	8800	9200	9600

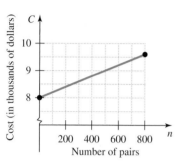

FIGURE 3.9

Graph the line as shown in Fig. 3.9. Because $C = 2n + 8000$ expresses C in terms of n, C is the dependent variable and the vertical axis is labeled C. To accommodate the large numbers, we let each unit on the n-axis represent 200 pairs and each unit on the C-axis represent $1000. ∎

Note how the axes in Fig. 3.9 are labeled. The n-axis starts at 0 and each tick mark represents 200 pairs. Because all of the costs were between $8000 and $9600 we omitted the tick marks for 1 through 7 and put a wave in the C-axis to indicate that some numbers are missing. Omitting the numbers from 1 through 7 makes the difference between the $8000 and $9600 costs look greater.

E X A M P L E   9

Writing a linear equation

A store manager is ordering shirts at $20 each and jackets at $30 each. The total cost of the order must be $1200. Write an equation for the total cost and graph it. If she orders 15 shirts, then how many jackets can she order?

Solution

Let s be the number of shirts in the order and j be the number of jackets in the order. Since the total cost is $1200 we can write

$$20s + 30j = 1200.$$

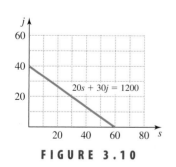

FIGURE 3.10

If $s = 0$, then $30j = 1200$ or $j = 40$. If $j = 0$, then $20s = 1200$ or $s = 60$. Graph the line through $(0, 40)$ and $(60, 0)$ as in Fig. 3.10. Note that we arbitrarily put s on the horizontal axis and j on the vertical axis. If $s = 15$, find j as follows:

$$20(15) + 30j = 1200$$
$$300 + 30j = 1200$$
$$30j = 900$$
$$j = 30$$

If she orders 15 shirts then she must order 30 jackets.

In Example 9, the numbers of shirts and jackets in the order must be whole numbers and every possible order corresponds to a point on the line in Fig. 3.10. However, points on the line whose coordinates are not whole numbers do not correspond to possible orders. Even though the line does not show the possible orders exactly, we draw it because it is more convenient than finding every possible order and then plotting just those points. ∎

WARM-UPS

True or false? Explain your answer.

1. The point $(2, 5)$ satisfies the equation $3y - 2x = -4$.
2. The vertical axis is usually called the x-axis.
3. The point $(0, 0)$ is in quadrant I.
4. The point $(0, 1)$ is on the y-axis.
5. The graph of $x = 7$ is a vertical line.
6. The graph of $8 - y = 0$ is a horizontal line.
7. The y-intercept for the line $y = 2x - 3$ is $(0, -3)$.
8. If $C = 3n + 4$, then $C = 10$ when $n = 2$.
9. If $P = 3x$ and $P = 12$, then $x = 36$.
10. The vertical axis should be A when graphing $A = \pi r^2$.

3.1 EXERCISES

Reading and Writing *After reading this section, write out the answers to these questions. Use complete sentences.*

1. What is the point called at the intersection of the x- and y-axis?

2. What is an ordered pair?

3. What are the x- and y-intercepts?

4. What type of equation has a graph that is a horizontal line?

5. What type of equation has a graph that is a vertical line?

6. Which variable usually goes on the vertical axis?

Plot the following points in a rectangular coordinate system. For each point, name the quadrant in which it lies or the axis on which it lies. See Example 1.

7. $(2, 5)$

8. $(-5, 1)$

9. $\left(-3, -\dfrac{1}{2}\right)$

10. $(-2, -6)$

11. $(0, 4)$

12. $(0, 2)$

13. $(\pi, -1)$

14. $\left(\dfrac{4}{3}, 0\right)$

15. $(-4, 3)$

16. $(0, -3)$

17. $\left(\dfrac{3}{2}, 0\right)$

18. $(3, 2)$

19. $\left(0, -\dfrac{7}{3}\right)$

20. $\left(4, -\dfrac{10}{3}\right)$

Find the midpoint and length of the line segment with the given endpoints. See Example 2.

21. $(2, 5)$ and $(5, 1)$

22. $(1, 7)$ and $(5, 10)$

23. $(-2, 4)$ and $(6, -2)$

24. $(-3, 5)$ and $(3, -3)$

25. $(3, 1)$ and $(-9, -4)$

26. $(-3, -4)$ and $(2, 8)$

27. $(-1, 4)$ and $(1, 1)$

28. $(-3, -4)$ and $(-6, 1)$

Graph each linear equation. Plot four points for each line.
See Examples 3–6.

29. $y = x + 1$

30. $y = x - 1$

31. $y = -2x + 3$

32. $y = 2x - 3$

33. $y = x$

34. $y = -x$

35. $y = 3$

36. $y = -2$

37. $y = 1 - x$

38. $y = 2 - x$

39. $x = 2$

40. $x = -3$

41. $y = \dfrac{1}{2}x - 1$

42. $y = \dfrac{1}{3}x - 2$

43. $y + 3 = 0$

44. $y + 4 = 0$

45. $x - 4 = 0$

46. $x + 5 = 0$

47. $y = \dfrac{1}{2}x$

48. $y = -\dfrac{2}{3}x$

57. $x - y + 5 = 0$

58. $x + y + 7 = 0$

49. $3x + y = 5$

50. $x + 2y = 4$

59. $2x + 3y = 5$

60. $3x - 4y = 7$

51. $6x + 3y = 0$

52. $2x + 4y = 0$

61. $2x - 3y = 60$

62. $2x + 3y = 30$

53. $y = 2x - 20$

54. $y = 40 - 2x$

63. $y = 2x - 4$

64. $y = -3x + 6$

Find the x- and y-intercepts for each line and use them to graph the line. See Example 7.

55. $4x - 3y = 12$

56. $2x + 5y = 20$

65. $y = -\dfrac{1}{2}x - 20$

66. $y = \dfrac{1}{3}x + 10$

Find all intercepts for each line. Some of these lines have only one intercept.

67. $3x - 5y = 15$

68. $9x + 8y = 72$

69. $y = 5x$

70. $y = -4x$

71. $6x + 3 = 0$

72. $40x + 5 = 0$

73. $12 + 18y = 0$

74. $2 - 10y = 0$

75. $2 - 4y = 8x$

76. $9x + 3 = 12y$

Complete the given ordered pairs so that each ordered pair satisfies the given equation.

77. $(2, \ \ ), (\ \ , -3), \quad y = -3x + 6$

78. $(-1, \ \ ), (\ \ , 4), \quad y = \dfrac{1}{2}x + 2$

79. $(-4, \ \ ), (\ \ , 6), \quad \dfrac{1}{2}x - \dfrac{1}{3}y = 9$

80. $(3, \ \ ), (\ \ , -1), \quad 2x - 3y = 5$

Solve each problem. See Examples 8 and 9.

81. *Camaro inflation.* The rising list price P (in dollars) for a new Camaro Z28 Coupe can be modeled by the equation $P = 320n + 22{,}765$, where n is the number of years since 2000 (www.edmunds.com).
a) What will be the list price for a new Z28 Coupe in 2008?
b) What is the annual increase in list price?
c) Graph the equation for $0 \le n \le 10$.

82. *Camaro Z28 depreciation.* The 2002 average retail price P (in dollars) for an n-year-old Camaro Z28 Coupe can be modeled by the equation $P = 23{,}405 - 2{,}530n$, where $0 \le n \le 4$ (www. edmunds.com).
a) What was the average retail price of a 4-year-old Z28 in 2002?

b) How much does this model depreciate each year?
c) Graph the equation for $0 \le n \le 4$.

83. *Rental cost.* For a one-day car rental the X-press Car Company charges C dollars, where C is determined by the formula $C = 0.26m + 42$ and m is the number of miles driven.
a) What is the charge for a car driven 400 miles?
b) Sketch a graph of the equation for m ranging from 0 to 1000.

84. *Measuring risk.* The Friendly Bob Loan Company gives each applicant a rating, t, from 0 to 10 according to the applicant's ability to repay, a higher rating indicating higher risk. The interest rate, r, is then determined by the formula $r = 0.02t + 0.15$.
a) If your rating were 8, then what would be your interest rate?
b) Sketch the graph of the equation for t ranging from 0 to 10.

85. *Little Chicago pizza.* The equation $C = 0.50t + 8.95$ gives the customer's cost in dollars for a pan pizza, where t is the number of toppings.
a) Find the cost of a five-topping pizza.
b) Find t if $C = 14.45$ and interpret your result.

86. *Long distance charges.* The formula $L = 0.10n + 4.95$ gives the monthly bill in dollars for AT&T's one-rate

We measure the steepness of a line in the same way that we measure steepness of a road or a roof. The slope of a line is the ratio of the change in y-coordinate, or the **rise,** to the change in x-coordinate, or the **run,** between two points on the line.

Slope

$$\text{Slope} = \frac{\text{change in } y\text{-coordinate}}{\text{change in } x\text{-coordinate}} = \frac{\text{rise}}{\text{run}}$$

Consider the line in Fig. 3.12(a). In going from (0, 1) to (1, 3), there is a change of $+1$ in the x-coordinate and a change of $+2$ in the y-coordinate, or a run of 1 and a rise of 2. So the slope is $\frac{2}{1}$ or 2. If we move from (1, 3) to (0, 1) as in Fig. 3.12(b) the rise is -2 and the run is -1. So the slope is $\frac{-2}{-1}$ or 2. If we start at either point and move to the other point, we get the same slope.

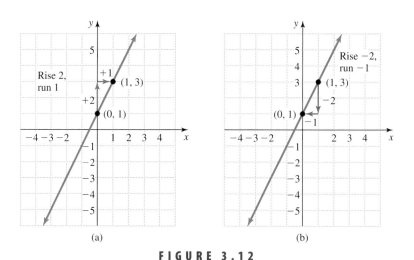

FIGURE 3.12

E X A M P L E   1

Finding the slope from a graph

Find the slope of each line by going from point A to point B.

a)
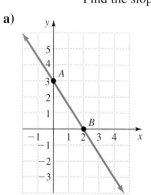

b)
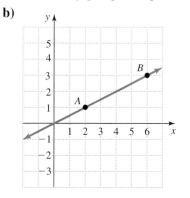

c)
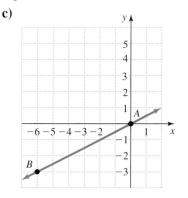

Solution

a) *A* is located at (0, 3) and *B* at (2, 0). In going from *A* to *B*, the change in *y* is -3 and the change in *x* is 2. So

$$\text{slope} = \frac{-3}{2} = -\frac{3}{2}.$$

b) In going from *A*(2, 1) to *B*(6, 3), we must rise 2 and run 4. So

$$\text{slope} = \frac{2}{4} = \frac{1}{2}.$$

c) In going from *A*(0, 0) to *B*(−6, −3), we find that the rise is -3 and the run is -6. So

$$\text{slope} = \frac{-3}{-6} = \frac{1}{2}.$$ ∎

Note that in Example 1(c) we found the slope of the line of Example 1(b) by using two different points. The slope is the ratio of the lengths of the two legs of a right triangle whose hypotenuse is on the line. See Fig. 3.13. As long as one leg is vertical and the other leg is horizontal, all such triangles for a given line have the same shape: They are similar triangles. Because ratios of corresponding sides in similar triangles are equal, the slope has the same value no matter which two points of the line are used to find it.

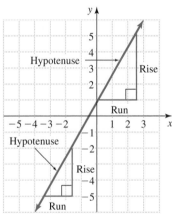

FIGURE 3.13

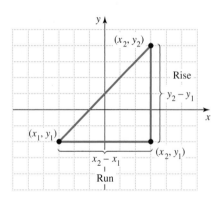

FIGURE 3.14

Using Coordinates to Find Slope

We can obtain the rise and run from a graph, or we can get them without a graph by subtracting the *y*-coordinates to get the rise and the *x*-coordinates to get the run for two points on the line. See Fig. 3.14.

Slope Using Coordinates

The slope *m* of the line containing the points (x_1, y_1) and (x_2, y_2) is given by

$$m = \frac{y_2 - y_1}{x_2 - x_1}, \qquad \text{provided that } x_2 - x_1 \neq 0.$$

E X A M P L E   2

Finding slope from coordinates

Find the slope of each line.

a) The line through $(2, 5)$ and $(6, 3)$

b) The line through $(-2, 3)$ and $(-5, -1)$

c) The line through $(-6, 4)$ and the origin

Solution

a) Let $(x_1, y_1) = (2, 5)$ and $(x_2, y_2) = (6, 3)$. The assignment of (x_1, y_1) and (x_2, y_2) is arbitrary.

$$m = \frac{y_2 - y_1}{x_2 - x_1} = \frac{3 - 5}{6 - 2} = \frac{-2}{4} = -\frac{1}{2}$$

b) Let $(x_1, y_1) = (-5, -1)$ and $(x_2, y_2) = (-2, 3)$:

$$m = \frac{y_2 - y_1}{x_2 - x_1} = \frac{3 - (-1)}{-2 - (-5)} = \frac{4}{3}$$

c) Let $(x_1, y_1) = (0, 0)$ and $(x_2, y_2) = (-6, 4)$:

$$m = \frac{4 - 0}{-6 - 0} = \frac{4}{-6} = -\frac{2}{3}$$

■

C A U T I O N   Do not reverse the order of subtraction from numerator to denominator when finding the slope. If you divide $y_2 - y_1$ by $x_1 - x_2$, you will get the wrong sign for the slope.

E X A M P L E   3

Slope for horizontal and vertical lines

Find the slope of each line.

a)

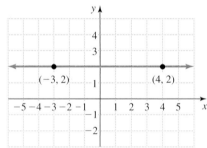

b)

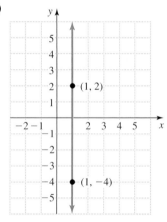

Solution

a) Using $(-3, 2)$ and $(4, 2)$ to find the slope of the horizontal line, we get

$$m = \frac{2 - 2}{-3 - 4}$$

$$= \frac{0}{-7} = 0.$$

Think about what slope means to skiers. No one skis on cliffs or even refers to them as slopes.

Zero slope

Small slope

Larger slope

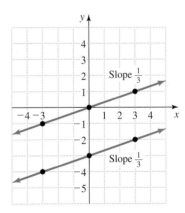

Undefined slope

b) Using $(1, -4)$ and $(1, 2)$ to find the slope of the vertical line, we get $x_2 - x_1 = 0$. Because the definition of slope using coordinates says that $x_2 - x_1$ must be nonzero, the slope is undefined for this line.   ∎

Since the y-coordinates are equal for any two points on a horizontal line, $y_2 - y_1 = 0$ and the slope is 0. Since the x-coordinates are equal for any two points on a vertical line, $x_2 - x_1 = 0$ and the slope is undefined.

Horizontal and Vertical Lines

The slope of any horizontal line is 0.
Slope is undefined for any vertical line.

CAUTION   Do not say that a vertical line has no slope because "no slope" could be confused with 0 slope, the slope of a horizontal line.

As you move the tip of your pencil from left to right along a line with positive slope, the y-coordinates are increasing. As you move the tip of your pencil from left to right along a line with negative slope, the y-coordinates are decreasing. See Fig. 3.15.

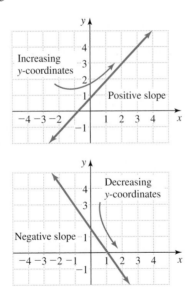

FIGURE 3.15

FIGURE 3.16

Parallel Lines

Consider the two lines shown in Fig. 3.16. Each of these lines has a slope of $\frac{1}{3}$, and these lines are parallel. In general, we have the following fact.

Parallel Lines

Nonvertical parallel lines have equal slopes.

Of course, any two vertical lines are parallel, but we cannot say that they have equal slopes because slope is not defined for vertical lines.

E X A M P L E   4

Parallel lines

Line *l* goes through the origin and is parallel to the line through $(-2, 3)$ and $(4, -5)$. Find the slope of line *l*.

Solution

The line through $(-2, 3)$ and $(4, -5)$ has slope

$$m = \frac{-5 - 3}{4 - (-2)} = \frac{-8}{6} = -\frac{4}{3}.$$

Because line *l* is parallel to a line with slope $-\frac{4}{3}$, the slope of line *l* is $-\frac{4}{3}$ also. ■

Perpendicular Lines

The lines shown in Fig. 3.17 have slopes 2 and $-\frac{1}{2}$. These two lines appear to be perpendicular to each other. It can be shown that *a line is perpendicular to another line if its slope is the negative of the reciprocal of the slope of the other.*

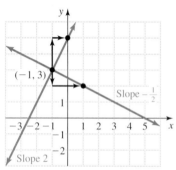

FIGURE 3.17

Perpendicular Lines

Two lines with slopes m_1 and m_2 are perpendicular if and only if

$$m_1 = -\frac{1}{m_2}.$$

Note that the relationship between slopes of perpendicular lines can also be expressed by the equation $m_1 \cdot m_2 = -1$. Of course, any vertical line and any horizontal line are perpendicular, but their slopes do not satisfy this equation because slope is undefined for vertical lines.

E X A M P L E   5

Perpendicular lines

Line *l* contains the point $(1, 6)$ and is perpendicular to the line through $(-4, 1)$ and $(3, -2)$. Find the slope of line *l*.

Solution

The line through $(-4, 1)$ and $(3, -2)$ has slope

$$m = \frac{1 - (-2)}{-4 - 3} = \frac{3}{-7} = -\frac{3}{7}.$$

Because line *l* is perpendicular to a line with slope $-\frac{3}{7}$, the slope of line *l* is $\frac{7}{3}$. ■

Applications of Slope

When a geometric figure is located in a coordinate system, we can use slope to determine whether it has any parallel or perpendicular sides.

E X A M P L E   6

Using slope with geometric figures

Determine whether $(-3, 2)$, $(-2, -1)$, $(4, 1)$, and $(3, 4)$ are the vertices of a rectangle.

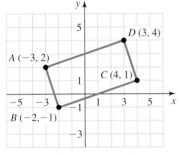

FIGURE 3.18

Solution

Figure 3.18 shows the quadrilateral determined by these points. If a parallelogram has at least one right angle, then it is a rectangle. Calculate the slope of each side.

$$m_{AB} = \frac{2 - (-1)}{-3 - (-2)}$$

$$= \frac{3}{-1} = -3$$

$$m_{CD} = \frac{1 - 4}{4 - 3}$$

$$= \frac{-3}{1} = -3$$

$$m_{BC} = \frac{-1 - 1}{-2 - 4}$$

$$= \frac{-2}{-6} = \frac{1}{3}$$

$$m_{AD} = \frac{2 - 4}{-3 - 3}$$

$$= \frac{-2}{-6} = \frac{1}{3}$$

Because the opposite sides have the same slope, they are parallel, and the figure is a parallelogram. Because $\frac{1}{3}$ is the opposite of the reciprocal of -3, the intersecting sides are perpendicular. Therefore the figure is a rectangle. ■

The slope of a line is a rate. The slope tells us how much the dependent variable changes for a change of 1 in the independent variable. For example, if the horizontal axis is hours and the vertical axis is miles, then the slope is miles per hour (mph). If the horizontal axis is days and the vertical axis is dollars, then the slope is dollars per day.

E X A M P L E   7

Interpreting slope

Worldwide carbon dioxide (CO_2) emissions have increased from 14 billion tons in 1970 to 26 billion tons in 2000 (World Resources Institute, www.wri.org).

a) Find and interpret the slope of the line in Fig. 3.19.

b) Use the slope to predict the amount of worldwide CO_2 emissions in 2010.

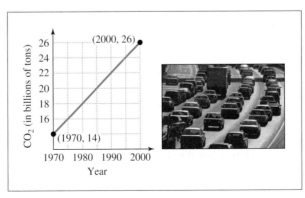

FIGURE 3.19

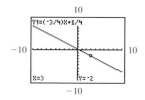

Solution

a) First find the slope:

$$m = \frac{y_2 - y_1}{x_2 - x_1} = \frac{7 - 5}{4-3} = 2$$

Now use the slope and one point, say $(3, 5)$, in the point-slope form:

$$y - y_1 = m(x - x_1) \quad \text{Point-slope form}$$
$$y - 5 = 2(x - 3) \quad \text{Substitute } m = 2, (x_1, y_1) = (3, 5).$$
$$y - 5 = 2x - 6 \quad \text{Distributive property}$$
$$y = 2x - 1 \quad \text{Solve for } y.$$

Because $(3, 5)$ and $(4, 7)$ both satisfy $y = 2x - 1$, we can be sure that we have the correct equation.

b) First find the slope of the line through $(3, -2)$ and $(-1, 1)$:

$$m = \frac{1 - (-2)}{-1 - 3}$$
$$= \frac{3}{-4} = -\frac{3}{4}$$

Now use this slope and one of the points, say $(3, -2)$, to write the equation in point-slope form:

$$y - (-2) = -\frac{3}{4}(x - 3) \quad \text{Point-slope form}$$
$$y + 2 = -\frac{3}{4}x + \frac{9}{4} \quad \text{Distributive property}$$
$$y = -\frac{3}{4}x + \frac{1}{4} \quad \text{Solve for } y: \frac{9}{4} - 2 = \frac{9}{4} - \frac{8}{4} = \frac{1}{4}.$$

Note that we would get the same equation if we had used slope $-\frac{3}{4}$ and the other point $(-1, 1)$. Try it. ∎

We know that if a line has slope m, then the slope of any line perpendicular to it is $-\frac{1}{m}$, provided $m \neq 0$. We also know that nonvertical parallel lines have equal slopes. These facts are used in Example 3.

E X A M P L E   3

Writing equations of perpendicular and parallel lines

In each case find the equation for line l and then solve it for y.

a) Line l goes through $(2, 0)$ and is perpendicular to the line through $(5, -1)$ and $(-1, 3)$.

b) Line l goes through $(-1, 6)$ and is parallel to the line through $(2, 4)$ and $(7, -11)$.

Solution

a) First find the slope of the line through $(5, -1)$ and $(-1, 3)$:

$$m = \frac{3 - (-1)}{-1 - 5} = \frac{4}{-6} = -\frac{2}{3}$$

Because line l is perpendicular to this line, line l has slope $\frac{3}{2}$. Now use $(2, 0)$ and the slope $\frac{3}{2}$ in the point-slope formula to get the equation of line l:

$$y - 0 = \frac{3}{2}(x - 2)$$

$$y = \frac{3}{2}x - 3 \quad \text{Distributive property}$$

b) First find the slope of the line through $(2, 4)$ and $(7, -11)$:

$$m = \frac{-11 - 4}{7 - 2} = \frac{-15}{5} = -3$$

Since parallel lines have equal slopes, use the slope -3 and the point $(-1, 6)$:

$$
\begin{aligned}
y - 6 &= -3(x - (-1)) \quad &\text{Point-slope form} \\
y - 6 &= -3(x + 1) \quad &\text{Simplify.} \\
y - 6 &= -3x - 3 \quad &\text{Distributive property} \\
y &= -3x + 3 \quad &\text{Solve for } y.
\end{aligned}
$$

■

Calculator Close-Up

With slope-intercept form and a graphing calculator, it is easy to see how the slope affects the steepness of a line. The graphs of $y_1 = \frac{1}{2}x$, $y_2 = x$, $y_3 = 2x$, and $y_4 = 3x$ are all shown on the accompanying screen.

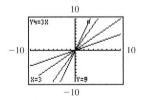

Slope-Intercept Form

The line $y = -3x - 1$ in Example 1 has slope -3. To find the y-intercept of this line, let $x = 0$ in $y = -3x - 1$: $y = -3(0) - 1 = -1$. The y-intercept is $(0, -1)$. Its y-coordinate appears in the equation:

$$y = -3x - 1$$

Slope y-intercept $(0, -1)$

Because the slope and y-intercept can be read from the equation when it is solved for y, this form of the equation of the line is called slope-intercept form.

> ### Slope-Intercept Form
>
> The equation of a line in **slope-intercept form** is
>
> $$y = mx + b,$$
>
> where m is the slope and $(0, b)$ is the y-intercept.

E X A M P L E   4

Writing an equation given its slope and y-intercept

Write the slope-intercept form of the equation of the line shown in Fig. 3.21.

Solution

From Fig. 3.21 we see that the y-intercept is $(0, 3)$. If we start at the y-intercept and move down 2 and 3 to the right, we get to another point on the line. So the slope is $-\frac{2}{3}$. The equation of this line in slope-intercept form is

$$y = -\frac{2}{3}x + 3.$$

■

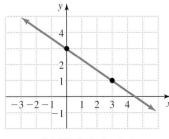

FIGURE 3.21

Standard Form

If x students paid \$5 each and y adults paid \$7 each to attend a play for which the ticket sales totaled \$1900, then we can write the equation $5x + 7y = 1900$. This form of a linear equation is common in applications. It is called standard form.

Standard Form

The equation of a line in **standard form** is

$$Ax + By = C,$$

where A, B, and C are real numbers with A and B not both zero.

The numbers A, B, and C in standard form can be any real numbers, but it is a common practice to write standard form using only integers and a positive coefficient for x.

E X A M P L E   5

Changing to standard form

Write the equation $y = \frac{1}{2}x - \frac{3}{4}$ in standard form using only integers and a positive coefficient for x.

Helpful Hint

Solve $Ax + By = C$ for y, to get

$$y = \frac{-A}{B}x + \frac{C}{B}.$$

So the slope of $Ax + By = C$ is $-\frac{A}{B}$. This fact can be used in checking standard form. The slope of $2x - 4y = 3$ in Example 5 is $\frac{-2}{-4}$ or $\frac{1}{2}$, which is the slope of the original equation.

Solution

Use the properties of equality to get the equation in the form $Ax + By = C$:

$$y = \frac{1}{2}x - \frac{3}{4} \qquad \text{Original equation}$$

$$-\frac{1}{2}x + y = -\frac{3}{4} \qquad \text{Subtract } \tfrac{1}{2}x \text{ from each side.}$$

$$4\left(-\frac{1}{2}x + y\right) = 4\left(-\frac{3}{4}\right) \qquad \begin{array}{l}\text{Multiply each side by 4 to}\\ \text{get integral coefficients.}\end{array}$$

$$-2x + 4y = -3 \qquad \text{Distributive property}$$

$$2x - 4y = 3 \qquad \begin{array}{l}\text{Multiply by } -1 \text{ to make the}\\ \text{coefficient of } x \text{ positive.}\end{array}$$ ∎

To find the slope and y-intercept of a line written in standard form, we convert the equation to slope-intercept form.

E X A M P L E   6

Changing to slope-intercept form

Find the slope and y-intercept of the line $3x - 2y = 5$.

Helpful Hint

Note that every term in a linear equation in two variables is either a constant or a multiple of a variable. That is why equations in one variable of the form $ax + b = 0$ were called linear equations in Chapter 2.

Solution

Solve for y to get slope-intercept form:

$$3x - 2y = 5 \qquad \text{Original equation}$$

$$-2y = -3x + 5 \qquad \text{Subtract } 3x \text{ from each side.}$$

$$y = \frac{3}{2}x - \frac{5}{2} \qquad \text{Divide each side by } -2.$$

The slope is $\frac{3}{2}$, and the y-intercept is $\left(0, -\frac{5}{2}\right)$. ∎

You learned in Section 3.1 that the graph of the equation $x = 4$ is a vertical line. Because slope is undefined for vertical lines, the equation of this line cannot be written in slope-intercept form or point-slope form. Only nonvertical lines can be written in those forms. However, a vertical line can be written in standard form. For example,

$$x = 4$$

can be written as

$$1 \cdot x + 0 \cdot y = 4.$$

Every line has an equation in standard form.

E X A M P L E   7

Finding the equation of a line

Write an equation in standard form with integral coefficients for the line l through $(2, 5)$ that is perpendicular to the line $2x + 3y = 1$.

Solution

First solve the equation $2x + 3y = 1$ for y to find its slope:

$$2x + 3y = 1$$
$$3y = -2x + 1$$
$$y = -\frac{2}{3}x + \frac{1}{3} \quad \text{The slope is } -\frac{2}{3}.$$

The slope of line l is the opposite of the reciprocal of $-\frac{2}{3}$. So line l has slope $\frac{3}{2}$ and goes through $(2, 5)$. Now use the point-slope form to write the equation:

$$y - 5 = \frac{3}{2}(x - 2) \quad \text{Point-slope form}$$
$$y - 5 = \frac{3}{2}x - 3 \quad \text{Distributive property}$$
$$y = \frac{3}{2}x + 2$$
$$-\frac{3}{2}x + y = 2$$
$$3x - 2y = -4 \quad \text{Multiply each side by } -2.$$

So $3x - 2y = -4$ is the standard form of the equation of the line through $(2, 5)$ that is perpendicular to $2x + 3y = 1$.   ∎

Calculator Close-Up

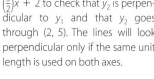

Graph $y_1 = \left(-\frac{2}{3}\right)x + \frac{1}{3}$ and $y_2 = \left(\frac{3}{2}\right)x + 2$ to check that y_2 is perpendicular to y_1 and that y_2 goes through $(2, 5)$. The lines will look perpendicular only if the same unit length is used on both axes.

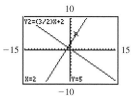

Some calculators have a feature that adjusts the window to get the same unit length on both axes.

Using Slope-Intercept Form for Graphing

In the slope-intercept form, a point on the line (the y-intercept) and the slope are readily available. To graph a line, we can start at the y-intercept and count off the rise and run to get a second point on the line.

E X A M P L E   8

Using slope and y-intercept to graph

Graph the line $2x - 3y = -3$.

Solution

First write the equation in slope-intercept form:

$$2x - 3y = -3$$
$$-3y = -2x - 3$$
$$y = \frac{2}{3}x + 1$$

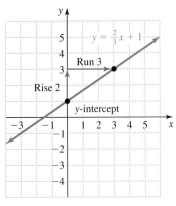

FIGURE 3.22

The slope is $\frac{2}{3}$, and the y-intercept is $(0, 1)$. Start at $(0, 1)$ on the y-axis, then rise 2 and run 3 to locate a second point on the line. Because there is only one line containing any two given points, these two points determine the line. See Fig. 3.22. ∎

The three methods that we used for graphing linear equations are summarized as follows.

> **Methods for Graphing a Linear Equation**
>
> **1.** Arbitrarily select some points that satisfy the equation, and draw a line through them.
>
> **2.** Find the x- and y-intercepts (provided that they are not the origin), and draw a line through them.
>
> **3.** Start at the y-intercept and use the slope to locate a second point, then draw a line through the two points.

If the y-coordinate of the y-intercept is an integer and the slope is a rational number, then it is usually the easiest to use the y-intercept and slope.

Applications

The linear equation $y = mx + b$ with $m \neq 0$ is a formula that expresses y in terms of x. In Example 9, we use the point-slope formula to write Fahrenheit temperature in terms of Celsius temperature.

E X A M P L E   9   **Writing a linear equation given two points**

The equation that expresses Fahrenheit temperature F in terms of Celsius temperature C is linear. Water freezes at $0°C$ or $32°F$ and boils at $100°C$ or $212°F$. Find the linear equation.

Solution

We want the equation of the line that contains the points $(0, 32)$ and $(100, 212)$ as shown in Fig. 3.23. Use C as the independent variable (x) and F as the dependent variable (y). The slope of the line is

$$m = \frac{F_2 - F_1}{C_2 - C_1} = \frac{212 - 32}{100 - 0} = \frac{180}{100} = \frac{9}{5}.$$

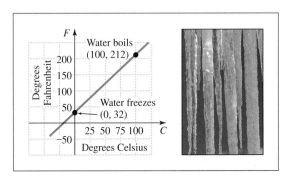

FIGURE 3.23

Using a slope of $\frac{9}{5}$ and the point $(100, 212)$ in the point-slope formula, we get

$$F - 212 = \frac{9}{5}(C - 100).$$

We can solve this equation for F to get the familiar formula relating Celsius and Fahrenheit temperature:

$$F = \frac{9}{5}C + 32$$

Because we knew the intercept $(0, 32)$, we could have used it and the slope $\frac{9}{5}$ in slope-intercept form to write $F = \frac{9}{5}C + 32$. ■

WARM-UPS

True or false? Explain your answer.

1. There is exactly one line through a given point with a given slope.
2. The line $y - a = m(x - b)$ goes through (a, b) and has slope m.
3. The equation of the line through (a, b) with slope m is $y = mx + b$.
4. The x-coordinate of the y-intercept of a nonvertical line is 0.
5. The y-coordinate of the x-intercept of a nonhorizontal line is 0.
6. Every line in the xy-plane has an equation in slope-intercept form.
7. The line $2y + 3x = 7$ has slope $-\frac{3}{2}$.
8. The line $y = 3x - 1$ is perpendicular to the line $y = \frac{1}{3}x - 1$.
9. The line $2y = 3x + 5$ has a y-intercept of $(0, 5)$.
10. Every line in the xy-plane has an equation in standard form.

3.3   EXERCISES

Reading and Writing   *After reading this section, write out the answers to these questions. Use complete sentences.*

1. What is point-slope form?

2. What is slope-intercept form?

3. What two bits of information must you have to write the equation of a line from a description of the line?

4. What is standard form?

5. How do you find the slope of a line when its equation is given in standard form?

6. How do you graph a line when its equation is given in slope-intercept form?

Find the equation of line l in each case and solve it for y. See Examples 1–3.

7. Line *l* goes through (2, −3) and has slope 2.

8. Line *l* goes through (−3, −1) and has slope 6.

9. Line *l* goes through (−2, 3) and has slope $-\frac{1}{2}$.

10. Line *l* goes through (3, 5) and has slope $\frac{2}{3}$.

11. Line *l* goes through (−2, −1) and (3, −6).

12. Line *l* goes through (−1, −5) and (2, 1).

13. Line *l* goes through (2, 2) and (−1, 1).

14. Line *l* goes through (2, 3) and (−5, 6).

15. Line *l* goes through (−1, −12) and is perpendicular to the line through (−3, 1) and (5, −1).

16. Line *l* goes through (0, 0) and is perpendicular to the line through (0, 6) and (−5, 0).

17. Line *l* goes through (0, 0) and is parallel to the line through (9, −3) and (−3, 6).

18. Line *l* goes through (2, −4) and is parallel to the line through (6, 2) and (−2, 6).

In Exercises 19–30, write an equation in slope-intercept form (if possible) for each of the lines shown. See Example 4.

19.

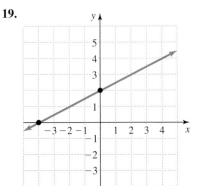

20.

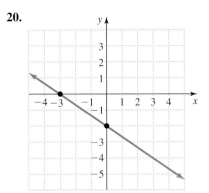

21.

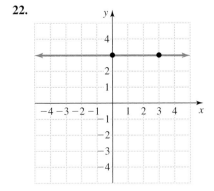

22.

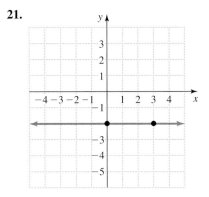

23.

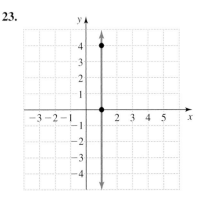

24.

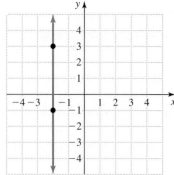

25.

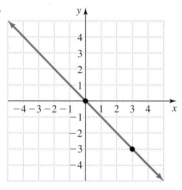

26.

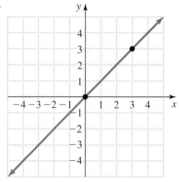

27.

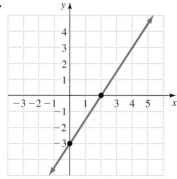

28.

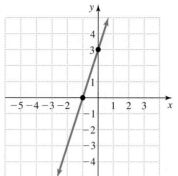

29.

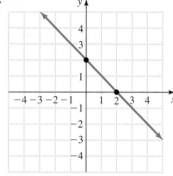

30.

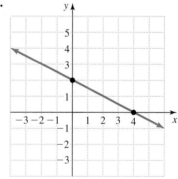

Write each equation in standard form using only integers and a positive coefficient for x. See Example 5.

31. $y = \dfrac{1}{3}x - 2$

32. $y = \dfrac{1}{2}x + 7$

33. $y - 5 = \dfrac{1}{2}(x + 3)$

34. $y - 1 = \dfrac{1}{4}(x - 6)$

35. $y + \dfrac{1}{2} = \dfrac{1}{3}(x - 4)$

36. $y + \dfrac{1}{3} = \dfrac{1}{4}(x - 3)$

37. $0.05x + 0.06y - 8.9 = 0$

38. $0.03x - 0.07y = 2$

Write each equation in slope-intercept form, and identify the slope and y-intercept. See Example 6.

39. $2x + 5y = 1$

40. $3x - 3y = 2$

41. $3x - y - 2 = 0$

42. $5 - x - 2y = 0$

43. $y + 3 = 5$

44. $y - 9 = 0$

45. $y - 2 = 3(x - 1)$

46. $y + 4 = -2(x - 5)$

47. $\dfrac{y - 5}{x + 4} = \dfrac{3}{2}$

48. $\dfrac{y - 6}{x - 2} = -\dfrac{3}{5}$

49. $y - \dfrac{1}{2} = \dfrac{1}{3}\left(x + \dfrac{1}{4}\right)$

50. $y - \dfrac{1}{3} = -\dfrac{1}{2}\left(x - \dfrac{1}{4}\right)$

51. $y - 6000 = 0.01(x + 5700)$

52. $y - 5000 = 0.05(x - 1990)$

Find the equation of line l in each case and then write it in standard form with integral coefficients. See Example 7.

53. Line *l* has slope $\dfrac{1}{2}$ and goes through $(0, 5)$.

54. Line *l* has slope 5 and goes through $\left(0, \dfrac{1}{2}\right)$.

55. Line *l* has x-intercept $(2, 0)$ and y-intercept $(0, 4)$.

56. Line *l* has y-intercept $(0, 5)$ and x-intercept $(4, 0)$.

57. Line *l* goes through $(-3, -1)$ and is parallel to $y = 2x + 6$.

58. Line *l* goes through $(1, -3)$ and is parallel to $y = -3x - 5$.

59. Line *l* is parallel to $2x + 4y = 1$ and goes through $(-3, 5)$.

60. Line *l* is parallel to $3x - 5y = -7$ and goes through $(-8, -2)$.

61. Line *l* goes through $(1, 1)$ and is perpendicular to $y = \dfrac{1}{2}x - 3$.

62. Line *l* goes through $(-1, -2)$ and is perpendicular to $y = -3x + 7$.

63. Line *l* goes through $(-4, -3)$ and is perpendicular to $x + 3y = 4$.

64. Line *l* is perpendicular to $2y + 5 - 3x = 0$ and goes through $(2, 7)$.

65. Line *l* goes through $(2, 5)$ and is parallel to the x-axis.

66. Line *l* goes through $(-1, 6)$ and is parallel to the y-axis.

Graph each line. Use the slope and y-intercept when possible. See Example 8.

67. $y = \dfrac{1}{2}x$

68. $y = -\dfrac{2}{3}x$

69. $y = 2x - 3$

70. $y = -x + 1$

71. $y = -\dfrac{2}{3}x + 2$

72. $y = 3x - 4$

73. $3y + x = 0$

74. $4y - x = 0$

81. $y = \dfrac{3}{4}x + 3$

$y = -\dfrac{4}{3}x + 1$

82. $y = \dfrac{2}{3}x + 1$

$y = -\dfrac{3}{2}x + 3$

Graph each pair of lines in the same coordinate system using the slope and y-intercept.

75. $y = x + 3$
$y = x + 2$

76. $y = -x + 2$
$y = -x - 2$

Determine whether each pair of lines is parallel, perpendicular, or neither.

83. $y = 3x - 8, x + 3y = 7$

84. $y = \dfrac{1}{2}x - 4, \dfrac{1}{2}x + \dfrac{1}{4}y = 1$

85. $2x - 4y = 9, \dfrac{1}{3}x = \dfrac{2}{3}y - 8$

86. $\dfrac{1}{4}x - \dfrac{1}{6}y = \dfrac{1}{3}, \dfrac{1}{3}y = \dfrac{1}{2}x - 2$

87. $2y = x + 6, y - 2x = 4$

88. $y - 3x = 5, 3x + y = 7$

89. $x - 6 = 9, y - 4 = 12$

90. $9 - x = 3, \dfrac{1}{2}x = 8$

77. $y = 3x + 1$
$y = -\dfrac{1}{3}x + 1$

78. $y = 2x + 3$
$y = -\dfrac{1}{2}x + 3$

Solve each problem. See Example 9.

91. ***Heating water.*** There is a linear equation that expresses the temperature, t, of a cup of water in terms of the number of seconds, s, that it is in the microwave. If the temperature at $s = 0$ second is $t = 60°F$ and the temperature at $s = 120$ seconds is $200°F$, find the linear equation that expresses t in terms of s. What should the temperature be after 30 seconds? (*Hint:* Write the equation of the line containing the points $(0, 60)$ and $(120, 200)$ in the form $t = ms + b$.) Draw a graph of this linear equation.

79. $y = \dfrac{2}{3}x - 1$

$y = \dfrac{2}{3}x + 1$

80. $y = -2x + 4$

$y = -2x + 2$

92. *Making circuit boards.* There is a linear equation that expresses the cost C per week in dollars for making circuit boards in terms of the number n of circuit boards per week. If $C = \$1500$ when $n = 1000$, and $C = \$2000$ when $n = 2000$, find the linear equation that expresses C in terms of n. What is the cost if only one circuit board is produced in a week? Draw a graph of this linear equation.

93. *Carbon dioxide emission.* Worldwide emission of carbon dioxide (CO_2) increased from 14 billion tons in 1970 to 26 billion tons in 2000 (World Resources Institute, www.wri.org).
a) Find the equation of the line through (1970, 14) and (2000, 26).
b) Use the equation to predict the worldwide emission of CO_2 in 2010.

94. *World energy use.* Worldwide energy use in all forms increased from the equivalent of 3.5 billion tons of oil in 1970 to the equivalent of 6.5 billion tons of oil in 2000 (World Resources Institute, www.wri.org).
a) Find the equation of the line through (1970, 3.5) and (2000, 6.5).
b) Use the equation to predict the worldwide energy use in 2010.

95. *Depth and flow.* On April 15, 2002, the depth of the water in the Tangipahoa River at Robert, Louisiana, was

9.14 feet and the flow was 1230 cubic feet per second (ft^3/sec). On April 8, 2002, the depth was 7.84 feet and the flow was 826 ft^3/sec. (U.S. Geological Survey, www.usgs.gov). Let w represent the flow in cubic feet per second and d represent the depth in feet.
a) Write the equation of the line through (9.14, 1230) and (7.84, 826) and express w in terms of d. Round to two decimal places.
b) What is the flow when the depth is 8.25 ft?
c) Is the flow increasing or decreasing as the depth increases?

96. *Buying stock.* On April 15, 2002, a mutual fund manager spent $484,375 on x shares of Ford Motor Company Stock at $15.50 per share and y shares of General Motors stock at $62.50 per share.
a) Write a linear equation that models this situation.
b) If 10,000 shares of Ford were purchased, then how many shares of GM were purchased?
c) Find and interpret the intercepts of the graph of the linear equation.
d) As the number of shares of Ford increases, does the number of shares of GM increase or decrease?

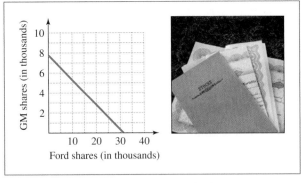

FIGURE FOR EXERCISE 96

GETTING MORE INVOLVED

97. *Exploration.* The **intercept form** for the equation of a line is

$$\frac{x}{a} + \frac{y}{b} = 1$$

where neither a nor b is zero.
a) Find the x- and y-intercepts for $\frac{x}{4} + \frac{y}{6} = 1$.

b) Find the x- and y-intercepts for $\frac{x}{a} + \frac{y}{b} = 1$.

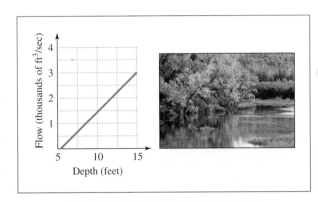

FIGURE FOR EXERCISE 95

c) Write the equation of the line through (0, 3) and (−5, 0) in intercept form.

d) Which lines cannot be written in intercept form?

GRAPHING CALCULATOR EXERCISES

98. Graph the equation $y = 0.5x - 1$ using the standard viewing window. Adjust the range of y-values so that the line goes from the lower left corner of your viewing window to the upper right corner.

99. Graph $y = x - 3000$, using a viewing window that shows both the x-intercept and the y-intercept.

100. Graph $y = 2x - 400$ and $y = -0.5x + 1$ on the same screen, using the viewing window $-500 \leq x \leq 500$ and $-1000 \leq y \leq 1000$. Should these lines be perpendicular? Explain.

101. The lines $y = 2x - 3$ and $y = 1.9x + 2$ are not parallel. Find a viewing window in which the lines intersect. Estimate the point of intersection.

In This Section

- Definition
- Graphing Linear Inequalities
- The Test Point Method
- Graphing Compound Inequalities
- Applications

 3.4

LINEAR INEQUALITIES AND THEIR GRAPHS

In the first three sections of this chapter you studied linear equations. We now turn our attention to linear inequalities.

Definition

A linear inequality is a linear equation with the equal sign replaced by an inequality symbol.

> **Linear Inequality**
>
> If A, B, and C are real numbers with A and B not both zero, then
>
> $$Ax + By \leq C$$
>
> is called a **linear inequality.** In place of $\leq$, we can also use $\geq$, $<$, or $>$.

Graphing Linear Inequalities

Consider the inequality $-x + y > 1$. If we solve the inequality for y, we get

$$y > x + 1.$$

Which points in the xy-plane satisfy this inequality? We want the points where the y-coordinate is larger than the x-coordinate plus 1. If we locate a point on the line $y = x + 1$, say (2, 3), then the y-coordinate is equal to the x-coordinate plus 1. If we move upward from that point, to say (2, 4), the y-coordinate is larger than the x-coordinate plus 1. Because this argument can be made at every point on the line, all points above the line satisfy $y > x + 1$. Likewise, points below the line satisfy $y < x + 1$. The solution sets, or graphs, for the inequality $y > x + 1$ and the inequality $y < x + 1$ are the shaded regions shown in Figs. 3.24(a) and 3.24(b) on the next page. In each case the line $y = x + 1$ is dashed to indicate that points on the line do not satisfy the inequality and so are not in the solution set. If the inequality symbol is $\leq$ or $\geq$, then points on the boundary line also satisfy the inequality, and the line is drawn solid.

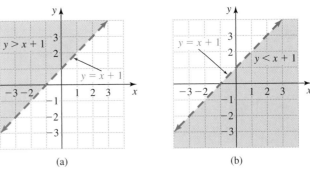

FIGURE 3.24

Every nonvertical line divides the xy-plane into two regions. One region is above the line, and the other is below the line. A vertical line also divides the plane into two regions, but one is on the left side of the line and the other is on the right side of the line. An inequality involving only x has a vertical boundary line, and its graph is one of those regions.

Graphing a Linear Inequality

1. Solve the inequality for y, then graph $y = mx + b$.

$y > mx + b$ is satisfied above the line.

$y = mx + b$ is satisfied on the line itself.

$y < mx + b$ is satisfied below the line.

2. If the inequality involves x and not y, then graph the vertical line $x = k$.

$x > k$ is satisfied to the right of the line.

$x = k$ is satisfied on the line itself.

$x < k$ is satisfied to the left of the line.

E X A M P L E   1

Graphing linear inequalities

Graph each inequality.

a) $y < \dfrac{1}{2}x - 1$ **b)** $y \geq -2x + 1$ **c)** $3x - 2y < 6$

Solution

a) The set of points satisfying this inequality is the region below the line $y = \frac{1}{2}x - 1$. To show this region, we first graph the boundary line $y = \frac{1}{2}x - 1$. The slope of the line is $\frac{1}{2}$, and the y-intercept is $(0, -1)$. Start at $(0, -1)$ on the y-axis, then rise 1 and run 2 to get a second point of the line. We draw the line dashed because points on the line do not satisfy this inequality. The solution set to the inequality is the shaded region shown in Fig. 3.25.

b) Because the inequality symbol is $\geq$, every point on or above the line $y = -2x + 1$ satisfies $y \geq -2x + 1$. To graph the line use y-intercept $(0, 1)$ and slope -2. Start at $(0, 1)$ and find a second point on the line using a rise of -2 and a run of 1. Draw a solid line through $(0, 1)$ and $(1, -1)$ to show that it is included in the solution set to the inequality. Shade above the line as in Fig. 3.26.

c) First solve for y:

$$3x - 2y < 6$$
$$-2y < -3x + 6$$
$$y > \frac{3}{2}x - 3 \quad \text{Divide by } -2 \text{ and reverse the inequality.}$$

To graph this inequality, first graph the boundary $y = \frac{3}{2}x - 3$ using its y-intercept $(0, -3)$ and slope $\frac{3}{2}$ or graph the line using its intercepts $(0, -3)$ and $(2, 0)$. Use a dashed line for the boundary and shade the region above the line as in Fig. 3.27.

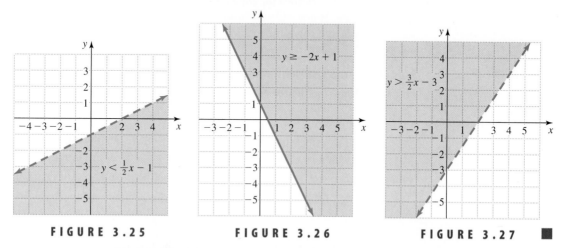

FIGURE 3.25 **FIGURE 3.26** **FIGURE 3.27** ■

CAUTION In Example 1(c) we solved the inequality for y before graphing the line. We did that because $<$ corresponds to the region below the line and $>$ corresponds to the region above the line only when the inequality is solved for y.

E X A M P L E   2 **Inequalities with horizontal and vertical boundaries**

Graph the inequalities.

a) $y \leq 5$ **b)** $x > 4$

Solution

a) The line $y = 5$ is the horizontal line with y-intercept $(0, 5)$. Draw a solid horizontal line and shade below it as in Fig. 3.28.

b) The points that satisfy $x > 4$ lie to the right of the vertical line $x = 4$. The solution set is shown in Fig. 3.29.

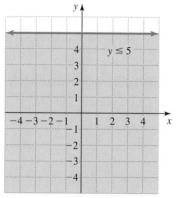

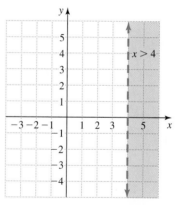

FIGURE 3.28 **FIGURE 3.29** ■

The Test Point Method

The graph of any line $Ax + By = C$ separates the xy-plane into two regions. Every point on one side of the line satisfies the inequality $Ax + By < C$, and every point on the other side satisfies the inequality $Ax + By > C$. We can use these facts to graph an inequality by the **test point method:**

1. Graph the corresponding equation.
2. Choose any point *not* on the line.
3. Test to see whether the point satisfies the inequality.

If the point satisfies the inequality, then the solution set is the region containing the test point. If not, then the solution set is the other region. With this method, it is not necessary to solve the inequality for y.

E X A M P L E 3

Study Tip

Students who have difficulty with algebra often schedule a class that meets one day per week so that they do not have to see it as often. However, students usually do better in classes that meet more often for shorter time periods.

Using the test point method

Graph the inequality $3x - 4y > 7$.

Solution

First graph the equation $3x - 4y = 7$ using the x-intercept and the y-intercept. If $x = 0$, then $y = -\frac{7}{4}$. If $y = 0$, then $x = \frac{7}{3}$. Use the x-intercept $\left(\frac{7}{3}, 0\right)$ and the y-intercept $\left(0, -\frac{7}{4}\right)$ to graph the line as shown in Fig. 3.30(a). Select a point on one side of the line, say $(0, 1)$, to test in the inequality. Because

$$3(0) - 4(1) > 7$$

is false, the region on the other side of the line satisfies the inequality. The graph of $3x - 4y > 7$ is shown in Fig. 3.30(b).

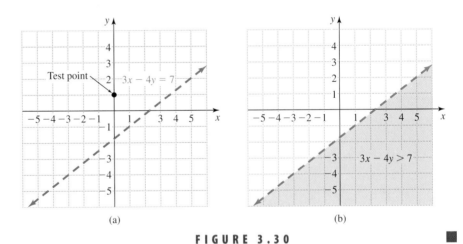

(a)   (b)

FIGURE 3.30

Graphing Compound Inequalities

We can write compound inequalities with two variables just as we do for one variable. For example,

$$y > x - 3 \qquad \text{and} \qquad y < -\frac{1}{2}x + 2$$

is a compound inequality. Because the inequalities are connected by the word *and,* a point is in the solution set to the compound inequality if and only if it is in the solution sets to *both* of the individual inequalities. So the graph of this compound inequality is the intersection of the solution sets to the individual inequalities.

EXAMPLE 4

Graphing a compound inequality with *and*

Graph the compound inequality $y > x - 3$ and $y < -\frac{1}{2}x + 2$.

Solution

We first graph the equations $y = x - 3$ and $y = -\frac{1}{2}x + 2$. These lines divide the plane into four regions as shown in Fig. 3.31(a). Now test one point of each region to determine which region satisfies the compound inequality. Test the points $(3, 3)$, $(0, 0)$, $(4, -5)$, and $(5, 0)$:

$$3 > 3 - 3 \quad \text{and} \quad 3 < -\frac{1}{2} \cdot 3 + 2 \quad \text{Second inequality is incorrect.}$$

$$0 > 0 - 3 \quad \text{and} \quad 0 < -\frac{1}{2} \cdot 0 + 2 \quad \text{Both inequalities are correct.}$$

$$-5 > 4 - 3 \quad \text{and} \quad -5 < -\frac{1}{2} \cdot 4 + 2 \quad \text{First inequality is incorrect.}$$

$$0 > 5 - 3 \quad \text{and} \quad 5 < -\frac{1}{2} \cdot 0 + 2 \quad \text{Both inequalities are incorrect.}$$

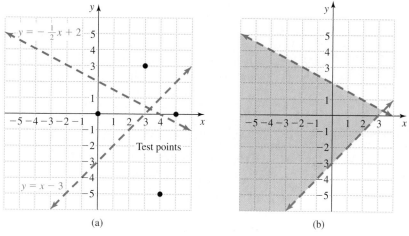

(a)   (b)

FIGURE 3.31

The only point that satisfies both inequalities is $(0, 0)$. So the solution set to the compound inequality consists of all points in the region containing $(0, 0)$. The graph of the compound inequality is shown in Fig. 3.31(b). ■

Compound inequalities are also formed by connecting individual inequalities with the word *or*. A point satisfies a compound inequality connected by *or* if and only if it satisfies one or the other or both of the individual inequalities. The graph is the union of the graphs of the individual inequalities.

EXAMPLE 5

Graphing a compound inequality with *or*

Graph the compound inequality

$$2x - 3y \le -6 \quad \text{or} \quad x + 2y \ge 4.$$

Helpful Hint

When graphing a compound inequality connected with "or," shade the region that satisfies the first inequality and then shade the region that satisfies the second inequality. If the inequalities are connected with "and," then you must be careful not to shade too much.

Solution

First graph the lines $2x - 3y = -6$ and $x + 2y = 4$. If we graph the lines using x- and y-intercepts, then we do not have to solve the equations for y. The lines are shown in Fig. 3.32(a). The graph of the compound inequality is the set of all points that satisfy either one inequality or the other (or both). Test the points (0, 0), (3, 2), (0, 5), and (−3, 2). You should verify that only (0, 0) fails to satisfy at least one of the inequalities. So only the region containing the origin is left unshaded. The graph of the compound inequality is shown in Fig. 3.32(b).

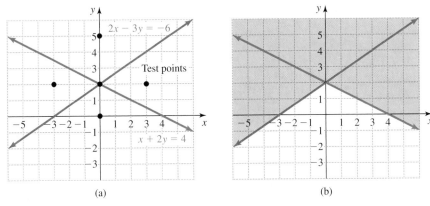

(a)   (b)

FIGURE 3.32

In Section 2.6 we learned that the absolute value inequality $|x| > 2$ is equivalent to the compound inequality $x < -2$ or $x > 2$. The absolute value inequality $|x| < 2$ is equivalent to the compound inequality $x > -2$ and $x < 2$. We can also write $|x| < 2$ as $-2 < x < 2$. We use these ideas with inequalities in two variables in Example 6.

E X A M P L E   6

Graphing absolute value inequalities

Graph each absolute value inequality.

a) $|y - 2x| \leq 3$ **b)** $|x - y| > 1$

Helpful Hint

Remember that absolute value of a quantity is its distance from 0 (Section 2.6). If $|w| < 3$, then w is less than 3 units from 0:

$$-3 < w < 3$$

If $|w| > 1$, then w is more than 1 unit away from 0:

$$w > 1 \quad \text{or} \quad w < -1$$

In Example 6 we are using an expression in place of w.

Solution

a) The inequality $|y - 2x| \leq 3$ is equivalent to $-3 \leq y - 2x \leq 3$, which is equivalent to the compound inequality

$$y - 2x \leq 3 \qquad \text{and} \qquad y - 2x \geq -3.$$

First graph the lines $y - 2x = 3$ and $y - 2x = -3$ as shown in Fig. 3.33(a). These lines divide the plane into three regions. Test a point from each region in the original inequality, say (−5, 0), (0, 1), and (5, 0):

$$|0 - 2(-5)| \leq 3 \qquad |1 - 2 \cdot 0| \leq 3 \qquad |0 - 2 \cdot 5| \leq 3$$
$$10 \leq 3 \qquad\qquad 1 \leq 3 \qquad\qquad 10 \leq 3$$

Only (0, 1) satisfies the original inequality. So the region satisfying the absolute value inequality is the shaded region containing (0, 1) as shown in Fig. 3.33(b). The boundary lines are solid because of the $\leq$ symbol.

b) The inequality $|x - y| > 1$ is equivalent to

$$x - y > 1 \quad \text{or} \quad x - y < -1.$$

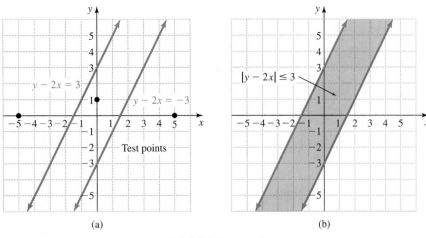

FIGURE 3.33

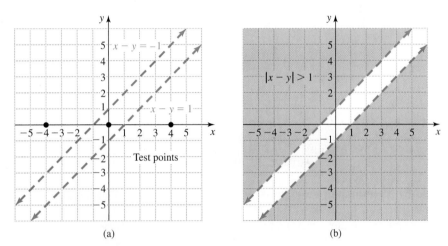

FIGURE 3.34

First graph the lines $x - y = 1$ and $x - y = -1$ as shown in Fig. 3.34(a). Test a point from each region in the original inequality, say $(-4, 0)$, $(0, 0)$, and $(4, 0)$:

$$|-4 - 0| > 1 \qquad |0 - 0| > 1 \qquad |4 - 0| > 1$$
$$4 > 1 \qquad\qquad 0 > 1 \qquad\qquad 4 > 1$$

Because $(-4, 0)$ and $(4, 0)$ satisfy the inequality, we shade those regions as shown in Fig. 3.34(b). The boundary lines are dashed because of the $>$ symbol. ∎

Applications

In real situations x and y often represent quantities or amounts, which cannot be negative. In this case our graphs are restricted to the first quadrant, where x and y are both nonnegative.

E X A M P L E   7   **Inequalities in business**

The manager of a furniture store can spend a maximum of $3000 on advertising per week. It costs $50 to run a 30-second ad on an AM radio station and $75 to run the ad on an FM station. Graph the region that shows the possible numbers of AM and FM ads that can be purchased and identify some possibilities.

Solution

If x represents the number of AM ads and y represents the number of FM ads, then x and y must satisfy the inequality $50x + 75y \leq 3000$. Because the number of ads cannot be negative, we also have $x \geq 0$ and $y \geq 0$. So we graph only points in the first quadrant that satisfy $50x + 75y \leq 3000$. The line $50x + 75y = 3000$ goes

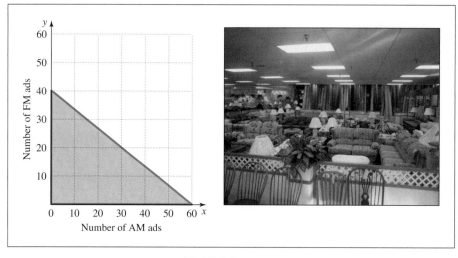

FIGURE 3.35

MATH AT WORK

MEDIA SALESPERSON

"We will return after these messages." We often hear these words on television and radio just before several minutes of commercials. Carolanne Johnson, Account Executive and Media Salesperson for WBOQ, a classical radio station, is involved in every step of creating such advertisements.

The first step is finding clients that are consistent with the station's image. Ms. Johnson generates her own leads from a number of sources, such as print ads and billboards. The next steps are sitting down with the client, gathering information about the product or service, assessing the competition, and finally determining how much of the client's advertising budget should be spent on radio. Typically, this can be 2% to 4% of the total budget.

Radio ads usually run for 60 seconds, but reminder ads can be as short as 30 seconds. Some of the radio spots are time-sensitive and run 40 to 60 times a month for a specific month. Other clients are concerned with image building and may sponsor one particular broadcast every day for the whole year.

Ms. Johnson is concerned that the clients receive an adequate return on their investment. She is constantly reviewing the budget and making sure that the commercials present what the client wishes to project.

Example 7 and Exercise 77 of this section give problems that involve allocation of advertising dollars.

through (0, 40) and (60, 0). The inequality is satisfied below this line. The region showing the possible numbers of AM ads and FM ads is shown in Fig. 3.35. We shade the entire region in Fig. 3.35, but only points in the shaded region in which both coordinates are whole numbers actually satisfy the given condition. For example, 40 AM ads and 10 FM ads could be purchased. Other possibilities are 30 AM ads and 20 FM ads, or 10 AM ads and 10 FM ads.

WARM-UPS

True or false? Explain your answer.

1. The point $(2, -3)$ satisfies the inequality $y > -3x + 2$.
2. The graph of $3x - y > 2$ is the region above the line $3x - y = 2$.
3. The graph of $3x + y < 5$ is the region below the line $y = -3x + 5$.
4. The graph of $x < -3$ is the region to the left of the vertical line $x = 3$.
5. The graph of $y > x + 3$ and $y < 2x - 6$ is the intersection of two regions.

6. The graph of $y \leq 2x - 3$ or $y \geq 3x + 5$ is the union of two regions.
7. The ordered pair $(2, -5)$ satisfies $y > -3x + 5$ and $y < 2x - 3$.
8. The ordered pair $(-3, 2)$ satisfies $y \leq 3x - 6$ or $y \leq x + 5$.
9. The inequality $|2x - y| \leq 4$ is equivalent to $2x - y \leq 4$ and $2x + y \leq 4$.

10. The inequality $|x - y| > 3$ is equivalent to $x - y > 3$ or $x - y < -3$.

3.4 EXERCISES

Reading and Writing   *After reading this section, write out the answers to these questions. Use complete sentences.*

1. What is a linear inequality?

2. How do we usually illustrate the solution set to a linear inequality in two variables.

3. How do you know whether the line should be solid or dashed when graphing a linear inequality?

4. How do you know which side of the line to shade when graphing a linear inequality?

5. What is the test point method used for?

6. How do you graph a compound inequality?

Graph each linear inequality. See Examples 1 and 2.

7. $y < x + 2$ 8. $y < x - 1$

9. $y \leq -2x + 1$ 10. $y \geq -3x + 4$

11. $x + y > 3$

12. $x + y \leq -1$

21. $y < 3$

22. $y > -1$

13. $2x + 3y < 9$

14. $-3x + 2y > 6$

Graph each linear inequality by using a test point. See Example 3.

23. $2x - 3y < 5$

24. $5x - 4y > 3$

15. $3x - 4y \leq 8$

16. $4x - 5y > 10$

25. $x + y + 3 \geq 0$

26. $x - y - 6 \leq 0$

17. $x - y > 0$

18. $2x - y < 0$

27. $y - 2x \leq 0$

28. $2y - x > 0$

19. $x \geq 1$

20. $x < 0$

29. $3x - 2y > 0$

30. $6x - 2y \leq 0$

31. $\frac{1}{2}x + \frac{1}{3}y < 1$ **32.** $2 - \frac{2}{5}y > \frac{1}{2}x$

39. $x + y \le 5$ and
$\quad\ x - y \le 3$

40. $2x - y < 3$ and
$\quad\ 3x - y > 0$

Graph each compound inequality. See Examples 4 and 5.

33. $y > x$ and $y > -2x + 3$ **34.** $y < x$ and $y < -3x + 2$

41. $x - 2y \le 4$ or
$\quad\ 2x - 3y \le 6$

42. $4x - 3y \le 3$ or
$\quad\ 2x + y \ge 2$

35. $y < x + 3$ or
$\quad\ y > -x + 2$

36. $y \ge x - 5$ or
$\quad\ y \le -2x + 1$

43. $y > 2$ and $x < 3$ **44.** $x \le 5$ and $y \ge -1$

37. $x - 4y < 0$ and
$\quad\ 3x + 2y \ge 6$

38. $x \ge -2y$ and
$\quad\ x - 3y < 6$

45. $y \ge x$ and $x \le 2$ **46.** $y < x$ and $y > 0$

47. $2x < y + 3$ or
     $y > 2 - x$

48. $3 - x < y + 2$ or
     $x > y + 5$

Graph the absolute value inequalities. See Example 6.

55. $|x + y| < 2$

56. $|2x + y| < 1$

49. $y > x - 1$ and
     $y < x + 3$

50. $y > x - 1$ and
     $y < 2x + 5$

57. $|2x + y| \geq 1$

58. $|x + 2y| \geq 6$

51. $0 \leq y \leq x$ and $x \leq 1$

52. $x \leq y \leq 1$ and $x \geq 0$

59. $|y - x| > 2$

60. $|2y - x| > 6$

53. $1 \leq x \leq 3$ and
     $2 \leq y \leq 5$

54. $-1 < x < 1$ and
     $-1 < y < 1$

61. $|x - 2y| \leq 4$

62. $|x - 3y| \leq 6$

63. $|x| > 2$

64. $|x| \le 3$

65. $|y| < 1$

66. $|y| \ge 2$

67. $|x| < 2$ and $|y| < 3$

68. $|x| \ge 3$ or $|y| \ge 1$

69. $|x - 3| < 1$ and
$|y - 2| < 1$

70. $|x - 2| \ge 3$ or
$|y - 5| \ge 2$

Solve each problem. See Example 7.

71. ***Budget planning.*** The Highway Patrol can spend a maximum of $120,000 on new vehicles this year. They can get a fully equipped compact car for $15,000 or a fully equipped full-size car for $20,000. Graph the region that shows the number of cars of each type that could be purchased.

72. ***Allocating resources.*** A furniture maker has a shop that can employ 12 workers for 40 hours per week at its maximum capacity. The shop makes tables and chairs. It takes 16 hours of labor to make a table and 8 hours of labor to make a chair. Graph the region that shows the possibilities for the number of tables and chairs that could be made in one week.

73. ***More restrictions.*** In Exercise 71, add the condition that the number of full-size cars must be greater than or equal to the number of compact cars. Graph the region showing the possibilities for the number of cars of each type that could be purchased.

74. ***Chairs per table.*** In Exercise 72, add the condition that the number of chairs must be at least four times the number of tables and at most six times the number of tables. Graph the region showing the possibilities for the number of tables and chairs that could be made in one week.

75. ***Building fitness.*** To achieve cardiovascular fitness, you should exercise so that your target heart rate is between 70% and 85% of its maximum rate. Your target heart rate h depends on your age a. For building fitness, you should have $h \leq 187 - 0.85a$ and $h \geq 154 - 0.70a$ (NordicTrack brochure). Graph this compound inequality for $20 \leq a \leq 75$ to see the heart rate target zone for building fitness.

76. ***Waist-to-hip ratio.*** A study by Dr. Aaron R. Folsom concluded that waist-to-hip ratios are a better predictor of 5-year survival than more traditional height-to-weight ratios. Dr. Folsom concluded that for good health the waist size of a woman aged 50 to 69 should be less than or equal to 80% of her hip size, $w \leq 0.80h$. Make a graph showing possible waist and hip sizes for good health for women in this age group for which hip size is no more than 50 inches.

77. ***Advertising dollars.*** A restaurant manager can spend at most $9000 on advertising per month and has two choices for advertising. The manager can purchase an ad in the *Daily Chronicle* (a 7-day-per-week newspaper) for $300 per day or a 30-second ad on WBTU television for $1000 each time the ad is aired. Graph the region that shows the possible number of days that an ad can be run in the newspaper and the possible number of times that an ad can be aired on television.

78. ***Shipping restrictions.*** The accompanying graph shows all of the possibilities for the number of refrigerators and the number of TVs that will fit into an 18-wheeler.
a) Write an inequality to describe this region.
b) Will the truck hold 71 refrigerators and 118 TVs?
c) Will the truck hold 51 refrigerators and 176 TVs?

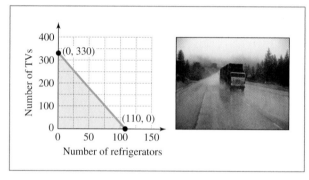

FIGURE FOR EXERCISE 78

GETTING MORE INVOLVED

 79. ***Writing.*** Explain the difference between a compound inequality using the word *and* and a compound inequality using the word *or*.

 80. ***Discussion.*** Explain how to write an absolute value inequality as a compound inequality.

3.5 FUNCTIONS AND RELATIONS

In this chapter we have been studying ordered pairs. In this section we will use ordered pairs in our study of functions and relations.

The Concept of a Function

If the value of the variable y is determined by the value of the variable x, then y **is a function of x.** So "is a function of" means "is uniquely determined by." But what does uniquely determined mean? According to the dictionary "determine" means "to settle conclusively." There can be no ambiguity. There is only one y for any x.

Consider all possible circles. Is the area of a circle A a function of the radius r? The well-known formula $A = \pi r^2$ tells us exactly how to determine the area from the radius. There is only one area for any given radius and A is a function of r.

Now consider all first-class letters mailed today in the United States. Is the weight W a function of the amount of postage P? That is, can W be determined from P? There are certainly letters that have the same amount of postage and different weights. So the weight cannot be determined from the postage and W is not a function of P. The weight cannot be determined conclusively if there is more than one weight for a given amount of postage.

E X A M P L E   1

Deciding if b is a function of a

In each situation decide whether b is a function of a.

a) Consider all students at Pasadena City College. Let b represent the weight of a student to the nearest pound and a represent the height of the same student to the nearest inch.

b) Consider all possible rectangles. Let b represent the area a rectangle and a represent the width.

c) Consider all cars sold at Bill Hood Ford this year where the sales tax rate is 9%. Let b represent the amount of sales tax and a represent the selling price of the car.

Solution

a) Can the weight of a student be determined from the height of the student? Imagine that we have a list containing weights and heights for all students. There will certainly be two 5 ft 9 in. students with different weights. So weight cannot be determined from the height and b is not a function of a.

b) Can the area of a rectangle be determined from the width? Among all possible rectangles there are infinitely many rectangles with width 1 ft and different areas. So the area is not determined by the width and b is not a function of a.

c) Can the amount of sales tax be determined from the price of the car? The formula $b = 0.09a$ is used to determine the amount of tax. For example, the tax on every $20,000 car is $1,800. So b is a function of a.   ■

Example 1 should help you understand the concept of function. However, answers to questions like those in Example 1 might vary depending on the interpretation of the situation. So we must have a mathematically precise definition of a function.

When discussing two variables, we can consider the set of all ordered pairs containing their possible values. If we are trying to decide whether weight is a function of height, then the ordered pairs have the form (height, weight). If we are considering whether p is a function of s, then the ordered pairs look like (s, p). The variable corresponding to the first coordinate is the **independent variable** and the variable corresponding to the second coordinate is the **dependent variable.** The dependent variable is a function of the independent variable if and only if the corresponding set of ordered pairs is a function according to the following definition.

Function—A Set of Ordered Pairs

A **function** is a set of ordered pairs in which no two ordered pairs have the same first coordinate and different second coordinates.

Note that in Example 1(a) we concluded that weight was not a function of height because there are certainly two students with the same height and different weights. There may be many more, but all it takes to fail to be a function is two ordered pairs with the same first coordinate and different second coordinates.

Identifying Functions

Any set of ordered pairs is called a **relation.** The ordered pairs of a relation may be given by a graph, list, or equation. In each case we can use the definition of function to decide whether the relation is a function.

If the ordered pairs of a relation are given by a graph, then we can use a simple visual test, the **vertical-line test,** to determine whether the relation is a function.

The Vertical-Line Test

A graph is the graph of a function if and only if there is no vertical line that crosses the graph more than once.

If there is a vertical line that crosses a graph twice (or more), then we have two points with the same *x*-coordinate and different *y*-coordinates, and the graph is not the graph of a function. If you mentally consider every possible vertical line and none of them crosses the graph more than once, then you can conclude that the graph is the graph of a function.

E X A M P L E 2   Using the vertical-line test

Which of these graphs are graphs of functions?

a)

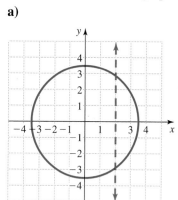

b)

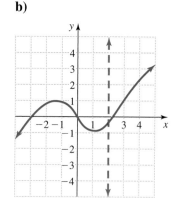

c)

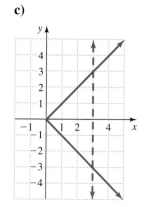

Solution

Neither (a) nor (c) is the graph of a function, since we can draw vertical lines that cross these graphs twice. The graph (b) is the graph of a function, since no vertical line crosses it more than once. ■

The vertical-line test illustrates the visual difference between a set of ordered pairs that is a function and one that is not. Because graphs are not precise, the vertical-line test might be inconclusive. When a relation is given as a list of ordered pairs we can decide conclusively whether the relation is a function, as in the next example.

E X A M P L E   3

Relations given as lists of ordered pairs

Determine whether each relation is a function.

a) $\{(1, 2), (1, 5), (3, 7)\}$

b) $\{(4, 5), (3, 5), (2, 6), (1, 7)\}$

Solution

a) This relation is not a function because $(1, 2)$ and $(1, 5)$ have the same first coordinate but different second coordinates.

b) This relation is a function. Note that the same second coordinate with different first coordinates is permitted in a function. ■

The solution set to any equation in x and y is the set of ordered pairs that satisfy the equation. Since any set of ordered pairs is called a relation, any equation in x and y is called a relation. If the solution set is a function, then the equation is also called a function.

E X A M P L E   4

Relations given as equations

Determine whether each relation is a function.

a) $x = y^2$ **b)** $y = 2x$ **c)** $x = |y|$

Solution

a) Is it possible to find two ordered pairs with the same first coordinate and different second coordinates that satisfy $x = y^2$? Since $(1, 1)$ and $(1, -1)$ both satisfy $x = y^2$, this relation is not a function.

b) The equation $y = 2x$ indicates that the y-coordinate is always twice the x-coordinate. Ordered pairs such as $(0, 0)$, $(2, 4)$, and $(3, 6)$ satisfy $y = 2x$. It is not possible to find two ordered pairs with the same first coordinate and different second coordinates. So $y = 2x$ is a function. Note that the graph of $y = 2x$ is a straight line with slope 2. Since no vertical line will cross that line more than once, we can also conclude that $y = 2x$ is a function by the vertical-line test.

c) The equation $x = |y|$ is satisfied by ordered pairs such as $(2, 2)$ and $(2, -2)$ because $2 = |2|$ and $2 = |-2|$ are both correct. So this relation is not a function. ■

Domain and Range

A relation or function is a set of ordered pairs. The **domain** of a relation or function is the set of first coordinates of the ordered pairs. The **range** is the set of second coordinates of the ordered pairs. If the ordered pairs are listed, then the domain and range can be simply read from the list. More often, a relation or function is given by an equation, with no domain stated. *When the domain is not stated we assume that the domain consists of all real numbers that, when substituted for the independent variable, produce real numbers for the dependent variable.*

E X A M P L E   5

Identifying the domain and range

Determine the domain and range of each relation.

a) $\{(2, 5), (2, 7), (4, 3)\}$ **b)** $y = 2x$ **c)** $y = \sqrt{x - 1}$

Solution

a) The domain is the set of first coordinates, $\{2, 4\}$. The range is the set of second coordinates, $\{3, 5, 7\}$.

b) Since any real number can be used in place of x in $y = 2x$, the domain is $(-\infty, \infty)$. Since any real number can be used in place of y in $y = 2x$, the range is also $(-\infty, \infty)$.

c) Since the square root of a negative number is not a real number, we must have $x - 1 \geq 0$ or $x \geq 1$. So the domain is the interval $[1, \infty)$. Since the square root of a nonnegative real number is a nonnegative real number, we must have $y \geq 0$. So the range is the interval $[0, \infty)$. ∎

Using domain and range we can write another definition of function that is equivalent to the ordered-pair definition that we have been using:

Function—A Rule

A **function** is a rule that assigns to each element of one set (the domain) exactly one element of another set (the range).

If a set of ordered pairs is a function, then the ordered pairs give us a rule for assigning each element of the domain with exactly one element of the range. Conversely, if we have a rule for assigning elements, then we could write all of the assignments as ordered pairs that satisfy the ordered-pair definition of function. So a function by one definition is also a function by the other definition.

Function Notation

If y is a function of x, we can use the notation $f(x)$ to represent y. The expression $f(x)$ is read as "f of x." The notation $f(x)$ is called **function notation.** So if x is the independent variable, then either y or $f(x)$ is the dependent variable. For example, the function $y = 2x + 3$ can be written as

$$f(x) = 2x + 3.$$

We use y and $f(x)$ interchangeably. We can think of f as the name of the function. We may use letters other than f. For example $g(x) = 2x + 3$ is the same function as $f(x) = 2x + 3$. The ordered pairs for each function are identical. Note that $f(x)$ does not mean f times x. The expression $f(x)$ represents the second coordinate when the first coordinate is x.

If $f(x) = 2x + 3$, then $f(4) = 2(4) + 3 = 11$. So the second coordinate is 11 if the first coordinate is 4. The ordered pair $(4, 11)$ is an ordered pair in the function f. Figure 3.36 illustrates this situation.

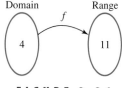

Domain   Range

f

4   11

FIGURE 3.36

EXAMPLE 6

Using function notation

Let $f(x) = 3x - 2$ and $g(x) = x^2 - x$. Evaluate each expression.

a) $f(-5)$ **b)** $g(-5)$ **c)** $f(0) + g(3)$

Solution

a) Replace x by -5 in the equation defining the function f:

$$f(x) = 3x - 2$$
$$f(-5) = 3(-5) - 2$$
$$= -17$$

So $f(-5) = -17$.

b) Replace x by -5 in the equation defining the function g:
$$g(x) = x^2 - x$$
$$g(-5) = (-5)^2 - (-5) = 30$$

So $g(-5) = 30$.

c) Since $f(0) = 3(0) - 2 = -2$ and $g(3) = 3^2 - 3 = 6$, we have $f(0) + g(3) = -2 + 6 = 4$.   ■

Linear Functions

A function of the form $f(x) = mx + b$ is called a **linear function** if $m \neq 0$ and a **constant function** if $m = 0$. So $f(x) = 3x - 1$ is a linear function and $f(x) = 5$ is a constant function. The graph of a linear function is a line with slope m and the graph of a constant function is a line with slope 0 (a horizontal line).

E X A M P L E   7   **Graphing linear and constant functions**

Graph each function.

a) $f(x) = 3x - 1$ **b)** $f(x) = 5$

Solution

a) The graph of $f(x) = 3x - 1$ is the same as the graph of $y = 3x - 1$, a line with y-intercept $(0, -1)$ and slope 3. See Fig. 3.37.

b) The graph of $f(x) = 5$ is the same as the graph of $y = 5$, a line with slope 0 and y-intercept $(0, 5)$. See Fig. 3.38.

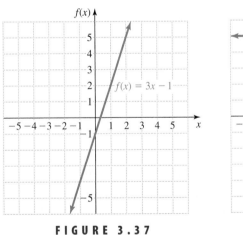

FIGURE 3.37   **FIGURE 3.38**   ■

In Example 8 we see function notation with a linear function in an applied setting.

E X A M P L E   8   **Using function notation in applications**

To determine the cost of an in-home repair, a computer technician uses the linear function $C(n) = 40n + 30$, where n is the time in hours and $C(n)$ is the cost in dollars. Find $C(2)$ and $C(4)$.

Midpoint formula	The midpoint of the line segment with endpoints (x_1, y_1) and (x_2, y_2) is $$(\bar{x}, \bar{y}) = \left(\frac{x_1 + x_2}{2}, \frac{y_1 + y_2}{2}\right).$$	If $(x_1, y_1) = (1, -2)$ and $(x_2, y_2) = (7, 8)$, then $(\bar{x}, \bar{y}) = (4, 3)$.
Distance formula	The distance between (x_1, y_1) and (x_2, y_2) is $\sqrt{(x_2 - x_1)^2 + (y_2 - y_1)^2}$.	The distance between $(3, 5)$ and $(-2, 9)$ is $\sqrt{41}$.

Slope

Examples

Slope of a line	$$\text{Slope} = \frac{\text{change in } y\text{-coordinate}}{\text{change in } x\text{-coordinate}}$$ $$= \frac{\text{rise}}{\text{run}}$$	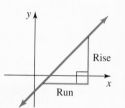
Slope using coordinates	Slope of line through (x_1, y_1) and (x_2, y_2) is $m = \dfrac{y_2 - y_1}{x_2 - x_1}$, provided that $x_2 - x_1 \neq 0$.	If $(x_1, y_1) = (4, -2)$ and $(x_2, y_2) = (3, -6)$, then $$m = \frac{-6 - (-2)}{3 - 4} = 4.$$
Types of slope	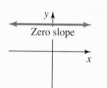 	
Perpendicular lines	The slope of one line is the negative of the reciprocal of the slope of the other line.	The lines $y = -\frac{1}{3}x + 5$ and $y = 3x - 9$ are perpendicular.
Parallel lines	Nonvertical parallel lines have equal slopes.	The lines $y = 2x - 3$ and $y = 2x + 7$ are parallel.

Forms of Linear Equations

Examples

Point-slope form	$y - y_1 = m(x - x_1)$ (x_1, y_1) is a point on the line, and m is the slope.	Line through $(5, -3)$ with slope 2: $y + 3 = 2(x - 5)$
Slope-intercept form	$y = mx + b$ m is the slope, $(0, b)$ is the y-intercept, and y is a linear function of x. We also write $f(x) = mx + b$.	Line through $(0, -3)$ with slope 2: $y = 2x - 3$ $f(x) = 2x - 3, f(4) = 5$
Standard form	$Ax + By = C$ A and B are not both 0.	$3x - 2y = 12$

| Vertical line | $x = k$, where k is any real number. Slope is undefined for vertical lines. | $x = 5$ |
| Horizontal line | $y = k$, where k is any real number. Slope is zero for horizontal lines. | $y = -2$ |

Graphing Linear Equations

Examples

Point-plotting	Arbitrarily select some points that satisfy the equation, and draw a line through them.	For $y = 2x + 1$, draw a line through $(0, 1)$, $(1, 3)$, and $(2, 5)$.
Intercepts	Find the x- and y-intercepts (provided that they are not the origin), and draw a line through them.	For $x + y = 4$ the intercepts are $(0, 4)$ and $(4, 0)$.
y-intercept and slope	Start at the y-intercept and use the slope to locate a second point, then draw a line through the two points.	For $y = 3x - 2$ start at $(0, -2)$, rise 3 and run 1 to get to $(1, 1)$. Draw a line through the two points.

Linear Inequalities

Examples

Linear inequality	$Ax + By \leq C$, where A and B are not both zero. The symbols $<$, $>$, and $\geq$ are also used.	$2x - 3y \leq 7$ $x - y > 6$
Graphing linear inequalities	Solve for y, then graph the line $y = mx + b$. $y > mx + b$ is the region above the line. $y < mx + b$ is the region below the line.	Graph of $y = x + 2$ is a line. $y > x + 2$ above $y = x + 2$. $y < x + 2$ below $y = x + 2$.
	For inequalities without y, graph $x = k$. $x > k$ is the region to the right of $x = k$. $x < k$ is the region to the left of $x = k$.	The graph of $x > 5$ is to the right of the vertical line $x = 5$, and the graph of $x < 5$ is to left of $x = 5$.
Test points	A linear inequality may also be graphed by graphing the corresponding line and then testing a point to determine which region satisfies the inequality.	
Compound inequalities	Simple inequalities connected by *and* or *or* For *and*, find the intersection of the regions. For *or*, find the union of the regions.	$x < 3$ and $y > x - 4$ $x + y \geq 1$ or $y \leq x - 1$

Relations and Functions

Examples

Relation	Any set of ordered pairs of real numbers	$\{(1, 2), (1, 3)\}$
Function	A relation in which no two ordered pairs have the same first coordinate and different second coordinates.	$\{(1, 2), (3, 5), (4, 5)\}$
	If y is a function of x, then y is uniquely determined by x. A function may be defined by a table, a listing of ordered pairs, or an equation.	
Domain	The set of first coordinates of the ordered pairs	Function: $y = x^2$ Domain: $(-\infty, \infty)$

Range	The set of second coordinates of the ordered pairs.	Range: $[0, \infty)$
Function notation	If y is a function of x, the expression $f(x)$ is used in place of y.	$y = 2x + 3$ $f(x) = 2x + 3$
Vertical-line test	If a graph can be crossed more than once by a vertical line, then it is not the graph of a function.	
Linear function	A function of the form $f(x) = mx + b$ with $m \neq 0$	$f(x) = 3x - 7$ $f(x) = -2x + 5$
Constant function	A function of the form $f(x) = b$, where b is a real number	$f(x) = 2$

ENRICHING YOUR MATHEMATICAL WORD POWER

For each mathematical term, choose the correct meaning.

1. **graph of an equation**
    a. the Cartesian coordinate system
    b. two number lines that intersect at a right angle
    c. the x-axis and y-axis
    d. an illustration in the coordinate plane that shows all ordered pairs that satisfy an equation

2. **origin**
    a. the point of intersection of the x- and y-axes
    b. the beginning of algebra
    c. the number 0
    d. the x-axis

3. **x-coordinate**
    a. the first number in an ordered pair
    b. the second number in an ordered pair
    c. a point on the x-axis
    d. a point where a graph crosses the x-axis

4. **y-intercept**
    a. the second number in an ordered pair
    b. a point at which a graph intersects the y-axis
    c. any point on the y-axis
    d. the point where the y-axis intersects the x-axis

5. **coordinate plane**
    a. a matching plane
    b. when the x-axis is coordinated with the y-axis
    c. a plane with a rectangular coordinate system
    d. a coordinated system for graphs

6. **independent variable**
    a. the first coordinate of an ordered pair
    b. the second coordinate of an ordered pair
    c. the x-axis
    d. the y-axis

7. **dependent variable**
    a. the first coordinate of an ordered pair
    b. the second coordinate of an ordered pair
    c. the x-axis
    d. the y-axis

8. **slope**
    a. the change in x divided by the change in y
    b. a measure of the steepness of a line
    c. the run divided by the rise
    d. the slope of a line

9. **slope-intercept form**
    a. $y = mx + b$
    b. rise over run
    c. the point at which a line crosses the y-axis
    d. $y - y_1 = m(x - x_1)$

10. **point-slope form**
    a. $Ax + By = C$
    b. rise over run
    c. $y - y_1 = m(x - x_1)$
    d. the slope of a line at a single point

11. **standard form**
    a. $y = mx + b$
    b. $Ax + By = C$, where A and B are not both 0
    c. $y - y_1 = m(x - x_1)$
    d. the most common form

12. **linear inequality in two variables**
    a. when two lines are not equal
    b. line segments that are unequal in length
    c. an inequality of the form $Ax + By \geq C$ or with another symbol of inequality
    d. an inequality of the form $Ax^2 + By^2 < C^2$

13. **function**
    a. a set of ordered pairs of real numbers
    b. a set of ordered pairs of real numbers in which no two have the same first coordinates and different second coordinates

c.   a set of ordered pairs of real numbers in which no two have the same second coordinates and different first coordinates

d.   an equation

14.   **relation**

a.   a set of ordered pairs of real numbers

b.   a set of ordered pairs of real numbers in which no two have the same first coordinates and different second coordinates

c.   cousins and second cousins

d.   a fraction

15.   **domain**

a.   the range

b.   the set of second coordinates of a relation

c.   the independent variable

d.   the set of first coordinates of a relation

16.   **function notation**

a.   a notation where $f(x)$ is used as the independent variable

b.   a notation where $f(x)$ is used as the dependent variable

c.   the notation of algebra

d.   the notation of exponents

Study Tip

Note how the review exercises are arranged according to the sections in this chapter. If you are having trouble with a certain type of problem, refer back to the appropriate section for examples and explanations.

REVIEW EXERCISES

3.1 *For each point, name the quadrant in which it lies or the axis on which it lies.*

1. $(-3, -2)$

2. $(0, \pi)$

3. $(\pi, 0)$

4. $(-5, 4)$

5. $(0, -1)$

6. $\left(\dfrac{\pi}{2}, 1\right)$

7. $(\sqrt{2}, -3)$

8. $(6, -3)$

Find the midpoint and length of the line segment with the given endpoints.

9. $(8, -2)$ and $(2, 6)$

10. $(-9, 4)$ and $(-3, -4)$

11. $(2, -2)$ and $(3, 1)$

12. $(0, 3)$ and $(-1, -1)$

Complete the given ordered pairs so that each ordered pair satisfies the given equation.

13. $(0, \ ), (\ , 0), (4, \ ), (\ , -3), y = -3x + 2$

14. $(0, \ ), (\ , 0), (-6, \ ), (\ , 5), 2x + 3y = 5$

3.2 *Find the slope of the line through each pair of points.*

15. $(-5, 6), (-2, 9)$

16. $(-2, 7), (3, -4)$

17. $(4, 1), (-3, -2)$

18. $(6, 0), (0, -3)$

Solve each problem.

19. What is the slope of any line that is parallel to the line through $(-3, -4)$ and $(5, -1)$?

20. What is the slope of the line through $(4, 6)$ that is parallel to the line through $(-2, 1)$ and $(7, 1)$?

21. What is the slope of any line that is perpendicular to the line through $(-3, 5)$ and $(4, -6)$?

22. What is the slope of the line through $(1, 2)$ that is perpendicular to the line through $(5, 4)$ and $(5, -2)$?

3.3 *Find the slope and y-intercept for each line.*

23. $y = -3x + 4$

24. $2y - 3x + 1 = 0$

25. $y - 3 = \dfrac{2}{3}(x - 1)$

26. $y - 3 = 5$

Write each equation in standard form with integral coefficients.

27. $y = \dfrac{2}{3}x - 4$

28. $y = -0.05x + 0.26$

29. $y - 1 = \dfrac{1}{2}(x + 3)$

30. $\dfrac{1}{2}x - \dfrac{1}{3}y = \dfrac{1}{4}$

Write the equation of the line containing the given point and having the given slope. Rewrite each equation in standard form with integral coefficients.

31. $(1, -3), m = \dfrac{1}{2}$

32. $(0, 2), m = 3$

33. $(-2, 6), m = -\dfrac{3}{4}$

34. $\left(2, \dfrac{1}{2}\right), m = \dfrac{1}{4}$

35. $(3, 5), m = 0$

36. $(0, 0), m = -1$

Graph each equation.

37. $y = 2x - 3$ **38.** $y = \dfrac{2}{3}x + 1$

39. $3x - 2y = -6$ **40.** $4x + 5y = 10$

41. $y - 3 = 10$ **42.** $2x = 8$

43. $5x - 3y = 7$ **44.** $3x + 4y = -1$

45. $5x + 4y = 100$ **46.** $2x - y = 120$

47. $x - 80y = 400$ **48.** $75x + y = 300$

3.4 *Graph each linear inequality.*

49. $y > 3x - 2$ **50.** $y \le 2x + 3$

51. $x - y \leq 5$

52. $2x + y > 1$

59. $5x - 2y < 9$

60. $3x + 4y \leq -1$

53. $3x > 2$

54. $x + 2 \leq 0$

Graph each compound or absolute value inequality.

61. $y > 3$ and
$\quad y - x < 5$

62. $x + y \leq 1$ or
$\quad y \leq 4$

55. $4y \leq 0$

56. $4y - 4 > 0$

63. $3x + 2y \geq 8$ or
$\quad 3x - 2y \leq 6$

64. $x + 8y > 8$ and
$\quad x - 2y < 10$

57. $4x - 2y \geq 6$

58. $-5x - 3y > 6$

65. $|x + 2y| < 10$

66. $|x - 3y| \geq 9$

67. $|x| \le 5$

68. $|y| > 6$

69. $|y - x| > 2$

70. $|x - y| \le 1$

MISCELLANEOUS

Write an equation in standard form with integral coefficients for each line described.

91. The line that crosses the *x*-axis at (2, 0) and the *y*-axis at (0, −6)

92. The line with an *x*-intercept of (4, 0) and slope $-\frac{1}{2}$

93. The line through (−1, 4) with slope $-\frac{1}{2}$

94. The line through (2, −3) with slope 0

95. The line through (2, −6) and (2, 5)

96. The line through (−3, 6) and (4, 2)

97. The line through (0, 0) perpendicular to $x = 5$

98. The line through (2, −3) perpendicular to $y = -3x + 5$

99. The line through (−1, 4) parallel to $y = 2x + 1$

100. The line through (2, 1) perpendicular to $y = 10$

3.5 *Determine whether each relation is a function.*

71. {(5, 7), (5, 10), (5, 3)}

72. {(1, 3), (4, 7), (1, 6)}

73. {(1, 1), (2, 1), (3, 3)}

74. {(2, 4), (4, 6), (6, 8)}

75. $y = x^2$

76. $x^2 = 1 + y^2$

77. $x = y^4$

78. $y = \sqrt{x - 1}$

Determine the domain and range of each relation.

79. {(3, 5), (4, 9), (5, 1)}

80. {(2, 6), (6, 7), (8, 9)}

81. $y = x + 1$

82. $y = 2x - 3$

83. $y = \sqrt{x + 5}$

84. $y = \sqrt{x - 1}$

Let $f(x) = 2x - 5$ *and* $g(x) = x^2 + x - 6$. *Evaluate each expression.*

85. $f(0)$

86. $f(-3)$

87. $g(0)$

88. $g(-2)$

89. $g\left(\frac{1}{2}\right)$

90. $g\left(-\frac{1}{2}\right)$

For Exercises 101–104, write an equation in standard form with integral coefficients for each line.

101.

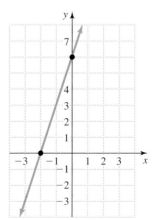

102.

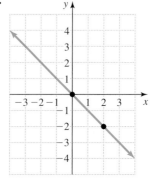

103.

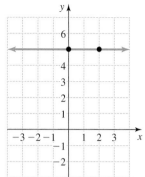

104.

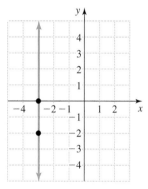

Use slope to solve each geometric problem.

105. Show that the points $(-5, -5)$, $(-3, -1)$, $(6, 2)$, and $(4, -2)$ are the vertices of a parallelogram.

106. Show that the points $(-5, -5)$, $(4, -2)$, and $(3, 1)$ are the vertices of a right triangle.

107. Show that the points $(-2, 2)$, $(0, 0)$, $(2, 6)$, and $(4, 4)$ are the vertices of a rectangle.

108. Determine whether the points $(2, 1)$, $(4, 7)$, and $(-3, -14)$ lie on a straight line.

Solve each problem.

109. *Maximum heart rate.* The maximum heart rate during exercise for a 20 year old is 200 beats per minute, and the maximum heart rate for a 70 year old is 150 (NordicTrack brochure) as shown in the accompanying figure.

a) Write the maximum heart rate h as a linear function of age a.

b) What is the maximum heart rate for a 40 year old?

c) Does your maximum heart rate increase or decrease as you get older?

110. *Resting heart rate.* A subject is given 3 milligrams (mg) of an experimental drug, and a resting heart rate of 82 is recorded. Another subject is given 5 mg of the same drug, and a resting heart rate of 89 is recorded. If we assume the heart rate, h, is a linear function of the dosage, d, find the linear equation expressing h in terms of d. If a subject is given 10 mg of the drug, what would be the expected heart rate?

111. *Rental costs.* The charge, C, in dollars, for renting an air hammer from the Tools Is Us Rental Company is determined from the formula $C = 26 + 17d$, where d is the number of days in the rental period. Graph this function for d from 1 to 30. If the air hammer is worth $1080, then in how many days would the rental charge equal the value of the air hammer?

112. *Waist-to-hip ratio.* Dr. Aaron R. Folsom, from the University of Minnesota School of Public Health, has concluded that for a man aged 50 to 69 to be in good health, his waist size w should be less than or equal to

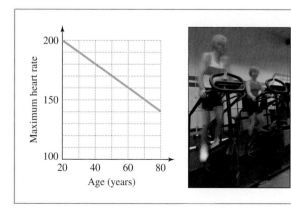

FIGURE FOR EXERCISE 109

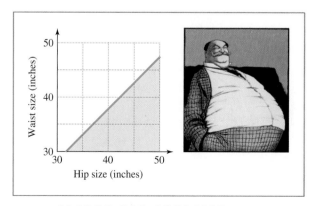

FIGURE FOR EXERCISE 112

95% of his hip size h as shown in the figure on the previous page.

a) Write an inequality that describes the region shown in the figure.

b) Is a man in this group with a 36-inch waist and 37-inch hips in good health?

c) If a man in this group has a waist of 38 inches, then what is his minimum hip size for good health?

CHAPTER 3 TEST

Complete each ordered pair so that it satisfies the given equation.

1. $(0, \ ), (\ , 0), (\ , -8), 2x + y = 5$

Solve each problem.

2. Find the slope of the line through $(-3, 7)$ and $(2, 1)$.

3. Find the midpoint and length of the line segment with endpoints $(2, 0)$ and $(-3, -1)$.

4. Determine the slope and y-intercept for the line $8x - 5y = -10$.

5. Show that $(-1, -2), (0, 0), (6, 2)$, and $(5, 0)$ are the vertices of a parallelogram.

6. Suppose the value, V, in dollars, of a boat is a linear function of its age, a, in years. If a boat was valued at \$22,000 brand new and it is worth \$16,000 when it is 3 years old, find the linear equation that expresses V in terms of a.

For each line described below, write its equation in standard form with integral coefficients.

7. The line with y-intercept $(0, 3)$ and slope $-\dfrac{1}{2}$

8. The line through $(-3, 5)$ with slope -4

9. The line through $(2, 3)$ that is perpendicular to $3x - 5y = 7$

10. The line shown in the graph:

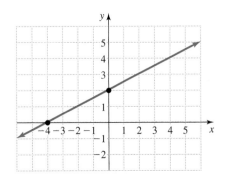

FIGURE FOR EXERCISE 10

Sketch the graph of each equation in the rectangular coordinate system.

11. $y = 4$

12. $x = 3$

13. $3x + 4y = 12$

14. $y = \dfrac{2}{3}x - 2$

Sketch the graph of each inequality.

15. $y > -\dfrac{1}{2}x + 3$

16. $x > 2$ and $x + y > 0$

17. $|2x + y| \geq 3$

Solve each problem.

18. Determine whether $\{(0, 5), (9, 5), (4, 5)\}$ is a function.

19. Let $f(x) = -2x + 5$. Find $f(-3)$.

20. Find the domain and range of the function $y = \sqrt{x - 7}$.

21. A mail-order firm charges its customers a shipping and handling fee of \$3.00 plus \$0.50 per pound for each order shipped. Express the shipping and handling fee S as a function of the weight of the order n.

22. If a ball is tossed into the air from a height of 6 feet with a velocity of 32 feet per second, then its altitude at time t (in seconds) can be described by the function

$$A(t) = -16t^2 + 32t + 6.$$

Find the altitude of the ball at 2 seconds.

Graph Paper

Use these grids for graphing. Make as many copies of this page as you need.

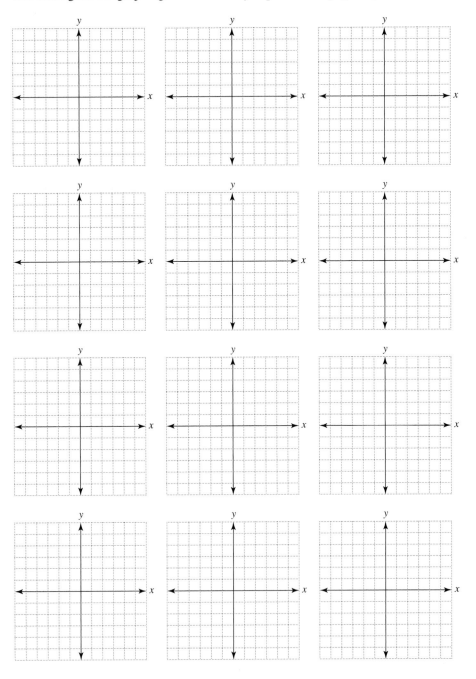

Evaluate each expression.

1. $2^3 \cdot 4^2$

2. $2^7 - 2^6$

3. $3^2 - 4(5)(-2)$

4. $3 - 2 \,|\, 5 - 7 \cdot 3 \,|$

5. $\dfrac{2 - (-3)}{5 - 6}$

6. $\dfrac{-3 - 7}{-1 - (-3)}$

Simplify each expression.

7. $3t \cdot 4t$

8. $3t + 4t$

9. $\dfrac{4x + 8}{4}$

10. $\dfrac{-8y}{-4} - \dfrac{10y}{-2}$

11. $3(x - 4) - 4(5 - x)$

12. $-2(3x^2 - x) + 3(2x - 5x^2)$

Solve each equation.

13. $15(b - 27) = 0$

14. $0.05a - 0.04(a - 50) = 4$

15. $|\, 3v - 7 \,| = 0$

16. $|\, 3u - 7 \,| = 3$

17. $|\, 3x - 7 \,| = -77$

18. $|\, 3x - 7 \,| + 1 = 8$

Graph the solution set to each inequality or compound inequality in one variable on the number line.

19. $2x - 1 > 7$

20. $5 - 3x \le -1$

21. $x - 5 \le 4$ and $3x - 1 < 8$

22. $2x \le -6$ or $5 - 2x < -7$

23. $|\, x - 3 \,| < 2$

24. $|\, 1 - 2x \,| \ge 7$

Graph the solution set to each linear inequality or compound inequality in a rectangular coordinate system.

25. $y < 2x - 1$

26. $3x - y \le 2$

27. $y > x$ and $y < 5 - 3x$

28. $y \le 2$ or $x \ge -3$

Study Tip

Don't wait until the final exam to review material. Do some review on a regular basis. The Making Connections exercises on this page can be used to review, compare, and contrast different concepts that you have studied. A good time to work these exercises is between a test and the start of new material.

Solve this problem.

29. *Social Security.* A person retiring in the year 2005 who earned a lifetime average annual salary of $25,000 will receive a benefit based on age (Social Security Administration, www.ssa.gov). For ages 62 through 64 the benefit in dollars is determined by $b = 7{,}000 + 500(a - 62)$, for ages 65 through 67 the benefit is determined by $b = 10{,}000 + 667(a - 67)$, and for ages 68 through 70 the benefit is determined by $b = 10{,}000 + 800(a - 67)$.

a) Write each benefit formula in slope-intercept form.

b) What will be the annual Social Security benefit for a person who retires in 2005 at age 64?

c) If a person retires in 2005 and gets an $11,600 benefit, then what is the age of that person in 2005?

d) Find the slope of each line segment in the accompanying figure and interpret your results.

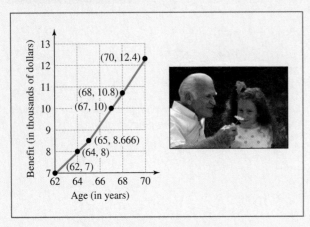

FIGURE FOR EXERCISE 29

Systems of Linear Equations

I n his letter to M. Leroy in 1789 Benjamin Franklin said, "In this world nothing is certain but death and taxes." Since that time taxes have become not only inevitable, but also intricate and complex.

Each year the U.S. Congress revises parts of the Federal Income Tax Code. To help clarify these revisions, the Internal Revenue Service issues frequent revenue rulings. In addition, there are seven tax courts that further interpret changes and revisions, sometimes in entirely different ways. Is it any wonder that tax preparation has become complicated and few individuals actually prepare their own taxes? Both corporate and individual tax preparation is a growing business, and there are over 500,000 tax counselors helping more than 60 million taxpayers to file their returns correctly.

Everyone knows that doing taxes involves a lot of arithmetic, but not everyone knows that computing taxes can also involve algebra. In fact, to find state and federal taxes for certain corporations, you must solve a system of equations. You will see an example of using algebra to find amounts of income taxes in Exercises 61 and 62 of Section 4.1.

4.1   SOLVING SYSTEMS BY GRAPHING AND SUBSTITUTION

In Chapter 3 we studied linear equations in two variables, but we have usually considered only one equation at a time. In this chapter we will see problems that involve more than one equation. Any collection of two or more equations is called a **system** of equations. If the equations of a system involve two variables, then the set of ordered pairs that satisfy all of the equations is the **solution set of the system.** In this section we solve systems of linear equations in two variables and use systems to solve problems.

Solving a System by Graphing

Because the graph of each linear equation is a line, points that satisfy both equations lie on both lines. For some systems these points can be found by graphing.

EXAMPLE 1

A system with only one solution

Solve the system by graphing:

$$y = x + 2$$
$$x + y = 4$$

Solution

First write the equations in slope-intercept form:

$$y = x + 2$$
$$y = -x + 4$$

Use the y-intercept and the slope to graph each line. The graph of the system is shown in Fig. 4.1. From the graph it appears that these lines intersect at $(1, 3)$. To be certain, we can check that $(1, 3)$ satisfies both equations. Let $x = 1$ and $y = 3$ in $y = x + 2$ to get

$$3 = 1 + 2.$$

Let $x = 1$ and $y = 3$ in $x + y = 4$ to get

$$1 + 3 = 4.$$

Because $(1, 3)$ satisfies both equations, the solution set to the system is $\{(1, 3)\}$.

Calculator Close-Up

To check Example 1, graph

$$y_1 = x + 2$$

and

$$y_2 = -x + 4.$$

From the CALC menu, choose intersect to have the calculator locate the point of intersection of the two lines. After choosing intersect, you must indicate which two lines you want to intersect and then guess the point of intersection.

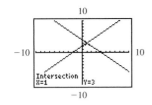

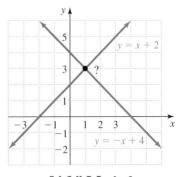

FIGURE 4.1

■

The graphs of the equations in Example 2 are parallel lines, and there is no point of intersection.

E X A M P L E   2

A system with no solution

Solve the system by graphing:

$$2x - 3y = 6$$
$$3y - 2x = 3$$

Solution

First write each equation in slope-intercept form:

$$2x - 3y = 6 \qquad\qquad 3y - 2x = 3$$
$$-3y = -2x + 6 \qquad\qquad 3y = 2x + 3$$
$$y = \frac{2}{3}x - 2 \qquad\qquad y = \frac{2}{3}x + 1$$

The graph of the system is shown in Fig. 4.2. Because the two lines in Fig. 4.2 are parallel, there is no ordered pair that satisfies both equations. The solution set to the system is the empty set, $\varnothing$.

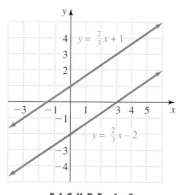

FIGURE 4.2   ■

The equations in Example 3 are two different equations for the same straight line.

E X A M P L E   3

A system with infinitely many solutions

Solve the system by graphing:

$$2(y + 2) = x$$
$$x - 2y = 4$$

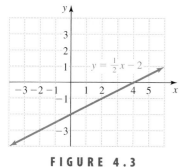

FIGURE 4.3

Solution

Write each equation in slope-intercept form:

$$2(y + 2) = x \qquad\qquad x - 2y = 4$$
$$2y + 4 = x \qquad\qquad -2y = -x + 4$$
$$y = \frac{1}{2}x - 2 \qquad\qquad y = \frac{1}{2}x - 2$$

Because the equations have the same slope-intercept form, the original equations are equivalent. Their graphs are the same straight line as shown in Fig. 4.3. Every point on the line satisfies both equations of the system. There are infinitely many points in the solution set. The solution set is $\{(x, y) \mid x - 2y = 4\}$.   ■

35. $2x + y = 9$
$2x - 5y = 15$

36. $3y - x = 0$
$x - 4y = -2$

37. $x - y = 0$
$2x + 3y = 35$

38. $2y = x + 6$
$-3x + 2y = -2$

39. $x + y = 40$
$0.2x + 0.8y = 23$

40. $x - y = 10$
$0.1x + 0.5y = 13$

41. $2x = 3y - 8$
$5y = 10x - 5$

42. $6x - 3y = 3$
$10x = y + 7$

43. $y = \dfrac{5}{7}x$
$x = -\dfrac{2}{3}y$

44. $y = \dfrac{5}{2}x$
$x + 3y = 3$

45. $x + y = 4$
$x - y = 5$

46. $3x - 6y = 5$
$2y = 4x - 6$

47. $3(y - 1) = 2(x - 3)$
$3y - 2x = -3$

48. $y = 3(x - 4)$
$3x - y = 12$

49. $y = 3x$
$y = 3x + 1$

50. $y = 2x - 3$
$y = 3x - 3$

51. $x - y = 0.1$
$2x - 3y = -0.5$

52. $y - 2x = -7.5$
$3x - 5y = 3.2$

In Exercises 53–66, write a system of two equations in two unknowns for each problem. Solve each system by substitution. See Examples 7 and 8.

53. *Perimeter of a rectangle.* The length of a rectangular swimming pool is 15 feet longer than the width. If the perimeter is 82 feet, then what are the length and width?

54. *Household income.* Alkena and Hsu together earn $84,326 per year. If Alkena earns $12,468 more per year than Hsu, then how much does each of them earn per year?

55. *Different interest rates.* Mrs. Brighton invested $30,000 and received a total of $2,300 in interest. If she invested part of the money at 10% and the remainder at 5%, then how much did she invest at each rate?

56. *Different growth rates.* The combined population of Marysville and Springfield was 25,000 in 1990. By 1995 the population of Marysville had increased by

10%, while Springfield had increased by 9%. If the total population increased by 2,380 people, then what was the population of each city in 1990?

57. *Finding numbers.* The sum of two numbers is 2, and their difference is 26. Find the numbers.

58. *Finding more numbers.* The sum of two numbers is -16, and their difference is 8. Find the numbers.

59. *Toasters and vacations.* During one week a land developer gave away Florida vacation coupons or toasters to 100 potential customers who listened to a sales presentation. It costs the developer $6 for a toaster and $24 for a Florida vacation coupon. If his bill for prizes that week was $708, then how many of each prize did he give away?

60. *Ticket sales.* Tickets for a concert were sold to adults for $3 and to students for $2. If the total receipts were $824 and twice as many adult tickets as student tickets were sold, then how many of each were sold?

61. *Corporate taxes.* According to Bruce Harrell, CPA, the amount of federal income tax for a class C corporation is deductible on the Louisiana state tax return, and the amount of state income tax for a class C corporation is deductible on the federal tax return. So for a state tax rate of 5% and a federal tax rate of 30%, we have

state tax $= 0.05$(taxable income $-$ federal tax)

and

federal tax $= 0.30$(taxable income $-$ state tax).

Find the amounts of state and federal income tax for a class C corporation that has a taxable income of $100,000.

62. *More taxes.* Use the information given in Exercise 61 to find the amounts of state and federal income tax for a class C corporation that has a taxable income of $300,000. Use a state tax rate of 6% and a federal tax rate of 40%.

63. *Cost accounting.* The problems presented in this exercise and the next are encountered in cost accounting. A company has agreed to distribute 20% of its net income N to its employees as a bonus; $B = 0.20N$. If the company has income of $120,000 before the bonus, the bonus B is deducted from the $120,000 as an expense to determine net income; $N = 120,000 - B$. Solve the system of two equations in N and B to find the amount of the bonus.

64. *Bonus and taxes.* A company has an income of $100,000 before paying taxes and a bonus. The bonus B is to be 20% of the income after deducting income taxes T but before deducting the bonus. So

$$B = 0.20(100,000 - T).$$

Because the bonus is a deductible expense, the amount of income tax T at a 40% rate is 40% of the income after deducting the bonus. So

$$T = 0.40(100,000 - B).$$

a) Use the accompanying graph to estimate the values of T and B that satisfy both equations.

b) Solve the system algebraically to find the bonus and the amount of tax.

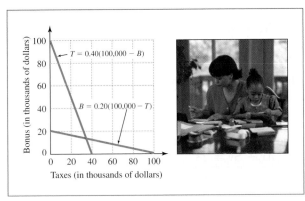

FIGURE FOR EXERCISE 64

65. *Textbook case.* The accompanying graph shows the cost of producing textbooks and the revenue from the sale of those textbooks.

a) What is the cost of producing 10,000 textbooks?

b) What is the revenue when 10,000 textbooks are sold?

c) For what number of textbooks is the cost equal to the revenue?

d) The cost of producing zero textbooks is called the *fixed cost*. Find the fixed cost.

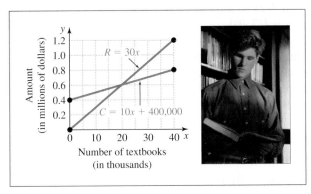

FIGURE FOR EXERCISE 65

66. *Free market.* The function $S = 5000 + 200x$ and $D = 9500 - 100x$ express the supply S and the demand D, respectively, for a popular compact disk brand as a function of its price x (in dollars).

a) Graph the functions on the same coordinate system.

b) What happens to the supply as the price increases?

c) What happens to the demand as the price increases?

d) The price at which supply and demand are equal is called the *equilibrium price*. What is the equilibrium price?

GETTING MORE INVOLVED

 67. *Discussion.* Which of the following equations is not equivalent to $2x - 3y = 6$?

a) $3y - 2x = 6$

b) $y = \dfrac{2}{3}x - 2$

c) $x = \dfrac{3}{2}y + 3$

d) $2(x - 5) = 3y - 4$

 68. *Discussion.* Which of the following equations is inconsistent with the equation $3x + 4y = 8$?

a) $y = \dfrac{3}{4}x + 2$

b) $6x + 8y = 16$

c) $y = -\dfrac{3}{4}x + 8$

d) $3x - 4y = 8$

 ## GRAPHING CALCULATOR EXERCISES

69. Solve each system by graphing each pair of equations on a graphing calculator and using the trace feature or intersect feature to estimate the point of intersection. Find the coordinates of the intersection to the nearest tenth.

a) $y = 3.5x - 7.2$
$\quad\; y = -2.3x + 9.1$

b) $2.3x - 4.1y = 3.3$
$\quad\; 3.4x + 9.2y = 1.3$

E X A M P L E   4

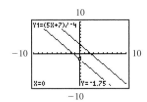
Using the addition method for an inconsistent system

Solve the system:

$$-4y = 5x + 7$$
$$4y = -5x + 12$$

Solution

If these equations are added, both variables are eliminated:

$$-4y = 5x + 7$$
$$\underline{4y = -5x + 12}$$
$$0 = 19$$

Because this equation is inconsistent, the original equations are inconsistent. The solution set to the system is the empty set, $\varnothing$. ■

Equations Involving Fractions or Decimals

When a system of equations involves fractions or decimals, we can use the multiplication property of equality to eliminate the fractions or decimals.

E X A M P L E   5

A system with fractions

Solve the system:

$$\frac{1}{2}x - \frac{2}{3}y = 7$$
$$\frac{2}{3}x - \frac{3}{4}y = 11$$

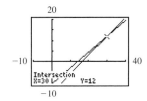
Solution

Multiply the first equation by 6 and the second equation by 12:

$$6\left(\frac{1}{2}x - \frac{2}{3}y\right) = 6(7) \qquad \rightarrow \qquad 3x - 4y = 42$$

$$12\left(\frac{2}{3}x - \frac{3}{4}y\right) = 12(11) \qquad \rightarrow \qquad 8x - 9y = 132$$

To eliminate x, multiply the first equation by -8 and the second by 3:

$$-8(3x - 4y) = -8(42) \qquad \rightarrow \qquad -24x + 32y = -336$$
$$3(8x - 9y) = 3(132) \qquad \rightarrow \qquad \underline{24x - 27y = 396}$$
$$5y = 60$$
$$y = 12$$

Substitute $y = 12$ into the first of the original equations:

$$\frac{1}{2}x - \frac{2}{3}(12) = 7$$

$$\frac{1}{2}x - 8 = 7$$

$$\frac{1}{2}x = 15$$

$$x = 30$$

Check (30, 12) in the original system. The solution set is $\{(30, 12)\}$. ■

E X A M P L E   6

A system with decimals

Solve the system:

$$0.05x + 0.7y = 40$$
$$x + 0.4y = 120$$

Solution

Multiply the first equation by 100 and the second by 10 to eliminate the decimals:

$$100(0.05x + 0.7y) = 100(40) \quad \rightarrow \quad 5x + 70y = 4000$$
$$10(x + 0.4y) = 10(120) \quad \rightarrow \quad 10x + 4y = 1200$$

To eliminate x by addition, multiply the first equation by -2:

$$-2(5x + 70y) = -2(4000) \quad \rightarrow \quad -10x - 140y = -8000$$
$$10x + 4y = 1200 \quad \rightarrow \quad \underline{10x + \quad 4y = 1200}$$
$$-136y = -6800$$
$$y = 50$$

Use $y = 50$ in $x + 0.4y = 120$ to find x:

$$x + 0.4(50) = 120$$
$$x + 20 = 120$$
$$x = 100$$

Check (100, 50) in the original system. The solution set is $\{(100, 50)\}$. ■

The strategy for solving an independent system by addition is summarized as follows.

The Addition Method

1. Write both equations in the same form (usually $Ax + By = C$).
2. Multiply one or both of the equations by appropriate numbers (if necessary) so that one of the variables will be eliminated by addition.
3. Add the equations to get an equation in one variable.
4. Solve the equation in one variable.
5. Substitute the value obtained for one variable into one of the original equations to obtain the value of the other variable.
6. Check the two values in both of the original equations.

Applications

Any system of two linear equations in two variables can be solved by either the addition method or substitution. In applications we use whichever method appears to be the simpler for the problem at hand.

E X A M P L E   7

Fajitas and burritos

At the Cactus Cafe the total price for four fajita dinners and three burrito dinners is $48, and the total price for three fajita dinners and two burrito dinners is $34. What is the price of each type of dinner?

Solution

Let x represent the price (in dollars) of a fajita dinner, and let y represent the price (in dollars) of a burrito dinner. We can write two equations to describe the given information:

$$4x + 3y = 48$$
$$3x + 2y = 34$$

Because 12 is the least common multiple of 4 and 3 (the coefficients of x), we multiply the first equation by -3 and the second by 4:

$$-3(4x + 3y) = -3(48) \quad \text{Multiply each side by } -3.$$
$$4(3x + 2y) = 4(34) \quad \text{Multiply each side by 4.}$$

$$\begin{aligned} -12x - 9y &= -144 \\ \underline{12x + 8y} &= \underline{136} \quad \text{Add.} \\ -y &= -8 \\ y &= 8 \end{aligned}$$

To find x, use $y = 8$ in the first equation $4x + 3y = 48$:

$$4x + 3(8) = 48$$
$$4x + 24 = 48$$
$$4x = 24$$
$$x = 6$$

So the fajita dinners are $6 each, and the burrito dinners are $8 each. Check this solution in the original problem. ■

E X A M P L E 8

Mixing cooking oil

Canola oil is 7% saturated fat, and corn oil is 14% saturated fat. Crisco sells a blend, Crisco Canola and Corn Oil, which is 11% saturated fat. How many gallons of each type of oil must be mixed to get 280 gallons of this blend?

Solution

Let x represent the number of gallons of canola oil, and let y represent the number of gallons of corn oil. Make a table to summarize all facts:

	Amount (gallons)	% fat	Amount of fat (gallons)
Canola oil	x	7	$0.07x$
Corn oil	y	14	$0.14y$
Canola and Corn Oil	280	11	0.11(280) or 30.8

We can write two equations to express the following facts: (1) the total amount of oil is 280 gallons and (2) the total amount of fat is 30.8 gallons. Then we can use multiplication and addition to solve the system.

$$(1) \qquad x + y = 280 \qquad \text{Multiply by } -0.07. \quad -0.07x - 0.07y = -19.6$$
$$(2) \quad 0.07x + 0.14y = 30.80 \qquad \qquad \underline{0.07x + 0.14y = \quad 30.8}$$
$$0.07y = \quad 11.2$$
$$y = \frac{11.2}{0.07} = 160$$

If $y = 160$ and $x + y = 280$, then $x = 120$. Check that $0.07(120) + 0.14(160) = 30.8$. So it takes 120 gallons of canola oil and 160 gallons of corn oil to make 280 gallons of Crisco Canola and Corn Oil. ■

WARM-UPS

True or false? Explain your answer.

Exercises 1–6 refer to the following systems.

a) $3x - y = 9$ **b)** $4x - 2y = 20$ **c)** $x - y = 6$
     $2x + y = 6$ $-2x + y = -10$ $x - y = 7$

1. To solve system (a) by addition, we simply add the equations.

2. To solve system (a) by addition, we can multiply the first equation by 2 and the second by 3 and then add.

3. To solve system (b) by addition, we can multiply the second equation by 2 and then add.

4. Both $(0, -10)$ and $(5, 0)$ are in the solution set to system (b).

5. The solution set to system (b) is the set of all real numbers.

6. System (c) has no solution.

7. Both the addition method and substitution method are used to eliminate a variable from a system of two linear equations in two variables.

8. For the addition method, both equations must be in standard form.

9. To eliminate fractions in an equation, we multiply each side by the least common denominator of all fractions involved.

10. We can eliminate either variable by using the addition method.

4.2 EXERCISES

Reading and Writing *After reading this section, write out the answers to these questions. Use complete sentences.*

1. What method is presented in this section for solving a system of linear equations?

2. What are we trying to accomplish by adding the equations?

3. What must we sometimes do before we add the equations?

4. How can you recognize an inconsistent system when solving by addition?

5. How can you recognize a dependent system when solving by addition?

6. For which systems is the addition method easier to use than substitution?

Solve each system by the addition method. See Examples 1–3.

7. $x + y = 7$
$x - y = 9$

8. $3x - 4y = 11$
$-3x + 2y = -7$

9. $x - y = 12$
$2x + y = 3$

10. $x - 2y = -1$
$-x + 5y = 4$

11. $3x - y = 5$
$5x + y = -2$

12. $-x + 2y = 4$
$x - 5y = 1$

13. $2x - y = -5$
$3x + 2y = 3$

14. $3x + 5y = -11$
$x - 2y = 11$

15. $-3x + 5y = 1$
$9x - 3y = 5$

16. $7x - 4y = -3$
$x + 2y = 3$

17. $2x - 5y = 13$
$3x + 4y = -15$

18. $3x + 4y = -5$
$5x + 6y = -7$

19. $2x = 3y + 11$
$7x - 4y = 6$

20. $2x = 2 - y$
$3x + y = -1$

21. $x + y = 48$
$12x + 14y = 628$

22. $x + y = 13$
$22x + 36y = 356$

Solve each system by the addition method. Determine whether the equations are independent, dependent, or inconsistent. See Example 4.

23. $3x - 4y = 9$
$-3x + 4y = 12$

24. $x - y = 3$
$-6x + 6y = 17$

25. $5x - y = 1$
$10x - 2y = 2$

26. $4x + 3y = 2$
$-12x - 9y = -6$

27. $2x - y = 5$
$2x + y = 5$

28. $-3x + 2y = 8$
$3x + 2y = 8$

Solve each system by the addition method. See Examples 5 and 6.

29. $\dfrac{1}{4}x + \dfrac{1}{3}y = 5$
$x - y = 6$

30. $\dfrac{3x}{2} - \dfrac{2y}{3} = 10$
$\dfrac{1}{2}x + \dfrac{1}{2}y = -1$

31. $\dfrac{x}{4} - \dfrac{y}{3} = -4$
$\dfrac{x}{8} + \dfrac{y}{6} = 0$

32. $\dfrac{x}{3} - \dfrac{y}{2} = \dfrac{5}{6}$
$\dfrac{x}{5} - \dfrac{y}{3} = -\dfrac{3}{5}$

33. $\dfrac{1}{8}x + \dfrac{1}{4}y = 5$
$\dfrac{1}{16}x + \dfrac{1}{2}y = 7$

34. $\dfrac{3}{7}x + \dfrac{5}{9}y = 27$
$\dfrac{1}{9}x + \dfrac{2}{7}y = 7$

35. $\dfrac{1}{3}x + \dfrac{1}{2}y = \dfrac{1}{3}$
$\dfrac{5}{6}x - \dfrac{3}{4}y = \dfrac{1}{6}$

36. $\dfrac{2}{3}x + \dfrac{5}{6}y = \dfrac{1}{4}$
$\dfrac{1}{5}x - \dfrac{1}{10}y = -\dfrac{1}{10}$

37. $0.05x + 0.10y = 1.30$
$x + y = 19$

38. $0.1x + 0.06y = 9$
$0.09x + 0.5y = 52.7$

39. $x + y = 1200$
$0.12x + 0.09y = 120$

40. $x - y = 100$
$0.20x + 0.06y = 150$

41. $1.5x - 2y = -0.25$
$3x + 1.5y = 6.375$

42. $3x - 2.5y = 7.125$
$2.5x - 3y = 7.3125$

43. $0.24x + 0.6y = 0.58$
$0.8x - 0.12y = 0.52$

44. $0.18x + 0.27y = 0.09$
$0.06x - 0.54y = -0.04$

Solve each system by substitution or addition, whichever is easier.

45. $y = x + 1$
$2x - 5y = -20$

46. $y = 3x - 4$
$x + y = 32$

47. $x - y = 19$
$2x + y = -13$

48. $x + y = 3$
$7x - y = 29$

49. $2y = x + 2$
$x = y - 1$

50. $2y - x = 3$
$x = 3y - 5$

51. $2y - 3x = -1$
$5y + 3x = 29$

52. $y - 5 = 2x$
$y - 9 = -2x$

53. $6x + 3y = 4$
$$y = \frac{2}{3}x$$

54. $3x - 2y = 2$
$$x = \frac{2}{9}y$$

55. $y = 3x + 1$
$$x = \frac{1}{3}y + 5$$

56. $y = -\frac{2}{3}x - 3$
$$x = -\frac{3}{2}y + 9$$

57. $x - y = 0$
$$x + y = 2x$$

58. $5x - 4y = 9$
$$8y - 10x = -18$$

Write a system of two equations in two unknowns for each problem. Solve each system by the method of your choice. See Examples 7 and 8.

59. *Coffee and doughnuts.* On Monday, Archie paid $3.40 for three doughnuts and two coffees. On Tuesday he paid $3.60 for two doughnuts and three coffees. On Wednesday he was tired of paying the tab and went out for coffee by himself. What was his bill for one doughnut and one coffee?

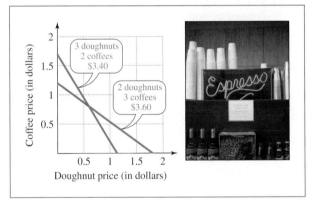

FIGURE FOR EXERCISE 59

60. *Books and magazines.* At Gwen's garage sale, all books were one price, and all magazines were another price. Harriet bought four books and three magazines for $1.45, and June bought two books and five magazines for $1.25. What was the price of a book and what was the price of a magazine?

61. *Boys and girls.* One-half of the boys and one-third of the girls of Freemont High attended the homecoming game, whereas one-third of the boys and one-half of the girls attended the homecoming dance. If there were 570 students at the game and 580 at the dance, then how many students are there at Freemont High?

62. *Girls and boys.* There are 385 surfers in Surf City. Two-thirds of the boys are surfers and one-twelfth of the girls are surfers. If there are two girls for every boy, then how many boys and how many girls are there in Surf City?

63. *Nickels and dimes.* Winborne has 35 coins consisting of dimes and nickels. If the value of his coins is $3.30, then how many of each type does he have?

64. *Pennies and nickels.* Wendy has 52 coins consisting of nickels and pennies. If the value of the coins is $1.20, then how many of each type does she have?

65. *Blending fudge.* The Chocolate Factory in Vancouver blends its double-dark-chocolate fudge, which is 35% fat, with its peanut butter fudge, which is 25% fat, to obtain double-dark-peanut fudge, which is 29% fat.
  a) Use the accompanying graph to estimate the number of pounds of each type that must be mixed to obtain 50 pounds of double-dark-peanut fudge.
  b) Write a system of equations and solve it algebraically to find the exact amount of each type that should be used to obtain 50 pounds of double-dark-peanut fudge.

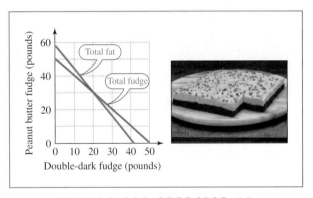

FIGURE FOR EXERCISE 65

66. *Low-fat yogurt.* Ziggy's Famous Yogurt blends regular yogurt that is 3% fat with its no-fat yogurt to obtain low-fat yogurt that is 1% fat. How many pounds of regular yogurt and how many pounds of no-fat yogurt should be mixed to obtain 60 pounds of low-fat yogurt?

67. *Keystone state.* Judy averaged 42 miles per hour (mph) driving from Allentown to Harrisburg and 51 mph driving from Harrisburg to Pittsburgh. See the figure on the next page. If she drove a total of 288 miles in 6 hours, then how long did it take her to drive from Harrisburg to Pittsburgh?

FIGURE FOR EXERCISE 67

68. *Empire state.* Spike averaged 45 mph driving from Rochester to Syracuse and 49 mph driving from Syracuse to Albany. If he drove a total of 237 miles in 5 hours, then how far is it from Syracuse to Albany?

69. *Probability of rain.* The probability of rain tomorrow is four times the probability that it does not rain tomorrow. The probability that it rains plus the probability that it does not rain is 1. What is the probability that it rains tomorrow?

70. *Super Bowl contender.* The probability that San Francisco plays in the next Super Bowl is nine times the probability that they do not play in the next Super Bowl. The probability that San Francisco plays in the next Super Bowl plus the probability that they do not play is 1. What is the probability that San Francisco plays in the next Super Bowl?

71. *Rectangular lot.* The width of a rectangular lot is 75% of its length. If the perimeter is 700 meters, then what are the length and width?

72. *Fence painting.* Darren and Douglas must paint the 792-foot fence that encircles their family home. Because Darren is older, he has agreed to paint 20% more than Douglas. How much of the fence will each boy paint?

GETTING MORE INVOLVED

73. *Discussion.* Explain how you decide whether it is easier to solve a system by substitution or addition.

74. *Exploration.* a) Write a linear equation in two variables that is satisfied by $(-3, 5)$.
  b) Write another linear equation in two variables that is satisfied by $(-3, 5)$.
  c) Are your equations independent or dependent?
  d) Explain how to select the second equation so that it will be independent of the first.

75. *Exploration.* a) Make up a system of two linear equations in two variables such that both $(-1, 2)$ and $(4, 5)$ are in the solution set.
  b) Are your equations independent or dependent?
  c) Is it possible to find an independent system that is satisfied by both ordered pairs? Explain.

In This Section

- Definition
- Solving a System by Elimination
- Graphs of Equations in Three Variables
- Applications

4.3 SYSTEMS OF LINEAR EQUATIONS IN THREE VARIABLES

The techniques that you learned in Section 4.2 can be extended to systems of equations in more than two variables. In this section we use elimination of variables to solve systems of equations in three variables.

Definition

The equation $5x - 4y = 7$ is called a linear equation in two variables because its graph is a straight line. The equation $2x + 3y - 4z = 12$ is similar in form, and so it is a linear equation in three variables. An equation in three variables is graphed in a three-dimensional coordinate system. The graph of a linear equation in three variables is a plane, not a line. We will not graph equations in three variables in this text, but we can solve systems without graphing. In general, we make the following definition.

Linear Equation in Three Variables

If A, B, C, and D are real numbers, with A, B, and C not all zero, then

$$Ax + By + Cz = D$$

is called a **linear equation in three variables.**

Study Tip

Everyone knows that you must practice to be successful with musical instruments, foreign languages, and sports. Success in algebra also requires regular practice. Thus budget your time so that you have a regular practice period for algebra.

Solving a System by Elimination

A solution to an equation in three variables is an **ordered triple** such as $(-2, 1, 5)$, where the first coordinate is the value of x, the second coordinate is the value of y, and the third coordinate is the value of z. There are infinitely many solutions to a linear equation in three variables.

The solution to a system of equations in three variables is the set of all ordered triples that satisfy all of the equations of the system. The techniques for solving a system of linear equations in three variables are similar to those used on systems of linear equations in two variables. We eliminate variables by either substitution or addition.

E X A M P L E   1   **A linear system with a single solution**

Solve the system:

$$(1) \qquad x + y - z = -1$$
$$(2) \qquad 2x - 2y + 3z = 8$$
$$(3) \qquad 2x - y + 2z = 9$$

Solution

We can eliminate y from Eqs. (1) and (2) by multiplying Eq. (1) by 2 and adding it to Eq. (2):

$$\begin{array}{ll} 2x + 2y - 2z = -2 & \text{Eq. (1) multiplied by 2} \\ \underline{2x - 2y + 3z = 8} & \text{Eq. (2)} \\ (4) \quad 4x + z = 6 & \end{array}$$

Now we must eliminate the same variable, y, from another pair of equations. Eliminate y from Eqs. (1) and (3) by simply adding them:

$$\begin{array}{ll} x + y - z = -1 & \text{Eq. (1)} \\ \underline{2x - y + 2z = 9} & \text{Eq. (3)} \\ (5) \quad 3x + z = 8 & \end{array}$$

Equations (4) and (5) give us a system with two variables. We now solve this system. Eliminate z by multiplying Eq. (4) by -1 and adding the equations:

$$\begin{array}{ll} -4x - z = -6 & \text{Eq. (4) multiplied by } -1 \\ \underline{3x + z = 8} & \text{Eq. (5)} \\ -x = 2 & \\ x = -2 & \end{array}$$

Now that we have x, we can replace x by -2 in Eq. (5) to find y:

$$\begin{array}{ll} 3x + z = 8 & \text{Eq. (5)} \\ 3(-2) + z = 8 & \\ -6 + z = 8 & \\ z = 14 & \end{array}$$

Now replace x by -2 and z by 14 in Eq. (1) to find y:

$$\begin{array}{ll} x + y - z = -1 & \text{Eq. (1)} \\ -2 + y - 14 = -1 & x = -2, z = 14 \\ y - 16 = -1 & \\ y = 15 & \end{array}$$

Calculator Close-Up

You can use a calculator to check that $(-2, 15, 14)$ satisfies all three equations of the original system.

```
-2+15-14
            -1
2* -2-2*15+3*14
             8
2* -2-15+2*14
             9
```

Check that $(-2, 15, 14)$ satisfies all three of the original equations. The solution set is $\{(-2, 15, 14)\}$. ∎

Note that we could have eliminated any one of the three variables in Example 1 to get a system of two equations in two variables. We chose to eliminate y first because it was the easiest to eliminate. The strategy that we follow for solving a system of three linear equations in three variables is stated as follows:

Solving a System in Three Variables

1. Use substitution or addition to eliminate any one of the variables from a pair of equations of the system. Look for the easiest variable to eliminate.
2. Eliminate the same variable from another pair of equations of the system.
3. Solve the resulting system of two equations in two unknowns.
4. After you have found the values of two of the variables, substitute into one of the original equations to find the value of the third variable.
5. Check the three values in all of the original equations.

In Example 2 we use a combination of addition and substitution.

E X A M P L E   2

Using addition and substitution

Solve the system:

$$\begin{aligned}
(1) \quad & x + y \phantom{{}- 3z} = 4 \\
(2) \quad & 2x \phantom{{}+ y} - 3z = 14 \\
(3) \quad & 2y + z = 2
\end{aligned}$$

Helpful Hint

In Example 2 we chose to eliminate y first. Try solving Example 2 by first eliminating z. Write $z = 2 - 2y$ and then substitute $2 - 2y$ for z in Eqs. (1) and (2).

Solution

From Eq. (1) we get $y = 4 - x$. If we substitute $y = 4 - x$ into Eq. (3), then Eqs. (2) and (3) will be equations involving x and z only.

$$\begin{aligned}
(3) \quad & 2y + z = 2 \\
& 2(4 - x) + z = 2 \quad \text{Replace } y \text{ by } 4 - x. \\
& 8 - 2x + z = 2 \quad \text{Simplify.} \\
(4) \quad & -2x + z = -6
\end{aligned}$$

Now solve the system consisting of Eqs. (2) and (4) by addition:

$$\begin{array}{rl}
2x - 3z = 14 & \text{Eq. (2)} \\
\underline{-2x + z = -6} & \text{Eq. (4)} \\
-2z = 8 & \\
z = -4 &
\end{array}$$

Use Eq. (3) to find y:

$$\begin{array}{rl}
2y + z = 2 & \text{Eq. (3)} \\
2y + (-4) = 2 & \text{Let } z = -4. \\
2y = 6 & \\
y = 3 &
\end{array}$$

Use Eq. (1) to find x:

$$\begin{array}{rl}
x + y = 4 & \text{Eq. (1)} \\
x + 3 = 4 & \text{Let } y = 3. \\
x = 1 &
\end{array}$$

Check that $(1, 3, -4)$ satisfies all three of the original equations. The solution set is $\{(1, 3, -4)\}$. ∎

Study Tip

When one student asks another for help, often the one who does the explaining is the one who learns the most. When you work together, don't let one person do all of the talking. If you must work alone, then try explaining things to yourself. You might even try talking to yourself.

CAUTION In solving a system in three variables it is essential to keep your work organized and neat. Writing short notes that explain your steps (as was done in the examples) will allow you to go back and check your work.

Graphs of Equations in Three Variables

The graph of any equation in three variables can be drawn on a three-dimensional coordinate system. The graph of a linear equation in three variables is a plane. To solve a system of three linear equations in three variables by graphing, we would have to draw the three planes and then identify the points that lie on all three of them. This method would be difficult even when the points have simple coordinates. So we will not attempt to solve these systems by graphing.

By considering how three planes might intersect, we can better understand the different types of solutions to a system of three equations in three variables. Figure 4.6 shows some of the possibilities for the positioning of three planes in three-dimensional space. In most of the problems that we will solve the planes intersect at a single point as in Fig. 4.6(a). The solution set consists of one ordered triple. However, the system may include two equations corresponding to parallel planes that have no intersection. In this case the equations are said to be **inconsistent.** If the system has at least two inconsistent equations, then the solution set is the empty set [see Figs. 4.6(b) and 4.6(c)].

There are two ways in which the intersection of three planes can consist of infinitely many points. The intersection could be a line or a plane. To get a line, we can have either three different planes intersecting along a line, as in Fig. 4.6(d) or two equations for the same plane, with the third plane intersecting that plane. If all three equations are equations of the same plane, we get that plane for the intersection. We will not solve systems corresponding to all of the possible configurations described. The following examples illustrate two of these cases.

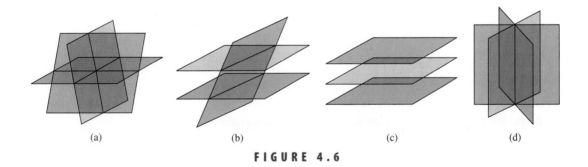

(a)　　　　　(b)　　　　　(c)　　　　　(d)

FIGURE 4.6

EXAMPLE 3

An inconsistent system of three linear equations

Solve the system:

$$(1) \qquad x + y - z = 5$$
$$(2) \qquad 3x - 2y + z = 8$$
$$(3) \qquad 2x + 2y - 2z = 7$$

Solution

We can eliminate the variable z from Eqs. (1) and (2) by adding them:

$$
\begin{array}{rl}
(1) & x + y - z = 5 \\
(2) & 3x - 2y + z = 8 \\
\hline
& 4x - y = 13
\end{array}
$$

To eliminate z from Eqs. (1) and (3), multiply Eq. (1) by -2 and add the resulting equation to Eq. (3):

$$
\begin{array}{rl}
-2x - 2y + 2z = -10 & \text{Eq. (1) multiplied by } -2 \\
2x + 2y - 2z = 7 & \text{Eq. (3)} \\
\hline
0 = -3
\end{array}
$$

Because the last equation is false, there are two inconsistent equations in the system. Therefore the solution set is the empty set.   ■

E X A M P L E   4

A dependent system of three equations

Solve the system:

$$
\begin{array}{rl}
(1) & 2x - 3y - z = 4 \\
(2) & -6x + 9y + 3z = -12 \\
(3) & 4x - 6y - 2z = 8
\end{array}
$$

Helpful Hint

If you recognize that multiplying Eq. (1) by -3 will produce Eq. (2), and multiplying Eq. (1) by 2 will produce Eq. (3), then you can conclude that all three equations are equivalent and there is no need to add the equations.

Solution

We will first eliminate x from Eqs. (1) and (2). Multiply Eq. (1) by 3 and add the resulting equation to Eq. (2):

$$
\begin{array}{rl}
6x - 9y - 3z = 12 & \text{Eq. (1) multiplied by 3} \\
-6x + 9y + 3z = -12 & \text{Eq. (2)} \\
\hline
0 = 0
\end{array}
$$

The last statement is an identity. The identity occurred because Eq. (2) is a multiple of Eq. (1). In fact, Eq. (3) is also a multiple of Eq. (1). These equations are dependent. They are all equations for the same plane. The solution set is the set of all points on that plane,

$$\{(x, y, z) \mid 2x - 3y - z = 4\}.$$ ■

Applications

Problems involving three unknown quantities can often be solved by using a system of three equations in three variables.

E X A M P L E   5

Finding three unknown rents

Theresa took in a total of $1240 last week from the rental of three condominiums. She had to pay 10% of the rent from the one-bedroom condo for repairs, 20% of the rent from the two-bedroom condo for repairs, and 30% of the rent from the three-bedroom condo for repairs. If the three-bedroom condo rents for twice as much as the one-bedroom condo and her total repair bill was $276, then what is the rent for each condo?

Solution

Let x, y, and z represent the rent on the one-bedroom, two-bedroom, and three-bedroom condos, respectively. We can write one equation for the total rent, another

Helpful Hint

A problem involving two unknowns can often be solved with one variable as in Chapter 2. Likewise, you can often solve a problem with three unknowns using only two variables. Solve Example 5 by letting a, b, and $2a$ be the rent for a one-bedroom, two-bedroom, and a three-bedroom condo.

equation for the total repairs, and a third equation expressing the fact that the rent for the three-bedroom condo is twice that for the one-bedroom condo:

$$x + y + z = 1240$$
$$0.1x + 0.2y + 0.3z = 276$$
$$z = 2x$$

Substitute $z = 2x$ into both of the other equations to eliminate z:

$$x + y + 2x = 1240$$
$$0.1x + 0.2y + 0.3(2x) = 276$$

$$3x + \quad y = 1240$$
$$0.7x + 0.2y = 276$$

$$-2(3x + y) = -2(1240) \qquad \text{Multiply each side by } -2.$$
$$10(0.7x + 0.2y) = 10(276) \qquad \text{Multiply each side by } 10.$$

$$-6x - 2y = -2480$$
$$\underline{7x + 2y = 2760} \qquad \text{Add.}$$
$$x \quad\quad = 280$$

$$z = 2(280) = 560 \qquad \text{Because } z = 2x$$
$$280 + y + 560 = 1240 \qquad \text{Because } x + y + z = 1240$$
$$y = 400$$

Check that $(280, 400, 560)$ satisfies all three of the original equations. The condos rent for $280, $400, and $560 per week. ∎

WARM-UPS

True or false? Explain your answer.

1. The point $(1, -2, 3)$ is in the solution set to the equation $x + y - z = 4$.

2. The point $(4, 1, 1)$ is the only solution to the equation $x + y - z = 4$.

3. The ordered triple $(1, -1, 2)$ satisfies $x + y + z = 2$, $x - y - z = 0$, and $2x + y - z = -1$.

4. Substitution cannot be used on three equations in three variables.

5. Two distinct planes are either parallel or intersect in a single point.

6. The equations $x - y + 2z = 6$ and $x - y + 2z = 4$ are inconsistent.

7. The equations $3x + 2y - 6z = 4$ and $-6x - 4y + 12z = -8$ are dependent.

8. The graph of $y = 2x - 3z + 4$ is a straight line.

9. The value of x nickels, y dimes, and z quarters is $0.05x + 0.10y + 0.25z$ cents.

10. If $x = -2$, $z = 3$, and $x + y + z = 6$, then $y = 7$.

4.3   EXERCISES

Reading and Writing   *After reading this section, write out the answers to these questions. Use complete sentences.*

1. What is a linear equation in three variables?

2. What is an ordered triple?

3. What is a solution to a system of linear equations in three variables?

4. How do we solve systems of linear equations in three variables?

5. What does the graph of a linear equation in three variables look like?

6. How are the planes positioned when a system of linear equations in three variables is inconsistent?

Solve each system of equations. See Examples 1 and 2.

7. $x + y + z = 2$
  $x + 2y - z = 6$
  $2x + y - z = 5$

8. $2x - y + 3z = 14$
  $x + y - 2z = -5$
  $3x + y - z = 2$

9. $x - 2y + 4z = 3$
  $x + 3y - 2z = 6$
  $x - 4y + 3z = -5$

10. $2x + 3y + z = 13$
  $-3x + 2y + z = -4$
  $4x - 4y + z = 5$

11. $2x - y + z = 10$
  $3x - 2y - 2z = 7$
  $x - 3y - 2z = 10$

12. $x - 3y + 2z = -11$
  $2x - 4y + 3z = -15$
  $3x - 5y - 4z = 5$

13. $2x - 3y + z = -9$
  $-2x + y - 3z = 7$
  $x - y + 2z = -5$

14. $3x - 4y + z = 19$
  $2x + 4y + z = 0$
  $x - 2y + 5z = 17$

15. $2x - 5y + 2z = 16$
  $3x + 2y - 3z = -19$
  $4x - 3y + 4z = 18$

16. $-2x + 3y - 4z = 3$
  $3x - 5y + 2z = 4$
  $-4x + 2y - 3z = 0$

17. $x + y = 4$
  $y - z = -2$
  $x + y + z = 9$

18. $x + y - z = 0$
  $x - y = -2$
  $y + z = 10$

19. $x + y = 7$
  $y - z = -1$
  $x + 3z = 18$

20. $2x - y = -8$
  $y + 3z = 22$
  $x - z = -8$

Solve each system. See Examples 3 and 4.

21. $x - y + 2z = 3$
  $2x + y - z = 5$
  $3x - 3y + 6z = 4$

22. $2x - 4y + 6z = 12$
  $6x - 12y + 18z = 36$
  $-x + 2y - 3z = -6$

23. $3x - y + z = 5$
  $9x - 3y + 3z = 15$
  $-12x + 4y - 4z = -20$

24. $4x - 2y - 2z = 5$
  $2x - y - z = 7$
  $-4x + 2y + 2z = 6$

25. $x - y = 3$
  $y + z = 8$
  $2x + 2z = 7$

26. $2x - y = 6$
  $2y + z = -4$
  $8x + 2z = 3$

27. $0.10x + 0.08y - 0.04z = 3$
  $5x + 4y - 2z = 150$
  $0.3x + 0.24y - 0.12z = 9$

28. $0.06x - 0.04y + z = 6$
  $3x - 2y + 50z = 300$
  $0.03x - 0.02y + 0.5z = 3$

   Use a calculator to solve each system.

29. $3x + 2y - 0.4z = 0.1$
  $3.7x - 0.2y + 0.05z = 0.41$
  $-2x + 3.8y - 2.1z = -3.26$

30. $3x - 0.4y + 9z = 1.668$
  $0.3x + 5y - 8z = -0.972$
  $5x - 4y - 8z = 1.8$

Solve each problem by using a system of three equations in three unknowns. See Example 5.

31. *Three cars.* The town of Springfield purchased a Chevrolet, a Ford, and a Toyota for a total of $66,000. The Ford was $2,000 more than the Chevrolet and the Toyota was $2,000 more than the Ford. What was the price of each car?

32. ***Buying texts.*** Melissa purchased an English text, a math text, and a chemistry text for a total of $276. The English text was $20 more than the math text and the chemistry text was twice the price of the math text. What was the price of each text?

33. ***Three-day drive.*** In three days, Carter drove 2196 miles in 36 hours behind the wheel. The first day he averaged 64 mph, the second day 62 mph, and the third day 58 mph. If he drove 4 more hours on the third day than on the first day, then how many hours did he drive each day?

34. ***Three-day trip.*** In three days, Katy traveled 146 miles down the Mississippi River in her kayak with 30 hours of paddling. The first day she averaged 6 mph, the second day 5 mph, and the third day 4 mph. If her distance on the third day was equal to her distance on the first day, then for how many hours did she paddle each day?

35. ***Diversification.*** Ann invested a total of $12,000 in stocks, bonds, and a mutual fund. She received a 10% return on her stock investment, an 8% return on her bond investment, and a 12% return on her mutual fund. Her total return was $1,230. If the total investment in stocks and bonds equaled her mutual fund investment, then how much did she invest in each?

36. ***Paranoia.*** Fearful of a bank failure, Norman split his life savings of $60,000 among three banks. He received 5%, 6%, and 7% on the three deposits. In the account earning 7% interest, he deposited twice as much as in the account earning 5% interest. If his total earnings were $3,760, then how much did he deposit in each account?

37. ***Weighing in.*** Anna, Bob, and Chris will not disclose their weights but agree to be weighed in pairs. Anna and Bob together weigh 226 pounds. Bob and Chris together weigh 210 pounds. Anna and Chris together weigh 200 pounds. How much does each student weigh?

Anna & Bob   Bob & Chris   Anna & Chris

FIGURE FOR EXERCISE 37

38. ***Big tipper.*** On Monday Headley paid $1.70 for two cups of coffee and one doughnut, including the tip. On Tuesday he paid $1.65 for two doughnuts and a cup of coffee, including the tip. On Wednesday he paid $1.30 for one coffee and one doughnut, including the tip. If he always tips the same amount, then what is the amount of each item?

39. ***Three coins.*** Nelson paid $1.75 for his lunch with 13 coins, consisting of nickels, dimes, and quarters. If the number of dimes was twice the number of nickels, then how many of each type of coin did he use?

40. ***Pocket change.*** Harry has $2.25 in nickels, dimes, and quarters. If he had twice as many nickels, half as many dimes, and the same number of quarters, he would have $2.50. If he has 27 coins altogether, then how many of each does he have?

41. ***Working overtime.*** To make ends meet, Ms. Farnsby works three jobs. Her total income last year was $48,000. Her income from teaching was just $6,000 more than her income from house painting. Royalties from her textbook sales were one-seventh of the total money she received from teaching and house painting. How much did she make from each source last year?

42. ***Lunch-box special.*** Salvador's Fruit Mart sells variety packs. The small pack contains three bananas, two apples, and one orange for $1.80. The medium pack contains four bananas, three apples, and three oranges for $3.05. The family size contains six bananas, five apples, and four oranges for $4.65. What price should Salvador charge for his lunch-box special that consists of one banana, one apple, and one orange?

43. ***Three generations.*** Edwin, his father, and his grandfather have an average age of 53. One-half of his grandfather's age, plus one-third of his father's age, plus one-fourth of Edwin's age is 65. If 4 years ago, Edwin's grandfather was four times as old as Edwin, then how old are they all now?

44. ***Three-digit number.*** The sum of the digits of a three-digit number is 11. If the digits are reversed, the new number is 46 more than five times the old number. If the hundreds digit plus twice the tens digit is equal to the units digit, then what is the number?

GETTING MORE INVOLVED

45. ***Exploration.*** Draw diagrams showing the possible ways to position three planes in three-dimensional space.

46. ***Discussion.*** Make up a system of three linear equations in three variables for which the solution set is {(0, 0, 0)}. A system with this solution set is called a *homogeneous* system. Why do you think it is given that name?

4.4 SOLVING LINEAR SYSTEMS USING MATRICES

You solved linear systems in two variables by substitution and addition in Sections 4.1 and 4.2. Those methods are done differently on each system. In this section you will learn the Gauss-Jordan elimination method, which is related to the addition method. The Gauss-Jordan elimination method is performed in the same way on every system. We first need to introduce some new terminology.

Matrices

A **matrix** is a rectangular array of numbers. The **rows** of a matrix run horizontally, and the **columns** of a matrix run vertically. A matrix with m rows and n columns has **order** $m \times n$ (read "m by n"). Each number in a matrix is called an **element** or **entry** of the matrix.

EXAMPLE 1

Order of a matrix

Determine the order of each matrix.

a) $\begin{bmatrix} -1 & 2 \\ 5 & \sqrt{2} \\ 0 & 3 \end{bmatrix}$

b) $\begin{bmatrix} 2 & 3 \\ -1 & 5 \end{bmatrix}$

c) $\begin{bmatrix} 1 & 2 & 3 \\ 4 & 5 & 6 \\ -1 & 0 & 2 \end{bmatrix}$

d) $[1 \quad 3 \quad 6]$

Study Tip

Solution

Because matrix (a) has 3 rows and 2 columns, its order is 3×2. Matrix (b) is a 2×2 matrix, matrix (c) is a 3×3 matrix, and matrix (d) is a 1×3 matrix. ∎

The Augmented Matrix

The solution to a system of linear equations such as

$$x - 2y = -5$$
$$3x + y = 6$$

depends on the coefficients of x and y and the constants on the right-hand side of the equation. The matrix of coefficients for this system is the 2×2 matrix

$$\begin{bmatrix} 1 & -2 \\ 3 & 1 \end{bmatrix}.$$

If we insert the constants from the right-hand side of the system into the matrix of coefficients, we get the 2×3 matrix

$$\left[\begin{array}{cc|c} 1 & -2 & -5 \\ 3 & 1 & 6 \end{array}\right].$$

We use a vertical line between the coefficients and the constants to represent the equal signs. This matrix is the **augmented matrix** of the system. Two systems of linear equations are **equivalent** if they have the same solution set. Two augmented matrices are **equivalent** if the systems they represent are equivalent.

E X A M P L E   2

Writing the augmented matrix

Write the augmented matrix for each system of equations.

a) $3x - 5y = 7$
$x + y = 4$

b) $x + y - z = 5$
$2x + z = 3$
$2x - y + 4z = 0$

c) $x + y = 1$
$y + z = 6$
$z = -5$

Solution

a) $\begin{bmatrix} 3 & -5 & | & 7 \\ 1 & 1 & | & 4 \end{bmatrix}$

b) $\begin{bmatrix} 1 & 1 & -1 & | & 5 \\ 2 & 0 & 1 & | & 3 \\ 2 & -1 & 4 & | & 0 \end{bmatrix}$

c) $\begin{bmatrix} 1 & 1 & 0 & | & 1 \\ 0 & 1 & 1 & | & 6 \\ 0 & 0 & 1 & | & -5 \end{bmatrix}$ ∎

E X A M P L E   3

Writing the system

Write the system of equations represented by each augmented matrix.

a) $\begin{bmatrix} 1 & 4 & | & -2 \\ 1 & -1 & | & 3 \end{bmatrix}$

b) $\begin{bmatrix} 1 & 0 & | & 5 \\ 0 & 1 & | & 1 \end{bmatrix}$

c) $\begin{bmatrix} 2 & 3 & 4 & | & 6 \\ -1 & 0 & 5 & | & -2 \\ 1 & -2 & 3 & | & 1 \end{bmatrix}$

Solution

a) Use the first two numbers in each row as the coefficients of x and y and the last number as the constant to get the following system:

$$x + 4y = -2$$
$$x - y = 3$$

b) Use the first two numbers in each row as the coefficients of x and y and the last number as the constant to get the following system:

$$x = 5$$
$$y = 1$$

c) Use the first three numbers in each row as the coefficients of x, y, and z and the last number as the constant to get the following system:

$$2x + 3y + 4z = 6$$
$$-x + 5z = -2$$
$$x - 2y + 3z = 1$$ ∎

The Gauss-Jordan Elimination Method

When we solve a single equation, we write simpler and simpler equivalent equations to get an equation whose solution is obvious. In the **Gauss-Jordan elimination method** we write simpler and simpler equivalent augmented matrices until we get an augmented matrix [like the one in Example 3(b)] in which the solution to the corresponding system is obvious.

Because each row of an augmented matrix represents an equation, we can perform the operations on the rows of the augmented matrix. These **row operations**, which follow, correspond to the usual operations with equations used in the addition method.

Row Operations

The following row operations on an augmented matrix give an equivalent augmented matrix:

1. Interchange two rows of the matrix.
2. Multiply every element in a row by a nonzero real number.
3. Add to a row a multiple of another row.

In the Gauss-Jordan elimination method our goal is to use row operations to obtain an augmented matrix that has ones on the **diagonal** in its matrix of coefficients and zeros elsewhere:

$$\begin{bmatrix} 1 & 0 & | & a \\ 0 & 1 & | & b \end{bmatrix}$$

The system corresponding to this augmented matrix is $x = a$ and $y = b$. So the solution set to the system is $\{(a, b)\}$.

E X A M P L E 4

Gauss-Jordan elimination with two equations in two variables

Use the Gauss-Jordan elimination method to solve the system:

$$x - 3y = 11$$
$$2x + y = 1$$

Solution

Start with the augmented matrix:

$$\begin{bmatrix} 1 & -3 & | & 11 \\ 2 & 1 & | & 1 \end{bmatrix}$$

Multiply row 1 by -2 and add the result to row 2 (in symbols, $-2R_1 + R_2 \rightarrow R_2$). Because $-2R_1 = [-2, 6, -22]$ and $R_2 = [2, 1, 1]$, $-2R_1 + R_2 = [0, 7, -21]$. Note that the coefficient of x in the second equation is now 0. We get the following matrix:

$$\begin{bmatrix} 1 & -3 & | & 11 \\ 0 & 7 & | & -21 \end{bmatrix} \quad -2R_1 + R_2 \rightarrow R_2$$

Multiply each element of row 2 by $\frac{1}{7}$ (in symbols, $\frac{1}{7}R_2 \rightarrow R_2$):

$$\begin{bmatrix} 1 & -3 & | & 11 \\ 0 & 1 & | & -3 \end{bmatrix} \quad \frac{1}{7}R_2 \rightarrow R_2$$

Multiply row 2 by 3 and add the result to row 1. Because $3R_2 = [0, 3, -9]$ and $R_1 = [1, -3, 11]$, $3R_2 + R_1 = [1, 0, 2]$. Note that the coefficient of y in the first equation is now 0. We get the following matrix:

$$\begin{bmatrix} 1 & 0 & | & 2 \\ 0 & 1 & | & -3 \end{bmatrix} \quad 3R_2 + R_1 \rightarrow R_1$$

This augmented matrix represents the system $x = 2$ and $y = -3$. So the solution set to the system is $\{(2, -3)\}$. Check in the original system. ∎

In Example 5 we use the row operations on the augmented matrix of a system of three linear equations in three variables.

E X A M P L E 5

Gauss-Jordan elimination with three equations in three variables

Use the Gauss-Jordan elimination method to solve the following system:

$$2x - y + z = -3$$
$$x + y - z = 6$$
$$3x - y - z = 4$$

Helpful Hint

It is not necessary to perform the row operations in exactly the same order as is shown in Example 5. As long as you use the legitimate row operations and get to the final form, you will get the solution to the system. Of course, you must double check your arithmetic at every step if you want to be successful at Gauss-Jordan elimination.

Solution

Start with the augmented matrix and interchange the first and second rows to get a 1 in the upper left position in the matrix:

$$\begin{bmatrix} 2 & -1 & 1 & | & -3 \\ 1 & 1 & -1 & | & 6 \\ 3 & -1 & -1 & | & 4 \end{bmatrix} \quad \text{The augmented matrix}$$

$$\begin{bmatrix} 1 & 1 & -1 & | & 6 \\ 2 & -1 & 1 & | & -3 \\ 3 & -1 & -1 & | & 4 \end{bmatrix} \quad R_1 \leftrightarrow R_2$$

Now multiply the first row by -2 and add the result onto the second row. Multiply the first row by -3 and add the result onto the third row. These two steps eliminate the variable x from the second and third rows:

$$\begin{bmatrix} 1 & 1 & -1 & | & 6 \\ 0 & -3 & 3 & | & -15 \\ 0 & -4 & 2 & | & -14 \end{bmatrix} \quad \begin{matrix} -2R_1 + R_2 \to R_2 \\ -3R_1 + R_3 \to R_3 \end{matrix}$$

Multiply the second row by $-\frac{1}{3}$ to get 1 in the second position on the diagonal:

$$\begin{bmatrix} 1 & 1 & -1 & | & 6 \\ 0 & 1 & -1 & | & 5 \\ 0 & -4 & 2 & | & -14 \end{bmatrix} \quad -\frac{1}{3}R_2 \to R_2$$

Use the second row to eliminate the variable y from the first and third rows:

$$\begin{bmatrix} 1 & 0 & 0 & | & 1 \\ 0 & 1 & -1 & | & 5 \\ 0 & 0 & -2 & | & 6 \end{bmatrix} \quad \begin{matrix} -1R_2 + R_1 \to R_1 \\ 4R_2 + R_3 \to R_3 \end{matrix}$$

Multiply the third row by $-\frac{1}{2}$ to get a 1 in the third position on the diagonal:

$$\begin{bmatrix} 1 & 0 & 0 & | & 1 \\ 0 & 1 & -1 & | & 5 \\ 0 & 0 & 1 & | & -3 \end{bmatrix} \quad -\frac{1}{2}R_3 \to R_3$$

Use the third row to eliminate the variable z from the second row:

$$\begin{bmatrix} 1 & 0 & 0 & | & 1 \\ 0 & 1 & 0 & | & 2 \\ 0 & 0 & 1 & | & -3 \end{bmatrix} \quad R_3 + R_2 \to R_2$$

This last augmented matrix represents the system $x = 1$, $y = 2$, and $z = -3$. So the solution set to the system is $\{(1, 2, -3)\}$. ∎

15. $x - y + z = 1$
$x + y - 2z = 3$
$y - 3z = 4$

16. $x + y = 2$
$y - 3z = 5$
$-3x + 2z = 8$

Write the system of equations represented by each augmented matrix. See Example 3.

17. $\begin{bmatrix} 5 & 1 & | & -1 \\ 2 & -3 & | & 0 \end{bmatrix}$

18. $\begin{bmatrix} 1 & 0 & | & 4 \\ 0 & 1 & | & -3 \end{bmatrix}$

19. $\begin{bmatrix} 1 & 0 & 0 & | & 6 \\ -1 & 0 & 1 & | & -3 \\ 1 & 1 & 0 & | & 1 \end{bmatrix}$

20. $\begin{bmatrix} 1 & 0 & 4 & | & 3 \\ 0 & 2 & 1 & | & -1 \\ 1 & 1 & 1 & | & 1 \end{bmatrix}$

Determine the row operation that was used to convert each given augmented matrix into the equivalent augmented matrix that follows it. See Example 4.

21. $\begin{bmatrix} 3 & 2 & | & 12 \\ 1 & -1 & | & -1 \end{bmatrix}, \begin{bmatrix} 1 & -1 & | & -1 \\ 3 & 2 & | & 12 \end{bmatrix}$

22. $\begin{bmatrix} 1 & -1 & | & -1 \\ 3 & 2 & | & 12 \end{bmatrix}, \begin{bmatrix} 1 & -1 & | & -1 \\ 0 & 5 & | & 15 \end{bmatrix}$

23. $\begin{bmatrix} 1 & -1 & | & -1 \\ 0 & 5 & | & 15 \end{bmatrix}, \begin{bmatrix} 1 & -1 & | & -1 \\ 0 & 1 & | & 3 \end{bmatrix}$

24. $\begin{bmatrix} 1 & -1 & | & -1 \\ 0 & 1 & | & 3 \end{bmatrix}, \begin{bmatrix} 1 & 0 & | & 2 \\ 0 & 1 & | & 3 \end{bmatrix}$

Solve each system using the Gauss-Jordan elimination method. See Examples 4–7.

25. $x + y = 3$
$-3x + y = -1$

26. $x - y = -1$
$2x - y = 2$

27. $2x - y = 3$
$x + y = 9$

28. $3x - 4y = -1$
$x - y = 0$

29. $3x - y = 4$
$2x + y = 1$

30. $2x - y = -3$
$3x + y = -2$

31. $6x - 7y = 0$
$2x + y = 20$

32. $2x + y = 11$
$2x - y = 1$

33. $2x - 3y = 4$
$-2x + 3y = 5$

34. $x - 3y = 8$
$2x - 6y = 1$

35. $x + 2y = 1$
$3x + 6y = 3$

36. $2x - 3y = 1$
$-6x + 9y = -3$

37. $x + y + z = 6$
$x - y + z = 2$
$2y - z = 1$

38. $x - y - z = 0$
$-x - y + z = -4$
$-x + y - z = -2$

39. $2x + y + z = 4$
$x + y - z = 1$
$x - y + 2z = 2$

40. $3x - y = 1$
$x + y + z = 4$
$x + 2z = 3$

41. $2x - y + z = 0$
$x + y - 3z = 3$
$x - y + z = -1$

42. $x - y - z = 0$
$-x - y + 2z = -1$
$-x + y - 2z = -3$

43. $-x + 3y + z = 0$
$x - y - 4z = -3$
$x + y + 2z = 3$

44. $-x + z = -2$
$2x - y = 5$
$y + 3z = 9$

45. $x - y + z = 1$
$2x - 2y + 2z = 2$
$-3x + 3y - 3z = -3$

46. $4x - 2y + 2z = 2$
$2x - y + z = 1$
$-2x + y - z = -1$

47. $x + y - z = 2$
$2x - y + z = 1$
$3x + 3y - 3z = 8$

48. $x + y + z = 5$
$x - y - z = 8$
$-x + y + z = 2$

GETTING MORE INVOLVED

49. *Cooperative learning.* Write a step-by-step procedure for solving any system of two linear equations in two variables by the Gauss-Jordan elimination method. Have a classmate evaluate your procedure by using it to solve a system.

50. *Cooperative learning.* Repeat Exercise 49 for a system of three linear equations in three variables.

In This Section

- Determinants
- Cramer's Rule (2 × 2)
- Minors
- Evaluating a 3 × 3 Determinant
- Cramer's Rule (3 × 3)

4.5

DETERMINANTS AND CRAMER'S RULE

The Gauss-Jordan elimination method of Section 4.4 can be performed the same way on every system. Another method that is applied the same way for every system is Cramer's rule, which we study in this section. Before you learn Cramer's rule, we need to introduce a new number associated with a matrix, called a **determinant**.

Determinants

The determinant of a square matrix is a real number corresponding to the matrix. For a 2×2 matrix the determinant is defined as follows.

Determinant of a 2 × 2 Matrix

The **determinant** of the matrix $\begin{bmatrix} a & b \\ c & d \end{bmatrix}$ is defined to be the real number $ad - bc$. We write

$$\begin{vmatrix} a & b \\ c & d \end{vmatrix} = ad - bc.$$

Note that the symbol for the determinant is a pair of vertical lines similar to the absolute value symbol, while a matrix is enclosed in brackets.

EXAMPLE 1

Using the definition of determinant

Find the determinant of each matrix.

a) $\begin{bmatrix} 1 & 3 \\ -2 & 5 \end{bmatrix}$

b) $\begin{bmatrix} 2 & 4 \\ 6 & 12 \end{bmatrix}$

Calculator Close-Up

With a graphing calculator you can define matrix A using MATRX EDIT.

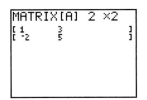

Then use the determinant function (det) found in MATRX MATH and the A from MATRX NAMES to find its determinant.

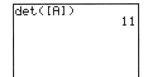

Solution

a) $\begin{vmatrix} 1 & 3 \\ -2 & 5 \end{vmatrix} = 1 \cdot 5 - 3(-2)$

$$= 5 + 6$$

$$= 11$$

b) $\begin{vmatrix} 2 & 4 \\ 6 & 12 \end{vmatrix} = 2 \cdot 12 - 4 \cdot 6$

$$= 24 - 24$$

$$= 0 \qquad \blacksquare$$

Cramer's Rule (2 × 2)

To understand Cramer's rule, we first solve a general system of two linear equations in two variables. Consider the system

$$(1) \qquad a_1 x + b_1 y = c_1$$
$$(2) \qquad a_2 x + b_2 y = c_2$$

where a_1, b_1, c_1, a_2, b_2, and c_2 represent real numbers. To eliminate y, we multiply Eq. (1) by b_2 and Eq. (2) by $-b_1$:

$$a_1 b_2 x + b_1 b_2 y = c_1 b_2 \qquad \text{Eq. (1) multiplied by } b_2$$
$$\underline{-a_2 b_1 x - b_1 b_2 y = -c_2 b_1} \qquad \text{Eq. (2) multiplied by } -b_1$$
$$a_1 b_2 x - a_2 b_1 x \qquad\quad = c_1 b_2 - c_2 b_1 \qquad \text{Add.}$$
$$(a_1 b_2 - a_2 b_1)x = c_1 b_2 - c_2 b_1$$
$$x = \frac{c_1 b_2 - c_2 b_1}{a_1 b_2 - a_2 b_1} \qquad \text{Provided that } a_1 b_2 - a_2 b_1 \neq 0$$

Using similar steps to eliminate x from the system, we get

$$y = \frac{a_1 c_2 - a_2 c_1}{a_1 b_2 - a_2 b_1},$$

provided that $a_1 b_2 - a_2 b_1 \neq 0$. These formulas for x and y can be written by using determinants. In the determinant form they are known as **Cramer's rule.**

Study Tip

Remember that everything we do in solving problems is based on principles (which are also called rules, theorems, and definitions). These principles justify the steps we take. Be sure that you understand the reasons. If you just memorize procedures without understanding, you will soon forget the procedures.

Determinant of a 3 × 3 Matrix

The determinant of a 3 × 3 matrix is defined as follows:

$$\begin{vmatrix} a_1 & b_1 & c_1 \\ a_2 & b_2 & c_2 \\ a_3 & b_3 & c_3 \end{vmatrix} = a_1 \cdot \begin{vmatrix} b_2 & c_2 \\ b_3 & c_3 \end{vmatrix} - a_2 \cdot \begin{vmatrix} b_1 & c_1 \\ b_3 & c_3 \end{vmatrix} + a_3 \cdot \begin{vmatrix} b_1 & c_1 \\ b_2 & c_2 \end{vmatrix}$$

Note that the determinants following a_1, a_2, and a_3 are the minors for a_1, a_2, and a_3, respectively. Writing the determinant of a 3 × 3 matrix in terms of minors is called **expansion by minors.** In the definition we expanded by minors about the first column. Later we will see how to expand by minors using any row or column and get the same value for the determinant.

E X A M P L E 4

Determinant of a 3 × 3 matrix

Find the determinant of the matrix by expansion by minors about the first column.

$$\begin{bmatrix} 1 & 3 & -5 \\ -2 & 4 & 6 \\ 0 & -7 & 9 \end{bmatrix}$$

Solution

$$\begin{vmatrix} 1 & 3 & -5 \\ -2 & 4 & 6 \\ 0 & -7 & 9 \end{vmatrix} = 1 \cdot \begin{vmatrix} 4 & 6 \\ -7 & 9 \end{vmatrix} - (-2) \cdot \begin{vmatrix} 3 & -5 \\ -7 & 9 \end{vmatrix} + 0 \cdot \begin{vmatrix} 3 & -5 \\ 4 & 6 \end{vmatrix}$$

$$= 1 \cdot [36 - (-42)] + 2 \cdot (27 - 35) + 0 \cdot [18 - (-20)]$$
$$= 1 \cdot 78 + 2 \cdot (-8) + 0$$
$$= 78 - 16$$
$$= 62$$

In Example 5 we evaluate a determinant using expansion by minors about the second row. In expanding about any row or column, the signs of the coefficients of the minors alternate according to the **sign array** that follows:

$$\begin{bmatrix} + & - & + \\ - & + & - \\ + & - & + \end{bmatrix}$$

The sign array is easily remembered by observing that there is a "+" sign in the upper left position and then alternating signs for all of the remaining positions.

E X A M P L E 5

Determinant of a 3 × 3 matrix

Evaluate the determinant of the matrix by expanding by minors about the second row.

$$\begin{bmatrix} 1 & 3 & -5 \\ -2 & 4 & 6 \\ 0 & -7 & 9 \end{bmatrix}$$

Solution

For expansion using the second row we prefix the signs "− + −" from the second row of the sign array to the corresponding numbers in the second row of the matrix, -2, 4, and 6. Note that the signs from the sign array are used in addition to any signs that occur on the numbers in the second row.

From the sign array, second row

$$\begin{vmatrix} 1 & 3 & -5 \\ -2 & 4 & 6 \\ 0 & -7 & 9 \end{vmatrix} = -(-2) \cdot \begin{vmatrix} 3 & -5 \\ -7 & 9 \end{vmatrix} + 4 \cdot \begin{vmatrix} 1 & -5 \\ 0 & 9 \end{vmatrix} - 6 \cdot \begin{vmatrix} 1 & 3 \\ 0 & -7 \end{vmatrix}$$

$$= 2(27 - 35) + 4(9 - 0) - 6(-7 - 0)$$
$$= 2(-8) + 4(9) - 6(-7)$$
$$= -16 + 36 + 42$$
$$= 62$$

Note that 62 is the same value that was obtained for this determinant in Example 4. ■

It can be shown that expanding by minors using any row or column prefixed by the corresponding signs from the sign array yields the same value for the determinant. Because we can use any row or column to evaluate a determinant of a 3×3 matrix, we can choose a row or column that makes the work easier. We can shorten the work considerably by picking a row or column with zeros in it.

Calculator Close-Up

A calculator is very useful for finding the determinant of a 3×3 matrix. Define A using MATRX EDIT.

Now use the determinant function from MATRX MATH and the A from MATRX NAMES to find the determinant.

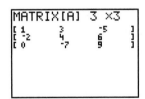

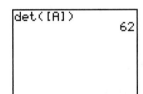

E X A M P L E   6   **Choosing the simplest row or column**

Find the determinant of the matrix

$$\begin{bmatrix} 3 & -5 & 0 \\ 4 & -6 & 0 \\ 7 & 9 & 2 \end{bmatrix}.$$

Solution

We choose to expand by minors about the third column of the matrix because the third column contains two zeros. Prefix the third-column entries 0, 0, 2 by the signs "+ − +" from the third column of the sign array:

$$\begin{vmatrix} 3 & -5 & 0 \\ 4 & -6 & 0 \\ 7 & 9 & 2 \end{vmatrix} = 0 \cdot \begin{vmatrix} 4 & -6 \\ 7 & 9 \end{vmatrix} - 0 \cdot \begin{vmatrix} 3 & -5 \\ 7 & 9 \end{vmatrix} + 2 \cdot \begin{vmatrix} 3 & -5 \\ 4 & -6 \end{vmatrix}$$

$$= 0 - 0 + 2[-18 - (-20)]$$
$$= 4$$

■

Cramer's Rule (3 × 3)

A system of three linear equations in three variables can be solved by using determinants and Cramer's rule.

Cramer's Rule for Three Equations in Three Unknowns

The solution to the system

$$a_1 x + b_1 y + c_1 z = d_1$$
$$a_2 x + b_2 y + c_2 z = d_2$$
$$a_3 x + b_3 y + c_3 z = d_3$$

is given by $x = \dfrac{D_x}{D}$, $y = \dfrac{D_y}{D}$, and $z = \dfrac{D_z}{D}$, where

$$D = \begin{vmatrix} a_1 & b_1 & c_1 \\ a_2 & b_2 & c_2 \\ a_3 & b_3 & c_3 \end{vmatrix}, \qquad D_x = \begin{vmatrix} d_1 & b_1 & c_1 \\ d_2 & b_2 & c_2 \\ d_3 & b_3 & c_3 \end{vmatrix},$$

$$D_y = \begin{vmatrix} a_1 & d_1 & c_1 \\ a_2 & d_2 & c_2 \\ a_3 & d_3 & c_3 \end{vmatrix}, \qquad D_z = \begin{vmatrix} a_1 & b_1 & d_1 \\ a_2 & b_2 & d_2 \\ a_3 & b_3 & d_3 \end{vmatrix},$$

provided that $D \neq 0$.

Note that D_x, D_y, and D_z are obtained from D by replacing the x-, y-, or z-column with the constants d_1, d_2, and d_3.

E X A M P L E   7

Solving an independent system with Cramer's rule

Use Cramer's rule to solve the system:

$$x + y + z = 4$$
$$x - y = -3$$
$$x + 2y - z = 0$$

Solution

We first calculate D, D_x, D_y, and D_z. To calculate D, expand by minors about the third column because the third column has a zero in it:

$$D = \begin{vmatrix} 1 & 1 & 1 \\ 1 & -1 & 0 \\ 1 & 2 & -1 \end{vmatrix} = 1 \cdot \begin{vmatrix} 1 & -1 \\ 1 & 2 \end{vmatrix} - 0 \cdot \begin{vmatrix} 1 & 1 \\ 1 & 2 \end{vmatrix} + (-1) \cdot \begin{vmatrix} 1 & 1 \\ 1 & -1 \end{vmatrix}$$

$$= 1 \cdot [2 - (-1)] - 0 + (-1)[-1 - 1]$$
$$= 3 - 0 + 2$$
$$= 5$$

Calculator Close-Up

When you see the amount of arithmetic required to solve the system in Example 7 by Cramer's rule, you can understand why computers and calculators have been programmed to perform this method. Some calculators can find determinants for matrices as large as 10×10. Try to solve Example 7 with a graphing calculator that has determinants.

For D_x, expand by minors about the first column:

$$D_x = \begin{vmatrix} 4 & 1 & 1 \\ -3 & -1 & 0 \\ 0 & 2 & -1 \end{vmatrix} = 4 \cdot \begin{vmatrix} -1 & 0 \\ 2 & -1 \end{vmatrix} - (-3) \cdot \begin{vmatrix} 1 & 1 \\ 2 & -1 \end{vmatrix} + 0 \cdot \begin{vmatrix} 1 & 1 \\ -1 & 0 \end{vmatrix}$$

$$= 4 \cdot (1 - 0) + 3 \cdot (-1 - 2) + 0$$

$$= 4 - 9 + 0 = -5$$

For D_y, expand by minors about the third row:

$$D_y = \begin{vmatrix} 1 & 4 & 1 \\ 1 & -3 & 0 \\ 1 & 0 & -1 \end{vmatrix} = 1 \cdot \begin{vmatrix} 4 & 1 \\ -3 & 0 \end{vmatrix} - 0 \cdot \begin{vmatrix} 1 & 1 \\ 1 & 0 \end{vmatrix} + (-1) \cdot \begin{vmatrix} 1 & 4 \\ 1 & -3 \end{vmatrix}$$

$$= 1 \cdot 3 - 0 + (-1)(-7) = 10$$

To get D_z, expand by minors about the third row:

$$D_z = \begin{vmatrix} 1 & 1 & 4 \\ 1 & -1 & -3 \\ 1 & 2 & 0 \end{vmatrix} = 1 \cdot \begin{vmatrix} 1 & 4 \\ -1 & -3 \end{vmatrix} - 2 \cdot \begin{vmatrix} 1 & 4 \\ 1 & -3 \end{vmatrix} + 0 \cdot \begin{vmatrix} 1 & 1 \\ 1 & -1 \end{vmatrix}$$

$$= 1 \cdot 1 - 2(-7) + 0 = 15$$

Now, by Cramer's rule,

$$x = \frac{D_x}{D} = \frac{-5}{5} = -1, \qquad y = \frac{D_y}{D} = \frac{10}{5} = 2, \qquad \text{and} \qquad z = \frac{D_z}{D} = \frac{15}{5} = 3.$$

Check $(-1, 2, 3)$ in the original equations. The solution set is $\{(-1, 2, 3)\}$. ■

If $D = 0$, Cramer's rule does not apply. Cramer's rule provides the solution only to a system of three equations with three variables that has a single point in the solution set. If $D = 0$, then the solution set either is empty or consists of infinitely many points, and we can use the methods discussed in Sections 4.3 or 4.4 to find the solution.

WARM-UPS

True or false? Explain your answer.

1. $\begin{vmatrix} -1 & 2 \\ 3 & -5 \end{vmatrix} = -1$ **2.** $\begin{vmatrix} 2 & 4 \\ -4 & 8 \end{vmatrix} = 0$

3. Cramer's rule solves any system of two linear equations in two variables.

4. The determinant of a 2×2 matrix is a real number.

5. If $D = 0$, then there might be no solution to the system.

6. Cramer's rule is used to solve systems of linear equations only.

7. If the graphs of a pair of linear equations intersect at exactly one point, then this point can be found by using Cramer's rule.

8. The determinant of a 3×3 matrix is found by using minors.

9. Expansion by minors about any row or any column gives the same value for the determinant of a 3×3 matrix.

10. The sign array is used in evaluating the determinant of a 3×3 matrix.

4.5 EXERCISES

Reading and Writing *After reading this section, write out the answers to these questions. Use complete sentences.*

1. What is a determinant?

2. What is Cramer's rule used for?

3. Which systems can be solved using Cramer's rule?

4. What is a minor?

5. How do you find the minor for an element of a 3×3 matrix?

6. What is the purpose of the sign array?

Find the value of each determinant. See Example 1.

7. $\begin{vmatrix} 2 & 5 \\ 3 & 7 \end{vmatrix}$

8. $\begin{vmatrix} -1 & 0 \\ 1 & 1 \end{vmatrix}$

9. $\begin{vmatrix} 0 & 3 \\ 1 & 5 \end{vmatrix}$

10. $\begin{vmatrix} 2 & 4 \\ 6 & 12 \end{vmatrix}$

11. $\begin{vmatrix} -3 & -2 \\ -4 & 2 \end{vmatrix}$

12. $\begin{vmatrix} -2 & 2 \\ -3 & -5 \end{vmatrix}$

13. $\begin{vmatrix} 0.05 & 0.06 \\ 10 & 20 \end{vmatrix}$

14. $\begin{vmatrix} 0.02 & -0.5 \\ 30 & 50 \end{vmatrix}$

Solve each system using Cramer's rule. See Example 2.

15. $2x - y = 5$
$3x + 2y = -3$

16. $3x + y = -1$
$x + 2y = 8$

17. $3x - 5y = -2$
$2x + 3y = 5$

18. $x - y = 1$
$3x - 2y = 0$

19. $4x - 3y = 5$
$2x + 5y = 7$

20. $2x - y = 2$
$3x - 2y = 1$

21. $0.5x + 0.2y = 8$
$0.4x - 0.6y = -5$

22. $0.6x + 0.5y = 18$
$0.5x - 0.25y = 7$

23. $\dfrac{1}{2}x + \dfrac{1}{4}y = 5$
$\dfrac{1}{3}x - \dfrac{1}{2}y = -1$

24. $\dfrac{1}{2}x + \dfrac{2}{3}y = 4$
$\dfrac{3}{4}x + \dfrac{1}{3}y = -2$

Find the indicated minors using the following matrix. See Example 3.

$$\begin{bmatrix} 3 & -2 & 5 \\ 4 & -3 & 7 \\ 0 & 1 & -6 \end{bmatrix}$$

25. Minor for 3

26. Minor for -2

27. Minor for 5

28. Minor for -3

29. Minor for 7

30. Minor for 0

31. Minor for 1

32. Minor for -6

Find the determinant of each 3×3 matrix by using expansion by minors about the first column. See Example 4.

33. $\begin{bmatrix} 1 & 1 & 2 \\ 2 & 3 & 1 \\ 3 & 1 & 5 \end{bmatrix}$

34. $\begin{bmatrix} 2 & 1 & 3 \\ 1 & 1 & 2 \\ 3 & 4 & 6 \end{bmatrix}$

35. $\begin{bmatrix} 2 & 1 & 0 \\ 1 & 0 & 1 \\ 3 & 1 & 2 \end{bmatrix}$

36. $\begin{bmatrix} 1 & 0 & 2 \\ 2 & 1 & 3 \\ 4 & 3 & 0 \end{bmatrix}$

37. $\begin{bmatrix} -2 & 1 & 2 \\ -3 & 3 & 1 \\ -5 & 4 & 0 \end{bmatrix}$

38. $\begin{bmatrix} -2 & 1 & 3 \\ -1 & 4 & 2 \\ 2 & 1 & 1 \end{bmatrix}$

39. $\begin{bmatrix} 1 & 1 & 5 \\ 0 & 3 & 2 \\ 0 & 2 & 3 \end{bmatrix}$

40. $\begin{bmatrix} 1 & 0 & 6 \\ 0 & 1 & 4 \\ 0 & 0 & 9 \end{bmatrix}$

Evaluate the determinant of each 3×3 matrix using expansion by minors about the row or column of your choice. See Examples 5 and 6.

41. $\begin{bmatrix} 3 & 1 & 5 \\ 2 & 0 & 6 \\ 4 & 0 & 1 \end{bmatrix}$

42. $\begin{bmatrix} 2 & 1 & 2 \\ 1 & 2 & 5 \\ 3 & 0 & 0 \end{bmatrix}$

43. $\begin{bmatrix} -2 & 1 & 3 \\ 0 & 1 & -1 \\ 2 & -4 & -3 \end{bmatrix}$

44. $\begin{bmatrix} -2 & 0 & 1 \\ -3 & 2 & -5 \\ 4 & -2 & 6 \end{bmatrix}$

45. $\begin{bmatrix} -2 & -3 & 0 \\ 4 & -1 & 0 \\ 0 & 3 & 5 \end{bmatrix}$

46. $\begin{bmatrix} -2 & 6 & 3 \\ 0 & 4 & 0 \\ -1 & -4 & 5 \end{bmatrix}$

47. $\begin{bmatrix} 2 & 1 & 1 \\ 0 & 0 & 5 \\ 5 & 0 & 4 \end{bmatrix}$

48. $\begin{bmatrix} 2 & 3 & 0 \\ 6 & 4 & 1 \\ 1 & 2 & 0 \end{bmatrix}$

Use Cramer's rule to solve each system. See Example 7.

49. $x + y + z = 6$
$x - y + z = 2$
$2x + y + z = 7$

50. $x + y + z = 2$
$x - y - 2z = -3$
$2x - y + z = 7$

51. $x - 3y + 2z = 0$
$x + y + z = 2$
$x - y + z = 0$

52. $3x + 2y + 2z = 0$
$x - y + z = 1$
$x + y - z = 3$

53. $x + y = -1$
$2y - z = 3$
$x + y + z = 0$

54. $x - y = 8$
$x - 2z = 0$
$x + y - z = 1$

55. $x + y - z = 0$
$2x + 2y + z = 6$
$x - 3y = 0$

56. $x + y + z = 1$
$5x - y = 0$
$3x + y + 2z = 0$

57. $x + y + z = 0$
$2y + 2z = 0$
$3x - y = -1$

58. $x + z = 0$
$x - 3y = 1$
$4y - 3z = 3$

Solve each problem by using two equations in two variables and Cramer's rule.

59. *Peas and beets.* One serving of canned peas contains 3 grams of protein and 11 grams of carbohydrates. One serving of canned beets contains 1 gram of protein and 8 grams of carbohydrates. A dietitian wants to determine the number of servings of each that would provide 38 grams of protein and 187 grams of carbohydrates.
a) Use the accompanying graph to estimate the number of servings of each.
b) Use Cramer's rule to find the number of servings of each.

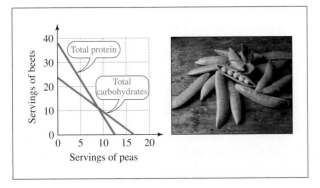

FIGURE FOR EXERCISE 59

60. *Protein and carbohydrates.* One serving of Cornies breakfast cereal contains 2 grams of protein and 25 grams of carbohydrates. One serving of Oaties breakfast cereal contains 4 grams of protein and 20 grams of carbohydrates. How many servings of each would provide exactly 24 grams of protein and 210 grams of carbohydrates?

61. *Milk and a magazine.* Althia bought a gallon of milk and a magazine for a total of $4.65, excluding tax. Including the tax, the bill was $4.95. If there is a 5% sales tax on milk and an 8% sales tax on magazines, then what was the price of each item?

62. *Washing machines and refrigerators.* A truck carrying 3600 cubic feet of cargo consisting of washing machines and refrigerators was hijacked. The washing machines are worth $300 each and are shipped in 36-cubic-foot cartons. The refrigerators are worth $900 each and are shipped in 45-cubic-foot cartons. If the total value of the cargo was $51,000, then how many of each were there on the truck?

63. *Singles and doubles.* Windy's Hamburger Palace sells singles and doubles. Toward the end of the evening, Windy himself noticed that he had on hand only 32 patties and 34 slices of tomatoes. If a single takes 1 patty and 2 slices, and a double takes 2 patties and 1 slice, then how many more singles and doubles must Windy sell to use up all of his patties and tomato slices?

64. *Valuable wrenches.* Carmen has a total of 28 wrenches, all of which are either box wrenches or open-end wrenches. For insurance purposes she values the box wrenches at $3.00 each and the open-end wrenches at $2.50 each. If the value of her wrench collection is $78, then how many of each type does she have?

65. *Gary and Harry.* Gary is 5 years older than Harry. Twenty-nine years ago, Gary was twice as old as Harry. How old are they now?

66. *Acute angles.* One acute angle of a right triangle is 3° more than twice the other acute angle. What are the sizes of the acute angles?

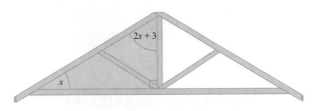

FIGURE FOR EXERCISE 66

67. *Equal perimeters.* A rope of length 80 feet is to be cut into two pieces. One piece will be used to form a square, and the other will be used to form an equilateral triangle. If the figures are to have equal perimeters, then what should be the length of a side of each?

FIGURE FOR EXERCISE 67

68. *Coffee and doughnuts.* For a cup of coffee and a doughnut, Thurrel spent $2.25, including a tip. Later he spent $4.00 for two coffees and three doughnuts, including a tip. If he always tips $1.00, then what is the price of a cup of coffee?

69. *Chlorine mixture.* A 10% chlorine solution is to be mixed with a 25% chlorine solution to obtain 30 gallons of 20% solution. How many gallons of each must be used?

70. *Safe drivers.* Emily and Camille started from the same city and drove in opposite directions on the freeway. After 3 hours they were 354 miles apart. If they had gone in the same direction, Emily would have been 18 miles ahead of Camille. How fast did each woman drive?

Write a system of three equations in three variables for each word problem. Use Cramer's rule to solve each system.

71. *Weighing dogs.* Cassandra wants to determine the weights of her two dogs, Mimi and Mitzi. However, neither dog will sit on the scale by herself. Cassandra, Mimi, and Mitzi altogether weigh 175 pounds. Cassandra and Mimi together weigh 143 pounds.

Cassandra   Cassandra   Cassandra
Mimi   Mimi   Mitzi
Mitzi

FIGURE FOR EXERCISE 71

Cassandra and Mitzi together weigh 139 pounds. How much does each weigh individually?

72. *Nickels, dimes, and quarters.* Bernard has 41 coins consisting of nickels, dimes, and quarters, and they are worth a total of $4.00. If the number of dimes plus the number of quarters is one more than the number of nickels, then how many of each does he have?

73. *Finding three angles.* If the two acute angles of a right triangle differ by 12°, then what are the measures of the three angles of this triangle?

74. *Two acute and one obtuse.* The obtuse angle of a triangle is twice as large as the sum of the two acute angles. If the smallest angle is only one-eighth as large as the sum of the other two, then what is the measure of each angle?

GETTING MORE INVOLVED

 75. *Writing.* Explain what to do when you are trying to use Cramer's rule and $D = 0$.

 76. *Exploration.* For what value of a does the system

$$ax - y = 3$$
$$x + 2y = 1$$

have a single solution?

77. *Exploration.* Can Cramer's rule be used to solve this system? Explain.

$$2x^2 - y = 3$$
$$3x^2 + 2y = 22$$

78. *Writing.* For what values of a, b, c, and d is the determinant of the matrix

$$\begin{bmatrix} a & b & 0 \\ c & d & 0 \\ b & a & 0 \end{bmatrix}$$

equal to zero? Explain your answer.

 GRAPHING CALCULATOR EXERCISES

79. Use the determinant feature on your graphing calculator to find the determinants in Exercises 7–14 and 33–40 of this section.

80. Solve the systems in Exercises 15–24 and 49–58 of this section by using your graphing calculator to find the necessary determinants.

4.6 LINEAR PROGRAMMING

In this section we graph the solution set to a system of several linear inequalities, much as we graphed compound linear inequalities in Chapter 3. We then use the solution set as the domain of a function for which we are seeking the maximum or minimum value. The method that we use is called **linear programming,** and it can be applied to problems such as finding maximum profit or minimum cost.

Graphing the Constraints

In linear programming we have two variables that must satisfy several linear inequalities. These inequalities are called the **constraints** because they restrict the variables to only certain values. A graph in the coordinate plane is used to indicate the points that satisfy all of the constraints.

EXAMPLE 1

Graphing the constraints

Graph the solution set to the system of inequalities and identify each vertex of the region:

$$x \geq 0, \quad y \geq 0$$
$$3x + 2y \leq 12$$
$$x + 2y \leq 8$$

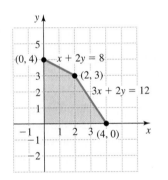

FIGURE 4.7

Solution

The points on or to the right of the y-axis satisfy $x \geq 0$. The points on or above the x-axis satisfy $y \geq 0$. The points on or below the line $3x + 2y = 12$ satisfy $3x + 2y \leq 12$. The points on or below the line $x + 2y = 8$ satisfy $x + 2y \leq 8$. Graph each straight line and shade the region that satisfies all four inequalities as shown in Fig. 4.7. Three of the vertices are easily identified as (0, 0), (0, 4), and (4, 0). The fourth vertex is found by solving the system $3x + 2y = 12$ and $x + 2y = 8$. The fourth vertex is (2, 3). ∎

In linear programming the constraints usually come from physical limitations in some problem. In Example 2 we write the constraints and then graph the points in the coordinate plane that satisfy all of the constraints.

EXAMPLE 2

Writing the constraints

Jules is in the business of constructing dog houses. A small dog house requires 8 square feet (ft^2) of plywood and 6 ft^2 of insulation. A large dog house requires 16 ft^2 of plywood and 3 ft^2 of insulation. Jules has available only 48 ft^2 of plywood and 18 ft^2 of insulation. Write the constraints on the number of small and large dog houses that he can build with the available supplies and graph the solution set to the system of constraints.

Solution

Let x represent the number of small dog houses and y represent the number of large dog houses. We have two natural constraints $x \geq 0$ and $y \geq 0$ since he cannot build a negative number of dog houses. Since the total plywood available for use is at most 48 ft^2, $8x + 16y \leq 48$. Since the total insulation available is at most 18 ft^2,

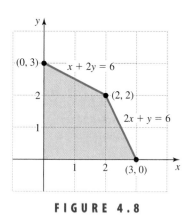

FIGURE 4.8

$6x + 3y \leq 18$. Simplify the inequalities to get the following constraints:

$$x \geq 0, \quad y \geq 0$$
$$x + 2y \leq 6$$
$$2x + y \leq 6$$

The graph of the solution set to the system of inequalities is shown in Fig. 4.8. ■

Maximizing or Minimizing a Linear Function

In Example 2 any ordered pair within the region is a possible solution to the number of dog houses of each type that could be built. If a small dog house sells for $15 and a large dog house sells for $20, then the total revenue in dollars from x small and y large dog houses is $R = 15x + 20y$. Since the revenue is a function of x and y, we write $R(x, y) = 15x + 20y$. The function R is a linear function of x and y. The domain of R is the region graphed in Fig. 4.8.

Linear Function of Two Variables

A function of the form $f(x, y) = Ax + By + C$, where A, B, and C are real numbers, is called a **linear function of two variables.**

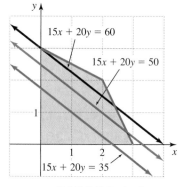

FIGURE 4.9

Naturally, we are interested in the maximum revenue subject to the constraints on x and y. To investigate some possible revenues, replace R in $R = 15x + 20y$ with, say 35, 50, and 60. The graphs of the parallel lines $15x + 20y = 35$, $15x + 20y = 50$, and $15x + 20y = 60$ are shown in Fig. 4.9. The revenue at any point on the line $15x + 20y = 35$ is $35. We get a larger revenue on a higher revenue line (and lower revenue on a lower line). The maximum revenue possible will be on the highest revenue line that still intersects the region. Because the sides of the region are straight-line segments, the intersection of the highest (or lowest) revenue line with the region must include a vertex of the region. This is the fundamental principle behind linear programming.

The Principle of Linear Programming

The maximum or minimum value of a linear function subject to linear constraints occurs at a vertex of the region determined by the constraints.

E X A M P L E   3   **Maximizing a linear function with linear constraints**

A small dog house requires 8 ft² of plywood and 6 ft² of insulation. A large dog house requires 16 ft² of plywood and 3 ft² of insulation. Only 48 ft² of plywood and 18 ft² of insulation are available. If a small dog house sells for $15 and a large dog house sells for $20, then how many dog houses of each type should be built to maximize the revenue and to satisfy the constraints?

Solution

Let x be the number of small dog houses and y be the number of large dog houses. We wrote and graphed the constraints for this problem in Example 2, so we will not repeat that here. The graph in Fig. 4.8 has four vertices: $(0, 0)$, $(0, 3)$, $(3, 0)$, and

(2, 2). The revenue function is $R(x, y) = 15x + 20y$. Since the maximum value of this function must occur at a vertex, we evaluate the function at each vertex:

$$R(0, 0) = 15(0) + 20(0) = \$0$$
$$R(0, 3) = 15(0) + 20(3) = \$60$$
$$R(3, 0) = 15(3) + 20(0) = \$45$$
$$R(2, 2) = 15(2) + 20(2) = \$70$$

From this list we can see that the maximum revenue is $70 when two small and two large dog houses are built. We also see that the minimum revenue is $0 when no dog houses of either type are built. ■

We can summarize the procedure for solving linear programming problems with the following strategy.

Strategy for Linear Programming

Use the following steps to find the maximum or minimum value of a linear function subject to linear constraints.

1. Graph the region that satisfies all of the constraints.

2. Determine the coordinates of each vertex of the region.

3. Evaluate the function at each vertex of the region.

4. Identify which vertex gives the maximum or minimum value of the function.

In Example 4 we solve another linear programming problem.

E X A M P L E   4

Minimizing a linear function with linear constraints

One serving of food A contains 2 grams of protein and 6 grams of carbohydrates. One serving of food B contains 4 grams of protein and 3 grams of carbohydrates. A dietitian wants a meal that contains at least 12 grams of protein and at least 18 grams of carbohydrates. If the cost of food A is 9 cents per serving and the cost of food B is 20 cents per serving, then how many servings of each food would minimize the cost and satisfy the constraints?

Solution

Let x equal the number of servings of food A and y equal the number of servings of food B. If the meal is to contain at least 12 grams of protein, then $2x + 4y \geq 12$. If the meal is to contain at least 18 grams of carbohydrates, then $6x + 3y \geq 18$. Simplify each inequality and use the two natural constraints to get the following system:

$$x \geq 0, \quad y \geq 0$$
$$x + 2y \geq 6$$
$$2x + y \geq 6$$

The graph of the constraints is shown in Fig. 4.10. The vertices are (0, 6), (6, 0), and (2, 2). The cost in cents for x servings of A and y servings of B is $C(x, y) = 9x + 20y$. Evaluate the cost at each vertex:

$$C(0, 6) = 9(0) + 20(6) = 120 \text{ cents}$$
$$C(6, 0) = 9(6) + 20(0) = 54 \text{ cents}$$
$$C(2, 2) = 9(2) + 20(2) = 58 \text{ cents}$$

The minimum cost of 54 cents is attained by using six servings of food A and no servings of food B.

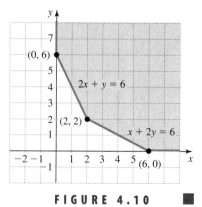

FIGURE 4.10

WARM-UPS

True or false? Explain your answer.

1. The graph of $x \geq 0$ in the coordinate plane consists of the points on or above the x-axis.

2. The graph of $y \geq 0$ in the coordinate plane consists of the points on or to the right of the y-axis.

3. The graph of $x + y \leq 6$ consists of the points below the line $x + y = 6$.

4. The graph of $2x + 3y = 30$ has x-intercept (0, 10) and y-intercept (15, 0).

5. The graph of a system of inequalities is a union of their individual solution sets.

6. In linear programming, constraints are inequalities that restrict the possible values that the variables can assume.

7. The function $F(x, y) = Ax^2 + By^2 + C$ is a linear function of x and y.

8. The value of $R(x, y) = 3x + 5y$ at the point (2, 4) is 26.

9. If $C(x, y) = 12x + 10y$, then $C(0, 5) = 62$.

10. In solving a linear programming problem, we must determine the vertices of the region defined by the constraints.

4.6 EXERCISES

Reading and Writing *After reading this section, write out the answers to these questions. Use complete sentences.*

1. What is a constraint?

2. What is linear programming?

3. Where do the constraints come from in a linear programming problem?

4. What is a linear function of two variables?

5. Where does the maximum or minimum value of a linear function subject to linear constraints occur?

6. What is the strategy for solving a linear programming problem?

Graph the solution set to each system of inequalities and identify each vertex of the region. See Example 1.

7. $x \geq 0, y \geq 0$
$x + y \leq 5$

8. $x \geq 0, y \geq 0$
$y \leq 5, y \geq x$

9. $x \geq 0, y \geq 0$
$2x + y \leq 4$
$x + y \leq 3$

10. $x \geq 0, y \geq 0$
$x + y \leq 4$
$x + 2y \leq 6$

11. $x \geq 0, y \geq 0$
$2x + y \geq 3$
$x + y \geq 2$

12. $x \geq 0, y \geq 0$
$3x + 2y \geq 12$
$2x + y \geq 7$

13. $x \geq 0, y \geq 0$
$x + 3y \leq 15$
$2x + y \leq 10$

14. $x \geq 0, y \geq 0$
$2x + 3y \leq 15$
$x + y \leq 7$

15. $x \geq 0, y \geq 0$
$x + y \geq 4$
$3x + y \geq 6$

16. $x \geq 0, y \geq 0$
$x + 3y \geq 6$
$2x + y \geq 7$

Solve each problem. See Examples 2–4.

17. *Phase I advertising.* The publicity director for Mercy Hospital is planning to bolster the hospital's image by running a TV ad and a radio ad. Due to budgetary and other constraints, the number of times that she can run the TV ad, x, and the number of times that she can run the radio ad, y, must be in the region shown in the figure on the next page. The function

$$A = 9000x + 4000y$$

gives the total number of people reached by the ads.
a) Find the total number of people reached by the ads at each vertex of the region.
b) What mix of TV and radio ads maximizes the number of people reached?

18. *Phase II advertising.* Suppose the radio station in Exercise 17 starts playing country music and the function for the total number of people changes to

$$A = 9000x + 2000y.$$

a) Find A at each vertex of the region using this function.

b) What mix of TV and radio ads maximizes the number of people reached?

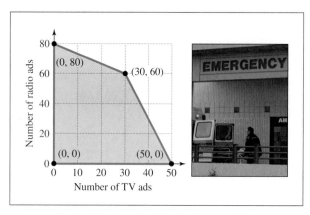

FIGURE FOR EXERCISES 17 AND 18

19. At Burger Heaven a double contains 2 meat patties and 6 pickles, whereas a triple contains 3 meat patties and 3 pickles. Near closing time one day, only 24 meat patties and 48 pickles are available. If a double burger sells for $1.20 and a triple burger sells for $1.50, then how many of each should be made to maximize the total revenue?

20. Sam and Doris manufacture rocking chairs and porch swings in the Ozarks. Each rocker requires 3 hours of work from Sam and 2 hours from Doris. Each swing requires 2 hours of work from Sam and 2 hours from Doris. Sam cannot work more than 48 hours per week, and Doris cannot work more than 40 hours per week. If a rocker sells for $160 and a swing sells for $100, then how many of each should be made per week to maximize the revenue?

21. If a double burger sells for $1.00 and a triple burger sells for $2.00, then how many of each should be made to maximize the total revenue subject to the constraints of Exercise 19?

22. If a rocker sells for $120 and a swing sells for $100, then how many of each should be made to maximize the total revenue subject to the constraints of Exercise 20?

23. One cup of Doggie Dinner contains 20 grams of protein and 40 grams of carbohydrates. One cup of Puppy Power contains 30 grams of protein and 20 grams of carbohydrates. Susan wants her dog to get at least 200 grams of protein and 180 grams of carbohydrates per

day. If Doggie Dinner costs 16 cents per cup and Puppy Power costs 20 cents per cup, then how many cups of each would satisfy the constraints and minimize the total cost?

24. Mammoth Muffler employs supervisors and helpers. According to the union contract, a supervisor does 2 brake jobs and 3 mufflers per day, whereas a helper does 6 brake jobs and 3 mufflers per day. The home office requires enough staff for at least 24 brake jobs and for at least 18 mufflers per day. If a supervisor makes $90 per day and a helper makes $100 per day, then how many of each should be employed to satisfy the constraints and to minimize the daily labor cost?

25. Suppose in Exercise 23 Doggie Dinner costs 4 cents per cup and Puppy Power costs 10 cents per cup. How many cups of each would satisfy the constraints and minimize the total cost?

26. Suppose in Exercise 24 the supervisor makes $110 per day and the helper makes $100 per day. How many of each should be employed to satisfy the constraints and to minimize the daily labor cost?

27. Anita has at most $24,000 to invest in her brother-in-law's laundromat and her nephew's car wash. Her brother-in-law has high blood pressure and heart disease but he will pay 18%, whereas her nephew is healthier but will pay only 12%. So the amount she will invest in the car wash will be at least twice the amount that she will invest in the laundromat but not more than three times as much. How much should she invest in each to maximize her total income from the two investments?

28. Herbert assembles computers in his shop. The parts for each economy model are shipped to him in a carton with a volume of 2 cubic feet (ft^3) and the parts for each deluxe model are shipped to him in a carton with a volume of 3 ft^3. After assembly, each economy model is shipped out in a carton with a volume of 4 ft^3, and each deluxe model is shipped out in a carton with a volume of 4 ft^3. The truck that delivers the parts has a maximum capacity of 180 ft^3, and the truck that takes out the completed computers has a maximum capacity of 280 ft^3. He can receive only one shipment of parts and send out one shipment of computers per week. If his profit on an economy model is $60 and his profit on a deluxe model is $100, then how many of each should he order per week to maximize his profit?

COLLABORATIVE ACTIVITIES

Types of Systems

Assign roles in your groups. Set up the system of equations for each scenario below and attempt to solve it. Analyze your results.

Part I: Talia's Tallitot. Talia plans to make tallitot (prayer shawls) and matching kipot (prayer hats) from a bolt of material. The fabric she plans to use is 250 yards long. She will need 2 yards of material for each tallit (prayer shawl) and $\frac{1}{6}$ of a yard for each kipah (prayer hat). She also plans to put tzitzit (fringes) on the tallit and will need 1 yard of cord for each tallit. The kipot will not have any fringes. She has 100 yards of cord to use for the tzitzit.

1. Write two equations to use to solve for how many kipot and tallitot she can make from the supplies on hand. Let t equal the number of tallitot made and k equal the number of kipot made.

2. Try to solve this system of equations. If you get a solution, state what it is. If not, describe what your result means.

Part II: Karif's Kerchiefs. Karif plans to make red and green kerchiefs in two sizes, medium and large. He has 60 yards of each color of material. He will need $\frac{1}{4}$ of a yard of the appropriate colored fabric for each medium kerchief and $\frac{1}{2}$ of a yard for each large kerchief. He also plans to trim each kerchief with the alternate color of ribbon. He has 240 yards of each color of ribbon. He will need 1 yard of ribbon for each medium kerchief and 2 yards for each large kerchief.

Grouping: Two to four students per group

Topic: Types of solutions to systems of equations

3. Let m equal the number of medium kerchiefs and l equal the number of large kerchiefs. Set up two equations to use to solve for the number of each color of kerchiefs Karif can make from the supplies on hand.

4. Try to solve this system of equations. If you get a solution, state what it is. If not, describe what your result means.

Part III: Maria's Mantillas. Maria plans to make two different kinds of mantillas (veils), some out of lace and some out of a sheer cotton fabric. She also plans to make two sizes of mantillas, one size for women and one size for young girls. She has 150 yards of the lace fabric and 200 yards of the cotton fabric. She will need 2 yards of either fabric for the smaller mantillas and $3\frac{1}{2}$ yards of either fabric for the larger mantillas.

5. Let w equal the number of mantillas for the women and y equal the number of mantillas for the young girls. Set up two equations to use to solve for the number of each mantilla Maria can make from each type of fabric.

6. Try to solve this system of equations. If you get a solution, state what it is. If not, describe what your result means.

Extension: Explain what you would need to do for the systems of equations you could not solve to make them solvable.

WRAP-UP   CHAPTER 4

SUMMARY

Systems of Linear Equations

Methods for solving systems in two variables	Graphing: Sketch the graphs to see the solution.
	Substitution: Solve one equation for one variable in terms of the other, then substitute into the other equation.
	Addition: Multiply each equation as necessary to eliminate a variable upon addition of the equations.

Examples

The graphs of
$y = x - 1$ and
$x + y = 3$ intersect
at $(2, 1)$.

Substitution:
$x + (x - 1) = 3$

$$-x + y = -1$$
$$\underline{x + y = 3}$$
$$2y = 2$$

Types of linear systems in two variables	Independent: One point in solution set The lines intersect at one point.	$y = x - 5$ $y = 2x + 3$
	Inconsistent: Empty solution set The lines are parallel.	$2x + y = 1$ $2x + y = 5$
	Dependent: Infinite solution set The lines are the same.	$2x + 3y = 4$ $4x + 6y = 8$
Linear equation in three variables	$Ax + By + Cz = D$ In a three-dimensional coordinate system the graph is a plane.	$2x - y + 3z = 5$
Linear systems in three variables	Use substitution or addition to eliminate variables in the system. The solution set may be a single point, the empty set, or an infinite set of points.	$x + y - z = 3$ $2x - 3y + z = 2$ $x - y - 4z = 14$

Matrices and Determinants

Examples

Matrix	A rectangular array of real numbers An $n \times m$ matrix has n rows and m columns.	$\begin{bmatrix} 1 & -3 \\ 2 & 5 \end{bmatrix}, \begin{bmatrix} 1 & 0 & 1 \\ 2 & 1 & 4 \end{bmatrix}$
Augmented matrix	The matrix of coefficients and constants from a system of linear equations	$x - 3y = -7$ $2x + 5y = 19$ Augmented matrix: $\begin{bmatrix} 1 & -3 & | & -7 \\ 2 & 5 & | & 19 \end{bmatrix}$
Gauss-Jordan elimination method	Use the row operations to get ones on the diagonal and zeros elsewhere for the coefficients in the augmented matrix.	$\begin{bmatrix} 1 & 0 & | & 2 \\ 0 & 1 & | & 3 \end{bmatrix}$ $x = 2$ and $y = 3$
Determinant	A real number corresponding to a square matrix	
Determinant of a 2×2 matrix	$\begin{vmatrix} a_1 & b_1 \\ a_2 & b_2 \end{vmatrix} = a_1 b_2 - a_2 b_1$	$\begin{vmatrix} 1 & -3 \\ 2 & 5 \end{vmatrix} = 5 - (-6)$ $= 11$
Determinant of a 3×3 matrix	Expand by minors about any row or column, using signs from the sign array. $\begin{vmatrix} a_1 & b_1 & c_1 \\ a_2 & b_2 & c_2 \\ a_3 & b_3 & c_3 \end{vmatrix} = a_1 \cdot \begin{vmatrix} b_2 & c_2 \\ b_3 & c_3 \end{vmatrix} - a_2 \cdot \begin{vmatrix} b_1 & c_1 \\ b_3 & c_3 \end{vmatrix} + a_3 \cdot \begin{vmatrix} b_1 & c_1 \\ b_2 & c_2 \end{vmatrix}$	Sign array: $\begin{bmatrix} + & - & + \\ - & + & - \\ + & - & + \end{bmatrix}$

Cramer's Rules

Two linear equations in two variables	The solution to the system $$a_1 x + b_1 y = c_1$$ $$a_2 x + b_2 y = c_2$$ is given by $x = \dfrac{D_x}{D}$ and $y = \dfrac{D_y}{D}$, where $$D = \begin{vmatrix} a_1 & b_1 \\ a_2 & b_2 \end{vmatrix}, \qquad D_x = \begin{vmatrix} c_1 & b_1 \\ c_2 & b_2 \end{vmatrix}, \qquad \text{and} \qquad D_y = \begin{vmatrix} a_1 & c_1 \\ a_2 & c_2 \end{vmatrix}$$ provided that $D \neq 0$.

Three linear equations
in three variables

The solution to the system

$$a_1x + b_1y + c_1z = d_1$$
$$a_2x + b_2y + c_2z = d_2$$
$$a_3x + b_3y + c_3z = d_3$$

is given by $x = \dfrac{D_x}{D}$, $y = \dfrac{D_y}{D}$, and $z = \dfrac{D_z}{D}$, where

$$D = \begin{vmatrix} a_1 & b_1 & c_1 \\ a_2 & b_2 & c_2 \\ a_3 & b_3 & c_3 \end{vmatrix}, \qquad D_x = \begin{vmatrix} d_1 & b_1 & c_1 \\ d_2 & b_2 & c_2 \\ d_3 & b_3 & c_3 \end{vmatrix},$$

$$D_y = \begin{vmatrix} a_1 & d_1 & c_1 \\ a_2 & d_2 & c_2 \\ a_3 & d_3 & c_3 \end{vmatrix}, \qquad D_z = \begin{vmatrix} a_1 & b_1 & d_1 \\ a_2 & b_2 & d_2 \\ a_3 & b_3 & d_3 \end{vmatrix},$$

provided that $D \neq 0$.

Linear Programming

Use the following steps to find the maximum or minimum value
of a linear function subject to linear constraints.
1. Graph the region that satisfies all of the constraints.
2. Determine the coordinates of each vertex of the region.
3. Evaluate the function at each vertex of the region.
4. Identify which vertex gives the maximum or minimum value of the function.

ENRICHING YOUR MATHEMATICAL WORD POWER

For each mathematical term, choose the correct meaning.

1. system of equations
   a. a systematic method for classifying equations
   b. a method for solving an equation
   c. two or more equations
   d. the properties of equality

2. independent linear system
   a. a system with exactly one solution
   b. an equation that is satisfied by every real number
   c. equations that are identical
   d. a system of lines

3. inconsistent system
   a. a system with no solution
   b. a system of inconsistent equations
   c. a system that is incorrect
   d. a system that we are not sure how to solve

4. dependent system
   a. a system that is independent
   b. a system that depends on a variable
   c. a system that has no solution
   d. a system for which the graphs coincide

5. substitution method
   a. replacing the variables by the correct answer
   b. a method of eliminating a variable by substituting
      one equation into the other
   c. the replacement method
   d. any method of solving a system

6. addition method
   a. adding the same number to each side of an equation
   b. adding fractions
   c. eliminating a variable by adding two equations
   d. the sum of a number and its additive inverse is zero

7. linear equation in three variables
   a. $Ax + By + Cz = D$ with A, B, and C not all zero
   b. $Ax + By = C$ with A and B not both zero
   c. the equation of a line
   d. $A/x + B/y = C$ with A and B not both zero

8. matrix
   a. a television screen
   b. a maze
   c. a rectangular array of numbers
   d. coordinates in four dimensions

9. **augmented matrix**
   a. a matrix with a power booster
   b. a matrix with no solution
   c. a square matrix
   d. a matrix containing the coefficients and constants of a system of equations

10. **order**
    a. the length of a matrix
    b. the number of rows and columns in a matrix
    c. the highest power of a matrix
    d. the lowest power of a matrix

11. **determinant**
    a. a number corresponding to a square matrix
    b. a number that is determined by any matrix
    c. the first entry of a matrix
    d. a number that determines whether a matrix has a solution

12. **sign array**
    a. the signs of the entries of a matrix
    b. the sign of the determinant
    c. the signs of the answers
    d. a matrix of $+$ and $-$ signs used in computing a determinant

REVIEW EXERCISES

4.1 *Solve by graphing. Indicate whether each system is independent, inconsistent, or dependent.*

1. $y = 2x - 1$
   $x + y = 2$

2. $y = 3x - 4$
   $y = -2x + 1$

3. $x + 2y = 4$
   $y = -\dfrac{1}{2}x + 2$

4. $2x - 3y = 12$
   $3y - 2x = -12$

5. $y = -x$
   $y = -x + 3$

6. $3x - y = 4$
   $3x - y = 0$

Solve each system by the substitution method. Indicate whether each system is independent, inconsistent, or dependent.

7. $y = 3x + 11$
   $3x + 3y = 0$

8. $x - y = 3$
   $3x - 2y = 3$

9. $x = y + 5$
   $2x - 2y = 12$

10. $3y = x + 5$
    $3x - 9y = -10$

11. $2x - y = 3$
    $6x - 9 = 3y$

12. $y = \dfrac{1}{2}x - 9$
    $3x - 6y = 54$

13. $y = \dfrac{1}{2}x - 3$
    $y = \dfrac{1}{3}x + 2$

14. $x = \dfrac{1}{8}y - 1$
    $y = \dfrac{1}{4}x + 39$

15. $x + 2y = 1$
    $8x + 6y = 4$

16. $x - 5y = 4$
    $4x + 8y = -5$

4.2 *Solve each system by the addition method. Indicate whether each system is independent, inconsistent, or dependent.*

17. $5x - 3y = -20$
    $3x + 2y = 7$

18. $-3x + y = 3$
    $2x - 3y = 5$

19. $2(y - 5) + 4 = 3(x - 6)$
    $3x - 2y = 12$

20. $x + 3(y - 1) = 11$
    $2(x - y) + 8y = 28$

Study Tip

Note how the review exercises are arranged according to the sections in this chapter. If you are having trouble with a certain type of problem, refer back to the appropriate section for examples and explanations.

21. $3x - 4(y - 5) = x + 2$
    $2y - x = 7$

22. $4(1 - x) + y = 3$
    $3(1 - y) - 4x = -4y$

23. $\dfrac{1}{4}x + \dfrac{3}{8}y = \dfrac{3}{8}$
    $\dfrac{5}{2}x - 6y = 7$

24. $\dfrac{1}{3}x - \dfrac{1}{6}y = \dfrac{1}{3}$
    $\dfrac{1}{6}x + \dfrac{1}{4}y = 0$

25. $0.4x + 0.06y = 11.6$
    $0.8x - 0.05y = 13$

26. $0.08x + 0.7y = 37.4$
    $0.06x - 0.05y = -0.7$

4.3 *Solve each system by elimination of variables.*

27. $x - y + z = 4$
    $-x + 2y - z = 0$
    $-x + y - 3z = -16$

28. $2x - y + z = 5$
    $x + y - 2z = -4$
    $3x - y + 3z = 10$

29. $2x - y - z = 3$
$3x + y + 2z = 4$
$4x + 2y - z = -4$

30. $2x + 3y - 2z = -11$
$3x - 2y + 3z = 7$
$x - 4y + 4z = 14$

31. $x - 3y + z = 5$
$2x - 4y - z = 7$
$2x - 6y + 2z = 6$

32. $x - y + z = 1$
$2x - 2y + 2z = 2$
$-3x + 3y - 3z = -3$

4.4 *Solve each system by the Gauss-Jordan elimination method.*

33. $x + y = 7$
$-x + 2y = 5$

34. $-x + y = 1$
$2x - 3y = -7$

35. $2x + y = 0$
$x - 3y = 14$

36. $2x - y = 8$
$3x + 2y = -2$

37. $x + y - z = 0$
$x - y + 2z = 4$
$2x + y - z = 1$

38. $2x - y + 2z = 9$
$x + 3y = 5$
$3x + z = 9$

4.5 *Evaluate each determinant.*

39. $\begin{vmatrix} 1 & 3 \\ 0 & 2 \end{vmatrix}$

40. $\begin{vmatrix} -1 & 2 \\ -3 & 5 \end{vmatrix}$

41. $\begin{vmatrix} 0.01 & 0.02 \\ 50 & 80 \end{vmatrix}$

42. $\begin{vmatrix} \dfrac{1}{2} & \dfrac{1}{3} \\ \dfrac{1}{4} & \dfrac{1}{5} \end{vmatrix}$

Solve each system. Use Cramer's rule.

43. $2x - y = 0$
$3x + y = -5$

44. $3x - 2y = 14$
$2x + 3y = -8$

45. $y = 2x - 3$
$3x - 2y = 4$

46. $y = 2x - 5$
$y = 3x - 3y$

Evaluate each determinant.

47. $\begin{vmatrix} 2 & 3 & 1 \\ -1 & 2 & 4 \\ 6 & 1 & 1 \end{vmatrix}$

48. $\begin{vmatrix} 1 & -1 & 0 \\ -2 & 0 & 0 \\ 3 & 1 & 5 \end{vmatrix}$

49. $\begin{vmatrix} 2 & 3 & -2 \\ 2 & 0 & 4 \\ -1 & 0 & 3 \end{vmatrix}$

50. $\begin{vmatrix} 3 & -1 & 4 \\ 2 & -1 & 1 \\ -2 & 0 & 1 \end{vmatrix}$

Solve each system. Use Cramer's rule.

51. $x + y = 3$
$x + y + z = 0$
$x - y - z = 2$

52. $2x - y + z = 0$
$4x + 6y - 2z = 0$
$x - 2y - z = -9$

4.6 *Graph eac\h system of inequalities and identify each vertex of the region.*

53. $x \geq 0, y \geq 0$
$x + 2y \leq 6$
$x + y \leq 5$

54. $x \geq 0, y \geq 0$
$3x + 2y \geq 12$
$x + 2y \geq 8$

Solve each problem by linear programming.

55. Find the maximum value of the function $R(x, y) = 6x + 9y$ subject to the following constraints:

$$x \geq 0, y \geq 0$$
$$2x + y \leq 6$$
$$x + 2y \leq 6$$

56. Find the minimum value of the function $C(x, y) = 9x + 10y$ subject to the following constraints:

$$x \geq 0, y \geq 0$$
$$x + y \geq 4$$
$$3x + y \geq 6$$

MISCELLANEOUS

Use a system of equations in two or three variables to solve each word problem. Solve by the method of your choice.

57. *Two-digit number.* The sum of the digits in a two-digit number is 15. When the digits are reversed, the new number is 9 more than the original number. What is the original number?

58. *Two-digit number.* The sum of the digits in a two-digit number is 8. When the digits are reversed, the new number is 18 less than the original number. What is the original number?

59. *Traveling by boat.* Alonzo can travel from his camp downstream to the mouth of the river in 30 minutes. If it takes him 45 minutes to come back, then how long would it take him to go that same distance in the lake with no current?

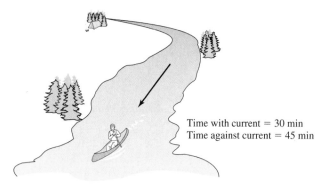

Time with current = 30 min
Time against current = 45 min

FIGURE FOR EXERCISE 59

60. *Driving and dating.* In 4 years Gasper will be old enough to drive. His parents said that he must have a driver's license for 2 years before he can date. Three years ago, Gasper's age was only one-half of the age necessary to date. How old must Gasper be to drive, and how old is he now?

61. *Three solutions.* A chemist has three solutions of acid that must be mixed to obtain 20 liters of a solution that is 38% acid. Solution A is 30% acid, solution B is 20% acid, and solution C is 60% acid. Because of another chemical in these solutions, the chemist must keep the ratio of solution C to solution A at 2 to 1. How many liters of each should she mix together?

62. *Mixing investments.* Darlene invested a total of $20,000. The part that she invested in Dell Computer stock returned 70% and the part that she invested in U.S. Treasury bonds returned 5%. Her total return on these two investments was $9,580.

a) Use the accompanying graph to estimate the amount that she put into each investment.

b) Solve a system of equations to find the exact amount that she put into each investment.

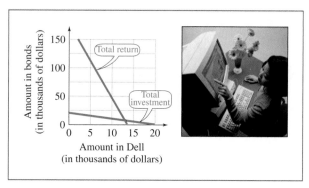

FIGURE FOR EXERCISE 62

63. *Beets and beans.* One serving of canned beets contains 1 gram of protein and 6 grams of carbohydrates. One serving of canned red beans contains 6 grams of protein and 20 grams of carbohydrates. How many servings of each would it take to get exactly 21 grams of protein and 78 grams of carbohydrates?

CHAPTER 4 TEST

Solve the system by graphing.

1. $x + y = 4$
  $y = 2x + 1$

Solve each system by substitution.

2. $y = 2x - 8$
  $4x + 3y = 1$

3. $y = x - 5$
  $3x - 4(y - 2) = 28 - x$

Solve each system by the addition method.

4. $3x + 2y = 3$
  $4x - 3y = -13$

5. $3x - y = 5$
  $-6x + 2y = 1$

Determine whether each system is independent, inconsistent, or dependent.

6. $y = 3x - 5$
  $y = 3x + 2$

7. $2x + 2y = 8$
  $x + y = 4$

8. $y = 2x - 3$
  $y = 5x - 14$

Solve the following system by elimination of variables.

9. $x + y - z = 2$
  $2x - y + 3z = -5$
  $x - 3y + z = 4$

Solve by the Gauss-Jordan elimination method.

10. $3x - y = 1$
  $x + 2y = 12$

11. $x - y - z = 1$
  $-x - y + 2z = -2$
  $-x - 3y + z = -5$

Evaluate each determinant.

12. $\begin{vmatrix} 2 & 3 \\ 4 & -3 \end{vmatrix}$

13. $\begin{vmatrix} 1 & -2 & -1 \\ 2 & 3 & 1 \\ 1 & 1 & 0 \end{vmatrix}$

Solve each system by using Cramer's rule.

14. $2x - y = -4$
  $3x + y = -1$

15. $x + y = 0$
  $x - y + 2z = 6$
  $2x + y - z = 1$

Study Tip

Before you take an in-class exam on this chapter, work the sample test given here. Set aside one hour to work this test and use the answers in the back of this book to grade yourself. Even though your instructor might not ask exactly the same questions, you will get a good idea of your test readiness.

For each problem, write a system of equations in two or three variables. Use the method of your choice to solve each system.

16. One night the manager of the Sea Breeze Motel rented 5 singles and 12 doubles for a total of $390. The next night he rented 9 singles and 10 doubles for a total of $412. What is the rental charge for each type of room?

17. Jill, Karen, and Betsy studied a total of 93 hours last week. Jill's and Karen's study time totaled only one-half as much as Betsy's. If Jill studied 3 hours more than Karen, then how many hours did each one of the girls spend studying?

Solve the following problem by linear programming.

18. Find the maximum value of the function

$$P(x, y) = 8x + 10y$$

subject to the following constraints:

$$x \geq 0, y \geq 0$$
$$2x + 3y \leq 12$$
$$x + y \leq 5$$

Simplify each expression.

1. -3^4

2. $\dfrac{1}{3}(3) + 6$

3. $(-5)^2 - 4(-2)(6)$

4. $6 - (0.2)(0.3)$

5. $5(t - 3) - 6(t - 2)$

6. $0.1(x - 1) - (x - 1)$

7. $\dfrac{-9x^2 - 6x + 3}{-3}$

8. $\dfrac{4y - 6}{2} - \dfrac{3y - 9}{3}$

Solve each equation for y.

9. $3x - 5y = 7$

10. $Cx - Dy = W$

11. $Cy = Wy - K$

12. $A = \dfrac{1}{2}b(w - y)$

Solve each system.

13. $y = x - 5$
   $2x + 3y = 5$

14. $0.05x + 0.06y = 67$
   $x + y = 1200$

15. $3x - 15y = -51$
   $x + 17 = 5y$

16. $0.07a + 0.3b = 6.70$
   $7a + 30b = 67$

Find the equation of each line.

17. The line through $(0, 55)$ and $(-99, 0)$

18. The line through $(2, -3)$ and $(-4, 8)$

19. The line through $(-4, 6)$ that is parallel to $y = 5x$

20. The line through $(4, 7)$ that is perpendicular to $y = -2x + 1$

21. The line through $(3, 5)$ that is parallel to the *x*-axis

22. The line through $(-7, 0)$ that is perpendicular to the *x*-axis

Study Tip

Don't wait until the final exam to review material. Do some review on a regular basis. The Making Connections exercises on this page can be used to review, compare, and contrast different concepts that you have studied. A good time to work these exercises is between a test and the start of new material.

Solve.

23. ***Comparing copiers.*** A self-employed consultant has prepared the accompanying graph to compare the total cost of purchasing and using two different copy machines.

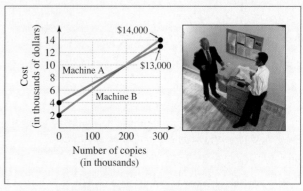

FIGURE FOR EXERCISE 23

a) Which machine has the larger purchase price?

b) What is the per copy cost for operating each machine, not including the purchase price?

c) Find the slope of each line and interpret your findings.

d) Find the equation of each line.

e) Find the number of copies for which the total cost is the same for both machines.

Exponents and Polynomials

O ne statistic that can be used to measure the general health of a nation or group within a nation is life expectancy. This data is considered more accurate than many other statistics because it is easy to determine the precise number of years in a person's lifetime.

According to the National Center for Health Statistics, an American born in 2002 has a life expectancy of 77.5 years. However, an American male born in 2002 has a life expectancy of only 74.5 years, whereas a female can expect 80.3 years. A male who makes it to 65 can expect to live 15.9 more years, whereas a female who makes it to 65 can expect 17.8 more years. In the next few years, thanks in part to advances in health care and science, longevity is expected to increase significantly worldwide. In fact, the World Health Organization predicts that by 2025 no country will have a life expectancy of less than 50 years.

In this chapter we study algebraic expressions involving exponents. In Exercises 95 and 96 of Section 5.2 you will see how formulas involving exponents can be used to find the life expectancies of men and women.

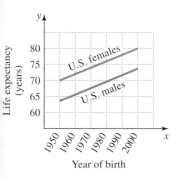

Year of birth

5.1 INTEGRAL EXPONENTS AND SCIENTIFIC NOTATION

In Chapter 1 we defined positive integral exponents and learned to evaluate expressions involving exponents. In this section we will extend the definition of exponents to include all integers and to learn some rules for working with integral exponents. In Chapter 7 we will see that any rational number can be used as an exponent.

Positive and Negative Exponents

Positive integral exponents provide a convenient way to write repeated multiplication or very large numbers. For example,

$$2 \cdot 2 \cdot 2 = 2^3, \qquad y \cdot y \cdot y \cdot y = y^4, \qquad \text{and} \qquad 1{,}000{,}000{,}000 = 10^9.$$

We refer to 2^3 as "2 cubed," "2 raised to the third power," or "a power of 2."

> **Positive Integral Exponents**
>
> If a is a nonzero real number and n is a positive integer, then
>
> $$a^n = \underbrace{a \cdot a \cdot a \cdot \ldots \cdot a}_{n \text{ factors of } a}.$$
>
> In the **exponential expression** a^n, the **base** is a, and the **exponent** is n.

We use 2^{-3} to represent the reciprocal of 2^3. Because $2^3 = 8$, we have $2^{-3} = \frac{1}{8}$. In general, a^{-n} is defined as the reciprocal of a^n.

> **Negative Integral Exponents**
>
> If a is a nonzero real number and n is a positive integer, then
>
> $$a^{-n} = \frac{1}{a^n}. \qquad \text{If } n \text{ is positive, } -n \text{ is negative.}$$

To evaluate 2^{-3}, you can first cube 2 to get 8 and then find the reciprocal to get $\frac{1}{8}$, or you can first find the reciprocal of 2 $\left(\text{which is } \frac{1}{2}\right)$ and then cube $\frac{1}{2}$ to get $\frac{1}{8}$. So

$$2^{-3} = \frac{1}{2^3} = \left(\frac{1}{2}\right)^3 = \frac{1}{8}.$$

The power and the reciprocal can be found in either order. If the exponent is -1, we simply find the reciprocal. For example,

$$2^{-1} = \frac{1}{2}, \qquad \left(\frac{2}{3}\right)^{-1} = \frac{3}{2}, \qquad \text{and} \qquad \left(-\frac{1}{4}\right)^{-1} = -4.$$

If an expression with a negative exponent is a denominator, then we can rewrite the expression as follows:

$$\frac{1}{2^{-3}} = \frac{1}{\dfrac{1}{2^3}} = 1 \cdot \frac{2^3}{1} = 2^3.$$

Helpful Hint

A negative exponent does not cause an expression to have a negative value. The negative exponent "causes" the reciprocal:

$$2^{-3} = \frac{1}{2^3} = \frac{1}{8},$$

$$(-3)^{-4} = \frac{1}{(-3)^4} = \frac{1}{81},$$

$$(-4)^{-3} = \frac{1}{(-4)^3} = -\frac{1}{64}.$$

So $2^{-3} = \dfrac{1}{2^3}$ and $\dfrac{1}{2^{-3}} = 2^3$. These examples illustrate the following rules.

Rules for Negative Exponents

If a and b are nonzero real numbers and n is a positive integer, then

$$\left(\frac{a}{b}\right)^{-n} = \left(\frac{b}{a}\right)^{n}, \qquad a^{-n} = \left(\frac{1}{a}\right)^{n}, \qquad a^{-1} = \frac{1}{a}, \qquad \text{and} \qquad \frac{1}{a^{-n}} = a^{n}.$$

E X A M P L E   1

Negative exponents

Evaluate each expression.

a) 3^{-2} b) $(-3)^{-2}$ c) -3^{-2} d) $\left(\dfrac{3}{4}\right)^{-3}$ e) $\dfrac{1}{5^{-3}}$

Solution

a) $3^{-2} = \dfrac{1}{3^2}$ Definition of negative exponent

$\phantom{3^{-2}} = \dfrac{1}{9}$ Since $3^2 = 9$

b) $(-3)^{-2} = \dfrac{1}{(-3)^2}$ Definition of negative exponent

$\phantom{(-3)^{-2}} = \dfrac{1}{9}$ Since $(-3)^2 = (-3)(-3) = 9$

c) $-3^{-2} = -\dfrac{1}{3^2}$ The negative exponent applies to 3 only.

$\phantom{-3^{-2}} = -\dfrac{1}{9}$ Since $3^2 = 9$

d) By the first rule of negative exponents we can find the reciprocal of $\frac{3}{4}$ and then cube:

$$\left(\frac{3}{4}\right)^{-3} = \left(\frac{4}{3}\right)^{3}$$

$$= \frac{64}{27}$$

e) Using the fourth rule for negative exponents we can simply write $\dfrac{1}{5^{-3}} = 5^3 = 125$. We could also evaluate as follows:

$$\frac{1}{5^{-3}} = \frac{1}{\dfrac{1}{5^3}}$$

$$= 1 \cdot \frac{5^3}{1}$$

$$= 125 \qquad \blacksquare$$

Calculator Close-Up

You can evaluate expressions with negative exponents using a graphing calculator. Use the fraction feature to get fractional answers.

```
3^-2▶Frac
              1/9
(-3)^-2▶Frac
              1/9
-3^-2▶Frac
             -1/9
```

C A U T I O N   In Chapter 1 we agreed to evaluate -3^2 by squaring 3 first and then taking the opposite. So $-3^2 = -9$, whereas $(-3)^2 = 9$. The same agreement also holds for negative exponents. That is why the answer to Example 1(c) is negative.

Calculator Close-Up

A graphing calculator cannot prove that the product rule is correct, but it can provide numerical support for the product rule.

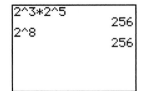

```
2^3*2^5
            256
2^8
            256
```

Product Rule

We can simplify an expression such as $2^3 \cdot 2^5$ using the definition of exponents.

$$2^3 \cdot 2^5 = \overbrace{(2 \cdot 2 \cdot 2)}^{\text{three 2's}}\overbrace{(2 \cdot 2 \cdot 2 \cdot 2 \cdot 2)}^{\text{five 2's}} = 2^8$$

$$\underbrace{\qquad\qquad\qquad\qquad\qquad}_{\text{eight 2's}}$$

Notice that the exponent 8 is the sum of the exponents 3 and 5. This example illustrates the **product rule for exponents.**

Product Rule for Exponents

If m and n are integers and $a \neq 0$, then

$$a^m \cdot a^n = a^{m+n}.$$

EXAMPLE 2

Using the product rule

Simplify each expression. Write answers with positive exponents and assume all variables represent nonzero real numbers.

a) $3^4 \cdot 3^6$ **b)** $4x^{-3} \cdot 5x$ **c)** $-2y^{-3}(-5y^{-4})$

Helpful Hint

The definitions of the different types of exponents are a really clever mathematical invention. The fact that we have rules for performing arithmetic with those exponents makes the notation of exponents even more amazing.

Solution

a) $3^4 \cdot 3^6 = 3^{4+6} = 3^{10}$ Product rule

b) $4x^{-3} \cdot 5x = 4 \cdot 5 \cdot x^{-3} \cdot x^1$

$\qquad = 20x^{-2}$ Product rule: $x^{-3} \cdot x^1 = x^{-3+1} = x^{-2}$

$\qquad = \dfrac{20}{x^2}$ Definition of negative exponent

c) $-2y^{-3}(-5y^{-4}) = (-2)(-5)y^{-3}y^{-4}$

$\qquad = 10y^{-7}$ Product rule: $-3 + (-4) = -7$

$\qquad = \dfrac{10}{y^7}$ Definition of negative exponent

CAUTION The product rule cannot be applied to $2^3 \cdot 3^2$ because the bases are not identical. Even when the bases are identical, we do not multiply the bases. For example, $2^5 \cdot 2^4 \neq 4^9$. Using the rule correctly, we get $2^5 \cdot 2^4 = 2^9$.

Zero Exponent

We have used positive and negative integral exponents, but we have not yet seen the integer 0 used as an exponent. Note that the product rule was stated to hold for *any* integers m and n. If we use the product rule on $2^3 \cdot 2^{-3}$, we get

$$2^3 \cdot 2^{-3} = 2^0.$$

However, $2^3 \cdot 2^{-3} = 2^3 \cdot \dfrac{1}{2^3} = 8 \cdot \dfrac{1}{8} = 1$. So for consistency we define 2^0 and the zero power of any nonzero number to be 1.

Zero Exponent

If a is any nonzero real number, then $a^0 = 1$.

E X A M P L E   3

Using zero as an exponent

Simplify each expression. Write answers with positive exponents and assume all variables represent nonzero real numbers.

a) -3^0 **b)** $\left(\dfrac{1}{4} - \dfrac{3}{2}\right)^0$ **c)** $-2a^5b^{-6} \cdot 3a^{-5}b^2$

Helpful Hint

Defining a^0 to be 1 gives a consistent pattern to exponents:

$$3^{-2} = \frac{1}{9}$$

$$3^{-1} = \frac{1}{3}$$

$$3^0 = 1$$

$$3^1 = 3$$

$$3^2 = 9$$

If the exponent is increased by 1 (with base 3) the value of the expression is multiplied by 3.

Solution

a) To evaluate -3^0, we find 3^0 and then take the opposite. So $-3^0 = -1$.

b) $\left(\dfrac{1}{4} - \dfrac{3}{2}\right)^0 = 1$ Definition of zero exponent

c) $-2a^5b^{-6} \cdot 3a^{-5}b^2 = -6a^5 \cdot a^{-5} \cdot b^{-6} \cdot b^2$

$$= -6a^0 b^{-4} \quad \text{Product rule}$$

$$= -\frac{6}{b^4} \quad \text{Definitions of negative and zero exponent} \qquad \blacksquare$$

Changing the Sign of an Exponent

Because a^{-n} and a^n are reciprocals of each other, we know that

$$a^{-n} = \frac{1}{a^n} \qquad \text{and} \qquad \frac{1}{a^{-n}} = a^n.$$

So a negative exponent in the numerator or denominator can be changed to positive by relocating the exponential expression. In Example 4 we use these facts to remove negative exponents from exponential expressions.

E X A M P L E   4

Simplifying expressions with negative exponents

Write each expression without negative exponents and simplify. All variables represent nonzero real numbers.

a) $\dfrac{5a^{-3}}{a^2 \cdot 2^{-2}}$ **b)** $\dfrac{-2x^{-3}}{y^{-2}z^3}$

Solution

a) $\dfrac{5a^{-3}}{a^2 \cdot 2^{-2}} = 5 \cdot a^{-3} \cdot \dfrac{1}{a^2} \cdot \dfrac{1}{2^{-2}}$ Rewrite division as multiplication.

$$= 5 \cdot \frac{1}{a^3} \cdot \frac{1}{a^2} \cdot 2^2 \quad \text{Change the signs of the negative exponents.}$$

$$= \frac{20}{a^5} \quad \text{Product rule: } a^3 \cdot a^2 = a^5$$

Note that in $5a^{-3}$ the negative exponent applies only to a.

b) $\dfrac{-2x^{-3}}{y^{-2}z^3} = -2 \cdot x^{-3} \cdot \dfrac{1}{y^{-2}} \cdot \dfrac{1}{z^3}$ Rewrite as multiplication.

$$= -2 \cdot \frac{1}{x^3} \cdot y^2 \cdot \frac{1}{z^3} \quad \text{Definition of negative exponent}$$

$$= \frac{-2y^2}{x^3 z^3} \quad \text{Simplify.} \qquad \blacksquare$$

In Example 4 we showed more steps than are necessary. For instance, in part (b) we could simply write

$$\frac{-2x^{-3}}{y^{-2}z^3} = \frac{-2y^2}{x^3z^3}.$$

Exponential expressions (that are factors) can be moved from numerator to denominator (or vice versa) as long as we change the sign of the exponent.

Calculator Close-Up

A graphing calculator cannot prove that the quotient rule is correct, but it can provide numerical support for the quotient rule.

```
2^15/2^5
              1024
2^10
              1024
```

CAUTION   If an exponential expression is *not* a factor, you *cannot* move it from numerator to denominator (or vice versa). For example,

$$\frac{2^{-1} + 1^{-1}}{1^{-1}} \neq \frac{1}{2 + 1}.$$

Because $2^{-1} = \frac{1}{2}$ and $1^{-1} = 1$, we get

$$\frac{2^{-1} + 1^{-1}}{1^{-1}} = \frac{\frac{1}{2} + 1}{1} = \frac{\frac{3}{2}}{1} = \frac{3}{2} \qquad \text{not} \qquad \frac{1}{2 + 1} = \frac{1}{3}.$$

Quotient Rule

We can use arithmetic to simplify the quotient of two exponential expressions. For example,

$$\frac{2^5}{2^3} = \frac{\cancel{2} \cdot \cancel{2} \cdot \cancel{2} \cdot 2 \cdot 2}{\cancel{2} \cdot \cancel{2} \cdot \cancel{2}} = 2^2.$$

There are five 2's in the numerator and three 2's in the denominator. After dividing, two 2's remain. The exponent in 2^2 can be obtained by subtracting the exponents 3 and 5. This example illustrates the **quotient rule for exponents.**

> **Quotient Rule for Exponents**
>
> If m and n are any integers and $a \neq 0$, then
>
> $$\frac{a^m}{a^n} = a^{m-n}.$$

CAUTION   Do not divide the bases when using the quotient rule. We cannot apply the quotient rule to $\frac{6^5}{2^4}$ even though 6 is divisible by 2.

EXAMPLE 5

Using the quotient rule

Simplify each expression. Write answers with positive exponents only. All variables represent nonzero real numbers.

a) $\dfrac{2^9}{2^4}$ **b)** $\dfrac{m^5}{m^{-3}}$ **c)** $\dfrac{y^{-4}}{y^{-2}}$

Study Tip

The keys to college success are motivation and time management. Students who tell you that they are making great grades without studying are probably not telling the truth. Success in college takes effort.

Solution

a) $\dfrac{2^9}{2^4} = 2^{9-4}$ Quotient rule

$= 2^5$ Simplify the exponent.

b) $\dfrac{m^5}{m^{-3}} = m^{5-(-3)}$ Quotient rule

$\qquad = m^8$ Simplify the exponent.

c) $\dfrac{y^{-4}}{y^{-2}} = y^{-4-(-2)}$ Quotient rule

$\qquad = y^{-2}$ Simplify the exponent.

$\qquad = \dfrac{1}{y^2}$ Rewrite with a positive exponent.   ■

Example 6 further illustrates the rules of exponents. Remember that the bases must be identical for the quotient rule or the product rule.

E X A M P L E   6

Using the product and quotient rules

Use the rules of exponents to simplify each expression. Write answers with positive exponents only. All variables represent nonzero real numbers.

a) $\dfrac{2x^{-7}}{x^{-7}}$ 　　　　　　　**b)** $\dfrac{w(2w^{-4})}{3w^{-2}}$ 　　　　　　　**c)** $\dfrac{x^{-1}x^{-3}y^5}{x^{-2}y^2}$

Solution

a) $\dfrac{2x^{-7}}{x^{-7}} = 2x^0$ Quotient rule: $-7 - (-7) = 0$

$\qquad = 2$ Definition of zero exponent

b) $\dfrac{w(2w^{-4})}{3w^{-2}} = \dfrac{2w^{-3}}{3w^{-2}}$ Product rule: $w^1 \cdot w^{-4} = w^{-3}$

$\qquad = \dfrac{2w^{-1}}{3}$ Quotient rule: $-3 - (-2) = -1$

$\qquad = \dfrac{2}{3w}$ Definition of negative exponent

c) $\dfrac{x^{-1}x^{-3}y^5}{x^{-2}y^2} = \dfrac{x^{-4}y^5}{x^{-2}y^2}$ Product rule

$\qquad = x^{-2}y^3$ Quotient rule

$\qquad = \dfrac{y^3}{x^2}$ Rewrite x^{-2} with a positive exponent.   ■

Scientific Notation

Many of the numbers that are encountered in science are either very large or very small. For example, the distance from the earth to the sun is 93,000,000 miles, and a hydrogen atom weighs 0.00000000000000000000000017 gram. Scientific notation provides a convenient way of writing very large and very small numbers. In scientific notation the distance from the earth to the sun is 9.3×10^7 miles and a hydrogen atom weighs 1.7×10^{-24} gram. In scientific notation the times symbol, $\times$, is used to indicate multiplication. Converting a number from scientific notation to standard notation is simply a matter of multiplication.

E X A M P L E   7

Scientific notation to standard notation

Write each number using standard notation.

a) 7.62×10^5 **b)** 6.35×10^{-4}

Calculator Close-Up

In normal mode, display a number in scientific notation and press ENTER to convert to standard notation. You can use a power of 10 or the EE key to get the E for the built-in scientific notation.

```
7.62E5
           762000
7.62*10^5
           762000
```

Solution

a) Multiplying a number by 10^5 moves the decimal point five places to the right:

$$7.62 \times 10^5 = 762000. = 762{,}000$$

b) Multiplying a number by 10^{-4} or 0.0001 moves the decimal point four places to the left:

$$6.35 \times 10^{-4} = 0.000635 = 0.000635 \quad \blacksquare$$

The procedure for converting a number from scientific notation to standard notation is summarized as follows.

> **Strategy for Converting from Scientific Notation to Standard Notation**
>
> 1. Determine the number of places to move the decimal point by examining the exponent on the 10.
> 2. Move to the right for a positive exponent and to the left for a negative exponent.

A positive number in scientific notation is written as a product of a number between 1 and 10, and a power of 10. Numbers in scientific notation are written with only one digit to the left of the decimal point. A number larger than 10 is written with a positive power of 10, and a positive number smaller than 1 is written with a negative power of 10. Note that 1000 (a power of 10) could be written as 1×10^3 or simply 10^3. Numbers between 1 and 10 are usually not written in scientific notation. To convert to scientific notation, we reverse the strategy for converting from scientific notation.

> **Strategy for Converting from Standard Notation to Scientific Notation**
>
> 1. Count the number of places (n) that the decimal point must be moved so that it will follow the first nonzero digit of the number.
> 2. If the original number was larger than 10, use 10^n.
> 3. If the original number was smaller than 1, use 10^{-n}.

E X A M P L E   8

Standard notation to scientific notation

Convert each number to scientific notation.

a) 934,000,000 **b)** 0.0000025

Solution

a) In 934,000,000 the decimal point must be moved eight places to the left to get it to follow 9, the first nonzero digit.

$$934{,}000{,}000 = 9.34 \times 10^8 \quad \text{Use 8 because } 934{,}000{,}000 > 10.$$

b) The decimal point in 0.0000025 must be moved six places to the right to get the 2 to the left of the decimal point.

$$0.0000025 = 2.5 \times 10^{-6} \quad \text{Use } -6 \text{ because } 0.0000025 < 1. \quad ∎$$

We can perform computations with numbers in scientific notation by using the rules of exponents on the powers of 10.

E X A M P L E   9

Using scientific notation in computations

Evaluate each expression without using a calculator. Express each answer in scientific notation.

a) $(2 \times 10^7)(6.3 \times 10^{-11})$

b) $\dfrac{7 \times 10^{13}}{2 \times 10^6}$

c) $\dfrac{(10{,}000)(0.000025)}{0.000005}$

Solution

a) $(2 \times 10^7)(6.3 \times 10^{-11}) = 2 \cdot 6.3 \cdot 10^7 \cdot 10^{-11}$

$$= 12.6 \times 10^{-4}$$
$$= 1.26 \times 10^1 \times 10^{-4}$$
$$= 1.26 \times 10^{-3}$$

b) $\dfrac{7 \times 10^{13}}{2 \times 10^6} = \dfrac{7}{2} \cdot \dfrac{10^{13}}{10^6} = 3.5 \times 10^7$

c) $\dfrac{(10{,}000)(0.000025)}{0.000005} = \dfrac{(1 \times 10^4)(2.5 \times 10^{-5})}{5 \times 10^{-6}}$

$$= \dfrac{2.5}{5} \cdot \dfrac{10^4 \cdot 10^{-5}}{10^{-6}}$$
$$= 0.5 \times 10^5$$
$$= 5 \times 10^{-1} \times 10^5$$
$$= 5 \times 10^4 \qquad ∎$$

E X A M P L E   10

Counting hydrogen atoms

If the weight of hydrogen is 1.7×10^{-24} gram per atom, then how many hydrogen atoms are there in one kilogram of hydrogen?

Solution

There are 1000 or 1×10^3 grams in one kilogram. So to find the number of hydrogen atoms in one kilogram of hydrogen, we divide 1×10^3 by 1.7×10^{-24}:

$$\frac{1 \times 10^3 \text{ g/kg}}{1.7 \times 10^{-24} \text{ g/atom}} \approx 5.9 \times 10^{26} \text{ atom per kilogram (atom/kg)}$$

To divide by grams per atom, we invert and multiply: $\dfrac{g}{kg} \cdot \dfrac{\text{atom}}{g} = \dfrac{\text{atom}}{kg}$. Keeping track of the units as we did here helps us to be sure that we performed the correct operation. So there are approximately 5.9×10^{26} hydrogen atoms in one kilogram of hydrogen. $\qquad ∎$

b) Bob, 30, and Ashley, 26, are an average white couple. How many years can Ashley expect to live as a widow?

c) Interpret the intersection of the life expectancy curves in the accompanying figure.

GETTING MORE INVOLVED

97. *Discussion.* For which values of a and b is it true that $(ab)^{-1} = a^{-1}b^{-1}$? Find a pair of nonzero values for a and b for which $(a + b)^{-1} \neq a^{-1} + b^{-1}$.

98. *Writing.* Explain how to evaluate $\left(-\frac{2}{3}\right)^{-3}$ in three different ways.

99. *Discussion.* Which of the following expressions has a value different from the others? Explain.
a) -1^{-1} **b)** -3^0 **c)** $-2^{-1} - 2^{-1}$
d) $(-1)^{-2}$ **e)** $(-1)^{-3}$

100. *True or False?* Explain your answer.
a) The square of a product is the product of the squares.
b) The square of a sum is the sum of the squares.

GRAPHING CALCULATOR EXERCISES

101. At 12% compounded annually the value of an investment of $10,000 after x years is given by

$$y = 10,000(1.12)^x.$$

a) Graph $y = 10,000(1.12)^x$ and the function $y = 20,000$ on a graphing calculator. Use a viewing window that shows the intersection of the two graphs.

b) Use the intersect feature of your calculator to find the point of intersection.

c) The x-coordinate of the point of intersection is the number of years that it will take for the $10,000 investment to double. What is that number of years?

102. The function $y = 72.2(1.002)^x$ gives the life expectancy y of a U.S. white male with present age x. (See Exercise 95.)

a) Graph $y = 72.2(1.002)^x$ and $y = 86$ on a graphing calculator. Use a viewing window that shows the intersection of the two graphs.

b) Use the intersect feature of your calculator to find the point of intersection.

c) What does the x-coordinate of the point of intersection tell you?

In This Section

- Polynomials
- Evaluating Polynomial Functions
- Addition and Subtraction of Polynomials
- Multiplication of Polynomials

5.3 POLYNOMIALS AND POLYNOMIAL FUNCTIONS

A polynomial is a particular type of algebraic expression that serves as a fundamental building block in algebra. We used polynomials in Chapters 1 and 2, but we did not identify them as polynomials. In this section you will learn to recognize polynomials and to add, subtract, and multiply them.

Polynomials

A **term** is a single number or the product of a number and one or more variables raised to whole number powers. For example, the expressions $3x^3$, $-15x^2$, $7x$, and -2 are terms. The number preceding the variable in each term is called the **coefficient** of that variable. The coefficient of x^3 is 3, the coefficient of x^2 is -15, and the coefficient of x is 7. In algebra a number is often referred to as a **constant,** and so the term -2 is called a **constant term.** A **polynomial** is defined as a single term or a sum of a finite number of terms. So the expression

$$3x^3 + (-15x^2) + 7x + (-2)$$

is a polynomial in one variable with four terms. For simplicity we will write this polynomial as $3x^3 - 15x^2 + 7x - 2$.

E X A M P L E   1   **Identifying polynomials**

Determine whether each algebraic expression is a polynomial.

a) -3 **b)** $3x + 2^{-1}$ **c)** $3x^{-2} + 4x^2$

d) $\dfrac{1}{x} + \dfrac{1}{x^2}$ **e)** $x^{49} - 8x^2 + 11x - 2$

Solution

a) The number -3 is a polynomial of one term, a constant term.

b) Since $3x + 2^{-1}$ can be written as $3x + \frac{1}{2}$, it is a polynomial of two terms.

c) The expression $3x^{-2} + 4x^2$ is not a polynomial because x has a negative exponent.

d) If this expression is rewritten as $x^{-1} + x^{-2}$, then it fails to be a polynomial because of the negative exponents. So a polynomial does not have variables in denominators, and

$$\frac{1}{x} + \frac{1}{x^2}$$

is not a polynomial.

e) The expression $x^{49} - 8x^2 + 11x - 2$ is a polynomial.   ■

For simplicity we usually write polynomials in one variable with the exponents in decreasing order from left to right. Thus we would write

$$3x^3 - 15x^2 + 7x - 2 \quad \text{rather than} \quad -15x^2 - 2 + 7x + 3x^3.$$

When a polynomial is written in decreasing order, the coefficient of the first term is called the **leading coefficient.**

Certain polynomials have special names depending on the number of terms. A **monomial** is a polynomial that has one term, a **binomial** is a polynomial that has two terms, and a **trinomial** is a polynomial that has three terms. The **degree** of a polynomial in one variable is the highest power of the variable in the polynomial. The number 0 is considered to be a monomial without degree because $0 = 0x^n$, where n could be any number.

E X A M P L E   2   **Identifying coefficients and degree**

State the degree of each polynomial and the coefficient of x^2. Determine whether the polynomial is monomial, binomial, or trinomial.

a) $\dfrac{x^2}{3} - 5x^3 + 7$ **b)** $x^{48} - x^2$ **c)** 6

Study Tip

Effective time management will allow adequate time for school, social life, and free time. However, at times you will have to sacrifice to do well.

Solution

a) The degree of this trinomial is 3, and the coefficient of x^2 is $\frac{1}{3}$.

b) The degree of this binomial is 48, and the coefficient of x^2 is -1.

c) Because $6 = 6x^0$, the number 6 is a monomial with degree 0. Because x^2 does not appear in this polynomial, the coefficient of x^2 is 0.   ■

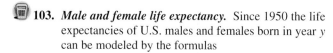

FIGURE FOR EXERCISE 102

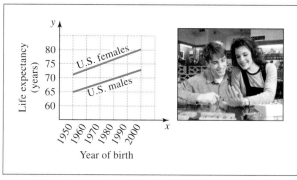

FIGURE FOR EXERCISES 103 AND 104

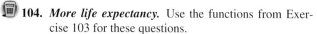

103. *Male and female life expectancy.* Since 1950 the life expectancies of U.S. males and females born in year y can be modeled by the formulas

$$M(y) = 0.16252y - 251.91$$

and

$$F(y) = 0.18268y - 284.98,$$

respectively (National Center for Health Statistics, www.cdc.gov/nchswww).
a) How much greater was the life expectancy of a female born in 1950 than a male born in 1950?
b) Are the lines in the accompanying figure parallel?
c) In what year will female life expectancy be 8 years greater than male life expectancy?

104. *More life expectancy.* Use the functions from Exercise 103 for these questions.
a) A male born in 1975 does not want his future wife to outlive him. What should be the year of birth for

his wife so that they both can be expected to die in the same year?
b) Find $\dfrac{M(y) + F(y)}{2}$ to get a formula for the life expectancy of a person born in year y.

GETTING MORE INVOLVED

105. *Discussion.* Is it possible for a binomial to have degree 4? If so, give an example.
106. *Discussion.* Give an example of two fourth-degree trinomials whose sum is a third-degree binomial.
107. *Cooperative learning.* Work in a group to find the product $(a + b)(c + d)$. How many terms does it have? Find the product $(a + b)(c + d)(e + f)$. How many terms does it have? How many terms are there in a product of four binomials in which there are no like terms to combine? How many terms are there in a product of n binomials in which there are no like terms?

In This Section

- The FOIL Method
- The Square of a Binomial
- Product of a Sum and a Difference

5.4 MULTIPLYING BINOMIALS

In Section 5.3 you learned to multiply polynomials. In this section you will learn rules to make multiplication of binomials simpler.

The FOIL Method

Consider how we find the product of two binomials $x + 3$ and $x + 5$ using the distributive property twice:

$$(x + 3)(x + 5) = (x + 3)x + (x + 3)5 \quad \text{Distributive property}$$
$$= x^2 + 3x + 5x + 15 \quad \text{Distributive property}$$
$$= x^2 + 8x + 15 \quad \text{Combine like terms.}$$

There are four terms in the product. The term x^2 is the product of the first term of each binomial. The term $5x$ is the product of the two outer terms, 5 and x. The term $3x$ is the product of the two inner terms, 3 and x. The term 15 is the product of the

Helpful Hint

The product of two binomials always has four terms before combining like terms. The product of two trinomials always has nine terms before combining like terms. How many terms are there in the product of a binomial and trinomial?

last two terms in each binomial, 3 and 5. It may be helpful to connect the terms multiplied by lines.

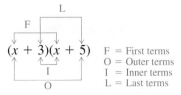

$$F = \text{First terms}$$
$$O = \text{Outer terms}$$
$$I = \text{Inner terms}$$
$$L = \text{Last terms}$$

So instead of writing out all of the steps in using the distributive property, we can get the result by finding the products of the first, outer, inner, and last terms. This method is called the **FOIL method.**

For example, let's apply FOIL to the product $(x - 3)(x + 4)$:

$$(x - 3)(x + 4) = x^2 + 4x - 3x - 12 = x^2 + x - 12$$

If the outer and inner products are like terms, you can save a step by writing down only their sum.

EXAMPLE 1

Multiplying binomials

Use FOIL to find the products of the binomials.

a) $(2x - 3)(3x + 4)$

b) $(2x^3 + 5)(2x^3 - 5)$

c) $(m + w)(2m - w)$

d) $(a + b)(a - 3)$

Solution

a) $(2x - 3)(3x + 4) = \overset{F}{6x^2} + \overset{O}{8x} - \overset{I}{9x} - \overset{L}{12}$
$$= 6x^2 - x - 12$$

b) $(2x^3 + 5)(2x^3 - 5) = 4x^6 - 10x^3 + 10x^3 - 25$
$$= 4x^6 - 25$$

c) $(m + w)(2m - w) = 2m^2 - mw + 2mw - w^2$
$$= 2m^2 + mw - w^2$$

d) $(a + b)(a - 3) = a^2 - 3a + ab - 3b$ There are no like terms.   ∎

Helpful Hint

To visualize the square of a sum, draw a square with sides of length $a + b$ as shown.

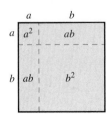

The area of the large square is $(a + b)^2$. It comes from four terms as stated in the rule for the square of a sum.

The Square of a Binomial

To find $(a + b)^2$, the square of a sum, we can use FOIL on $(a + b)(a + b)$:

$$(a + b)(a + b) = a^2 + ab + ab + b^2$$
$$= a^2 + 2ab + b^2$$

You can use the result $a^2 + 2ab + b^2$ that we obtained from FOIL to quickly find the square of *any* sum. *To square a sum, we square the first term* (a^2), *add twice the product of the two terms* ($2ab$), *then add the square of the last term* (b^2).

Rule for the Square of a Sum

$$(a + b)^2 = a^2 + 2ab + b^2$$

In general, the square of a sum $(a + b)^2$ is not equal to the sum of the squares $a^2 + b^2$. The square of a sum has the middle term $2ab$.

E X A M P L E 2

Squaring a binomial

Square each sum, using the new rule.

a) $(x + 5)^2$ **b)** $(2w + 3)^2$ **c)** $(2y^4 + 3)^2$

Solution

a) $(x + 5)^2 = x^2 + 2(x)(5) + 5^2 = x^2 + 10x + 25$

$\quad\quad\quad\quad\quad\quad\uparrow\quad\quad\quad\uparrow\quad\quad\quad\uparrow$
$\quad\quad\quad\quad\quad$ Square Twice Square
$\quad\quad\quad\quad\quad$ of the of
$\quad\quad\quad\quad\quad$ first product last

b) $(2w + 3)^2 = (2w)^2 + 2(2w)(3) + 3^2$
$\quad\quad\quad\quad\quad\quad = 4w^2 + 12w + 9$

c) $(2y^4 + 3)^2 = (2y^4)^2 + 2(2y^4)(3) + 3^2$
$\quad\quad\quad\quad\quad\quad = 4y^8 + 12y^4 + 9$ ∎

CAUTION   Squaring $x + 5$ correctly, as in Example 2(a), gives us the identity

$$(x + 5)^2 = x^2 + 10x + 25,$$

which is satisfied by any x. If you forget the middle term and write $(x + 5)^2 = x^2 + 25$, then you have an equation that is satisfied only if $x = 0$.

To find $(a - b)^2$, the square of a difference, we can use FOIL:

$$(a - b)(a - b) = a^2 - ab - ab + b^2$$
$$= a^2 - 2ab + b^2$$

As in squaring a sum, it is simply better to remember the result of using FOIL. *To square a difference, square the first term, subtract twice the product of the two terms, and add the square of the last term.*

Rule for the Square of a Difference
$$(a - b)^2 = a^2 - 2ab + b^2$$

E X A M P L E 3

Squaring a binomial

Square each difference, using the new rule.

a) $(x - 6)^2$ **b)** $(3w - 5y)^2$
c) $(-4 - st)^2$ **d)** $(3 - 5a^3)^2$

Helpful Hint

Many students keep using FOIL to find the square of a sum or a difference. However, you will be greatly rewarded if you learn the new rules for squaring a sum or a difference.

Solution

a) $(x - 6)^2 = x^2 - 2(x)(6) + 6^2$ For the middle term, subtract twice the product: $2(x)(6)$.

$\quad\quad\quad\quad\quad = x^2 - 12x + 36$

b) $(3w - 5y)^2 = (3w)^2 - 2(3w)(5y) + (5y)^2$
$\quad\quad\quad\quad\quad\quad = 9w^2 - 30wy + 25y^2$

c) $(-4 - st)^2 = (-4)^2 - 2(-4)(st) + (st)^2$
$$= 16 + 8st + s^2t^2$$
d) $(3 - 5a^3)^2 = 3^2 - 2(3)(5a^3) + (5a^3)^2$
$$= 9 - 30a^3 + 25a^6$$ ■

Product of a Sum and a Difference

If we multiply the sum $a + b$ and the difference $a - b$ by using FOIL, we get
$$(a + b)(a - b) = a^2 - ab + ab - b^2$$
$$= a^2 - b^2.$$

The inner and outer products add up to zero, canceling each other out. So *the product of a sum and a difference is the difference of two squares,* as shown in the following rule.

> **Rule for the Product of a Sum and a Difference**
> $$(a + b)(a - b) = a^2 - b^2$$

E X A M P L E   4 **Finding the product of a sum and a difference**
Find the products.
a) $(x + 3)(x - 3)$ **b)** $(a^3 + 8)(a^3 - 8)$ **c)** $(3x^2 - y^3)(3x^2 + y^3)$

Solution
a) $(x + 3)(x - 3) = x^2 - 9$
b) $(a^3 + 8)(a^3 - 8) = a^6 - 64$
c) $(3x^2 - y^3)(3x^2 + y^3) = 9x^4 - y^6$ ■

The square of a sum, the square of a difference, and the product of a sum and a difference are referred to as **special products.** Although the special products can be found by using the distributive property or FOIL, they occur so frequently in algebra that it is essential to learn the new rules. In the next example we use the special product rules to multiply two trinomials and to square a trinomial.

E X A M P L E   5 **Using special product rules to multiply trinomials**
Find the products.
a) $[(x + y) + 3][(x + y) - 3]$ **b)** $[(m - n) + 5]^2$

Solution
a) Use the rule $(a + b)(a - b) = a^2 - b^2$ with $a = x + y$ and $b = 3$:
$$[(x + y) + 3][(x + y) - 3] = (x + y)^2 - 3^2$$
$$= x^2 + 2xy + y^2 - 9$$
b) Use the rule $(a + b)^2 = a^2 + 2ab + b^2$ with $a = m - n$ and $b = 5$:
$$[(m - n) + 5]^2 = (m - n)^2 + 2(m - n)5 + 5^2$$
$$= m^2 - 2mn + n^2 + 10m - 10n + 25$$ ■

True or false? Explain your answer.

1. $(x + 2)(x + 5) = x^2 + 7x + 10$ for any value of x.
2. $(2x - 3)(3x + 5) = 6x^2 + x - 15$ for any value of x.
3. $(2 + 3)^2 = 2^2 + 3^2$
4. $(x + 7)^2 = x^2 + 14x + 49$ for any value of x.
5. $(8 - 3)^2 = 64 - 9$
6. The product of a sum and a difference of the same two terms is equal to the difference of two squares.
7. $(60 - 1)(60 + 1) = 3600 - 1$
8. $(x - y)^2 = x^2 - 2xy + y^2$ for any values of x and y.
9. $(x - 3)^2 = x^2 - 3x + 9$ for any value of x.
10. The expression $3x \cdot 5x$ is a product of two binomials.

5.4 EXERCISES

Reading and Writing *After reading this section, write out the answers to these questions. Use complete sentences.*

1. What property of the real numbers is used in multiplying two binomials?

2. What does FOIL stand for?

3. What is the purpose of the FOIL method?

4. How do you square a sum of two terms?

5. How do you square a difference of two terms?

6. How do you find the product of a sum and a difference?

7. Why is $(a + b)^2$ not equivalent to $a^2 + b^2$?

8. Why is $(a - b)^2$ not equivalent to $a^2 - b^2$?

Find each product. When possible, write down only the answer. See Example 1.

9. $(x - 2)(x + 4)$
10. $(x - 3)(x + 5)$

11. $(1 + 2x)(3 + x)$
12. $(3 + 2y)(y + 2)$
13. $(-2a - 3)(-a + 5)$
14. $(-3x - 5)(-x + 6)$
15. $(2x^2 - 7)(2x^2 + 7)$
16. $(3y^3 + 8)(3y^3 - 8)$
17. $(2x^3 - 1)(x^3 + 4)$
18. $(3t^2 - 4)(2t^2 + 3)$
19. $(6z + w)(w - z)$
20. $(4y + w)(w - 2y)$
21. $(3k - 2t)(4t + 3k)$
22. $(7a - 2x)(x + a)$
23. $(x - 3)(y + w)$
24. $(z - 1)(y + 2)$

Find the square of each sum or difference. When possible, write down only the answer. See Examples 2 and 3.

25. $(m + 3)^2$
26. $(a + 2)^2$
27. $(4 - a)^2$
28. $(3 - b)^2$
29. $(2w + 1)^2$
30. $(3m + 4)^2$
31. $(3t - 5u)^2$

32. $(3w - 2x)^2$

33. $(-x - 1)^2$

34. $(-d - 5)^2$

35. $(a - 3y^3)^2$

36. $(3m - 5n^3)^2$

Find each product. See Example 4.

37. $(w - 9)(w + 9)$

38. $(m - 4)(m + 4)$

39. $(w^3 + y)(w^3 - y)$

40. $(a^3 - x)(a^3 + x)$

41. $(7 - 2x)(7 + 2x)$

42. $(3 + 5x)(3 - 5x)$

43. $(3x^2 - 2)(3x^2 + 2)$

44. $(4y^2 + 1)(4y^2 - 1)$

45. $(5a^3 - 2b)(5a^3 + 2b)$

46. $(6w^4 + 5y^3)(6w^4 - 5y^3)$

Use the special product rules to find each product. See Example 5.

47. $[(m + t) + 5][(m + t) - 5]$

48. $[(2x + 3) - y][(2x + 3) + y]$

49. $[y - (r + 5)][y + (r + 5)]$

50. $[x + (3 - k)][x - (3 - k)]$

51. $[(2y - t) + 3]^2$

52. $[(u - 3v) - 4]^2$

53. $[3h + (k - 1)]^2$

54. $[2p - (3q + 6)]^2$

Perform the operations and simplify.

55. $(x - 6)(x + 9)$

56. $(2x^2 - 3)(3x^2 + 4)$

57. $(5 - x)(5 + x)$

58. $(4 - ab)(4 + ab)$

59. $(3x - 4a)(2x + 5a)$

60. $(x^5 + 2)(x^5 - 2)$

61. $(2t - 3)(t + w)$

62. $(5x - 9)(ax + b)$

63. $(3x^2 + 2y^3)^2$

64. $(5a^4 - 2b)^2$

65. $(2 + 2y)(3y - 5)$

66. $(3b - 3)(3 + 2b)$

67. $(2m - 7)^2$

68. $(5a + 4)^2$

69. $(3 + 7x)^2$

70. $(1 - pq)^2$

71. $4y\left(3y + \dfrac{1}{2}\right)^2$

72. $25y\left(2y - \dfrac{1}{5}\right)^2$

73. $(a + h)^2 - a^2$

74. $\dfrac{(x + h)^2 - x^2}{h}$

75. $(x + 2)(x + 2)^2$

76. $(a + 1)^2(a + 1)^2$

77. $(y + 3)^3$

78. $(2x - 3y)^3$

79. $4x - 3(x - 5)^2$

80. $2(x + 3)(x - 2) - (2x - 1)^2$

 Use a calculator to help you perform the following operations.

81. $(3.2x - 4.5)(5.1x + 3.9)$

82. $(5.3x - 9.2)^2$

83. $(3.6y + 4.4)^2$

84. $(3.3a - 7.9b)(3.3a + 7.9b)$

Find the products. Assume all variables are nonzero and variables used in exponents represent integers.

85. $(x^m + 2)(x^{2m} + 3)$

86. $(a^n - b)(a^n + b)$

87. $a^{n+1}(a^{2n} + a^n - 3)$

88. $x^{3b}(x^{-3b} + 3x^{-b} + 5)$

89. $(a^m + a^n)^2$

90. $(x^w - x^t)^2$

91. $(5y^m + 8z^k)(3y^{2m} + 4z^{3-k})$

92. $(4x^{a-1} + 3y^{b+5})(x^{2a-3} - 2y^{4-b})$

Solve each problem.

93. *Area of a room.* Suppose the length of a rectangular room is $x + 3$ meters and the width is $x + 1$ meters. Find a trinomial that can be used to represent the area of the room.

94. *House plans.* Barbie and Ken planned to build a square house with area x^2 square feet. Then they revised the plan so that one side was lengthened by 20 feet and the other side was shortened by 6 feet. (See the figure on the next page.) Find a trinomial that can be used to represent the area of the revised house.

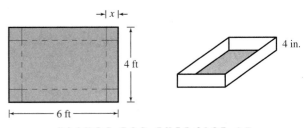

FIGURE FOR EXERCISE 94

FIGURE FOR EXERCISE 97

95. Available habitat. A wild animal will generally stay more than x kilometers from the edge of a forest preserve. So the available habitat for the animal excludes an area of uniform width x on the edge of the rectangular forest preserve shown in the figure. The value of x depends on the animal. Find a trinomial in x that gives the area of the available habitat in square kilometers (km²) for the forest preserve shown. What is the available habitat in this forest preserve for a bobcat for which $x = 0.4$ kilometers?

98. Energy efficient. A manufacturer of mobile homes makes a custom model that is x feet long, 12 feet wide, and 8 feet high (all inside dimensions). The insulation is 3 inches thick in the walls, 6 inches thick in the floor, and 8 inches thick in the ceiling. Given that the insulation costs the manufacturer 25 cents per cubic foot and doors and windows take up 80 square feet of wall space, find a polynomial in x that gives the cost in dollars for insulation in this model. State any assumptions that you are making to solve this problem.

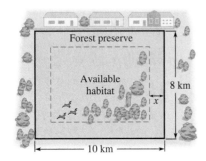

FIGURE FOR EXERCISE 95

96. Cubic coating. A cubic metal box x inches on each side is designed for transporting frozen specimens. The box is surrounded on all sides by a 2-inch-thick layer of styrofoam insulation. Find a polynomial that represents the total volume of the cube and styrofoam.

97. Overflow pan. An air conditioning contractor makes an overflow pan for a condenser by cutting squares with side of length x feet from the corners of a 4 foot by 6 foot piece of galvanized sheet metal as shown in the figure. The sides are then folded up, and the corners are sealed. Find a polynomial that gives the volume of the pan in cubic feet (ft³). What is the volume of the pan if $x = 4$ inches?

GETTING MORE INVOLVED

 99. Exploration.   a) Find $(a + b)^3$ by multiplying $(a + b)^2$ by $a + b$.
  b) Next find $(a + b)^4$ and $(a + b)^5$.
  c) How many terms are in each of these powers of $a + b$ after combining like terms?
  d) Make a general statement about the number of terms in $(a + b)^n$.

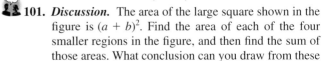 **100. Cooperative learning.** Make a four-column table with columns for a, b, $(a + b)^2$, and $a^2 + b^2$. Work with a group to fill in the table with five pairs of numbers for a and b for which $(a + b)^2 \neq a^2 + b^2$. For what values of a and b does $(a + b)^2 = a^2 + b^2$?

101. Discussion. The area of the large square shown in the figure is $(a + b)^2$. Find the area of each of the four smaller regions in the figure, and then find the sum of those areas. What conclusion can you draw from these areas about $(a + b)^2$?

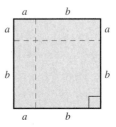

FIGURE FOR EXERCISE 101

5.5 FACTORING POLYNOMIALS

In Sections 5.3 and 5.4 we multiplied polynomials. In this section and Sections 5.6 and 5.7 we will learn to factor polynomials. Factoring will then be used for solving equations and problems in the last section of this chapter.

Factoring Out the Greatest Common Factor (GCF)

A natural number larger than 1 that has no factors other than itself and 1 is called a **prime number.** The numbers

$$2, 3, 5, 7, 11, 13, 17, 19, 23$$

are the first nine prime numbers. There are infinitely many prime numbers.

To factor a natural number **completely** means to write it as a product of prime numbers. In factoring 12 we might write $12 = 4 \cdot 3$. However, 12 is not factored completely as $4 \cdot 3$ because 4 is not a prime. To factor 12 completely, we write $12 = 2 \cdot 2 \cdot 3$ (or $2^2 \cdot 3$).

We use the distributive property to multiply a monomial and a binomial:

$$6x(2x - 1) = 12x^2 - 6x$$

If we start with $12x^2 - 6x$, we can use the distributive property to get

$$12x^2 - 6x = 6x(2x - 1).$$

We have **factored out** $6x$, which is a common factor of $12x^2$ and $-6x$. We could have factored out just 3 to get

$$12x^2 - 6x = 3(4x^2 - 2x),$$

but this would not be factoring out the *greatest* common factor. The **greatest common factor** (GCF) is a monomial that includes every number or variable that is a factor of all of the terms of the polynomial.

We can use the following strategy for finding the greatest common factor of a group of terms.

> **Strategy for Finding the Greatest Common Factor (GCF)**
>
> 1. Factor each term completely.
> 2. Write a product using each factor that is common to all of the terms.
> 3. On each of these factors, use an exponent equal to the smallest exponent that appears on that factor in any of the terms.

EXAMPLE 1

The greatest common factor

Find the greatest common factor (GCF) for each group of terms.

a) $8x^2y, 20xy^3$ b) $30a^2, 45a^3b^2, 75a^4b$

Solution

a) First factor each term completely:

$$8x^2y = 2^3x^2y$$
$$20xy^3 = 2^2 \cdot 5xy^3$$

The factors common to both terms are 2, x, and y. In the GCF we use the smallest exponent that appears on each factor in either of the terms. So the GCF is 2^2xy or $4xy$.

b) First factor each term completely:

$$30a^2 = 2 \cdot 3 \cdot 5a^2$$
$$45a^3b^2 = 3^2 \cdot 5a^3b^2$$
$$75a^4b = 3 \cdot 5^2a^4b$$

The GCF is $3 \cdot 5a^2$ or $15a^2$.   ◼

To factor out the GCF from a polynomial, find the GCF for the terms, then use the distributive property to factor it out.

E X A M P L E   2

Factoring out the greatest common factor

Factor each polynomial by factoring out the GCF.

a) $5x^4 - 10x^3 + 15x^2$ **b)** $8xy^2 + 20x^2y$ **c)** $60x^5 + 24x^3 + 36x^2$

Study Tip

Everyone has a different attention span. Start by studying 10 to 15 minutes at a time and then build up to longer periods over time. In your senior year you should be able to concentrate on one task for 30 to 45 minutes without a break. Be realistic. When you cannot remember what you have read and can no longer concentrate, take a break.

Solution

a) First factor each term completely:

$$5x^4 = 5x^4, \qquad 10x^3 = 2 \cdot 5x^3, \qquad 15x^2 = 3 \cdot 5x^2.$$

The GCF of the three terms is $5x^2$. Now factor $5x^2$ out of each term:

$$5x^4 - 10x^3 + 15x^2 = 5x^2(x^2 - 2x + 3)$$

b) The GCF for $8xy^2$ and $20x^2y$ is $4xy$:

$$8xy^2 + 20x^2y = 4xy(2y + 5x)$$

c) First factor each coefficient in $60x^5 + 24x^3 + 36x^2$:

$$60 = 2^2 \cdot 3 \cdot 5, \qquad 24 = 2^3 \cdot 3, \qquad 36 = 2^2 \cdot 3^2.$$

The GCF of the three terms is $2^2 \cdot 3x^2$ or $12x^2$:

$$60x^5 + 24x^3 + 36x^2 = 12x^2(5x^3 + 2x + 3)$$ ◼

In the next example the common factor in each term is a binomial.

E X A M P L E   3

Factoring out a binomial

Factor.

a) $(x + 3)w + (x + 3)a$ **b)** $x(x - 9) - 4(x - 9)$

Solution

a) We treat $x + 3$ like a common monomial when factoring:

$$(x + 3)w + (x + 3)a = (x + 3)(w + a)$$

b) Factor out the common binomial $x - 9$:

$$x(x - 9) - 4(x - 9) = (x - 4)(x - 9)$$ ◼

Factoring Out the Opposite of the GCF

In Example 4 we factor each polynomial twice. First we factor out the greatest common factor. Then we factor out the opposite of the GCF.

EXAMPLE 4

Factoring out the opposite of the GCF

Factor out the GCF, then factor out the opposite of the GCF.

a) $5x - 5y$ b) $-x^2 - 3$ c) $-x^3 + 3x^2 - 5x$

Solution

a) $5x - 5y = 5(x - y)$ Factor out 5.

$\qquad\qquad = -5(-x + y)$ Factor out -5.

b) $-x^2 - 3 = 1(-x^2 - 3)$ The GCF is 1.

$\qquad\qquad = -1(x^2 + 3)$ Factor out -1.

c) $-x^3 + 3x^2 - 5x = x(-x^2 + 3x - 5)$ Factor out x.

$\qquad\qquad\qquad = -x(x^2 - 3x + 5)$ Factor out $-x$. ∎

Factoring by Grouping

In Example 5 we factor a four-term polynomial by factoring out a common factor from the first group of two terms and a common factor from the last group of two terms. We then proceed to factor out a common binomial as in Example 3. This method is called **factoring by grouping.** To factor by grouping it is sometimes necessary to factor out the opposite of the greatest common factor as was shown in Example 4.

EXAMPLE 5

Factoring by grouping

Factor each four-term polynomial by grouping

a) $2x + 2y + ax + ay$ b) $wa - wb + a - b$

c) $4am - 4an - bm + bn$

Solution

a) The first group of two terms has 2 as a common factor and the second group of two terms has a as a common factor:

$$2x + 2y + ax + ay = 2(x + y) + a(x + y)$$
$$= (2 + a)(x + y)$$

b) Factor w out of the first two terms and 1 out of the last two terms:

$$wa - wb + a - b = w(a - b) + 1(a - b)$$
$$= (w + 1)(a - b)$$

c) Factor out $4a$ from the first two terms and $-b$ (the opposite of the greatest common factor) from the last two terms:

$$4am - 4an - bm + bn = 4a(m - n) - b(m - n)$$
$$= (4a - b)(m - n)$$ ∎

Factoring the Difference of Two Squares

A first-degree polynomial in one variable, such as $3x - 5$, is called a linear polynomial. (The equation $3x - 5 = 0$ is a linear equation.)

Linear Polynomial

If a and b are real numbers with $a \neq 0$, then $ax + b$ is called a **linear polynomial.**

A second-degree polynomial such as $x^2 + 5x - 6$ is called a quadratic polynomial.

Quadratic Polynomial

If a, b, and c are real numbers with $a \neq 0$, then $ax^2 + bx + c$ is called a **quadratic polynomial.**

One of the main goals of this chapter is to write a quadratic polynomial (when possible) as a product of linear factors.

Consider the quadratic polynomial $x^2 - 25$. We recognize that $x^2 - 25$ is a difference of two squares, $x^2 - 5^2$. We recall that the product of a sum and a difference is a difference of two squares: $(a + b)(a - b) = a^2 - b^2$. If we reverse this special product rule, we get a rule for factoring the difference of two squares.

Factoring the Difference of Two Squares

$$a^2 - b^2 = (a + b)(a - b)$$

The difference of two squares factors as the product of a sum and a difference. To factor $x^2 - 25$, we replace a by x and b by 5 to get

$$x^2 - 25 = (x + 5)(x - 5).$$

This equation expresses a quadratic polynomial as a product of two linear factors.

E X A M P L E   6

Factoring the difference of two squares

Factor each polynomial.

a) $y^2 - 36$ **b)** $9x^2 - 1$ **c)** $4x^2 - y^2$

Helpful Hint

Using the power of a power rule, we can see that any even power is a perfect square:

$$x^{2n} = (x^n)^2$$

Solution

Each of these binomials is a difference of two squares. Each binomial factors into a product of a sum and a difference.

a) $y^2 - 36 = (y + 6)(y - 6)$ We could also write $(y - 6)(y + 6)$ because
                                       the factors can be written in any order.

b) $9x^2 - 1 = (3x + 1)(3x - 1)$

c) $4x^2 - y^2 = (2x + y)(2x - y)$ ∎

Factoring Perfect Square Trinomials

The trinomial that results from squaring a binomial is called a **perfect square trinomial.** We can reverse the rules from Section 5.4 for the square of a sum or a difference to get rules for factoring.

Factoring Perfect Square Trinomials

$$a^2 + 2ab + b^2 = (a + b)^2$$
$$a^2 - 2ab + b^2 = (a - b)^2$$

Consider the polynomial $x^2 + 6x + 9$. If we recognize that

$$x^2 + 6x + 9 = x^2 + 2 \cdot x \cdot 3 + 3^2,$$

then we can see that it is a perfect square trinomial. It fits the rule if $a = x$ and $b = 3$:

$$x^2 + 6x + 9 = (x + 3)^2$$

Perfect square trinomials can be identified by using the following strategy.

> **Strategy for Identifying Perfect Square Trinomials**
>
> A trinomial is a perfect square trinomial if
> **1.** the first and last terms are of the form a^2 and b^2,
> **2.** the middle term is 2 or -2 times the product of a and b.

We use this strategy in Example 7.

EXAMPLE 7

Factoring perfect square trinomials
Factor each polynomial.
a) $x^2 - 8x + 16$ **b)** $a^2 + 14a + 49$ **c)** $4x^2 + 12x + 9$

Solution

a) Because the first term is x^2, the last is 4^2, and $-2(x)(4)$ is equal to the middle term $-8x$, the trinomial $x^2 - 8x + 16$ is a perfect square trinomial:

$$x^2 - 8x + 16 = (x - 4)^2$$

b) Because $49 = 7^2$ and $14a = 2(a)(7)$, we have a perfect square trinomial:

$$a^2 + 14a + 49 = (a + 7)^2$$

c) Because $4x^2 = (2x)^2$, $9 = 3^2$, and the middle term $12x$ is equal to $2(2x)(3)$, the trinomial $4x^2 + 12x + 9$ is a perfect square trinomial:

$$4x^2 + 12x + 9 = (2x + 3)^2$$ ∎

Factoring a Difference or Sum of Two Cubes

To factor $a^3 - b^3$, a difference of two cubes, examine the following product:

$$
\begin{aligned}
(a - b)(a^2 + ab + b^2) &= a(a^2 + ab + b^2) - b(a^2 + ab + b^2) \\
&= a^3 + a^2b + ab^2 - a^2b - ab^2 - b^3 \\
&= a^3 - b^3
\end{aligned}
$$

To factor $a^3 + b^3$, a sum of two cubes, examine the following product:

$$
\begin{aligned}
(a + b)(a^2 - ab + b^2) &= a(a^2 - ab + b^2) + b(a^2 - ab + b^2) \\
&= a^3 - a^2b + ab^2 + a^2b - ab^2 + b^3 \\
&= a^3 + b^3
\end{aligned}
$$

By finding these products, we have verified the following formulas for factoring $a^3 - b^3$ and $a^3 + b^3$.

> **Factoring a Difference or a Sum of Two Cubes**
>
> $$a^3 - b^3 = (a - b)(a^2 + ab + b^2)$$
> $$a^3 + b^3 = (a + b)(a^2 - ab + b^2)$$

EXAMPLE 8

Factoring a difference or a sum of two cubes
Factor each polynomial.
a) $x^3 - 8$ **b)** $y^3 + 1$ **c)** $8z^3 - 27$

Solution

a) Because $8 = 2^3$, we can use the formula for factoring the difference of two cubes. In the formula $a^3 - b^3 = (a - b)(a^2 + ab + b^2)$, let $a = x$ and $b = 2$:

$$x^3 - 8 = (x - 2)(x^2 + 2x + 4)$$

b) $y^3 + 1 = y^3 + 1^3$ Recognize a sum of two cubes.

     $= (y + 1)(y^2 - y + 1)$ Let $a = y$ and $b = 1$ in the formula for the sum of two cubes.

c) $8z^3 - 27 = (2z)^3 - 3^3$ Recognize a difference of two cubes.

     $= (2z - 3)(4z^2 + 6z + 9)$ Let $a = 2z$ and $b = 3$ in the formula for a difference of two cubes. ∎

Factoring a Polynomial Completely

Polynomials that cannot be factored are called **prime polynomials.** Because binomials such as $x + 5$, $a - 6$, and $3x + 1$ cannot be factored, they are prime polynomials. A polynomial is **factored completely** when it is written as a product of prime polynomials. To factor completely, always factor out the GCF (or its opposite) first. Then continue to factor until all of the factors are prime.

E X A M P L E 9

Factoring completely

Factor each polynomial completely.

a) $5x^2 - 20$ b) $3a^3 - 30a^2 + 75a$ c) $-2b^4 + 16b$

Solution

a) $5x^2 - 20 = 5(x^2 - 4)$ Greatest common factor

     $= 5(x - 2)(x + 2)$ Difference of two squares

b) $3a^3 - 30a^2 + 75a = 3a(a^2 - 10a + 25)$ Greatest common factor

     $= 3a(a - 5)^2$ Perfect square trinomial

c) $-2b^4 + 16b = -2b(b^3 - 8)$ Factor out $-2b$ to make the next step easier.

     $= -2b(b - 2)(b^2 + 2b + 4)$ Difference of two cubes ∎

WARM-UPS

True or false? Explain your answer.

1. For the polynomial $3x^2y - 6xy^2$ we can factor out either $3xy$ or $-3xy$.

2. The greatest common factor for the polynomial $8a^3 - 15b^2$ is 1.

3. $2x - 4 = -2(2 - x)$ for any value of x.

4. $x^2 - 16 = (x - 4)(x + 4)$ for any value of x.

5. The polynomial $x^2 + 6x + 36$ is a perfect square trinomial.

6. The polynomial $y^2 + 16$ is a perfect square trinomial.

7. $9x^2 + 21x + 49 = (3x + 7)^2$ for any value of x.

8. The polynomial $x + 1$ is a factor of $x^3 + 1$.

9. $x^3 - 27 = (x - 3)(x^2 + 6x + 9)$ for any value of x.

10. $x^3 - 8 = (x - 2)^3$ for any value of x.

5.5 EXERCISES

Reading and Writing *After reading this section, write out the answers to these questions. Use complete sentences.*

1. What is a prime number?

2. When is a natural number factored completely?

3. What is the greatest common factor for the terms of a polynomial?

4. What are the two ways to factor out the greatest common factor?

5. What is a linear polynomial?

6. What is a quadratic polynomial?

7. What is a prime polynomial?

8. When is a polynomial factored completely?

Find the greatest common factor for each group of terms. See Example 1.

9. $48, 36x$

10. $42a, 28a^2$

11. $9wx, 21wy, 15xy$

12. $70x^2, 84x, 42x^3$

13. $24x^2y, 42xy^2, 66xy^3$

14. $60a^2b^5, 140a^9b^2, 40a^3b^6$

Factor out the greatest common factor in each expression. See Examples 2 and 3.

15. $x^3 - 5x$

16. $10x^2 - 20y^3$

17. $48wx + 36wy$

18. $42wz + 28wa$

19. $2x^3 - 4x^2 + 6x$

20. $6x^3 - 12x^2 + 18x$

21. $36a^3b^6 - 24a^4b^2 + 60a^5b^3$

22. $44x^8y^6z - 110x^6y^9z^2$

23. $(x - 6)a + (x - 6)b$

24. $(y - 4)3 + (y - 4)b$

25. $(y - 1)^2y + (y - 1)^2z$

26. $(w - 2)^2 \cdot w + (w - 2)^2 \cdot 3$

Factor out the greatest common factor, then factor out the opposite of the greatest common factor. See Example 4.

27. $2x - 2y$

28. $-3x + 6$

29. $6x^2 - 3x$

30. $10x^2 + 5x$

31. $-w^3 + 3w^2$

32. $-2w^4 + 6w^3$

33. $-a^3 + a^2 - 7a$

34. $-2a^4 - 4a^3 + 6a^2$

Factor each polynomial by grouping. See Example 5.

35. $ax + ay + 3x + 3y$

36. $2a + 2b + wa + wb$

37. $xy - 3y + x - 3$

38. $2wt - 2wa + t - a$

39. $4a - 4b - ca + cb$

40. $pr - 2r - ap + 2a$

41. $xy - y - 6x + 6$

42. $-3a + 3 + ax - x$

Factor each polynomial. See Example 6.

43. $x^2 - 100$

44. $81 - y^2$

45. $4y^2 - 49$

46. $16b^2 - 1$

47. $9x^2 - 25a^2$

48. $121a^2 - b^2$

49. $144w^2z^2 - h^2$

50. $x^2y^2 - 9c^2$

Factor each polynomial. See Example 7.

51. $x^2 - 20x + 100$

52. $y^2 + 10y + 25$

53. $4m^2 - 4m + 1$

54. $9t^2 + 30t + 25$

55. $w^2 - 2wt + t^2$

56. $4r^2 + 20rt + 25t^2$

Factor. See Example 8.

57. $a^3 - 1$

58. $w^3 + 1$

59. $w^3 + 27$

60. $x^3 - 64$

61. $8x^3 - 1$

62. $27x^3 + 1$

63. $64x^3 + 125$

64. $27a^3 + 1000$

65. $8a^3 - 27b^3$

66. $27w^3 - 125y^3$

Factor each polynomial completely. See Example 9.

67. $2x^2 - 8$

68. $3x^3 - 27x$

69. $x^3 + 10x^2 + 25x$

70. $5a^4m - 45a^2m$

71. $4x^2 + 4x + 1$

72. $ax^2 - 8ax + 16a$

73. $(x + 3)x + (x + 3)7$

74. $(x - 2)x - (x - 2)5$

75. $6y^2 + 3y$

76. $4y^2 - y$

77. $4x^2 - 20x + 25$

78. $a^3x^3 - 6a^2x^2 + 9ax$

79. $2m^4 - 2mn^3$

80. $5x^3y^2 - y^5$

81. $(2x - 3)x - (2x - 3)2$

82. $(2x + 1)x + (2x + 1)3$

83. $9a^3 - aw^2$

84. $2bn^2 - 4b^2n + 2b^3$

85. $-5a^2 + 30a - 45$

86. $-2x^2 + 50$

87. $16 - 54x^3$

88. $27x^2y - 64x^2y^4$

89. $-3y^3 - 18y^2 - 27y$

90. $-2m^2n - 8mn - 8n$

91. $-7a^2b^2 + 7$

92. $-17a^2 - 17a$

93. $7x - 7h - hx + h^2$

94. $6a - 6y - ax + xy$

95. $a^2x + 3a^2 - 4x - 12$

96. $x^2y - 2x^2 - y + 2$

Replace k in each trinomial by a number that makes the trinomial a perfect square trinomial.

97. $x^2 + 6x + k$ **98.** $y^2 - 8y + k$

99. $4a^2 - ka + 25$

100. $9u^2 + kuv + 49v^2$

101. $km^2 - 24m + 9$ **102.** $kz^2 + 40z + 16$

103. $81y^2 - 180y + k$ **104.** $36a^2 + 60a + k$

Solve each problem.

105. *Volume of a bird cage.* A company makes rectangular shaped bird cages with height b inches and square

bottoms. The volume of these cages is given by the function

$$V = b^3 - 6b^2 + 9b.$$

a) Find an expression for the length of each side of the square bottom by factoring the expression on the right side of the function.

b) Use the function to find the volume of a cage with a height of 18 inches.

c) Use the accompanying graph to estimate the height of a cage for which the volume is 20,000 cubic inches.

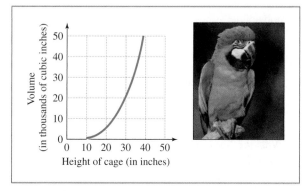

FIGURE FOR EXERCISE 105

106. *Pyramid power.* A powerful crystal pyramid has a square base and a volume of $3y^3 + 12y^2 + 12y$ cubic centimeters. If its height is y centimeters, then what polynomial represents the length of a side of the square base? $\left(\text{The volume of a pyramid with a square base of area } a^2 \text{ and height } h \text{ is given by } V = \frac{ha^2}{3}.\right)$

FIGURE FOR EXERCISE 106

GETTING MORE INVOLVED

107. *Cooperative learning.* List the perfect square trinomials corresponding to $(x + 1)^2, (x + 2)^2, (x + 3)^2, \ldots,$ $(x + 12)^2$. Use your list to quiz a classmate. Read a perfect square trinomial at random from your list and ask your classmate to write its factored form. Repeat until both of you have mastered these 12 perfect square trinomials.

5.6   **FACTORING** $ax^2 + bx + c$

In Section 5.5 you learned to factor certain special polynomials. In this section you will learn to factor general quadratic polynomials. We first factor $ax^2 + bx + c$ with $a = 1$, and then we consider the case $a \neq 1$.

Factoring Trinomials with Leading Coefficient 1

Let's look closely at an example of finding the product of two binomials using the distributive property:

$$(x + 3)(x + 4) = (x + 3)x + (x + 3)4 \quad \text{Distributive property}$$
$$= x^2 + 3x + 4x + 12 \quad \text{Distributive property}$$
$$= x^2 + 7x + 12$$

To factor $x^2 + 7x + 12$, we need to reverse these steps. First observe that the coefficient 7 is the sum of two numbers that have a product of 12. The only numbers that have a product of 12 and a sum of 7 are 3 and 4. So write $7x$ as $3x + 4x$:

$$x^2 + 7x + 12 = x^2 + 3x + 4x + 12$$

Now factor the common factor x out of the first two terms and the common factor 4 out of the last two terms.

$$x^2 + 7x + 12 = \overbrace{x^2 + 3x}^{\text{Factor out } x} + \overbrace{4x + 12}^{\text{Factor out } 4} \quad \text{Rewrite } 7x \text{ as } 3x + 4x.$$
$$= (x + 3)x + (x + 3)4 \quad \text{Factor out common factors.}$$
$$= (x + 3)(x + 4) \quad \text{Factor out the common factor } x + 3.$$

EXAMPLE 1

Factoring $ax^2 + bx + c$ with $a = 1$ by grouping

Factor each trinomial by grouping.

a) $x^2 + 9x + 18$ **b)** $x^2 - 2x - 24$

Solution

a) We need to find two integers with a product of 18 and a sum of 9. For a product of 18 we could use 1 and 18, 2 and 9, or 3 and 6. Only 3 and 6 have a sum of 9. So we replace $9x$ with $3x + 6x$ and factor by grouping:

$$x^2 + 9x + 18 = x^2 + 3x + 6x + 18 \quad \text{Replace } 9x \text{ by } 3x + 6x.$$
$$= (x + 3)x + (x + 3)6 \quad \text{Factor out common factors.}$$
$$= (x + 3)(x + 6) \quad \text{Check by using FOIL.}$$

b) We need to find two integers with a product of -24 and a sum of -2. For a product of 24 we have 1 and 24, 2 and 12, 3 and 8, or 4 and 6. To get a product of -24 and a sum of -2, we must use 4 and -6:

$$x^2 - 2x - 24 = x^2 - 6x + 4x - 24 \quad \text{Replace } -2x \text{ with } -6x + 4x.$$
$$= (x - 6)x + (x - 6)4 \quad \text{Factor out common factors.}$$
$$= (x - 6)(x + 4) \quad \text{Check by using FOIL.}$$

We factored the trinomials in Example 1 by grouping to show that we could reverse the steps in the multiplication of binomials. However, it is not necessary to write down all of the details shown in Example 1. In Example 2 we simply write the factors.

E X A M P L E   2

A simpler way to factor $ax^2 + bx + c$ with $a = 1$

Factor each quadratic polynomial.

a) $x^2 + 4x + 3$ **b)** $x^2 + 3x - 10$ **c)** $a^2 - 5a + 6$

Study Tip

Set short-term goals and reward yourself for accomplishing them. When you have solved 10 problems, take a short break and listen to your favorite music.

Solution

a) Two integers with a product of 3 and a sum of 4 are 1 and 3:

$$x^2 + 4x + 3 = (x + 1)(x + 3)$$

Check by using FOIL.

b) Two integers with a product of -10 and a sum of 3 are 5 and -2:

$$x^2 + 3x - 10 = (x + 5)(x - 2)$$

Check by using FOIL.

c) Two integers with a product of 6 and a sum of -5 are -3 and -2:

$$a^2 - 5a + 6 = (a - 3)(a - 2)$$

Check by using FOIL. ◼

Factoring Trinomials with Leading Coefficient Not 1

If the leading coefficient of $ax^2 + bx + c$ is not 1 there are two ways to proceed: the *ac* method or the trial-and-error method. The *ac* method is a slight variation of the grouping method shown in Example 1 and there is a definite procedure to follow. The trial-and-error method is not as definite. We write down possible factors. If they check you are done and if not you try again. We will present the *ac* method first.

Consider the trinomial $2x^2 + 11x + 12$, for which $a = 2$, $b = 11$, and $c = 12$. First find *ac*, the product of the leading coefficient and the constant term. In this case $ac = 2 \cdot 12 = 24$. Now find two integers with a product of 24 and a sum of 11. The pairs of integers with a product of 24 are 1 and 24, 2 and 12, 3 and 8, and 4 and 6. Only 3 and 8 have a product of 24 and a sum of 11. Now replace $11x$ by $3x + 8x$ and factor by grouping:

$$2x^2 + 11x + 12 = 2x^2 + 3x + 8x + 12$$
$$= (2x + 3)x + (2x + 3)4$$
$$= (2x + 3)(x + 4)$$

This strategy for factoring a quadratic trinomial, known as the ***ac* method,** is summarized in the following box. The *ac* method works also when $a = 1$.

Strategy for Factoring $ax^2 + bx + c$ by the *ac* Method

To factor the trinomial $ax^2 + bx + c$

1. find two integers that have a product equal to *ac* and a sum equal to *b*,

2. replace *bx* by two terms using the two new integers as coefficients,

3. then factor the resulting four-term polynomial by grouping.

E X A M P L E   3

Factoring $ax^2 + bx + c$ with $a \neq 1$

Factor each trinomial.

a) $2x^2 + 9x + 4$ **b)** $2x^2 + 5x - 12$ **c)** $6w^2 - w - 15$

Solution

a) Because $2 \cdot 4 = 8$, we need two numbers with a product of 8 and a sum of 9. The numbers are 1 and 8. Replace $9x$ by $x + 8x$ and factor by grouping:

$$2x^2 + 9x + 4 = 2x^2 + x + 8x + 4$$
$$= (2x + 1)x + (2x + 1)4$$
$$= (2x + 1)(x + 4) \quad \text{Check by FOIL.}$$

Note that if you start with $2x^2 + 8x + x + 4$, and factor by grouping, you get the same result.

b) Because $2(-12) = -24$, we need two numbers with a product of -24 and a sum of 5. The pairs of numbers with a product of 24 are 1 and 24, 2 and 12, 3 and 8, and 4 and 6. To get a product of -24, one of the numbers must be negative and the other positive. To get a sum of positive 5, we need -3 and 8:

$$2x^2 + 5x - 12 = 2x^2 - 3x + 8x - 12$$
$$= (2x - 3)x + (2x - 3)4$$
$$= (2x - 3)(x + 4) \quad \text{Check by FOIL.}$$

c) To factor $6w^2 - w - 15$ we first find that $ac = 6(-15) = -90$. Now we need two numbers that have a product of -90 and a sum of -1. The numbers are -10 and 9. Replace $-w$ with $-10w + 9w$ and factor by grouping:

$$6w^2 - w - 15 = 6w^2 - 10w + 9w - 15$$
$$= 2w(3w - 5) + 3(3w - 5)$$
$$= (2w + 3)(3w - 5) \quad \text{Check by FOIL.} \quad ■$$

Helpful Hint

The *ac* method has more written work and less guesswork than trial and error. However, many students enjoy the challenge of trying to write only the answer without any other written work.

Trial and Error

After we have gained some experience at factoring by grouping, we can often find the factors without going through the steps of grouping. Consider the polynomial

$$2x^2 - 7x + 6.$$

The factors of $2x^2$ can only be $2x$ and x. The factors of 6 could be 2 and 3 or 1 and 6. We can list all of the possibilities that give the correct first and last terms without putting in the signs:

$$(2x \quad 2)(x \quad 3) \qquad (2x \quad 6)(x \quad 1)$$
$$(2x \quad 3)(x \quad 2) \qquad (2x \quad 1)(x \quad 6)$$

Before actually trying these out, we make an important observation. If $(2x \quad 2)$ or $(2x \quad 6)$ were one of the factors, then there would be a common factor 2 in the original trinomial, but there is not. *If the original trinomial has no common factor, there can be no common factor in either of its linear factors.* Since 6 is positive and the middle term is $-7x$, both of the missing signs must be negative. So the only possibilities are $(2x - 1)(x - 6)$ and $(2x - 3)(x - 2)$. The middle term of the first product is $-13x$, and the middle term of the second product is $-7x$. So we have found the factors:

$$2x^2 - 7x + 6 = (2x - 3)(x - 2)$$

Even though there may be many possibilities in some factoring problems, often we find the correct factors without writing down every possibility. We can use a bit of guesswork in factoring trinomials. *Try* whichever possibility you think might work. *Check* it by multiplying. If it is not right, then *try again*. That is why this method is called **trial and error.**

E X A M P L E   4   **Trial and error**

Factor each quadratic trinomial using trial and error.

a) $2x^2 + 5x - 3$ **b)** $3x^2 - 11x + 6$ **c)** $6m^2 + 17m + 10$

Solution

a) Because $2x^2$ factors only as $2x \cdot x$ and 3 factors only as $1 \cdot 3$, there are only two possible ways to factor this trinomial to get the correct first and last terms:

$$(2x \quad 1)(x \quad 3) \qquad \text{and} \qquad (2x \quad 3)(x \quad 1)$$

Because the last term of the trinomial is negative, one of the missing signs must be $+$, and the other must be $-$. Now we try the various possibilities until we get the correct middle term:

$$(2x + 1)(x - 3) = 2x^2 - 5x - 3$$
$$(2x + 3)(x - 1) = 2x^2 + x - 3$$
$$(2x - 1)(x + 3) = 2x^2 + 5x - 3$$

Since the last product has the correct middle term, the trinomial is factored as

$$2x^2 + 5x - 3 = (2x - 1)(x + 3).$$

b) There are four possible ways to factor $3x^2 - 11x + 6$:

$$(3x \quad 1)(x \quad 6) \qquad (3x \quad 2)(x \quad 3)$$
$$(3x \quad 6)(x \quad 1) \qquad (3x \quad 3)(x \quad 2)$$

Because the last term is positive and the middle term is negative, both signs must be negative. Now try possible factors until we get the correct middle term:

$$(3x - 1)(x - 6) = 3x^2 - 19x + 6$$
$$(3x - 2)(x - 3) = 3x^2 - 11x + 6$$

The trinomial is factored correctly as

$$3x^2 - 11x + 6 = (3x - 2)(x - 3).$$

c) Because all of the signs in $6m^2 + 17m + 10$ are positive, all of the signs in the factors are positive. There are eight possible products that will start with $6m^2$ and end with 10:

$$(2m + 2)(3m + 5) \qquad (6m + 2)(m + 5)$$
$$(2m + 5)(3m + 2) \qquad (6m + 5)(m + 2)$$
$$(2m + 1)(3m + 10) \qquad (6m + 1)(m + 10)$$
$$(2m + 10)(3m + 1) \qquad (6m + 10)(m + 1)$$

Only $(6m + 5)(m + 2)$ has a middle term of $17m$. So

$$6m^2 + 17m + 10 = (6m + 5)(m + 2). \qquad \blacksquare$$

Factoring by Substitution

So far, the polynomials that we have factored, without common factors, have all been of degree 2 or 3. Some polynomials of higher degree can be factored by substituting a single variable for a variable with a higher power. After factoring, we replace the single variable by the higher-power variable. This method is called **substitution.**

EXAMPLE 5

Factoring by substitution

Factor each polynomial.

a) $x^4 - 9$ **b)** $y^8 - 14y^4 + 49$

Solution

a) We recognize $x^4 - 9$ as a difference of two squares in which $x^4 = (x^2)^2$ and $9 = 3^2$. If we let $w = x^2$, then $w^2 = x^4$. So we can replace x^4 by w^2 and factor:

$$
\begin{aligned}
x^4 - 9 &= w^2 - 9 && \text{Replace } x^4 \text{ by } w^2. \\
&= (w + 3)(w - 3) && \text{Difference of two squares} \\
&= (x^2 + 3)(x^2 - 3) && \text{Replace } w \text{ by } x^2.
\end{aligned}
$$

b) We recognize $y^8 - 14y^4 + 49$ as a perfect square trinomial in which $y^8 = (y^4)^2$ and $49 = 7^2$. We let $w = y^4$ and $w^2 = y^8$:

$$
\begin{aligned}
y^8 - 14y^4 + 49 &= w^2 - 14w + 49 && \text{Replace } y^4 \text{ by } w \text{ and } y^8 \text{ by } w^2. \\
&= (w - 7)^2 && \text{Perfect square trinomial} \\
&= (y^4 - 7)^2 && \text{Replace } w \text{ by } y^4.
\end{aligned}
$$
■

CAUTION   Polynomials that we factor by substitution must contain just the right exponents. We can factor $y^8 - 14y^4 + 49$ because y^8 is a perfect square: $y^8 = (y^4)^2$. Note that even powers such as x^4, y^{14}, and w^{20} are perfect squares, because $x^4 = (x^2)^2$, $y^{14} = (y^7)^2$, and $w^{20} = (w^{10})^2$.

In Example 6 we use substitution to factor polynomials that have variables as exponents.

EXAMPLE 6

Polynomials with variable exponents

Factor completely. The variables used in the exponents represent positive integers.

a) $x^{2m} - y^2$ **b)** $z^{2n+1} - 6z^{n+1} + 9z$

Solution

a) Notice that $x^{2m} = (x^m)^2$. So if we let $w = x^m$, then $w^2 = x^{2m}$:

$$
\begin{aligned}
x^{2m} - y^2 &= w^2 - y^2 && \text{Substitution} \\
&= (w + y)(w - y) && \text{Difference of two squares} \\
&= (x^m + y)(x^m - y) && \text{Replace } w \text{ by } x^m.
\end{aligned}
$$

b) First factor out the common factor z:

$$
\begin{aligned}
z^{2n+1} - 6z^{n+1} + 9z &= z(z^{2n} - 6z^n + 9) \\
&= z(a^2 - 6a + 9) && \text{Let } a = z^n. \\
&= z(a - 3)^2 && \text{Perfect square trinomial} \\
&= z(z^n - 3)^2 && \text{Replace } a \text{ by } z^n.
\end{aligned}
$$
■

It is not absolutely necessary to use substitution in factoring polynomials with higher degrees or variable exponents as we did in Examples 5 and 6. In Example 7 we use trial and error to factor similar polynomials. Remember to always look for a common factor first.

E X A M P L E 7

Higher-degree and variable exponent trinomials

Factor each polynomial completely. Variables used as exponents represent positive integers.

a) $x^8 - 2x^4 - 15$ **b)** $-18y^7 + 21y^4 + 15y$ **c)** $2u^{2m} - 5u^m - 3$

Solution

a) To factor by trial and error, notice that $x^8 = x^4 \cdot x^4$. Now 15 is $3 \cdot 5$ or $1 \cdot 15$. Using 1 and 15 will not give the required -2 for the coefficient of the middle term. So choose 3 and -5 to get the -2 in the middle term:

$$x^8 - 2x^4 - 15 = (x^4 - 5)(x^4 + 3)$$

b) $-18y^7 + 21y^4 + 15y = -3y(6y^6 - 7y^3 - 5)$ Factor out the common factor $-3y$ first.

$$= -3y(2y^3 + 1)(3y^3 - 5)$$ Factor the trinomial by trial and error.

c) Notice that $2u^{2m} = 2u^m \cdot u^m$ and $3 = 3 \cdot 1$. Using trial and error, we get

$$2u^{2m} - 5u^m - 3 = (2u^m + 1)(u^m - 3). \blacksquare$$

WARM-UPS

True or false? Answer true if the polynomial is factored correctly and false otherwise.

1. $x^2 + 9x + 18 = (x + 3)(x + 6)$

2. $y^2 + 2y - 35 = (y + 5)(y - 7)$

3. $x^2 + 4 = (x + 2)(x + 2)$

4. $x^2 - 5x - 6 = (x - 3)(x - 2)$

5. $x^2 - 4x - 12 = (x - 6)(x + 2)$

6. $x^2 + 15x + 36 = (x + 4)(x + 9)$

7. $3x^2 + 4x - 15 = (3x + 5)(x - 3)$

8. $4x^2 + 4x - 3 = (4x - 1)(x + 3)$

9. $4x^2 - 4x - 3 = (2x + 1)(2x - 3)$

10. $4x^2 + 8x + 3 = (2x + 1)(2x + 3)$

5.6 EXERCISES

Reading and Writing *After reading this section, write out the answers to these questions. Use complete sentences.*

1. How do we factor trinomials that have a leading coefficient of 1?

2. How do we factor trinomials in which the leading coefficient is not 1?

3. What is trial-and-error factoring?

4. What should you always first look for when factoring a polynomial?

Factor each polynomial. See Examples 1 and 2.

5. $x^2 + 4x + 3$ **6.** $y^2 + 5y + 6$

7. $a^2 + 15a + 50$ **8.** $t^2 + 11t + 24$

9. $y^2 - 5y - 14$ **10.** $x^2 - 3x - 18$

11. $x^2 - 6x + 8$ **12.** $y^2 - 13y + 30$

13. $a^2 - 12a + 27$ **14.** $x^2 - x - 30$

15. $a^2 + 7a - 30$ **16.** $w^2 + 29w - 30$

Factor each polynomial. See Example 3.
17. $6w^2 + 5w + 1$ **18.** $4x^2 + 11x + 6$

19. $2x^2 - 5x - 3$ **20.** $2a^2 + 3a - 2$

21. $4x^2 + 16x + 15$ **22.** $6y^2 + 17y + 12$

23. $6x^2 - 5x + 1$ **24.** $6m^2 - m - 12$

25. $12y^2 + y - 1$ **26.** $12x^2 + 5x - 2$

27. $6a^2 + a - 5$ **28.** $30b^2 - b - 3$

Factor each polynomial. See Example 4.
29. $2x^2 + 15x - 8$ **30.** $3a^2 + 20a + 12$

31. $3b^2 - 16b - 35$ **32.** $2y^2 - 17y + 21$

33. $6w^2 + w - 12$ **34.** $15x^2 - x - 6$

35. $4x^2 - 5x + 1$ **36.** $4x^2 + 7x + 3$

37. $5m^2 + 13m - 6$ **38.** $5t^2 - 9t - 2$

39. $6y^2 - 7y - 20$ **40.** $7u^2 + 11u - 6$

Factor each polynomial completely. See Example 5.
41. $x^{10} - 9$
42. $y^8 - 4$
43. $z^{12} - 6z^6 + 9$
44. $a^6 + 10a^3 + 25$
45. $2x^7 + 8x^4 + 8x$
46. $x^{13} - 6x^7 + 9x$
47. $4x^5 + 4x^3 + x$
48. $18x^6 + 24x^3 + 8$
49. $x^6 - 8$
50. $y^6 - 27$

Factor each polynomial completely. The variables used as exponents represent positive integers. See Example 6.
51. $a^{2n} - 1$
52. $b^{4n} - 9$
53. $a^{2r} + 6a^r + 9$
54. $u^{6n} - 4u^{3n} + 4$

55. $x^{3m} - 8$
56. $y^{3n} + 1$
57. $a^{3m} - b^3$
58. $r^{3m} + 8t^3$
59. $k^{2w+1} - 10k^{w+1} + 25k$
60. $4a^{2t+1} + 4a^{t+1} + a$

Factor each polynomial completely. See Example 7. The variables used in exponents represent positive integers.
61. $x^6 - 2x^3 - 35$ **62.** $x^4 + 7x^2 - 30$

63. $a^{20} - 20a^{10} + 100$ **64.** $b^{16} + 22b^8 + 121$

65. $-12a^5 - 10a^3 - 2a$ **66.** $-4b^7 + 4b^4 + 3b$

67. $x^{2a} + 2x^a - 15$ **68.** $y^{2b} + y^b - 20$

69. $x^{2a} - y^{2b}$ **70.** $w^{4m} - a^2$

71. $x^8 - x^4 - 6$ **72.** $m^{10} - 5m^5 - 6$

73. $x^{a+2} - x^a$ **74.** $y^{2a+1} - y$

75. $x^{2a} + 6x^a + 9$ **76.** $x^{2a} - 2x^ay^b + y^{2b}$

Factor each polynomial completely.
77. $2x^2 + 20x + 50$ **78.** $3a^2 + 6a + 3$

79. $a^3 - 36a$ **80.** $x^3 + 5x^2 - 6x$

81. $10a^2 + 55a - 30$ **82.** $6a^2 + 22a - 84$

83. $2x^2 - 128y^2$ **84.** $a^3 - 6a^2 + 9a$

85. $-9x^2 + 33x + 12$ **86.** $2xy^2 - 27xy + 70x$

87. $m^5 + 20m^4 + 100m^3$ **88.** $4a^2 - 16a + 16$

89. $6x^2 + 23x + 20$ **90.** $2y^2 - 13y + 6$

91. $9y^3 - 24y^2 + 16y$ **92.** $25m^3 - 10m^2 + m$

93. $r^2 - 6rs + 8s^2$ **94.** $7z^2 + 15zy + 2y^2$

95. $m^3 + 2m + 3m^2$ **96.** $7w^2 - 18w + w^3$

97. $6m^3 - m^2n - 2mn^2$ **98.** $3a^3 + 3a^2b - 18ab^2$

99. $9m^2 - 25n^2$ **100.** $m^2n^2 - 2mn^3 + n^4$

101. $5a^2 + 20a - 60$

102. $-3y^2 + 9y + 30$

103. $-2w^2 + 18w + 20$

104. $x^2z + 2xyz + y^2z$

105. $w^2x^2 - 100x^2$

106. $9x^2 + 30x + 25$

107. $81x^2 - 9$

108. $12w^2 - 38w - 72$

109. $8x^2 - 2x - 15$

110. $4w^2 + 12w + 9$

111. $3m^4 - 24m$
112. $6w^3z + 6z$

GETTING MORE INVOLVED

 113. *Discussion.* Which of the following is not a perfect square trinomial? Explain.
  a) $4a^6 - 6a^3b^4 + 9b^8$ **b)** $1000x^2 + 200ax + a^2$
  c) $900y^4 - 60y^2 + 1$ **d)** $36 - 36z^7 + 9z^{14}$

 114. *Discussion.* Which of the following is not a difference of two squares? Explain.
  a) $16a^8y^4 - 25c^{12}$ **b)** $a^9 - b^4$
  c) $t^{90} - 1$ **d)** $x^2 - 196$

115. *Writing.* Factor each polynomial and explain how you decided which method to use.
  a) $x^2 + 10x + 25$
  b) $x^2 - 10x + 25$
  c) $x^2 + 26x + 25$
  d) $x^2 - 25$
  e) $x^2 + 25$

 116. *Discussion.* On an exam, a student factored $2x^2 - 6x + 4$ as $(2x - 4)(x - 1)$. Even though the student carefully checked that

$$(2x - 4)(x - 1) = 2x^2 - 6x + 4,$$

the student lost some points. What went wrong?

In This Section

- Prime Polynomials
- Factoring Polynomials Completely
- Summary

5.7   FACTORING STRATEGY

In previous sections we established the general idea of factoring and many special cases. In this section we will see that a polynomial can have as many factors as its degree, and we will factor higher-degree polynomials completely. We will also see a general strategy for factoring polynomials.

Prime Polynomials

A polynomial that cannot be factored is a prime polynomial. Binomials with no common factors, such as $2x + 1$ and $a - 3$, are prime polynomials. To determine whether a polynomial such as $x^2 + 1$ is a prime polynomial, we must try all possibilities for factoring it. If $x^2 + 1$ could be factored as a product of two binomials, the only possibilities that would give a first term of x^2 and a last term of 1 are $(x + 1)(x + 1)$ and $(x - 1)(x - 1)$. However,

$$(x + 1)(x + 1) = x^2 + 2x + 1 \qquad \text{and} \qquad (x - 1)(x - 1) = x^2 - 2x + 1.$$

Both products have an x-term. Of course, $(x + 1)(x - 1)$ has no x-term, but

$$(x + 1)(x - 1) = x^2 - 1.$$

Because none of these possibilities results in $x^2 + 1$, the polynomial $x^2 + 1$ is a prime polynomial. Note that $x^2 + 1$ is a sum of two squares. A sum of two squares of the form $a^2 + b^2$ is always a prime polynomial.

E X A M P L E   1   **Prime polynomials**
Determine whether the polynomial $x^2 + 3x + 4$ is a prime polynomial.

Solution

To factor $x^2 + 3x + 4$, we must find two integers with a product of 4 and a sum of 3. The only pairs of positive integers with a product of 4 are 1 and 4, and 2 and 2. Because the product is positive 4, both numbers must be negative or both positive. Under these conditions it is impossible to get a sum of positive 3. The polynomial is prime. ∎

Factoring Polynomials Completely

So far, a typical polynomial has been a product of two factors, with possibly a common factor removed first. However, it is possible that the factors can still be factored again. A polynomial in a single variable may have as many factors as its degree. We have factored a polynomial completely when all of the factors are prime polynomials.

E X A M P L E   2

Factoring higher-degree polynomials completely

Factor $x^4 + x^2 - 2$ completely.

Solution

Two numbers with a product of -2 and a sum of 1 are 2 and -1:

$$x^4 + x^2 - 2 = (x^2 + 2)(x^2 - 1)$$
$$= (x^2 + 2)(x - 1)(x + 1) \quad \text{Difference of two squares}$$

Since $x^2 + 2$, $x - 1$, and $x + 1$ are prime, the polynomial is factored completely. ∎

In Example 3 we factor a sixth-degree polynomial.

E X A M P L E   3

Study Tip
_____

Find a clean, comfortable, well-lit place to study. But don't get too comfortable. Sitting at a desk is preferable to lying in bed. Where you study can influence your concentration and your study habits.

Factoring completely

Factor $3x^6 - 3$ completely.

Solution

To factor $3x^6 - 3$, we must first factor out the common factor 3 and then recognize that x^6 is a perfect square: $x^6 = (x^3)^2$:

$$3x^6 - 3 = 3(x^6 - 1) \qquad\qquad \text{Factor out the common factor.}$$
$$= 3((x^3)^2 - 1) \qquad\quad \text{Write } x^6 \text{ as a perfect square.}$$
$$= 3(x^3 - 1)(x^3 + 1) \qquad \text{Difference of two squares}$$
$$= 3(x - 1)(x^2 + x + 1)(x + 1)(x^2 - x + 1) \quad \text{Difference of two cubes and sum of two cubes}$$

Since $x^2 + x + 1$ and $x^2 - x + 1$ are prime, the polynomial is factored completely. ∎

In Example 3 we recognized $x^6 - 1$ as a difference of two squares. However, $x^6 - 1$ is also a difference of two cubes, and we can factor it using the rule for the difference of two cubes:

$$x^6 - 1 = (x^2)^3 - 1 = (x^2 - 1)(x^4 + x^2 + 1)$$

Now we can factor $x^2 - 1$, but it is difficult to see how to factor $x^4 + x^2 + 1$. (It is not prime.) Although x^6 can be thought of as a perfect square or a perfect cube, in this case thinking of it as a perfect square is better.

In Example 4 we use substitution to simplify the polynomial before factoring. This fourth-degree polynomial has four factors.

E X A M P L E   4   **Using substitution to simplify**

Factor $(w^2 - 1)^2 - 11(w^2 - 1) + 24$ completely.

Solution

Let $a = w^2 - 1$ to simplify the polynomial:

$$(w^2 - 1)^2 - 11(w^2 - 1) + 24 = a^2 - 11a + 24 \qquad \text{\small Replace } w^2 - 1 \text{ by } a.$$
$$= (a - 8)(a - 3)$$
$$= (w^2 - 1 - 8)(w^2 - 1 - 3) \quad \text{\small Replace } a \text{ by } w^2 - 1.$$
$$= (w^2 - 9)(w^2 - 4)$$
$$= (w + 3)(w - 3)(w + 2)(w - 2) \qquad \blacksquare$$

Example 5 shows two four-term polynomials that can be factored by grouping. In the first part, the terms must be rearranged before the polynomial can be factored by grouping. In the second part the polynomial is grouped in a new manner.

E X A M P L E   5   **More factoring by grouping**

Factor completely.

a) $x^2 - 3w - 3x + xw$ **b)** $x^2 - 6x + 9 - y^2$

Solution

a) Since the first two terms do not have a common factor, we rearrange the terms as follows:

$$x^2 - 3w - 3x + xw = x^2 - 3x + xw - 3w$$
$$= x(x - 3) + w(x - 3)$$
$$= (x + w)(x - 3)$$

b) We cannot factor this polynomial by grouping pairs of terms. However, $x^2 - 6x + 9$ is a perfect square, $(x - 3)^2$. So we can group the first three terms and then factor the difference of two squares:

$$x^2 - 6x + 9 - y^2 = (x - 3)^2 - y^2 \quad \text{\small Perfect square trinomial}$$
$$= (x - 3 + y)(x - 3 - y) \quad \text{\small Difference of two squares} \qquad \blacksquare$$

Summary

A strategy for factoring polynomials is given in the following box.

Strategy for Factoring Polynomials

1. If there are any common factors, factor them out first.

2. When factoring a binomial, look for the special cases: difference of two squares, difference of two cubes, and sum of two cubes. Remember that a sum of two squares $a^2 + b^2$ is prime.

3. When factoring a trinomial, check to see whether it is a perfect square trinomial.

4. When factoring a trinomial that is not a perfect square, use grouping or trial and error.

5. When factoring a polynomial of high degree, use substitution to get a polynomial of degree 2 or 3, or use trial and error.

6. If the polynomial has four terms, try factoring by grouping.

E X A M P L E 6

Using the factoring strategy

Factor each polynomial completely.

a) $3w^3 - 3w^2 - 18w$ **b)** $10x^2 + 160$

c) $16a^2b - 80ab + 100b$ **d)** $aw + mw + az + mz$

e) $a^4b + 125ab$ **f)** $12x^2y - 26xy - 30y$

Helpful Hint

When factoring integers, we write $4 = 2 \cdot 2$. However, when factoring polynomials we usually do not factor any of the integers that appear. So we say that $4b(2a - 5)^2$ is factored completely.

Solution

a) The greatest common factor (GCF) for the three terms is $3w$:

$$3w^3 - 3w^2 - 18w = 3w(w^2 - w - 6) \quad \text{Factor out } 3w.$$
$$= 3w(w - 3)(w + 2) \quad \text{Factor completely.}$$

b) The GCF in $10x^2 + 160$ is 10:

$$10x^2 + 160 = 10(x^2 + 16)$$

Because $x^2 + 16$ is prime, the polynomial is factored completely.

c) The GCF in $16a^2b - 80ab + 100b$ is $4b$:

$$16a^2b - 80ab + 100b = 4b(4a^2 - 20a + 25)$$
$$= 4b(2a - 5)^2$$

d) The polynomial has four terms, and we can factor it by grouping:

$$aw + mw + az + mz = w(a + m) + z(a + m)$$
$$= (w + z)(a + m)$$

e) The GCF in $a^4b + 125ab$ is ab:

$$a^4b + 125ab = ab(a^3 + 125) \quad \text{Factor out } ab.$$
$$= ab(a + 5)(a^2 - 5a + 25) \quad \text{Factor the sum of two cubes.}$$

f) The GCF in $12x^2y - 26xy - 30y$ is $2y$:

$$12x^2y - 26xy - 30y = 2y(6x^2 - 13x - 15) \quad \text{Factor out } 2y.$$
$$= 2y(x - 3)(6x + 5) \quad \text{Trial and error}$$

WARM-UPS

True or false? Explain your answer.

1. $x^2 - 9 = (x - 3)^2$ for any value of x.

2. The polynomial $4x^2 + 12x + 9$ is a perfect square trinomial.

3. The sum of two squares $a^2 + b^2$ is prime.

4. The polynomial $x^4 - 16$ is factored completely as $(x^2 - 4)(x^2 + 4)$.

5. $y^3 - 27 = (y + 3)(y^2 + 3y - 9)$ for any value of y.

6. The polynomial $y^6 - 1$ is a difference of two squares.

7. The polynomial $2x^2 + 2x - 12$ is factored completely as $(2x - 4)(x + 3)$.

8. The polynomial $x^2 - 4x - 4$ is a prime polynomial.

9. The polynomial $a^6 - 1$ is the difference of two cubes.

10. The polynomial $x^2 + 3x - ax + 3a$ can be factored by grouping.

5.7   EXERCISES

Reading and Writing   *After reading this section, write out the answers to these questions. Use complete sentences.*

1. What should you do first when factoring a polynomial?

2. If you are factoring a binomial, then what should you look for?

3. When factoring a trinomial what should you look for?

4. What should you look for when factoring a four-term polynomial?

Determine whether each polynomial is a prime polynomial. See Example 1.

5. $y^2 + 100$

6. $3x^2 + 27$

7. $-9w^2 - 9$

8. $25y^2 + 36$

9. $x^2 - 2x - 3$

10. $x^2 - 2x + 3$

11. $x^2 + 2x + 3$

12. $x^2 + 4x + 3$

13. $x^2 - 4x - 3$

14. $x^2 + 4x - 3$

15. $6x^2 + 3x - 4$

16. $4x^2 - 5x - 3$

Factor each polynomial completely. See Examples 2–4.

17. $a^4 - 10a^2 + 25$

18. $9y^4 + 12y^2 + 4$

19. $x^4 - 6x^2 + 8$

20. $x^6 + 2x^3 - 3$

21. $(3x - 5)^2 - 1$

22. $(2x + 1)^2 - 4$

23. $2y^6 - 128$

24. $6 - 6y^6$

25. $32a^4 - 18$

26. $2a^4 - 32$

27. $x^4 - (x - 6)^2$

28. $y^4 - (2y + 1)^2$

29. $(m + 2)^2 + 2(m + 2) - 3$

30. $(2w - 3)^2 - 2(2w - 3) - 15$

31. $3(y - 1)^2 + 11(y - 1) - 20$

32. $2(w + 2)^2 + 5(w + 2) - 3$

33. $(y^2 - 3)^2 - 4(y^2 - 3) - 12$

34. $(m^2 - 8)^2 - 4(m^2 - 8) - 32$

Factor completely. See Example 5.

35. $x^2 - 2b - 2x + bx$

36. $y^2 - c - y + cy$

37. $x^2 - ay - xy + ax$

38. $ax - by + bx - ay$

39. $x^2 + 2x + 1 - a^2$

40. $x^2 + 10x + 25 - b^2$

41. $x^2 - 4x + 4 - w^2$

42. $x^2 - 8x + 16 - c^2$

43. $x^2 - z^2 + 4x + 4$

44. $x^2 + 36 - m^2 - 12x$

Use the factoring strategy to factor each polynomial completely. See Example 6.

45. $9x^2 - 24x + 16$

46. $-3x^2 + 18x + 48$

47. $12x^2 - 13x + 3$

48. $2x^2 - 3x - 6$

49. $3a^4 + 81a$

50. $-a^3 + 25a$

51. $32 + 2x^2$

52. $x^3 + 4x^2 + 4x$

53. $6x^2 - 5x + 12$

54. $x^4 + 2x^3 - x - 2$

55. $(x + y)^2 - 1$

56. $x^3 + 9x$

57. $a^3b - ab^3$

58. $2m^3 - 250n^3$

59. $x^4 + 2x^3 - 8x - 16$

60. $(x + 5)^2 - 4$

61. $m^2n + 2mn^2 + n^3$

62. $a^2b - 2ab^2 + b^3$

63. $2m + wn + 2n + wm$

64. $aw - 5b + bw - 5a$

65. $4w^2 + 4w - 3$

66. $4w^2 + 8w - 63$

67. $t^4 + 4t^2 - 21$

68. $m^4 + 5m^2 + 4$

69. $-a^3 - 7a^2 + 30a$

70. $2y^4 + 3y^3 - 20y^2$

71. $(y + 5)^2 - 2(y + 5) - 3$

72. $(2t - 1)^2 + 7(2t - 1) + 10$

73. $-2w^4 + 1250$

74. $5a^5 - 5a$

75. $4a^2 + 16$

76. $9w^2 + 81$

77. $8a^3 + 8a$

78. $awx + ax$

79. $(w + 5)^2 - 9$

80. $(a - 6)^2 - 1$

81. $4aw^2 - 12aw + 9a$

82. $9an^3 + 15an^2 - 14an$

83. $x^2 - 6xy + 9y^2$

84. $x^3 + 12x^2y + 36xy^2$

85. $3x^4 - 75x^2$

86. $3x^2 + 9x + 12$

87. $m^3n - n$

88. $m^4 + 16m^2$

89. $12x^2 + 2x - 30$

90. $90x^2 + 3x - 60$

91. $2a^3 - 32$

92. $12x^2 - 28x + 15$

Factor completely. Assume variables used as exponents represent positive integers.

93. $a^{3m} - 1$

94. $x^{6a} + 8$

95. $a^{3w} - b^{6n}$

96. $x^{2n} - 9$

97. $t^{4n} - 16$

98. $a^{3n+2} + a^2$

99. $a^{2n+1} - 2a^{n+1} - 15a$

100. $x^{3m} + x^{2m} - 6x^m$

101. $a^{2n} - 3a^n + a^nb - 3b$

102. $x^mz + 5z + x^{m+1} + 5x$

GETTING MORE INVOLVED

 103. *Cooperative learning.* Write down 10 trinomials of the form $ax^2 + bx + c$ "at random" using integers for a, b, and c. What percent of your 10 trinomials are prime? Would you say that prime trinomials are the exception or the rule? Compare your results with those of your classmates.

 104. *Writing.* The polynomial

$$x^3 + 5x^2 + 7x + 3$$

is a product of three factors of the form $x \pm n$, where n is a natural number smaller than 4. Factor this polynomial completely and explain your procedure.

In This Section

- The Zero Factor Property
- Applications

Helpful Hint

Note that the zero factor property is our second example of getting an equivalent equation without "doing the same thing to each side." What was the first?

5.8 SOLVING EQUATIONS BY FACTORING

The techniques of factoring can be used to solve equations involving polynomials that cannot be solved by the other methods that you have learned. After you learn to solve equations by factoring, we will use this technique to solve some new applied problems in this section and in Chapters 6 and 8.

The Zero Factor Property

The equation $ab = 0$ indicates that the product of two unknown numbers is 0. But the product of two real numbers is zero only when one or the other of the numbers is 0. So even though we do not know exactly the values of a and b from $ab = 0$, we do know that $a = 0$ or $b = 0$. This idea is called the **zero factor property.**

> **Zero Factor Property**
>
> The equation $ab = 0$ is equivalent to the compound equation
>
> $$a = 0 \qquad \text{or} \qquad b = 0.$$

Example 1 shows how to use the zero factor property to solve an equation in one variable.

EXAMPLE 1   **Using the zero factor property**

Solve $x^2 + x - 12 = 0$.

Solution

We factor the left-hand side of the equation to get a product of two factors that are equal to 0. Then we write an equivalent equation using the zero factor property.

$$x^2 + x - 12 = 0$$

$$(x + 4)(x - 3) = 0 \quad \text{Factor the left-hand side.}$$

$$x + 4 = 0 \quad \text{or} \quad x - 3 = 0 \quad \text{Zero factor property}$$

$$x = -4 \quad \text{or} \quad x = 3 \quad \text{Solve each part of the compound equation.}$$

Check that both -4 and 3 satisfy $x^2 + x - 12 = 0$. If $x = -4$, we get

$$(-4)^2 + (-4) - 12 = 16 - 4 - 12 = 0.$$

If $x = 3$, we get

$$(3)^2 + 3 - 12 = 9 + 3 - 12 = 0.$$

So the solution set is $\{-4, 3\}$. ∎

The zero factor property is used only in solving polynomial equations that have zero on one side and a polynomial that can be factored on the other side. The polynomials that we factored most often were the quadratic polynomials. The equations that we will solve most often using the zero factor property will be quadratic equations.

Quadratic Equation

If a, b, and c are real numbers, with $a \neq 0$, then the equation

$$ax^2 + bx + c = 0$$

is called a **quadratic equation.**

M A T H A T W O R K

Seamas Mercado, professional bodyboarder and 1988 National Champion, charges the waves off Hawaii, Tahiti, Indonesia, Mexico, and California. In choosing a board for competition and for the maneuvers he wants to perform, Mercado factors in his height and weight as well as the size, power, and temperature of the waves he will be riding. In colder water a softer, more flexible board is used; in warmer water a stiffer board is chosen. When waves crash on shore, the ride usually lasts 3 to 5 seconds, and a shorter board with a narrow tail is chosen for greater control. When waves break along a sand bar or reef, the ride can sometimes last as long as 2 minutes, and a straighter board with more surface area is chosen so that the board will move faster and allow the rider to pull off more maneuvers. Basic maneuvers include bottom turns, aerials, forward and reverse 360's, and el rollos.

BODYBOARD DESIGNER

As one of the top 10 bodyboarders in the world, Mercado helps to design the boards he uses. "Performance levels are greatly increased with fine-tuned equipment and techniques," he says. In Exercise 75 of Section 5.8 you will find the dimensions of a given bodyboard.

In Chapter 8 we will study quadratic equations further and solve quadratic equations that cannot be solved by factoring. Keep the following strategy in mind when solving equations by factoring.

> **Strategy for Solving Equations by Factoring**
>
> 1. Write the equation with 0 on the right-hand side.
> 2. Factor the left-hand side.
> 3. Use the zero factor property to get simpler equations. (Set each factor equal to 0.)
> 4. Solve the simpler equations.
> 5. Check the answers in the original equation.

E X A M P L E   2

Solving a quadratic equation by factoring

Solve each equation.

a) $10x^2 = 5x$ 　　　　　　　　　**b)** $3x - 6x^2 = -9$

Solution

a) Use the steps in the strategy for solving equations by factoring:

$$10x^2 = 5x \qquad \text{Original equation}$$

$$10x^2 - 5x = 0 \qquad \text{Rewrite with zero on the right-hand side.}$$

$$5x(2x - 1) = 0 \qquad \text{Factor the left-hand side.}$$

$$5x = 0 \quad \text{or} \quad 2x - 1 = 0 \qquad \text{Zero factor property}$$

$$x = 0 \quad \text{or} \quad x = \frac{1}{2} \qquad \text{Solve for } x.$$

The solution set is $\left\{0, \frac{1}{2}\right\}$. Check each solution in the original equation.

b) First rewrite the equation with 0 on the right-hand side and the left-hand side in order of descending exponents:

$$3x - 6x^2 = -9 \qquad \text{Original equation}$$

$$-6x^2 + 3x + 9 = 0 \qquad \text{Add 9 to each side.}$$

$$2x^2 - x - 3 = 0 \qquad \text{Divide each side by } -3.$$

$$(2x - 3)(x + 1) = 0 \qquad \text{Factor.}$$

$$2x - 3 = 0 \quad \text{or} \quad x + 1 = 0 \qquad \text{Zero factor property}$$

$$x = \frac{3}{2} \quad \text{or} \quad x = -1 \qquad \text{Solve for } x.$$

The solution set is $\left\{-1, \frac{3}{2}\right\}$. Check each solution in the original equation. ∎

C A U T I O N   If we divide each side of $10x^2 = 5x$ by $5x$, we get $2x = 1$, or $x = \frac{1}{2}$. We do not get $x = 0$. By dividing by $5x$ we have lost one of the factors and one of the solutions.

In Example 3 there are more than two factors, but we can still write an equivalent equation by setting each factor equal to 0.

E X A M P L E   3

Solving a cubic equation by factoring

Solve $2x^3 - 3x^2 - 8x + 12 = 0$.

Solution

First notice that the first two terms have the common factor x^2 and the last two terms have the common factor -4.

$$x^2(2x - 3) - 4(2x - 3) = 0 \quad \text{Factor by grouping.}$$
$$(x^2 - 4)(2x - 3) = 0 \quad \text{Factor out } 2x - 3.$$
$$(x - 2)(x + 2)(2x - 3) = 0 \quad \text{Factor completely.}$$

$x - 2 = 0 \quad$ or $\quad x + 2 = 0 \quad$ or $\quad 2x - 3 = 0 \quad$ Set each factor equal to 0.

$x = 2 \quad$ or $\quad x = -2 \quad$ or $\quad x = \dfrac{3}{2}$

The solution set is $\left\{-2, \dfrac{3}{2}, 2\right\}$. Check each solution in the original equation. ■

The equation in the next example involves absolute value.

Calculator Close-Up

To check, use Y= to enter

$y_1 = 2x^3 - 3x^2 - 8x + 12$.

Then use the variables feature (VARS) to find $y_1(-2)$, $y_1(3/2)$, and $y_1(2)$.

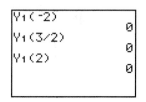

E X A M P L E   4

Solving an absolute value equation by factoring

Solve $| x^2 - 2x - 16 | = 8$.

Solution

First write an equivalent compound equation without absolute value:

$$x^2 - 2x - 16 = 8 \quad \text{or} \quad x^2 - 2x - 16 = -8$$
$$x^2 - 2x - 24 = 0 \quad \text{or} \quad x^2 - 2x - 8 = 0$$
$$(x - 6)(x + 4) = 0 \quad \text{or} \quad (x - 4)(x + 2) = 0$$

$x - 6 = 0 \quad$ or $\quad x + 4 = 0 \quad$ or $\quad x - 4 = 0 \quad$ or $\quad x + 2 = 0$

$x = 6 \quad$ or $\quad x = -4 \quad$ or $\quad x = 4 \quad$ or $\quad x = -2$

The solution set is $\{-2, -4, 4, 6\}$. Check each solution. ■

Applications

Many applied problems can be solved by using equations such as those we have been solving.

E X A M P L E   5

Area of a room

Ronald's living room is 2 feet longer than it is wide, and its area is 168 square feet. What are the dimensions of the room?

Solution

Let x be the width and $x + 2$ be the length. See Fig. 5.1. Because the area of a rectangle is the length times the width, we can write the equation

$$x(x + 2) = 168.$$

We solve the equation by factoring:

$$x^2 + 2x - 168 = 0$$
$$(x - 12)(x + 14) = 0$$

$x - 12 = 0 \quad$ or $\quad x + 14 = 0$

$x = 12 \quad$ or $\quad x = -14$

Helpful Hint

To prove the Pythagorean theorem, draw two squares with sides of length $a + b$, and partition them as shown.

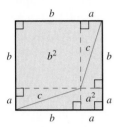

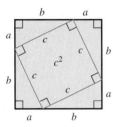

Erase the four triangles in each picture. Since we started with equal areas, we must have equal areas after erasing the triangles:

$$a^2 + b^2 = c^2$$

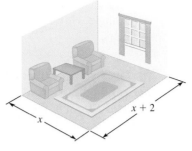

FIGURE 5.1

Because the width of a room is a positive number, we disregard the solution $x = -14$. We use $x = 12$ and get a width of 12 feet and a length of 14 feet. Check this answer by multiplying 12 and 14 to get 168. ∎

Applications involving quadratic equations often require a theorem called the **Pythagorean theorem.** This theorem states that *in any right triangle the sum of the squares of the lengths of the legs is equal to the length of the hypotenuse squared.*

The Pythagorean Theorem

The triangle shown is a right triangle if and only if

$$a^2 + b^2 = c^2.$$

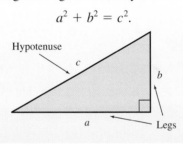

We use the Pythagorean theorem in Example 6.

EXAMPLE 6

Using the Pythagorean theorem

Shirley used 14 meters of fencing to enclose a rectangular region. To be sure that the region was a rectangle, she measured the diagonals and found that they were 5 meters each. (If the opposite sides of a quadrilateral are equal and the diagonals are equal, then the quadrilateral is a rectangle.) What are the length and width of the rectangle?

Solution

The perimeter of a rectangle is twice the length plus twice the width, $P = 2L + 2W$. Because the perimeter is 14 meters, the sum of one length and one width is 7 meters. If we let x represent the width, then $7 - x$ is the length. We use the Pythagorean theorem to get a relationship among the length, width, and diagonal. See Fig. 5.2.

$$x^2 + (7 - x)^2 = 5^2 \qquad \text{Pythagorean theorem}$$
$$x^2 + 49 - 14x + x^2 = 25 \qquad \text{Simplify.}$$
$$2x^2 - 14x + 24 = 0 \qquad \text{Simplify.}$$
$$x^2 - 7x + 12 = 0 \qquad \text{Divide each side by 2.}$$
$$(x - 3)(x - 4) = 0 \qquad \text{Factor the left-hand side.}$$
$$x - 3 = 0 \quad \text{or} \quad x - 4 = 0 \qquad \text{Zero factor property}$$
$$x = 3 \quad \text{or} \quad x = 4$$
$$7 - x = 4 \quad \text{or} \quad 7 - x = 3$$

FIGURE 5.2

Solving the equation gives two possible rectangles: a 3 by 4 rectangle or a 4 by 3 rectangle. However, those are identical rectangles. The rectangle is 3 meters by 4 meters. ■

Example 7 involves a formula from physics for the height of a projectile where the only force acting on the object is gravity. If an object is projected upward at v_0 feet/sec from h_0 feet above the ground, then its height in feet at time t in seconds is given by $h(t) = -16t^2 + v_0t + h_0$.

E X A M P L E   7

Height of a projectile

A construction worker accidentally fires a nail gun upward from a height of 144 feet. The nail is propelled upward at 128 feet/sec, as shown in Fig. 5.3. The height of the nail in feet at time t in seconds is given by the function $h(t) = -16t^2 + 128t + 144$. How long does it take for the nail to fall to the ground?

Solution

On the ground the height is 0 feet. So we want to solve the quadratic equation $-16t^2 + 128t + 144 = 0$:

$$-16t^2 + 128t + 144 = 0$$
$$-16(t^2 - 8t - 9) = 0 \quad \text{Factor out the GCF.}$$
$$-16(t - 9)(t + 1) = 0 \quad \text{Factor the trinomial.}$$
$$t - 9 = 0 \quad \text{or} \quad t + 1 = 0 \quad \text{Zero factor property}$$
$$t = 9 \quad \text{or} \quad t = -1$$

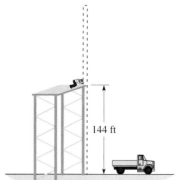

FIGURE 5.3

Since $t = -1$ does not make sense, the nail takes 9 seconds to fall to the ground. ■

WARM-UPS

True or false? Explain your answer.

1. The equation $(x - 1)(x + 3) = 12$ is equivalent to $x - 1 = 3$ or $x + 3 = 4$.

2. Equations solved by factoring may have two solutions.

3. The equation $c \cdot d = 0$ is equivalent to $c = 0$ or $d = 0$.

4. The equation $|x^2 + 4| = 5$ is equivalent to the compound equation $x^2 + 4 = 5$ or $x^2 - 4 = 5$.

5. The solution set to the equation $(2x - 1)(3x + 4) = 0$ is $\left\{\dfrac{1}{2}, -\dfrac{4}{3}\right\}$.

6. The Pythagorean theorem states that the sum of the squares of any two sides of any triangle is equal to the square of the third side.

7. If the perimeter of a rectangular room is 38 feet, then the sum of the length and width is 19 feet.

8. Two numbers that have a sum of 8 can be represented by x and $8 - x$.

9. The solution set to the equation $x(x - 1)(x - 2) = 0$ is $\{1, 2\}$.

10. The solution set to the equation $3(x + 2)(x - 5) = 0$ is $\{3, -2, 5\}$.

5.8   EXERCISES

Reading and Writing   *After reading this section, write out the answers to these questions. Use complete sentences.*

1. What is the zero factor property?

2. What is a quadratic equation?

3. Where is the hypotenuse in a right triangle?

4. Where are the legs in a right triangle?

5. What is the Pythagorean theorem?

6. Where is the diagonal of a rectangle?

Solve each equation. See Examples 1–3.

7. $(x - 5)(x + 4) = 0$

8. $(a - 6)(a + 5) = 0$

9. $(2x - 5)(3x + 4) = 0$

10. $(3k + 8)(4k - 3) = 0$

11. $4(x - 2)(x + 5) = 0$

12. $8(x - 9)(x + 9) = 0$

13. $x(x - 5)(x + 5) = 0$

14. $x(x - 4)(x + 7) = 0$

15. $w^2 + 5w - 14 = 0$

16. $t^2 - 6t - 27 = 0$

17. $m^2 - 7m = 0$

18. $h^2 - 5h = 0$

19. $a^2 - a = 20$

20. $p^2 - p = 42$

21. $2a^2 + 7a = 15$

22. $6p^2 + p = 1$

23. $10a^2 + 38a - 8 = 0$

24. $-48b^2 + 28b + 6 = 0$

25. $3x^2 - 3x - 36 = 0$

26. $-2x^2 - 16x - 24 = 0$

27. $z^2 + \dfrac{3}{2}z = 10$

28. $m^2 + \dfrac{11}{3}m = -2$

29. $x^3 - 4x = 0$

30. $16x - x^3 = 0$

31. $-4x^3 + x = 3x^2$

32. $2x - 11x^2 = 6x^3$

33. $w^3 + 4w^2 - 25w - 100 = 0$

34. $a^3 + 2a^2 - 16a - 32 = 0$

35. $n^3 - 2n^2 - n + 2 = 0$

36. $w^3 - w^2 - 25w + 25 = 0$

Solve each equation. See Example 4.

37. $\lvert x^2 - 5 \rvert = 4$

38. $\lvert x^2 - 17 \rvert = 8$

39. $\lvert x^2 + 2x - 36 \rvert = 12$

40. $\lvert x^2 + 2x - 19 \rvert = 16$

41. $\lvert x^2 + 4x + 2 \rvert = 2$

42. $\lvert x^2 + 8x + 8 \rvert = 8$

43. $\lvert x^2 + 6x + 1 \rvert = 8$

44. $\lvert x^2 - x - 21 \rvert = 9$

Solve each equation.

45. $2x^2 - x = 6$

46. $3x^2 + 14x = 5$

47. $\lvert x^2 + 5x \rvert = 6$

48. $\lvert x^2 + 6x - 4 \rvert = 12$

49. $x^2 + 5x = 6$

50. $x + 5x = 6$

51. $(x + 2)(x + 1) = 12$

52. $(x + 2)(x + 3) = 20$

53. $y^3 + 9y^2 + 20y = 0$

54. $m^3 - 2m^2 - 3m = 0$

55. $5a^3 = 45a$

56. $5x^3 = 125x$

57. $(2x - 1)(x^2 - 9) = 0$

58. $(3x - 5)(25x^2 - 4)$

59. $(2x - 1)(3x + 1)(4x - 1) = 0$

60. $(x - 1)(x + 3)(x - 9) = 0$

61. $4x^2 - 12x + 9 = 0$

62. $16x^2 + 8x + 1 = 0$

Solve each equation for y. Assume a and b are positive numbers.

63. $y^2 + by = 0$

64. $y^2 + ay + by + ab = 0$

65. $a^2y^2 - b^2 = 0$

66. $9y^2 + 6ay + a^2 = 0$

67. $4y^2 + 4by + b^2 = 0$

68. $y^2 - b^2 = 0$

69. $ay^2 + 3y - ay = 3$

70. $a^2y^2 + 2aby + b^2 = 0$

Solve each problem. See Examples 5, 6, and 7.

71. Color print. The length of a new "super size" color print is 2 inches more than the width. If the area is 24 square inches, what are the length and width?

72. Tennis court dimensions. In singles competition, each player plays on a rectangular area of 117 square yards. Given that the length of that area is 4 yards greater than its width, find the length and width.

73. Missing numbers. The sum of two numbers is 13 and their product is 36. Find the numbers.

74. More missing numbers. The sum of two numbers is 6.5, and their product is 9. Find the numbers.

75. Bodyboarding. The Seamas Channel pro bodyboard shown in the figure has a length that is 21 inches greater than its width. Any rider weighing up to 200 pounds can use it because its surface area is 946 square inches. Assume that it is rectangular in shape and find the length and width.

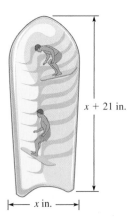

$x + 21$ in.

x in.

FIGURE FOR EXERCISE 75

76. New dimensions in gardening. Mary Gold has a rectangular flower bed that measures 4 feet by 6 feet. If she wants to increase the length and width by the same

amount to have a flower bed of 48 square feet, then what will be the new dimensions?

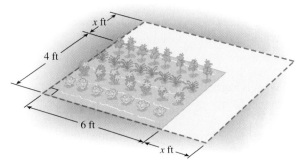

x ft

4 ft

6 ft

x ft

FIGURE FOR EXERCISE 76

77. Shooting arrows. An archer shoots an arrow straight upward at 64 feet per second. The height of the arrow $h(t)$ (in feet) at time t seconds is given by the function

$$h(t) = -16t^2 + 64t.$$

a) Use the accompanying graph to estimate the amount of time that the arrow is in the air.

b) Algebraically find the amount of time that the arrow is in the air.

c) Use the accompanying graph to estimate the maximum height reached by the arrow.

d) At what time does the arrow reach its maximum height?

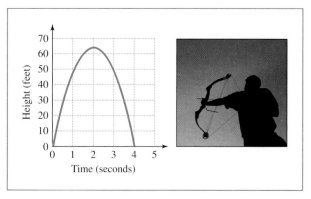

FIGURE FOR EXERCISE 77

78. Time until impact. If an object is dropped from a height of s_0 feet, then its altitude after t seconds is given by the formula $S = -16t^2 + s_0$. If a pack of emergency supplies is dropped from an airplane at a height of 1600 feet, then how long does it take for it to reach the ground?

79. Firing an M-16. If an M-16 is fired straight upward, then the height $h(t)$ of the bullet in feet at time t in seconds is given by

$$h(t) = -16t^2 + 325t.$$

a) What is the height of the bullet 5 seconds after it is fired?

b) How long does it take for the bullet to return to the earth?

80. *Firing a howitzer.* If an 8-in. (diameter) howitzer is fired straight into the air, then the height $h(t)$ of the projectile in feet at time t in seconds is given by

$$h(t) = -16t^2 + 1332t.$$

a) What is the height of the projectile 10 seconds after it is fired?

b) How long does it take for the projectile to return to the earth?

81. *Tossing a ball.* A boy tosses a ball upward at 32 feet per second from a window that is 48 feet above the ground. The height of the ball above the ground (in feet) at time t (in seconds) is given by

$$h(t) = -16t^2 + 32t + 48.$$

Find the time at which the ball strikes the ground.

82. *Firing a slingshot.* A girl uses a slingshot to propel a stone upward at 64 feet per second from a window that is 80 feet above the ground. The height of the stone above the ground (in feet) at time t (in seconds) is given by

$$h(t) = -16t^2 + 64t + 80.$$

Find the time at which the stone strikes the ground.

83. *Yolanda's closet.* The length of Yolanda's closet is 2 feet longer than twice its width. If the diagonal measures 13 feet, then what are the length and width?

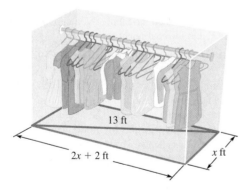

FIGURE FOR EXERCISE 83

84. *Ski jump.* The base of a ski ramp forms a right triangle. One leg of the triangle is 2 meters longer than the other. If the hypotenuse is 10 meters, then what are the lengths of the legs?

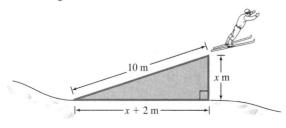

FIGURE FOR EXERCISE 84

85. *Trimming a gate.* A total of 34 feet of 1 × 4 lumber is used around the perimeter of the gate shown in the figure. If the diagonal brace is 13 feet long, then what are the length and width of the gate?

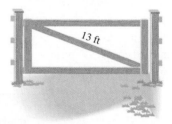

FIGURE FOR EXERCISE 85

86. *Maria's kids.* The sum of the squares of the ages of Maria's two kids is 289. If the boy is seven years older than the girl, then what are their ages?

87. *Leaning ladder.* A 15-foot ladder is leaning against a wall. If the distance from the top of the ladder to the ground is 3 feet more than the distance from the bottom of the ladder to the wall, then what is the distance from the top of the ladder to the ground?

88. *Laying tile.* Lorinda is planning to redo the floor in her bedroom, which has an area of 192 square feet. If the width of the rectangular room is 4 feet less than the length, then what are its dimensions?

89. *Finding numbers.* If the square of a number decreased by the number is 12, then what is the number?

90. *Perimeter of a rectangle.* The perimeter of a rectangle is 28 inches, and the diagonal measures 10 inches. What are the length and width of the rectangle?

91. *Consecutive integers.* The sum of the squares of two consecutive integers is 25. Find the integers.

92. *Pete's garden.* Each row in Pete's garden is 3 feet wide. If the rows run north and south, he can have two more rows than if they run east and west. If the area of Pete's garden is 135 square feet, then what are the length and width?

93. *House plans.* In the plans for their dream house the Baileys have a master bedroom that is 240 square feet in area. If they increase the width by 3 feet, they must decrease the length by 4 feet to keep the original area. What are the original dimensions of the bedroom?

94. *Arranging the rows.* Mr. Converse has 112 students in his algebra class with an equal number in each row. If he arranges the desks so that he has one fewer rows, he will have two more students in each row. How many rows did he have originally?

GETTING MORE INVOLVED

95. *Writing.* If you divide each side of $x^2 = x$ by x, you get $x = 1$. If you subtract x from each side of $x^2 = x$,

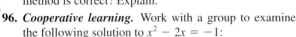

you get $x^2 - x = 0$, which has two solutions. Which method is correct? Explain.

96. *Cooperative learning.* Work with a group to examine the following solution to $x^2 - 2x = -1$:

$$x(x - 2) = -1$$
$$x = -1 \quad \text{or} \quad x - 2 = -1$$
$$x = -1 \quad \text{or} \quad x = 1$$

Is this method correct? Explain.

97. *Cooperative learning.* Work with a group to examine the following steps in the solution to $5x^2 - 5 = 0$

$$5(x^2 - 1) = 0$$
$$5(x - 1)(x + 1) = 0$$
$$x - 1 = 0 \quad \text{or} \quad x + 1 = 0$$
$$x = 1 \quad \text{or} \quad x = -1$$

What happened to the 5? Explain.

COLLABORATIVE ACTIVITIES

Magic Tricks

Jim and Sadar are talking one day after class.

Sadar: Jim, I have a trick for you. Think of a number between 1 and 10. I will ask you to do some things to this number. Then at the end tell me your result, and I will tell you your number.

Jim: Oh, yeah you probably rig it so the result is my number.

Sadar: Come on Jim, give it a try and see.

Jim: Okay, okay, I thought of a number.

Sadar: Good, now write it down, and don't let me see your paper. Now add x. Got that? Now multiply everything by 2.

Jim: Hey, I didn't know you were going to make me think! This is algebra!

Sadar: I know, now just do it. Okay, now square the polynomial. Got that? Now subtract $4x^2$.

Jim: How did you know I had a $4x^2$? I told you this was rigged!

Sadar: Of course it's rigged, or it wouldn't work. Do you want to finish or not?

Jim: Yeah, I guess so. Go ahead, what do I do next?

Sadar: Divide by 4. Okay, now subtract the x-term.

Grouping: Two students per group

Topic: Practice with exponent rules, multiplying polynomials

Jim: Just any old x-term? Got any particular coefficient in mind?

Sadar: Now stop teasing me. I know you only have one x-term left, so subtract it.

Jim: Ha, ha, I *could* give you a hint about the coefficient, but that wouldn't be fair, would it?

Sadar: Well you could, and then I could tell you your number, or you could just tell me the number you have left after subtracting.

Jim: Okay, the number I had left at the end was 25. Let's see if you can tell me what the coefficient of the x-term I subtracted is.

Sadar: Aha, then the number you chose at the beginning was 5, and the coefficient was 10!

Jim: Hey, you're right! How did you do that?

In your group, follow Sadar's instructions and determine why she knew Jim's number. Make up another set of instructions to use as a magic trick. Be sure to use variables and some of the exponent rules or rules for multiplying polynomials that you learned in this chapter. Exchange instructions with another group and see whether you can figure out how their trick works.

WRAP-UP   CHAPTER 5

SUMMARY

Definitions

Definition of negative integral exponents

If a is a nonzero real number and n is a positive integer, then

$$a^{-n} = \frac{1}{a^n}.$$

Examples

$$2^{-3} = \frac{1}{2^3} = \frac{1}{8}$$

Definition of zero exponent	If a is any nonzero real number, then $a^0 = 1$. The expression 0^0 is undefined.	$3^0 = 1$

Rules of Exponents

Examples

If a and b are nonzero real numbers and m and n are integers, then the following rules hold.

Negative exponent rules	$a^{-n} = \left(\dfrac{1}{a}\right)^n$, $\quad a^{-1} = \dfrac{1}{a}$, $\quad$ and $\quad \dfrac{1}{a^{-n}} = a^n$	$5^{-1} = \dfrac{1}{5}, \dfrac{1}{5^{-3}} = 5^3$
	Find the power and reciprocal in either order.	$\left(\dfrac{2}{3}\right)^{-2} = \left(\dfrac{3}{2}\right)^2$
Product rule	$a^m \cdot a^n = a^{m+n}$	$3^5 \cdot 3^7 = 3^{12}, 2^{-3} \cdot 2^{10} = 2^7$
Quotient rule	$\dfrac{a^m}{a^n} = a^{m-n}$	$\dfrac{x^8}{x^5} = x^3, \dfrac{5^4}{5^{-7}} = 5^{11}$
Power of a power rule	$(a^m)^n = a^{mn}$	$(5^2)^3 = 5^6$
Power of a product rule	$(ab)^n = a^n b^n$	$(2x)^3 = 8x^3$ $(2x^3)^4 = 16x^{12}$
Power of a quotient rule	$\left(\dfrac{a}{b}\right)^n = \dfrac{a^n}{b^n}$	$\left(\dfrac{x}{3}\right)^2 = \dfrac{x^2}{9}$

Scientific Notation

Examples

Converting from scientific notation	1. Determine the number of places to move the decimal point by examining the exponent on the 10.	$4 \times 10^3 = 4000$
	2. Move to the right for a positive exponent and to the left for a negative exponent.	$3 \times 10^{-4} = 0.0003$
Converting to scientific notation	1. Count the number of places (n) that the decimal point must be moved so that it will follow the first nonzero digit of the number.	
	2. If the original number was larger than 10, use 10^n.	$67{,}000 = 6.7 \times 10^4$
	3. If the original number was smaller than 1, use 10^{-n}.	$0.009 = 9 \times 10^{-3}$

Polynomials

Examples

Term of a polynomial	The product of a number (coefficient) and one or more variables raised to whole number powers	$3x^4, -2xy^2, 5$
Polynomial	A single term or a finite sum of terms	$x^5 - 3x^2 + 7$
Adding or subtracting polynomials	Add or subtract the like terms.	$(x + 3) + (x - 7) = 2x - 4$ $(x^2 - 2x) - (3x^2 - x) = -2x^2 - x$

| Multiplying two polynomials | Multiply each term of the first polynomial by each term of the second polynomial, then combine like terms. | $\begin{aligned}(x^2 + 2x &+ 3)(x + 1)\\ &= (x^2 + 2x + 3)x + (x^2 + 2x + 3)1\\ &= x^3 + 2x^2 + 3x + x^2 + 2x + 3\\ &= x^3 + 3x^2 + 5x + 3\end{aligned}$ |

Shortcuts for Multiplying Two Binomials

Examples

FOIL	The product of two binomials can be found quickly by multiplying their **F**irst, **O**uter, **I**nner, and **L**ast terms.	$(x + 2)(x + 3) = x^2 + 5x + 6$
Square of a sum	$(a + b)^2 = a^2 + 2ab + b^2$	$(x + 5)^2 = x^2 + 10x + 25$
Square of a difference	$(a - b)^2 = a^2 - 2ab + b^2$	$(m - 3)^2 = m^2 - 6m + 9$
Product of a sum and a difference	$(a + b)(a - b) = a^2 - b^2$	$(x + 3)(x - 3) = x^2 - 9$

Factoring

Examples

Factoring a polynomial	Write a polynomial as a product of two or more polynomials. A polynomial is factored completely if it is a product of prime polynomials.	$\begin{aligned}3x^2 - 3 &= 3(x^2 - 1)\\ &= 3(x + 1)(x - 1)\end{aligned}$
Common factors	Factor out the greatest common factor (GCF).	$2x^3 - 6x = 2x(x^2 - 3)$
Difference of two squares	$a^2 - b^2 = (a + b)(a - b)$ (The sum of two squares $a^2 + b^2$ is prime.)	$m^2 - 25 = (m + 5)(m - 5)$ $m^2 + 25$ is prime.
Perfect square trinomials	$a^2 + 2ab + b^2 = (a + b)^2$ $a^2 - 2ab + b^2 = (a - b)^2$	$x^2 + 10x + 25 = (x + 5)^2$ $x^2 - 6x + 9 = (x - 3)^2$
Difference of two cubes	$a^3 - b^3 = (a - b)(a^2 + ab + b^2)$	$x^3 - 8 = (x - 2)(x^2 + 2x + 4)$
Sum of two cubes	$a^3 + b^3 = (a + b)(a^2 - ab + b^2)$	$x^3 + 27 = (x + 3)(x^2 - 3x + 9)$
Grouping	Factor out common factors from groups of terms.	$\begin{aligned}3x + 3w &+ bx + bw\\ &= 3(x + w) + b(x + w)\\ &= (3 + b)(x + w)\end{aligned}$
Factoring $ax^2 + bx + c$	By the *ac* method: 1. Find two numbers that have a product equal to *ac* and a sum equal to *b*. 2. Replace *bx* by two terms using the two new numbers as coefficients. 3. Factor the resulting four-term polynomial by grouping.	$2x^2 + 7x + 3$ $ac = 6, b = 7, 1 \cdot 6 = 6, 1 + 6 = 7$ $2x^2 + 7x + 3$ $\begin{aligned}&= 2x^2 + x + 6x + 3\\ &= (2x + 1)x + (2x + 1)3\\ &= (2x + 1)(x + 3)\end{aligned}$

48. $(x + 5)(x^2 - 2x + 10)$

49. $xy + 7z - 5(xy - 3z)$

50. $7 - 4(x - 3)$

51. $m^2(5m^3 - m + 2)$

52. $(a + 2)^3$

5.4 *Perform the following computations mentally. Write down only the answers.*

53. $(x - 3)(x + 7)$ **54.** $(k - 5)(k + 4)$

55. $(z - 5y)(z + 5y)$ **56.** $(m - 3)(m + 3)$

57. $(m + 8)^2$ **58.** $(b + 2a)^2$

59. $(w - 6x)(w - 4x)$ **60.** $(2w - 3)(w + 6)$

61. $(k - 3)^2$ **62.** $(n - 5)^2$

63. $(m^2 - 5)(m^2 + 5)$ **64.** $(3k^2 - 5t)(2k^2 + 6t)$

5.5 *Complete the factoring by filling in the parentheses.*

65. $3x - 6 = 3($ $)$

66. $7x^2 - x = x($ $)$

67. $4a - 20 = -4($ $)$

68. $w^2 - w = -w($ $)$

69. $3w - w^2 = -w($ $)$

70. $3x - 6 = ($ $)(2 - x)$

Factor each polynomial.

71. $y^2 - 81$

72. $r^2t^2 - 9v^2$

73. $4x^2 + 28x + 49$

74. $y^2 - 20y + 100$

75. $t^2 - 18t + 81$

76. $4w^2 + 4ws + s^2$

77. $t^3 - 125$

78. $8y^3 + 1$

5.6 *Factor each polynomial.*

79. $x^2 - 7x - 30$

80. $y^2 + 4y - 32$

81. $w^2 - 3w - 28$

82. $6t^2 - 5t + 1$

83. $2m^2 + 5m - 7$

84. $12x^2 - 17x + 6$

85. $m^7 - 3m^4 - 10m$

86. $6w^5 - 7w^3 - 5w$

5.7 *Factor each polynomial completely.*

87. $5x^3 + 40$

88. $w^3 - 6w^2 + 9w$

89. $9x^2 + 9x + 2$

90. $ax^3 + a$

91. $x^3 + x^2 - x - 1$

92. $16x^2 - 4x - 2$

93. $-x^2y + 16y$

94. $-5m^2 + 5$

95. $-a^3b^2 + 2a^2b^2 - ab^2$

96. $-2w^2 - 16w - 32$

97. $x^3 - x^2 + 9x - 9$

98. $w^4 + 2w^2 - 3$

99. $x^4 - x^2 - 12$

100. $8x^3 - 1$

101. $a^6 - a^3$

102. $a^2 - ab + 2a - 2b$

103. $-8m^2 - 24m - 18$

104. $-3x^2 - 9x + 30$

105. $(2x - 3)^2 - 16$

106. $(m - 6)^2 - (m - 6) - 12$

107. $x^6 + 7x^3 - 8$

108. $32a^5 - 2a$

109. $(a^2 - 9)^2 - 5(a^2 - 9) + 6$

110. $x^3 - 9x + x^2 - 9$

Factor each polynomial completely. Variables used as exponents represent positive integers.

111. $x^{2k} - 49$

112. $x^{6k} - 1$

113. $m^{2a} - 2m^a - 3$

114. $2y^{2n} - 7y^n + 6$

115. $9z^{2k} - 12z^k + 4$

116. $25z^{6m} + 20z^{3m} + 4$

117. $y^{2a} - by^a + cy^a - bc$

118. $x^3y^b - xy^b + 2x^3 - 2x$

5.8 Solve each equation.

119. $x^3 - 5x^2 = 0$

120. $2m^2 + 10m + 12 = 0$

121. $(a - 2)(a - 3) = 6$

122. $(w - 2)(w + 3) = 50$

123. $2m^2 - 9m - 5 = 0$

124. $m^3 + 4m^2 - 9m - 36 = 0$

125. $w^3 + 5w^2 - w - 5 = 0$

126. $12x^2 + 5x - 3 = 0$

127. $|x^2 - 5| = 4$

128. $|x^2 - 3x - 7| = 3$

MISCELLANEOUS

Solve each problem.

129. *Roadrunner and the coyote.* The roadrunner has just taken a position atop a giant saguaro cactus. While positioning a 10-foot Acme ladder against the cactus, Wile E. Coyote notices a warning label on the ladder. For safety, Acme recommends that the distance from the ground to the top of the ladder, measured vertically along the cactus, must be 2 feet longer than the distance between the bottom of the ladder and the cactus. How far from the cactus should he place the bottom of this ladder?

130. *Three consecutive integers.* Find three consecutive integers such that the sum of their squares is 50.

131. *Playground dimensions.* It took 32 meters of fencing to enclose the rectangular playground at Kiddie Kare. If the area of the playground is 63 square meters, then what are its dimensions?

132. *Landscape design.* Rico is planting red tulips in a rectangular flower bed that is 2 feet longer than it is wide. He plans to surround the tulips with a border of daffodils that is 2 feet wide. If the total area is 224 square feet and he plants 36 daffodils per square foot, then how many daffodils does he need?

133. *Panoramic screen.* Engineers are designing a new 25-inch diagonal measure television. The new rectangular screen will have a length that is 17 inches larger than its width. What are the dimensions of the screen?

134. *Less panoramic.* The engineers are also experimenting with a 25-inch diagonal measure television that has a width that is 5 inches less than the length. What are the dimensions of this rectangular screen?

 135. *Life expectancy of black males.* The age at which people die is precisely measured and provides an indication of the health of the population as a whole. The formula

$$L = 64.3(1.0033)^a$$

can be used to model life expectancy L for U.S. black males with present age a (National Center for Health Statistics, www.cdc.gov/nchswww).

a) To what age can a 20-year-old black male expect to live?

b) How many more years is a 20-year-old white male expected to live than a 20-year-old black male? (See Section 5.2 Exercise 95.)

 136. *Life expectancy of black females.* The formula

$$L = 72.9(1.002)^a$$

can be used to model life expectancy for U.S. black females with present age a. How long can a 20-year-old black female expect to live?

 137. *Golden years.* A person earning $80,000 per year should expect to receive 21% of her retirement income from Social Security and the rest from personal savings. To calculate the amount of regular savings, we use the formula

$$S = R \cdot \frac{(1 + i)^n - 1}{i},$$

where S is the amount at the end of n years of n investments of R dollars each year earning interest rate i compounded annually.

a) Use the accompanying graph to estimate the interest rate needed to get an investment of $1 per year for 20 years to amount to $100.

b) Use the formula to determine the annual savings for 20 years that would amount to $500,000 at 7% compounded annually.

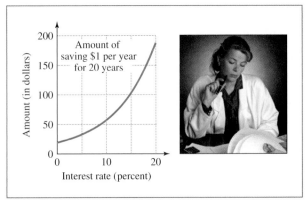

FIGURE FOR EXERCISE 137

 138. *Costly education.* The cost of attending Tulane University for one year is approximately $35,414 (www.tulane.edu). Use the formula in Exercise 137 to find the annual savings for 18 years that would amount to $35,414 with an annual return of 8%.

CHAPTER 5 TEST

Simplify each expression. Assume all variables represent nonzero real numbers. Exponents in your answers should be positive exponents.

1. 3^{-2}

2. $\dfrac{1}{6^{-2}}$

3. $\left(\dfrac{1}{2}\right)^{-3}$

4. $3x^4 \cdot 4x^3$

5. $\dfrac{8y^9}{2y^{-3}}$

6. $(4a^2b)^3$

7. $\left(\dfrac{x^2}{3}\right)^{-3}$

8. $\dfrac{(2^{-1}a^2b)^{-3}}{4a^{-9}}$

Convert to standard notation.

9. 3.24×10^9

10. 8.673×10^{-4}

Perform each computation by converting each number to scientific notation. Give the answer in scientific notation.

11. $\dfrac{(80,000)(0.0006)}{2,000,000}$

12. $\dfrac{(0.00006)^2(500)}{(30,000)^2(0.01)}$

Perform the indicated operations.

13. $(3x^3 - x^2 + 6) + (4x^2 - 2x - 3)$

14. $(x^2 - 6x - 7) - (3x^2 + 2x - 4)$

15. $(x^2 - 3x + 7)(x - 2)$

16. $(x - 2)^3$

Find the products.

17. $(x - 7)(2x + 3)$

18. $(x - 6)^2$

19. $(2x + 5)^2$

20. $(3y^2 - 5)(3y^2 + 5)$

Factor completely.

21. $a^2 - 2a - 24$

22. $4x^2 + 28x + 49$

23. $3m^3 - 24$

24. $2x^2y - 32y$

25. $12m^2 + 28m + 15$

26. $2x^{10} + 5x^5 - 12$

27. $2xa + 3a - 10x - 15$

28. $x^4 + 3x^2 - 4$

Solve each equation.

29. $2m^2 + 7m - 15 = 0$

30. $x^3 - 4x = 0$

31. $|x^2 + x - 9| = 3$

Write a complete solution for each problem.

32. A portable television is advertised as having a 10-inch diagonal measure screen. If the width of the screen is 2 inches more than the height, then what are the dimensions of the screen?

33. The infant mortality rate for the United States, the number of deaths per 100,000 live births, has decreased dramatically since 1950. The formula

$$d = (1.8 \times 10^{28})(1.032)^{-y}$$

gives the infant mortality rate d as a function of the year y (National Center for Health Statistics, www.cdc.gov/nchswww). Find the infant mortality rates in 1950, 1990, and 2000.

34. If a boy uses a slingshot to propel a stone straight upward, then the height $h(t)$ of the stone in feet at time t in seconds is given by

$$h(t) = -16t^2 + 80t.$$

a) What is the height of the stone at 2 seconds and at 3 seconds?

b) For how long is the stone in the air?

35. *Room dimensions.* The perimeter of the den in the Bailey's house is 88 feet. If the area is 480 square feet, then what are the dimensions of this rectangular room?

Simplify each expression.

1. 4^2

2. $4(-2)$

3. 4^{-2}

4. $2^3 \cdot 4^{-1}$

5. $2^{-1} + 2^{-1}$

6. $2^{-1} \cdot 3^{-1}$

7. $3^{-1} - 2^{-2}$

8. $3^2 - 4(5)(-2)$

9. $2^7 - 2^6$

10. $0.08(32) + 0.08(68)$

11. $3 - 2|5 - 7 \cdot 3|$

12. $5^{-1} + 6^{-1}$

Solve each equation.

13. $0.05a - 0.04(a - 50) = 4$

14. $15b - 27 = 0$

15. $2c^2 + 15c - 27 = 0$

16. $2t^2 + 15t = 0$

17. $|15u - 27| = 3$

18. $|15v - 27| = 0$

19. $|15x - 27| = -78$

20. $|x^2 + x - 4| = 2$

21. $(2x - 1)(x + 5) = 0$

22. $|3x - 1| + 6 = 9$

23. $(1.5 \times 10^{-4})w - 5 \times 10^5 = 7 \times 10^6$

24. $(3 \times 10^7)(y - 5 \times 10^3) = 6 \times 10^{12}$

Solve each problem.

25. *Negative income tax.* In a negative income tax proposal, the function

$$D = 0.75E + 5000$$

is used to determine the disposable income D (the amount available for spending) for an earned income E (the amount earned). If $E > D$, then the difference is paid in federal taxes. If $D > E$, then the difference is paid to the wage earner by Uncle Sam.

a) Find the amount of tax paid by a person who earns $100,000.

b) Find the amount received from Uncle Sam by a person who earns $10,000.

c) The accompanying graph shows the lines $D = 0.75E + 5000$ and $D = E$. Find the intersection of these lines.

d) How much tax does a person pay whose earned income is at the intersection found in part (c)?

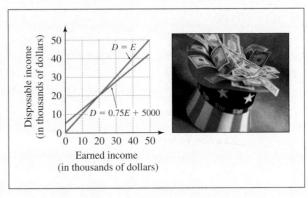

FIGURE FOR EXERCISE 25

Rational Expressions and Functions

Helpful

Most students lea
into $\frac{4}{6}$ by dividing
and then multiply
In algebra it is bett
version by multipl
tor and denomin
shown here.

Information is everywhere—in the newspapers and magazines we read, the televisions we watch, and the computers we use. And now people are talking about the Information Superhighway, which will deliver vast amounts of information directly to consumers' homes. In the future the combination of telephone, television, and computer will give us on-the-spot health care recommendations, video conferences, home shopping, and perhaps even electronic voting and driver's license renewal, to name just a few. There is even talk of 500 television channels!

Some experts are concerned that the consumer will give up privacy for this technology. Others worry about regulation, access, and content of the enormous international computer network.

Whatever the future of this technology, few people understand how all their electronic devices work. However, this vast array of electronics rests on physical principles, which are described by mathematical formulas. In Exercises 49 and 50 of Section 6.7 we will see that the formula governing resistance for receivers connected in parallel involves rational expressions, which are the subject of this chapter.

C A U T I O N Although it is true that

$$\frac{5}{6} = \frac{2 + 3}{2 + 4},$$

we cannot divide out the 2's in this expression because the 2's are not factors. We can divide out only common *factors* when reducing fractions.

Just as a rational number has infinitely many equivalent forms, a rational expression also has infinitely many equivalent forms. To reduce rational expressions to lowest terms, we follow exactly the same procedure as we do for rational numbers: *Factor the numerator and denominator completely, then divide out all common factors.*

E X A M P L E 2 Reducing

Reduce each rational expression to its lowest terms.

a) $\dfrac{18}{42}$

b) $\dfrac{-2a^7 b}{a^2 b^3}$

Helpful Hint

A negative sign in a fraction can be placed in three locations:

$$\frac{-1}{2} = \frac{1}{-2} = -\frac{1}{2}$$

The same goes for rational expressions:

$$\frac{-3x^2}{5y} = \frac{3x^2}{-5y} = -\frac{3x^2}{5y}$$

Solution

a) Factor 18 as $2 \cdot 3^2$ and 42 as $2 \cdot 3 \cdot 7$:

$$\frac{18}{42} = \frac{2 \cdot 3^2}{2 \cdot 3 \cdot 7} \qquad \text{Factor.}$$

$$= \frac{3}{7} \qquad \text{Divide out the common factors.}$$

b) Because this expression is already factored, we use the quotient rule for exponents to reduce:

$$\frac{-2a^7 b}{a^2 b^3} = \frac{-2a^5}{b^2}$$

∎

In Example 3 we use the techniques for factoring polynomials that we learned in Chapter 5.

E X A M P L E 3 Reducing

Reduce each rational expression to its lowest terms.

a) $\dfrac{2x^2 - 18}{x^2 + x - 6}$

b) $\dfrac{w - 2}{2 - w}$

c) $\dfrac{2a^3 - 16}{16 - 4a^2}$

Solution

a) $\dfrac{2x^2 - 18}{x^2 + x - 6} = \dfrac{2(x^2 - 9)}{(x - 2)(x + 3)} \qquad \text{Factor.}$

$$= \frac{2(x - 3)(x + 3)}{(x - 2)(x + 3)} \qquad \text{Factor completely.}$$

$$= \frac{2x - 6}{x - 2} \qquad \text{Divide out the common factors.}$$

b) Factor out -1 from the numerator to get a common factor:

$$\frac{w - 2}{2 - w} = \frac{-1(2 - w)}{(2 - w)} = -1$$

c) $\dfrac{2a^3 - 16}{16 - 4a^2} = \dfrac{2(a^3 - 8)}{-4(a^2 - 4)}$ Factoring out -4 will give the common factor $a - 2$.

$$= \frac{2(a - 2)(a^2 + 2a + 4)}{-2 \cdot 2(a - 2)(a + 2)} \qquad \text{Difference of two cubes, difference of two squares}$$

$$= -\frac{a^2 + 2a + 4}{2a + 4} \qquad \text{Divide out common factors.} \qquad ■$$

The rational expressions in Example 3(a) are equivalent because they have the same value for any replacement of the variables, provided that the replacement is in the domain of both expressions. In other words, the equation

$$\frac{2x^2 - 18}{x^2 + x - 6} = \frac{2x - 6}{x - 2}$$

is an identity. It is true for any value of x except 2 and -3.

The main points to remember for reducing rational expressions are summarized as follows.

Study Tip

Studying in a quiet place is better than studying in a noisy place. There are very few people who can listen to music or a conversation and study at the same time.

Helpful Hint

Since $-1(a - b) = b - a$, placement of a negative sign in a rational expression changes the appearance of the expression:

$$-\frac{3 - x}{x - 2} = \frac{-(3 - x)}{x - 2}$$
$$= \frac{x - 3}{x - 2}$$
$$-\frac{3 - x}{x - 2} = \frac{3 - x}{-(x - 2)}$$
$$= \frac{3 - x}{2 - x}$$

> ### Strategy for Reducing Rational Expressions
>
> **1.** All reducing is done by dividing out common factors.
>
> **2.** Factor the numerator and denominator completely to see the common factors.
>
> **3.** Use the quotient rule to reduce a ratio of two monomials involving exponents.
>
> **4.** We may have to factor out a common factor with a negative sign to get identical factors in the numerator and denominator.

Building Up the Denominator

In Section 6.3 we will see that only rational expressions with identical denominators can be added or subtracted. Fractions without identical denominators can be converted to equivalent fractions with a common denominator by reversing the procedure for reducing fractions to lowest terms. This procedure is called **building up the denominator.**

Consider converting the fraction $\frac{1}{3}$ into an equivalent fraction with a denominator of 51. Any fraction that is equivalent to $\frac{1}{3}$ can be obtained by multiplying the numerator and denominator of $\frac{1}{3}$ by the same nonzero number. Because $51 = 3 \cdot 17$, we multiply the numerator and denominator of $\frac{1}{3}$ by 17 to get an equivalent fraction with a denominator of 51:

$$\frac{1}{3} = \frac{1}{3} \cdot 1 = \frac{1}{3} \cdot \frac{17}{17} = \frac{17}{51}$$

E X A M P L E   4

Building up the denominator

Convert each rational expression into an equivalent rational expression that has the indicated denominator.

a) $\dfrac{2}{7}, \dfrac{?}{42}$ **b)** $\dfrac{5}{3a^2b}, \dfrac{?}{9a^3b^4}$

Solution

a) Factor 42 as $42 = 2 \cdot 3 \cdot 7$, then multiply the numerator and denominator of $\frac{2}{7}$ by the missing factors, 2 and 3:

$$\frac{2}{7} = \frac{2 \cdot 2 \cdot 3}{7 \cdot 2 \cdot 3} = \frac{12}{42}$$

b) Because $9a^3b^4 = 3ab^3 \cdot 3a^2b$, we multiply the numerator and denominator by $3ab^3$:

$$\frac{5}{3a^2b} = \frac{5 \cdot 3ab^3}{3a^2b \cdot 3ab^3}$$
$$= \frac{15ab^3}{9a^3b^4}$$

When building up a denominator to match a more complicated denominator, we factor both denominators completely to see which factors are missing from the simpler denominator. Then we multiply the numerator and denominator of the simpler expression by the missing factors.

E X A M P L E   5

Building up the denominator

Convert each rational expression into an equivalent rational expression that has the indicated denominator.

a) $\dfrac{5}{2a - 2b}, \dfrac{?}{6b - 6a}$ **b)** $\dfrac{x + 2}{x + 3}, \dfrac{?}{x^2 + 7x + 12}$

Solution

a) Factor both $2a - 2b$ and $6b - 6a$ to see which factor is missing in $2a - 2b$. Note that we factor out -6 from $6b - 6a$ to get the factor $a - b$:

$$2a - 2b = 2(a - b)$$
$$6b - 6a = -6(a - b) = -3 \cdot 2(a - b)$$

Now multiply the numerator and denominator by the missing factor, -3:

$$\frac{5}{2a - 2b} = \frac{5(-3)}{(2a - 2b)(-3)} = \frac{-15}{6b - 6a}$$

b) Because $x^2 + 7x + 12 = (x + 3)(x + 4)$, multiply the numerator and denominator by $x + 4$:

$$\frac{x + 2}{x + 3} = \frac{(x + 2)(x + 4)}{(x + 3)(x + 4)} = \frac{x^2 + 6x + 8}{x^2 + 7x + 12}$$

Rational Functions

A rational expression can be used to determine the value of a variable. For example, if

$$y = \frac{3x - 1}{x^2 - 4},$$

then we say that y is a **rational function** of x. We can also use function notation as shown in Example 6. The domain of a rational function is the same as the domain of the rational expression used to define the function.

E X A M P L E 6

Evaluating a rational function

Find $R(3)$, $R(-1)$, and $R(2)$ for the rational function

$$R(x) = \frac{3x - 1}{x^2 - 4}.$$

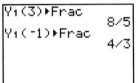

Calculator Close-Up

To check, use Y= to enter

$y_1 = (3x - 1)/(x^2 - 4)$.

Then use the variables feature (VARS) to find $y_1(3)$ and $y_1(-1)$.

```
Y₁(3)▸Frac
              8/5
Y₁(-1)▸Frac
              4/3
```

Solution

To find $R(3)$, replace x by 3 in the formula:

$$R(3) = \frac{3 \cdot 3 - 1}{3^2 - 4} = \frac{8}{5}$$

To find $R(-1)$, replace x by -1 in the formula:

$$R(-1) = \frac{3(-1) - 1}{(-1)^2 - 4}$$

$$= \frac{-4}{-3} = \frac{4}{3}$$

We cannot find $R(2)$ because 2 is not in the domain of the rational expression. ∎

Applications

A rational expression can occur in finding an average cost. The average cost of making a product is the total cost divided by the number of products made.

E X A M P L E 7

Average cost function

A car maker spent $700 million to develop a new SUV, which will sell for $40,000. If the cost of manufacturing the SUV is $30,000 each, then what rational function gives the average cost of developing and manufacturing x vehicles? Compare the average cost per vehicle for manufacturing levels of 10,000 vehicles and 100,000 vehicles.

Solution

The polynomial $30,000x + 700,000,000$ gives the cost in dollars of developing and manufacturing x vehicles. The average cost per vehicle is given by the rational function

$$AC(x) = \frac{30,000x + 700,000,000}{x}.$$

If $x = 10,000$, then

$$AC(10,000) = \frac{30,000(10,000) + 700,000,000}{10,000} = 100,000.$$

If $x = 100,000$, then

$$AC(100,000) = \frac{30,000(100,000) + 700,000,000}{100,000} = 37,000.$$

The average cost per vehicle when 10,000 vehicles are made is $100,000, whereas the average cost per vehicle when 100,000 vehicles are made is $37,000. ∎

True or false? Explain.

1. A rational number is a rational expression.
2. The expression $\frac{2 + x}{x - 1}$ is a rational expression.
3. The domain of the rational expression $\frac{3}{x - 2}$ is $\{2\}$.
4. The domain of $\frac{2x + 5}{(x - 9)(2x + 1)}$ is $\left\{x \mid x \neq 9 \text{ and } x \neq -\frac{1}{2}\right\}$.
5. The domain of $\frac{x - 1}{x + 2}$ is $(-\infty, -2) \cup (-2, 1) \cup (1, \infty)$.
6. The rational expression $\frac{5x + 2}{15}$ reduces to $\frac{x + 2}{3}$.
7. Multiplying the numerator and denominator of $\frac{x}{x - 1}$ by x yields $\frac{x^2}{x^2 - 1}$.
8. The expression $\frac{2}{3 - x}$ is equivalent to $\frac{-2}{x - 3}$.
9. The equation $\frac{4x^3}{6x} = \frac{2x^2}{3}$ is an identity.
10. The expression $\frac{x^2 - y^2}{x - y}$ reduced to its lowest terms is $x - y$.

6.1 EXERCISES

Reading and Writing *After reading this section, write out the answers to these questions. Use complete sentences.*

1. What is a rational expression?

2. What is the domain of a rational expression?

3. What is the basic principle of rational numbers?

4. How do we reduce a rational expression to lowest terms?

5. How do you build up the denominator of a rational expression?

6. What is average cost?

Find the domain of each rational expression. See Example 1.

7. $\frac{3x}{x - 1}$

8. $\frac{x}{x + 5}$

9. $\frac{2z - 5}{7z}$

10. $\frac{z - 12}{4z}$

11. $\frac{5y - 1}{y^2 - 4}$

12. $\frac{2y - 1}{y^2 - 9}$

13. $\frac{2a - 3}{a^2 + 5a + 6}$

14. $\frac{3b + 1}{b^2 - 3b - 4}$

15. $\frac{x - 1}{x^2 + 4}$

16. $\frac{y + 5}{y^2 + 9}$

17. $\frac{x + 1}{x^3 + x^2 - 6x}$

18. $\frac{x^2 - 3x - 4}{2x^5 - 2x}$

Reduce each rational expression to its lowest terms. See Examples 2 and 3.

19. $\frac{6}{57}$

20. $\frac{14}{91}$

21. $\dfrac{42}{210}$

22. $\dfrac{242}{154}$

23. $\dfrac{2x + 2}{4}$

24. $\dfrac{3a + 3}{3}$

25. $\dfrac{3x - 6y}{10y - 5x}$

26. $\dfrac{5b - 10a}{2a - b}$

27. $\dfrac{ab^2}{a^3b}$

28. $\dfrac{36y^3z^8}{54y^2z^9}$

29. $\dfrac{-2w^2x^3y}{6wx^5y^2}$

30. $\dfrac{6a^3b^{12}c^5}{-8ab^4c^9}$

31. $\dfrac{a^3b^2}{a^3 + a^4}$

32. $\dfrac{b^8 - ab^5}{ab^5}$

33. $\dfrac{a - b}{2b - 2a}$

34. $\dfrac{2m - 2n}{4n - 4m}$

35. $\dfrac{3x + 6}{3x}$

36. $\dfrac{7x - 14}{7x}$

37. $\dfrac{a^3 - b^3}{a - b}$

38. $\dfrac{27x^3 + y^3}{6x + 2y}$

39. $\dfrac{4x^2 - 4}{4x^2 + 4}$

40. $\dfrac{2a^2 - 2b^2}{2a^2 + 2b^2}$

41. $\dfrac{12x^2 - 26x - 10}{4x^2 - 25}$

42. $\dfrac{9x^2 - 15x - 6}{81x^2 - 9}$

43. $\dfrac{x^3 + 7x^2 - 4x}{x^3 - 16x}$

44. $\dfrac{2x^4 - 32}{4x - 8}$

45. $\dfrac{2ab + 2by + 3a + 3y}{2b^2 - 7b - 15}$

46. $\dfrac{3m^2 + 3mn + m + n}{12m^2 - 5m - 3}$

47. $\dfrac{4x^2 - 10x - 6}{2x^2 + 11x + 5}$

48. $\dfrac{6x^2 + x - 1}{8x^2 - 2x - 3}$

49. $\dfrac{2a^2 + 5ab + 3b^2}{4a^2 + 12ab + 9b^2}$

50. $\dfrac{3x^2 + 2xy - y^2}{9x^2 - 6xy + y^2}$

Convert each rational expression into an equivalent rational expression that has the indicated denominator. See Examples 4 and 5.

51. $\dfrac{1}{5}, \dfrac{?}{50}$

52. $\dfrac{2}{3}, \dfrac{?}{9}$

53. $\dfrac{1}{xy}, \dfrac{?}{3x^2y^3}$

54. $\dfrac{3}{ab^2}, \dfrac{?}{a^3b^5}$

55. $\dfrac{5}{x - 1}, \dfrac{?}{x^2 - 2x + 1}$

56. $\dfrac{7}{2x + 1}, \dfrac{?}{4x^2 + 4x + 1}$

57. $\dfrac{3}{2x - 5}, \dfrac{?}{4x^2 - 25}$

58. $\dfrac{x}{x - 3}, \dfrac{?}{x^2 - 9}$

59. $\dfrac{1}{2x + 2}, \dfrac{?}{-6x - 6}$

60. $\dfrac{-2}{-3x + 4}, \dfrac{?}{15x - 20}$

61. $5, \dfrac{?}{a}$

62. $3, \dfrac{?}{a + 1}$

63. $\dfrac{x + 2}{x + 3}, \dfrac{?}{x^2 + 2x - 3}$

64. $\dfrac{x}{x - 5}, \dfrac{?}{x^2 - x - 20}$

65. $\dfrac{7}{x - 1}, \dfrac{?}{1 - x}$

66. $\dfrac{1}{a - b}, \dfrac{?}{2b - 2a}$

67. $\dfrac{3}{x + 2}, \dfrac{?}{x^3 + 8}$

68. $\dfrac{x}{x - 2}, \dfrac{?}{x^3 - 8}$

69. $\dfrac{x+2}{3x-1}, \dfrac{?}{6x^2+13x-5}$ **70.** $\dfrac{a}{2a+1}, \dfrac{?}{4a^2-16a-9}$

91. $\dfrac{3a+3}{3a} = \dfrac{?}{a}$ **92.** $\dfrac{x-3}{x^2-9} = \dfrac{1}{?}$

Find the indicated value for each given rational expression, if possible. See Example 6.

71. $R(x) = \dfrac{3x-5}{x+4}, \ R(3)$

72. $T(x) = \dfrac{5-x}{x-5}, \ T(-9)$

73. $H(y) = \dfrac{y^2-5}{3y-4}, \ H(-2)$

74. $G(a) = \dfrac{3-5a}{2a+7}, \ G(5)$

75. $W(b) = \dfrac{4b^3-1}{b^2-b-6}, \ W(-2)$

76. $N(x) = \dfrac{x+3}{x^3-2x^2-2x-3}, \ N(3)$

In place of each question mark in Exercises 77–94, put an expression that will make the rational expressions equivalent.

77. $\dfrac{1}{3} = \dfrac{?}{21}$ **78.** $4 = \dfrac{?}{3}$

79. $5 = \dfrac{10}{?}$ **80.** $\dfrac{3}{4} = \dfrac{12}{?}$

81. $\dfrac{3}{a} = \dfrac{?}{a^2}$ **82.** $\dfrac{5}{y} = \dfrac{10}{?}$

83. $\dfrac{2}{a-b} = \dfrac{?}{b-a}$ **84.** $\dfrac{3}{x-4} = \dfrac{?}{4-x}$

85. $\dfrac{2}{x-1} = \dfrac{?}{x^2-1}$ **86.** $\dfrac{5}{x+3} = \dfrac{?}{x^2-9}$

87. $\dfrac{2}{w-3} = \dfrac{-2}{?}$ **88.** $\dfrac{-2}{5-x} = \dfrac{2}{?}$

89. $\dfrac{2x+4}{6} = \dfrac{?}{3}$ **90.** $\dfrac{2x-3}{4x-6} = \dfrac{1}{?}$

93. $\dfrac{1}{x-1} = \dfrac{?}{x^3-1}$ **94.** $\dfrac{x^2+2x+4}{x+2} = \dfrac{?}{x^2-4}$

Reduce each rational expression to its lowest terms. Variables used in exponents represent integers.

95. $\dfrac{x^{2a}-4}{x^a+2}$ **96.** $\dfrac{x^{2b}+3x^b-18}{x^{2b}-36}$

97. $\dfrac{x^a+m+wx^a+wm}{x^{2a}-m^2}$ **98.** $\dfrac{x^{3a}-8}{x^{2a}+2x^a+4}$

99. $\dfrac{x^{3b+1}-x}{x^{2b+1}-x}$ **100.** $\dfrac{2x^{2a+1}+3x^{a+1}+x}{4x^{2a+1}-x}$

Solve each problem. See Example 7.

101. *Driving speed.* If Jeremy drives 500 miles in $2x$ hours, then what rational expression represents his speed in miles per hour (mph)?

102. *Filing suit.* If Marsha files 48 suits in $2x + 2$ work days, then what rational expression represents the rate (in suits per day) at which she is filing suits?

103. *Wedding bells.* Wheeler Printing Co. charges $45 plus $0.50 per invitation to print wedding invitations.
 a) Write a rational function that gives the average cost in dollars per invitation for printing n invitations.

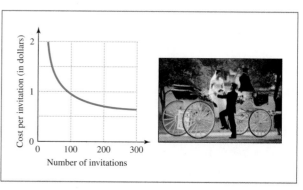

FIGURE FOR EXERCISE 103

b) How much less does it cost per invitation to print 300 invitations rather than 200 invitations?

c) As the number of invitations increases, does the average cost per invitation increase or decrease?

d) As the number of invitations increases, does the total cost of the invitations increase or decrease?

104. *Rose Bowl bound.* A travel agent offers a Rose Bowl package including hotel, tickets, and transportation. It costs the travel agent $50,000 plus $300 per person to charter the airplane. Find a rational function that gives the average cost in dollars per person for the charter flight. How much lower is the average cost per person when 200 people go compared to 100 people?

 105. *Solid waste recovery.* The amount of municipal solid waste generated in the United States in the year 1960 + n is given by the polynomial

$$3.43n + 87.24,$$

whereas the amount recycled is given by the polynomial

$$0.053n^2 - 0.64n + 6.71,$$

where the amounts are in millions of tons (U.S. Environmental Protection Agency, www.epa.gov).

a) Write a rational function $p(n)$ that gives the fraction of solid waste that is recovered in the year 1960 + n.

b) Find $p(0)$, $p(30)$, and $p(50)$.

106. *Higher education.* The total number of degrees awarded in U.S. higher education in the year 1990 + n is given in thousands by the polynomial $41.7n + 1429$, whereas the number of bachelor's degrees awarded is given in thousands by the polynomial $25.2n + 1069$ (National Center for Education Statistics, www.nces.ed.gov).

a) Write a rational function $p(n)$ that gives the percentage of bachelor's degrees among the total number of degrees conferred for the year 1990 + n.

b) What percentage of the degrees awarded in 2010 will be bachelor's degrees?

GETTING MORE INVOLVED

107. *Exploration.* Use a calculator to find $R(2)$, $R(30)$, $R(500)$, $R(9,000)$, and $R(80,000)$ for the rational expression

$$R(x) = \frac{x - 3}{2x + 1}.$$

Round answers to four decimal places. What can you conclude about the value of $R(x)$ as x gets larger and larger without bound?

108. *Exploration.* Use a calculator to find $H(1,000)$, $H(100,000)$, $H(1,000,000)$, and $H(10,000,000)$ for the rational expression

$$H(x) = \frac{7x - 50}{3x + 91}.$$

Round answers to four decimal places. What can you conclude about the value of $H(x)$ as x gets larger and larger without bound?

In This Section

- Multiplying Rational Expressions
- Dividing $a - b$ by $b - a$
- Dividing Rational Expressions

6.2 # MULTIPLICATION AND DIVISION

In Chapter 5 you learned to add, subtract, multiply, and divide polynomials. In this chapter you will learn to perform the same operations with rational expressions. We begin in this section with multiplication and division.

Multiplying Rational Expressions

We multiply two rational numbers by multiplying their numerators and multiplying their denominators. For example,

$$\frac{6}{7} \cdot \frac{14}{15} = \frac{84}{105} = \frac{21 \cdot 4}{21 \cdot 5} = \frac{4}{5}.$$

Instead of reducing the rational number after multiplying, it is often easier to reduce before multiplying. We first factor all terms, then divide out the common factors, then multiply:

$$\frac{6}{7} \cdot \frac{14}{15} = \frac{2 \cdot 3 \cdot 2 \cdot 7}{7 \cdot 3 \cdot 5} = \frac{4}{5}$$

When we multiply rational numbers, we use the following definition.

Multiplication of Rational Numbers

If $\frac{a}{b}$ and $\frac{c}{d}$ are rational numbers, then $\frac{a}{b} \cdot \frac{c}{d} = \frac{ac}{bd}$.

We multiply rational expressions in the same way that we multiply rational numbers: Factor all polynomials, divide out the common factors, then multiply the remaining factors.

EXAMPLE 1

Multiplying rational expressions

Find each product of rational expressions.

a) $\dfrac{3a^8b^3}{6b} \cdot \dfrac{10a}{a^2b^6}$

b) $\dfrac{x^2 + 7x + 12}{x^2 + 3x} \cdot \dfrac{x^2}{x^2 - 16}$

Solution

a) First factor the coefficients in each numerator and denominator:

$$\frac{3a^8b^3}{6b} \cdot \frac{10a}{a^2b^6} = \frac{3a^8b^3}{2 \cdot 3b} \cdot \frac{2 \cdot 5a}{a^2b^6} \qquad \text{Factor.}$$

$$= \frac{5a^9b^3}{a^2b^7} \qquad \text{Divide out the common factors.}$$

$$= \frac{5a^7}{b^4} \qquad \text{Quotient rule}$$

b) $\dfrac{x^2 + 7x + 12}{x^2 + 3x} \cdot \dfrac{x^2}{x^2 - 16} = \dfrac{(x+3)(x+4)}{x(x+3)} \cdot \dfrac{x \cdot x}{(x-4)(x+4)} = \dfrac{x}{x-4}$ ∎

CAUTION Do not attempt to divide out the x in $\frac{x}{x-4}$. This expression cannot be reduced because x is not a factor of *both* terms in the denominator. Compare this expression to the following:

$$\frac{3x}{x - xy} = \frac{x \cdot 3}{x(1 - y)} = \frac{3}{1 - y}$$

In Example 2(a) we will multiply a rational expression and a polynomial. For Example 2(b) we will use the rule for factoring the difference of two cubes.

EXAMPLE 2

Multiplying rational expressions

Find each product.

a) $(a^2 - 1) \cdot \dfrac{6}{2a^2 + 4a + 2}$

b) $\dfrac{a^3 - b^3}{b - a} \cdot \dfrac{6}{2a^2 + 2ab + 2b^2}$

Solution

a) First factor the polynomials completely:

$$(a^2 - 1) \cdot \frac{6}{2a^2 + 4a + 2} = \frac{(a + 1)(a - 1)}{1} \cdot \frac{2 \cdot 3}{2(a + 1)(a + 1)}$$

$$= \frac{3(a - 1)}{a + 1} \quad \text{Divide out the common factors.}$$

$$= \frac{3a - 3}{a + 1} \quad \text{Multiply.}$$

b) First factor the polynomials completely:

$$\frac{a^3 - b^3}{b - a} \cdot \frac{6}{2a^2 + 2ab + 2b^2} = \frac{(a - b)(a^2 + ab + b^2)}{b - a} \cdot \frac{2 \cdot 3}{2(a^2 + ab + b^2)}$$

$$= \frac{(a - b)3}{b - a}$$

$$= \frac{-1(b - a)3}{b - a} \quad \begin{array}{l}\text{Factor out } -1 \text{ to get}\\ \text{a common } b - a.\end{array}$$

$$= -3 \quad \blacksquare$$

Dividing $a - b$ by $b - a$

Since $a - b = -1(b - a)$ we have $\frac{a-b}{b-a} = -1$. So instead of factoring out -1 as in Example 2(b) we can simply divide $a - b$ by $b - a$ to get -1 as shown in Example 3.

E X A M P L E 3

Dividing $a - b$ by $b - a$

Find the product:

$$\frac{m - 4}{3} \cdot \frac{6}{4 - m}$$

Solution

Instead of factoring out -1 from $m - 4$, we divide $m - 4$ by $4 - m$ to get -1:

$$\frac{m - 4}{3} \cdot \frac{6}{4 - m} = \frac{\overset{-1}{m - 4}}{3} \cdot \frac{\overset{2}{6}}{4 - m} \quad \text{Note that } (m - 4) \div (4 - m) = -1.$$

$$= -2 \quad \blacksquare$$

Dividing Rational Expressions

We divide rational numbers by multiplying by the reciprocal or multiplicative inverse of the divisor. For example,

$$\frac{3}{4} \div \frac{15}{2} = \frac{3}{4} \cdot \frac{2}{15} = \frac{3}{2 \cdot 2} \cdot \frac{2 \cdot 1}{3 \cdot 5} = \frac{1}{10}.$$

When we divide rational numbers, we use the following definition.

Division of Rational Numbers

If $\frac{a}{b}$ and $\frac{c}{d}$ are rational numbers with $\frac{c}{d} \neq 0$, then

$$\frac{a}{b} \div \frac{c}{d} = \frac{a}{b} \cdot \frac{d}{c}.$$

We use the same method to divide rational expressions: We invert the divisor and multiply.

E X A M P L E   4   **Dividing rational expressions**

Find each quotient.

a) $\dfrac{10}{3x} \div \dfrac{6}{5x}$

b) $\dfrac{5a^2b^8}{c^3} \div (4ab^3c)$

Solution

a) The reciprocal of the divisor $\dfrac{6}{5x}$ is $\dfrac{5x}{6}$.

$$\frac{10}{3x} \div \frac{6}{5x} = \frac{10}{3x} \cdot \frac{5x}{6} \qquad \text{Invert and multiply.}$$

$$= \frac{2 \cdot 5}{3x} \cdot \frac{5x}{2 \cdot 3} = \frac{25}{9}$$

b) The reciprocal of $4ab^3c$ is $\dfrac{1}{4ab^3c}$.

$$\frac{5a^2b^8}{c^3} \div (4ab^3c) = \frac{5a^2b^8}{c^3} \cdot \frac{1}{4ab^3c} = \frac{5ab^5}{4c^4} \qquad \text{Quotient rule}$$

In Example 5 we factor the polynomials in the rational expressions.

E X A M P L E   5   **Dividing rational expressions**

Find the quotient:

$$\frac{25 - x^2}{x^2 + x} \div \frac{x - 5}{x^2 - 1}$$

Solution

$$\frac{25 - x^2}{x^2 + x} \div \frac{x - 5}{x^2 - 1} = \frac{25 - x^2}{x^2 + x} \cdot \frac{x^2 - 1}{x - 5} \qquad \text{Invert and multiply.}$$

$$= \frac{\overset{-1}{(5 - x)}(5 + x)}{x(x + 1)} \cdot \frac{(x + 1)(x - 1)}{x - 5} \qquad (5 - x) \div (x - 5) = -1.$$

$$= \frac{-1(5 + x)(x - 1)}{x} \qquad \begin{array}{l}\text{Divide out the common}\\\text{factors.}\end{array}$$

$$= \frac{-x^2 - 4x + 5}{x} \qquad \begin{array}{l}\text{Multiply the factors}\\\text{in the numerator.}\end{array}$$

CAUTION   When dividing rational expressions, you can factor the polynomials at any time, but do not reduce until after you have inverted the divisor.

In Example 6 division is indicated by a fraction bar.

E X A M P L E   6   **Dividing rational expressions**

Perform the operations indicated.

a) $\dfrac{\dfrac{a + b}{3}}{\dfrac{1}{2}}$

b) $\dfrac{\dfrac{x^2 - 4}{2}}{\dfrac{x - 2}{3}}$

c) $\dfrac{\dfrac{m^2 + 1}{5}}{3}$

Solution

a) $\dfrac{\frac{a+b}{3}}{\frac{1}{2}} = \dfrac{a+b}{3} \div \dfrac{1}{2}$

$= \dfrac{a+b}{3} \cdot \dfrac{2}{1}$ Invert the divisor.

$= \dfrac{2a+2b}{3}$ Multiply.

b) $\dfrac{\frac{x^2-4}{2}}{\frac{x-2}{3}} = \dfrac{x^2-4}{2} \cdot \dfrac{3}{x-2}$ Invert and multiply.

$= \dfrac{(x-2)(x+2)}{2} \cdot \dfrac{3}{x-2}$ Factor.

$= \dfrac{3x+6}{2}$ Reduce.

c) $\dfrac{\frac{m^2+1}{5}}{3} = \dfrac{m^2+1}{5} \cdot \dfrac{1}{3} = \dfrac{m^2+1}{15}$ Multiply by $\frac{1}{3}$, the reciprocal of 3.

WARM-UPS

True or false? Explain.

1. We can multiply only fractions that have identical denominators.

2. $\frac{2}{7} \cdot \frac{3}{7} = \frac{6}{7}$

3. To divide rational expressions, invert the divisor and multiply.

4. $a \div b = \frac{1}{a} \cdot b$ for any nonzero a and b.

5. $\frac{1}{2x} \cdot 8x^2 = 4x$ for any nonzero real number x.

6. One-half of one-third is one-sixth.

7. One-third divided by one-half is two-thirds.

8. The quotient of $w-z$ divided by $z-w$ is -1, provided that $z-w \neq 0$.

9. $\frac{x}{3} \div 2 = \frac{x}{6}$ for any real number x.

10. $\frac{a}{b} \div \frac{b}{a} = 1$ for any nonzero real numbers a and b.

6.2   EXERCISES

Reading and Writing   *After reading this section, write out the answers to these questions. Use complete sentences.*

1. How do you multiply rational numbers?

2. What is the procedure for multiplying rational expressions?

3. What is the relationship between $a - b$ and $b - a$?

4. How do we divide rational numbers?

In Exercises 5–20, perform the indicated operations. See Examples 1–3.

5. $\dfrac{12}{42} \cdot \dfrac{35}{22}$

6. $\dfrac{3}{8} \cdot \dfrac{20}{21}$

7. $\dfrac{3a}{10b} \cdot \dfrac{5b^2}{6}$

8. $\dfrac{3x}{7y} \cdot \dfrac{14y^2}{9x}$

9. $\dfrac{3x - 3}{6} \cdot \dfrac{x}{x^2 - x}$

10. $\dfrac{-2x - 4}{2} \cdot \dfrac{6}{3x + 6}$

11. $\dfrac{10x + 5}{5x^2 + 5} \cdot \dfrac{2x^2 + x - 1}{4x^2 - 1}$

12. $\dfrac{x^3 + x}{5} \cdot \dfrac{5x - 5}{x^3 - x}$

13. $\dfrac{ax + aw + bx + bw}{x^2 - w^2} \cdot \dfrac{x - w}{a^2 - b^2}$

14. $\dfrac{3a - 3y}{3a - 3y - ab + by} \cdot \dfrac{b^2 - 9}{6b + 18}$

15. $\dfrac{a^2 - 2a + 4}{a^3 + 8} \cdot \dfrac{(a + 2)^3}{2a + 4}$

16. $\dfrac{w^3 - 1}{(w - 1)^2} \cdot \dfrac{w^2 - 1}{w^2 + w + 1}$

17. $\dfrac{x - 9}{12y} \cdot \dfrac{8y}{9 - x}$

18. $\dfrac{19x^2}{12y - 1} \cdot \dfrac{1 - 12y}{3x}$

19. $(a^2 - 4) \cdot \dfrac{7}{2 - a}$

20. $\dfrac{10x - 4x^2}{4x^2 - 20x + 25} \cdot (2x^3 - 5x^2)$

21. $\dfrac{(3x + 1)^3}{2x - 1} \cdot \dfrac{4x^2 - 4x + 1}{9x^2 + 6x + 1}$

22. $\dfrac{a^2 - 2ab + b^2}{a - b} \cdot \dfrac{(a + b)^3}{a^2 + 2ab + b^2}$

Perform the indicated operations. See Examples 4 and 5.

23. $\dfrac{15}{17} \div \dfrac{10}{17}$

24. $\dfrac{3}{4} \div \dfrac{1}{8}$

25. $\dfrac{36x}{5y} \div \dfrac{20x}{35y}$

26. $\dfrac{18a^3b^4}{c^9} \div \dfrac{12ab^6}{7c^2}$

27. $\dfrac{24a^5b^2}{5c^3} \div (4a^5bc^5)$

28. $\dfrac{60x^9y^2}{z} \div (48x^4y^3)$

29. $(w + 1) \div \dfrac{w^2 - 1}{w}$

30. $(a - 3) \div \dfrac{9 - a^2}{4}$

31. $\dfrac{x - y}{5} \div \dfrac{x^2 - 2xy + y^2}{10}$

32. $\dfrac{x^2 + 6x + 9}{18} \div \dfrac{(x + 3)^2}{36}$

33. $\dfrac{4x - 2}{x^2 - 5x} \div \dfrac{2x^2 + 9x - 5}{x^2 - 25}$

34. $\dfrac{2x^2 - 5x - 12}{6 + 4x} \div \dfrac{x^2 - 16}{2}$

Perform the indicated operations. See Example 6.

35. $\dfrac{\dfrac{x - y}{3}}{\dfrac{1}{6}}$

36. $\dfrac{\dfrac{2a - b}{10}}{\dfrac{1}{5}}$

37. $\dfrac{\dfrac{x^2 - 25}{3}}{\dfrac{x - 5}{6}}$

38. $\dfrac{\dfrac{3x^2 + 3}{5}}{\dfrac{3x + 3}{5}}$

39. $\dfrac{\dfrac{a - b}{2}}{3}$

40. $\dfrac{\dfrac{10}{a + b}}{5}$

41. $\dfrac{\dfrac{a^2 - b^2}{a + b}}{3}$

42. $\dfrac{\dfrac{x^2 + 5x + 6}{x + 2}}{x + 3}$

Perform the indicated operations. When possible write down only the answer.

43. $\dfrac{5x}{2} \div 3$

44. $\dfrac{x}{a} \div 2$

45. $\dfrac{3}{4} \div \dfrac{1}{4}$

46. $\dfrac{1}{4} \div \dfrac{1}{2}$

47. One-half of $\dfrac{1}{6}$

48. One-half of $\dfrac{b}{a}$

49. One-half of $\dfrac{4x}{3}$

50. One-third of $\dfrac{6x}{y}$

51. $(a - b) \div (b - a)$

52. $(a - b) \div (-1)$

53. $\dfrac{x - y}{3} \cdot \dfrac{6}{y - x}$ **54.** $\dfrac{5x - 5y}{x} \cdot \dfrac{1}{x - y}$

55. $\dfrac{2a + 2b}{a} \cdot \dfrac{1}{2}$ **56.** $\dfrac{x - y}{y - x} \cdot \dfrac{1}{2}$

57. $-1\left(\dfrac{9 - x}{2}\right)$ **58.** $\dfrac{-1}{x - 1} \cdot \dfrac{1 - x}{2}$

59. $\dfrac{4}{y - 7} \div \dfrac{2}{7 - y}$ **60.** $\dfrac{1}{3 - m} \div \dfrac{1}{2m - 6}$

61. $\dfrac{a + b}{\frac{1}{2}}$ **62.** $\dfrac{x + 3}{\frac{1}{3}}$

63. $\dfrac{\frac{3x}{5}}{y}$ **64.** $\dfrac{\frac{b^2 - 4a}{2}}{a}$

65. $\dfrac{\frac{3a}{5b}}{2}$ **66.** $\dfrac{\frac{6x}{a}}{x}$

Perform the indicated operations.

67. $\dfrac{3x^2 + 13x - 10}{x} \cdot \dfrac{x^3}{9x^2 - 4} \cdot \dfrac{7x - 35}{x^2 - 25}$

68. $\dfrac{x^2 + 5x + 6}{x} \cdot \dfrac{x^2}{3x + 6} \cdot \dfrac{9}{x^2 - 4}$

69. $\dfrac{(a^2b^3c)^2}{(-2ab^2c)^3} \cdot \dfrac{(a^3b^2c)^3}{(abc)^4}$

70. $\dfrac{(-wy^2)^3}{3w^2y} \cdot \dfrac{(2wy)^2}{4wy^3}$

71. $\dfrac{(2mn)^3}{6mn^2} \div \dfrac{2m^2n^3}{(m^2n)^4}$

72. $\dfrac{(rt)^3}{rt^4} \div \dfrac{(rt^2)^3}{r^2t^3}$

73. $\dfrac{2x^2 + 7x - 15}{4x^2 - 100} \cdot \dfrac{2x^2 - 9x - 5}{4x^2 - 1}$

74. $\dfrac{x^3 + 1}{x^2 - 1} \cdot \dfrac{3x - 3}{x^3 - x^2 + x}$

75. $\dfrac{2h^2 - 5h - 3}{5h^2 - 4h - 1} \div \dfrac{2h^2 + 7h + 3}{h^2 + 2h - 3}$

76. $\dfrac{9w^2 - 64}{3w^2 - 5w - 8} \cdot \dfrac{5w^2 + 3w - 2}{25w^2 - 4}$

77. $\dfrac{9a - 3}{1 - 9a^2} \cdot \dfrac{9a^2 + 6a + 1}{6}$

78. $\dfrac{5 - 10k}{k^2 - 2k} \div \dfrac{2k^2 + 7k - 4}{k^2 + 2k - 8}$

79. $\dfrac{k^2 + 2km + m^2}{k^2 - 2km + m^2} \cdot \dfrac{m^2 + 3m - mk - 3k}{m^2 + mk + 3m + 3k}$

80. $\dfrac{a^2 + 2ab + b^2}{ac + bc - ad - bd} \div \dfrac{ac + ad - bc - bd}{c^2 - d^2}$

Perform the indicated operations. Variables in exponents represent integers.

81. $\dfrac{x^a}{y^2} \cdot \dfrac{y^{b+2}}{x^{2a}}$ **82.** $\dfrac{x^{3a+1}}{y^{2b-3}} \cdot \dfrac{y^{3b+4}}{x^{2a-1}}$

83. $\dfrac{x^{2a} + x^a - 6}{x^{2a} + 6x^a + 9} \div \dfrac{x^{2a} - 4}{x^{2a} + 2x^a - 3}$

84. $\dfrac{w^{2b} + 2w^b - 8}{w^{2b} + 3w^b - 4} \div \dfrac{w^{2b} - w^b - 2}{w^{2b} - 1}$

85. $\dfrac{m^k v^k + 3v^k - 2m^k - 6}{m^{2k} - 9} \cdot \dfrac{m^{2k} - 2m^k - 3}{v^k m^k - 2m^k + 2v^k - 4}$

86. $\dfrac{m^{3k} - 1}{m^{3k} + 1} \cdot \dfrac{m^{2k+1} - m^{k+1} + m}{m^{3k} + m^{2k} + m^k}$

Solve each problem.

87. *School enrollment.* In 2005, $\frac{1}{50}$ of the children enrolled in U.S. schools will be enrolled in private secondary schools (National Center for Education Statistics, www.nces.ed.gov). Use the accompanying figure to determine the percentage of secondary school children who will be in private schools in 2005.

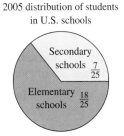

2005 distribution of students in U.S. schools

Secondary schools $\frac{7}{25}$

Elementary schools $\frac{18}{25}$

FIGURE FOR EXERCISE 87

88. *The golden state.* In 2000, $\frac{3}{25}$ of the U.S. population was living in California (U.S. Census Bureau). Use the figure on the next page to determine the percentage of the population of the western region living in California in 2000.

Helpful Hint

The product of 24 and 126 is 3024 and 3024 is a common multiple but not the least common multiple of 24 and 126. If you divide 3024 by 6, the greatest common factor of 24 and 126, you get 504.

Any number that is a multiple of both 24 and 126 must have all of the factors of 24 and all of the factors of 126 in its factored form. So in the LCM we use the factors 2, 3, and 7, and for each factor we use the highest power that appears on that factor. The highest power of 2 is 3, the highest power of 3 is 2, and the highest power of 7 is 1. So the LCM is $2^3 \cdot 3^2 \cdot 7$. If we write this product without exponents, we can see clearly that it is a multiple of both 24 and 126:

$$\underbrace{2 \cdot 2 \cdot \overbrace{2 \cdot 3 \cdot 3 \cdot 7}^{126}}_{24} = 504 \qquad \begin{array}{l} 504 = 126 \cdot 4 \\ 504 = 24 \cdot 21 \end{array}$$

The strategy for finding the LCM for a group of polynomials can be stated as follows.

Strategy for Finding the LCM for Polynomials

1. Factor each polynomial completely. Use exponents to express repeated factors.
2. Write the product of all of the different factors that appear in the polynomials.
3. For each factor, use the highest power of that factor in any of the polynomials.

E X A M P L E   2   **Finding the LCM**

Find the least common multiple for each group of polynomials.

a) $4x^2y$, $6y$ b) a^2bc, ab^3c^2, a^3bc

c) $x^2 + 5x + 6$, $x^2 + 6x + 9$

Solution

a) Factor $4x^2y$ and $6y$ as follows:

$$4x^2y = 2^2 \cdot x^2y, \qquad 6y = 2 \cdot 3y$$

To get the LCM, we use 2, 3, x, and y the maximum number of times that each appears in either of the expressions. The LCM is $2^2 \cdot 3 \cdot x^2y$, or $12x^2y$.

b) The expressions a^2bc, ab^3c^2, and a^3bc are already factored. To get the LCM, we use a, b, and c the maximum number of times that each appears in any of the expressions. The LCM is $a^3b^3c^2$.

c) Factor $x^2 + 5x + 6$ and $x^2 + 6x + 9$ completely:

$$x^2 + 5x + 6 = (x + 2)(x + 3), \qquad x^2 + 6x + 9 = (x + 3)^2$$

The LCM is $(x + 2)(x + 3)^2$. ∎

Adding and Subtracting with Different Denominators

To add or subtract rational expressions with different denominators, we must build up each rational expression to equivalent forms with identical denominators, as we did in Section 6.1. Of course, it is most efficient to use the LCD as in the following examples.

E X A M P L E   3

Different denominators

Perform the indicated operations.

a) $\dfrac{3}{a^2b} + \dfrac{5}{ab^3}$

b) $\dfrac{x + 1}{6} - \dfrac{2x - 3}{4}$

Solution

a) The LCD for a^2b and ab^3 is a^2b^3. To build up each denominator to a^2b^3, multiply the numerator and denominator of the first expression by b^2, and multiply the numerator and denominator of the second expression by a:

$$\frac{3}{a^2b} + \frac{5}{ab^3} = \frac{3(b^2)}{a^2b(b^2)} + \frac{5(a)}{ab^3(a)} \qquad \text{Build up each denominator to the LCD.}$$

$$= \frac{3b^2}{a^2b^3} + \frac{5a}{a^2b^3}$$

$$= \frac{3b^2 + 5a}{a^2b^3} \qquad \text{Add the numerators.}$$

b) $\dfrac{x + 1}{6} - \dfrac{2x - 3}{4} = \dfrac{(x + 1)(2)}{6(2)} - \dfrac{(2x - 3)(3)}{4(3)}$ $\quad$ Build up each denominator to the LCD 12.

$$= \frac{2x + 2}{12} - \frac{6x - 9}{12} \qquad \text{Distributive property}$$

$$= \frac{2x + 2 - (6x - 9)}{12} \qquad \begin{array}{l}\text{Subtract the numerators.}\\ \text{Note that } 6x - 9 \text{ is put in}\\ \text{parentheses.}\end{array}$$

$$= \frac{2x + 2 - 6x + 9}{12} \qquad \text{Remove the parentheses.}$$

$$= \frac{-4x + 11}{12} \qquad \text{Combine like terms.} \qquad ■$$

C A U T I O N $\quad$ Before you add or subtract rational expressions, they must be written with identical denominators. For multiplication and division it is not necessary to have identical denominators.

In Example 4 we must first factor polynomials to find the LCD.

E X A M P L E   4

Different denominators

Perform the indicated operations.

a) $\dfrac{1}{x^2 - 1} + \dfrac{2}{x^2 + x}$

b) $\dfrac{5}{a - 2} - \dfrac{3}{2 - a}$

Helpful Hint

It is not actually necessary to identify the LCD. Once the denominators are factored, simply look at each denominator and ask, "What factor does the other denominator have that is missing from this one?" Then use the missing factor to build up the denominator and you will obtain the LCD.

Solution

a) Because $x^2 - 1 = (x + 1)(x - 1)$ and $x^2 + x = x(x + 1)$, the LCD is $x(x - 1)(x + 1)$. The first denominator is missing the factor x, and the second denominator is missing the factor $x - 1$.

$$\frac{1}{x^2 - 1} + \frac{2}{x^2 + x} = \underbrace{\frac{1}{(x - 1)(x + 1)}}_{\text{Missing } x} + \underbrace{\frac{2}{x\,(x + 1)}}_{\text{Missing } x - 1}$$

The LCD is $x(x - 1)(x + 1)$.

$$= \frac{1(x)}{(x - 1)(x + 1)(x)} + \frac{2(x - 1)}{x(x + 1)(x - 1)}$$

Build up the denominators to the LCD.

$$= \frac{x}{x(x - 1)(x + 1)} + \frac{2x - 2}{x(x - 1)(x + 1)}$$

$$= \frac{3x - 2}{x(x - 1)(x + 1)}$$

Add the numerators.

For this type of answer we usually leave the denominator in factored form. That way, if we need to work with the expression further, we do not have to factor the denominator again.

b) Because $-1(2 - a) = a - 2$, we can convert the denominator $2 - a$ to $a - 2$.

$$\frac{5}{a - 2} - \frac{3}{2 - a} = \frac{5}{a - 2} - \frac{3(-1)}{(2 - a)(-1)}$$

$$= \frac{5}{a - 2} - \frac{-3}{a - 2}$$

The LCD is $a - 2$.

$$= \frac{5 - (-3)}{a - 2}$$

Subtract the numerators.

$$= \frac{8}{a - 2}$$

Simplify.

Note that we get an equivalent answer if we multiply the numerator and denominator by -1:

$$\frac{8}{a - 2} = \frac{8(-1)}{(a - 2)(-1)} = \frac{-8}{2 - a}$$

This is the answer that we would have gotten if we had used $2 - a$ as the common denominator in the beginning. ∎

If the rational expressions in a sum or difference are not in lowest terms, then they should be reduced before finding the least common denominator.

E X A M P L E   5   **Reducing before finding the LCD**
Perform the indicated operations.

a) $\dfrac{2xy}{4x} + \dfrac{x^2}{xy}$

b) $\dfrac{8x - 8}{4x^2 - 4} - \dfrac{9x}{3x^2 - 3x - 6}$

Solution

a) Notice that the rational expressions can be reduced:

$$\frac{2xy}{4x} + \frac{x^2}{xy} = \frac{y}{2} + \frac{x}{y} \qquad \text{Reduce each rational expression.}$$

$$= \frac{y \cdot y}{2 \cdot y} + \frac{x \cdot 2}{y \cdot 2} \qquad \text{Build up each denominator to } 2y.$$

$$= \frac{y^2 + 2x}{2y} \qquad \text{Add the rational expressions.}$$

b) Notice that $3x^2 - 3x - 6 = 3(x^2 - x - 2) = 3(x - 2)(x + 1)$ and $4x^2 - 4 = 4(x^2 - 1) = 4(x - 1)(x + 1)$:

$$\frac{8x - 8}{4x^2 - 4} - \frac{9x}{3x^2 - 3x - 6}$$

$$= \frac{8(x - 1)}{4(x - 1)(x + 1)} - \frac{9x}{3(x - 2)(x + 1)} \qquad \text{Factor.}$$

$$= \frac{2}{x + 1} - \frac{3x}{(x - 2)(x + 1)} \qquad \text{Reduce.}$$

$$= \frac{2(x - 2)}{(x + 1)(x - 2)} - \frac{3x}{(x - 2)(x + 1)} \qquad \text{Build up to get the LCD.}$$

$$= \frac{2x - 4 - 3x}{(x + 1)(x - 2)} \qquad \text{Subtract the expressions.}$$

$$= \frac{-x - 4}{(x + 1)(x - 2)} \qquad \text{Simplify. Leave denominator factored.}$$

Shortcuts

Consider the following addition:

$$\frac{a}{b} + \frac{c}{d} = \frac{a(d)}{b(d)} + \frac{c(b)}{d(b)} = \frac{ad + bc}{bd} \qquad \text{The LCD is } bd.$$

We can use this result as a rule for adding simple fractions in which the LCD is the product of the denominators. A similar rule works for subtraction.

Adding or Subtracting Simple Fractions

If $b \neq 0$ and $d \neq 0$, then

$$\frac{a}{b} + \frac{c}{d} = \frac{ad + bc}{bd} \qquad \text{and} \qquad \frac{a}{b} - \frac{c}{d} = \frac{ad - bc}{bd}.$$

E X A M P L E   6   **Adding and subtracting simple fractions**

Use the rules for adding and subtracting simple fractions to find the sums and differences.

a) $\dfrac{1}{2} + \dfrac{1}{3}$

b) $\dfrac{1}{a} - \dfrac{1}{x}$

c) $\dfrac{a}{5} + \dfrac{a}{3}$

d) $x - \dfrac{2}{3}$

Solution

a) For the numerator, compute $ad + bc = 1 \cdot 3 + 2 \cdot 1 = 5$. Use $2 \cdot 3$ or 6 for the denominator:

$$\frac{1}{2} + \frac{1}{3} = \frac{5}{6}$$

b) $\dfrac{1}{a} - \dfrac{1}{x} = \dfrac{1 \cdot x - 1 \cdot a}{ax} = \dfrac{x - a}{ax}$

c) $\dfrac{a}{5} + \dfrac{a}{3} = \dfrac{3a + 5a}{15} = \dfrac{8a}{15}$

d) $x - \dfrac{2}{3} = \dfrac{x}{1} - \dfrac{2}{3} = \dfrac{3x - 2}{3}$

■

C A U T I O N   The rules for adding or subtracting simple fractions can be applied to any rational expressions, but they work best when the LCD is the product of the two denominators. Always make sure that the answer is in its lowest terms. If the product of the two denominators is too large, these rules are not helpful because then reducing can be difficult.

Applications

Rational expressions occur often in expressing rates. For example, if you can process one application in 2 hours, then you are working at the rate of $\frac{1}{2}$ of an application per hour. If you can complete one task in x hours, then you are working at the rate of $\frac{1}{x}$ task per hour.

E X A M P L E   7

Work rates

Susan takes an average of x hours to process a mortgage application, whereas Betty's average is 1 hour longer. Write a rational expression for the number of applications that they can process in 40 hours.

Solution

The number of applications processed by Susan is the product of her rate and her time:

$$\frac{1}{x} \frac{\text{application}}{\text{hr}} \cdot 40 \text{ hr} = \frac{40}{x} \text{ applications}$$

The number of applications processed by Betty is the product of her rate and her time:

$$\frac{1}{x + 1} \frac{\text{application}}{\text{hr}} \cdot 40 \text{ hr} = \frac{40}{x + 1} \text{ applications}$$

Find the sum of the rational expressions:

$$\frac{40}{x} + \frac{40}{x + 1} = \frac{40x + 40 + 40x}{x(x + 1)} = \frac{80x + 40}{x(x + 1)}$$

So together in 40 hours they process $\frac{80x + 40}{x(x + 1)}$ applications.   ■

WARM-UPS

True or false? Explain.

1. The LCM of 6 and 10 is 60.
2. The LCM of $6a^2b$ and $8ab^3$ is $24ab$.
3. The LCM of $x^2 - 1$ and $x - 1$ is $x^2 - 1$.
4. The LCD for the rational expressions $\frac{5}{x}$ and $\frac{x-3}{x+1}$ is $x + 1$.
5. $\frac{1}{2} + \frac{2}{3} = \frac{3}{5}$
6. $5 + \frac{1}{x} = \frac{6}{x}$ for any nonzero real number x.
7. $\frac{7}{a} + 3 = \frac{7 + 3a}{a}$ for any $a \neq 0$.
8. $\frac{c}{3} - \frac{d}{5} = \frac{5c - 3d}{15}$ for any real numbers c and d.
9. $\frac{2}{3} + \frac{3}{4} = \frac{17}{12}$
10. If Jamal uses x reams of paper in one day, then he uses $\frac{1}{x}$ ream per day.

6.3   EXERCISES

Reading and Writing   *After reading this section, write out the answers to these questions. Use complete sentences.*

1. How do you add rational numbers?

2. What is the least common denominator (LCD)?

3. What is the least common multiple?

4. How do we find the LCM for a group of polynomials?

5. How do we add or subtract rational expressions with different denominators?

6. For which operations with rational expressions is it not necessary to have identical denominators?

Perform the indicated operations. Reduce answers to their lowest terms. See Example 1.

7. $\dfrac{3x}{2} + \dfrac{5x}{2}$

8. $\dfrac{5x^2}{3} + \dfrac{4x^2}{3}$

9. $\dfrac{x - 3}{2x} - \dfrac{3x - 5}{2x}$

10. $\dfrac{9 - 4y}{3y} - \dfrac{6 - y}{3y}$

11. $\dfrac{3x - 4}{2x - 4} + \dfrac{2x - 6}{2x - 4}$

12. $\dfrac{a^3}{a + b} + \dfrac{b^3}{a + b}$

13. $\dfrac{x^2 + 4x - 6}{x^2 - 9} - \dfrac{x^2 + 2x - 12}{x^2 - 9}$

14. $\dfrac{x^2 + 3x - 3}{x - 4} - \dfrac{x^2 + 4x - 7}{x - 4}$

15. $\dfrac{2x^2 - 8x - 4}{2x^2 + 7x + 3} + \dfrac{4x^2 + x - 1}{2x^2 + 7x + 3}$

16. $\dfrac{5x^2 - 2x - 5}{2x^2 + 3x - 2} - \dfrac{x^2 - 9x - 3}{2x^2 + 3x - 2}$

Find the least common multiple for each group of polynomials. See Example 2.

17. 24, 20

18. 12, 18, 22

19. $10x^3y, 15x$

20. $12a^3b^2, 18ab^5$

21. a^3b, ab^4c, ab^5c^2

22. x^2yz, xy^2z^3, xy^6

23. $x, x + 2, x - 2$

24. $y, y - 5, y + 2$

25. $4a + 8, 6a + 12$

26. $4a - 6, 2a^2 - 3a$

27. $x^2 - 1, x^2 + 2x + 1$

28. $y^2 - 2y - 15, y^2 + 6y + 9$

29. $x^2 - 4x, x^2 - 16, x^2 + 6x + 8$

30. $z^2 - 25, 5z - 25, 5z + 25$

31. $6x^2 + 17x + 12, 9x^2 - 16$

32. $16x^2 - 8x - 3, 4x^2 - 7x + 3$

Perform the indicated operations. Reduce answers to lowest terms. See Examples 3, 4, and 5.

33. $\dfrac{1}{28} + \dfrac{3}{35}$

34. $\dfrac{7}{24} - \dfrac{4}{15}$

35. $\dfrac{7}{48} - \dfrac{5}{36}$

36. $\dfrac{7}{52} + \dfrac{3}{40}$

37. $\dfrac{3}{wz^2} + \dfrac{5}{w^2z}$

38. $\dfrac{2}{a^2b} - \dfrac{3}{ab^2}$

39. $\dfrac{2x - 3}{8} - \dfrac{x - 2}{6}$

40. $\dfrac{a - 5}{10} + \dfrac{3 - 2a}{15}$

41. $\dfrac{xa^3}{2a^4} + \dfrac{21x^2}{35ax}$

42. $\dfrac{5x^2}{30xy} - \dfrac{30x}{80y}$

43. $\dfrac{9}{4y} - x$

44. $\dfrac{b^2}{4a} - c$

45. $\dfrac{5}{a + 2} - \dfrac{7}{a}$

46. $\dfrac{2}{x + 1} - \dfrac{3}{x}$

47. $\dfrac{1}{a - b} + \dfrac{2}{a + b}$

48. $\dfrac{5}{x + 2} + \dfrac{3}{x - 2}$

49. $\dfrac{2x^2}{2x^3 - 18x} + \dfrac{15}{5x - 15}$

50. $\dfrac{5x}{5x^2 - 125} + \dfrac{5x - 5}{x^2 - 6x + 5}$

51. $\dfrac{1}{a - b} + \dfrac{1}{b - a}$

52. $\dfrac{3}{x - 5} + \dfrac{7}{5 - x}$

53. $\dfrac{10}{4x - 8} - \dfrac{15}{10 - 5x}$

54. $\dfrac{8}{6x - 18} - \dfrac{14}{6 - 2x}$

55. $\dfrac{5}{x^2 + x - 2} - \dfrac{6}{x^2 + 2x - 3}$

56. $\dfrac{2}{x^2 - 4} - \dfrac{5}{x^2 - 3x - 10}$

57. $\dfrac{x}{2x^2 + x - 1} + \dfrac{3}{3x^2 + 2x - 1}$

58. $\dfrac{x + 1}{3x^2 - 2x - 1} + \dfrac{x - 1}{3x^2 + 4x + 1}$

59. $\dfrac{1}{x} + \dfrac{2}{x - 1} - \dfrac{3}{x + 2}$

60. $\dfrac{2}{a} - \dfrac{3}{a + 1} + \dfrac{5}{a - 1}$

Perform the following operations. Write down only the answer. See Example 6.

61. $\dfrac{1}{3} + \dfrac{1}{4}$

62. $\dfrac{3}{5} + \dfrac{1}{4}$

63. $\dfrac{1}{8} - \dfrac{3}{5}$

64. $\dfrac{a}{2} + \dfrac{5}{3}$

65. $\dfrac{x}{3} + \dfrac{x}{2}$

66. $\dfrac{y}{4} - \dfrac{y}{3}$

67. $\dfrac{a}{b} - \dfrac{2}{3}$

68. $\dfrac{3}{x} + \dfrac{1}{9}$

69. $a + \dfrac{2}{3}$

70. $\dfrac{m}{3} + y$

71. $\dfrac{3}{a} + 1$

72. $\dfrac{1}{x} + 1$

73. $\dfrac{3 + x}{x} - 1$　　　　**74.** $\dfrac{a + 2}{a} + 3$

75. $\dfrac{2}{3} + \dfrac{1}{4x}$　　　　**76.** $\dfrac{1}{5} + \dfrac{1}{5x}$

Perform the indicated operations.

77. $\dfrac{w^2 - 3w + 6}{w - 5} + \dfrac{9 - w^2}{w - 5}$

78. $\dfrac{2z^2 - 3z + 6}{z^2 - 1} - \dfrac{z^2 - 5z + 9}{z^2 - 1}$

79. $\dfrac{1}{3x - 6} - \dfrac{6}{5x - 10}$

80. $\dfrac{3}{6x^2 - 4x} - \dfrac{x - 2}{9x - 6}$

81. $\dfrac{x - 1}{2x^2 + 3x + 1} - \dfrac{x + 1}{2x^2 - x - 1}$

82. $\dfrac{2x + 1}{6x^2 - 5x + 1} + \dfrac{2x - 1}{6x^2 + x - 1}$

83. $\dfrac{(a^2 b^3)^4}{(ab^4)^3} \cdot \dfrac{(ab)^3}{(a^4 b)^2}$

84. $\dfrac{(ab)^2}{(a + b)^2} \cdot \dfrac{(a + b)^3}{(ab)^3}$

85. $\dfrac{x^2 + 4}{25x^2 - 20x + 4} + \dfrac{10x + 4}{25x^2 - 4}$

86. $\dfrac{8a}{2a^2 + 4a + 2} - \dfrac{3a - 3}{a^2 - 1}$

87. $\dfrac{4x^2 + 9}{4x^2 - 9} \cdot \dfrac{4x^2 + 12x + 9}{2x^2 + 3x}$

88. $\dfrac{3a^2 - 2a - 16}{2a^2 + 3a - 2} \cdot \dfrac{6a + 16}{9a^2 - 64}$

89. $\dfrac{w^2 - 3}{3w^3 + 81} - \dfrac{2}{6w + 18} - \dfrac{w - 4}{w^2 - 3w + 9}$

90. $\dfrac{a - 3}{a^3 + 8} - \dfrac{2}{a + 2} - \dfrac{a - 3}{a^2 - 2a + 4}$

91. $\dfrac{a^2 - 6a + 9}{a^3 - 8} \div \dfrac{a^2 - a - 6}{a^2 - 4}$

92. $\dfrac{1}{z^2 + 4} \div \dfrac{z^3 - 8}{z^4 - 16}$

93. $\dfrac{w^2 + 3}{w^3 - 8} - \dfrac{2w}{w^2 - 4}$

94. $\dfrac{x + 5}{x^3 + 27} - \dfrac{x - 1}{x^2 - 9}$

95. $\dfrac{1}{x^3 - 1} - \dfrac{1}{x^2 - 1} + \dfrac{1}{x - 1}$

96. $\dfrac{x - 4}{x^3 - 1} + \dfrac{x - 2}{x^2 - 1}$

In Exercises 97–102, solve each problem. See Example 7.

97. *Processing.* Joe takes x hours on the average to process a claim, whereas Ellen averages $x + 1$ hours to process a claim. Write a rational expression for the number of claims that they will process while working together for an 8-hour shift.

98. *Roofing.* Bill attaches one bundle of shingles in an average of x minutes using a hammer, whereas Julio can attach one bundle in an average of $x - 6$ minutes using a pneumatic stapler. Write a rational expression for the number of bundles that they can attach while working together for 10 hours.

FIGURE FOR EXERCISE 98

99. *Selling.* George sells one magazine subscription every 20 minutes, whereas Theresa sells one every x minutes. Write a rational expression for the number of magazine subscriptions that they will sell when working together for one hour.

100. *Painting.* Harry can paint his house by himself in 6 days. His wife Judy can paint the house by herself in x days. Write a rational expression for the portion of the house that they paint when working together for 2 days.

101. *Driving.* Joan drove for 100 miles at one speed and then increased her speed by 5 miles per hour and drove 200 additional miles. Write a rational expression for her total travel time.

102. *Running.* Willard jogged for 3 miles at one speed and then doubled his speed for an additional mile. Write a rational expression for his total running time.

GETTING MORE INVOLVED

 103. *Discussion.* Explain why fractions must have common denominators for addition but not for multiplication.

 104. *Discussion.* Find each "infinite sum" and explain your answer.

a) $\dfrac{3}{10} + \dfrac{3}{10^2} + \dfrac{3}{10^3} + \dfrac{3}{10^4} + \cdots$

b) $\dfrac{9}{10} + \dfrac{9}{10^2} + \dfrac{9}{10^3} + \dfrac{9}{10^4} + \cdots$

In This Section

- Simplifying Complex Fractions
- Simplifying Expressions with Negative Exponents
- Applications

6.4   COMPLEX FRACTIONS

In this section we will use the techniques of Section 6.3 to simplify complex fractions. As their name suggests, complex fractions are rather messy-looking expressions.

Simplifying Complex Fractions

A **complex fraction** is a fraction that has rational expressions in the numerator, the denominator, or both. For example,

$$\frac{\dfrac{1}{2} + \dfrac{1}{3}}{\dfrac{1}{4} + \dfrac{1}{5}}, \qquad \frac{3 - \dfrac{2}{x}}{\dfrac{1}{x^2} - \dfrac{1}{4}}, \qquad \text{and} \qquad \frac{\dfrac{x+2}{x^2-9}}{\dfrac{x}{x^2-6x+9} + \dfrac{4}{x-3}}$$

are complex fractions. In the next example we show two methods for simplifying a complex fraction.

E X A M P L E   1   **A complex fraction without variables**

Simplify $\dfrac{\dfrac{1}{2} + \dfrac{1}{3}}{\dfrac{1}{4} + \dfrac{1}{5}}$.

Calculator Close-Up

You can use a calculator to find the value of a complex fraction.

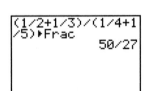

Solution

Method A   For this method we perform the computations of the numerator and denominator separately and then divide:

$$\frac{\dfrac{1}{2} + \dfrac{1}{3}}{\dfrac{1}{4} + \dfrac{1}{5}} = \frac{\dfrac{5}{6}}{\dfrac{9}{20}} = \frac{5}{6} \div \frac{9}{20} = \frac{5}{6} \cdot \frac{20}{9} = \frac{5 \cdot 2 \cdot 10}{2 \cdot 3 \cdot 9} = \frac{50}{27}$$

Method B   For this method we find the LCD for all of the fractions in the complex fraction. Then we multiply the numerator and denominator of the complex fraction by the LCD. The LCD for the denominators 2, 3, 4, and 5 is 60. So we multiply the numerator and denominator of the complex fraction by 60:

$$\frac{\frac{1}{2} + \frac{1}{3}}{\frac{1}{4} + \frac{1}{5}} = \frac{\left(\frac{1}{2} + \frac{1}{3}\right)60}{\left(\frac{1}{4} + \frac{1}{5}\right)60} = \frac{30 + 20}{15 + 12} = \frac{50}{27} \qquad \frac{1}{2} \cdot 60 = 30, \frac{1}{3} \cdot 60 = 20$$
$$\frac{1}{4} \cdot 60 = 15, \frac{1}{5} \cdot 60 = 12$$

$\blacksquare$

In most cases Method B of Example 1 is the faster method for simplifying complex fractions, and we will continue to use it.

E X A M P L E   2   **A complex fraction with variables**

Simplify $\dfrac{3 - \frac{2}{x}}{\frac{1}{x^2} - \frac{1}{4}}$.

Helpful Hint

When students see addition or sub-traction in a complex fraction, they often convert all of the fractions to the same denominator. This is not wrong, but it is not necessary. Simply multiplying every fraction by the LCD eliminates the denomi-nators of the original fractions.

Solution

The LCD of x, x^2, and 4 is $4x^2$. Multiply the numerator and denominator by $4x^2$:

$$\frac{3 - \frac{2}{x}}{\frac{1}{x^2} - \frac{1}{4}} = \frac{\left(3 - \frac{2}{x}\right)(4x^2)}{\left(\frac{1}{x^2} - \frac{1}{4}\right)(4x^2)}$$

$$= \frac{3(4x^2) - \frac{2}{x}(4x^2)}{\frac{1}{x^2}(4x^2) - \frac{1}{4}(4x^2)} \qquad \text{Distributive property}$$

$$= \frac{12x^2 - 8x}{4 - x^2}$$

$\blacksquare$

E X A M P L E   3   **More complicated denominators**

Simplify $\dfrac{\frac{x + 2}{x^2 - 9}}{\frac{x}{x^2 - 6x + 9} + \frac{4}{x - 3}}$.

Study Tip

Your mood for studying should match the mood in which you are tested. Being too relaxed during studying will not match the increased level of activation you attain during a test. Likewise, if you get too tensed-up during a test, you will not do well because your test-taking mood will not match your studying mood.

Solution

Because $x^2 - 9 = (x - 3)(x + 3)$ and $x^2 - 6x + 9 = (x - 3)^2$, the LCD is $(x - 3)^2(x + 3)$. Multiply the numerator and denominator by the LCD:

$$\frac{\frac{x + 2}{x^2 - 9}}{\frac{x}{x^2 - 6x + 9} + \frac{4}{x - 3}} = \frac{\frac{x + 2}{(x - 3)(x + 3)}(x - 3)^2(x + 3)}{\frac{x}{(x - 3)^2}(x - 3)^2(x + 3) + \frac{4}{x - 3}(x - 3)^2(x + 3)}$$

$$= \frac{(x + 2)(x - 3)}{x(x + 3) + 4(x - 3)(x + 3)} \qquad \text{Simplify.}$$

$$= \frac{(x + 2)(x - 3)}{(x + 3)[x + 4(x - 3)]} \qquad \text{Factor out } x + 3.$$

$$= \frac{(x + 2)(x - 3)}{(x + 3)(5x - 12)}$$

$\blacksquare$

Simplifying Expressions with Negative Exponents

Consider the expression

$$\frac{3a^{-1} - 2^{-1}}{1 - b^{-1}}.$$

Using the definition of negative exponents, we can rewrite this expression as a complex fraction:

$$\frac{3a^{-1} - 2^{-1}}{1 - b^{-1}} = \frac{\dfrac{3}{a} - \dfrac{1}{2}}{1 - \dfrac{1}{b}}$$

The LCD for the complex fraction is $2ab$. Note that $2ab$ could be obtained from a^{-1}, 2^{-1}, and b^{-1} in the original expression. To simplify the complex fraction we can multiply the numerator and denominator of either of the above expressions by $2ab$. To gain more experience with negative exponents, we will work with the first expression in Example 4.

E X A M P L E   4   **A complex fraction with negative exponents**

Simplify the complex fraction $\frac{3a^{-1} - 2^{-1}}{1 - b^{-1}}$.

Solution

Multiply the numerator and denominator by $2ab$, the LCD of the fractions. Remember that $a^{-1} \cdot a = a^0 = 1$.

$$\frac{3a^{-1} - 2^{-1}}{1 - b^{-1}} = \frac{(3a^{-1} - 2^{-1})2ab}{(1 - b^{-1})2ab}$$

$$= \frac{3a^{-1}(2ab) - 2^{-1}(2ab)}{1(2ab) - b^{-1}(2ab)} \quad \text{Distributive property}$$

$$= \frac{6b - ab}{2ab - 2a} \qquad\qquad \blacksquare$$

E X A M P L E   5   **A complex fraction with negative exponents**

Simplify the complex fraction $\frac{a^{-1} + b^{-2}}{ab^{-2} + ba^{-3}}$.

Helpful Hint

In Examples 4, 5, and 6 we are simplifying the expressions without first removing the negative exponents to gain experience in working with negative exponents. Of course, each expression with a negative exponent could be rewritten with a positive exponent and then the complex fraction could be simplified as in Examples 2 and 3.

Solution

If we rewrote a^{-1}, b^{-2}, b^{-2}, and a^{-3}, then the denominators would be a, b^2, b^2, and a^3. So the LCD is a^3b^2. If we multiply the numerator and denominator by a^3b^2, the negative exponents will be eliminated:

$$\frac{a^{-1} + b^{-2}}{ab^{-2} + ba^{-3}} = \frac{(a^{-1} + b^{-2})a^3b^2}{(ab^{-2} + ba^{-3})a^3b^2}$$

$$= \frac{a^{-1} \cdot a^3b^2 + b^{-2} \cdot a^3b^2}{ab^{-2} \cdot a^3b^2 + ba^{-3} \cdot a^3b^2} \quad \text{Distributive property}$$

$$= \frac{a^2b^2 + a^3}{a^4 + b^3} \qquad\qquad \begin{array}{l} b^{-2}b^2 = b^0 = 1 \\ a^{-3}a^3 = a^0 = 1 \end{array}$$

Note that the positive exponents of a^3b^2 are just large enough to eliminate all of the negative exponents when we multiply. $\blacksquare$

Example 6 is not exactly a complex fraction, but we can use the same technique as in the previous example.

E X A M P L E   6

More negative exponents

Eliminate negative exponents and simplify $p + p^{-1}q^{-2}$.

Solution

If we multiply the numerator and denominator by pq^2, we will eliminate the negative exponents:

$$p + p^{-1}q^{-2} = \frac{(p + p^{-1}q^{-2})}{1} \cdot \frac{pq^2}{pq^2}$$

$$= \frac{p^2q^2 + 1}{pq^2} \quad \begin{array}{l} p \cdot pq^2 = p^2q^2 \\ p^{-1}q^{-2} \cdot pq^2 = 1 \end{array}$$ ∎

Applications

Example 7 illustrates how complex fractions can occur in a problem.

E X A M P L E   7

An application of complex fractions

Eastside Elementary has the same number of students as Westside Elementary. One-half of the students at Eastside ride buses to school, and two-thirds of the students at Westside ride buses to school. One-sixth of the students at Eastside are female, and one-third of the students at Westside are female. If all of the female students ride the buses, then what percentage of the students who ride the buses are female?

Solution

To find the required percentage, we must divide the number of females who ride the buses by the total number of students who ride the buses. Let

$$x = \text{the number of students at Eastside.}$$

Because the number of students at Westside is also x, we have

$$\frac{1}{2}x + \frac{2}{3}x = \text{the total number of students who ride the buses}$$

and

$$\frac{1}{6}x + \frac{1}{3}x = \text{the total number of female students.}$$

Because all of the female students ride the buses, we can express the percentage of riders who are female by the following rational expression:

$$\frac{\dfrac{1}{6}x + \dfrac{1}{3}x}{\dfrac{1}{2}x + \dfrac{2}{3}x}$$

Multiply the numerator and denominator by 6, the LCD for 2, 3, and 6:

$$\frac{\left(\dfrac{1}{6}x + \dfrac{1}{3}x\right)6}{\left(\dfrac{1}{2}x + \dfrac{2}{3}x\right)6} = \frac{x + 2x}{3x + 4x} = \frac{3x}{7x} = \frac{3}{7} \approx 0.43 = 43\%$$

So 43% of the students who ride the buses are female.   ∎

WARM-UPS

True or false? Explain.

1. The LCM for 2, x, 6, and x^2 is $6x^3$.

2. The LCM for $a - b$, $2b - 2a$, and 6 is $6a - 6b$.

3. The LCD is the LCM of the denominators.

4. $\dfrac{\dfrac{1}{2} + \dfrac{1}{3}}{1 + \dfrac{1}{2}} = \dfrac{5}{6} \div \dfrac{3}{2}$

5. $2^{-1} + 3^{-1} = (2 + 3)^{-1}$

6. $(2^{-1} + 3^{-1})^{-1} = 2 + 3$

7. $2 + 3^{-1} = 5^{-1}$

8. $x + 2^{-1} = \dfrac{x}{2}$ for any real number x.

9. To simplify $\dfrac{a^{-1} - b^{-1}}{a - b}$, multiply the numerator and denominator by ab.

10. To simplify $\dfrac{ab^{-2} + a^{-5}b^2}{a^{-3}b - a^5b^{-1}}$, multiply the numerator and denominator by a^5b^2.

6.4   EXERCISES

Reading and Writing *After reading this section, write out the answers to these questions. Use complete sentences.*

1. What is a complex fraction?

2. What are the two methods for simplifying complex fractions?

Simplify each complex fraction. Use either method. See Example 1.

3. $\dfrac{\dfrac{1}{2} - \dfrac{1}{3}}{\dfrac{1}{4} - \dfrac{1}{5}}$

4. $\dfrac{\dfrac{1}{3} + \dfrac{1}{4}}{\dfrac{1}{5} + \dfrac{1}{6}}$

5. $\dfrac{\dfrac{2}{3} + \dfrac{5}{6} - \dfrac{1}{2}}{\dfrac{1}{8} - \dfrac{1}{3} + \dfrac{1}{12}}$

6. $\dfrac{\dfrac{2}{5} - \dfrac{x}{9} - \dfrac{1}{3}}{\dfrac{1}{3} + \dfrac{x}{5} + \dfrac{2}{15}}$

Simplify the complex fractions. Use Method B. See Example 2.

7. $\dfrac{\dfrac{a + b}{b}}{\dfrac{a - b}{ab}}$

8. $\dfrac{\dfrac{m - n}{m^2}}{\dfrac{m - 3}{mn^3}}$

9. $\dfrac{a + \dfrac{3}{b}}{\dfrac{b}{a} + \dfrac{1}{b}}$

10. $\dfrac{m - \dfrac{2}{n}}{\dfrac{1}{m} - \dfrac{3}{n}}$

11. $\dfrac{\dfrac{x - 3y}{xy}}{\dfrac{1}{x} + \dfrac{1}{y}}$

12. $\dfrac{\dfrac{2}{w} + \dfrac{3}{t}}{\dfrac{w - t}{4wt}}$

13. $\dfrac{3 - \dfrac{m - 2}{6}}{\dfrac{4}{9} + \dfrac{2}{m}}$

14. $\dfrac{6 - \dfrac{2 - z}{z}}{\dfrac{1}{3z} - \dfrac{1}{6}}$

15. $\dfrac{\dfrac{a^2 - b^2}{a^2b^3}}{\dfrac{a + b}{a^3b}}$

16. $\dfrac{\dfrac{4x^2 - 1}{x^2y}}{\dfrac{4x - 2}{xy^2}}$

17. $\dfrac{\dfrac{1}{x^2y^2} + \dfrac{1}{xy^3}}{\dfrac{1}{x^3y} - \dfrac{1}{xy}}$

18. $\dfrac{\dfrac{1}{2a^3b} - \dfrac{1}{ab^4}}{\dfrac{1}{6a^2b^2} + \dfrac{1}{3a^4b}}$

Simplify each complex fraction. See Examples 1–3.

19. $\dfrac{x + \dfrac{4}{x + 4}}{x - \dfrac{4x + 4}{x + 4}}$

20. $\dfrac{x - \dfrac{x + 6}{x + 2}}{x - \dfrac{4x + 15}{x + 2}}$

21. $\dfrac{1 - \dfrac{1}{y - 1}}{3 + \dfrac{1}{y + 1}}$

22. $\dfrac{2 - \dfrac{3}{a - 2}}{4 - \dfrac{1}{a + 2}}$

23. $\dfrac{\dfrac{2}{3 - x} - 4}{\dfrac{1}{x - 3} - 1}$

24. $\dfrac{\dfrac{x}{x - 5} - 2}{\dfrac{2x}{5 - x} - 1}$

25. $\dfrac{\dfrac{w + 2}{w - 1} - \dfrac{w - 3}{w}}{\dfrac{w + 4}{w} + \dfrac{w - 2}{w - 1}}$

26. $\dfrac{\dfrac{x - 1}{x + 2} - \dfrac{x - 2}{x + 3}}{\dfrac{x - 3}{x + 3} + \dfrac{x + 1}{x + 2}}$

27. $\dfrac{\dfrac{1}{a - b} - \dfrac{3}{a + b}}{\dfrac{2}{b - a} + \dfrac{4}{b + a}}$

28. $\dfrac{\dfrac{3}{2 + x} - \dfrac{4}{2 - x}}{\dfrac{1}{x + 2} - \dfrac{3}{x - 2}}$

29. $\dfrac{\dfrac{4}{y} - \dfrac{y + 4}{y - 3}}{\dfrac{2}{y - 3} + \dfrac{y + 1}{y}}$

30. $\dfrac{\dfrac{x + 4}{x + 1} + \dfrac{4}{x}}{\dfrac{x + 1}{x} - \dfrac{1}{x + 1}}$

31. $\dfrac{3 - \dfrac{4}{a - 1}}{5 - \dfrac{3}{1 - a}}$

32. $\dfrac{\dfrac{x}{3} - \dfrac{x - 1}{9 - x}}{\dfrac{x}{6} - \dfrac{2 - x}{x - 9}}$

33. $\dfrac{\dfrac{2}{m - 3} + \dfrac{4}{m}}{\dfrac{3}{m - 2} + \dfrac{1}{m}}$

34. $\dfrac{\dfrac{1}{y + 2} - \dfrac{4}{3y}}{\dfrac{3}{y} - \dfrac{2}{y + 3}}$

35. $\dfrac{\dfrac{3}{x^2 - 1} - \dfrac{x - 2}{x^3 - 1}}{\dfrac{3}{x^2 + x + 1} + \dfrac{x - 3}{x^3 - 1}}$

36. $\dfrac{\dfrac{2}{a^3 + 8} - \dfrac{3}{a^2 - 2a + 4}}{\dfrac{4}{a^2 - 4} + \dfrac{a - 3}{a^3 + 8}}$

Simplify. See Examples 4–6.

37. $\dfrac{w^{-1} + y^{-1}}{z^{-1} + y^{-1}}$

38. $\dfrac{a^{-1} - b^{-1}}{a^{-1} + b^{-1}}$

39. $\dfrac{1 - x^{-1}}{1 - x^{-2}}$

40. $\dfrac{4 - a^{-2}}{2 - a^{-1}}$

41. $\dfrac{a^{-2} + b^{-2}}{a^{-1}b}$

42. $\dfrac{m^{-3} + n^{-3}}{mn^{-2}}$

43. $1 - a^{-1}$

44. $m^{-1} - a^{-1}$

45. $\dfrac{x^{-1} + x^{-2}}{x + x^{-2}}$

46. $\dfrac{x - x^{-2}}{1 - x^{-2}}$

47. $\dfrac{2m^{-1} - 3m^{-2}}{m^{-2}}$

48. $\dfrac{4x^{-3} - 6x^{-5}}{2x^{-5}}$

49. $\dfrac{a^{-1} - b^{-1}}{a - b}$

50. $\dfrac{a^2 - b^2}{a^{-2} - b^{-2}}$

51. $\dfrac{x^3 - y^3}{x^{-3} - y^{-3}}$

52. $\dfrac{(a - b)^2}{a^{-2} - b^{-2}}$

53. $\dfrac{1 - 8x^{-3}}{x^{-1} + 2x^{-2} + 4x^{-3}}$

54. $\dfrac{a + 27a^{-2}}{1 - 3a^{-1} + 9a^{-2}}$

55. $(x^{-1} + y^{-1})^{-1}$

56. $(a^{-1} - b^{-1})^{-2}$

Use a calculator to evaluate each complex fraction. Round answers to four decimal places. If your calculator does fractions, then also find the fractional answer.

57. $\dfrac{\dfrac{5}{3} - \dfrac{4}{5}}{\dfrac{1}{3} - \dfrac{5}{6}}$

58. $\dfrac{\dfrac{1}{12} + \dfrac{1}{2} - \dfrac{3}{4}}{\dfrac{3}{5} + \dfrac{5}{6}}$

59. $\dfrac{4^{-1} - 9^{-1}}{2^{-1} + 3^{-1}}$

60. $\dfrac{2^{-1} + 3^{-1} - 6^{-1}}{3^{-1} - 5^{-1} + 4^{-1}}$

Solve each problem. See Example 7.

61. Racial balance. Clarksville has three elementary schools. Northside has one-half as many students as Central, and Southside has two-thirds as many students as Central. One-third of the students at Northside are African-American, three-fourths of the students at Central are African-American, and one-sixth of the students at Southside are African-American. What percent of the city's elementary students are African-American?

62. Explosive situation. All of the employees at Acme Explosives are in either development, manufacturing, or sales. One-fifth of the employees in development are women, one-third of the employees in manufacturing are women, and one-half of the employees in sales are women. Use the accompanying figure to determine the percentage of workers at Acme who are women. What percent of the women at Acme are in sales?

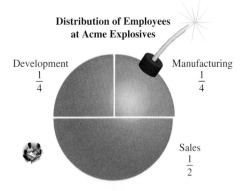

Distribution of Employees at Acme Explosives

Development $\dfrac{1}{4}$ Manufacturing $\dfrac{1}{4}$ Sales $\dfrac{1}{2}$

FIGURE FOR EXERCISE 62

63. Average speed. Mary drove from Clarksville to Leesville at 45 miles per hour (mph). At Leesville she discovered that she had forgotten her purse. She immediately returned to Clarksville at 55 mph. What was her average speed for the entire trip? (The answer is *not* 50 mph.)

64. Average price. On her way to New York, Jenny spent the same amount for gasoline each time she stopped for gas. She paid 139.9 cents per gallon the first time, 149.9 cents per gallon the second time, and 159.9 cents per gallon the third time. What was the average price per gallon to the nearest tenth of a cent for the gasoline that she bought?

FIGURE FOR EXERCISE 64

GETTING MORE INVOLVED

65. Cooperative learning. Write a step-by-step strategy for simplifying complex fractions with negative exponents. Have a classmate use your strategy to simplify some complex fractions from Exercises 37–56.

66. Discussion. **a)** Find the exact value of each expression.

i) $\dfrac{1}{1 + \dfrac{1}{1 + \dfrac{1}{1 + \dfrac{1}{2}}}}$

ii) $\dfrac{1}{1 + \dfrac{1}{1 + \dfrac{1}{1 + \dfrac{1}{1 + \dfrac{1}{3}}}}}$

b) Explain why in each case the exact value must be less than 1.

67. Cooperative learning. Work with a group to simplify the complex fraction. For what values of x is the complex fraction undefined?

$$\dfrac{1}{1 + \dfrac{1}{1 + \dfrac{1}{1 + \dfrac{1}{x}}}}$$

6.5   DIVISION OF POLYNOMIALS

We began our study of polynomials in Section 5.3 by learning how to add, subtract, and multiply polynomials. In this section we will study division of polynomials.

Dividing a Polynomial by a Monomial

You learned how to divide monomials in Section 5.1. For example,

$$6x^3 \div (3x) = \frac{6x^3}{3x} = 2x^2.$$

We check by multiplying. Because $2x^2 \cdot 3x = 6x^3$, this answer is correct. Recall that $a \div b = c$ if and only if $c \cdot b = a$. We call a the **dividend,** b the **divisor,** and c the **quotient.** We may also refer to $a \div b$ and $\frac{a}{b}$ as quotients.

We can use the distributive property to find that

$$3x(2x^2 + 5x - 4) = 6x^3 + 15x^2 - 12x.$$

So if we divide $6x^3 + 15x^2 - 12x$ by the monomial $3x$, we must get $2x^2 + 5x - 4$. We can perform this division by dividing $3x$ into *each term* of $6x^3 + 15x^2 - 12x$:

$$\frac{6x^3 + 15x^2 - 12x}{3x} = \frac{6x^3}{3x} + \frac{15x^2}{3x} - \frac{12x}{3x}$$
$$= 2x^2 + 5x - 4$$

In this case the divisor is $3x$, the dividend is $6x^3 + 15x^2 - 12x$, and the quotient is $2x^2 + 5x - 4$.

E X A M P L E   1

Dividing a polynomial by a monomial

Find the quotient.

a) $-12x^5 \div (2x^3)$ **b)** $(-20x^6 + 8x^4 - 4x^2) \div (4x^2)$

Solution

a) When dividing x^5 by x^3, we subtract the exponents:

$$-12x^5 \div (2x^3) = \frac{-12x^5}{2x^3} = -6x^2$$

The quotient is $-6x^2$. Check:

$$-6x^2 \cdot 2x^3 = -12x^5$$

b) Divide each term of $-20x^6 + 8x^4 - 4x^2$ by $4x^2$:

$$\frac{-20x^6 + 8x^4 - 4x^2}{4x^2} = \frac{-20x^6}{4x^2} + \frac{8x^4}{4x^2} - \frac{4x^2}{4x^2}$$
$$= -5x^4 + 2x^2 - 1$$

The quotient is $-5x^4 + 2x^2 - 1$. Check:

$$4x^2(-5x^4 + 2x^2 - 1) = -20x^6 + 8x^4 - 4x^2$$

In Example 1 we found the quotient of a polynomial and a monomial and the remainder was zero. If the remainder is zero, then the dividend is equal to the divisor times the quotient. If the remainder is not zero, then the degree of the remainder must be less than the degree of the divisor and

$$\textbf{dividend} = (\textbf{divisor})(\textbf{quotient}) + (\textbf{remainder}).$$

If we divide each side of this equation by the divisor, we get

$$\frac{\textbf{dividend}}{\textbf{divisor}} = \textbf{quotient} + \frac{\textbf{remainder}}{\textbf{divisor}}.$$

The remainder in Example 1 was zero, because the degree of the monomial denominator was less than or equal to the degree of every term in the numerator. If the degree of the monomial denominator is larger than the degree of at least one term in the numerator, then there will be a remainder, as shown in Example 2.

E X A M P L E   2   **Dividing a polynomial by a monomial (remainder $\neq 0$)**

Find the quotient and remainder.

a) $\dfrac{6x - 1}{2x}$

b) $\dfrac{x^3 - 4x^2 + 5x - 3}{2x^2}$

Solution

a) Divide each term of $6x - 1$ by $2x$:

$$\frac{6x - 1}{2x} = \frac{6x}{2x} + \frac{-1}{2x} = 3 + \frac{-1}{2x}$$

Now $3 + \frac{-1}{2x}$ has the form quotient $+ \frac{\text{remainder}}{\text{divisor}}$. So the quotient is 3 and the remainder is -1. Check that (divisor)(quotient) + remainder = dividend:

$$(2x)(3) + (-1) = 6x - 1$$

b) The first two terms in the numerator have a degree that is greater than or equal to the degree of the denominator. So divide the first two terms of the numerator by the monomial denominator:

$$\frac{x^3 - 4x^2 + 5x - 3}{2x^2} = \frac{x^3}{2x^2} - \frac{4x^2}{2x^2} + \frac{5x - 3}{2x^2}$$

$$= \frac{1}{2}x - 2 + \frac{5x - 3}{2x^2}$$

The last expression has the form quotient $+ \frac{\text{remainder}}{\text{divisor}}$. So the quotient is $\frac{1}{2}x - 2$ and the remainder is $5x - 3$. Check that

$$(2x^2)\left(\frac{1}{2}x - 2\right) + 5x - 3 = x^3 - 4x^2 + 5x - 3. \qquad \blacksquare$$

Dividing a Polynomial by a Binomial

We can multiply $x - 2$ and $x + 5$ to get

$$(x - 2)(x + 5) = x^2 + 3x - 10.$$

So if we divide $x^2 + 3x - 10$ by the factor $x - 2$, we should get the other factor $x + 5$. This division is not done like division by a monomial; it is done like long division of whole numbers. We get the first term of the quotient by dividing the first term of $x - 2$ into the first term of $x^2 + 3x - 10$. Divide x^2 by x to get x.

$$
\begin{array}{r}
x \\
x - 2 \overline{)x^2 + 3x - 10} \\
\underline{x^2 - 2x} \\
5x
\end{array}
$$

$x^2 \div x = x$

Multiply: $x(x - 2) = x^2 - 2x$.

Subtract: $3x - (-2x) = 5x$.

Now bring down -10. We get the second term of the quotient (below) by dividing the first term of $x - 2$ into the first term of $5x - 10$. Divide $5x$ by x to get 5.

$$
\begin{array}{r}
x + 5 \\
x - 2 \overline{)x^2 + 3x - 10} \\
\underline{x^2 - 2x} \\
5x - 10 \\
\underline{5x - 10} \\
0
\end{array}
$$

$5x \div x = 5$

Multiply: $5(x - 2) = 5x - 10$.

Subtract: $-10 - (-10) = 0$.

So the quotient is $x + 5$ and the remainder is 0.

When dividing polynomials, we must write the terms of the divisor and the dividend in descending order of the exponents. If any terms are missing, as in Example 3, we insert terms with a coefficient of 0 as placeholders. When dividing polynomials, we stop the process when the degree of the remainder is smaller than the degree of the divisor.

EXAMPLE 3

Helpful Hint

Students usually have the most difficulty with the subtraction part of long division. So pay particular attention to that step and double check your work.

Dividing polynomials

Find the quotient and remainder for $(3x^4 - 2 - 5x) \div (x^2 - 3x)$.

Solution

Rearrange $3x^4 - 2 - 5x$ as $3x^4 - 5x - 2$ and insert the terms $0x^3$ and $0x^2$:

$$
\begin{array}{r}
3x^2 + 9x + 27 \\
x^2 - 3x \overline{)3x^4 + 0x^3 + 0x^2 - 5x - 2} \\
\underline{3x^4 - 9x^3} \\
9x^3 + 0x^2 \\
\underline{9x^3 - 27x^2} \\
27x^2 - 5x \\
\underline{27x^2 - 81x} \\
76x - 2
\end{array}
$$

$0x^3 - (-9x^3) = 9x^3$

The quotient is $3x^2 + 9x + 27$, and the remainder is $76x - 2$. Note that the degree of the remainder is 1, and the degree of the divisor is 2. To check, verify that

$$(x^2 - 3x)(3x^2 + 9x + 27) + 76x - 2 = 3x^4 - 5x - 2.$$ ∎

EXAMPLE 4

Rewriting a ratio of two polynomials

Write $\dfrac{4x^3 - x - 9}{2x - 3}$ in the form

$$\text{quotient} + \frac{\text{remainder}}{\text{divisor}}.$$

Solution

Divide $4x^3 - x - 9$ by $2x - 3$. Insert $0 \cdot x^2$ for the missing term.

$$
\begin{array}{r}
2x^2 + 3x + 4 \\
2x - 3 \overline{\smash{)}4x^3 + 0x^2 - x - 9} \\
\underline{4x^3 - 6x^2} \\
6x^2 - x \\
\underline{6x^2 - 9x} \\
8x - 9 \\
\underline{8x - 12} \\
3
\end{array}
$$

$4x^3 \div (2x) = 2x^2$

$0x^2 - (-6x^2) = 6x^2$

$-x - (-9x) = 8x$

$-9 - (-12) = 3$

Since the quotient is $2x^2 + 3x + 4$ and the remainder is 3, we have

$$\frac{4x^3 - x - 9}{2x - 3} = 2x^2 + 3x + 4 + \frac{3}{2x - 3}.$$

To check the answer, we must verify that

$$(2x - 3)(2x^2 + 3x + 4) + 3 = 4x^3 - x - 9.$$

Synthetic Division

When dividing a polynomial by a binomial of the form $x - c$, we can use **synthetic division** to speed up the process. For synthetic division we write only the essential parts of ordinary division. For example, to divide $x^3 - 5x^2 + 4x - 3$ by $x - 2$, we write only the coefficients of the dividend 1, -5, 4, and -3 in order of descending exponents. From the divisor $x - 2$ we use 2 and start with the following arrangement:

$$2 \,\big|\, 1 \;\; -5 \;\; 4 \;\; -3 \qquad (1 \cdot x^3 - 5x^2 + 4x - 3) \div (x - 2)$$

Next we bring the first coefficient, 1, straight down:

$$
\begin{array}{c|cccc}
2 & 1 & -5 & 4 & -3 \\
& \downarrow & \text{Bring down} \\
\hline
& 1
\end{array}
$$

We then multiply the 1 by the 2 from the divisor, place the answer under the -5, and then add that column. Using 2 for $x - 2$ allows us to add the column rather than subtract as in ordinary division:

$$
\begin{array}{c|cccc}
2 & 1 & -5 & 4 & -3 \\
& & 2 & & \text{Add} \\
\hline
& 1 & -3
\end{array}
$$

Multiply

We then repeat the multiply-and-add step for each of the remaining columns:

$$
\begin{array}{c|cccc}
2 & 1 & -5 & 4 & -3 \\
& & 2 & -6 & -4 \\
\hline
& 1 & -3 & -2 & -7 \;\; \leftarrow \text{Remainder}
\end{array}
$$

Multiply

Quotient

From the bottom row we can read the quotient and remainder. Since the degree of the quotient is one less than the degree of the dividend, the quotient is $1x^2 - 3x - 2$. The remainder is -7.

The strategy for getting the quotient $Q(x)$ and remainder R by synthetic division can be stated as follows.

> ### Strategy for Using Synthetic Division
>
> 1. List the coefficients of the polynomial (the dividend).
> 2. Be sure to include zeros for any missing terms in the dividend.
> 3. For dividing by $x - c$, place c to the left.
> 4. Bring the first coefficient down.
> 5. Multiply by c and add for each column.
> 6. Read $Q(x)$ and R from the bottom row.

CAUTION   Synthetic division is used only for dividing a polynomial by the binomial $x - c$, where c is a constant. If the binomial is $x - 7$, then $c = 7$. For the binomial $x + 7$ we have $x + 7 = x - (-7)$ and $c = -7$.

EXAMPLE 5

Using synthetic division

Find the quotient and remainder when $2x^4 - 5x^2 + 6x - 9$ is divided by $x + 2$.

Solution

Since $x + 2 = x - (-2)$, we use -2 for the divisor. Because x^3 is missing in the dividend, use a zero for the coefficient of x^3:

$$
\begin{array}{r}
-2 \;\big|\; \begin{array}{rrrrr} 2 & 0 & -5 & 6 & -9 \end{array} \qquad \leftarrow 2x^4 + 0 \cdot x^3 - 5x^2 + 6x - 9 \\
\underline{\begin{array}{rrrrr} & -4 & 8 & -6 & 0 \end{array}} \quad \Big\} \text{ Add} \\
\begin{array}{rrrrr} 2 & -4 & 3 & 0 & -9 \end{array} \qquad \leftarrow \text{Quotient and remainder}
\end{array}
$$

Because the degree of the dividend is 4, the degree of the quotient is 3. The quotient is $2x^3 - 4x^2 + 3x$, and the remainder is -9. We can also express the results of this division in the form quotient $+ \frac{\text{remainder}}{\text{divisor}}$:

$$
\frac{2x^4 - 5x^2 + 6x - 9}{x + 2} = 2x^3 - 4x^2 + 3x + \frac{-9}{x + 2}
$$

∎

Division and Factoring

To **factor** a polynomial means to write it as a product of two or more simpler polynomials. If we divide two polynomials and get 0 remainder, then we can write

$$\text{dividend} = (\text{divisor})(\text{quotient})$$

and we have factored the dividend. *The dividend factors as the divisor times the quotient if and only if the remainder is* 0. We can use division to help us discover factors of polynomials. To use this idea, however, we must know a factor or a possible factor to use as the divisor.

E X A M P L E   6   **Using synthetic division to determine factors**

Is $x - 1$ a factor of $6x^3 - 5x^2 - 4x + 3$?

Solution

We can use synthetic division to divide $6x^3 - 5x^2 - 4x + 3$ by $x - 1$:

$$
\begin{array}{r|rrrr}
1 & 6 & -5 & -4 & 3 \\
  & \downarrow & 6 & 1 & -3 \\
\hline
  & 6 & 1 & -3 & 0
\end{array}
$$

Because the remainder is 0, $x - 1$ is a factor, and

$$6x^3 - 5x^2 - 4x + 3 = (x - 1)(6x^2 + x - 3).$$ ∎

The Remainder Theorem

If a polynomial $P(x)$ is divided by $x - c$ we get a quotient and a remainder that satisfy

$$P(x) = (x - c)(\text{quotient}) + \text{remainder}$$

Now replace x by c:

$$P(c) = (c - c)(\text{quotient}) + \text{remainder}$$
$$= 0(\text{quotient}) + \text{remainder}$$
$$= \text{remainder}$$

This computation proves the remainder theorem.

The Remainder Theorem

If the polynomial $P(x)$ is divided by $x - c$, then the remainder is equal to $P(c)$.

The remainder theorem gives us a new way to evaluate a polynomial. Note that we could use long division or synthetic division to find the remainder, but it easier to use synthetic division.

E X A M P L E   7   **Using synthetic division to evaluate a polynomial**

Use synthetic division to find $P(2)$ when $P(x) = 4x^3 - 5x^2 + 6x - 7$.

Solution

Find the remainder when $P(x)$ is divided by $x - 2$:

$$
\begin{array}{r|rrrr}
2 & 4 & -5 & 6 & -7 \\
  & \downarrow & 8 & 6 & 24 \\
\hline
  & 4 & 3 & 12 & 17
\end{array}
$$

Since 17 is the remainder, $P(2) = 17$. Check by replacing x with 2 in $P(x)$:

$$P(2) = 4 \cdot 2^3 - 5 \cdot 2^2 + 6 \cdot 2 - 7$$
$$= 32 - 20 + 12 - 7$$
$$= 17$$ ∎

True or false? Explain your answer.

1. If $a \div b = c$, then c is the dividend.
2. The quotient times the dividend plus the remainder equals the divisor.
3. $(x + 2)(x + 3) + 1 = x^2 + 5x + 7$ is true for any value of x.
4. The quotient of $(x^2 + 5x + 7) \div (x + 3)$ is $x + 2$.
5. If $x^2 + 5x + 7$ is divided by $x + 2$, the remainder is 1.
6. To divide $x^3 - 4x + 1$ by $x - 3$, we use -3 in synthetic division.
7. We can use synthetic division to divide $x^3 - 4x^2 - 6$ by $x^2 - 5$.
8. If $3x^5 - 4x^2 - 3$ is divided by $x + 2$, the quotient has degree 4.
9. If the remainder is zero, then the divisor is a factor of the dividend.
10. If the remainder is zero, then the quotient is a factor of the dividend.

6.5   EXERCISES

Reading and Writing   After reading this section, write out the answers to these questions. Use complete sentences.

1. What are the dividend, divisor, and quotient?

2. In what form should polynomials be written for long division?

3. What do you do about missing terms when dividing polynomials?

4. When do you stop the long division process for dividing polynomials?

5. What is synthetic division used for?

6. What is the relationship between division of polynomials and factoring polynomials?

Find the quotient. See Example 1.

7. $36x^7 \div (3x^3)$
8. $-30x^3 \div (-5x)$
9. $16x^2 \div (-8x^2)$
10. $-22a^3 \div (11a^2)$
11. $(6b - 9) \div 3$

12. $(8x^2 - 6x) \div 2$
13. $(3x^2 + 3x) \div (3x)$
14. $(5x^3 - 10x^2 - 5x) \div (5x)$
15. $(10x^4 - 8x^3 + 6x^2) \div (-2x^2)$
16. $(-9x^3 + 6x^2 - 12x) \div (-3x)$

17. $(7x^3 - 4x^2) \div (2x)$

18. $(6x^3 - 5x^2) \div (4x^2)$

Find the quotient and remainder. See Example 2.

19. $(8x - 3) \div (4x)$
20. $(9x - 5) \div (3x)$

21. $(2x^3 + x^2 + 4x - 3) \div (3x^2)$

22. $(5x^3 - 6x^2 + 4x - 1) \div (5x^2)$

23. $(-10x^4 - 5x^3 - 6x - 7) \div (-5x^2)$
24. $(-12x^5 - 8x^4 - 6x^2 + x - 4) \div (3x^3)$

Find the quotient and remainder as in Example 3. Check by using the formula

$$dividend = (divisor)(quotient) + remainder.$$

25. $(x^2 + 8x + 13) \div (x + 3)$
26. $(x^2 + 5x + 7) \div (x + 3)$
27. $(x^2 - 2x) \div (x + 2)$
28. $(3x) \div (x - 1)$
29. $(x^3 + 8) \div (x + 2)$
30. $(y^3 - 1) \div (y - 1)$

31. $(a^3 + 4a - 5) \div (a - 2)$

32. $(w^3 + w^2 - 3) \div (w - 2)$

33. $(x^3 - x^2 + x - 3) \div (x + 1)$

34. $(a^3 - a^2 + a - 4) \div (a + 2)$

35. $(x^4 - x + x^3 - 1) \div (x - 2)$

36. $(3x^4 + 6 - x^2 + 3x) \div (x + 2)$

37. $(5x^2 - 3x^4 + x - 2) \div (x^2 - 2)$

38. $(x^4 - 2 + x^3) \div (x^2 + 3)$

39. $(6x^2 + x - 16) \div (2x - 3)$

40. $(12x^2 - x - 9) \div (3x + 2)$

41. $(10b^2 - 17b - 22) \div (5b + 4)$

42. $(20a^2 + 2a - 7) \div (4a - 2)$

43. $(2x^3 + 3x^2 - 3x - 2) \div (2x + 1)$

44. $(6x^3 - 7x^2 + 5x + 6) \div (3x - 2)$

45. $(x^3 - 4x^2 - 3x - 10) \div (x^2 + x + 2)$

46. $(2x^3 - 3x^2 + 7x - 3) \div (x^2 - x + 3)$

Write each expression in the form

$$\text{quotient} + \frac{\text{remainder}}{\text{divisor}}.$$

See Example 4.

47. $\dfrac{2x}{x - 5}$ **48.** $\dfrac{x}{x - 1}$

49. $\dfrac{2x^2 - x}{2x + 1}$ **50.** $\dfrac{8x^2 - 3}{4x - 6}$

51. $\dfrac{x^3}{x + 2}$ **52.** $\dfrac{x^3 - 1}{x - 2}$

53. $\dfrac{x^3 + 2x}{x^2}$ **54.** $\dfrac{2x^2 + 3}{2x}$

55. $\dfrac{2x^2 - 11x - 4}{2x + 1}$ **56.** $\dfrac{5x^2 - 13x + 13}{5x - 3}$

57. $\dfrac{3x^3 - 4x^2 + 7}{x - 1}$ **58.** $\dfrac{-2x^3 + x^2 - 3}{x + 2}$

59. $\dfrac{6x^3 - 4x + 5}{x - 2}$ **60.** $\dfrac{-x^3 - x + 2}{x + 3}$

61. $\dfrac{x^3 + x}{x + 1}$ **62.** $\dfrac{x^3 - x}{x - 3}$

Use synthetic division to find the quotient and remainder when the first polynomial is divided by the second. See Example 5.

63. $x^3 - 5x^2 + 6x - 3, \quad x - 2$

64. $x^3 + 6x^2 - 3x - 5, \quad x - 3$

65. $2x^2 - 4x + 5, \quad x + 1$

66. $3x^2 - 7x + 4, \quad x + 2$

67. $3x^4 - 15x^2 + 7x - 9, \quad x - 3$

68. $-2x^4 + 3x^2 - 5, \quad x - 2$

69. $x^5 - 1, \quad x - 1$

70. $x^6 - 1, \quad x + 1$

71. $x^3 - 5x + 6, \quad x + 2$

72. $x^3 - 3x - 7, \quad x - 4$

73. $x^3 - 3x^2 + 5, \quad x - 5$

74. $3x^3 + 20x^2 + 2, \quad x + 7$

For each pair of polynomials, use division to determine whether the first polynomial is a factor of the second. Use synthetic division when possible. If the first polynomial is a factor, then factor the second polynomial. See Example 6.

75. $x + 4, x^3 + x^2 - 11x + 8$

76. $x - 1, x^3 + 3x^2 - 5x$

77. $x - 4, x^2 - 6x + 8$

78. $x + 8, x^2 + 3x - 40$

79. $w - 3, w^3 - 27$

80. $w + 5, w^3 + 125$

81. $2x - 3, 2x^3 - 3x^2 - 4x + 7$

82. $3x - 5, 3x^3 + x^2 - 7x + 6$

83. $y - 2, y^3 - 4y^2 + 6y - 4$

84. $z + 1, 2z^3 + 5z + 7$

Use synthetic division and the remainder theorem to find $P(c)$ for the given polynomial and given value of c. See Example 7.

85. $P(x) = x^2 - 5x - 9, c = 3$

86. $P(x) = x^3 + 3x^2 - 7x + 2, c = 2$

87. $P(y) = 4y^3 - 6y + 7, c = -1$

88. $P(y) = 2y^3 - y^2 - 1, c = -4$

89. $P(w) = -w^3 + 5w^2 + 3w, c = 4$

90. $P(w) = -2w^3 - w^2 - 15, c = -3$

Solve each problem.

91. *Average cost.* The total cost in dollars for manufacturing x professional racing bicycles in one week is given by the polynomial function

$$C(x) = 0.03x^2 + 300x.$$

The average cost per bicycle is given by

$$AC(x) = \frac{C(x)}{x}.$$

a) Find a formula for $AC(x)$.

b) Is $AC(x)$ a constant function?

c) Why does the average cost look constant in the accompanying figure?

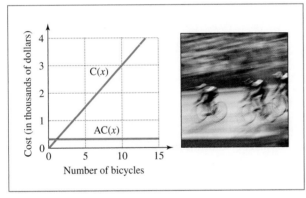

FIGURE FOR EXERCISE 91

92. *Average profit.* The weekly profit in dollars for manufacturing x bicycles is given by the polynomial $P(x) = 100x + 2x^2$. The average profit per bicycle is given by $AP(x) = \frac{P(x)}{x}$. Find $AP(x)$. Find the average profit per bicycle when 12 bicycles are manufactured.

93. *Area of a poster.* The area of a rectangular poster advertising a Pearl Jam concert is $x^2 - 1$ square feet. If the length is $x + 1$ feet, then what is the width?

94. *Volume of a box.* The volume of a shipping crate is $h^3 + 5h^2 + 6h$. If the height is h and the length is $h + 2$, then what is the width?

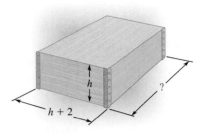

FIGURE FOR EXERCISE 94

95. *Volume of a pyramid.* Ancient Egyptian pyramid builders knew that the volume of the truncated pyramid shown in the figure is given by

$$V = \frac{H(a^3 - b^3)}{3(a - b)},$$

where a^2 is the area of the square base, b^2 is the area of the square top, and H is the distance from the base to the top. Find the volume of a truncated pyramid that has a base of 900 square meters, a top of 400 square meters, and a height H of 10 meters.

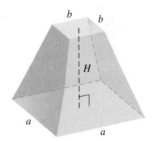

FIGURE FOR EXERCISE 95

96. *Egyptian pyramid formula.* Simplify the expression in Exercise 95.

GETTING MORE INVOLVED

97. *Discussion.* On a test a student divided $3x^3 - 5x^2 - 3x + 7$ by $x - 3$ and got a quotient of $3x^2 + 4x$ and remainder $9x + 7$. Verify that the divisor times the quotient plus the remainder is equal to the dividend. Why was the student's answer incorrect?

98. *Exploration.* Use synthetic division to find the quotient when $x^5 - 1$ is divided by $x - 1$ and the quotient when $x^6 - 1$ is divided by $x - 1$. Observe the pattern in the first two quotients and then write the quotient for $x^9 - 1$ divided by $x - 1$ without dividing.

6.6 SOLVING EQUATIONS INVOLVING RATIONAL EXPRESSIONS

Many problems in algebra are modeled by equations involving rational expressions. In this section you will learn how to solve equations that have rational expressions, and in Section 6.7 we will solve problems using these equations.

Multiplying by the LCD

To solve equations having rational expressions, we multiply each side of the equation by the LCD of the rational expressions.

E X A M P L E   1

An equation with rational expressions

Solve $\frac{1}{x} + \frac{1}{4} = \frac{1}{6}$.

Helpful Hint

Note that it is not necessary to convert each fraction into an equivalent fraction with a common denominator here. Since we can multiply both sides of an equation by any expression we choose, we choose to multiply by the LCD. This tactic eliminates the fractions in one step and that is good.

Solution

The LCD for the denominators 4, 6, and x is $12x$:

$$12x\left(\frac{1}{x} + \frac{1}{4}\right) = 12x\left(\frac{1}{6}\right) \quad \text{Multiply each side by } 12x.$$

$$12x \cdot \frac{1}{x} + \overset{3}{12}x \cdot \frac{1}{4} = \overset{2}{12}x \cdot \frac{1}{6} \quad \text{Distributive property}$$

$$12 + 3x = 2x \qquad \text{Divide out the common factors.}$$

$$12 + x = 0$$

$$x = -12$$

Check -12 in the original equation. The solution set is $\{-12\}$.   ∎

E X A M P L E   2

An equation with rational expressions

Solve $\frac{1}{x} + \frac{2}{3x} = \frac{1}{5}$.

Solution

Multiply each side by $15x$, the LCD for x, $3x$, and 5:

$$15x\left(\frac{1}{x} + \frac{2}{3x}\right) = 15x\left(\frac{1}{5}\right)$$

$$15x \cdot \frac{1}{x} + 15x \cdot \frac{2}{3x} = 3x$$

$$15 + 10 = 3x$$

$$25 = 3x$$

$$\frac{25}{3} = x$$

Check $\frac{25}{3}$ in the original equation. The solution set is $\left\{\frac{25}{3}\right\}$.   ∎

CAUTION   To solve an equation with rational expressions, we do *not* convert the rational expressions to ones with a common denominator. Instead, we multiply each side by the LCD to *eliminate* the denominators.

EXAMPLE 3

An equation with two solutions

Solve $\frac{200}{x} + \frac{300}{x + 20} = 10$.

Solution

$$x(x + 20)\left(\frac{200}{x} + \frac{300}{x + 20}\right) = x(x + 20)10 \qquad \text{Multiply each side by } x(x + 20).$$

$$x(x + 20)\frac{200}{x} + x(x + 20)\frac{300}{x + 20} = x(x + 20)10 \qquad \text{Distributive property}$$

$$(x + 20)200 + x(300) = (x^2 + 20x)10 \qquad \text{Simplify.}$$

$$200x + 4000 + 300x = 10x^2 + 200x$$

$$4000 + 300x = 10x^2 \qquad \text{Combine like terms.}$$

$$400 + 30x = x^2 \qquad \text{Divide each side by 10.}$$

$$0 = x^2 - 30x - 400$$

$$0 = (x - 40)(x + 10) \qquad \text{Factor.}$$

$$x - 40 = 0 \quad \text{or} \quad x + 10 = 0 \qquad \text{Set each factor equal to 0.}$$

$$x = 40 \quad \text{or} \qquad x = -10$$

Check these values in the original equation. The solution set is $\{-10, 40\}$. ■

Extraneous Roots

Because equations involving rational expressions have variables in denominators, a root to the equation might cause a 0 to appear in a denominator. In this case the root does not satisfy the original equation, and so it is called an **extraneous root.**

EXAMPLE 4

An equation with an extraneous root

Solve $\frac{3}{x} + \frac{6}{x - 2} = \frac{12}{x^2 - 2x}$.

Solution

Because $x^2 - 2x = x(x - 2)$, the LCD for x, $x - 2$, and $x^2 - 2x$ is $x(x - 2)$.

$$x(x - 2)\frac{3}{x} + x(x - 2)\frac{6}{x - 2} = x(x - 2)\frac{12}{x(x - 2)} \qquad \text{Multiply each side by } x(x - 2).$$

$$3(x - 2) + 6x = 12$$

$$3x - 6 + 6x = 12$$

$$9x - 6 = 12$$

$$9x = 18$$

$$x = 2$$

Neither 0 nor 2 could be a solution because replacing x by either 0 or 2 would cause 0 to appear in a denominator in the original equation. So 2 is an extraneous root and the solution set is the empty set, $\varnothing$. ■

E X A M P L E   5

An equation with an extraneous root

Solve $x + 2 + \dfrac{x}{x - 2} = \dfrac{2}{x - 2}$.

Solution

Because the LCD is $x - 2$, we multiply each side by $x - 2$:

$$(x - 2)(x + 2) + (x - 2)\dfrac{x}{x - 2} = (x - 2)\dfrac{2}{x - 2}$$

$$x^2 - 4 + x = 2$$

$$x^2 + x - 6 = 0$$

$$(x + 3)(x - 2) = 0$$

$$x + 3 = 0 \quad \text{or} \quad x - 2 = 0$$

$$x = -3 \quad \text{or} \quad x = 2$$

Replacing x by 2 in the original equation would cause 0 to appear in a denominator. So 2 is an extraneous root. Check that the original equation is satisfied if $x = -3$. The solution set is $\{-3\}$. ∎

Proportions

An equation that expresses the equality of two rational expressions is called a **proportion.** The equation

$$\frac{a}{b} = \frac{c}{d}$$

is a proportion. The terms in the position of b and c are called the **means.** The terms in the position of a and d are called the **extremes.** If we multiply this proportion by the LCD, bd, we get

$$bd \cdot \frac{a}{b} = bd \cdot \frac{c}{d}$$

or

$$ad = bc.$$

> ### Helpful Hint
>
> The extremes-means property is often referred to as *cross-multiplying.* Whatever you call it, remember that it is nothing new. You can accomplish the same thing by multiplying each side of the equation by the LCD.

The equation $ad = bc$ says that *the product of the extremes is equal to the product of the means.* When solving a proportion, we can omit multiplication by the LCD and just remember the result, $ad = bc$, as the **extremes-means property.**

> **Extremes-Means Property**
>
> If $\frac{a}{b} = \frac{c}{d}$, then $ad = bc$.

The extremes-means property makes it easier to solve proportions.

E X A M P L E   6

A proportion with one solution

Solve $\dfrac{20}{x} = \dfrac{30}{x + 20}$.

Solution

Rather than multiplying by the LCD, we use the extremes-means property to eliminate the denominators:

$$\frac{20}{x} = \frac{30}{x + 20}$$

$$20(x + 20) = 30x \qquad \text{Extremes-means property}$$

$$20x + 400 = 30x$$

$$400 = 10x$$

$$40 = x$$

Check 40 in the original equation. The solution set is $\{40\}$. ■

E X A M P L E   7

A proportion with two solutions

Solve $\frac{2}{x} = \frac{x + 3}{5}$.

Solution

Use the extremes-means property to write an equivalent equation:

$$x(x + 3) = 2 \cdot 5 \qquad \text{Extremes-means property}$$

$$x^2 + 3x = 10$$

$$x^2 + 3x - 10 = 0$$

$$(x + 5)(x - 2) = 0 \qquad \text{Factor.}$$

$$x + 5 = 0 \quad \text{or} \quad x - 2 = 0 \qquad \text{Zero factor property}$$

$$x = -5 \quad \text{or} \qquad x = 2$$

Both -5 and 2 satisfy the original equation. The solution set is $\{-5, 2\}$. ■

C A U T I O N   Use the extremes-means property only when solving a *proportion*. It cannot be used on an equation such as

$$\frac{3}{x} = \frac{2}{x + 1} + 5.$$

E X A M P L E   8

Ratios and proportions

The ratio of men to women at a football game was 4 to 3. If there were 12,000 more men than women in attendance, then how many men and how many women were in attendance?

Solution

Let x represent the number of men in attendance and $x - 12{,}000$ represent the number of women in attendance. Because the ratio of men to women was 4 to 3, we can write the following proportion:

$$\frac{4}{3} = \frac{x}{x - 12{,}000}$$

$$4x - 48{,}000 = 3x$$

$$x = 48{,}000$$

So there were 48,000 men and 36,000 women at the game. ■

M A T H   A T   W O R K

Cargo has been lost, or the hull of a ship has been damaged. What is the amount of money that should be paid to the insured party? Lisa M. Paccione, Ocean Marine Claim Representative for the St. Paul Insurance Company, investigates, evaluates, resolves, and pays these types of claims. Ms. Paccione does this by gathering data, occasionally doing a visual inspection, interviewing witnesses, and negotiating with attorneys.

MARINE INSURANCE AGENT

Decisions about losses are based on the insured party's individual policy as well as traditional marine practices and maritime law. When consignees suffer a cargo loss, they not only are compensated for the actual amount of the damaged goods, but also receive an additional "advance" in the settlement. Customarily, the advance is 10% over the value of the goods. The amount that St. Paul pays the insured party for a valid claim is computed by using a proportion. In Exercises 73 and 74 of this section you will solve problems involving this proportion.

WARM-UPS

True or false? Explain.

1. In solving an equation involving rational expressions, multiply each side by the LCD for all of the denominators.

2. To solve $\frac{1}{x} + \frac{1}{2x} = \frac{1}{3}$, first change each rational expression to an equivalent rational expression with a denominator of $6x$.

3. Extraneous roots are not real numbers.

4. To solve $\frac{1}{x-2} + 3 = \frac{1}{x+2}$, multiply each side by $x^2 - 4$.

5. The solution set to $\frac{x}{3x+4} - \frac{6}{2x+1} = \frac{7}{5}$ is $\left\{ -\frac{4}{3}, -\frac{1}{2} \right\}$.

6. The solution set to $\frac{3}{x} = \frac{2}{5}$ is $\left\{ \frac{15}{2} \right\}$.

7. We should use the extremes-means property to solve $\frac{x-2}{x+3} + 1 = \frac{1}{x}$.

8. The equation $x^2 = x$ is equivalent to the equation $x = 0$.

9. The solution set to $(2x - 3)(3x + 4) = 0$ is $\left\{ \frac{3}{2}, \frac{4}{3} \right\}$.

10. The equation $\frac{2}{x+1} = \frac{x-1}{4}$ is equivalent to $x^2 - 1 = 8$.

6.6   EXERCISES

Reading and Writing *After reading this section, write out the answers to these questions. Use complete sentences.*

1. What is the usual first step in solving an equation involving rational expressions?

2. How can an equation involving rational expressions have an extraneous root?

3. What is a proportion?

4. What are the means?

5. What are the extremes?

6. What is the extremes-means property?

Find the solution set to each equation. See Examples 1–5.

7. $\dfrac{1}{x} + \dfrac{1}{6} = \dfrac{1}{8}$

8. $\dfrac{3}{x} + \dfrac{1}{5} = \dfrac{1}{2}$

9. $\dfrac{2}{3x} + \dfrac{1}{15x} = \dfrac{1}{2}$

10. $\dfrac{5}{6x} - \dfrac{1}{8x} = \dfrac{17}{24}$

11. $\dfrac{3}{x-2} + \dfrac{5}{x} = \dfrac{10}{x}$

12. $\dfrac{5}{x-1} + \dfrac{1}{2x} = \dfrac{1}{x}$

13. $\dfrac{x}{x-2} + \dfrac{3}{x} = 2$

14. $\dfrac{x}{x-5} + \dfrac{5}{x} = \dfrac{11}{6}$

15. $\dfrac{100}{x} = \dfrac{150}{x+5} - 1$

16. $\dfrac{30}{x} = \dfrac{50}{x+10} + \dfrac{1}{2}$

17. $\dfrac{3x-5}{x-1} = 2 - \dfrac{2x}{x-1}$

18. $\dfrac{x-3}{x+2} = 3 - \dfrac{1-2x}{x+2}$

19. $x + 1 + \dfrac{2x-5}{x-5} = \dfrac{x}{x-5}$

20. $\dfrac{x-3}{2} - \dfrac{1}{x-3} = \dfrac{8-3x}{x-3}$

21. $5 + \dfrac{9}{x-2} = 2 + \dfrac{x+7}{x-2}$

22. $3 + \dfrac{x+1}{x-3} = 2 - \dfrac{5-3x}{x-3}$

23. $\dfrac{2}{x+2} + \dfrac{x}{x-3} + \dfrac{1}{x^2-x-6} = 0$

24. $\dfrac{x-4}{x^2+2x-15} = 2 - \dfrac{2}{x-3}$

Find the solution set to each equation. See Examples 6 and 7.

25. $\dfrac{2}{x} = \dfrac{3}{4}$

26. $\dfrac{5}{x} = \dfrac{7}{9}$

27. $\dfrac{a}{3} = \dfrac{-1}{4}$

28. $\dfrac{b}{5} = \dfrac{-3}{7}$

29. $-\dfrac{5}{7} = \dfrac{2}{x}$

30. $-\dfrac{3}{8} = \dfrac{5}{x}$

31. $\dfrac{10}{x} = \dfrac{20}{x+20}$

32. $\dfrac{x}{5} = \dfrac{x+2}{3}$

33. $\dfrac{2}{x+1} = \dfrac{x-1}{4}$

34. $\dfrac{3}{x-2} = \dfrac{x+2}{7}$

35. $\dfrac{x}{6} = \dfrac{5}{x-1}$

36. $\dfrac{x+5}{2} = \dfrac{3}{x}$

37. $\dfrac{x+7}{x+4} = \dfrac{x+1}{x-2}$

38. $\dfrac{x+1}{x-5} = \dfrac{x+2}{x-4}$

39. $\dfrac{x-2}{x-3} = \dfrac{x+5}{x+2}$

40. $\dfrac{a-5}{a+6} = \dfrac{a-7}{a+8}$

41. $\dfrac{3w}{3w-5} = \dfrac{w}{w+2}$

42. $\dfrac{x}{x+5} = \dfrac{x}{x-2}$

Solve each equation.

43. $\dfrac{a}{9} = \dfrac{4}{a}$

44. $\dfrac{y}{3} = \dfrac{27}{y}$

45. $\dfrac{1}{2x-4} + \dfrac{1}{x-2} = \dfrac{1}{4}$

46. $\dfrac{7}{3x-9} - \dfrac{1}{x-3} = \dfrac{4}{9}$

47. $\dfrac{x-2}{4} = \dfrac{x-2}{x}$

48. $\dfrac{y+5}{2} = \dfrac{y+5}{y}$

49. $\dfrac{5}{2x+4} - \dfrac{1}{x-1} = \dfrac{3}{x+2}$

50. $\dfrac{5}{2w+6} - \dfrac{1}{w-1} = \dfrac{1}{w+3}$

51. $\dfrac{5}{x-3} = \dfrac{x}{x-3}$

52. $\dfrac{6}{a+2} = \dfrac{a}{a+2}$

53. $\dfrac{w}{6} = \dfrac{3}{2w}$

54. $\dfrac{2m}{5} = \dfrac{10}{m}$

55. $\dfrac{5}{4x-2} - \dfrac{1}{1-2x} = \dfrac{7}{3x+6}$

56. $\dfrac{5}{x+1} - \dfrac{1}{1-x} = \dfrac{1}{x^2-1}$

57. $\dfrac{5}{x} = \dfrac{2}{5}$

58. $\dfrac{-3}{2x} = \dfrac{1}{-5}$

59. $\dfrac{x}{x-2} - \dfrac{x+2}{x^2-2x} = \dfrac{1}{x}$

60. $\dfrac{x-2}{x-6} - \dfrac{4}{x} = \dfrac{24}{x^2-6x}$

61. $\dfrac{5}{x^2-9} + \dfrac{2}{x+3} = \dfrac{1}{x-3}$

62. $\dfrac{1}{x-2} - \dfrac{2}{x+3} = \dfrac{11}{x^2+x-6}$

63. $\dfrac{9}{x^3-1} - \dfrac{1}{x-1} = \dfrac{2}{x^2+x+1}$

64. $\dfrac{x+4}{x^3+8} + \dfrac{x+2}{x^2-2x+4} = \dfrac{11}{2x+4}$

Either solve the given equation or perform the indicated operation(s), whichever is appropriate.

65. $\dfrac{4}{x} = \dfrac{3}{4}$

66. $\dfrac{5}{h} = \dfrac{h}{5}$

67. $\dfrac{4}{x} + \dfrac{3}{4}$

68. $\dfrac{5}{h} - \dfrac{h}{5}$

69. $\dfrac{2}{x} - \dfrac{3}{4} = \dfrac{1}{2}$

70. $\dfrac{1}{2x} - \dfrac{5}{3x} = \dfrac{1}{4}$

71. $\dfrac{2}{x} - \dfrac{3}{4} - \dfrac{1}{2}$

72. $\dfrac{1}{2x} - \dfrac{5}{3x} + \dfrac{1}{4}$

In Exercises 73–82, solve each problem. See Example 8.

73. *Maritime losses.* The amount paid to an insured party by the American Insurance Company is computed by using the proportion

$$\frac{\text{value shipped}}{\text{amount of loss}} = \frac{\text{amount of declared premium}}{\text{amount insured party gets paid}}.$$

If the value shipped was $300,000, the amount of loss was $250,000, and the amount of declared premium was $200,000, then what amount is paid to the insured party?

74. *Maritime losses.* Suppose the value shipped was $400,000, the amount of loss was $300,000, and the amount that the insured party got paid was $150,000. Use the proportion of Exercise 73 to find the amount of declared premium.

75. *Capture-recapture method.* To estimate the size of the grizzly bear population in a national park, rangers tagged and released 12 bears. Later it was observed that in 23 sightings of grizzly bears, only two had been tagged. Assuming the proportion of tagged bears in the later sightings is the same as the proportion of tagged bears in the population, estimate the number of bears in the population.

76. *Please rewind.* In a sample of 24 returned videotapes, it was found that only 3 were rewound as requested. If 872 videos are returned in a day, then how many of them would you expect to find that are not rewound?

77. *Pleasing painting.* The ancient Greeks often used the ratio of length to width for a rectangle as 7 to 6 to give the rectangle a pleasing shape. If the length of a pleasantly shaped Greek painting is 22 centimeters (cm) longer than its width, then what are its length and width?

78. *Pickups and cars.* The ratio of pickups to cars sold at a dealership is 2 to 3. If the dealership sold 142 more cars than pickups in 1999, then how many of each did it sell?

79. *Cleaning up the river.* Pollution in the Tickfaw River has been blamed primarily on pesticide runoff from area farms. The formula

$$C = \frac{4{,}000{,}000p}{100 - p}$$

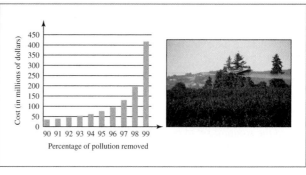

FIGURE FOR EXERCISE 79

has been used to model the cost in dollars for removing $p\%$ of the pollution in the river. If the state gets a $1 million federal grant for cleaning up the river, then what percentage of the pollution can be removed? Use the bar graph to estimate the percentage that can be cleaned up with a $100 million grant.

80. *Campaigning for governor.* A campaign manager for a gubernatorial candidate estimates that the cost in dollars for an advertising campaign that will get his candidate $p\%$ of the votes is given by

$$C = \frac{1{,}000{,}000 + 2{,}000{,}000p}{100 - p}.$$

If the candidate can spend only $2 million for advertising, then what percentage of the votes can she expect to receive? Use the bar graph to estimate the percentage of votes expected if $4 million is spent.

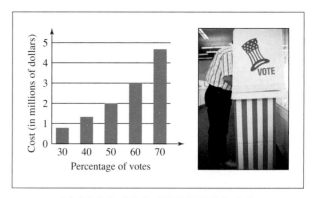

FIGURE FOR EXERCISE 80

81. *Wealth-building portfolio.* Misty decided to invest her annual bonus in a wealth-building portfolio as shown in the figure on the next page *(Fidelity Investments, Boston)*.

a) If the amount that she invested in stocks was $20,000 greater than her investment in bonds, then how much did she invest in bonds?

b) What was the amount of her annual bonus?

Designing a retirement portfolio

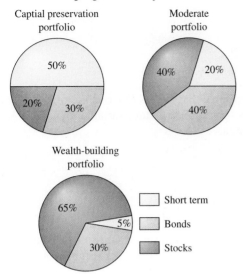

Captial preservation portfolio

Moderate portfolio

50%

20% 30%

40% 20%

40%

Wealth-building portfolio

65%

5%

30%

☐ Short term

☐ Bonds

■ Stocks

FIGURE FOR EXERCISE 81

82. *Estimating weapons.* When intelligence agents obtain enemy weapons marked with serial numbers, they use the formula $N = (1 + 1/C)B - 1$ to estimate the total number of such weapons N that the enemy has produced. B is the biggest serial number obtained and C is the number of weapons obtained. It is assumed the weapons are numbered 1 through N.

a) Find N if agents obtain five nerve gas containers numbered 45, 143, 258, 301, and 465.

b) Find C if agents estimate that the enemy has 255 tanks from a group of captured tanks on which the biggest serial number is 224.

GETTING MORE INVOLVED

 83. *Writing.* In this chapter the LCD is used to add rational expressions and to solve equations. Explain the difference between using the LCD to solve the equation

$$\frac{3}{x - 2} + \frac{7}{x + 2} = 2$$

and using the LCD to find the sum

$$\frac{3}{x - 2} + \frac{7}{x + 2}.$$

 84. *Discussion.* For each equation, find the values for x that *cannot* be solutions to the equation. Do not solve the equations.

a) $\dfrac{1}{x} + \dfrac{1}{x - 1} = \dfrac{1}{2}$ **b)** $\dfrac{x}{x - 1} = \dfrac{1}{2}$

c) $\dfrac{1}{x^2 + 1} = \dfrac{1}{x + 1}$

In This Section

- Formulas
- Uniform Motion Problems
- Work Problems
- Miscellaneous Problems

6.7 **APPLICATIONS**

In this section we will use the techniques of Section 6.6 to rewrite formulas involving rational expressions and to solve some problems.

Formulas

Rewriting formulas having rational expressions is similar to solving equations having rational expressions. Generally, the first step is to multiply each side by the LCD for the rational expressions.

E X A M P L E   1   **Solving a formula**

In Chapter 3, we wrote the equation of a line by starting with an equation involving a rational expression:

$$\frac{y - y_1}{x - x_1} = m$$

Solve the equation for y.

Solution

$$(x - x_1)\frac{y - y_1}{x - x_1} = (x - x_1)m \quad \text{Multiply each side by the denominator } x - x_1.$$

$$y - y_1 = (x - x_1)m \quad \text{Reduce.}$$

$$y = (x - x_1)m + y_1 \quad \blacksquare$$

In Example 2 we solve for a variable that occurs twice in the original formula. Remember that when a formula is solved for a certain variable, that variable must appear only once in the final formula.

E X A M P L E   2

Solving for a variable

The formula

$$\frac{P}{P_W} = \frac{2L}{2L + d}$$

is used in physics to find the relative density of a substance. Since P_W has subscript W, we treat P and P_W as two different variables. Solve the formula for L.

Solution

$$\frac{P}{P_W} = \frac{2L}{2L + d}$$

$$P(2L + d) = P_W(2L) \qquad \text{The extremes-means property}$$

$$2PL + Pd = 2LP_W \qquad \text{Simplify.}$$

$$Pd = 2LP_W - 2PL \qquad \text{Get all terms involving } L \text{ onto the same side.}$$

$$Pd = (2P_W - 2P)L \qquad \text{Factor out } L.$$

$$\frac{Pd}{2P_W - 2P} = L \qquad \blacksquare$$

In Example 3 we find the value of one variable when given the values of the remaining variables.

E X A M P L E   3

Evaluating a formula

Find x if $x_1 = 2$, $y_1 = -3$, $y = -1$, $m = \frac{1}{2}$, and

$$\frac{y - y_1}{x - x_1} = m.$$

Solution

Substitute all of the values into the formula and solve for x:

$$\frac{-1 - (-3)}{x - 2} = \frac{1}{2} \qquad \text{Substitute.}$$

$$\frac{2}{x - 2} = \frac{1}{2}$$

$$x - 2 = 4 \qquad \text{Extremes-means property}$$

$$x = 6 \qquad \text{Check in the original formula.} \qquad \blacksquare$$

Uniform Motion Problems

The uniform motion problems here are similar to those of Chapter 2, but in this chapter the equations have rational expressions.

E X A M P L E   4

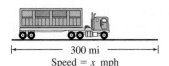

300 mi
Speed = x mph

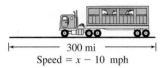

300 mi
Speed = $x - 10$ mph

F I G U R E   6 . 1

Uniform motion

Michele drove her empty rig 300 miles to Salina to pick up a load of cattle. When her rig was fully loaded, her average speed was 10 miles per hour less than when the rig was empty. If the return trip took her 1 hour longer, then what was her average speed with the rig empty? (See Fig. 6.1.)

Solution

Let x be Michele's average speed empty and let $x - 10$ be her average speed full. Because the time can be determined from the distance and the rate, $T = \dfrac{D}{R}$, we can make the following table.

	Rate	Time	Distance
Empty	$x \dfrac{\text{mi}}{\text{hr}}$	$\dfrac{300}{x}$ hr	300 mi
Full	$x - 10 \dfrac{\text{mi}}{\text{hr}}$	$\dfrac{300}{x - 10}$ hr	300 mi

We now write an equation expressing the fact that her time empty was 1 hour less than her time full:

$$\frac{300}{x} = \frac{300}{x - 10} - 1$$

$$x(x - 10)\frac{300}{x} = x(x - 10)\frac{300}{x - 10} - x(x - 10)1 \quad \text{Multiply each side by } x(x-10).$$

$$300x - 3000 = 300x - x^2 + 10x \quad \text{Reduce.}$$

$$-3000 = -x^2 + 10x$$

$$x^2 - 10x - 3000 = 0 \quad \text{Get 0 on one side.}$$

$$(x + 50)(x - 60) = 0 \quad \text{Factor.}$$

$$x + 50 = 0 \quad \text{or} \quad x - 60 = 0 \quad \text{Zero factor property}$$

$$x = -50 \quad \text{or} \quad x = 60$$

The equation is satisfied if $x = -50$, but because -50 is negative, it cannot be the speed of the truck. Michele's average speed empty was 60 miles per hour (mph). Checking this answer, we find that if she traveled 300 miles at 60 mph, it would take her 5 hours. If she traveled 300 miles at 50 mph with the loaded rig, it would take her 6 hours. Because Michele's time with the empty rig was 1 hour less than her time with the loaded rig, 60 mph is the correct answer. ∎

Work Problems

Problems involving different rates for completing a task are referred to as **work problems.** We did not solve work problems earlier because they usually require equations with rational expressions. Work problems are similar to uniform motion problems in which $RT = D$. The product of a person's time and rate is the amount of work completed. For example, if your puppy gains 1 pound every 3 days, then he is growing at the rate of $\frac{1}{3}$ pound per day. If he grows at the rate of $\frac{1}{3}$ pound per day for a period of 30 days, then he gains 10 pounds.

E X A M P L E   5   **Working together**

Linda can mow a certain lawn with her riding lawn mower in 4 hours. When Linda uses the riding mower and Rebecca operates the push mower, it takes them 3 hours to mow the lawn. How long would it take Rebecca to mow the lawn by herself using the push mower?

Solution

If x is the number of hours it takes for Rebecca to complete the lawn alone, then her rate is $\frac{1}{x}$ of the lawn per hour. Because Linda can mow the entire lawn in 4 hours, her rate is $\frac{1}{4}$ of the lawn per hour. In the 3 hours that they work together, Rebecca completes $\frac{3}{x}$ of the lawn while Linda completes $\frac{3}{4}$ of the lawn. We can classify all of the necessary information in a table that looks a lot like the one we used in Example 4.

	Rate	Time	Amount of Work
Linda	$\dfrac{1}{4}\dfrac{\text{lawn}}{\text{hr}}$	3 hr	$\dfrac{3}{4}$ lawn
Rebecca	$\dfrac{1}{x}\dfrac{\text{lawn}}{\text{hr}}$	3 hr	$\dfrac{3}{x}$ lawn

Because the lawn is finished in 3 hours, the two portions of the lawn (in the work column) mowed by each girl have a sum of 1:

$$\frac{3}{4} + \frac{3}{x} = 1$$

$$4x \cdot \frac{3}{4} + 4x \cdot \frac{3}{x} = 4x \cdot 1 \quad \text{Multiply each side by } 4x.$$

$$3x + 12 = 4x$$

$$12 = x$$

If $x = 12$, then in the 3 hours that they work together, Rebecca does $\frac{3}{12}$ or $\frac{1}{4}$ of the job while Linda does $\frac{3}{4}$ of the job. So it would take Rebecca 12 hours to mow the lawn by herself using the push mower. ■

The methods in Examples 4 and 5 are the same. One table uses $RT = D$ and the other uses $RT = W$. Making a table will help you understand a problem. Another method for solving Example 5 is to use only the rates. Since Linda's rate is $\frac{1}{4}$ lawn/hr and Rebecca's rate is $\frac{1}{x}$ lawn/hr, together their rate is $\left(\frac{1}{4} + \frac{1}{x}\right)$ lawn/hr. Since their rate together is $\frac{1}{3}$ lawn/hr, we have $\frac{1}{4} + \frac{1}{x} = \frac{1}{3}$. Solving this equation also yields $x = 12$.

Miscellaneous Problems

E X A M P L E   6   **Hamburger and steak**

Patrick bought 50 pounds of meat consisting of hamburger and steak. Steak costs twice as much per pound as hamburger. If he bought $30 worth of hamburger and $90 worth of steak, then how many pounds of each did he buy?

Solution

Let x be the number of pounds of hamburger and $50 - x$ be the number of pounds of steak. Because Patrick got x pounds of hamburger for \$30, he paid $\frac{30}{x}$ dollars per pound for the hamburger. We can classify all of the given information in a table.

	Price per pound	Amount	Total price
Hamburger	$\frac{30}{x}$ $\frac{\text{dollars}}{\text{lb}}$	x lb	30 dollars
Steak	$\frac{90}{50-x}$ $\frac{\text{dollars}}{\text{lb}}$	$50 - x$ lb	90 dollars

Because the price per pound of steak is twice that of hamburger, we can write the following equation:

$$2\left(\frac{30}{x}\right) = \frac{90}{50 - x}$$

$$\frac{60}{x} = \frac{90}{50 - x}$$

$$90x = 3000 - 60x \quad \text{The extremes-means property}$$

$$150x = 3000$$

$$x = 20$$

$$50 - x = 30$$

Patrick purchased 20 pounds of hamburger and 30 pounds of steak. Check this answer. ■

WARM-UPS

True or false? Explain.

1. The formula $w = \frac{1-t}{t}$, solved for t, is $t = \frac{1-t}{w}$.

2. To solve $\frac{1}{p} + \frac{1}{q} = \frac{1}{s}$ for s, multiply each side by pqs.

3. If 50 pounds of steak cost x dollars, then the price is $\frac{50}{x}$ dollars per pound.

4. If Claudia drives x miles in 3 hours, then her rate is $\frac{x}{3}$ miles per hour.

5. If Takenori mows his entire lawn in $x + 2$ hours, then he mows $\frac{1}{x+2}$ of the lawn per hour.

6. If Kareem drives 200 nails in 12 hours, then he is driving $\frac{200}{12}$ nails per hour.

7. If x hours is 1 hour less than y hours, then $x - 1 = y$.

8. If $A = \frac{mv^2}{B}$ and m and B are nonzero, then $v^2 = \frac{AB}{m}$.

9. If a and y are nonzero and $a = \frac{x}{y}$, then $y = ax$.

10. If x hours is 3 hours more than y hours, then $x + 3 = y$.

6.7   EXERCISES

Solve each equation for y. See Example 1.

1. $\dfrac{y - 3}{x - 2} = 5$

2. $\dfrac{y - 4}{x - 7} = -6$

3. $\dfrac{y + 1}{x - 6} = -\dfrac{1}{3}$

4. $\dfrac{y + 7}{x - 2} = \dfrac{-2}{3}$

5. $\dfrac{y - a}{x - b} = m$

6. $\dfrac{y - h}{x - k} = a$

7. $\dfrac{y - 2}{x + 5} = -\dfrac{7}{3}$

8. $\dfrac{y - 3}{x + 1} = -\dfrac{9}{4}$

Solve each formula for the indicated variable. See Example 2.

9. $M = \dfrac{F}{f}$ for f

10. $P = \dfrac{A}{1 + rt}$ for A

11. $A = \dfrac{\pi}{4} \cdot D^2$ for D^2

12. $V = \pi r^2 h$ for r^2

13. $F = k\dfrac{m_1 m_2}{r^2}$ for m_1

14. $F = \dfrac{mv^2}{r}$ for v^2

15. $\dfrac{1}{p} + \dfrac{1}{q} = \dfrac{1}{f}$ for q

16. $\dfrac{1}{R} = \dfrac{1}{R_1} + \dfrac{1}{R_2}$ for R_1

17. $e^2 = 1 - \dfrac{b^2}{a^2}$ for a^2

18. $e^2 = 1 - \dfrac{b^2}{a^2}$ for b^2

19. $\dfrac{P_1 V_1}{T_1} = \dfrac{P_2 V_2}{T_2}$ for T_1

20. $\dfrac{P_1 V_1}{T_1} = \dfrac{P_2 V_2}{T_2}$ for P_2

21. $V = \dfrac{4}{3}\pi r^2 h$ for h

22. $h = \dfrac{S - 2\pi r^2}{2\pi r}$ for S

Use the formula from the indicated exercise to find the value of the indicated variable. See Example 3. For calculator problems, round answers to three decimal places.

23. If $M = 10$ and $F = 5$ in Exercise 9, find f.

24. If $A = 550$, $P = 500$, and $t = 2$ in Exercise 10, find r.

25. If $A = 6\pi$ in Exercise 11, find D^2.

26. If $V = 12\pi$ and $r = 3$ in Exercise 12, find h.

27. If $F = 32$, $r = 4$, $m_1 = 6$, and $m_2 = 8$ in Exercise 13, find k.

28. If $F = 10$, $m = 8$, and $v = 6$ in Exercise 14, find r.

29. If $f = 2.3$ and $q = 1.7$ in Exercise 15, find p.

30. If $R = 1.29$ and $R_1 = 0.045$ in Exercise 16, find R_2.

31. If $e = 0.62$ and $b = 3.5$ in Exercise 17, find a^2.

32. If $a = 3.61$ and $e = 2.4$ in Exercise 18, find b^2.

33. If $V = 25.6$ and $h = 3.2$ in Exercise 21, find r^2.

34. If $h = 3.6$ and $r = 2.45$ in Exercise 22, find S.

Solve each problem. See Examples 4–6.

35. *Walking and riding.* Karen can ride her bike from home to school in the same amount of time as she can walk from home to the post office. She rides 10 miles per hour (mph) faster than she walks. The distance from her home to school is 7 miles, and the distance from her home to the post office is 2 miles. How fast does Karen walk?

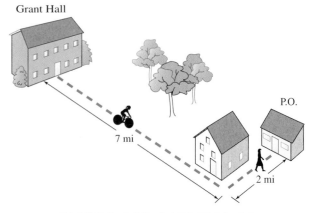

FIGURE FOR EXERCISE 35

36. *Fast driving.* Beverly can drive 600 miles in the same time as it takes Susan to drive 500 miles. If Beverly drives 10 mph faster than Susan, then how fast does Beverly drive?

37. *Faster driving.* Patrick drives 40 miles to work, and Guy drives 60 miles to work. Guy claims that he drives at the same speed as Patrick, but it takes him only 12 minutes longer to get to work. If this is true, then how long does it take each of them to get to work? What are their speeds? Do you think that Guy's claim is correct?

38. *Route drivers.* David and Keith are route drivers for a fast-photo company. David's route is 80 miles, and Keith's is 100 miles. Keith averages 10 mph more than David and finishes his route 10 minutes before David. What is David's speed?

39. *Physically fit.* Every morning, Yong Yi runs 5 miles, then walks one mile. He runs 6 mph faster than he walks. If his total time yesterday was 45 minutes, then how fast did he run?

40. *Row, row, row your boat.* Norma can row her boat 12 miles in the same time as it takes Marietta to cover 36 miles in her motorboat. If Marietta's boat travels 15 mph faster than Norma's boat, then how fast is Norma rowing her boat?

41. *Pumping out the pool.* A large pump can drain an 80,000-gallon pool in 3 hours. With a smaller pump also operating, the job takes only 2 hours. How long would it take the smaller pump to drain the pool by itself?

42. *Trimming hedges.* Lourdes can trim the hedges around her property in 8 hours by using an electric hedge trimmer. Rafael can do the same job in 15 hours by using a manual trimmer. How long would it take them to trim the hedges working together?

43. *Filling the tub.* It takes 10 minutes to fill Alisha's bathtub and 12 minutes to drain the water out. How long would it take to fill it with the drain accidentally left open?

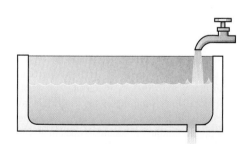

FIGURE FOR EXERCISE 43

44. *Eating machine.* Charles can empty the cookie jar in $1\frac{1}{2}$ hours. It takes his mother 2 hours to bake enough cookies to fill it. If the cookie jar is full when Charles comes home from school, and his mother continues baking and restocking the cookie jar, then how long will it take him to empty the cookie jar?

45. *Filing the invoices.* It takes Gina 90 minutes to file the monthly invoices. If Hilda files twice as fast as Gina does, how long will it take them working together?

46. *Painting alone.* Julie can paint a fence by herself in 12 hours. With Betsy's help, it takes only 5 hours. How long would it take Betsy by herself?

47. *Buying fruit.* Molly bought $5.28 worth of oranges and $8.80 worth of apples. She bought 2 more pounds of oranges than apples. If apples cost twice as much per pound as oranges, then how many pounds of each did she buy?

48. *Raising rabbits.* Luke raises rabbits and raccoons to sell for meat. The price of raccoon meat is three times the price of rabbit meat. One day Luke sold 160 pounds of meat, $72 worth of each type. What is the price per pound of each type of meat?

49. *Total resistance.* If two receivers with resistances R_1 and R_2 are connected in parallel, then the formula

$$\frac{1}{R} = \frac{1}{R_1} + \frac{1}{R_2}$$

relates the total resistance for the circuit R with R_1 and R_2. Given that R_1 is 3 ohms and R is 2 ohms, find R_2.

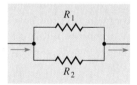

FIGURE FOR EXERCISE 49

50. *More resistance.* Use the formula from Exercise 49 to find R_1 and R_2 given that the total resistance is 1.2 ohms and R_1 is 1 ohm larger than R_2.

51. *Las Vegas vacation.* Brenda of Horizon Travel has arranged for a group of gamblers to share the $24,000 cost of a charter flight to Las Vegas. If Brenda can get 40 more people to share the cost, then the cost per person will decrease by $100. See the figure on the next page.
  a) How many people were in the original group?
  b) Write the cost per person as a function of the number of people sharing the cost.

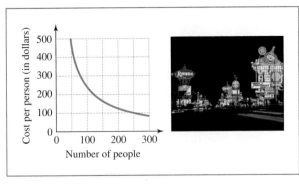

FIGURE FOR EXERCISE 51

52. White-water rafting. Adventures, Inc. has a $1500 group rate for an overnight rafting trip on the Colorado River. For the last trip five people failed to show, causing the price per person to increase by $25. How many were originally scheduled for the trip?

 53. Doggie bag. Muffy can eat a 25-pound bag of dog food in 28 days, whereas Missy eats a 25-pound bag in 23 days. How many days would it take them together to finish a 50-pound bag of dog food.

 54. Rodent food. A pest control specialist has found that 6 rats can eat an entire box of sugar-coated breakfast cereal in 13.6 minutes, and it takes a dozen mice 34.7 minutes to devour the same size box of cereal. How long would it take all 18 rodents, in a cooperative manner, to finish off a box of cereal?

COLLABORATIVE ACTIVITIES

Beorg's Business

In manufacturing or other businesses in which time is money and tasks are easily shared, problems involving work appear. An owner or manager who wants to know how to bid a job often develops a table of times needed to complete the job as determined by how much work is required and who could be assigned to the job.

Beorg owns a kaleidoscope-manufacturing company with two employees, Scott and Salina. It takes Scott one hour to make one kaleidoscope, and it takes Salina $\frac{1}{2}$ hour to make one kaleidoscope. Beorg wants to know how long it would take to complete a certain number of kaleidoscopes. Using the information given and answering the questions below, fill in the following table for Beorg.

Name of Employee	Time for one kaleidoscope	Time for 20 kaleidoscopes
Scott	1 hr	
Salina	$\frac{1}{2}$ hr	
Scott & Salina		
Sammy		
Scott & Sammy	$\frac{3}{4}$ hr	
Salina & Sammy		
Scott, Salina, & Sammy		

Grouping: Four students per group

Topic: Applications of work problems

1. How long will it take Scott and Salina working together to make one kaleidoscope?

2. Beorg hires a third person, Sammy, and has him and Scott make one kaleidoscope. Working together, it takes them $\frac{3}{4}$ hour to make one kaleidoscope. How long would it take Sammy by himself to make one kaleidoscope?

3. How long would it take Salina and Sammy working together to make one kaleidoscope? How long would it take for all three working together?

Now Beorg wants to finish his time table. He would like to have 20 kaleidoscopes completed each day.

4. Finish the preceding table, and find the best combination or combinations of employees to use to have 20 kaleidoscopes at the end of an 8-hour day.

Extension: Is Sammy in the combination or combinations you found in the last question? Is it worth having Sammy work? Remember that when someone is starting a new job, he or she may work more slowly until he or she learns how to do the job more efficiently. Find out how fast Sammy would need to work for production to double (40 kaleidoscopes in an 8-hour day).

Equations with Rational Expressions

Solving equations with rational expressions	Multiply each side by the LCD to eliminate all denominators.	**Examples** $$\frac{1}{x} - \frac{1}{3} = \frac{1}{2x} - \frac{1}{6}$$ $$6x\left(\frac{1}{x} - \frac{1}{3}\right) = 6x\left(\frac{1}{2x} - \frac{1}{6}\right)$$ $$6 - 2x = 3 - x$$
Solving proportions by the extremes-means property	If $\frac{a}{b} = \frac{c}{d}$, then $ad = bc$.	$$\frac{2}{x - 3} = \frac{5}{6}$$ $$12 = 5x - 15$$

ENRICHING YOUR MATHEMATICAL WORD POWER

For each mathematical term, choose the correct meaning.

1. **rational expression**
   a. a ratio of integers
   b. a ratio of two polynomials with the denominator not equal to zero
   c. an expression involving fractions
   d. a fraction in which the numerator and denominator contain fractions

2. **domain of a rational expression**
   a. all real numbers
   b. the denominator of the rational expression
   c. the set of all real numbers that cannot be used in place of the variable
   d. the set of all real numbers that can be used in place of the variable

3. **lowest terms**
   a. the numerator is smaller than the denominator
   b. no common factors
   c. the best interest rate
   d. when the numerator is 1

4. **reducing**
   a. less than
   b. losing weight
   c. making equivalent
   d. dividing out common factors

5. **equivalent fractions**
   a. identical fractions
   b. fractions that represent the same number
   c. fractions with the same denominator
   d. fractions with the same numerator

6. **complex fraction**
   a. a fraction having rational expressions in the numerator, denominator, or both
   b. a fraction with a large denominator
   c. the sum of two fractions
   d. a fraction with a variable in the denominator

7. **building up the denominator**
   a. the opposite of reducing a fraction
   b. finding the least common denominator
   c. adding the same number to the numerator and denominator
   d. writing a fraction larger

8. **least common denominator**
   a. the largest number that is a multiple of all denominators
   b. the sum of the denominators
   c. the product of the denominators
   d. the smallest number that is a multiple of all denominators

9. **extraneous root**
   a. a number that appears to be a solution to an equation but does not satisfy the equation
   b. an extra solution to an equation
   c. the second solution
   d. a nonreal solution

10. **ratio of a to b**
    a. b/a
    b. a/b
    c. $a/(a + b)$
    d. ab

11. **synthetic division**
    a. division of nonreal numbers
    b. division by zero
    c. multiplication that looks like division
    d. a quick method for dividing by $x - c$

12. **proportion**
    a. a ratio
    b. two ratios
    c. the product of the means equals the product of the extremes
    d. a statement expressing the equality of two rational expressions

13. **extremes**
   a. a and d in $a/b = c/d$
   b. b and c in $a/b = c/d$
   c.   the extremes-means property
   d.   if $a/b = c/d$, then $ad = bc$

14. **means**
   a.   the average of a, b, c, and d
   b. a and d in $a/b = c/d$

   c. b and c in $a/b = c/d$
   d.   if $a/b = c/d$, then $(a + b)/2 = (c + d)/2$

15. **extremes-means property**
   a. $ab = ba$ for any real numbers a and b
   b. $(a - b)^2 = (b - a)^2$ for any real numbers a and b
   c.   if $a/b = c/d$, then $ab = cd$
   d.   if $a/b = c/d$, then $ad = bc$

REVIEW EXERCISES

6.1 *State the domain of each rational expression.*

1. $\dfrac{5 - x}{3x - 3}$

2. $\dfrac{x - 4}{x^2 - 25}$

3. $\dfrac{x}{x^2 - x - 2}$

4. $\dfrac{1}{x^3 - x^2}$

Reduce each rational expression to its lowest terms.

5. $\dfrac{a^3 b c^3}{a^5 b^2 c}$

6. $\dfrac{x^4 - 1}{3x^2 - 3}$

7. $\dfrac{68x^3}{51xy}$

8. $\dfrac{5x^2 - 15x + 10}{5x - 10}$

6.2 *Perform the indicated operations.*

9. $\dfrac{a^3 b^2}{b^3 a} \cdot \dfrac{ab - b^2}{ab - a^2}$

10. $\dfrac{x^3 - 1}{3x} \cdot \dfrac{6x^2}{x - 1}$

11. $\dfrac{w - 4}{3w} \div \dfrac{2w - 8}{9w}$

12. $\dfrac{x^3 - xy^2}{y} \div \dfrac{x^3 + 2x^2 y + xy^2}{3y}$

6.3 *Find the least common multiple for each group of polynomials.*

13. $6x$, $3x - 6$, $x^2 - 2x$

14. $x^3 - 8$, $x^2 - 4$, $2x + 4$

15. $6ab^3$, $4a^5 b^2$

16. $4x^2 - 9$, $4x^2 + 12x + 9$

Perform the indicated operations.

17. $\dfrac{3}{2x - 6} + \dfrac{1}{x^2 - 9}$

18. $\dfrac{3}{x - 3} - \dfrac{5}{x + 4}$

19. $\dfrac{w}{ab^2} - \dfrac{5}{a^2 b}$

20. $\dfrac{x}{x - 1} + \dfrac{3x}{x^2 - 1}$

6.4 *Simplify the complex fractions.*

21. $\dfrac{\dfrac{3}{2x} - \dfrac{4}{5x}}{\dfrac{1}{3} - \dfrac{2}{x}}$

22. $\dfrac{\dfrac{5}{x - 2} - \dfrac{4}{4 - x^2}}{\dfrac{3}{x + 2} - \dfrac{1}{2 - x}}$

23. $\dfrac{\dfrac{1}{y - 2} - 3}{\dfrac{5}{y - 2} + 4}$

24. $\dfrac{\dfrac{a}{b^2} - \dfrac{b}{a^3}}{\dfrac{a}{b} + \dfrac{b}{a^2}}$

25. $\dfrac{a^{-2} - b^{-3}}{a^{-1} b^{-2}}$

26. $p^{-1} + pq^{-2}$

6.5 *Find the quotient and remainder.*

27. $(x^3 + x^2 - 11x + 10) \div (x - 2)$

28. $(2x^3 + 5x^2 + 9) \div (x + 3)$

29. $(m^4 - 1) \div (m + 1)$

30. $(x^4 - 1) \div (x - 1)$

31. $(a^9 - 8) \div (a^3 - 2)$

32. $(a^2 - b^2) \div (a - b)$

33. $(3m^3 + 6m^2 - 18m) \div (3m)$

34. $(w - 3) \div (3 - w)$

Rewrite each expression in the form

$$quotient + \frac{remainder}{divisor}.$$

Use synthetic division.

35. $\dfrac{x^2 - 5}{x - 1}$

36. $\dfrac{x^2 + 3x + 2}{x + 3}$

37. $\dfrac{3x}{x - 2}$

38. $\dfrac{4x}{x - 5}$

Use division to determine whether the first polynomial is a factor of the second. Use synthetic division when possible.

39. $x + 2, \quad x^3 - 2x^2 + 3x + 22$

40. $x - 2, \quad x^3 + x - 10$

41. $x - 5, \quad x^3 - x - 120$

42. $x + 3, \quad x^3 + 2x + 15$

43. $x - 1, \quad x^3 + x^2 - 3$

44. $x - 1, \quad x^3 + 1$

45. $x^2 + 2, \quad x^4 + x^3 + 5x^2 + 2x + 6$

46. $x^2 + 1, \quad x^4 - 1$

6.6 *Solve each equation.*

47. $\dfrac{-3}{8} = \dfrac{2}{x}$

48. $\dfrac{2}{x} + \dfrac{5}{2x} = 1$

49. $5 + \dfrac{x + 1}{x - 1} = 3 + \dfrac{5x - 3}{x - 1}$

50. $2 + \dfrac{7}{x - 5} = 3 + \dfrac{x + 2}{x - 5}$

51. $\dfrac{15}{a^2 - 25} + \dfrac{1}{a - 5} = \dfrac{6}{a + 5}$

52. $2 + \dfrac{3}{x - 5} = \dfrac{x - 1}{x - 5}$

6.7 *Solve each formula for the indicated variable.*

53. $\dfrac{y - b}{m} = x$ for y

54. $\dfrac{2A}{h} = b_1 + b_2$ for A

55. $F = \dfrac{mv^2}{r}$ for m

56. $P = \dfrac{A}{1 + rt}$ for r

57. $A = \dfrac{2}{3}\pi rh$ for r

58. $\dfrac{a}{w^2} = \dfrac{2}{b}$ for b

59. $\dfrac{y + 3}{x - 7} = 2$ for y

60. $\dfrac{y - 5}{x + 4} = \dfrac{-1}{2}$ for y

MISCELLANEOUS

Either perform the indicated operation or solve the equation, whichever is appropriate.

61. $\dfrac{5x}{3x^2 y} + \dfrac{7a^2}{6a^2 x}$

62. $\dfrac{4}{2x - 4} - \dfrac{15}{5x}$

63. $\dfrac{5}{a - 5} - \dfrac{3}{-a - 5}$

64. $\dfrac{2}{x - 2} - \dfrac{3}{x} = \dfrac{-1}{5x}$

65. $\dfrac{1}{x - 2} - \dfrac{1}{x + 2} = \dfrac{1}{15}$

66. $\dfrac{2}{x - 3} \cdot \dfrac{6x - 18}{30}$

67. $\dfrac{-3}{x + 2} \cdot \dfrac{5x + 10}{10}$

68. $\dfrac{x}{10} = \dfrac{10}{x}$

69. $\dfrac{x}{-3} = \dfrac{-27}{x}$

70. $\dfrac{x^2 - 4}{x} \div \dfrac{x^3 - 8}{x}$

71. $\dfrac{wx + wm + 3x + 3m}{w^2 - 9} \div \dfrac{x^2 - m^2}{w - 3}$

72. $\dfrac{-5}{7} = \dfrac{3}{x}$

73. $\dfrac{5}{a^2 - 25} + \dfrac{3}{a^2 - 4a - 5}$

74. $\dfrac{3}{w^2 - 1} + \dfrac{2}{2w + 2}$

75. $\dfrac{-7}{2a^2 - 18} - \dfrac{4}{a^2 + 5a + 6}$

76. $\dfrac{-5}{3a^2 - 12} - \dfrac{1}{a^2 - 3a + 2}$

77. $\dfrac{7}{a^2 - 1} + \dfrac{2}{1 - a} = \dfrac{1}{a + 1}$

78. $2 + \dfrac{4}{x - 1} = \dfrac{3x + 1}{x - 1}$

79. $\dfrac{2x}{x - 3} + \dfrac{3}{x - 2} = \dfrac{6}{(x - 2)(x - 3)}$

80. $\dfrac{a-3}{a+3} \div \dfrac{9-a^2}{3}$

81. $\dfrac{x-2}{6} \div \dfrac{2-x}{2}$

82. $\dfrac{x}{x+4} - \dfrac{2}{x+1} = \dfrac{-2}{(x+1)(x+4)}$

83. $\dfrac{x-3}{x^2+3x+2} \cdot \dfrac{x^2-4}{3x-9}$

84. $\dfrac{x^2-1}{x^2+2x+1} \cdot \dfrac{x^3+1}{2x-2}$

85. $\dfrac{a+4}{a^3-8} - \dfrac{3}{2-a}$

86. $\dfrac{x+2}{5} = \dfrac{3}{x}$

87. $\dfrac{x^3-9x}{1-x^2} \div \dfrac{x^3+6x^2+9x}{x-1}$

88. $\dfrac{x+3}{2x+3} = \dfrac{x-3}{x-1}$

89. $\dfrac{a^2+3a+3w+aw}{a^2+6a+8} \cdot \dfrac{a^2-aw-2w+2a}{a^2+3a-3w-aw}$

90. $\dfrac{3}{4-2y} + \dfrac{6}{y^2-4} + \dfrac{3}{2+y}$

91. $\dfrac{5}{x} - \dfrac{4}{x+2} = \dfrac{1}{5} + \dfrac{1}{5x}$

92. $\dfrac{1}{x} + \dfrac{1}{x-5} = \dfrac{2x+1}{x^2-25} + \dfrac{9}{x^2+5x}$

Replace each question mark by an expression that makes the equation an identity.

93. $\dfrac{6}{x} = \dfrac{?}{3x}$

94. $\dfrac{?}{a} = \dfrac{8}{4a}$

95. $\dfrac{3}{a-b} = \dfrac{?}{b-a}$

96. $\dfrac{-2}{a-x} = \dfrac{2}{?}$

97. $4 = \dfrac{?}{x}$

98. $5a = \dfrac{?}{b}$

99. $5x \div \dfrac{1}{2} = ?$

100. $3a \div \dfrac{1}{a} = ?$

101. $4a \div ? = 12a$

102. $14x \div ? = 28x^2$

103. $\dfrac{a-3}{a^2-9} = \dfrac{1}{?}$

104. $\dfrac{?}{x^2-4} = \dfrac{1}{x-2}$

105. $\dfrac{1}{2} - \dfrac{1}{5} = ?$

106. $\dfrac{1}{4} - \dfrac{1}{5} = ?$

107. $\dfrac{a}{3} + \dfrac{a}{2} = ?$

108. $\dfrac{x}{5} + \dfrac{x}{3} = ?$

Solve each problem.

109. *AIDS by gender.* The ratio of new reported male AIDS cases to female AIDS cases in 2002 was 7 to 3 (Center for Disease Control, www.cdc.gov). See the accompanying figure. If there were 16,000 more male AIDS cases than female AIDS cases, then how many reported male AIDS cases were there in 2002?

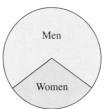

Distribution of new AIDS cases

FIGURE FOR EXERCISE 109

110. *Aggressive portfolio.* In an aggressive portfolio the ratio of money invested in stocks to money invested in bonds should be 5 to 1. If Halle has an aggressive portfolio with $20,972 more invested in stocks than bonds, then how much does she have in her portfolio?

111. *Just passing through.* Nikita drove 310 miles on his way to Louisville in the same amount of time that he drove 360 miles after passing through Louisville. If his average speed after passing Louisville was 10 miles per hour (mph) more than his average speed on his way to Louisville, then for how many hours did he drive?

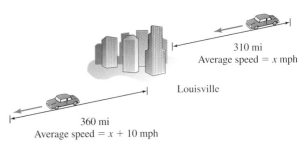

310 mi
Average speed = x mph

Louisville

360 mi
Average speed = $x + 10$ mph

FIGURE FOR EXERCISE 111

112. *Pushing a barge.* A tug can push a barge 144 miles down the Mississippi River in the same time that it takes to push the barge 84 miles in the Gulf of Mexico. If the tug's speed

FIGURE FOR EXERCISE 112

is 5 mph greater going down the river, then what is its speed in the Gulf of Mexico?

113. *Quilting bee.* Debbie can make a hand-sewn quilt in 2,000 hours, and Rosalina can make an identical quilt in 1,000 hours. If Cheryl works just as fast as Rosalina, then how long will it take all three of them working together to make one quilt?

114. *Blood out of a turnip.* A small pump can pump all of the blood out of an average turnip in 30 minutes. A larger pump can pump all of the blood from the same turnip in 20 minutes. If both pumps are hooked to the turnip, then how long would it take to get all of the blood out?

CHAPTER 6 TEST

State the domain of each rational expression.

1. $\dfrac{5}{4 - 3x}$

2. $\dfrac{2x - 1}{x^2 - 9}$

3. $\dfrac{17}{x^2 + 9}$

Reduce to lowest terms.

4. $\dfrac{12a^9b^8}{(2a^2b^3)^3}$

5. $\dfrac{y^2 - x^2}{2x^2 - 4xy + 2y^2}$

Perform the indicated operations. Write answers in lowest terms.

6. $\dfrac{5y}{12y} - \dfrac{4x}{9x}$

7. $\dfrac{3}{y} + 7y$

8. $\dfrac{4}{a - 9} - \dfrac{1}{9 - a}$

9. $\dfrac{1}{6ab^2} + \dfrac{1}{8a^2b}$

10. $\dfrac{3a^3b}{20ab} \cdot \dfrac{2a^2b}{9ab^3}$

11. $\dfrac{a - b}{7} \div \dfrac{b^2 - a^2}{21}$

12. $\dfrac{x - 3}{x - 1} \div (x^2 - 2x - 3)$

13. $\dfrac{2}{x^2 - 4} - \dfrac{6}{x^2 - 3x - 10}$

14. $\dfrac{m^3 - 1}{(m - 1)^2} \cdot \dfrac{m^2 - 1}{3m^2 + 3m + 3}$

Find the solution set to each equation.

15. $\dfrac{3}{x} = \dfrac{7}{4}$

16. $\dfrac{x}{x - 2} - \dfrac{5}{x} = \dfrac{3}{4}$

17. $\dfrac{3m}{2} = \dfrac{6}{m}$

Solve each formula for the indicated variable.

18. $W = \dfrac{a^2}{t}$ for t

19. $\dfrac{1}{a} + \dfrac{1}{b} = \dfrac{1}{2}$ for b

Simplify.

20. $\dfrac{\dfrac{1}{x} + \dfrac{1}{3x}}{\dfrac{3}{4x} - \dfrac{1}{2}}$

21. $\dfrac{m^{-2} - w^{-2}}{m^{-2}w^{-1} + m^{-1}w^{-2}}$

22. $\dfrac{\dfrac{a^2b^3}{4a}}{\dfrac{ab^3}{6a^2}}$

Find the quotient and remainder.

23. $(6x^2 + 7x - 6) \div (2x + 1)$

24. $(x - 3) \div (3 - x)$

Rewrite each expression in the form

$$quotient + \dfrac{remainder}{divisor}.$$

Use synthetic division.

25. $\dfrac{5x}{x + 3}$

26. $\dfrac{x^2 + 3x - 6}{x - 2}$

Solve each problem.

27. When Jane's wading pool was new, it could be filled in 6 minutes with water from the hose. Now that the pool has several leaks, it takes only 8 minutes for all of the water to leak out of a full pool. How long does it take to fill the leaky pool?

28. Milton and Bonnie are hiking the Appalachian Trail together. Milton averages 4 miles per hour (mph), and Bonnie averages 3 mph. If they start out together in the morning, but Milton gets to camp 2 hours and 30 minutes ahead of Bonnie, then how many miles did they hike that day?

29. A group of sailors plans to share equally the cost and use of a $72,000 boat. If they can get three more sailors to join their group, then the cost per person will be reduced by $2,000. How many sailors are in the original group?

Find the solution set to each equation.

1. $\dfrac{3}{x} = \dfrac{4}{5}$

2. $\dfrac{2}{x} = \dfrac{x}{8}$

3. $\dfrac{x}{3} = \dfrac{4}{5}$

4. $\dfrac{3}{x} = \dfrac{x+3}{6}$

5. $\dfrac{1}{x} = 4$

6. $\dfrac{2}{3}x = 4$

7. $2x + 3 = 4$

8. $2x + 3 = 4x$

9. $\dfrac{2a}{3} = \dfrac{6}{a}$

10. $\dfrac{12}{x} - \dfrac{14}{x+1} = \dfrac{1}{2}$

11. $|6x - 3| = 1$

12. $\dfrac{x}{2x+9} = \dfrac{3}{x}$

13. $4(6x - 3)(2x + 9) = 0$

14. $\dfrac{x-1}{x+2} - \dfrac{1}{5(x+2)} = 1$

Solve each equation for y. Assume A, B, and C are constants for which all expressions are defined.

15. $Ax + By = C$

16. $\dfrac{y-3}{x+5} = -\dfrac{1}{3}$

17. $Ay = By + C$

18. $\dfrac{A}{y} = \dfrac{y}{A}$

19. $\dfrac{A}{y} - \dfrac{1}{2} = \dfrac{B}{y}$

20. $\dfrac{A}{y} - \dfrac{1}{2} = \dfrac{B}{C}$

21. $3x - 4y = 6$

22. $y^2 - 2y - Ay + 2A = 0$

23. $A = \dfrac{1}{2}B(C + y)$

24. $y^2 + Cy = BC + By$

Simplify each expression.

25. $3x^5 \cdot 4x^8$

26. $3x^2(x^3 + 5x^6)$

27. $(5x^6)^2$

28. $(3a^3b^2)^3$

29. $\dfrac{12a^9b^4}{-3a^3b^{-2}}$

30. $\left(\dfrac{x^{-2}}{2}\right)^5$

31. $\left(\dfrac{2x^{-4}}{3y^5}\right)^{-3}$

32. $(-2a^{-1}b^3c)^{-2}$

33. $\dfrac{a^{-1} + b^3}{a^{-2} + b^{-1}}$

34. $\dfrac{(a+b)^{-1}}{(a+b)^{-2}}$

Solve.

35. *Basic energy requirement.* Clinical dietitians must design diets that meet patients' energy requirements and are suitable for the condition of their health (*Snapshots of Applications in Mathematics*). The basic energy requirement B (in calories) for a male is a function of three variables,

$$B = 655 + 9.56W + 1.85H - 4.68A,$$

where W is the patient's weight in kilograms, H is the height in centimeters, and A is the age in years.

a) Find the basic energy requirement for Chicago Bulls' center Luc Longley. Longley is 30 years old, has a height of 7 ft 2 in., and weight of 292 pounds (www.nba.com). (1 in. $\approx$ 2.54 cm, 1 kg $\approx$ 2.2 lb.)

b) The accompanying graph shows the basic energy requirement for a 7 ft 2 in. male at age 30 as a function of his weight. As the weight increases, does the basic energy requirement increase or decrease?

c) What is the equation for the line in the accompanying figure?

d) Write the basic energy requirement for Luc Longley as a function of his age and graph this function for $20 \leq A \leq 70$. Assume his size stays fixed.

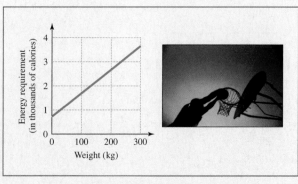

FIGURE FOR EXERCISE 35

CHAPTER 7

Radicals and Rational Exponents

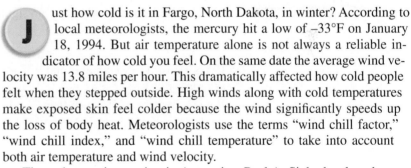

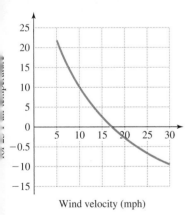

Wind velocity (mph)

Just how cold is it in Fargo, North Dakota, in winter? According to local meteorologists, the mercury hit a low of –33°F on January 18, 1994. But air temperature alone is not always a reliable indicator of how cold you feel. On the same date the average wind velocity was 13.8 miles per hour. This dramatically affected how cold people felt when they stepped outside. High winds along with cold temperatures make exposed skin feel colder because the wind significantly speeds up the loss of body heat. Meteorologists use the terms "wind chill factor," "wind chill index," and "wind chill temperature" to take into account both air temperature and wind velocity.

Through experimentation in Antarctica, Paul A. Siple developed a formula in the 1940s that measures the wind chill from the velocity of the wind and the air temperature. His complex formula involving the square root of the velocity of the wind is still used today to calculate wind chill temperatures. Siple's formula is unlike most scientific formulas in that it is not based on theory. Siple experimented with various formulas involving wind velocity and temperature until he found a formula that seemed to predict how cold the air felt. His formula is stated and used in Exercises 107 and 108 of Section 7.1.

7.1 RADICALS

In Section 5.1 you learned the basic facts about powers. In this section you will study roots and see how powers and roots are related.

Roots

We use the idea of roots to reverse powers. Because $3^2 = 9$ and $(-3)^2 = 9$, both 3 and -3 are square roots of 9. Because $2^4 = 16$ and $(-2)^4 = 16$, both 2 and -2 are fourth roots of 16. Because $2^3 = 8$ and $(-2)^3 = -8$, there is only one real cube root of 8 and only one real cube root of -8. The cube root of 8 is 2 and the cube root of -8 is -2.

> **nth Roots**
>
> If $a = b^n$ for a positive integer n, then b is an **nth root of a**. If $a = b^2$, then b is a **square root** of a. If $a = b^3$, then b is the **cube root** of a.

If n is a positive even integer and a is positive, then there are two real nth roots of a. We call these roots **even roots.** The positive even root of a positive number is called the **principal root.** The principal square root of 9 is 3 and the principal fourth root of 16 is 2 and these roots are even roots.

If n is a positive odd integer and a is any real number, there is only one real nth root of a. We call that root an **odd root.** Because $2^5 = 32$, the fifth root of 32 is 2 and 2 is an odd root.

We use the **radical symbol** $\sqrt{}$ to signify roots.

$$\sqrt[n]{a}$$

If n is a positive *even* integer and a is positive, then $\sqrt[n]{a}$ denotes the *principal nth root of a.*

If n is a positive *odd* integer, then $\sqrt[n]{a}$ denotes the nth root of a.

If n is any positive integer, then $\sqrt[n]{0} = 0$.

We read $\sqrt[n]{a}$ as "the nth root of a." In the notation $\sqrt[n]{a}$, n is the **index of the radical** and a is the **radicand.** For square roots the index is omitted, and we simply write $\sqrt{a}$.

E X A M P L E   1

Evaluating radical expressions

Find the following roots:

a) $\sqrt{25}$ b) $\sqrt[3]{-27}$ c) $\sqrt[6]{64}$ d) $-\sqrt{4}$

Solution

a) Because $5^2 = 25$, $\sqrt{25} = 5$.

b) Because $(-3)^3 = -27$, $\sqrt[3]{-27} = -3$.

c) Because $2^6 = 64$, $\sqrt[6]{64} = 2$.

d) Because $\sqrt{4} = 2$, $-\sqrt{4} = -(\sqrt{4}) = -2$.   ∎

> **CAUTION**   In radical notation, $\sqrt{4}$ represents the *principal square root of 4*, so $\sqrt{4} = 2$. Note that -2 is also a square root of 4, but $\sqrt{4} \neq -2$.

Note that even roots of negative numbers are omitted from the definition of *n*th roots because even powers of real numbers are never negative. So no real number can be an even root of a negative number. Expressions such as

Note that even roots of negative numbers are omitted from the definition of *n*th roots because even powers of real numbers are never negative. So no real number can be an even root of a negative number. Expressions such as

$$\sqrt{-9}, \quad \sqrt[4]{-81}, \quad \text{and} \quad \sqrt[6]{-64}$$

are not real numbers. Square roots of negative numbers will be discussed in Section 7.6 when we discuss the imaginary numbers.

Roots and Variables

Consider the result of squaring a power of *x*:

$$(x^1)^2 = x^2, \quad (x^2)^2 = x^4, \quad (x^3)^2 = x^6, \quad \text{and} \quad (x^4)^2 = x^8.$$

When a power of *x* is squared, the exponent is multiplied by 2. So any even power of *x* is a perfect square.

Perfect Squares

The following expressions are perfect squares:

$$x^2, \quad x^4, \quad x^6, \quad x^8, \quad x^{10}, \quad x^{12}, \quad \ldots$$

Since taking a square root reverses the operation of squaring, the square root of an even power of *x* is found by dividing the exponent by 2. Provided *x* is nonnegative (see Caution below), we have:

$$\sqrt{x^2} = x^1 = x, \quad \sqrt{x^4} = x^2, \quad \sqrt{x^6} = x^3, \quad \text{and} \quad \sqrt{x^8} = x^4.$$

CAUTION   If *x* is negative, equations like $\sqrt{x^2} = x$ and $\sqrt{x^6} = x^3$ are not correct because the radical represents the nonnegative square root but *x* and x^3 are negative. That is why we assume *x* is nonnegative.

If a power of *x* is cubed, the exponent is multiplied by 3:

$$(x^1)^3 = x^3, \quad (x^2)^3 = x^6, \quad (x^3)^3 = x^9, \quad \text{and} \quad (x^4)^3 = x^{12}.$$

So if the exponent is a multiple of 3, we have a perfect cube.

Perfect Cubes

The following expressions are perfect cubes:

$$x^3, \quad x^6, \quad x^9, \quad x^{12}, \quad x^{15}, \quad \ldots$$

Since the cube root reverses the operation of cubing, the cube root of any of these perfect cubes is found by dividing the exponent by 3:

$$\sqrt[3]{x^3} = x^1 = x, \quad \sqrt[3]{x^6} = x^2, \quad \sqrt[3]{x^9} = x^3, \quad \text{and} \quad \sqrt[3]{x^{12}} = x^4.$$

If the exponent is divisible by 4, we have a perfect fourth power, and so on.

E X A M P L E 2   **Roots of exponential expressions**

Find each root. Assume that all variables represent nonnegative real numbers.

a) $\sqrt{x^{22}}$
b) $\sqrt[3]{t^{18}}$
c) $\sqrt[5]{s^{30}}$

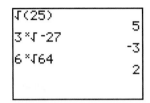

This example illustrates the quotient rule for radicals.

> ### Quotient Rule for Radicals
>
> The nth root of a quotient is equal to the quotient of the nth roots. In symbols,
>
> $$\sqrt[n]{\frac{a}{b}} = \frac{\sqrt[n]{a}}{\sqrt[n]{b}},$$
>
> provided that all of these roots are real numbers and $b \neq 0$.

EXAMPLE 6

Using the quotient rule for radicals

Simplify each radical. Assume that all variables represent positive real numbers.

a) $\sqrt{\dfrac{25}{9}}$ b) $\dfrac{\sqrt{15}}{\sqrt{3}}$ c) $\sqrt[3]{\dfrac{b}{125}}$ d) $\sqrt[3]{\dfrac{x^{21}}{y^6}}$

Solution

a) $\sqrt{\dfrac{25}{9}} = \dfrac{\sqrt{25}}{\sqrt{9}}$ Quotient rule for radicals

$\qquad = \dfrac{5}{3}$ Simplify.

b) $\dfrac{\sqrt{15}}{\sqrt{3}} = \sqrt{\dfrac{15}{3}}$ Quotient rule for radicals

$\qquad = \sqrt{5}$ Simplify.

c) $\sqrt[3]{\dfrac{b}{125}} = \dfrac{\sqrt[3]{b}}{\sqrt[3]{125}} = \dfrac{\sqrt[3]{b}}{5}$

d) $\sqrt[3]{\dfrac{x^{21}}{y^6}} = \dfrac{\sqrt[3]{x^{21}}}{\sqrt[3]{y^6}} = \dfrac{x^7}{y^2}$

In Example 7 we use the product and quotient rule to simplify radical expressions.

EXAMPLE 7

Using the product and quotient rules for radicals

Simplify each radical. Assume that all variables represent positive real numbers.

a) $\sqrt{\dfrac{50}{49}}$ b) $\sqrt[3]{\dfrac{x^5}{8}}$ c) $\sqrt[4]{\dfrac{a^5}{b^8}}$

Solution

a) $\sqrt{\dfrac{50}{49}} = \dfrac{\sqrt{25} \cdot \sqrt{2}}{\sqrt{49}}$ Product and quotient rules for radicals

$\qquad = \dfrac{5\sqrt{2}}{7}$ Simplify.

b) $\sqrt[3]{\dfrac{x^5}{8}} = \dfrac{\sqrt[3]{x^3} \cdot \sqrt[3]{x^2}}{\sqrt[3]{8}} = \dfrac{x\sqrt[3]{x^2}}{2}$

c) $\sqrt[4]{\dfrac{a^5}{b^8}} = \dfrac{\sqrt[4]{a^4} \cdot \sqrt[4]{a}}{\sqrt[4]{b^8}} = \dfrac{a\sqrt[4]{a}}{b^2}$

Radical Functions

Functions such as $f(x) = \sqrt{x - 5}$ and $g(x) = \sqrt[3]{x}$ that are defined by radicals are called **radical functions.** The radicand in an odd root can be any real number but in an even root the radicand must be nonnegative. So the domain for g is all real numbers, $(-\infty, \infty)$. For $f(x) = \sqrt{x - 5}$ we must have $x - 5 \geq 0$, or $x \geq 5$. So the domain of f is $[5, \infty)$.

E X A M P L E 8

Finding the domain of a square root function

For each function find $f(2)$ and the domain of the function.

a) $f(x) = \sqrt{2x + 12}$ **b)** $f(x) = \sqrt{x - 7}$

Solution

a) Let $x = 2$ in $f(x) = \sqrt{2x + 12}$ to get $f(x) = \sqrt{2(2) + 12} = 4$. Find the domain using the fact that $2x + 12$ must be nonnegative:

$$2x + 12 \geq 0$$
$$2x \geq -12$$
$$x \geq -6$$

So $f(2) = 4$ and the domain is the interval $[-6, \infty)$.

b) Let $x = 2$ to get $f(2) = \sqrt{2 - 7} = \sqrt{-5}$, which is not a real number. So 2 is not in the domain of the function and $f(2)$ does not exist. We must have $x - 7 \geq 0$, or $x \geq 7$. So the domain is the interval $[7, \infty)$. ∎

M A T H A T W O R K

Ernie Godshalk, avid sailor and owner of the sloop *Golden Eye,* has competed in races all over the world. He has learned that success in a race depends on the winds, a good crew, lots of skill, and knowing what makes his boat go fast.

Because of its shape and hull design, the maximum speed (in knots) of a sailboat can be calculated by finding the value 1.3 times the square root of her waterline (in feet). Thus Godshalk knows the maximum possible speed of the *Golden Eye.* But decisions made while she is

YACHTSMAN

under sail make the difference between attaining her maximum speed and only approaching it. For example, Godshalk knows that the pressure on the sails is what makes the boat move at a certain speed. It is especially important to sail where the wind is the strongest. This means that choosing the correct tack, as well as "going where the wind is" can make the difference between coming in first and just finishing the race. In Exercise 111 of this section you will calculate the maximum speed of the *Golden Eye.*

WARM-UPS

True or false? Explain your answer.

1. $\sqrt{2} \cdot \sqrt{2} = 2$ 2. $\sqrt[3]{2} \cdot \sqrt[3]{2} = 2$

3. $\sqrt[3]{-27} = -3$ 4. $\sqrt{-25} = -5$

5. $\sqrt[4]{16} = 2$ 6. $\sqrt{9} = \pm 3$

7. $\sqrt{2^9} = 2^3$ 8. $\dfrac{\sqrt{10}}{2} = \sqrt{5}$

9. $\sqrt{\dfrac{1}{4}} = \dfrac{1}{2}$ 10. $\dfrac{\sqrt{6}}{\sqrt{3}} = \sqrt{2}$

7.1 EXERCISES

Reading and Writing   *After reading this section, write out the answers to these questions. Use complete sentences.*

1. How do you know if b is an nth root of a?

2. What is a principal root?

3. What is the difference between an even root and an odd root?

4. What symbol is used to indicate an nth root?

5. What is the product rule for radicals?

6. What is the quotient rule for radicals?

For all of the exercises in this section assume that all variables represent positive real numbers.

Find each root. See Example 1.

7. $\sqrt{36}$ 8. $\sqrt{49}$

9. $\sqrt{100}$ 10. $\sqrt{81}$

11. $-\sqrt{9}$ 12. $-\sqrt{25}$

13. $\sqrt[3]{8}$ 14. $\sqrt[3]{27}$

15. $\sqrt[3]{-8}$ 16. $\sqrt[3]{-1}$

17. $\sqrt[5]{32}$ 18. $\sqrt[4]{81}$

19. $\sqrt[3]{1000}$ 20. $\sqrt[4]{16}$

21. $\sqrt[4]{-16}$ 22. $\sqrt{-1}$

23. $\sqrt[5]{-32}$ 24. $\sqrt[3]{-125}$

Find each root. See Example 2.

25. $\sqrt{m^2}$ 26. $\sqrt{m^6}$

27. $\sqrt{x^{16}}$ 28. $\sqrt{y^{36}}$

29. $\sqrt[5]{y^{15}}$ 30. $\sqrt[4]{m^8}$

31. $\sqrt[3]{y^{15}}$ 32. $\sqrt{m^8}$

33. $\sqrt[3]{m^3}$ 34. $\sqrt[4]{x^4}$

35. $\sqrt[4]{w^{12}}$ 36. $\sqrt[5]{a^{30}}$

Use the product rule for radicals to simplify each expression. See Example 3.

37. $\sqrt{9y}$ 38. $\sqrt{16n}$

39. $\sqrt{4a^2}$ 40. $\sqrt{36n^2}$

41. $\sqrt{x^4 y^2}$ 42. $\sqrt{w^6 t^2}$

43. $\sqrt{5m^{12}}$ 44. $\sqrt{7z^{16}}$

45. $\sqrt[3]{8y}$ 46. $\sqrt[3]{27z^2}$

47. $\sqrt[3]{3a^6}$ 48. $\sqrt[3]{5b^9}$

Use the product rule to simplify. See Example 4.

49. $\sqrt{20}$ 50. $\sqrt{18}$

51. $\sqrt{50}$ 52. $\sqrt{45}$

53. $\sqrt{72}$ 54. $\sqrt{98}$

55. $\sqrt[3]{40}$ 56. $\sqrt[3]{24}$

57. $\sqrt[4]{81}$ 58. $\sqrt[3]{250}$

59. $\sqrt[4]{48}$ 60. $\sqrt[5]{32}$

61. $\sqrt[5]{96}$ 62. $\sqrt[5]{2430}$

Use the product rule to simplify. See Example 5.

63. $\sqrt{a^3}$ 64. $\sqrt{b^5}$

65. $\sqrt{18a^6}$ 66. $\sqrt{12x^8}$

67. $\sqrt{20x^5 y}$ 68. $\sqrt{8w^3 y^3}$

69. $\sqrt[3]{24m^4}$ 70. $\sqrt[3]{54ab^5}$

71. $\sqrt[4]{32a^5}$ 72. $\sqrt[4]{162b^4}$

73. $\sqrt[5]{64x^6}$ **74.** $\sqrt[5]{96a^8}$

75. $\sqrt{48x^3y^8z^7}$ **76.** $\sqrt[3]{48x^3y^8z^7}$

Simplify each radical. See Example 6.

77. $\sqrt{\dfrac{t}{4}}$ **78.** $\sqrt{\dfrac{w}{36}}$

79. $\sqrt{\dfrac{625}{16}}$ **80.** $\sqrt{\dfrac{9}{144}}$

81. $\dfrac{\sqrt{30}}{\sqrt{3}}$ **82.** $\dfrac{\sqrt{50}}{\sqrt{2}}$

83. $\sqrt[3]{\dfrac{t}{8}}$ **84.** $\sqrt[3]{\dfrac{a}{27}}$

85. $\sqrt[3]{\dfrac{-8x^6}{y^3}}$ **86.** $\sqrt[3]{\dfrac{-27y^{36}}{1000}}$

87. $\sqrt{\dfrac{4a^6}{9}}$ **88.** $\sqrt{\dfrac{9a^2}{49b^4}}$

Use the product and quotient rules to simplify. See Example 7.

89. $\sqrt{\dfrac{12}{25}}$ **90.** $\sqrt{\dfrac{8}{81}}$

91. $\sqrt{\dfrac{27}{16}}$ **92.** $\sqrt{\dfrac{98}{9}}$

93. $\sqrt[3]{\dfrac{a^4}{125}}$ **94.** $\sqrt[3]{\dfrac{b^7}{1000}}$

95. $\sqrt[3]{\dfrac{81}{8b^3}}$ **96.** $\sqrt[3]{\dfrac{a^3b^4}{125}}$

97. $\sqrt[4]{\dfrac{x^7}{y^8}}$ **98.** $\sqrt[4]{\dfrac{x^5y^4}{z^{12}}}$

99. $\sqrt[4]{\dfrac{a^5}{16b^{12}}}$ **100.** $\sqrt[4]{\dfrac{a^7b}{81c^{16}}}$

For each function find f(3) and the domain of the function.

101. $f(x) = \sqrt{x - 2}$

102. $f(x) = \sqrt{x + 6}$

103. $f(x) = \sqrt{2x + 8}$

104. $f(x) = \sqrt{3x - 2}$

105. $f(x) = \sqrt{3 - 3x}$

106. $f(x) = \sqrt{4 - 2x}$

In Exercises 107–114, solve each problem.

107. **Factoring in the wind.** Through experimentation in Antarctica, Paul Siple developed the formula

$$W = 91.4 - \dfrac{(10.5 + 6.7\sqrt{v} - 0.45v)(457 - 5t)}{110}$$

to calculate the wind chill temperature W (in degrees Fahrenheit) from the wind velocity v [in miles per hour (mph)] and the air temperature t (in degrees Fahrenheit). Find the wind chill temperature when the air temperature is 25°F and the wind velocity is 20 mph. Use the accompanying graph to estimate the wind chill temperature when the air temperature is 25°F and the wind velocity is 30 mph.

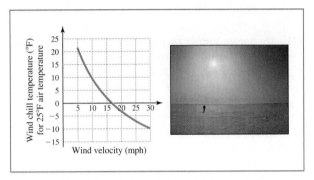

FIGURE FOR EXERCISE 107

108. **Comparing wind chills.** Use the formula from Exercise 107 to determine who will feel colder: a person in Minneapolis at 10°F with a 15-mph wind or a person in Chicago at 20°F with a 25-mph wind.

109. **Diving time.** The time t (in seconds) that it takes for a cliff diver to reach the water is a function of the height h (in feet) from which he dives:

$$t = \sqrt{\dfrac{h}{16}}$$

a) Use the properties of radicals to simplify this formula.

b) Find the exact time (according to the formula) that it takes for a diver to hit the water when diving from a height of 40 feet.

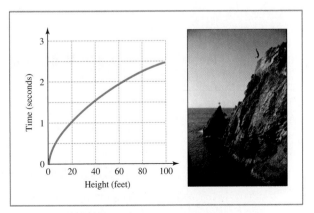

FIGURE FOR EXERCISE 109

c) Use the graph on page 401 to estimate the height if a diver takes 2.5 seconds to reach the water?

110. Sky diving. The formula in Exercise 109 accounts for the effect of gravity only on a falling object. According to that formula, how long would it take a sky diver to reach the earth when jumping from 17,000 feet? (A sky diver can actually get about twice as much falling time by spreading out and using the air to slow the fall.)

111. Maximum sailing speed. To find the maximum possible speed in knots (nautical miles per hour) for a sailboat, sailors use the function $M = 1.3\sqrt{w}$, where w is the length of the waterline in feet. If the waterline for the sloop *Golden Eye* is 20 feet, then what is the maximum speed of the *Golden Eye*?

112. America's Cup. Since 1988 basic yacht dimensions for the America's Cup competition have satisfied the inequality

$$L + 1.25\sqrt{S} - 9.8\sqrt[3]{D} \le 16.296,$$

where L is the boat's length in meters (m), S is the sail area in square meters, and D is the displacement in cubic meters (www.sailing.com). A team of naval architects is planning to build a boat with a displacement of 21.44 cubic meters (m^3), a sail area of 320.13 square meters (m^2), and a length of 21.22 m. Does this boat satisfy the inequality? If the length and displacement of this boat cannot be changed, then how many square meters of sail area must be removed so that the boat satisfies the inequality?

113. Landing a Piper Cheyenne. Aircraft design engineers determine the proper landing speed V [in feet per second (ft/sec)] for an airplane from the formula

$$V = \sqrt{\frac{841L}{CS}},$$

where L is the gross weight of the aircraft in pounds (lb), C is the coefficient of lift, and S is the wing surface area in square feet. According to Piper Aircraft of Vero Beach, Florida, the Piper Cheyenne has a gross weight of 8700 lb, a coefficient of lift of 2.81, and a wing surface area of 200 ft^2. Find the proper landing speed for this plane. What is the landing speed in miles per hour (mph)?

114. Landing speed and weight. Because the gross weight of the Piper Cheyenne depends on how much fuel and cargo are on board, the proper landing speed (from Exercise 113) is not always the same. The function $V = \sqrt{1.496L}$ gives the landing speed as a function of the gross weight only.
a) Find the landing speed if the gross weight is 7000 lb.
b) What gross weight corresponds to a landing speed of 115 ft/sec?

GETTING MORE INVOLVED

115. Cooperative learning. Work in a group to determine whether each equation is an identity. Explain your answers.
a) $\sqrt{x^2} = |x|$ b) $\sqrt[3]{x^3} = |x|$
c) $\sqrt{x^4} = x^2$ d) $\sqrt[4]{x^4} = |x|$

For which values of n is $\sqrt[n]{x^n} = x$ an identity?

116. Cooperative learning. Work in a group to determine whether each inequality is correct.
a) $\sqrt{0.9} > 0.9$ b) $\sqrt{1.01} > 1.01$
c) $\sqrt[3]{0.99} > 0.99$ d) $\sqrt[3]{1.001} > 1.001$

For which values of x and n is $\sqrt[n]{x} > x$?

117. Discussion. If your test scores are 80 and 100, then the arithmetic mean of your scores is 90. The geometric mean of the scores is a number h such that

$$\frac{80}{h} = \frac{h}{100}.$$

Are you better off with the arithmetic mean or the geometric mean?

7.2 **RATIONAL EXPONENTS**

You have learned how to use exponents to express powers of numbers and radicals to express roots. In this section you will see that roots can be expressed with exponents also. The advantage of using exponents to express roots is that the rules of exponents can be applied to the expressions.

Rational Exponents

The nth root of a number can be expressed by using radical notation or the exponent $1/n$. For example, $8^{1/3}$ and $\sqrt[3]{8}$ both represent the cube root of 8, and we have

$$8^{1/3} = \sqrt[3]{8} = 2.$$

Calculator Close-Up

You can find the fifth root of 2 using radical notation or exponent notation. Note that the fractional exponent 1/5 must be in parentheses.

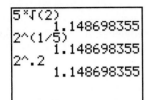

```
5*√(2)
        1.148698355
2^(1/5)
        1.148698355
2^.2
        1.148698355
```

Definition of $a^{1/n}$

If n is any positive integer, then

$$a^{1/n} = \sqrt[n]{a},$$

provided that $\sqrt[n]{a}$ is a real number.

Later in this section we will see that using exponent $1/n$ for nth root is compatible with the rules for integral exponents that we already know.

EXAMPLE 1

Radicals or exponents

Write each radical expression using exponent notation and each exponential expression using radical notation.

a) $\sqrt[3]{35}$ b) $\sqrt[4]{xy}$

c) $5^{1/2}$ d) $a^{1/5}$

Solution

a) $\sqrt[3]{35} = 35^{1/3}$ b) $\sqrt[4]{xy} = (xy)^{1/4}$

c) $5^{1/2} = \sqrt{5}$ d) $a^{1/5} = \sqrt[5]{a}$ ■

In the next example we evaluate some exponential expressions.

EXAMPLE 2

Finding roots

Evaluate each expression.

a) $4^{1/2}$ b) $(-8)^{1/3}$ c) $81^{1/4}$

d) $(-9)^{1/2}$ e) $-9^{1/2}$

Solution

a) $4^{1/2} = \sqrt{4} = 2$

b) $(-8)^{1/3} = \sqrt[3]{-8} = -2$

c) $81^{1/4} = \sqrt[4]{81} = 3$

d) Because $(-9)^{1/2}$ or $\sqrt{-9}$ is an even root of a negative number, it is not a real number.

e) Because the exponent in $-a^n$ is applied only to the base a (Section 1.4), we have $-9^{1/2} = -\sqrt{9} = -3$. ■

We now extend the definition of exponent $1/n$ to include any rational number as an exponent. The numerator of the rational number indicates the power, and the denominator indicates the root. For example, the expression

$$8^{2/3} \begin{array}{l} \longleftarrow \text{Power} \\ \longleftarrow \text{Root} \end{array}$$

represents the square of the cube root of 8. So we have

$$8^{2/3} = (8^{1/3})^2 = (2)^2 = 4.$$

Definition of $a^{m/n}$

If m and n are positive integers and $a^{1/n}$ is a real number, then

$$a^{m/n} = (a^{1/n})^m.$$

Using radical notation, $a^{m/n} = (\sqrt[n]{a})^m$.

By definition $a^{m/n}$ is the mth power of the nth root of a. However, $a^{m/n}$ is also equal to the nth root of the mth power of a. For example,

$$8^{2/3} = (8^2)^{1/3} = 64^{1/3} = 4.$$

Evaluating $a^{m/n}$ in Either Order

If m and n are positive integers and $a^{1/n}$ is a real number, then

$$a^{m/n} = (a^{1/n})^m = (a^m)^{1/n}.$$

Using radical notation, $a^{m/n} = (\sqrt[n]{a})^m = \sqrt[n]{a^m}$.

A negative rational exponent indicates a reciprocal:

Definition of $a^{-m/n}$

If m and n are positive integers, $a \neq 0$, and $a^{1/n}$ is a real number, then

$$a^{-m/n} = \frac{1}{a^{m/n}}.$$

Using radical notation, $a^{-m/n} = \frac{1}{(\sqrt[n]{a})^m}$.

E X A M P L E   3

Radicals or exponents

Write each radical expression using exponent notation and each exponential expression using radical notation.

a) $\sqrt[3]{x^2}$ **b)** $\dfrac{1}{\sqrt[4]{m^3}}$ **c)** $5^{2/3}$ **d)** $a^{-2/5}$

Solution

a) $\sqrt[3]{x^2} = x^{2/3}$ **b)** $\dfrac{1}{\sqrt[4]{m^3}} = \dfrac{1}{m^{3/4}} = m^{-3/4}$

c) $5^{2/3} = \sqrt[3]{5^2}$ **d)** $a^{-2/5} = \dfrac{1}{\sqrt[5]{a^2}}$ ∎

To evaluate an expression with a negative rational exponent, remember that the denominator indicates root, the numerator indicates power, and the negative sign indicates reciprocal:

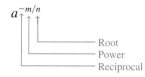

The root, power, and reciprocal can be evaluated in any order. However, to evaluate $a^{-m/n}$ mentally it is usually simplest to use the following strategy.

> **Strategy for Evaluating $a^{-m/n}$ Mentally**
>
> **1.** Find the nth root of a.
> **2.** Raise your result to the mth power.
> **3.** Find the reciprocal.

For example, to evaluate $8^{-2/3}$ mentally, we find the cube root of 8 (which is 2), square 2 to get 4, then find the reciprocal of 4 to get $\frac{1}{4}$. In print $8^{-2/3}$ could be written for evaluation as $((8^{1/3})^2)^{-1}$ or $\frac{1}{(8^{1/3})^2}$.

EXAMPLE 4

Rational exponents

Evaluate each expression.

a) $27^{2/3}$ **b)** $4^{-3/2}$

c) $81^{-3/4}$ **d)** $(-8)^{-5/3}$

Calculator Close-Up

A negative fractional exponent indicates a reciprocal, a root, and a power. To find $4^{-3/2}$ you can find the reciprocal first, the square root first, or the third power first as shown here.

```
(1/4)^(3/2)
               .125
(√(4))^-3
               .125
(4³)^(-1/2)
               .125
```

Solution

a) Because the exponent is $2/3$, we find the cube root of 27 and then square it:

$$27^{2/3} = (27^{1/3})^2 = 3^2 = 9$$

b) Because the exponent is $-3/2$, we find the square root of 4, cube it, and find the reciprocal:

$$4^{-3/2} = \frac{1}{(4^{1/2})^3} = \frac{1}{2^3} = \frac{1}{8}$$

c) Because the exponent is $-3/4$, we find the fourth root of 81, cube it, and find the reciprocal:

$$81^{-3/4} = \frac{1}{(81^{1/4})^3} = \frac{1}{3^3} = \frac{1}{27} \quad \text{Definition of negative exponent}$$

d) $(-8)^{-5/3} = \dfrac{1}{((-8)^{1/3})^5} = \dfrac{1}{(-2)^5} = \dfrac{1}{-32} = -\dfrac{1}{32}$ ■

> **CAUTION**   An expression with a negative base and a negative exponent can have a positive or a negative value. For example,
>
> $$(-8)^{-5/3} = -\frac{1}{32} \quad \text{and} \quad (-8)^{-2/3} = \frac{1}{4}.$$

Using the Rules of Exponents

All of the rules for exponents hold for rational exponents as well as integral exponents. Of course, we cannot apply the rules of exponents to expressions that are not real numbers.

Rules for Rational Exponents

The following rules hold for any nonzero real numbers a and b and rational numbers r and s for which the expressions represent real numbers.

1. $a^r a^s = a^{r+s}$ Product rule

2. $\dfrac{a^r}{a^s} = a^{r-s}$ Quotient rule

3. $(a^r)^s = a^{rs}$ Power of a power rule

4. $(ab)^r = a^r b^r$ Power of a product rule

5. $\left(\dfrac{a}{b}\right)^r = \dfrac{a^r}{b^r}$ Power of a quotient rule

We can use the product rule to add rational exponents. For example,

$$16^{1/4} \cdot 16^{1/4} = 16^{2/4}.$$

The fourth root of 16 is 2, and 2 squared is 4. So $16^{2/4} = 4$. Because we also have $16^{1/2} = 4$, we see that a rational exponent can be reduced to its lowest terms. If an exponent can be reduced, it is usually simpler to reduce the exponent before we evaluate the expression. We can simplify $16^{1/4} \cdot 16^{1/4}$ as follows:

$$16^{1/4} \cdot 16^{1/4} = 16^{2/4} = 16^{1/2} = 4$$

E X A M P L E   5

Using the product and quotient rules with rational exponents
Simplify each expression.

a) $27^{1/6} \cdot 27^{1/2}$

b) $\dfrac{5^{3/4}}{5^{1/4}}$

Solution

a) $27^{1/6} \cdot 27^{1/2} = 27^{1/6+1/2}$ Product rule for exponents

$\phantom{27^{1/6} \cdot 27^{1/2}} = 27^{2/3}$

$\phantom{27^{1/6} \cdot 27^{1/2}} = 9$

b) $\dfrac{5^{3/4}}{5^{1/4}} = 5^{3/4-1/4} = 5^{2/4} = 5^{1/2} = \sqrt{5}$ We used the quotient rule to subtract the exponents.

E X A M P L E   6

Using the power rules with rational exponents
Simplify each expression.

a) $3^{1/2} \cdot 12^{1/2}$ **b)** $(3^{10})^{1/2}$ **c)** $\left(\dfrac{2^6}{3^9}\right)^{-1/3}$

Solution

a) Because the bases 3 and 12 are different, we cannot use the product rule to add the exponents. Instead, we use the power of a product rule to place the $1/2$ power outside the parentheses:

$$3^{1/2} \cdot 12^{1/2} = (3 \cdot 12)^{1/2} = 36^{1/2} = 6$$

b) Use the power of a power rule to multiply the exponents:

$$(3^{10})^{1/2} = 3^5$$

c) $\left(\dfrac{2^6}{3^9}\right)^{-1/3} = \dfrac{(2^6)^{-1/3}}{(3^9)^{-1/3}}$ Power of a quotient rule

$$= \dfrac{2^{-2}}{3^{-3}}$$ Power of a power rule

$$= \dfrac{3^3}{2^2}$$ Definition of negative exponent

$$= \dfrac{27}{4}$$ ∎

Helpful Hint

We usually think of squaring and taking a square root as inverse operations, which they are as long as we stick to positive numbers. We can square 3 to get 9, and then find the square root of 9 to get 3—what we started with. We don't get back to where we began if we start with -3.

Simplifying Expressions Involving Variables

When simplifying expressions involving rational exponents and variables, we must be careful to write equivalent expressions. For example, in the equation

$$(x^2)^{1/2} = x$$

it looks as if we are correctly applying the power of a power rule. However, this statement is false if x is negative because the $1/2$ power on the left-hand side indicates the positive square root of x^2. For example, if $x = -3$, we get

$$[(-3)^2]^{1/2} = 9^{1/2} = 3,$$

which is not equal to -3. To write a simpler equivalent expression for $(x^2)^{1/2}$, we use absolute value as follows.

Square Root of x^2

$$(x^2)^{1/2} = |x| \text{ for any real number } x.$$

Note that $(x^2)^{1/2} = |x|$ is also written as $\sqrt{x^2} = |x|$. Both of these equations are identities.

It is also necessary to use absolute value when writing identities for other even roots of expressions involving variables.

E X A M P L E   7

Using absolute value symbols with roots

Simplify each expression. Assume the variables represent any real numbers and use absolute value symbols as necessary.

a) $(x^8 y^4)^{1/4}$ **b)** $\left(\dfrac{x^9}{8}\right)^{1/3}$

Solution

a) Apply the power of a product rule to get the equation $(x^8 y^4)^{1/4} = x^2 y$. The left-hand side is nonnegative for any choices of x and y, but the right-hand side is negative when y is negative. So for any real values of x and y we have

$$(x^8 y^4)^{1/4} = x^2 \, |y|.$$

b) Using the power of a quotient rule, we get

$$\left(\frac{x^9}{8}\right)^{1/3} = \frac{x^3}{2}.$$

This equation is valid for every real number x, so no absolute value signs are used.   ■

Because there are no real even roots of negative numbers, the expressions

$$a^{1/2}, \quad x^{-3/4}, \quad \text{and} \quad y^{1/6}$$

are not real numbers if the variables have negative values. To simplify matters, we sometimes assume the variables represent only positive numbers when we are working with expressions involving variables with rational exponents. That way we do not have to be concerned with undefined expressions and absolute value.

E X A M P L E   8   **Expressions involving variables with rational exponents**

Use the rules of exponents to simplify the following. Write your answers with positive exponents. Assume all variables represent *positive* real numbers.

a) $x^{2/3}x^{4/3}$

b) $\dfrac{a^{1/2}}{a^{1/4}}$

c) $(x^{1/2}y^{-3})^{1/2}$

d) $\left(\dfrac{x^2}{y^{1/3}}\right)^{-1/2}$

Solution

a) $x^{2/3}x^{4/3} = x^{6/3}$ Use the product rule to add the exponents.

$\qquad\qquad = x^2$ Reduce the exponent.

b) $\dfrac{a^{1/2}}{a^{1/4}} = a^{1/2-1/4}$ Use the quotient rule to subtract the exponents.

$\qquad\quad = a^{1/4}$ Simplify.

c) $(x^{1/2}y^{-3})^{1/2} = (x^{1/2})^{1/2}(y^{-3})^{1/2}$ Power of a product rule

$\qquad\qquad\quad = x^{1/4}y^{-3/2}$ Power of a power rule

$\qquad\qquad\quad = \dfrac{x^{1/4}}{y^{3/2}}$ Definition of negative exponent

d) Because this expression is a negative power of a quotient, we can first find the reciprocal of the quotient, then apply the power of a power rule:

$$\left(\frac{x^2}{y^{1/3}}\right)^{-1/2} = \left(\frac{y^{1/3}}{x^2}\right)^{1/2} = \frac{y^{1/6}}{x} \qquad \frac{1}{3}\cdot\frac{1}{2} = \frac{1}{6}$$ ■

WARM-UPS

True or false? Explain your answer.

1. $9^{1/3} = \sqrt[3]{9}$

2. $8^{5/3} = \sqrt[5]{8^3}$

3. $(-16)^{1/2} = -16^{1/2}$

4. $9^{-3/2} = \dfrac{1}{27}$

5. $6^{-1/2} = \dfrac{\sqrt{6}}{6}$

6. $\dfrac{2}{2^{1/2}} = 2^{1/2}$

7. $2^{1/2} \cdot 2^{1/2} = 4^{1/2}$

8. $16^{-1/4} = -2$

9. $6^{1/6} \cdot 6^{1/6} = 6^{1/3}$

10. $(2^8)^{3/4} = 2^6$

7.2 EXERCISES

Reading and Writing *After reading this section, write out the answers to these questions. Use complete sentences.*

1. How do we indicate an *n*th root using exponents?

2. How do we indicate the *m*th power of the *n*th root using exponents?

3. What is the meaning of a negative rational exponent?

4. Which rules of exponents hold for rational exponents?

5. In what order must you perform the operations indicated by a negative rational exponent?

6. When is $a^{-m/n}$ a real number?

Write each radical expression using exponent notation. See Example 1.

7. $\sqrt[4]{7}$

8. $\sqrt[5]{cbs}$

9. $\sqrt{5x}$

10. $\sqrt{3y}$

Write each exponential expression using radical notation. See Example 1.

11. $9^{1/5}$

12. $3^{1/2}$

13. $a^{1/2}$

14. $(-b)^{1/5}$

Evaluate each expression. See Example 2.

15. $25^{1/2}$

16. $16^{1/2}$

17. $(-125)^{1/3}$

18. $(-32)^{1/5}$

19. $16^{1/4}$

20. $8^{1/3}$

21. $(-4)^{1/2}$

22. $(-16)^{1/4}$

Write each radical expression using exponent notation and each exponential expression using radical notation. See Example 3.

23. $\sqrt[3]{w^7}$

24. $\sqrt{a^5}$

25. $\dfrac{1}{\sqrt[3]{2^{10}}}$

26. $\sqrt[3]{\dfrac{1}{a^2}}$

27. $w^{-3/4}$

28. $6^{-5/3}$

29. $(ab)^{3/2}$

30. $(3m)^{-1/5}$

Evaluate each expression. See Example 4.

31. $125^{2/3}$

32. $1000^{2/3}$

33. $25^{3/2}$

34. $16^{3/2}$

35. $27^{-4/3}$

36. $16^{-3/4}$

37. $16^{-3/2}$

38. $25^{-3/2}$

39. $(-27)^{-1/3}$

40. $(-8)^{-4/3}$

41. $(-16)^{-1/4}$

42. $(-100)^{-3/2}$

Use the rules of exponents to simplify each expression. See Examples 5 and 6.

43. $3^{1/3}3^{1/4}$

44. $2^{1/2}\,2^{1/3}$

45. $3^{1/3}3^{-1/3}$

46. $5^{1/4}5^{-1/4}$

47. $\dfrac{8^{1/3}}{8^{2/3}}$

48. $\dfrac{27^{-2/3}}{27^{-1/3}}$

49. $4^{3/4} \div 4^{1/4}$

50. $9^{1/4} \div 9^{3/4}$

51. $18^{1/2}2^{1/2}$

52. $8^{1/2}2^{1/2}$

53. $(2^6)^{1/3}$

54. $(3^{10})^{1/5}$

55. $(3^8)^{1/2}$

56. $(3^{-6})^{1/3}$

57. $(2^{-4})^{1/2}$

58. $(5^4)^{1/2}$

59. $\left(\dfrac{3^4}{2^6}\right)^{1/2}$

60. $\left(\dfrac{5^4}{3^6}\right)^{1/2}$

Simplify each expression. Assume the variables represent any real numbers and use absolute value as necessary. See Example 7.

61. $(x^4)^{1/4}$

62. $(y^6)^{1/6}$

63. $(a^8)^{1/2}$

64. $(b^{10})^{1/2}$

65. $(y^3)^{1/3}$

66. $(w^9)^{1/3}$

67. $(9x^6y^2)^{1/2}$

68. $(16a^8b^4)^{1/4}$

69. $\left(\dfrac{81x^{12}}{y^{20}}\right)^{1/4}$

70. $\left(\dfrac{144a^8}{9y^{18}}\right)^{1/2}$

Simplify. Assume all variables represent positive numbers. Write answers with positive exponents only. See Example 8.

71. $x^{1/2}x^{1/4}$

72. $y^{1/3}y^{1/3}$

73. $(x^{1/2}y)(x^{-3/4}y^{1/2})$

74. $(a^{1/2}b^{-1/3})(ab)$

75. $\dfrac{w^{1/3}}{w^3}$

76. $\dfrac{a^{1/2}}{a^2}$

77. $(144x^{16})^{1/2}$

78. $(125a^8)^{1/3}$

79. $\left(\dfrac{a^{-1/2}}{b^{-1/4}}\right)^{-4}$

80. $\left(\dfrac{2a^{1/2}}{b^{1/3}}\right)^6$

81. $\left(\dfrac{2w^{1/3}}{w^{-3/4}}\right)^3$

82. $\left(\dfrac{a^{-1/2}}{3a^{2/3}}\right)^{-3}$

83. $\dfrac{9^{1/4}h^{1/2}k^{3/2}}{9^{3/4}h^{1/3}k^2}$

84. $\dfrac{4^{1/4}s^{1/3}t^{-1/2}}{(4s^2t^{-3})^{-1/4}}$

Simplify each expression. Write your answers with positive exponents. Assume that all variables represent positive real numbers.

85. $(9^2)^{1/2}$

86. $(4^{16})^{1/2}$

87. $-16^{-3/4}$

88. $-25^{-3/2}$

89. $125^{-4/3}$

90. $27^{-2/3}$

91. $2^{1/2}2^{-1/4}$

92. $9^{-1}9^{1/2}$

93. $3^{0.26}3^{0.74}$

94. $2^{1.5}2^{0.5}$

95. $3^{1/4}27^{1/4}$

96. $3^{2/3}9^{2/3}$

97. $\left(-\dfrac{8}{27}\right)^{2/3}$

98. $\left(-\dfrac{8}{27}\right)^{-1/3}$

99. $\left(-\dfrac{1}{16}\right)^{-3/4}$

100. $\left(-\dfrac{5}{9}\right)^{-7/2}$

101. $\left(\dfrac{9}{16}\right)^{-1/2}$

102. $\left(\dfrac{16}{81}\right)^{-1/4}$

103. $-\left(\dfrac{25}{36}\right)^{-3/2}$

104. $\left(-\dfrac{27}{8}\right)^{-4/3}$

105. $(9x^9)^{1/2}$

106. $(-27x^9)^{1/3}$

107. $(3a^{-2/3})^{-3}$

108. $(5x^{-1/2})^{-2}$

109. $(a^{1/2}b)^{1/2}(ab^{1/2})$

110. $(m^{1/4}n^{1/2})^2(m^2n^3)^{1/2}$

111. $(km^{1/2})^3(k^3m^5)^{1/2}$

112. $(tv^{1/3})^2(t^2v^{-3})^{-1/2}$

 Use a scientific calculator with a power key (x^y) to find the decimal value of each expression. Round answers to four decimal places.

113. $2^{1/3}$

114. $5^{1/2}$

115. $-2^{1/2}$

116. $(-3)^{1/3}$

117. $1024^{1/10}$

118. $7776^{0.2}$

119. $\left(\dfrac{64}{15,625}\right)^{-1/6}$

120. $\left(\dfrac{32}{243}\right)^{-3/5}$

Simplify each expression. Assume a and b are positive real numbers and m and n are rational numbers.

121. $a^{m/2} \cdot a^{m/4}$

122. $b^{n/2} \cdot b^{-n/3}$

123. $\dfrac{a^{-m/5}}{a^{-m/3}}$

124. $\dfrac{b^{-n/4}}{b^{-n/3}}$

125. $(a^{-1/m}b^{-1/n})^{-mn}$

126. $(a^{-m/2}b^{-n/3})^{-6}$

127. $\left(\dfrac{a^{-3m}b^{-6n}}{a^{9m}}\right)^{-1/3}$

128. $\left(\dfrac{a^{-3/m}b^{6n}}{a^{-6/m}b^{9/n}}\right)^{-1/3}$

In Exercises 129–136, solve each problem.

129. Diagonal of a box. The length of the diagonal of a box can be found from the formula

$$D = (L^2 + W^2 + H^2)^{1/2},$$

where L, W, and H represent the length, width, and height of the box, respectively. If the box is 12 inches long, 4 inches wide, and 3 inches high, then what is the length of the diagonal?

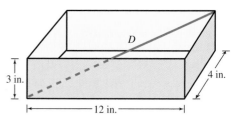

FIGURE FOR EXERCISE 129

130. Radius of a sphere. The radius of a sphere is a function of its volume, given by the formula

$$r = \left(\dfrac{0.75V}{\pi}\right)^{1/3}.$$

Find the radius of a spherical tank that has a volume of $\dfrac{32\pi}{3}$ cubic meters.

FIGURE FOR EXERCISE 130

131. Maximum sail area. According to the new International America's Cup Class Rules, the maximum sail area in square meters for a yacht in the America's Cup race is given by

$$S = (13.0368 + 7.84D^{1/3} - 0.8L)^2,$$

where D is the displacement in cubic meters (m^3), and L is the length in meters (m). (www.sailing.com).

Find the maximum sail area for a boat that has a displacement of 18.42 m³ and a length of 21.45 m.

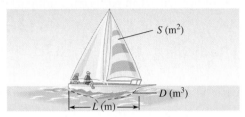

FIGURE FOR EXERCISE 131

 132. *Orbits of the planets.* According to Kepler's third law of planetary motion, the average radius R of the orbit of a planet around the sun is determined by $R = T^{2/3}$, where T is the number of years for one orbit and R is measured in astronomical units or AUs (Windows to the Universe, www.windows.umich.edu).
  a) It takes Mars 1.881 years to make one orbit of the sun. What is the average radius (in AUs) of the orbit of Mars?
  b) The average radius of the orbit of Saturn is 9.05 AU. Use the accompanying graph to estimate the number of years it takes Saturn to make one orbit of the sun.

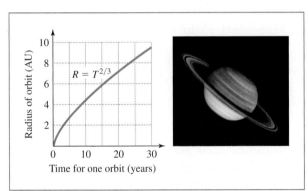

FIGURE FOR EXERCISE 132

133. *Top stock fund.* The average annual return r for an investment is given by the formula

$$r = \left(\frac{S}{P}\right)^{1/n} - 1,$$

where P is the initial investment and S is the amount it is worth after n years. An investment of $10,000 in 1999 in the Shroeder Ultra Investors Fund was worth $20,130 in 2002 (www.money.com). Find the 3-year average annual return.

134. *Top bond fund.* An investment of $10,000 in 1997 in the Spartan Investment Grade Bond Fund grew to $14,309.61 in 2002 (www.fidelity.com). Use the formula from the previous exercise to find the 5-year average annual return.

135. *Overdue loan payment.* In 1777 a wealthy Pennsylvania merchant, Jacob DeHaven, lent $450,000 to the Continental Congress to rescue the troops at Valley Forge. The loan was not repaid. In 1990 DeHaven's descendants filed suit for $141.6 billion (*New York Times*, May 27, 1990). What average annual rate of return were they using to calculate the value of the debt after 213 years? (See Exercise 133.)

136. *California growin'.* The population of California grew from 19.9 million in 1970 to 32.5 million in 2000 (U.S. Census Bureau, www.census.gov). Find the average annual rate of growth for that time period. (Use the formula from Exercise 133 with P being the initial population and S being the population n years later.)

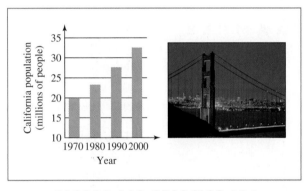

FIGURE FOR EXERCISE 136

GETTING MORE INVOLVED

 137. *Discussion.* If we use the product rule to simplify $(-1)^{1/2} \cdot (-1)^{1/2}$, we get

$$(-1)^{1/2} \cdot (-1)^{1/2} = (-1)^1 = -1.$$

If we use the power of a product rule, we get

$$(-1)^{1/2} \cdot (-1)^{1/2} = (-1 \cdot -1)^{1/2} = 1^{1/2} = 1.$$

Which of these computations is incorrect? Explain your answer.

 138. *Discussion.* Determine whether each equation is an identity. Explain.
  a) $(w^2x^2)^{1/2} = |w| \cdot |x|$
  b) $(w^2x^2)^{1/2} = |wx|$
  c) $(w^2x^2)^{1/2} = w|x|$

7.3 OPERATIONS WITH RADICALS

In this section we will use the ideas of Section 7.1 in performing arithmetic operations with radical expressions.

Adding and Subtracting Radicals

To find the sum of $\sqrt{2}$ and $\sqrt{3}$, we can use a calculator to get $\sqrt{2} \approx 1.414$ and $\sqrt{3} \approx 1.732$. (The symbol $\approx$ means "is approximately equal to.") We can then add the decimal numbers and get

$$\sqrt{2} + \sqrt{3} \approx 1.414 + 1.732 = 3.146.$$

We cannot write an exact decimal form for $\sqrt{2} + \sqrt{3}$; the number 3.146 is an approximation of $\sqrt{2} + \sqrt{3}$. To represent the exact value of $\sqrt{2} + \sqrt{3}$, we just use the form $\sqrt{2} + \sqrt{3}$. This form cannot be simplified any further. However, a sum of like radicals can be simplified. **Like radicals** are radicals that have the same index and the same radicand.

To simplify the sum $3\sqrt{2} + 5\sqrt{2}$, we can use the fact that $3x + 5x = 8x$ is true for any value of x. Substituting $\sqrt{2}$ for x gives us $3\sqrt{2} + 5\sqrt{2} = 8\sqrt{2}$. So like radicals can be combined just as like terms are combined.

E X A M P L E 1

Adding and subtracting like radicals

Simplify the following expressions. Assume the variables represent positive numbers.

a) $3\sqrt{5} + 4\sqrt{5}$ **b)** $\sqrt[4]{w} - 6\sqrt[4]{w}$

c) $\sqrt{3} + \sqrt{5} - 4\sqrt{3} + 6\sqrt{5}$ **d)** $3\sqrt[3]{6x} + 2\sqrt[3]{x} + \sqrt[3]{6x} + \sqrt[3]{x}$

Solution

a) $3\sqrt{5} + 4\sqrt{5} = 7\sqrt{5}$ **b)** $\sqrt[4]{w} - 6\sqrt[4]{w} = -5\sqrt[4]{w}$

c) $\sqrt{3} + \sqrt{5} - 4\sqrt{3} + 6\sqrt{5} = -3\sqrt{3} + 7\sqrt{5}$ Only like radicals are combined.

d) $3\sqrt[3]{6x} + 2\sqrt[3]{x} + \sqrt[3]{6x} + \sqrt[3]{x} = 4\sqrt[3]{6x} + 3\sqrt[3]{x}$ ■

Remember that *only radicals with the same index and same radicand can be combined by addition or subtraction.* If the radicals are not in simplified form, then they must be simplified before you can determine whether they can be combined.

E X A M P L E 2

Simplifying radicals before combining

Perform the indicated operations. Assume the variables represent positive numbers.

a) $\sqrt{8} + \sqrt{18}$ **b)** $\sqrt{2x^3} - \sqrt{4x^2} + 5\sqrt{18x^3}$

c) $\sqrt[3]{16x^4y^3} - \sqrt[3]{54x^4y^3}$

Solution

a) $\sqrt{8} + \sqrt{18} = \sqrt{4} \cdot \sqrt{2} + \sqrt{9} \cdot \sqrt{2}$

$\qquad\qquad\quad = 2\sqrt{2} + 3\sqrt{2}$ Simplify each radical.

$\qquad\qquad\quad = 5\sqrt{2}$ Add like radicals.

Note that $\sqrt{8} + \sqrt{18} \neq \sqrt{26}$.

Calculator Close-Up

Check that
$$\sqrt{8} + \sqrt{18} = 5\sqrt{2}.$$

```
√(8)+√(18)
        7.071067812
5√(2)
        7.071067812
```

b) $\sqrt{2x^3} - \sqrt{4x^2} + 5\sqrt{18x^3} = \sqrt{x^2} \cdot \sqrt{2x} - 2x + 5 \cdot \sqrt{9x^2} \cdot \sqrt{2x}$

$$= x\sqrt{2x} - 2x + 15x\sqrt{2x} \quad \text{Simplify each radical.}$$

$$= 16x\sqrt{2x} - 2x \quad \text{Add like radicals only.}$$

c) $\sqrt[3]{16x^4y^3} - \sqrt[3]{54x^4y^3} = \sqrt[3]{8x^3y^3} \cdot \sqrt[3]{2x} - \sqrt[3]{27x^3y^3} \cdot \sqrt[3]{2x}$

$$= 2xy\sqrt[3]{2x} - 3xy\sqrt[3]{2x} \quad \text{Simplify each radical.}$$

$$= -xy\sqrt[3]{2x} \qquad ■$$

Multiplying Radicals

The product rule for radicals, $\sqrt[n]{a} \cdot \sqrt[n]{b} = \sqrt[n]{ab}$, allows multiplication of radicals with the same index, such as

$$\sqrt{5} \cdot \sqrt{3} = \sqrt{15}, \qquad \sqrt[3]{2} \cdot \sqrt[3]{5} = \sqrt[3]{10}, \qquad \text{and} \qquad \sqrt[5]{x^2} \cdot \sqrt[5]{x} = \sqrt[5]{x^3}.$$

C A U T I O N   The product rule does not allow multiplication of radicals that have different indices. We cannot use the product rule to multiply $\sqrt{2}$ and $\sqrt[3]{5}$.

E X A M P L E   3

Multiplying radicals with the same index

Multiply and simplify the following expressions. Assume the variables represent positive numbers.

a) $5\sqrt{6} \cdot 4\sqrt{3}$

b) $\sqrt{3a^2} \cdot \sqrt{6a}$

c) $\sqrt[3]{4} \cdot \sqrt[3]{4}$

d) $\sqrt[4]{\dfrac{x^3}{2}} \cdot \sqrt[4]{\dfrac{x^2}{8}}$

Helpful Hint

Students often write
$$\sqrt{15} \cdot \sqrt{15} = \sqrt{225} = 15.$$
Although this is correct, you should get used to the idea that
$$\sqrt{15} \cdot \sqrt{15} = 15.$$
Because of the definition of a square root, $\sqrt{a} \cdot \sqrt{a} = a$ for any positive number a.

Solution

a) $5\sqrt{6} \cdot 4\sqrt{3} = 5 \cdot 4 \cdot \sqrt{6} \cdot \sqrt{3}$

$$= 20\sqrt{18} \qquad \text{Product rule for radicals}$$

$$= 20 \cdot 3\sqrt{2} \qquad \sqrt{18} = \sqrt{9} \cdot \sqrt{2} = 3\sqrt{2}$$

$$= 60\sqrt{2}$$

b) $\sqrt{3a^2} \cdot \sqrt{6a} = \sqrt{18a^3} \qquad \text{Product rule for radicals}$

$$= \sqrt{9a^2} \cdot \sqrt{2a}$$

$$= 3a\sqrt{2a} \qquad \text{Simplify.}$$

c) $\sqrt[3]{4} \cdot \sqrt[3]{4} = \sqrt[3]{16}$

$$= \sqrt[3]{8} \cdot \sqrt[3]{2} \qquad \text{Simplify.}$$

$$= 2\sqrt[3]{2}$$

d) $\sqrt[4]{\dfrac{x^3}{2}} \cdot \sqrt[4]{\dfrac{x^2}{8}} = \sqrt[4]{\dfrac{x^5}{16}} \qquad \text{Product rule for radicals}$

$$= \dfrac{\sqrt[4]{x^4} \cdot \sqrt[4]{x}}{\sqrt[4]{16}} \qquad \text{Product and quotient rules for radicals}$$

$$= \dfrac{x\sqrt[4]{x}}{2} \qquad \text{Simplify.}$$

$$■$$

We find a product such as $3\sqrt{2}(4\sqrt{2} - \sqrt{3})$ by using the distributive property as we do when multiplying a monomial and a binomial. A product such as $(2\sqrt{3} + \sqrt{5})(3\sqrt{3} - 2\sqrt{5})$ can be found by using FOIL as we do for the product of two binomials.

E X A M P L E 4

Multiplying radicals

Multiply and simplify.

a) $3\sqrt{2}\,(4\sqrt{2} - \sqrt{3})$ **b)** $\sqrt[3]{a}\,(\sqrt[3]{a} - \sqrt[3]{a^2})$

c) $(2\sqrt{3} + \sqrt{5})(3\sqrt{3} - 2\sqrt{5})$ **d)** $(3 + \sqrt{x - 9})^2$

Solution

a) $3\sqrt{2}(4\sqrt{2} - \sqrt{3}) = 3\sqrt{2} \cdot 4\sqrt{2} - 3\sqrt{2} \cdot \sqrt{3}$ Distributive property

$$= 12 \cdot 2 - 3\sqrt{6}$$ Because $\sqrt{2} \cdot \sqrt{2} = 2$ and $\sqrt{2} \cdot \sqrt{3} = \sqrt{6}$

$$= 24 - 3\sqrt{6}$$

b) $\sqrt[3]{a}\,(\sqrt[3]{a} - \sqrt[3]{a^2}) = \sqrt[3]{a^2} - \sqrt[3]{a^3}$ Distributive property

$$= \sqrt[3]{a^2} - a$$

c) $(2\sqrt{3} + \sqrt{5})(3\sqrt{3} - 2\sqrt{5})$

$$\overset{F}{\overbrace{= 2\sqrt{3} \cdot 3\sqrt{3}}} \overset{O}{\overbrace{- 2\sqrt{3} \cdot 2\sqrt{5}}} \overset{I}{\overbrace{+ \sqrt{5} \cdot 3\sqrt{3}}} \overset{L}{\overbrace{- \sqrt{5} \cdot 2\sqrt{5}}}$$

$$= 18 - 4\sqrt{15} + 3\sqrt{15} - 10$$

$$= 8 - \sqrt{15}$$ Combine like radicals.

d) To square a sum, we use $(a + b)^2 = a^2 + 2ab + b^2$:

$$(3 + \sqrt{x - 9})^2 = 3^2 + 2 \cdot 3\sqrt{x - 9} + (\sqrt{x - 9})^2$$

$$= 9 + 6\sqrt{x - 9} + x - 9$$

$$= x + 6\sqrt{x - 9}$$ ∎

In the next example we multiply radicals that have different indices.

E X A M P L E 5

Multiplying radicals with different indices

Write each product as a single radical expression.

a) $\sqrt[3]{2} \cdot \sqrt[4]{2}$ **b)** $\sqrt[3]{2} \cdot \sqrt{3}$

Calculator Close-Up

Check that
$$\sqrt[3]{2} \cdot \sqrt[4]{2} = \sqrt[12]{128}.$$

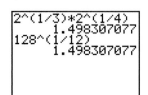

```
2^(1/3)*2^(1/4)
        1.498307077
128^(1/12)
        1.498307077
```

Solution

a) $\sqrt[3]{2} \cdot \sqrt[4]{2} = 2^{1/3} \cdot 2^{1/4}$ Write in exponential notation.

$$= 2^{7/12}$$ Product rule for exponents: $\frac{1}{3} + \frac{1}{4} = \frac{7}{12}$

$$= \sqrt[12]{2^7}$$ Write in radical notation.

$$= \sqrt[12]{128}$$

b) $\sqrt[3]{2} \cdot \sqrt{3} = 2^{1/3} \cdot 3^{1/2}$ Write in exponential notation.

$$= 2^{2/6} \cdot 3^{3/6}$$ Write the exponents with the LCD of 6.

$$= \sqrt[6]{2^2} \cdot \sqrt[6]{3^3}$$ Write in radical notation.

$$= \sqrt[6]{2^2 \cdot 3^3}$$ Product rule for radicals

$$= \sqrt[6]{108}$$ $2^2 \cdot 3^3 = 4 \cdot 27 = 108$ ∎

CAUTION   Because the bases in $2^{1/3} \cdot 2^{1/4}$ are identical, we can add the exponents [Example 5(a)]. Because the bases in $2^{2/6} \cdot 3^{3/6}$ are not the same, we cannot add the exponents [Example 5(b)]. Instead, we write each factor as a sixth root and use the product rule for radicals.

Helpful Hint

The word "conjugate" is used in many contexts in mathematics. According to the dictionary, conjugate means joined together, especially as in a pair.

Conjugates

Recall the special product rule $(a + b)(a - b) = a^2 - b^2$. The product of the sum $4 + \sqrt{3}$ and the difference $4 - \sqrt{3}$ can be found by using this rule:

$$(4 + \sqrt{3})(4 - \sqrt{3}) = 4^2 - (\sqrt{3})^2 = 16 - 3 = 13$$

The product of the irrational number $4 + \sqrt{3}$ and the irrational number $4 - \sqrt{3}$ is the rational number 13. For this reason the expressions $4 + \sqrt{3}$ and $4 - \sqrt{3}$ are called **conjugates** of one another. We will use conjugates in Section 7.4 to rationalize some denominators.

EXAMPLE 6   **Multiplying conjugates**

Find the products. Assume the variables represent positive real numbers.

a) $(2 + 3\sqrt{5})(2 - 3\sqrt{5})$
b) $(\sqrt{3} - \sqrt{2})(\sqrt{3} + \sqrt{2})$
c) $(\sqrt{2x} - \sqrt{y})(\sqrt{2x} + \sqrt{y})$

Solution

a) $(2 + 3\sqrt{5})(2 - 3\sqrt{5}) = 2^2 - (3\sqrt{5})^2$ $\quad (a + b)(a - b) = a^2 - b^2$

$\qquad\qquad\qquad\qquad\qquad = 4 - 45$ $\quad (3\sqrt{5})^2 = 9 \cdot 5 = 45$

$\qquad\qquad\qquad\qquad\qquad = -41$

b) $(\sqrt{3} - \sqrt{2})(\sqrt{3} + \sqrt{2}) = 3 - 2$

$\qquad\qquad\qquad\qquad\qquad\quad = 1$

c) $(\sqrt{2x} - \sqrt{y})(\sqrt{2x} + \sqrt{y}) = 2x - y$ ■

WARM-UPS

True or false? Explain your answer.

1. $\sqrt{3} + \sqrt{3} = \sqrt{6}$
2. $\sqrt{8} + \sqrt{2} = 3\sqrt{2}$
3. $2\sqrt{3} \cdot 3\sqrt{3} = 6\sqrt{3}$
4. $\sqrt[3]{2} \cdot \sqrt[3]{2} = 2$
5. $2\sqrt{5} \cdot 3\sqrt{2} = 6\sqrt{10}$
6. $2\sqrt{5} + 3\sqrt{5} = 5\sqrt{10}$
7. $\sqrt{2}(\sqrt{3} - \sqrt{2}) = \sqrt{6} - 2$
8. $\sqrt{12} = 2\sqrt{6}$
9. $(\sqrt{2} + \sqrt{3})^2 = 2 + 3$
10. $(\sqrt{3} - \sqrt{2})(\sqrt{3} + \sqrt{2}) = 1$

7.3 EXERCISES

Reading and Writing *After reading this section, write out the answers to these questions. Use complete sentences.*

1. What are like radicals?

2. How do we combine like radicals?

3. Does the product rule allow multiplication of unlike radicals?

4. How do we multiply radicals of different indices?

All variables in the following exercises represent positive numbers.

Simplify the sums and differences. Give exact answers. See Example 1.

5. $\sqrt{3} - 2\sqrt{3}$

6. $\sqrt{5} - 3\sqrt{5}$

7. $5\sqrt{7x} + 4\sqrt{7x}$

8. $3\sqrt{6a} + 7\sqrt{6a}$

9. $2\sqrt[3]{2} + 3\sqrt[3]{2}$

10. $\sqrt[3]{4} + 4\sqrt[3]{4}$

11. $\sqrt{3} - \sqrt{5} + 3\sqrt{3} - \sqrt{5}$

12. $\sqrt{2} - 5\sqrt{3} - 7\sqrt{2} + 9\sqrt{3}$

13. $\sqrt[3]{2} + \sqrt[3]{x} - \sqrt[3]{2} + 4\sqrt[3]{x}$

14. $\sqrt[3]{5y} - 4\sqrt[3]{5y} + \sqrt[3]{x} + \sqrt[3]{x}$

15. $\sqrt[3]{x} - \sqrt[3]{2x} + \sqrt[3]{x}$

16. $\sqrt[3]{ab} + \sqrt{a} + 5\sqrt{a} + \sqrt[3]{ab}$

Simplify each expression. Give exact answers. See Example 2.

17. $\sqrt{8} + \sqrt{28}$

18. $\sqrt{12} + \sqrt{24}$

19. $\sqrt{8} + \sqrt{18}$

20. $\sqrt{12} + \sqrt{27}$

21. $2\sqrt{45} - 3\sqrt{20}$

22. $3\sqrt{50} - 2\sqrt{32}$

23. $\sqrt{2} - \sqrt{8}$

24. $\sqrt{20} - \sqrt{125}$

25. $\sqrt{45x^3} - \sqrt{18x^2} + \sqrt{50x^2} - \sqrt{20x^3}$

26. $\sqrt{12x^5} - \sqrt{18x} - \sqrt{300x^5} + \sqrt{98x}$

27. $2\sqrt[3]{24} + \sqrt[3]{81}$

28. $5\sqrt[3]{24} + 2\sqrt[3]{375}$

29. $\sqrt[4]{48} - 2\sqrt[4]{243}$

30. $\sqrt[5]{64} + 7\sqrt[5]{2}$

31. $\sqrt[3]{54t^4y^3} - \sqrt[3]{16t^4y^3}$

32. $\sqrt[3]{2000w^2z^5} - \sqrt[3]{16w^2z^5}$

Simplify the products. Give exact answers. See Examples 3 and 4.

33. $\sqrt{3} \cdot \sqrt{5}$

34. $\sqrt{5} \cdot \sqrt{7}$

35. $2\sqrt{5} \cdot 3\sqrt{10}$

36. $(3\sqrt{2})(-4\sqrt{10})$

37. $2\sqrt{7a} \cdot 3\sqrt{2a}$

38. $2\sqrt{5c} \cdot 5\sqrt{5}$

39. $\sqrt[4]{9} \cdot \sqrt[4]{27}$

40. $\sqrt[3]{5} \cdot \sqrt[3]{100}$

41. $(2\sqrt{3})^2$

42. $(-4\sqrt{2})^2$

43. $2\sqrt{3}(\sqrt{6} + 3\sqrt{3})$

44. $2\sqrt{5}(\sqrt{3} + 3\sqrt{5})$

45. $\sqrt{5}(\sqrt{10} - 2)$

46. $\sqrt{6}(\sqrt{15} - 1)$

47. $\sqrt[3]{3t}(\sqrt[3]{9t} - \sqrt[3]{t^2})$

48. $\sqrt[3]{2}(\sqrt[3]{12x} - \sqrt[3]{2x})$

49. $(\sqrt{3} + 2)(\sqrt{3} - 5)$

50. $(\sqrt{5} + 2)(\sqrt{5} - 6)$

51. $(\sqrt{11} - 3)(\sqrt{11} + 3)$

52. $(\sqrt{2} + 5)(\sqrt{2} + 5)$

53. $(2\sqrt{5} - 7)(2\sqrt{5} + 4)$

54. $(2\sqrt{6} - 3)(2\sqrt{6} + 4)$

55. $(2\sqrt{3} - \sqrt{6})(\sqrt{3} + 2\sqrt{6})$

56. $(3\sqrt{3} - \sqrt{2})(\sqrt{2} + \sqrt{3})$

Write each product as a single radical expression. See Example 5.

57. $\sqrt[3]{3} \cdot \sqrt{3}$ **58.** $\sqrt{3} \cdot \sqrt[4]{3}$

59. $\sqrt[3]{5} \cdot \sqrt[4]{5}$ **60.** $\sqrt[3]{2} \cdot \sqrt[5]{2}$

61. $\sqrt[3]{2} \cdot \sqrt{5}$ **62.** $\sqrt{6} \cdot \sqrt[3]{2}$

63. $\sqrt[3]{2} \cdot \sqrt[4]{3}$ **64.** $\sqrt[3]{3} \cdot \sqrt[4]{2}$

Find the product of each pair of conjugates. See Example 6.

65. $(\sqrt{3} - 2)(\sqrt{3} + 2)$

66. $(7 - \sqrt{3})(7 + \sqrt{3})$

67. $(\sqrt{5} + \sqrt{2})(\sqrt{5} - \sqrt{2})$

68. $(\sqrt{6} + \sqrt{5})(\sqrt{6} - \sqrt{5})$

69. $(2\sqrt{5} + 1)(2\sqrt{5} - 1)$

70. $(3\sqrt{2} - 4)(3\sqrt{2} + 4)$

71. $(3\sqrt{2} + \sqrt{5})(3\sqrt{2} - \sqrt{5})$

72. $(2\sqrt{3} - \sqrt{7})(2\sqrt{3} + \sqrt{7})$

73. $(5 - 3\sqrt{x})(5 + 3\sqrt{x})$

74. $(4\sqrt{y} + 3\sqrt{z})(4\sqrt{y} - 3\sqrt{z})$

Simplify each expression.

75. $\sqrt{300} + \sqrt{3}$

76. $\sqrt{50} + \sqrt{2}$

77. $2\sqrt{5} \cdot 5\sqrt{6}$

78. $3\sqrt{6} \cdot 5\sqrt{10}$

79. $(3 + 2\sqrt{7})(\sqrt{7} - 2)$

80. $(2 + \sqrt{7})(\sqrt{7} - 2)$

81. $4\sqrt{w} \cdot 4\sqrt{w}$

82. $3\sqrt{m} \cdot 5\sqrt{m}$

83. $\sqrt{3x^3} \cdot \sqrt{6x^2}$

84. $\sqrt{2t^5} \cdot \sqrt{10t^4}$

85. $(2\sqrt{5} + \sqrt{2})(3\sqrt{5} - \sqrt{2})$

86. $(3\sqrt{2} - \sqrt{3})(2\sqrt{2} + 3\sqrt{3})$

87. $\dfrac{\sqrt{2}}{3} + \dfrac{\sqrt{2}}{5}$

88. $\dfrac{\sqrt{2}}{4} + \dfrac{\sqrt{3}}{5}$

89. $(5 + 2\sqrt{2})(5 - 2\sqrt{2})$

90. $(3 - 2\sqrt{7})(3 + 2\sqrt{7})$

91. $(3 + \sqrt{x})^2$

92. $(1 - \sqrt{x})^2$

93. $(5\sqrt{x} - 3)^2$

94. $(3\sqrt{a} + 2)^2$

95. $(1 + \sqrt{x + 2})^2$

96. $(\sqrt{x - 1} + 1)^2$

97. $\sqrt{4w} - \sqrt{9w}$

98. $10\sqrt{m} - \sqrt{16m}$

99. $2\sqrt{a^3} + 3\sqrt{a^3} - 2a\sqrt{4a}$

100. $5\sqrt{w^2y} - 7\sqrt{w^2y} + 6\sqrt{w^2y}$

101. $\sqrt{x^5} + 2x\sqrt{x^3}$

102. $\sqrt{8x^3} + \sqrt{50x^3} - x\sqrt{2x}$

103. $\sqrt[3]{-16x^4} + 5x\sqrt[3]{54x}$

104. $\sqrt[3]{3x^5y^7} - \sqrt[3]{24x^5y^7}$

105. $\sqrt[3]{2x} \cdot \sqrt[3]{2x}$

106. $\sqrt[4]{2m} \cdot \sqrt[4]{2n}$

In Exercises 107–110, solve each problem.

107. *Area of a rectangle.* Find the exact area of a rectangle that has a length of $\sqrt{6}$ feet and a width of $\sqrt{3}$ feet.

108. *Volume of a cube.* Find the exact volume of a cube with sides of length $\sqrt{3}$ meters.

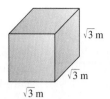

FIGURE FOR EXERCISE 108

109. *Area of a trapezoid.* Find the exact area of a trapezoid with a height of $\sqrt{6}$ feet and bases of $\sqrt{3}$ feet and $\sqrt{12}$ feet.

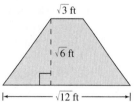

FIGURE FOR EXERCISE 109

110. *Area of a triangle.* Find the exact area of a triangle with a base of $\sqrt{30}$ meters and a height of $\sqrt{6}$ meters.

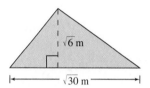

FIGURE FOR EXERCISE 110

GETTING MORE INVOLVED

111. *Discussion.* Is $\sqrt{a} + \sqrt{b} = \sqrt{a + b}$ for all values of a and b?

112. *Discussion.* Which of the following equations are identities? Explain your answers.

a) $\sqrt{9x} = 3\sqrt{x}$

b) $\sqrt{9 + x} = 3 + \sqrt{x}$

c) $\sqrt{x - 4} = \sqrt{x} - 2$

d) $\sqrt{\dfrac{x}{4}} = \dfrac{\sqrt{x}}{2}$

113. *Exploration.* Because 3 is the square of $\sqrt{3}$, a binomial such as $y^2 - 3$ is a difference of two squares.

a) Factor $y^2 - 3$ and $2a^2 - 7$ using radicals.

b) Use factoring with radicals to solve the equation $x^2 - 8 = 0$.

c) Assuming a is a positive real number, solve the equation $x^2 - a = 0$.

7.4 QUOTIENTS, POWERS, AND RATIONALIZING DENOMINATORS

In this section we will continue studying operations with radicals. We will first learn how to rationalize denominators, then we will find quotients and powers with radicals.

Rationalizing the Denominator

Square roots such as $\sqrt{2}$, $\sqrt{3}$, and $\sqrt{5}$ are irrational numbers. If roots of this type appear in the denominator of a fraction, it is customary to rewrite the fraction with a rational number in the denominator, or **rationalize** it. We rationalize a denominator by multiplying both the numerator and denominator by another radical that makes the denominator rational.

You can find products of radicals in two ways. By definition, $\sqrt{2}$ is the positive number that you multiply by itself to get 2. So

$$\sqrt{2} \cdot \sqrt{2} = 2.$$

By the product rule, $\sqrt{2} \cdot \sqrt{2} = \sqrt{4} = 2$. Note that $\sqrt[3]{2} \cdot \sqrt[3]{2} = \sqrt[3]{4}$ by the product rule, but $\sqrt[3]{4} \neq 2$. By definition of a cube root,

$$\sqrt[3]{2} \cdot \sqrt[3]{2} \cdot \sqrt[3]{2} = 2.$$

EXAMPLE 1

Rationalizing the denominator

Rewrite each expression with a rational denominator.

a) $\dfrac{\sqrt{3}}{\sqrt{5}}$
b) $\dfrac{3}{\sqrt[3]{2}}$

Solution

a) Because $\sqrt{5} \cdot \sqrt{5} = 5$, multiplying both the numerator and denominator by $\sqrt{5}$ will rationalize the denominator:

$$\frac{\sqrt{3}}{\sqrt{5}} = \frac{\sqrt{3}}{\sqrt{5}} \cdot \frac{\sqrt{5}}{\sqrt{5}} = \frac{\sqrt{15}}{5} \qquad \text{By the product rule, } \sqrt{3} \cdot \sqrt{5} = \sqrt{15}.$$

b) We must build up the denominator to be the cube root of a perfect cube. So we multiply by $\sqrt[3]{4}$ to get $\sqrt[3]{4} \cdot \sqrt[3]{2} = \sqrt[3]{8}$:

$$\frac{3}{\sqrt[3]{2}} = \frac{3}{\sqrt[3]{2}} \cdot \frac{\sqrt[3]{4}}{\sqrt[3]{4}} = \frac{3\sqrt[3]{4}}{\sqrt[3]{8}} = \frac{3\sqrt[3]{4}}{2} \qquad ■$$

CAUTION To rationalize a denominator with a single square root, you simply multiply by that square root. If the denominator has a cube root, you build the denominator to a cube root of a perfect cube, as in Example 1(b). For a fourth root you build to a fourth root of a perfect fourth power, and so on.

Simplifying Radicals

When simplifying a radical expression, we have three specific conditions to satisfy. First, we use the product rule to factor out perfect nth powers from the radicand in nth roots. That is, we factor out perfect squares in square roots, perfect cubes in cube roots, and so on. For example,

$$\sqrt{72} = \sqrt{36} \cdot \sqrt{2} = 6\sqrt{2} \qquad \text{and} \qquad \sqrt[3]{24} = \sqrt[3]{8} \cdot \sqrt[3]{3} = 2\sqrt[3]{3}.$$

Second, we use the quotient rule to remove all fractions from inside a radical. For example,

$$\sqrt{\frac{2}{3}} = \frac{\sqrt{2}}{\sqrt{3}}.$$

Third, we remove radicals from denominators by rationalizing the denominator:

$$\sqrt{\frac{2}{3}} = \frac{\sqrt{2} \cdot \sqrt{3}}{\sqrt{3} \cdot \sqrt{3}} = \frac{\sqrt{6}}{3}.$$

A radical expression that satisfies the three conditions is in *simplified radical form*.

> **Simplified Radical Form for Radicals of Index *n***
>
> A radical expression of index *n* is in **simplified radical form** if it has
> 1. *no* perfect *n*th powers as factors of the radicand,
> 2. *no* fractions inside the radical, and
> 3. *no* radicals in the denominator.

E X A M P L E   2   **Writing radical expressions in simplified radical form**

Simplify.

a) $\dfrac{\sqrt{10}}{\sqrt{6}}$

b) $\sqrt[3]{\dfrac{5}{9}}$

Solution

a) To rationalize the denominator, multiply the numerator and denominator by $\sqrt{6}$:

$$\frac{\sqrt{10}}{\sqrt{6}} = \frac{\sqrt{10}}{\sqrt{6}} \cdot \frac{\sqrt{6}}{\sqrt{6}} \qquad \text{Rationalize the denominator.}$$

$$= \frac{\sqrt{60}}{6}$$

$$= \frac{\sqrt{4}\sqrt{15}}{6} \qquad \text{Remove the perfect square from } \sqrt{60}.$$

$$= \frac{2\sqrt{15}}{6}$$

$$= \frac{\sqrt{15}}{3} \qquad \text{Reduce } \tfrac{2}{6} \text{ to } \tfrac{1}{3}. \text{ Note that } \sqrt{15} \div 3 \neq \sqrt{5}.$$

b) To rationalize the denominator, build up the denominator to a cube root of a perfect cube. Because $\sqrt[3]{9} \cdot \sqrt[3]{3} = \sqrt[3]{27} = 3$, we multiply by $\sqrt[3]{3}$:

$$\sqrt[3]{\frac{5}{9}} = \frac{\sqrt[3]{5}}{\sqrt[3]{9}} \qquad \text{Quotient rule for radicals}$$

$$= \frac{\sqrt[3]{5}}{\sqrt[3]{9}} \cdot \frac{\sqrt[3]{3}}{\sqrt[3]{3}} \qquad \text{Rationalize the denominator.}$$

$$= \frac{\sqrt[3]{15}}{\sqrt[3]{27}}$$

$$= \frac{\sqrt[3]{15}}{3}$$

E X A M P L E   3

Rationalizing the denominator with variables

Simplify each expression. Assume all variables represent positive real numbers.

a) $\sqrt{\dfrac{a}{b}}$ 　　　　　　**b)** $\sqrt{\dfrac{x^3}{y^5}}$ 　　　　　　**c)** $\sqrt[3]{\dfrac{x}{y}}$

Study Tip

Write about what you read in the text. Sum things up in your own words. Write out important facts on note cards. When you have a few spare minutes in between classes review your note cards. Try to memorize all the information on the cards.

Solution

a) $\sqrt{\dfrac{a}{b}} = \dfrac{\sqrt{a}}{\sqrt{b}}$ 　　　　　Quotient rule for radicals

$= \dfrac{\sqrt{a} \cdot \sqrt{b}}{\sqrt{b} \cdot \sqrt{b}}$ 　　　　Rationalize the denominator.

$= \dfrac{\sqrt{ab}}{b}$

b) $\sqrt{\dfrac{x^3}{y^5}} = \dfrac{\sqrt{x^3}}{\sqrt{y^5}}$ 　　　　　Quotient rule for radicals

$= \dfrac{\sqrt{x^2} \cdot \sqrt{x}}{\sqrt{y^4} \cdot \sqrt{y}}$ 　　　　Product rule for radicals

$= \dfrac{x\sqrt{x}}{y^2\sqrt{y}}$ 　　　　　Simplify.

$= \dfrac{x\sqrt{x} \cdot \sqrt{y}}{y^2\sqrt{y} \cdot \sqrt{y}}$ 　　　　Rationalize the denominator.

$= \dfrac{x\sqrt{xy}}{y^2 \cdot y} = \dfrac{x\sqrt{xy}}{y^3}$

c) Multiply by $\sqrt[3]{y^2}$ to rationalize the denominator:

$$\sqrt[3]{\dfrac{x}{y}} = \dfrac{\sqrt[3]{x}}{\sqrt[3]{y}} = \dfrac{\sqrt[3]{x}}{\sqrt[3]{y}} \cdot \dfrac{\sqrt[3]{y^2}}{\sqrt[3]{y^2}} = \dfrac{\sqrt[3]{xy^2}}{\sqrt[3]{y^3}} = \dfrac{\sqrt[3]{xy^2}}{y}$$

■

Dividing Radicals

In Section 7.3 you learned how to add, subtract, and multiply radical expressions. To divide two radical expressions, simply write the quotient as a ratio and then simplify. In general, we have

$$\sqrt[n]{a} \div \sqrt[n]{b} = \dfrac{\sqrt[n]{a}}{\sqrt[n]{b}} = \sqrt[n]{\dfrac{a}{b}},$$

provided that all expressions represent real numbers. Note that the quotient rule is applied only to radicals that have the same index.

E X A M P L E   4

Dividing radicals with the same index

Divide and simplify. Assume the variables represent positive numbers.

a) $\sqrt{10} \div \sqrt{5}$

b) $(3\sqrt{2}) \div (2\sqrt{3})$

c) $\sqrt[3]{10x^2} \div \sqrt[3]{5x}$

Solution

a) $\sqrt{10} \div \sqrt{5} = \dfrac{\sqrt{10}}{\sqrt{5}}$ $a \div b = \dfrac{a}{b}$, provided that $b \neq 0$.

$= \sqrt{\dfrac{10}{5}}$ Quotient rule for radicals

$= \sqrt{2}$ Reduce.

b) $(3\sqrt{2}) \div (2\sqrt{3}) = \dfrac{3\sqrt{2}}{2\sqrt{3}}$

$= \dfrac{3\sqrt{2}}{2\sqrt{3}} \cdot \dfrac{\sqrt{3}}{\sqrt{3}}$ Rationalize the denominator.

$= \dfrac{3\sqrt{6}}{2 \cdot 3}$

$= \dfrac{\sqrt{6}}{2}$ Note that $\sqrt{6} \div 2 \neq \sqrt{3}$.

c) $\sqrt[3]{10x^2} \div \sqrt[3]{5x} = \dfrac{\sqrt[3]{10x^2}}{\sqrt[3]{5x}}$

$= \sqrt[3]{\dfrac{10x^2}{5x}}$ Quotient rule for radicals

$= \sqrt[3]{2x}$ Reduce.   ∎

Note that in Example 4(a) we applied the quotient rule to get $\sqrt{10} \div \sqrt{5} = \sqrt{2}$. In Example 4(b) we did not use the quotient rule because 2 is not evenly divisible by 3. Instead, we rationalized the denominator to get the result in simplified form.

When working with radicals it is usually best to write them in simplified radical form before doing any operations with the radicals.

E X A M P L E   5   **Simplifying before dividing**

Divide and simplify. Assume the variables represent positive numbers.

a) $\sqrt{12} \div \sqrt{72x}$ **b)** $\sqrt[4]{16a} \div \sqrt[4]{a^5}$

Solution

a) $\sqrt{12} \div \sqrt{72x} = \dfrac{\sqrt{4} \cdot \sqrt{3}}{\sqrt{36} \cdot \sqrt{2x}}$ Factor out perfect squares.

$= \dfrac{2\sqrt{3}}{6\sqrt{2x}}$ Simplify.

$= \dfrac{\sqrt{3} \cdot \sqrt{2x}}{3\sqrt{2x} \cdot \sqrt{2x}}$ Reduce $\dfrac{2}{6}$ to $\dfrac{1}{3}$ and rationalize.

$= \dfrac{\sqrt{6x}}{6x}$ Multiply the radicals.

b) $\sqrt[4]{16a} \div \sqrt[4]{a^5} = \dfrac{\sqrt[4]{16} \cdot \sqrt[4]{a}}{\sqrt[4]{a^4} \cdot \sqrt[4]{a}}$ Factor out perfect fourth powers.

$= \dfrac{\sqrt[4]{16}}{\sqrt[4]{a^4}}$ Reduce.

$= \dfrac{2}{a}$ Simplify the radicals.   ∎

In Chapter 8 it will be necessary to simplify expressions of the type found in Example 6.

E X A M P L E   6   **Simplifying radical expressions**

Simplify.

a) $\dfrac{4 - \sqrt{12}}{4}$ b) $\dfrac{-6 + \sqrt{20}}{-2}$

Solution

a) First write $\sqrt{12}$ in simplified form. Then simplify the expression.

$$\frac{4 - \sqrt{12}}{4} = \frac{4 - 2\sqrt{3}}{4} \qquad \text{Simplify } \sqrt{12}.$$

$$= \frac{2(2 - \sqrt{3})}{2 \cdot 2} \qquad \text{Factor.}$$

$$= \frac{2 - \sqrt{3}}{2} \qquad \text{Divide out the common factor.}$$

b) $\dfrac{-6 + \sqrt{20}}{-2} = \dfrac{-6 + 2\sqrt{5}}{-2}$

$$= \frac{-2(3 - \sqrt{5})}{-2}$$

$$= 3 - \sqrt{5} \qquad\qquad\qquad\qquad ■$$

C A U T I O N   To simplify the expressions in Example 6, you must simplify the radical, factor the numerator, and then divide out the common factors. You cannot simply "cancel" the 4's in $\dfrac{4 - \sqrt{12}}{4}$ or the 2's in $\dfrac{2 - \sqrt{3}}{2}$ because they are not common factors.

Rationalizing Denominators Using Conjugates

A simplified expression involving radicals does not have radicals in the denominator. If an expression such as $4 - \sqrt{3}$ appears in a denominator, we can multiply both the numerator and denominator by its conjugate $4 + \sqrt{3}$ to get a rational number in the denominator.

E X A M P L E   7   **Rationalizing the denominator using conjugates**

Write in simplified form.

a) $\dfrac{2 + \sqrt{3}}{4 - \sqrt{3}}$ b) $\dfrac{\sqrt{5}}{\sqrt{6} + \sqrt{2}}$

Solution

a) $\dfrac{2 + \sqrt{3}}{4 - \sqrt{3}} = \dfrac{(2 + \sqrt{3})(4 + \sqrt{3})}{(4 - \sqrt{3})(4 + \sqrt{3})}$ Multiply the numerator and denominator by $4 + \sqrt{3}$.

$$= \frac{8 + 6\sqrt{3} + 3}{13} \qquad (4 - \sqrt{3})(4 + \sqrt{3}) = 16 - 3 = 13$$

$$= \frac{11 + 6\sqrt{3}}{13} \qquad\qquad \text{Simplify.}$$

b) $\dfrac{\sqrt{5}}{\sqrt{6} + \sqrt{2}} = \dfrac{\sqrt{5}(\sqrt{6} - \sqrt{2})}{(\sqrt{6} + \sqrt{2})(\sqrt{6} - \sqrt{2})}$ Multiply the numerator and denominator by $\sqrt{6} - \sqrt{2}$.

$= \dfrac{\sqrt{30} - \sqrt{10}}{4}$ $(\sqrt{6} + \sqrt{2})(\sqrt{6} - \sqrt{2}) = 6 - 2 = 4$ ∎

Powers of Radical Expressions

In Example 8 we use the power of a product rule $((ab)^n = a^n b^n)$ and the power of a power rule $((a^m)^n = a^{mn})$ with radical expressions. We also use the fact that a root and a power can be found in either order. That is, $(\sqrt[n]{a})^m = \sqrt[n]{a^m}$.

EXAMPLE 8

Finding powers of rational expressions

Simplify. Assume the variables represent positive numbers.

a) $(5\sqrt{2})^3$ **b)** $(2\sqrt[3]{x^3})^4$ **c)** $(3w\sqrt[3]{2w})^3$ **d)** $(2t\sqrt[4]{3t})^3$

Solution

a) $(5\sqrt{2})^3 = 5^3(\sqrt{2})^3$ Power of a product rule

$= 125\sqrt{8}$ $(\sqrt{2})^3 = \sqrt{2^3} = \sqrt{8}$

$= 125 \cdot 2\sqrt{2}$ $\sqrt{8} = \sqrt{4}\sqrt{2} = 2\sqrt{2}$

$= 250\sqrt{2}$

b) $(2\sqrt[3]{x^3})^4 = 2^4(\sqrt[3]{x^3})^4$ Power of a product rule

$= 2^4\sqrt[3]{(x^3)^4}$ $(\sqrt[n]{a})^m = \sqrt[n]{a^m}$

$= 16\sqrt[3]{x^{12}}$ $(a^m)^n = a^{mn}$

$= 16x^6$

c) $(3w\sqrt[3]{2w})^3 = 3^3 w^3(\sqrt[3]{2w})^3$

$= 27w^3(2w)$

$= 54w^4$

d) $(2t\sqrt[4]{3t})^3 = 2^3 t^3(\sqrt[4]{3t})^3 = 8t^3\sqrt[4]{27t^3}$ ∎

True or false? Explain your answer.

1. $\dfrac{\sqrt{6}}{\sqrt{2}} = \sqrt{3}$ **2.** $\dfrac{2}{\sqrt{2}} = \sqrt{2}$

3. $\dfrac{4 - \sqrt{10}}{2} = 2 - \sqrt{10}$ **4.** $\dfrac{1}{\sqrt{3}} = \dfrac{\sqrt{3}}{3}$

5. $\dfrac{8\sqrt{7}}{2\sqrt{7}} = 4\sqrt{7}$ **6.** $\dfrac{2(2 + \sqrt{3})}{(2 - \sqrt{3})(2 + \sqrt{3})} = 4 + 2\sqrt{3}$

7. $\dfrac{\sqrt{12}}{3} = \sqrt{4}$ **8.** $\dfrac{\sqrt{20}}{\sqrt{5}} = 2$

9. $(2\sqrt{4})^2 = 16$ **10.** $(3\sqrt{5})^3 = 27\sqrt{125}$

7.4   EXERCISES

All variables in the following exercises represent positive numbers.

Rewrite each expression with a rational denominator. See Example 1.

1. $\dfrac{2}{\sqrt{5}}$ **2.** $\dfrac{5}{\sqrt{3}}$

3. $\dfrac{\sqrt{3}}{\sqrt{7}}$ **4.** $\dfrac{\sqrt{6}}{\sqrt{5}}$

5. $\dfrac{1}{\sqrt[3]{4}}$ **6.** $\dfrac{7}{\sqrt[3]{3}}$

7. $\dfrac{\sqrt[3]{6}}{\sqrt[3]{5}}$ **8.** $\dfrac{\sqrt[4]{2}}{\sqrt[4]{27}}$

Write each radical expression in simplified radical form. See Example 2.

9. $\dfrac{\sqrt{5}}{\sqrt{12}}$ **10.** $\dfrac{\sqrt{7}}{\sqrt{18}}$

11. $\dfrac{\sqrt{3}}{\sqrt{12}}$ **12.** $\dfrac{\sqrt{2}}{\sqrt{18}}$

13. $\sqrt{\dfrac{1}{2}}$ **14.** $\sqrt{\dfrac{3}{8}}$

15. $\sqrt[3]{\dfrac{2}{3}}$ **16.** $\sqrt[3]{\dfrac{3}{5}}$

17. $\sqrt[3]{\dfrac{7}{4}}$ **18.** $\sqrt[4]{\dfrac{1}{5}}$

Simplify. See Example 3.

19. $\sqrt{\dfrac{x}{y}}$ **20.** $\sqrt{\dfrac{x^2}{a}}$

21. $\sqrt{\dfrac{a^3}{b^7}}$ **22.** $\sqrt{\dfrac{w^5}{y^3}}$

23. $\sqrt{\dfrac{a}{3b}}$ **24.** $\sqrt{\dfrac{5x}{2y}}$

25. $\sqrt[3]{\dfrac{a}{b}}$ **26.** $\sqrt[3]{\dfrac{4a}{b}}$

27. $\sqrt[3]{\dfrac{5}{2b^2}}$ **28.** $\sqrt[3]{\dfrac{3}{4a^2}}$

Divide and Simplify. See Examples 4 and 5.

29. $\sqrt{15} \div \sqrt{5}$ **30.** $\sqrt{14} \div \sqrt{7}$

31. $\sqrt{3} \div \sqrt{5}$ **32.** $\sqrt{5} \div \sqrt{7}$

33. $(3\sqrt{3}) \div (5\sqrt{6})$ **34.** $(2\sqrt{2}) \div (4\sqrt{10})$

35. $(2\sqrt{3}) \div (3\sqrt{6})$ **36.** $(5\sqrt{12}) \div (4\sqrt{6})$

37. $\sqrt{24a^2} \div \sqrt{72a}$

38. $\sqrt{32x^3} \div \sqrt{48x^2}$

39. $\sqrt[3]{20} \div \sqrt[3]{2}$ **40.** $\sqrt[3]{8x^7} \div \sqrt[3]{2x}$

41. $\sqrt[4]{48} \div \sqrt[4]{3}$ **42.** $\sqrt[4]{4a^{10}} \div \sqrt[4]{2a^2}$

43. $\sqrt[4]{16w} \div \sqrt[4]{w^5}$ **44.** $\sqrt[4]{81b^5} \div \sqrt[4]{b}$

Simplify. See Example 6.

45. $\dfrac{6 + \sqrt{45}}{3}$ **46.** $\dfrac{10 + \sqrt{50}}{5}$

47. $\dfrac{-2 + \sqrt{12}}{-2}$ **48.** $\dfrac{-6 + \sqrt{72}}{-6}$

Simplify each expression by rationalizing the denominator. See Example 7.

49. $\dfrac{4}{2 + \sqrt{8}}$ **50.** $\dfrac{6}{3 - \sqrt{18}}$

51. $\dfrac{3}{\sqrt{11} - \sqrt{5}}$ **52.** $\dfrac{6}{\sqrt{5} - \sqrt{14}}$

53. $\dfrac{1 + \sqrt{2}}{\sqrt{3} - 1}$

54. $\dfrac{2 - \sqrt{3}}{\sqrt{2} + \sqrt{6}}$

55. $\dfrac{\sqrt{2}}{\sqrt{6} + \sqrt{3}}$

56. $\dfrac{5}{\sqrt{7} - \sqrt{5}}$

57. $\dfrac{2\sqrt{3}}{3\sqrt{2} - \sqrt{5}}$

58. $\dfrac{3\sqrt{5}}{5\sqrt{2} + \sqrt{6}}$

Simplify. See Example 8.

59. $(2\sqrt{2})^5$ **60.** $(3\sqrt{3})^4$

61. $(\sqrt{x})^5$ **62.** $(2\sqrt{y})^3$

63. $\left(-3\sqrt{x^3}\right)^3$ **64.** $\left(-2\sqrt{x^3}\right)^4$

65. $\left(2x\sqrt[3]{x^2}\right)^3$ **66.** $\left(2y\sqrt[3]{4y}\right)^3$

67. $(-2\sqrt[3]{5})^2$

68. $(-3\sqrt[3]{4})^2$

69. $(\sqrt[3]{x^2})^6$

70. $(2\sqrt[4]{y^3})^3$

Simplify.

71. $\dfrac{\sqrt{3}}{\sqrt{2}} + \dfrac{2}{\sqrt{2}}$

72. $\dfrac{2}{\sqrt{7}} + \dfrac{5}{\sqrt{7}}$

73. $\dfrac{\sqrt{3}}{\sqrt{2}} + \dfrac{3\sqrt{6}}{2}$

74. $\dfrac{\sqrt{3}}{2\sqrt{2}} + \dfrac{\sqrt{5}}{3\sqrt{2}}$

75. $\dfrac{\sqrt{6}}{2} \cdot \dfrac{1}{\sqrt{3}}$

76. $\dfrac{\sqrt{6}}{\sqrt{7}} \cdot \dfrac{\sqrt{14}}{\sqrt{3}}$

77. $(2\sqrt{w}) \div (3\sqrt{w})$

78. $2 \div (3\sqrt{a})$

79. $\dfrac{8 - \sqrt{32}}{20}$

80. $\dfrac{4 - \sqrt{28}}{6}$

81. $\dfrac{5 + \sqrt{75}}{10}$

82. $\dfrac{3 + \sqrt{18}}{6}$

83. $\sqrt{a}(\sqrt{a} - 3)$

84. $3\sqrt{m}(2\sqrt{m} - 6)$

85. $4\sqrt{a}(a + \sqrt{a})$

86. $\sqrt{3ab}(\sqrt{3a} + \sqrt{3})$

87. $(2\sqrt{3m})^2$

88. $(-3\sqrt{4y})^2$

89. $\left(-2\sqrt{xy^2z}\right)^2$

90. $(5a\sqrt{ab})^2$

91. $\sqrt[3]{m}(\sqrt[3]{m^2} - \sqrt[3]{m^5})$

92. $\sqrt[4]{w}(\sqrt[4]{w^3} - \sqrt[4]{w^7})$

93. $\sqrt[3]{8x^4} + \sqrt[3]{27x^4}$

94. $\sqrt[3]{16a^4} + a\sqrt[3]{2a}$

95. $(2m\sqrt[4]{2m^2})^3$

96. $(-2t\sqrt[6]{2t^2})^5$

97. $\dfrac{x - 9}{\sqrt{x} - 3}$

98. $\dfrac{x - y}{\sqrt{x} - \sqrt{y}}$

99. $\dfrac{3\sqrt{k}}{\sqrt{k} + \sqrt{7}}$

100. $\dfrac{\sqrt{hk}}{\sqrt{h} + 3\sqrt{k}}$

101. $\dfrac{5}{\sqrt{2} - 1} + \dfrac{3}{\sqrt{2} + 1}$

102. $\dfrac{\sqrt{3}}{\sqrt{6} - 1} - \dfrac{\sqrt{3}}{\sqrt{6} + 1}$

103. $\dfrac{1}{\sqrt{2}} + \dfrac{1}{\sqrt{3}}$

104. $\dfrac{4}{2\sqrt{3}} + \dfrac{1}{\sqrt{5}}$

105. $\dfrac{3}{\sqrt{2} - 1} + \dfrac{4}{\sqrt{2} + 1}$

106. $\dfrac{3}{\sqrt{5} - \sqrt{3}} - \dfrac{2}{\sqrt{5} + \sqrt{3}}$

107. $\dfrac{\sqrt{x}}{\sqrt{x} + 2} + \dfrac{3\sqrt{x}}{\sqrt{x} - 2}$

108. $\dfrac{\sqrt{5}}{3 - \sqrt{y}} - \dfrac{\sqrt{5y}}{3 + \sqrt{y}}$

109. $\dfrac{1}{\sqrt{x}} + \dfrac{1}{1 - \sqrt{x}}$

110. $\dfrac{\sqrt{x}}{\sqrt{x} - 3} + \dfrac{5}{\sqrt{x}}$

GETTING MORE INVOLVED

111. *Exploration.* A polynomial is prime if it cannot be factored by using integers, but many prime polynomials can be factored if we use radicals.

  a) Find the product $(x - \sqrt[3]{2})(x^2 + \sqrt[3]{2}x + \sqrt[3]{4})$.

  b) Factor $x^3 + 5$ using radicals.

  c) Find the product

$$(\sqrt[3]{5} - \sqrt[3]{2})(\sqrt[3]{25} + \sqrt[3]{10} + \sqrt[3]{4}).$$

  d) Use radicals to factor $a + b$ as a sum of two cubes and $a - b$ as a difference of two cubes.

112. *Discussion.* Which one of the following expressions is not equivalent to the others?

  a) $(\sqrt[3]{x})^4$ **b)** $\sqrt[4]{x^3}$ **c)** $\sqrt[3]{x^4}$

  d) $x^{4/3}$ **e)** $(x^{1/3})^4$

7.5 SOLVING EQUATIONS WITH RADICALS AND EXPONENTS

One of our goals in algebra is to keep increasing our knowledge of solving equations because the solutions to equations can give us the answers to various applied questions. In this section we will apply our knowledge of radicals and exponents to solving some new types of equations.

The Odd-Root Property

Because $(-2)^3 = -8$ and $2^3 = 8$, the equation $x^3 = 8$ is equivalent to $x = 2$. The equation $x^3 = -8$ is equivalent to $x = -2$. Because there is only one real odd root of each real number, there is a simple rule for writing an equivalent equation in this situation.

> **Odd-Root Property**
>
> If n is an odd positive integer,
>
> $$x^n = k \quad \text{is equivalent to} \quad x = \sqrt[n]{k}$$
>
> for any real number k.

EXAMPLE 1

Using the odd-root property

Solve each equation.

a) $x^3 = 27$ **b)** $x^5 + 32 = 0$ **c)** $(x - 2)^3 = 24$

Solution

a) $x^3 = 27$

$\quad x = \sqrt[3]{27}$ Odd-root property

$\quad x = 3$

Check 3 in the original equation. The solution set is $\{3\}$.

b) $x^5 + 32 = 0$

$\quad\quad x^5 = -32$ Isolate the variable.

$\quad\quad\; x = \sqrt[5]{-32}$ Odd-root property

$\quad\quad\; x = -2$

Check -2 in the original equation. The solution set is $\{-2\}$.

c) $(x - 2)^3 = 24$

$\quad x - 2 = \sqrt[3]{24}$ Odd-root property

$\quad\quad x = 2 + 2\sqrt[3]{3}$ $\sqrt[3]{24} = \sqrt[3]{8} \cdot \sqrt[3]{3} = 2\sqrt[3]{3}$

Check. The solution set is $\{2 + 2\sqrt[3]{3}\}$. ∎

The Even-Root Property

In solving the equation $x^2 = 4$, you might be tempted to write $x = 2$ as an equivalent equation. But $x = 2$ is not equivalent to $x^2 = 4$ because $2^2 = 4$ and $(-2)^2 = 4$. So the solution set to $x^2 = 4$ is $\{-2, 2\}$. The equation $x^2 = 4$ is equivalent to the compound sentence $x = 2$ or $x = -2$, which we can abbreviate as $x = \pm 2$. The equation $x = \pm 2$ is read "x equals positive or negative 2."

Equations involving other even powers are handled like the squares. Because $2^4 = 16$ and $(-2)^4 = 16$, the equation $x^4 = 16$ is equivalent to $x = \pm 2$. So $x^4 = 16$ has two real solutions. Note that $x^4 = -16$ has no real solutions. The equation $x^6 = 5$ is equivalent to $x = \pm\sqrt[6]{5}$. We can now state a general rule.

> **Even-Root Property**
>
> Suppose n is a positive even integer.
> If $k > 0$, then $x^n = k$ is equivalent to $x = \pm\sqrt[n]{k}$.
> If $k = 0$, then $x^n = k$ is equivalent to $x = 0$.
> If $k < 0$, then $x^n = k$ has no real solution.

E X A M P L E   2

Using the even-root property

Solve each equation.

a) $x^2 = 10$ **b)** $w^8 = 0$ **c)** $x^4 = -4$

Solution

a) $x^2 = 10$

$\quad x = \pm\sqrt{10}$ Even-root property

The solution set is $\{-\sqrt{10}, \sqrt{10}\}$, or $\{\pm\sqrt{10}\}$.

b) $w^8 = 0$

$\quad w = 0$ Even-root property

The solution set is $\{0\}$.

c) By the even-root property, $x^4 = -4$ has no real solution. (The fourth power of any real number is nonnegative.) ■

Helpful Hint

We do not say, "take the square root of each side." We are not doing the same thing to each side of $x^2 = 9$ when we write $x = \pm 3$. This is the third time that we have seen a rule for obtaining an equivalent equation without "doing the same thing to each side." (What were the other two?) Because there is only one odd root of every real number, you can actually take an odd root of each side.

Whether an equation has a solution depends on the domain of the variable. For example, $2x = 5$ has no solution in the set of integers and $x^2 = -9$ has no solution in the set of real numbers. We can say that the solution set to both of these equations is the empty set, $\varnothing$, as long as the domain of the variable is clear. In the next section we introduce a new set of numbers, the *imaginary numbers,* in which $x^2 = -9$ will have two solutions. So in this section it is best to say that $x^2 = -9$ has no real solution, because in the next section its solution set will *not* be $\varnothing$. An equation such as $x = x + 1$ never has a solution and so saying that its solution set is $\varnothing$ is clear.

In Example 3 the even-root property is used to solve some equations that are a bit more complicated than those of Example 2.

E X A M P L E   3

Using the even-root property

Solve each equation.

a) $(x - 3)^2 = 4$ **b)** $2(x - 5)^2 - 7 = 0$ **c)** $x^4 - 1 = 80$

Solution

a) $(x - 3)^2 = 4$

$\quad\quad x - 3 = 2$ or $x - 3 = -2$ Even-root property

$\quad\quad\quad\quad x = 5$ or $x = 1$ Add 3 to each side.

The solution set is $\{1, 5\}$.

67. $(3a - 1)^{-2/5} = 1$

68. $(r - 1)^{-2/3} = 1$

69. $(t - 1)^{-2/3} = 2$

70. $(w + 3)^{-1/3} = \dfrac{1}{3}$

71. $(x - 3)^{2/3} = -4$

72. $(x + 2)^{3/2} = -1$

Solve each equation.

73. $2x^2 + 3 = 7$

74. $3x^2 - 5 = 16$

75. $\sqrt[3]{2w + 3} = \sqrt[3]{w - 2}$

76. $\sqrt[3]{2 - w} = \sqrt[3]{2w - 28}$

77. $(w + 1)^{2/3} = -3$

78. $(x - 2)^{4/3} = -2$

79. $(a + 1)^{1/3} = -2$

80. $(a - 1)^{1/3} = -3$

81. $(4y - 5)^7 = 0$

82. $(5x)^9 = 0$

83. $\sqrt{5x^2 + 4x + 1} - x = 0$

84. $3 + \sqrt{x^2 - 8x} = 0$

85. $\sqrt{4x^2} = x + 2$

86. $\sqrt{9x^2} = x + 6$

87. $(t + 2)^4 = 32$

88. $(w + 1)^4 = 48$

89. $\sqrt{x^2 - 3x} = x$

90. $\sqrt[4]{4x^4 - 48} = -x$

91. $x^{-3} = 8$

92. $x^{-2} = 4$

Solve each problem by writing an equation and solving it. Find the exact answer and simplify it using the rules for radicals. See Example 8.

93. *Side of a square.* Find the length of the side of a square whose diagonal is 8 feet.

94. *Diagonal of a patio.* Find the length of the diagonal of a square patio with an area of 40 square meters.

95. *Side of a sign.* Find the length of the side of a square sign whose area is 50 square feet.

96. *Side of a cube.* Find the length of the side of a cubic box whose volume is 80 cubic feet.

97. *Diagonal of a rectangle.* If the sides of a rectangle are 30 feet and 40 feet in length, find the length of the diagonal of the rectangle.

98. *Diagonal of a sign.* What is the length of the diagonal of a rectangular billboard whose sides are 5 meters and 12 meters?

99. *Sailboat stability.* To be considered safe for ocean sailing, the capsize screening value C should be less than 2 (www.sailing.com). For a boat with a beam (or width) b in feet and displacement d in pounds, C is determined by the formula

$$C = 4d^{-1/3}b.$$

a) Find the capsize screening value for the Tartan 4100, which has a displacement of 23,245 pounds and a beam of 13.5 feet.

b) Solve this formula for d.

c) The accompanying graph shows C as a function of d for the Tartan 4100 ($b = 13.5$). For what displacement is the Tartan 4100 safe for ocean sailing?

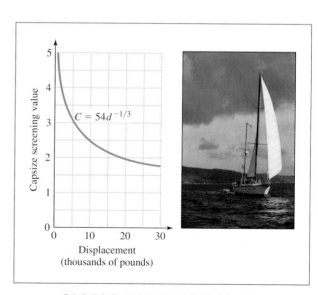

FIGURE FOR EXERCISE 99

100. *Sailboat speed.* The sail area-displacement ratio S provides a measure of the sail power available to drive a boat. For a boat with a displacement of d pounds and a sail area of A square feet

$$S = 16Ad^{-2/3}.$$

a) Find S for the Tartan 4100, which has a sail area of 810 square feet and a displacement of 23,245 pounds.

b) Solve the formula for d.

101. *Diagonal of a side.* Find the length of the diagonal of a side of a cubic packing crate whose volume is 2 cubic meters.

102. *Volume of a cube.* Find the volume of a cube on which the diagonal of a side measures 2 feet.

103. *Length of a road.* An architect designs a public park in the shape of a trapezoid. Find the length of the diagonal road marked a in the figure.

104. *Length of a boundary.* Find the length of the border of the park marked b in the trapezoid shown in the figure.

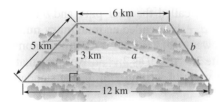

FIGURE FOR EXERCISES 103 AND 104

105. *Average annual return.* The formula

$$r = \left(\frac{S}{P}\right)^{1/n} - 1$$

was used to find the average annual return on an investment in Exercise 133 in Section 7.2. Solve the formula for S (the amount). Solve it for P (the original principal).

106. *Surface area of a cube.* The formula $A = 6V^{2/3}$ gives the surface area of a cube in terms of its volume V. What is the volume of a cube with surface area 12 square feet?

 107. *Kepler's third law.* According to Kepler's third law of planetary motion, the ratio $\frac{T^2}{R^3}$ has the same value for every planet in our solar system. R is the average radius of the orbit of the planet measured in astronomical units (AU), and T is the number of years it takes for one complete orbit of the sun. Jupiter orbits the sun in 11.86 years with an average radius of 5.2 AU, whereas Saturn orbits the sun in 29.46 years. Find the average radius of the orbit of Saturn. (One AU is the distance from the earth to the sun.)

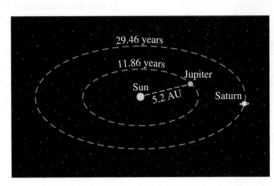

FIGURE FOR EXERCISE 107

 108. *Orbit of Venus.* If the average radius of the orbit of Venus is 0.723 AU, then how many years does it take for Venus to complete one orbit of the sun? Use the information in Exercise 107.

 Use a calculator to find approximate solutions to the following equations. Round your answers to three decimal places.

109. $x^2 = 3.24$

110. $(x + 4)^3 = 7.51$

111. $\sqrt{x - 2} = 1.73$

112. $\sqrt[3]{x - 5} = 3.7$

113. $x^{2/3} = 8.86$

114. $(x - 1)^{-3/4} = 7.065$

GETTING MORE INVOLVED

 115. *Cooperative learning.* Work in a small group to write a formula that gives the side of a cube in terms of the volume of the cube and explain the formula to the other groups.

 116. *Cooperative learning.* Work in a small group to write a formula that gives the side of a square in terms of the diagonal of the square and explain the formula to the other groups.

EXAM

EXAM

Calculat

Many graphing
form operatio
numbers.

2i(1+i)
(2+3i)(
(3+i)(3

We can find powers of i using the fact that $i^2 = -1$. For example,

$$i^3 = i^2 \cdot i = -1 \cdot i = -i.$$

The value of i^4 is found from the value of i^3:

$$i^4 = i^3 \cdot i = -i \cdot i = -i^2 = 1.$$

In Example 3 we find more powers of imaginary numbers.

E X A M P L E   3

Powers of imaginary numbers

Write each expression in the form $a + bi$.

a) $(2i)^2$ **b)** $(-2i)^2$ **c)** i^6

Solution

a) $(2i)^2 = 2^2 \cdot i^2 = 4(-1) = -4$

b) $(-2i)^2 = (-2)^2 \cdot i^2 = 4i^2 = 4(-1) = -4$

c) $i^6 = i^2 \cdot i^4 = -1 \cdot 1 = -1$ ∎

For completeness we give the following symbolic definition of multiplication of complex numbers. However, it is simpler to find products as we did in Examples 2 and 3 than to use this definition.

Multiplication of Complex Numbers

The complex numbers $a + bi$ and $c + di$ are multiplied as follows:

$$(a + bi)(c + di) = (ac - bd) + (ad + bc)i$$

Division of Complex Numbers

To divide a complex number by a real number, divide each term by the real number, just as we would divide a binomial by a number. For example,

$$\frac{4 + 6i}{2} = \frac{2(2 + 3i)}{2}$$
$$= 2 + 3i.$$

Helpful Hint

Here is that word "conjugate" again. It is generally used to refer to two things that go together in some way.

To understand division by a complex number, we first look at imaginary numbers that have a real product. The product of the two imaginary numbers in Example 2(c) is a real number:

$$(3 + i)(3 - i) = 10$$

We say that $3 + i$ and $3 - i$ are complex conjugates of each other.

Complex Conjugates

The complex numbers $a + bi$ and $a - bi$ are called **complex conjugates** of one another. Their product is the real number $a^2 + b^2$.

Make sure th
instructor e
can determi
feels is impc
examples
works in cla
assignment:
your instruc
responsible
answer.

E X A M P L E   4

Products of conjugates

Find the product of the given complex number and its conjugate.

a) $2 + 3i$ **b)** $5 - 4i$

Solution

a) The conjugate of $2 + 3i$ is $2 - 3i$.

$$(2 + 3i)(2 - 3i) = 4 - 9i^2$$
$$= 4 + 9$$
$$= 13$$

b) The conjugate of $5 - 4i$ is $5 + 4i$.

$$(5 - 4i)(5 + 4i) = 25 + 16$$
$$= 41 \qquad \blacksquare$$

We use the idea of complex conjugates to divide complex numbers. The process is similar to rationalizing the denominator. Multiply the numerator and denominator of the quotient by the complex conjugate of the denominator.

E X A M P L E   5

Dividing complex numbers

Find each quotient. Write the answer in the form $a + bi$.

a) $\dfrac{5}{3 - 4i}$ **b)** $\dfrac{3 - i}{2 + i}$

c) $\dfrac{3 + 2i}{i}$

Solution

a) Multiply the numerator and denominator by $3 + 4i$, the conjugate of $3 - 4i$:

$$\frac{5}{3 - 4i} = \frac{5(3 + 4i)}{(3 - 4i)(3 + 4i)}$$

$$= \frac{15 + 20i}{9 - 16i^2}$$

$$= \frac{15 + 20i}{25} \qquad 9 - 16i^2 = 9 - 16(-1) = 25$$

$$= \frac{15}{25} + \frac{20}{25}i$$

$$= \frac{3}{5} + \frac{4}{5}i$$

b) Multiply the numerator and denominator by $2 - i$, the conjugate of $2 + i$:

$$\frac{3 - i}{2 + i} = \frac{(3 - i)(2 - i)}{(2 + i)(2 - i)}$$

$$= \frac{6 - 5i + i^2}{4 - i^2}$$

$$= \frac{6 - 5i - 1}{4 - (-1)}$$

$$= \frac{5 - 5i}{5}$$

$$= 1 - i$$

c) Multiply the numerator and denominator by $-i$, the conjugate of i:

$$\frac{3 + 2i}{i} = \frac{(3 + 2i)(-i)}{i(-i)}$$

$$= \frac{-3i - 2i^2}{-i^2}$$

$$= \frac{-3i + 2}{1}$$

$$= 2 - 3i \qquad \blacksquare$$

The symbolic definition of division of complex numbers follows.

Division of Complex Numbers

We divide the complex number $a + bi$ by the complex number $c + di$ as follows:

$$\frac{a + bi}{c + di} = \frac{(a + bi)(c - di)}{(c + di)(c - di)}$$

Square Roots of Negative Numbers

In Examples 3(a) and 3(b) we saw that both

$$(2i)^2 = -4 \quad \text{and} \quad (-2i)^2 = -4.$$

Because the square of each of these complex numbers is -4, both $2i$ and $-2i$ are square roots of -4. We write $\sqrt{-4} = 2i$. In the complex number system the square root of any negative number is an imaginary number.

Square Root of a Negative Number

For any positive real number b,

$$\sqrt{-b} = i\sqrt{b}.$$

For example, $\sqrt{-9} = i\sqrt{9} = 3i$ and $\sqrt{-7} = i\sqrt{7}$. Note that the expression $\sqrt{7}i$ could easily be mistaken for the expression $\sqrt{7i}$, where i is under the radical. For this reason, when the coefficient of i is a radical, we write i preceding the radical.

Note that the product rule $(\sqrt{a} \cdot \sqrt{b} = \sqrt{ab})$ does not apply to negative numbers. For example $\sqrt{-2} \cdot \sqrt{-3} \neq \sqrt{6}$:

$$\sqrt{-2} \cdot \sqrt{-3} = i\sqrt{2} \cdot i\sqrt{3} = i^2\sqrt{6} = -\sqrt{6}$$

Square roots of negative numbers must written in terms of i before operations are performed.

EXAMPLE 6   **Square roots of negative numbers**

Write each expression in the form $a + bi$, where a and b are real numbers.

a) $3 + \sqrt{-9}$ 　　　　　　**b)** $\sqrt{-12} + \sqrt{-27}$

c) $\dfrac{-1 - \sqrt{-18}}{3}$ 　　　**d)** $\sqrt{-4} \cdot \sqrt{-9}$

Solution

a) $3 + \sqrt{-9} = 3 + i\sqrt{9}$
$$= 3 + 3i$$

b) $\sqrt{-12} + \sqrt{-27} = i\sqrt{12} + i\sqrt{27}$
$$= 2i\sqrt{3} + 3i\sqrt{3}$$
$$= 5i\sqrt{3}$$

$\sqrt{12} = \sqrt{4} \sqrt{3} = 2\sqrt{3}$
$\sqrt{27} = \sqrt{9} \sqrt{3} = 3\sqrt{3}$

c) $\dfrac{-1 - \sqrt{-18}}{3} = \dfrac{-1 - i\sqrt{18}}{3}$
$$= \dfrac{-1 - 3i\sqrt{2}}{3}$$
$$= -\dfrac{1}{3} - i\sqrt{2}$$

d) $\sqrt{-4} \cdot \sqrt{-9} = i\sqrt{4} \cdot i\sqrt{9} = 2i \cdot 3i = 6i^2 = -6$ ∎

Imaginary Solutions to Equations

In the complex number system the even-root property can be restated so that $x^2 = k$ is equivalent to $x = \pm\sqrt{k}$ for any $k \neq 0$. So an equation such as $x^2 = -9$ that has no real solutions has two imaginary solutions in the complex numbers.

E X A M P L E   7

Complex solutions to equations

Find the complex solutions to each equation.

a) $x^2 = -9$ **b)** $3x^2 + 2 = 0$

Solution

a) First apply the even-root property:

$$x^2 = -9$$
$$x = \pm\sqrt{-9} \quad \text{Even-root property}$$
$$= \pm i\sqrt{9}$$
$$= \pm 3i$$

Check these solutions in the original equation:

$$(3i)^2 = 9i^2 = 9(-1) = -9$$
$$(-3i)^2 = 9i^2 = -9$$

The solution set is $\{\pm 3i\}$.

b) First solve the equation for x^2:

$$3x^2 + 2 = 0$$
$$x^2 = -\frac{2}{3}$$
$$x = \pm\sqrt{-\frac{2}{3}} = \pm i\sqrt{\frac{2}{3}} = \pm i\frac{\sqrt{6}}{3}$$

Check these solutions in the original equation. The solution set is $\left\{\pm i\dfrac{\sqrt{6}}{3}\right\}$. ∎

The basic facts about complex numbers are listed in the following box.

> ### Complex Numbers
>
> 1. Definition of i: $i = \sqrt{-1}$, and $i^2 = -1$.
> 2. A complex number has the form $a + bi$, where a and b are real numbers.
> 3. The complex number $a + 0i$ is the real number a.
> 4. If b is a positive real number, then $\sqrt{-b} = i\sqrt{b}$.
> 5. The numbers $a + bi$ and $a - bi$ are called complex conjugates of each other. Their product is the real number $a^2 + b^2$.
> 6. Add, subtract, and multiply complex numbers as if they were algebraic expressions with i being the variable, and replace i^2 by -1.
> 7. Divide complex numbers by multiplying the numerator and denominator by the conjugate of the denominator.
> 8. In the complex number system $x^2 = k$ for any real number k is equivalent to $x = \pm\sqrt{k}$.

WARM-UPS

True or false? Explain your answer.

1. The set of real numbers is a subset of the set of complex numbers.
2. $2 - \sqrt{-6} = 2 - 6i$ 3. $\sqrt{-9} = \pm 3i$
4. The solution set to the equation $x^2 = -9$ is $\{\pm 3i\}$.
5. $2 - 3i - (4 - 2i) = -2 - i$
6. $i^4 = 1$ 7. $(2 - i)(2 + i) = 5$
8. $i^3 = i$ 9. $i^{48} = 1$
10. The equation $x^2 = k$ has two complex solutions for any real number k.

7.6   EXERCISES

Reading and Writing   *After reading this section, write out the answers to these questions. Use complete sentences.*

1. What are complex numbers?

2. What is an imaginary number?

3. What is the relationship among the real numbers, the imaginary numbers, and the complex numbers?

4. How do we add, subtract, and multiply complex numbers?

5. What is the conjugate of a complex number?

6. How do we divide complex numbers?

Find the indicated sums and differences of complex numbers. See Example 1.

7. $(2 + 3i) + (-4 + 5i)$ 8. $(-1 + 6i) + (5 - 4i)$

9. $(2 - 3i) - (6 - 7i)$ 10. $(2 - 3i) - (6 - 2i)$

11. $(-1 + i) + (-1 - i)$ 12. $(-5 + i) + (-5 - i)$

13. $(-2 - 3i) - (6 - i)$ 14. $(-6 + 4i) - (2 - i)$

Find each product. Express each answer in the form a + bi.
See Example 2.

15. $3(2 + 5i)$ **16.** $4(1 - 3i)$ **17.** $2i(i - 5)$

18. $3i(2 - 6i)$ **19.** $-4i(3 - i)$ **20.** $-5i(2 + 3i)$

21. $(2 + 3i)(4 + 6i)$ **22.** $(2 + i)(3 + 4i)$

23. $(-1 + i)(2 - i)$ **24.** $(3 - 2i)(2 - 5i)$

25. $(-1 - 2i)(2 + i)$ **26.** $(1 - 3i)(1 + 3i)$

27. $(5 - 2i)(5 + 2i)$ **28.** $(4 + 3i)(4 + 3i)$

29. $(1 - i)(1 + i)$ **30.** $(2 + 6i)(2 - 6i)$

31. $(4 + 2i)(4 - 2i)$ **32.** $(4 - i)(4 + i)$

Find the indicated powers of complex numbers. See Example 3.

33. $(3i)^2$ **34.** $(5i)^2$ **35.** $(-5i)^2$

36. $(-9i)^2$ **37.** $(2i)^4$ **38.** $(-2i)^3$

39. i^9 **40.** i^{12}

Find the product of the given complex number and its conjugate. See Example 4.

41. $3 + 5i$ **42.** $3 + i$ **43.** $1 - 2i$

44. $4 - 6i$ **45.** $-2 + i$ **46.** $-3 - 2i$

47. $2 - i\sqrt{3}$ **48.** $\sqrt{5} - 4i$

Find each quotient. Express each answer in the form a + bi.
See Example 5.

49. $\dfrac{3}{4 + i}$ **50.** $\dfrac{6}{7 - 2i}$

51. $\dfrac{2 + i}{3 - 2i}$ **52.** $\dfrac{3 + 5i}{2 - i}$

53. $\dfrac{4 + 3i}{i}$ **54.** $\dfrac{5 - 6i}{3i}$

55. $\dfrac{2 + 6i}{2}$ **56.** $\dfrac{9 - 3i}{-6}$

57. $\dfrac{1 + i}{3i - 2}$ **58.** $\dfrac{2 + i}{i + 5}$

59. $\dfrac{6}{3i}$ **60.** $\dfrac{8}{-2i}$

Write each expression in the form a + bi, where a and b are
real numbers. See Example 6.

61. $2 + \sqrt{-4}$ **62.** $3 + \sqrt{-9}$ **63.** $2\sqrt{-9} + 5$

64. $3\sqrt{-16} + 2$ **65.** $7 - \sqrt{-6}$ **66.** $\sqrt{-5} + 3$

67. $\sqrt{-8} + \sqrt{-18}$ **68.** $2\sqrt{-20} - \sqrt{-45}$

69. $\dfrac{2 + \sqrt{-12}}{2}$ **70.** $\dfrac{-6 - \sqrt{-18}}{3}$

71. $\dfrac{-4 - \sqrt{-24}}{4}$ **72.** $\dfrac{8 + \sqrt{-20}}{-4}$

73. $\sqrt{-2} \cdot \sqrt{-6}$ **74.** $\sqrt{-3} \cdot \sqrt{-15}$

75. $\sqrt{-3} \cdot \sqrt{-27}$ **76.** $\sqrt{-3} \cdot \sqrt{-7}$

77. $\dfrac{\sqrt{8}}{\sqrt{-4}}$ **78.** $\dfrac{\sqrt{6}}{\sqrt{-2}}$

Find the complex solutions to each equation. See Example 7.

79. $x^2 = -36$ **80.** $x^2 + 4 = 0$

81. $x^2 = -12$ **82.** $x^2 = -25$

83. $2x^2 + 5 = 0$ **84.** $3x^2 + 4 = 0$

85. $3x^2 + 6 = 0$ **86.** $x^2 + 1 = 0$

Write each expression in the form a + bi, where a and b
are real numbers.

87. $(2 - 3i)(3 + 4i)$ **88.** $(2 - 3i)(2 + 3i)$

89. $(2 - 3i) + (3 + 4i)$ **90.** $(3 - 5i) - (2 - 7i)$

91. $\dfrac{2 - 3i}{3 + 4i}$ **92.** $\dfrac{-3i}{3 - 6i}$

93. $i(2 - 3i)$ **94.** $-3i(4i - 1)$

95. $(-3i)^2$ **96.** $(-2i)^6$

97. $\sqrt{-12} + \sqrt{-3}$ **98.** $\sqrt{-49} - \sqrt{-25}$

99. $(2 - 3i)^2$ **100.** $(5 + 3i)^2$

101. $\dfrac{-4 + \sqrt{-32}}{2}$ **102.** $\dfrac{-2 - \sqrt{-27}}{-6}$

GETTING MORE INVOLVED

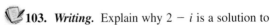

103. *Writing.* Explain why $2 - i$ is a solution to
$$x^2 - 4x + 5 = 0.$$

104. *Cooperative learning.* Work with a group to verify
that $-1 + i\sqrt{3}$ and $-1 - i\sqrt{3}$ satisfy the equation
$$x^3 - 8 = 0.$$
In the complex number system there are three cube
roots of 8. What are they?

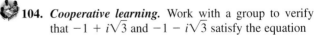

105. *Discussion.* What is wrong with using the product
rule for radicals to get
$$\sqrt{-4} \cdot \sqrt{-4} = \sqrt{(-4)(-4)} = \sqrt{16} = 4?$$
What is the correct product?

137. Long guy wires. The manufacturer of an antenna recommends that guy wires from the top of the antenna to the ground be attached to the ground at a distance from the base equal to the height of the antenna. How long would the guy wires be for a 200-foot antenna?

138. Height of a post. Betty observed that the lamp post in front of her house casts a shadow of length 8 feet when the angle of inclination of the sun is 60 degrees. How tall is the lamp post? (In a 30-60-90 right triangle, the side opposite 30 is one-half the length of the hypotenuse.)

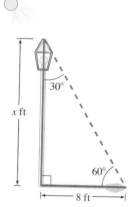

FIGURE FOR EXERCISE 138

139. Manufacturing a box. A cubic box has a volume of 40 cubic feet. The amount of recycled cardboard that it takes to make the six-sided box is 10% larger than the surface area of the box. Find the exact amount of recycled cardboard used in manufacturing the box.

140. Shipping parts. A cubic box with a volume of 32 cubic feet is to be used to ship some machine parts. All of the parts are small except for a long, straight steel connecting rod. What is the maximum length of a connecting rod that will fit into this box?

141. Health care costs. Total annual cost of health care in the United States grew from $993.3 billion in 1995 to $1392.7 billion in 2002 (Statistical Abstract of the United States, www.census.gov).

a) Find the average annual rate of growth r for that period by solving $1392.7 = 993.3(1 + r)^7$.

b) Estimate the total annual cost of health care in 2005 by reading the accompanying graph.

142. Population growth rate. The formula $P = P_0(1 + r)^n$ gives the population P at the end of an n-year time period, where P_0 is the initial population and r is the average annual growth rate. The U.S. population grew from 248.7 million in 1990 to 287.1 million in 2002 (U.S. Census Bureau). Find the average annual rate of growth for the U.S. population for that period.

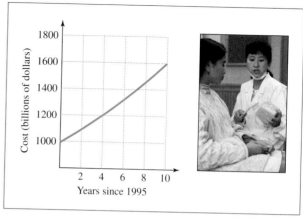

FIGURE FOR EXERCISE 141

143. Landing speed. Aircraft engineers determine the proper landing speed V (in feet per second) for an airplane from the formula

$$V = \sqrt{\frac{841L}{CS}},$$

where L is the gross weight of the aircraft in pounds, C is the coefficient of lift, and S is the wing surface area in square feet. Rewrite the formula so that the expression on the right-hand side is in simplified radical form.

144. Spillway capacity. Civil engineers use the formula

$$Q = 3.32LH^{3/2}$$

to find the maximum discharge that the dam (a broad-crested weir) shown in the figure can pass before the water breaches its abutments (Standard Handbook for Civil Engineers, 1968). In the formula Q is the discharge in cubic feet per second, L is the length of the spillway in feet, and H is the depth of the spillway. Find Q given that $L = 60$ feet and $H = 5$ feet. Find H given that $Q = 3000$ cubic feet per second and $L = 70$ feet.

FIGURE FOR EXERCISE 144

CHAPTER 7 TEST

Simplify each expression. Assume all variables represent positive numbers.

1. $8^{2/3}$

2. $4^{-3/2}$

3. $\sqrt{21} \div \sqrt{7}$

4. $2\sqrt{5} \cdot 3\sqrt{5}$

5. $\sqrt{20} + \sqrt{5}$

6. $\sqrt{5} + \dfrac{1}{\sqrt{5}}$

7. $2^{1/2} \cdot 2^{1/2}$

8. $\sqrt{72}$

9. $\sqrt{\dfrac{5}{12}}$

10. $\dfrac{6 + \sqrt{18}}{6}$

11. $(2\sqrt{3} + 1)(\sqrt{3} - 2)$

12. $\sqrt[4]{32a^5 y^8}$

13. $\dfrac{1}{\sqrt[3]{2x^2}}$

14. $\sqrt{\dfrac{8a^9}{b^3}}$

15. $\sqrt[3]{-27x^9}$

16. $\sqrt{20m^3}$

17. $x^{1/2} \cdot x^{1/4}$

18. $(9y^4 x^{1/2})^{1/2}$

19. $\sqrt[3]{40x^7}$

20. $(4 + \sqrt{3})^2$

Rationalize the denominator and simplify.

21. $\dfrac{2}{5 - \sqrt{3}}$

22. $\dfrac{\sqrt{6}}{4\sqrt{3} + \sqrt{2}}$

Write each expression in the form a + bi.

23. $(3 - 2i)(4 + 5i)$

24. $i^4 - i^5$

25. $\dfrac{3 - i}{1 + 2i}$

26. $\dfrac{-6 + \sqrt{-12}}{8}$

Find all real or imaginary solutions to each equation.

27. $(x - 2)^2 = 49$

28. $2\sqrt{x + 4} = 3$

29. $w^{2/3} = 4$

30. $9y^2 + 16 = 0$

31. $\sqrt{2x^2 + x - 12} = x$

32. $\sqrt{x - 1} + \sqrt{x + 4} = 5$

Show a complete solution to each problem.

33. Find the exact length of the side of a square whose diagonal is 3 feet.

34. Two positive numbers differ by 11, and their square roots differ by 1. Find the numbers.

35. If the perimeter of a rectangle is 20 feet and the diagonal is $2\sqrt{13}$ feet, then what are the length and width?

36. The average radius R of the orbit of a planet around the sun is determined by $R = T^{2/3}$, where T is the number of years for one orbit and R is measured in astronomical units (AU). If it takes Pluto 248.530 years to make one orbit of the sun, then what is the average radius of the orbit of Pluto? If the average radius of the orbit of Neptune is 30.08 AU, then how many years does it take Neptune to complete one orbit of the sun?

Find all real solutions to each equation or inequality. For the inequalities, also sketch the graph of the solution set.

1. $3(x - 2) + 5 = 7 - 4(x + 3)$

2. $\sqrt{6x + 7} = 4$

3. $|2x + 5| > 1$

4. $8x^3 - 27 = 0$

5. $2x - 3 > 3x - 4$

6. $\sqrt{2x - 3} - \sqrt{3x + 4} = 0$

7. $\dfrac{w}{3} + \dfrac{w - 4}{2} = \dfrac{11}{2}$

8. $2(x + 7) - 4 = x - (10 - x)$

9. $(x + 7)^2 = 25$

10. $a^{-1/2} = 4$

11. $x - 3 > 2$ or $x < 2x + 6$

12. $a^{-2/3} = 16$ **13.** $3x^2 - 1 = 0$

14. $5 - 2(x - 2) = 3x - 5(x - 2) - 1$

15. $|3x - 4| < 5$

16. $3x - 1 = 0$ **17.** $\sqrt{y - 1} = 9$

18. $|5(x - 2) + 1| = 3$

19. $0.06x - 0.04(x - 20) = 2.8$

20. $|3x - 1| > -2$ **21.** $\dfrac{3\sqrt{2}}{x} = \dfrac{\sqrt{3}}{4\sqrt{5}}$

22. $\dfrac{\sqrt{x} - 4}{x} = \dfrac{1}{\sqrt{x} + 5}$

23. $\dfrac{3\sqrt{2} + 4}{\sqrt{2}} = \dfrac{x\sqrt{18}}{3\sqrt{2} + 2}$

24. $\dfrac{x}{2\sqrt{5} - \sqrt{2}} = \dfrac{2\sqrt{5} + \sqrt{2}}{x}$

25. $\dfrac{\sqrt{2x} - 5}{x} = \dfrac{-3}{\sqrt{2x} + 5}$

26. $\dfrac{\sqrt{6} + 2}{x} = \dfrac{2}{\sqrt{6} + 4}$

27. $\dfrac{x - 1}{\sqrt{6}} = \dfrac{\sqrt{6}}{x}$ **28.** $\dfrac{x + 3}{\sqrt{10}} = \dfrac{\sqrt{10}}{x}$

29. $\dfrac{1}{x} - \dfrac{1}{x - 1} = -\dfrac{1}{6}$

30. $\dfrac{1}{x^2 - 2x} + \dfrac{1}{x} = \dfrac{2}{3}$

The expression $\dfrac{-b + \sqrt{b^2 - 4ac}}{2a}$ will be used in Chapter 8 to solve quadratic equations. Evaluate it for the given values of a, b, and c.

31. $a = 1, b = 2, c = -15$ **32.** $a = 1, b = 8, c = 12$

33. $a = 2, b = 5, c = -3$ **34.** $a = 6, b = 7, c = -3$

Solve each problem.

35. *Popping corn.* If 1 gram of popcorn with moisture content $x\%$ is popped in a hot-air popper, then the volume of popped corn v (in cubic centimeters) that results is modeled by the formula

$$v = -94.8 + 21.4x - 0.761x^2.$$

a) Use the formula to find the volume that results when 1 gram of popcorn with moisture content 11% is popped.

b) Use the accompanying graph to estimate the moisture content that will produce the maximum volume of popped corn.

c) Use the graph to estimate the maximum possible volume for popping 1 gram of popcorn in a hot-air popper.

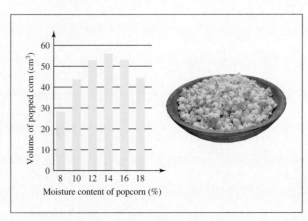

FIGURE FOR EXERCISE 35

Quadratic Equations, Functions, and Inequalities

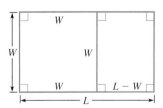

s it possible to measure beauty? For thousands of years artists and philosophers have been challenged to answer this question. The seventeenth-century philosopher John Locke said, "Beauty consists of a certain composition of color and figure causing delight in the beholder." Over the centuries many architects, sculptors, and painters have searched for beauty in their work by exploring numerical patterns in various art forms.

Today many artists and architects still use the concepts of beauty given to us by the ancient Greeks. One principle, called the Golden Rectangle, concerns the most pleasing proportions of a rectangle. The Golden Rectangle appears in nature as well as in many cultures. Examples of it can be seen in Leonardo da Vinci's *Proportions of the Human Figure* as well as in Indonesian temples and Chinese pagodas. Perhaps one of the best-known examples of the Golden Rectangle is in the façade and floor plan of the Parthenon, built in Athens in the fifth century B.C. In Exercise 63 of Section 8.4 we will see that the principle of the Golden Rectangle is based on a proportion that we can solve using the quadratic formula.

E X A M P L E   3

Two irrational solutions

Solve $2x^2 + 6x + 3 = 0$.

Calculator Close-Up

The two irrational solutions to
$$2x^2 + 6x + 3 = 0$$
correspond to the two x-intercepts for the graph of
$$y = 2x^2 + 6x + 3.$$

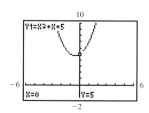

Solution

Let $a = 2$, $b = 6$, and $c = 3$ in the quadratic formula:

$$x = \frac{-6 \pm \sqrt{(6)^2 - 4(2)(3)}}{2(2)}$$

$$= \frac{-6 \pm \sqrt{36 - 24}}{4}$$

$$= \frac{-6 \pm \sqrt{12}}{4}$$

$$= \frac{-6 \pm 2\sqrt{3}}{4}$$

$$= \frac{2(-3 \pm \sqrt{3})}{2 \cdot 2}$$

$$= \frac{-3 \pm \sqrt{3}}{2}$$

Check these values in the original equation. The solution set is $\left\{ \dfrac{-3 \pm \sqrt{3}}{2} \right\}$. ∎

E X A M P L E   4

Two imaginary solutions, no real solutions

Find the complex solutions to $x^2 + x + 5 = 0$.

Calculator Close-Up

Because $x^2 + x + 5 = 0$ has no real solutions, the graph of
$$y = x^2 + x + 5$$
has no x-intercepts.

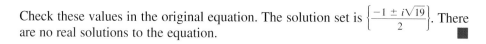

Solution

Let $a = 1$, $b = 1$, and $c = 5$ in the quadratic formula:

$$x = \frac{-1 \pm \sqrt{(1)^2 - 4(1)(5)}}{2(1)}$$

$$= \frac{-1 \pm \sqrt{-19}}{2}$$

$$= \frac{-1 \pm i\sqrt{19}}{2}$$

Check these values in the original equation. The solution set is $\left\{ \dfrac{-1 \pm i\sqrt{19}}{2} \right\}$. There are no real solutions to the equation. ∎

    You have learned to solve quadratic equations by four different methods: the even-root property, factoring, completing the square, and the quadratic formula. The even-root property and factoring are limited to certain special equations, but you should use those methods when possible. Any quadratic equation can be solved by completing the square or using the quadratic formula. Because the quadratic formula is usually faster, it is used more often than completing the square. However, completing the square is an important skill to learn. It will be used in the study of conic sections later in this text.

M A T H   A T   W O R K

Remodeling a kitchen can be an expensive undertaking. Choosing the correct style of cabinets, doors, and floor covering is just a small part of the process. Joe Prendergast, designer for Lee Kimball Kitchens, is involved in every step of creating a new kitchen for a client.

KITCHEN DESIGNER

The process begins with customers visiting the store to see what products are available. Once the client has decided on material and style, he or she fills out an extensive questionnaire so that Prendergast can get a sense of the client's lifestyle. Design plans are drawn using a scale of $\frac{1}{2}$ inch to 1 foot. Consideration is given to traffic patterns, doorways, and especially work areas where the cook would want to work unencumbered. Storage areas are a big consideration, as are lighting and color.

A new kitchen can take anywhere from 5 weeks to a few months or more, depending on how complicated the design and construction is. In Exercise 87 of this section we will find the dimensions of a border around a countertop.

Methods for Solving $ax^2 + bx + c = 0$

Method	Comments	Examples
Even-root property	Use when $b = 0$.	$(x - 2)^2 = 8$ $x - 2 = \pm\sqrt{8}$
Factoring	Use when the polynomial can be factored.	$x^2 + 5x + 6 = 0$ $(x + 2)(x + 3) = 0$
Quadratic formula	Solves any quadratic equation	$x^2 + 5x + 3 = 0$ $x = \dfrac{-5 \pm \sqrt{25 - 4(3)}}{2}$
Completing the square	Solves any quadratic equation, but quadratic formula is faster	$x^2 - 6x + 7 = 0$ $x^2 - 6x + 9 = -7 + 9$ $(x - 3)^2 = 2$

Number of Solutions

The quadratic equations in Examples 1 and 3 had two real solutions each. In each of those examples the value of $b^2 - 4ac$ was positive. In Example 2 the quadratic equation had only one solution because the value of $b^2 - 4ac$ was zero. In Example 4 the quadratic equation had no real solutions because $b^2 - 4ac$ was negative. Because $b^2 - 4ac$ determines the kind and number of solutions to a quadratic equation, it is called the **discriminant.**

Solve each equation by using the quadratic formula. See Example 1.

7. $x^2 + 5x + 6 = 0$ **8.** $x^2 - 7x + 12 = 0$

9. $y^2 + y = 6$ **10.** $m^2 + 2m = 8$

11. $-6z^2 + 7z + 3 = 0$ **12.** $-8q^2 - 2q + 1 = 0$

Solve each equation by using the quadratic formula. See Example 2.

13. $4x^2 - 4x + 1 = 0$ **14.** $4x^2 - 12x + 9 = 0$

15. $-9x^2 + 6x - 1 = 0$ **16.** $-9x^2 + 24x - 16 = 0$

17. $9 + 24x + 16x^2 = 0$ **18.** $4 + 20x = -25x^2$

Solve each equation by using the quadratic formula. See Example 3.

19. $v^2 + 8v + 6 = 0$ **20.** $p^2 + 6p + 4 = 0$

21. $-x^2 - 5x + 1 = 0$ **22.** $-x^2 - 3x + 5 = 0$

23. $2t^2 - 6t + 1 = 0$ **24.** $3z^2 - 8z + 2 = 0$

Solve each equation by using the quadratic formula. See Example 4.

25. $2t^2 - 6t + 5 = 0$ **26.** $2y^2 + 1 = 2y$

27. $-2x^2 + 3x = 6$ **28.** $-3x^2 - 2x - 5 = 0$

29. $\dfrac{1}{2}x^2 + 13 = 5x$ **30.** $\dfrac{1}{4}x^2 + \dfrac{17}{4} = 2x$

Find $b^2 - 4ac$ and the number of real solutions to each equation. See Example 5.

31. $x^2 - 6x + 2 = 0$ **32.** $x^2 + 6x + 9 = 0$

33. $-2x^2 + 5x - 6 = 0$ **34.** $-x^2 + 3x - 4 = 0$

35. $4m^2 + 25 = 20m$ **36.** $v^2 = 3v + 5$

37. $y^2 - \dfrac{1}{2}y + \dfrac{1}{4} = 0$ **38.** $\dfrac{1}{2}w^2 - \dfrac{1}{3}w + \dfrac{1}{4} = 0$

39. $-3t^2 + 5t + 6 = 0$ **40.** $9m^2 + 16 = 24m$

41. $9 - 24z + 16z^2 = 0$ **42.** $12 - 7x + x^2 = 0$

43. $5x^2 - 7 = 0$ **44.** $-6x^2 - 5 = 0$

45. $x^2 = x$ **46.** $-3x^2 + 7x = 0$

Solve each equation by the method of your choice.

47. $\dfrac{1}{4}y^2 + y = 1$ **48.** $\dfrac{1}{2}x^2 + x = 1$

49. $\dfrac{1}{3}x^2 + \dfrac{1}{2}x = \dfrac{1}{3}$ **50.** $\dfrac{4}{9}w^2 + 1 = \dfrac{5}{3}w$

51. $3y^2 + 2y - 4 = 0$ **52.** $2y^2 - 3y - 6 = 0$

53. $\dfrac{w}{w - 2} = \dfrac{w}{w - 3}$ **54.** $\dfrac{y}{3y - 4} = \dfrac{2}{y + 4}$

55. $\dfrac{9(3x - 5)^2}{4} = 1$ **56.** $\dfrac{25(2x + 1)^2}{9} = 0$

57. $25 - \dfrac{1}{3}x^2 = 0$ **58.** $\dfrac{49}{2} - \dfrac{1}{4}x^2 = 0$

59. $1 + \dfrac{20}{x^2} = \dfrac{8}{x}$ **60.** $\dfrac{34}{x^2} = \dfrac{6}{x} - 1$

61. $(x - 8)(x + 4) = -42$

62. $(x - 10)(x - 2) = -20$

63. $y = \dfrac{3(2y + 5)}{8(y - 1)}$ **64.** $z = \dfrac{7z - 4}{12(z - 1)}$

 Use the quadratic formula and a calculator to solve each equation. Round answers to three decimal places and check your answers.

65. $x^2 + 3.2x - 5.7 = 0$

66. $x^2 + 7.15x + 3.24 = 0$

67. $x^2 - 7.4x + 13.69 = 0$

68. $1.44x^2 + 5.52x + 5.29 = 0$

69. $1.85x^2 + 6.72x + 3.6 = 0$

70. $3.67x^2 + 4.35x - 2.13 = 0$

71. $3x^2 + 14,379x + 243 = 0$

72. $x^2 + 12,347x + 6741 = 0$

73. $x^2 + 0.00075x - 0.0062 = 0$

74. $4.3x^2 - 9.86x - 3.75 = 0$

Find the exact solution(s) to each problem. If the solution(s) are irrational, then also find approximate solution(s) to the nearest tenth. See Example 6.

75. *Missing numbers.* Find two positive real numbers that differ by 1 and have a product of 16.

76. *Missing numbers.* Find two positive real numbers that differ by 2 and have a product of 10.

77. *More missing numbers.* Find two real numbers that have a sum of 6 and a product of 4.

78. *More missing numbers.* Find two real numbers that have a sum of 8 and a product of 2.

79. *Bulletin board.* The length of a bulletin board is one foot more than the width. The diagonal has a length of $\sqrt{3}$ feet (ft). Find the length and width of the bulletin board.

80. *Diagonal brace.* The width of a rectangular gate is 2 meters (m) larger than its height. The diagonal brace measures $\sqrt{6}$ m. Find the width and height.

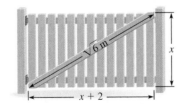

FIGURE FOR EXERCISE 80

81. *Area of a rectangle.* The length of a rectangle is 4 ft longer than the width, and its area is 10 square feet (ft²). Find the length and width.

82. *Diagonal of a square.* The diagonal of a square is 2 m longer than a side. Find the length of a side.

If an object is given an initial velocity of v_0 feet per second from a height of s_0 feet, then its height S after t seconds is given by the formula $S = -16t^2 + v_0t + s_0$.

83. *Projected pine cone.* If a pine cone is projected upward at a velocity of 16 ft/sec from the top of a 96-foot pine tree, then how long does it take to reach the earth?

84. *Falling pine cone.* If a pine cone falls from the top of a 96-foot pine tree, then how long does it take to reach the earth?

85. *Penny tossing.* If a penny is thrown downward at 30 ft/sec from the bridge at Royal Gorge, Colorado, how long does it take to reach the Arkansas River 1000 ft below?

86. *Foul ball.* Suppose Charlie O'Brian of the Braves hits a baseball straight upward at 150 ft/sec from a height of 5 ft.

   a) Use the formula to determine how long it takes the ball to return to the earth.

   b) Use the accompanying graph to estimate the maximum height reached by the ball.

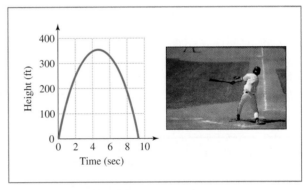

FIGURE FOR EXERCISE 86

In Exercises 87–90, solve each problem.

87. *Kitchen countertop.* A 30 in. by 40 in. countertop for a work island is to be covered with green ceramic tiles, except for a border of uniform width as shown in the figure. If the area covered by the green tiles is 704 square inches (in.²), then how wide is the border?

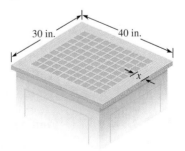

FIGURE FOR EXERCISE 87

88. *Recovering an investment.* The manager at Cream of the Crop bought a load of watermelons for $200. She priced the melons so that she would make $1.50 profit on each melon. When all but 30 had been sold, the manager had recovered her initial investment. How many did she buy originally?

89. *Baby shower.* A group of office workers plans to share equally the $100 cost of giving a baby shower for a coworker. If they can get six more people to share the cost then the cost per person will decrease by $15. How many people are in the original group?

90. *Sharing cost.* The members of a flying club plan to share equally the cost of a $200,000 airplane. The members want to find five more people to join the club so that the cost per person will decrease by $2000. How many members are currently in the club?

GETTING MORE INVOLVED

 91. *Discussion.* Find the solutions to $6x^2 + 5x - 4 = 0$. Is the sum of your solutions equal to $-\frac{b}{a}$? Explain why the sum of the solutions to any quadratic equation is $-\frac{b}{a}$. (*Hint:* Use the quadratic formula.)

 92. *Discussion.* Use the result of Exercise 91 to check whether $\left\{\frac{2}{3}, \frac{1}{3}\right\}$ is the solution set to $9x^2 - 3x - 2 = 0$. If

this solution set is not correct, then what is the correct solution set?

 93. *Discussion.* What is the product of the two solutions to $6x^2 + 5x - 4 = 0$? Explain why the product of the solutions to any quadratic equation is $\frac{c}{a}$.

94. *Discussion.* Use the result of the previous exercise to check whether $\left\{\frac{9}{2}, -2\right\}$ is the solution set to $2x^2 - 13x + 18 = 0$. If this solution set is not correct, then what is the correct solution set?

GRAPHING CALCULATOR EXERCISES

Determine the number of real solutions to each equation by examining the calculator graph of the corresponding function. Use the discriminant to check your conclusions.

95. $x^2 - 6.33x + 3.7 = 0$

96. $1.8x^2 + 2.4x - 895 = 0$

97. $4x^2 - 67.1x + 344 = 0$

98. $-2x^2 - 403 = 0$

99. $-x^2 + 30x - 226 = 0$

100. $16x^2 - 648x + 6562 = 0$

QUADRATIC FUNCTIONS AND THEIR GRAPHS

In This Section

- Definition
- Graphing Quadratic Functions
- The Vertex and Intercepts
- Applications

We have seen *quadratic functions* on several occasions in this text, but we have not yet defined the term. In this section we study quadratic functions and their graphs.

Definition

If y is determined from x by a formula involving a quadratic polynomial, then we say that y is a *quadratic function of x*. Recall that we can use $f(x)$ or y for the dependent variable.

> **Quadratic Function**
>
> A **quadratic function** is a function of the form
>
> $$f(x) = ax^2 + bx + c,$$
>
> where a, b, and c are real numbers and $a \neq 0$.

Without the term ax^2, this function would be a linear function. That is why we specify that $a \neq 0$.

EXAMPLE 1 Finding ordered pairs of a quadratic function

Complete each ordered pair so that it satisfies the given equation.

a) $f(x) = x^2 - x - 6$; (2,), (, 0)

b) $s = -16t^2 + 48t + 84$; (0,), (, 20)

Solution

a) If $x = 2$, then $f(2) = 2^2 - 2 - 6 = -4$. So the ordered pair is $(2, -4)$. To find x when $y = 0$, replace $f(x)$ by 0 and solve the resulting quadratic equation:

$$x^2 - x - 6 = 0$$
$$(x - 3)(x + 2) = 0$$
$$x - 3 = 0 \quad \text{or} \quad x + 2 = 0$$
$$x = 3 \quad \text{or} \quad x = -2$$

The ordered pairs are $(-2, 0)$ and $(3, 0)$.

b) If $t = 0$, then $s = -16 \cdot 0^2 + 48 \cdot 0 + 84 = 84$. The ordered pair is $(0, 84)$. To find t when $s = 20$, replace s by 20 and solve the equation for t:

$$-16t^2 + 48t + 84 = 20$$
$$-16t^2 + 48t + 64 = 0 \qquad \text{Subtract 20 from each side.}$$
$$t^2 - 3t - 4 = 0 \qquad \text{Divide each side by } -16.$$
$$(t - 4)(t + 1) = 0 \qquad \text{Factor.}$$
$$t - 4 = 0 \quad \text{or} \quad t + 1 = 0 \qquad \text{Zero factor property}$$
$$t = 4 \quad \text{or} \quad t = -1$$

The ordered pairs are $(-1, 20)$ and $(4, 20)$. ∎

CAUTION When variables other than x and y are used, the independent variable is the first coordinate of an ordered pair, and the dependent variable is the second coordinate. In Example 1(b), t is the independent variable and first coordinate because s depends on t by the formula $s = -16t^2 + 48t + 84$.

Graphing Quadratic Functions

Any real number may be used for x in $f(x) = ax^2 + bx + c$. So the domain (the set of x-coordinates) for any quadratic function is the set of all real numbers, $(-\infty, \infty)$. The range (the set of y-coordinates) can be determined from the graph. All quadratic functions have graphs that are similar in shape. The graph of any quadratic function is called a **parabola.**

E X A M P L E   2

Graphing the simplest quadratic function
Graph the function $f(x) = x^2$, and state the domain and range.

Solution

Make a table of values for x and y:

x	-2	-1	0	1	2
$y = x^2$	4	1	0	1	4

See Fig. 8.2 on the next page for the graph. The domain is the set of all real numbers, $(-\infty, \infty)$, because we can use any real number for x. From the graph we see that the smallest y-coordinate of the function is 0. So the range is the set of real numbers that are greater than or equal to 0, $[0, \infty)$.

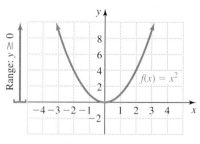

FIGURE 8.2

Calculator Close-Up

This close-up view of $y = x^2$ shows how rounded the curve is at the bottom. When drawing a parabola by hand, be sure to draw it smoothly.

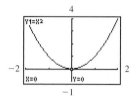

The parabola in Fig. 8.2 is said to **open upward.** In the next example we see a parabola that **opens downward.** If $a > 0$ in the equation $y = ax^2 + bx + c$, then the parabola opens upward. If $a < 0$, then the parabola opens downward.

E X A M P L E   3

A quadratic function

Graph the function $g(x) = 4 - x^2$, and state the domain and range.

Solution

We plot enough points to get the correct shape of the graph:

x	-2	-1	0	1	2
$y = 4 - x^2$	0	3	4	3	0

See Fig. 8.3 for the graph. The domain is the set of all real numbers, $(-\infty, \infty)$. From the graph we see that the largest y-coordinate is 4. So the range is $(-\infty, 4]$.

FIGURE 8.3

The Vertex and Intercepts

The lowest point on a parabola that opens upward or the highest point on a parabola that opens downward is called the **vertex.** The y-coordinate of the vertex is the **minimum value** of the function if the parabola opens upward, and it is the **maximum value** of the function if the parabola opens downward. For $f(x) = x^2$ the vertex is $(0, 0)$, and 0 is the minimum value of the function. For $g(x) = 4 - x^2$ the vertex is $(0, 4)$, and 4 is the maximum value of the function.

If $y = ax^2 + bx + c$ has x-intercepts, they can be found by solving $ax^2 + bx + c = 0$ by the quadratic formula. The vertex is midway between the x-intercepts as shown in Fig. 8.4. Note that in the quadratic formula

$$x = \frac{-b \pm \sqrt{b^2 - 4ac}}{2a},$$

$\sqrt{b^2 - 4ac}$ is added and subtracted from the numerator of $\frac{-b}{2a}$. So $\left(\frac{-b}{2a}, 0\right)$ is the point midway between the x-intercepts and the vertex has the same x-coordinate. Even if the parabola has no x-intercepts, the x-coordinate of the vertex is still $\frac{-b}{2a}$.

Vertex of a Parabola

The x-coordinate of the vertex of $y = ax^2 + bx + c$ is $\frac{-b}{2a}$, provided that $a \neq 0$.

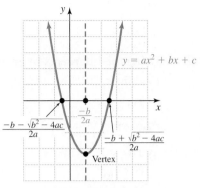

FIGURE 8.4

When you graph a parabola, you should always locate the vertex because it is the point at which the graph "turns around." With the vertex and several nearby points you can see the correct shape of the parabola.

E X A M P L E   4

Using the vertex in graphing a quadratic function

Graph $f(x) = -x^2 - x + 2$, and state the domain and range.

Solution

First find the x-coordinate of the vertex:

$$x = \frac{-b}{2a} = \frac{-(-1)}{2(-1)} = \frac{1}{-2} = -\frac{1}{2}$$

Now find $f\left(-\frac{1}{2}\right)$:

$$f\left(-\frac{1}{2}\right) = -\left(-\frac{1}{2}\right)^2 - \left(-\frac{1}{2}\right) + 2 = -\frac{1}{4} + \frac{1}{2} + 2 = \frac{9}{4}$$

The vertex is $\left(-\frac{1}{2}, \frac{9}{4}\right)$. Now find a few points on either side of the vertex:

x	-2	-1	$-\frac{1}{2}$	0	1
$f(x) = -x^2 - x + 2$	0	2	$\frac{9}{4}$	2	0

Sketch a parabola through these points as in Fig. 8.5. The domain is $(-\infty, \infty)$. Because the graph goes no higher than $\frac{9}{4}$, the range is $\left(-\infty, \frac{9}{4}\right]$.

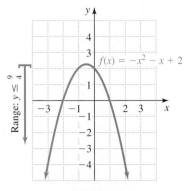

FIGURE 8.5

The *y*-intercept of a parabola is the point that has 0 as the first coordinate. The *x*-intercepts are the points that have 0 as their second coordinates.

E X A M P L E   5

Using the intercepts in graphing a quadratic function

Find the vertex and intercepts, and sketch the graph of each function.

a) $f(x) = x^2 - 2x - 8$ **b)** $s = -16t^2 + 64t$

Solution

a) Use $x = \dfrac{-b}{2a}$ to get $x = 1$ as the *x*-coordinate of the vertex. If $x = 1$, then

$$f(1) = 1^2 - 2 \cdot 1 - 8$$
$$= -9.$$

So the vertex is $(1, -9)$. If $x = 0$, then

$$f(0) = 0^2 - 2 \cdot 0 - 8$$
$$= -8.$$

The *y*-intercept is $(0, -8)$. To find the *x*-intercepts, replace $f(x)$ by 0:

$$x^2 - 2x - 8 = 0$$
$$(x - 4)(x + 2) = 0$$
$$x - 4 = 0 \quad \text{or} \quad x + 2 = 0$$
$$x = 4 \quad \text{or} \quad x = -2$$

The *x*-intercepts are $(-2, 0)$ and $(4, 0)$. The graph is shown in Fig. 8.6.

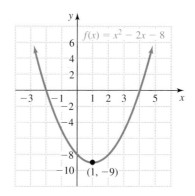

FIGURE 8.6

b) Because *s* is expressed as a function of *t*, the first coordinate is *t*. Use $t = \dfrac{-b}{2a}$ to get

$$t = \frac{-64}{2(-16)} = 2.$$

If $t = 2$, then

$$s = -16 \cdot 2^2 + 64 \cdot 2$$
$$= 64.$$

So the vertex is $(2, 64)$. If $t = 0$, then

$$s = -16 \cdot 0^2 + 64 \cdot 0$$
$$= 0.$$

So the s-intercept is $(0, 0)$. To find the t-intercepts, replace s by 0:

$$-16t^2 + 64t = 0$$
$$-16t(t - 4) = 0$$
$$-16t = 0 \quad \text{or} \quad t - 4 = 0$$
$$t = 0 \quad \text{or} \quad t = 4$$

The t-intercepts are $(0, 0)$ and $(4, 0)$. The graph is shown in Fig. 8.7.

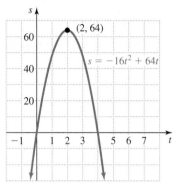

FIGURE 8.7

Calculator Close-Up

You can find the vertex of a parabola with a calculator by using either the maximum or minimum feature. First graph the parabola as shown.

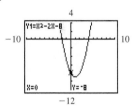

Because this parabola opens upward, the y-coordinate of the vertex is the minimum y-coordinate on the graph. Press CALC and choose minimum.

The calculator will ask for a left bound, a right bound, and a guess. For the left bound choose a point to the left of the vertex by

moving the cursor to the point and pressing ENTER. For the right bound choose a point to the right of the vertex. For the guess choose a point close to the vertex.

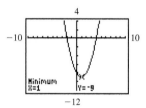

Applications

In applications we are often interested in finding the maximum or minimum value of a variable. If the graph of a quadratic function opens downward, then the maximum value of the second coordinate is the second coordinate of the vertex. If the parabola opens upward, then the minimum value of the second coordinate is the second coordinate of the vertex.

EXAMPLE 6

Finding the maximum height

If a projectile is launched with an initial velocity of v_0 feet per second from an initial height of s_0 feet, then its height $s(t)$ in feet is determined by the quadratic function $s(t) = -16t^2 + v_0 t + s_0$, where t is the time in seconds. If a ball is tossed upward with velocity 64 feet per second from a height of 5 feet, then what is the maximum height reached by the ball?

Solution

The height $s(t)$ of the ball for any time t is given by $s(t) = -16t^2 + 64t + 5$. Because the maximum height occurs at the vertex of the parabola, we use $t = \dfrac{-b}{2a}$ to find the vertex:

$$t = \frac{-64}{2(-16)} = 2$$

Now use $t = 2$ to find the second coordinate of the vertex:

$$s(2) = -16(2)^2 + 64(2) + 5 = 69$$

The maximum height reached by the ball is 69 feet. See Fig. 8.8. ■

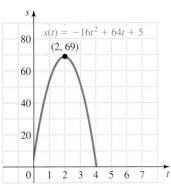

FIGURE 8.8

WARM-UPS

True or false? Explain your answer.

1. The ordered pair $(-2, -1)$ satisfies $f(x) = x^2 - 5$.
2. The y-intercept for $g(x) = x^2 - 3x + 9$ is $(9, 0)$.
3. The x-intercepts for $y = x^2 - 5$ are $(\sqrt{5}, 0)$ and $(-\sqrt{5}, 0)$.
4. The graph of $f(x) = x^2 - 12$ opens upward.
5. The graph of $y = 4 + x^2$ opens downward.
6. The vertex of $y = x^2 + 2x$ is $(-1, -1)$.
7. The parabola $y = x^2 + 1$ has no x-intercepts.
8. The y-intercept for $g(x) = ax^2 + bx + c$ is $(0, c)$.
9. If $w = -2v^2 + 9$, then the maximum value of w is 9.
10. If $y = 3x^2 - 7x + 9$, then the maximum value of y occurs when $x = \dfrac{7}{6}$.

8.3 EXERCISES

Reading and Writing *After reading this section, write out the answers to these questions. Use complete sentences.*

1. What is a quadratic function?

2. What is a parabola?

3. When does a parabola open upward and when does a parabola open downward?

4. What is the domain of any quadratic function?

5. What is the vertex of a parabola?

6. How can you find the vertex of a parabola?

Complete each ordered pair so that it satisfies the given equation. See Example 1.

7. $f(x) = x^2 - x - 12$ $(3,\ \ )$, $(\ \ , 0)$

8. $f(x) = -\dfrac{1}{2}x^2 - x + 1$ $(0,\ \ )$, $(\ \ , -3)$

9. $s = -16t^2 + 32t$ (4,), (, 0)

10. $a = b^2 + 4b + 5$ (−2,), (, 2)

Graph each quadratic function, and state its domain and range. See Examples 2 and 3.

11. $f(x) = x^2 + 2$

12. $g(x) = x^2 - 4$

13. $y = \dfrac{1}{2}x^2 - 4$

14. $y = \dfrac{1}{3}x^2 - 6$

15. $f(x) = -2x^2 + 5$

16. $g(x) = -x^2 - 1$

17. $y = -\dfrac{1}{3}x^2 + 5$

18. $y = -\dfrac{1}{2}x^2 + 3$

19. $h(x) = (x - 2)^2$

20. $h(x) = (x + 3)^2$

Find the vertex and intercepts for each quadratic function. Sketch the graph, and state the domain and range. See Examples 4 and 5.

21. $f(x) = x^2 - x - 2$

22. $f(x) = x^2 + 2x - 3$

28. $h(x) = -x^2 - 2x + 8$

23. $g(x) = x^2 + 2x - 8$

29. $a = b^2 - 6b - 16$

24. $g(x) = x^2 + x - 6$

30. $v = -u^2 - 8u + 9$

25. $y = -x^2 - 4x - 3$

Find the maximum or minimum value of y for each function.

31. $y = x^2 - 8$ **32.** $y = 33 - x^2$

33. $y = -3x^2 + 14$ **34.** $y = 6 + 5x^2$

35. $y = x^2 + 2x + 3$ **36.** $y = x^2 - 2x + 5$

37. $y = -2x^2 - 4x$ **38.** $y = -3x^2 + 24x$

26. $y = -x^2 - 5x - 4$

Solve each problem. See Example 6.

39. *Maximum height.* If a baseball is projected upward from ground level with an initial velocity of 64 feet per second, then its height is a function of time, given by $s(t) = -16t^2 + 64t$. Graph this function for $0 \leq t \leq 4$. What is the maximum height reached by the ball?

27. $h(x) = -x^2 + 3x + 4$

40. *Maximum height.* If a soccer ball is kicked straight up with an initial velocity of 32 feet per second, then its height above the earth is a function of time given by $s(t) = -16t^2 + 32t$. Graph this function for $0 \leq t \leq 2$. What is the maximum height reached by this ball?

41. *Minimum cost.* It costs Acme Manufacturing C dollars per hour to operate its golf ball division. An analyst has determined that C is related to the number of golf balls produced per hour, x, by the equation $C = 0.009x^2 - 1.8x + 100$. What number of balls per hour should Acme produce to minimize the cost per hour of manufacturing these golf balls?

42. *Maximum profit.* A chain store manager has been told by the main office that daily profit, P, is related to the number of clerks working that day, x, according to the equation $P = -25x^2 + 300x$. What number of clerks will maximize the profit, and what is the maximum possible profit?

43. *Maximum area.* Jason plans to fence a rectangular area with 100 meters of fencing. He has written the formula $A = w(50 - w)$ to express the area in terms of the width w. What is the maximum possible area that he can enclose with his fencing?

FIGURE FOR EXERCISE 43

44. *Minimizing cost.* A company uses the function $C(x) = 0.02x^2 - 3.4x + 150$ to model the unit cost in dollars for producing x stabilizer bars. For what number of bars

is the unit cost at its minimum? What is the unit cost at that level of production?

45. *Air pollution.* The amount of nitrogen dioxide A in parts per million (ppm) that was present in the air in the city of Homer on a certain day in June is modeled by the function

$$A(t) = -2t^2 + 32t + 12,$$

where t is the number of hours after 6:00 A.M. Use this function to find the time at which the nitrogen dioxide level was at its maximum.

46. *Stabilization ratio.* The stabilization ratio (births/deaths) for South and Central America can be modeled by the function

$$y = -0.0012x^2 + 0.074x + 2.69$$

where y is the number of births divided by the number of deaths in the year $1950 + x$ (World Resources Institute, www.wri.org).

a) Use the graph to estimate the year in which the stabilization ratio was at its maximum.

b) Use the function to find the year in which the stabilization ratio was at its maximum.

c) What was the maximum stabilization ratio from part (b)?

d) What is the significance of a stabilization ratio of 1?

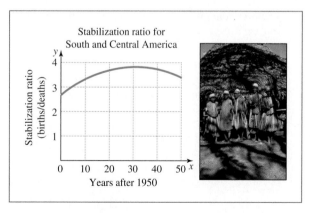

FIGURE FOR EXERCISE 46

47. *Suspension bridge.* The cable of the suspension bridge shown in the figure on the next page hangs in the shape of a parabola with equation $y = 0.0375x^2$, where x and y are in meters. What is the height of each tower above the roadway? What is the length z for the cable bracing the tower?

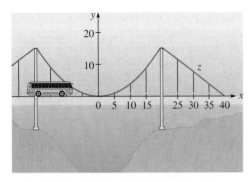

FIGURE FOR EXERCISE 47

GETTING MORE INVOLVED

 48. *Exploration.*

   a) Write the function $y = 3(x - 2)^2 + 6$ in the form $y = ax^2 + bx + c$, and find the vertex of the parabola using the formula $x = \frac{-b}{2a}$.

   b) Repeat part (a) with the functions $y = -4(x - 5)^2 - 9$ and $y = 3(x + 2)^2 - 6$.

   c) What is the vertex for a parabola that is written in the form $y = a(x - h)^2 + k$? Explain your answer.

51. The equation $x = y^2$ is equivalent to $y = \pm\sqrt{x}$. Graph both $y = \sqrt{x}$ and $y = -\sqrt{x}$ on a graphing calculator. How does the graph of $x = y^2$ compare to the graph of $y = x^2$?

52. Graph each of the following equations by solving for y.

   a) $x = y^2 - 1$

   b) $x = -y^2$

   c) $x^2 + y^2 = 4$

 GRAPHING CALCULATOR EXERCISES

49. Graph $y = x^2$, $y = \frac{1}{2}x^2$, and $y = 2x^2$ on the same coordinate system. What can you say about the graph of $y = kx^2$?

50. Graph $y = x^2$, $y = (x - 3)^2$, and $y = (x + 3)^2$ on the same coordinate system. How does the graph of $y = (x - k)^2$ compare to the graph of $y = x^2$?

53. Determine the approximate vertex, domain, range, and x-intercepts for each quadratic function.

   a) $y = 3.2x^2 - 5.4x + 1.6$

   b) $y = -1.09x^2 + 13x + 7.5$

In This Section

- Using the Discriminant in Factoring
- Writing a Quadratic with Given Solutions
- Equations Quadratic in Form
- Applications

8.4   MORE ON QUADRATIC EQUATIONS

In this section we use the ideas and methods of the previous sections to explore additional topics involving quadratic equations.

Using the Discriminant in Factoring

Consider $ax^2 + bx + c$, where a, b, and c are integers with a greatest common factor of 1. If $b^2 - 4ac$ is a perfect square, then $\sqrt{b^2 - 4ac}$ is a whole number, and the solutions to $ax^2 + bx + c = 0$ are rational numbers. If the solutions to a quadratic equation are rational numbers, then they could be found by the factoring method. So if $b^2 - 4ac$ is a perfect square, then $ax^2 + bx + c$ factors. It is also true that if $b^2 - 4ac$ is not a perfect square, then $ax^2 + bx + c$ is prime.

E X A M P L E   1   **Using the discriminant**

Use the discriminant to determine whether each polynomial can be factored.

a) $6x^2 + x - 15$ **b)** $5x^2 - 3x + 2$

Solution

a) Use $a = 6$, $b = 1$, and $c = -15$ to find $b^2 - 4ac$:

$$b^2 - 4ac = 1^2 - 4(6)(-15) = 361$$

Because $\sqrt{361} = 19$, $6x^2 + x - 15$ can be factored. Using the ac method, we get

$$6x^2 + x - 15 = (2x - 3)(3x + 5).$$

b) Use $a = 5$, $b = -3$, and $c = 2$ to find $b^2 - 4ac$:

$$b^2 - 4ac = (-3)^2 - 4(5)(2) = -31$$

Because the discriminant is not a perfect square, $5x^2 - 3x + 2$ is prime.   ■

Writing a Quadratic with Given Solutions

Not every quadratic equation can be solved by factoring, but the factoring method can be used (in reverse) to write a quadratic equation with any given solutions. For example, if the solutions to a quadratic equation are 5 and -3, we can reverse the steps in the factoring method as follows:

$$x = 5 \quad \text{or} \quad x = -3$$
$$x - 5 = 0 \quad \text{or} \quad x + 3 = 0$$
$$(x - 5)(x + 3) = 0 \quad \text{Zero factor property}$$
$$x^2 - 2x - 15 = 0 \quad \text{Multiply the factors.}$$

This method will produce the equation even if the solutions are irrational or imaginary.

E X A M P L E   2   **Writing a quadratic given the solutions**

Write a quadratic equation that has each given pair of solutions.

a) $4, -6$ **b)** $-\sqrt{2}, \sqrt{2}$ **c)** $-3i, 3i$

Solution

a) Reverse the factoring method using solutions 4 and -6:

$$x = 4 \quad \text{or} \quad x = -6$$
$$x - 4 = 0 \quad \text{or} \quad x + 6 = 0$$
$$(x - 4)(x + 6) = 0 \quad \text{Zero factor property}$$
$$x^2 + 2x - 24 = 0 \quad \text{Multiply the factors.}$$

Solution

Note that the square of $x^{1/2}$ is x. Let $w = x^{1/2}$; then $w^2 = (x^{1/2})^2 = x$. Now substitute w and w^2 into the original equation:

$$w^2 - 9w + 14 = 0$$
$$(w - 7)(w - 2) = 0$$
$$w - 7 = 0 \quad \text{or} \quad w - 2 = 0$$
$$w = 7 \quad \text{or} \quad w = 2$$
$$x^{1/2} = 7 \quad \text{or} \quad x^{1/2} = 2 \quad \text{\scriptsize Replace w by $x^{1/2}$.}$$
$$x = 49 \quad \text{or} \quad x = 4 \quad \text{\scriptsize Square each side.}$$

Because we squared each side, we must check for extraneous roots. First evaluate $x - 9x^{1/2} + 14$ for $x = 49$:

$$49 - 9 \cdot 49^{1/2} + 14 = 49 - 9 \cdot 7 + 14 = 0$$

Now evaluate $x - 9x^{1/2} + 14$ for $x = 4$:

$$4 - 9 \cdot 4^{1/2} + 14 = 4 - 9 \cdot 2 + 14 = 0$$

Because each solution checks, the solution set is $\{4, 49\}$. ■

CAUTION   An equation of quadratic form must have a term that is the square of another. Equations such as $x^4 - 5x^3 + 6 = 0$ or $x^{1/2} - 3x^{1/3} - 18 = 0$ are not quadratic in form and cannot be solved by substitution.

Applications

Applied problems often result in quadratic equations that cannot be factored. For such equations we use the quadratic formula to find exact solutions and a calculator to find decimal approximations for the exact solutions.

E X A M P L E 7   Changing area

Marvin's flower bed is rectangular in shape with a length of 10 feet and a width of 5 feet (ft). He wants to increase the length and width by the same amount to obtain a flower bed with an area of 75 square feet (ft^2). What should the amount of increase be?

Solution

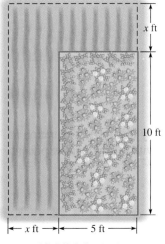

Let x be the amount of increase. The length and width of the new flower bed are $x + 10$ ft and $x + 5$ ft, as shown in Fig. 8.9. Because the area is to be 75 ft^2, we have

$$(x + 10)(x + 5) = 75.$$

Write this equation in the form $ax^2 + bx + c = 0$:

$$x^2 + 15x + 50 = 75$$
$$x^2 + 15x - 25 = 0 \quad \text{\scriptsize Get 0 on the right.}$$
$$x = \frac{-15 \pm \sqrt{225 - 4(1)(-25)}}{2(1)}$$
$$= \frac{-15 \pm \sqrt{325}}{2} = \frac{-15 \pm 5\sqrt{13}}{2}$$

Because the value of x must be positive, the exact increase is

$$\frac{-15 + 5\sqrt{13}}{2} \text{ feet.}$$

x ft   5 ft

x ft

10 ft

FIGURE 8.9

28. $(3a + 2)^2 - 3(3a + 2) = 10$

29. $(w - 1)^2 + 5(w - 1) + 5 = 0$

30. $(2x - 1)^2 - 4(2x - 1) + 2 = 0$

Find all real solutions to each equation. See Example 4.
31. $x^4 - 14x^2 + 45 = 0$ **32.** $x^4 + 2x^2 = 15$

33. $x^6 + 7x^3 = 8$ **34.** $a^6 + 6a^3 = 16$

Find all real solutions to each equation. See Example 5.
35. $(x^2 + 2x)^2 - 7(x^2 + 2x) + 12 = 0$
36. $(x^2 + 3x)^2 + (x^2 + 3x) - 20 = 0$
37. $(y^2 + y)^2 - 8(y^2 + y) + 12 = 0$
38. $(w^2 - 2w)^2 + 24 = 11(w^2 - 2w)$

Find all real solutions to each equation. See Example 6.
39. $x^{1/2} - 5x^{1/4} + 6 = 0$ **40.** $2x - 5\sqrt{x} + 2 = 0$

41. $2x - 5x^{1/2} - 3 = 0$ **42.** $x^{1/4} + 2 = x^{1/2}$

Find all real solutions to each equation.
43. $x^{-2} + x^{-1} - 6 = 0$ **44.** $x^{-2} - 2x^{-1} = 8$

45. $x^{1/6} - x^{1/3} + 2 = 0$ **46.** $x^{2/3} - x^{1/3} - 20 = 0$

47. $\left(\dfrac{1}{y - 1}\right)^2 + \left(\dfrac{1}{y - 1}\right) = 6$

48. $\left(\dfrac{1}{w + 1}\right)^2 - 2\left(\dfrac{1}{w + 1}\right) - 24 = 0$

49. $2x^2 - 3 - 6\sqrt{2x^2 - 3} + 8 = 0$

50. $x^2 + x + \sqrt{x^2 + x} - 2 = 0$

51. $x^{-2} - 2x^{-1} - 1 = 0$ **52.** $x^{-2} - 6x^{-1} + 6 = 0$

Find the exact solution to each problem. If the exact solution is an irrational number, then also find an approximate decimal solution. See Examples 7 and 8.

53. Country singers. Harry and Gary are traveling to Nashville to make their fortunes. Harry leaves on the train at 8:00 A.M. and Gary travels by car, starting at 9:00 A.M. To complete the 300-mile trip and arrive at the same time as Harry, Gary travels 10 miles per hour (mph) faster than the train. At what time will they both arrive in Nashville?

54. Gon
to fi
it to
How

55. Cro
des
60 n
one
spe
spe

56. Ex
7:3
sta
tha
ho

57. A
to
pe
tal

58. O
C
a
ta

Using a calculator, we can find that x is approximately 1.51 ft. If $x = 1.51$ ft, then the new length is 11.51 ft, and the new width is 6.51 ft. The area of a rectangle with these dimensions is 74.93 ft². Of course, the approximate dimensions do not give exactly 75 ft². ∎

EXAMPLE 8   **Mowing the lawn**

It takes Carla 1 hour longer to mow the lawn than it takes Sharon to mow the lawn. If they can mow the lawn in 5 hours working together, then how long would it take each girl by herself?

Solution

If Sharon can mow the lawn by herself in x hours, then she works at the rate of $\dfrac{1}{x}$ of the lawn per hour. If Carla can mow the lawn by herself in $x + 1$ hours, then she works at the rate of $\dfrac{1}{x + 1}$ of the lawn per hour. We can use a table to list all of the important quantities.

	Rate	Time	Work
Sharon	$\dfrac{1}{x} \dfrac{\text{lawn}}{\text{hr}}$	5 hr	$\dfrac{5}{x}$ lawn
Carla	$\dfrac{1}{x + 1} \dfrac{\text{lawn}}{\text{hr}}$	5 hr	$\dfrac{5}{x + 1}$ lawn

Because they complete the lawn in 5 hours, the portion of the lawn done by Sharon and the portion done by Carla have a sum of 1:

$$\frac{5}{x} + \frac{5}{x + 1} = 1$$

$$x(x + 1)\frac{5}{x} + x(x + 1)\frac{5}{x + 1} = x(x + 1)1 \quad \text{Multiply by the LCD.}$$

$$5x + 5 + 5x = x^2 + x$$

$$10x + 5 = x^2 + x$$

$$-x^2 + 9x + 5 = 0$$

$$x^2 - 9x - 5 = 0$$

$$x = \frac{9 \pm \sqrt{(-9)^2 - 4(1)(-5)}}{2(1)}$$

$$= \frac{9 \pm \sqrt{101}}{2}$$

Using a calculator, we find that $\dfrac{9 - \sqrt{101}}{2}$ is negative. So Sharon's time alone is

$$\frac{9 + \sqrt{101}}{2} \text{ hours.}$$

To find Carla's time alone, we add one hour to Sharon's time. So Carla's time alone is

$$\frac{9 + \sqrt{101}}{2} + 1 = \frac{9 + \sqrt{101}}{2} + \frac{2}{2} = \frac{11 + \sqrt{101}}{2} \text{ hours.}$$

Sharon's time alone is approximately 9.525 hours, and Carla's time alone is approximately 10.525 hours. ∎

Helpful Hint

Note that the equation concerns the portion of the job done by each girl. We could have written an equation about the rates at which the two girls work. Because they can finish the lawn together in 5 hours, they are mowing together at the rate of $\frac{1}{5}$ lawn per hour. So

$$\frac{1}{x} + \frac{1}{x + 1} = \frac{1}{5}.$$

WARM-UPS

True or false? Explain your a[...]

1. To solve $x^4 - 5x^2 + 6 = 0$[...]

2. We can solve $x^5 - 3x^3 - 1$[...]

3. We always use the quadratic[...]

4. If $w = x^{1/6}$, then $w^2 = x^{1/3}$[...]

5. To solve $x - 7\sqrt{x} + 10 =$[...]

6. If $y = 2^{1/2}$, then $y^2 = 2^{1/4}$.

7. If John paints a 100-foot fe[...] per hour.

8. If Elvia drives 300 miles [...] (mph).

9. If Ann's boat goes 10 mph i[...] go 2 mph.

10. If squares with sides of leng[...] by 14-inch rectangular piece[...] a box, then the dimensions [...]

8.4 EXERCISES

Reading and Writing *After reading this section, write out the answers to these questions. Use complete sentences.*

1. How can you use the discriminant to determine if a quadratic polynomial can be factored?

2. What is the relationship between solutions to a quadratic equation and factors of a quadratic polynomial?

3. How do we write a quadratic equation with given solutions?

4. What is an equation quadratic in form?

Use the discriminant to determine whether each quadratic polynomial can be factored, then factor the ones that are not prime. See Example 1.

5. $2x^2 - x + 4$

6. $2x^2 + 3x - 5$

7. $2x^2 + 6x - 5$

8. $3x^2 + 5x - 1$

9.

11.

13.

W[...] tio[...]

15.

17

19

21

23

25

F[...]

2[...]

---

59. *The growing garden.* Eric's garden is 20 ft by 30 ft. He wants to increase the length and width by the same amount to have a 1000-ft^2 garden. What should be the new dimensions of the garden?

60. *Open-top box.* Thomas is going to make an open-top box by cutting equal squares from the four corners of an 11 inch by 14 inch sheet of cardboard and folding up the sides. If the area of the base is to be 80 square inches, then what size square should be cut from each corner?

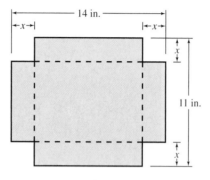
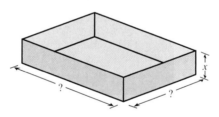

FIGURE FOR EXERCISE 60

61. *Pumping the pool.* It takes pump A 2 hours less time than pump B to empty a certain swimming pool. Pump A is started at 8:00 A.M., and pump B is started at 11:00 A.M. If the pool is still half full at 5:00 P.M., then how long would it take pump A working alone?

62. *Time off for lunch.* It usually takes Eva 3 hours longer to do the monthly payroll than it takes Cicely. They start working on it together at 9:00 A.M. and at 5:00 P.M. they have 90% of it done. If Eva took a 2-hour lunch break while Cicely had none, then how much longer will it take for them to finish the payroll working together?

 63. *Golden Rectangle.* One principle used by the ancient Greeks to get shapes that are pleasing to the eye in art and architecture was the Golden Rectangle. If a square is removed from one end of a Golden Rectangle, as shown in the figure, the sides of the remaining rectangle are

---

proportional to the original rectangle. So the length and width of the original rectangle satisfy

$$\frac{L}{W} = \frac{W}{L - W}.$$

If the length of a Golden Rectangle is 10 meters, then what is its width?

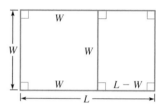

FIGURE FOR EXERCISE 63

GETTING MORE INVOLVED

64. *Exploration.*
   a) Given that $P(x) = x^4 + 6x^2 - 27$, find $P(3i)$, $P(-3i)$, $P(\sqrt{3})$, and $P(-\sqrt{3})$.
   b) What can you conclude about the values $3i$, $-3i$, $\sqrt{3}$, and $-\sqrt{3}$ and their relationship to each other?

65. *Cooperative learning.* Work with a group to write a quadratic equation that has each given pair of solutions.
   a) $3 + \sqrt{5}, 3 - \sqrt{5}$ b) $4 - 2i, 4 + 2i$
   c) $\dfrac{1 + i\sqrt{3}}{2}, \dfrac{1 - i\sqrt{3}}{2}$

GRAPHING CALCULATOR EXERCISES

Solve each equation by locating the x-intercepts on the graph of a corresponding function. Round approximate answers to two decimal places.

66. $(5x - 7)^2 - (5x - 7) - 6 = 0$

67. $x^4 - 116x^2 + 1600 = 0$

68. $(x^2 + 3x)^2 - 7(x^2 + 3x) + 9 = 0$

69. $x^2 - 3x^{1/2} - 12 = 0$

8.5 # QUADRATIC AND RATIONAL INEQUALITIES

In this section we solve inequalities involving quadratic polynomials. We use a new technique based on the rules for multiplying real numbers.

Solving Quadratic Inequalities with a Sign Graph

An inequality involving a quadratic polynomial is called a **quadratic** inequality.

> ### Quadratic Inequality
>
> A quadratic inequality is an inequality of the form
>
> $$ax^2 + bx + c > 0,$$
>
> where a, b, and c are real numbers with $a \neq 0$. The inequality symbols $<$, $\leq$, and $\geq$ may also be used.

If we can factor a quadratic inequality, then the inequality can be solved with a **sign graph,** which shows where each factor is positive, negative, or zero.

E X A M P L E   1

Solving a quadratic inequality

Use a sign graph to solve the inequality $x^2 + 3x - 10 > 0$.

Solution

Because the left-hand side can be factored, we can write the inequality as

$$(x + 5)(x - 2) > 0.$$

This inequality says that the product of $x + 5$ and $x - 2$ is positive. If both factors are negative or both are positive, the product is positive. To analyze the signs of each factor, we make a sign graph as follows. First consider the possible values of the factor $x + 5$:

Value	Where	On the number line
$x + 5 = 0$	if $x = -5$	Put a 0 above -5.
$x + 5 > 0$	if $x > -5$	Put $+$ signs to the right of -5.
$x + 5 < 0$	if $x < -5$	Put $-$ signs to the left of -5.

The sign graph shown in Fig. 8.10 for the factor $x + 5$ is made from the information in the preceding table.

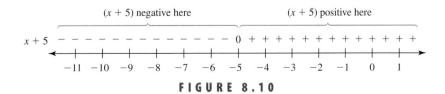

FIGURE 8.10

Calculator Close-Up

Use Y= to set $y_1 = x + 5$ and $y_2 = x - 2$. Now make a table and scroll through the table. The table numerically supports the sign graph in Fig. 8.11.

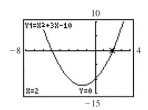

Note that the graph of $y = x^2 + 3x - 10$ is above the x-axis when $x < -5$ or when $x > 2$.

Now consider the possible values of the factor $x - 2$:

Value	Where	On the number line
$x - 2 = 0$	if $x = 2$	Put a 0 above 2.
$x - 2 > 0$	if $x > 2$	Put + signs to the right of 2.
$x - 2 < 0$	if $x < 2$	Put − signs to the left of 2.

We put the information for the factor $x - 2$ on the sign graph for the factor $x + 5$ as shown in Fig. 8.11. We can see from Fig. 8.11 that the product is positive if $x < -5$ and the product is positive if $x > 2$. The solution set for the quadratic inequality is shown in Fig. 8.12. Note that -5 and 2 are not included in the graph because for those values of x the product is zero. The solution set is $(-\infty, -5) \cup (2, \infty)$.

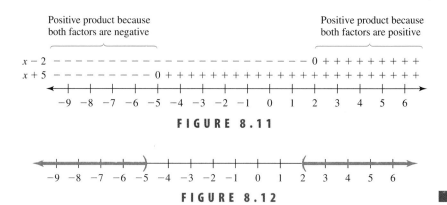

FIGURE 8.11

FIGURE 8.12

In Example 2 we will make the procedure from Example 1 a bit more efficient.

E X A M P L E   2

Solving a quadratic inequality

Solve $2x^2 + 5x \leq 3$ and graph the solution set.

Solution

Rewrite the inequality with 0 on one side:

$$2x^2 + 5x - 3 \leq 0$$
$$(2x - 1)(x + 3) \leq 0 \quad \text{Factor.}$$

Examine the signs of each factor:

$$2x - 1 = 0 \quad \text{if} \quad x = \frac{1}{2}$$

$$2x - 1 > 0 \quad \text{if} \quad x > \frac{1}{2}$$

$$2x - 1 < 0 \quad \text{if} \quad x < \frac{1}{2}$$

$$x + 3 = 0 \quad \text{if} \quad x = -3$$
$$x + 3 > 0 \quad \text{if} \quad x > -3$$
$$x + 3 < 0 \quad \text{if} \quad x < -3$$

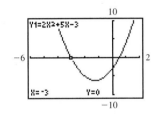
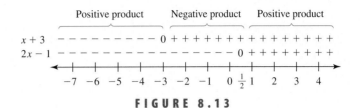

Make a sign graph as shown in Fig. 8.13. The product of the factors is negative between -3 and $\frac{1}{2}$, when one factor is negative and the other is positive. The product is 0 at -3 and at $\frac{1}{2}$. So the solution set is the interval $\left[-3, \frac{1}{2}\right]$. The graph of the solution set is shown in Fig. 8.14.

FIGURE 8.13

FIGURE 8.14

We summarize the strategy used for solving a quadratic inequality as follows.

> ### Strategy for Solving a Quadratic Inequality with a Sign Graph
>
> **1.** Write the inequality with 0 on the right.
> **2.** Factor the quadratic polynomial on the left.
> **3.** Make a sign graph showing where each factor is positive, negative, or zero.
> **4.** Use the rules for multiplying signed numbers to determine which intervals satisfy the original inequality.
> **5.** Write the solution set using interval notation.

Solving Rational Inequalities with a Sign Graph

The inequalities

$$\frac{x + 2}{x - 3} \le 2, \qquad \frac{2x - 3}{x + 5} \le 0 \qquad \text{and} \qquad \frac{2}{x + 4} \ge \frac{1}{x + 1}$$

are called **rational inequalities.** When we solve *equations* that involve rational expressions, we usually multiply each side by the LCD. However, if we multiply each side of any inequality by a negative number, we must reverse the inequality, and when we multiply by a positive number, we do not reverse the inequality. For this reason we generally *do not multiply inequalities by expressions involving variables.* The values of the expressions might be positive or negative. Examples 3 and 4 show how to use a sign graph to solve rational inequalities that have variables in the denominator.

EXAMPLE 3   **Solving a rational inequality**

Solve $\dfrac{x+2}{x-3} \le 2$ and graph the solution set.

Helpful Hint

Solution

We *do not* multiply each side by $x-3$. Instead, subtract 2 from each side to get 0 on the right:

$$\frac{x+2}{x-3} - 2 \le 0$$

$$\frac{x+2}{x-3} - \frac{2(x-3)}{x-3} \le 0 \quad \text{Get a common denominator.}$$

$$\frac{x+2}{x-3} - \frac{2x-6}{x-3} \le 0 \quad \text{Simplify.}$$

$$\frac{x+2-2x+6}{x-3} \le 0 \quad \text{Subtract the rational expressions.}$$

$$\frac{-x+8}{x-3} \le 0 \quad \begin{array}{l}\text{The quotient of } -x+8 \text{ and } x-3 \text{ is less} \\ \text{than or equal to 0.}\end{array}$$

Examine the signs of the numerator and denominator:

$$x - 3 = 0 \quad \text{if} \quad x = 3 \qquad -x + 8 = 0 \quad \text{if} \quad x = 8$$
$$x - 3 > 0 \quad \text{if} \quad x > 3 \qquad -x + 8 > 0 \quad \text{if} \quad x < 8$$
$$x - 3 < 0 \quad \text{if} \quad x < 3 \qquad -x + 8 < 0 \quad \text{if} \quad x > 8$$

Calculator Close-Up

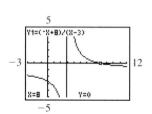

Graph $y = \dfrac{-x+8}{x-3}$ to support the conclusion that $y \le 0$ when $x < 3$ or $x \ge 8$.

Make a sign graph as shown in Fig. 8.15. Using the rule for dividing signed numbers and the sign graph, we can identify where the quotient is negative or zero. The solution set is $(-\infty, 3) \cup [8, \infty)$. Note that 3 is not in the solution set because the quotient is undefined if $x = 3$. The graph of the solution set is shown in Fig. 8.16.

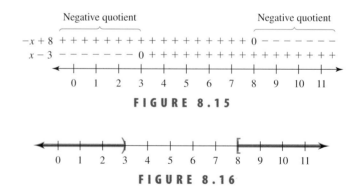

FIGURE 8.15

FIGURE 8.16

CAUTION   Remember to reverse the inequality sign when multiplying or dividing by a negative number. For example, $x - 3 > 0$ is equivalent to $x > 3$. But $-x + 8 > 0$ is equivalent to $-x > -8$, or $x < 8$.

EXAMPLE 4   **Solving a rational inequality**

Solve $\dfrac{2}{x+4} \ge \dfrac{1}{x+1}$ and graph the solution set.

Solution

We do not multiply by the LCD as we do in solving equations. Instead, subtract $\frac{1}{x+1}$ from each side:

$$\frac{2}{x+4} - \frac{1}{x+1} \geq 0$$

$$\frac{2(x+1)}{(x+4)(x+1)} - \frac{1(x+4)}{(x+1)(x+4)} \geq 0 \quad \text{Get a common denominator.}$$

$$\frac{2x+2-x-4}{(x+1)(x+4)} \geq 0 \quad \text{Simplify.}$$

$$\frac{x-2}{(x+1)(x+4)} \geq 0$$

Make a sign graph as shown in Fig. 8.17.

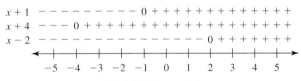

FIGURE 8.17

The computation of

$$\frac{x-2}{(x+1)(x+4)}$$

involves multiplication and division. The result of this computation is positive if all of the three binomials are positive or if only one is positive and the other two are negative. The sign graph shows that this rational expression will have a positive value when x is between -4 and -1 and again when x is larger than 2. The solution set is $(-4, -1) \cup [2, \infty)$. Note that -1 and -4 are not in the solution set because they make the denominator zero. The graph of the solution set is shown in Fig. 8.18.

FIGURE 8.18

Solving rational inequalities with a sign graph is summarized below.

Calculator Close-Up

Graph $y = \frac{x-2}{(x+1)(x+4)}$ to support the conclusion that $y \geq 0$ when x is between -4 and -1 or when $x \geq 2$.

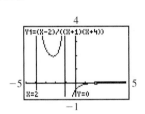

> **Strategy for Solving a Rational Inequality with a Sign Graph**
>
> 1. Rewrite the inequality with 0 on the right-hand side.
> 2. Use only addition and subtraction to get an equivalent inequality.
> 3. Factor the numerator and denominator if possible.
> 4. Make a sign graph showing where each factor is positive, negative, or zero.
> 5. Use the rules for multiplying and dividing signed numbers to determine the intervals that satisfy the original inequality.
> 6. Write the solution set using interval notation.

Another method for solving quadratic and rational inequalities will be shown in Example 5. This method, called the **test point method,** can be used instead of the sign graph to solve the inequalities of Examples 1, 2, 3, and 4.

Quadratic Inequalities That Cannot Be Factored

Example 5 shows how to solve a quadratic inequality that involves a prime polynomial.

E X A M P L E   5   **Solving a quadratic inequality using the quadratic formula**

Solve $x^2 - 4x - 6 > 0$ and graph the solution set.

Solution

The quadratic polynomial is prime, but we can solve $x^2 - 4x - 6 = 0$ by the quadratic formula:

$$x = \frac{4 \pm \sqrt{16 - 4(1)(-6)}}{2(1)} = \frac{4 \pm \sqrt{40}}{2} = \frac{4 \pm 2\sqrt{10}}{2} = 2 \pm \sqrt{10}$$

As in the previous examples, the solutions to the equation divide the number line into the intervals $(-\infty, 2 - \sqrt{10})$, $(2 - \sqrt{10}, 2 + \sqrt{10})$, and $(2 + \sqrt{10}, \infty)$ on which the quadratic polynomial has either a positive or negative value. To determine which, we select an arbitrary **test point** in each interval. Because $2 + \sqrt{10} \approx 5.2$ and $2 - \sqrt{10} \approx -1.2$, we choose a test point that is less than -1.2, one between -1.2 and 5.2, and one that is greater than 5.2. We have selected $-2, 0$, and 7 for test points, as shown in Fig. 8.19. Now evaluate $x^2 - 4x - 6$ at each test point.

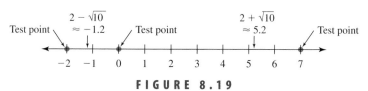

FIGURE 8.19

Test point	Value of $x^2 - 4x - 6$ at the test point	Sign of $x^2 - 4x - 6$ in interval of test point
-2	6	Positive
0	-6	Negative
7	15	Positive

Calculator Close-Up

Notice that the graph of

$$y = x^2 - 4x - 6$$

lies above the x-axis when

$$x < 2 - \sqrt{10}$$

or $$x > 2 + \sqrt{10}.$$

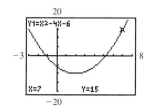

Because $x^2 - 4x - 6$ is positive at the test points -2 and 7, it is positive at every point in the intervals containing those test points. So the solution set to the inequality $x^2 - 4x - 6 > 0$ is

$$(-\infty, 2 - \sqrt{10}) \cup (2 + \sqrt{10}, \infty),$$

and its graph is shown in Fig. 8.20.

FIGURE 8.20

The test point method used in Example 5 can be used also on inequalities that do factor. We summarize the strategy for solving inequalities using test points in the following box.

> **Strategy for Solving Quadratic Inequalities Using Test Points**
>
> 1. Rewrite the inequality with 0 on the right.
> 2. Solve the quadratic equation that results from replacing the inequality symbol with the equals symbol.
> 3. Locate the solutions to the quadratic equation on a number line.
> 4. Select a test point in each interval determined by the solutions to the quadratic equation.
> 5. Test each point in the original quadratic inequality to determine which intervals satisfy the inequality.
> 6. Write the solution set using interval notation.

Applications

Example 6 shows how a quadratic inequality can be used to solve a problem.

E X A M P L E   6

Making a profit

Charlene's daily profit P (in dollars) for selling x magazine subscriptions is determined by the formula

$$P = -x^2 + 80x - 1500.$$

For what values of x is her profit positive?

Solution

We can find the values of x for which $P > 0$ by solving a quadratic inequality:

$$-x^2 + 80x - 1500 > 0$$
$$x^2 - 80x + 1500 < 0 \quad \text{Multiply each side by } -1.$$
$$(x - 30)(x - 50) < 0 \quad \text{Factor.}$$

Make a sign graph as shown in Fig. 8.21. The product of the two factors is negative for x between 30 and 50. Because the last inequality is equivalent to the first, the profit is positive when the number of magazine subscriptions sold is greater than 30 and less than 50.

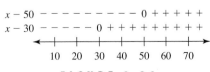

F I G U R E   8 . 2 1

WARM-UPS

True or false? Explain.

1. The solution set to $x^2 > 4$ is $(2, \infty)$.
2. The inequality $\frac{x}{x-3} > 2$ is equivalent to $x > 2x - 6$.
3. The inequality $(x - 1)(x + 2) < 0$ is equivalent to $x - 1 < 0$ or $x + 2 < 0$.
4. We cannot solve quadratic inequalities that do not factor.
5. One technique for solving quadratic inequalities is based on the rules for multiplying signed numbers.
6. Multiplying each side of an inequality by a variable should be avoided.
7. In solving quadratic or rational inequalities, we always get 0 on one side.
8. The inequality $\frac{x}{2} > 3$ is equivalent to $x > 6$.
9. The inequality $\frac{x-3}{x+2} < 1$ is equivalent to $\frac{x-3}{x+2} - 1 < 0$.
10. The solution set to $\frac{x+2}{x-4} \geq 0$ is $(-\infty, -2] \cup [4, \infty)$.

8.5 EXERCISES

Reading and Writing *After reading this section, write out the answers to these questions. Use complete sentences.*

1. What is a quadratic inequality?

2. What is a sign graph?

3. What is a rational inequality?

4. Why don't we usually multiply each side of an inequality by an expression involving a variable?

Solve each inequality. Graph the solution set and state the solution set using interval notation. See Examples 1 and 2.

5. $x^2 + x - 6 < 0$

6. $x^2 - 3x - 4 \geq 0$

7. $y^2 - 4 > 0$

8. $z^2 - 16 < 0$

9. $2u^2 + 5u \geq 12$

10. $2v^2 + 7v < 4$

11. $4x^2 - 8x \geq 0$

12. $x^2 + x > 0$

13. $5x - 10x^2 < 0$

14. $3x - x^2 > 0$

15. $x^2 + 6x + 9 \geq 0$

16. $x^2 + 25 < 10x$

Solve each rational inequality. State and graph the solution set. See Examples 3 and 4.

17. $\dfrac{x}{x-3} > 0$

18. $\dfrac{a}{a+2} > 0$

19. $\dfrac{x+2}{x} \le 0$

20. $\dfrac{w-6}{w} \le 0$

21. $\dfrac{t-3}{t+6} > 0$

22. $\dfrac{x-2}{2x+5} < 0$

23. $\dfrac{x}{x+2} > -1$

24. $\dfrac{x+3}{x} \le -2$

25. $\dfrac{2}{x-5} > \dfrac{1}{x+4}$

26. $\dfrac{3}{x+2} > \dfrac{2}{x-1}$

27. $\dfrac{m}{m-5} + \dfrac{3}{m-1} > 0$

28. $\dfrac{p}{p-16} + \dfrac{2}{p-6} \le 0$

29. $\dfrac{x}{x-3} \le \dfrac{-8}{x-6}$

30. $\dfrac{x}{x+20} > \dfrac{2}{x+8}$

Solve each inequality. State and graph the solution set. See Example 5.

31. $x^2 - 2x - 4 > 0$

32. $x^2 - 2x - 5 \le 0$

33. $2x^2 - 6x + 3 \ge 0$

34. $2x^2 - 8x + 3 < 0$

35. $y^2 - 3y - 9 \le 0$

36. $z^2 - 5z - 7 < 0$

In Exercises 37–60, solve each inequality. State the solution set using interval notation.

37. $x^2 \le 9$

38. $x^2 \ge 36$

39. $16 - x^2 > 0$

40. $9 - x^2 < 0$

41. $x^2 - 4x \ge 0$

42. $4x^2 - 9 > 0$

43. $3(2w^2 - 5) < w$

44. $6(y^2 - 2) + y < 0$

45. $z^2 \geq 4(z + 3)$

46. $t^2 < 3(2t - 3)$

47. $(q + 4)^2 > 10q + 31$

48. $(2p + 4)(p - 1) < (p + 2)^2$

49. $\frac{1}{2}x^2 \geq 4 - x$

50. $\frac{1}{2}x^2 \leq x + 12$

51. $\frac{x - 4}{x + 3} \leq 0$

52. $\frac{2x - 1}{x + 5} \geq 0$

53. $(x - 2)(x + 1)(x - 5) \geq 0$

54. $(x - 1)(x + 2)(2x - 5) < 0$

55. $x^3 + 3x^2 - x - 3 < 0$

56. $x^3 + 5x^2 - 4x - 20 \geq 0$

57. $0.23x^2 + 6.5x + 4.3 < 0$

58. $0.65x^2 + 3.2x + 5.1 > 0$

59. $\frac{x}{x - 2} > \frac{-1}{x + 3}$

60. $\frac{x}{3 - x} > \frac{2}{x + 5}$

Solve each problem by using a quadratic inequality. See Example 6.

61. *Positive profit.* The monthly profit P (in dollars) that Big Jim makes on the sale of x mobile homes is determined by the formula $P = x^2 + 5x - 50$. For what values of x is his profit positive?

62. *Profitable fruitcakes.* Sharon's revenue R (in dollars) on the sale of x fruitcakes is determined by the formula $R = 50x - x^2$. Her cost C (in dollars) for producing x fruitcakes is given by the formula $C = 2x + 40$. For what values of x is Sharon's profit positive? (Profit = revenue − cost.)

If an object is given an initial velocity straight upward of v_0 feet per second from a height of s_0 feet, then its altitude S after t seconds is given by the formula

$$S = -16t^2 + v_0 t + s_0.$$

63. *Flying high.* An arrow is shot straight upward with a velocity of 96 feet per second (ft/sec) from an altitude of 6 feet. For how many seconds is this arrow more than 86 feet high?

 64. *Putting the shot.* In 1978 Udo Beyer (East Germany) set a world record in the shot-put of 72 ft 8 in. If Beyer had projected the shot straight upward with a velocity of 30 ft/sec from a height of 5 ft, then for what values of t would the shot be under 15 ft high?

If a projectile is fired at a 45° angle from a height of s_0 feet with initial velocity v_0 ft/sec, then its altitude S in feet after t seconds is given by

$$S = -16t^2 + \frac{v_0}{\sqrt{2}}t + s_0.$$

65. *Siege and garrison artillery.* An 8-inch mortar used in the Civil War fired a 44.5-lb projectile from ground level a distance of 3600 ft when aimed at a 45° angle (Harold R. Peterson, *Notes on Ordinance of the American Civil War*). The accompanying graph shows the altitude of the projectile when it is fired with a velocity of $240\sqrt{2}$ ft/sec.

a) Use the graph to estimate the maximum altitude reached by the projectile.

b) Use the graph to estimate approximately how long the altitude of the projectile was greater than 864 ft.

c) Use the formula to determine the length of time for which the projectile had an altitude of more than 864 ft.

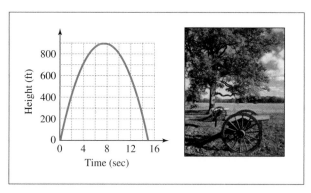

FIGURE FOR EXERCISE 65

 66. *Seacoast artillery.* The 13-inch mortar used in the Civil War fired a 220-lb projectile a distance of 12,975 ft when aimed at a 45° angle. If the 13-inch mortar was fired from a hill 100 ft above sea level with an initial velocity of 644 ft/sec, then for how long was the projectile more than 800 ft above sea level?

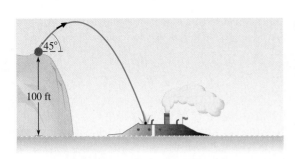

FIGURE FOR EXERCISE 66

GETTING MORE INVOLVED

 67. *Cooperative learning.* Work in a small group to solve each inequality for x, given that h and k are real numbers with $h < k$.

a) $(x - h)(x - k) < 0$

b) $(x - h)(x - k) > 0$

c) $(x + h)(x + k) < 0$

d) $(x + h)(x + k) \geq 0$

e) $\dfrac{x - h}{x - k} \geq 0$

f) $\dfrac{x + h}{x + k} \leq 0$

68. *Cooperative learning.* Work in a small group to solve $ax^2 + bx + c > 0$ for x in each case.

a) $b^2 - 4ac = 0$ and $a > 0$

b) $b^2 - 4ac = 0$ and $a < 0$

c) $b^2 - 4ac < 0$ and $a > 0$

d) $b^2 - 4ac < 0$ and $a < 0$

e) $b^2 - 4ac > 0$ and $a > 0$

f) $b^2 - 4ac > 0$ and $a < 0$

 ## GRAPHING CALCULATOR EXERCISES

Match the given inequalities with their solution sets (a through d) by examining a table or a graph.

69. $x^2 - 2x - 8 < 0$ **a.** $(-2, 2) \cup (8, \infty)$

70. $x^2 - 3x > 54$ **b.** $(2, 4)$

71. $\dfrac{x}{x - 2} > 2$ **c.** $(-2, 4)$

72. $\dfrac{3}{x - 2} < \dfrac{5}{x + 2}$ **d.** $(-\infty, -6) \cup (9, \infty)$

COLLABORATIVE ACTIVITIES

Completing the Square

Al-Khwarizmi, an Arab mathematician who lived in Baghdad in the mid-800s, wrote the first book on algebra that is more analytic than geometric. It looks like our algebra books today. The word "algebra" comes from his book called *The Book of Algebra and Almucabola.* His book describes methods of solving quadratic equations that are based on a geometric understanding of what the equations represent. In this activity you will explore how to derive the quadratic formula geometrically and learn why the method is called "completing the square."

Consider the equation $2x^2 + 4x = 8$. To solve it geometrically, we first divide by the leading coefficient, 2, to get

$$x^2 + 2x = 4.$$

Grouping: 3 students per group

Topic: A geometric solution to a quadratic

Now this equation can be viewed geometrically as an x by x square and an x by 2 rectangle having a total area of 4:

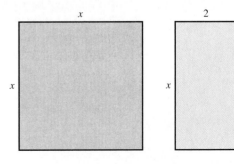

To complete the square, divide the x by 2 rectangle into four x by $\frac{1}{2}$ rectangles and add them to the sides of the x by x square:

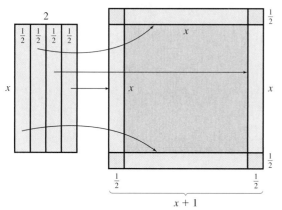

The square is complete except for the four $\frac{1}{2}$ by $\frac{1}{2}$ squares in the corners, each of which has area $\frac{1}{4}$. Filling those in will add

1 square unit of area to the 4 we had already for a total of 5. Since the sides of the completed square are $x + 1$, we have

$$(x + 1)^2 = 5.$$

Solve for x to get $x + 1 = \pm\sqrt{5}$ or $x = -1 \pm \sqrt{5}$.

Complete the following in your groups:

1. Verify and write down the steps for the geometric method of completing the square.

2. Use the geometric method of completing the square to solve each equation for x:
   a) $3x^2 + 12x = 18$
   b) $2x^2 + 6x = 5$
   c) $3x^2 + 4x = 9$

3. Solve $ax^2 + bx = c$ by the geometric method. Explain why the formula found in this general case is not quite the quadratic formula.

WRAP-UP   CHAPTER 8

SUMMARY

Quadratic Equations		Examples

Quadratic equation

An equation of the form
$ax^2 + bx + c = 0$,
where a, b, and c are real numbers, with $a \neq 0$

$$x^2 = 11$$
$$(x - 5)^2 = 99$$
$$x^2 + 3x - 20 = 0$$

Methods for solving quadratic equations

Factoring:
Factor the quadratic polynomial, then set each factor equal to 0.

$$x^2 + x - 6 = 0$$
$$(x + 3)(x - 2) = 0$$
$$x + 3 = 0 \text{ or } x - 2 = 0$$

The even-root property:
If $x^2 = k$ ($k > 0$), then $x = \pm\sqrt{k}$.
If $x^2 = 0$, then $x = 0$.
There are no real solutions to $x^2 = k$ for $k < 0$.

$$(x - 5)^2 = 10$$
$$x - 5 = \pm\sqrt{10}$$

Completing the square:
Take one-half of middle term, square it, then add it to each side.

$$x^2 + 6x = -4$$
$$x^2 + 6x + 9 = -4 + 9$$
$$(x + 3)^2 = 5$$

Quadratic formula:
Solves $ax^2 + bx + c = 0$ with $a \neq 0$:

$$x = \frac{-b \pm \sqrt{b^2 - 4ac}}{2a}$$

$$2x^2 + 3x - 5 = 0$$

$$x = \frac{-3 \pm \sqrt{3^2 - 4(2)(-5)}}{2(2)}$$

Number of solutions	Determined by the discriminant $b^2 - 4ac$:	
	$b^2 - 4ac > 0$ 2 real solutions	$x^2 + 6x - 12 = 0$ $6^2 - 4(1)(-12) > 0$
	$b^2 - 4ac = 0$ 1 real solution	$x^2 + 10x + 25 = 0$ $10^2 - 4(1)(25) = 0$
	$b^2 - 4ac < 0$ no real solutions, 2 imaginary solutions	$x^2 + 2x + 20 = 0$ $2^2 - 4(1)(20) < 0$
Factoring	The quadratic polynomial $ax^2 + bx + c$ (with integral coefficients) can be factored if and only if $b^2 - 4ac$ is a perfect square.	$2x^2 - 11x + 12$ $b^2 - 4ac = 25$ $(2x - 3)(x - 4)$
Writing equations	To write an equation with given solutions, reverse the steps in solving an equation by factoring.	$x = 2$ or $x = -3$ $(x - 2)(x + 3) = 0$ $x^2 + x - 6 = 0$
Equations quadratic in form	Use substitution to convert to a quadratic.	$x^4 + 3x^2 - 10 = 0$ Let $a = x^2$ $a^2 + 3a - 10 = 0$

Quadratic Functions

Examples

Quadratic function	A function of the form $f(x) = ax^2 + bx + c$, where a, b, and c are real numbers and $a \neq 0$	$f(x) = 3x^2 - 8x + 9$ $p = -3q^2 - 8q + 1$
Graphing a quadratic function	The graph is a parabola opening upward if $a > 0$ and downward if $a < 0$. The first coordinate of the vertex is $\frac{-b}{2a}$. The second coordinate of the vertex is either the minimum value of the function if $a > 0$ or the maximum value of the function if $a < 0$.	$y = x^2 - 2x + 5$ Opens upward Vertex: $(1, 4)$ Minimum value of y is 4.

Quadratic and Rational Inequalities

Examples

Quadratic inequality	An inequality involving a quadratic polynomial	$2x^2 - 7x + 6 \geq 0$ $x^2 - 4x - 5 < 0$
Rational inequality	An inequality involving a rational expression	$\dfrac{1}{x - 1} < \dfrac{3}{x - 2}$
Solving quadratic and rational inequalities	Get 0 on one side and express the other side as a product and/or quotient of linear factors. Make a sign graph showing the signs of the factors. Use test points if the quadratic polynomial is prime.	$(x - 5)(x + 1) < 0$ $x + 1$ $-\ -\ 0\ +\ +\ +\ +\ +\ +\ +$ $x - 5$ $-\ -\ -\ -\ -\ -\ -\ 0\ +\ +$ $-3\ -2\ -1\ 0\ 1\ 2\ 3\ 4\ 5\ 6\ 7$

For each mathematical term, choose the correct meaning.

1. quadratic equation
   a. $ax + b = c$ with $a \neq 0$
   b. $ax^2 + bx + c = 0$ with $a \neq 0$
   c. $ax + b = 0$ with $a \neq 0$
   d. $a/x^2 + b/x = c$ with $x \neq 0$

2. perfect square trinomial
   a. a trinomial of the form $a^2 + 2ab + b^2$
   b. a trinomial of the form $a^2 + b^2$
   c. a trinomial of the form $a^2 + ab + b^2$
   d. a trinomial of the form $a^2 - 2ab - b^2$

3. completing the square
   a. drawing a perfect square
   b. evaluating $(a + b)^2$
   c. drawing the fourth side when given three sides of a square
   d. finding the third term of a perfect square trinomial

4. quadratic formula
   a. $x = \dfrac{-b \pm \sqrt{b^2 - 4ac}}{2}$
   b. $x = -b \pm \dfrac{\sqrt{b^2 - 4ac}}{2a}$
   c. $x = \dfrac{-b \pm \sqrt{b^2 - 4ac}}{2a}$
   d. $x = \dfrac{b \pm \sqrt{b^2 - 4ac}}{2a}$

5. discriminant
   a. the vertex of a parabola
   b. the radicand in the quadratic formula
   c. the leading coefficient in $ax^2 + bx + c$
   d. to treat unfairly

6. quadratic function
   a. $y = ax + b$ with $a \neq 0$
   b. a parabola
   c. $y = ax^2 + bx + c$ with $a \neq 0$
   d. the quadratic formula

7. quadratic in form
   a. $ax^2 + bx + c = 0$
   b. a parabola
   c. an equation that is quadratic after a substitution
   d. having four equal sides

8. quadratic inequality
   a. $ax^2 + bx + c > 0$ with $a \neq 0$ or with $\geq$, $<$, or $\leq$
   b. $ax + b > 0$ with $a \neq 0$ or with $\geq$, $<$, or $\leq$
   c. completing the square
   d. the Pythagorean theorem

9. sign graph
   a. a graph showing the sign of x
   b. a sign on which a graph is drawn
   c. a number line showing the signs of factors
   d. to graph in sign language

10. rational inequality
   a. an inequality involving a rational expression(s)
   b. a quadratic inequality
   c. an inequality with rational exponents
   d. an inequality that compares two fractions

11. test point
   a. the end of a chapter
   b. to check if a point is in the right location
   c. a number that is used to check if an inequality is satisfied
   d. a positive integer

8.1 *Solve by factoring.*

1. $x^2 - 2x - 15 = 0$

2. $x^2 - 2x - 24 = 0$

3. $2x^2 + x = 15$

4. $2x^2 + 7x = 4$

5. $w^2 - 25 = 0$

6. $a^2 - 121 = 0$

7. $4x^2 - 12x + 9 = 0$

8. $x^2 - 12x + 36 = 0$

Solve by using the even-root property.

9. $x^2 = 12$

10. $x^2 = 20$

11. $(x - 1)^2 = 9$

12. $(x + 4)^2 = 4$

13. $(x - 2)^2 = \dfrac{3}{4}$

14. $(x - 3)^2 = \dfrac{1}{4}$

15. $4x^2 = 9$ **16.** $2x^2 = 3$

Solve by completing the square.

17. $x^2 - 6x + 8 = 0$ **18.** $x^2 + 4x + 3 = 0$

19. $x^2 - 5x + 6 = 0$ **20.** $x^2 - x - 6 = 0$

21. $2x^2 - 7x + 3 = 0$ **22.** $2x^2 - x = 6$

23. $x^2 + 4x + 1 = 0$ **24.** $x^2 + 2x - 2 = 0$

8.2 *Solve by the quadratic formula.*

25. $x^2 - 3x - 10 = 0$ **26.** $x^2 - 5x - 6 = 0$

27. $6x^2 - 7x = 3$ **28.** $6x^2 = x + 2$

29. $x^2 + 4x + 2 = 0$ **30.** $x^2 + 6x = 2$

31. $3x^2 + 1 = 5x$

32. $2x^2 + 3x - 1 = 0$

Find the value of the discriminant and the number of real solutions to each equation.

33. $25x^2 - 20x + 4 = 0$ **34.** $16x^2 + 1 = 8x$

35. $x^2 - 3x + 7 = 0$ **36.** $3x^2 - x + 8 = 0$

37. $2x^2 + 1 = 5x$ **38.** $-3x^2 + 6x - 2 = 0$

Find the complex solutions to the quadratic equations.

39. $2x^2 - 4x + 3 = 0$

40. $2x^2 - 6x + 5 = 0$

41. $2x^2 + 3 = 3x$

42. $x^2 + x + 1 = 0$

43. $3x^2 + 2x + 2 = 0$

44. $x^2 + 2 = 2x$

45. $\frac{1}{2}x^2 + 3x + 8 = 0$

46. $\frac{1}{2}x^2 - 5x + 13 = 0$

8.3 *Find the vertex and intercepts for each quadratic function, and sketch its graph.*

47. $f(x) = x^2 - 6x$

48. $f(x) = x^2 + 4x$

49. $g(x) = x^2 - 4x - 12$

50. $g(x) = x^2 + 2x - 24$

51. $h(x) = -2x^2 + 8x$

52. $h(x) = -3x^2 + 6x$

53. $y = -x^2 + 2x + 3$

54. $y = -x^2 - 3x - 2$

Find the domain and range of each quadratic function.
55. $f(x) = x^2 + 4x + 1$

56. $f(x) = x^2 - 6x + 2$

57. $y = -2x^2 - x + 4$

58. $y = -3x^2 + 2x + 7$

8.4 *Use the discriminant to determine whether each quadratic polynomial can be factored, then factor the ones that are not prime.*

59. $8x^2 - 10x - 3$ **60.** $18x^2 + 9x - 2$

61. $4x^2 - 5x + 2$ **62.** $6x^2 - 7x - 4$

63. $8y^2 + 10y - 25$ **64.** $25z^2 - 15z - 18$

Write a quadratic equation that has each given pair of solutions.
65. $-3, -6$ **66.** $4, -9$

67. $-5\sqrt{2}, 5\sqrt{2}$ **68.** $-2i\sqrt{3}, 2i\sqrt{3}$

Find all real solutions to each equation.
69. $x^6 + 7x^3 - 8 = 0$

70. $8x^6 + 63x^3 - 8 = 0$

71. $x^4 - 13x^2 + 36 = 0$
72. $x^4 + 7x^2 + 12 = 0$
73. $(x^2 + 3x)^2 - 28(x^2 + 3x) + 180 = 0$
74. $(x^2 + 1)^2 - 8(x^2 + 1) + 15 = 0$
75. $x^2 - 6x + 6\sqrt{x^2 - 6x} - 40 = 0$
76. $x^2 - 3x - 3\sqrt{x^2 - 3x} + 2 = 0$
77. $t^{-2} + 5t^{-1} - 36 = 0$

78. $a^{-2} + a^{-1} - 6 = 0$

79. $w - 13\sqrt{w} + 36 = 0$

80. $4a - 5\sqrt{a} + 1 = 0$

8.5 *Solve each inequality. State the solution set using interval notation and graph it.*
81. $a^2 + a > 6$

82. $x^2 - 5x + 6 > 0$

83. $x^2 - x - 20 \leq 0$

84. $a^2 + 2a \leq 15$

85. $w^2 - w < 0$

86. $x - x^2 \leq 0$

87. $\dfrac{x-4}{x+2} \geq 0$

88. $\dfrac{x-3}{x+5} < 0$

89. $\dfrac{x-2}{x+3} < 1$

90. $\dfrac{x-3}{x+4} > 2$

91. $\dfrac{3}{x+2} > \dfrac{1}{x+1}$

92. $\dfrac{1}{x+1} < \dfrac{1}{x-1}$

MISCELLANEOUS

In Exercises 93–104, find all real or imaginary solutions to each equation.

93. $144x^2 - 120x + 25 = 0$

94. $49x^2 + 9 = 42x$

95. $(2x+3)^2 + 7 = 12$

96. $6x = -\dfrac{19x+25}{x+1}$

97. $1 + \dfrac{20}{9x^2} = \dfrac{8}{3x}$

98. $\dfrac{x-1}{x+2} = \dfrac{2x-3}{x+4}$

99. $\sqrt{3x^2 + 7x - 30} = x$

100. $\dfrac{x^4}{3} = x^2 + 6$

101. $2(2x+1)^2 + 5(2x+1) = 3$

102. $(w^2-1)^2 + 2(w^2-1) = 15$

103. $x^{1/2} - 15x^{1/4} + 50 = 0$

104. $x^{-2} - 9x^{-1} + 18 = 0$

Find exact and approximate solutions to each problem.

105. *Missing numbers.* Find two positive real numbers that differ by 4 and have a product of 4.

106. *One on one.* Find two positive real numbers that differ by 1 and have a product of 1.

107. *Big screen TV.* On a 19-inch diagonal measure television picture screen, the height is 4 inches less than the width. Find the height and width.

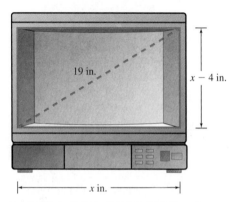

19 in.

$x - 4$ in.

x in.

FIGURE FOR EXERCISE 107

108. *Boxing match.* A boxing ring is in the shape of a square, 20 ft on each side. How far apart are the fighters when they are in opposite corners of the ring?

109. *Students for a Clean Environment.* A group of environmentalists plans to print a message on an 8 inch by 10 inch

STOP THE POLLUTION!

10 in.

8 in.

FIGURE FOR EXERCISE 109

paper. If the typed message requires 24 square inches of paper and the group wants an equal border on all sides, then how wide should the border be?

110. *Winston works faster.* Winston can mow his dad's lawn in 1 hour less than it takes his brother Willie. If they take 2 hours to mow it when working together, then how long would it take Winston working alone?

111. *Ping Pong.* The table used for table tennis is 4 ft longer than it is wide and has an area of 45 ft^2. What are the dimensions of the table?

FIGURE FOR EXERCISE 111

112. *Swimming pool design.* An architect has designed a motel pool within a rectangular area that is fenced on three sides as shown in the figure. If she uses 60 yards of fencing to enclose an area of 352 square yards, then what are the dimensions marked L and W in the figure? Assume L is greater than W.

FIGURE FOR EXERCISE 112

113. *Minimizing cost.* The unit cost in dollars for manufacturing n starters is given by $C(n) = 0.004n^2 - 3.2n + 660$. What is the unit cost when 390 starters are manufactured? For what number of starters is the unit cost at a minimum?

114. *Maximizing profit.* The total profit (in dollars) for sales of x rowing machines is given by $P(x) = -0.2x^2 + 300x - 200$. What is the profit if 500 are sold? For what value of x will the profit be at a maximum?

115. *Decathlon champion.* For 1989 and 1990 Dave Johnson had the highest decathlon score in the world. When Johnson reached a speed of 32 ft/sec on the pole vault runway, his height above the ground t seconds after leaving the ground was given by $h = -16t^2 + 32t$. (The elasticity of the pole converts the horizontal speed into vertical speed.) Find the value of t for which his height was 12 ft.

116. *Time of flight.* Use the information from Exercise 115 to determine how long Johnson was in the air. For how long was he more than 14 ft in the air?

CHAPTER 8 TEST

Calculate the value of $b^2 - 4ac$, and state how many real solutions each equation has.

1. $2x^2 - 3x + 2 = 0$

2. $-3x^2 + 5x - 1 = 0$

3. $4x^2 - 4x + 1 = 0$

Solve by using the quadratic formula.

4. $2x^2 + 5x - 3 = 0$

5. $x^2 + 6x + 6 = 0$

Solve by completing the square.

6. $x^2 + 10x + 25 = 0$

7. $2x^2 + x - 6 = 0$

Solve by any method.

8. $x(x + 1) = 12$

9. $a^4 - 5a^2 + 4 = 0$

10. $x - 2 - 8\sqrt{x - 2} + 15 = 0$

Find the complex solutions to the quadratic equations.

11. $x^2 + 36 = 0$

12. $x^2 + 6x + 10 = 0$

13. $3x^2 - x + 1 = 0$

Graph each quadratic function. State the domain and range.

14. $f(x) = 16 - x^2$

15. $g(x) = x^2 - 3x$

Write a quadratic equation that has each given pair of solutions.

16. $-4, 6$

17. $-5i, 5i$

Solve each inequality. State and graph the solution set.

18. $w^2 + 3w < 18$

19. $\dfrac{2}{x - 2} < \dfrac{3}{x + 1}$

Find the exact solution to each problem.

20. The length of a rectangle is 2 ft longer than the width. If the area is 16 ft², then what are the length and width?

21. A new computer can process a company's monthly payroll in 1 hour less time than the old computer. To really save time, the manager used both computers and finished the payroll in 3 hours. How long would it take the new computer to do the payroll by itself?

Solve each problem.

22. Find the x-intercepts for the parabola $y = x^2 - 6x + 5$.

23. The height in feet for a ball thrown upward at 48 feet per second is given by $s(t) = -16t^2 + 48t$, where t is the time in seconds after the ball is tossed. What is the maximum height that the ball will reach?

Solve each equation.

1. $2x - 15 = 0$ **2.** $2x^2 - 15 = 0$

3. $2x^2 + x - 15 = 0$

4. $2x^2 + 4x - 15 = 0$

5. $|4x + 11| = 3$

6. $|4x^2 + 11x| = 3$

7. $\sqrt{x} = x - 6$

8. $(2x - 5)^{2/3} = 4$

Solve each inequality. State the solution set using interval notation.

9. $1 - 2x < 5 - x$

10. $(1 - 2x)(5 - x) \leq 0$

11. $\dfrac{1 - 2x}{5 - x} \leq 0$

12. $|5 - x| < 3$

13. $3x - 1 < 5$ and $-3 \leq x$

14. $x - 3 < 1$ or $2x \geq 8$

Solve each equation for y.

15. $2x - 3y = 9$

16. $\dfrac{y - 3}{x + 2} = -\dfrac{1}{2}$

17. $3y^2 + cy + d = 0$

18. $my^2 - ny = w$

19. $\dfrac{1}{3}x - \dfrac{2}{5}y = \dfrac{5}{6}$

20. $y - 3 = -\dfrac{2}{3}(x - 4)$

Let $m = \dfrac{y_2 - y_1}{x_2 - x_1}$. Find the value of m for each of the following choices of $x_1, x_2, y_1,$ and y_2.

21. $x_1 = 2, x_2 = 5, y_1 = 3, y_2 = 7$

22. $x_1 = -3, x_2 = 4, y_1 = 5, y_2 = -6$

23. $x_1 = 0.3, x_2 = 0.5, y_1 = 0.8, y_2 = 0.4$

24. $x_1 = \dfrac{1}{2}, x_2 = \dfrac{1}{3}, y_1 = \dfrac{3}{5}, y_2 = -\dfrac{4}{3}$

510

Solve each problem.

25. *Ticket prices.* If the price of a concert ticket goes up, then the number sold will go down, as shown in the figure. If you use the formula $n = 48{,}000 - 400p$ to predict the number sold depending on the price p, then how many will be sold at $20 per ticket? How many will be sold at $25 per ticket? Use the bar graph to estimate the price if 35,000 tickets were sold.

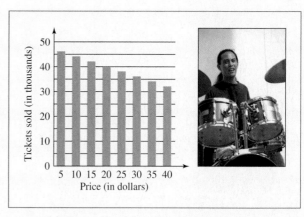

FIGURE FOR EXERCISE 25

26. *Increasing revenue.* Even though the number of tickets sold for a concert decreases with increasing price, the revenue generated does not necessarily decrease. Use the formula $R = p(48{,}000 - 400p)$ to determine the revenue when the price is $20 and when the price is $25. What price would produce a revenue of $1.28 million? Use the graph to find the price that determines the maximum revenue.

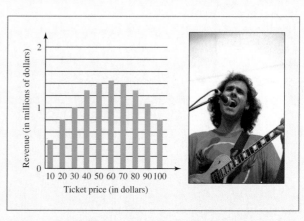

FIGURE FOR EXERCISE 26

Additional Function Topics

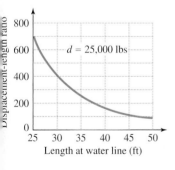

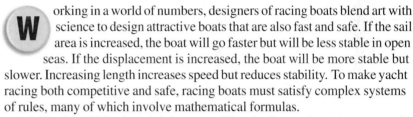

W orking in a world of numbers, designers of racing boats blend art with science to design attractive boats that are also fast and safe. If the sail area is increased, the boat will go faster but will be less stable in open seas. If the displacement is increased, the boat will be more stable but slower. Increasing length increases speed but reduces stability. To make yacht racing both competitive and safe, racing boats must satisfy complex systems of rules, many of which involve mathematical formulas.

After the 1988 mismatch between Dennis Conner's catamaran and New Zealander Michael Fay's 133-foot monohull, an international group of yacht designers rewrote the America's Cup rules to ensure the fairness of the race. In addition to hundreds of pages of other rules, every yacht must satisfy the basic inequality

$$\frac{L + 1.25\sqrt{S} - 9.8\sqrt[3]{D}}{0.679} \le 24.000,$$

which balances the length L, the sail area S, and the displacement D.

In the 1979 Fastnet Race 15 sailors lost their lives. After *Exide Challenger*'s carbon-fiber keel snapped off, Tony Bullimore spent 4 days inside the overturned hull before being rescued by the Australian navy. Yacht racing is a dangerous sport. To determine the general performance and safety of a yacht, designers calculate the displacement-length ratio, the sail area-displacement ratio, the ballast-displacement ratio, and the capsize screening value. In Exercises 73 and 74 of Section 9.3 we will see how composition of functions is used to define the displacement-length ratio and the sail area-displacement ratio.

9.1 GRAPHS OF FUNCTIONS AND RELATIONS

Functions were introduced in Section 3.5. In this section we will study the graphs of several types of functions. We graphed linear functions in Chapter 3 and quadratic functions in Chapter 8, but for completeness we will review them here.

Linear and Constant Functions

Linear functions get their name from the fact that their graphs are straight lines.

> **Linear Function**
>
> A **linear function** is a function of the form
> $$f(x) = mx + b,$$
> where m and b are real numbers with $m \neq 0$.

The graph of the linear function $f(x) = mx + b$ is exactly the same as the graph of the linear equation $y = mx + b$. If $m = 0$, then we get $f(x) = b$, which is called a **constant function.** If $m = 1$ and $b = 0$, then we get the function $f(x) = x$, which is called the **identity function.** When we graph a function given in function notation, we usually label the vertical axis as $f(x)$ rather than y.

E X A M P L E   1   **Graphing a constant function**

Graph $f(x) = 3$ and state the domain and range.

Solution

The graph of $f(x) = 3$ is the same as the graph of $y = 3$, which is the horizontal line in Fig. 9.1. Since any real number can be used for x in $f(x) = 3$ and since the line in Fig. 9.1 extends without bounds to the left and right, the domain is the set of all real numbers, $(-\infty, \infty)$. Since the only y-coordinate for $f(x) = 3$ is 3, the range is $\{3\}$. ■

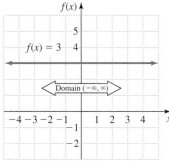

FIGURE 9.1

The domain and range of a function can be determined from the formula or the graph. However, the graph is usually very helpful for understanding domain and range.

E X A M P L E   2   **Graphing a linear function**

Graph the function $f(x) = 3x - 4$ and state the domain and range.

Solution

The y-intercept is $(0, -4)$ and the slope of the line is 3. We can use the y-intercept and the slope to draw the graph in Fig. 9.2. Since any real number can be used for x in $f(x) = 3x - 4$, and since the line in Fig. 9.2 extends without bounds to the left and right, the domain is the set of all real numbers, $(-\infty, \infty)$. Since the graph extends without bounds upward and downward, the range is the set of all real numbers, $(-\infty, \infty)$.

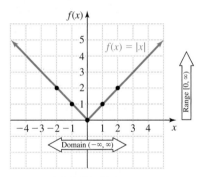

FIGURE 9.2

Absolute Value Functions

The equation $y = |x|$ defines a function because every value of x determines a unique value of y. We call this function the absolute value function.

> **Absolute Value Function**
>
> The **absolute value function** is the function defined by
>
> $$f(x) = |x|.$$

To graph the absolute value function, we simply plot enough ordered pairs of the function to see what the graph looks like.

EXAMPLE 3

The absolute value function

Graph $f(x) = |x|$ and state the domain and range.

Solution

To graph this function, we find points that satisfy the equation $f(x) = |x|$.

x	-2	-1	0	1	2
$f(x) = |x|$	2	1	0	1	2

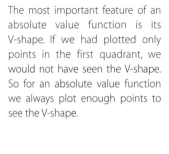

Helpful Hint

The most important feature of an absolute value function is its V-shape. If we had plotted only points in the first quadrant, we would not have seen the V-shape. So for an absolute value function we always plot enough points to see the V-shape.

Plotting these points, we see that they lie along the V-shaped graph shown in Fig. 9.3. Since any real number can be used for x in $f(x) = |x|$ and since the graph extends without bounds to the left and right, the domain is $(-\infty, \infty)$. Because the graph does not go below the x-axis and because $|x|$ is never negative, the range is the set of nonnegative real numbers, $[0, \infty)$.

FIGURE 9.3

Many functions involving absolute value have graphs that are V-shaped, as in Fig. 9.3. To graph functions involving absolute value, we must choose points that determine the correct shape and location of the V-shaped graph.

E X A M P L E   4   Other functions involving absolute value

Graph each function and state the domain and range.

a) $f(x) = |x| - 2$ **b)** $g(x) = |2x - 6|$

Calculator Close-Up

To check Example 4(a) set

$$y_1 = \text{abs}(x) - 2$$

and then press GRAPH.

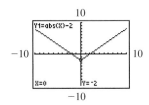

To check Example 4(b) set

$$y_2 = \text{abs}(2x - 6)$$

and then press GRAPH.

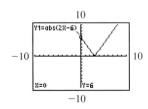

Solution

a) Choose values for x and find $f(x)$.

x	-2	-1	0	1	2
$f(x) = |x| - 2$	0	-1	-2	-1	0

Plot these points and draw a V-shaped graph through them as shown in Fig. 9.4. The domain is $(-\infty, \infty)$, and the range is $[-2, \infty)$.

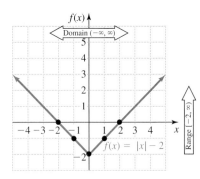

FIGURE 9.4

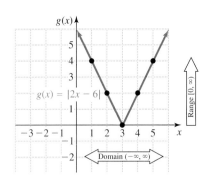

FIGURE 9.5

b) Make a table of values for x and $g(x)$.

x	1	2	3	4	5
$g(x) = |2x - 6|$	4	2	0	2	4

Draw the graph as shown in Fig. 9.5. The domain is $(-\infty, \infty)$, and the range is $[0, \infty)$.   ■

Quadratic Functions

In Chapter 8 we learned that the graph of any quadratic function is a parabola, which opens upward or downward. The vertex of a parabola is the lowest point on a parabola that opens upward or the highest point on a parabola that opens downward. Parabolas will be discussed again when we study conic sections later in this text.

Quadratic Function

A **quadratic function** is a function of the form

$$f(x) = ax^2 + bx + c,$$

where a, b, and c are real numbers, with $a \neq 0$.

E X A M P L E   5

A quadratic function

Graph the function $g(x) = 4 - x^2$ and state the domain and range.

Calculator Close-Up

You can find the vertex of a parabola with a calculator. For example, graph

$$y = -x^2 - x + 2.$$

Then use the maximum feature, which is found in the CALC menu. For the left bound pick a point to the left of the vertex; for the right bound pick a point to the right of the vertex; and for the guess pick a point near the vertex.

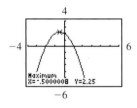

Solution

We plot enough points to get the correct shape of the graph.

x	-2	-1	0	1	2
$g(x) = 4 - x^2$	0	3	4	3	0

See Fig. 9.6 for the graph. The domain is $(-\infty, \infty)$. From the graph we see that the largest y-coordinate is 4. So the range is $(-\infty, 4]$.

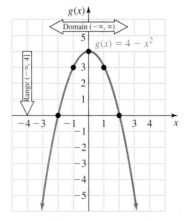

F I G U R E   9 . 6

Square-Root Functions

Functions involving square roots typically have graphs that look like half a parabola.

> **Square-Root Function**
>
> The **square-root function** is the function defined by
>
> $$f(x) = \sqrt{x}.$$

E X A M P L E   6

Square-root functions

Graph each equation and state the domain and range.

a) $y = \sqrt{x}$ **b)** $y = \sqrt{x + 3}$

Solution

a) The graph of the equation $y = \sqrt{x}$ and the graph of the function $f(x) = \sqrt{x}$ are the same. Because $\sqrt{x}$ is a real number only if $x \geq 0$, the domain of this function is the set of nonnegative real numbers. The following ordered pairs are on the graph:

x	0	1	4	9
$y = \sqrt{x}$	0	1	2	3

The graph goes through these ordered pairs as shown in Fig. 9.7. Note that x is chosen from the nonnegative numbers. The domain is $[0, \infty)$ and the range is $[0, \infty)$.

b) Note that $\sqrt{x + 3}$ is a real number only if $x + 3 \geq 0$, or $x \geq -3$. So we make a table of ordered pairs in which $x \geq -3$:

x	-3	-2	1	6
$y = \sqrt{x + 3}$	0	1	2	3

The graph goes through these ordered pairs as shown in Fig. 9.8. The domain is $[-3, \infty)$ and the range is $[0, \infty)$.

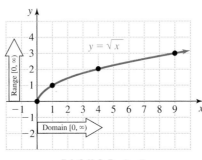

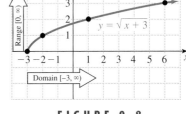

FIGURE 9.7   **FIGURE 9.8**

Graphing Relations

A function is a set of ordered pairs in which no two have the same first coordinate and different second coordinates. A relation is any set of ordered pairs. The domain of a relation is the set of x-coordinates of the ordered pairs and the range of a relation is the set of y-coordinates of the ordered pairs. In Example 7 we graph the relation $x = y^2$. Note that this relation is not a function because ordered pairs such as $(4, 2)$ and $(4, -2)$ satisfy $x = y^2$.

E X A M P L E   7

Graphing relations that are not functions

Graph each relation and state the domain and range.

a) $x = y^2$ **b)** $x = |y - 3|$

Solution

a) Because the equation $x = y^2$ expresses x in terms of y, it is easier to choose the y-coordinate first and then find the x-coordinate:

$x = y^2$	4	1	0	1	4
y	-2	-1	0	1	2

Figure 9.9 shows the graph. The domain is $[0, \infty)$ and the range is $(-\infty, \infty)$.

b) Again we select values for y first and find the corresponding x-coordinates:

$x = |y - 3|$	2	1	0	1	2
y	1	2	3	4	5

Plot these points as shown in Fig. 9.10. The domain is $[0, \infty)$ and the range is $(-\infty, \infty)$.

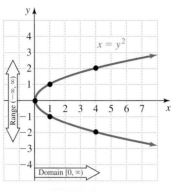

FIGURE 9.9

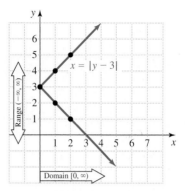

FIGURE 9.10

WARM-UPS

True or false? Explain your answer.

1. The graph of a function is a picture of all ordered pairs of the function.

2. The graph of every linear function is a straight line.

3. The absolute value function has a V-shaped graph.

4. The domain of $f(x) = 3$ is $(-\infty, \infty)$.

5. The graph of a quadratic function is a parabola.

6. The range of any quadratic function is $(-\infty, \infty)$.

7. The y-axis and the $f(x)$-axis are the same.

8. The domain of $x = y^2$ is $[0, \infty)$.

9. The domain of $f(x) = \sqrt{x - 1}$ is $(1, \infty)$.

10. The domain of any quadratic function is $(-\infty, \infty)$.

9.1   EXERCISES

Reading and Writing   *After reading this section, write out the answers to these questions. Use complete sentences.*

1. What is a linear function?

2. What is a constant function?

3. What is the graph of a constant function?

4. What shape is the graph of an absolute value function?

5. What is the graph of quadratic function called?

6. What is the identity function?

Graph each function and state its domain and range. See Examples 1 and 2.

7. $h(x) = -2$ **8.** $f(x) = 4$

9. $f(x) = 2x - 1$

10. $g(x) = x + 2$

19. $h(x) = |x + 1|$

20. $f(x) = |x - 2|$

11. $g(x) = \dfrac{1}{2}x + 2$

12. $h(x) = \dfrac{2}{3}x - 4$

21. $g(x) = |3x|$

22. $h(x) = |-2x|$

23. $f(x) = |2x - 1|$

24. $y = |2x - 3|$

13. $y = -\dfrac{2}{3}x + 3$

14. $y = -\dfrac{3}{4}x + 4$

25. $f(x) = |x - 2| + 1$

26. $y = |x - 1| + 2$

15. $y = -0.3x + 6.5$

16. $y = 0.25x - 0.5$

Graph each absolute value function and state its domain and range. See Examples 3 and 4.

17. $f(x) = |x| + 1$

18. $g(x) = |x| - 3$

Graph each quadratic function and state its domain and range. See Example 5.

27. $g(x) = x^2 + 2$

28. $f(x) = x^2 - 4$

29. $f(x) = 2x^2$

30. $h(x) = -3x^2$

39. $y = \sqrt{x} + 2$

40. $y = 2\sqrt{x} + 1$

31. $y = 6 - x^2$

32. $y = -2x^2 + 3$

Graph each relation and state its domain and range. See Example 7.

41. $x = |y|$

42. $x = -|y|$

Graph each square-root function and state its domain and range. See Example 6.

33. $g(x) = 2\sqrt{x}$

34. $g(x) = \sqrt{x} - 1$

43. $x = -y^2$

44. $x = 1 - y^2$

45. $x = 5$

46. $x = -3$

35. $f(x) = \sqrt{x - 1}$

36. $f(x) = \sqrt{x + 1}$

47. $x + 9 = y^2$

48. $x + 3 = |y|$

37. $h(x) = -\sqrt{x}$

38. $h(x) = -\sqrt{x - 1}$

49. $x = \sqrt{y}$

50. $x = -\sqrt{y}$

59. $y = \sqrt{x} - 3$

60. $y = 2\,|x|$

51. $x = (y - 1)^2$

52. $x = (y + 2)^2$

61. $y = 3x - 5$

62. $g(x) = (x + 2)^2$

Graph each function and state the domain and range.

53. $f(x) = 1 - |x|$

54. $h(x) = \sqrt{x - 3}$

63. $y = -x^2 + 4x - 4$

64. $y = -2\,|x - 1| + 4$

55. $y = (x - 3)^2 - 1$

56. $y = x^2 - 2x - 3$

GRAPHING CALCULATOR EXERCISES

65. Graph the function $f(x) = \sqrt{x^2}$ and explain what this graph illustrates.

66. Graph the function $f(x) = \dfrac{1}{x}$ and state the domain and range.

57. $y = |x + 3| + 1$

58. $f(x) = -2x + 4$

67. Graph $y = x^2$, $y = \frac{1}{2}x^2$, and $y = 2x^2$ on the same coordinate system. What can you say about the graph of $y = kx^2$?

68. Graph $y = x^2$, $y = x^2 + 2$, and $y = x^2 - 3$ on the same screen. What can you say about the position of $y = x^2 + k$ relative to $y = x^2$.

69. Graph $y = x^2$, $y = (x + 5)^2$, and $y = (x - 2)^2$ on the same screen. What can you say about the position of $y = (x - k)^2$ relative to $y = x^2$.

70. You can graph the relation $x = y^2$ by graphing the two functions $y = \sqrt{x}$ and $y = -\sqrt{x}$. Try it and explain why this works.

71. Graph $y = (x - 3)^2$, $y = |x - 3|$, and $y = \sqrt{x - 3}$ on the same coordinate system. How does the graph of $y = f(x - k)$ compare to the graph of $y = f(x)$?

In This Section

- Reflecting
- Translating
- Stretching and Shrinking
- Multiple Transformations

Calculator Close-Up

With a graphing calculator, you can quickly see the result of modifying the formula for a function. If you have a graphing calculator, use it to graph the functions in the examples. Experimenting with it will help you to understand the ideas in this section.

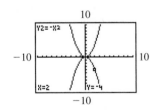

9.2   TRANSFORMATIONS OF GRAPHS

We can discover what the graph of almost any function looks like if we plot enough points. However, it is helpful to know something about a graph so that we do not have to plot very many points. In this section we will learn how one graph can be transformed into another by modifying the formula that defines the function.

Reflecting

Consider the graphs of $f(x) = x^2$ and $g(x) = -x^2$ shown in Fig. 9.11. Notice that the graph of g is a mirror image of the graph of f. For any value of x we compute the y-coordinate of an ordered pair of f by squaring x. For an ordered pair of g we square first and then find the opposite because of the order of operations. This gives a correspondence between the ordered pairs of f and the ordered pairs of g. For every ordered pair on the graph of f there is a corresponding ordered pair directly below it on the graph of g, and these ordered pairs are the same distance from the x-axis. We say that the graph of g is obtained by reflecting the graph of f in the x-axis or that g is a reflection of the graph of f.

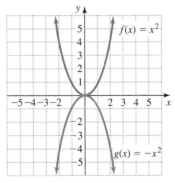

FIGURE 9.11

> **Reflection**
>
> The graph of $y = -f(x)$ is a **reflection** in the x-axis of the graph of $y = f(x)$.

EXAMPLE 1

Reflection

Sketch the graphs of each pair of functions on the same coordinate system.

a) $f(x) = \sqrt{x}$, $g(x) = -\sqrt{x}$ **b)** $f(x) = |x|$, $g(x) = -|x|$

Solution

In each case the graph of g is a reflection of the graph of f. Recall that we graphed the square root function and the absolute value function in the last section. Figures 9.12 and 9.13 show the graphs for these functions.

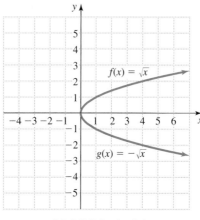

FIGURE 9.12

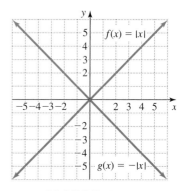

FIGURE 9.13

Translating

Consider the graphs of the functions $f(x) = \sqrt{x}$, $g(x) = \sqrt{x} + 2$, and $h(x) = \sqrt{x} - 6$ shown in Fig. 9.14. In the expression $\sqrt{x} + 2$, adding 2 is the last operation to perform. So every point on the graph of g is exactly two units above a corresponding point on the graph of f, and g has the same shape as the graph of f. Every point on the graph of h is exactly six units below a corresponding point on the graph of f. The graph of g is an upward translation of the graph of f, and the graph of h is a downward translation of the graph of f.

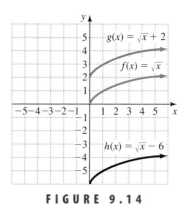

FIGURE 9.14

Translating Upward or Downward

If $k > 0$, then the graph of $y = f(x) + k$ is an **upward translation** of the graph of $y = f(x)$ and the graph of $y = f(x) - k$ is a **downward translation** of the graph of $y = f(x)$.

Consider the graphs of $f(x) = \sqrt{x}$, $g(x) = \sqrt{x - 2}$, and $h(x) = \sqrt{x + 6}$ shown in Fig. 9.15. In the expression $\sqrt{x - 2}$ subtracting 2 is the first operation to

Calculator Close-Up

Note that for a translation of six units to the left, $x + 6$ must be written in parentheses on a graphing calculator.

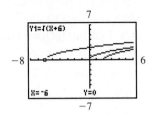

perform. So every point on the graph of g is exactly two units to the right of a corresponding point on the graph of f. (We must start with a larger value of x to get the same y-coordinate because we first subtract 2.) Every point on the graph of h is exactly six units to the left of a corresponding point on the graph of f.

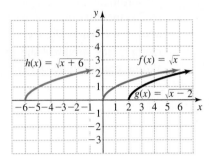

FIGURE 9.15

Translating to the Right or Left

If $h > 0$, then the graph of $y = f(x - h)$ is a **translation to the right** of the graph of $y = f(x)$, and the graph of $y = f(x + h)$ is a **translation to the left** of the graph of $y = f(x)$.

E X A M P L E   2

Translation

Sketch the graph of each function.

a) $f(x) = |x| - 6$ **b)** $f(x) = (x - 2)^2$ **c)** $f(x) = |x + 3|$

Solution

a) The graph of $f(x) = |x| - 6$ is a translation six units downward of the familiar graph of $f(x) = |x|$. Calculate a few ordered pairs to get an accurate graph. The pairs $(0, -6)$, $(1, -5)$, and $(-1, -5)$ are on the graph shown in Fig. 9.16.

b) The graph of $f(x) = (x - 2)^2$ is a translation two units to the right of the familiar graph of $f(x) = x^2$. Calculate a few ordered pairs to get an accurate graph. The pairs $(2, 0)$, $(0, 4)$, and $(4, 4)$ are on the graph shown in Fig. 9.17.

c) The graph of $f(x) = |x + 3|$ is a translation three units to the left of the familiar graph of $f(x) = |x|$. The pairs $(0, 3)$, $(-3, 0)$, and $(-6, 3)$ are on the graph shown in Fig. 9.18.

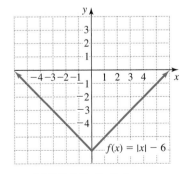

FIGURE 9.16

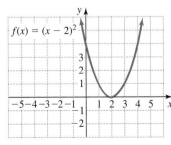

FIGURE 9.17

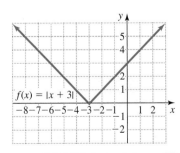

FIGURE 9.18

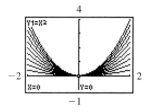
Stretching and Shrinking

Consider the graphs of $f(x) = x^2$, $g(x) = 2x^2$, and $h(x) = \frac{1}{2}x^2$ shown in Fig. 9.19. Every point on $g(x) = 2x^2$ corresponds to a point directly below on the graph of $f(x) = x^2$. The y-coordinate on g is exactly twice as large as the corresponding y-coordinate on f. This situation occurs because in the expression $2x^2$, multiplying by 2 is the last operation performed. Every point on h corresponds to a point directly above on f, where the y-coordinate on h is half as large as the y-coordinate on f. The factor 2 has stretched the graph of f to form the graph of g, and the factor $\frac{1}{2}$ has shrunk the graph of f to form the graph of h.

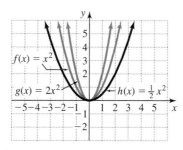

FIGURE 9.19

Stretching and Shrinking

If $a > 1$, then the graph of $y = af(x)$ is obtained by **stretching** the graph of $y = f(x)$. If $0 < a < 1$, then the graph of $y = af(x)$ is obtained by **shrinking** the graph of $y = f(x)$.

Note that the last operation to be performed in stretching or shrinking is multiplication by a. Whereas the function $g(x) = 2\sqrt{x}$ is obtained by stretching $f(x) = \sqrt{x}$ by a factor of 2, $h(x) = \sqrt{2x}$ is not.

EXAMPLE 3   Stretching and shrinking

Graph the functions $f(x) = \sqrt{x}$, $g(x) = 2\sqrt{x}$, and $h(x) = \frac{1}{2}\sqrt{x}$ on the same coordinate system.

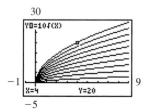
Solution

The graph of g is obtained by stretching the graph of f, and the graph of h is obtained by shrinking the graph of f. The graph of f includes the points $(0, 0)$, $(1, 1)$, and $(4, 2)$. The graph of g includes the points $(0, 0)$, $(1, 2)$, and $(4, 4)$. The graph of h includes the points $(0, 0)$, $(1, 0.5)$, and $(4, 1)$. The graphs are shown in Fig. 9.20.

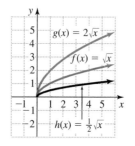

FIGURE 9.20

Multiple Transformations

When graphing a function containing more than one transformation perform the transformations in the following order:

1. Left or right translation
2. Stretching or shrinking
3. Reflection in the x-axis
4. Upward or downward translation

For example, the graph of $y = -2|x + 3| + 5$ is obtained by translating $y = |x|$ to the left 3 units, then stretching by a factor of 2, reflecting in the x-axis, and finally translating 5 units upward.

E X A M P L E   4

A multiple transformation of $y = \sqrt{x}$

Graph the function $y = -2\sqrt{x - 3}$.

Calculator Close-Up

You can check Example 4 by graphing $y = -2\sqrt{x - 3}$ with a graphing calculator.

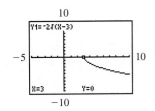

Solution

Start with the graph of $y = \sqrt{x}$ through $(0, 0)$, $(1, 1)$, and $(4, 2)$, as shown in Fig. 9.21. Translate it three units to the right to get the graph of $y = \sqrt{x - 3}$. Stretch this graph by a factor of two to get the graph of $y = 2\sqrt{x - 3}$ shown in Fig. 9.21. Now reflect in the x-axis to get the graph of $y = -2\sqrt{x - 3}$. To get an accurate graph calculate a few points on the final graph as follows:

x	3	4	7
$y = -2\sqrt{x - 3}$	0	-2	-4

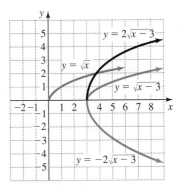

F I G U R E   9 . 2 1

The graph of $y = x^2$ is a parabola opening upward with vertex $(0, 0)$. The graph of a function of the form $y = a(x - h)^2 + k$ is a transformation of $y = x^2$ and is also a parabola. It opens upward if $a > 0$ and downward if $a < 0$. Its vertex is (h, k). In Example 5 we graph a transformation of $y = x^2$.

E X A M P L E   5

A multiple transformation of the parabola $y = x^2$

Graph the function $y = -2(x + 3)^2 + 4$.

Solution

Think of the parabola $y = x^2$ through $(-1, 1)$, $(0, 0)$, and $(1, 1)$. To get the graph of $y = -2(x + 3)^2 + 4$, translate it three units to the left, stretch by a factor of two, reflect in the *x*-axis, and finally translate upward four units. The graph is a stretched parabola opening downward from the vertex $(-3, 4)$ as shown in Fig. 9.22. To get an accurate graph calculate a few points around the vertex as follows:

x	-5	-4	-3	-2	-1
$y = -2(x + 3)^2 + 4$	-4	2	4	2	-4

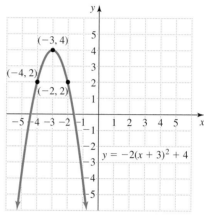

FIGURE 9.22

Understanding transformations helps us to see the location of the graph of a function. To get an accurate graph we must still calculate ordered pairs that satisfy the equation. However, if we know where to expect the graph it is easier to choose appropriate ordered pairs.

E X A M P L E   6

A multiple transformation of the absolute value function $y = |x|$

Graph the function $y = \frac{1}{2}|x - 4| - 1$.

Solution

Think of the V-shaped graph of $y = |x|$ through $(-1, 1)$, $(0, 0)$, and $(1, 1)$. To get the graph of $y = \frac{1}{2}|x - 4| - 1$, translate $y = |x|$ to the right four units, shrink by a factor of $\frac{1}{2}$, and finally translate downward one unit. The graph is shown in Fig. 9.23. To get an accurate graph calculate a few points around the lowest point on the V-shaped graph as follows:

x	2	4	6
$y = \frac{1}{2}|x - 4| - 1$	0	-1	0

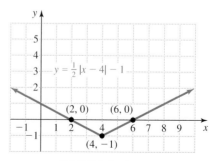

FIGURE 9.23

True or false? Explain your answer.

1. The graph of $f(x) = (-x)^2$ is a reflection in the x-axis of the graph of $g(x) = x^2$.

2. The graph of $f(x) = -2$ is a reflection in the x-axis of the graph of $f(x) = 2$.

3. The graph of $f(x) = x + 3$ lies three units to the left of the graph of $f(x) = x$.

4. The graph of $y = |x - 3|$ lies three units to the left of the graph of $y = |x|$.

5. The graph of $y = |x| - 3$ lies three units below the graph of $y = |x|$.

6. The graph of $y = -2x^2$ can be obtained by stretching and reflecting the graph of $y = x^2$.

7. The graph of $f(x) = (x - 2)^2$ is symmetric about the y-axis.

8. For each point on the graph of $y = \sqrt{x}/9$ there is a corresponding point on $y = \sqrt{x}$ that has a y-coordinate three times as large.

9. The graph of $y = \sqrt{x - 3} + 5$ has the same shape as the graph of $y = \sqrt{x}$.

10. The graph of $y = -(x + 2)^2 - 7$ can be obtained by moving $y = x^2$ two units to the left and down seven units and then reflecting in the x-axis.

9.2   EXERCISES

Reading and Writing   After reading this section, write out the answers to these questions. Use complete sentences.

1. What is a reflection in the x-axis of a graph?

2. What is an upward translation of a graph?

3. What is a downward translation of a graph?

4. What is a translation to the right of a graph?

5. What is a translation to the left of a graph?

6. What is stretching and shrinking of a graph?

Sketch the graphs of each pair of functions on the same coordinate system. See Example 1.

7. $f(x) = \sqrt{2x}$,
   $g(x) = -\sqrt{2x}$

8. $y = x, y = -x$

47. $y = -2x + 3$

48. $y = 3x - 1$

a)

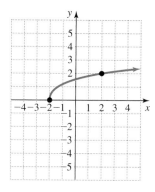

b)

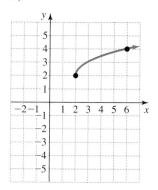

49. $y = 2(x + 3)^2 + 1$

50. $y = 2(x + 1)^2 - 2$

c)

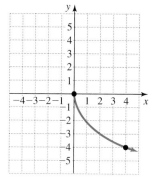

d)

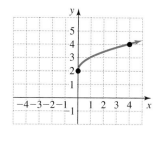

51. $y = -2(x - 4)^2 + 2$

52. $y = -2(x - 1)^2 + 3$

e)

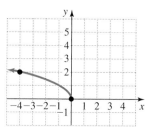

f)

53. $y = -3(x - 1)^2 + 6$

54. $y = 3(x + 2)^2 - 6$

g)

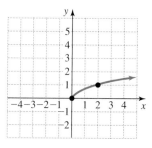

h)

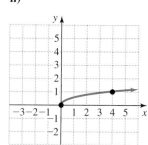

Match each function with its graph a–h.

55. $y = 2 + \sqrt{x}$

56. $y = \sqrt{2 + x}$

57. $y = 2\sqrt{x}$

58. $y = \sqrt{\dfrac{x}{2}}$

59. $y = \dfrac{1}{2}\sqrt{x}$

60. $y = 2 + \sqrt{x - 2}$

61. $y = -2\sqrt{x}$

62. $y = \sqrt{-x}$

GETTING MORE INVOLVED

63. If the graph of $y = x^2$ is translated eight units upward, then what is the equation of the curve at that location?

64. If the graph of $y = x^2$ is translated six units to the right, then what is the equation of the curve at that location?

65. If the graph of $y = \sqrt{x}$ is translated five units to the left, then what is the equation of the curve at that location?

66. If the graph of $y = \sqrt{x}$ is translated four units downward, then what is the equation of the curve at that location?

67. If the graph of $y = |x|$ is translated three units to the left and then five units upward, then what is the equation of the curve at that location?

68. If the graph of $y = |x|$ is translated four units downward and then nine units to the right, then what is the equation of the curve at that location?

 GRAPHING CALCULATOR EXERCISES

69. Graph $f(x) = |x|$ and $g(x) = |x - 20| + 30$ on the same screen of your calculator. What transformations will transform the graph of f into the graph of g?

70. Graph $f(x) = (x + 3)^2$, $g(x) = x^2 + 3^2$, and $h(x) = x^2 + 6x + 9$ on the same screen of your calculator.

   a) Which two of these functions has the same graph? Why are they the same?

   b) Is it true that $(x + 3)^2 = x^2 + 9$ for all real numbers x?

   c) Describe each graph in terms of a transformation of the graph of $y = x^2$.

In This Section

- Basic Operations with Functions
- Composition

 9.3   COMBINING FUNCTIONS

In this section you will learn how to combine functions to obtain new functions.

Basic Operations with Functions

An entrepreneur plans to rent a stand at a farmers market for \$25 per day to sell strawberries. If she buys x flats of berries for \$5 per flat and sells them for \$9 per flat, then her daily cost in dollars can be written as a function of x:

$$C(x) = 5x + 25$$

Assuming she sells as many flats as she buys, her revenue in dollars is also a function of x:

$$R(x) = 9x$$

Because profit is revenue minus cost, we can find a function for the profit by subtracting the functions for cost and revenue:

$$
\begin{aligned}
P(x) &= R(x) - C(x) \\
&= 9x - (5x + 25) \\
&= 4x - 25
\end{aligned}
$$

The function $P(x) = 4x - 25$ expresses the daily profit as a function of x. Since $P(6) = -1$ and $P(7) = 3$, the profit is negative if 6 or fewer flats are sold and positive if 7 or more flats are sold.

   In the example of the entrepreneur we subtracted two functions to find a new function. In other cases we may use addition, multiplication, or division to combine two functions. For any two given functions we can define the sum, difference, product, and quotient functions as follows.

Sum, Difference, Product, and Quotient Functions

Given two functions f and g, the functions $f + g$, $f - g$, $f \cdot g$, and $\frac{f}{g}$ are defined as follows:

Sum function:	$(f + g)(x) = f(x) + g(x)$
Difference function:	$(f - g)(x) = f(x) - g(x)$
Product function:	$(f \cdot g)(x) = f(x) \cdot g(x)$
Quotient function:	$\left(\dfrac{f}{g}\right)(x) = \dfrac{f(x)}{g(x)}$ provided that $g(x) \neq 0$

The domain of the function $f + g$, $f - g$, $f \cdot g$, or $\frac{f}{g}$ is the intersection of the domain of f and the domain of g. For the function $\frac{f}{g}$ we also rule out any values of x for which $g(x) = 0$.

E X A M P L E 1

Operations with functions

Let $f(x) = 4x - 12$ and $g(x) = x - 3$. Find the following.

a) $(f + g)(x)$ **b)** $(f - g)(x)$

c) $(f \cdot g)(x)$ **d)** $\left(\dfrac{f}{g}\right)(x)$

Helpful Hint

Note that we use $f + g, f - g, f \cdot g$, and f/g to name these functions only because there is no application in mind here. We generally use a single letter to name functions after they are combined as we did when using P for the profit function rather than $R - C$.

Solution

a) $(f + g)(x) = f(x) + g(x)$
$$= 4x - 12 + x - 3$$
$$= 5x - 15$$

b) $(f - g)(x) = f(x) - g(x)$
$$= 4x - 12 - (x - 3)$$
$$= 3x - 9$$

c) $(f \cdot g)(x) = f(x) \cdot g(x)$
$$= (4x - 12)(x - 3)$$
$$= 4x^2 - 24x + 36$$

d) $\left(\dfrac{f}{g}\right)(x) = \dfrac{f(x)}{g(x)} = \dfrac{4x - 12}{x - 3} = \dfrac{4(x - 3)}{x - 3} = 4$ for $x \neq 3$. ∎

E X A M P L E 2

Evaluating a sum function

Let $f(x) = 4x - 12$ and $g(x) = x - 3$. Find $(f + g)(2)$.

Solution

In Example 1(a) we found a general formula for the function $f + g$, namely, $(f + g)(x) = 5x - 15$. If we replace x by 2, we get

$$(f + g)(2) = 5(2) - 15$$
$$= -5.$$

We can also find $(f + g)(2)$ by evaluating each function separately and then adding the results. Because $f(2) = -4$ and $g(2) = -1$, we get

$$(f + g)(2) = f(2) + g(2)$$
$$= -4 + (-1)$$
$$= -5.$$ ∎

Helpful Hint

The difference between the first four operations with functions and composition is like the difference between parallel and series in electrical connections. Components connected in parallel operate simultaneously and separately. If components are connected in series, then electricity must pass through the first component to get to the second component.

Composition

A salesperson's monthly salary is a function of the number of cars he sells: $1000 plus $50 for each car sold. If we let S be his salary and n be the number of cars sold, then S in dollars is a function of n:

$$S = 1000 + 50n$$

Each month the dealer contributes $100 plus 5% of his salary to a profit-sharing plan. If P represents the amount put into profit sharing, then P (in dollars) is a function of S:

$$P = 100 + 0.05S$$

Now P is a function of S, and S is a function of n. Is P a function of n? The value of n certainly determines the value of P. In fact, we can write a formula for P in terms of n by substituting one formula into the other:

$$P = 100 + 0.05S$$
$$= 100 + 0.05(1000 + 50n) \quad \text{Substitute } S = 1000 + 50n.$$
$$= 100 + 50 + 2.5n \qquad\qquad \text{Distributive property}$$
$$= 150 + 2.5n$$

Now P is written as a function of n, bypassing S. We call this idea **composition of functions**.

E X A M P L E   3

The composition of two functions
Given that $y = x^2 - 2x + 3$ and $z = 2y - 5$, write z as a function of x.

Solution
Replace y in $z = 2y - 5$ by $x^2 - 2x + 3$:

$$z = 2y - 5$$
$$= 2(x^2 - 2x + 3) - 5 \quad \text{Replace } y \text{ by } x^2 - 2x + 3.$$
$$= 2x^2 - 4x + 1$$

The equation $z = 2x^2 - 4x + 1$ expresses z as a function of x. ∎

The composition of two functions using function notation is defined as follows.

Composition of Functions

The **composition** of f and g is denoted $f \circ g$ and is defined by the equation

$$(f \circ g)(x) = f(g(x)),$$

provided that $g(x)$ is in the domain of f.

The notation $f \circ g$ is read as "the composition of f and g" or "f compose g." The diagram in Fig. 9.24 shows a function g pairing numbers in its domain with numbers in its range. If the range of g is contained in or equal to the domain of f, then f pairs the second coordinates of g with numbers in the range of f. The composition function $f \circ g$ is a rule for pairing numbers in the domain of g directly with numbers in the range of f, bypassing the middle set. The domain of the function $f \circ g$ is the domain of g (or a subset of it) and the range of $f \circ g$ is the range of f (or a subset of it).

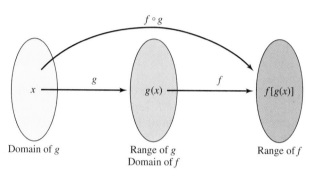

FIGURE 9.24

CAUTION The order in which functions are written is important in composition. For the function $f \circ g$ the function f is applied to $g(x)$. For the function $g \circ f$ the function g is applied to $f(x)$. The function closest to the variable x is applied first.

EXAMPLE 4

Evaluating compositions

Let $f(x) = 3x - 2$ and $g(x) = x^2 + 2x$. Evaluate each of the following expressions.

a) $g(f(3))$ **b)** $f(g(-4))$ **c)** $(g \circ f)(2)$ **d)** $(f \circ g)(2)$

Calculator Close-Up

Set $y_1 = 3x - 2$ and $y_2 = x^2 + 2x$. You can find the composition for Examples 4(a) and 4(b) by evaluating $y_2(y_1(2))$ and $y_1(y_2(2))$. Note that the order in which you evaluate the functions is critical.

```
Y2(Y1(2))
                    24
Y1(Y2(2))
                    22
```

Solution

a) Because $f(3) = 3(3) - 2 = 7$, we have

$$g(f(3)) = g(7) = 7^2 + 2 \cdot 7 = 63.$$

So $g(f(3)) = 63$.

b) Because $g(-4) = (-4)^2 + 2(-4) = 8$, we have

$$f(g(-4)) = f(8) = 3(8) - 2 = 22.$$

So $f(g(-4)) = 22$.

c) Because $(g \circ f)(2) = g(f(2))$ we first find $f(2)$:

$$f(2) = 3(2) - 2 = 4$$

Because $f(2) = 4$, we have

$$(g \circ f)(2) = g(f(2)) = g(4) = 4^2 + 2(4) = 24.$$

So $(g \circ f)(2) = 24$.

d) Because $(f \circ g)(2) = f(g(2))$, we first find $g(2)$:

$$g(2) = 2^2 + 2(2) = 8.$$

Because $g(2) = 8$, we have

$$(f \circ g)(2) = f(g(2)) = f(8) = 3(8) - 2 = 22.$$

So $(f \circ g)(2) = 22.$ ∎

In Example 4 we found specific values of compositions of two functions. In Example 5 we find a general formula for the two functions from Example 4.

E X A M P L E   5

Finding formulas for compositions

Let $f(x) = 3x - 2$ and $g(x) = x^2 + 2x$. Find the following.

a) $(g \circ f)(x)$

b) $(f \circ g)(x)$

Solution

a) Since $f(x) = 3x - 2$ we replace $f(x)$ with $3x - 2$:

$$\begin{aligned}
(g \circ f)(x) &= g(f(x)) \\
&= g(3x - 2) \\
&= (3x - 2)^2 + 2(3x - 2) \\
&= 9x^2 - 12x + 4 + 6x - 4 \\
&= 9x^2 - 6x
\end{aligned}$$

So $(g \circ f)(x) = 9x^2 - 6x$.

b) Since $g(x) = x^2 + 2x$ we replace $g(x)$ with $x^2 + 2x$:

$$\begin{aligned}
(f \circ g)(x) &= f(g(x)) \\
&= f(x^2 + 2x) \\
&= 3(x^2 + 2x) - 2 \\
&= 3x^2 + 6x - 2
\end{aligned}$$

So $(f \circ g)(x) = 3x^2 + 6x - 2.$ ∎

Helpful Hint

A composition of functions can be viewed as two function machines where the output of the first is the input of the second.

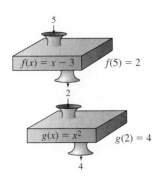

Notice that in Example 4(c) and (d), $(g \circ f)(2) \neq (f \circ g)(2)$. In Example 5(a) and (b) we see that $(g \circ f)(x)$ and $(f \circ g)(x)$ have different formulas defining them. In general, $f \circ g \neq g \circ f$. However, in Section 9.4 we will see some functions for which the composition in either order results in the same function.

It is often useful to view a complicated function as a composition of simpler functions. For example, the function $Q(x) = (x - 3)^2$ consists of two operations, subtracting 3 and squaring. So Q can be described as a composition of the functions $f(x) = x - 3$ and $g(x) = x^2$. To check this, we find $(g \circ f)(x)$:

$$\begin{aligned}
(g \circ f)(x) &= g(f(x)) \\
&= g(x - 3) \\
&= (x - 3)^2
\end{aligned}$$

We can express the fact that Q is the same as the composition function $g \circ f$ by writing $Q = g \circ f$ or $Q(x) = (g \circ f)(x)$.

E X A M P L E   6

Expressing a function as a composition of simpler functions

Let $f(x) = x - 2$, $g(x) = 3x$, and $h(x) = \sqrt{x}$. Write each of the following functions as a composition, using f, g, and h.

a) $F(x) = \sqrt{x - 2}$

b) $H(x) = x - 4$

c) $K(x) = 3x - 6$

Study Tip

Solution

a) The function F consists of first subtracting 2 from x and then taking the square root of that result. So $F = h \circ f$. Check this result by finding $(h \circ f)(x)$:

$$(h \circ f)(x) = h(f(x)) = h(x - 2) = \sqrt{x - 2}$$

b) Subtracting 4 from x can be accomplished by subtracting 2 from x and then subtracting 2 from that result. So $H = f \circ f$. Check by finding $(f \circ f)(x)$:

$$(f \circ f)(x) = f(f(x)) = f(x - 2) = x - 2 - 2 = x - 4$$

c) Notice that $K(x) = 3(x - 2)$. The function K consists of subtracting 2 from x and then multiplying the result by 3. So $K = g \circ f$. Check by finding $(g \circ f)(x)$:

$$(g \circ f)(x) = g(f(x)) = g(x - 2) = 3(x - 2) = 3x - 6$$ ■

> **C A U T I O N**   In Example 6(a) we have $F = h \circ f$ because in F we subtract 2 before taking the square root. If we had the function $G(x) = \sqrt{x} - 2$, we would take the square root before subtracting 2. So $G = f \circ h$. Notice how important the order of operations is here.

In Example 7 we see functions for which the composition is the identity function. Each function undoes what the other function does. We will study functions of this type further in Section 9.4.

E X A M P L E   7

Composition of functions

Show that $(f \circ g)(x) = x$ for each pair of functions.

a) $f(x) = 2x - 1$ and $g(x) = \dfrac{x + 1}{2}$

b) $f(x) = x^3 + 5$ and $g(x) = (x - 5)^{1/3}$

Solution

a) $(f \circ g)(x) = f(g(x)) = f\left(\dfrac{x + 1}{2}\right)$

$$= 2\left(\dfrac{x + 1}{2}\right) - 1$$

$$= x + 1 - 1$$

$$= x$$

b) $(f \circ g)(x) = f(g(x)) = f((x - 5)^{1/3})$

$$= ((x - 5)^{1/3})^3 + 5$$

$$= x - 5 + 5$$

$$= x$$ ■

WARM-UPS

True or false? Explain your answer.

1. If $f(x) = x - 2$ and $g(x) = x + 3$, then $(f - g)(x) = -5$.
2. If $f(x) = x + 4$ and $g(x) = 3x$, then $\left(\dfrac{f}{g}\right)(2) = 1$.
3. The functions $f \circ g$ and $g \circ f$ are always the same.
4. If $f(x) = x^2$ and $g(x) = x + 2$, then $(f \circ g)(x) = x^2 + 2$.
5. The functions $f \circ g$ and $f \cdot g$ are always the same.
6. If $f(x) = \sqrt{x}$ and $g(x) = x - 9$, then $g(f(x)) = f(g(x))$ for every x.
7. If $f(x) = 3x$ and $g(x) = \frac{x}{3}$, then $(f \circ g)(x) = x$.
8. If $a = 3b^2 - 7b$, and $c = a^2 + 3a$, then c is a function of b.
9. The function $F(x) = \sqrt{x - 5}$ is a composition of two functions.
10. If $F(x) = (x - 1)^2$, $h(x) = x - 1$, and $g(x) = x^2$, then $F = g \circ h$.

9.3   EXERCISES

Reading and Writing   *After reading this section, write out the answers to these questions. Use complete sentences.*

1. What are the basic operations with functions?

2. How do we perform the basic operations with functions?

3. What is the composition of two functions?

4. How is the order of operations related to composition of functions?

Let $f(x) = 4x - 3$, and $g(x) = x^2 - 2x$. Find the following. See Examples 1 and 2.

5. $(f + g)(x)$
6. $(f - g)(x)$

7. $(f \cdot g)(x)$
8. $\left(\dfrac{f}{g}\right)(x)$

9. $(f + g)(3)$
10. $(f + g)(2)$
11. $(f - g)(-3)$
12. $(f - g)(-2)$
13. $(f \cdot g)(-1)$
14. $(f \cdot g)(-2)$
15. $\left(\dfrac{f}{g}\right)(4)$
16. $\left(\dfrac{f}{g}\right)(-2)$

For Exercises 17–24, use the two functions to write y as a function of x. See Example 3.

17. $y = 3a - 2$, $a = 2x - 6$
18. $y = 2c + 3$, $c = -3x + 4$
19. $y = 2d + 1$, $d = \dfrac{x + 1}{2}$
20. $y = -3d + 2$, $d = \dfrac{2 - x}{3}$
21. $y = m^2 - 1$, $m = x + 1$
22. $y = n^2 - 3n + 1$, $n = x + 2$
23. $y = \dfrac{a - 3}{a + 2}$, $a = \dfrac{2x + 3}{1 - x}$
24. $y = \dfrac{w + 2}{w - 5}$, $w = \dfrac{5x + 2}{x - 1}$

Let $f(x) = 2x - 3$, $g(x) = x^2 + 3x$, and $h(x) = \frac{x + 3}{2}$. Find the following. See Examples 4 and 5.

25. $(g \circ f)(1)$
26. $(f \circ g)(-2)$
27. $(f \circ g)(1)$
28. $(g \circ f)(-2)$
29. $(f \circ f)(4)$
30. $(h \circ h)(3)$
31. $(h \circ f)(5)$
32. $(f \circ h)(0)$
33. $(f \circ h)(5)$
34. $(h \circ f)(0)$
35. $(g \circ h)(-1)$
36. $(h \circ g)(-1)$
37. $(f \circ g)(2.36)$
38. $(h \circ f)(23.761)$
39. $(g \circ f)(x)$
40. $(g \circ h)(x)$

41. $(f \circ g)(x)$ **42.** $(h \circ g)(x)$

43. $(h \circ f)(x)$ **44.** $(f \circ h)(x)$

45. $(f \circ f)(x)$ **46.** $(g \circ g)(x)$

47. $(h \circ h)(x)$ **48.** $(f \circ f \circ f)(x)$

Let $f(x) = \sqrt{x}$, $g(x) = x^2$, and $h(x) = x - 3$. Write each of the following functions as a composition using f, g, or h. See Example 6.

49. $F(x) = \sqrt{x - 3}$ **50.** $N(x) = \sqrt{x} - 3$

51. $G(x) = x^2 - 6x + 9$ **52.** $P(x) = x$ for $x \geq 0$

53. $H(x) = x^2 - 3$ **54.** $M(x) = x^{1/4}$

55. $J(x) = x - 6$ **56.** $R(x) = \sqrt{x^2 - 3}$

57. $K(x) = x^4$ **58.** $Q(x) = \sqrt{x^2 - 6x + 9}$

Show that $(f \circ g)(x) = x$ and $(g \circ f)(x) = x$ for each given pair of functions. See Example 7.

59. $f(x) = 3x + 5$, $g(x) = \dfrac{x - 5}{3}$

60. $f(x) = 3x - 7$, $g(x) = \dfrac{x + 7}{3}$

61. $f(x) = x^3 - 9$, $g(x) = \sqrt[3]{x + 9}$

62. $f(x) = x^3 + 1$, $g(x) = \sqrt[3]{x - 1}$

63. $f(x) = \dfrac{x - 1}{x + 1}$, $g(x) = \dfrac{x + 1}{1 - x}$

64. $f(x) = \dfrac{x + 1}{x - 3}$, $g(x) = \dfrac{3x + 1}{x - 1}$

65. $f(x) = \dfrac{1}{x}$, $g(x) = \dfrac{1}{x}$

66. $f(x) = 2x^3$, $g(x) = \left(\dfrac{x}{2}\right)^{1/3}$

Solve each problem.

67. *Area.* A square gate in a wood fence has a diagonal brace with a length of 10 feet.

  a) Find the area of the square gate.

  b) Write a formula for the area of a square as a function of the length of its diagonal.

68. *Perimeter.* Write a formula for the perimeter of a square as a function of its area.

69. *Profit function.* A plastic bag manufacturer has determined that the company can sell as many bags as it can produce each month. If it produces x thousand bags in a month, the revenue is $R(x) = x^2 - 10x + 30$ dollars, and the cost is $C(x) = 2x^2 - 30x + 200$ dollars. Use the fact that profit is revenue minus cost to write the profit as a function of x.

70. *Area of a sign.* A sign is in the shape of a square with a semicircle of radius x adjoining one side and a semicircle of diameter x removed from the opposite side. If the sides of the square are length $2x$, then write the area of the sign as a function of x.

FIGURE FOR EXERCISE 70

71. *Junk food expenditures.* Suppose the average family spends 25% of its income on food, $F = 0.25I$, and 10% of each food dollar on junk food, $J = 0.10F$. Write J as a function of I.

72. *Area of an inscribed circle.* A pipe of radius r must pass through a square hole of area M as shown in the figure. Write the cross-sectional area of the pipe A as a function of M.

FIGURE FOR EXERCISE 72

73. *Displacement-length ratio.* To find the displacement-length ratio D for a sailboat, first find x, where $x = (L/100)^3$ and L is the length at the water line in feet (www.sailing.com). Next find D, where $D = (d/2240)/x$ and d is the displacement in pounds.

  a) For the Pacific Seacraft 40, $L = 30$ ft 3 in. and $d = 24{,}665$ pounds. Find D.

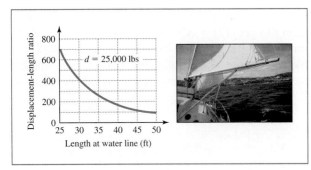

FIGURE FOR EXERCISE 73

b) For a boat with a displacement of 25,000 pounds, write D as a function of L.

c) The graph for the function in part (b) is shown in the accompanying figure. For a fixed displacement, does the displacement-length ratio increase or decrease as the length increases?

74. Sail area-displacement ratio. To find the sail area-displacement ratio S, first find y, where $y = (d/64)^{2/3}$ and d is the displacement in pounds. Next find S, where $S = A/y$ and A is the sail area in square feet.

a) For the Pacific Seacraft 40, $A = 846$ square feet (ft^2) and $d = 24{,}665$ pounds. Find S.

b) For a boat with a sail area of 900 ft^2, write S as a function of d.

c) For a fixed sail area, does S increase or decrease as the displacement increases?

GETTING MORE INVOLVED

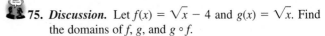

75. Discussion. Let $f(x) = \sqrt{x} - 4$ and $g(x) = \sqrt{x}$. Find the domains of f, g, and $g \circ f$.

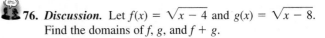

76. Discussion. Let $f(x) = \sqrt{x - 4}$ and $g(x) = \sqrt{x - 8}$. Find the domains of f, g, and $f + g$.

GRAPHING CALCULATOR EXERCISES

77. Graph $y_1 = x$, $y_2 = \sqrt{x}$, and $y_3 = x + \sqrt{x}$ in the same screen. Find the domain and range of $y_3 = x + \sqrt{x}$ by examining its graph. (On some graphing calculators you can enter y_3 as $y_3 = y_1 + y_2$.)

78. Graph $y_1 = |x|$, $y_2 = |x - 3|$, and $y_3 = |x| + |x - 3|$. Find the domain and range of $y_3 = |x| + |x - 3|$ by examining its graph.

9.4 INVERSE FUNCTIONS

In Section 9.3 we introduced the idea of a pair of functions such that $(f \circ g)(x) = x$ and $(g \circ f)(x) = x$. Each function reverses what the other function does. In this section we explore that idea further.

Inverse of a Function

You can buy a 6-, 7-, or 8-foot conference table in the K-LOG Catalog for $299, $329, or $349, respectively. The set

$$f = \{(6, 299), (7, 329), (8, 349)\}$$

gives the price as a function of the length. We use the letter f as a name for this set or function, just as we use the letter f as a name for a function in the function notation. In the function f, lengths in the domain $\{6, 7, 8\}$ are paired with prices in the range $\{299, 329, 349\}$. The **inverse** of the function f, denoted f^{-1}, is a function whose ordered pairs are obtained from f by interchanging the x- and y-coordinates:

$$f^{-1} = \{(299, 6), (329, 7), (349, 8)\}$$

We read f^{-1} as "f inverse." The domain of f^{-1} is $\{299, 329, 349\}$, and the range of f^{-1} is $\{6, 7, 8\}$. The inverse function reverses what the function does: it pairs prices

In This Section

- Inverse of a Function
- Identifying Inverse Functions
- Switch-and-Solve Strategy
- Even Roots or Even Powers
- Graphs of f and f^{-1}

in the range of f with lengths in the domain of f. For example, to find the cost of a 7-foot table, we use the function f to get $f(7) = 329$. To find the length of a table, that costs $349, we use the function f^{-1} to get $f^{-1}(349) = 8$. Of course, we could find the length of a $349 table by looking at the function f, but f^{-1} is a function whose input is price and whose output is length. In general, *the domain of f^{-1} is the range of f, and the range of f^{-1} is the domain of f.* See Fig. 9.25.

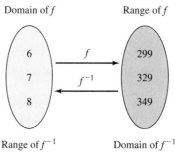

FIGURE 9.25

CAUTION The -1 in f^{-1} is not read as an exponent. It does not mean $\frac{1}{f}$.

The cost per ribbon for Apple Imagewriter ribbons is a function of the number of boxes purchased:

$$g = \{(1, 4.85), (2, 4.60), (3, 4.60), (4, 4.35)\}$$

If we interchange the first and second coordinates in the ordered pairs of this function, we get

$$\{(4.85, 1), (4.60, 2), (4.60, 3), (4.35, 4)\}.$$

This set of ordered pairs is not a function because it contains ordered pairs with the same first coordinates and different second coordinates. So g does not have an inverse function. A function is **invertible** if you obtain a function when the coordinates of all ordered pairs are reversed. So f is invertible and g is not invertible. The function g is not invertible because the definition of function allows more than one number of the domain to be paired with the same number in the range. Of course, when this pairing is reversed, the definition of function is violated.

One-to-One Function

If a function is such that no two ordered pairs have different x-coordinates and the same y-coordinate, then the function is called a **one-to-one** function.

In a one-to-one function each member of the domain corresponds to just one member of the range, and each member of the range corresponds to just one member of the domain. *Functions that are one-to-one are invertible functions.*

Inverse Function

The inverse of a one-to-one function f is the function f^{-1}, which is obtained from f by interchanging the coordinates in each ordered pair of f.

Helpful Hint

Consider the universal product codes (UPC) and the prices for all of the items in your favorite grocery store. The price of an item is a function of the UPC because every UPC determines a price. This function is not invertible because you cannot determine the UPC from a given price.

E X A M P L E   1

Identifying invertible functions

Determine whether each function is invertible. If it is invertible, then find the inverse function.

a) $f = \{(2, 4), (-2, 4), (3, 9)\}$

b) $g = \left\{\left(2, \dfrac{1}{2}\right), \left(5, \dfrac{1}{5}\right), \left(7, \dfrac{1}{7}\right)\right\}$

c) $h = \{(3, 5), (7, 9)\}$

Solution

a) Since (2, 4) and (−2, 4) have the same y-coordinate, this function is not one-to-one, and it is not invertible.

b) This function is one-to-one, and so it is invertible.

$$g^{-1} = \left\{\left(\dfrac{1}{2}, 2\right), \left(\dfrac{1}{5}, 5\right), \left(\dfrac{1}{7}, 7\right)\right\}$$

c) This function is invertible, and $h^{-1} = \{(5, 3), (9, 7)\}$. ■

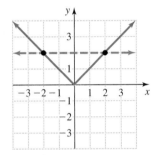

FIGURE 9.26

You learned to use the vertical-line test in Section 3.5 to determine whether a graph is the graph of a function. The **horizontal-line test** is a similar visual test for determining whether a function is invertible. If a horizontal line crosses a graph two (or more) times, as in Fig. 9.26, then there are two points on the graph, say (x_1, y) and (x_2, y), that have different x-coordinates and the same y-coordinate. So the function is not one-to-one, and the function is not invertible.

> **Horizontal-Line Test**
>
> A function is invertible if and only if no horizontal line crosses its graph more than once.

E X A M P L E   2

Using the horizontal-line test

Determine whether each function is invertible by examining its graph.

a)

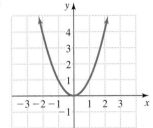

b)

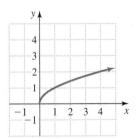

Solution

a) This function is not invertible because a horizontal line can be drawn so that it crosses the graph at (2, 4) and (−2, 4).

b) This function is invertible because every horizontal line that crosses the graph crosses it only once. ■

Identifying Inverse Functions

Consider the one-to-one function $f(x) = 3x$. The inverse function must reverse the ordered pairs of the function. Because division by 3 undoes multiplication by 3, we could guess that $g(x) = \frac{x}{3}$ is the inverse function. To verify our guess, we can use the following rule for determining whether two given functions are inverses of each other.

Identifying Inverse Functions

Functions f and g are inverses of each other if and only if

$(g \circ f)(x) = x$ for every number x in the domain of f and

$(f \circ g)(x) = x$ for every number x in the domain of g.

In the next example we verify that $f(x) = 3x$ and $g(x) = \frac{x}{3}$ are inverses.

E X A M P L E   3   **Identifying inverse functions**

Determine whether the functions f and g are inverses of each other.

a) $f(x) = 3x$ and $g(x) = \dfrac{x}{3}$

b) $f(x) = 2x - 1$ and $g(x) = \dfrac{1}{2}x + 1$

c) $f(x) = x^2$ and $g(x) = \sqrt{x}$

Study Tip

Personal issues can have a tremendous effect on your progress in any course. So do not hesitate to deal with personal problems. If you need help, get it. Most schools have counseling centers that can help you to overcome personal issues that are affecting your studies.

Solution

a) Find $g \circ f$ and $f \circ g$:

$$(g \circ f)(x) = g(f(x)) = g(3x) = \frac{3x}{3} = x$$

$$(f \circ g)(x) = f(g(x)) = f\left(\frac{x}{3}\right) = 3 \cdot \frac{x}{3} = x$$

Because each of these equations is true for any real number x, f and g are inverses of each other. We write $g = f^{-1}$ or $f^{-1}(x) = \frac{x}{3}$.

b) Find the composition of g and f:

$$(g \circ f)(x) = g(f(x))$$

$$= g(2x - 1) = \frac{1}{2}(2x - 1) + 1 = x + \frac{1}{2}$$

So f and g are not inverses of each other.

c) If x is any real number, we can write

$$(g \circ f)(x) = g(f(x))$$

$$= g(x^2) = \sqrt{x^2} = |x|.$$

The domain of f is $(-\infty, \infty)$, and $|x| \neq x$ if x is negative. So g and f are not inverses of each other. Note that $f(x) = x^2$ is not a one-to-one function, since both $(3, 9)$ and $(-3, 9)$ are ordered pairs of this function. Thus $f(x) = x^2$ does not have an inverse. ∎

Switch-and-Solve Strategy

If an invertible function is defined by a list of ordered pairs, as in Example 1, then the inverse function is found by simply interchanging the coordinates in the ordered pairs. If an invertible function is defined by a formula, then the inverse function must reverse or undo what the function does. Because the inverse function interchanges the roles of x and y, we interchange x and y in the formula and then solve the new formula for y to undo what the original function did. This **switch-and-solve** strategy is illustrated in Examples 4 and 5.

EXAMPLE 4

The switch-and-solve strategy

Find the inverse of $h(x) = 2x + 1$.

Solution

First write the function as $y = 2x + 1$, then interchange x and y:

$$y = 2x + 1$$
$$x = 2y + 1 \quad \text{Interchange } x \text{ and } y.$$
$$x - 1 = 2y \quad \text{Solve for } y.$$
$$\frac{x - 1}{2} = y$$
$$h^{-1}(x) = \frac{x - 1}{2} \quad \text{Replace } y \text{ by } h^{-1}(x).$$

We can verify that h and h^{-1} are inverses by using composition:

$$(h^{-1} \circ h)(x) = h^{-1}(h(x)) = h^{-1}(2x + 1) = \frac{2x + 1 - 1}{2} = \frac{2x}{2} = x$$

$$(h \circ h^{-1})(x) = h(h^{-1}(x)) = h\left(\frac{x - 1}{2}\right) = 2 \cdot \frac{x - 1}{2} + 1 = x - 1 + 1 = x \quad ■$$

EXAMPLE 5

The switch-and-solve strategy

If $f(x) = \dfrac{x + 1}{x - 3}$, find $f^{-1}(x)$.

Solution

Replace $f(x)$ by y, interchange x and y, then solve for y:

$$y = \frac{x + 1}{x - 3} \quad \text{Use } y \text{ in place of } f(x).$$
$$x = \frac{y + 1}{y - 3} \quad \text{Switch } x \text{ and } y.$$
$$x(y - 3) = y + 1 \quad \text{Multiply each side by } y - 3.$$
$$xy - 3x = y + 1 \quad \text{Distributive property}$$
$$xy - y = 3x + 1$$
$$y(x - 1) = 3x + 1 \quad \text{Factor out } y.$$
$$y = \frac{3x + 1}{x - 1} \quad \text{Divide each side by } x - 1.$$
$$f^{-1}(x) = \frac{3x + 1}{x - 1} \quad \text{Replace } y \text{ by } f^{-1}(x).$$

You should check that $(f \circ f^{-1})(x) = x$ and $(f^{-1} \circ f)(x) = x$. ■

The strategy for finding the inverse of a function $f(x)$ is summarized as follows.

Switch-and-Solve Strategy for Finding f^{-1}

1. Replace $f(x)$ by y.
2. Interchange x and y.
3. Solve the equation for y.
4. Replace y by $f^{-1}(x)$.

If we use the switch-and-solve strategy to find the inverse of $f(x) = x^3$, then we get $f^{-1}(x) = x^{1/3}$. For $h(x) = 6x$ we have $h^{-1}(x) = \frac{x}{6}$. The inverse of $k(x) = x - 9$ is $k^{-1}(x) = x + 9$. For each of these functions there is an appropriate operation of arithmetic that undoes what the function does.

If a function involves two operations, the inverse function undoes those operations in the opposite order from which the function does them. For example, the function $g(x) = 3x - 5$ multiplies x by 3 and then subtracts 5 from that result. To undo these operations, we add 5 and then divide the result by 3. So

$$g^{-1}(x) = \frac{x + 5}{3}.$$

Note that $g^{-1}(x) \neq \frac{x}{3} + 5$.

Even Roots or Even Powers

We need to use special care in finding inverses for functions that involve even roots or even powers. We saw in Example 3(c) that $f(x) = x^2$ is not the inverse of $g(x) = \sqrt{x}$. However, because $g(x) = \sqrt{x}$ is a one-to-one function, it has an inverse. The domain of g is $[0, \infty)$, and the range is $[0, \infty)$. So the inverse of g must have domain $[0, \infty)$ and range $[0, \infty)$. See Fig. 9.27. The only reason that $f(x) = x^2$ is not the inverse of g is that it has the wrong domain. So to write the inverse function, we must use the appropriate domain:

$$g^{-1}(x) = x^2 \qquad \text{for} \quad x \geq 0$$

Note that by restricting the domain of g^{-1} to $[0, \infty)$, g^{-1} is one-to-one. With this restriction it is true that $(g \circ g^{-1})(x) = x$ and $(g^{-1} \circ g)(x) = x$ for every nonnegative number x.

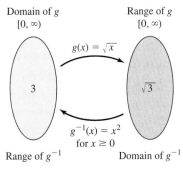

FIGURE 9.27

When a serious automobile accident occurs in Massachusetts, Stephen Benanti, the Commanding Officer of the Accident Reconstruction Section of the State Police, may be called to examine the physical evidence at the scene. Physical evidence can consist of debris, scrapes, and gouges on the road; damage to fixed objects such as utility poles, trees, or guardrails; and the final resting position of and damage to the vehicles.

STATE POLICE OFFICER

One critical type of evidence that is sometimes found are skid marks on the road. Sergeant Benanti can use the lengths of the skid marks to calculate the speeds of accident vehicles. Using a sophisticated laser measuring device, Benanti can store data that later can be downloaded into a computer to reconstruct the accident scene. He must also conduct tests on the road surface to calculate the drag factor, which is the resistance between the tire and the road surface. A smooth, icy surface yields a much lower drag factor than a dry asphalt surface. The minimum speed formula that state troopers use to determine vehicles' speeds is a function of the drag factor and the skid distance: $S = \sqrt{30DF}$, where S = speed, D = distance skidded, and F = drag factor.

In Exercise 73 of this section you will use this minimum speed formula with a given length of skid marks to determine the speed of a vehicle.

EXAMPLE 6   Inverse of a function with an even exponent

Find the inverse of the function $f(x) = (x - 3)^2$ for $x \geq 3$.

Solution

Because of the restriction $x \geq 3$, f is a one-to-one function with domain $[3, \infty)$ and range $[0, \infty)$. The domain of the inverse function is $[0, \infty)$, and its range is $[3, \infty)$. Use the switch-and-solve strategy to find the formula for the inverse:

$$y = (x - 3)^2$$
$$x = (y - 3)^2$$
$$y - 3 = \pm\sqrt{x}$$
$$y = 3 \pm \sqrt{x}$$

Because the inverse function must have range $[3, \infty)$, we use the formula $f^{-1}(x) = 3 + \sqrt{x}$. Because the domain of f^{-1} is assumed to be $[0, \infty)$, no restriction is required on x.   ■

Graphs of f and f^{-1}

Consider $f(x) = x^2$ for $x \geq 0$ and $f^{-1}(x) = \sqrt{x}$. Their graphs are shown in Fig. 9.28. Notice the symmetry. If we folded the paper along the line $y = x$, the two graphs would coincide.

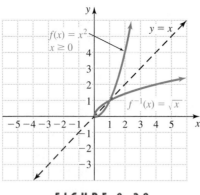

FIGURE 9.28

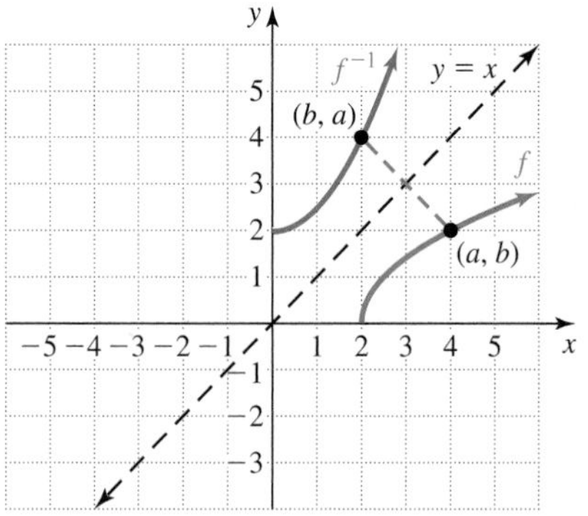

FIGURE 9.29

If a point (a, b) is on the graph of the function f, then (b, a) must be on the graph of $f^{-1}(x)$. See Fig. 9.29. The points (a, b) and (b, a) lie on opposite sides of the diagonal line $y = x$ and are the same distance from it. For this reason the graphs of f and f^{-1} are symmetric with respect to the line $y = x$.

EXAMPLE 7   Inverses and their graphs

Find the inverse of the function $f(x) = \sqrt{x - 1}$ and graph f and f^{-1} on the same pair of axes.

Solution

To find f^{-1}, first switch x and y in the formula $y = \sqrt{x - 1}$:

$$x = \sqrt{y - 1}$$

$$x^2 = y - 1 \qquad \text{Square both sides.}$$

$$x^2 + 1 = y$$

Because the range of f is the set of nonnegative real numbers $[0, \infty)$, we must restrict the domain of f^{-1} to be $[0, \infty)$. Thus $f^{-1}(x) = x^2 + 1$ for $x \geq 0$. The two graphs are shown in Fig. 9.30.

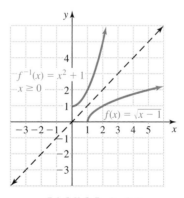

FIGURE 9.30

WARM-UPS

True or false? Explain your answer.

1. The inverse of $\{(1, 3), (2, 5)\}$ is $\{(3, 1), (2, 5)\}$.
2. The function $f(x) = 3$ is a one-to-one function.
3. If $g(x) = 2x$, then $g^{-1}(x) = \dfrac{1}{2x}$.
4. Only one-to-one functions are invertible.
5. The domain of g is the same as the range of g^{-1}.
6. The function $f(x) = x^4$ is invertible.
7. If $f(x) = -x$, then $f^{-1}(x) = -x$.
8. If h is invertible and $h(7) = -95$, then $h^{-1}(-95) = 7$.
9. If $k(x) = 3x - 6$, then $k^{-1}(x) = \frac{1}{3}x + 2$.
10. If $f(x) = 3x - 4$, then $f^{-1}(x) = x + 4$.

9.4 EXERCISES

Reading and Writing *After reading this section, write out the answers to these questions. Use complete sentences.*

1. What is the inverse of a function?

2. What is the domain of f^{-1}?

3. What is the range of f^{-1}?

4. What does the -1 in f^{-1} mean?

5. What is a one-to-one function?

6. What is the horizontal-line test?

7. What is the switch-and-solve strategy?

8. How are the graphs of f and f^{-1} related?

Determine whether each function is invertible. If it is invertible, then find the inverse. See Example 1.

9. $\{(-3, 3), (-2, 2), (0, 0), (2, 2)\}$
10. $\{(1, 1), (2, 8), (3, 27)\}$
11. $\{(16, 4), (9, 3), (0, 0)\}$
12. $\{(-1, 1), (-3, 81), (3, 81)\}$
13. $\{(0, 5), (5, 0), (6, 0)\}$
14. $\{(3, -3), (-2, 2), (1, -1)\}$
15. $\{(0, 0), (2, 2), (9, 9)\}$
16. $\{(9, 1), (2, 1), (7, 1), (0, 1)\}$

Determine whether each function is invertible by examining the graph of the function. See Example 2.

17.

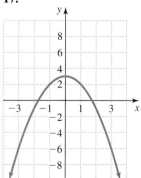

18.

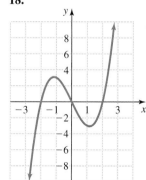

Solve each problem.

73. Accident reconstruction. The distance that it takes a car to stop is a function of the speed and the drag factor. The drag factor is a measure of the resistance between the tire and the road surface. The formula $S = \sqrt{30LD}$ is used to determine the minimum speed S [in miles per hour (mph)] for a car that has left skid marks of length L feet (ft) on a surface with drag factor D.

a) Find the minimum speed for a car that has left skid marks of length 50 ft where the drag factor is 0.75.

b) Does the drag factor increase or decrease for a road surface when it gets wet?

c) Write L as a function of S for a road surface with drag factor 1 and graph the function.

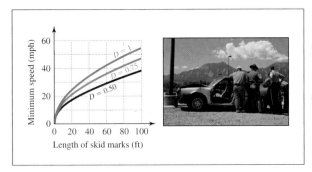

FIGURE FOR EXERCISE 73

74. Area of a circle. Let x be the radius of a circle and $h(x)$ be the area of the circle. Write a formula for $h(x)$ in terms of x. What does x represent in the notation $h^{-1}(x)$? Write a formula for $h^{-1}(x)$.

75. Vehicle cost. At Bill Hood Ford in Hammond a sales tax of 9% of the selling price x and a $125 title and license fee are added to the selling price to get the total cost of a vehicle. Find the function $T(x)$ that the dealer uses to get the total cost as a function of the selling

price x. Citizens National Bank will not include sales tax or fees in a loan. Find the function $T^{-1}(x)$ that the bank can use to get the selling price as a function of the total cost x.

76. Carpeting cost. At the Windrush Trace apartment complex all living rooms are square, but the length of x feet may vary. The cost of carpeting a living room is $18 per square yard plus a $50 installation fee. Find the function $C(x)$ that gives the total cost of carpeting a living room of length x. The manager has an invoice for the total cost of a living room carpeting job but does not know in which apartment it was done. Find the function $C^{-1}(x)$ that gives the length of a living room as a function of the total cost of the carpeting job x.

GETTING MORE INVOLVED

77. Discussion. Let $f(x) = x^n$ for n a positive integer. For which values of n is f an invertible function? Explain.

78. Discussion. Suppose f is a function with range $(-\infty, \infty)$ and g is a function with domain $(0, \infty)$. Is it possible that g and f are inverse functions? Explain.

GRAPHING CALCULATOR EXERCISES

79. Most graphing calculators can form compositions of functions. Let $f(x) = x^2$ and $g(x) = \sqrt{x}$. To graph the composition $g \circ f$, let $y_1 = x^2$ and $y_2 = \sqrt{y_1}$. The graph of y_2 is the graph of $g \circ f$. Use the graph of y_2 to determine whether f and g are inverse functions.

80. Let $y_1 = x^3 - 4$, $y_2 = \sqrt[3]{x + 4}$, and $y_3 = \sqrt[3]{y_1 + 4}$. The function y_3 is the composition of the first two functions. Graph all three functions on the same screen. What do the graphs indicate about the relationship between y_1 and y_2?

In This Section

- Direct Variation
- Finding the Proportionality Constant
- Inverse Variation
- Joint Variation
- More Variation

9.5   VARIATION

If $y = 3x$, then as x varies so does y. Certain functions are customarily expressed in terms of variation. In this section you will learn to write formulas for those functions from verbal descriptions of the functions.

Direct Variation

In a community with an 8% sales tax rate, the amount of tax, t (in dollars), is a function of the amount of the purchase, a (in dollars). This function is expressed by the formula

$$t = 0.08a.$$

If the amount increases, then the tax increases. If a decreases, then t decreases. In this situation we say that t *varies directly with a, or t is directly proportional to a.* The constant tax rate, 0.08, is called the **variation constant** or **proportionality constant.** Notice that t is just a simple linear function of a. We are merely introducing some new terms to express an old idea.

> ### Direct Variation
>
> The statement y **varies directly as** x**,** or y **is directly proportional to** x**,** means that
>
> $$y = kx$$
>
> for some constant, k. The constant, k, is a fixed nonzero real number.

Finding the Proportionality Constant

If y varies directly as x and we know corresponding values for x and y, then we can find the proportionality constant.

E X A M P L E   1   **Finding the proportionality constant**

Joyce is traveling by car, and the distance she travels, d, varies directly with the amount of time, t, that she drives. In 3 hours she drove 120 miles. Find the proportionality constant and write d as a function of t.

Solution

Because d varies directly as t, we must have a constant k such that

$$d = kt.$$

Because $d = 120$ when $t = 3$, we can write

$$120 = k \cdot 3,$$

or

$$40 = k.$$

So the proportionality constant is 40 mph, and $d = 40t$.   ■

Calculator Close-Up

The graph of $d = 40t$ is a straight line through the origin.

E X A M P L E   2   **Direct variation**

In a downtown office building the monthly rent for an office is directly proportional to the size of the office. If a 420-square-foot office rents for $1260 per month, then what is the rent for a 900-square-foot office?

Solution

Because the rent, R, varies directly with the area of the office, A, we have

$$R = kA.$$

Because a 420-square-foot office rents for $1260, we can substitute to find k:

$$1260 = k \cdot 420$$

$$3 = k$$

E X A M P L E   5

An application of joint variation

The labor cost for installing ceramic floor tile varies jointly with the length and width of the room in which it is installed. If the labor cost for a 9 foot by 12 foot room is $324, then what is the labor cost for a 6 foot by 8 foot room?

Solution

Since the labor cost C varies jointly with the length L and width W we have $C = kLW$ for some constant k. Use $C = 324$, $L = 12$, and $W = 9$ in this formula to find k:

$$324 = k \cdot 12 \cdot 9$$
$$324 = 108k$$
$$k = \frac{324}{108} = 3$$

So the labor cost is $3 per square foot and the formula is $C = 3LW$. Now find C when $L = 8$ and $W = 6$:

$$C = 3LW$$
$$= 3 \cdot 8 \cdot 6 = 144$$

So the labor cost for a 6 foot by 8 foot room is $144. ■

More Variation

We frequently combine the ideas of direct, inverse, and joint variation with powers and roots. A combination of direct and inverse variation is referred to as **combined variation.** Study the examples that follow.

Helpful Hint

The language of variation is popular in science. Instead of saying $V = kT/P$, a chemist would say that the volume of a gas varies directly with the temperature and inversely with the pressure.

More Variation Examples

Statement	Formula
y varies directly as the square root of x.	$y = k\sqrt{x}$
y is directly proportional to the cube of x.	$y = kx^3$
y is inversely proportional to x^2.	$y = \dfrac{k}{x^2}$
y varies inversely as the square root of x.	$y = \dfrac{k}{\sqrt{x}}$
y varies jointly as x and the square of z.	$y = kxz^2$
y varies directly with x and inversely with the square root of z (combined variation).	$y = \dfrac{kx}{\sqrt{z}}$

C A U T I O N   The variation terms never signify addition or subtraction. We always use multiplication unless we see the word "inversely." In that case we divide.

E X A M P L E   6

Newton's law of gravity

According to Newton's law of gravity, the gravitational attraction F between two objects with masses m_1 and m_2 is directly proportional to the product of their masses and inversely proportional to the square of the distance r between their centers. Write a formula for Newton's law of gravity.

Solution

Letting k be the constant of proportionality, we have

$$F = \frac{km_1m_2}{r^2}.$$

■

E X A M P L E   7

House framing

The time t that it takes to frame a house varies directly with the size of the house s in square feet and inversely with the number of framers n working on the job. If three framers can complete a 2500-square-foot house in 6 days, then how long will it take six framers to complete a 4500-square-foot house?

Solution

Because t varies directly with s and inversely with n, we have

$$t = \frac{ks}{n}.$$

Substitute $t = 6$, $s = 2500$, and $n = 3$ into this equation to find k:

$$6 = \frac{k \cdot 2500}{3}$$

$$18 = 2500k$$

$$0.0072 = k$$

Now use $k = 0.0072$, $s = 4500$, and $n = 6$ to find t:

$$t = \frac{0.0072 \cdot 4500}{6}$$

$$t = 5.4$$

So six framers can frame a 4500-square-foot house in 5.4 days.

■

WARM-UPS

True or false? Explain your answer.

1. If a varies directly as b, then $a = kb$.
2. If a is inversely proportional to b, then $a = bk$.
3. If a is jointly proportional to b and c, then $a = bc$.
4. If a is directly proportional to the square root of c, then $a = k\sqrt{c}$.
5. If b is directly proportional to a, then $b = ka^2$.
6. If a varies directly as b and inversely as c, then $a = \frac{kb}{c}$.
7. If a is jointly proportional to c and the square of b, then $a = \frac{kc}{b^2}$.
8. If a varies directly as c and inversely as the square root of b, then $a = \frac{kc}{b}$.
9. If b varies directly as a and inversely as the square of c, then $b = ka\sqrt{c}$.
10. If b varies inversely with the square of c, then $b = \frac{k}{c^2}$.

Reading and Writing *After reading this section, write out the answers to these questions. Use complete sentences.*

1. What does it mean that y varies directly as x?

2. What is the constant of proportionality in a direct variation?

3. What does it mean that y is inversely proportional to x?

4. What is the difference between direct and inverse variation?

5. What does it mean that y is jointly proportional to x and z?

6. What is the difference between varies directly and directly proportional?

Write a formula that expresses the relationship described by each statement. Use k as a constant of variation. See Examples 1–7.

7. a varies directly as m.

8. w varies directly with P.

9. d varies inversely with e.

10. y varies inversely as x.

11. I varies jointly as r and t.

12. q varies jointly as w and v.

13. m is directly proportional to the square of p.

14. g is directly proportional to the cube of r.

15. B is directly proportional to the cube root of w.

16. F is directly proportional to the square of m.

17. t is inversely proportional to the square of x.

18. y is inversely proportional to the square root of z.

19. v varies directly as m and inversely as n.

20. b varies directly as the square of n and inversely as the square root of v.

Find the proportionality constant and write a formula that expresses the indicated variation. See Example 1.

21. y varies directly as x, and $y = 6$ when $x = 4$.

22. m varies directly as w, and $m = \frac{1}{3}$ when $w = \frac{1}{4}$.

23. A varies inversely as B, and $A = 10$ when $B = 3$.

24. c varies inversely as d, and $c = 0.31$ when $d = 2$.

25. m varies inversely as the square root of p, and $m = 12$ when $p = 9$.

26. s varies inversely as the square root of v, and $s = 6$ when $v = \frac{3}{2}$.

27. A varies jointly as t and u, and $A = 6$ when $t = 5$ and $u = 3$.

28. N varies jointly as the square of p and the cube of q, and $N = 72$ when $p = 3$ and $q = 2$.

29. y varies directly as x and inversely as z, and $y = 2.37$ when $x = \pi$ and $z = \sqrt{2}$.

30. a varies directly as the square root of m and inversely as the square of n, and $a = 5.47$ when $m = 3$ and $n = 1.625$.

Solve each variation problem. See Examples 2–7.

31. If y varies directly as x, and $y = 7$ when $x = 5$, find y when $x = -3$.

32. If n varies directly as p, and $n = 0.6$ when $p = 0.2$, find n when $p = \sqrt{2}$.

33. If w varies inversely as z, and $w = 6$ when $z = 2$, find w when $z = -8$.

34. If p varies inversely as q, and $p = 5$ when $q = \sqrt{3}$, find p when $q = 5$.

35. If A varies jointly as F and T, and $A = 6$ when $F = 3\sqrt{2}$ and $T = 4$, find A when $F = 2\sqrt{2}$ and $T = \frac{1}{2}$.

36. If j varies jointly as the square of r and the cube of v, and $j = -3$ when $r = 2\sqrt{3}$ and $v = \frac{1}{2}$, find j when $r = 3\sqrt{5}$ and $v = 2$.

37. If D varies directly with t and inversely with the square of s, and $D = 12.35$ when $t = 2.8$ and $s = 2.48$, find D when $t = 5.63$ and $s = 6.81$.

38. If M varies jointly with x and the square of v, and $M = 39.5$ when $x = \sqrt{10}$ and $v = 3.87$, find M when $x = \sqrt{30}$ and $v = 7.21$.

Determine whether each equation represents direct, inverse, joint, or combined variation.

39. $y = \dfrac{78}{x}$

40. $y = \dfrac{\pi}{x}$

41. $y = \dfrac{1}{2}x$

42. $y = \dfrac{x}{4}$

43. $y = \dfrac{3x}{w}$

44. $y = \dfrac{4t^2}{\sqrt{x}}$

45. $y = \dfrac{1}{3}xz$

46. $y = 99qv$

In Exercises 47–61, solve each problem.

47. *Lawn maintenance.* At Larry's Lawn Service the cost of lawn maintenance varies directly with the size of the lawn. If the monthly maintenance on a 4000-square-foot lawn is $280, then what is the maintenance fee for a 6000-square-foot lawn?

48. *Weight of the iguana.* The weight of an iguana is directly proportional to its length. If a 4-foot iguana weighs 30 pounds, then how much should a 5-foot iguana weigh?

49. *Gas laws.* The volume of a gas in a cylinder at a fixed temperature is inversely proportional to the weight on the piston. If the gas has a volume of 6 cubic centimeters (cm^3) for a weight of 30 kilograms (kg), then what would the volume be for a weight of 20 kg?

50. *Selling software.* A software vendor sells a software package at a price that is inversely proportional to the number of packages sold per month. When they are selling 900 packages per month, the price is $80 each. If they sell 1000 packages per month, then what should the new price be?

51. *Costly culvert.* The price of an aluminum culvert is jointly proportional to its radius and length. If a 12-foot culvert with a 6-inch radius costs $324, then what is the price of a 10-foot culvert with an 8-inch radius?

52. *Pricing plastic.* The cost of a piece of PVC water pipe varies jointly as its diameter and length. If a 20-foot pipe with a diameter of 1 inch costs $6.80, then what will be the cost of a 10-foot pipe with a $\frac{3}{4}$-inch diameter?

53. *Reinforcing rods.* The price of a steel rod varies jointly as the length and the square of the diameter. If an 18-foot rod with a 2-inch diameter costs $12.60, then what is the cost of a 12-foot rod with a 3-inch diameter?

54. *Pea soup.* The weight of a cylindrical can of pea soup varies jointly with the height and the square of the radius. If a 4-inch-high can with a 1.5-inch radius weighs 16 ounces, then what is the weight of a 5-inch-high can with a radius of 3 inches?

55. *Falling objects.* The distance an object falls in a vacuum varies directly with the square of the time it is falling. In the first 0.1 second after an object is dropped, it falls 0.16 feet.

   a) Find the formula that expresses the distance d an object falls as a function of the time it is falling t.

   b) How far does an object fall in the first 0.5 second after it is dropped?

   c) How long does it take for a watermelon to reach the ground when dropped from a height of 100 feet?

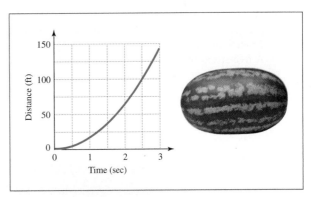

FIGURE FOR EXERCISE 55

56. *Making Frisbees.* The cost of material used in making a Frisbee varies directly with the square of the diameter. If it costs the manufacturer $0.45 for the material in a Frisbee with a 9-inch diameter, then what is the cost for the material in a 12-inch-diameter Frisbee?

57. *Using leverage.* The basic law of leverage is that the force required to lift an object is inversely proportional to the length of the lever. If a force of 2000 pounds applied 2 feet from the pivot point would lift a car, then what force would be required at 10 feet to lift the car?

58. *Resistance.* The resistance of a wire varies directly with the length and inversely as the square of the diameter. If a wire of length 20 feet and diameter 0.1 inch has a resistance of 2 ohms, then what is the resistance of a 30-foot wire with a diameter of 0.2 inch?

59. *Computer programming.* The time t required to complete a programming job varies directly with the complexity of the job and inversely with the number n of programmers working on the job. The complexity c is an arbitrarily assigned number between 1 and 10, with 10 being the most complex. It takes 8 days for a team of three programmers to complete a job with complexity 6. How long will it take five programmers to complete a job with complexity 9?

60. *Shock absorbers.* The volume of gas in a gas shock absorber varies directly with the temperature and inversely with the pressure. The volume is 10 cubic centimeters (cm^3) when the temperature is 20°C and the pressure is 40 kg. What is the volume when the temperature is 30°C and the pressure is 25 kg?

61. *Bicycle gear ratio.* A bicycle's gear ratio G varies jointly with the number of teeth on the chain ring N (by the pedals) and the diameter of the wheel d, and inversely with the number of teeth on the cog c (on the rear wheel). A bicycle with 27-inch-diameter wheels, 26 teeth on the cog, and 52 teeth on the chain ring has a gear ratio of 54.

   a) Find a formula that expresses the gear ratio as a function of N, d, and c.

   b) What is the gear ratio for a bicycle with 26-inch-diameter wheels, 42 teeth on the chain ring, and 13 teeth on the cog?

   c) A five-speed bicycle with 27-inch-diameter wheels and 44 teeth on the chain ring has gear ratios of 52, 59, 70, 79, and 91. Find the number of teeth on the cog for each gear ratio.

   d) For a fixed wheel size and chain ring, does the gear ratio increase or decrease as the number of teeth on the cog increases?

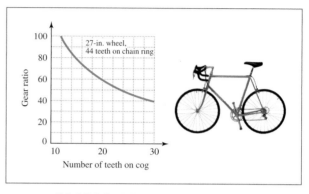

FIGURE FOR EXERCISE 61

 GRAPHING CALCULATOR EXERCISES

62. To see the difference between direct and inverse variation, graph $y_1 = 2x$ and $y_2 = \frac{2}{x}$ using $0 \le x \le 5$ and $0 \le y \le 10$. Which of these functions is increasing and which is decreasing?

63. Graph $y_1 = 2\sqrt{x}$ and $y_2 = \frac{2}{\sqrt{x}}$ by using $0 \le x \le 5$ and $0 \le y \le 10$. At what point in the first quadrant do the curves cross? Which function is increasing and which is decreasing? Which represents direct variation and which represents inverse variation?

COLLABORATIVE ACTIVITIES

Life's a Function of What?

Suppose that alertness is a function of the number of cups of coffee consumed. Let x (the independent variable) represent the number of cups of coffee consumed in a morning and y (the dependent variable) represent alertness (as a percent). Suppose an average coffee drinker drinks between 0 and 5 cups in a morning. Let's say that a person is 20% alert for 0 cups and 100% alert for 5 cups. Then the domain is the interval [0, 5] and the range is [0, 1].

If our function is linear, we need only two points to draw its graph. Plot the pairs (0, 0.2) and (5, 1), and draw a line through them.

Grouping: Three students per group

Topic: Functions, dependence, domain, and range

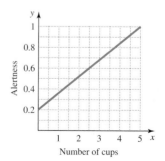

Find the slope of the line through $(5, 1)$ and $(0, 0.2)$:

$$m = \frac{1 - 0.2}{5 - 0} = \frac{0.8}{5} = 0.16$$

Using slope-intercept form the equation is $y = 0.16x + 0.2$. So the linear function that gives alertness in terms of cups of coffee is $f(x) = 0.16x + 0.2$.

In your groups do the following:

1. Decide on something in your life that could be modeled by a function of one variable.
2. Determine the domain and range of your function using interval notation.

3. Find two points that would make sense in your function. Graph a line through these points.
4. Find a linear equation for your graph. Write it in function notation.
5. Trade with a group near you and add, subtract, multiply, divide, and compose your functions. Discuss in your groups if these operations make sense for your functions. What would need to be true for composition to make sense? Write down the things your group discovers about operations on functions.
6. Assuming that your function is nonlinear, plot at least four points that you think would be in your function. Use the different regression programs on a graphing calculator to find the function that fits your data points the best.

W R A P - U P

CHAPTER 9

SUMMARY

Types of Functions		**Examples**
Linear function	$y = mx + b$ or $f(x) = mx + b$ for $m \neq 0$ Domain $(-\infty, \infty)$, range $(-\infty, \infty)$ If $m = 0$, $y = b$ is a constant function. Domain $(-\infty, \infty)$, range $\{b\}$	$f(x) = 2x - 3$
Absolute value function	$y = \lvert x \rvert$ or $f(x) = \lvert x \rvert$ Domain $(-\infty, \infty)$, range $[0, \infty)$	$f(x) = \lvert x + 5 \rvert$
Quadratic function	$f(x) = ax^2 + bx + c$ for $a \neq 0$	$f(x) = x^2 - 4x + 3$
Square-root function	$f(x) = \sqrt{x}$ Domain $[0, \infty)$, range $[0, \infty)$	$f(x) = \sqrt{x - 4}$

Transformations of Graphs

Reflecting	The graph of $y = -f(x)$ is a reflection in the x-axis of the graph of $y = f(x)$.	The graph of $y = -x^2$ is a reflection of the graph of $y = x^2$.
Translating	If $k > 0$, the graph of $y = f(x) + k$ is k units above $y = f(x)$ and $y = f(x) - k$ is k units below $y = f(x)$. If $h > 0$, the graph of $y = f(x - h)$ is h units to the right of $y = f(x)$ and $y = f(x + h)$ is h units to the left of $y = f(x)$.	The graph of $y = x^2 + 3$ is three units above $y = x^2$, and $y = x^2 - 3$ is three units below $y = x^2$. The graph of $y = (x - 3)^2$ is three units to the right of $y = x^2$, and $y = (x + 3)^2$ is three units to the left.

Stretching and shrinking	The graph of $y = af(x)$ is obtained by stretching (if $a > 1$) or shrinking (if $0 < a < 1$) the graph of $y = f(x)$.	The graph of $y = 5x^2$ is obtained by stretching $y = x^2$, and $y = 0.1x^2$ is obtained by shrinking $y = x^2$.

Combining Functions

Examples

Sum	$(f + g)(x) = f(x) + g(x)$	For $f(x) = x^2$ and $g(x) = x + 1$ $(f + g)(x) = x^2 + x + 1$
Difference	$(f - g)(x) = f(x) - g(x)$	$(f - g)(x) = x^2 - x - 1$
Product	$(f \cdot g)(x) = f(x) \cdot g(x)$	$(f \cdot g)(x) = x^3 + x^2$
Quotient	$\left(\dfrac{f}{g}\right)(x) = \dfrac{f(x)}{g(x)}$	$\left(\dfrac{f}{g}\right)(x) = \dfrac{x^2}{x + 1}$
Composition of functions	$(g \circ f)(x) = g(f(x))$ $(f \circ g)(x) = f(g(x))$	$(g \circ f)(x) = g(x^2) = x^2 + 1$ $(f \circ g)(x) = f(x + 1)$ $\qquad = x^2 + 2x + 1$

Inverse Functions

Examples

One-to-one function	A function in which no two ordered pairs have different x-coordinates and the same y-coordinate.	$f = \{(2, 20), (3, 30)\}$
Inverse function	The inverse of a one-to-one function f is the function f^{-1}, which is obtained from f by interchanging the coordinates in each ordered pair of f. The domain of f^{-1} is the range of f, and the range of f^{-1} is the domain of f.	$f^{-1} = \{(20, 2), (30, 3)\}$
Horizontal-line test	If there is a horizontal line that crosses the graph of a function more than once, then the function is not invertible.	
Function notation for inverse	Two functions f and g are inverses of each other if and only if both of the following conditions are met. 1. $(g \circ f)(x) = x$ for every number x in the domain of f. 2. $(f \circ g)(x) = x$ for every number x in the domain of g.	$f(x) = x^3 + 1$ $f^{-1}(x) = \sqrt[3]{x - 1}$
Switch-and-solve strategy for finding f^{-1}	1. Replace $f(x)$ by y. 2. Interchange x and y. 3. Solve for y. 4. Replace y by $f^{-1}(x)$.	$y = x^3 + 1$ $x = y^3 + 1$ $x - 1 = y^3$ $y = \sqrt[3]{x - 1}$ $f^{-1}(x) = \sqrt[3]{x - 1}$
Graphs of f and f^{-1}	Graphs of inverse functions are symmetric with respect to the line $y = x$.	

The Language of Variation   **Examples**

Direct y varies directly as x, $y = kx$ $z = 5m$

Inverse y varies inversely as x, $y = \dfrac{k}{x}$ $a = \dfrac{1}{c}$

Joint y varies jointly as x and z, $y = kxz$ $V = 6LW$

Combined y varies directly as x and inversely as z, $y = \dfrac{kx}{z}$ $S = \dfrac{3A}{B}$

ENRICHING YOUR MATHEMATICAL WORD POWER

For each mathematical term, choose the correct meaning.

1. **composition of f and g**
   a. the function $f \circ g$ where $(f \circ g)(x) = f(g(x))$
   b. the function $f \circ g$ where $(f \circ g)(x) = g(f(x))$
   c. the function $f \cdot g$ where $(f \cdot g)(x) = f(x) \cdot g(x)$
   d. a diagram showing f and g

2. **sum of f and g**
   a. the function $f \cdot g$ where $(f \cdot g)(x) = f(x) \cdot g(x)$
   b. the function $f + g$ where $(f + g)(x) = f(x) + g(x)$
   c. the function $f \circ g$ where $(f \circ g)(x) = g(f(x))$
   d. the function obtained by adding the domains of f and g

3. **inverse of the function f**
   a. a function with the same ordered pairs as f
   b. the opposite of the function f
   c. the function $1/f$
   d. a function in which the ordered pairs of f are reversed

4. **one-to-one function**
   a. a constant function
   b. a function that pairs 1 with 1
   c. a function in which no two ordered pairs have the same first coordinate and different second coordinates
   d. a function in which no two ordered pairs have the same second coordinate and different first coordinates

5. **vertical-line test**
   a. a visual method for determining whether a graph is a graph of a function
   b. a visual method for determining whether a function is one-to-one
   c. using a vertical line to check a graph
   d. a test on vertical lines

6. **horizontal-line test**
   a. a test that horizontal lines must pass
   b. a visual method for determining whether a function is one-to-one

   c. a graph that does not cross the x-axis
   d. a visual method for determining whether a graph is a graph of a function

7. **proportionality constant**
   a. a direct variation
   b. a constant proportion
   c. a ratio that is constant
   d. the constant k in $y = kx$

8. **y varies directly as x**
   a. $y = kx^2$ where k is a constant
   b. $y = mx + b$ where m and b are nonzero constants
   c. $y = kx$ where k is a nonzero constant
   d. $y = k/x$ where k is a nonzero constant

9. **y varies inversely as x**
   a. $y = x/k$ where k is a nonzero constant
   b. $y = -x$
   c. $y = kx$ where k is a nonzero constant
   d. $y = k/x$ where k is a nonzero constant

10. **reflection in the x-axis**
    a. the graph of $y = f(-x)$
    b. the graph of $y = -f(x)$
    c. the graph of $y = -f(-x)$
    d. the line of symmetry

11. **upward translation**
    a. the graph of $y = f(x) + c$ for $c > 0$
    b. the graph of $y = f(x + c)$ for $c < 0$
    c. the graph of $y = f(x - c)$ for $c > 0$
    d. the graph of $y = f(x) + c$ for $c < 0$

12. **translation to the left**
    a. the graph of $y = f(x) - c$ for $c > 0$
    b. the graph of $y = f(x) + c$ for $c > 0$
    c. the graph of $y = f(x - c)$ for $c > 0$
    d. the graph of $y = f(x + c)$ for $c > 0$

9.1 *Graph each function and state the domain and range.*

1. $f(x) = 3x - 4$

2. $y = 0.3x$

3. $h(x) = |x| - 2$

4. $y = |x - 2|$

5. $y = x^2 - 2x + 1$

6. $g(x) = x^2 - 2x - 15$

7. $k(x) = \sqrt{x} + 2$

8. $y = \sqrt{x - 2}$

9. $y = 30 - x^2$

10. $y = 4 - x^2$

Graph each relation and state its domain and range.
11. $x = 2$

16. $y = -\sqrt{x}$

17. $y = -2\sqrt{x}$

12. $x = y^2 - 1$

18. $y = 2\sqrt{x}$

13. $x = |y| + 1$

19. $y = \sqrt{x - 2}$

20. $y = \sqrt{x + 2}$

14. $x = \sqrt{y - 1}$

21. $y = \frac{1}{2}\sqrt{x}$

9.2 *Sketch the graph of each function.*
15. $y = \sqrt{x}$

22. $y = \sqrt{x - 1} + 2$

23. $y = -\sqrt{x + 1} + 3$

47. $g(x) = 13x - 6$ **48.** $h(x) = \sqrt[3]{x - 6}$

49. $j(x) = \dfrac{x + 1}{x - 1}$ **50.** $k(x) = |x| + 7$

51. $m(x) = (x - 1)^2$ **52.** $n(x) = \dfrac{3}{x}$

24. $y = 3\sqrt{x + 4} - 5$

Find the inverse of each function, and graph f and f^{-1} on the same pair of axes.

53. $f(x) = 3x - 1$ **54.** $f(x) = 2 - x^2$ for $x \geq 0$

9.3 *Let* $f(x) = 3x + 5$, $g(x) = x^2 - 2x$, *and* $h(x) = \frac{x - 5}{3}$.
Find the following.

25. $f(-3)$ **26.** $h(-4)$

27. $(h \circ f)(\sqrt{2})$ **28.** $(f \circ h)(\pi)$

29. $(g \circ f)(2)$ **30.** $(g \circ f)(x)$

55. $f(x) = \dfrac{x^3}{2}$ **56.** $f(x) = -\dfrac{1}{4}x$

31. $(f + g)(3)$ **32.** $(f - g)(x)$

33. $(f \cdot g)(x)$ **34.** $\left(\dfrac{f}{g}\right)(1)$

35. $(f \circ f)(0)$ **36.** $(f \circ f)(x)$

Let $f(x) = |x|$, $g(x) = x + 2$, *and* $h(x) = x^2$. *Write each of the following functions as a composition of functions, using f, g, or h.*

37. $F(x) = |x + 2|$ **38.** $G(x) = |x| + 2$

9.5 *Solve each variation problem.*

57. If y varies directly as m and $y = -3$ when $m = \frac{1}{4}$, find y when $m = -2$.

39. $H(x) = x^2 + 2$ **40.** $K(x) = x^2 + 4x + 4$

58. If a varies inversely as b and $a = 6$ when $b = -3$, find a when $b = 4$.

41. $I(x) = x + 4$ **42.** $J(x) = x^4 + 2$

59. If c varies directly as m and inversely as n, and $c = 20$ when $m = 10$ and $n = 4$, find c when $m = 6$ and $n = -3$.

9.4 *Determine whether each function is invertible. If it is invertible, find the inverse.*

43. $\{(-2, 4), (2, 4)\}$ **44.** $\{(1, 1), (3, 3)\}$

60. If V varies jointly as h and the square of r, and $V = 32$ when $h = 6$ and $r = 3$, find V when $h = 3$ and $r = 4$.

45. $f(x) = 8x$ **46.** $i(x) = -\dfrac{x}{3}$

MISCELLANEOUS

61. Falling object. If a ball is dropped from a tall building, then the distance traveled by the ball in t seconds varies directly as the square of the time t. If the ball travels 144 feet (ft) in 3 seconds, then how far does it travel in 4 seconds?

62. Studying or partying. Evelyn's grade on a math test varies directly with the number of hours spent studying and inversely with the number of hours spent partying during the 24 hours preceding the test. If she scored a 90 on a test after she studied 10 hours and partied 2 hours, then what should she score after studying 4 hours and partying 6 hours?

63. Inscribed square. Given that B is the area of a square inscribed in a circle of radius r and area A, write B as a function of A.

64. Area of a window. A window is in the shape of a square of side s, with a semicircle of diameter s above it. Write a function that expresses the total area of the window as a function of s.

65. Composition of functions. Given that $a = 3k + 2$ and $k = 5w - 6$, write a as a function of w.

66. Volume of a cylinder. The volume of a cylinder with a fixed height of 10 centimeters (cm) is given by $V = 10\pi r^2$,

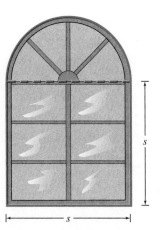

FIGURE FOR EXERCISE 64

where r is the radius of the circular base. Write the volume as a function of the area of the base, A.

67. Square formulas. Write the area of a square A as a function of the length of a side of the square s. Write the length of a side of a square as a function of the area.

68. Circle formulas. Write the area of a circle A as a function of the radius of the circle r. Write the radius of a circle as a function of the area of the circle. Write the area as a function of the diameter d.

CHAPTER 9 TEST

Sketch the graph of each function or relation.

1. $f(x) = -\dfrac{2}{3}x + 1$

2. $y = |x| - 4$

3. $g(x) = x^2 + 2x - 8$

4. $x = y^2$

5. $y = -|x - 2|$

6. $y = \sqrt{x + 5} - 2$

Let $f(x) = -2x + 5$ *and* $g(x) = x^2 + 4$. *Find the following.*

7. $f(-3)$ **8.** $(g \circ f)(-3)$

9. $f^{-1}(11)$ **10.** $f^{-1}(x)$

11. $(g + f)(x)$ **12.** $(f \cdot g)(1)$

13. $(f^{-1} \circ f)(1776)$ **14.** $(f/g)(2)$

15. $(f \circ g)(x)$ **16.** $(g \circ f)(x)$

Let $f(x) = x - 7$ *and* $g(x) = x^2$. *Write each of the following functions as a composition of functions using f and g.*

17. $H(x) = x^2 - 7$

18. $W(x) = x^2 - 14x + 49$

Determine whether each function is invertible. If it is invertible, find the inverse.

19. $\{(2, 3), (4, 3)\}$

20. $f(x) = \sqrt[3]{x} + 9$

Solve each problem.

21. Find the domain and range of the function $f(x) = |x|$.

22. Find the inverse of $f(x) = \frac{2x + 1}{x - 1}$.

23. The volume of a sphere varies directly as the cube of the radius. If a sphere with radius 3 feet (ft) has a volume of 36π cubic feet (ft³), then what is the volume of a sphere with a radius of 2 ft?

24. Suppose y varies directly as x and inversely as the square root of z. If $y = 12$ when $x = 7$ and $z = 9$, then what is the proportionality constant?

25. The cost of a Persian rug varies jointly as the length and width of the rug. If the cost is $2256 for a 6 foot by 8 foot rug, then what is the cost of a 9 foot by 12 foot rug?

Simplify each expression.

1. $125^{-2/3}$

2. $\left(\dfrac{8}{27}\right)^{-1/3}$

3. $\sqrt{18} - \sqrt{8}$

4. $x^5 \cdot x^3$

5. $16^{1/4}$

6. $\dfrac{x^{12}}{x^3}$

Find the real solution set to each equation.

7. $x^2 = 9$

8. $x^2 = 8$

9. $x^2 = x$

10. $x^2 - 4x - 6 = 0$

11. $x^{1/4} = 3$

12. $x^{1/6} = -2$

13. $|x| = 8$

14. $|5x - 4| = 21$

15. $x^3 = 8$

16. $(3x - 2)^3 = 27$

17. $\sqrt{2x - 3} = 9$

18. $\sqrt{x - 2} = x - 8$

Sketch the graph of each set.

19. $\{(x, y) \mid y = 5\}$

20. $\{(x, y) \mid y = 2x - 5\}$

21. $\{(x, y) \mid x = 5\}$

22. $\{(x, y) \mid 3y = x\}$

23. $\{(x, y) \mid y = 5x^2\}$

24. $\{(x, y) \mid y = -2x^2\}$

Find the missing coordinates in each ordered pair so that the ordered pair satisfies the given equation.

25. $(2, \ ), (3, \ ), (\ , 2), (\ , 16), \quad 2^x = y$

26. $\left(\dfrac{1}{2}, \ \right), (-1, \ ), (\ , 16), (\ , 1), \quad 4^x = y$

Find the domain of each expression.

27. $\sqrt{x}$

28. $\sqrt{6 - 2x}$

29. $\dfrac{5x - 3}{x^2 + 1}$

30. $\dfrac{x - 3}{x^2 - 10x + 9}$

Solve each problem.

31. *Capital cost and operating cost.* To decide when to replace company cars, an accountant looks at two cost components: capital cost and operating cost. The capital cost C (the difference between the original cost and the salvage value) for a certain car is $3000 plus $0.12 for each mile that the car is driven.

a) Write the capital cost C as a linear function of x, the number of miles that the car is driven.

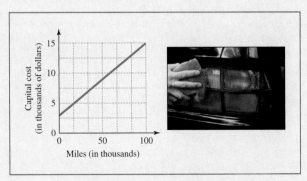

FIGURE FOR EXERCISE 31(a)

b) The operating cost P is \$0.15 per mile initially and increases linearly to \$0.25 per mile when the car reaches 100,000 miles. Write P as a function of x, the number of miles that the car is driven.

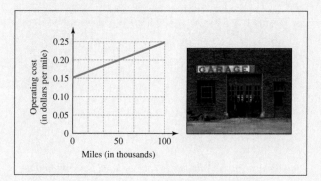

FIGURE FOR EXERCISE 31(b)

32. *Total cost.* The accountant in the previous exercise uses the function $T = \frac{C}{x} + P$ to find the total cost per mile.

a) Find T for $x = 20{,}000$, $30{,}000$, and $90{,}000$.

b) Sketch a graph of the total cost function.

c) The accountant has decided to replace the car when T reaches \$0.38 for the second time. At what mileage will the car be replaced?

d) For what values of x is T less than or equal to \$0.38?

Polynomial and Rational Functions

N ew products are coming to market daily. Television ads are constantly touting the features and benefits of new exercise devices, diets, can openers, bag sealers, vacuum cleaners, cars, trucks, drugs, makeup, toothpaste, and so on. By some estimates 90% of new products are failures. But how can products fail to make money? The answer to that question lies in the tremendous cost of research, development, manufacturing, distribution, and advertising.

It now takes an average of 14.8 years and $350 million to get a new drug to market. However, the payoff can be quick and tremendous. At around $9 per pill sales of a new miracle drug can top $1 billion in the first year.

Mercedes-Benz introduced a new sport utility vehicle in 1998 that took 5 years to design. Mercedes-Benz spent $700 million on design, $300 million to build the Alabama plant for manufacturing the SUV, $400 million to design the engine, and $450 million to construct a plant for making the engine—not to mention the cost of manufacturing each car. Mercedes-Benz expects to sell 40,000 of these vehicles the first year at around $35,000 each. Making a profit will take a while.

For any product, profits are made when the average cost of the product is below the price at which the company sells the product. In Exercises 55 and 56 of Section 10.5 we will see how rational functions can be used to model average cost.

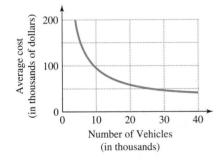

10.1 **THE FACTOR THEOREM**

We have worked with polynomials on many occassions in this text. In this section we study functions defined by polynomials and learn to solve some higher-degree polynomial equations.

The Factor Theorem

If a polynomial is used to define a function, then the function is called a **polynomial function.** For example, the functions

$$m(x) = 2, \quad n(x) = 3x - 6, \quad h(x) = 5x^2 - 2x + 6, \quad \text{and} \quad j(x) = x^3$$

are polynomial functions. The degree of a polynomial function is the degree of the polynomial used to define it. The polynomials m, n, h, and j have degrees 0, 1, 2, and 3, respectively. If $f(c) = 0$, then c is called a **root** or **zero** of the function f.

Consider the polynomial function $P(x) = x^2 + 2x - 15$. We can find the zeros of the function by solving the equation $P(x) = 0$:

$$x^2 + 2x - 15 = 0$$
$$(x + 5)(x - 3) = 0$$
$$x + 5 = 0 \quad \text{or} \quad x - 3 = 0$$
$$x = -5 \quad \text{or} \quad x = 3$$

Helpful Hint

Note that the zeros of the polynomial function are factors of the constant term 15.

Because $x + 5$ is a factor of $x^2 + 2x - 15$, -5 is a solution to the equation $x^2 + 2x - 15 = 0$ and a zero of the function $P(x) = x^2 + 2x - 15$. We can check that -5 is a zero of $P(x) = x^2 + 2x - 15$ as follows:

$$P(-5) = (-5)^2 + 2(-5) - 15$$
$$= 25 - 10 - 15$$
$$= 0$$

Because $x - 3$ is a factor of the polynomial, 3 is also a solution to the equation $x^2 + 2x - 15 = 0$ and a zero of the polynomial function. Check that $P(3) = 0$:

$$P(3) = 3^2 + 2 \cdot 3 - 15$$
$$= 9 + 6 - 15$$
$$= 0$$

Every linear factor of the polynomial corresponds to a zero of the polynomial function, and every zero of the polynomial function corresponds to a linear factor.

Now suppose $P(x)$ represents an arbitrary polynomial. If $x - c$ is a factor of the polynomial $P(x)$, then c is a solution to the equation $P(x) = 0$, and so $P(c) = 0$. If we divide $P(x)$ by $x - c$ and the remainder is 0, we must have

$$P(x) = (x - c)(\text{quotient}). \quad \text{Dividend equals the divisor times the quotient.}$$

If the remainder is 0, then $x - c$ is a factor of $P(x)$.

The **factor theorem** summarizes these ideas.

The Factor Theorem

The following statements are equivalent for any polynomial $P(x)$.

1. The remainder is zero when $P(x)$ is divided by $x - c$.
2. $x - c$ is a factor of $P(x)$.
3. c is a solution to $P(x) = 0$.
4. c is a zero of the function $P(x)$, or $P(c) = 0$.

To say that statements are equivalent means that the truth of any one of them implies that the others are true.

According to the factor theorem, if we want to determine whether a given number c is a zero of a polynomial function, we can divide the polynomial by $x - c$. The remainder is zero if and only if c is a zero of the polynomial function. The quickest way to divide by $x - c$ is to use synthetic division from Section 6.5.

E X A M P L E   1

Calculator Close-Up

You can perform the multiply-and-add steps for synthetic division with a graphing calculator as shown here.

```
Ans*2+ -3          1
                  -1
Ans*2+5
                   3
Ans*2+ -2
                   4
```

Using the factor theorem

Use synthetic division to determine whether 2 is a zero of
$P(x) = x^3 - 3x^2 + 5x - 2$.

Solution

By the factor theorem, 2 is a zero of the function if and only if the remainder is zero when $P(x)$ is divided by $x - 2$. We can use synthetic division to determine the remainder. If we divide by $x - 2$, we use 2 on the left in synthetic division along with the coefficients $1, -3, 5, -2$ from the polynomial:

$$
\begin{array}{r|rrrr}
2 & 1 & -3 & 5 & -2 \\
  &   & 2 & -2 & 6 \\
\hline
  & 1 & -1 & 3 & 4
\end{array}
$$

Because the remainder is 4, 2 is not a zero of the function. ∎

E X A M P L E   2

Using the factor theorem

Use synthetic division to determine whether -4 is a solution to the equation $2x^4 - 28x^2 + 14x - 8 = 0$.

Solution

By the factor theorem, -4 is a solution to the equation if and only if the remainder is zero when $P(x)$ is divided by $x + 4$. When dividing by $x + 4$, we use -4 in the synthetic division:

$$
\begin{array}{r|rrrrr}
-4 & 2 & 0 & -28 & 14 & -8 \\
   &   & -8 & 32 & -16 & 8 \\
\hline
   & 2 & -8 & 4 & -2 & 0
\end{array}
$$

Because the remainder is zero, -4 is a solution to $2x^4 - 28x^2 + 14x - 8 = 0$. ∎

In Example 3 we use the factor theorem to determine whether a given binomial is a factor of a polynomial.

E X A M P L E   3

Using the factor theorem

Use synthetic division to determine whether $x + 4$ is a factor of $x^3 + 3x^2 + 16$.

29. $x - 0.5$, $2x^3 - 3x^2 - 11x + 6$

30. $x - \dfrac{1}{3}$, $3x^3 - 10x^2 - 27x + 10$

Solve each equation, given that at least one of the solutions to each equation is an integer between -5 and 5. See Example 4.

31. $x^3 - 13x + 12 = 0$

32. $x^3 + 2x^2 - 5x - 6 = 0$

33. $2x^3 - 9x^2 + 7x + 6 = 0$

34. $6x^3 + 13x^2 - 4 = 0$

35. $2x^3 - 3x^2 - 50x - 24 = 0$

36. $x^3 - 7x^2 + 2x + 40 = 0$

37. $x^3 + 5x^2 + 3x - 9 = 0$

38. $x^3 + 6x^2 + 12x + 8 = 0$

39. $x^4 - 4x^3 + 3x^2 + 4x - 4 = 0$

40. $x^4 + x^3 - 7x^2 - x + 6 = 0$

GETTING MORE INVOLVED

 41. *Exploration.* We can find the zeros of a polynomial function by solving a polynomial equation. We can also work backward to find a polynomial function that has given zeros.

   a) Write a first-degree polynomial function whose zero is -2.

b) Write a second-degree polynomial function whose zeros are 5 and -5.

c) Write a third-degree polynomial function whose zeros are 1, -3, and 4.

d) Is there a polynomial function with any given number of zeros? What is its degree?

GRAPHING CALCULATOR EXERCISES

42. The x-coordinate of each x-intercept on the graph of a polynomial function is a zero of the polynomial function. Find the zeros of each function from its graph. Use synthetic division to check that the zeros found on your calculator really are zeros of the function.

   a) $P(x) = x^3 - 2x^2 - 5x + 6$

   b) $P(x) = 12x^3 - 20x^2 + x + 3$

43. With a graphing calculator an equation can be solved without the kind of hint that was given for Exercises 31–40. Solve each of the following equations by examining the graph of a corresponding function. Use synthetic division to check.

   a) $x^3 - 4x^2 - 7x + 10 = 0$

   b) $8x^3 - 20x^2 - 18x + 45 = 0$

In This Section

- The Remainder Theorem
- The Fundamental Theorem of Algebra
- The Rational Root Theorem

10.2 ZEROS OF A POLYNOMIAL FUNCTION

In this section we continue our study of zeros of polynomial functions, which we began in Section 10.1. An essential theorem in this regard is the remainder theorem, which was introduced in Section 6.5. For completeness we review and restate the remainder theorem here.

The Remainder Theorem

The factor theorem in Section 10.1 indicates what happens when a polynomial is divided by $x - c$ and the remainder is zero. The remainder theorem gives us more information about the remainder.

> **The Remainder Theorem**
>
> If R is the remainder when a polynomial $P(x)$ is divided by $x - c$, then $R = P(c)$.

E X A M P L E   1

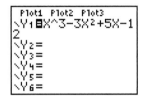
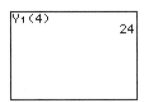
Evaluating a polynomial function

Let $f(x) = x^3$ and $g(x) = x^3 - 3x^2 + 5x - 12$. Use synthetic division to find the following function values.

a) $f(-2)$ **b)** $g(4)$

Solution

a) Use synthetic division to divide x^3 by $x + 2$ as follows:

$$
\begin{array}{r|rrrr}
-2 & 1 & 0 & 0 & 0 \\
   &   & -2 & 4 & -8 \\
\hline
   & 1 & -2 & 4 & -8
\end{array}
$$

The synthetic division shows that the quotient is $x^2 - 2x + 4$ and the remainder is -8. So $f(-2) = -8$. The answer is correct because $f(-2) = (-2)^3 = -8$.

b) Use synthetic division to divide $x^3 - 3x^2 + 5x - 12$ by $x - 4$ as follows:

$$
\begin{array}{r|rrrr}
4 & 1 & -3 & 5 & -12 \\
  &   & 4 & 4 & 36 \\
\hline
  & 1 & 1 & 9 & 24
\end{array}
$$

The synthetic division shows that the quotient is $x^2 + x + 9$ and the remainder is 24. So $g(4) = 24$. We can check this answer by evaluating the polynomial $x^3 - 3x^2 + 5x - 12$ for $x = 4$. We get $4^3 - 3(4^2) + 5(4) - 12 = 24$.   ■

Note that we now have two different ways to find the value of a polynomial $P(x)$ when $x = c$. We can find the remainder when the polynomial is divided by $x - c$, or we can evaluate the polynomial by using c in place of x. In Example 1(a) it is easier to find $(-2)^3$ than to do synthetic division to get $f(-2) = -8$. In Example 1(b) synthetic division is easier because there are fewer arithmetic operations in the synthetic division than in evaluating the polynomial. For polynomials of higher degree there may be an even bigger difference between the number of operations in evaluating the polynomial and finding the remainder of synthetic division.

In Example 2 we use synthetic division and the remainder theorem to determine whether a given number is a zero to a polynomial function.

E X A M P L E   2

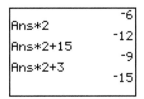
Zeros of polynomial functions

Determine whether each given number is a zero of the polynomial function following the number.

a) $2, f(x) = -6x^3 + 15x + 3$ **b)** $-2, g(x) = x^4 - 3x^3 + 5x^2 - 6x - 72$

Solution

a) Use synthetic division to find $f(2)$ as follows:

$$
\begin{array}{r|rrrr}
2 & -6 & 0 & 15 & 3 \\
  &   & -12 & -24 & -18 \\
\hline
  & -6 & -12 & -9 & -15
\end{array}
$$

So $f(2) = -15$, and 2 is not a zero of the polynomial function.

b) Use synthetic division to find $g(-2)$ as follows:

$$
\begin{array}{r|rrrrr}
-2 & 1 & -3 & 5 & -6 & -72 \\
   &   & -2 & 10 & -30 & 72 \\
\hline
   & 1 & -5 & 15 & -36 & 0
\end{array}
$$

So $g(-2) = 0$, and -2 is a zero of the polynomial function.   ■

b) If the rational number p/q is a zero of $g(x)$, then p must be a factor of 8 and q must be a factor of 3. The factors of 8 are 1, 2, 4, and 8. The factors of 3 are 1 and 3. If we take all possible ratios of a factor of 8 over a factor of 3, we get

$$\pm 1, \quad \pm 2, \quad \pm 4, \quad \pm 8, \quad \pm \frac{1}{3}, \quad \pm \frac{2}{3}, \quad \pm \frac{4}{3}, \quad \text{and} \quad \pm \frac{8}{3}$$

as the possible rational zeros of the function $g(x)$.   ■

A polynomial function might or might not have any rational zeros, but with the rational root theorem we have a place to start in the problem of finding all of the zeros of a polynomial function. Synthetic division is used to determine whether a possible rational zero is actually a zero of the function.

E X A M P L E   5

Finding all zeros of a polynomial function

Find all of the real and imaginary zeros for each polynomial function of Example 4.
a) $f(x) = 2x^3 - 3x^2 - 11x + 6$
b) $g(x) = 3x^3 - 8x^2 - 8x + 8$

Calculator Close-Up

The graph of a polynomial function can give us a good idea of which possible rational zeros are actually zeros of the function. The graph can also be used to support the answers that are obtained algebraically. In this case the graph has x-intercepts at $(-2, 0)$, $(0.5, 0)$, and $(3, 0)$, which supports the algebraic answers.

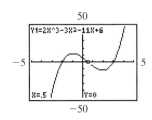

Solution

a) The possible rational zeros are listed in Example 4(a) for the function $f(x)$. Now use synthetic division to check each possible zero to see whether it is actually a zero. Try $\frac{1}{2}$ first. (If $\frac{1}{2}$ does not produce a remainder of 0, then we would try another number from the list of possible rational zeros.)

$$\begin{array}{r|rrrr} \frac{1}{2} & 2 & -3 & -11 & 6 \\ & & 1 & -1 & -6 \\ \hline & 2 & -2 & -12 & 0 \end{array}$$

Since the remainder is 0, the remainder theorem indicates that $\frac{1}{2}$ is a zero of the function and a root of the equation $2x^3 - 3x^2 - 11x + 6 = 0$. By the factor theorem, $x - \frac{1}{2}$ is a factor of the polynomial, and the other factor is the quotient:

$$2x^3 - 3x^2 - 11x + 6 = 0$$

$$\left(x - \frac{1}{2}\right)(2x^2 - 2x - 12) = 0$$

$$(2x - 1)(x^2 - x - 6) = 0$$

$$(2x - 1)(x - 3)(x + 2) = 0$$

$$2x - 1 = 0 \quad \text{or} \quad x - 3 = 0 \quad \text{or} \quad x + 2 = 0$$

$$x = \frac{1}{2} \quad \text{or} \quad x = 3 \quad \text{or} \quad x = -2$$

The zeros of the function f are $\frac{1}{2}$, 3, and -2.

b) We listed the possible rational roots in Example 4(b) for the function $g(x)$. We will first check $\frac{2}{3}$ to see whether it produces a remainder of 0:

$$\begin{array}{r|rrrr} \frac{2}{3} & 3 & -8 & -8 & 8 \\ & & 2 & -4 & -8 \\ \hline & 3 & -6 & -12 & 0 \end{array}$$

Calculator Close-Up

Note how the graph of the function supports the solutions obtained algebraically. When the function is evaluated at $1 + \sqrt{5}$, or approximately 3.236068, the calculator does not get exactly 0 because it cannot perform this computation exactly. However, the answer 2×10^{-12} is very close to 0.

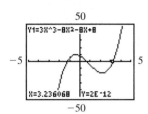

Since the remainder is 0, by the remainder theorem $\frac{2}{3}$ is a zero of the function and a root of the equation $3x^3 - 8x^2 - 8x + 8 = 0$. By the factor theorem we know that $x - \frac{2}{3}$ is a factor of the polynomial and the quotient is the other factor:

$$3x^3 - 8x^2 - 8x + 8 = 0$$

$$\left(x - \frac{2}{3}\right)(3x^2 - 6x - 12) = 0$$

$$(3x - 2)(x^2 - 2x - 4) = 0$$

$$3x - 2 = 0 \quad \text{or} \quad x^2 - 2x - 4 = 0$$

$$x = \frac{2}{3} \quad \text{or} \quad x = \frac{2 \pm \sqrt{20}}{2}$$

$$x = \frac{2}{3} \quad \text{or} \quad x = 1 \pm \sqrt{5}$$

There is one rational root and two irrational roots to the equation. So the zeros of the function $g(x)$ are $\frac{2}{3}$, $1 + \sqrt{5}$, and $1 - \sqrt{5}$. ∎

Note that in Example 5(a) all of the zeros were rational. We could have found all three by continuing to check the possible rational roots using synthetic division. In Example 5(b) we would be wasting time if we continued to check the possible rational roots because there is only one. When we get to the point in the equation at which one of the factors of the polynomial is a quadratic polynomial, it is best either to factor the quadratic polynomial or to use the quadratic formula to find the remaining solutions to the equation.

WARM-UPS

True or false? Explain your answer.

1. The function $f(x) = x^{-1}$ is a polynomial function.
2. To find the value of $f(x) = x^3 - 4x^2 + 3x - 7$ when $x = 3$, we use -3 in the synthetic division.
3. If we divide $P(x) = x^3 - 6x^2 + 3x - 7$ by $x - 5$, then $P(5)$ is equal to the remainder.
4. If we divide $x^4 - 1$ by $x - 2$, then the remainder is 15.
5. The polynomial function $P(x) = 5$ has at least one zero.
6. If $P(x) = x^3 - 7x + 3$ and c is a number such that $P(c) = 0$, then $c^3 - 7c + 3 = 0$.
7. If $P(x) = x^3 - 3x^2 + 5x - 14$, then $P(3) = 0$.
8. If $P(x) = 5x^3 - 5x^2 + 7x - 9$, then $\frac{1}{3}$ is not a zero of the polynomial.
9. The polynomial $x - 1$ is a factor of $x^4 - x^3 + x^2 - x + 1$.
10. The polynomial $x + 3$ is a factor of $3x^5 - 5x^4 - 6x^3 + 8x^2 + 9x - 2$.

10.2 EXERCISES

Reading and Writing *After reading this section, write out the answers to these questions. Use complete sentences.*

1. What is a polynomial function?

2. What is a root of a function?

3. What is a zero of a function?

4. What is the remainder theorem?

5. What is the rational root theorem?

6. What is the fundamental theorem of algebra?

Let $f(x) = x^4 - 1$, $g(x) = x^3 - 3x^2 + 5$, and $h(x) = 4x^4 - 3x^2 + 3x - 1$. Find the following function values by using two different methods. See Example 1.

7. $f(1)$ **8.** $f(-3)$

9. $f(-2)$ **10.** $f(5)$

11. $g(1)$ **12.** $g(-1)$

13. $g(-2)$ **14.** $g(2)$

15. $h\left(\dfrac{1}{2}\right)$ **16.** $h\left(-\dfrac{1}{2}\right)$

17. $h\left(\dfrac{3}{2}\right)$ **18.** $h\left(-\dfrac{3}{2}\right)$

Determine whether each given number is a zero of the polynomial function following the number. See Example 2.

19. $3, f(x) = 3x^3 - 6x^2 - 4x - 15$

20. $-2, f(x) = 3x^3 - 6x^2 - 4x - 15$

21. $-2, P(x) = x^3 + 2x^2 + 3x + 2$

22. $-1, P(x) = x^3 + 2x^2 + 3x + 2$

23. $-1, g(x) = x^4 + 3x^3 + 5x^2 + 5x + 2$

24. $3, g(x) = x^4 + 3x^3 + 5x^2 + 5x + 2$

25. $\dfrac{1}{2}, h(x) = x^3 + 3x^2 - 4x + 1$

26. $-\dfrac{1}{2}, h(x) = x^3 + 3x^2 - 4x + 1$

Find all real and imaginary zeros of each polynomial function. See Example 3.

27. $f(x) = 5x - 9$

28. $h(x) = 3x + 12$

29. $k(x) = x^2 - 5x + 6$

30. $m(x) = x^2 - x - 12$

31. $P(t) = t^2 + 9$

32. $W(t) = t^2 - 2t + 6$

33. $H(x) = x^3 - 3x^2 + 4x - 12$

34. $A(x) = x^3 + x^2 + x + 1$

35. $K(s) = 2s^3 - 5s^2 - 3s$

36. $J(s) = 2s^3 + s^2 - 3s$

37. $L(x) = -x^3 - x^2 + 7x + 7$

38. $Q(x) = -3x^3 + 3x^2 + 2x - 2$

39. $M(x) = x^3 - 1$

40. $N(x) = x^3 - 8$

Find all possible rational zeros for each polynomial function. See Example 4.

41. $P(x) = 2x^3 - 5x^2 + x + 2$

42. $P(x) = x^3 - 2x^2 - 5x + 6$

43. $P(x) = x^3 + 9x^2 + 26x + 24$

44. $P(x) = 3x^3 + 4x^2 - 5x - 2$

45. $P(x) = x^3 + 5x^2 - 6$

46. $P(x) = 3x^3 + 16x^2 - 8$

Find all of the real and imaginary zeros for each polynomial function. See Example 5.

47. $P(x) = 2x^3 - 5x^2 + x + 2$

48. $P(x) = x^3 - 2x^2 - 5x + 6$

49. $P(x) = x^3 + 9x^2 + 26x + 24$

50. $P(x) = 3x^3 + 4x^2 - 5x - 2$

51. $P(x) = x^3 + 5x^2 - 6$

52. $P(x) = 3x^3 + 16x^2 - 8$

53. $P(x) = x^3 + 2x^2 - 16$
54. $P(x) = x^3 + 6x^2 + 13x + 10$

55. $P(x) = 24x^3 - 26x^2 + 9x - 1$

56. $P(x) = 12x^3 - 20x^2 + x + 3$

Solve each problem.

57. The total profit in dollars on the sale of x Electronic Tummy Trimmers is given by the polynomial function $P(x) = x^3 - 40x^2 + 400x$. Find the profit when 10 are sold. How many must be sold to get a profit of 0 dollars?

58. The velocity in feet per second (ft/sec) of a rocket t seconds (sec) after launching is given by the polynomial function $v(t) = t^3 - 20t^2 + 110t$. What is the velocity of the rocket 10 sec after launching? For what value of t does the rocket have 0 velocity?

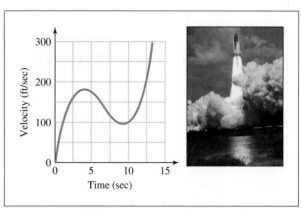

FIGURE FOR EXERCISE 58

 GRAPHING CALCULATOR EXERCISES

Find all real zeros to each polynomial function by graphing the function and locating the x-intercepts.

59. $f(x) = x^3 - 0.2x^2 - 0.05x + 0.006$
60. $f(x) = x^3 - 13x^2 + 32x - 20$
61. $f(x) = x^3 - 60x^2 + 1100x - 6000$
62. $f(x) = x^3 - 3x^2 - 2200x + 50,000$

In This Section

- The Number of Roots to a Polynomial Equation
- The Conjugate Pairs Theorem
- Descartes' Rule of Signs
- Bounds on the Roots

 10.3   THE THEORY OF EQUATIONS

The zeros of a polynomial function $P(x)$ are the same as the roots of the polynomial equation $P(x) = 0$. Remember that one of our main goals in algebra is to keep expanding our knowledge of solving equations. In this section we will learn several facts that are useful in solving polynomial equations.

The Number of Roots to a Polynomial Equation

In solving a polynomial equation by factoring, we find that a factor may occur more than once.

> **Multiplicity**
>
> If the factor $x - c$ occurs n times in the complete factorization of the polynomial $P(x)$, then we say that c is a root of the equation $P(x) = 0$ with **multiplicity** n.

For example, the equation $x^2 - 10x + 25 = 0$ is equivalent to $(x - 5)(x - 5) = 0$. The only root to this equation is 5. Since the factor $x - 5$ occurs twice, we say that 5 is a root with multiplicity 2. Counting multiplicity, every quadratic equation has two roots.

Consider a polynomial equation $P(x) = 0$ of positive degree n. By the fundamental theorem of algebra there is at least one complex root c_1 to this equation. By the factor theorem $P(x) = 0$ is equivalent to $(x - c_1)Q_1(x) = 0$, where $Q_1(x)$ is a polynomial with degree $n - 1$ (the quotient when $P(x)$ is divided by $x - c_1$). By the fundamental theorem of algebra there is at least one complex root c_2 to $Q_1(x) = 0$. By the factor theorem $P(x) = 0$ can be written as $(x - c_1)(x - c_2)Q_2(x) = 0$, where $Q_2(x)$ is a polynomial with degree $n - 2$. Continuing this reasoning n times, we get a quotient polynomial that has 0 degree, n factors for $P(x)$, and n complex roots, not necessarily all different. We have just proved the following theorem.

n-Root Theorem

If $P(x) = 0$ is a polynomial equation with real or complex coefficients and positive degree n, then counting multiplicities, $P(x) = 0$ has n complex roots.

Note that the n-root theorem also means that a polynomial function of positive degree n has n zeros, counting multiplicities.

E X A M P L E 1

Finding all roots to a polynomial equation

State the degree of each polynomial equation. Find all of the real and imaginary roots to each equation, stating multiplicity when it is greater than 1.

a) $6x^5 + 24x^3 = 0$

b) $(x - 3)^2(x + 4)^5 = 0$

Calculator Close-Up

You can check Example 1 by examining the graphs shown here.

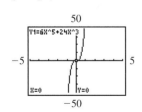

The roots to the equations correspond to the *x*-intercepts.

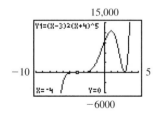

Solution

a) The equation is a fifth-degree equation. We can solve it by factoring:

$$6x^3(x^2 + 4) = 0$$

$$6x^3 = 0 \quad \text{or} \quad x^2 + 4 = 0$$

$$x^3 = 0 \quad \text{or} \quad x^2 = -4$$

$$x = 0 \quad \text{or} \quad x = \pm2i$$

The roots are $\pm2i$ and 0. Since 0 is a root with multiplicity 3, counting multiplicities there are five roots.

b) If we would multiply the factors in this polynomial equation, then the highest power of x would be 7. So the degree of the equation is 7. There are only two distinct roots to the equation, 3 and -4. We say that 3 is a root with multiplicity 2 and -4 is a root with multiplicity 5. So counting multiplicities, there are seven roots to the equation. ∎

The Conjugate Pairs Theorem

The solutions to the quadratic equation $x^2 - 2x + 5 = 0$ are the complex numbers $1 - 2i$ and $1 + 2i$. These numbers are conjugates of one another. The quadratic formula guarantees that complex solutions of quadratic equations with real coefficients occur in conjugate pairs. This situation also occurs for polynomial equations of higher degree.

Conjugate Pairs Theorem

If $P(x) = 0$ is a polynomial equation with real coefficients and the complex number $a + bi$ $(b \neq 0)$ is a root, then the complex number $a - bi$ is also a root.

E X A M P L E   2

Finding an equation with given roots

Find a polynomial equation with real coefficients that has 2 and $1 - i$ as roots.

Calculator Close-Up

You can check Example 2 by examining the graph shown here. The graph should cross the x-axis only once because the function has only one real root.

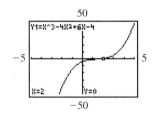

Solution

Since the polynomial is to have real coefficients, the imaginary roots occur in conjugate pairs. So a polynomial with these two roots actually must have at least three roots: 2, $1 - i$, and $1 + i$. Since each root of the equation comes from a factor of the polynomial, we can write the following equation:

$$(x - 2)(x - [1 - i])(x - [1 + i]) = 0$$
$$(x - 2)(x^2 - 2x + 2) = 0 \quad {\scriptstyle (1 - i)(1 + i) = 1 - i^2 = 2}$$
$$x^3 - 4x^2 + 6x - 4 = 0$$

This equation has the required solutions and the smallest degree. Any multiple of this equation would also have the required solutions but would not be as simple. ∎

Descartes' Rule of Signs

None of the theorems in this chapter tells us how to find all of the n roots to a polynomial equation of degree n. The theorems and rules presented here add to our knowledge of polynomial equations and help us to solve more equations. Descartes' rule of signs is a method for looking at a polynomial equation and estimating the number of positive, negative, and imaginary solutions.

   When a polynomial is written in descending order, a variation of sign occurs when the signs of consecutive terms change. For example, if $P(x) = 3x^5 - 7x^4 - 8x^3 - x^2 + 3x - 9$, there are sign changes in going from the first to the second terms, from the fourth to the fifth terms, and from the fifth to the sixth terms. So there are three variations in sign for $P(x)$. Descartes' rule requires that we also count the variations in sign for $P(-x)$ after it is simplified:

$$P(-x) = 3(-x)^5 - 7(-x)^4 - 8(-x)^3 - (-x)^2 + 3(-x) - 9$$
$$= -3x^5 - 7x^4 + 8x^3 - x^2 - 3x - 9$$

In the polynomial $P(-x)$ the signs of the terms change from the second to the third terms, and then the signs change again from the third to the fourth terms. So there are two variations in sign for $P(-x)$.

Descartes' Rule of Signs

If $P(x) = 0$ is a polynomial equation with real coefficients, then the number of positive roots of the equation is either equal to the number of variations of sign of $P(x)$ or less than that by an even number. The number of negative roots of the equation is either equal to the number of variations in sign of $P(-x)$ or less than that by an even number.

E X A M P L E   3

Discussing the possibilities for the roots

Discuss the possibilities for the roots to $2x^3 - 5x^2 - 6x + 4 = 0$.

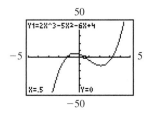

Solution

The number of variations of sign in $P(x) = 2x^3 - 5x^2 - 6x + 4$ is 2. According to Descartes' rule, the number of positive roots is either 2 or 0. Since $P(-x) = 2(-x)^3 - 5(-x)^2 - 6(-x) + 4 = -2x^3 - 5x^2 + 6x + 4$, there is only one variation of sign in $P(-x)$. So there is exactly one negative root. If only one negative root exists, then the other two roots must be positive or imaginary. The number of imaginary roots is determined by the number of positive and negative roots because the total number of roots must be three. The following table summarizes these two possibilities.

Number of Positive Roots	Number of Negative Roots	Number of Imaginary Roots
2	1	0
0	1	2

EXAMPLE 4

Discussing the possibilities for the roots

Discuss the possibilities for the roots to $3x^4 - 5x^3 - x^2 - 8x + 4 = 0$.

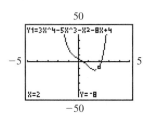

Solution

The number of variations of sign in $P(x) = 3x^4 - 5x^3 - x^2 - 8x + 4$ is two. According to Descartes' rule, there are either two or no positive roots to the equation. Since $P(-x) = 3(-x)^4 - 5(-x)^3 - (-x)^2 - 8(-x) + 4 = 3x^4 + 5x^3 - x^2 + 8x + 4$, there are two variations of sign in $P(-x)$. So the number of negative roots is either two or zero. Each line of the following table gives a possible distribution of the type of roots to the equation.

Number of Positive Roots	Number of Negative Roots	Number of Imaginary Roots
2	2	0
2	0	2
0	2	2
0	0	4

Descartes' rule of signs adds to our knowledge of the roots of an equation. It is especially helpful when the number of variations of sign is zero or one. If there are no variations in sign for $P(x)$, then there are no positive roots. If there is one variation of sign in $P(x)$, then we know that one positive root exists.

Bounds on the Roots

The next theorem on roots has to do with determining the size of the roots.

Theorem on Bounds

Suppose $P(x)$ is a polynomial with real coefficients and a positive leading coefficient, and synthetic division with c is performed.

- If $c > 0$ and all terms in the bottom row are nonnegative, then no number greater than c can be a root of $P(x) = 0$.
- If $c < 0$ and the terms in the bottom row alternate in sign, then no number less than c can be a root of $P(x) = 0$.

If there are no roots greater than c, then c is called an **upper bound** for the roots. If there are no roots less than c, then c is called a **lower bound** for the roots. If 0 appears in the bottom row of the synthetic division, we may consider it as positive or negative term in determining whether the signs alternate.

E X A M P L E   5

Integral bounds for the roots

Use the theorem on bounds to establish the best integral bounds for the roots of $2x^3 - 5x^2 - 6x + 4 = 0$.

Solution

Try synthetic division with the integers 1, 2, 3, and so on. The first integer for which all terms on the bottom row are nonnegative is the best upper bound for the roots:

$$
\begin{array}{r|rrrr}
1 & 2 & -5 & -6 & 4 \\
  &   & 2 & -3 & -9 \\
\hline
  & 2 & -3 & -9 & -5 \\
\end{array}
\qquad
\begin{array}{r|rrrr}
2 & 2 & -5 & -6 & 4 \\
  &   & 4 & -2 & -16 \\
\hline
  & 2 & -1 & -8 & -12 \\
\end{array}
$$

$$
\begin{array}{r|rrrr}
3 & 2 & -5 & -6 & 4 \\
  &   & 6 & 3 & -9 \\
\hline
  & 2 & 1 & -3 & -5 \\
\end{array}
\qquad
\begin{array}{r|rrrr}
4 & 2 & -5 & -6 & 4 \\
  &   & 8 & 12 & 24 \\
\hline
  & 2 & 3 & 6 & 28 \\
\end{array}
$$

By the theorem on bounds no number greater than 4 can be a root to the equation. Now try synthetic division with the integers -1, -2, -3, and so on. The first negative integer for which the terms on the bottom row alternate in sign is the best lower bound for the roots:

$$
\begin{array}{r|rrrr}
-1 & 2 & -5 & -6 & 4 \\
   &   & -2 & 7 & -1 \\
\hline
   & 2 & -7 & 1 & 3 \\
\end{array}
\qquad
\begin{array}{r|rrrr}
-2 & 2 & -5 & -6 & 4 \\
   &   & -2 & 14 & -16 \\
\hline
   & 2 & -7 & 8 & -12 \\
\end{array}
$$

By the theorem on bounds no number less than -2 can be a root to the equation. So all of the real roots to this equation are between -2 and 4. ■

In Example 6 we will use all of the information available to find all of the solutions to a polynomial equation.

E X A M P L E   6

Finding all solutions to a polynomial equation

Find all of the solutions to $2x^3 - 5x^2 - 6x + 4 = 0$.

Solution

In Example 3 we saw that this equation has either two positive roots and one negative root or one negative root and two imaginary roots. In Example 5 we saw that all of the real roots to this equation are between -2 and 4. From the rational root theorem we have ± 1, ± 2, ± 4, and $\pm \frac{1}{2}$ as the possible rational roots. Since there must be one negative root and it must be greater than -2, the only possible

Calculator Close-Up

Because all x-intercepts are between -2 and 4, the graph supports the conclusion that all of the roots to the equation are between -2 and 4.

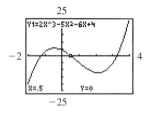

numbers from the list are -1 and $-\frac{1}{2}$. So start by checking $-\frac{1}{2}$ and -1 with synthetic division:

$$
\begin{array}{r|rrrr}
-\frac{1}{2} & 2 & -5 & -6 & 4 \\
             &   & -1 & 3 & \frac{3}{2} \\
\hline
             & 2 & -6 & -3 & \frac{11}{2}
\end{array}
\qquad
\begin{array}{r|rrrr}
-1 & 2 & -5 & -6 & 4 \\
   &   & -2 & 7 & -1 \\
\hline
   & 2 & -7 & 1 & 3
\end{array}
$$

Since neither -1 nor $-\frac{1}{2}$ is a root, the negative root must be irrational. Since there might be two positive roots smaller than 4, we check $\frac{1}{2}$, 1, and 2:

$$
\begin{array}{r|rrrr}
\frac{1}{2} & 2 & -5 & -6 & 4 \\
            &   & 1 & -2 & -4 \\
\hline
            & 2 & -4 & -8 & 0
\end{array}
$$

Since $\frac{1}{2}$ is a root of the equation, $x - \frac{1}{2}$ is a factor of the polynomial:

$$\left(x - \frac{1}{2}\right)(2x^2 - 4x - 8) = 0$$

$$(2x - 1)(x^2 - 2x - 4) = 0$$

$$2x - 1 = 0 \quad\text{ or }\quad x^2 - 2x - 4 = 0$$

$$x = \frac{1}{2} \quad\text{ or }\quad x = \frac{2 \pm \sqrt{4 - 4(1)(-4)}}{2} = 1 \pm \sqrt{5}$$

There are two positive roots, $\frac{1}{2}$ and $1 + \sqrt{5}$. The negative root is $1 - \sqrt{5}$. Note that the roots guaranteed by Descartes' rule of signs are real numbers but not necessarily rational numbers.   ∎

WARM-UPS

True or false? Explain your answer.

1. The number 3 is a root of $x^2 - 9 = 0$ with multiplicity 2.

2. Counting multiplicities, the equation $x^8 = 1$ has eight solutions in the set of complex numbers.

3. The number $\frac{2}{3}$ is a root of multiplicity 4 for the equation $(3x - 2)^4(x^2 + 2x + 1) = 0$.

4. The number 2 is a root of multiplicity 3 for the equation $(x - 2)^3(x^2 + x - 6) = 0$.

5. If $2 - 3i$ is a solution to a polynomial equation with real coefficients, then $-2 + 3i$ is also a solution to the equation.

6. If $P(x) = 0$ is a polynomial equation with real coefficients and $5 - 4i$ and $3 + 6i$ are solutions to $P(x) = 0$, then the degree of $P(x)$ is at least 4.

7. Both $-1 - i\sqrt{2}$ and $1 - i\sqrt{2}$ are solutions to $7x^3 - 5x^2 + 6x - 8 = 0$.

8. If $P(x) = x^3 - 6x^2 + 3x - 2$, then $P(-x) = -x^3 + 6x^2 - 3x + 2$.

9. The equation $x^3 + 5x^2 + 6x + 1 = 0$ has no positive solutions.

10. The equation $x^3 - 5 = 0$ has two imaginary solutions.

10.3   EXERCISES

Reading and Writing   After reading this section, write out the answers to these questions. Use complete sentences.

1. What is multiplicity?

2. What is the *n*-root theorem?

3. What is the conjugate pairs theorem?

4. What is Descartes' rule of signs?

5. What is an upper bound for the roots of a polynomial?

6. What is a lower bound for the roots?

State the degree of each polynomial equation. Find all of the real and imaginary roots to each equation. State the multiplicity of a root when it is greater than 1. See Example 1.

7. $x^5 - 4x^3 = 0$

8. $x^6 + 9x^4 = 0$

9. $x^4 + 2x^3 + x^2 = 0$

10. $x^5 - 4x^4 + 4x^3 = 0$

11. $x^4 - 6x^2 + 9 = 0$

12. $x^4 - 8x^2 + 16 = 0$

13. $(x - 1)^2(x + 2)^2 = 0$

14. $(2x + 1)^2(3x - 5)^4 = 0$

15. $x^4 - 2x^2 + 1 = 0$

16. $4x^4 - 4x^2 + 1 = 0$

Find a polynomial equation with real coefficients that has the given roots. See Example 2.

17. $3, 2 - i$

18. $-4, 3 + i$

19. $-2, i$

20. $4, -i$

21. $0, i\sqrt{2}$

22. $-3, i\sqrt{3}$

23. $i, 1 - i$

24. $2i, -i$

25. $1, 2$

26. $\dfrac{1}{2}, -1$

27. $-1, 2, 3$

28. $-2, 3, 2$

Discuss the possibilities for the roots to each equation. Do not solve the equation. See Examples 3 and 4.

29. $x^3 + 3x^2 + 5x + 7 = 0$

30. $2x^3 - 3x^2 + 5x - 6 = 0$

31. $-2x^3 - x^2 + 3x + 2 = 0$

32. $x^3 + x^2 - 5x - 1 = 0$

33. $x^4 - x^3 + x^2 - x + 1 = 0$

34. $x^4 - 1 = 0$

35. $x^4 + x^2 + 1 = 0$

36. $x^6 + 3x^4 + 2x^2 + 6 = 0$

37. $x^3 + x - 1 = 0$

38. $-x^4 + 3x^3 + 5x + 5 = 0$

39. $x^5 + x^3 + 3x = 0$

40. $x^3 - 5x^2 + 6x = 0$

Establish the best integral bounds for the roots of each equation according to the theorem on bounds. See Example 5.

41. $x^4 - 5x^2 + 7 = 0$

42. $2x^3 - x^2 - 7x + 7 = 0$

43. $2x^3 - 5x^2 + 9x - 18 = 0$

44. $x^2 - 7x - 16 = 0$

45. $x^2 + x - 13 = 0$

46. $x^3 - 15x + 25 = 0$

47. $2x^3 - 13x^2 + 25x - 14 = 0$

48. $x^3 - 6x^2 + 11x - 6 = 0$

Use the rational root theorem, Descartes' rule of signs, and the theorem on bounds as aids in finding all solutions to each equation. See Example 6.

49. $x^3 + x + 10 = 0$

50. $x^3 - 7x^2 + 17x - 15 = 0$

51. $2x^3 - 5x^2 - 6x + 4 = 0$

52. $3x^3 - 17x^2 + 12x + 6 = 0$

53. $4x^3 - 6x^2 - 2x + 1 = 0$

54. $x^3 + 5x^2 - 20x - 42 = 0$

55. $x^4 - 5x^3 + 5x^2 + 5x - 6 = 0$

56. $x^4 - 2x^3 + 5x^2 - 8x + 4 = 0$

57. $x^4 - 7x^3 + 17x^2 - 17x + 6 = 0$

58. $x^4 + 7x^3 + 17x^2 + 17x + 6 = 0$

59. $x^6 - x^5 + 2x^4 - 2x^3 - 15x^2 + 15x = 0$

60. $2x^6 + 4x^5 + x^4 + 2x^3 - x^2 - 2x = 0$

Solve each problem.

61. Willard is designing a cylindrical tank with cone-shaped ends. The length of the cylinder is to be 20 feet (ft) larger than the radius of the cylinder, and the height of the cone is 2 ft. If the volume of the tank is 984π cubic feet (ft^3), then what is the radius of the cylinder?

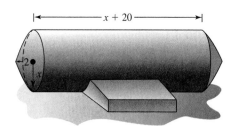

FIGURE FOR EXERCISE 61

62. Dr. Hu is designing a chemical storage tank in the shape of a cylinder with hemispherical ends. If the length of the cylinder is to be 20 ft larger than its radius and the volume is to be $3{,}321\pi$ ft^3, then what is the radius?

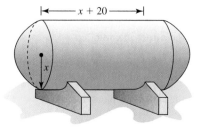

FIGURE FOR EXERCISE 62

63. A box of frozen specimens measures 4 inches by 5 inches by 3 inches. It is wrapped in an insulating material of uniform thickness for shipment. The volume of the box including the insulating material is 120 cubic inches (in.^{3}). How thick is the insulation?

64. An independent marketing research agency has determined that the best box for breakfast cereal has a height that is 6 inches (in.) larger than its thickness and a width that is 5 in. larger than its thickness. If such a box is to have a volume of 112 in.^{3}, then what should the thickness be?

GRAPHING CALCULATOR EXERCISES

Find all real roots to each polynomial equation by graphing the corresponding function and locating the x-intercepts.

65. $x^4 - 12x^2 + 10 = 0$

66. $x^5 + x^4 - 7x^3 - 7x^2 + 12x + 12 = 0$

67. $x^6 - 9x^4 + 20x^2 - 12 = 0$

68. $4x^5 + 16x^4 - 5x^3 - 20x^2 + x + 8 = 0$

In This Section

- Symmetry
- Behavior at the x-Intercepts
- Sketching Some Graphs

10.4 # GRAPHS OF POLYNOMIAL FUNCTIONS

The graph of a polynomial function of degree 0 or 1 is a straight line and the graph of a second-degree polynomial function is a parabola. In this section we will concentrate on graphs of polynomial functions of degree larger than 2.

Symmetry

Consider the graph of the quadratic function $f(x) = x^2$ shown in Fig. 10.1. Notice that both $(2, 4)$ and $(-2, 4)$ are on the graph. In fact, $f(x) = f(-x)$ for any value of x. We get the same y-coordinate whether we evaluate the function at a number or its opposite. This fact causes the graph to be symmetric about the y-axis. If we folded the paper along the y-axis, the two halves of the graph would coincide.

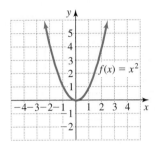

FIGURE 10.1

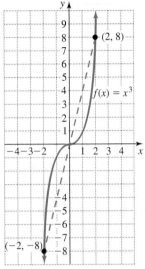

FIGURE 10.2

Symmetric about the y-Axis

If $f(x)$ is a function such that $f(x) = f(-x)$ for any value of x in its domain, then the graph of the function is said to be **symmetric about the y-axis.**

Consider the graph of $f(x) = x^3$ shown in Fig. 10.2. It is not symmetric about the y-axis like the graph of $f(x) = x^2$, but it has a different kind of symmetry. On the graph of $f(x) = x^3$ we find the points $(2, 8)$ and $(-2, -8)$. In this case $f(x)$ and $f(-x)$ are not equal, but $f(-x) = -f(x)$. Notice that the points $(2, 8)$ and $(-2, -8)$ are the same distance from the origin and lie on a line through the origin.

Symmetric about the Origin

If $f(x)$ is a function such that $f(-x) = -f(x)$ for any value of x in its domain, then the graph of the function is said to be **symmetric about the origin.**

EXAMPLE 1

Determining the symmetry of a graph

Discuss the symmetry of the graph of each polynomial function.

a) $f(x) = 5x^3 - x$

b) $f(x) = 2x^4 - 3x^2$

c) $f(x) = x^2 - 3x + 6$

Solution

a) Since $f(-x) = 5(-x)^3 - (-x) = -5x^3 + x$, we have $f(-x)$ equal to the opposite of $f(x)$. So the graph is symmetric about the origin.

b) Since $f(-x) = 2(-x)^4 - 3(-x)^2 = 2x^4 - 3x^2$, we have $f(x) = f(-x)$. So the graph is symmetric about the y-axis.

c) In this case $f(-x) = (-x)^2 - 3(-x) + 6 = x^2 + 3x + 6$. So $f(-x) \neq f(x)$ and $f(-x) \neq -f(x)$. This graph has neither type of symmetry. ■

Calculator Close-Up

We can use graphs to check the conclusions about symmetry that were arrived at algebraically in Example 1. The graph of $f(x) = 5x^3 - x$ appears to be symmetric about the origin.

The graph of $f(x) = 2x^4 - 3x^2$ appears to be symmetric about the y-axis.

The graph of $f(x) = x^2 - 3x + 6$ does not appear to have either type of symmetry.

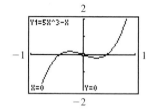

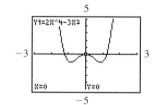

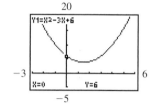

Behavior at the x-Intercepts

Each of the graphs of $f(x) = x^2$ and $f(x) = x^3$ has one x-intercept $(0, 0)$. If we use a positive or negative number very close to 0 for x in $f(x) = x^2$, the y-coordinate is positive because the power on x is even. That is why the graph just touches the x-axis at $(0, 0)$ but does not cross the x-axis there. If we use a positive number very close to 0 for x in $f(x) = x^3$, we get a positive y-coordinate. If we use a negative number very close to 0 for x in $f(x) = x^3$, we get a negative y-coordinate because the power on x is odd. That is why the graph crosses the x-axis at $(0, 0)$. In general, the graph crosses the x-axis at an x-intercept if the factor that produces that intercept has an odd power and the graph does not cross if the factor has an even power.

E X A M P L E   2   **Behavior at the x-intercepts**

Find the x-intercepts and discuss the behavior of the graph of each polynomial function at its x-intercepts.

a) $f(x) = (x - 1)^2(x - 3)$ **b)** $f(x) = x^3 + 2x^2 - 3x$

Solution

a) The x-intercepts are found by solving $(x - 1)^2(x - 3) = 0$. The x-intercepts are $(1, 0)$ and $(3, 0)$. The graph does not cross the x-axis at $(1, 0)$ but does cross the x-axis at $(3, 0)$.

b) The x-intercepts are found by solving $x^3 + 2x^2 - 3x = 0$. By factoring, we get $x(x + 3)(x - 1) = 0$. The x-intercepts are $(0, 0)$, $(-3, 0)$, and $(1, 0)$. Since each factor occurs an odd number of times, the graph crosses the x-axis at each of the x-intercepts. ∎

Calculator Close-Up

The graphs of the functions in Example 2 support the conclusions about the behavior at the x-intercepts.

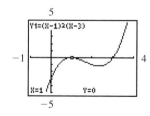

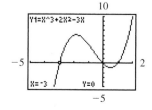

Sketching Some Graphs

We can use our knowledge of symmetry and the behavior at the x-intercepts to sketch some graphs of polynomial functions. To find the x-intercepts, we might have to use the ideas of Section 10.2 to find the roots of a polynomial equation.

E X A M P L E   3

Graphing a polynomial function

Sketch the graph of each polynomial function.

a) $f(x) = x^3 - 5x^2 + 7x - 3$

b) $f(x) = x^4 - 2x^2 + 1$

Calculator Close-Up

This calculator graph supports the conclusions made in Example 3(a).

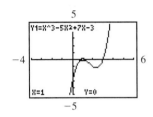

Solution

a) Since $f(-x) = -x^3 - 5x^2 - 7x - 3$, the graph has neither type of symmetry. By Descartes' rule of signs there are no negative roots to the equation $x^3 - 5x^2 + 7x - 3 = 0$, and the number of positive roots is either 3 or 1. So the only possible rational roots are 1 and 3:

$$
\begin{array}{r|rrr}
1 & 1 & -5 & 7 & -3 \\
  &   & 1 & -4 & 3 \\
\hline
  & 1 & -4 & 3 & 0
\end{array}
$$

From the synthetic division we get $f(x) = (x - 1)(x^2 - 4x + 3)$, and if we factor again, we get $f(x) = (x - 1)^2(x - 3)$. The x-intercepts are $(1, 0)$ and $(3, 0)$. The discussion of Example 2(a) applies to this function. The points $(0, -3)$, $(2, -1)$, and $(4, 9)$ are also on the graph. The graph is shown in Fig. 10.3.

b) Since $f(-x) = (-x)^4 - 2(-x)^2 + 1 = x^4 - 2x^2 + 1$, we have $f(x) = f(-x)$. So the graph is symmetric about the y-axis. We can factor the polynomial as follows:

$$
\begin{aligned}
f(x) &= x^4 - 2x^2 + 1 \\
     &= (x^2 - 1)(x^2 - 1) \\
     &= (x - 1)(x + 1)(x - 1)(x + 1) \\
     &= (x - 1)^2(x + 1)^2
\end{aligned}
$$

Calculator Close-Up

This calculator graph supports the conclusions made in Example 3(b).

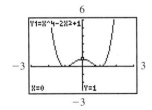

The x-intercepts are $(1, 0)$ and $(-1, 0)$. Since each factor for these intercepts has an even power, the graph does not cross the x-axis at the intercepts. The points $(0, 1)$, $(2, 9)$, and $(-2, 9)$ are also on the graph shown in Fig. 10.4.

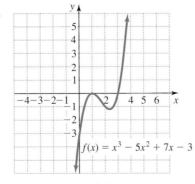

FIGURE 10.3

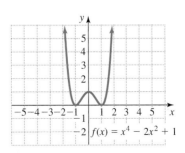

FIGURE 10.4

True or false? Explain your answer.

1. The graph of $f(x) = x^3 - x$ is symmetric about the y-axis.
2. The graph of $y = 2x - 1$ is symmetric about the origin.
3. If the graph of a polynomial function $y = P(x)$ is symmetric about the y-axis and $P(3) = 16$, then $P(-3) = -16$.
4. For the function $f(x) = 3x$ we have $f(x) = f(-x)$ for any value of x.
5. If $f(x) = 3x^4 - 5x^3 + 2x^2 - 6x + 7$, then
   $f(-x) = 3x^4 + 5x^3 + 2x^2 + 6x + 7$.
6. There is only one x-intercept for the graph of $f(x) = x^2 - 4x + 4$.
7. The points $(0, 2)$ and $(0, -3)$ are the x-intercepts for the graph of the function $P(x) = (x - 2)^2(x + 3)$.
8. The y-intercept for the graph of $P(x) = 3x^3 - 7x^2 + 8x - 9$ is $(0, 9)$.
9. The graph of $f(x) = (x - 1)^2(x + 4)^2$ does not cross the x-axis at either of its x-intercepts.
10. The graph of $f(x) = x^3 - 8$ has three x-intercepts.

10.4   EXERCISES

Reading and Writing   *After reading this section, write out the answers to these questions. Use complete sentences.*

1. What does symmetric about the y-axis mean?

2. What does symmetric about the origin mean?

3. What is an x-intercept?

4. How can you determine whether the graph of a polynomial function crosses the x-axis at an x-intercept?

Discuss the symmetry of the graph of each polynomial function. See Example 1.

5. $f(x) = x^4$
6. $f(x) = x^4 - x$
7. $f(x) = x^3 - 5x + 1$
8. $f(x) = 5x^3 + 7x$
9. $f(x) = 6x^6 - 3x^2 - x$
10. $f(x) = x^6 - x^4 + x^2 - 8$
11. $f(x) = (x - 3)^2$

12. $f(x) = 3(x + 2)^2$
13. $f(x) = (x^2 - 5)^3$
14. $f(x) = (x^2 + 1)^2$
15. $f(x) = x$
16. $f(x) = -3x$

Find the x-intercepts and discuss the behavior of the graph of each polynomial function at its x-intercepts. See Example 2.

17. $f(x) = (x - 5)^2$
18. $f(x) = 3x - 2$

19. $f(x) = x^2 - 3x - 4$
20. $f(x) = 9x^2 - 12x + 4$
21. $f(x) = x^4$
22. $f(x) = x^4 - 1$
23. $f(x) = (x - 3)^2(x + 5)$

24. $f(x) = (2x + 1)^3$
25. $f(x) = x^3 - x^2$

26. $f(x) = x^3 - x^2 - x + 1$

27. $f(x) = 2x^3 + 3x^2 - 1$

28. $f(x) = x^3 + 3x^2 - 4$

Match each polynomial function with its graph a–h.

29. $f(x) = -2x + 3$

30. $f(x) = -2x^2 + 3$

31. $f(x) = -2x^3 + 3$

32. $f(x) = -2x^2 + 4x + 3$

33. $f(x) = -x^4 + 3$

34. $f(x) = x^3 - 3x^2$

35. $f(x) = x^3 + 3x^2 - x - 3$

36. $f(x) = \dfrac{1}{2}x^4 - 3$

(a)

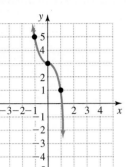

(b)

(c)

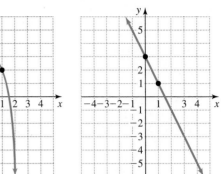

(d)

(e)

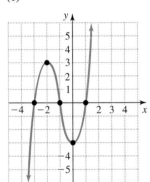

(f)

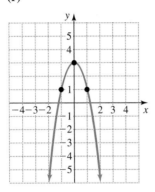

(g)

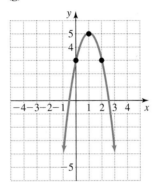

(h)

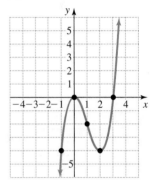

Sketch the graph of each polynomial function. See Example 3.

37. $f(x) = 2x - 6$

38. $f(x) = -3x + 3$

39. $f(x) = -x^2$

40. $f(x) = x^2 - 3$

41. $f(x) = x^3 - 2x^2$

42. $f(x) = x^3 - 4x$

43. $f(x) = (x - 1)^2(x + 1)^2$

44. $f(x) = (x + 2)^2(x - 1)$

45. $f(x) = x^3 - 5x^2 + 7x - 3$

46. $f(x) = x^3 + 2x^2 - 3x$

47. $f(x) = x^4 - 4x^3 + 4x^2$

48. $f(x) = -x^4 + 6x^3 - 9x^2$

GRAPHING CALCULATOR EXERCISES

Sketch the graph of each polynomial function. First graph the function on a calculator and use the calculator graph as a guide.

49. $f(x) = x - 20$

50. $f(x) = (x - 20)^2$

51. $f(x) = (x - 20)^2(x + 30)$

52. $f(x) = (x - 20)^2(x + 30)^2$

53. $f(x) = (x - 20)^2(x + 30)^2x$

54. $f(x) = (x - 20)^2(x + 30)^2x^2$

10.5 GRAPHS OF RATIONAL FUNCTIONS

We first studied rational expressions in Chapter 6. In this section we will study functions that are defined by rational expressions.

Domain

A rational expression was defined in Chapter 6 as a ratio of two polynomials. If a ratio of two polynomials is used to define a function, then the function is called a rational function.

> **Rational Function**
>
> If $P(x)$ and $Q(x)$ are polynomials with no common factor and $f(x) = \dfrac{P(x)}{Q(x)}$ for $Q(x) \neq 0$, then $f(x)$ is called a **rational function.**

The domain of a rational function is the set of all real numbers except those that cause the denominator to have a value of 0.

EXAMPLE 1

Domain of a rational function

Find the domain of each rational function.

a) $f(x) = \dfrac{x - 3}{x - 1}$

b) $g(x) = \dfrac{2x - 3}{x^2 - 4}$

Solution

a) Since $x - 1 = 0$ only for $x = 1$, the domain of f is the set of all real numbers except 1, $(-\infty, 1) \cup (1, \infty)$.

b) Since $x^2 - 4 = 0$ for $x = \pm 2$, the domain of g is the set of all real numbers excluding 2 and -2, $(-\infty, -2) \cup (-2, 2) \cup (2, \infty)$. ∎

Horizontal and Vertical Asymptotes

Consider the simplest rational function $f(x) = 1/x$. Its domain does not include 0, but 0 is an important number for the graph of this function. The behavior of the graph of f when x is very close to 0 is what interests us. For this function the y-coordinate is the reciprocal of the x-coordinate. When the x-coordinate is close

Calculator Close-Up

If the viewing window is too large, a rational function will appear to touch its asymptotes.

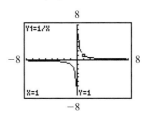

Because the asymptotes are an important feature of a rational function, we should draw it so that it approaches but does not touch its asymptotes.

> ### Strategy for Finding Asymptotes for a Rational Function
>
> Suppose $f(x) = \frac{P(x)}{Q(x)}$ is a rational function with the degree of $Q(x)$ at least 1.
>
> 1. Solve the equation $Q(x) = 0$. The graph of f has a vertical asymptote corresponding to each solution to the equation.
>
> 2. If the degree of $P(x)$ is less than the degree of $Q(x)$, then the x-axis is a horizontal asymptote.
>
> 3. If the degree of $P(x)$ is equal to the degree of $Q(x)$, then find the ratio of the leading coefficients. The horizontal line through that ratio is the horizontal asymptote.
>
> 4. If the degree of $P(x)$ is one larger than the degree of $Q(x)$, then use division to rewrite the function as
>
> $$\text{quotient} + \frac{\text{remainder}}{\text{divisor}}.$$
>
> The equation formed by setting y equal to the quotient gives us an oblique asymptote.

M A T H   A T   W O R K

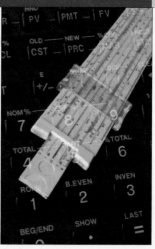

Machines that do computations have been around for thousands of years. The abacus, the slide rule, and the calculator have simplified computations. However, recent calculators have gone way beyond numerical computations. Graphing calculators now draw two- and three-dimensional graphs and even do symbolic computations. Modern calculators are great, but to use one effectively you must still learn the underlying principles of mathematics.

Consider the fairly simple process of drawing a graph of a function. The graph of a function is a picture of all ordered pairs of the function. When we graph a function, we typically plot a few ordered pairs and then use our knowledge about the function to draw a graph that shows all of the important features

MATHEMATICS MACHINES

of the function. A typical graphing calculator plots 96 ordered pairs of a function on a screen that is not much bigger than a postage stamp. The calculator does not generalize and does not make conclusions. We are still responsible for looking at what the calculator shows and making conclusions. For example, if we graphed $y = 1/(x - 100)$ with the window set for $-10 \le x \le 10$, we would not see the vertical asymptote $x = 100$. Would we believe the calculator and conclude that the graph has no vertical asymptote? If we graph $y = 1/x$ with the window set for $-500 \le x \le 500$ and $-500 \le y \le 500$, the graph will be too close to its horizontal and vertical asymptotes for us to see it. Would we conclude that there is no graph for $y = 1/x$?

If you have a graphing calculator, use it to help you graph the functions in this chapter and to reinforce your understanding of the properties of functions that we are learning. Do not attempt to use it as a substitute for learning.

Sketching the Graphs

We now use asymptotes and symmetry to help us sketch the graphs of some rational functions.

E X A M P L E   4

Graphing a rational function

Sketch the graph of each rational function.

a) $f(x) = \dfrac{3}{x^2 - 1}$

b) $g(x) = \dfrac{x}{x^2 - 4}$

Calculator Close-Up

This calculator graph supports the graph drawn in Fig. 10.7. Remember that the calculator graph can be misleading. The vertical lines drawn by the calculator are not part of the graph of the function.

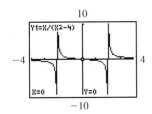

Solution

a) From Example 2(a) we know that the lines $x = 1$ and $x = -1$ are vertical asymptotes and the x-axis is a horizontal asymptote. Draw the vertical asymptotes on the graph with dashed lines. Since all of the powers of x are even, $f(x) = f(-x)$, and the graph is symmetric about the y-axis. The ordered pairs $(0, -3)$, $(0.9, -15.789)$, $(1.1, 14.286)$, $(2, 1)$, and $\left(3, \dfrac{3}{8}\right)$ are also on the graph. Use the symmetry to sketch the graph shown in Fig. 10.6.

b) Draw the vertical asymptotes $x = 2$ and $x = -2$ from Example 2(b) as dashed lines. The x-axis is a horizontal asymptote. Because $f(-x) = -f(x)$, the graph is symmetric about the origin. The ordered pairs $(0, 0)$, $\left(1, -\dfrac{1}{3}\right)$, $(1.9, -4.872)$, $(2.1, 5.122)$, $\left(3, \dfrac{3}{5}\right)$, and $\left(4, \dfrac{1}{3}\right)$ are on the graph. Use the symmetry to get the graph shown in Fig. 10.7.

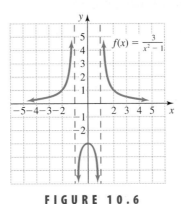

FIGURE 10.6

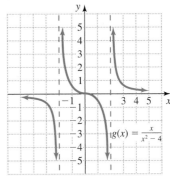

FIGURE 10.7

E X A M P L E   5

Graphing a rational function

Sketch the graph of each rational function.

a) $h(x) = \dfrac{2x + 1}{x + 3}$

b) $g(x) = \dfrac{2x^2 + 3x - 5}{x + 2}$

Calculator Close-Up

This calculator graph supports the graph drawn in Fig. 10.8. Note that if x is -3, there is no y-coordinate because $x = -3$ is the vertical asymptote.

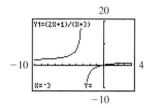

Solution

a) Draw the vertical asymptote $x = -3$ and the horizontal asymptote $y = 2$ from Example 2(c) as dashed lines. The points $(-2, -3)$, $\left(0, \frac{1}{3}\right)$, $\left(-\frac{1}{2}, 0\right)$, $(7, 1.5)$, $(-4, 7)$, and $(-13, 2.5)$ are on the graph shown in Fig. 10.8.

b) Draw the vertical asymptote $x = -2$ and the oblique asymptote $y = 2x - 1$ from Example 3 as dashed lines. The points $(-1, -6)$, $\left(0, -\frac{5}{2}\right)$, $(1, 0)$, $(4, 6.5)$, and $(-2.5, 0)$ are on the graph shown in Fig. 10.9.

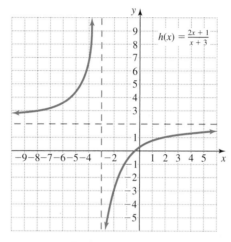

FIGURE 10.8

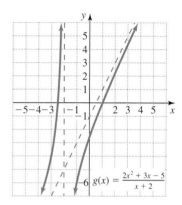

FIGURE 10.9

WARM-UPS

True or false? Explain your answer.

1. The domain of $f(x) = \dfrac{1}{x - 9}$ is $x = 9$.

2. The domain of $f(x) = \dfrac{x - 1}{x + 2}$ is $(-\infty, -2) \cup (-2, 1) \cup (1, \infty)$.

3. The domain of $f(x) = \dfrac{1}{x^2 + 1}$ is $(-\infty, -1) \cup (-1, 1) \cup (1, \infty)$.

4. The line $x = 2$ is the only vertical asymptote for the graph of $f(x) = \dfrac{1}{x^2 - 4}$.

5. The x-axis is a horizontal asymptote for the graph of $f(x) = \dfrac{x^2 - 3x + 5}{x^3 - 9x}$.

6. The x-axis is a horizontal asymptote for the graph of $f(x) = \dfrac{3x - 5}{x - 2}$.

7. The line $y = 2x - 5$ is an asymptote for the graph of $f(x) = 2x - 5 + \dfrac{1}{x}$.

8. The line $y = 2x - 5$ is an asymptote for the graph of $f(x) = 2x - 5 + x^2$.

9. The graph of $f(x) = \dfrac{x^2}{x^2 - 9}$ is symmetric about the y-axis.

10. The graph of $f(x) = \dfrac{3x}{x^2 - 25}$ is symmetric about the origin.

10.5   EXERCISES

Reading and Writing   *After reading this section, write out the answers to these questions. Use complete sentences.*

1. What is a rational function?

2. What is the domain of a rational function?

3. What is a vertical asymptote?

4. What is a horizontal asymptote?

5. What is an oblique asymptote?

6. What is a slant asymptote?

Find the domain of each rational function. See Example 1.

7. $f(x) = \dfrac{2}{x - 1}$

8. $f(x) = \dfrac{-2}{x + 3}$

9. $f(x) = \dfrac{x^2 - 1}{x}$

10. $f(x) = \dfrac{-2x + 3}{x^2}$

11. $f(x) = \dfrac{5}{x^2 - 16}$

12. $f(x) = \dfrac{x + 12}{x^2 - x - 6}$

Determine all asymptotes for the graph of each rational function. See Examples 2 and 3.

13. $f(x) = \dfrac{7}{x + 4}$

14. $f(x) = \dfrac{-8}{x - 9}$

15. $f(x) = \dfrac{1}{x^2 - 16}$

16. $f(x) = \dfrac{-2}{x^2 - 5x + 6}$

17. $f(x) = \dfrac{5x}{x - 7}$

18. $f(x) = \dfrac{3x + 8}{x - 2}$

19. $f(x) = \dfrac{2x^2}{x - 3}$

20. $f(x) = \dfrac{3x^2 + 2}{x + 1}$

Match each rational function with its graph a–h.

21. $f(x) = -\dfrac{2}{x}$

22. $f(x) = -\dfrac{1}{x - 2}$

23. $f(x) = \dfrac{x}{x - 2}$

24. $f(x) = \dfrac{x - 2}{x}$

25. $f(x) = \dfrac{1}{x^2 - 2x}$

26. $f(x) = \dfrac{x^2}{x^2 - 4}$

27. $f(x) = -\dfrac{x + 4}{2}$

28. $f(x) = \dfrac{x^2 + 2x + 1}{x}$

(a)

(b)

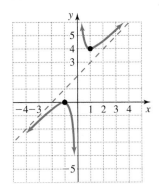

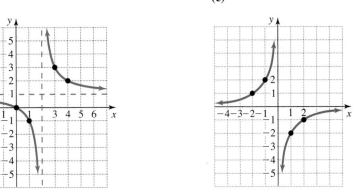

(c)

(d)

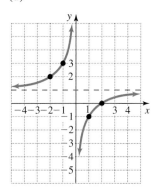

(e)

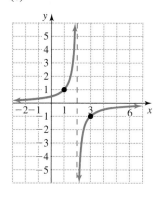

(f)

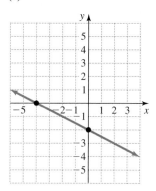

(g)

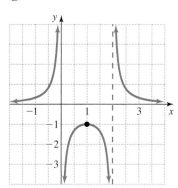

(h)

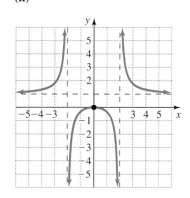

Determine all asymptotes and sketch the graph of each function. See Examples 4 and 5.

29. $f(x) = \dfrac{2}{x + 4}$

30. $f(x) = \dfrac{-3}{x - 1}$

31. $f(x) = \dfrac{x}{x^2 - 9}$

32. $f(x) = \dfrac{-2}{x^2 + x - 2}$

33. $f(x) = \dfrac{2x - 1}{x + 3}$

38. $f(x) = \dfrac{-x^2 + 5x - 5}{x - 3}$

34. $f(x) = \dfrac{5 - 2x}{x - 2}$

Find all asymptotes, x-intercepts, and y-intercepts for the graph of each rational function and sketch the graph of the function.

39. $f(x) = \dfrac{1}{x^2}$

35. $f(x) = \dfrac{x^2 - 3x + 1}{x}$

40. $f(x) = \dfrac{2}{x^2 - 4x + 4}$

36. $f(x) = \dfrac{x^3 + 1}{x^2}$

41. $f(x) = \dfrac{2x - 3}{x^2 + x - 6}$

37. $f(x) = \dfrac{3x^2 - 2x}{x - 1}$

42. $f(x) = \dfrac{x}{x^2 + 4x + 4}$

43. $f(x) = \dfrac{x + 1}{x^2}$

44. $f(x) = \dfrac{x - 1}{x^2}$

45. $f(x) = \dfrac{2x - 1}{x^3 - 9x}$

46. $f(x) = \dfrac{2x^2 + 1}{x^3 - x}$

47. $f(x) = \dfrac{x}{x^2 - 1}$

48. $f(x) = \dfrac{x}{x^2 + x - 2}$

49. $f(x) = \dfrac{2}{x^2 + 1}$

50. $f(x) = \dfrac{x}{x^2 + 1}$

51. $f(x) = \dfrac{x^2}{x + 1}$

52. $f(x) = \dfrac{x^2}{x-1}$

Solve each problem.

53. *Oscillating modulators.* The number of oscillating modulators produced by a factory in t hours is given by the polynomial function $n(t) = t^2 + 6t$ for $t \geq 1$. The cost in dollars of operating the factory for t hours is given by the function $c(t) = 36t + 500$ for $t \geq 1$. The average cost per modulator is given by the rational function $f(t) = \dfrac{36t + 500}{t^2 + 6t}$ for $t \geq 1$. Graph the function f. What is the average cost per modulator at time $t = 20$ and time $t = 30$? What can you conclude about the average cost per modulator after a long period of time?

54. *Nonoscillating modulators.* The number of nonoscillating modulators produced by a factory in t hours is given by the polynomial function $n(t) = 16t$ for $t \geq 1$. The cost in dollars of operating the factory for t hours is given by the function $c(t) = 64t + 500$ for $t \geq 1$. The average cost per modulator is given by the rational function $f(t) = \dfrac{64t + 500}{16t}$ for $t \geq 1$. Graph the function f. What is the average cost per modulator at time $t = 10$ and $t = 20$? What can you conclude about the average cost per modulator after a long period of time?

55. *Average cost of an SUV.* Mercedes-Benz spent $700 million to design its new 1998 SUV (Motor Trend, www.motortrend.com). If it costs $25,000 to manufacture each SUV, then the average cost per vehicle in dollars when x vehicles are manufactured is given by the rational function

$$A(x) = \frac{25{,}000x + 700{,}000{,}000}{x}.$$

a) What is the horizontal asymptote for the graph of this function?

b) What is the average cost per vehicle when 50,000 vehicles are made?

c) For what number of vehicles is the average cost $30,000?

d) Graph this function for x ranging from 0 to 100,000.

56. *Average cost of a pill.* Assuming Pfizer spent a typical $350 million to develop its latest miracle drug and $0.10 each to make the pills, then the average cost per pill in

FIGURE FOR EXERCISE 56

dollars when x pills are made is given by the rational function

$$A(x) = \frac{0.10x + 350,000,000}{x}.$$

a) What is the horizontal asymptote for the graph of this function?

b) What is the average cost per pill when 100 million pills are made?

c) For what number of pills is the average cost per pill $2?

d) Graph this function for x ranging from 0 to 100 million.

GRAPHING CALCULATOR EXERCISES

Sketch the graph of each pair of functions in the same coordinate system. What do you observe in each case?

57. $f(x) = x^2$, $g(x) = x^2 + 1/x$

58. $f(x) = x^2$, $g(x) = x^2 + 1/x^2$

59. $f(x) = |x|$, $g(x) = |x| + 1/x$

60. $f(x) = |x|$, $g(x) = |x| + 1/x^2$

61. $f(x) = \sqrt{x}$, $g(x) = \sqrt{x} + 1/x$

62. $f(x) = x^3$, $g(x) = x^3 + 1/x^2$

COLLABORATIVE ACTIVITIES

Betting on Rockets

Gretchen and Rafael are launching model rockets in the park. They have a bet to see whose rocket can go the highest. Both have taken this math course and have some clues on how to use algebra to find out whose went the highest. Below is the formula that they will use to determine whose rocket has gone the highest:

$$h = -16t^2 + v_0 t,$$

where h is the distance (feet) of the rocket above the ground, t is the time passed (seconds) since the rocket was launched, and v_0 is the speed of the rocket when launched (initial velocity).

They have decided to do three trials and to see whose is the highest two out of the three times.

From the following list, have each member of your group choose a different trial.

- **First Trial:** On the first launch Gretchen's rocket has a time in the air of 14 seconds, and Rafael's rocket has a time of 10 seconds.

Grouping: 3 students per group

Topic: Applications of maximum and minimum of a parabola

- **Second Trial:** On the second launch Gretchen's rocket was in the air 11.5 seconds, and Rafael's rocket was in the air 12 seconds.

- **Third Trial:** On the third launch Gretchen's rocket was in the air 11.25 seconds, and Rafael's rocket was in the air 11.3 seconds.

Individually, complete the following for the trial you selected.

1. Find the initial velocity for each rocket using the formula $h = -16t^2 + v_0 t$.

2. Graph the two quadratic functions. What is the h-value for each vertex? Whose rocket went the highest?

Together in your groups, compare your results and decide who wins the bet.

WRAP-UP

CHAPTER 10

SUMMARY

Polynomial Functions		Examples
Polynomial function	A function defined by a polynomial	$P(x) = x^2 - x - 12$
Root or zero of a function	A number c such that $f(c) = 0$	Since $P(4) = 4^2 - 4 - 12 = 0$, 4 is a root or zero of the function P.
Factor theorem	The following are equivalent for $P(x)$ a polynomial in x. 1. The remainder is zero when $P(x)$ is divided by $x - c$. 2. $x - c$ is a factor of $P(x)$. 3. c is a solution to $P(x) = 0$. 4. c is a zero of the function $P(x)$, or $P(c) = 0$.	$P(x) = x^2 - x - 2$ $P(x) = (x - 2)(x + 1)$ $P(-1) = 0$, $P(2) = 0$ -1 and 2 both satisfy $x^2 - x - 2 = 0$
Remainder theorem	If R is the remainder when a polynomial $P(x)$ is divided by $x - c$, then $R = P(c)$.	$P(x) = x^2 - x - 12$, $P(2) = -\mathbf{10}$ $\dfrac{x^2 - x - 12}{x - 2} = x + 1 + \dfrac{-\mathbf{10}}{x - 2}$
Fundamental theorem of algebra	If $P(x)$ is a polynomial function of positive degree, then $P(x)$ has at least one complex zero.	$H(x) = x^7 - \pi x^6 + 99x^5 + x - \sqrt{2}$ has at least one complex zero.
Rational root theorem	If $P(x)$ is a polynomial with integral coefficients, then any rational zero is a factor of the constant term divided by a factor of the leading coefficient.	The possible rational zeros for $P(x) = 2x^2 - 3x + 1$ are ± 1 and $\pm \dfrac{1}{2}$.
Multiplicity	If $x - c$ occurs n times in the complete factorization of $P(x)$, then c is a root of $P(x) = 0$ with multiplicity n.	If $P(x) = (x - 2)^2$, then 2 is a root of $(x - 2)^2 = 0$ with multiplicity 2.
n-root theorem	If $P(x) = 0$ is a polynomial equation with real or complex coefficients and positive degree n, then counting multiplicity $P(x) = 0$ has n complex roots.	$x^3 - 5x = 0$ has three roots. $x^4 - 1 = 0$ has four roots.
Conjugate pairs theorem	If $P(x) = 0$ is a polynomial equation with real coefficients and $a + bi$ ($b \neq 0$) is a root, then $a - bi$ is also a root.	The roots to $x^2 - 6x + 13 = 0$ are $3 + 2i$ and $3 - 2i$.

10.2 *For each polynomial find $P(-2)$ and $P\left(\frac{1}{2}\right)$ in two different ways.*

9. $P(x) = 4x^3 - 2x^2 + 3x + 1$

10. $P(x) = 2x^3 - 3x^2 + 5x - 2$

Use the rational root theorem to list all possible rational roots for each polynomial function.

11. $f(x) = 3x^3 - 5x^2 + 7x - 4$

12. $f(x) = 2x^4 - 5x^2 + 3x - 5$

13. $f(x) = 4x^4 - 5x^2 - 3x + 3$

14. $f(x) = 6x^3 + x^2 - 25x - 9$

Find all real and imaginary zeros for each polynomial function.

15. $f(x) = 2x - 3$

16. $f(x) = 5$

17. $f(x) = x^2 - 100$

18. $f(x) = 2x^2 - 1$

19. $f(x) = x^3 - 64$

20. $f(x) = x^3 - 27$

21. $f(x) = x^4 - 64$

22. $f(x) = 4x^4 - 1$

23. $f(x) = 12x^3 - 4x^2 - 3x + 1$

24. $f(x) = 18x^3 + 9x^2 - 2x - 1$

10.3 *Find a polynomial equation with real coefficients that has the given roots.*

25. $\frac{1}{2}, 2$

26. $\frac{1}{3}, -4$

27. $5 - 2i$

28. $3 + 2i$

29. $3, 1 + 3i$

30. $-5, 2 - 4i$

Use Descartes' rule of signs to discuss the possibilities for the roots to each equation. Do not solve the equation.

31. $x^6 + x^4 + x^2 = 0$

32. $2x^3 - 3x^2 - 5x - 9 = 0$

33. $x^3 - 5x^2 + 3x - 9 = 0$

34. $x^5 + x^3 + 5x = 0$

Establish the best integral bounds for the roots of each equation according to the theorem on bounds.

35. $x^2 - 2x - 4 = 0$

36. $x^2 - 2x - 6 = 0$

37. $x^3 - 3x^2 - 5x - 6 = 0$

38. $2x^3 - 4x^2 - 12x - 7 = 0$

Find all real and imaginary solutions to each equation, stating multiplicity when it is greater than 1.

39. $2x^3 - 19x^2 + 49x - 20 = 0$

40. $3x^3 + 2x^2 - 37x + 12 = 0$

41. $8x^3 - 12x^2 - 26x + 15 = 0$

42. $12x^3 - 16x^2 - 5x + 3 = 0$

43. $4x^3 - 24x^2 + 25x - 25 = 0$

44. $2x^3 + 4x^2 - 5x + 3 = 0$

45. $4x^4 - 28x^3 + 59x^2 - 30x - 9 = 0$

46. $2x^4 - 6x^3 + 5x^2 - 1 = 0$

47. $x^3 - 3x^2 + 3x - 1 = 0$

48. $x^4 - 4x^3 + 6x^2 - 4x + 1 = 0$

10.4 *Discuss the symmetry of the graph of each function.*

49. $f(x) = 3x^4 - 2x^2$

50. $f(x) = x^7 - 3x^5 + x^3$

51. $f(x) = -x^3 + 3x$

52. $f(x) = -2x^4 + 6x^2 + 3$

Find the x-intercepts and y-intercept for the graph of each function, and sketch the graph.

53. $f(x) = x^3 - 3x + 2$

54. $f(x) = -x^3 - 3x^2 + 4$

55. $f(x) = -x^4 + 2x^2 - 1$

56. $f(x) = x^4 - 2x^2$

57. $f(x) = \frac{1}{2}x^3 - 2x$

58. $f(x) = x^3 - 6x^2 + 8x$

10.5 *Find the domain of each rational function.*

59. $f(x) = \frac{x^2 - 1}{2x + 3}$

60. $f(x) = \frac{3x + 2}{x^2 - x - 12}$

61. $f(x) = \frac{1}{x^2 + 9}$

62. $f(x) = \frac{x - 4}{x^2 - 9}$

Find all asymptotes for each rational function and sketch the graph of the function.

63. $f(x) = \frac{2}{x - 3}$

64. $f(x) = \frac{-1}{x + 1}$

65. $f(x) = \frac{x}{x^2 - 4}$

66. $f(x) = \frac{x^2}{x^2 - 4}$

67. $f(x) = \dfrac{2x - 1}{x - 1}$ **68.** $f(x) = \dfrac{-x - 1}{x}$ **75.** $f(x) = \dfrac{1}{x^2 - 3}$ **76.** $f(x) = \dfrac{x}{(x - 1)(x + 2)}$

77. $f(x) = x(x - 1)(x + 2)$

69. $f(x) = \dfrac{x^2 - 2x + 1}{x - 2}$ **70.** $f(x) = \dfrac{-x^2 + x + 2}{x - 1}$

78. $f(x) = x^3 - 4x^2 + 4x$

MISCELLANEOUS

Sketch the graph of each function.

71. $f(x) = 3$ **72.** $f(x) = 2x - 3$

Solve each problem.

79. Tanya is designing a trophy for a golf tournament. The trophy consists of a solid bronze sphere mounted on a solid bronze square base. The diameter of the sphere will equal

73. $f(x) = x^2 - 3$ **74.** $f(x) = 3 - x^2$

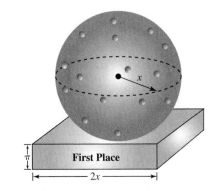

FIGURE FOR EXERCISE 79

the length of the side of the square, and the thickness of the base will be π inches (in.). If she wants to use 72π cubic inches (in.^{3}) of bronze for the trophy, then what is the radius of the sphere?

80. Joshua is designing a metal silo for storing grain. The silo consists of a cylindrical base with a cone-shaped roof. He wants the radius of the base to be equal to its height and the height of the cone to be 5 feet (ft). If the silo is to have a volume of 864π ft^3, then what is the radius of the base?

FIGURE FOR EXERCISE 80

CHAPTER 10 TEST

Find the following values for $f(x) = 3x^4 + 5x^3 - 10x^2 + 3x - 2$ using two different methods.

1. $f(2)$

2. $f(-3)$

Find all possible rational zeros for each polynomial function.

3. $f(x) = x^4 + x^3 - 7x^2 + 5x - 6$

4. $f(x) = 2x^3 - 5x^2 + 9x - 3$

Find all of the real and imaginary zeros for each polynomial function.

5. $f(x) = x^3 - 13x + 12$

6. $f(x) = 2x^3 - 9x^2 + 14x - 5$

Write a polynomial equation with real coefficients that has the given roots.

7. $-1, 1, 2$

8. $2, 3 - i$

Solve each problem.

9. Is $x + 1$ a factor of $2x^4 - 5x^3 + 3x^2 + 6x - 4$? Explain.

10. Factor $x^3 - 12x^2 + 47x - 60$ completely.

Use Descartes' rule of signs to discuss the possibilities for the roots to each equation. Do not solve the equation.

11. $2x^3 - 6x^2 + 5x - 9 = 0$

12. $x^5 + 5x^3 + x = 0$

Establish the best integral bounds for the roots of each equation according to the theorem on bounds.

13. $4x^2 - 4x - 15 = 0$

14. $2x^3 - 3x^2 - 7x + 4 = 0$

Determine whether the graph of each function is symmetric about the y-axis or the origin.

15. $f(x) = x^3 - 16x$

16. $f(x) = x^4 - 25x^2 + 1$

Graph each function.

17. $f(x) = (x + 2)(x - 2)^2$

18. $f(x) = \dfrac{1}{x^2 - 4x + 4}$

19. $f(x) = \dfrac{2x - 3}{x - 2}$

20. $f(x) = x^3 - x^2 - 4x + 4$

Find all real and imaginary solutions to each equation.

1. $2x - 3 = x - 5$

2. $(2x - 3)(x - 5) = 0$

3. $\dfrac{2x - 3}{x - 5} = 0$

4. $2x^2 - 3 = 0$

5. $\dfrac{3}{2x - 3} = \dfrac{2}{x - 5}$

6. $2x^4 + 7x^2 - 15 = 0$

7. $\dfrac{1}{x} + \dfrac{3}{x - 5} = -\dfrac{1}{2}$

8. $30x^3 - 29x^2 - 22x - 3 = 0$

Sketch the graph of each function.

9. $y = 2x$

10. $y = 2 - x$

11. $y = x - 2$

12. $y = \dfrac{1}{x - 2}$

13. $y = x^2 - 2$

14. $y = (x - 2)^2$

15. $y = \dfrac{1}{(x - 2)^2}$

16. $y = x^3 - 2$

17. $y = x^3 - x$

18. $y = x^4 - x^2$

19. $y = \sqrt{x + 5} - 2$

20. $y = -|x - 2|$

CHAPTER 11

Exponential and Logarithmic Functions

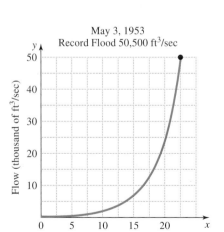

Water is one of the essentials of life, yet it is something that most of us take for granted. Among other things, the U.S. Geological Survey (U.S.G.S.) studies freshwater. For over 50 years the Water Resources Division of the U.S.G.S. has been gathering basic data about the flow of both freshwater and saltwater from streams and groundwater surfaces. This division collects, compiles, analyzes, verifies, organizes, and publishes data gathered from groundwater data collection networks in each of the 50 states, Puerto Rico, and the Trust Territories. Records of stream flow, groundwater levels, and water quality provide hydrological information needed by local, state, and federal agencies as well as the private sector.

There are many instances of the importance of the data collected by the U.S.G.S. For example, before 1987 the Tangipahoa River in Louisiana was used extensively for swimming and boating. In 1987 data gathered by the U.S.G.S. showed that fecal coliform levels in the river exceeded safe levels. Consequently, Louisiana banned recreational use of the river. Other studies by the Water Resources Division include the results of pollutants on salt marsh environments and the effect that salting highways in winter has on our drinking water supply.

In Exercises 85 and 86 of Section 11.2 you will see how data from the U.S.G.S. is used in a logarithmic function to measure water quality.

May 3, 1953
Record Flood 50,500 ft³/sec

Flow (thousand of ft³/sec) vs. Water depth (ft)

In This Section

- Definition
- Domain
- Graphing Exponential Functions
- Exponential Equations
- Applications

11.1   # EXPONENTIAL FUNCTIONS AND THEIR APPLICATIONS

We have studied functions such as

$$f(x) = x^2, \qquad g(x) = x^3, \qquad \text{and} \qquad h(x) = x^{1/2}.$$

For these functions the variable is the base. In this section we discuss functions that have a variable as an exponent. These functions are called *exponential functions*.

Definition

Some examples of exponential functions are

$$f(x) = 2^x, \qquad f(x) = \left(\frac{1}{2}\right)^x, \qquad \text{and} \qquad f(x) = 3^x.$$

> **Exponential Function**
>
> An **exponential function** is a function of the form
>
> $$f(x) = a^x,$$
>
> where $a > 0$ and $a \neq 1$.

We rule out the base 1 in the definition because $f(x) = 1^x$ is the same as the constant function $f(x) = 1$. Zero is not used as a base because $0^x = 0$ for any positive x and nonpositive powers of 0 are undefined. Negative numbers are not used as bases because an expression such as $(-4)^x$ is not a real number if $x = \frac{1}{2}$.

E X A M P L E   1   **Evaluating exponential functions**

Let $f(x) = 2^x$, $g(x) = \left(\frac{1}{4}\right)^{1-x}$, and $h(x) = -3^x$. Find the following.

a) $f\left(\dfrac{3}{2}\right)$ **b)** $f(-3)$ **c)** $g(3)$ **d)** $h(2)$

Solution

a) $f\left(\dfrac{3}{2}\right) = 2^{3/2} = \sqrt{2^3} = \sqrt{8} = 2\sqrt{2}$

b) $f(-3) = 2^{-3} = \dfrac{1}{2^3} = \dfrac{1}{8}$

c) $g(3) = \left(\dfrac{1}{4}\right)^{1-3} = \left(\dfrac{1}{4}\right)^{-2} = 4^2 = 16$

d) $h(2) = -3^2 = -9$ Note that $-3^2 \neq (-3)^2$.   ■

For many applications of exponential functions we use base 10 or another base called e. The number e is an irrational number that is approximately 2.718. We will see how e is used in compound interest in Example 10 of this section. Base 10 will be used in the next section. Base 10 is called the **common base,** and base e is called the **natural base.**

E X A M P L E   2

Base 10 and base e

Let $f(x) = 10^x$ and $g(x) = e^x$. Find the following and round approximate answers to four decimal places.

a) $f(3)$ **b)** $f(1.51)$ **c)** $g(0)$ **d)** $g(2)$

Solution

a) $f(3) = 10^3 = 1000$

b) $f(1.51) = 10^{1.51} \approx 32.3594$ Use the 10^x key on a calculator.

c) $g(0) = e^0 = 1$

d) $g(2) = e^2 \approx 7.3891$ Use the e^x key on a calculator. ■

Domain

In the definition of an exponential function no restrictions were placed on the exponent x because the domain of an exponential function is the set of all real numbers. So both rational and irrational numbers can be used as the exponent. We have been using rational numbers for exponents since Chapter 7, but we have not yet seen an irrational number as an exponent. Even though we do not formally define irrational exponents in this text, an irrational number such as π can be used as an exponent, and you can evaluate an expression such as 2^π by using a calculator. Try it:

$$2^\pi \approx 8.824977827$$

Graphing Exponential Functions

Even though the domain of an exponential function is the set of all real numbers, we can graph an exponential function by evaluating it for just a few integers.

E X A M P L E   3

Exponential functions with base greater than 1

Sketch the graph of each function.

a) $f(x) = 2^x$ **b)** $g(x) = 3^x$

Solution

a) We first make a table of ordered pairs that satisfy $f(x) = 2^x$:

x	-2	-1	0	1	2	3
$f(x) = 2^x$	$\frac{1}{4}$	$\frac{1}{2}$	1	2	4	8

As x increases, 2^x increases and 2^x is always positive. Because the domain of the function is $(-\infty, \infty)$, we draw the graph in Fig. 11.1 as a smooth curve through these points. From the graph we can see that the range is $(0, \infty)$.

Calculator Close-Up

Most graphing calculators have keys for the functions 10^x and e^x.

```
10^(1.51)
         32.35936569
e^(0)
                   1
e^(2)
         7.389056099
```

Calculator Close-Up

The graph of $f(x) = 2^x$ on a calculator appears to touch the x-axis. When drawing this graph by hand, make sure that it does not touch the x-axis.

```
         10
Y1=2^X

-5  |         |         5


X=0       Y=1
        -10
```

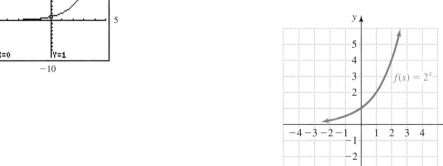

FIGURE 11.1

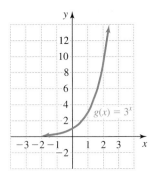

FIGURE 11.2

b) Make a table of ordered pairs that satisfy $g(x) = 3^x$:

x	-2	-1	0	1	2	3
$g(x) = 3^x$	$\frac{1}{9}$	$\frac{1}{3}$	1	3	9	27

As x increases, 3^x increases and 3^x is always positive. The graph is shown in Fig. 11.2. From the graph we see that the range is $(0, \infty)$. ∎

Because $e \approx 2.718$, the graph of $f(x) = e^x$ lies between the graphs of $f(x) = 2^x$ and $g(x) = 3^x$, as shown in Fig. 11.3. Note that all three functions have the same domain and range and the same y-intercept. In general, the function $f(x) = a^x$ for $a > 1$ has the following characteristics:

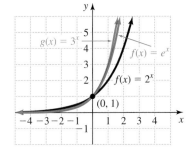

FIGURE 11.3

1. The y-intercept of the curve is $(0, 1)$.
2. The domain is $(-\infty, \infty)$, and the range is $(0, \infty)$.
3. The curve approaches the negative x-axis but does not touch it.
4. The y-values are increasing as we go from left to right along the curve.

E X A M P L E   4

Exponential functions with base between 0 and 1

Graph each function.

a) $f(x) = \left(\frac{1}{2}\right)^x$

b) $f(x) = 4^{-x}$

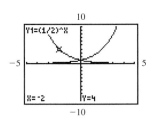
Solution

a) First make a table of ordered pairs that satisfy $f(x) = \left(\frac{1}{2}\right)^x$:

x	-2	-1	0	1	2	3
$f(x) = \left(\frac{1}{2}\right)^x$	4	2	1	$\frac{1}{2}$	$\frac{1}{4}$	$\frac{1}{8}$

As x increases, $\left(\frac{1}{2}\right)^x$ decreases, getting closer and closer to 0. Draw a smooth curve through these points as shown in Fig. 11.4.

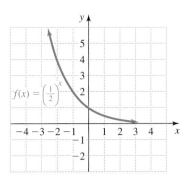

FIGURE 11.4

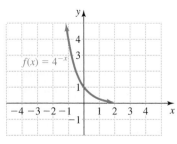

FIGURE 11.5

b) Because $4^{-x} = \left(\frac{1}{4}\right)^x$, we make a table for $f(x) = \left(\frac{1}{4}\right)^x$:

x	-2	-1	0	1	2	3
$f(x) = \left(\frac{1}{4}\right)^x$	16	4	1	$\frac{1}{4}$	$\frac{1}{16}$	$\frac{1}{64}$

As x increases, $\left(\frac{1}{4}\right)^x$, or 4^{-x}, decreases, getting closer and closer to 0. Draw a smooth curve through these points as shown in Fig. 11.5. ■

Notice the similarities and differences between the exponential function with $a > 1$ and with $0 < a < 1$. The function $f(x) = a^x$ for $0 < a < 1$ has the following characteristics:

1. The y-intercept of the curve is $(0, 1)$.
2. The domain is $(-\infty, \infty)$, and the range is $(0, \infty)$.
3. The curve approaches the positive x-axis but does not touch it.
4. The y-values are decreasing as we go from left to right along the curve.

CAUTION An exponential function can be written in more than one form. For example, $f(x) = \left(\frac{1}{2}\right)^x$ is the same as $f(x) = \frac{1}{2^x}$, or $f(x) = 2^{-x}$.

Although exponential functions have the form $f(x) = a^x$, other functions that have similar forms are also called exponential functions. Notice how changing the form $f(x) = a^x$ in Examples 5 and 6 changes the shape and location of the graph.

EXAMPLE 5

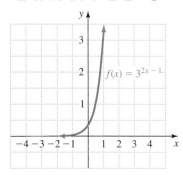

FIGURE 11.6

Changing the shape and location

Sketch the graph of $f(x) = 3^{2x-1}$.

Solution

Make a table of ordered pairs:

x	-1	0	$\frac{1}{2}$	1	2
$f(x) = 3^{2x-1}$	$\frac{1}{27}$	$\frac{1}{3}$	1	3	27

The graph through these points is shown in Fig. 11.6. ■

EXAMPLE 6

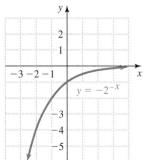

FIGURE 11.7

Changing the shape and location

Sketch the graph of $y = -2^{-x}$.

Solution

Because $-2^{-x} = -(2^{-x})$, all y-coordinates are negative. Make a table of ordered pairs:

x	-2	-1	0	1	2
$f(x) = -2^{-x}$	-4	-2	-1	$-\frac{1}{2}$	$-\frac{1}{4}$

The graph through these points is shown in Fig. 11.7. ■

Exponential Equations

In Chapter 9 we used the horizontal-line test to determine whether a function is one-to-one. Because no horizontal line can cross the graph of an exponential function more than once, exponential functions are one-to-one functions. For an exponential function one-to-one means that *if two exponential expressions with the same base are equal, then the exponents are equal.*

> ### One-to-One Property of Exponential Functions
>
> For $a > 0$ and $a \neq 1$,
> $$\text{if} \quad a^m = a^n, \quad \text{then} \quad m = n.$$

In the next example we use the one-to-one property to solve equations involving exponential functions.

E X A M P L E   7

Using the one-to-one property
Solve each equation.

a) $2^{2x-1} = 8$ **b)** $9^{|x|} = 3$ **c)** $\dfrac{1}{8} = 4^x$

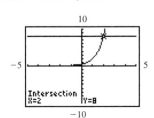
Solution
a) Because 8 is 2^3, we can write each side as a power of the same base, 2:

$$2^{2x-1} = 8 \qquad \text{Original equation}$$
$$2^{2x-1} = 2^3 \qquad \text{Write each side as a power of the same base.}$$
$$2x - 1 = 3 \qquad \text{One-to-one property}$$
$$2x = 4$$
$$x = 2$$

Check: $2^{2 \cdot 2 - 1} = 2^3 = 8$. The solution set is $\{2\}$.

b) Because $9 = 3^2$, we can write each side as a power of 3:

$$9^{|x|} = 3 \qquad \text{Original equation}$$
$$(3^2)^{|x|} = 3^1$$
$$3^{2|x|} = 3^1 \qquad \text{Power of a power rule}$$
$$2|x| = 1 \qquad \text{One-to-one property}$$
$$|x| = \frac{1}{2}$$
$$x = \pm\frac{1}{2}$$

Check $x = \pm\frac{1}{2}$ in the original equation. The solution set is $\left\{-\frac{1}{2}, \frac{1}{2}\right\}$.

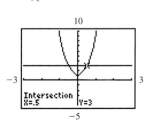
c) Because $\dfrac{1}{8} = 2^{-3}$ and $4 = 2^2$, we can write each side as a power of 2:

$$\frac{1}{8} = 4^x \qquad \text{Original equation}$$
$$2^{-3} = (2^2)^x \qquad \text{Write each side as a power of 2.}$$
$$2^{-3} = 2^{2x} \qquad \text{Power of a power rule}$$
$$2x = -3 \qquad \text{One-to-one property}$$
$$x = -\frac{3}{2}$$

Check $x = -\frac{3}{2}$ in the original equation. The solution set is $\left\{-\frac{3}{2}\right\}$.

The one-to-one property is also used to find the first coordinate when given the second coordinate of an exponential function.

E X A M P L E   8

Finding the x-coordinate in an exponential function

Let $f(x) = 2^x$ and $g(x) = \left(\frac{1}{2}\right)^{1-x}$. Find x if:

a) $f(x) = 32$
b) $g(x) = 8$

Solution

a) Because $f(x) = 2^x$ and $f(x) = 32$, we can find x by solving $2^x = 32$:

$$2^x = 32$$
$$2^x = 2^5 \quad \text{Write both sides as a power of the same base.}$$
$$x = 5 \quad \text{One-to-one property}$$

b) Because $g(x) = \left(\frac{1}{2}\right)^{1-x}$ and $g(x) = 8$, we can find x by solving $\left(\frac{1}{2}\right)^{1-x} = 8$:

$$\left(\frac{1}{2}\right)^{1-x} = 8$$
$$(2^{-1})^{1-x} = 2^3 \quad \text{Because } \frac{1}{2} = 2^{-1} \text{ and } 8 = 2^3$$
$$2^{x-1} = 2^3 \quad \text{Power of a power rule}$$
$$x - 1 = 3 \quad \text{One-to-one property}$$
$$x = 4$$

■

Study Tip

Although you should avoid cramming, there are times when you have no other choice. In this case concentrate on what is in your class notes and the homework assignments. Try to work one or two problems of each type. Instructors often ask some relatively easy questions on a test to see if you have understood the major ideas.

Applications

Exponential functions are used to describe phenomena such as population growth, radioactive decay, and compound interest. Here we discuss compound interest. If an investment is earning **compound interest,** then interest is periodically paid into the account and the interest that is paid also earns interest. If a bank pays 6% compounded quarterly on an account, then the interest is computed four times per year (every 3 months) at 1.5% (one-quarter of 6%). Suppose an account has $5000 in it at the beginning of a quarter. We can apply the simple interest formula $A = P + Prt$, with $r = 6\%$ and $t = \frac{1}{4}$, to find how much is in the account at the end of the first quarter.

$$A = P + Prt$$
$$= P(1 + rt) \qquad \text{Factor.}$$
$$= 5000\left(1 + 0.06 \cdot \frac{1}{4}\right) \qquad \text{Substitute.}$$
$$= 5000(1.015)$$
$$= \$5075$$

To repeat this computation for another quarter, we multiply $5075 by 1.015. If A represents the amount in the account at the end of n quarters, we can write A as an exponential function of n:

$$A = \$5000(1.015)^n$$

In general, the amount A is given by the following formula.

Compound Interest Formula

If P represents the principal, i the interest rate per period, n the number of periods, and A the amount at the end of n periods, then

$$A = P(1 + i)^n.$$

E X A M P L E 9

Compound interest formula

If \$350 is deposited in an account paying 12% compounded monthly, then how much is in the account at the end of 6 years and 6 months?

Calculator Close-Up

Graph $y = 350(1.01)^x$ to see the growth of the \$350 deposit in Example 9 over time. After 360 months it is worth \$12,582.37.

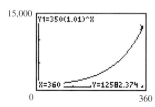

Solution

Interest is paid 12 times per year, so the account earns $\frac{1}{12}$ of 12%, or 1% each month, for 78 months. So $i = 0.01$, $n = 78$, and $P = \$350$:

$$A = P(1 + i)^n$$
$$A = \$350(1.01)^{78}$$
$$\approx \$760.56 \qquad \blacksquare$$

If we shorten the length of the time period (yearly, quarterly, monthly, daily, hourly, etc.), the number of periods n increases while the interest rate for the period decreases. As n increases, the amount A also increases but will not exceed a certain amount. That certain amount is the amount obtained from *continuous compounding* of the interest. It is shown in more advanced courses that the following formula gives the amount when interest is compounded continuously.

Helpful Hint

Compare Examples 9 and 10 to see the difference between compounded monthly and compounded continuously. Although there is not much difference to an individual investor, there could be a large difference to the bank. Rework Examples 9 and 10 using \$50 million as the deposit.

Continuous-Compounding Formula

If P is the principal or beginning balance, r is the annual percentage rate compounded continuously, t is the time in years, and A is the amount or ending balance, then

$$A = Pe^{rt}.$$

C A U T I O N   The value of t in the continuous-compounding formula must be in years. For example, if the time is 1 year and 3 months, then $t = 1.25$ years. If the time is 3 years and 145 days, then

$$t = 3 + \frac{145}{365}$$
$$\approx 3.3973 \text{ years.}$$

EXAMPLE 10

Continuous-compounding formula

If $350 is deposited in an account paying 12% compounded continuously, then how much is in the account after 6 years and 6 months?

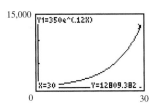
Solution

Use $r = 12\%$, $t = 6.5$ years, and $P = \$350$ in the formula for compounding interest continuously:

$$A = Pe^{rt}$$
$$= 350e^{(0.12)(6.5)}$$
$$= 350e^{0.78}$$
$$\approx \$763.52 \quad \text{Use the } e^x \text{ key on a scientific calculator.}$$

Note that compounding continuously amounts to a few dollars more than compounding monthly did in Example 9. ∎

MATH AT WORK

Neal Driscoll, a geophysicist at the Lamont-Doherty Earth Observatory of Columbia University, explores both the ocean and the continents to understand the processes that shape the earth. What he finds fascinating is the interaction between the ocean and the land—not just at the shoreline, but underneath the sea as well.

To get a preliminary picture of the ocean floor, Dr. Driscoll has worked with the U.S.G.S., studying the effects of storms on beaches and underwater landscapes. The results of these studies can be used as a baseline to provide help to coastal planners who are building waterfront homes. Other information obtained can be used to direct transporters of dredged material to places where the material is least likely to affect plant, fish, and human life. The most recent study found many different types of ocean floor, ranging from sand and mud to large tracts of algae.

GEOPHYSICIST

Imaging the seafloor is a difficult problem. It can be a costly venture, and there are numerous logistical problems. Recently developed technology, such as towable undersea cameras and satellite position systems, has made the task easier. Dr. Driscoll and his team use this new technology and sound reflection to gather data about how the sediment on the ocean floor changes in response to storm events. This research is funded by the Office of Naval Research (ONR).

In Exercise 28 of the Making Connections exercises you will see how a geophysicist uses sound to measure the depth of the ocean.

WARM-UPS

True or false? Explain your answer.

1. If $f(x) = 4^x$, then $f\left(-\frac{1}{2}\right) = -2$.

2. If $f(x) = \left(\frac{1}{3}\right)^x$, then $f(-1) = 3$.

3. The function $f(x) = x^4$ is an exponential function.

4. The functions $f(x) = \left(\frac{1}{2}\right)^x$ and $g(x) = 2^{-x}$ have the same graph.

5. The function $f(x) = 2^x$ is invertible.

6. The graph of $y = \left(\frac{1}{3}\right)^x$ has an x-intercept.

7. The y-intercept for $f(x) = e^x$ is $(0, 1)$.

8. The expression $2^{\sqrt{2}}$ is undefined.

9. The functions $f(x) = 2^{-x}$ and $g(x) = \frac{1}{2^x}$ have the same graph.

10. If \$500 earns 6% compounded monthly, then at the end of 3 years the investment is worth $500(1.005)^3$ dollars.

11.1   EXERCISES

Reading and Writing   After reading this section, write out the answers to these questions. Use complete sentences.

1. What is an exponential function?

2. What is the domain of every exponential function?

3. What are the two most popular bases?

4. What is the one-to-one property of exponential functions?

5. What is the compound interest formula?

6. What does compounded continuously mean?

Let $f(x) = 4^x$, $g(x) = \left(\frac{1}{3}\right)^{x+1}$, and $h(x) = -2^x$. Find the following. See Example 1.

7. $f(2)$ 8. $f(-1)$ 9. $f\left(\frac{1}{2}\right)$

10. $f\left(-\frac{3}{2}\right)$ 11. $g(-2)$ 12. $g(1)$

13. $g(0)$ 14. $g(-3)$ 15. $h(0)$

16. $h(3)$ 17. $h(-2)$ 18. $h(-4)$

Let $h(x) = 10^x$ and $j(x) = e^x$. Find the following. Use a calculator as necessary and round approximate answers to three decimal places. See Example 2.

19. $h(0)$ 20. $h(-1)$

21. $h(2)$ 22. $h(3.4)$

23. $j(1)$ 24. $j(3.5)$

25. $j(-2)$ 26. $j(0)$

Sketch the graph of each function. See Examples 3 and 4.

27. $f(x) = 4^x$ 28. $g(x) = 5^x$

29. $h(x) = \left(\frac{1}{3}\right)^x$ 30. $i(x) = \left(\frac{1}{5}\right)^x$

31. $y = 10^x$

32. $y = (0.1)^x$

43. $P = 5000(1.05)^t$

44. $d = 800 \cdot 10^{-4t}$

Sketch the graph of each function. See Examples 5 and 6.

33. $y = 10^{x+2}$

34. $y = 3^{2x+1}$

35. $f(x) = -2^x$

36. $k(x) = -2^{x-2}$

37. $g(x) = 2^{-x}$

38. $A(x) = 10^{1-x}$

39. $f(x) = -e^x$

40. $g(x) = e^{-x}$

41. $H(x) = 10^{|x|}$

42. $s(x) = 2^{(x^2)}$

Solve each equation. See Example 7.

45. $2^x = 64$

46. $3^x = 9$

47. $10^x = 0.001$

48. $10^{2x} = 0.1$

49. $2^x = \dfrac{1}{4}$

50. $3^x = \dfrac{1}{9}$

51. $\left(\dfrac{2}{3}\right)^{x-1} = \dfrac{9}{4}$

52. $\left(\dfrac{1}{4}\right)^{3x} = 16$

53. $5^{-x} = 25$

54. $10^{-x} = 0.01$

55. $-2^{1-x} = -8$

56. $-3^{2-x} = -81$

57. $10^{|x|} = 1000$

58. $3^{|2x-5|} = 81$

Let $f(x) = 2^x$, $g(x) = \left(\dfrac{1}{3}\right)^x$, and $h(x) = 4^{2x-1}$. Find x in each case. See Example 8.

59. $f(x) = 4$

60. $f(x) = \dfrac{1}{4}$

61. $f(x) = 4^{2/3}$

62. $f(x) = 1$

63. $g(x) = 9$

64. $g(x) = \dfrac{1}{9}$

65. $g(x) = 1$

66. $g(x) = \sqrt{3}$

67. $h(x) = 16$

68. $h(x) = \dfrac{1}{2}$

69. $h(x) = 1$

70. $h(x) = \sqrt{2}$

 Solve each problem. See Example 9.

71. *Compounding quarterly.* If $6000 is deposited in an account paying 5% compounded quarterly, then what amount will be in the account after 10 years?

72. *Compounding quarterly.* If $400 is deposited in an account paying 10% compounded quarterly, then what amount will be in the account after 7 years?

73. *Outstanding performance.* The top growth fund at Fidelity Investments from 1992 to 2002 was the Low-Priced Stock Fund (www.fidelity.com), which returned an average of 18.21% annually for those 10 years.

a) How much was an investment of $10,000 in this fund in 1992 worth in 2002 at 18.21% compounded annually?

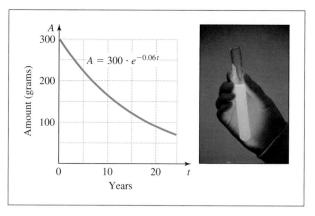

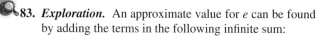

FIGURE FOR EXERCISE 73

b) Use the accompanying graph to estimate the year in which the $10,000 investment would be worth $200,000 if it continued to grow at 18.21% annually.

74. Second place. The second best growth fund at Fidelity Investments from 1992 to 2002 was the Contrafund Fund, which returned an average of 13.47% annually for those 10 years. How much was an investment of $10,000 in this fund in 1992 worth in 2002?

75. Depreciating knowledge. The value of a certain textbook seems to decrease according to the formula $V = 45 \cdot 2^{-0.9t}$, where V is the value in dollars and t is the age of the book in years. What is the book worth when it is new? What is it worth when it is 2 years old?

76. Mosquito abatement. In a Minnesota swamp in the springtime the number of mosquitoes per acre appears to grow according to the formula $N = 10^{0.1t+2}$, where t is the number of days since the last frost. What is the size of the mosquito population at times $t = 10$, $t = 20$, and $t = 30$?

 In Exercises 77–82, solve each problem. See Example 10.

77. Compounding continuously. If $500 is deposited in an account paying 7% compounded continuously, then how much will be in the account after 3 years?

78. Compounding continuously. If $7000 is deposited in an account paying 8% compounded continuously, then what will it amount to after 4 years?

79. One year's interest. How much interest will be earned the first year on $80,000 on deposit in an account paying 7.5% compounded continuously?

80. Partial year. If $7500 is deposited in an account paying 6.75% compounded continuously, then how much will be in the account after 5 years and 215 days?

81. Radioactive decay. The number of grams of a certain radioactive substance present at time t is given by the

FIGURE FOR EXERCISE 81

formula $A = 300 \cdot e^{-0.06t}$, where t is the number of years. Find the amount present at time $t = 0$. Find the amount present after 20 years. Use the accompanying graph to estimate the number of years that it takes for one-half of the substance to decay. Will the substance ever decay completely?

82. Population growth. The population of a certain country appears to be growing according to the formula $P = 20 \cdot e^{0.1t}$, where P is the population in millions and t is the number of years since 1990. What was the population in 1990? What will the population be in the year 2010?

GETTING MORE INVOLVED

83. Exploration. An approximate value for e can be found by adding the terms in the following infinite sum:

$$1 + \frac{1}{1} + \frac{1}{2 \cdot 1} + \frac{1}{3 \cdot 2 \cdot 1} + \frac{1}{4 \cdot 3 \cdot 2 \cdot 1} + \cdots$$

Use a calculator to find the sum of the first four terms. Find the difference between the sum of the first four terms and e. (For e, use all of the digits that your calculator gives for e^1.) What is the difference between e and the sum of the first eight terms?

GRAPHING CALCULATOR EXERCISES

84. Graph $y_1 = 2^x$, $y_2 = e^x$, and $y_3 = 3^x$ on the same coordinate system. Which point do all three graphs have in common?

85. Graph $y_1 = 3^x$, $y_2 = 3^{x-1}$, and $y_3 = 3^{x-2}$ on the same coordinate system. What can you say about the graph of $y = 3^{x-k}$ for any real number k?

In This Section

- Definition
- Domain and Range
- Graphing Logarithmic Functions
- Logarithmic Equations
- Applications

11.2 LOGARITHMIC FUNCTIONS AND THEIR APPLICATIONS

In Section 11.1 you learned that exponential functions are one-to-one functions. Because they are one-to-one functions, they have inverse functions. In this section we study the inverses of the exponential functions.

Definition

We define $\log_a(x)$ as *the exponent that is used on the base a to obtain x.* Read $\log_a(x)$ as "the base *a* logarithm of *x*." The expression $\log_a(x)$ is called a **logarithm.** Because $2^3 = 8$, the exponent is 3 and $\log_2(8) = 3$. Because $5^2 = 25$, the exponent is 2 and $\log_5(25) = 2$. Because $2^{-5} = \frac{1}{32}$, the exponent is -5 and $\log_2\left(\frac{1}{32}\right) = -5$. So the logarithmic equation $y = \log_a(x)$ is equivalent to the exponential equation $a^y = x$.

$\log_a(x)$

For any $a > 0$ and $a \neq 1$,

$$y = \log_a(x) \qquad \text{if and only if} \qquad a^y = x.$$

EXAMPLE 1

Using the definition of logarithm

Write each logarithmic equation as an exponential equation and each exponential equation as a logarithmic equation.

a) $\log_5(125) = 3$ **b)** $6 = \log_{1/4}(x)$ **c)** $\left(\frac{1}{2}\right)^m = 8$ **d)** $7 = 3^z$

Solution

a) "The base-5 logarithm of 125 equals 3" means that 3 is the exponent on 5 that produces 125. So $5^3 = 125$.

b) The equation $6 = \log_{1/4}(x)$ is equivalent to $\left(\frac{1}{4}\right)^6 = x$ by the definition of logarithm.

c) The equation $\left(\frac{1}{2}\right)^m = 8$ is equivalent to $\log_{1/2}(8) = m$.

d) The equation $7 = 3^z$ is equivalent to $\log_3(7) = z$. ■

The inverse of the base-*a* exponential function $f(x) = a^x$ is the **base-*a* logarithmic function** $f^{-1}(x) = \log_a(x)$. For example, $f(x) = 2^x$ and $f^{-1}(x) = \log_2(x)$ are inverse functions as shown in Fig. 11.8. Each function undoes the other.

$$f(5) = 2^5 = 32 \quad \text{and} \quad g(32) = \log_2(32) = 5.$$

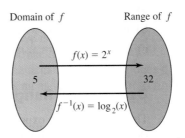

FIGURE 11.8

Use a calculator to solve each equation. Round answers to four decimal places.

71. $3 = 10^x$

72. $10^x = 0.03$

73. $10^x = \dfrac{1}{2}$

74. $75 = 10^x$

75. $e^x = 7.2$

76. $e^{3x} = 0.4$

Solve each problem. See Example 8. Use a calculator as necessary.

77. Double your money. How long does it take $5000 to grow to $10,000 at 12% compounded continuously?

78. Half the rate. How long does it take $5000 to grow to $10,000 at 6% compounded continuously?

79. Earning interest. How long does it take to earn $1000 in interest on a deposit of $6000 at 8% compounded continuously?

80. Lottery winnings. How long does it take to earn $1000 interest on a deposit of one million dollars at 9% compounded continuously?

81. Investing. An investment of $10,000 in Bonavista Petroleum in 1997 grew to $20,733 in 2002.

   a) Assuming that the investment grew continuously, what was the annual growth rate?

   b) If Bonavista Petroleum continued to grow continuously at the rate from part (a), then what would the investment be worth in 2010?

82. Investing. An investment of $10,000 in Baytex Energy in 1997 was worth $19,568 in 2002.

   a) Assuming that the investment grew continuously, what was the annual rate?

   b) If Baytex Energy continued to grow continuously at the rate from part (a), then what would the investment be worth in 2012?

In chemistry the pH *of a solution is defined by*

$$pH = -\log_{10} [H+],$$

where H+ is the hydrogen ion concentration of the solution in moles per liter. Distilled water has a pH *of approximately 7. A solution with a* pH *under 7 is called an acid, and one with a* pH *over 7 is called a base.*

83. Tomato juice. Tomato juice has a hydrogen ion concentration of $10^{-4.1}$ mole per liter (mol/L). Find the pH of tomato juice.

84. Stomach acid. The gastric juices in your stomach have a hydrogen ion concentration of 10^{-1} mol/L. Find the pH of your gastric juices.

85. Neuse River pH. The pH of a water sample is one of the many measurements of water quality done by the U.S. Geological Survey. The hydrogen ion concentration of the water in the Neuse River at New Bern, North Carolina, was 1.58×10^{-7} mol/L on April 8, 2002 (Water Resources for North Carolina, wwwnc.usgs.gov). What was the pH of the water at that time?

86. Roanoke River pH. On April 8, 2002, the hydrogen ion concentration of the water in the Roanoke River at Janesville, North Carolina, was 1.995×10^{-7} mol/L (Water Resources for North Carolina, wwwnc.usgs.gov). What was the pH of the water at that time?

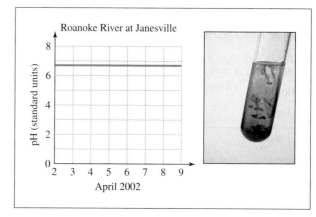

FIGURE FOR EXERCISE 86

Solve each problem.

87. Sound level. The level of sound in decibels (db) is given by the formula

$$L = 10 \cdot \log(I \times 10^{12}),$$

where I is the intensity of the sound in watts per square meter. If the intensity of the sound at a rock concert is 0.001 watt per square meter at a distance of 75 meters from the stage, then what is the level of the sound at this point in the audience?

88. Logistic growth. If a rancher has one cow with a contagious disease in a herd of 1000, then the time in days t for n of the cows to become infected is modeled by

$$t = -5 \cdot \ln\!\left(\frac{1000 - n}{999n}\right).$$

Find the number of days that it takes for the disease to spread to 100, 200, 998, and 999 cows. This model, called a *logistic growth model*, describes how a disease can spread very rapidly at first and then very slowly as nearly all of the population has become infected.

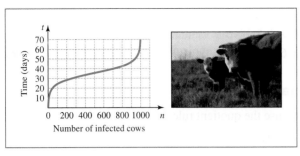

 90. *Discussion.* Find the inverse of the function $f(x) = 2 + e^{x+4}$. State the domain and range of the inverse function.

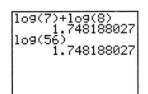

FIGURE FOR EXERCISE 88

GRAPHING CALCULATOR EXERCISES

91. *Composition of inverses.* Graph the functions $y = \ln(e^x)$ and $y = e^{\ln(x)}$. Explain the similarities and differences between the graphs.

GETTING MORE INVOLVED

89. *Discussion.* Use the switch-and-solve method from Chapter 9 to find the inverse of the function $f(x) = 5 + \log_2(x - 3)$. State the domain and range of the inverse function.

92. *The population bomb.* The population of the earth is growing continuously with an annual rate of about 1.6%. If the present population is 6 billion, then the function $y = 6e^{0.016x}$ gives the population in billions x years from now. Graph this function for $0 \leq x \leq 200$. What will the population be in 100 years and in 200 years?

In This Section

- Product Rule for Logarithms
- Quotient Rule for Logarithms
- Power Rule for Logarithms
- Inverse Properties
- Using the Properties

11.3 **PROPERTIES OF LOGARITHMS**

The properties of logarithms are very similar to the properties of exponents because *logarithms are exponents.* In this section we use the properties of exponents to write some properties of logarithms. The properties will be used in solving logarithmic equations in Section 11.4.

Product Rule for Logarithms

If $M = a^x$ and $N = a^y$, we can use the product rule for exponents to write

$$MN = a^x \cdot a^y = a^{x+y}.$$

The equation $MN = a^{x+y}$ is equivalent to

$$\log_a(MN) = x + y.$$

Because $M = a^x$ and $N = a^y$ are equivalent to $x = \log_a(M)$ and $y = \log_a(N)$, we can replace x and y in $\log_a(MN) = x + y$ to get

$$\log_a(MN) = \log_a(M) + \log_a(N).$$

So *the logarithm of a product is the sum of the logarithms,* provided that all of the logarithms are defined. This rule is called the **product rule for logarithms.**

Calculator Close-Up

You can illustrate the product rule for logarithms with a graphing calculator.

```
log(7)+log(8)
          1.748188027
log(56)
          1.748188027
```

> **Product Rule for Logarithms**
> $$\log_a(MN) = \log_a(M) + \log_a(N)$$

EXAMPLE 1 **Using the product rule for logarithms**

Write each expression as a single logarithm.

a) $\log_2(7) + \log_2(5)$ **b)** $\ln(\sqrt{2}) + \ln(\sqrt{3})$

Note that there is more than one way to simplify the expressions in Example 4. Using the power rule for logarithms and the fact that $\ln(e) = 1$, we have $\ln(e^5) = 5 \cdot \ln(e) = 5$. Using $\log_2(8) = 3$, we have $2^{\log_2(8)} = 2^3 = 8$.

Using the Properties

We have already seen many properties of logarithms. There are three properties that we have not yet formally stated. Because $a^1 = a$ and $a^0 = 1$, we have $\log_a(a) = 1$ and $\log_a(1) = 0$ for any positive number a. If we apply the quotient rule to $\log_a(1/N)$, we get

$$\log_a\left(\frac{1}{N}\right) = \log_a(1) - \log_a(N) = 0 - \log_a(N) = -\log_a(N).$$

So $\log_a\left(\frac{1}{N}\right) = -\log_a(N)$. These three new properties along with all of the other properties of logarithms are summarized as follows.

Properties of Logarithms

If M, N, and a are positive numbers, $a \neq 1$, then

1. $\log_a(a) = 1$ **2.** $\log_a(1) = 0$

3. $\log_a(a^M) = M$ Inverse properties   **4.** $a^{\log_a(M)} = M$

5. $\log_a(MN) = \log_a(M) + \log_a(N)$ Product rule

6. $\log_a\left(\frac{M}{N}\right) = \log_a(M) - \log_a(N)$ Quotient rule

7. $\log_a\left(\frac{1}{N}\right) = -\log_a(N)$ **8.** $\log_a(M^N) = N \cdot \log_a(M)$ Power rule

---

We have already seen several ways in which to use the properties of logarithms. In Examples 5, 6, and 7 we see more uses of the properties. First we use the rules of logarithms to write the logarithm of a complicated expression in terms of logarithms of simpler expressions.

E X A M P L E 5   Using the properties of logarithms

Rewrite each expression in terms of $\log(2)$ and/or $\log(3)$.

a) $\log(6)$ **b)** $\log(16)$ **c)** $\log\left(\frac{9}{2}\right)$ **d)** $\log\left(\frac{1}{3}\right)$

Solution

a) $\log(6) = \log(2 \cdot 3)$

$= \log(2) + \log(3)$ Product rule

b) $\log(16) = \log(2^4)$

$= 4 \cdot \log(2)$ Power rule

c) $\log\left(\frac{9}{2}\right) = \log(9) - \log(2)$ Quotient rule

$= \log(3^2) - \log(2)$

$= 2 \cdot \log(3) - \log(2)$ Power rule

d) $\log\left(\frac{1}{3}\right) = -\log(3)$ Property 7

CAUTION Do not confuse $\frac{\log(9)}{\log(2)}$ with $\log\left(\frac{9}{2}\right)$. We can use the quotient rule to write $\log\left(\frac{9}{2}\right) = \log(9) - \log(2)$, but $\frac{\log(9)}{\log(2)} \neq \log(9) - \log(2)$. The expression $\frac{\log(9)}{\log(2)}$ means $\log(9) \div \log(2)$. Use your calculator to verify these two statements.

The properties of logarithms can be used to combine several logarithms into a single logarithm (as in Examples 1 and 2) or to write a logarithm of a complicated expression in terms of logarithms of simpler expressions.

E X A M P L E   6 **Using the properties of logarithms**

Rewrite each expression as a sum or difference of multiples of logarithms.

a) $\log\left(\dfrac{xz}{y}\right)$

b) $\log_3\left(\dfrac{(x-3)^{2/3}}{\sqrt{x}}\right)$

Solution

a) $\log\left(\dfrac{xz}{y}\right) = \log(xz) - \log(y)$ Quotient rule

$\qquad\qquad\quad = \log(x) + \log(z) - \log(y)$ Product rule

b) $\log_3\left(\dfrac{(x-3)^{2/3}}{\sqrt{x}}\right) = \log_3\left((x-3)^{2/3}\right) - \log_3\left(x^{1/2}\right)$ Quotient rule

$\qquad\qquad\qquad\qquad = \dfrac{2}{3}\log_3(x-3) - \dfrac{1}{2}\log_3(x)$ Power rule ∎

In Example 7 we use the properties of logarithms to convert expressions involving several logarithms into a single logarithm. The skills we are learning here will be used to solve logarithmic equations in Section 11.4.

E X A M P L E   7 **Combining logarithms**

Rewrite each expression as a single logarithm.

a) $\dfrac{1}{2}\log(x) - 2 \cdot \log(x+1)$

b) $3 \cdot \log(y) + \dfrac{1}{2}\log(z) - \log(x)$

Solution

a) $\dfrac{1}{2}\log(x) - 2 \cdot \log(x+1) = \log\left(x^{1/2}\right) - \log\left((x+1)^2\right)$ Power rule

$\qquad\qquad\qquad\qquad = \log\left(\dfrac{\sqrt{x}}{(x+1)^2}\right)$ Quotient rule

b) $3 \cdot \log(y) + \dfrac{1}{2}\log(z) - \log(x) = \log(y^3) + \log\left(\sqrt{z}\right) - \log(x)$ Power rule

$\qquad\qquad\qquad\qquad = \log\left(y^3 \cdot \sqrt{z}\right) - \log(x)$ Product rule

$\qquad\qquad\qquad\qquad = \log\left(\dfrac{y^3 \cdot \sqrt{z}}{x}\right)$ Quotient rule ∎

WARM-UPS

True or false? Explain your answer.

1. $\log_2\left(\dfrac{x^2}{8}\right) = \log_2(x^2) - 3$

2. $\dfrac{\log(100)}{\log(10)} = \log(100) - \log(10)$

3. $\ln(\sqrt{2}) = \dfrac{\ln(2)}{2}$

4. $3^{\log_3(17)} = 17$

5. $\log_2\left(\dfrac{1}{8}\right) = \dfrac{1}{\log_2(8)}$

6. $\ln(8) = 3 \cdot \ln(2)$

7. $\ln(1) = e$

8. $\dfrac{\log(100)}{10} = \log(10)$

9. $\dfrac{\log_2(8)}{\log_2(2)} = \log_2(4)$

10. $\ln(2) + \ln(3) - \ln(7) = \ln\left(\dfrac{6}{7}\right)$

11.3 EXERCISES

Reading and Writing *After reading this section, write out the answers to these questions. Use complete sentences.*

1. What is the product rule for logarithms?

2. What is the quotient rule for logarithms?

3. What is the power rule for logarithms?

4. Why is it true that $\log_a(a^M) = M$?

5. Why is it true that $a^{\log_a(M)} = M$?

6. Why is it true that $\log_a(1) = 0$ for $a > 0$ and $a \neq 1$?

Assume all variables involved in logarithms represent numbers for which the logarithms are defined.

Write each expression as a single logarithm and simplify. See Example 1.

7. $\log(3) + \log(7)$

8. $\ln(5) + \ln(4)$

9. $\log_3(\sqrt{5}) + \log_3(\sqrt{x})$

10. $\ln(\sqrt{x}) + \ln(\sqrt{y})$

11. $\log(x^2) + \log(x^3)$

12. $\ln(a^3) + \ln(a^5)$

13. $\ln(2) + \ln(3) + \ln(5)$

14. $\log_2(x) + \log_2(y) + \log_2(z)$

15. $\log(x) + \log(x + 3)$

16. $\ln(x - 1) + \ln(x + 1)$

17. $\log_2(x - 3) + \log_2(x + 2)$

18. $\log_3(x - 5) + \log_3(x - 4)$

Write each expression as a single logarithm. See Example 2.

19. $\log(8) - \log(2)$

20. $\ln(3) - \ln(6)$

21. $\log_2(x^6) - \log_2(x^2)$

22. $\ln(w^9) - \ln(w^3)$

23. $\log(\sqrt{10}) - \log(\sqrt{2})$

24. $\log_3(\sqrt{6}) - \log_3(\sqrt{3})$

25. $\ln(4h - 8) - \ln(4)$

26. $\log(3x - 6) - \log(3)$

27. $\log_2(w^2 - 4) - \log_2(w + 2)$

28. $\log_3(k^2 - 9) - \log_3(k - 3)$

29. $\ln(x^2 + x - 6) - \ln(x + 3)$

30. $\ln(t^2 - t - 12) - \ln(t - 4)$

Write each expression in terms of $\log(3)$. *See Example 3.*

31. $\log(27)$

32. $\log\left(\dfrac{1}{9}\right)$

33. $\log(\sqrt{3})$

34. $\log(\sqrt[4]{3})$

35. $\log(3^x)$

36. $\log(3^{-99})$

Simplify each expression. See Example 4.

37. $\log_2(2^{10})$

38. $\ln(e^9)$

39. $5^{\log_5(19)}$

40. $10^{\log(2.3)}$

41. $\log(10^8)$

42. $\log_4(4^5)$

43. $e^{\ln(4.3)}$

44. $3^{\log_3(5.5)}$

Rewrite each expression in terms of $\log(3)$ *and/or* $\log(5)$. *See Example 5.*

45. $\log(15)$

46. $\log(9)$

47. $\log\left(\dfrac{5}{3}\right)$

48. $\log\left(\dfrac{3}{5}\right)$

49. $\log(25)$

50. $\log\left(\dfrac{1}{27}\right)$

51. $\log(75)$

52. $\log(0.6)$

53. $\log\left(\dfrac{1}{3}\right)$

54. $\log(45)$

55. $\log(0.2)$

56. $\log\left(\dfrac{9}{25}\right)$

Rewrite each expression as a sum or a difference of multiples of logarithms. See Example 6.

57. $\log(xyz)$

58. $\log(3y)$

59. $\log_2(8x)$

60. $\log_2(16y)$

61. $\ln\left(\dfrac{x}{y}\right)$

62. $\ln\left(\dfrac{z}{3}\right)$

63. $\log(10x^2)$

64. $\log(100\sqrt{x})$

65. $\log_5\left(\dfrac{(x-3)^2}{\sqrt{w}}\right)$

66. $\log_3\left(\dfrac{(y+6)^3}{y-5}\right)$

67. $\ln\left(\dfrac{yz\sqrt{x}}{w}\right)$

68. $\ln\left(\dfrac{(x-1)\sqrt{w}}{x^3}\right)$

Rewrite each expression as a single logarithm. See Example 7.

69. $\log(x) + \log(x - 1)$

70. $\log_2(x - 2) + \log_2(5)$

71. $\ln(3x - 6) - \ln(x - 2)$

72. $\log_3(x^2 - 1) - \log_3(x - 1)$

73. $\ln(x) - \ln(w) + \ln(z)$

74. $\ln(x) - \ln(3) - \ln(7)$

75. $3 \cdot \ln(y) + 2 \cdot \ln(x) - \ln(w)$

76. $5 \cdot \ln(r) + 3 \cdot \ln(t) - 4 \cdot \ln(s)$

77. $\dfrac{1}{2}\log(x - 3) - \dfrac{2}{3}\log(x + 1)$

78. $\dfrac{1}{2}\log(y - 4) + \dfrac{1}{2}\log(y + 4)$

79. $\dfrac{2}{3}\log_2(x - 1) - \dfrac{1}{4}\log_2(x + 2)$

80. $\dfrac{1}{2}\log_3(y + 3) + 6 \cdot \log_3(y)$

Determine whether each equation is true or false.

81. $\log(56) = \log(7) \cdot \log(8)$

82. $\log\left(\dfrac{5}{9}\right) = \dfrac{\log(5)}{\log(9)}$

83. $\log_2(4^2) = (\log_2(4))^2$

84. $\ln(4^2) = (\ln(4))^2$

85. $\ln(25) = 2 \cdot \ln(5)$

86. $\ln(3e) = 1 + \ln(3)$

87. $\dfrac{\log_2(64)}{\log_2(8)} = \log_2(8)$

88. $\dfrac{\log_2(16)}{\log_2(4)} = \log_2(4)$

89. $\log\left(\dfrac{1}{3}\right) = -\log(3)$

90. $\log_2(8 \cdot 2^{59}) = 62$

91. $\log_2(16^5) = 20$

92. $\log_2\left(\dfrac{5}{2}\right) = \log_2(5) - 1$

93. $\log(10^3) = 3$ **94.** $\log_3(3^7) = 7$

95. $\log(100 + 3) = 2 + \log(3)$ **96.** $\dfrac{\log_7(32)}{\log_7(8)} = \dfrac{5}{3}$

Solve each problem.

97. *Richter scale.* The Richter scale rating of an earthquake is given by the formula $r = \log(I) - \log(I_0)$, where I is the *intensity* of the earthquake and I_0 is the intensity of a small "benchmark" earthquake. Use the appropriate property of logarithms to rewrite this formula using a single logarithm. Find r if $I = 100 \cdot I_0$.

98. *Diversity index.* The U.S.G.S. measures the quality of a water sample by using the diversity index d, given by

$$d = -[p_1 \cdot \log_2(p_1) + p_2 \cdot \log_2(p_2) + \cdots + p_n \cdot \log_2(p_n)],$$

where n is the number of different taxons (biological classifications) represented in the sample and p_1 through p_n are the percentages of organisms in each of the n taxons. The value of d ranges from 0 when all organisms in the water sample are the same to some positive number when all organisms in the sample are different. If two-thirds of the organisms in a water sample are in one taxon and one-third of the organisms are in a second taxon, then $n = 2$ and

$$d = -\left[\frac{2}{3}\log_2\left(\frac{2}{3}\right) + \frac{1}{3}\log_2\left(\frac{1}{3}\right)\right].$$

Use the properties of logarithms to write the expression on the right-hand side as $\log_2\left(\frac{3\sqrt[3]{2}}{2}\right)$. (In Section 11.4 you will learn how to evaluate a base-2 logarithm using a calculator.)

GETTING MORE INVOLVED

99. *Discussion.* Which of the following equations is an identity? Explain.
   a) $\ln(3x) = \ln(3) \cdot \ln(x)$
   b) $\ln(3x) = \ln(3) + \ln(x)$
   c) $\ln(3x) = 3 \cdot \ln(x)$
   d) $\ln(3x) = \ln(x^3)$

100. *Discussion.* Which of the following expressions is not equal to $\log(5^{2/3})$? Explain.
   a) $\dfrac{2}{3}\log(5)$ **b)** $\dfrac{\log(5) + \log(5)}{3}$
   c) $(\log(5))^{2/3}$ **d)** $\dfrac{1}{3}\log(25)$

GRAPHING CALCULATOR EXERCISES

101. Graph the functions $y_1 = \ln(\sqrt{x})$ and $y_2 = 0.5 \cdot \ln(x)$ on the same screen. Explain your results.

102. Graph the functions $y_1 = \log(x)$, $y_2 = \log(10x)$, $y_3 = \log(100x)$, and $y_4 = \log(1000x)$ using the viewing window $-2 \le x \le 5$ and $-2 \le y \le 5$. Why do these curves appear as they do?

103. Graph the function $y = \log(e^x)$. Explain why the graph is a straight line. What is its slope?

11.4

SOLVING EQUATIONS AND APPLICATIONS

We solved some equations involving exponents and logarithms in Sections 11.1 and 11.2. In this section we use the properties of exponents and logarithms to solve more complex equations.

Logarithmic Equations

The main tool that we have for solving logarithmic equations is the definition of logarithms: $y = \log_a(x)$ if and only if $a^y = x$. We can use the definition to rewrite any equation that has only one logarithm as an equivalent exponential equation.

EXAMPLE 1

A logarithmic equation with only one logarithm

Solve $\log(x + 3) = 2$.

Solution

Write the equivalent exponential equation:

$$\log(x + 3) = 2 \qquad \text{Original equation}$$
$$10^2 = x + 3 \qquad \text{Definition of logarithm}$$
$$100 = x + 3$$
$$97 = x$$

Check: $\log(97 + 3) = \log(100) = 2$. The solution set is $\{97\}$. ■

In Example 2 we use the product rule for logarithms to write a sum of two logarithms as a single logarithm.

EXAMPLE 2

Using the product rule to solve an equation

Solve $\log_2(x + 3) + \log_2(x - 3) = 4$.

Solution

Rewrite the sum of the logarithms as the logarithm of a product:

$$\log_2(x + 3) + \log_2(x - 3) = 4 \qquad \text{Original equation}$$
$$\log_2[(x + 3)(x - 3)] = 4 \qquad \text{Product rule}$$
$$\log_2[x^2 - 9] = 4 \qquad \text{Multiply the binomials.}$$
$$x^2 - 9 = 2^4 \qquad \text{Definition of logarithm}$$
$$x^2 - 9 = 16$$
$$x^2 = 25$$
$$x = \pm 5 \qquad \text{Even-root property}$$

To check, first let $x = -5$ in the original equation:

$$\log_2(-5 + 3) + \log_2(-5 - 3) = 4$$
$$\log_2(-2) + \log_2(-8) = 4 \qquad \text{Incorrect}$$

Because the domain of any logarithm function is the set of positive real numbers, these logarithms are undefined. Now check $x = 5$ in the original equation:

$$\log_2(5 + 3) + \log_2(5 - 3) = 4$$
$$\log_2(8) + \log_2(2) = 4$$
$$3 + 1 = 4 \qquad \text{Correct}$$

The solution set is $\{5\}$. ■

CAUTION   Always check that your solutions to a logarithmic equation do not produce undefined logarithms in the original equation.

EXAMPLE 3

Using the one-to-one property of logarithms
Solve $\log(x) + \log(x - 1) = \log(8x - 12) - \log(2)$.

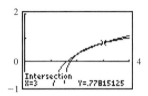

Calculator Close-Up

Graph

$$y_1 = \log(x) + \log(x - 1)$$

and

$$y_2 = \log(8x - 12) - \log(2)$$

to see the two solutions to the equation in Example 3.

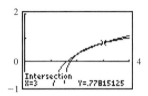

Solution

Apply the product rule to the left-hand side and the quotient rule to the right-hand side to get a single logarithm on each side:

$$\log(x) + \log(x - 1) = \log(8x - 12) - \log(2).$$

$$\log[x(x - 1)] = \log\left(\frac{8x - 12}{2}\right) \quad \text{Product rule; quotient rule}$$

$$\log(x^2 - x) = \log(4x - 6) \quad \text{Simplify.}$$

$$x^2 - x = 4x - 6 \quad \text{One-to-one property of logarithms}$$

$$x^2 - 5x + 6 = 0$$

$$(x - 2)(x - 3) = 0$$

$$x - 2 = 0 \quad \text{or} \quad x - 3 = 0$$

$$x = 2 \quad \text{or} \quad x = 3$$

Neither $x = 2$ nor $x = 3$ produces undefined terms in the original equation. Use a calculator to check that they both satisfy the original equation. The solution set is $\{2, 3\}$. ∎

CAUTION The product rule, quotient rule, and power rule do not eliminate logarithms from equations. To do so, we use the definition to change $y = \log_a(x)$ into $a^y = x$ or the one-to-one property to change $\log_a(m) = \log_a(n)$ into $m = n$.

Exponential Equations

If an equation has a single exponential expression, we can write the equivalent logarithmic equation.

EXAMPLE 4

A single exponential expression
Find the exact solution to $2^x = 10$.

Solution

The equivalent logarithmic equation is

$$x = \log_2(10).$$

The solution set is $\{\log_2(10)\}$. The number $\log_2(10)$ is the exact solution to the equation. Later in this section you will learn how to use the base-change formula to find an approximate value for an expression of this type. ∎

In Section 11.1 we solved some exponential equations by writing each side as a power of the same base and then applying the one-to-one property of exponential functions. We review that method in Example 5.

EXAMPLE 5

Powers of the same base

Solve $2^{(x^2)} = 4^{3x-4}$.

Solution

We can write each side as a power of the same base:

$$2^{(x^2)} = \left(2^2\right)^{3x-4} \qquad \text{Because } 4 = 2^2$$
$$2^{(x^2)} = 2^{6x-8} \qquad \text{Power of a power rule}$$
$$x^2 = 6x - 8 \qquad \text{One-to-one property of exponential functions}$$
$$x^2 - 6x + 8 = 0$$
$$(x - 4)(x - 2) = 0$$
$$x - 4 = 0 \quad \text{or} \quad x - 2 = 0$$
$$x = 4 \quad \text{or} \quad x = 2$$

Check $x = 2$ and $x = 4$ in the original equation. The solution set is $\{2, 4\}$. ■

For some exponential equations we cannot write each side as a power of the same base as we did in Example 5. In this case we take a logarithm of each side and simplify, using the rules for logarithms.

EXAMPLE 6

Exponential equation with two different bases

Find the exact and approximate solution to $2^{x-1} = 3^x$.

Solution

We first take the base-10 logarithm of each side:

$$2^{x-1} = 3^x \qquad \text{Original equation}$$
$$\log(2^{x-1}) = \log(3^x) \qquad \text{Take log of each side.}$$
$$(x - 1)\log(2) = x \cdot \log(3) \qquad \text{Power rule}$$
$$x \cdot \log(2) - \log(2) = x \cdot \log(3) \qquad \text{Distributive property}$$
$$x \cdot \log(2) - x \cdot \log(3) = \log(2) \qquad \text{Get all } x\text{-terms on one side.}$$
$$x[\log(2) - \log(3)] = \log(2) \qquad \text{Factor out } x.$$
$$x = \frac{\log(2)}{\log(2) - \log(3)} \qquad \text{Exact solution}$$
$$x \approx -1.7095 \qquad \text{Approximate solution}$$

You can use a calculator to check -1.7095 in the original equation. As the first step of the solution, we could have taken the logarithm of each side using any base. We chose base 10 so that we could use a calculator to find an approximate solution from the exact solution. ■

Changing the Base

Scientific calculators have an x^y key for computing any power of any base, in addition to the function keys for computing 10^x and e^x. For logarithms we have the keys ln and log, but there are no function keys for logarithms using other bases. To solve this problem, we develop a formula for expressing a base-a logarithm in terms of base-b logarithms.

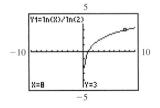

If $y = \log_a(M)$, then $a^y = M$. Now we solve $a^y = M$ for y, using base-b logarithms:

$$a^y = M$$

$$\log_b(a^y) = \log_b(M) \quad \text{Take the base-}b\text{ logarithm of each side.}$$

$$y \cdot \log_b(a) = \log_b(M) \quad \text{Power rule}$$

$$y = \frac{\log_b(M)}{\log_b(a)} \quad \text{Divide each side by } \log_b(a).$$

Because $y = \log_a(M)$, we can write $\log_a(M)$ in terms of base-b logarithms.

Base-Change Formula

If a and b are positive numbers not equal to 1 and M is positive, then

$$\log_a(M) = \frac{\log_b(M)}{\log_b(a)}.$$

In words, we take the logarithm with the new base and divide by the logarithm of the old base. The most important use of the base-change formula is to find base-a logarithms using a calculator. If the new base is 10 or e, then

$$\log_a(M) = \frac{\log(M)}{\log(a)} = \frac{\ln(M)}{\ln(a)}.$$

E X A M P L E   7   **Using the base-change formula**

Find $\log_7(99)$ to four decimal places.

Solution

Use the base-change formula with $a = 7$ and $b = 10$:

$$\log_7(99) = \frac{\log(99)}{\log(7)} \approx 2.3614$$

Check by finding $7^{2.3614}$ with your calculator. Note that we also have

$$\log_7(99) = \frac{\ln(99)}{\ln(7)} \approx 2.3614.$$ ∎

Strategy for Solving Equations

There is no formula that will solve every equation in this section. However, we have a strategy for solving exponential and logarithmic equations. The following list summarizes the ideas that we need for solving these equations.

Solving Exponential and Logarithmic Equations

1. If the equation has a single logarithm or a single exponential expression, rewrite the equation using the definition $y = \log_a(x)$ if and only if $a^y = x$.
2. Use the properties of logarithms to combine logarithms as much as possible.
3. Use the one-to-one properties:
   a) If $\log_a(m) = \log_a(n)$, then $m = n$.
   b) If $a^m = a^n$, then $m = n$.
4. To get an approximate solution of an exponential equation, take the common or natural logarithm of each side of the equation.

Applications

In compound interest problems, logarithms are used to find the time it takes for money to grow to a specified amount.

E X A M P L E   8

Finding the time

If $500 is deposited into an account paying 8% compounded quarterly, then in how many quarters will the account have $1000 in it?

Solution

We use the compound interest formula $A = P(1 + i)^n$ with a principal of $500, an amount of $1000, and an interest rate of 2% each quarter:

$$A = P(1 + i)^n$$
$$1000 = 500(1.02)^n \quad \text{Substitute.}$$
$$2 = (1.02)^n \quad \text{Divide each side by 500.}$$
$$n = \log_{1.02}(2) \quad \text{Definition of logarithm}$$
$$= \frac{\ln(2)}{\ln(1.02)} \quad \text{Base-change formula}$$
$$\approx 35.0028 \quad \text{Use a calculator.}$$

It takes approximately 35 quarters, or 8 years and 9 months, for the initial investment to be worth $1000. Note that we could also solve $2 = (1.02)^n$ by taking the common or natural logarithm of each side. Try it. ■

Helpful Hint

When we get $2 = (1.02)^n$, we can use the definition of log as in Example 8 or take the natural log of each side:

$$\ln(2) = \ln(1.02^n)$$
$$\ln(2) = n \cdot \ln(1.02)$$
$$n = \frac{\ln(2)}{\ln(1.02)}$$

In either way we arrive at the same solution.

In Example 9 we find the rate in a radioactive decay problem.

E X A M P L E   9

Finding the rate in radioactive decay

The number of grams of a radioactive substance that is present in an old bone after t years is given by

$$A = 8e^{rt},$$

where r is the decay rate. How many grams of the radioactive substance were present when the bone was in a living organism at time $t = 0$? If it took 6300 years for the radioactive substance to decay from 8 grams to 4 grams, then what is the decay rate?

Solution

If $t = 0$, then $A = 8e^{r \cdot 0} = 8e^0 = 8 \cdot 1 = 8$. So the bone contained 8 grams of the substance when it was in a living organism. Now use $A = 4$ and $t = 6300$ in the formula $A = 8e^{rt}$ and solve for r:

$$4 = 8e^{6300r}$$
$$0.5 = e^{6300r} \quad \text{Divide each side by 8.}$$
$$6300r = \ln(0.5) \quad \text{Definition of logarithm}$$
$$r = \frac{\ln(0.5)}{6300} \quad \text{Divide each side by 6300.}$$
$$r \approx -1.1 \times 10^{-4} \text{ or } -0.00011$$

Note that the rate is negative because the substance is decaying. ■

WARM-UPS

True or false? Explain your answer.

1. If $\log(x - 2) + \log(x + 2) = 7$, then $\log(x^2 - 4) = 7$.
2. If $\log(3x + 7) = \log(5x - 8)$, then $3x + 7 = 5x - 8$.
3. If $e^{x-6} = e^{x^2-5x}$, then $x - 6 = x^2 - 5x$.
4. If $2^{3x-1} = 3^{5x-4}$, then $3x - 1 = 5x - 4$.
5. If $\log_2(x^2 - 3x + 5) = 3$, then $x^2 - 3x + 5 = 8$.
6. If $2^{2x-1} = 3$, then $2x - 1 = \log_2(3)$.
7. If $5^x = 23$, then $x \cdot \ln(5) = \ln(23)$.
8. $\log_3(5) = \dfrac{\ln(3)}{\ln(5)}$
9. $\dfrac{\ln(2)}{\ln(6)} = \dfrac{\log(2)}{\log(6)}$
10. $\log(5) = \ln(5)$

11.4 EXERCISES

Reading and Writing *After reading this section, write out the answers to these questions. Use complete sentences.*

1. What exponential equation is equivalent to $\log_a(x) = y$?

2. How can you find a logarithm with a base other than 10 or e using a calculator?

Solve each equation. See Examples 1 and 2.

3. $\log_2(x + 1) = 3$
4. $\log_3(x^2) = 4$
5. $3 \log_2(x + 1) - 2 = 13$

6. $4 \log_3(2x) - 1 = 7$

7. $12 + 2 \ln(x) = 14$
8. $23 = 3 \ln(x - 1) + 14$
9. $\log(x) + \log(5) = 1$
10. $\ln(x) + \ln(3) = 0$

11. $\log_2(x - 1) + \log_2(x + 1) = 3$
12. $\log_3(x - 4) + \log_3(x + 4) = 2$
13. $\log_2(x - 1) - \log_2(x + 2) = 2$
14. $\log_4(8x) - \log_4(x - 1) = 2$
15. $\log_2(x - 4) + \log_2(x + 2) = 4$
16. $\log_6(x + 6) + \log_6(x - 3) = 2$

Solve each equation. See Example 3.

17. $\ln(x) + \ln(x + 5) = \ln(x + 1) + \ln(x + 3)$
18. $\log(x) + \log(x + 5) = 2 \cdot \log(x + 2)$
19. $\log(x + 3) + \log(x + 4) = \log(x^3 + 13x^2) - \log(x)$

20. $\log(x^2 - 1) - \log(x - 1) = \log(6)$
21. $2 \cdot \log(x) = \log(20 - x)$
22. $2 \cdot \log(x) + \log(3) = \log(2 - 5x)$

Solve each equation. See Examples 4 and 5.

23. $3^x = 7$
24. $2^{x-1} = 5$

25. $e^{2x} = 7$
26. $e^{x+3} = 2$

27. $2^{3x+4} = 4^{x-1}$
28. $9^{2x-1} = 27^{1/2}$

29. $\left(\dfrac{1}{3}\right)^x = 3^{1+x}$
30. $4^{3x} = \left(\dfrac{1}{2}\right)^{1-x}$

 Find the exact solution and approximate solution to each equation. See Example 6.

31. $2^x = 3^{x+5}$

32. $e^x = 10^x$

33. $5^{x+2} = 10^{x-4}$

34. $3^{2x} = 6^{x+1}$

35. $8^x = 9^{x-1}$

36. $5^{x+1} = 8^{x-1}$

Use the base-change formula to find each logarithm to four decimal places. See Example 7.

37. $\log_2(3)$ **38.** $\log_3(5)$

39. $\log_3\left(\dfrac{1}{2}\right)$ **40.** $\log_5(2.56)$

41. $\log_{1/2}(4.6)$ **42.** $\log_{1/3}(3.5)$

43. $\log_{0.1}(0.03)$ **44.** $\log_{0.2}(1.06)$

For each equation, find the exact solution and an approximate solution when appropriate. Round approximate answers to three decimal places.

45. $x \cdot \ln(2) = \ln(7)$

46. $x \cdot \log(3) = \log(5)$

47. $3x - x \cdot \ln(2) = 1$

48. $2x + x \cdot \log(5) = \log(7)$

49. $3^x = 5$

50. $2^x = \dfrac{1}{3}$

51. $2^{x-1} = 9$

52. $10^{x-2} = 6$

53. $3^x = 20$

54. $2^x = 128$

55. $\log_3(x) + \log_3(5) = 1$

56. $\log(x) - \log(3) = \log(6)$

57. $8^x = 2^{x+1}$

58. $2^x = 5^{x+1}$

In Exercises 59–74, solve each problem. See Examples 8 and 9.

59. *Finding the time.* How many months does it take for $1000 to grow to $1500 in an account paying 12% compounded monthly?

60. *Finding the time.* How many years does it take for $25 to grow to $100 in an account paying 8% compounded annually?

61. *Finding days.* How many days does it take for a deposit of $100 to grow to $105 at 3% annual percentage rate compounded daily? Round to the nearest day.

62. *Finding quarters.* How many quarters does it take for a deposit of $500 to grow to $600 at 2% annual percentage rate compounded quarterly? Round to the nearest quarter.

63. *Radioactive decay.* The number of grams of a radioactive substance that is present in an old piece of cloth after t years is given by

$$A = 10e^{-0.0001t}.$$

How many grams of the radioactive substance did the cloth contain when it was made at time $t = 0$? If the cloth now contains only 4 grams of the substance then when was the cloth made?

64. *Finding the decay rate.* The number of grams of a radioactive substance that is present in an old log after t years is given by

$$A = 5e^{rt},$$

where r is the decay rate. How many grams of the radioactive substance were present when the log was alive at time $t = 0$? If it took 5000 years for the substance to decay from 5 grams to 2 grams, then what is the decay rate?

65. *Going with the flow.* The flow y [in cubic feet per second (ft^3/sec)] of the Tangipahoa River at Robert, Louisiana, is modeled by the exponential function $y = 114.308e^{0.265x}$, where x is the depth in feet. Find the flow when the depth is 15.8 feet.

FIGURE FOR EXERCISES 65 AND 66

66. *Record flood.* Use the formula of the previous exercise to find the depth of the Tangipahoa River at Robert, Louisiana, on May 3, 1953 when the flow reached an all-time record of 50,500 ft^3/sec (U.S.G.S., waterdata.usgs.gov).

67. *Above the poverty level.* In a certain country the number of people above the poverty level is currently 28 million and growing 5% annually. Assuming the population is growing continuously, the population P (in millions), t years from now, is determined by the formula $P = 28e^{0.05t}$. In how many years will there be 40 million people above the poverty level?

68. Below the poverty level. In the same country as in Exercise 67, the number of people below the poverty level is currently 20 million and growing 7% annually. This population (in millions), t years from now, is determined by the formula $P = 20e^{0.07t}$. In how many years will there be 40 million people below the poverty level?

69. Fifty-fifty. For this exercise, use the information given in Exercises 67 and 68. In how many years will the number of people above the poverty level equal the number of people below the poverty level?

70. Golden years. In a certain country there are currently 100 million workers and 40 million retired people. The population of workers is decreasing according to the formula $W = 100e^{-0.01t}$, where t is in years and W is in millions. The population of retired people is increasing according to the formula $R = 40e^{0.09t}$, where t is in years and R is in millions. In how many years will the number of workers equal the number of retired people?

71. Ions for breakfast. Orange juice has a pH of 3.7. What is the hydrogen ion concentration of orange juice? (See Exercises 83–86 of Section 11.2.)

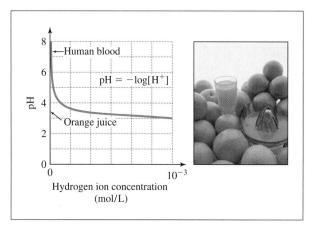

FIGURE FOR EXERCISES 71 AND 72

72. Ions in your veins. Normal human blood has a pH of 7.4. What is the hydrogen ion concentration of normal human blood?

73. Diversity index. In Exercise 98 of Section 11.3 we expressed the diversity index d for a certain water sample as

$$d = \log_2\left(\frac{3\sqrt[3]{2}}{2}\right).$$

Use the base-change formula and a calculator to calculate the value of d. Round the answer to four decimal places.

74. Quality water. In a certain water sample, 5% of the organisms are in one taxon, 10% are in a second taxon, 20% are in a third taxon, 15% are in a fourth taxon, 23% are in a fifth taxon, and the rest are in a sixth taxon. Use the formula given in Exercise 98 of Section 11.3 with $n = 6$ to find the diversity index of the water sample.

GETTING MORE INVOLVED

75. Exploration. Logarithms were designed to solve equations that have variables in the exponents, but logarithms can be used to solve certain polynomial equations. Consider the following example:

$$x^5 = 88$$
$$5 \cdot \ln(x) = \ln(88)$$
$$\ln(x) = \frac{\ln(88)}{5} \approx 0.895467$$
$$x = e^{0.895467} \approx 2.4485$$

Solve $x^3 = 12$ by taking the natural logarithm of each side. Round the approximate solution to four decimal places. Solve $x^3 = 12$ without using logarithms and compare with your previous answer.

76. Discussion. Determine whether each logarithm is positive or negative without using a calculator. Explain your answers.

a) $\log_2(0.45)$

b) $\ln(1.01)$

c) $\log_{1/2}(4.3)$

d) $\log_{1/3}(0.44)$

GRAPHING CALCULATOR EXERCISES

77. Graph $y_1 = 2^x$ and $y_2 = 3^{x-1}$ on the same coordinate system. Use the intersect feature of your calculator to find the point of intersection of the two curves. Round to two decimal places.

78. Bob invested $1000 at 6% compounded continuously. At the same time Paula invested $1200 at 5% compounded monthly. Write two functions that give the amounts of Bob's and Paula's investments after x years. Graph these functions on a graphing calculator. Use the intersect feature of your graphing calculator to find the approximate value of x for which the investments are equal in value.

79. Graph the functions $y_1 = \log_2(x)$ and $y_2 = 3^{x-4}$ on the same coordinate system and use the intersect feature to find the points of intersection of the curves. Round to two decimal places. (*Hint:* To graph $y = \log_2(x)$, use the base-change formula to write the function as $y = \ln(x)/\ln(2)$.)

COLLABORATIVE ACTIVITIES

In How Much Space Could We Live?

The formula for population growth is $P(t) = P_0 e^{kt}$, where $P(t)$ is the population after t years, P_0 is the initial population, k is the growth rate per year, and t is the number of years. In the following exercises you will find out how long it would take to cover the habitable part of the earth if the human population grows exponentially.

1. The population of the earth in 2000 was 6.06×10^9 people. If the population was 2.75×10^9 in 1964, then what is the current growth rate to the nearest tenth of a percent?

2. The earth has a total surface area of 5.1×10^{14} square meters. Seventy percent of this surface area is rock, ice, sand, and ocean. Another 8% is tundra, lakes and streams, continental shelves, algal beds and reefs, and estuaries. Assuming that the remaining area is suitable for growing food and living space find that area.

Grouping: 2 students per group

Topic: Exponential and logarithmic functions

3. If 100 square meters of the earth's surface is needed for each person to grow food and live, in how many years after 2000 will all of the available surface of the earth be used?

4. Does 100 square meters per person for living space and growing food seem reasonable? Remember that tall apartment buildings use less surface area than single family dwellings.

5. Think about the land use issues for different types of foods. Would it take more surface area to grow animals for food? Would food grow better on some parts of the earth's surface than on others? Would there be any space left for wild animals or natural plant life? Would there be any space left for shopping malls, movie theaters, concert halls, factories, office buildings, or parking lots?

WRAP-UP   CHAPTER 11

SUMMARY

Exponential and Logarithmic Functions

		Examples
Exponential function	A function of the form $f(x) = a^x$ for $a > 0$ and $a \neq 1$	$f(x) = 3^x$
Logarithm function	A function of the form $f(x) = \log_a(x)$ for $a > 0$ and $a \neq 1$	$f(x) = \log_2(x)$
	$y = \log_a(x)$ if and only if $a^y = x$.	$\log_3(8) = x \leftrightarrow 3^x = 8$
Common logarithm	Base-10: $f(x) = \log(x)$	$\log(100) = 2$ because $100 = 10^2$.
Natural logarithm	Base-e: $f(x) = \ln(x)$ $e \approx 2.718$	$\ln(e) = 1$ because $e^1 = e$.
Inverse functions	$f(x) = a^x$ and $g(x) = \log_a(x)$ are inverse functions.	If $f(x) = e^x$, then $f^{-1}(x) = \ln(x)$.

Properties   **Examples**

M, N, and a are positive numbers with $a \neq 1$.

$$\log_a(a) = 1 \qquad \log_a(1) = 0$$

$$\log_5(5) = 1, \log_5(1) = 0$$

Inverse properties	$\log_a(a^M) = M \qquad a^{\log_a(M)} = M$	$\log(10^7) = 7,\ e^{\ln(3.4)} = 3.4$
Product rule	$\log_a(MN) = \log_a(M) + \log_a(N)$	$\ln(3x) = \ln(3) + \ln(x)$
Quotient rule	$\log_a\!\left(\dfrac{M}{N}\right) = \log_a(M) - \log_a(N)$	$\ln\!\left(\dfrac{2}{3}\right) = \ln(2) - \ln(3)$
	$\log_a\!\left(\dfrac{1}{N}\right) = -\log_a(N)$	$\ln\!\left(\dfrac{1}{3}\right) = -\ln(3)$
Power rule	$\log_a(M^N) = N \cdot \log_a(M)$	$\log(x^3) = 3 \cdot \log(x)$
Base-change formula	$\log_a(M) = \dfrac{\log_b(M)}{\log_b(a)}$	$\log_3(5) = \dfrac{\ln(5)}{\ln(3)}$

Equations Involving Logarithms and Exponents **Examples**

Strategy

1. If there is a single logarithm or a single exponential expression, rewrite the equation using the definition of logarithms:
   $y = \log_a(x)$ if and only if $a^y = x$.

   $2^x = 3$ and $x = \log_2(3)$ are equivalent.

2. Use the properties of logarithms to combine logarithms as much as possible.

   $\log(x) + \log(x - 3) = 1$
   $\log(x^2 - 3x) = 1$

3. Use the one-to-one properties:
   a) If $\log_a(m) = \log_a(n)$, then $m = n$.
   b) If $a^m = a^n$, then $m = n$.

   $\ln(x) = \ln(5 - x)$,
   $x = 5 - x$
   $2^{3x} = 2^{5x-7},\ 3x = 5x - 7$

4. To get an approximate solution, take the common or natural logarithm of each side of an exponential equation.

   $2^x = 3,\ \ln(2^x) = \ln(3)$
   $x \cdot \ln(2) = \ln(3)$
   $x = \dfrac{\ln(3)}{\ln(2)}$

ENRICHING YOUR MATHEMATICAL WORD POWER

For each mathematical term, choose the correct meaning.

1. **exponential function**
   a. $f(x) = a^x$ where $a > 0$ and $a \neq 1$
   b. $f(x) = ax^2$ where $a \neq 0$
   c. $f(x) = ax + b$ where $a \neq 0$
   d. $f(x) = x^n$ where n is an integer

2. **common base**
   a. base 2
   b. base e
   c. base π
   d. base 10

3. **natural base**
   a. base 2
   b. base e
   c. base π
   d. base 10

4. **domain**
   a. the range
   b. the set of second coordinates of a relation
   c. the independent variable
   d. the set of first coordinates of a relation

5. **compound interest**
   a. simple interest
   b. $A = Prt$
   c. an irrational interest rate
   d. interest is periodically paid into the account and the interest earns interest

6. **continuous compounding**
   a. compound interest
   b. using $A = Pe^{rt}$ to compute the amount
   c. frequent compounding
   d. using $A = P(1 + i)^n$ to compute the amount

7. base-*a* logarithm of *x*
   a. the exponent that is used on the base *a* to obtain *x*
   b. the exponent that is used on *x* to obtain *a*
   c. the power of 10 that produces *x*
   d. the power of *e* that produces *a*

8. base-*a* logarithm function
   a. $f(x) = a^x$ where $a > 0$ and $a \neq 1$
   b. $f(x) = \log_a(x)$ where $a > 0$ and $a \neq 1$
   c. $f(x) = \log_x(a)$ where $a > 0$ and $a \neq 1$
   d. $f(x) = \log(x)$ where $x > 0$

9. common logarithm
   a. $\log_2(x)$
   b. $\log(x)$
   c. $\ln(x)$
   d. $\log_3(x)$

10. natural logarithm
   a. $\log_2(x)$
   b. $\log(x)$
   c. $\ln(x)$
   d. $\log_3(x)$

REVIEW EXERCISES

11.1 *Use* $f(x) = 5^x$, $g(x) = 10^{x-1}$, *and* $h(x) = \left(\frac{1}{4}\right)^x$ *for Exercises 1–28. Find the following.*

1. $f(-2)$

2. $f(0)$

3. $f(3)$

4. $f(4)$

5. $g(1)$

6. $g(-1)$

7. $g(0)$

8. $g(3)$

9. $h(-1)$

10. $h(2)$

11. $h\left(\frac{1}{2}\right)$

12. $h\left(-\frac{1}{2}\right)$

Find x in each case.

13. $f(x) = 25$

14. $f(x) = -\dfrac{1}{125}$

15. $g(x) = 1000$

16. $g(x) = 0.001$

17. $h(x) = 32$

18. $h(x) = 8$

19. $h(x) = \dfrac{1}{16}$

20. $h(x) = 1$

 Find the following.

21. $f(1.34)$

22. $f(-3.6)$

23. $g(3.25)$

24. $g(4.87)$

25. $h(2.82)$

26. $h(\pi)$

27. $h(\sqrt{2})$

28. $h\left(\dfrac{1}{3}\right)$

Sketch the graph of each function.

29. $f(x) = 5^x$

30. $g(x) = e^x$

31. $y = \left(\dfrac{1}{5}\right)^x$

32. $y = e^{-x}$

33. $f(x) = 3^{-x}$

34. $f(x) = -3^{x-1}$

35. $y = 1 + 2^x$

36. $y = 1 - 2^x$

58. $f(x) = \log_8(x)$

59. $f(x) = e^x$

60. $f(x) = \log_3(x)$

11.2 *Write each exponential equation as a logarithmic equation and each logarithmic equation as an exponential equation.*

37. $10^m = n$ **38.** $b = a^5$

39. $h = \log_k(t)$ **40.** $\log_v(5) = u$

Let $f(x) = \log_2(x)$, $g(x) = \log(x)$, *and* $h(x) = \log_{1/2}(x)$. *Find the following.*

41. $f\left(\dfrac{1}{8}\right)$ **42.** $f(64)$

43. $g(0.1)$ **44.** $g(1)$

45. $g(100)$ **46.** $h\left(\dfrac{1}{8}\right)$

47. $h(1)$ **48.** $h(4)$

49. x, if $f(x) = 8$ **50.** x, if $g(x) = 3$

51. $f(77)$ **52.** $g(88.4)$

53. $h(33.9)$ **54.** $h(0.05)$

55. x, if $f(x) = 2.475$ **56.** x, if $g(x) = 1.426$

For each function f, find f^{-1} *and sketch the graphs of f and* f^{-1} *on the same set of axes.*

57. $f(x) = 10^x$

11.3 *Rewrite each expression as a sum or a difference of multiples of logarithms.*

61. $\log(x^2 y)$

62. $\log_3(x^2 + 2x)$

63. $\ln(16)$

64. $\log\left(\dfrac{y}{\sqrt{x}}\right)$

65. $\log_5\left(\dfrac{1}{x}\right)$

66. $\ln\left(\dfrac{xy}{z}\right)$

Rewrite each expression as a single logarithm.

67. $\dfrac{1}{2}\log(x + 2) - 2 \cdot \log(x - 1)$

68. $3 \cdot \ln(x) + 2 \cdot \ln(y) - \dfrac{1}{3}\ln(z)$

11.4 *Find the exact solution to each equation.*

69. $\log_2(x) = 8$

70. $\log_3(x) = 0.5$

71. $\log_2(8) = x$

72. $3^x = 8$

73. $x^3 = 8$

74. $3^2 = x$

75. $\log_x(27) = 3$

76. $\log_x(9) = -\dfrac{1}{3}$

77. $x \cdot \ln(3) - x = \ln(7)$

78. $x \cdot \log(8) = x \cdot \log(4) + \log(9)$

79. $3^x = 5^{x-1}$

80. $5^{(2x^2)} = 5^{3-5x}$

81. $4^{2x} = 2^{x+1}$

82. $\log(12) = \log(x) + \log(7 - x)$

83. $\ln(x + 2) - \ln(x - 10) = \ln(2)$

84. $2 \cdot \ln(x + 3) = 3 \cdot \ln(4)$

85. $\log(x) - \log(x - 2) = 2$

86. $\log_2(x) = \log_2(x + 16) - 1$

 Use a calculator to find an approximate solution to each of the following. Round your answers to four decimal places.

87. $6^x = 12$

88. $5^x = 8^{3x+2}$

89. $3^{x+1} = 5$

90. $\log_3(x) = 2.634$

MISCELLANEOUS

 Solve each problem.

91. *Compounding annually.* What does $10,000 invested at 11.5% compounded annually amount to after 15 years?

92. *Doubling time.* How many years does it take for an investment to double at 6.5% compounded annually?

93. *Decaying substance.* The amount, A, of a certain radioactive substance remaining after t years, is given by the formula $A = A_0 e^{-0.0003t}$, where A_0 is the initial amount. If we have 218 grams of this substance today, then how much of it will be left 1000 years from now?

94. *Wildlife management.* The number of white-tailed deer in the Hiawatha National Forest is believed to be growing according to the function

$$P = 517 + 10 \cdot \ln(8t + 1),$$

where t is the time in years from the year 2000.

a) What is the size of the population in 2000?

b) In what year will the population reach 600?

c) Does the population as shown on the accompanying graph appear to be growing faster during the period 2000 to 2005 or during the period 2005 to 2010?

d) What is the average rate of change of the population for each period in part (c)?

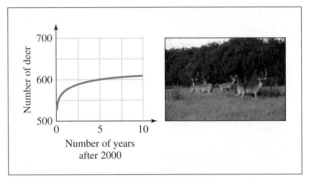

FIGURE FOR EXERCISE 94

95. *Comparing investments.* Melissa deposited $1000 into an account paying 5% annually; on the same day Frank deposited $900 into an account paying 7% compounded continuously. Find the number of years that it will take for the amounts in the accounts to be equal.

96. *Imports and exports.* The value of imports for a small Central American country is believed to be growing according to the function

$$I = 15 \cdot \log(16t + 33),$$

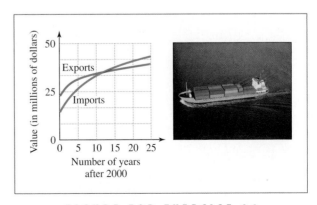

FIGURE FOR EXERCISE 96

and the value of exports appears to be growing according to the function

$$E = 30 \cdot \log(t + 3),$$

where I and E are in millions of dollars and t is the number of years after 2000.

a) What are the values of imports and exports in 2000?

b) Use the accompanying graph to estimate the year in which imports will equal exports.

c) Algebraically find the year in which imports will equal exports.

97. Finding river flow. The U.S.G.S. measures the water height h (in feet above sea level) for the Tangipahoa River at Robert, Louisiana, and then finds the flow y [in cubic feet per second (ft^3/sec)], using the formula

$$y = 114.308 e^{0.265(h-6.87)}.$$

Find the flow when the river at Robert is 20.6 ft above sea level.

98. Finding the height. Rewrite the formula in Exercise 97 to express h as a function of y. Use the new formula to find the water height above sea level when the flow is 10,000 ft^3/sec.

CHAPTER 11 TEST

Let $f(x) = 5^x$ and $g(x) = \log_5(x)$. Find the following.

1. $f(2)$

2. $f(-1)$

3. $f(0)$

4. $g(125)$

5. $g(1)$

6. $g\left(\dfrac{1}{5}\right)$

Sketch the graph of each function.

7. $y = 2^x$

8. $f(x) = \log_2(x)$

9. $y = \left(\dfrac{1}{3}\right)^x$

10. $g(x) = \log_{1/3}(x)$

Suppose $\log_a(M) = 6$ and $\log_a(N) = 4$. Find the following.

11. $\log_a(MN)$

12. $\log_a\left(\dfrac{M^2}{N}\right)$

13. $\dfrac{\log_a(M)}{\log_a(N)}$

14. $\log_a(a^3 M^2)$

15. $\log_a\left(\dfrac{1}{N}\right)$

Find the exact solution to each equation.

16. $3^x = 12$

17. $\log_3(x) = \dfrac{1}{2}$

18. $5^x = 8^{x-1}$

19. $\log(x) + \log(x + 15) = 2$

20. $2 \cdot \ln(x) = \ln(3) + \ln(6 - x)$

 Use a scientific calculator to find an approximate solution to each of the following. Round your answers to four decimal places.

21. Solve $20^x = 5$.

22. Solve $\log_3(x) = 2.75$.

23. The number of bacteria present in a culture at time t is given by the formula $N = 10 e^{0.4t}$, where t is in hours. How many bacteria are present initially? How many are present after 24 hours?

24. How many hours does it take for the bacteria population of Problem 23 to double?

Find the exact solution to each equation.

1. $(x - 3)^2 = 8$

2. $\log_2(x - 3) = 8$

3. $2^{x-3} = 8$

4. $2x - 3 = 8$

5. $|x - 3| = 8$

6. $\sqrt{x - 3} = 8$

7. $\log_2(x - 3) + \log_2(x) = \log_2(18)$

8. $2 \cdot \log_2(x - 3) = \log_2(5 - x)$

9. $\dfrac{1}{2}x - \dfrac{2}{3} = \dfrac{3}{4}x + \dfrac{1}{5}$

10. $3x^2 - 6x + 2 = 0$

Find the inverse of each function.

11. $f(x) = \dfrac{1}{3}x$

12. $g(x) = \log_3(x)$

13. $f(x) = 2x - 4$

14. $h(x) = \sqrt{x}$

15. $j(x) = \dfrac{1}{x}$

16. $k(x) = 5^x$

17. $m(x) = e^{x-1}$

18. $n(x) = \ln(x)$

Sketch the graph of each equation.

19. $y = 2x$

20. $y = 2^x$

21. $y = x^2$

22. $y = \log_2(x)$

23. $y = \dfrac{1}{2}x - 4$

24. $y = |2 - x|$

25. $y = 2 - x^2$

26. $y = e^2$

Solve each problem.

27. *Civilian labor force.* The number of workers in the civilian labor force can be modeled by the linear function

$$n(t) = 1.51t + 125.5$$

or by the exponential function

$$n(t) = 125.6e^{0.011t},$$

where t is the number of years since 1990 and $n(t)$ is in millions of workers (Bureau of Labor Statistics, www.bls.gov).

a) Graph both functions on the same coordinate system for $0 \leq t \leq 30$.

b) What does each model predict for the value of n in 2010?

c) What does each model predict for the value of n in the present year? Which model's prediction is closest to the actual size of the present civilian labor force?

28. *Measuring ocean depths.* In this exercise you will see how a geophysicist uses sound reflection to measure the depth of the ocean. Let v be the speed of sound through the water and d_1 be the depth of the ocean below the ship, as shown in the accompanying figure.

a) The time it takes for sound to travel from the ship at point S straight down to the ocean floor at point B_1 and back to point S is 0.270 second. Write d_1 as a function of v.

b) It takes 0.432 second for sound to travel from point S to point B_2 and then to a receiver at R, which is towed 500 meters behind the ship. Assuming $d_2 = d_3$, write d_2 as a function of v.

c) Use the Pythagorean theorem to find v. Then find the ocean depth d_1.

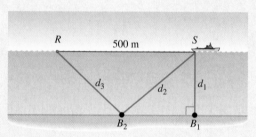

FIGURE FOR EXERCISE 28

Nonlinear Systems and the Conic Sections

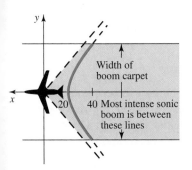

Width of boom carpet

20 | 40 Most intense sonic boom is between these lines

t a cruising speed of 1540 miles per hour, the Concorde can fly from London to New York in about 3 hours. So why isn't the same aircraft used for a fast flight from New York to Los Angeles? Concerns about cost efficiency and pollution are two reasons. However, most people agree that the biggest problem is noise. Traveling at Mach 2, the supersonic jet is flying faster than the speed of sound. At this speed the Concorde creates a cone-shaped wave in the air, on which there is a momentary change in air pressure. This change in air pressure causes a thunderlike sonic boom. When the jet is traveling parallel to the ground, the cone-shaped wave intersects the ground along one branch of a hyperbola. People on the ground hear the boom as the hyperbola passes them.

Sonic booms not only are noisy, but they have also been known to cause physical destruction such as broken windows and cracked plaster. For this reason supersonic jets are restricted from flying over land areas in the United States and much of the world. Some engineers believe that changing the silhouette of the plane can lessen the sonic boom, but most agree that it is impossible to eliminate the noise altogether.

In this chapter we discuss curves, including the hyperbola, that occur when a geometric plane intersects a cone. In Exercise 60 of Section 12.4 you will see how the altitude of the aircraft is related to the width of the area where the sonic boom is heard.

12.1 # NONLINEAR SYSTEMS OF EQUATIONS

We studied systems of linear equations in Chapter 4. In this section we turn our attention to nonlinear systems of equations.

Solving by Elimination

Equations such as

$$y = x^2, \qquad y = \sqrt{x}, \qquad y = |x|, \qquad y = 2^x, \qquad \text{and} \qquad y = \log_2(x)$$

are **nonlinear equations** because their graphs are not straight lines. We say that a system of equations is nonlinear if at least one equation in the system is nonlinear. We solve a nonlinear system just like a linear system, by elimination of variables. However, because the graphs of nonlinear equations may intersect at more than one point, there may be more than one ordered pair in the solution set to the system.

E X A M P L E   1   **A parabola and a line**

Solve the system of equations and draw the graph of each equation on the same coordinate system:

$$y = x^2 - 1$$
$$x + y = 1$$

Solution

We can eliminate y by substituting $y = x^2 - 1$ into $x + y = 1$:

$$x + y = 1$$
$$x + (x^2 - 1) = 1 \qquad \text{Substitute } x^2 - 1 \text{ for } y.$$
$$x^2 + x - 2 = 0$$
$$(x - 1)(x + 2) = 0$$
$$x - 1 = 0 \qquad \text{or} \qquad x + 2 = 0$$
$$x = 1 \qquad \text{or} \qquad x = -2$$

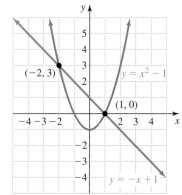

Replace x by 1 and -2 in $y = x^2 - 1$ to find the corresponding values of y:

$$y = (1)^2 - 1 \qquad y = (-2)^2 - 1$$
$$y = 0 \qquad\qquad y = 3$$

Check that each of the points $(1, 0)$ and $(-2, 3)$ satisfies both of the original equations. The solution set is $\{(1, 0), (-2, 3)\}$. If we solve $x + y = 1$ for y, we get $y = -x + 1$. The line $y = -x + 1$ has y-intercept $(0, 1)$ and slope -1. The graph of $y = x^2 - 1$ is a parabola with vertex $(0, -1)$. Of course, $(1, 0)$ and $(-2, 3)$ are on both graphs. The two graphs are shown in Fig. 12.1. ■

FIGURE 12.1

Graphing is not an accurate method for solving any system of equations. However, the graphs of the equations in a nonlinear system help us to understand how many solutions we should have for the system. It is not necessary to graph a system to solve it. Even when the graphs are too difficult to sketch, we can solve the system.

E X A M P L E   2   **Solving a system algebraically with substitution**

Solve the system:

$$x^2 + y^2 + 2y = 3$$
$$x^2 - y = 5$$

Solution

If we substitute $y = x^2 - 5$ into the first equation to eliminate y, we will get a fourth-degree equation to solve. Instead, we can eliminate the variable x by writing $x^2 - y = 5$ as $x^2 = y + 5$. Now replace x^2 by $y + 5$ in the first equation:

$$x^2 + y^2 + 2y = 3$$
$$(y + 5) + y^2 + 2y = 3$$
$$y^2 + 3y + 5 = 3$$
$$y^2 + 3y + 2 = 0$$
$$(y + 2)(y + 1) = 0 \quad \text{Solve by factoring.}$$
$$y + 2 = 0 \quad \text{or} \quad y + 1 = 0$$
$$y = -2 \quad \text{or} \quad y = -1$$

Let $y = -2$ in the equation $x^2 = y + 5$ to find the corresponding x:

$$x^2 = -2 + 5$$
$$x^2 = 3$$
$$x = \pm\sqrt{3}$$

Now let $y = -1$ in the equation $x^2 = y + 5$ to find the corresponding x:

$$x^2 = -1 + 5$$
$$x^2 = 4$$
$$x = \pm 2$$

Check these values in the original equations. The solution set is

$$\{(\sqrt{3}, -2), (-\sqrt{3}, -2), (2, -1), (-2, -1)\}.$$

The graphs of these two equations intersect at four points. ∎

E X A M P L E   3

Solving a system with the addition method

Solve each system:

a) $x^2 - y^2 = 5$
$\quad x^2 + y^2 = 7$

b) $\dfrac{2}{x} + \dfrac{1}{y} = \dfrac{1}{5}$
$\quad \dfrac{1}{x} - \dfrac{3}{y} = \dfrac{1}{3}$

Solution

a) We can eliminate y by adding the equations:

$$x^2 - y^2 = 5$$
$$\underline{x^2 + y^2 = 7}$$
$$2x^2 \quad\quad = 12$$
$$x^2 = 6$$
$$x = \pm\sqrt{6}$$

Since $x^2 = 6$, the second equation yields $6 + y^2 = 7$, $y^2 = 1$, and $y = \pm 1$. If $x^2 = 6$ and $y^2 = 1$, then both of the original equations are satisfied. The solution set is

$$\{(\sqrt{6}, 1)(\sqrt{6}, -1), (-\sqrt{6}, 1), (-\sqrt{6}, -1)\}$$

b) Usually with equations involving rational expressions we first multiply by the least common denominator (LCD), but this would make the given system more complicated. So we will just use the addition method to eliminate y:

$$\frac{6}{x} + \frac{3}{y} = \frac{3}{5} \qquad \text{Eq. (1) multiplied by 3}$$

$$\frac{1}{x} - \frac{3}{y} = \frac{1}{3} \qquad \text{Eq. (2)}$$

$$\frac{7}{x} = \frac{14}{15} \qquad \frac{3}{5} + \frac{1}{3} = \frac{14}{15}$$

$$14x = 7 \cdot 15$$

$$x = \frac{7 \cdot 15}{14} = \frac{15}{2}$$

To find y, substitute $x = \frac{15}{2}$ into Eq. (1):

$$\frac{2}{\frac{15}{2}} + \frac{1}{y} = \frac{1}{5}$$

$$\frac{4}{15} + \frac{1}{y} = \frac{1}{5} \qquad \frac{2}{\frac{15}{2}} = 2 \cdot \frac{2}{15} = \frac{4}{15}$$

$$15y \cdot \frac{4}{15} + 15y \cdot \frac{1}{y} = 15y \cdot \frac{1}{5} \qquad \text{Multiply each side by the LCD, } 15y.$$

$$4y + 15 = 3y$$

$$y = -15$$

Check that $x = \frac{15}{2}$ and $y = -15$ satisfy both original equations. The solution set is $\left\{ \left(\frac{15}{2}, -15 \right) \right\}$. ■

A system of nonlinear equations might involve exponential or logarithmic functions. To solve such systems, you will need to recall some facts about exponents and logarithms.

E X A M P L E   4   **A system involving logarithms**

Solve the system

$$y = \log_2(x + 28)$$
$$y = 3 + \log_2(x)$$

Solution

Eliminate y by substituting $\log_2(x + 28)$ for y in the second equation:

$$\log_2(x + 28) = 3 + \log_2(x) \qquad \text{Eliminate } y.$$

$$\log_2(x + 28) - \log_2(x) = 3 \qquad \text{Subtract } \log_2(x) \text{ from each side.}$$

$$\log_2\left(\frac{x + 28}{x} \right) = 3 \qquad \text{Quotient rule for logarithms}$$

$$\frac{x + 28}{x} = 8 \qquad \text{Definition of logarithm}$$

$$x + 28 = 8x \qquad \text{Multiply each side by } x.$$

$$28 = 7x \qquad \text{Subtract } x \text{ from each side.}$$

$$4 = x \qquad \text{Divide each side by 7.}$$

If $x = 4$, then $y = \log_2(4 + 28) = \log_2(32) = 5$. Check $(4, 5)$ in both equations. The solution to the system is $\{(4, 5)\}$. ∎

Applications

Example 5 shows a geometric problem that can be solved with a system of non-linear equations.

EXAMPLE 5

Nonlinear equations in applications

A 15-foot ladder is leaning against a wall so that the distance from the bottom of the ladder to the wall is one-half of the distance from the top of the ladder to the ground. Find the distance from the top of the ladder to the ground.

Calculator Close-Up

To see the solutions, graph
$$y_1 = \sqrt{15^2 - x^2},$$
$$y_2 = -\sqrt{15^2 - x^2},$$
and $y_3 = 2x$.

The line intersects the circle twice.

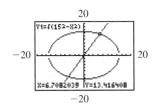

Solution

Let x be the number of feet from the bottom of the ladder to the wall and y be the number of feet from the top of the ladder to the ground (see Fig. 12.2). We can write two equations involving x and y:

$$x^2 + y^2 = 15^2 \quad \text{Pythagorean theorem}$$
$$y = 2x$$

Solve by substitution:

$$x^2 + (2x)^2 = 225 \quad \text{Replace } y \text{ by } 2x.$$
$$x^2 + 4x^2 = 225$$
$$5x^2 = 225$$
$$x^2 = 45$$
$$x = \pm\sqrt{45} = \pm 3\sqrt{5}$$

Because x represents distance, x must be positive. So $x = 3\sqrt{5}$. Because $y = 2x$, we get $y = 6\sqrt{5}$. The distance from the top of the ladder to the ground is $6\sqrt{5}$ feet.

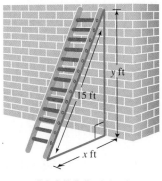

FIGURE 12.2 ∎

Example 6 shows how a nonlinear system can be used to solve a problem involving work.

EXAMPLE 6

Nonlinear equations in applications

A large fish tank at the Gulf Aquarium can usually be filled in 10 minutes using pumps A and B. However, pump B can pump water in or out at the same rate. If pump B is inadvertently run in reverse, then the tank will be filled in 30 minutes. How long would it take each pump to fill the tank by itself?

Helpful Hint

Note that we could write equations about the rates. Pump A's rate is $\frac{1}{a}$ tank per minute, B's rate is $\frac{1}{b}$ tank per minute, and together their rate is $\frac{1}{10}$ tank per minute or $\frac{1}{30}$ tank per minute.

$$\frac{1}{a} + \frac{1}{b} = \frac{1}{10}$$

$$\frac{1}{a} - \frac{1}{b} = \frac{1}{30}$$

Solution

Let a represent the number of minutes that it takes pump A to fill the tank alone and b represent the number of minutes it takes pump B to fill the tank alone. The rate at which pump A fills the tank is $\frac{1}{a}$ of the tank per minute, and the rate at which pump B fills the tank is $\frac{1}{b}$ of the tank per minute. Because the work completed is the product of the rate and time, we can make the following table when the pumps work together to fill the tank:

	Rate	Time	Work
Pump A	$\frac{1}{a} \dfrac{\text{tank}}{\text{min}}$	10 min	$\frac{10}{a}$ tank
Pump B	$\frac{1}{b} \dfrac{\text{tank}}{\text{min}}$	10 min	$\frac{10}{b}$ tank

Note that each pump fills a fraction of the tank and those fractions have a sum of 1:

$$(1) \qquad \frac{10}{a} + \frac{10}{b} = 1$$

In the 30 minutes in which pump B is working in reverse, A puts in $\frac{30}{a}$ of the tank whereas B takes out $\frac{30}{b}$ of the tank. Since the tank still gets filled, we can write the following equation:

$$(2) \qquad \frac{30}{a} - \frac{30}{b} = 1$$

Multiply Eq. (1) by 3 and add the result to Eq. (2) to eliminate b:

$$\frac{30}{a} + \frac{30}{b} = 3 \quad \text{\small Eq. (1) multiplied by 3}$$

$$\frac{30}{a} - \frac{30}{b} = 1 \quad \text{\small Eq. (2)}$$

$$\overline{\phantom{\frac{30}{a}}}$$

$$\frac{60}{a} = 4$$

$$4a = 60$$

$$a = 15$$

Use $a = 15$ in Eq. (1) to find b:

$$\frac{10}{15} + \frac{10}{b} = 1$$

$$\frac{10}{b} = \frac{1}{3} \quad \text{\small Subtract } \tfrac{10}{15} \text{ from each side.}$$

$$b = 30$$

So pump A fills the tank in 15 minutes working alone, and pump B fills the tank in 30 minutes working alone. ■

WARM-UPS

True or false? Explain your answer.

1. The graph of $y = x^2$ is a parabola.
2. The graph of $y = |x|$ is a straight line.
3. The point $(3, -4)$ satisfies both $x^2 + y^2 = 25$ and $y = \sqrt{5x + 1}$.
4. The graphs of $y = \sqrt{x}$ and $y = -x - 2$ do not intersect.
5. Substitution is the only method for eliminating a variable when solving a nonlinear system.
6. If Bob paints a fence in x hours, then he paints $\frac{1}{x}$ of the fence per hour.
7. In a triangle whose angles are $30°$, $60°$, and $90°$, the length of the side opposite the $30°$ angle is one-half the length of the hypotenuse.
8. The formula $V = LWH$ gives the volume of a rectangular box in which the sides have lengths L, W, and H.
9. The surface area of a rectangular box is $2LW + 2WH + 2LH$.
10. The area of a right triangle is one-half the product of the lengths of its legs.

12.1 EXERCISES

Reading and Writing *After reading this section, write out the answers to these questions. Use complete sentences.*

1. Why are some equations called nonlinear?

2. Why do we graph the equations in a nonlinear system?

3. Why don't we solve systems by graphing?

4. What techniques do we use to solve nonlinear systems?

Solve each system and graph both equations on the same set of axes. See Example 1.

5. $y = x^2$
   $x + y = 6$

6. $y = x^2 - 1$
   $x + y = 11$

7. $y = |x|$
   $2y - x = 6$

8. $y = |x|$
   $3y = x + 6$

9. $y = \sqrt{2x}$
   $x - y = 4$

10. $y = \sqrt{x}$
    $x - y = 6$

11. $4x - 9y = 9$
$xy = 1$

12. $2x + 2y = 3$
$xy = -1$

25. $\dfrac{1}{x} - \dfrac{1}{y} = 5$
$\dfrac{2}{x} + \dfrac{1}{y} = -3$

26. $\dfrac{2}{x} - \dfrac{3}{y} = \dfrac{1}{2}$
$\dfrac{3}{x} + \dfrac{1}{y} = \dfrac{1}{2}$

27. $\dfrac{2}{x} - \dfrac{1}{y} = \dfrac{5}{12}$
$\dfrac{1}{x} - \dfrac{3}{y} = -\dfrac{5}{12}$

28. $\dfrac{3}{x} - \dfrac{2}{y} = 5$
$\dfrac{4}{x} + \dfrac{3}{y} = 18$

13. $y = -x^2 + 1$
$y = x^2$

14. $y = x^2$
$y = \sqrt{x}$

29. $x^2y = 20$
$xy + 2 = 6x$

30. $y^2x = 3$
$xy + 1 = 6x$

31. $x^2 + xy - y^2 = -11$
$x + y = 7$

32. $x^2 + xy + y^2 = 3$
$y = 2x - 5$

33. $3y - 2 = x^4$
$y = x^2$

34. $y - 3 = 2x^4$
$y = 7x^2$

Solve each system. See Examples 2 and 3.

15. $x^2 + y^2 = 25$
$y = x^2 - 5$

16. $x^2 + y^2 = 25$
$y = x + 1$

17. $xy - 3x = 8$
$y = x + 1$

18. $xy + 2x = 9$
$x - y = 2$

19. $xy - x = 8$
$xy + 3x = -4$

20. $2xy - 3x = -1$
$xy + 5x = -7$

21. $x^2 + y^2 = 8$
$x^2 - y^2 = 2$

22. $y^2 - 2x^2 = 1$
$y^2 + 2x^2 = 5$

23. $x^2 + 2y^2 = 8$
$2x^2 - y^2 = 1$

24. $2x^2 + 3y^2 = 8$
$3x^2 + 2y^2 = 7$

Solve the following systems involving logarithmic and exponential functions. See Example 4.

35. $y = \log_2(x - 1)$
$y = 3 - \log_2(x + 1)$

36. $y = \log_3(x - 4)$
$y = 2 - \log_3(x + 4)$

37. $y = \log_2(x - 1)$
$y = 2 + \log_2(x + 2)$

38. $y = \log_4(8x)$
$y = 2 + \log_4(x - 1)$

39. $y = 2^{3x+4}$
$y = 4^{x-1}$

40. $y = 4^{3x}$
$y = \left(\dfrac{1}{2}\right)^{1-x}$

Solve each problem by using a system of two equations in two unknowns. See Examples 5 and 6.

41. *Known hypotenuse.* Find the lengths of the legs of a right triangle whose hypotenuse is $\sqrt{15}$ feet and whose area is 3 square feet.

42. *Known diagonal.* A small television is advertised to have a picture with a diagonal measure of 5 inches and a viewing area of 12 square inches (in.²). What are the length and width of the screen?

FIGURE FOR EXERCISE 42

43. *House of seven gables.* Vincent has plans to build a house with seven gables. The plans call for an attic vent in the shape of an isosceles triangle in each gable. Because of the slope of the roof, the ratio of the height to the base of each triangle must be 1 to 4. If the vents are to provide a total ventilating area of 3500 in.², then what should be the height and base of each triangle?

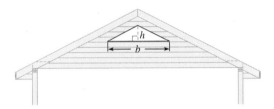

FIGURE FOR EXERCISE 43

44. *Known perimeter.* Find the lengths of the sides of a triangle whose perimeter is 6 feet (ft) and whose angles are 30°, 60°, and 90° (see Appendix A).

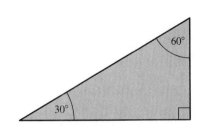

FIGURE FOR EXERCISE 44

45. *Filling a tank.* Pump A can either fill a tank or empty it in the same amount of time. If pump A and pump B are working together, the tank can be filled in 6 hours. When pump A was inadvertently left in the drain position while pump B was trying to fill the tank, it took 12 hours to fill the tank. How long would it take either pump working alone to fill the tank?

46. *Cleaning a house.* Roxanne either cleans the house or messes it up at the same rate. When Roxanne is cleaning with her mother, they can clean up a completely messed up house in 6 hours. If Roxanne is not cooperating, it takes her mother 9 hours to clean the house,

with Roxanne continually messing it up. How long would it take her mother to clean the entire house if Roxanne were sent to her grandmother's house?

47. *Cleaning fish.* Jan and Beth work in a seafood market that processes 200 pounds of catfish every morning. On Monday, Jan started cleaning catfish at 8:00 A.M. and finished cleaning 100 pounds just as Beth arrived. Beth then took over and finished the job at 8:50 A.M. On Tuesday they both started at 8 A.M. and worked together to finish the job at 8:24 A.M. On Wednesday, Beth was sick. If Jan is the faster worker, then how long did it take Jan to complete all of the catfish by herself?

FIGURE FOR EXERCISE 47

48. *Building a patio.* Richard has already formed a rectangular area for a flagstone patio, but his wife Susan is unsure of the size of the patio they want. If the width is increased by 2 ft, then the area is increased by 30 square feet (ft²). If the width is increased by 1 ft and the length by 3 ft, then the area is increased by 54 ft². What are the dimensions of the rectangle that Richard has already formed?

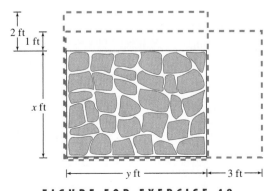

FIGURE FOR EXERCISE 48

49. *Fencing a rectangle.* If 34 ft of fencing are used to enclose a rectangular area of 72 ft², then what are the dimensions of the area?

50. *Real numbers.* Find two numbers that have a sum of 8 and a product of 10.

51. *Imaginary numbers.* Find two complex numbers whose sum is 8 and whose product is 20.

52. *Imaginary numbers.* Find two complex numbers whose sum is −6 and whose product is 10.

53. *Making a sign.* Rico's Sign Shop has a contract to make a sign in the shape of a square with an isosceles triangle on top of it, as shown in the figure. The contract calls for a total height of 10 ft with an area of 72 ft². How long should Rico make the side of the square and what should be the height of the triangle?

54. *Designing a box.* Angelina is designing a rectangular box of 120 cubic inches that is to contain new Eaties breakfast cereal. The box must be 2 inches thick so that it is easy to hold. It must have 184 square inches of surface area to provide enough space for all of the special offers and coupons. What should be the dimensions of the box?

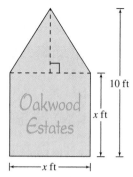

FIGURE FOR EXERCISE 53

 GRAPHING CALCULATOR EXERCISES

55. Solve each system by graphing each pair of equations on a graphing calculator and using the intersect feature to estimate the point of intersection. Find the coordinates of each intersection to the nearest hundredth.

a) $y = e^x - 4$
$y = \ln(x + 3)$

b) $3^{y-1} = x$
$y = x^2$

c) $x^2 + y^2 = 4$
$y = x^3$

In This Section

- The Distance Formula
- The Geometric Definition of Parabola
- Developing the Equation
- Parabolas in the Form $y = a(x − h)^2 + k$
- Finding the Vertex, Focus, and Directrix
- Axis of Symmetry
- Changing Forms
- Parabolas Opening to the Right or Left

12.2 THE PARABOLA

The **conic sections** are the four curves that are obtained by intersecting a cone and a plane as in Fig. 12.3. The figure explains why the parabola, ellipse, circle, and hyperbola are called conic sections, but it does not help us find equations for the curves. To develop equations for these curves we will redefine them more precisely using distance between points. So we will first review the distance formula that we used in Section 3.1.

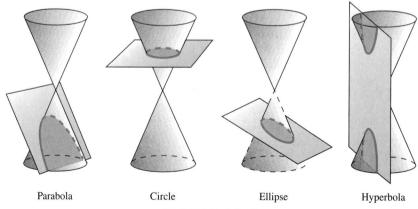

Parabola   Circle   Ellipse   Hyperbola

FIGURE 12.3

The Distance Formula

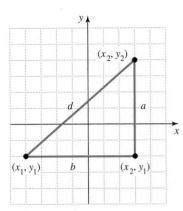

FIGURE 12.4

Consider the points (x_1, y_1) and (x_2, y_2) as shown in Fig. 12.4. The distance between these points is the length of the hypotenuse of a right triangle as shown in the figure. The length of side a is $y_2 - y_1$ and the length of side b is $x_2 - x_1$. Using the Pythagorean theorem, we can write

$$d^2 = (x_2 - x_1)^2 + (y_2 - y_1)^2.$$

If we apply the even-root property and omit the negative square root (because the distance is positive), we can express this formula as follows.

> **Distance Formula**
>
> The distance d between (x_1, y_1) and (x_2, y_2) is given by the formula
>
> $$d = \sqrt{(x_2 - x_1)^2 + (y_2 - y_1)^2}.$$

E X A M P L E   1

Using the distance formula

Find the length of the line segment with endpoints $(-8, -10)$ and $(6, -4)$.

Solution

Let $(x_1, y_1) = (-8, -10)$ and $(x_2, y_2) = (6, -4)$. Now substitute the appropriate values into the distance formula:

$$\begin{aligned}
d &= \sqrt{[6 - (-8)]^2 + [-4 - (-10)]^2} \\
&= \sqrt{(14)^2 + (6)^2} \\
&= \sqrt{196 + 36} \\
&= \sqrt{232} \\
&= \sqrt{4 \cdot 58} \\
&= 2\sqrt{58} \quad \text{Simplified form}
\end{aligned}$$

The exact length of the segment is $2\sqrt{58}$. ∎

The Geometric Definition of Parabola

In Section 8.3 we called the graph of $y = ax^2 + bx + c$ a parabola. This equation is the **standard equation** of a parabola. In this section you will see that the following geometric definition describes the same curve as the equation.

> **Parabola**
>
> Given a line (the **directrix**) and a point not on the line (the **focus**), the set of all points in the plane that are equidistant from the point and the line is called a **parabola.**

In Section 8.3 we defined the vertex as the highest point on a parabola that opens downward or the lowest point on a parabola that opens upward. We learned that $x = -b/(2a)$ gives the x-coordinate of the vertex. We can also describe the vertex of a parabola as the midpoint of the line segment that joins the focus and directrix, perpendicular to the directrix. See Fig. 12.5.

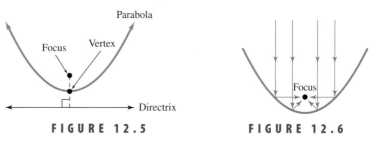

FIGURE 12.5   FIGURE 12.6

The focus of a parabola is important in applications. When parallel rays of light travel into a parabolic reflector, they are reflected toward the focus as in Fig. 12.6. This property is used in telescopes to see the light from distant stars. If the light source is at the focus, as in a searchlight, the light is reflected off the parabola and projected outward in a narrow beam. This reflecting property is also used in camera lenses, satellite dishes, and eavesdropping devices.

Developing the Equation

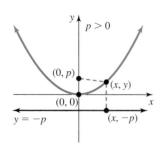

FIGURE 12.7

To develop an equation for a parabola, given the focus and directrix, choose the point $(0, p)$, where $p > 0$ as the focus and the line $y = -p$ as the directrix, as shown in Fig. 12.7. The vertex of this parabola is $(0, 0)$. For an arbitrary point (x, y) on the parabola the distance to the directrix is the distance from (x, y) to $(x, -p)$. The distance to the focus is the distance between (x, y) and $(0, p)$. We use the fact that these distances are equal to write the equation of the parabola:

$$\sqrt{(x - 0)^2 + (y - p)^2} = \sqrt{(x - x)^2 + (y - (-p))^2}$$

To simplify the equation, first remove the parentheses inside the radicals:

$$\sqrt{x^2 + y^2 - 2py + p^2} = \sqrt{y^2 + 2py + p^2}$$

$$x^2 + y^2 - 2py + p^2 = y^2 + 2py + p^2 \qquad \text{Square each side.}$$

$$x^2 = 4py \qquad \text{Subtract } y^2 \text{ and } p^2 \text{ from each side.}$$

$$y = \frac{1}{4p}x^2$$

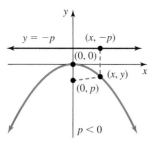

FIGURE 12.8

So the parabola with focus $(0, p)$ and directrix $y = -p$ for $p > 0$ has equation $y = \frac{1}{4p}x^2$. This equation has the form $y = ax^2 + bx + c$, where $a = \frac{1}{4p}$, $b = 0$, and $c = 0$.

If the focus is $(0, p)$ with $p < 0$ and the directrix is $y = -p$, then the parabola opens downward as shown in Fig. 12.8. Deriving the equation using the distance formula again yields $y = \frac{1}{4p}x^2$.

Parabolas in the Form $y = a(x - h)^2 + k$

The simplest parabola, $y = x^2$, has vertex $(0, 0)$. The transformation $y = a(x - h)^2 + k$ is also a parabola and its vertex is (h, k). The focus and directrix of the transformation are found as follows:

> **Parabolas in the Form $y = a(x - h)^2 + k$**
>
> The graph of the equation $y = a(x - h)^2 + k$ $(a \neq 0)$ is a parabola with vertex (h, k), focus $(h, k + p)$, and directrix $y = k - p$, where $a = \frac{1}{4p}$. If $a > 0$, the parabola opens upward; if $a < 0$, the parabola opens downward.

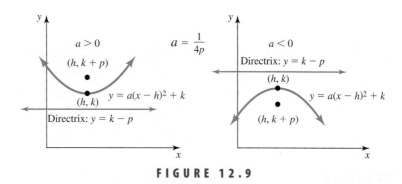

FIGURE 12.9

Figure 12.9 shows the location of the focus and directrix for parabolas with vertex (h, k) and opening either upward or downward. Note that the location of the focus and directrix determine the value of a and the shape and opening of the parabola.

CAUTION   For a parabola that opens upward, $p > 0$, and the focus $(h, k + p)$ is above the vertex (h, k). For a parabola that opens downward, $p < 0$, and the focus $(h, k + p)$ is below the vertex (h, k). In either case the distance from the vertex to the focus and the vertex to the directrix is $|p|$.

Finding the Vertex, Focus, and Directrix

In Example 2 we find the vertex, focus, and directrix from an equation of a parabola. In Example 3 we find the equation given the focus and directrix.

E X A M P L E   2   **Finding the vertex, focus, and directrix, given an equation**

Find the vertex, focus, and directrix for the parabola $y = x^2$.

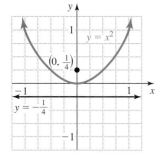

FIGURE 12.10

Solution

Compare $y = x^2$ to the general formula $y = a(x - h)^2 + k$. We see that $h = 0$, $k = 0$, and $a = 1$. So the vertex is $(0, 0)$. Because $a = 1$, we can use $a = \frac{1}{4p}$ to get

$$1 = \frac{1}{4p},$$

or $p = \frac{1}{4}$. Use $(h, k + p)$ to get the focus $\left(0, \frac{1}{4}\right)$. Use the equation $y = k - p$ to get $y = -\frac{1}{4}$ as the equation of the directrix. See Fig. 12.10.   ■

E X A M P L E   3   **Finding an equation, given a focus and directrix**

Find the equation of the parabola with focus $(-1, 4)$ and directrix $y = 3$.

Solution

Because the vertex is halfway between the focus and directrix, the vertex is $\left(-1, \frac{7}{2}\right)$. See Fig. 12.11 on the next page. The distance from the vertex to the focus is $\frac{1}{2}$. Because the focus is above the vertex, p is positive. So $p = \frac{1}{2}$, and $a = \frac{1}{4p} = \frac{1}{2}$. The equation is

$$y = \frac{1}{2}(x - (-1))^2 + \frac{7}{2}.$$

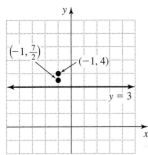

FIGURE 12.11

Convert to $y = ax^2 + bx + c$ form as follows:

$$y = \frac{1}{2}(x + 1)^2 + \frac{7}{2}$$

$$y = \frac{1}{2}(x^2 + 2x + 1) + \frac{7}{2}$$

$$y = \frac{1}{2}x^2 + x + 4$$

■

Axis of Symmetry

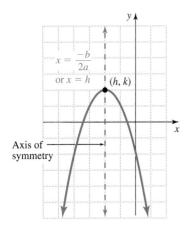

FIGURE 12.12

The graph of $y = x^2$ shown in Fig. 12.10 is **symmetric about the y-axis** because the two halves of the parabola would coincide if the paper were folded on the y-axis. In general, the vertical line through the vertex is the **axis of symmetry** for the parabola. See Fig. 12.12. In the form $y = ax^2 + bx + c$ the x-coordinate of the vertex is $-b/(2a)$ and the equation of the axis of symmetry is $x = -b/(2a)$. In the form $y = a(x - h)^2 + k$ the vertex is (h, k) and the equation for the axis of symmetry is $x = h$.

Changing Forms

Since there are two forms for the equation of a parabola, it is sometimes useful to change from one form to the other. To change from $y = a(x - h)^2 + k$ to the form $y = ax^2 + bx + c$, we square the binomial and combine like terms, as in Example 3. To change from $y = ax^2 + bx + c$ to the form $y = a(x - h)^2 + k$, we complete the square, as in Example 4.

E X A M P L E   4   **Converting $y = ax^2 + bx + c$ to $y = a(x - h)^2 + k$**

Write $y = 2x^2 - 4x + 5$ in the form $y = a(x - h)^2 + k$ and identify the vertex, focus, directrix, and axis of symmetry of the parabola.

Solution

Use completing the square to rewrite the equation:

$$y = 2(x^2 - 2x) + 5$$
$$y = 2(x^2 - 2x + 1 - 1) + 5 \quad \text{Complete the square.}$$
$$y = 2(x^2 - 2x + 1) - 2 + 5 \quad \text{Move } 2(-1) \text{ outside the parentheses.}$$
$$y = 2(x - 1)^2 + 3$$

The vertex is $(1, 3)$. Because $a = \frac{1}{4p}$, we have

$$\frac{1}{4p} = 2,$$

and $p = \frac{1}{8}$. Because the parabola opens upward, the focus is $\frac{1}{8}$ unit above the vertex at $\left(1, 3\frac{1}{8}\right)$, or $\left(1, \frac{25}{8}\right)$, and the directrix is the horizontal line $\frac{1}{8}$ unit below the vertex, $y = 2\frac{7}{8}$ or $y = \frac{23}{8}$. The axis of symmetry is $x = 1$.

■

Calculator Close-Up

The graphs of

$$y_1 = 2x^2 - 4x + 5$$

and

$$y_2 = 2(x - 1)^2 + 3$$

appear to be identical. This supports the conclusion that the equations are equivalent.

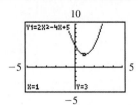

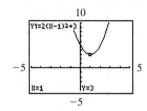

C A U T I O N   Be careful when you complete a square within parentheses as in Example 4. For another example, consider the equivalent equations

$$y = -3(x^2 + 4x),$$
$$y = -3(x^2 + 4x + 4 - 4),$$

and

$$y = -3(x + 2)^2 + 12.$$

E X A M P L E   5

Finding the features of a parabola from standard form

Find the vertex, focus, directrix, and axis of symmetry of the parabola $y = -3x^2 + 9x - 5$, and determine whether the parabola opens upward or downward.

Calculator Close-Up

A calculator graph can be used to check the vertex and opening of a parabola.

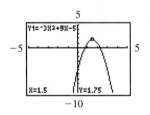

Solution

The x-coordinate of the vertex is

$$x = \frac{-b}{2a} = \frac{-9}{2(-3)} = \frac{-9}{-6} = \frac{3}{2}.$$

To find the y-coordinate of the vertex, let $x = \frac{3}{2}$ in $y = -3x^2 + 9x - 5$:

$$y = -3\left(\frac{3}{2}\right)^2 + 9\left(\frac{3}{2}\right) - 5 = -\frac{27}{4} + \frac{27}{2} - 5 = \frac{7}{4}$$

The vertex is $\left(\frac{3}{2}, \frac{7}{4}\right)$. Because $a = -3$, the parabola opens downward. To find the focus, use $-3 = \frac{1}{4p}$ to get $p = -\frac{1}{12}$. The focus is $\frac{1}{12}$ of a unit below the vertex at $\left(\frac{3}{2}, \frac{7}{4} - \frac{1}{12}\right)$ or $\left(\frac{3}{2}, \frac{5}{3}\right)$. The directrix is the horizontal line $\frac{1}{12}$ of a unit above the vertex, $y = \frac{7}{4} + \frac{1}{12}$ or $y = \frac{11}{6}$. The equation of the axis of symmetry is $x = \frac{3}{2}$. ■

Parabolas Opening to the Right or Left

If we interchange x and y in the equation $y = a(x - h)^2 + k$ we get the equation $x = a(y - k)^2 + h$, which is a parabola opening to the right or left.

> **Parabolas in the Form $x = a(y - k)^2 + h$**
>
> The graph of $x = a(y - k)^2 + h$ ($a \neq 0$) is a parabola with vertex (h, k), focus $(h + p, k)$, and directrix $x = h - p$, where $a = \frac{1}{4p}$. If $a > 0$, the parabola opens to the right; if $a < 0$, the parabola opens to the left.

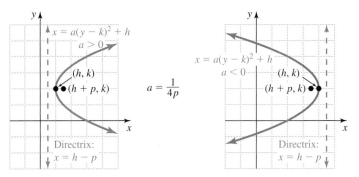

FIGURE 12.13

Figure 12.13 shows the location of the focus and directrix for parabolas with vertex (h, k) and opening either right or left. The location of the focus and directrix determine the value of a and the shape and opening of the parabola. Note that a and p have the same sign because $a = \dfrac{1}{4p}$.

The equation $x = ay^2 + by + c$ could be converted to the form $x = a(y - k)^2 + h$ from which the vertex, focus, and directrix could be determined. Without converting we can determine that the graph of $x = ay^2 + by + c$ opens to the right for $a > 0$ and to the left for $a < 0$. The y-coordinate of the vertex is $\dfrac{-b}{2a}$. The x-coordinate of the vertex can be determined by substituting $\dfrac{-b}{2a}$ for y in $x = ay^2 + by + c$.

EXAMPLE 6

Graphing a parabola opening to the right

Find the vertex, focus, and directrix for the parabola $x = \frac{1}{2}(y - 2)^2 + 1$ and sketch the graph.

Solution

In the form $x = a(y - k)^2 + h$ the vertex is (h, k). So the vertex for $x = \frac{1}{2}(y - 2)^2 + 1$ is $(1, 2)$. Since $a = \dfrac{1}{4p}$ and $a = \frac{1}{2}$, we have $p = \frac{1}{2}$ and the focus is $\left(\frac{3}{2}, 2\right)$. The directrix is the vertical line $x = \frac{1}{2}$. Find a few points that satisfy $x = \frac{1}{2}(y - 2)^2 + 1$ as follows:

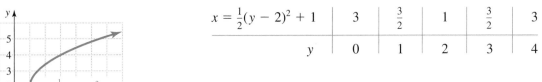

$x = \frac{1}{2}(y - 2)^2 + 1$	3	$\frac{3}{2}$	1	$\frac{3}{2}$	3
y	0	1	2	3	4

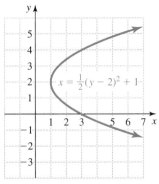

FIGURE 12.14

Sketch the graph through these points, as shown in Fig. 12.14.

The equation $x = ay^2 + by + c$ could be converted to the form $x = a(y - k)^2 + h$ from which the vertex, focus, and directrix could be determined. Without converting we can determine that the graph of $x = ay^2 + by + c$ opens to the right for $a > 0$ and to the left for $a < 0$. The y-coordinate of the vertex is $\dfrac{-b}{2a}$. The x-coordinate of the vertex can be determined by substituting $\dfrac{-b}{2a}$ for y in $x = ay^2 + by + c$.

WARM-UPS

True or false? Explain your answer.

1. There is a parabola with focus (2, 3), directrix $y = 1$, and vertex (0, 0).

2. The focus for the parabola $y = \frac{1}{4}x^2 + 1$ is (0, 2).

3. The graph of $y - 3 = 5(x - 4)^2$ is a parabola with vertex (4, 3).

4. The graph of $y = 6x + 3x + 2$ is a parabola.

5. The graph of $y = 2x - x^2 + 9$ is a parabola opening upward.

6. For $y = x^2$ the vertex and y-intercept are the same point.

7. A parabola with vertex (2, 3) and focus (2, 4) has no x-intercepts.

8. The parabola with focus (0, 2) and directrix $y = 1$ opens upward.

9. The axis of symmetry for $y = a(x - 2)^2 + k$ is $x = 2$.

10. If $a = \frac{1}{(4p)}$ and $a = 1$, then $p = \frac{1}{4}$.

12.2   EXERCISES

Reading and Writing   *After reading this section, write out the answers to these questions. Use complete sentences.*

1. What is the definition of a parabola given in this section?

2. What is the location of the vertex?

3. What are the two forms of the equation of a parabola?

4. What is the distance from the focus to the vertex in any parabola of the form $y = ax^2 + bx + c$?

5. How do we convert an equation of the form $y = ax^2 + bx + c$ into the form $y = a(x - h)^2 + k$?

6. How do we convert an equation of the form $y = a(x - h)^2 + k$ into the form $y = ax^2 + bx + c$?

Find the distance between each given pair of points. See Example 1.

7. (6, 5), (4, 2)

8. (7, 3), (5, 1)

9. (3, 5), (1, −3)

10. (6, 2), (3, −5)

11. (4, −2), (−3, −6)

12. (−2, 3), (1, −4)

Find the vertex, focus, and directrix for each parabola. See Example 2.

13. $y = 2x^2$

14. $y = \frac{1}{2}x^2$

15. $y = -\frac{1}{4}x^2$

16. $y = -\frac{1}{12}x^2$

17. $y = \frac{1}{2}(x - 3)^2 + 2$

18. $y = \frac{1}{4}(x + 2)^2 - 5$

19. $y = -(x + 1)^2 + 6$

20. $y = -3(x - 4)^2 + 1$

Find the equation of the parabola with the given focus and directrix. See Example 3.

21. Focus (0, 2), directrix $y = -2$

22. Focus (0, −3), directrix $y = 3$

23. Focus $\left(0, -\frac{1}{2}\right)$, directrix $y = \frac{1}{2}$

24. Focus $\left(0, \frac{1}{8}\right)$, directrix $y = -\frac{1}{8}$

25. Focus $(3, 2)$, directrix $y = 1$

26. Focus $(-4, 5)$, directrix $y = 4$

27. Focus $(1, -2)$, directrix $y = 2$

28. Focus $(2, -3)$, directrix $y = 1$

29. Focus $(-3, 1.25)$, directrix $y = 0.75$

30. Focus $\left(5, \dfrac{17}{8}\right)$, directrix $y = \dfrac{15}{8}$

Write each equation in the form $y = a(x - h)^2 + k$. Identify the vertex, focus, directrix, and axis of symmetry of each parabola. See Example 4.

31. $y = x^2 - 6x + 1$

32. $y = x^2 + 4x - 7$

33. $y = 2x^2 + 12x + 5$

34. $y = 3x^2 + 6x - 7$

35. $y = -2x^2 + 16x + 1$

36. $y = -3x^2 - 6x + 7$

37. $y = 5x^2 + 40x$

38. $y = -2x^2 + 10x$

Find the vertex, focus, directrix, and axis of symmetry of each parabola (without completing the square), and determine whether the parabola opens upward or downward. See Example 5.

39. $y = x^2 - 4x + 1$

40. $y = x^2 - 6x - 7$

41. $y = -x^2 + 2x - 3$

42. $y = -x^2 + 4x + 9$

43. $y = 3x^2 - 6x + 1$

44. $y = 2x^2 + 4x - 3$

45. $y = -x^2 - 3x + 2$

46. $y = -x^2 + 3x - 1$

47. $y = 3x^2 + 5$

48. $y = -2x^2 - 6$

Find the vertex, focus, and directrix for each parabola. See Example 6.

49. $x = (y - 2)^2 + 3$

50. $x = (y + 3)^2 - 1$

51. $x = \dfrac{1}{4}(y - 1)^2 - 2$

52. $x = \dfrac{1}{4}(y + 1)^2 + 2$

53. $x = -\dfrac{1}{2}(y - 2)^2 + 4$

54. $x = -\dfrac{1}{2}(y + 1)^2 - 1$

Sketch the graph of each parabola.

55. $y = (x - 2)^2 + 3$ **56.** $y = (x + 3)^2 - 1$

57. $y = -2(x - 1)^2 + 3$ **58.** $y = -\dfrac{1}{2}(x + 1)^2 + 5$

the vertex at the origin and the focus at (0, 15). Find the equation of the parabola.

64. ***Arecibo Observatory.*** The largest radio telescope in the world uses a 1000-ft parabolic dish, suspended in a valley in Arecibo, Puerto Rico. The antenna hangs above the vertex of the dish on cables stretching from two towers. The accompanying figure shows a cross section of the parabolic dish and the towers. Assuming the vertex is at (0, 0), find the equation for the parabola. Find the distance from the vertex to the antenna located at the focus.

59. $x = (y - 2)^2 + 3$ **60.** $x = (y + 3)^2 - 1$

61. $x = -2(y - 1)^2 + 3$ **62.** $x = -\dfrac{1}{2}(y + 1)^2 + 5$

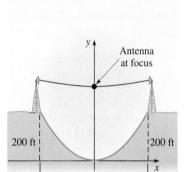

FIGURE FOR EXERCISE 64

Graph both equations of each system on the same coordinate axes. Use elimination of variables to find all points of intersection.

65. $y = -x^2 + 3$
$y = x^2 + 1$

Solve each problem.

63. ***World's largest telescope.*** The largest reflecting telescope in the world is the 6-meter (m) reflector on Mount Pastukhov in Russia. The accompanying figure shows a cross section of a parabolic mirror 6 m in diameter with

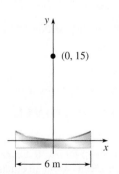

FIGURE FOR EXERCISE 63

66. $y = x^2 - 3$
$y = -x^2 + 5$

67. $y = x^2 - 2$
$y = 2x - 3$

68. $y = x^2 + x - 6$
$y = 7x - 15$

69. $y = x^2 + 3x - 4$
$y = -x^2 - 2x + 8$

70. $y = x^2 + 2x - 8$
$y = -x^2 - x + 12$

71. $y = x^2 + 3x - 4$
$y = 2x + 2$

72. $y = x^2 + 5x + 6$
$y = x + 11$

Solve each problem.

73. Find all points of intersection of the parabola $y = x^2 - 2x - 3$ and the *x*-axis.

74. Find all points of intersection of the parabola $y = 80x^2 - 33x + 255$ and the *y*-axis.

75. Find all points of intersection of the parabola $y = 0.01x^2$ and the line $y = 4$.

76. Find all points of intersection of the parabola $y = 0.02x^2$ and the line $y = x$.

77. Find all points of intersection of the parabolas $y = x^2$ and $x = y^2$.

78. Find all points of intersection of the parabolas $y = x^2$ and $y = (x - 3)^2$.

GETTING MORE INVOLVED

79. *Exploration.* Consider the parabola with focus $(p, 0)$ and directrix $x = -p$ for $p > 0$. Let (x, y) be an arbitrary point on the parabola. Write an equation expressing the fact that the distance from (x, y) to the focus is equal to the distance from (x, y) to the directrix. Rewrite the equation in the form $x = ay^2$, where $a = \dfrac{1}{4p}$.

80. *Exploration.* In general, the graph of $x = a(y - k)^2 + h$ for $a \neq 0$ is a parabola opening left or right with vertex at (h, k).

  a) For which values of a does the parabola open to the right, and for which values of a does it open to the left?

  b) What is the equation of its axis of symmetry?

  c) Sketch the graphs $x = 2(y - 3)^2 + 1$ and $x = -(y + 1)^2 + 2$.

GRAPHING CALCULATOR EXERCISES

81. Graph $y = x^2$ using the viewing window with $-1 \leq x \leq 1$ and $0 \leq y \leq 1$. Next graph $y = 2x^2 - 1$ using the viewing window $-2 \leq x \leq 2$ and $-1 \leq y \leq 7$. Explain what you see.

82. Graph $y = x^2$ and $y = 6x - 9$ in the viewing window $-5 \leq x \leq 5$ and $-5 \leq y \leq 20$. Does the line appear to be tangent to the parabola? Solve the system $y = x^2$ and $y = 6x - 9$ to find all points of intersection for the parabola and the line.

In This Section

- Developing the Equation
- Equations Not in Standard Form
- Systems of Equations

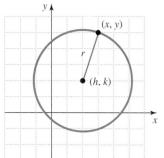

FIGURE 12.15

12.3   THE CIRCLE

In this section we continue the study of the conic sections with a discussion of the circle.

Developing the Equation

A circle is obtained by cutting a cone, as was shown in Fig. 12.3. We can also define a circle using points and distance, as we did for the parabola.

> **Circle**
>
> A **circle** is the set of all points in a plane that lie a fixed distance from a given point in the plane. The fixed distance is called the **radius,** and the given point is called the **center.**

We can use the distance formula of Section 12.2 to write an equation for the circle with center (h, k) and radius r, shown in Fig. 12.15. If (x, y) is a point on the circle, its distance from the center is r. So

$$\sqrt{(x - h)^2 + (y - k)^2} = r.$$

We square both sides of this equation to get the **standard form** for the equation of a circle.

> **Standard Equation for a Circle**
>
> The graph of the equation
>
> $$(x - h)^2 + (y - k)^2 = r^2$$
>
> with $r > 0$, is a circle with center (h, k) and radius r.

Note that a circle centered at the origin with radius r $(r > 0)$ has the standard equation

$$x^2 + y^2 = r^2.$$

E X A M P L E   1

Finding the equation, given the center and radius

Write the standard equation for the circle with the given center and radius.

a) Center $(0, 0)$, radius 2

b) Center $(-1, 2)$, radius 4

Solution

a) The center at $(0, 0)$ means that $h = 0$ and $k = 0$ in the standard equation. So the equation is $(x - 0)^2 + (y - 0)^2 = 2^2$, or $x^2 + y^2 = 4$. The circle with radius 2 centered at the origin is shown in Fig. 12.16.

b) The center at $(-1, 2)$ means that $h = -1$ and $k = 2$. So

$$[x - (-1)]^2 + [y - 2]^2 = 4^2.$$

Simplify this equation to get

$$(x + 1)^2 + (y - 2)^2 = 16.$$

The circle with center $(-1, 2)$ and radius 4 is shown in Fig. 12.17.

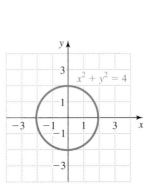

FIGURE 12.16

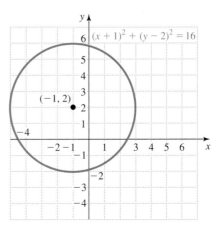

FIGURE 12.17

■

CAUTION   The equations $(x - 1)^2 + (y + 3)^2 = -9$ and $(x - 1)^2 + (y + 3)^2 = 0$ might look like equations of circles, but they are not. The first equation is not satisfied by any ordered pair of real numbers because the left-hand side is nonnegative for any x and y. The second equation is satisfied only by the point $(1, -3)$.

E X A M P L E   2

Finding the center and radius, given the equation

Determine the center and radius of the circle $x^2 + (y + 5)^2 = 2$.

Solution

We can write this equation as

$$(x - 0)^2 + [y - (-5)]^2 = (\sqrt{2})^2.$$

In this form we see that the center is $(0, -5)$ and the radius is $\sqrt{2}$.

■

E X A M P L E 3

Graphing a circle

Find the center and radius of $(x - 1)^2 + (y + 2)^2 = 9$, and sketch the graph.

Solution

The graph of this equation is a circle with center at $(1, -2)$ and radius 3. See Fig. 12.18 for the graph. ■

FIGURE 12.18

Calculator Close-Up

To graph the circle in Example 3, graph

$$y_1 = -2 + \sqrt{9 - (x - 1)^2}$$

and

$$y_2 = -2 - \sqrt{9 - (x - 1)^2}.$$

To get the circle to look round, you must use the same unit length on each axis. Most calculators have a *square* feature that automatically adjusts the window to use the same unit length on each axis.

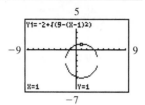

Equations Not in Standard Form

It is not easy to recognize that $x^2 - 6x + y^2 + 10y = -30$ is the equation of a circle, but it is. In Example 4 we convert this equation into the standard form for a circle by completing the squares for the variables x and y.

E X A M P L E 4

Converting to standard form

Find the center and radius of the circle given by the equation

$$x^2 - 6x + y^2 + 10y = -30.$$

Solution

To complete the square for $x^2 - 6x$, we add 9, and for $y^2 + 10y$, we add 25. To get an equivalent equation, we must add on both sides:

$$x^2 - 6x + \qquad y^2 + 10y \qquad = -30$$
$$x^2 - 6x + 9 + y^2 + 10y + 25 = -30 + 9 + 25 \quad \text{Add 9 and 25 to both sides.}$$
$$(x - 3)^2 + (y + 5)^2 = 4 \quad \text{Factor the trinomials on the left-hand side.}$$

From the standard form we see that the center is $(3, -5)$ and the radius is 2. ■

Systems of Equations

We first solved systems of nonlinear equations in two variables in Section 12.1. We found the points of intersection of two graphs without drawing the graphs. Here we will solve systems involving circles, parabolas, and lines. In the next example we find the points of intersection of a line and a circle.

E X A M P L E 5

Intersection of a line and a circle

Graph both equations of the system

$$(x - 3)^2 + (y + 1)^2 = 9$$
$$y = x - 1$$

on the same coordinate axes, and solve the system by elimination of variables.

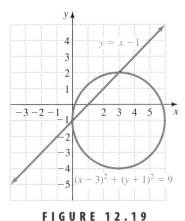

FIGURE 12.19

Solution

The graph of the first equation is a circle with center at $(3, -1)$ and radius 3. The graph of the second equation is a straight line with slope 1 and y-intercept $(0, -1)$. Both graphs are shown in Fig. 12.19. To solve the system by elimination, we substitute $y = x - 1$ into the equation of the circle:

$$(x - 3)^2 + (x - 1 + 1)^2 = 9$$
$$(x - 3)^2 + x^2 = 9$$
$$x^2 - 6x + 9 + x^2 = 9$$
$$2x^2 - 6x = 0$$
$$x^2 - 3x = 0$$
$$x(x - 3) = 0$$

$$x = 0 \quad \text{or} \quad x = 3$$
$$y = -1 \qquad\quad y = 2 \quad \text{Because } y = x - 1$$

Check $(0, -1)$ and $(3, 2)$ in the original system and with the graphs in Fig. 12.19. The solution set is $\{(0, -1), (3, 2)\}$. ■

MATH AT WORK

Friedrich von Huene, a flautist and recorder player, has been crafting woodwind instruments in his family business for over 30 years. Because it is best to play music of earlier centuries on the instruments of their time, von Huene is using many originals as models for his flutes, recorders, and oboes of different sizes.

EARLY MUSICAL INSTRUMENT MAKER

Because museum instruments have many different pitch standards, their dimensions frequently have to be changed to accommodate pitch standards that musicians use today. For a lower pitch the length of the instrument as well as the inside diameter must be increased. For a higher pitch the length has to be shortened and the diameter decreased. However, the factor for changing the length will be different from the factor for changing the diameter. A row of organ pipes demonstrates that the larger and longer pipes are proportionately more slender than the shorter high-pitched pipes. A pipe an octave higher in pitch is about half as long as the pipe an octave lower, but its diameter will be about 0.6 as large as the diameter of the lower pipe.

When making a very large recorder, von Huene carefully chooses the length, the position of the tone holes, and the bore to get the proper volume of air inside the instrument. In Exercises 57 and 58 of this section you will make the kinds of calculations von Huene makes when he crafts a modern reproduction of a Renaissance flute.

WARM-UPS

True or false? Explain your answer.

1. The radius of a circle can be any nonzero real number.
2. The coordinates of the center must satisfy the equation of the circle.
3. The circle $x^2 + y^2 = 4$ has its center at the origin.
4. The graph of $x^2 + y^2 = 9$ is a circle centered at $(0, 0)$ with radius 9.

5. The graph of $(x - 2)^2 + (y - 3)^2 + 4 = 0$ is a circle of radius 2.
6. The graph of $(x - 3) + (y + 5) = 9$ is a circle of radius 3.
7. There is only one circle centered at $(-3, -1)$ passing through the origin.

8. The center of the circle $(x - 3)^2 + (y - 4)^2 = 10$ is $(-3, -4)$.
9. The center of the circle $x^2 + y^2 + 6y - 4 = 0$ is on the y-axis.
10. The radius of the circle $x^2 - 3x + y^2 = 4$ is 2.

12.3   EXERCISES

Reading and Writing   *After reading this section, write out the answers to these questions. Use complete sentences.*

1. What is the definition of a circle?

2. What is the standard equation of a circle?

Write the standard equation for each circle with the given center and radius. See Example 1.

3. Center $(0, 3)$, radius 5
4. Center $(2, 0)$, radius 3
5. Center $(1, -2)$, radius 9
6. Center $(-3, 5)$, radius 4
7. Center $(0, 0)$, radius $\sqrt{3}$
8. Center $(0, 0)$, radius $\sqrt{2}$
9. Center $(-6, -3)$, radius $\dfrac{1}{2}$
10. Center $(-3, -5)$, radius $\dfrac{1}{4}$
11. Center $\left(\dfrac{1}{2}, \dfrac{1}{3}\right)$, radius 0.1
12. Center $\left(-\dfrac{1}{2}, 3\right)$, radius 0.2

Find the center and radius for each circle. See Example 2.

13. $(x - 3)^2 + (y - 5)^2 = 2$
14. $(x + 3)^2 + (y - 7)^2 = 6$

15. $x^2 + \left(y - \dfrac{1}{2}\right)^2 = \dfrac{1}{2}$
16. $5x^2 + 5y^2 = 5$
17. $4x^2 + 4y^2 = 9$
18. $9x^2 + 9y^2 = 49$
19. $3 - y^2 = (x - 2)^2$
20. $9 - x^2 = (y + 1)^2$

Sketch the graph of each equation. See Example 3.

21. $x^2 + y^2 = 9$ 22. $x^2 + y^2 = 16$

23. $x^2 + (y - 3)^2 = 9$ 24. $(x - 4)^2 + y^2 = 16$

25. $(x + 1)^2 + (y - 1)^2 = 2$ **26.** $(x - 2)^2 + (y + 2)^2 = 8$

38. $x^2 - 3x + y^2 = 0$

39. $x^2 - 3x + y^2 - y = 1$

40. $x^2 - 5x + y^2 + 3y = 2$

27. $(x - 4)^2 + (y + 3)^2 = 16$ **28.** $(x - 3)^2 + (y - 7)^2 = 25$

41. $x^2 - \dfrac{2}{3}x + y^2 + \dfrac{3}{2}y = 0$

42. $x^2 + \dfrac{1}{3}x + y^2 - \dfrac{2}{3}y = \dfrac{1}{9}$

29. $\left(x - \dfrac{1}{2}\right)^2 + \left(y + \dfrac{1}{2}\right)^2 = \dfrac{1}{4}$ **30.** $\left(x + \dfrac{1}{3}\right)^2 + y^2 = \dfrac{1}{9}$

Graph both equations of each system on the same coordinate axes. Solve the system by elimination of variables to find all points of intersection of the graphs. See Example 5.

43. $x^2 + y^2 = 10$ **44.** $x^2 + y^2 = 4$
$\quad\ y = 3x$ $\quad\ y = x - 2$

Rewrite each equation in the standard form for the equation of a circle, and identify its center and radius. See Example 4.

31. $x^2 + 4x + y^2 + 6y = 0$

32. $x^2 - 10x + y^2 + 8y = 0$

33. $x^2 - 2x + y^2 - 4y - 3 = 0$

45. $x^2 + y^2 = 9$ **46.** $x^2 + y^2 = 4$
$\quad\ y = x^2 - 3$ $\quad\ y = x^2 - 2$

34. $x^2 - 6x + y^2 - 2y + 9 = 0$

35. $x^2 + y^2 = 8y + 10x - 32$

36. $x^2 + y^2 = 8x - 10y$

37. $x^2 - x + y^2 + y = 0$

47. $(x - 2)^2 + (y + 3)^2 = 4$
$y = x - 3$

48. $(x + 1)^2 + (y - 4)^2 = 17$
$y = x + 2$

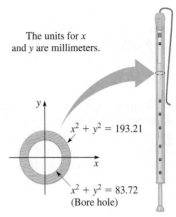

The units for x and y are millimeters.

$x^2 + y^2 = 193.21$

$x^2 + y^2 = 83.72$
(Bore hole)

FIGURE FOR EXERCISES 57 AND 58

In Exercises 49–58, solve each problem.

49. Determine all points of intersection of the circle $(x - 1)^2 + (y - 2)^2 = 4$ with the y-axis.

50. Determine the points of intersection of the circle $x^2 + (y - 3)^2 = 25$ with the x-axis.

51. Find the radius of the circle that has center $(2, -5)$ and passes through the origin.

52. Find the radius of the circle that has center $(-2, 3)$ and passes through $(3, -1)$.

53. Determine the equation of the circle that is centered at $(2, 3)$ and passes through $(-2, -1)$.

54. Determine the equation of the circle that is centered at $(3, 4)$ and passes through the origin.

55. Find all points of intersection of the circles $x^2 + y^2 = 9$ and $(x - 5)^2 + y^2 = 9$.

56. A donkey is tied at the point $(2, -3)$ on a rope of length 12. Turnips are growing at the point $(6, 7)$. Can the donkey reach them?

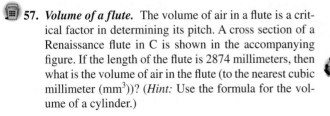 **57.** *Volume of a flute.* The volume of air in a flute is a critical factor in determining its pitch. A cross section of a Renaissance flute in C is shown in the accompanying figure. If the length of the flute is 2874 millimeters, then what is the volume of air in the flute (to the nearest cubic millimeter (mm^3))? (*Hint:* Use the formula for the volume of a cylinder.)

58. *Flute reproduction.* To make the smaller C# flute, Friedrich von Huene multiplies the length and cross-sectional area of the flute of Exercise 57 by 0.943. Find the equation for the bore hole (centered at the origin) and the volume of air in the C# flute.

Graph each equation.

59. $x^2 + y^2 = 0$

60. $x^2 - y^2 = 0$

61. $y = \sqrt{1 - x^2}$

62. $y = -\sqrt{1 - x^2}$

GETTING MORE INVOLVED

63. *Cooperative learning.* The equation of a circle is a special case of the general equation $Ax^2 + Bx + Cy^2 + Dy = E$, where A, B, C, D, and E are real numbers. Working in small groups, find restrictions that must be placed on A, B, C, D, and E so that the graph of this equation is a circle. What does the graph of $x^2 + y^2 = -9$ look like?

64. **Discussion.** Suppose lighthouse A is located at the origin and lighthouse B is located at coordinates (0, 6). The captain of a ship has determined that the ship's distance from lighthouse A is 2 and its distance from lighthouse B is 5. What are the possible coordinates for the location of the ship?

GRAPHING CALCULATOR EXERCISES

Graph each relation on a graphing calculator by solving for y and graphing two functions.

65. $x^2 + y^2 = 4$

66. $(x - 1)^2 + (y + 2)^2 = 1$

67. $x = y^2$

68. $x = (y + 2)^2 - 1$

69. $x = y^2 + 2y + 1$

70. $x = 4y^2 + 4y + 1$

In This Section

- The Ellipse
- The Hyperbola

12.4 THE ELLIPSE AND HYPERBOLA

In this section we study the remaining two conic sections: the ellipse and the hyperbola.

The Ellipse

An ellipse can be obtained by intersecting a plane and a cone, as was shown in Fig. 12.3. We can also give a definition of an ellipse in terms of points and distance.

FIGURE 12.20

> **Ellipse**
>
> An **ellipse** is the set of all points in a plane such that the sum of their distances from two fixed points is a constant. Each fixed point is called a **focus** (plural: foci).

An easy way to draw an ellipse is illustrated in Fig. 12.20. A string is attached at two fixed points, and a pencil is used to take up the slack. As the pencil is moved around the paper, the sum of the distances of the pencil point from the two fixed points remains constant. Of course, the length of the string is that constant. You may wish to try this.

Like the parabola, the ellipse also has interesting reflecting properties. All light or sound waves emitted from one focus are reflected off the ellipse to concentrate at the other focus (see Fig. 12.21). This property is used in light fixtures where a concentration of light at a point is desired or in a whispering gallery such as Statuary Hall in the U.S. Capitol Building.

The orbits of the planets around the sun and satellites around the earth are elliptical. For the orbit of the earth around the sun, the sun is at one focus. For the elliptical path of an earth satellite, the earth is at one focus and a point in space is the other focus.

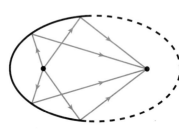

FIGURE 12.21

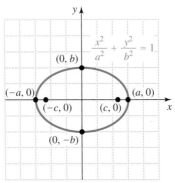

FIGURE 12.22

Figure 12.22 shows an ellipse with foci $(c, 0)$ and $(-c, 0)$. The origin is the center of this ellipse. In general, the **center** of an ellipse is a point midway between the foci. The ellipse in Fig. 12.22 has x-intercepts at $(a, 0)$ and $(-a, 0)$ and y-intercepts at $(0, b)$ and $(0, -b)$. The distance formula can be used to write the following equation for this ellipse. (See Exercise 55.)

Equation of an Ellipse Centered at the Origin

An ellipse centered at $(0, 0)$ with foci at $(\pm c, 0)$ and constant sum $2a$ has equation

$$\frac{x^2}{a^2} + \frac{y^2}{b^2} = 1,$$

where a, b, and c are positive real numbers with $c^2 = a^2 - b^2$.

To draw a "nice-looking" ellipse, we would locate the foci and use string as shown in Fig. 12.20. We can get a rough sketch of an ellipse centered at the origin by using the x- and y-intercepts only.

E X A M P L E   1

Graphing an ellipse

Find the x- and y-intercepts for the ellipse and sketch its graph.

$$\frac{x^2}{9} + \frac{y^2}{4} = 1$$

To graph the ellipse in Example 1, graph

$$y_1 = \sqrt{4 - 4x^2/9}$$

and

$$y_2 = -\sqrt{4 - 4x^2/9}.$$

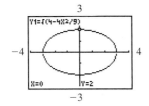

Solution

To find the y-intercepts, let $x = 0$ in the equation:

$$\frac{0}{9} + \frac{y^2}{4} = 1$$

$$\frac{y^2}{4} = 1$$

$$y^2 = 4$$

$$y = \pm 2$$

To find the x-intercepts, let $y = 0$. We get $x = \pm 3$. The four intercepts are $(0, 2)$, $(0, -2)$, $(3, 0)$, and $(-3, 0)$. Plot the intercepts and draw an ellipse through them as in Fig. 12.23.

Helpful Hint

When sketching ellipses or circles by hand, use your hand like a compass and rotate your paper as you draw the curve.

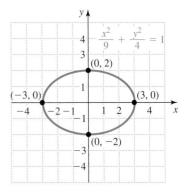

FIGURE 12.23

Ellipses, like circles, may be centered at any point in the plane. To get the equation of an ellipse centered at (h, k), we replace x by $x - h$ and y by $y - k$ in the equation of the ellipse centered at the origin.

Equation of an Ellipse Centered at (h, k)

An ellipse centered at (h, k) has equation

$$\frac{(x - h)^2}{a^2} + \frac{(y - k)^2}{b^2} = 1,$$

where a and b are positive real numbers.

E X A M P L E   2   **An ellipse with center (h, k)**

Sketch the graph of the ellipse:

$$\frac{(x - 1)^2}{9} + \frac{(y + 2)^2}{4} = 1$$

Solution

The graph of this ellipse is exactly the same size and shape as the ellipse

$$\frac{x^2}{9} + \frac{y^2}{4} = 1,$$

which was graphed in Example 1. However, the center for

$$\frac{(x - 1)^2}{9} + \frac{(y + 2)^2}{4} = 1$$

is $(1, -2)$. The denominator 9 is used to determine that the ellipse passes through points that are three units to the right and three units to the left of the center: $(4, -2)$ and $(-2, -2)$. See Fig. 12.24. The denominator 4 is used to determine that the ellipse passes through points that are two units above and two units below the center: $(1, 0)$ and $(1, -4)$. We draw an ellipse using these four points, just as we did for an ellipse centered at the origin.

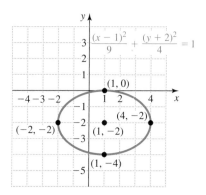

F I G U R E   1 2 . 2 4

The Hyperbola

A hyperbola is the curve that occurs at the intersection of a cone and a plane, as was shown in Fig. 12.3 in Section 12.2. A hyperbola can also be defined in terms of points and distance.

Hyperbola

A **hyperbola** is the set of all points in the plane such that the difference of their distances from two fixed points (foci) is constant.

Like the parabola and the ellipse, the hyperbola also has reflecting properties. If a light ray is aimed at one focus, it is reflected off the hyperbola and goes to the other focus, as shown in Fig. 12.25. Hyperbolic mirrors are used in conjunction with parabolic mirrors in telescopes.

The definitions of a hyperbola and an ellipse are similar, and so are their equations. However, their graphs are very different. Figure 12.26 shows a hyperbola in which the distance from a point on the hyperbola to the closer focus is N and the distance to the farther focus is M. The value $M - N$ is the same for every point on the hyperbola.

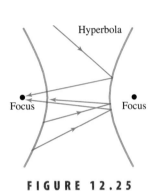

FIGURE 12.25

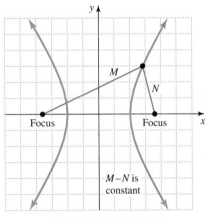

FIGURE 12.26

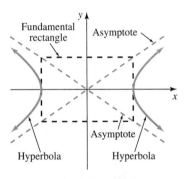

FIGURE 12.27

A hyperbola has two parts called **branches.** These branches look like parabolas, but they are not parabolas. The branches of the hyperbola shown in Fig. 12.27 get closer and closer to the dashed lines, called **asymptotes,** but they never intersect them. The asymptotes are used as guidelines in sketching a hyperbola. The asymptotes are found by extending the diagonals of the **fundamental rectangle,** shown in Fig. 12.27. The key to drawing a hyperbola is getting the fundamental rectangle and extending its diagonals to get the asymptotes. You will learn how to find the fundamental rectangle from the equation of a hyperbola. The hyperbola in Fig. 12.27 opens to the left and right.

If we start with foci at $(\pm c, 0)$ and a positive number a, then we can use the definition of a hyperbola to derive the following equation of a hyperbola in which the constant difference between the distances to the foci is $2a$.

Equation of a Hyperbola Centered at (0, 0) Opening Left and Right

A hyperbola centered at $(0, 0)$ with foci $(c, 0)$ and $(-c, 0)$ and constant difference $2a$ has equation

$$\frac{x^2}{a^2} - \frac{y^2}{b^2} = 1,$$

where a, b, and c are positive real numbers such that $c^2 = a^2 + b^2$.

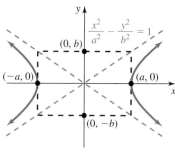

FIGURE 12.28

The graph of a general equation for a hyperbola is shown in Fig. 12.28. Notice that the fundamental rectangle extends to the x-intercepts along the x-axis and extends b units above and below the origin along the y-axis. Use the following procedure for graphing a hyperbola centered at the origin and opening to the left and to the right.

> ### Graphing a Hyperbola Centered at the Origin, Opening Left and Right
>
> To graph the hyperbola $\frac{x^2}{a^2} - \frac{y^2}{b^2} = 1$:
> 1. Locate the x-intercepts at $(a, 0)$ and $(-a, 0)$.
> 2. Draw the fundamental rectangle through $(\pm a, 0)$ and $(0, \pm b)$.
> 3. Draw the extended diagonals of the rectangle to use as asymptotes.
> 4. Draw the hyperbola to the left and right approaching the asymptotes.

EXAMPLE 3

A hyperbola opening left and right

Sketch the graph of $\frac{x^2}{36} - \frac{y^2}{9} = 1$, and find the equations of its asymptotes.

Calculator Close-Up

To graph the hyperbola and its asymptotes from Example 3, graph
$$y_1 = \sqrt{x^2/4 - 9}, y_2 = -y_1,$$
$$y_3 = 0.5x, \quad \text{and} \quad y_4 = -y_3.$$

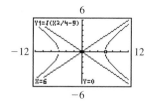

Solution

The x-intercepts are $(6, 0)$ and $(-6, 0)$. Draw the fundamental rectangle through these x-intercepts and the points $(0, 3)$ and $(0, -3)$. Extend the diagonals of the fundamental rectangle to get the asymptotes. Now draw a hyperbola passing through the x-intercepts and approaching the asymptotes as shown in Fig. 12.29. From the graph in Fig. 12.29 we see that the slopes of the asymptotes are $\frac{1}{2}$ and $-\frac{1}{2}$. Because the y-intercept for both asymptotes is the origin, their equations are $y = \frac{1}{2}x$ and $y = -\frac{1}{2}x$.

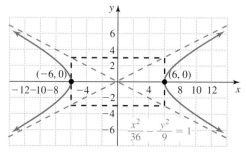

FIGURE 12.29

If the variables x and y are interchanged in the equation of the hyperbola, then the hyperbola opens up and down.

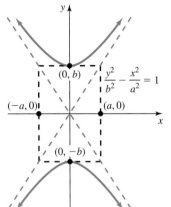

FIGURE 12.30

Equation of a Hyperbola Centered at (0, 0) Opening Up and Down

A hyperbola centered at $(0, 0)$ with foci $(0, c)$ and $(0, -c)$ and constant difference $2a$ has equation

$$\frac{y^2}{b^2} - \frac{x^2}{a^2} = 1,$$

where a, b, and c are positive real numbers such that $c^2 = a^2 + b^2$.

The graph of the general equation for a hyperbola opening up and down is shown in Fig. 12.30. Notice that the fundamental rectangle extends to the y-intercepts along the y-axis and extends a units to the left and right of the origin along the x-axis. The procedure for graphing a hyperbola opening up and down follows.

Graphing a Hyperbola Centered at the Origin, Opening Up and Down

To graph the hyperbola $\frac{y^2}{b^2} - \frac{x^2}{a^2} = 1$:

1. Locate the y-intercepts at $(0, b)$ and $(0, -b)$.
2. Draw the fundamental rectangle through $(0, \pm b)$ and $(\pm a, 0)$.
3. Draw the extended diagonals of the rectangle to use as asymptotes.
4. Draw the hyperbola opening up and down approaching the asymptotes.

EXAMPLE 4

Helpful Hint

We could include here general formulas for the equations of the asymptotes, but that is not necessary. It is easier first to draw the asymptotes as suggested and then to figure out their equations by looking at the graph.

A hyperbola opening up and down

Graph the hyperbola $\frac{y^2}{9} - \frac{x^2}{4} = 1$ and find the equations of its asymptotes.

Solution

If $y = 0$, we get

$$-\frac{x^2}{4} = 1$$
$$x^2 = -4.$$

Because this equation has no real solution, the graph has no x-intercepts. Let $x = 0$ to find the y-intercepts:

$$\frac{y^2}{9} = 1$$
$$y^2 = 9$$
$$y = \pm 3$$

The y-intercepts are $(0, 3)$ and $(0, -3)$, and the hyperbola opens up and down. From $a^2 = 4$ we get $a = 2$. So the fundamental rectangle extends to the intercepts $(0, 3)$ and $(0, -3)$ on the y-axis and to the points $(2, 0)$ and $(-2, 0)$ along the x-axis. We extend the diagonals of the rectangle and draw the graph of the hyperbola as shown

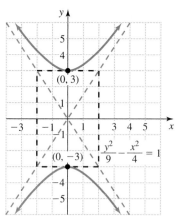

FIGURE 12.31

in Fig. 12.31. From the graph in Fig. 12.31 we see that the asymptotes have slopes $\frac{3}{2}$ and $-\frac{3}{2}$. Because the y-intercept for both asymptotes is the origin, their equations are $y = \frac{3}{2}x$ and $y = -\frac{3}{2}x$. ∎

Like circles and ellipses, hyperbolas may be centered at any point in the plane. To get the equation of a hyperbola centered at (h, k), we replace x by $x - h$ and y by $y - k$ in the equation of the hyperbola centered at the origin.

Equation of a Hyperbola Centered at (h, k)

A hyperbola centered at (h, k) has one of the following equations depending on which way it opens.

Opening left and right:

$$\frac{(x - h)^2}{a^2} - \frac{(y - k)^2}{b^2} = 1$$

Opening up and down:

$$\frac{(y - k)^2}{b^2} - \frac{(x - h)^2}{a^2} = 1$$

E X A M P L E   5

Graphing a hyperbola centered at (h, k)

Graph the hyperbola $\frac{(x - 3)^2}{16} - \frac{(y + 1)^2}{4} = 1$.

Solution

This hyperbola is centered at $(3, -1)$ and opens left and right. It is a transformation of the graph of $\frac{x^2}{16} - \frac{y^2}{4} = 1$. The fundamental rectangle for $\frac{x^2}{16} - \frac{y^2}{4} = 1$ is centered at the origin and goes through $(\pm 4, 0)$ and $(0, \pm 2)$. So draw a fundamental rectangle centered at $(3, -1)$ that extends four units to the right and left and two units up and down as shown in Fig. 12.32. Draw the asymptotes through the vertices of the fundamental rectangle and the hyperbola opening to the left and right.

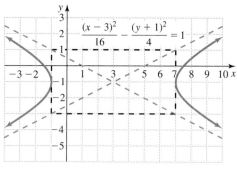

FIGURE 12.32 ∎

E X A M P L E   6

A hyperbola not in standard form

Sketch the graph of the hyperbola $4x^2 - y^2 = 4$.

Solution

First write the equation in standard form. Divide each side by 4 to get

$$x^2 - \frac{y^2}{4} = 1.$$

There are no y-intercepts. If $y = 0$, then $x = \pm 1$. The hyperbola opens left and right with x-intercepts at $(1, 0)$ and $(-1, 0)$. The fundamental rectangle extends to the intercepts along the x-axis and to the points $(0, 2)$ and $(0, -2)$ along the y-axis. We extend the diagonals of the rectangle for the asymptotes and draw the graph as shown in Fig. 12.33.

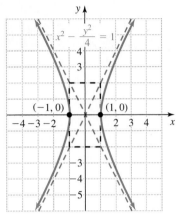

FIGURE 12.33

WARM-UPS

True or false? Explain your answer.

1. The x-intercepts of the ellipse $\frac{x^2}{36} + \frac{y^2}{25} = 1$ are $(5, 0)$ and $(-5, 0)$.
2. The graph of $\frac{x^2}{9} + \frac{y}{4} = 1$ is an ellipse.
3. If the foci of an ellipse coincide, then the ellipse is a circle.
4. The graph of $2x^2 + y^2 = 2$ is an ellipse centered at the origin.
5. The y-intercepts of $x^2 + \frac{y^2}{3} = 1$ are $(0, \sqrt{3})$ and $(0, -\sqrt{3})$.
6. The graph of $\frac{x^2}{9} + \frac{y}{4} = 1$ is a hyperbola.
7. The graph of $\frac{x^2}{25} - \frac{y^2}{16} = 1$ has y-intercepts at $(0, 4)$ and $(0, -4)$.
8. The hyperbola $\frac{y^2}{9} - x^2 = 1$ opens up and down.
9. The graph of $4x^2 - y^2 = 4$ is a hyperbola.
10. The asymptotes of a hyperbola are the extended diagonals of a rectangle.

12.4 EXERCISES

Reading and Writing *After reading this section, write out the answers to these questions. Use complete sentences.*

1. What is the definition of an ellipse?

2. How can you draw an ellipse with a pencil and string?

3. Where is the center of an ellipse?

4. What is the equation of an ellipse centered at the origin?

5. What is the equation of an ellipse centered at (h, k)?

6. What is the definition of a hyperbola?

7. How do you find the asymptotes of a hyperbola?

8. What is the equation of a hyperbola centered at the origin and opening left and right?

Sketch the graph of each ellipse. See Example 1.

9. $\dfrac{x^2}{9} + \dfrac{y^2}{4} = 1$

10. $\dfrac{x^2}{9} + \dfrac{y^2}{16} = 1$

11. $\dfrac{x^2}{9} + y^2 = 1$

12. $x^2 + \dfrac{y^2}{4} = 1$

13. $\dfrac{x^2}{36} + \dfrac{y^2}{25} = 1$

14. $\dfrac{x^2}{25} + \dfrac{y^2}{49} = 1$

15. $\dfrac{x^2}{24} + \dfrac{y^2}{5} = 1$

16. $\dfrac{x^2}{6} + \dfrac{y^2}{17} = 1$

17. $9x^2 + 16y^2 = 144$

18. $9x^2 + 25y^2 = 225$

19. $25x^2 + y^2 = 25$

20. $x^2 + 16y^2 = 16$

21. $4x^2 + 9y^2 = 1$

22. $25x^2 + 16y^2 = 1$

Sketch the graph of each ellipse. See Example 2.

23. $\dfrac{(x-3)^2}{4} + \dfrac{(y-1)^2}{9} = 1$

24. $\dfrac{(x+5)^2}{49} + \dfrac{(y-2)^2}{25} = 1$

25. $\dfrac{(x+1)^2}{16} + \dfrac{(y-2)^2}{25} = 1$

26. $\dfrac{(x-3)^2}{36} + \dfrac{(y+4)^2}{64} = 1$

27. $(x - 2)^2 + \dfrac{(y + 1)^2}{36} = 1$ **28.** $\dfrac{(x + 3)^2}{9} + (y + 1)^2 = 1$ **35.** $x^2 - \dfrac{y^2}{25} = 1$ **36.** $\dfrac{x^2}{9} - y^2 = 1$

Sketch the graph of each hyperbola and write the equations of its asymptotes. See Examples 3–6.

29. $\dfrac{x^2}{4} - \dfrac{y^2}{9} = 1$ **30.** $\dfrac{x^2}{16} - \dfrac{y^2}{9} = 1$

37. $9x^2 - 16y^2 = 144$

31. $\dfrac{y^2}{4} - \dfrac{x^2}{25} = 1$ **32.** $\dfrac{y^2}{9} - \dfrac{x^2}{16} = 1$

38. $9x^2 - 25y^2 = 225$

33. $\dfrac{x^2}{25} - y^2 = 1$ **34.** $x^2 - \dfrac{y^2}{9} = 1$

39. $x^2 - y^2 = 1$

40. $y^2 - x^2 = 1$

45. $\dfrac{(y-2)^2}{9} - \dfrac{(x-4)^2}{4} = 1$

Sketch the graph of each hyperbola.

41. $\dfrac{(x-2)^2}{4} - (y+1)^2 = 1$

46. $\dfrac{(y+3)^2}{16} - \dfrac{(x+1)^2}{9} = 1$

42. $(x+3)^2 - \dfrac{(y-1)^2}{4} = 1$

Graph both equations of each system on the same coordinate axes. Use elimination of variables to find all points of intersection.

47. $\dfrac{x^2}{4} + \dfrac{y^2}{9} = 1$

$\quad\ \ x^2 - \dfrac{y^2}{9} = 1$

43. $\dfrac{(x+1)^2}{16} - \dfrac{(y-1)^2}{9} = 1$

48. $x^2 - \dfrac{y^2}{4} = 1$

$\quad\ \dfrac{x^2}{9} + \dfrac{y^2}{4} = 1$

44. $\dfrac{(x-2)^2}{9} - \dfrac{(y+2)^2}{16} = 1$

49. $\dfrac{x^2}{4} + \dfrac{y^2}{16} = 1$
$x^2 + y^2 = 1$

50. $x^2 + \dfrac{y^2}{9} = 1$
$x^2 + y^2 = 4$

51. $x^2 + y^2 = 4$
$x^2 - y^2 = 1$

52. $x^2 + y^2 = 16$
$x^2 - y^2 = 4$

53. $x^2 + 9y^2 = 9$
$x^2 + y^2 = 4$

54. $x^2 + y^2 = 25$
$x^2 + 25y^2 = 25$

55. $x^2 + 9y^2 = 9$
$y = x^2 - 1$

56. $4x^2 + y^2 = 4$
$y = 2x^2 - 2$

57. $9x^2 - 4y^2 = 36$
$2y = x - 2$

58. $25y^2 - 9x^2 = 225$
$y = 3x + 3$

Solve each problem.

59. Marine navigation. The loran (long-range navigation) system is used by boaters to determine their location at sea. The loran unit on a boat measures the difference in time that it takes for radio signals from pairs of fixed points to reach the boat. The unit then finds the equations of two hyperbolas that pass through the location of the boat. Suppose a boat is located in the first quadrant at the intersection of $x^2 - 3y^2 = 1$ and $4y^2 - x^2 = 1$.

a) Use the accompanying graph to approximate the location of the boat.

b) Algebraically find the exact location of the boat.

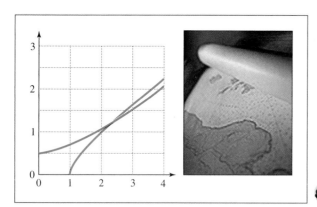

FIGURE FOR EXERCISE 59

60. Sonic boom. An aircraft traveling at supersonic speed creates a cone-shaped wave that intersects the ground along a hyperbola, as shown in the accompanying figure. A thunderlike sound is heard at any point on the hyperbola. This sonic boom travels along the ground, following the aircraft. The area where the sonic boom is most noticeable is called the *boom carpet*. The width of the boom carpet is roughly five times the altitude of the aircraft. Suppose the equation of the hyperbola in

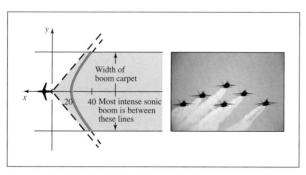

FIGURE FOR EXERCISE 60

the figure is

$$\frac{x^2}{400} - \frac{y^2}{100} = 1,$$

where the units are miles and the width of the boom carpet is measured 40 miles behind the aircraft. Find the altitude of the aircraft.

GETTING MORE INVOLVED

61. Cooperative learning. Let (x, y) be an arbitrary point on an ellipse with foci $(c, 0)$ and $(-c, 0)$ for $c > 0$. The following equation expresses the fact that the distance from (x, y) to $(c, 0)$ plus the distance from (x, y) to $(-c, 0)$ is the constant value $2a$ (for $a > 0$):

$$\sqrt{(x - c)^2 + (y - 0)^2} + \sqrt{(x - (-c))^2 + (y - 0)^2} = 2a$$

Working in groups, simplify this equation. First get the radicals on opposite sides of the equation, then square both sides twice to eliminate the square roots. Finally, let $b^2 = a^2 - c^2$ to get the equation

$$\frac{x^2}{a^2} + \frac{y^2}{b^2} = 1.$$

62. Cooperative learning. Let (x, y) be an arbitrary point on a hyperbola with foci $(c, 0)$ and $(-c, 0)$ for $c > 0$. The following equation expresses the fact that the distance from (x, y) to $(c, 0)$ minus the distance from (x, y) to $(-c, 0)$ is the constant value $2a$ (for $a > 0$):

$$\sqrt{(x - c)^2 + (y - 0)^2} - \sqrt{(x - (-c))^2 + (y - 0)^2} = 2a$$

Working in groups, simplify the equation. You will need to square both sides twice to eliminate the square roots. Finally, let $b^2 = c^2 - a^2$ to get the equation

$$\frac{x^2}{a^2} - \frac{y^2}{b^2} = 1.$$

GRAPHING CALCULATOR EXERCISES

63. Graph $y_1 = \sqrt{x^2 - 1}$, $y_2 = -\sqrt{x^2 - 1}$, $y_3 = x$, and $y_4 = -x$ to get the graph of the hyperbola $x^2 - y^2 = 1$ along with its asymptotes. Use the viewing window $-3 \le x \le 3$ and $-3 \le y \le 3$. Notice how the branches of the hyperbola approach the asymptotes.

64. Graph the same four functions in Exercise 63, but use $-30 \le x \le 30$ and $-30 \le y \le 30$ as the viewing window. What happened to the hyperbola?

12.5   SECOND-DEGREE INEQUALITIES

In this section we graph second-degree inequalities and systems of inequalities involving second-degree inequalities.

Graphing a Second-Degree Inequality

A second-degree inequality is an inequality involving squares of at least one of the variables. Changing the equal sign to an inequality symbol for any of the equations of the conic sections gives us a second-degree inequality. Second-degree inequalities are graphed in the same manner as linear inequalities.

E X A M P L E   1

A second-degree inequality

Graph the inequality $y < x^2 + 2x - 3$.

Solution

We first graph $y = x^2 + 2x - 3$. This parabola has x-intercepts at $(1, 0)$ and $(-3, 0)$, y-intercept at $(0, -3)$, and vertex at $(-1, -4)$. The graph of the parabola is drawn with a dashed line, as shown in Fig. 12.34. The graph of the parabola divides the plane into two regions. Every point on one side of the parabola satisfies the inequality $y < x^2 + 2x - 3$, and every point on the other side satisfies the inequality $y > x^2 + 2x - 3$. To determine which side is which, we test a point that is not on the parabola, say $(0, 0)$. Because

$$0 < 0^2 + 2 \cdot 0 - 3$$

is false, the region not containing the origin is shaded, as in Fig. 12.34.

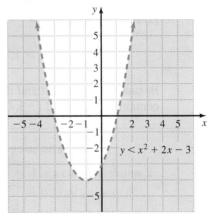

$$y < x^2 + 2x - 3$$

F I G U R E   1 2 . 3 4   ■

E X A M P L E   2

A second-degree inequality

Graph the inequality $x^2 + y^2 < 9$.

Solution

The graph of $x^2 + y^2 = 9$ is a circle of radius 3 centered at the origin. The circle divides the plane into two regions. Every point in one region satisfies $x^2 + y^2 < 9$,

12.5   EXERCISES

Graph each inequality. See Examples 1–3.

1. $y > x^2$

2. $y \le x^2 + 1$

3. $y < x^2 - x$

4. $y > x^2 + x$

5. $y > x^2 - x - 2$

6. $y < x^2 + x - 6$

7. $x^2 + y^2 \le 9$

8. $x^2 + y^2 > 16$

9. $x^2 + 4y^2 > 4$

10. $4x^2 + y^2 \le 4$

11. $4x^2 - 9y^2 < 36$

12. $25x^2 - 4y^2 > 100$

13. $(x - 2)^2 + (y - 3)^2 < 4$

14. $(x + 1)^2 + (y - 2)^2 > 1$

15. $x^2 + y^2 > 1$

16. $x^2 + y^2 < 25$

17. $4x^2 - y^2 > 4$

18. $x^2 - 9y^2 \le 9$

19. $y^2 - x^2 \leq 1$

20. $x^2 - y^2 > 1$

27. $y > x^2 + x$
$y < 5$

28. $y > x^2 + x - 6$
$y < x + 3$

21. $x > y$

22. $x < 2y - 1$

29. $y \geq x + 2$
$y \leq 2 - x$

30. $y \geq 2x - 3$
$y \leq 3 - 2x$

Graph the solution set to each system of inequalities. See Example 4.

23. $x^2 + y^2 < 9$
$y > x$

24. $x^2 + y^2 > 1$
$x > y$

31. $4x^2 - y^2 < 4$
$x^2 + 4y^2 > 4$

32. $x^2 - 4y^2 < 4$
$x^2 + 4y^2 > 4$

25. $x^2 - y^2 > 1$
$x^2 + y^2 < 4$

26. $y^2 - x^2 < 1$
$x^2 + y^2 > 9$

33. $x - y < 0$
$y + x^2 < 1$

34. $y + 1 > x^2$
$x + y < 2$

35. $y < 5x - x^2$
$x^2 + y^2 < 9$

36. $y < x^2 + 5x$
$x^2 + y^2 < 16$

Solve the problem.

43. ***Buried treasure.*** An old pirate on his deathbed gave the following description of where he had buried some treasure on a deserted island: "Starting at the large palm tree, I walked to the north and then to the east, and there I buried the treasure. I walked at least 50 paces to get to that spot, but I was not more than 50 paces, as the crow flies, from the large palm tree. I am sure that I walked farther in the northerly direction than in the easterly direction." With the large palm tree at the origin and the positive y-axis pointing to the north, graph the possible locations of the treasure.

37. $y \geq 3$
$x \leq 1$

38. $x > -3$
$y < 2$

39. $4y^2 - 9x^2 < 36$
$x^2 + y^2 < 16$

40. $25y^2 - 16x^2 < 400$
$x^2 + y^2 > 4$

FIGURE FOR EXERCISE 43

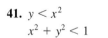 **GRAPHING CALCULATOR EXERCISES**

41. $y < x^2$
$x^2 + y^2 < 1$

42. $y > x^2$
$4x^2 + y^2 < 4$

44. Use graphs to find an ordered pair that is in the solution set to the system of inequalities:

$$y > x^2 - 2x + 1$$
$$y < -1.1(x - 4)^2 + 5$$

Verify that your answer satisfies both inequalities.

45. Use graphs to find the solution set to the system of inequalities:

$$y > 2x^2 - 3x + 1$$
$$y < -2x^2 - 8x - 1$$

COLLABORATIVE ACTIVITIES

Focus on Comets

Conic sections are used to model many different things in the natural world. Astronomers use mirrors in the shape of parabolas in telescopes. They have learned that planets can have elliptical as well as circular orbits around the sun and that comets may have orbits that resemble hyperbolas, parabolas, or ellipses. In this activity we will consider comets with these three types of orbits.

The orbit that a comet will take as it approaches the sun depends on its velocity (as well as other factors). If it has enough velocity to escape from the pull of the sun, it may take either a parabolic orbit or a hyperbolic orbit. If it doesn't have enough velocity, then it will take an elliptical orbit. Of course, a comet that has a parabolic or hyperbolic orbit will not come back again around our sun. Only comets with elliptical orbits do we see again.

For the problems below, round all your answers to two decimal places.

1. Halley's comet is in an elliptical orbit about the sun with the sun at one of the foci. In this problem we will make a scale model of the orbit of Halley's comet about the sun. We will choose our coordinate system so that the ellipse is centered at (0, 0). Halley's comet comes within 0.6 astronomical unit[1] from the sun at its closest point and 35 astronomical units at its farthest point. The position of the comet at these points

[1] An astronomical unit is the distance of the earth from the sun. The earth's orbit is almost circular and so is about the same distance from the sun at any point in its orbit.

Grouping: 2 students per group

Topic: Conic sections

will correspond to the horizontal vertices. Find the equation for the ellipse. Determine where the foci should be. On a piece of cardboard, put thumbtacks at the foci. Determine the length of string you will need to draw the ellipse using the scale 1 centimeter = 1 astronomical unit (AU). Draw the comet's orbit, indicating which focus is the sun.

2. If the velocity of a comet equals the escape velocity (it is going just fast enough to get away), then its orbit will be parabolic. The sun will be at the focus of the parabola. We will place the vertex at the point (0, 0); in this case the vertex will be where the comet is the closest to the sun. Suppose we have a comet that is 0.75 AU from the sun at its closest point. Find the equation for the parabola. Graph the parabola.

3. If the velocity of a comet is greater than the escape velocity (it can easily escape from the sun's gravitational pull), its path will resemble one-half of a hyperbola with the sun as one focus. Assuming we have a left- and right-opening hyperbola, we can model the path of such a comet along one of its branches. We will center the hyperbola at (0, 0), and place the sun at the left focus and draw the path of the comet as it approaches from the left. Suppose that the comet will be 1.5 AUs from the sun at its closest point. Assume the sun is at the point (−3, 0). Draw a sketch of this scenario. What is the equation for the hyperbola? Graph the hyperbola.

Extension: Graph all three equations on a graphing calculator or computer.

WRAP-UP   CHAPTER 12

SUMMARY

Nonlinear Systems

		Examples
Nonlinear systems in two variables	Use substitution or addition to eliminate variables. Nonlinear systems may have several points in the solution set.	$y = x^2$ $x^2 + y^2 = 4$ Substitution: $y + y^2 = 4$

The Distance Formula

		Examples
Distance formula	The distance between (x_1, y_1) and (x_2, y_2) is $\sqrt{(x_2 - x_1)^2 + (y_2 - y_1)^2}$.	Distance between $(1, -2)$ and $(3, -4)$ is $\sqrt{2^2 + (-2)^2}$ or $2\sqrt{2}$.

Parabola

Examples

$y = a(x - h)^2 + k$

Opens upward for $a > 0$, downward for $a < 0$
Vertex at (h, k)
To find focus and directrix, use $a = \dfrac{1}{4p}$.
Distance from vertex to focus or directrix is $|p|$.

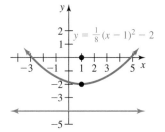

$x = a(y - k)^2 + h$

Opens right for $a > 0$, left for $a < 0$
Vertex at (h, k)
To find focus and directrix use $a = \dfrac{1}{4p}$.
Distance from vertex to focus or directrix is $|p|$.

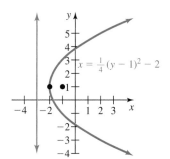

$y = ax^2 + bx + c$

Opens upward for $a > 0$, downward for $a < 0$
The x-coordinate of the vertex is $\dfrac{-b}{2a}$.
Find the y-coordinate of the vertex by evaluating
$y = ax^2 + bx + c$ for $x = \dfrac{-b}{2a}$.

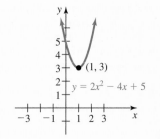

$x = ay^2 + by + c$

Opens right for $a > 0$, left for $a < 0$
The y-coordinate of the vertex is $\dfrac{-b}{2a}$.
Find the x-coordinate of the vertex by evaluating
$x = ay^2 + by + c$ for $y = \dfrac{-b}{2a}$.

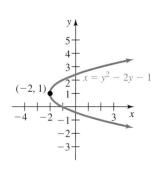

Circle

Examples

$(x - h)^2 + (y - k)^2 = r^2$ Center (h, k)
Radius r (for $r > 0$)

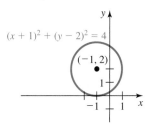

Centered at origin
$x^2 + y^2 = r^2$

Center $(0, 0)$
Radius r (for $r > 0$)

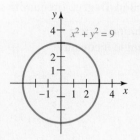

Ellipse

Examples

Centered at origin

$$\frac{x^2}{a^2} + \frac{y^2}{b^2} = 1$$

Center: $(0, 0)$
x-intercepts: $(a, 0)$ and $(-a, 0)$
y-intercepts: $(0, b)$ and $(0, -b)$
Foci: $(\pm c, 0)$ if $a^2 > b^2$ and $c^2 = a^2 - b^2$
$(0, \pm c)$ if $b^2 > a^2$ and $c^2 = b^2 - a^2$

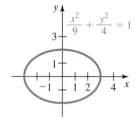

Arbitrary center

$$\frac{(x - h)^2}{a^2} + \frac{(y - k)^2}{b^2} = 1$$

Center: (h, k)

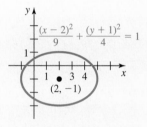

Hyperbola

Examples

Opening left and right

Centered at origin: $\dfrac{x^2}{a^2} - \dfrac{y^2}{b^2} = 1$
   Center: $(0, 0)$
   x-intercepts: $(a, 0)$ and $(-a, 0)$
   y-intercepts: none

Centered at (h, k): $\dfrac{(x - h)^2}{a^2} - \dfrac{(y - k)^2}{b^2} = 1$

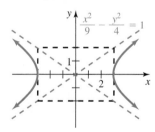

Opening up and down

Centered at origin: $\dfrac{y^2}{b^2} - \dfrac{x^2}{a^2} = 1$
   Center: $(0, 0)$
   x-intercepts: none
   y-intercepts: $(0, b)$ and $(0, -b)$

Centered at (h, k): $\dfrac{(y - k)^2}{b^2} - \dfrac{(x - h)^2}{a^2} = 1$

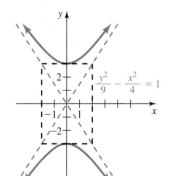

Second-Degree Inequalities

Examples

Solution set for
a single inequality

Graph the boundary curve obtained by replacing
the inequality symbol by the equal sign.
Use test points to determine which regions satisfy
the inequality.

$x^2 + y^2 < 16$

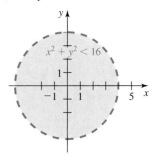

Solution set for a system
of inequalities

Graph the boundary curves. Then select a test
point in each region. Shade only the regions for
which the test point satisfies all inequalities of
the system.

$x^2 + y^2 < 16$
$y > x^2 - 1$

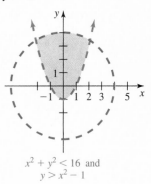

$x^2 + y^2 < 16$ and
$y > x^2 - 1$

ENRICHING YOUR MATHEMATICAL WORD POWER

For each mathematical term, choose the correct meaning.

1. **nonlinear equation**
   a. an equation that is not lined up
   b. an equation whose graph is a straight line
   c. an equation whose graph is not a straight line
   d. an exponential equation

2. **parabola**
   a. the points in a plane that are equidistant from a point and a line
   b. the points in a plane that are a fixed distance from a fixed point
   c. the points in a plane that are equidistant from two fixed points
   d. the points in a plane the sum of whose distances from two fixed points is a constant

3. **directrix**
   a. the line $y = x$
   b. the line of symmetry of a parabola
   c. the x-axis
   d. the fixed line in the definition of parabola

4. **vertex of a parabola**
   a. the midpoint of the line segment joining the focus and directrix perpendicular to the directrix
   b. the focus
   c. the x-intercept
   d. the endpoint

5. **conic sections**
   a. the two halves of a cone
   b. the vertex and focus
   c. the curves obtained at the intersection of a cone and a plane
   d. the asymptotes

6. **axis of symmetry**
   a. the x-axis
   b. the y-axis
   c. the directrix
   d. the line of symmetry of a parabola

7. **circle**
   a. the points in a plane that are equidistant from a point and a line

b. the points in a plane that are a fixed distance from a fixed point

c. the points in a plane that are equidistant from two fixed points

d. the points in a plane the sum of whose distances from two fixed points is a constant

8. ellipse

a. the points in a plane that are equidistant from a point and a line

b. the points in a plane that are a fixed distance from a fixed point

c. the points in a plane that are equidistant from two fixed points

d. the points in a plane such that the sum of their distances from two fixed points is constant

9. hyperbola

a. the points in a plane that are equidistant from a point and a line

b. the points in a plane that are a fixed distance from a fixed point

c. the points in a plane such that the difference of their distances from two fixed points is constant

d. the points in a plane such that the sum of their distances from two fixed points is a constant

10. asymptotes

a. lines approached by a hyperbola

b. lines approached by parabolas

c. tangent lines to a circle

d. lines that pass through the vertices of an ellipse

REVIEW EXERCISES

12.1 *Graph both equations on the same set of axes, then determine the points of intersection of the graphs by solving the system.*

1. $y = x^2$
$y = -2x + 15$

2. $y = \sqrt{x}$
$y = \frac{1}{3}x$

3. $y = 3x$
$y = \frac{1}{x}$

4. $y = |x|$
$y = -3x + 5$

Solve each system.

5. $x^2 + y^2 = 4$
$y = \frac{1}{3}x^2$

6. $12y^2 - 4x^2 = 9$
$x = y^2$

7. $x^2 + y^2 = 34$
$y = x + 2$

8. $y = 2x + 1$
$xy - y = 5$

9. $y = \log(x - 3)$
$y = 1 - \log(x)$

10. $y = \left(\frac{1}{2}\right)^x$
$y = 2^{x-1}$

11. $x^4 = 2(12 - y)$
$y = x^2$

12. $x^2 + 2y^2 = 7$
$x^2 - 2y^2 = -5$

12.2 *Find the distance between each pair of points.*

13. $(1, 1), (3, 3)$

14. $(1, 2), (4, 5)$

15. $(-4, 6), (2, -8)$

16. $(-3, -5), (5, -7)$

Determine the vertex, axis of symmetry, focus, and directrix for each parabola.

17. $y = x^2 + 3x - 18$

18. $y = x - x^2$

19. $y = x^2 + 3x + 2$

20. $y = -x^2 - 3x + 4$

21. $y = -\dfrac{1}{2}(x - 2)^2 + 3$

22. $y = \dfrac{1}{4}(x + 1)^2 - 2$

Write each equation in the form $y = a(x - h)^2 + k$, and identify the vertex of the parabola.

23. $y = 2x^2 - 8x + 1$

24. $y = -2x^2 - 6x - 1$

25. $y = -\dfrac{1}{2}x^2 - x + \dfrac{1}{2}$

26. $y = \dfrac{1}{4}x^2 + x - 9$

12.3 *Determine the center and radius of each circle, and sketch its graph.*

27. $x^2 + y^2 = 100$ **28.** $x^2 + y^2 = 20$

29. $(x - 2)^2 + (y + 3)^2 = 81$

30. $x^2 + 2x + y^2 = 8$

31. $9y^2 + 9x^2 = 4$

32. $x^2 + 4x + y^2 - 6y - 3 = 0$

Write the standard equation for each circle with the given center and radius.

33. Center $(0, 3)$, radius 6

34. Center $(0, 0)$, radius $\sqrt{6}$

35. Center $(2, -7)$, radius 5

36. Center $\left(\dfrac{1}{2}, -3\right)$, radius $\dfrac{1}{2}$

12.4 *Sketch the graph of each ellipse.*

37. $\dfrac{x^2}{36} + \dfrac{y^2}{49} = 1$ **38.** $\dfrac{x^2}{25} + y^2 = 1$

44. $6y^2 - 16x^2 = 96$

39. $25x^2 + 4y^2 = 100$ **40.** $6x^2 + 4y^2 = 24$

12.5 *Graph each inequality.*

45. $4x - 2y > 3$

Sketch the graph of each hyperbola.

41. $\dfrac{x^2}{49} - \dfrac{y^2}{36} = 1$

46. $y < x^2 - 3x$

42. $\dfrac{y^2}{25} - \dfrac{x^2}{49} = 1$

47. $y^2 < x^2 - 1$

43. $4x^2 - 25y^2 = 100$

48. $y^2 < 1 - x^2$

49. $4x^2 + 9y^2 > 36$ **50.** $x^2 + y > 2x - 1$

63. $\dfrac{x^2}{3} - \dfrac{y^2}{5} = 1$ **64.** $x^2 + \dfrac{y^2}{3} = 1$

65. $4y^2 - x^2 = 8$ **66.** $9x^2 + y = 9$

Sketch the graph of each equation.

67. $x^2 = 4 - y^2$ **68.** $x^2 = 4y^2 + 4$

Graph the solution set to each system of inequalities.

51. $y < 3x - x^2$ **52.** $x^2 - y^2 < 1$
    $x^2 + y^2 < 9$ $y < 1$

69. $x^2 = 4y + 4$ **70.** $x = 4y + 4$

53. $4x^2 + 9y^2 > 36$ **54.** $y^2 - x^2 > 4$
    $x^2 + y^2 < 9$ $y^2 + 16x^2 < 16$

71. $x^2 = 4 - 4y^2$ **72.** $x^2 = 4y - y^2$

MISCELLANEOUS

Identify each equation as the equation of a straight line, parabola, circle, hyperbola, or ellipse. Try to do these without rewriting the equations.

73. $x^2 = 4 - (y - 4)^2$ **74.** $(x - 2)^2 + (y - 4)^2 = 4$

55. $x^2 = y^2 + 1$ **56.** $x = y + 1$

57. $x^2 = 1 - y^2$ **58.** $x^2 = y + 1$

59. $x^2 + x = 1 - y^2$ **60.** $(x - 3)^2 + (y + 2)^2 = 7$

61. $x^2 + 4x = 6y - y^2$ **62.** $4x + 6y = 1$

Write the equation of the circle with the given features.

75. Centered at the origin and passing through $(3, 4)$

76. Centered at $(2, -3)$ and passing through $(-1, 4)$

77. Centered at $(-1, 5)$ with radius 6

78. Centered at $(0, -3)$ and passing through the origin

Write the equation of the parabola with the given features.

79. Focus $(1, 4)$ and directrix $y = 2$

80. Focus $(-2, 1)$ and directrix $y = 5$

81. Vertex $(0, 0)$ and focus $\left(0, \frac{1}{4}\right)$

82. Vertex $(1, 2)$ and focus $\left(1, \frac{3}{2}\right)$

83. Vertex $(0, 0)$, passing through $(3, 2)$, and opening upward

84. Vertex $(1, 3)$, passing through $(0, 0)$, and opening downward

Solve each system of equations.

85. $x^2 + y^2 = 25$
$y = -x + 1$

86. $x^2 - y^2 = 1$
$x^2 + y^2 = 7$

87. $4x^2 + y^2 = 4$
$x^2 - y^2 = 21$

88. $y = x^2 + x$
$y = -x^2 + 3x + 12$

Solve each problem.

89. *Perimeter of a rectangle.* A rectangle has a perimeter of 16 feet and an area of 12 square feet. Find its length and width.

90. *Tale of two circles.* Find the radii of two circles such that the difference in areas of the two is 10π square inches and the difference in radii of the two is 2 inches.

CHAPTER 12 TEST

Sketch the graph of each equation.

1. $x^2 + y^2 = 25$

2. $\dfrac{x^2}{16} - \dfrac{y^2}{25} = 1$

5. $y^2 - 4x^2 = 4$

6. $y = -x^2 - 2x + 3$

3. $y^2 + 4x^2 = 4$

4. $y = x^2 + 4x + 4$

Sketch the graph of each inequality.

7. $x^2 - y^2 < 9$

8. $x^2 + y^2 > 9$

9. $y > x^2 - 9$

Graph the solution set to each system of inequalities.

10. $x^2 + y^2 < 9$
$x^2 - y^2 > 1$

11. $y < -x^2 + x$
$y < x - 4$

Solve each system of equations.

12. $y = x^2 - 2x - 8$
$y = 7 - 4x$

13. $x^2 + y^2 = 12$
$y = x^2$

Solve each problem.

14. Find the distance between $(-1, 4)$ and $(1, 6)$.

15. Find the center and radius of the circle $x^2 + 2x + y^2 + 10y = 10$.

16. Find the vertex, focus, and directrix of the parabola $y = x^2 + x + 3$. State the axis of symmetry and whether the parabola opens up or down.

17. Write the equation $y = \frac{1}{2}x^2 - 3x - \frac{1}{2}$ in the form $y = a(x - h)^2 + k$.

18. Write the equation of a circle with center $(-1, 3)$ that passes through $(2, 5)$.

19. Find the length and width of a rectangular room that has an area of 108 square feet and a perimeter of 42 ft.

Sketch the graph of each equation.

1. $y = 9x - x^2$

2. $y = 9x$

3. $y = (x - 9)^2$

4. $y^2 = 9 - x^2$

5. $y = 9x^2$

6. $y = |9x|$

7. $4x^2 + 9y^2 = 36$

8. $4x^2 - 9y^2 = 36$

9. $y = 9 - x$

10. $y = 9^x$

Find the following products.

11. $(x + 2y)^2$

12. $(x + y)(x^2 + 2xy + y^2)$

13. $(a + b)^3$

14. $(a - 3b)^2$

15. $(2a + 1)(3a - 5)$

16. $(x - y)(x^2 + xy + y^2)$

Solve each system of equations.

17. $2x - 3y = -4$
$x + 2y = 5$

18. $x^2 + y^2 = 25$
$x + y = 7$

19. $2x - y + z = 7$
$x - 2y - z = 2$
$x + y + z = 2$

20. $y = x^2$
$y - 2x = 3$

Solve each formula for the specified variable.

21. $ax + b = 0$, for x

22. $wx^2 + dx + m = 0$, for x

23. $A = \dfrac{1}{2}h(B + b)$, for B

24. $\dfrac{1}{x} + \dfrac{1}{y} = \dfrac{1}{2}$, for x

25. $L = m + mxt$, for m

26. $y = 3a\sqrt{t}$, for t

Solve each problem.

27. Write the equation of the line in slope-intercept form that goes through the points $(2, -3)$ and $(-4, 1)$.

28. Write the equation of the line in slope-intercept form that contains the origin and is perpendicular to the line $2x - 4y = 5$.

29. Write the equation of the circle that has center $(2, 5)$ and passes through the point $(-1, -1)$.

30. Find the center and radius of the circle $x^2 + 3x + y^2 - 6y = 0$.

Perform the computations with complex numbers.

31. $2i(3 + 5i)$ **32.** i^6

33. $(2i - 3) + (6 - 7i)$ **34.** $(3 + i\sqrt{2})^2$

35. $(2 - 3i)(5 - 6i)$ **36.** $(3 - i) + (-6 + 4i)$

37. $(5 - 2i)(5 + 2i)$ **38.** $(2 - 3i) \div (2i)$

39. $(4 + 5i) \div (1 - i)$ **40.** $\dfrac{4 - \sqrt{-8}}{2}$

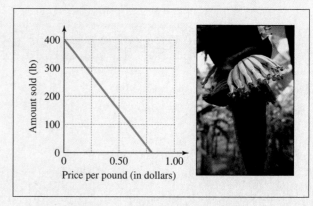

FIGURE FOR EXERCISE 41

Solve.

41. *Going bananas.* Salvadore has observed that when bananas are \$0.30 per pound (lb), he sells 250 lb per day, and when bananas are \$0.40 per lb, he sells only 200 lb per day.

a) Assume the number of pounds sold, q, is a linear function of the price per pound, x, and find that function.

b) Salvadore's daily revenue in dollars is the product of the number of pounds sold and the price per pound. Write the revenue as a function of x.

c) Graph the revenue function.

d) What price per pound maximizes his revenue?

e) What is his maximum possible revenue?

Sequences and Series

Growth of $5000
investment per year

veryone realizes the importance of investing for the future. Some people go to great pains to study the markets and to make wise investment decisions. Some stay away from investing because they do not want to take chances. However, the most important factor in investing is making regular investments (*Money,* www.money.com). According to *Money,* if you had invested $5000 in the stock market every year at the market high for that year (the worst time to invest) for the last 40 years, your investment would be worth $2.8 million today.

A sequence of periodic investments earning a fixed rate of interest can be thought of as a geometric sequence. In this chapter you will learn how to find the sum of a geometric sequence and to calculate the future value of a sequence of periodic investments. In Exercise 58 of Section 13.4 you will calculate the value of $5000 invested each year for 10 years in Fidelity's Magellan fund.

13.1 SEQUENCES

The word "sequence" is a familiar word. We may speak of a sequence of events or say that something is out of sequence. In this section we give the mathematical definition of a sequence.

Definition

In mathematics we think of a sequence as a list of numbers. Each number in the sequence is called a **term** of the sequence. There is a first term, a second term, a third term, and so on. For example, the daily high temperature readings in Minot, North Dakota, for the first 10 days in January can be thought of as a finite sequence with 10 terms:

$$-9, -2, 8, -11, 0, 6, 14, 1, -5, -11$$

The set of all positive even integers,

$$2, 4, 6, 8, 10, 12, 14, \ldots,$$

can be thought of as an infinite sequence.

To give a precise definition of sequence, we use the terminology of functions. The list of numbers is the range of the function.

> **Sequence**
>
> A **finite sequence** is a function whose domain is the set of positive integers less than or equal to some fixed positive integer. An **infinite sequence** is a function whose domain is the set of all positive integers.

When the domain is apparent, we will refer to either a finite sequence or an infinite sequence simply as a sequence. For the independent variable of the function we will usually use n (for natural number) rather than x. For the dependent variable we write a_n (read "a sub n") rather than y. We call a_n the **nth term,** or the **general term** of the sequence. Rather than use the $f(x)$ notation for functions, we will define sequences with formulas. When n is used as a variable, we will assume it represents natural numbers only.

EXAMPLE 1

Listing terms of a finite sequence

List all of the terms of each finite sequence.

a) $a_n = n^2$ for $1 \leq n \leq 5$ **b)** $a_n = \dfrac{1}{n+2}$ for $1 \leq n \leq 4$

Solution

a) Using the natural numbers from 1 through 5 in $a_n = n^2$, we get

$$a_1 = 1^2 = 1,$$
$$a_2 = 2^2 = 4,$$
$$a_3 = 3^2 = 9,$$
$$a_4 = 4^2 = 16,$$

and

$$a_5 = 5^2 = 25.$$

The five terms of this sequence are 1, 4, 9, 16, and 25. We often refer to the listing of the terms of the sequence as the sequence.

Calculator Close-Up

We can define the sequence with the Y= key and make a list of the terms.

X	Y1
1	1
2	4
3	9
4	16
5	25
6	36
7	49

Y1■X²

b) Using the natural numbers from 1 through 4 in $a_n = \frac{1}{n+2}$, we get the terms

$$a_1 = \frac{1}{1+2} = \frac{1}{3},$$

$$a_2 = \frac{1}{2+2} = \frac{1}{4},$$

$$a_3 = \frac{1}{5},$$

and

$$a_4 = \frac{1}{6}.$$

The four terms of the sequence are $\frac{1}{3}, \frac{1}{4}, \frac{1}{5},$ and $\frac{1}{6}$. ∎

E X A M P L E   2   **Listing terms of an infinite sequence**

List the first three terms of the infinite sequence whose nth term is

$$a_n = \frac{(-1)^n}{2^{n+1}}.$$

Calculator Close-Up

Some calculators have a sequence feature that allows you to specify the formula and which terms to evaluate. We can even get the terms as fractions.

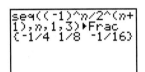

```
seq((-1)^n/2^(n+
1),n,1,3)▶Frac
{-1/4 1/8 -1/16}
```

Solution

Using the natural numbers 1, 2, and 3 in the formula for the nth term yields

$$a_1 = \frac{(-1)^1}{2^{1+1}} = -\frac{1}{4}, \qquad a_2 = \frac{(-1)^2}{2^{2+1}} = \frac{1}{8}, \qquad \text{and} \qquad a_3 = \frac{(-1)^3}{2^{3+1}} = -\frac{1}{16}.$$

We write the sequence as follows:

$$-\frac{1}{4}, \frac{1}{8}, -\frac{1}{16}, \dots$$

∎

Finding a Formula for the *n*th Term

We often know the terms of a sequence and want to write a formula that will produce those terms. To write a formula for the nth term of a sequence, examine the terms and look for a pattern. Each term is a function of the term number. The first term corresponds to $n = 1$, the second term corresponds to $n = 2$, and so on.

E X A M P L E   3   **A familiar sequence**

Write the general term for the infinite sequence

$$3, 5, 7, 9, 11, \dots.$$

Solution

The even numbers are all multiples of 2 and can be represented as $2n$. Because each odd number is 1 more than an even number, a formula for the nth term might be

$$a_n = 2n + 1.$$

Helpful Hint

Finding a formula for a sequence could be extremely difficult. For example, there is no known formula that will produce the sequence of prime numbers:

2, 3, 5, 7, 11, 13, 17, 19, ...

To be sure, we write out a few terms using the formula:

$$a_1 = 2(1) + 1 = 3$$
$$a_2 = 2(2) + 1 = 5$$
$$a_3 = 2(3) + 1 = 7$$

So the general term is $a_n = 2n + 1$. ∎

CAUTION There can be more than one formula that produces the given terms of a sequence. For example, the sequence

$$1, 2, 4, \ldots$$

could have *n*th term $a_n = 2^{n-1}$ or $a_n = \frac{1}{2}n^2 - \frac{1}{2}n + 1$. The first three terms for both of these sequences are identical, but their fourth terms are different.

EXAMPLE 4

A sequence with alternating signs

Write the general term for the infinite sequence

$$1, -\frac{1}{4}, \frac{1}{9}, -\frac{1}{16}, \ldots.$$

Solution

To obtain the alternating signs, we use powers of -1. Because any even power of -1 is positive and any odd power of -1 is negative, we use $(-1)^{n+1}$. The denominators are the squares of the positive integers. So the *n*th term of this infinite sequence is given by the formula

$$a_n = \frac{(-1)^{n+1}}{n^2}.$$

Check this sequence by using this formula to find the first four terms. ■

In Example 5 we use a sequence to model a physical situation.

EXAMPLE 5

The bouncing ball

Suppose a ball always rebounds $\frac{2}{3}$ of the height from which it falls and the ball is dropped from a height of 6 feet. Write a sequence whose terms are the heights from which the ball falls. What is a formula for the *n*th term of this sequence?

Solution

On the first fall the ball travels 6 feet (ft), as shown in Fig. 13.1. On the second fall it travels $\frac{2}{3}$ of 6, or 4 ft. On the third fall it travels $\frac{2}{3}$ of 4, or $\frac{8}{3}$ ft, and so on. We write

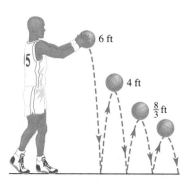

FIGURE 13.1

M A T H   A T   W O R K

Most of us find an upholstered chair, sink into it, and remark on the comfort. Before design consultant Audrey Jordan sits down, she often looks at the fabric to observe the color and texture—and especially to see whether the fabric is one of her original designs. Fabric design is more than just an idea that is printed on a piece of cloth. Consideration must be given to the end product, which could be anything from a handbag to a large sofa. Colors and themes must be chosen with both

FABRIC DESIGNER

current trends and styles in mind. Sometimes a design will be an overall or nondirectional pattern, such as polka dots, which can be cut randomly. More often, it will have a specific theme, such as fruit, which can be cut and sewn in only one direction.

For all products one of the main considerations is the vertical repeat. A good portion of textile machinery is standardized for vertical repeats of 27 inches or fractions thereof. For example, the vertical repeat could be every $13\frac{1}{2}$ inches or every 9 inches. Even though the horizontal repeat can vary, Ms. Jordan must consider both the horizontal and vertical repeats for a particular end product.

In Exercise 45 of this section you will find the standard vertical repeats for a textile machine.

the sequence as follows:

$$6, 4, \frac{8}{3}, \frac{16}{9}, \frac{32}{27}, \ldots$$

The nth term can be written by using powers of $\frac{2}{3}$:

$$a_n = 6\left(\frac{2}{3}\right)^{n-1}$$

WARM-UPS

True or false? Explain your answer.

1. The nth term of the sequence 2, 4, 6, 8, 10, . . . is $a_n = 2n$.
2. The nth term of the sequence 1, 3, 5, 7, 9, . . . is $a_n = 2n - 1$.
3. A sequence is a function.
4. The domain of a finite sequence is the set of positive integers.
5. The nth term of $-1, 4, -9, 16, -25, \ldots$ is $a_n = (-1)^{n+1}n^2$.
6. For the infinite sequence $b_n = \frac{1}{n}$, the independent variable is $\frac{1}{n}$.
7. For the sequence $c_n = n^3$, the dependent variable is c_n.
8. The sixth term of the sequence $a_n = (-1)^{n+1}2^n$ is 64.
9. The symbol a_n is used for the dependent variable of a sequence.
10. The tenth term of the sequence 2, 4, 8, 16, 32, 64, 128, . . . is 1024.

13.1 EXERCISES

Reading and Writing *After reading this section, write out the answers to these questions. Use complete sentences.*

1. What is a sequence?

2. What is a term of a sequence?

3. What is a finite sequence?

4. What is an infinite sequence?

List all terms of each finite sequence. See Example 1.

5. $a_n = n^2$ for $1 \leq n \leq 8$

6. $a_n = -n^2$ for $1 \leq n \leq 4$

7. $b_n = \dfrac{(-1)^n}{n}$ for $1 \leq n \leq 10$

8. $b_n = \dfrac{(-1)^{n+1}}{n}$ for $1 \leq n \leq 6$

9. $c_n = (-2)^{n-1}$ for $1 \leq n \leq 5$

10. $c_n = (-3)^{n-2}$ for $1 \leq n \leq 5$

11. $a_n = 2^{-n}$ for $1 \leq n \leq 6$

12. $a_n = 2^{-n+2}$ for $1 \leq n \leq 5$

13. $b_n = 2n - 3$ for $1 \leq n \leq 7$

14. $b_n = 2n + 6$ for $1 \leq n \leq 7$

15. $c_n = n^{-1/2}$ for $1 \leq n \leq 5$

16. $c_n = n^{1/2}2^{-n}$ for $1 \leq n \leq 4$

Write the first four terms of the infinite sequence whose nth term is given. See Example 2.

17. $a_n = \dfrac{1}{n^2 + n}$

18. $b_n = \dfrac{1}{(n + 1)(n + 2)}$

19. $b_n = \dfrac{1}{2n - 5}$

20. $a_n = \dfrac{4}{2n + 5}$

21. $c_n = (-1)^n(n - 2)^2$

22. $c_n = (-1)^n(2n - 1)^2$

23. $a_n = \dfrac{(-1)^{2n}}{n^2}$

24. $a_n = (-1)^{2n+1}2^{n-1}$

Write a formula for the general term of each infinite sequence. See Examples 3 and 4.

25. $1, 3, 5, 7, 9, \ldots$

26. $5, 7, 9, 11, 13, \ldots$

27. $1, -1, 1, -1, \ldots$

28. $-1, 1, -1, 1, \ldots$

29. $0, 2, 4, 6, 8, \ldots$

30. $4, 6, 8, 10, 12, \ldots$

31. $3, 6, 9, 12, \ldots$

32. $4, 8, 12, 16, \ldots$

33. $4, 7, 10, 13, \ldots$

34. $3, 7, 11, 15, \ldots$

35. $-1, 2, -4, 8, -16, \ldots$

36. $1, -3, 9, -27, \ldots$

37. $0, 1, 4, 9, 16, \ldots$

38. $0, 1, 8, 27, 64, \ldots$

Solve each problem. See Example 5.

39. *Football penalties.* A football is on the 8-yard line, and five penalties in a row are given that move the ball half the distance to the (closest) goal. Write a sequence of five terms that specify the location of the ball after each penalty.

40. *Infestation.* Leona planted 9 acres of soybeans, but by the end of each week, insects had destroyed one-third of the acreage that was healthy at the beginning of the week. How many acres does she have left after 6 weeks?

41. *Constant rate of increase.* The MSRP for the 2002 Ford F-250 Lariat 4WD Super Duty Super Cab was $34,940 (Edmund's New Car Prices, www.edmunds.com). Suppose the price of this truck increases by 5% each year. Find the prices to the nearest dollar for the 2003 through 2008 models.

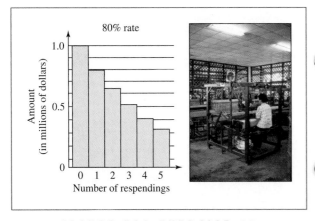

FIGURE FOR EXERCISE 41

42. Constant increase. The MSRP for a new 2002 Mercury Cougar was $20,395 (Edmund's New Car Prices, www.edmunds.com). Suppose the price of this car increases by $1000 each year. Find the prices of the 2003 through 2008 models.

43. Economic impact. To assess the economic impact of a factory on a community, economists consider the annual amount the factory spends in the community, then the portion of the money that is respent in the community, then the portion of the respent money that is respent in the community, and so on. Suppose a garment manufacturer spends $1 million annually in its community and 80% of all money received in the community is respent in the community. Find the first four terms of the economic impact sequence.

80% rate

FIGURE FOR EXERCISE 43

44. Less impact. The rate at which money is respent in a community varies from community to community. Find the first four terms of the economic impact sequence for the manufacturer in Exercise 43, assuming only 50% of money received in the community is respent in the community.

45. Fabric design. A fabric designer must take into account the capability of textile machines to produce material with vertical repeats. A textile machine can be set up for a vertical repeat every $\frac{27}{n}$ inches (in.), where n is a natural number. Write the first five terms of the sequence $a_n = \frac{27}{n}$, which gives the possible vertical repeats for a textile machine.

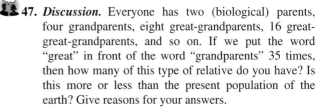

46. Musical tones. The note middle C on a piano is tuned so that the string vibrates at 262 cycles per second, or 262 Hertz (Hz). The C note one octave higher is tuned to 524 Hz. The tuning for the 11 notes in between using the method called *equal temperament* is determined by the sequence $a_n = 262 \cdot 2^{n/12}$. Find the tuning for the 11 notes in between.

GETTING MORE INVOLVED

47. Discussion. Everyone has two (biological) parents, four grandparents, eight great-grandparents, 16 great-great-grandparents, and so on. If we put the word "great" in front of the word "grandparents" 35 times, then how many of this type of relative do you have? Is this more or less than the present population of the earth? Give reasons for your answers.

48. Discussion. If you deposit 1 cent into your piggy bank on September 1 and each day thereafter deposit twice as much as on the previous day, then how much will you be depositing on September 30? The total amount deposited for the month can be found without adding up all 30 deposits. Look at how the amount on deposit is increasing each day and see whether you can find the total for the month. Give reasons for your answers.

49. Cooperative learning. Working in groups, have someone in each group make up a formula for a_n, the nth term of a sequence, but do not show it to the other group members. Write the terms of the sequence on a piece of paper one at a time. After each term is given, ask whether anyone knows the next term. When the group can correctly give the next term, ask for a formula for the nth term.

50. Exploration. Find a real-life sequence in which all of the terms are the same. Find one in which each term after the first is one larger than the previous term. Find out what the sequence of fines is on your campus for your first, second, third, and fourth parking ticket.

51. Exploration. Consider the sequence whose nth term is $a_n = (0.999)^n$.

a) Calculate a_{100}, a_{1000}, and $a_{10,000}$.

b) What happens to a_n as n gets larger and larger?

13.2 **SERIES**

If you make a sequence of bank deposits, then you might be interested in the total value of the terms of the sequence. Of course, if the sequence has only a few terms, you can simply add them. In Sections 13.3 and 13.4 we will develop formulas that give the sum of the terms for certain finite and infinite sequences. In this section you will first learn a notation for expressing the sum of the terms of a sequence.

Summation Notation

To describe the sum of the terms of a sequence, we use **summation notation.** The Greek letter Σ (sigma) is used to indicate sums. For example, the sum of the first five terms of the sequence $a_n = n^2$ is written as

$$\sum_{n=1}^{5} n^2.$$

You can read this notation as "the sum of n^2 for n between 1 and 5, inclusive." To find the sum, we let n take the values 1 through 5 in the expression n^2:

$$\sum_{n=1}^{5} n^2 = 1^2 + 2^2 + 3^2 + 4^2 + 5^2$$
$$= 1 + 4 + 9 + 16 + 25$$
$$= 55$$

In this context the letter n is the **index of summation.** Other letters may also be used. For example, the expressions

$$\sum_{n=1}^{5} n^2, \quad \sum_{j=1}^{5} j^2, \quad \text{and} \quad \sum_{i=1}^{5} i^2$$

all have the same value. Note that i is used as a variable here and not as an imaginary number.

E X A M P L E   1

Evaluating a sum in summation notation

Find the value of the expression

$$\sum_{i=1}^{3} (-1)^i (2i + 1).$$

Solution

Replace i by 1, 2, and 3, and then add the results:

$$\sum_{i=1}^{3} (-1)^i (2i + 1) = (-1)^1 [2(1) + 1] + (-1)^2 [2(2) + 1] + (-1)^3 [2(3) + 1]$$
$$= -3 + 5 - 7$$
$$= -5 \qquad \blacksquare$$

Series

The sum of the terms of the sequence 1, 4, 9, 16, 25 is written as

$$1 + 4 + 9 + 16 + 25.$$

This expression is called a *series*. It indicates that we are to add the terms of the given sequence. The sum, 55, is the sum of the series.

> **Series**
>
> The indicated sum of the terms of a sequence is called a **series.**

Just as a sequence may be finite or infinite, a series may be finite or infinite. In this section we discuss finite series only. In Section 13.4 we will discuss one type of infinite series.

Summation notation is a convenient notation for writing a series.

E X A M P L E   2   **Converting to summation notation**

Write the series in summation notation:

$$2 + 4 + 6 + 8 + 10 + 12 + 14$$

Solution

The general term for the sequence of positive even integers is $2n$. If we let n take the values from 1 through 7, then $2n$ ranges from 2 through 14. So

$$2 + 4 + 6 + 8 + 10 + 12 + 14 = \sum_{n=1}^{7} 2n. \qquad \blacksquare$$

E X A M P L E   3   **Converting to summation notation**

Write the series

$$\frac{1}{2} - \frac{1}{3} + \frac{1}{4} - \frac{1}{5} + \frac{1}{6} - \frac{1}{7} + \cdots + \frac{1}{50}$$

in summation notation.

Helpful Hint

A series is called an *indicated sum* because the addition is indicated but not actually being performed. The sum of a series is the real number obtained by actually performing the indicated addition.

Solution

For this series we let n be 2 through 50. The expression $(-1)^n$ produces alternating signs. The series is written as

$$\sum_{n=2}^{50} \frac{(-1)^n}{n}. \qquad \blacksquare$$

Changing the Index

In Example 3 we saw the index go from 2 through 50, but this is arbitrary. A series can be written with the index starting at any given number.

E X A M P L E   4   **Changing the index**

Rewrite the series

$$\sum_{i=1}^{6} \frac{(-1)^i}{i^2}$$

with an index j, where j starts at 0.

Solution

Because i starts at 1 and j starts at 0, we have $i = j + 1$. Because i ranges from 1 through 6 and $i = j + 1$, j must range from 0 through 5. Now replace i by $j + 1$ in the summation notation:

$$\sum_{j=0}^{5} \frac{(-1)^{j+1}}{(j + 1)^2}$$

Check that these two series have exactly the same six terms. $\qquad \blacksquare$

True or false? Explain your answer.

1. A series is the indicated sum of the terms of a sequence.

2. The sum of a series can never be negative.

3. There are eight terms in the series $\displaystyle\sum_{i=2}^{10} i^3$.

4. The series $\displaystyle\sum_{i=1}^{9} (-1)^i i^2$ and $\displaystyle\sum_{j=0}^{8} (-1)^j (j+1)^2$ have the same sum.

5. The ninth term of the series $\displaystyle\sum_{i=1}^{100} \frac{(-1)^i}{(i+1)(i+2)}$ is $\dfrac{1}{110}$.

6. $\displaystyle\sum_{i=1}^{2} (-1)^i 2^i = 2$

7. $\displaystyle\sum_{i=1}^{5} 3i = 3\left(\sum_{i=1}^{5} i\right)$

8. $\displaystyle\sum_{i=1}^{5} 4 = 20$

9. $\displaystyle\sum_{i=1}^{5} 2i + \sum_{i=1}^{5} 7i = \sum_{i=1}^{5} 9i$

10. $\displaystyle\sum_{i=1}^{3} (2i+1) = \left(\sum_{i=1}^{3} 2i\right) + 1$

13.2   EXERCISES

Reading and Writing   *After reading this section, write out the answers to these questions. Use complete sentences.*

1. What is summation notation?

2. What is the index of summation?

3. What is a series?

4. What is a finite series?

Find the sum of each series. See Example 1.

5. $\displaystyle\sum_{i=1}^{4} i^2$

6. $\displaystyle\sum_{j=0}^{3} (j+1)^2$

7. $\displaystyle\sum_{j=0}^{5} (2j-1)$

8. $\displaystyle\sum_{i=1}^{6} (2i-3)$

9. $\displaystyle\sum_{i=1}^{5} 2^{-i}$

10. $\displaystyle\sum_{i=1}^{5} (-2)^{-i}$

11. $\displaystyle\sum_{i=1}^{10} 5i^0$

12. $\displaystyle\sum_{j=1}^{20} 3$

13. $\displaystyle\sum_{i=1}^{3} (i-3)(i+1)$

14. $\displaystyle\sum_{i=0}^{5} i(i-1)(i-2)(i-3)$

15. $\displaystyle\sum_{j=1}^{10} (-1)^j$

16. $\displaystyle\sum_{j=1}^{11} (-1)^j$

Write each series in summation notation. Use the index i, and let i begin at 1 in each summation. See Examples 2 and 3.

17. $1 + 2 + 3 + 4 + 5 + 6$

18. $2 + 4 + 6 + 8 + 10$

19. $-1 + 3 - 5 + 7 - 9 + 11$

20. $1 - 3 + 5 - 7 + 9$

21. $1 + 4 + 9 + 16 + 25 + 36$

22. $1 + 8 + 27 + 64 + 125$

23. $\dfrac{1}{3} + \dfrac{1}{4} + \dfrac{1}{5} + \dfrac{1}{6}$

24. $1 - \dfrac{1}{2} + \dfrac{1}{3} - \dfrac{1}{4} + \dfrac{1}{5} - \dfrac{1}{6}$

25. $\ln(2) + \ln(3) + \ln(4)$

26. $e^1 + e^2 + e^3 + e^4$

27. $a_1 + a_2 + a_3 + a_4$

28. $a^2 + a^3 + a^4 + a^5$

29. $x_3 + x_4 + x_5 + \cdots + x_{50}$

30. $y_1 + y_2 + y_3 + \cdots + y_{30}$

31. $w_1 + w_2 + w_3 + \cdots + w_n$

32. $m_1 + m_2 + m_3 + \cdots + m_k$

Complete the rewriting of each series using the new index as indicated. See Example 4.

33. $\displaystyle\sum_{i=1}^{5} i^2 = \sum_{j=0}$

34. $\displaystyle\sum_{i=1}^{6} i^3 = \sum_{j=0}$

35. $\displaystyle\sum_{i=0}^{12} (2i - 1) = \sum_{j=1}$

36. $\displaystyle\sum_{i=1}^{3} (3i + 2) = \sum_{j=0}$

37. $\displaystyle\sum_{i=4}^{8} \frac{1}{i} = \sum_{j=1}$

38. $\displaystyle\sum_{i=5}^{10} 2^{-i} = \sum_{j=1}$

39. $\displaystyle\sum_{i=1}^{4} x^{2i+3} = \sum_{j=0}$

40. $\displaystyle\sum_{i=0}^{2} x^{3-2i} = \sum_{j=1}$

41. $\displaystyle\sum_{i=1}^{n} x^i = \sum_{j=0}$

42. $\displaystyle\sum_{i=0}^{n} x^{-i} = \sum_{j=1}$

Write out the terms of each series.

43. $\displaystyle\sum_{i=1}^{6} x^i$

44. $\displaystyle\sum_{i=1}^{5} (-1)^i x^{i-1}$

45. $\displaystyle\sum_{j=0}^{3} (-1)^j x_j$

46. $\displaystyle\sum_{j=1}^{5} \frac{1}{x_j}$

47. $\displaystyle\sum_{i=1}^{3} i x^i$

48. $\displaystyle\sum_{i=1}^{5} \frac{x}{i}$

A series can be used to model the situation in each of the following problems.

49. *Leap frog.* A frog with a vision problem is 1 yard away from a dead cricket. He spots the cricket and jumps halfway to the cricket. After the frog realizes that he has not reached the cricket, he again jumps halfway to the cricket. Write a series in summation notation to describe how far the frog has moved after nine such jumps.

50. *Compound interest.* Cleo deposited $1000 at the beginning of each year for 5 years into an account paying 10% interest compounded annually. Write a series using summation notation to describe how much she has in the account at the end of the fifth year. Note that the first $1000 will receive interest for 5 years, the second $1000 will receive interest for 4 years, and so on.

51. *Total economic impact.* In Exercise 43 of Section 13.1 we described a factory that spends $1 million annually in a community in which 80% of all money received in the community is respent in the community. Use summation notation to write the sum of the first four terms of the economic impact sequence for the factory.

52. *Total earnings.* Suppose you earn $1 on January 1, $2 on January 2, $3 on January 3, and so on. Use summation notation to write the sum of your earnings for the entire month of January.

GETTING MORE INVOLVED

53. *Discussion.* What is the difference between a sequence and a series?

54. *Discussion.* For what values of n is $\displaystyle\sum_{i=1}^{n} \frac{1}{i} > 4$?

In This Section

- Arithmetic Sequences
- Arithmetic Series

Helpful Hint

Arithmetic used as an adjective (ar-ith-met'-ic) is pronounced differently from arithmetic used as a noun (a-rith'-me-tic). Arithmetic (the adjective) is accented similarly to geometric.

13.3 ARITHMETIC SEQUENCES AND SERIES

We defined sequences and series in Sections 13.1 and 13.2. In this section you will study a special type of sequence known as an arithmetic sequence. You will also study the series corresponding to this sequence.

Arithmetic Sequences

Consider the following sequence:

$$5, 9, 13, 17, 21, \ldots$$

This sequence is called an arithmetic sequence because of the pattern for the terms. Each term is 4 larger than the previous term.

> **Arithmetic Sequence**
>
> A sequence in which each term after the first is obtained by adding a fixed amount to the previous term is called an **arithmetic sequence.**

The fixed amount is called the **common difference** and is denoted by the letter d. If a_1 is the first term, then the second term is $a_1 + d$. The third term is $a_1 + 2d$, the fourth term is $a_1 + 3d$, and so on.

> **Formula for the nth Term of an Arithmetic Sequence**
>
> The nth term, a_n, of an arithmetic sequence with first term a_1 and common difference d is
>
> $$a_n = a_1 + (n - 1)d.$$

E X A M P L E   1

The nth term of an arithmetic sequence

Write a formula for the nth term of the arithmetic sequence

$$5, 9, 13, 17, 21, \ldots.$$

Solution

Each term of the sequence after the first is 4 more than the previous term. Because the common difference is 4 and the first term is 5, the nth term is given by

$$a_n = 5 + (n - 1)4.$$

We can simplify this expression to get

$$a_n = 4n + 1.$$

Check a few terms: $a_1 = 4(1) + 1 = 5$, $a_2 = 4(2) + 1 = 9$, and $a_3 = 4(3) + 1 = 13$. ∎

In the next example the common difference is negative.

E X A M P L E   2

An arithmetic sequence of decreasing terms

Write a formula for the nth term of the arithmetic sequence

$$4, 1, -2, -5, -8, \ldots.$$

Solution

Each term is 3 less than the previous term, so $d = -3$. Because $a_1 = 4$, we can write the nth term as

$$a_n = 4 + (n - 1)(-3),$$

or

$$a_n = -3n + 7.$$

Check a few terms: $a_1 = -3(1) + 7 = 4$, $a_2 = -3(2) + 7 = 1$, and $a_3 = -3(3) + 7 = -2$. ■

In Example 3 we find some terms of an arithmetic sequence using a given formula for the nth term.

EXAMPLE 3

Writing terms of an arithmetic sequence

Write the first five terms of the sequence in which $a_n = 3 + (n - 1)6$.

Solution

Let n take the values from 1 through 5, and find a_n:

$$a_1 = 3 + (1 - 1)6 = 3$$
$$a_2 = 3 + (2 - 1)6 = 9$$
$$a_3 = 3 + (3 - 1)6 = 15$$
$$a_4 = 3 + (4 - 1)6 = 21$$
$$a_5 = 3 + (5 - 1)6 = 27$$

Notice that $a_n = 3 + (n - 1)6$ gives the general term for an arithmetic sequence with first term 3 and common difference 6. Because each term after the first is 6 more than the previous term, the first five terms that we found are correct. ■

The formula $a_n = a_1 + (n - 1)d$ involves four variables: a_1, a_n, n, and d. If we know the values of any three of these variables, we can find the fourth.

EXAMPLE 4

Finding a missing term of an arithmetic sequence

Find the twelfth term of the arithmetic sequence whose first term is 2 and whose fifth term is 14.

Study Tip

Stay alert for the entire class period. The first 20 minutes are the easiest and the last 20 minutes are the hardest. Some students put down their pencils, fold up their notebooks, and daydream for those last 20 minutes. Don't give in. Recognize when you are losing it and force yourself to stay alert. Think of how much time you will have to spend outside of class figuring out what happened during those last 20 minutes.

Solution

Before finding the twelfth term, we use the given information to find the missing common difference. Let $n = 5$, $a_1 = 2$, and $a_5 = 14$ in the formula $a_n = a_1 + (n - 1)d$ to find d:

$$14 = 2 + (5 - 1)d$$
$$14 = 2 + 4d$$
$$12 = 4d$$
$$3 = d$$

Now use $a_1 = 2$, $d = 3$ and $n = 12$ in $a_n = a_1 + (n - 1)d$ to find a_{12}:

$$a_{12} = 2 + (12 - 1)3$$
$$a_{12} = 35$$

■

Arithmetic Series

The indicated sum of an arithmetic sequence is called an **arithmetic series.** For example, the series

$$2 + 4 + 6 + 8 + 10 + \cdots + 54$$

is an arithmetic series because there is a common difference of 2 between the terms.

We can find the actual sum of this arithmetic series without adding all of the terms. Write the series in increasing order, and below that write the series in decreasing order. We then add the corresponding terms:

$$
\begin{array}{llllllll}
S = & 2 + & 4 + & 6 + & 8 + \cdots + 52 + 54 \\
S = & 54 + & 52 + & 50 + & 48 + \cdots + \ 4 + \ 2 \\
\hline
2S = & 56 + & 56 + & 56 + & 56 + \cdots + 56 + 56
\end{array}
$$

Now, how many times does 56 appear in the sum on the right? Because

$$2 + 4 + 6 + \cdots + 54 = 2 \cdot 1 + 2 \cdot 2 + 2 \cdot 3 + \cdots + 2 \cdot 27,$$

there are 27 terms in this sum. Because 56 appears 27 times on the right, we have $2S = 27 \cdot 56$, or

$$S = \frac{27 \cdot 56}{2} = 27 \cdot 28 = 756.$$

If $S_n = a_1 + a_2 + a_3 + \cdots + a_n$ is any arithmetic series, then we can find its sum using the same technique. Rewrite S_n as follows:

$$
\begin{array}{lll}
S_n = a_1 & + (a_1 + d) \ + (a_1 + 2d) + \cdots + a_n \\
S_n = a_n & + (a_n - d) \ + (a_n - 2d) + \cdots + a_1 \\
\hline
2S_n = (a_1 + a_n) + (a_1 + a_n) + (a_1 + a_n) + \cdots + (a_1 + a_n) & \text{Add.}
\end{array}
$$

Because $(a_1 + a_n)$ appears n times on the right, we have $2S_n = n(a_1 + a_n)$. Divide each side by 2 to get the following formula.

Sum of an Arithmetic Series

The sum, S_n, of the first n terms of an arithmetic series with first term a_1 and nth term a_n, is given by

$$S_n = \frac{n}{2}(a_1 + a_n).$$

E X A M P L E   5

The sum of an arithmetic series

Find the sum of the positive integers from 1 to 100 inclusive.

Helpful Hint

Legend has it that Carl F. Gauss knew this formula when he was in grade school. Gauss's teacher told him to add up the numbers from 1 through 100 for busy work. He immediately answered 5050.

Solution

The described series, $1 + 2 + 3 + \cdots + 100$, has 100 terms. So we can use $n = 100$, $a_1 = 1$, and $a_n = 100$ in the formula for the sum of an arithmetic series:

$$S_n = \frac{n}{2}(a_1 + a_n)$$

$$S_{100} = \frac{100}{2}(1 + 100)$$

$$= 50(101)$$

$$= 5050$$

E X A M P L E   6   **The sum of an arithmetic series**

Find the sum of the series

$$12 + 16 + 20 + \cdots + 84.$$

Solution

This series is an arithmetic series with $a_n = 84$, $a_1 = 12$, and $d = 4$. To get the number of terms, n, we use $a_n = a_1 + (n - 1)d$:

$$84 = 12 + (n - 1)4$$
$$84 = 8 + 4n$$
$$76 = 4n$$
$$19 = n$$

Now find the sum of these 19 terms:

$$S_{19} = \frac{19}{2}(12 + 84) = 912$$

■

WARM-UPS

True or false? Explain your answer.

1. The arithmetic sequence 3, 1, −1, −3, −5, . . . has common difference 2.

2. The sequence 2, 5, 9, 14, 20, 27, . . . is an arithmetic sequence.

3. The sequence 2, 4, 2, 0, 2, 4, 2, 0, . . . is an arithmetic sequence.

4. The nth term of an arithmetic sequence with first term a_1 and common difference d is given by the formula $a_n = a_1 + nd$.

5. If $a_1 = 5$ and $a_3 = 10$ in an arithmetic sequence, then $a_4 = 15$.

6. If $a_1 = 6$ and $a_3 = 2$ in an arithmetic sequence, then $a_2 = 10$.

7. An arithmetic series is the indicated sum of an arithmetic sequence.

8. The series $\sum_{i=1}^{5}(3 + 2i)$ is an arithmetic series.

9. The sum of the first n counting numbers is $\frac{n(n + 1)}{2}$.

10. The sum of the even integers from 8 through 28 inclusive is $5(8 + 28)$.

13.3   EXERCISES

Reading and Writing   *After reading this section, write out the answers to these questions. Use complete sentences.*

1. What is an arithmetic sequence?

2. What is the nth term of an arithmetic sequence?

3. What is an arithmetic series?

4. What is the formula for the sum of the first n terms of an arithmetic series?

Write a formula for the nth term of each arithmetic sequence. See Examples 1 and 2.

5. 0, 6, 12, 18, 24, . . .

6. 0, 5, 10, 15, 20, . . .

7. 7, 12, 17, 22, 27, . . .

8. 4, 15, 26, 37, 48, . . .

9. −4, −2, 0, 2, 4, . . .

10. $-3, 0, 3, 6, 9, \ldots$

11. $5, 1, -3, -7, -11, \ldots$

12. $8, 5, 2, -1, -4, \ldots$

13. $-2, -9, -16, -23, \ldots$

14. $-5, -7, -9, -11, -13, \ldots$

15. $-3, -2.5, -2, -1.5, -1, \ldots$

16. $-2, -1.25, -0.5, 0.25, \ldots$

17. $-6, -6.5, -7, -7.5, -8, \ldots$

18. $1, 0.5, 0, -0.5, -1, \ldots$

In Exercises 19–32, write the first five terms of the arithmetic sequence whose nth term is given. See Example 3.

19. $a_n = 9 + (n-1)4$

20. $a_n = 13 + (n-1)6$

21. $a_n = 7 + (n-1)(-2)$

22. $a_n = 6 + (n-1)(-3)$

23. $a_n = -4 + (n-1)3$

24. $a_n = -19 + (n-1)12$

25. $a_n = -2 + (n-1)(-3)$

26. $a_n = -1 + (n-1)(-2)$

27. $a_n = -4n - 3$

28. $a_n = -3n + 1$

29. $a_n = 0.5n + 4$

30. $a_n = 0.3n + 1$

31. $a_n = 20n + 1000$

32. $a_n = -600n + 4000$

Find the indicated part of each arithmetic sequence. See Example 4.

33. Find the eighth term of the sequence that has a first term of 9 and a common difference of 6.

34. Find the twelfth term of the sequence that has a first term of -2 and a common difference of -3.

35. Find the common difference if the first term is 6 and the twentieth term is 82.

36. Find the common difference if the first term is -8 and the ninth term is -64.

37. If the common difference is -2 and the seventh term is 14, then what is the first term?

38. If the common difference is 5 and the twelfth term is -7, then what is the first term?

39. Find the sixth term of the sequence that has a fifth term of 13 and a first term of -3.

40. Find the eighth term of the sequence that has a sixth term of -42 and a first term of 3.

Find the sum of each given series. See Examples 5 and 6.

41. $1 + 2 + 3 + \cdots + 48$

42. $1 + 2 + 3 + \cdots + 12$

43. $8 + 10 + 12 + \cdots + 36$

44. $9 + 12 + 15 + \cdots + 72$

45. $-1 + (-7) + (-13) + \cdots + (-73)$

46. $-7 + (-12) + (-17) + \cdots + (-72)$

47. $-6 + (-1) + 4 + 9 + \cdots + 64$

48. $-9 + (-1) + 7 + \cdots + 103$

49. $20 + 12 + 4 + (-4) + \cdots + (-92)$

50. $19 + 1 + (-17) + \cdots + (-125)$

51. $\displaystyle\sum_{i=1}^{12} (3i - 7)$

52. $\displaystyle\sum_{i=1}^{7} (-4i + 6)$

53. $\displaystyle\sum_{i=1}^{11} (-5i + 2)$

54. $\displaystyle\sum_{i=1}^{19} (3i - 5)$

Solve each problem using the ideas of arithmetic sequences and series.

55. **Increasing salary.** If a lab technician has a salary of $22,000 her first year and is due to get a $500 raise each year, then what will her salary be in her seventh year?

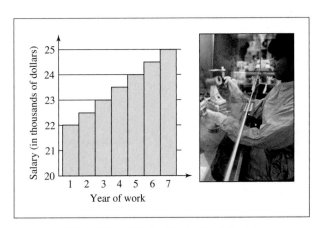

FIGURE FOR EXERCISE 55

56. **Seven years of salary.** What is the total salary for 7 years of work for the lab technician of Exercise 55?

57. **Light reading.** On the first day of October an English teacher suggests to his students that they read five pages

of a novel and every day thereafter increase their daily reading by two pages. If his students follow this suggestion, then how many pages will they read during October?

58. *Heavy penalties.* If an air-conditioning system is not completed by the agreed upon date, the contractor pays a penalty of $500 for the first day that it is overdue, $600 for the second day, $700 for the third day, and so on. If the system is completed 10 days late, then what is the total amount of the penalties that the contractor must pay?

GETTING MORE INVOLVED

59. *Discussion.* Which of the following sequences is not an arithmetic sequence? Explain your answer.

a) $\dfrac{1}{2}, 1, \dfrac{3}{2}, \ldots$ b) $\dfrac{1}{2}, \dfrac{1}{3}, \dfrac{1}{4}, \ldots$

c) $5, 0, -5, \ldots$ d) $2, 3, 4, \ldots$

60. *Discussion.* What is the smallest value of n for which

$$\sum_{i=1}^{n} \dfrac{i}{2} > 50?$$

In This Section

- Geometric Sequences
- Finite Geometric Series
- Infinite Geometric Series
- Annuities

13.4 GEOMETRIC SEQUENCES AND SERIES

In Section 13.3 you studied the arithmetic sequences and series. In this section you will study sequences in which each term is a *multiple* of the term preceding it. You will also learn how to find the sum of the corresponding series.

Geometric Sequences

In an arithmetic sequence such as 2, 4, 6, 8, 10, . . . there is a common difference between consecutive terms. In a geometric sequence there is a common ratio between consecutive terms. The following table contains several geometric sequences and the common ratios between consecutive terms.

Geometric Sequence	Common Ratio
3, 6, 12, 24, 48, . . .	2
27, 9, 3, 1, $\frac{1}{3}$, . . .	$\frac{1}{3}$
1, -10, 100, -1000, . . .	-10

Note that every term after the first term of each geometric sequence can be obtained by multiplying the previous term by the common ratio.

> **Geometric Sequence**
>
> A sequence in which each term after the first is obtained by multiplying the preceding term by a constant is called a **geometric sequence.**

The constant is denoted by the letter r and is called the **common ratio.** If a_1 is the first term, then the second term is $a_1 r$. The third term is $a_1 r^2$, the fourth term is $a_1 r^3$, and so on. We can write a formula for the nth term of a geometric sequence by following this pattern.

Formula for the *n*th Term of a Geometric Sequence

The *n*th term, a_n, of a geometric sequence with first term a_1 and common ratio *r* is

$$a_n = a_1 r^{n-1}.$$

The first term and the common ratio determine all of the terms of a geometric sequence.

E X A M P L E   1

Finding the *n*th term

Write a formula for the *n*th term of the geometric sequence

$$6, 2, \frac{2}{3}, \frac{2}{9}, \ldots.$$

Solution

We can obtain the common ratio by dividing any term after the first by the term preceding it. So

$$r = 2 \div 6 = \frac{1}{3}.$$

Because each term after the first is $\frac{1}{3}$ of the term preceding it, the *n*th term is given by

$$a_n = 6\left(\frac{1}{3}\right)^{n-1}.$$

Check a few terms: $a_1 = 6\left(\frac{1}{3}\right)^{1-1} = 6$, $a_2 = 6\left(\frac{1}{3}\right)^{2-1} = 2$, and $a_3 = 6\left(\frac{1}{3}\right)^{3-1} = \frac{2}{3}$. ■

E X A M P L E   2

Finding the *n*th term

Find a formula for the *n*th term of the geometric sequence

$$2, -1, \frac{1}{2}, -\frac{1}{4}, \ldots.$$

Solution

We obtain the ratio by dividing a term by the term preceding it:

$$r = -1 \div 2 = -\frac{1}{2}$$

Each term after the first is obtained by multiplying the preceding term by $-\frac{1}{2}$. The formula for the *n*th term is

$$a_n = 2\left(-\frac{1}{2}\right)^{n-1}.$$

Check a few terms: $a_1 = 2\left(-\frac{1}{2}\right)^{1-1} = 2$, $a_2 = 2\left(-\frac{1}{2}\right)^{2-1} = -1$, and $a_3 = 2\left(-\frac{1}{2}\right)^{3-1} = \frac{1}{2}$. ■

In Example 3 we use the formula for the *n*th term to write some terms of a geometric sequence.

EXAMPLE 3

Writing the terms

Write the first five terms of the geometric sequence whose nth term is

$$a_n = 3(-2)^{n-1}.$$

Solution

Let n take the values 1 through 5 in the formula for the nth term:

$$a_1 = 3(-2)^{1-1} = 3$$
$$a_2 = 3(-2)^{2-1} = -6$$
$$a_3 = 3(-2)^{3-1} = 12$$
$$a_4 = 3(-2)^{4-1} = -24$$
$$a_5 = 3(-2)^{5-1} = 48$$

Notice that $a_n = 3(-2)^{n-1}$ gives the general term for a geometric sequence with first term 3 and common ratio -2. Because every term after the first can be obtained by multiplying the previous term by -2, the terms 3, -6, 12, -24, and 48 are correct.   ∎

The formula for the nth term involves four variables: a_n, a_1, r, and n. If we know the value of any three of them, we can find the value of the fourth.

EXAMPLE 4

Finding a missing term

Find the first term of a geometric sequence whose fourth term is 8 and whose common ratio is $\frac{1}{2}$.

Solution

Let $a_4 = 8$, $r = \frac{1}{2}$, and $n = 4$ in the formula $a_n = a_1 r^{n-1}$:

$$8 = a_1 \left(\frac{1}{2}\right)^{4-1}$$

$$8 = a_1 \cdot \frac{1}{8}$$

$$64 = a_1$$

So the first term is 64.   ∎

Finite Geometric Series

Consider the following series:

$$1 + 2 + 4 + 8 + 16 + \cdots + 512$$

The terms of this series are the terms of a finite geometric sequence. The indicated sum of a geometric sequence is called a **geometric series.**

We can find the actual sum of this finite geometric series by using a technique similar to the one used for the sum of an arithmetic series. Let

$$S = 1 + 2 + 4 + 8 + \cdots + 256 + 512.$$

Because the common ratio is 2, multiply each side by -2:

$$-2S = -2 - 4 - 8 - \cdots - 512 - 1024$$

Adding the last two equations eliminates all but two of the terms on the right:

$$
\begin{array}{llll}
S = 1 + 2 + 4 + 8 + \cdots & + 256 + 512 & \\
-2S = \quad -2 - 4 - 8 - \cdots & \quad\quad - 512 - 1024 & \\
\hline
-S = 1 & \quad\quad\quad\quad - 1024 & \text{Add.} \\
-S = -1023 & & \\
S = 1023 & &
\end{array}
$$

If $S_n = a_1 + a_1 r + a_1 r^2 + \cdots + a_1 r^{n-1}$ is any geometric series, we can find the sum in the same manner. Multiplying each side of this equation by $-r$ yields

$$-r S_n = -a_1 r - a_1 r^2 - a_1 r^3 - \cdots - a_1 r^n.$$

If we add S_n and $-r S_n$, all but two of the terms on the right are eliminated:

$$
\begin{array}{lll}
S_n = a_1 + a_1 r + a_1 r^2 + \cdots & \quad + a_1 r^{n-1} & \\
-r S_n = \quad\ - a_1 r - a_1 r^2 - a_1 r^3 - \cdots & \quad - a_1 r^n & \\
\hline
S_n - r S_n = a_1 & \quad - a_1 r^n & \text{Add.} \\
(1 - r) S_n = a_1 (1 - r^n) & & \begin{array}{l}\text{Factor out}\\\text{common factors.}\end{array}
\end{array}
$$

Now divide each side of this equation by $1 - r$ to get the formula for S_n.

Sum of n Terms of a Geometric Series

If S_n represents the sum of the first n terms of a geometric series with first term a_1 and common ratio r ($r \neq 1$), then

$$S_n = \frac{a_1(1 - r^n)}{1 - r}.$$

E X A M P L E 5

The sum of a finite geometric series

Find the sum of the series

$$\frac{1}{3} + \frac{1}{9} + \frac{1}{27} + \cdots + \frac{1}{729}.$$

Solution

The first term is $\frac{1}{3}$, and the common ratio is $\frac{1}{3}$. So the nth term can be written as

$$a_n = \frac{1}{3}\left(\frac{1}{3}\right)^{n-1}.$$

We can use this formula to find the number of terms in the series:

$$\frac{1}{729} = \frac{1}{3}\left(\frac{1}{3}\right)^{n-1}$$

$$\frac{1}{729} = \left(\frac{1}{3}\right)^n$$

Because $3^6 = 729$, we have $n = 6$. (Of course, you could use logarithms to solve for n.) Now use the formula for the sum of six terms of this geometric series:

$$S_6 = \frac{\frac{1}{3}\left[1 - \left(\frac{1}{3}\right)^6\right]}{1 - \frac{1}{3}} = \frac{\frac{1}{3}\left[1 - \frac{1}{729}\right]}{\frac{2}{3}}$$

$$= \frac{1}{3} \cdot \frac{728}{729} \cdot \frac{3}{2}$$

$$= \frac{364}{729}$$

$\blacksquare$

E X A M P L E   6

The sum of a finite geometric series

Find the sum of the series

$$\sum_{i=1}^{12} 3(-2)^{i-1}.$$

Solution

This series is geometric with first term 3, ratio -2, and $n = 12$. We use the formula for the sum of the first 12 terms of a geometric series:

$$S_{12} = \frac{3[1 - (-2)^{12}]}{1 - (-2)} = \frac{3[-4095]}{3} = -4095$$

$\blacksquare$

Calculator Close-Up

Experiment with your calculator to see what happens to r^n as n gets larger and larger.

```
.99^100
       .3660323413
.99^1000
      4.317124741E-5
.99^10000
      2.24877485E-44
```

Infinite Geometric Series

Consider how a very large value of n affects the formula for the sum of a finite geometric series,

$$S_n = \frac{a_1(1 - r^n)}{1 - r}.$$

If $|r| < 1$, then the value of r^n gets closer and closer to 0 as n gets larger and larger. For example, if $r = \frac{2}{3}$ and $n = 10$, 20, and 100, then

$$\left(\frac{2}{3}\right)^{10} \approx 0.0173415, \quad \left(\frac{2}{3}\right)^{20} \approx 0.0003007, \quad \text{and} \quad \left(\frac{2}{3}\right)^{100} \approx 2.460 \times 10^{-18}.$$

Because r^n is approximately 0 for large values of n, $1 - r^n$ is approximately 1. If we replace $1 - r^n$ by 1 in the expression for S_n, we get

$$S_n \approx \frac{a_1}{1 - r}.$$

So as n gets larger and larger, the sum of the first n terms of the infinite geometric series

$$a_1 + a_1 r + a_1 r^2 + \cdots$$

gets closer and closer to $\frac{a_1}{1 - r}$, provided that $|r| < 1$. Therefore we say that $\frac{a_1}{1 - r}$ is the sum of *all* of the terms of the infinite geometric series.

> **Sum of an Infinite Geometric Series**
>
> If $a_1 + a_1 r + a_1 r^2 + \cdots$ is an infinite geometric series, with $|r| < 1$, then the sum S of all of the terms of this series is given by
>
> $$S = \frac{a_1}{1 - r}.$$

E X A M P L E 7

Sum of an infinite geometric series

Find the sum

$$\frac{1}{2} + \frac{1}{4} + \frac{1}{8} + \frac{1}{16} + \cdots .$$

Helpful Hint

You can imagine this series in a football game. The Bears have the ball on the Lions' 1-yard line. The Lions continually get penalties that move the ball one-half of the distance to the goal. Theoretically, the ball will never reach the goal, but the total distance it moves will get closer and closer to 1 yard.

Solution

This series is an infinite geometric series with $a_1 = \frac{1}{2}$ and $r = \frac{1}{2}$. Because $r < 1$, we have

$$S = \frac{\dfrac{1}{2}}{1 - \dfrac{1}{2}} = 1.$$

For an infinite series the index of summation i takes the values 1, 2, 3, and so on, without end. To indicate that the values for i keep increasing without bound, we say that i *takes the values from* 1 *through* ∞ (infinity). Note that the symbol "∞" does not represent a number. Using the ∞ symbol, we can write the indicated sum of an infinite geometric series (with $|r| < 1$) by using summation notation as follows:

$$a_1 + a_1 r + a_1 r^2 + \cdots = \sum_{i=1}^{\infty} a_1 r^{i-1}$$

E X A M P L E 8

Sum of an infinite geometric series

Find the value of the sum

$$\sum_{i=1}^{\infty} 8 \left(\frac{3}{4} \right)^{i-1} .$$

Solution

This series is an infinite geometric series with first term 8 and ratio $\frac{3}{4}$. So

$$S = \frac{8}{1 - \dfrac{3}{4}} = 8 \cdot \frac{4}{1} = 32.$$

E X A M P L E 9

Follow the bouncing ball

Suppose a ball always rebounds $\frac{2}{3}$ of the height from which it falls and the ball is dropped from a height of 6 feet. Find the total distance that the ball travels.

Solution

The ball falls 6 feet (ft) and rebounds 4 ft, then falls 4 ft and rebounds $\frac{8}{3}$ ft. The following series gives the total distance that the ball falls:

$$F = 6 + 4 + \frac{8}{3} + \frac{16}{9} + \cdots$$

The distance that the ball rebounds is given by the following series:

$$R = 4 + \frac{8}{3} + \frac{16}{9} + \cdots$$

Each of these series is an infinite geometric series with ratio $\frac{2}{3}$. Use the formula for an infinite geometric series to find each sum:

$$F = \frac{6}{1 - \frac{2}{3}} = 6 \cdot \frac{3}{1} = 18 \text{ ft}, \qquad R = \frac{4}{1 - \frac{2}{3}} = 4 \cdot \frac{3}{1} = 12 \text{ ft}$$

The total distance traveled by the ball is the sum of F and R, 30 ft. ■

Annuities

One of the most important applications of geometric series is in calculating the value of an annuity. An **annuity** is a sequence of periodic payments. The payments might be loan payments or investments.

EXAMPLE 10 **Value of an annuity**

A deposit of $1000 is made at the beginning of each year for 30 years and earns 6% interest compounded annually. What is the value of this annuity at the end of the thirtieth year?

Solution

The last deposit earns interest for only one year. So at the end of the thirtieth year it amounts to $1000(1.06)$. The next to last deposit earns interest for 2 years and amounts to $1000(1.06)^2$. The first deposit earns interest for 30 years and amounts to $1000(1.06)^{30}$. So the value of the annuity at the end of the thirtieth year is the sum of the finite geometric series

$$1000(1.06) + 1000(1.06)^2 + 1000(1.06)^3 + \cdots + 1000(1.06)^{30}.$$

Use the formula for the sum of 30 terms of a finite geometric series with $a_1 = 1000(1.06)$ and $r = 1.06$:

$$S_{30} = \frac{1000(1.06)(1 - (1.06)^{30})}{1 - 1.06} \approx \$83,801.68$$

So 30 annual deposits of $1000 each amount to $83,801.68. ■

WARM-UPS

True or false? Explain your answer.

1. The sequence 2, 6, 24, 120, . . . is a geometric sequence.
2. For $a_n = 2^n$ there is a common difference between adjacent terms.
3. The common ratio for the geometric sequence $a_n = 3(0.5)^{n-1}$ is 0.5.
4. If $a_n = 3(2)^{-n+3}$, then $a_1 = 12$.
5. In the geometric sequence $a_n = 3(2)^{-n+3}$ we have $r = \frac{1}{2}$.
6. The terms of a geometric series are the terms of a geometric sequence.

(continued)

7. To evaluate $\sum\limits_{i=1}^{10} 2^i$, we must list all of the terms.

8. $\sum\limits_{i=1}^{5} 6\left(\dfrac{3}{4}\right)^{i-1} = \dfrac{9\left[1 - \left(\dfrac{3}{4}\right)^5\right]}{1 - \dfrac{3}{4}}$

9. $10 + 5 + \dfrac{5}{2} + \cdots = \dfrac{10}{1 - \dfrac{1}{2}}$

10. $2 + 4 + 8 + 16 + \cdots = \dfrac{2}{1 - 2}$

13.4 EXERCISES

Reading and Writing *After reading this section, write out the answers to these questions. Use complete sentences.*

1. What is a geometric sequence?

2. What is the *n*th term of a geometric sequence?

3. What is a geometric series?

4. What is the formula for the sum of the first *n* terms of a geometric series?

5. What is the approximate value of r^n when *n* is large and $|r| < 1$?

6. What is the formula for the sum of an infinite geometric series?

Write a formula for the nth term of each geometric sequence. See Examples 1 and 2.

7. $\dfrac{1}{3}, 1, 3, 9, \ldots$

8. $\dfrac{1}{4}, 2, 16, \ldots$

9. $64, 8, 1, \ldots$

10. $100, 10, 1, \ldots$

11. $8, -4, 2, -1, \ldots$

12. $-9, 3, -1, \ldots$

13. $2, -4, 8, -16, \ldots$

14. $-\dfrac{1}{2}, 2, -8, 32, \ldots$

15. $-\dfrac{1}{3}, -\dfrac{1}{4}, -\dfrac{3}{16}, \ldots$

16. $-\dfrac{1}{4}, -\dfrac{1}{5}, -\dfrac{4}{25}, \ldots$

Write the first five terms of the geometric sequence with the given nth term. See Example 3.

17. $a_n = 2\left(\dfrac{1}{3}\right)^{n-1}$

18. $a_n = -5\left(\dfrac{1}{2}\right)^{n-1}$

19. $a_n = (-2)^{n-1}$

20. $a_n = \left(-\dfrac{1}{3}\right)^{n-1}$

21. $a_n = 2^{-n}$

22. $a_n = 3^{-n}$

23. $a_n = (0.78)^n$

24. $a_n = (-0.23)^n$

Find the required part of each geometric sequence. See Example 4.

25. Find the first term of the geometric sequence that has fourth term 40 and common ratio 2.

26. Find the first term of the geometric sequence that has fifth term 4 and common ratio $\frac{1}{2}$.

27. Find r for the geometric sequence that has $a_1 = 6$ and $a_4 = \frac{2}{9}$.

28. Find r for the geometric sequence that has $a_1 = 1$ and $a_4 = -27$.

29. Find a_4 for the geometric sequence that has $a_1 = -3$ and $r = \frac{1}{3}$.

30. Find a_5 for the geometric sequence that has $a_1 = -\frac{2}{3}$ and $r = -\frac{2}{3}$.

Find the sum of each geometric series. See Examples 5 and 6.

31. $\frac{1}{2} + \frac{1}{4} + \frac{1}{8} + \cdots + \frac{1}{512}$

32. $1 + \frac{1}{3} + \frac{1}{9} + \cdots + \frac{1}{81}$

33. $\frac{1}{2} - \frac{1}{4} + \frac{1}{8} - \frac{1}{16} + \frac{1}{32}$

34. $3 - 1 + \frac{1}{3} - \frac{1}{9} + \frac{1}{27} - \frac{1}{81}$

35. $30 + 20 + \frac{40}{3} + \cdots + \frac{1280}{729}$

36. $9 - 6 + 4 - \cdots - \frac{128}{243}$

37. $\sum_{i=1}^{10} 5(2)^{i-1}$

38. $\sum_{i=1}^{7} (10{,}000)(0.1)^{i-1}$

39. $\sum_{i=1}^{6} (0.1)^i$

40. $\sum_{i=1}^{5} (0.2)^i$

41. $\sum_{i=1}^{6} 100(0.3)^i$

42. $\sum_{i=1}^{7} 36(0.5)^i$

Find the sum of each infinite geometric series. See Examples 7 and 8.

43. $\frac{1}{8} + \frac{1}{16} + \frac{1}{32} + \cdots$

44. $\frac{1}{9} + \frac{1}{27} + \frac{1}{81} + \cdots$

45. $3 + 2 + \frac{4}{3} + \cdots$

46. $2 + 1 + \frac{1}{2} + \cdots$

47. $4 - 2 + 1 - \frac{1}{2} + \cdots$

48. $16 - 12 + 9 - \frac{27}{4} + \cdots$

49. $\sum_{i=1}^{\infty} (0.3)^i$

50. $\sum_{i=1}^{\infty} (0.2)^i$

51. $\sum_{i=1}^{\infty} 3(0.5)^{i-1}$

52. $\sum_{i=1}^{\infty} 7(0.4)^{i-1}$

53. $\sum_{i=1}^{\infty} 3(0.1)^i$

54. $\sum_{i=1}^{\infty} 6(0.1)^i$

55. $\sum_{i=1}^{\infty} 12(0.01)^i$

56. $\sum_{i=1}^{\infty} 72(0.01)^i$

Use the ideas of geometric series to solve each problem. See Examples 9 and 10.

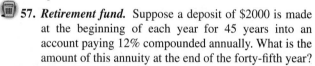

57. *Retirement fund.* Suppose a deposit of $2000 is made at the beginning of each year for 45 years into an account paying 12% compounded annually. What is the amount of this annuity at the end of the forty-fifth year?

58. *World's largest mutual fund.* If you had invested $5000 at the beginning of each year for the past 10 years in the Fidelity's Magellan Fund you would have averaged 12.46% compounded annually (www.fidelity.com). Find the amount of this annuity at the end of the tenth year.

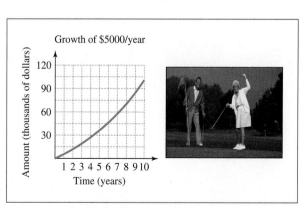

Growth of $5000/year

FIGURE FOR EXERCISE 58

59. *Big saver.* Suppose you deposit one cent into your piggy bank on the first day of December and, on each day of December after that, you deposit twice as much as on the previous day. How much will you have in the bank after the last deposit?

 60. *Big family.* Consider yourself, your parents, your grandparents, your great-grandparents, your great-great-grandparents, and so on, back to your grandparents with the word "great" used in front 40 times. What is the total number of people you are considering?

61. *Total economic impact.* In Exercise 43 of Section 13.1 we described a factory that spends $1 million annually in a community in which 80% of the money received is respent in the community. Economists assume the money is respent again and again at the 80% rate. The total economic impact of the factory is the total of all of this spending. Find an approximation for the total by using the formula for the sum of an infinite geometric series with a rate of 80%.

62. *Less impact.* Repeat Exercise 61, assuming money is respent again and again at the 50% rate.

GETTING MORE INVOLVED

 63. *Discussion.* Which of the following sequences is not a geometric sequence? Explain your answer.
a) 1, 2, 4, . . .
b) 0.1, 0.01, 0.001, . . .
c) −1, 2, −4, . . .
d) 2, 4, 6, . . .

 64. *Discussion.* The repeating decimal number 0.44444 . . . can be written as

$$\frac{4}{10} + \frac{4}{100} + \frac{4}{1000} + \cdots,$$

an infinite geometric series. Find the sum of this geometric series.

 65. *Discussion.* Write the repeating decimal number 0.24242424 . . . as an infinite geometric series. Find the sum of the geometric series.

In This Section

- Some Examples
- Obtaining the Coefficients
- The Binomial Theorem

13.5 BINOMIAL EXPANSIONS

In Chapter 5 you learned how to square a binomial. In this section you will study higher powers of binomials.

Some Examples

We know that $(x + y)^2 = x^2 + 2xy + y^2$. To find $(x + y)^3$, we multiply $(x + y)^2$ by $x + y$:

$$(x + y)^3 = (x^2 + 2xy + y^2)(x + y)$$
$$= (x^2 + 2xy + y^2)x + (x^2 + 2xy + y^2)y$$
$$= x^3 + 2x^2y + xy^2 + x^2y + 2xy^2 + y^3$$
$$= x^3 + 3x^2y + 3xy^2 + y^3$$

The sum $x^3 + 3x^2y + 3xy^2 + y^3$ is called the **binomial expansion** of $(x + y)^3$. If we again multiply by $x + y$, we will get the binomial expansion of $(x + y)^4$. This method is rather tedious. However, if we examine these expansions, we can find a pattern and learn how to find binomial expansions without multiplying.

Consider the following binomial expansions:

$$(x + y)^0 = 1$$
$$(x + y)^1 = x + y$$
$$(x + y)^2 = x^2 + 2xy + y^2$$
$$(x + y)^3 = x^3 + 3x^2y + 3xy^2 + y^3$$
$$(x + y)^4 = x^4 + 4x^3y + 6x^2y^2 + 4xy^3 + y^4$$
$$(x + y)^5 = x^5 + 5x^4y + 10x^3y^2 + 10x^2y^3 + 5xy^4 + y^5$$

Observe that the exponents on the variable x are decreasing, whereas the exponents on the variable y are increasing, as we read from left to right. Also notice that the sum of the exponents in each term is the same for that entire line. For instance, in the fourth expansion the terms x^4, x^3y, x^2y^2, xy^3, and y^4 all have exponents with a sum of 4. If we continue the pattern, the expansion of $(x + y)^6$ will have seven terms containing x^6, x^5y, x^4y^2, x^3y^3, x^2y^4, xy^5, and y^6. Now we must find the pattern for the coefficients of these terms.

Obtaining the Coefficients

If we write out only the coefficients of the expansions that we already have, we can easily see a pattern. This triangular array of coefficients for the binomial expansions is called **Pascal's triangle.**

$$
\begin{array}{ccccccccccc}
 & & & & & 1 & & & & & \\
 & & & & 1 & & 1 & & & & \\
 & & & 1 & & 2 & & 1 & & & \\
 & & 1 & & 3 & & 3 & & 1 & & \\
 & 1 & & 4 & & 6 & & 4 & & 1 & \\
1 & & 5 & & 10 & & 10 & & 5 & & 1
\end{array}
$$

$(x + y)^0 = 1$

$(x + y)^1 = 1x + 1y$

$(x + y)^2 = 1x^2 + 2xy + 1y^2$

$(x + y)^3 = 1x^3 + 3x^2y + 3xy^2 + 1y^3$

$(x + y)^4 = 1x^4 + 4x^3y + 6x^2y^2 + 4xy^3 + 1y^4$

Coefficients in $(x + y)^5$

Notice that each line starts and ends with a 1 and that each entry of a line is the sum of the two entries above it in the previous line. For instance, $4 = 3 + 1$, and $10 = 6 + 4$. Following this pattern, the sixth and seventh lines of coefficients are

$$
\begin{array}{ccccccccccccc}
1 & & 6 & & 15 & & 20 & & 15 & & 6 & & 1 \\
 & 1 & & 7 & & 21 & & 35 & & 35 & & 21 & & 7 & & 1
\end{array}
$$

Pascal's triangle gives us an easy way to get the coefficients for the binomial expansion with small powers, but it is impractical for larger powers. For larger powers we use a formula involving **factorial notation.**

n! (n factorial)

If n is a positive integer, $n!$ (read "n factorial") is defined to be the product of all of the positive integers from 1 through n.

Calculator Close-Up

You can evaluate the coefficients using either the factorial notation or $_nC_r$. The factorial symbol and $_nC_r$ are found in the MATH menu under PRB.

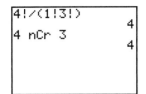

```
4!/(1!3!)
                    4
4 nCr 3
                    4
```

For example, $3! = 3 \cdot 2 \cdot 1 = 6$, and $5! = 5 \cdot 4 \cdot 3 \cdot 2 \cdot 1 = 120$. We also define 0! to be 1.

Before we state a general formula, consider how the coefficients for $(x + y)^4$ are found by using factorials:

$$\frac{4!}{4!\,0!} = \frac{4 \cdot 3 \cdot 2 \cdot 1}{4 \cdot 3 \cdot 2 \cdot 1 \cdot 1} = 1 \quad \text{Coefficient of } x^4 \text{ (or } x^4y^0)$$

$$\frac{4!}{3!\,1!} = \frac{4 \cdot 3 \cdot 2 \cdot 1}{3 \cdot 2 \cdot 1 \cdot 1} = 4 \quad \text{Coefficient of } 4x^3y$$

$$\frac{4!}{2!\,2!} = \frac{4 \cdot 3 \cdot 2 \cdot 1}{2 \cdot 1 \cdot 2 \cdot 1} = 6 \quad \text{Coefficient of } 6x^2y^2$$

$$\frac{4!}{1!\,3!} = \frac{4 \cdot 3 \cdot 2 \cdot 1}{1 \cdot 3 \cdot 2 \cdot 1} = 4 \quad \text{Coefficient of } 4xy^3$$

$$\frac{4!}{0!\,4!} = \frac{4 \cdot 3 \cdot 2 \cdot 1}{1 \cdot 4 \cdot 3 \cdot 2 \cdot 1} = 1 \quad \text{Coefficient of } y^4 \text{ (or } x^0y^4)$$

Note that each expression has 4! in the numerator, with factorials in the denominator corresponding to the exponents on x and y.

The Binomial Theorem

We now summarize these ideas in the **binomial theorem.**

The Binomial Theorem

In the expansion of $(x + y)^n$ for a positive integer n, there are $n + 1$ terms, given by the following formula:

$$(x + y)^n = \frac{n!}{n!\,0!}x^n + \frac{n!}{(n-1)!\,1!}x^{n-1}y + \frac{n!}{(n-2)!\,2!}x^{n-2}y^2 + \cdots + \frac{n!}{0!\,n!}y^n$$

The notation $\binom{n}{r}$ is often used in place of $\frac{n!}{(n-r)!r!}$ in the binomial expansion. Using this notation, we write the expansion as

$$(x + y)^n = \binom{n}{0}x^n + \binom{n}{1}x^{n-1}y + \binom{n}{2}x^{n-2}y^2 + \cdots + \binom{n}{n}y^n.$$

Another notation for $\frac{n!}{(n-r)!r!}$ is $_nC_r$. Using this notation, we have

$$(x + y)^n = {_nC_0}x^n + {_nC_1}x^{n-1}y + {_nC_2}x^{n-2}y^2 + \cdots + {_nC_n}y^n.$$

E X A M P L E   1

Calculating the binomial coefficients

Evaluate each expression.

a) $\dfrac{7!}{4!\,3!}$

b) $\dfrac{10!}{8!\,2!}$

Solution

a) $\dfrac{7!}{4!\,3!} = \dfrac{7 \cdot 6 \cdot 5 \cdot \cancel{4} \cdot \cancel{3} \cdot \cancel{2} \cdot \cancel{1}}{\cancel{4} \cdot \cancel{3} \cdot \cancel{2} \cdot \cancel{1} \cdot 3 \cdot 2 \cdot 1} = \dfrac{7 \cdot 6 \cdot 5}{3 \cdot 2 \cdot 1} = 35$

b) $\dfrac{10!}{8!\,2!} = \dfrac{10 \cdot 9 \cdot \cancel{8} \cdot \cancel{7} \cdot \cancel{6} \cdot \cancel{5} \cdot \cancel{4} \cdot \cancel{3} \cdot \cancel{2} \cdot \cancel{1}}{\cancel{8} \cdot \cancel{7} \cdot \cancel{6} \cdot \cancel{5} \cdot \cancel{4} \cdot \cancel{3} \cdot \cancel{2} \cdot \cancel{1} \cdot 2 \cdot 1} = \dfrac{10 \cdot 9}{2 \cdot 1} = 45$ ∎

E X A M P L E   2

Using the binomial theorem

Write out the first three terms of $(x + y)^9$.

Solution

$$(x + y)^9 = \dfrac{9!}{9!\,0!}x^9 + \dfrac{9!}{8!\,1!}x^8y + \dfrac{9!}{7!\,2!}x^7y^2 + \cdots = x^9 + 9x^8y + 36x^7y^2 + \cdots$$ ∎

E X A M P L E   3

Using the binomial theorem

Write the binomial expansion for $(x^2 - 2a)^5$.

Solution

We expand a difference by writing it as a sum and using the binomial theorem:

$$(x^2 - 2a)^5 = (x^2 + (-2a))^5$$

$$= \dfrac{5!}{5!\,0!}(x^2)^5 + \dfrac{5!}{4!\,1!}(x^2)^4(-2a)^1 + \dfrac{5!}{3!\,2!}(x^2)^3(-2a)^2 + \dfrac{5!}{2!\,3!}(x^2)^2(-2a)^3$$

$$+ \dfrac{5!}{1!\,4!}(x^2)(-2a)^4 + \dfrac{5!}{0!\,5!}(-2a)^5$$

$$= x^{10} - 10x^8a + 40x^6a^2 - 80x^4a^3 + 80x^2a^4 - 32a^5$$ ∎

E X A M P L E   4

Finding a specific term

Find the fourth term of the expansion of $(a + b)^{12}$.

Calculator Close-Up

Because $_nC_r = \dfrac{n!}{(n-r)!\,r!}$, we have

$_{12}C_9 = \dfrac{12!}{3!\,9!}$ and $_{12}C_3 = \dfrac{12!}{9!\,3!}$.

So there is more than one way to compute $12!/(9!\,3!)$:

```
12!/(9!3!)
                220
12 nCr 9
                220
12 nCr 3
                220
```

Solution

The variables in the first term are $a^{12}b^0$, those in the second term are $a^{11}b^1$, those in the third term are $a^{10}b^2$, and those in the fourth term are a^9b^3. So

$$\dfrac{12!}{9!\,3!}a^9b^3 = 220a^9b^3.$$

The fourth term is $220a^9b^3$.   ∎

   Using the ideas of Example 4, we can write a formula for any term of a binomial expansion.

> **Formula for the kth Term of $(x + y)^n$**
>
> For k ranging from 1 to $n + 1$, the kth term of the expansion of $(x + y)^n$ is given by the formula
>
> $$\dfrac{n!}{(n - k + 1)!\,(k - 1)!}x^{n-k+1}y^{k-1}.$$

E X A M P L E   5   **Finding a specific term**

Find the sixth term of the expansion of $(a^2 - 2b)^7$.

Solution

Use the formula for the kth term with $k = 6$ and $n = 7$:

$$\frac{7!}{(7 - 6 + 1)!(6 - 1)!}(a^2)^2(-2b)^5 = 21a^4(-32b^5) = -672a^4b^5 \quad \blacksquare$$

We can think of the binomial expansion as a finite series. Using summation notation, we can write the binomial theorem as follows.

The Binomial Theorem (Using Summation Notation)

For any positive integer n,

$$(x + y)^n = \sum_{i=0}^{n} \frac{n!}{(n - i)!i!}x^{n-i}y^i \quad \text{or} \quad (x + y)^n = \sum_{i=0}^{n}\binom{n}{i}x^{n-i}y^i.$$

E X A M P L E   6   **Using summation notation**

Write $(a + b)^5$ using summation notation.

Solution

Use $n = 5$ in the binomial theorem:

$$(a + b)^5 = \sum_{i=0}^{5} \frac{5!}{(5 - i)!i!}a^{5-i}b^i \quad \blacksquare$$

WARM-UPS

True or false? Explain your answer.

1. There are 12 terms in the expansion of $(a + b)^{12}$.
2. The seventh term of $(a + b)^{12}$ is a multiple of a^5b^7.
3. For all values of x, $(x + 2)^5 = x^5 + 32$.
4. In the expansion of $(x - 5)^8$ the signs of the terms alternate.
5. The eighth line of Pascal's triangle is
$$1\ 8\ 28\ 56\ 70\ 56\ 28\ 8\ 1.$$
6. The sum of the coefficients in the expansion of $(a + b)^4$ is 2^4.
7. $(a + b)^3 = \sum_{i=0}^{3} \frac{3!}{(3 - i)!\,i!}a^{3-i}b^i$
8. The sum of the coefficients in the expansion of $(a + b)^n$ is 2^n.
9. $0! = 1!$
10. $\dfrac{7!}{5!2!} = 21$

13.5   EXERCISES

Reading and Writing   *After reading this section, write out the answers to these questions. Use complete sentences.*

1. What is a binomial expansion?

2. What is Pascal's triangle and how do you make it?

3. What does $n!$ mean?

4. What is the binomial theorem?

Evaluate each expression. See Example 1.

5. $\dfrac{5!}{2!\,3!}$

6. $\dfrac{6!}{5!\,1!}$

7. $\dfrac{8!}{5!\,3!}$

8. $\dfrac{9!}{2!\,7!}$

Use the binomial theorem to expand each binomial. See Examples 2 and 3.

9. $(r + t)^5$

10. $(r + t)^6$

11. $(m - n)^3$

12. $(m - n)^4$

13. $(x + 2a)^3$

14. $(a + 3b)^4$

15. $\left(x^2 - 2\right)^4$

16. $\left(x^2 - a^2\right)^5$

17. $(x - 1)^7$

18. $(x + 1)^6$

Write out the first four terms in the expansion of each binomial. See Examples 2 and 3.

19. $(a - 3b)^{12}$

20. $(x - 2y)^{10}$

21. $\left(x^2 + 5\right)^9$

22. $\left(x^2 + 1\right)^{20}$

23. $(x - 1)^{22}$

24. $(2x - 1)^8$

25. $\left(\dfrac{x}{2} + \dfrac{y}{3}\right)^{10}$

26. $\left(\dfrac{a}{2} + \dfrac{b}{5}\right)^8$

Find the indicated term of the binomial expansion. See Examples 4 and 5.

27. $(a + w)^{13}$, 6th term

28. $(m + n)^{12}$, 7th term

29. $(m - n)^{16}$, 8th term

30. $(a - b)^{14}$, 6th term

31. $(x + 2y)^8$, 4th term

32. $(3a + b)^7$, 4th term

33. $(2a^2 - b)^{20}$, 7th term

34. $(a^2 - w^2)^{12}$, 5th term

Write each expansion using summation notation. See Example 6.

35. $(a + m)^8$

36. $(z + w)^{13}$

37. $(a - 2x)^5$

38. $(w - 3m)^7$

GETTING MORE INVOLVED

39. *Discussion.* Find the trinomial expansion for $(a + b + c)^3$ by using $x = a$ and $y = b + c$ in the binomial theorem.

40. *Discussion.* What problem do you encounter when trying to find the fourth term in the binomial expansion for $(x + y)^{120}$? How can you overcome this problem? Find the fifth term in the binomial expansion for $(x - 2y)^{100}$.

COLLABORATIVE ACTIVITIES

A Sequence of Investments can be Series(ous)

Grouping: 2 to 4 students per group

Topic: Sequences and series

Roberto, his brother Horatio, and his sister Genevieve each have a three-year-old child. Each would like to save money for his or her child's college expenses and decide to set aside $5 each week to the cause. Horatio plans to use his $5 to buy lottery tickets each week for the next 15 years, hoping to win and use the money for his child's college expenses. Genevieve plans to invest her $5 in a mutual fund and Roberto plans to invest in an education Individual Retirement Account (IRA).

1. Write the first 10 terms of the sequence in which the *n*th term is the total amount that Horatio has spent after *n* weeks. What type of sequence is this? How much money will Horatio spend on lottery tickets after 15 years? Assume that there are 52 weeks per year.

2. For every $5.00 Horatio spends each week on lottery tickets, his average winnings are $3.00 per week. He decides to buy a new certificate of deposit (CD) with his winnings at the end of each year. How much money will he put into a CD each year? At the end of the 15th year he has purchased 15 CDs.

Assume his CDs pay 3.75% annual interest compounded annually. Write a sequence of 15 terms that gives the amounts of each of the 15 CDs at the end of the 15th year. What type of sequence is this? Find the sum of the 15 terms.

3. Roberto sets aside $5 per week and pays into his IRA at the end of each quarter. The education IRA pays 4.5% annual interest compounded quarterly. Assume that there are 13 weeks per quarter. Determine the amount Roberto will have at the end of the 15 years.

4. Genevieve sets aside $5 per week and pays into her mutual fund at the end of each year. If her mutual fund pays 7.375% annual interest compounded annually, then what amount will Genevieve have at the end of the 15 years?

5. Discuss in your groups the amount of risk in each of the investment strategies. Do Horatio's chances increase the longer he buys lottery tickets? What should he do if he "wins big"? Are Genevieve's and Roberto's investment strategies sure things?

WRAP-UP CHAPTER 13

SUMMARY

Sequences and Series

		Examples
Sequence	Finite—A function whose domain is the set of positive integers less than or equal to a fixed positive integer	3, 5, 7, 9, 11 $a_n = 2n + 1$ $1 \le n \le 5$
	Infinite—A function whose domain is the set of positive integers	2, 4, 6, 8, ... $a_n = 2n$
Series	The indicated sum of a sequence	$2 + 4 + 6 + \cdots + 50$
Summation notation	$\displaystyle\sum_{i=1}^{n} a_i = a_1 + a_2 + a_3 + \cdots + a_n$	$\displaystyle\sum_{i=1}^{25} 2i = 2 + 4 + \cdots + 50$

Arithmetic Sequences and Series

		Examples
Arithmetic sequence	Each term after the first is obtained by adding a fixed amount to the previous term.	6, 11, 16, 21, ... Fixed amount, *d*, is 5.

nth term	The nth term of an arithmetic sequence is $a_n = a_1 + (n - 1)d$.	If $a_1 = 6$ and $d = 5$, then $a_n = 6 + (n - 1)5$.
Arithmetic series	The sum of an arithmetic sequence	$6 + 11 + 16 + 21$
Sum of first n terms	$S_n = \dfrac{n}{2}(a_1 + a_n)$	$S_4 = \dfrac{4}{2}(6 + 21) = 54$

Geometric Sequences and Series   **Examples**

Geometric sequence	Each term after the first is obtained by multiplying the preceding term by a constant.	$2, 6, 18, 54, \ldots$ Constant, r, is 3.
nth term	The nth term of a geometric sequence is $$a_n = a_1 r^{n-1}.$$	$a_1 = 2, r = 3$ $a_n = 2 \cdot 3^{n-1}$
Geometric series (finite)	The indicated sum of a finite geometric sequence. $a_1 + a_1 r + a_1 r^2 + \cdots + a_1 r^{n-1}$	$2 + 6 + 18 + 54 + 162$
Sum of first n terms	$S_n = \dfrac{a_1(1 - r^n)}{1 - r}$	$a_1 = 2, r = 3, n = 5$ $S_5 = \dfrac{2(1 - 3^5)}{1 - 3} = 242$
Geometric series (infinite)	$a_1 + a_1 r + a_1 r^2 + a_1 r^3 + \cdots$	$8 + 4 + 2 + 1 + \dfrac{1}{2} + \cdots$
Sum of an infinite geometric series	$S = \dfrac{a_1}{1 - r}$, provided that $|r| < 1$	$a_1 = 8, r = \dfrac{1}{2}$ $S = \dfrac{8}{1 - \dfrac{1}{2}} = 16$
Factorial notation	The notation $n!$ represents the product of the positive integers from 1 through n.	$5! = 5 \cdot 4 \cdot 3 \cdot 2 \cdot 1 = 120$
Binomial theorem	$(x + y)^n = \dfrac{n!}{n!\,0!}x^n + \dfrac{n!}{(n - 1)!\,1!}x^{n-1}y$ $+ \dfrac{n!}{(n - 2)!\,2!}x^{n-2}y^2 + \cdots + \dfrac{n!}{0!\,n!}y^n$ Using summation notation: $(x + y)^n = \displaystyle\sum_{i=0}^{n} \dfrac{n!}{(n - i)!\,i!} x^{n-i}y^i = \sum_{i=0}^{n} \binom{n}{i} x^{n-i}y^i$	$(x + y)^3 = x^3 + 3x^2 y$ $+ 3xy^2 + y^3$
kth term of $(x + y)^n$	$\dfrac{n!}{(n - k + 1)!(k - 1)!} x^{n-k+1}y^{k-1}$	Third term of $(a + b)^{10}$ is $\dfrac{10!}{8!\,2!}a^8 b^2 = 45a^8 b^2.$

ENRICHING YOUR MATHEMATICAL WORD POWER

For each mathematical term, choose the correct meaning.

1. **sequence**
    a. a list of numbers
    b. a procedure for getting the answer
    c. events that happen in order
    d. a linear function

2. **finite sequence**
    a. a short sequence
    b. a sequence of whole numbers
    c. a function whose domain is the set of positive integers
    d. a function whose domain is the set of positive integers less than or equal to a fixed positive integer

3. **infinite sequence**
    a. a short sequence
    b. a sequence of whole numbers
    c. a function whose domain is the set of positive integers
    d. a function whose domain is the set of positive integers less than or equal to a fixed positive integer

4. **series**
    a. a special sequence
    b. the indicated sum of the terms of a sequence
    c. a sequence of positive numbers
    d. a show with many episodes

5. **arithmetic sequence**
    a. a sequence in which each term after the first is obtained by adding a fixed amount to the previous term
    b. a sequence of fractions

c. a sequence found in arithmetic
d. a finite sequence

6. **geometric sequence**
    a. a sequence of rectangles
    b. a sequence of geometric formulas
    c. a sequence in which each term after the first is obtained by multiplying the preceding term by a constant
    d. a sequence in which the terms are geometric

7. **geometric series**
    a. a series of geometric shapes
    b. the indicated sum of an arithmetic sequence
    c. a series of ratios
    d. the indicated sum of a geometric sequence

8. **binomial expansion**
    a. the trinomial obtained when a binomial is stretched
    b. the expression obtained from raising a binomial to a whole number power
    c. the coefficients of a binomial
    d. the various powers of a binomial

9. **Pascal's triangle**
    a. an equilateral triangle
    b. a triangle formed by the graphs of three linear equations
    c. the right triangle in the Pythagorean theorem
    d. a triangular array of coefficients for the binomial expansions

10. **$n!$**
    a. the product of the positive integers from 1 through n
    b. the binomial coefficients
    c. the n vertices of Pascal's triangle
    d. 3.141592654

REVIEW EXERCISES

13.1 *List all terms of each finite sequence.*

1. $a_n = n^3$ for $1 \le n \le 5$

2. $b_n = (n - 1)^4$ for $1 \le n \le 4$

3. $c_n = (-1)^n(2n - 3)$ for $1 \le n \le 6$

4. $d_n = (-1)^{n-1}(3 - n)$ for $1 \le n \le 7$

Write the first three terms of the infinite sequence whose nth term is given.

5. $a_n = -\dfrac{1}{n}$

6. $b_n = \dfrac{(-1)^n}{n^2}$

7. $b_n = \dfrac{(-1)^{2n}}{2n + 1}$

8. $a_n = \dfrac{-1}{2n - 3}$

9. $c_n = \log_2(2^{n+3})$

10. $c_n = \ln(e^{2n})$

13.2 *Find the sum of each series.*

11. $\displaystyle\sum_{i=1}^{3} i^3$

12. $\displaystyle\sum_{i=0}^{4} 6$

13. $\displaystyle\sum_{n=1}^{5} n(n - 1)$

14. $\displaystyle\sum_{j=0}^{3} (-2)^j$

Write each series in summation notation. Use the index i, and let i begin at 1.

15. $\dfrac{1}{4} + \dfrac{1}{6} + \dfrac{1}{8} + \cdots$

16. $\dfrac{1}{3} + \dfrac{1}{4} + \dfrac{1}{5} + \cdots$

17. $0 + 1 + 4 + 9 + 16 + \cdots$

18. $-1 + 2 - 3 + 4 - 5 + 6 - \cdots$

19. $x_1 - x_2 + x_3 - x_4 + \cdots$

20. $-x^2 + x^3 - x^4 + x^5 - \cdots$

13.3 *Write the first four terms of the arithmetic sequence with the given nth term.*

21. $a_n = 6 + (n - 1)5$

22. $a_n = -7 + (n - 1)4$

23. $a_n = -20 + (n - 1)(-2)$

24. $a_n = 10 + (n - 1)(-2.5)$

25. $a_n = 1000n + 2000$

26. $a_n = -500n + 5000$

Write a formula for the nth term of each arithmetic sequence.

27. $\dfrac{1}{3}, \dfrac{2}{3}, 1, \dfrac{4}{3}, \ldots$

28. $10, 6, 2, -2, \ldots$

29. $2, 4, 6, 8, \ldots$

30. $20, 10, 0, -10, \ldots$

Find the sum of each arithmetic series.

31. $1 + 2 + 3 + \cdots + 24$

32. $-5 + (-2) + 1 + 4 + \cdots + 34$

33. $\dfrac{1}{6} + \dfrac{1}{2} + \dfrac{5}{6} + \dfrac{7}{6} + \cdots + \dfrac{11}{2}$

34. $-3 - 6 - 9 - 12 - \cdots - 36$

35. $\displaystyle\sum_{i=1}^{7} (2i - 3)$

36. $\displaystyle\sum_{i=1}^{6} [12 + (i - 1)5]$

13.4 *Write the first four terms of the geometric sequence with the given nth term.*

37. $a_n = 3\left(\dfrac{1}{2}\right)^{n-1}$

38. $a_n = 6\left(-\dfrac{1}{3}\right)^{n}$

39. $a_n = 2^{1-n}$

40. $a_n = 5(10)^{n-1}$

41. $a_n = 23(10)^{-2n}$

42. $a_n = 4(10)^{-n}$

Write a formula for the nth term of each geometric sequence.

43. $\dfrac{1}{2}, 3, 18, \ldots$

44. $-6, 2, -\dfrac{2}{3}, \dfrac{2}{9}, \ldots$

45. $\dfrac{7}{10}, \dfrac{7}{100}, \dfrac{7}{1000}, \ldots$

46. $2, 2x, 2x^2, 2x^3, \ldots$

Find the sum of each geometric series.

47. $\dfrac{1}{3} + \dfrac{1}{9} + \dfrac{1}{27} + \dfrac{1}{81}$

48. $2 + 4 + 8 + 16 + \cdots + 512$

49. $\displaystyle\sum_{i=1}^{10} 3(10)^{-i}$

50. $\displaystyle\sum_{i=1}^{5} (0.1)^i$

51. $\dfrac{1}{4} + \dfrac{1}{12} + \dfrac{1}{36} + \dfrac{1}{108} + \cdots$

52. $12 + (-6) + 3 + \left(-\dfrac{3}{2}\right) + \cdots$

53. $\displaystyle\sum_{i=1}^{\infty} 18\left(\dfrac{2}{3}\right)^{i-1}$

54. $\displaystyle\sum_{i=1}^{\infty} 9(0.1)^i$

13.5 *Use the binomial theorem to expand each binomial.*

55. $(m + n)^5$

56. $(2m - y)^4$

57. $(a^2 - 3b)^3$

58. $\left(\dfrac{x}{2} + 2a\right)^5$

Find the indicated term of the binomial expansion.

59. $(x + y)^{12}$, 5th term

60. $(x - 2y)^9$, 5th term

61. $(2a - b)^{14}$, 3rd term

62. $(a + b)^{10}$, 4th term

Write each expression in summation notation.

63. $(a + w)^7$

64. $(m - 3y)^9$

MISCELLANEOUS

Identify each sequence as an arithmetic sequence, a geometric sequence, or neither.

65. $1, 3, 6, 10, 15, \ldots$

66. $9, 12, 16, \dfrac{64}{3}, \ldots$

67. 9, 12, 15, 18, . . .   **68.** 2, 4, 8, 16, . . .

69. 0, 2, 4, 6, 8, . . .   **70.** 0, 3, 9, 27, 81, . . .

Solve each problem.

71. Find the common ratio for the geometric sequence with first term 6 and fourth term $\frac{1}{30}$.

72. Find the common difference for an arithmetic sequence with first term 6 and fourth term 36.

73. Write out all of the terms of the series
$$\sum_{i=1}^{5} \frac{(-1)^i}{i!}.$$

74. Write out the first eight rows of Pascal's triangle.

75. Write out all of the terms of the series
$$\sum_{i=0}^{5} \frac{5!}{(5-i)!\,i!} a^{5-i} b^i.$$

76. Write out all of the terms of the series
$$\sum_{i=0}^{8} \frac{8!}{(8-i)!\,i!} x^{8-i} y^i.$$

77. How many terms are there in the expansion of $(a + b)^{25}$?

78. Calculate $\frac{12!}{8!4!}$.

79. If \$3000 is deposited at the beginning of each year for 16 years into an account paying 10% compounded annually, then what is the value of the annuity at the end of the 16th year?

80. If \$3000 is deposited at the beginning of each year for 8 years into an account paying 10% compounded annually, then what is the value of the annuity at the end of the eighth year? How does the value of the annuity in this exercise compare to that of Exercise 79?

81. If one deposit of \$3000 is made into an account paying 10% compounded annually, then how much will be in the account at the end of 16 years? Note that a single deposit is not an annuity.

CHAPTER 13 TEST

List the first four terms of the sequence whose nth term is given.

1. $a_n = -10 + (n - 1)6$ **2.** $a_n = 5(0.1)^{n-1}$

3. $a_n = \frac{(-1)^n}{n!}$ **4.** $a_n = \frac{2n - 1}{n^2}$

Write a formula for the nth term of each sequence.

5. 7, 4, 1, −2, . . .

6. −25, 5, −1, $\frac{1}{5}$, . . .

7. 2, −4, 6, −8, 10, −12, . . .

8. 1, 4, 9, 16, 25, . . .

Write out all of the terms of each series.

9. $\sum_{i=1}^{5} (2i + 3)$

10. $\sum_{i=1}^{6} 5(2)^{i-1}$

11. $\sum_{i=0}^{4} \frac{4!}{(4-i)!\,i!} m^{4-i} q^i$

Find the sum of each series.

12. $\sum_{i=1}^{20} (6 + 3i)$ **13.** $\sum_{i=1}^{5} 10 \left(\frac{1}{2}\right)^{i-1}$

14. $\sum_{i=1}^{\infty} 0.35(0.93)^{i-1}$

15. $2 + 4 + 6 + \cdots + 200$

16. $\frac{1}{4} + \frac{1}{8} + \frac{1}{16} + \cdots$

17. $2 + 1 + \frac{1}{2} + \frac{1}{4} + \cdots + \frac{1}{128}$

Solve each problem.

18. Find the common ratio for the geometric sequence that has first term 3 and fifth term 48.

19. Find the common difference for the arithmetic sequence that has first term 1 and twelfth term 122.

20. Find the fifth term in the expansion of $(r - t)^{15}$.

21. Find the fourth term in the expansion of $(a^2 - 2b)^8$.

22. If \$800 is deposited at the beginning of each year for 25 years into an account earning 10% compounded annually, then what is the value of this annuity at the end of the 25th year?

Let $f(x) = x^2 - 3$, $g(x) = 2x - 1$, $h(x) = 2^x$, and $m(x) = \log_2(x)$. Find the following.

1. $f(3)$

2. $f(n)$

3. $f(x + h)$

4. $f(x) - g(x)$

5. $g(f(3))$

6. $(f \circ g)(2)$

7. $m(16)$

8. $(h \circ m)(32)$

9. $h(-1)$

10. $h^{-1}(8)$

11. $m^{-1}(0)$

12. $(m \circ h)(x)$

Solve each variation problem.

13. If y varies directly as x, and $y = -6$ when $x = 4$, find y when $x = 9$.

14. If a varies inversely as b, and $a = 2$ when $b = -4$, find a when $b = 3$.

15. If y varies directly as w and inversely as t, and $y = 16$ when $w = 3$ and $t = -4$, find y when $w = 2$ and $t = 3$.

16. If y varies jointly as h and the square of r, and $y = 12$ when $h = 2$ and $r = 3$, find y when $h = 6$ and $r = 2$.

Sketch the graph of each inequality or system of inequalities.

17. $x > 3$ and $x + y < 0$

18. $|x - y| \geq 2$

19. $y < -2x + 3$ and $y > 2^x$

20. $|y + 2x| < 1$

21. $x^2 + y^2 < 4$

22. $x^2 - y^2 < 1$

23. $y < \log_2(x)$

24. $x^2 + 2y < 4$

25. $\dfrac{x^2}{4} + \dfrac{y^2}{9} < 1$ and $y > x^2$

Perform the indicated operation and simplify. Write answers with positive exponents.

26. $\dfrac{a}{b} + \dfrac{b}{a}$

27. $1 - \dfrac{3}{y}$

28. $\dfrac{x-2}{x^2-9} - \dfrac{x-4}{x^2-2x-3}$

29. $\dfrac{x^2-16}{2x+8} \cdot \dfrac{4x^2+16x+64}{x^3-16}$

30. $\dfrac{(a^2b)^3}{(ab^2)^4} \cdot \dfrac{ab^3}{a^{-4}b^2}$

31. $\dfrac{x^2y}{(xy)^3} \div \dfrac{xy^2}{x^2y^4}$

Simplify.

32. $8^{2/3}$

33. $16^{-5/4}$

34. $-4^{1/2}$

35. $27^{-2/3}$

36. -2^{-3}

37. $2^{-3/5} \cdot 2^{-7/5}$

38. $5^{-2/3} \div 5^{1/3}$

39. $(9^{1/2} + 4^{1/2})^2$

Solve.

40. ***Predicting heights of preschoolers.*** A popular model in pediatrics for predicting the height of preschoolers is the JENNS model. According to this model, if $h(x)$ is the height [in centimeters (cm)] at age x (in years) for $0.25 \le x \le 6$, then
$$h(x) = 79.041 + 6.39x - e^{(3.261-0.993x)}.$$

a) Find the predicted height in inches for a child of age 4 years, 3 months.

b) If you have a graphing calculator, graph the function as shown in the accompanying figure.

c) Use your graphing calculator to find the age to the nearest tenth of a year for a child who has a height of 80 cm.

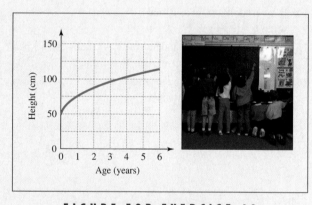

FIGURE FOR EXERCISE 40

Counting and Probability

L otteries and gaming are as old as history records. Homer described how Agamemnon had his soldiers cast lots to see who would face Hector. In the Bible, Moses divided the lands among the tribes by casting lots.

Today 36 of the 50 states have lotteries and they are prosperous. Nationwide, state-run lotteries generate $26.6 billion in income annually—sales minus commissions. Available proceeds—money left over for the states after paying out prizes and paying for administration of the games totals $10.1 billion.

But what are your chances of winning a lottery? In this chapter we will study the basic ideas of counting and probability. We will find the probability of winning a lottery when we do Exercises 43 and 44 in Section 14.3.

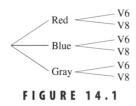

FIGURE 14.1

14.1 COUNTING AND PERMUTATIONS

Although the main topic of this chapter is probability, we first study counting. We all know how to count, but here we will learn methods for counting the number of ways in which a sequence of events can occur.

The Fundamental Counting Principle

A new car is available in 3 different colors with 2 optional engines, V6 or V8. For example, you can get a red car with a V6 engine or a red car with a V8 engine. If the car comes in red, blue, or gray, then how many different cars are available? We can make a diagram showing all of the different possibilities. See Fig. 14.1. This diagram is called a **tree diagram.** Considering only color and engine type, we count 6 different cars that are available from the tree diagram. Of course, we can obtain 6 by multiplying 3 and 2. This example illustrates the fundamental counting principle.

> **Fundamental Counting Principle**
>
> If event A has m different outcomes and event B has n different outcomes, then there are mn different ways for events A and B to occur.

The fundamental counting principle can also be used for more than two events.

EXAMPLE 1

The fundamental counting principle

At Windy's Hamburger Palace you can get a single, double, or triple burger. You also have a choice of whether to include pickles, mustard, ketchup, onions, tomatoes, lettuce, or cheese. How many different hamburgers are available at Windy's?

Solution

There are 3 outcomes to the event of choosing the amount of meat. For each of the condiments there are 2 outcomes: whether or not to include it. So the number of different hamburgers is $3 \cdot 2 \cdot 2 \cdot 2 \cdot 2 \cdot 2 \cdot 2 \cdot 2 = 384$. ∎

Helpful Hint

When counting the number of different possibilities, it must be clear what "different" means. In one problem we might count a hamburger and fries differently from fries and a hamburger because we are interested in the order in which they occur. In another problem we will consider them as the same because they are the same meal.

EXAMPLE 2

The fundamental counting principle

How many different license plates are possible if each plate consists of 2 letters followed by a 4-digit number? Assume repetitions in the letters or numbers are allowed and any of the 10 digits may be used in each place of the 4-digit number.

Solution

Since there are 26 choices for each of the 2 letters and 10 choices for each of the numbers, by the fundamental counting principle the number of license plates is $26 \cdot 26 \cdot 10 \cdot 10 \cdot 10 \cdot 10 = 6,760,000$. ∎

Permutations

The number of ways in which an event can occur often depends on what has already occurred. In Examples 1 and 2 each choice was independent of the previous choices. In Example 3 we will count permutations in which the number of choices depends on what has already been chosen. A **permutation** is any ordering or arrangement of distinct objects in a linear manner.

EXAMPLE 3

Permutations of *n* objects

How many different ways are there for 10 people to stand in line to buy basketball tickets?

Solution

For the event of choosing the first person in line we have 10 outcomes. For the event of choosing the second person to put in line only 9 people are left, so we have only 9 outcomes. For the third person we have 8 outcomes, and so on. So the number of permutations of 10 people is $10 \cdot 9 \cdot 8 \cdot 7 \cdot 6 \cdot 5 \cdot 4 \cdot 3 \cdot 2 \cdot 1 = 10! = 3{,}628{,}800$. ∎

Calculator Close-Up

You can use factorial notation on a calculator or the calculator's built-in formula for permutations to find $P(10, 3)$.

```
10!/7!
              720
10 nPr 3
              720
```

The number of arrangements of the 10 people in Example 3 is referred to as the number of permutations of 10 people taken 10 at a time, and we use the notation $P(10, 10)$ to represent this number. We have the following theorem.

> **Permutations of *n* Things *n* at a Time**
>
> The notation $P(n, n)$ represents the number of permutations of *n* things taken *n* at a time, and $P(n, n) = n!$.

Sometimes we are interested in permutations in which all of the objects are not used. For example, how many ways are there to fill the offices of president, vice-president, and treasurer in a club of 10 people, assuming no one holds more than one office? For the event of choosing the president there are 10 possible outcomes. Since no one can hold 2 offices, there are only 9 possibilities for vice-president, and only 8 possibilities for treasurer. So the number of ways to fill the offices is $10 \cdot 9 \cdot 8 = 720$. We say that the number of permutations of 10 people taken 3 at a time is 720. We use the notation $P(10, 3)$ to represent the number of permutations of 10 things taken 3 at a time. Notice that

$$P(10, 3) = \frac{10!}{7!} = \frac{\mathbf{10 \cdot 9 \cdot 8} \cdot 7 \cdot 6 \cdot 5 \cdot 4 \cdot 3 \cdot 2 \cdot 1}{7 \cdot 6 \cdot 5 \cdot 4 \cdot 3 \cdot 2 \cdot 1} = 10 \cdot 9 \cdot 8 = 720.$$

In general, we have the following theorem.

Study Tip

Be sure to ask your instructor what to expect on the final exam. Will it be written in the same format as the other tests? Will it be multiple choice? Are there any sample final exams available? Knowing what to expect will decrease your anxiety about the final exam.

> **Permutations of *n* Things *r* at a Time**
>
> The notation $P(n, r)$ represents the number of permutations of *n* things taken *r* at a time, and $P(n, r) = \frac{n!}{(n-r)!}$ for $0 \leq r \leq n$.

Even though we do not usually take *n* things 0 at a time, we allow 0 in the formula. For example,

$$P(8, 0) = \frac{8!}{8!} = 1 \qquad \text{and} \qquad P(0, 0) = \frac{0!}{0!} = \frac{1}{1} = 1.$$

EXAMPLE 4 **Permutations of *n* things *r* at a time**

Eight prize winners will be randomly selected from 25 people attending a sales meeting. There will be a first, second, third, fourth, fifth, sixth, seventh, and eighth prize, each prize being of lesser value than the one before it. In how many different ways can the prizes be awarded, assuming no one gets more than one prize?

Solution

The number of ways in which these prizes can be awarded is precisely the number of permutations of 25 things taken 8 at a time,

$$P(25, 8) = \frac{25!}{(25 - 8)!} = \frac{25!}{17!} = 25 \cdot 24 \cdot 23 \cdot 22 \cdot 21 \cdot 20 \cdot 19 \cdot 18$$
$$\approx 4.3609 \times 10^{10}.$$

■

WARM-UPS

True or false? Explain your answer.

1. If a manufacturer codes its products using a single letter followed by a single-digit number (0–9), then 36 different codes are available.

2. If a sorority name consists of 3 Greek letters chosen from the 24 letters in the Greek alphabet, with repetitions allowed, then $24 \cdot 23 \cdot 22$ different sorority names are possible.

3. If an outfit consists of a skirt, a blouse, and a hat and Mirna has 4 skirts, 5 blouses, and 4 hats, then she has 80 different outfits in her wardrobe.

4. The number of ways in which 4 people can line up for a group photo is 24.

5. $\frac{100!}{98!} = 9900$

6. $P(100, 98) = 9900$

7. The number of permutations of 5 things taken 2 at a time is 20.

8. $P(18, 0) = 1$

9. The number of different ways to mark the answers to a 10-question multiple-choice test in which each question has 5 choices is 10^5.

10. The number of different ways to mark the answers to this sequence of 10 Warm-up questions is 2^{10}.

14.1 EXERCISES

Reading and Writing *After reading this section, write out the answers to these questions. Use complete sentences.*

1. What is a tree diagram?

2. What is the fundamental counting principle?

3. What is a permutation?

4. How many permutations are there for *n* things taken *r* at a time?

Solve each problem. See Examples 1 and 2.

5. A parcel delivery truck can take any one of 3 different roads from Clarksville to Leesville and any one of 4 different roads from Leesville to Jonesboro. How many different routes are available from Clarksville to Jonesboro?

6. A car can be ordered in any one of 8 different colors, with 3 different engine sizes, 2 different transmissions, 3 different body styles, 4 different interior designs, and 5 different stereos. How many different cars are available?

7. A poker hand consists of 5 cards drawn from a deck of 52. How many different poker hands are there consisting of an ace, king, queen, jack, and ten?

FIGURE FOR EXERCISE 7

8. A certain card game consists of 3 cards drawn from a poker deck of 52. How many different 3-card hands are there containing one heart, one diamond, and one club?

9. Wendy's Hamburgers once advertised that there were 256 different hamburgers available at Wendy's. This number was obtained by using the fundamental counting principle and considering whether to include each one of several different options on the burger. How many different optional items were used to get this number?

10. A pizza can be ordered with your choice of one of 4 different meats or no meat. You also have a choice of whether to include green peppers, onions, mushrooms, anchovies, or black olives. How many different pizzas can be ordered?

Solve each problem. See Examples 3 and 4.

11. Randall has homework in mathematics, history, art, literature, and chemistry but cannot decide in which order to attack these subjects. How many different orders are possible?

12. Zita has packages to pick up at 8 different locations. How many different ways are there for her to pick up the packages?

13. Yesha has 12 schools to visit this week. In how many different ways can she pick a first, second, and third school to visit on Monday?

14. In how many ways can a history professor randomly assign exactly one A, and B, one C, one D, and six F's to a class of 10 students?

15. The program director for an independent television station has 34 one-hour shows available for Monday night prime time. How many different schedules are possible for the 7:00 to 10:00 P.M. time period?

16. A disc jockey must choose 8 songs from the top 40 to play in the next 30-minute segment of his show. How many different arrangements are possible for this segment?

Solve each counting problem.

17. How many different ways are there to mark the answers to a 20-question multiple-choice test in which each question has 4 possible answers?

18. A bookstore manager wants to make a window display that consists of a mathematics book, a history book, and an economics book in that order. He has 13 different mathematics books, 10 different history books, and 5 different economics books from which to choose. How many different displays are possible?

19. In how many ways can the 37 seats on a commuter flight be filled from the 39 people holding tickets?

20. If a couple has decided on 6 possible first names for their baby and 5 possible middle names, then how many ways are there for them to name their baby?

21. A developer builds houses with 3 different exterior styles. You have your choice of 3, 4, or 5 bedrooms, a fireplace, 2 or 3 baths, and 5 different kitchen designs. How many different houses are available?

22. How many different seven-digit phone numbers are available in Wentworth if the first 3 digits must be 286?

23. How many different seven-digit phone numbers are available in Creekside if the first digit cannot be a 0?

24. In how many different ways can a Mercedes, a Cadillac, and a Ford be awarded to 3 people chosen from the 9 finalists in a contest?

FIGURE FOR EXERCISE 10

25. How many different ways are there to seat 7 students in a row?

FIGURE FOR EXERCISE 25

26. A supply boat must stop at 9 oil rigs in the Gulf of Mexico. How many different routes are possible?

27. How many different license plates can be formed by using 3 digits followed by a single letter followed by 3 more digits? How many if the single letter can occur anywhere except last?

28. How many different license plates can be formed by using any 3 letters followed by any 3 digits? How many if we allow either the 3 digits or the 3 letters to come first?

29. Make a list of all of the subsets of the set $\{a, b, c\}$. How many are there?

30. Use the fundamental counting principle to find the number of subsets of the set $\{a, b, c, d, e, f\}$.

31. How many ways are there to mark the answers to a test that consists of 10 true-false questions followed by 10 multiple-choice questions with 5 options each?

32. A fraternity votes on whether to accept each of 5 pledges. How many different outcomes are possible for the vote?

33. Make a list of all of the ways to arrange the letters in the word MILK. How many arrangements should be in your list?

34. Make a list of all of the permutations of the letters A, B, C, D, and E taken 3 at a time. How many permutations should be in your list?

Evaluate each expression.

35. $P(8, 3)$ **36.** $P(17, 4)$ **37.** $P(52, 0)$ **38.** $P(34, 1)$

39. $\dfrac{P(10, 4)}{4!}$ **40.** $\dfrac{P(8, 3)}{3!}$ **41.** $\dfrac{P(12, 3)}{3!}$ **42.** $\dfrac{P(15, 6)}{6!}$

43. $\dfrac{14!}{3! \, 11!}$ **44.** $\dfrac{18!}{17! \, 1!}$ **45.** $\dfrac{98!}{95! \, 3!}$ **46.** $\dfrac{87!}{83! \, 4!}$

14.2 COMBINATIONS

In Section 14.1 we learned the fundamental counting principle and applied it to finding the number of permutations of *n* objects taken *r* at a time. We will now learn how to count the number of combinations of *n* objects taken *r* at a time.

Combinations of *n* Things *r* at a Time

Consider the problem of awarding 2 identical scholarships to 2 students among 4 finalists: Ahmadi, Butler, Chen, and Davis. Since the scholarships are identical, we do not count Ahmadi and Butler as different from Butler and Ahmadi. We can easily list all possible choices of 2 students from the 4 possibilities A, B, C, and D:

$$\{A, B\} \quad \{A, C\} \quad \{A, D\} \quad \{B, C\} \quad \{B, D\} \quad \{C, D\}$$

It is convenient to use set notation to list these choices because in set notation we have $\{A, B\} = \{B, A\}$. Actually, we want the number of subsets or **combinations** of size 2 from a set of 4 elements. This number is referred to as the number of combinations of 4 things taken 2 at a time, and we use the notation $C(4, 2)$ to represent it. We have $C(4, 2) = 6$.

If we had a first and second prize to give to 2 of 4 finalists, then $P(4, 2) = 4 \cdot 3 = 12$ is the number of ways to award the prizes. If the prizes are identical, then we do not count AB as different from BA, or AC as different from CA, and so on. So we divide $P(4, 2)$ by $2!$, the number of permutations of the 2 prize winners, to get $C(4, 2)$.

In general, the number of subsets of size r taken from a set of size n can be found by dividing $P(n, r)$ by $r!$:

$$C(n, r) = \frac{P(n, r)}{r!}$$

Since $P(n, r) = \frac{n!}{(n - r)!}$, we can write this expression as follows:

$$C(n, r) = \frac{P(n, r)}{r!} = \frac{\dfrac{n!}{(n - r)!}}{r!} = \frac{n!}{(n - r)!\, r!}$$

The notation $\binom{n}{r}$ is also used for $C(n, r)$. We summarize these results in the following theorem.

> **Combinations of n Things r at a Time**
>
> The number of combinations of n things taken r at a time (or the number of subsets of size r from a set of n elements) is given by the formula
>
> $$C(n, r) = \binom{n}{r} = \frac{n!}{(n - r)!\, r!} \qquad \text{for} \qquad 0 \le r \le n.$$

E X A M P L E   1

Combinations of n things r at a time

In how many ways can a committee of 4 people be chosen from a group of 12?

Solution

Choosing 4 people from a group of 12 is the same as choosing a subset of size 4 from a set of 12 elements. So the number of ways to choose the committee is the number of combinations of 12 things taken 4 at a time:

$$C(12, 4) = \frac{12!}{8!\,4!} = \frac{12 \cdot 11 \cdot 10 \cdot 9 \cdot 8 \cdot 7 \cdot 6 \cdot 5 \cdot 4 \cdot 3 \cdot 2 \cdot 1}{8 \cdot 7 \cdot 6 \cdot 5 \cdot 4 \cdot 3 \cdot 2 \cdot 1 \cdot 4 \cdot 3 \cdot 2 \cdot 1} = 495 \qquad ■$$

E X A M P L E   2

Finding a binomial coefficient

What is the coefficient of $a^4 b^2$ in the binomial expansion of $(a + b)^6$?

Calculator Close-Up

You can use factorial notation to calculate $C(12, 4)$ or your calculator's built-in formula for combinations. With factorial notation you must use parentheses around the denominator.

```
12!/(8!*4!)
            495
12 nCr 4
            495
```

Solution

Write $(a + b)^6 = (a + b)(a + b)(a + b)(a + b)(a + b)(a + b)$. The terms of the product come from all of the different ways there are to select either a or b from each of the 6 factors and to multiply the selections. The number of ways to pick 4 factors for the selection of a is $C(6, 4) = \frac{6!}{2!\,4!} = 15$. From the remaining 2 we select b. So in the binomial expansion of $(a + b)^6$ we find the term $15a^4 b^2$. ■

Note that as in Example 2, the coefficients of the terms in any binomial expansion are combinations. The coefficient of $a^r b^{n-r}$ in $(a + b)^n$ is $C(n, r)$.

Permutations, Combinations, or Neither

How do you know when to use the permutation formula and when to use the combination formula? The key to answering this question is understanding what each formula counts. In either case we are choosing from a group of distinct objects. Compare the following examples.

EXAMPLE 3

Permutations of *n* things *r* at a time

How many ways are there to choose a president, a vice-president, and a treasurer from a group of 9 people, assuming no one holds more than one office?

Solution

There are 9 choices for the president, 8 choices for the vice-president, and 7 choices for the treasurer. The number of ways to make these choices is $P(9, 3) = 9 \cdot 8 \cdot 7 = 504$. ■

Note that in Example 3 we are not just counting the number of ways to select 3 people from 9. In the number $P(9, 3)$ every permutation of the 3 people selected is counted.

EXAMPLE 4

Combinations of *n* things *r* at a time

How many ways are there to choose 3 people to receive a $100 prize from a group of 9, assuming no one receives more than one prize?

Solution

Since each person chosen from the 9 is given the same treatment, the number of choices is the same as the number of subsets of size 3 from a set of 9 elements.

$$C(9, 3) = \frac{9!}{6!\,3!} = \frac{9 \cdot 8 \cdot 7}{3 \cdot 2 \cdot 1} = 84.$$ ■

Note that in Example 4 we do not count different arrangements of the 3 people selected. Example 5 is neither a permutation nor a combination.

EXAMPLE 5

The fundamental counting principle

How many ways are there to answer a 9-question multiple-choice test in which each question has 3 possible answers?

Solution

There are 3 outcomes to the event of choosing the first answer, 3 outcomes to the event of choosing the second answer, and so on. By the fundamental counting principle there are $3^9 = 19,683$ ways to answer the 9 questions. ■

Note that in choosing the answer to each question in Example 5 we may repeat answers, so we are not choosing from a set of distinct objects as in permutations and combinations. In Example 6 we use both the fundamental counting principle and the permutation formula.

EXAMPLE 6

The fundamental counting principle and permutations

Josephine has 4 different mathematics books, 3 different art books, and 5 different music books that she plans to display on a shelf. If she plans to keep each type of book together and put the types in the order mathematics–art–music, then how many different arrangements are possible?

Helpful Hint

You cannot solve counting problems by picking out the numbers in the problem and performing a computation to get the answer. This approach to Example 5 will lead you to wrong answers, such as $\frac{9!}{3!6!}$, 9^3, or $3 \cdot 9$. You must think about the problem.

Solution

First observe that the mathematics books can be arranged in $P(4, 4) = 4! = 24$ ways, the art books in $P(3, 3) = 3! = 6$ ways, and the music books in $P(5, 5) = 5! = 120$ ways. Now we use the fundamental counting principle to get $24 \cdot 6 \cdot 120 = 17,280$ as the number of ways to arrange the books on the shelf. ∎

Labeling

In a labeling problem we count the number of ways to put labels on distinct objects.

E X A M P L E 7

The fundamental counting principle and combinations

Twelve students have volunteered to help clean up a small oil spill. The project director needs 3 bird washers, 4 rock wipers, and 5 sand cleaners. In how many ways can these jobs (labels) be assigned to these 12 students?

Solution

Since the 3 bird washers all get the same label, the number of ways to select the 3 students is $C(12, 3)$. The number of ways to select 4 rock wipers from the remaining 9 students is $C(9, 4)$. The number of ways to select the 5 sand cleaners from the remaining 5 students is $C(5, 5)$. By the fundamental counting principle the number of ways to make all 3 selections is

$$C(12, 3) \cdot C(9, 4) \cdot C(5, 5) = \frac{12!}{9!\,3!} \cdot \frac{9!}{5!\,4!} \cdot \frac{5!}{0!\,5!} = \frac{12!}{3!\,4!\,5!} = 27,720. \quad ∎$$

Note that in Example 7 there were 12 distinct objects to be labeled with 3 labels of one type, 4 labels of another type, and 5 labels of a third type, and the number of ways to assign those labels was found to be $\frac{12!}{3!\,4!\,5!}$. Instead of using combinations and the fundamental counting principle as in Example 7, we can use the following theorem.

> **Labeling**
>
> In a **labeling problem** n distinct objects are each to be given a label with each object getting exactly one label. If there are r_1 labels of the first type, r_2 labels of the second type, . . . , and r_k labels of the kth type, where $r_1 + r_2 + \cdots + r_k = n$, then the number of ways to assign the labels to the objects is $\frac{n!}{r_1!\,r_2! \cdots r_k!}$.

E X A M P L E 8

A labeling problem

How many different arrangements are there for the 11 letters in the word MISSISSIPPI?

Solution

This problem is a labeling problem if we think of the 11 positions for the letters as 11 distinct objects to be labeled. There are 1 M-label, 4 S-labels, 4 I-labels, and 2 P-labels. So the number of ways to arrange the letters in MISSISSIPPI is $\frac{11!}{1!\,4!\,4!\,2!} = 34,650$. ∎

EXAMPLE 9 **Coefficients in a trinomial expansion**

What is the coefficient of a^3b^2c in the expansion of $(a + b + c)^6$?

Solution

The terms of the product $(a + b + c)^6$ come from all of the different ways there are to select a, b, or c from each of the 6 distinct factors and to multiply the selections. The number of ways to pick 3 factors from which we select a, 2 factors from which we select b, and 1 factor from which we select c is $\frac{6!}{3!2!1!} = \frac{6 \cdot 5 \cdot 4 \cdot 3 \cdot 2 \cdot 1}{3 \cdot 2 \cdot 1 \cdot 2 \cdot 1 \cdot 1} = 60$. So in the expansion we have the term $60a^3b^2c$. ∎

The coefficients of the terms in an expansion such as that of Example 9 are called **multinomial coefficients.** Determining the coefficients is a labeling problem.

We may think of permutation and combination problems as being very different, but they are both labeling problems. For example, to find the number of subsets of size 3 from a set of size 5, we are assigning 3 I-labels and 2 O-labels (I for in and O for out) to the 5 distinct objects of the set. Note that $\frac{5!}{3!2!} = C(5, 3)$. To find the number of ways to give a **F**irst, **S**econd, and **T**hird prize to 3 of 10 people, we are assigning 1 F-label, 1 S-label, 1 T-label, and 7 N-labels (N for no prize) to the 10 distinct people. Note that $\frac{10!}{1!1!1!7!} = P(10, 3)$.

WARM-UPS

True or false? Explain your answer.

1. The number of ways to choose 2 questions to answer out of 3 questions on an essay test is $C(3, 2)$.

2. The number of ways to choose 1 question to omit out of 3 questions on an essay test is $C(3, 1)$.

3. $C(12, 4) = C(4, 12)$

4. $P(10, 6) < C(10, 6)$

5. There are $P(10, 3)$ ways to label randomly 3 of the top 10 restaurants in Philadelphia as "superior."

6. There are $\binom{20}{16}$ ways to select 4 of 20 students to stay after school.

7. $P(9, 4) = (4!) \cdot C(9, 4)$

8. $P(8, 3) = \binom{8}{5}$

9. $C(100, 1) = 100$

10. $\frac{8!}{1!1!1!5!} = P(8, 3)$

14.2 EXERCISES

Reading and Writing *After reading this section, write out the answers to these questions. Use complete sentences.*

1. What is a combination?

2. How many combinations are there for n things taken r at a time?

3. What is a labeling problem?

4. What are multinomial coefficients?

Solve each problem. See Examples 1 and 2.

5. How many 5-card poker hands are possible when you are dealt 5 cards from a deck of 52?

6. How many 13-card bridge hands are possible when you are dealt 13 cards from a deck of 52?

7. How many ways are there to select 3 candidates from the 5 finalists for an in-depth interview?

8. How many ways are there to select 12 welders to be laid off from 30 welders employed at the Ingalls Shipyard?

9. How many ways are there for a health inspector to select 5 restaurants to visit from a list of 20 restaurants?

10. The water inspector in drought-stricken Marin County randomly selects 10 homes for inspection from a list of 25 suspected violators of the rationing laws. How many ways are there to pick the 10 homes?

11. In the Florida Lottery you can win a lot of money for merely selecting 6 different numbers from the numbers 1 through 49. How many different ways are there to select the 6 numbers?

12. In the game Fantasy Five you can win by selecting 5 different numbers from the numbers 1 through 39. How many ways are there to select the 5 numbers?

13. What is the coefficient of $w^3 y^4$ in the expansion of $(w + y)^7$?

14. What is the coefficient of $a^5 z^9$ in the expansion of $(a + z)^{14}$?

Solve each problem. See Examples 3–5.

15. The Dean's Search Committee must choose 3 candidates from a list of 6 and rank them as first, second, and third. How many different outcomes are possible?

16. The Provost's Search Committee must choose 3 candidates from a list of 8 and submit the names to the president unranked. How many different outcomes are possible?

17. Charlotte must write on any 3 of the 8 essay questions on the final exam in History 201. How many ways are there for her to pick the questions?

18. How many ways are there for Murphy to mark the answers to 8 multiple-choice questions, each of which has 5 possible answers?

19. In how many different ways can Professor Reyes return his examination papers to a class of 12 students?

20. In how many different ways can Professor Lee return her examination papers to a class of 12 students if she always returns the best paper first and the worst paper last?

21. How many ways are there to select 5 seats from a 150-seat auditorium to be occupied by 5 plain-clothes officers?

22. For her final exam in Literature 302 Charlotte is allowed to omit any 5 of the 8 essay questions. How many ways are there for her to omit the 5 questions?

23. How many distinct chords (line segments with endpoints on the circle) are determined by 3 points lying on a circle? By 4 points? By 5 points? By n points?

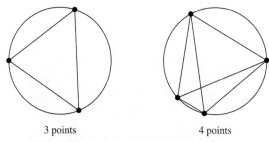

3 points   4 points

FIGURE FOR EXERCISE 23

24. How many distinct triangles are determined by 5 points lying on a circle, where the vertices of each triangle are chosen from the 5 points?

25. If the outcome of tossing a pair of dice is thought of as an ordered pair of numbers, then how many ordered pairs are there?

26. Francene is eligible to take 4 different mathematics classes, 5 different history classes, 6 different psychology classes, and 3 different literature classes. If her schedule is to consist of one class from each category, then how many different schedules are possible for her?

27. The outcome "heads" or "tails" is recorded on each toss of a coin. If we think of the outcome for 3 tosses as an ordered triple, then how many outcomes are there for 3 tosses of a coin?

28. A coin and a die are tossed. How many different outcomes are possible?

29. Explain why $C(n, r) = C(n, n - r)$.

30. Is $P(n, r) = P(n, n - r)$? Explain your answer.

Solve each problem. See Example 6.

31. Juanita is eligible to take 4 different mathematics classes and 5 different history classes. If her schedule is to consist of two classes from each category, then how many different schedules are possible for her?

32. A committee consisting of 2 men and 1 woman is to be formed from a department consisting of 8 men and 3 women. How many different committees are possible?

33. In a class of 20 students the teacher randomly assigns 4 A's, 5 B's, and 11 C's. In how many ways can these grades be assigned?

34. How many ways are there to seat 3 boys and 3 girls in a row with no 2 boys and no 2 girls sitting next to each other?

35. How many different orders are there for 4 marching bands and 4 floats to parade if a marching band must lead the parade and we cannot have 2 bands in a row or 2 floats in a row?

FIGURE FOR EXERCISE 35

36. In how many ways can 8 students be seated in a row if 2 of them must be seated next to one another?

Solve each problem. See Examples 7–9.

37. A teacher randomly assigns 6 A's, 3 B's, and 7 C's to a batch of 16 term papers. In how many different ways can she do this?

38. The 15 volunteers for the annual Bluegrass Festival are to be divided into 3 groups of 5 each and assigned to tickets, parking, and cleanup. In how many ways can these assignments be made?

39. Bob, Carol, Ted, and Alice are playing bridge. How many different ways are there to give each of them 13 cards from the deck of 52? Is the answer larger or smaller than the number of seconds in a trillion years?

40. Bret, Bart, and Mad Dog are playing poker. How many different ways are there to give each of them 5 cards from a deck of 52?

41. How many different arrangements are there for the letters in the word TOYOTA? ALGEBRA? STATISTICS?

42. How many different orders are possible for 3 identical contemporary, 4 identical traditional, and 6 identical colonial homes to march in a parade of homes?

43. Twenty salespeople are getting new cars. How many ways are there to assign 6 identical Chevrolets, 5 identical Fords, 8 identical Buicks, and 1 Lincoln to them?

44. Twenty different Fords are being sent to 4 Ford dealers. In how many ways can Bill Poole Ford get 3 cars, Heritage Ford get 5 cars, Mid-City Ford get 5 cars, and Northside Ford get 7 cars?

45. Nine sofas are to be discounted at Sofa City with discounts as large as 75% off the manufacturers suggested retail price. (Sorry, none sold to dealers.) How many ways are there to mark 4 of the sofas 10% off, 4 of them 15% off, and 1 of them 75% off?

46. A combination for a safe is a sequence of 4 numbers with no repetitions selected from the integers 1 through 99. How many combinations are possible? Is combination the proper word to use here?

FIGURE FOR EXERCISE 46

47. What is the coefficient of $a^3b^2c^5$ in the expansion of $(a + b + c)^{10}$?

48. What is the coefficient of $wx^2y^3z^9$ in the expansion of $(w + x + y + z)^{15}$?

49. What is the coefficient of a^3b^5 in the expansion of $(a + b + c)^8$?

50. What is the coefficient of x^2z^5 in the expansion of $(x + y + z)^7$?

14.3   PROBABILITY

In Sections 14.1 and 14.2 we were concerned with counting the number of different outcomes to an experiment. We now use those counting techniques to find probabilities.

The Probability of an Event

In probability an **experiment** is a process such as tossing a coin, tossing a die, drawing a poker hand from a deck, or arranging people in a line. A **sample space** is the set of all possible outcomes to an experiment. An **event** is a subset of a sample space. For example, if we toss a coin, then the sample space consists of two equally likely outcomes, heads and tails. We write $S = \{H, T\}$. The subset $E = \{H\}$ is the event of getting heads when the coin is tossed. We use $n(S)$ to represent the number of equally likely outcomes in the sample space S and $n(E)$ to represent the number of outcomes in the event E. For the example of tossing a coin, $n(S) = 2$ and $n(E) = 1$.

> **The Probability of an Event**
>
> If S is a sample space of equally likely outcomes to an experiment and the event E is a subset of S, then the probability of E, $P(E)$, is defined to be
>
> $$P(E) = \frac{n(E)}{n(S)}.$$

When $S = \{H, T\}$ and $E = \{H\}$,

$$P(E) = \frac{n(E)}{n(S)} = \frac{1}{2}.$$

So the probability of getting heads on a single toss of a coin is $\frac{1}{2}$. If E is the event of getting 2 heads on a single toss of a coin, then $n(E) = 0$ and $P(E) = \frac{0}{2} = 0$. If E is the event of getting fewer than 2 heads on a single toss of a coin, then for either outcome H or T we have fewer than 2 heads. So $E = \{H, T\}$, $n(E) = 2$, and $P(E) = \frac{2}{2} = 1$. Note that the probability of an event is a number between 0 and 1 inclusive, 1 being the probability of an event that is certain to occur and 0 being the probability of an event that is impossible to occur.

E X A M P L E   1

Rolling a die

What is the probability of getting a number larger than 4 when a single die is rolled?

Solution

When we roll a die, we count the number of dots showing on the upper face of the die. So the sample space of equally likely outcomes is $S = \{1, 2, 3, 4, 5, 6\}$. Since only 5 and 6 are larger than 4, $E = \{5, 6\}$. According to the definition of probability,

$$P(E) = \frac{n(E)}{n(S)} = \frac{2}{6} = \frac{1}{3}.$$

∎

MATH AT WORK

LOTTERIES

The probability experiments discussed in this chapter are not just textbook examples that have no relationship to real life. For example, if a couple plans to have 6 children and the probability of having a girl on each try is $\frac{1}{2}$, then the couple can expect to have 3 girls. If you guess at the answer to each question of a 100-question, 5-choice multiple-choice test, then you have $\frac{1}{5}$ probability of getting each question correct, and you can expect to get 20 questions correct. Try it. The expected number of successes is the product of the probability of success and the number of tries.

Lotteries provide us an opportunity to observe massive probability experiments. In the Florida Lottery you can win by choosing 6 numbers from the numbers 1 through 49 and matching the 6 numbers chosen by the Florida Lottery. There are $C(49, 6)$ ways to choose 6 numbers from 49, so the probability of winning on any individual try is

$$\frac{1}{C(49, 6)} = \frac{1}{13{,}983{,}816}.$$

In the fall of 1990 the weekly drawing frequently had relatively few participants, and consequently there was no winner for many weeks. When the prize got up to $106.5 million, the lottery got national attention. People came from everywhere to participate. During the week prior to September 15, 1990, 109,163,978 tickets were sold. We expected $\frac{1}{13{,}983{,}816} \cdot 109{,}163{,}978 = 7.8$ winners. On September 15 the winning numbers were announced, and 6 winners shared the prize. Of course, probability cannot predict the future like a fortune-teller, but the power of probability to tell us what to expect is truly amazing.

EXAMPLE 2 **Tossing coins**

What is the probability of getting at least one head when a pair of coins is tossed?

Solution

Since there are 2 equally likely outcomes for the first coin and 2 equally likely outcomes for the second coin, by the fundamental counting principle there are 4 equally likely outcomes to the experiment of tossing a pair of coins. We can list the outcomes as ordered pairs: $S = \{(H, H), (H, T), (T, H), (T, T)\}$. Since 3 of these outcomes result in at least one head, $E = \{(H, H), (H, T), (T, H)\}$, and $n(E) = 3$. So

$$P(E) = \frac{n(E)}{n(S)} = \frac{3}{4}.$$

∎

EXAMPLE 3 **Rolling a pair of dice**

What is the probability of getting a sum of 6 when a pair of dice is rolled?

Solution

Since there are 6 equally likely outcomes for each die, there are 36 equally likely outcomes to the experiment of rolling the pair. We can list the 36 outcomes as ordered pairs:

$$S = \{(1, 1), (1, 2), (1, 3), (1, 4), \mathbf{(1, 5)}, (1, 6),$$
$$(2, 1), (2, 2), (2, 3), \mathbf{(2, 4)}, (2, 5), (2, 6),$$
$$(3, 1), (3, 2), \mathbf{(3, 3)}, (3, 4), (3, 5), (3, 6),$$
$$(4, 1), \mathbf{(4, 2)}, (4, 3), (4, 4), (4, 5), (4, 6),$$
$$\mathbf{(5, 1)}, (5, 2), (5, 3), (5, 4), (5, 5), (5, 6),$$
$$(6, 1), (6, 2), (6, 3), (6, 4), (6, 5), (6, 6)\}$$

The sum of the numbers is 6, describes the event $E = \{(5, 1), (4, 2), (3, 3), (2, 4), (1, 5)\}$. So

$$P(E) = \frac{n(E)}{n(S)} = \frac{5}{36}.$$

The Addition Rule

In tossing a pair of dice, let A be the event that doubles occurs and B be the event that the sum is 4. We can list the following events and their probabilities:

$$A = \{(1, 1), (2, 2), (3, 3), (4, 4), (5, 5), (6, 6)\} \text{ and } P(A) = \frac{6}{36}$$
$$B = \{(3, 1), (2, 2), (1, 3)\} \text{ and } P(B) = \frac{3}{36}$$
$$A \cup B = \{(1, 1), (2, 2), (3, 3), (4, 4), (5, 5), (6, 6), (3, 1), (1, 3)\}$$
$$\text{and } P(A \cup B) = \frac{8}{36}$$
$$A \cap B = \{(2, 2)\} \text{ and } P(A \cap B) = \frac{1}{36}$$

Note that the probability of doubles or a sum of 4, $P(A \cup B)$, is $\frac{8}{36}$ and

$$\frac{8}{36} = \frac{6}{36} + \frac{3}{36} - \frac{1}{36}.$$

This equation makes sense because there is one outcome, (2, 2), that is in both the events A and B. This example illustrates the addition rule.

> **The Addition Rule**
>
> If A and B are any events in a sample space, then
>
> $$P(A \cup B) = P(A) + P(B) - P(A \cap B).$$
>
> If $P(A \cap B) = 0$, then A and B are called **mutually exclusive** events and
>
> $$P(A \cup B) = P(A) + P(B).$$

Note that for mutually exclusive events it is impossible for both events to occur. The addition rule for mutually exclusive events is a special case of the general addition rule.

E X A M P L E 4

The addition rule

At Downtown College 60% of the students are commuters (C), 50% are female (F), and 30% are female commuters. If a student is selected at random, what is the probability that the student is either a female or a commuter?

Solution

By the addition rule the probability of selecting either a female or a commuter is $P(F \cup C) = P(F) + P(C) - P(F \cap C) = 0.50 + 0.60 - 0.30 = 0.80$. ■

E X A M P L E 5

The addition rule with dice

In rolling a pair of dice, what is the probability that the sum is 12 or at least one die shows a 2?

Solution

Let A be the event that the sum is 12 and B be the event that at least one die shows a 2. Since A occurs on only one of the 36 equally likely outcomes (see Example 3), $P(A) = \frac{1}{36}$. Since B occurs on 11 of the equally likely outcomes, $P(B) = \frac{11}{36}$. Since A and B are mutually exclusive, we have

$$P(A \cup B) = P(A) + P(B)$$
$$= \frac{1}{36} + \frac{11}{36} = \frac{12}{36} = \frac{1}{3}.$$

■

Complementary Events

If the probability of rain today is 60%, then the probability that it does not rain is 40%. Rain and not rain are called complementary events. There is no possibility that both occur, and one of them must occur. If A is an event, then $\overline{A}$ (read "A bar" or "A complement") represents the complement of the event A. Note that complementary events are mutually exclusive, but mutually exclusive events are not necessarily complementary.

> **Complementary Events**
>
> Two events A and $\overline{A}$ are called **complementary events** if $A \cap \overline{A} = \varnothing$ and $P(A) + P(\overline{A}) = 1$.

E X A M P L E 6

Complementary events

What is the probability of getting a number less than or equal to 4 when rolling a single die?

Solution

We saw in Example 1 that getting a number larger than 4 when rolling a single die has probability $\frac{1}{3}$. The complement to getting a number larger than 4 is getting a number less than or equal to 4. So the probability of getting a number less than or equal to 4 is $\frac{2}{3}$. ■

EXAMPLE 7

Complementary events

If the probability that White Lightning will win the Kentucky Derby is 0.15, then what is the probability that White Lightning does not win the Kentucky Derby?

Solution

Let W be winning the Kentucky Derby and N be not winning the Kentucky Derby. Since W and N are complementary events, we have $P(W) + P(N) = 1$. So $P(N) = 1 - P(W) = 1 - 0.15 = 0.85$. ∎

Odds

If the probability is $\frac{2}{3}$ that the Giants win the Super Bowl and $\frac{1}{3}$ that they lose, then they are twice as likely to win as they are to lose. We say that the odds in favor of the Giants winning the Super Bowl are 2 to 1. Notice that odds are not probabilities. Odds are ratios of probabilities. We usually write odds as ratios of whole numbers.

> **Odds**
>
> If A is any event, then the **odds in favor of A** is the ratio $P(A)$ to $P(\overline{A})$ and the **odds against A** is the ratio of $P(\overline{A})$ to $P(A)$.

EXAMPLE 8

Determining odds

What are the odds in favor of getting a sum of 6 when rolling a pair of dice? What are the odds against a sum of 6?

Solution

In Example 3 we found the probability of a sum of 6 to be $\frac{5}{36}$. So the probability of the complement (the sum is not 6) is $\frac{31}{36}$. The odds in favor of getting a sum of 6 are $\frac{5}{36}$ to $\frac{31}{36}$. Multiply each fraction by 36 to get the odds 5 to 31. The odds against a sum of 6 are 31 to 5. ∎

EXAMPLE 9

Determining probability given the odds

If the odds in favor of Daddy's Darling winning the third race at Delta Downs are 4 to 1, then what is the probability that Daddy's Darling wins the third race?

Solution

Since 4 to 1 is the ratio of the probability of winning to not winning, the probability of winning is four times as large as the probability of not winning. Let $P(\overline{W}) = x$ and $P(W) = 4x$. Since $P(W) + P(\overline{W}) = 1$, we have $4x + x = 1$, or $5x = 1$, or $x = \frac{1}{5}$. So the probability of winning is $\frac{4}{5}$. ∎

We can write the idea found in Example 9 as a strategy for converting from odds to probabilities.

> **Strategy for Converting from Odds to Probability**
>
> If the odds in favor of event E are a to b, then
>
> $$P(E) = \frac{a}{a+b} \quad \text{and} \quad P(\overline{E}) = \frac{b}{a+b}.$$

WARM-UPS

True or false? Explain your answer.

1. If S is a sample space of equally likely outcomes and E is a subset of S, then $P(E) = n(E)$.

2. If an experiment consists of tossing 3 coins, then the sample space consists of 6 equally likely outcomes.

3. The probability of getting at least one tail when a coin is tossed twice is 0.75.

4. The probability of getting at least one 4 when a pair of dice is tossed is $\frac{11}{36}$.

5. The probability of getting at least one head when 5 coins are tossed is $\frac{33}{32}$.

6. If 3 coins are tossed, then getting exactly 3 heads and getting exactly 3 tails are complementary events.

7. If the probability of getting exactly 3 tails in a toss of 3 coins is $\frac{1}{8}$, then the probability of getting at least one head is $\frac{7}{8}$.

8. If the probability of snow today is 80%, then the odds in favor of snow are 8 to 10.

9. If the odds in favor of an event E are 2 to 3, then $P(E) = \frac{2}{3}$.

10. The ratio of $\frac{1}{2}$ to $\frac{1}{3}$ is equivalent to the ratio of 2 to 3.

14.3 EXERCISES

Reading and Writing *After reading this section, write out the answers to these questions. Use complete sentences.*

1. What is an experiment?

2. What is a sample space?

3. What is an event?

4. What is the probability of an event?

5. What is the addition rule?

6. What are the odds in favor of an event?

Solve each probability problem. See Examples 1–3.

7. If a single die is tossed, then what is the probability of getting
 a) a number larger than 3?
 b) a number less than or equal to 5?
 c) a number other than 6?
 d) a number larger than 7?
 e) a number smaller than 9?

8. If a single coin is tossed once, then what is the probability of getting
 a) tails?
 b) fewer than two heads?
 c) exactly three heads?

9. If a pair of coins is tossed, then what is the probability of getting
 a) exactly two heads?
 b) at least one tail?
 c) exactly two tails?
 d) at most one tail?

10. If a single coin is tossed twice, then what is the probability of getting
 a) heads followed by tails?
 b) two heads in a row?
 c) a tail on the second toss?
 d) exactly one tail?

11. If a pair of dice is tossed, then what is the probability of getting
 a) a pair of 2's?
 b) at least one 2?
 c) a sum of 7?
 d) a sum greater than 1?
 e) a sum less than 2?

12. If a single die is tossed twice, then what is the probability of getting
 a) a 1 followed by a 2?
 b) a sum of 3?
 c) a 6 on the second toss?
 d) no more than two 5's?
 e) an even number followed by an odd number?

13. A ball is selected at random from a jar containing 3 red balls, 4 yellow balls, and 5 green balls. What is the probability that
 a) the ball is red?
 b) the ball is not yellow?
 c) the ball is either red or green?
 d) the ball is neither red nor green?

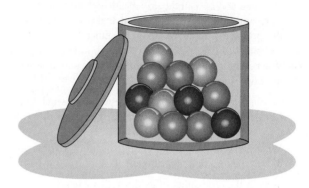

FIGURE FOR EXERCISE 13

14. A committee consists of 1 Democrat, 5 Republicans, and 6 independents. If one person is randomly selected from the committee to be the chairperson, then what is the probability that
 a) the person is a Democrat?
 b) the person is either a Democrat or a Republican?
 c) the person is not a Republican?

15. A jar contains 10 balls numbered 1 through 10. Two balls are randomly selected one at a time without replacement. What is the probability that
 a) 1 is selected first and 2 is selected second?
 b) the sum of the numbers selected is 3?
 c) the sum of the numbers selected is 6?

16. A small company consists of a president, a vice-president, and 14 salespeople. If 2 of the 16 people are randomly selected to win a Hawaiian vacation, then what is the probability that none of the salespeople is a winner?

17. If a 5-card poker hand is drawn from a deck of 52, then what is the probability that
 a) the hand contains the ace, king, queen, jack, and ten of spades?
 b) the hand contains one 2, one 3, one 4, one 5, and one 6?

18. If 5 people with different names and different weights randomly line up to buy concert tickets, then what is the

probability that

a) they line up in alphabetical order?

b) they line up in order of increasing weight?

Use the addition rule to solve each problem. See Examples 4 and 5.

19. Among the drivers insured by American Insurance, 65% are women, 38% of the drivers are in a high-risk category, and 24% of the drivers are high-risk women. If a driver is randomly selected from that company, what is the probability that the driver is either high-risk or a woman?

20. What is the probability of getting either a sum of 7 or at least one 4 in the toss of a pair of dice?

21. A couple plans to have 3 children. Assuming males and females are equally likely, what is the probability that they have either 3 boys or 3 girls.

22. What is the probability of getting a sum of 10 or a sum of 5 in the toss of a pair of dice?

23. What is the probability of getting either a heart or an ace when drawing a single card from a deck of 52 cards?

24. What is the probability of getting either a heart or a spade when drawing a single card from a deck of 52 cards?

Solve each problem. See Examples 6 and 7.

25. If the probability of surviving a head-on car accident at 55 mph is 0.005, then what is the probability of not surviving?

26. If the probability of a tax return not being audited by the IRS is 0.97, then what is the probability of a tax return being audited?

27. A pair of dice is tossed. What is the probability of

a) getting a pair of 4's?

b) not getting a pair of 4's?

c) getting at least one number that is not a 4?

28. Three coins are tossed. What is the probability of

a) getting three heads?

b) not getting three heads?

c) getting at least one tail?

Solve each problem. See Examples 8 and 9.

29. If the probability is 60% that the eye of Hurricane Edna comes ashore within 30 miles of Charleston, then what are the odds in favor of the eye of Edna coming ashore within 30 miles of Charleston?

30. If the probability that a Sidewinder missile hits its target is $\frac{8}{9}$, then what are the odds

a) in favor of the Sidewinder hitting its target?

b) against the Sidewinder hitting its target?

FIGURE FOR EXERCISE 29

31. If the probability that the stock market goes up tomorrow is $\frac{3}{5}$, then what are the odds

a) in favor of the stock market going up tomorrow?

b) against the stock market going up tomorrow?

32. If the probability of a coal miners' strike this year is $\frac{9}{10}$, then what are the odds

a) in favor of a strike?

b) against a strike?

33. If the odds are 3 to 1 in favor of the Black Hawks winning their next game, then

a) what are the odds against the Black Hawks winning their next game?

b) what is the probability that the Black Hawks win their next game?

34. If the odds are 5 to 1 against the Democratic presidential nominee winning the election, then

a) what are the odds in favor of the Democrat winning the election?

b) what is the probability that the Democrat wins the election?

35. What are the odds in favor of getting exactly 2 heads in 3 tosses of a coin?

36. What are the odds in favor of getting a 6 in a single toss of a die?

37. What are the odds in favor of getting a sum of 8 when tossing a pair of dice?

38. What are the odds in favor of getting at least one 6 when tossing a pair of dice?

FIGURE FOR EXERCISE 38

39. If one million lottery tickets are sold and only one of them is the winning ticket, then what are the odds in favor of winning if you hold a single ticket?

40. What are the odds in favor of winning a lottery where you must choose 6 numbers from the numbers 1 through 49?

41. If the odds in favor of getting 5 heads in 5 tosses of a coin are 1 to 31, then what is the probability of getting 5 heads in 5 tosses of a coin?

42. If the odds against Smith winning the election are 2 to 5, then what is the probability that Smith wins the election?

GETTING MORE INVOLVED

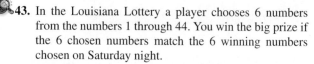

43. In the Louisiana Lottery a player chooses 6 numbers from the numbers 1 through 44. You win the big prize if the 6 chosen numbers match the 6 winning numbers chosen on Saturday night.

   a) What is the probability that you choose all 6 winning numbers?

   b) What is the probability that you do not get all 6 winning numbers?

   c) What are the odds in favor of winning the big prize with a single entry?

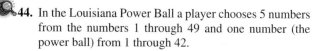

44. In the Louisiana Power Ball a player chooses 5 numbers from the numbers 1 through 49 and one number (the power ball) from 1 through 42.

   a) How many ways are there to choose the 5 numbers and, choose the power ball?

   b) What is the probability of winning the big prize in the Power Ball Lottery?

   c) What are the odds in favor of winning the big prize?

COLLABORATIVE ACTIVITIES

Extra Sensory Perception (ESP)

In this activity we will test each student in the class for ESP. Working in groups of three or four, start with a well-shuffled deck of ordinary playing cards. Place the stack of cards face down on a table. Have one student (the subject) try to guess whether the top card is a heart, diamond, spade, or club. After the student has guessed, remove the card and record whether the student was correct or incorrect. Do not let the subject know whether the guess was correct. Repeat the experiment for each of the 52 cards in the deck. The subject's score is the number of times he or she correctly guessed the suit of the card. Now choose a new subject and start over.

Answer the following questions in your group.

1. What is the probability that the subject will guess the correct suit of any card?

2. What score would you expect for each subject?

3. How many correct guesses would a subject have to make for you to think he or she was unusual?

Grouping: 3 or 4 students per group

Topic: Applications of probability

4. How many correct guesses would a subject have to make for you to be convinced he or she has ESP?

Using the results of all of the groups, make a bar graph with the possible scores (0 through 52) along the *x*-axis. The height of each bar should correspond to the number of subjects in the class who obtained the score.

5. Is there anyone in the class with an unusual score according to your answer to question 3?

6. Is there anyone in your class who has ESP according to your answer to question 4?

7. What percent of the class scored above 13 and what percent scored below 13? Would you say that the high scores have ESP and the low scores are unlucky?

8. Retest the student with the highest score and see what happens.

WRAP-UP

CHAPTER 14

SUMMARY

Counting		Examples
Fundamental counting principle	If event A has m different outcomes and event B has n different outcomes, then there are mn different ways for events A and B to occur.	If a pie can be ordered with 2 different crusts and 5 fillings, then 10 pies are available.
Permutations of n things r at a time	The number of permutations of n things taken r at a time is $P(n, r) = \dfrac{n!}{(n-r)!}$ for $0 \le r \le n$. $P(n, n) = n!$ and $P(n, 0) = 1$.	The number of ways to choose Miss America and the First Runner Up from 5 finalists is $P(5, 2) = 5 \cdot 4$. The number of ways for 5 people to stand in line is $P(5, 5) = 5!$.
Combinations of n things r at a time	The number of combinations of n things taken r at a time is $C(n, r) = \dfrac{n!}{(n-r)!\, r!}$ for $0 \le r \le n$. $C(n, n) = 1$ and $C(n, 0) = 1$.	The number of ways to rate 2 of 5 people as excellent is $C(5, 2) = \dfrac{5!}{3!\,2!}$. $C(5, 5) = \dfrac{5!}{0!\,5!} = 1$, $C(5, 0) = \dfrac{5!}{5!\,0!} = 1$
Labeling	One label is given to each of n distinct objects. If there are r_1 labels of type 1, r_2 labels of type 2, . . . , and r_k labels of type k, then the number of ways to label is $\dfrac{n!}{r_1!\,r_2! \ldots r_k!}$.	If 5 students are randomly given 2 A's, 2 B's, and 1 C, then the number of ways to assign these grades is $\dfrac{5!}{2!\,2!\,1!}$.

Coefficients		Examples
Binomial coefficients	The coefficient of the term $a^r b^{n-r}$ in the expansion of $(a + b)^n$ is $C(n, r)$ for $0 \le r \le n$.	The coefficient of $a^3 b^2$ in $(a + b)^5$ is $C(5, 3) = \dfrac{5!}{3!\,2!} = 10$.
Multinomial coefficients	Determining the coefficients in a multinominal expansion is a labeling problem.	The coefficient of $a^2 b^2 c^3$ in $(a + b + c)^7$ is $\dfrac{7!}{2!\,2!\,3!} = 210$.

Probability		Examples
Probability of an event	If S is a sample space of equally likely outcomes to an experiment and E is a subset of S, then $P(E) = \dfrac{n(E)}{n(S)}$.	If a single die is tossed, then $S = \{1, 2, 3, 4, 5, 6\}$. If $A = \{4, 5, 6\}$, then $P(A) = \dfrac{3}{6}$.

Mutually exclusive events	Two events are called mutually exclusive when it is impossible for both to occur.	If a die is tossed once, then $\{1\}$ and $\{2\}$ are mutually exclusive.
Addition rule	If A and B are any events in a sample space, then $P(A \cup B) = P(A) + P(B) - P(A \cap B)$.	If $A = \{4, 5, 6\}$ and $B = \{3, 4\}$, then $P(A \cup B) = \dfrac{3}{6} + \dfrac{2}{6} - \dfrac{1}{6} = \dfrac{4}{6}$.
	If A and B are mutually exclusive events in a sample space, then $P(A \cup B) = P(A) + P(B)$.	If $C = \{1\}$ and $D = \{2\}$, then $P(C \cup D) = \dfrac{1}{6} + \dfrac{1}{6} = \dfrac{2}{6}$.
Complementary events	Two events A and $\overline{A}$ are complementary events if $A \cap \overline{A} = \varnothing$ and $P(A) + P(\overline{A}) = 1$.	If $C = \{1\}$, then $\overline{C} = \{2, 3, 4, 5, 6\}$ and $P(C) + P(\overline{C}) = \dfrac{1}{6} + \dfrac{5}{6} = 1$.

Odds

Examples

Odds	For an event A the odds in favor of A is the ratio of $P(A)$ to $P(\overline{A})$, and the odds against A is the ratio $P(\overline{A})$ to $P(A)$.	The odds in favor of getting 1 on a single toss of a die are 1 to 5, and the odds against getting 1 are 5 to 1.
Converting from odds to probability	If the odds in favor of E are a to b, then $$P(E) = \frac{a}{a + b} \text{ and } P(\overline{E}) = \frac{b}{a + b}.$$	Odds in favor of $E = \{1, 2, 3, 4\}$ in tossing a die are 2 to 1. So $$P(E) = \frac{2}{2 + 1} = \frac{2}{3} \text{ and } P(\overline{E}) = \frac{1}{3}.$$

ENRICHING YOUR MATHEMATICAL WORD POWER

For each mathematical term, choose the correct meaning.

1. **tree diagram**
   a. a prehistoric tree carving
   b. a family tree
   c. a diagram showing all possibilities
   d. a diagram of numbers and their square roots

2. **permutation**
   a. a linear rearrangement
   b. a distortion of the facts
   c. $P(n, r)$
   d. a factorial

3. **combination**
   a. a padlock
   b. a group or subset
   c. a factorial
   d. $C(n, r)$

4. **multinomial coefficients**
   a. multiple coefficients
   b. coefficients involving many numbers
   c. binomial coefficients
   d. the coefficients in the expansion of a power of a polynomial of more than 2 terms

5. **experiment**
   a. a chemistry problem
   b. a process with an uncertain outcome
   c. a guess
   d. trial and error

6. **sample space**
   a. the set of all possible outcomes to an experiment
   b. a space reserved for free samples
   c. to choose a space
   d. a typical outcome to an experiment

7. **event**
   a. an outcome to an experiment
   b. winning a lottery
   c. an experiment
   d. a subset of a sample space

8. **mutually exclusive events**
   a. events to which you would not go even if you were invited
   b. two events that cannot both occur
   c. two events that always occur together
   d. events that cannot happen

9. **complementary events**
    a. events where everyone says nice things
    b. events that cannot both occur
    c. events that must occur
    d. two events that cannot both occur but one of them must occur

10. **odds in favor of an event**
    a. the ratio of $P(A)$ to $P(\overline{A})$
    b. the probability of the event
    c. the probability that an event does not occur
    d. 2 to 1

REVIEW EXERCISES

14.1 *Solve each problem.*

1. How many different ways are there to mark the answers to a 15-question multiple-choice test in which each question has 3 possible answers?

2. Eight airplanes are scheduled to depart at 1 o'clock. In how many ways can they line up for departure?

3. John is trying to find all 3-letter words that can be formed without repetition using the letters in the word UNITED. He plans to write down all "possible" 3-letter words and then check each one with a dictionary to see whether it is actually a word in the English language. How many "possible" 3-letter words are there?

4. The sales manager for an insurance company must select a team of 2 agents to give a presentation. If the manager has 9 male agents and 7 female agents available, and the team must consist of one man and one woman, then how many different teams are possible?

5. A candidate for city council is going to place one newspaper advertisement, one radio advertisement, and one television advertisement. If there are 3 newspapers, 12 radio stations, and 4 television stations available, then in how many ways can the advertisements be placed?

6. A ship has 11 different flags available. A signal consists of 3 flags displayed on a vertical pole. How many different signals are possible?

FIGURE FOR EXERCISE 6

14.2 *Solve each problem.*

7. A travel agent offers a vacation in which you can visit any 4 cities, chosen from Paris, Rome, London, Istanbul, Monte Carlo, Vienna, Madrid, and Berlin. How many different vacations are possible, if the order in which the cities are visited is not important?

8. How many 5-element subsets are there from the set $\{a, b, c, d, e, f, g\}$?

9. A city council consists of 5 Democrats and 4 Republicans. In how many ways can 4 council members be selected by the mayor to go to a convention in San Diego if the mayor
    a) may choose any 4?
    b) must choose 4 Democrats?
    c) must choose 2 Democrats and 2 Republicans?

10. In a 5-card poker hand a full house is 3 cards of one kind and 2 cards of another. How many full houses are there consisting of three kings and two jacks?

11. What is the coefficient of x^7y^3 in the expansion of $(x + y)^{10}$?

12. What is the coefficient of a^4b^3 in the expansion of $(a + b)^7$?

13. What is the coefficient of $w^2x^3y^6$ in the expansion of $(w + x + y)^{11}$?

14. What is the coefficient of x^5y^7 in the expansion of $(w + x + y)^{12}$?

15. How many different arrangements are there for the letters in the word ARKANSAS? MARCH?

16. Eight Toyota pickups of different colors are on sale through Saturday only. How many ways are there for the dealer to mark 2 of them $7,000, 3 of them $8,000, and 3 of them $9,000?

17. A couple plans to have 6 children. How many different families are possible, considering the sex of each child and the order of birth?

18. The Galaxy Theater has 3 horror films to show on Saturday night. How many different triple features are possible?

14.3 *Solve each problem.*

19. If Miriam randomly marks the answers to a 12-question true-false test, then what is the probability that she gets all 12 correct? What is the probability that she gets all 12 wrong?

20. If a couple plans to have 6 children, then what is the probability that they will have 6 girls?

21. There are 6 red, 5 green, and 3 yellow jelly beans in a jar. If a jelly bean is selected at random, then what is the probability that

   a) the selected bean is green?

   b) the selected bean is either yellow or red?

   c) the selected bean is blue?

   d) the selected bean is not purple?

22. A pair of dice is tossed. What is the probability that

   a) at least one die shows an even number?

   b) the sum is an even number?

   c) the sum is 6?

   d) the sum is 6 and at least one die shows an even number?

   e) the sum is 6 or at least one die shows an even number?

23. Suppose a couple plans to have 3 children. What are the odds in favor of having 3 boys?

24. Suppose a pair of dice is tossed. What are the odds in favor of the sum being 6?

25. If 60% of the voters in Massachusetts are Democrats and a single voter is drawn at random, then what are the odds in favor of that voter being a Democrat?

26. Seventy percent of the students at Wellknown University have money as their primary goal in life. If a student is selected at random, then what are the odds against selecting one who has money as his or her primary goal in life?

27. At Wellknown University 60% of the students are enrolled in an English class, 70% are enrolled in a mathematics class, and 40% are enrolled in both. If a student is selected at random, then what is the probability that the student is enrolled in either mathematics or English?

28. If a pair of dice is tossed, then what is the probability that the sum is either 5 or 7?

MISCELLANEOUS

Evaluate each expression.

29. $8!$

30. $1!$

31. $\dfrac{5!}{3!}$

32. $\dfrac{7!}{(7-3)!}$

33. $\dfrac{9!}{3!\,3!\,3!}$

34. $\dfrac{10!}{0!\,2!\,3!\,5!}$

35. $C(8, 6)$

36. $\dbinom{12}{3}$

37. $P(8, 4)$

38. $P(4, 4)$

39. $C(8, 1)$

40. $C(12, 0)$

Rectangular Solid

Volume: $V = LWH$

Surface Area: $A = 2LW + 2WH + 2LH$

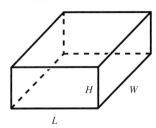

Square: A four-sided figure with four equal sides and four right angles

Area: $A = s^2$

Perimeter: $P = 4s$

Sphere

Volume: $V = \frac{4}{3}\pi r^3$

Surface Area: $S = 4\pi r^2$

Right Circular Cylinder

Volume: $V = \pi r^2 h$

Lateral Surface Area: $S = 2\pi rh$

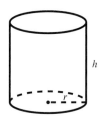

Geometric Terms

An **angle** is a union of two rays with a common endpoint.

A **right angle** is an angle with a measure of 90°.

Two angles are **complementary** if the sum of their measures is 90°.

An **isosceles triangle** is a triangle that has two equal sides.

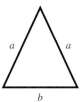

Similar triangles are triangles that have the same shape. Their corresponding angles are equal and corresponding sides are proportional:

$$\frac{a}{d} = \frac{b}{e} = \frac{c}{f}$$

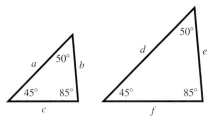

An **acute angle** is an angle with a measure between 0° and 90°.

An **obtuse angle** is an angle with a measure between 90° and 180°.

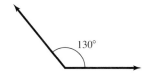

Two angles are **supplementary** if the sum of their measures is 180°.

An **equilateral triangle** is a triangle that has three equal sides.

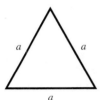

Geometry Review Exercises

(Answers are at the end of the answer section in this text.)

1. Find the perimeter of a triangle whose sides are 3 in., 4 in., and 5 in.

2. Find the area of a triangle whose base is 4 ft and height is 12 ft.

3. If two angles of a triangle are 30° and 90°, then what is the third angle?

4. If the area of a triangle is 36 ft^2 and the base is 12 ft, then what is the height?

5. If the side opposite 30° in a 30-60-90 right triangle is 10 cm, then what is the length of the hypotenuse?

6. Find the area of a trapezoid whose height is 12 cm and whose parallel sides are 4 cm and 20 cm.

7. Find the area of the right triangle that has sides of 6 ft, 8 ft, and 10 ft.

8. If a right triangle has sides of 5 ft, 12 ft, and 13 ft, then what is the length of the hypotenuse?

9. If the hypotenuse of a right triangle is 50 cm and the length of one leg is 40 cm, then what is the length of the other leg?

10. Is a triangle with sides of 5 ft, 10 ft, and 11 ft a right triangle?

11. What is the area of a triangle with sides of 7 yd, 24 yd, and 25 yd?

12. Find the perimeter of a parallelogram in which one side is 9 in. and another side is 6 in.

13. Find the area of a parallelogram which has a base of 8 ft and a height of 4 ft.

14. If one side of a rhombus is 5 km, then what is its perimeter?

15. Find the perimeter and area of a rectangle whose width is 18 in. and length is 2 ft.

16. If the width of a rectangle is 8 yd and its perimeter is 60 yd, then what is its length?

17. The radius of a circle is 4 ft. Find its area to the nearest tenth of a square foot.

18. The diameter of a circle is 12 ft. Find its circumference to the nearest tenth of a foot.

19. A right circular cone has radius 4 cm and height 9 cm. Find its volume to the nearest hundredth of a cubic centimeter.

20. A right circular cone has a radius 12 ft and a height of 20 ft. Find its lateral surface area to the nearest hundredth of a square foot.

21. A shoe box has a length of 12 in., a width of 6 in., and a height of 4 in. Find its volume and surface area.

22. The volume of a rectangular solid is 120 cm^3. If the area of its bottom is 30 cm^2, then what is its height?

23. What is the area and perimeter of a square in which one of the sides is 10 mi long?

24. Find the perimeter of a square whose area is 25 km^2.

25. Find the area of a square whose perimeter is 26 cm.

26. A sphere has a radius of 2 ft. Find its volume to the nearest thousandth of a cubic foot and its surface area to the nearest thousandth of a square foot.

27. A can of soup (right circular cylinder) has a radius of 2 in. and a height of 6 in. Find its volume to the nearest tenth of a cubic inch and total surface area to the nearest tenth of a square inch.

28. If one of two complementary angles is 34°, then what is the other angle?

29. If the perimeter of an isosceles triangle is 29 cm and one of the equal sides is 12 cm, then what is the length of the shortest side of the triangle?

30. A right triangle with sides of 6 in., 8 in., and 10 in., is similar to another right triangle that has a hypotenuse of 25 in. What are the lengths of the other two sides in the second triangle?

31. If one of two supplementary angles is 31°, then what is the other angle?

32. Find the perimeter of an equilateral triangle in which one of the sides is 4 km.

33. Find the length of a side of an equilateral triangle that has a perimeter of 30 yd.

n	n^2	$\sqrt{n}$	n	n^2	$\sqrt{n}$	n	n^2	$\sqrt{n}$
1	1	1.0000	41	1681	6.4031	81	6561	9.0000
2	4	1.4142	42	1764	6.4807	82	6724	9.0554
3	9	1.7321	43	1849	6.5574	83	6889	9.1104
4	16	2.0000	44	1936	6.6332	84	7056	9.1652
5	25	2.2361	45	2025	6.7082	85	7225	9.2195
6	36	2.4495	46	2116	6.7823	86	7396	9.2736
7	49	2.6458	47	2209	6.8557	87	7569	9.3274
8	64	2.8284	48	2304	6.9282	88	7744	9.3808
9	81	3.0000	49	2401	7.0000	89	7921	9.4340
10	100	3.1623	50	2500	7.0711	90	8100	9.4868
11	121	3.3166	51	2601	7.1414	91	8281	9.5394
12	144	3.4641	52	2704	7.2111	92	8464	9.5917
13	169	3.6056	53	2809	7.2801	93	8649	9.6437
14	196	3.7417	54	2916	7.3485	94	8836	9.6954
15	225	3.8730	55	3025	7.4162	95	9025	9.7468
16	256	4.0000	56	3136	7.4833	96	9216	9.7980
17	289	4.1231	57	3249	7.5498	97	9409	9.8489
18	324	4.2426	58	3364	7.6158	98	9604	9.8995
19	361	4.3589	59	3481	7.6811	99	9801	9.9499
20	400	4.4721	60	3600	7.7460	100	10000	10.0000
21	441	4.5826	61	3721	7.8102	101	10201	10.0499
22	484	4.6904	62	3844	7.8740	102	10404	10.0995
23	529	4.7958	63	3969	7.9373	103	10609	10.1489
24	576	4.8990	64	4096	8.0000	104	10816	10.1980
25	625	5.0000	65	4225	8.0623	105	11025	10.2470
26	676	5.0990	66	4356	8.1240	106	11236	10.2956
27	729	5.1962	67	4489	8.1854	107	11449	10.3441
28	784	5.2915	68	4624	8.2462	108	11664	10.3923
29	841	5.3852	69	4761	8.3066	109	11881	10.4403
30	900	5.4772	70	4900	8.3666	110	12100	10.4881
31	961	5.5678	71	5041	8.4261	111	12321	10.5357
32	1024	5.6569	72	5184	8.4853	112	12544	10.5830
33	1089	5.7446	73	5329	8.5440	113	12769	10.6301
34	1156	5.8310	74	5476	8.6023	114	12996	10.6771
35	1225	5.9161	75	5625	8.6603	115	13225	10.7238
36	1296	6.0000	76	5776	8.7178	116	13456	10.7703
37	1369	6.0828	77	5929	8.7750	117	13689	10.8167
38	1444	6.1644	78	6084	8.8318	118	13924	10.8628
39	1521	6.2450	79	6241	8.8882	119	14161	10.9087
40	1600	6.3246	80	6400	8.9443	120	14400	10.9545

This table gives the common logarithms for numbers between 1 and 10. The common logarithms for other numbers can be found by using scientific notation and the properties of logarithms. For example, to find log(1230) we write

$$\log(1230) = \log(1.23 \times 10^3) = \log(1.23) + \log(10^3)$$
$$= 0.0899 + 3 = 3.0899$$

n	0	1	2	3	4	5	6	7	8	9
1.0	.0000	.0043	.0086	.0128	.0170	.0212	.0253	.0294	.0334	.0374
1.1	.0414	.0453	.0492	.0531	.0569	.0607	.0645	.0682	.0719	.0755
1.2	.0792	.0828	.0864	.0899	.0934	.0969	.1004	.1038	.1072	.1106
1.3	.1139	.1173	.1206	.1239	.1271	.1303	.1335	.1367	.1399	.1430
1.4	.1461	.1492	.1523	.1553	.1584	.1614	.1644	.1673	.1703	.1732
1.5	.1761	.1790	.1818	.1847	.1875	.1903	.1931	.1959	.1987	.2014
1.6	.2041	.2068	.2095	.2122	.2148	.2175	.2201	.2227	.2253	.2279
1.7	.2304	.2330	.2355	.2380	.2405	.2430	.2455	.2480	.2504	.2529
1.8	.2553	.2577	.2601	.2625	.2648	.2672	.2695	.2718	.2742	.2765
1.9	.2788	.2810	.2833	.2856	.2878	.2900	.2923	.2945	.2967	.2989
2.0	.3010	.3032	.3054	.3075	.3096	.3118	.3139	.3160	.3181	.3201
2.1	.3222	.3243	.3263	.3284	.3304	.3324	.3345	.3365	.3385	.3404
2.2	.3424	.3444	.3464	.3483	.3502	.3522	.3541	.3560	.3579	.3598
2.3	.3617	.3636	.3655	.3674	.3692	.3711	.3729	.3747	.3766	.3784
2.4	.3802	.3820	.3838	.3856	.3874	.3892	.3909	.3927	.3945	.3962
2.5	.3979	.3997	.4014	.4031	.4048	.4065	.4082	.4099	.4116	.4133
2.6	.4150	.4166	.4183	.4200	.4216	.4232	.4249	.4265	.4281	.4298
2.7	.4314	.4330	.4346	.4362	.4378	.4393	.4409	.4425	.4440	.4456
2.8	.4472	.4487	.4502	.4518	.4533	.4548	.4564	.4579	.4594	.4609
2.9	.4624	.4639	.4654	.4669	.4683	.4698	.4713	.4728	.4742	.4757
3.0	.4771	.4786	.4800	.4814	.4829	.4843	.4857	.4871	.4886	.4900
3.1	.4914	.4928	.4942	.4955	.4969	.4983	.4997	.5011	.5024	.5038
3.2	.5051	.5065	.5079	.5092	.5105	.5119	.5132	.5145	.5159	.5172
3.3	.5185	.5198	.5211	.5224	.5237	.5250	.5263	.5276	.5289	.5302
3.4	.5315	.5328	.5340	.5353	.5366	.5378	.5391	.5403	.5416	.5428
3.5	.5441	.5453	.5465	.5478	.5490	.5502	.5514	.5527	.5539	.5551
3.6	.5563	.5575	.5587	.5599	.5611	.5623	.5635	.5647	.5658	.5670
3.7	.5682	.5694	.5705	.5717	.5729	.5740	.5752	.5763	.5775	.5786
3.8	.5798	.5809	.5821	.5832	.5843	.5855	.5866	.5877	.5888	.5899
3.9	.5911	.5922	.5933	.5944	.5955	.5966	.5977	.5988	.5999	.6010
4.0	.6021	.6031	.6042	.6053	.6064	.6075	.6085	.6096	.6107	.6117
4.1	.6128	.6138	.6149	.6160	.6170	.6180	.6191	.6201	.6212	.6222
4.2	.6232	.6243	.6253	.6263	.6274	.6284	.6294	.6304	.6314	.6325
4.3	.6335	.6345	.6355	.6365	.6375	.6385	.6395	.6405	.6415	.6425
4.4	.6435	.6444	.6454	.6464	.6474	.6484	.6493	.6503	.6513	.6522
4.5	.6532	.6542	.6551	.6561	.6571	.6580	.6590	.6599	.6609	.6618
4.6	.6628	.6637	.6646	.6656	.6665	.6675	.6684	.6693	.6702	.6712
4.7	.6721	.6730	.6739	.6749	.6758	.6767	.6776	.6785	.6794	.6803
4.8	.6812	.6821	.6830	.6839	.6848	.6857	.6866	.6875	.6884	.6893
4.9	.6902	.6911	.6920	.6928	.6937	.6946	.6955	.6964	.6972	.6981
n	0	1	2	3	4	5	6	7	8	9

n	0	1	2	3	4	5	6	7	8	9
5.0	.6990	.6998	.7007	.7016	.7024	.7033	.7042	.7050	.7059	.7067
5.1	.7076	.7084	.7093	.7101	.7110	.7118	.7126	.7135	.7143	.7152
5.2	.7160	.7168	.7177	.7185	.7193	.7202	.7210	.7218	.7226	.7235
5.3	.7243	.7251	.7259	.7267	.7275	.7284	.7292	.7300	.7308	.7316
5.4	.7324	.7332	.7340	.7348	.7356	.7364	.7372	.7380	.7388	.7396
5.5	.7404	.7412	.7419	.7427	.7435	.7443	.7451	.7459	.7466	.7474
5.6	.7482	.7490	.7497	.7505	.7513	.7520	.7528	.7536	.7543	.7551
5.7	.7559	.7566	.7574	.7582	.7589	.7597	.7604	.7612	.7619	.7627
5.8	.7634	.7642	.7649	.7657	.7664	.7672	.7679	.7686	.7694	.7701
5.9	.7709	.7716	.7723	.7731	.7738	.7745	.7752	.7760	.7767	.7774
6.0	.7782	.7789	.7796	.7803	.7810	.7818	.7825	.7832	.7839	.7846
6.1	.7853	.7860	.7868	.7875	.7882	.7889	.7896	.7903	.7910	.7917
6.2	.7924	.7931	.7938	.7945	.7952	.7959	.7966	.7973	.7980	.7987
6.3	.7993	.8000	.8007	.8014	.8021	.8028	.8035	.8041	.8048	.8055
6.4	.8062	.8069	.8075	.8082	.8089	.8096	.8102	.8109	.8116	.8122
6.5	.8129	.8136	.8142	.8149	.8156	.8162	.8169	.8176	.8182	.8189
6.6	.8195	.8202	.8209	.8215	.8222	.8228	.8235	.8241	.8248	.8254
6.7	.8261	.8267	.8274	.8280	.8287	.8293	.8299	.8306	.8312	.8319
6.8	.8325	.8331	.8338	.8344	.8351	.8357	.8363	.8370	.8376	.8382
6.9	.8388	.8395	.8401	.8407	.8414	.8420	.8426	.8432	.8439	.8445
7.0	.8451	.8457	.8463	.8470	.8476	.8482	.8488	.8494	.8500	.8506
7.1	.8513	.8519	.8525	.8531	.8537	.8543	.8549	.8555	.8561	.8567
7.2	.8573	.8579	.8585	.8591	.8597	.8603	.8609	.8615	.8621	.8627
7.3	.8633	.8639	.8645	.8651	.8657	.8663	.8669	.8675	.8681	.8686
7.4	.8692	.8698	.8704	.8710	.8716	.8722	.8727	.8733	.8739	.8745
7.5	.8751	.8756	.8762	.8768	.8774	.8779	.8785	.8791	.8797	.8802
7.6	.8808	.8814	.8820	.8825	.8831	.8837	.8842	.8848	.8854	.8859
7.7	.8865	.8871	.8876	.8882	.8887	.8893	.8899	.8904	.8910	.8915
7.8	.8921	.8927	.8932	.8938	.8943	.8949	.8954	.8960	.8965	.8971
7.9	.8976	.8982	.8987	.8993	.8998	.9004	.9009	.9015	.9020	.9025
8.0	.9031	.9036	.9042	.9047	.9053	.9058	.9063	.9069	.9074	.9079
8.1	.9085	.9090	.9096	.9101	.9106	.9112	.9117	.9122	.9128	.9133
8.2	.9138	.9143	.9149	.9154	.9159	.9165	.9170	.9175	.9180	.9186
8.3	.9191	.9196	.9201	.9206	.9212	.9217	.9222	.9227	.9232	.9238
8.4	.9243	.9248	.9253	.9258	.9263	.9269	.9274	.9279	.9284	.9289
8.5	.9294	.9299	.9304	.9309	.9315	.9320	.9325	.9330	.9335	.9340
8.6	.9345	.9350	.9355	.9360	.9365	.9370	.9375	.9380	.9385	.9390
8.7	.9395	.9400	.9405	.9410	.9415	.9420	.9425	.9430	.9435	.9440
8.8	.9445	.9450	.9455	.9460	.9465	.9469	.9474	.9479	.9484	.9489
8.9	.9494	.9499	.9504	.9509	.9513	.9518	.9523	.9528	.9533	.9538
9.0	.9542	.9547	.9552	.9557	.9562	.9566	.9571	.9576	.9581	.9586
9.1	.9590	.9595	.9600	.9605	.9609	.9614	.9619	.9624	.9628	.9633
9.2	.9638	.9643	.9647	.9652	.9657	.9661	.9666	.9671	.9675	.9680
9.3	.9685	.9689	.9694	.9699	.9703	.9708	.9713	.9717	.9722	.9727
9.4	.9731	.9736	.9741	.9745	.9750	.9754	.9759	.9763	.9768	.9773
9.5	.9777	.9782	.9786	.9791	.9795	.9800	.9805	.9809	.9814	.9818
9.6	.9823	.9827	.9832	.9836	.9841	.9845	.9850	.9854	.9859	.9863
9.7	.9868	.9872	.9877	.9881	.9886	.9890	.9894	.9899	.9903	.9908
9.8	.9912	.9917	.9921	.9926	.9930	.9934	.9939	.9943	.9948	.9952
9.9	.9956	.9961	.9965	.9969	.9974	.9978	.9983	.9987	.9991	.9996
n	0	1	2	3	4	5	6	7	8	9

Chapter 1

Section 1.1 Warm-ups F F F F T T T F T T
1. A set is a collection of objects.
3. A Venn diagram is used to illustrate relationships between sets.
5. Every member of set A is also a member of set B.
7. F   **9.** T   **11.** T   **13.** F   **15.** F   **17.** F   **19.** $\varnothing$
21. $\{1, 3, 5\}$ **23.** $\{1, 2, 3, 4, 5, 6, 8\}$ **25.** A **27.** $\varnothing$
29. A **31.** $=$ **33.** $\cup$ **35.** $\cap$ **37.** $\notin$ **39.** $\in$
41. T   **43.** T   **45.** T   **47.** T   **49.** F   **51.** T
53. $\{2, 3, 4, 5, 6, 7, 8\}$ **55.** $\{3, 5\}$ **57.** $\{1, 2, 3, 4, 5, 6, 8\}$
59. $\{2, 3, 4, 5\}$ **61.** $\{2, 3, 4, 5, 7\}$ **63.** $\{2, 3, 4, 5\}$
65. $\{2, 3, 4, 5, 7\}$ **67.** $\subseteq$ **69.** $\in$ **71.** $\cap$
73. $\subseteq$ **75.** $\cap$ **77.** $\cup$ **79.** $\{2, 4, 6, \ldots, 18\}$
81. $\{13, 15, 17, \ldots\}$ **83.** $\{6, 8, 10, \ldots, 78\}$
85. $\{x \mid x$ is a natural number between 2 and 7$\}$
87. $\{x \mid x$ is an odd natural number greater than 4$\}$
89. $\{x \mid x$ is an even natural number between 5 and 83$\}$
91. No
93. a) $3 \in \{1, 2, 3\}$ **b)** $\{3\} \subseteq \{1, 2, 3\}$ **c)** $\varnothing \neq \{\varnothing\}$

Section 1.2 Warm-ups F T F F T F T F T F
1. The integers consist of the positive and negative counting numbers and zero.
3. The repeating or terminating decimal numbers are rational numbers.
5. The set of real numbers is the union of the rational and irrational numbers.
7. T   **9.** F   **11.** T   **13.** T
15. $\{0, 1, 2, 3, 4, 5\}$

17. $\{-4, -3, -2, -1, 0, 1, \ldots\}$

19. $\{1, 2, 3, 4\}$

21. $\{-2, -1, 0, 1, 2, 3, 4\}$

23. All   **25.** $\left\{0, \dfrac{8}{2}\right\}$ **27.** $\left\{-3, -\dfrac{5}{2}, -0.025, 0, 3\dfrac{1}{2}, \dfrac{8}{2}\right\}$
29. T   **31.** F   **33.** T   **35.** F   **37.** F   **39.** F   **41.** T
43. $\subseteq$ **45.** $\not\subseteq$ **47.** $\subseteq$ **49.** $\subseteq$ **51.** $\subseteq$ **53.** $\in$
55. $\in$ **57.** $\in$ **59.** $\notin$ **61.** $\subseteq$ **63.** $\subseteq$
65. $(1, \infty)$ **67.** $(-\infty, -1)$

69. $(3, 4)$ **71.** $[0, 2]$

73. $[1, 3)$

75. $[5, 7]$ **77.** $(-3, 0]$ **79.** $[60, \infty)$ **81.** $(-\infty, -5)$
83. $(1, 9)$ **85.** $(2, 3)$ **87.** $(-2, \infty)$ **89.** $(0, 2)$
91. $[2, 9]$ **93.** $[2, 6)$

Section 1.3 Warm-ups T T F T T F F F F T
1. The absolute value of a number is the number's distance from 0 on the number line.
3. Subtract their absolute values and use the sign of the number with the larger absolute value.
5. Multiply their absolute values, then affix a positive sign if the original numbers have the same sign and a negative sign if the original numbers have opposite signs.
7. 34   **9.** 0   **11.** 0   **13.** -9 **15.** 9   **17.** -3 **19.** 4
21. -7 **23.** -2 **25.** -10 **27.** -26 **29.** -2
31. -5 **33.** 0   **35.** $\dfrac{1}{10}$ **37.** $-\dfrac{1}{6}$ **39.** -14.98
41. -2.71 **43.** 2.803   **45.** -0.2649 **47.** -3
49. -11 **51.** 13   **53.** -6 **55.** -9 **57.** 23   **59.** 1
61. $-\dfrac{1}{2}$ **63.** 1.97   **65.** 7.3   **67.** -50.73 **69.** 1.27
71. -75 **73.** $\dfrac{1}{6}$ **75.** -0.09 **77.** 0.2   **79.** $\dfrac{1}{20}$ or 0.05
81. $-\dfrac{5}{6}$ **83.** $-\dfrac{10}{3}$ **85.** -2 **87.** -37.5 **89.** -0.08
91. 0.25   **93.** -12 **95.** $\dfrac{3}{5}$ **97.** -91.25 **99.** 17,000
101. -49 **103.** -7 **105.** 15   **107.** -342
109. $\dfrac{3}{4}$ **111.** -3 **113.** 20   **115.** 0   **117.** -180
119. $-\dfrac{1}{6}$ **121.** -55 **123.** -1 **125.** $-\dfrac{39}{2}$
127. 27.99   **129.** -29.3 **131.** -0.7 **133.** 2
135. $44,400   **137.** 20°F   **139.** 1014 ft

Section 1.4 Warm-ups F T T F F F T T F F
1. An arithmetic expression is the result of writing numbers in a meaningful combination with the ordinary operations of arithmetic.
3. Grouping symbols are used to indicate the order in which operations are to be performed.
5. The order of operations tells us the order in which to perform operations when we omit grouping symbols.

7. -22 **9.** -8 **11.** -14 **13.** 32 **15.** 1 **17.** $\dfrac{1}{9}$

19. 7 **21.** 10 **23.** 8 **25.** -8 **27.** 17 **29.** $\dfrac{1}{24}$

31. 58 **33.** -25 **35.** -200 **37.** 40 **39.** -25

41. -7.5 **43.** -22.4841 **45.** -1.9602 **47.** -276.48

49. -2 **51.** -1 **53.** -6 **55.** 0 **57.** -7 **59.** $-\dfrac{4}{3}$

61. -8 **63.** 5 **65.** $-\dfrac{5}{2}$ **67.** 4 **69.** $\dfrac{10}{9}$ **71.** $\dfrac{3}{4}$

73. -2.67 **75.** 41 **77.** 27 **79.** 1 **81.** 9 **83.** -1

85. 26 **87.** $-\dfrac{3}{2}$ **89.** -2 **91.** $\dfrac{5}{12}$ **93.** 17

95. -46 **97.** 3 **99.** -8

101. 26 beats per minute, age 43   **103.** 104 feet

105. a) \$60,000   **b)** \$60,776.47

107. \$5500, \$5441.96   **109.** \$24,169

Section 1.5 Warm-ups T F F F F F T T F T

1. The commutative property of addition states that $a + b = b + a$ and the commutative property of multiplication states that $a \cdot b = b \cdot a$.

3. The commutative property of addition states that you get the same result when you add two numbers in either order. The associative property of addition has to do with which two numbers are added first when adding three numbers.

5. Zero is the additive identity because adding zero to a number does not change the number.

7. 1 **9.** -14 **11.** -24 **13.** -1.7 **15.** -19.8

17. $4x - 24$ **19.** $2(m + 5)$ **21.** $3a + at$

23. $-2w + 10$ **25.** $-6 + 2y$ **27.** $5(x - 1)$

29. $2x + y$ **31.** $6w + 9y$ **33.** $3(y - 5)$ **35.** $3(a + 3)$

37. $2x + 4$ **39.** $-x + 2$ **41.** 2 **43.** 1 **45.** $\dfrac{1}{6}$

47. 4 **49.** $-\dfrac{10}{7}$ **51.** $-\dfrac{5}{9}$ **53.** 0.6200

55. 0.7326 **57.** 1450 mph   **59.** 217 buttons per hour

61. Commutative property of addition

63. Distributive property

65. Associative property of multiplication

67. Multiplicative inverse property

69. Commutative property of multiplication

71. Multiplicative identity property

73. Distributive property

75. Additive inverse property

77. Multiplication property of zero

79. Distributive property

81. $w + 5$ **83.** $(5x)y$ **85.** $\dfrac{1}{2}(x - 1)$

87. $3(2x + 3)$ **89.** 1 **91.** 0 **93.** 4

Section 1.6 Warm-ups T F T T F T F F F T

1. A term is a single number or a product of a number and one or more variables.

3. The coefficient of a term is the number preceding the variables.

5. You can multiply and divide unlike terms.

7. 9000 **9.** 1 **11.** 527 **13.** 470 **15.** 38

17. $48,000$ **19.** 0 **21.** 398 **23.** 1 **25.** 1700

27. 374 **29.** 0 **31.** $2n$ **33.** $7w$ **35.** $-11mw^2$

37. $-3x$ **39.** $-4 - 7z$ **41.** $9t^2$ **43.** $-4ab + 3a^2b$

45. $8mn$ **47.** $-2x^3y$ **49.** $-2kz^6$ **51.** $28t$ **53.** $10x^2$

55. h^2 **57.** $-28w$ **59.** $-x + x^2$ **61.** $25k^2$ **63.** y

65. $2y$ **67.** $3x^3$ **69.** $x^2y + 5x$ **71.** $-x + 2$

73. $\dfrac{1}{2}xt - 5$ **75.** $-3a + 1$ **77.** $10 - x$

79. $3m + 1$ **81.** $-12b + at$ **83.** $2t^2 - 3w$

85. $y^2 + z$ **87.** $9x + 8$ **89.** $2x - 2$ **91.** $-2a^2 + 2c$

93. $7t^2 - 9w$ **95.** $m - 12$ **97.** $-7k^3 - 17$

99. $0.96x - 2$ **101.** $0.06x - 1.5$ **103.** $-4k + 16$

105. $-4.5x + 17.83$ **107.** $-4xy - 22$ **109.** $-29w^2$

111. $-6a^2w^2$ **113.** $2x^2y + \dfrac{1}{3}$ **115.** $\dfrac{1}{4}m^2 - m$

117. $4t^3 + 3t^2 - 1$ **119.** $2xyz + xy - 3z$ **121.** $3s + 6$ ft

123. $\dfrac{13}{3}x$ m, $\dfrac{7}{6}x^2$ m^2

Chapter 1 Wrap-Up

Enriching Your Mathematical Word Power

1. a   **2.** c   **3.** a   **4.** d   **5.** a   **6.** c   **7.** a   **8.** d

9. b   **10.** a   **11.** b   **12.** a   **13.** b   **14.** c

Review Exercises

1. T   **3.** F   **5.** T   **7.** F   **9.** T   **11.** T   **13.** F

15. T   **17.** F   **19.** T   **21.** $\{0, 1, 31\}$

23. $\{-1, 0, 1, 31\}$ **25.** $\{-\sqrt{2}, \sqrt{3}, \pi\}$

27. $(0, \infty)$ **29.** $(5, 6)$

31. $[-1, 2)$

33. $(0, 5)$ **35.** $(3, 4)$ **37.** $[2, 8)$ **39.** 5 **41.** -12

43. -24 **45.** 2 **47.** $-\dfrac{1}{6}$ **49.** 10 **51.** 9.96

53. -4 **55.** 0 **57.** -4 **59.** 0 **61.** 39 **63.** 121

65. 23 **67.** 2 **69.** 23 **71.** -96 **73.** 5 **75.** -1

77. 0.76 **79.** 1 **81.** -3 **83.** 4 **85.** 1 **87.** -8

89. 1 **91.** -35 **93.** 2 **95.** 5 **97.** -1

99. Commutative property of addition

101. Distributive property

103. Associative property of multiplication

105. Multiplicative identity property

107. Multiplicative inverse property

109. Multiplication property of zero

111. Additive identity property

113. Additive inverse property

115. $3(x - a)$ **117.** $3w + 3$ **119.** $7(x + 1)$

121. $5x - 25$ **123.** $-6x + 15$ **125.** $p(1 - t)$

127. $7a + 2$ **129.** $-t - 2$ **131.** $-2a + 4$

133. $4x + 33$ **135.** $-0.8x - 0.48$ **137.** $-0.05x - 1.85$

139. $\frac{1}{4}x + 4$ **141.** $-3x^2 - 2x + 1$

143. 0, additive inverse, multiplication property of zero
145. 7680, distributive
147. 48, associative property of addition, additive inverse, additive identity
149. 0, distributive, additive inverse
151. 47, associative property of multiplication, multiplicative inverse
153. -24, commutative property of multiplication, associative property of multiplication
155. 0, additive inverse, multiplication property of zero
157. Seven shingles per minute
159. a) $41,013   **b)** 2015

Chapter 1 Test

1. $\{2, 3, 4, 5, 6, 7, 8, 10\}$ **2.** $\{6, 7\}$ **3.** $\{4, 6, 8, 10\}$
4. $\{0, 8\}$ **5.** $\{-4, 0, 8\}$ **6.** $\left\{-4, -\frac{1}{2}, 0, 1.65, 8\right\}$
7. $\{-\sqrt{3}, \sqrt{5}, \pi\}$ **8.**

9.

10. $(-\infty, 4)$ **11.** $[4, 8)$ **12.** -9 **13.** 8
14. -11 **15.** -1.98 **16.** -2 **17.** -4
18. $\frac{1}{18}$ **19.** -12 **20.** 7   **21.** -3 **22.** 0
23. 4780   **24.** 240   **25.** 40   **26.** 7   **27.** 0
28. Distributive property
29. Commutative property of multiplication
30. Associative property of addition
31. Additive inverse property
32. Commutative property of multiplication
33. $11m - 3$ **34.** $0.95x + 2.9$
35. $\frac{3}{4}x - \frac{5}{4}$ **36.** $5x^2$ **37.** $3x^2 + 2x - 1$
38. $5(x - 8)$ **39.** $7(t - 1)$ **40.** 16 trees per hour
41. $4x - 8, x^2 - 4x$, 28 ft, 45 ft^2
42. 12.6 billion

Chapter 2

Section 2.1 Warm-ups F T F T T T T T T T
1. An equation is a sentence that expresses the equality of two algebraic expressions.
3. Equivalent equations are equations that have the same solution set.
5. If the equation involves fractions then multiply each side by the LCD.
7. A conditional equation is an equation that has at least one solution but is not an identity.
9. Yes   **11.** Yes   **13.** No   **15.** No   **17.** $\{-87\}$
19. $\{-24\}$ **21.** $\left\{\frac{3}{2}\right\}$ **23.** $\{-1\}$ **25.** $\{-3\}$ **27.** $\left\{\frac{5}{2}\right\}$
29. $\{18\}$ **31.** $\{18\}$ **33.** $\{0\}$ **35.** $\left\{-\frac{28}{3}\right\}$ **37.** $\left\{-\frac{28}{5}\right\}$

39. $\{2\}$ **41.** $\{12\}$ **43.** $\{-7\}$ **45.** $\{12\}$ **47.** $\{6\}$
49. $\{90\}$ **51.** $\{1000\}$ **53.** $\{800\}$ **55.** $\varnothing$, inconsistent
57. R, identity   **59.** $\{1\}$, conditional   **61.** R, identity
63. R, identity   **65.** $\varnothing$, inconsistent   **67.** R, identity
69. $\{-4\}$, conditional   **71.** $\{1\}$ **73.** $\left\{\frac{5}{18}\right\}$ **75.** $\left\{\frac{121}{48}\right\}$
77. $\left\{\frac{19}{13}\right\}$ **79.** $\left\{\frac{10}{29}\right\}$ **81.** $\{3\}$ **83.** $\{16\}$ **85.** $\left\{\frac{3}{4}\right\}$
87. $\{-15\}$ **89.** $\{6\}$ **91.** $\{6\}$ **93.** $\{-2\}$
95. $\{53,191.49\}$ **97.** $\{4.7\}$
99. a) 42.2 million   **b)** 2010   **c)** increasing

Section 2.2 Warm-ups F F F T F T F T T F
1. A formula is an equation involving two or more variables.
3. Solving for a variable means to rewrite the formula by isolating the indicated variable.
5. To find the value of a variable, solve for that variable, then replace all other variables with the given numbers.
7. $t = \frac{I}{Pr}$ **9.** $C = \frac{5}{9}(F - 32)$ **11.** $W = \frac{A}{L}$
13. $b_1 = 2A - b_2$ **15.** $L = \frac{P - 2W}{2}$ or $L = \frac{1}{2}P - W$
17. $h = \frac{V}{\pi r^2}$ **19.** $y = -\frac{2}{3}x + 3$ **21.** $y = x - 4$
23. $y = \frac{3}{2}x - 6$ **25.** $y = \frac{1}{2}x + \frac{1}{2}$ **27.** $t = \frac{A - P}{Pr}$
29. $a = \frac{1}{b + 1}$ **31.** $y = \frac{12}{1 - x}$ **33.** $x = \frac{6}{w^2 - y^2 - z^2}$
35. $R_1 = \frac{RR_2}{R_2 - R}$ **37.** 12.472   **39.** 34.932   **41.** 0.539
43. $\frac{1}{3}$ **45.** $\frac{13}{2}$ **47.** -1 **49.** 4   **51.** -4.4507
53. $\frac{5}{8}$ **55.** $-\frac{7}{2}$ **57.** -10 **59.** $-\frac{8}{3}$ **61.** 4
63. $A = \pi r^2$ **65.** $r = \frac{C}{2\pi}$ **67.** $W = \frac{P - 2L}{2}$ **69.** 15%
71. 5.75 yards   **73.** 7.2 feet   **75.** 5 feet   **77.** 15 feet
79. 14 inches   **81.** 168 feet   **83.** 1.5 meters
85. 3979 miles   **87.** 4.24 inches   **89.** 95,232 pounds
91. a) 2457   **b)** 420   **93.** 200 feet   **95.** $1200

Section 2.3 Warm-ups F T F F T T F T F F
1. Three unknown consecutive integers are represented by x, $x + 1$, and $x + 2$.
3. The formula $P = 2L + 2W$ expresses the perimeter in terms of length and width.
5. The commission is a percentage of the selling price.
7. $x, x + 2$ **9.** $x, 10 - x$ **11.** $0.85x$ **13.** $3x$ miles
15. $4x + 10$ **17.** 27, 28, 29   **19.** 82, 84, 86   **21.** 63, 65
23. Width 46 meters, length 93 meters
25. 161 feet, 312 feet, 211 feet
27. Width 11.25 feet, length 27.5 feet
29. $1500 at 6%, $2500 at 10%   **31.** $80,000
33. $\frac{40}{3}$ gallons   **35.** 1.36 ounces   **37.** 40 mph

39. 15 mph **41.** $86,957

43. $8450 **45.** 18 feet **47.** Packers 35, Chiefs 10

49. $8.67 per pound **51.** 30 pounds **53.** $\frac{40}{7}$ quarts

55. $10,720 million

57. Brian $14,400, Daniel $7,200, Raymond $3,800

59. 22, 23 **61.** 7.5 hours **63.** 20 meters by 20 meters

65. $500 at 8%, $2500 at 10%

67. 2 gallons of 5% solution, 3 gallons of 10% solution

69. Todd 46, Darla 32

Section 2.4 Warm-ups F F T F F F T T T T

1. An inequality is a sentence that expresses inequality between two algebraic expressions.

3. If a is less than b, then a lies to the left of b on the number line.

5. When you multiply or divide by a negative number, the inequality symbol is reversed.

7. F **9.** T **11.** T **13.** T **15.** Yes **17.** No

19. No

21. $(-\infty, -1]$

23. $(20, \infty)$

25. $[3, \infty)$

27. $(-\infty, 2.3)$

29. > **31.** > **33.** ≤ **35.** >

37. $(-2, \infty)$

39. $[-4, \infty)$

41. $(5, \infty)$

43. $[-3, \infty)$

45. $(13, \infty)$

47. $[-1, \infty)$

49. $(-\infty, 4]$

51. $\left(\frac{2}{3}, \infty\right)$

53. $\left(\frac{13}{3}, \infty\right)$

55. $(-\infty, \infty)$

57. ∅ **59.** $(-\infty, \infty)$

61. ∅ **63.** x = Tony's height, $x > 6$ feet

65. s = Wilma's salary, $s < $80,000

67. v = speed of the Concorde, $v \le 1450$ mph

69. a = amount Julie can afford, $a \le $400

71. b = Burt's height, $b \le 5$ feet

73. t = Tina's hourly wage, $t \le $8.20

75. x = price of car, $x < $9100

77. x = price of truck, $x \ge $9100.92

79. a) Decreasing **b)** 2011

81. x = final exam score, $x \ge 77$

83. x = the price of A-Mart jeans, $x < $16.67

85. a) $[8, \infty)$ **b)** $(-\infty, -6)$ **c)** $(2, \infty)$
d) $(-\infty, -12)$ **e)** $(2, \infty)$

Section 2.5 Warm-ups T T F T T T F T F T

1. A compound inequality consists of two inequalities joined with the words "and" or "or."

3. A compound inequality using "or" is true when either one or the other or both inequalities is true.

5. The inequality $a < b < c$ means that $a < b$ and $b < c$.

7. No **9.** Yes **11.** No **13.** No **15.** Yes **17.** Yes

19.

21.

23.

25. ∅

27.

29. ∅

31. $(-\infty, 1) \cup (10, \infty)$

33. $(9, \infty)$

35. $(-6, \infty)$

37. $(1, 4]$

39. $(-\infty, \infty)$

41. ∅

43. $(4, 7)$

45. $[-3, 2)$

47. $\left(-\frac{7}{3}, 3\right]$

49. $(-1, 5)$

51. $[2, 3]$

53. $(2, \infty)$ **55.** $(-\infty, 5)$

57. $[2, 4]$ **59.** $(-\infty, \infty)$ **61.** ∅ **63.** $[4, 5)$

65. $[1, 6]$ **67.** $x > 2$ **69.** $x < 3$

71. $x > 2$ or $x \le -1$ **73.** $-2 \le x < 3$ **75.** $x \ge -3$

77. x = final exam score, $73 \le x \le 86.5$

79. $x = $ price of truck, $\$11{,}033 \le x \le \$13{,}811$
81. $x = $ number of cigarettes on the run, $4 \le x \le 18$
83. a) 1,226,950   **b)** 2011   **c)** 2019   **d)** 2011
85. $-b < x < -a$ provided $a < b$
87. a) $(12, 32)$ **b)** $(-20, 10]$ **c)** $(0, 9)$ **d)** $[-3, -1]$

Section 2.6 Warm-ups T F F T F T F F T F
1. Absolute value of a number is the number's distance from 0 on the number line.
3. Since both 4 and -4 are four units from 0, $|x| = 4$ has two solutions.
5. Since the distance from 0 for every number on the number line is greater than or equal to 0, $|x| \ge 0$.
7. $\{-5, 5\}$ **9.** $\{2, 4\}$ **11.** $\{-3, 9\}$ **13.** $\left\{-\dfrac{8}{3}, \dfrac{16}{3}\right\}$
15. $\{12\}$ **17.** $\{-20, 80\}$ **19.** $\varnothing$ **21.** $\{0, 5\}$
23. $\{0.143, 1.298\}$ **25.** $\{-2, 2\}$ **27.** $\{-11, 5\}$
29. $\{0, 3\}$ **31.** $\left\{-6, \dfrac{4}{3}\right\}$ **33.** $\{1, 3\}$ **35.** $(-\infty, \infty)$
37. $|x| < 2$ **39.** $|x| > 3$ **41.** $|x| \le 1$ **43.** $|x| \ge 2$
45. No   **47.** Yes   **49.** No   **51.** Yes
53. $(-\infty, -6) \cup (6, \infty)$ **55.** $(-3, 3)$
57. $(-\infty, -1] \cup [5, \infty)$ **59.** $\left(-\dfrac{1}{2}, \dfrac{9}{2}\right)$
61. $[-2, 12]$ **63.** $\left(-\infty, -\dfrac{9}{2}\right] \cup \left[\dfrac{15}{2}, \infty\right)$
65. $(-\infty, 2) \cup (2, \infty)$
67. $(-\infty, \infty)$ **69.** $\varnothing$ **71.** $(-\infty, \infty)$
73. $(-\infty, -3) \cup (-1, \infty)$ **75.** $(-4, 4)$ **77.** $(-1, 1)$
79. $(0.255, 0.847)$ **81.** 1401 or 1429
83. Between 121 and 133 pounds
85. a) 1 sec   **b)** 1 sec   **c)** $0.5 < t < 1.5$
87. a) $(-\infty, \infty)$ **b)** $(-\infty, \infty)$ **c)** all reals except $n = 0$

Chapter 2 Wrap-Up

Enriching Your Mathematical Word Power
1. c   **2.** b   **3.** d   **4.** c   **5.** c   **6.** d   **7.** d   **8.** a
9. d   **10.** d   **11.** d   **12.** c   **13.** d

Review Exercises
1. $\{8\}$ **3.** $\left\{-\dfrac{3}{2}\right\}$ **5.** R **7.** $\varnothing$ **9.** $\{0\}$ **11.** $\{20\}$
13. $\{5\}$ **15.** $\{5\}$ **17.** $x = \dfrac{-b}{a}$ **19.** $x = \dfrac{2}{c-a}$

21. $x = \dfrac{P}{mw}$ **23.** $x = \dfrac{2}{2w-1}$ **25.** $y = \dfrac{3}{2}x + 3$
27. $y = -\dfrac{1}{3}x + 4$ **29.** $y = 2x - 20$
31. Length 8.5 inches, width 14 inches
33. Wife $\$27{,}000$, Roy $\$35{,}000$ **35.** $\$9500$
37. 11 nickels, 4 dimes   **39.** 15 miles
41. $(-3, \infty)$ **43.** $(0, \infty)$
45. $(-\infty, -8]$ **47.** $\left(-\infty, \dfrac{11}{2}\right)$
49. $[48, \infty)$ **51.** $(-\infty, -4) \cup (1, \infty)$
53. $(0, 9)$ **55.** $(0, \infty)$
57. $(-\infty, 4)$
59. $\varnothing$ **61.** $(-\infty, \infty)$
63. $\left[-\dfrac{17}{2}, \dfrac{13}{2}\right]$
65. $[1, \infty)$ **67.** $(3, 6)$
69. $(-\infty, \infty)$ **71.** $[-2, -1]$
73. $\{-14, 14\}$
75. $\{3\}$
77. $\varnothing$ **79.** $\{-1, 2\}$
81. $(-\infty, -4] \cup [4, \infty)$
83. $(-\infty, -4) \cup (14, \infty)$
85. $\varnothing$ **87.** $(-\infty, \infty)$
89. $(-\infty, 1) \cup (3, \infty)$
91. $x = $ rental price, $\$3 \le x \le \$5$
93. $(40.2, 53.6)$ **95.** 81 or 91
97. $\$50{,}000$ accountant, $\$60{,}000$ employees
99. Washington County 1200, Cade County 2400
101. $x > 1$ **103.** $|x - 2| = 0$ **105.** $|x| = 3$

107. $x \leq -1$ **109.** $|x| \leq 2$ **111.** $x \leq 2$ or $x \geq 7$
113. $|x| > 3$ **115.** $5 < x < 7$ **117.** $|x| > 0$

Chapter 2 Test

1. $\{-4\}$ **2.** R **3.** $\{-6, 6\}$ **4.** $\{2, 5\}$ **5.** $y = \frac{2}{5}x - 4$

6. $y = \dfrac{5}{1 - 3x}$ **7.** $[4, 8]$

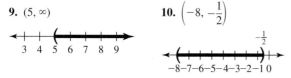

8. $(-\infty, -7) \cup (13, \infty)$

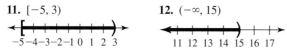

9. $(5, \infty)$ **10.** $\left(-8, -\dfrac{1}{2}\right)$

11. $[-5, 3)$ **12.** $(-\infty, 15)$

13. $\varnothing$ **14.** $(-\infty, \infty)$ **15.** $\varnothing$ **16.** $\{2.5\}$ **17.** $\varnothing$
18. R **19.** $\varnothing$ **20.** R **21.** $\{100\}$ **22.** 13 meters
23. 14 inches   **24.** \$300   **25.** 30 liters
26. $|x - 28{,}000| > 3{,}000$, Brenda makes more than \$31,000
   or less than \$25,000.

Making Connections Chapters 1–2

1. $11x$ **2.** $30x^2$ **3.** $3x + 1$ **4.** $4x - 3$ **5.** 899
6. 961   **7.** 841   **8.** 25   **9.** 13   **10.** -25 **11.** 5
12. -4 **13.** $-2x + 13$ **14.** 60   **15.** 72   **16.** -9
17. $-3x^3$ **18.** 1   **19.** $\{0\}$ **20.** R **21.** $\{0\}$ **22.** $\{1\}$

23. $\left\{-\dfrac{1}{3}\right\}$ **24.** $\{1\}$ **25.** R **26.** $\{1000\}$ **27.** $\left\{-\dfrac{17}{5}, 1\right\}$

28. a) 87,500   **b)** $C_r = 4{,}500 + 0.06x$, $C_b = 8{,}000 + 0.02x$
   c) 87,500   **d)** Buying is \$1,300 cheaper.
   e) $(75{,}000, 100{,}000)$

Chapter 3

Section 3.1 Warm-ups F F F T T T T T F T
1. The origin is the point where the x-axis and y-axis intersect.
3. Intercepts are points where a graph crosses the axes.
5. The graph of an equation of the type $x = k$, where k is a
   fixed number is a vertical line.
7. I   **9.** III   **11.** y-axis   **13.** IV   **15.** II   **17.** x-axis
19. y-axis

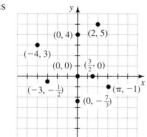

21. $\left(\dfrac{7}{2}, 3\right), 5$ **23.** $(2, 1), 10$

25. $\left(-3, -\dfrac{3}{2}\right), 13$ **27.** $\left(0, \dfrac{5}{2}\right), \sqrt{13}$

29.

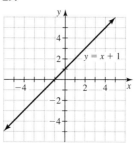

31.

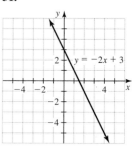

33.

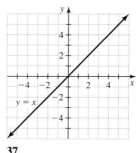

35.

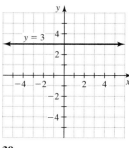

37.

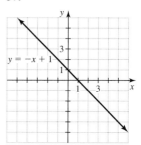

39.

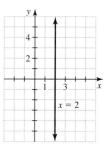

41.

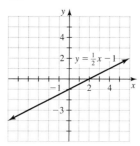

43.

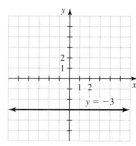

45.

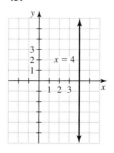

47.

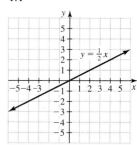

49.

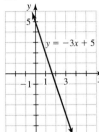

$y = -3x + 5$

51.

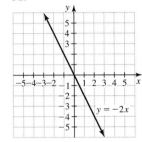

$y = -2x$

53.

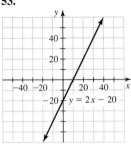

$y = 2x - 20$

55.

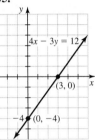

$4x - 3y = 12$

$(3, 0)$

$(0, -4)$

57.

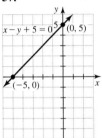

$x - y + 5 = 0$ $(0, 5)$

$(-5, 0)$

59.

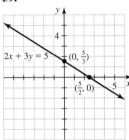

$2x + 3y = 5$ $(0, \frac{5}{3})$

$(\frac{5}{2}, 0)$

61.

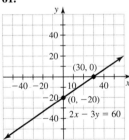

$(30, 0)$

$(0, -20)$

$2x - 3y = 60$

63.

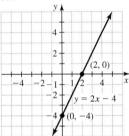

$(2, 0)$

$y = 2x - 4$

$(0, -4)$

65.

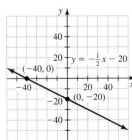

$y = -\frac{1}{2}x - 20$

$(-40, 0)$

$(0, -20)$

67. $(5, 0), (0, -3)$

69. $(0, 0)$ **71.** $\left(-\frac{1}{2}, 0\right)$ **73.** $\left(0, -\frac{2}{3}\right)$ **75.** $\left(\frac{1}{4}, 0\right)\left(0, \frac{1}{2}\right)$

77. $(2, 0), (3, -3)$ **79.** $(-4, -33), (22, 6)$

81. a) \$25,325   **b)** \$320

c)

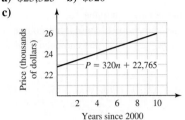

$P = 320n + 22,765$

Price (thousands of dollars)

Years since 2000

83. a) \$146   **b)**

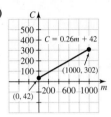

$C = 0.26m + 42$

$(1000, 302)$

$(0, 42)$

85. a) \$11.45.

b) The number of toppings on a \$14.45 pizza is 11.

87. $n + 2b = 100$, 35 binders

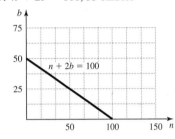

$n + 2b = 100$

89. a) Her weekly cost, revenue, and profit are \$517.50, \$1275, and \$757.50.

b) 1100. She had a profit of \$995 on selling 1100 roses.

c) 995. The difference between revenue and cost is \$995, which is her profit.

91.

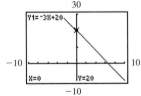

Y1=-3X+20

X=0   Y=20

93.

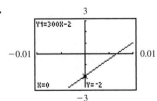

Y1=300X-2

X=0   Y=-2

95.

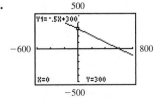

Y1=-.5X+300

X=0   Y=300

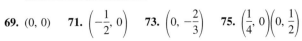

Section 3.2 Warm-ups T F F T F F F T F F
1. Slope measures the steepness of a line.
3. A horizontal line has zero slope because it has no rise.
5. If m_1 and m_2 are the slopes of perpendicular lines, then $m_1 = -\dfrac{1}{m_2}$.

7. $\dfrac{2}{3}$ **9.** Undefined   **11.** 0   **13.** -1 **15.** $\dfrac{3}{2}$ **17.** -1

19. $-\dfrac{5}{3}$ **21.** $\dfrac{4}{7}$ **23.** 5   **25.** $-\dfrac{5}{3}$ **27.** $-\dfrac{3}{5}$ **29.** $-\dfrac{2}{5}$

31. -3 **33.** 0   **35.** Undefined   **37.** 0.169   **39.** -1.273

41. $\dfrac{8}{3}$ **43.** $\dfrac{3}{7}$

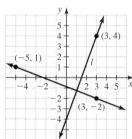 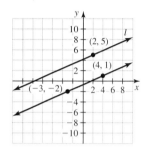

45. $-\dfrac{5}{4}$

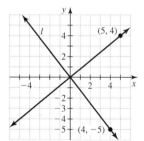

47. Yes   **49.** No   **51.** No
53. a) \$625 per year   **b)** Approximately \$29,000
    c) \$28,635

55. $(3, 5), (0, -7)$ **57.** $-\dfrac{5}{2}$ **59.** -4.049

61. A horizontal line has zero slope and a vertical line has undefined slope.

63. $-2, \dfrac{1}{2}$, perpendicular

65. Increasing m makes the graph increase faster. The slopes of these lines are 1, 2, 3, and 4.

Section 3.3 Warm-ups T F F T T F T F F T
1. Point-slope form is $y - y_1 = m(x - x_1)$, where m is the slope and (x_1, y_1) is a point on the line.
3. We need the slope and a point on the line. (We might have to find the slope from two points or from knowing the line is parallel or perpendicular to another line.)
5. To find the slope from standard form solve the equation for y to get the form $y = mx + b$, where m is the slope.

7. $y = 2x - 7$ **9.** $y = -\dfrac{1}{2}x + 2$ **11.** $y = -x - 3$

13. $y = \dfrac{1}{3}x + \dfrac{4}{3}$ **15.** $y = 4x - 8$ **17.** $y = -\dfrac{3}{4}x$

19. $y = \dfrac{1}{2}x + 2$ **21.** $y = -2$ **23.** $x = 1$

25. $y = -x$ **27.** $y = \dfrac{3}{2}x - 3$ **29.** $y = -x + 2$

31. $x - 3y = 6$ **33.** $x - 2y = -13$

35. $2x - 6y = 11$ **37.** $5x + 6y = 890$

39. $y = -\dfrac{2}{5}x + \dfrac{1}{5}, -\dfrac{2}{5}, \left(0, \dfrac{1}{5}\right)$

41. $y = 3x - 2, 3, (0, -2)$ **43.** $y = 2, 0, (0, 2)$

45. $y = 3x - 1, 3, (0, -1)$ **47.** $y = \dfrac{3}{2}x + 11, \dfrac{3}{2}, (0, 11)$

49. $y = \dfrac{1}{3}x + \dfrac{7}{12}, \dfrac{1}{3}, \left(0, \dfrac{7}{12}\right)$

51. $y = 0.01x + 6057, 0.01, (0, 6057)$
53. $x - 2y = -10$ **55.** $2x + y = 4$
57. $2x - y = -5$ **59.** $x + 2y = 7$
61. $2x + y = 3$ **63.** $3x - y = -9$
65. $y = 5$

67. 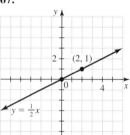   **69.**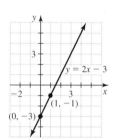

71. 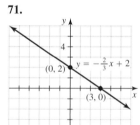   **73.**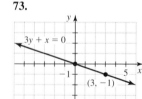

75. 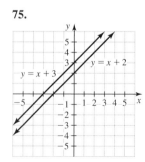   **77.**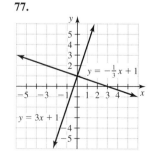

79.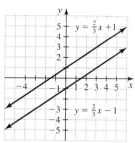

81.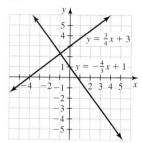

83. Perpendicular   **85.** Parallel

87. Neither   **89.** Perpendicular

91. $t = \dfrac{7}{6}s + 60$, 95°F

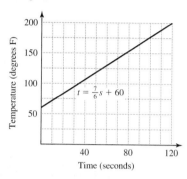

93. a) $y = 0.4x - 774$ **b)** 30 billion tons

95. a) $w = 310.77d - 1610.44$ **b)** 953 ft³/sec
   c) increasing

97. a) $(4, 0), (0, 6)$ **b)** $(a, 0), (0, b)$

   c) $\dfrac{x}{-5} + \dfrac{y}{3} = 1$

   d) Horizontal lines, vertical lines, and lines through $(0, 0)$

101. The lines intersect at $(50, 97)$.

Section 3.4 Warm-ups T F T F T T F T F T

1. A linear inequality is an inequality of the form $Ax + By \leq C$ (or using $<$, $>$, or $\geq$), where A, B, and C are real numbers and A and B are not both zero.

3. If the inequality includes equality then the line should be solid.

5. The test point method is used to determine which side of the boundary line to shade.

7.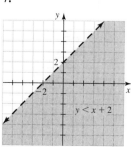

9.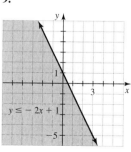

11.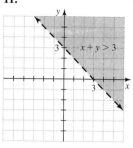

13.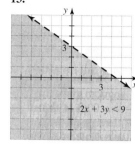

15.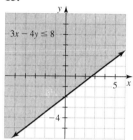

17.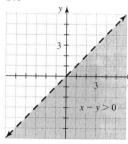

19.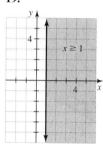

21.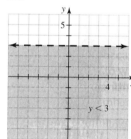

23.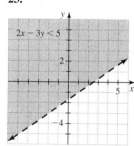

25.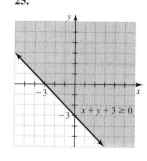

27.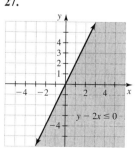

29.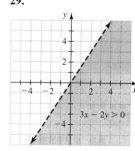

49.
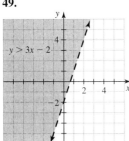

51.
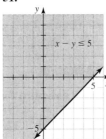

69.
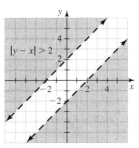

71. No   **73.** Yes   **75.** Yes   **77.** No
79. $\{3, 4, 5\}, \{1, 5, 9\}$ **81.** $(-\infty, \infty), (-\infty, \infty)$
83. $[-5, \infty), [0, \infty)$ **85.** -5 **87.** -6
89. $-\dfrac{21}{4}$ **91.** $3x - y = 6$ **93.** $x + 2y = 7$
95. $x = 2$ **97.** $y = 0$ **99.** $2x - y = -6$
101. $3x - y = -6$ **103.** $y = 5$
109. a) $h = 220 - a$ **b)** 180   **c)** Decreases
111. 62 days
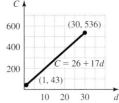

53.
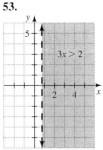

55.
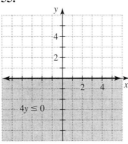

57.
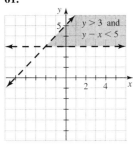

59.
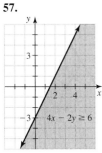

Chapter 3 Test

1. $(0, 5), \left(\dfrac{5}{2}, 0\right), \left(\dfrac{13}{2}, -8\right)$ **2.** $-\dfrac{6}{5}$ **3.** $\left(-\dfrac{1}{2}, -\dfrac{1}{2}\right), \sqrt{26}$

4. $\dfrac{8}{5}, (0, 2)$ **6.** $V = -2{,}000a + 22{,}000$ **7.** $x + 2y = 6$

8. $4x + y = -7$ **9.** $5x + 3y = 19$ **10.** $x - 2y = -4$

11.
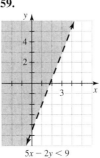

12.
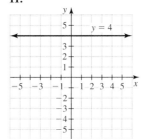

61.
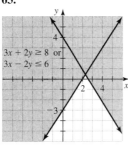

63.
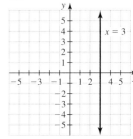

13.
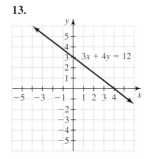

14.
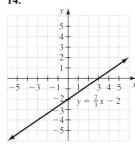

65.
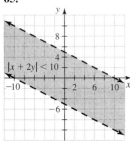

67.
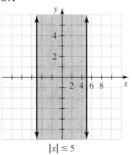

15.

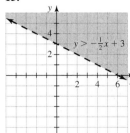

$y > -\frac{1}{2}x + 3$

16.

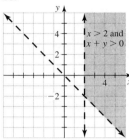

$x > 2$ and $x + y > 0$

27.

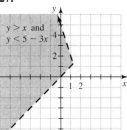

$y > x$ and $y < 5 - 3x$

28.

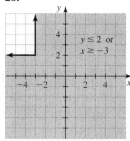

$y \le 2$ or $x \ge -3$

17.

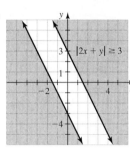

$|2x + y| \ge 3$

18. Yes   **19.** 11

20. $[7, \infty)$, $[0, \infty)$ **21.** $S = 0.50n + 3$ **22.** 6 ft

29. a) $b = 500a - 24{,}000$, $b = 667a - 34{,}689$, $b = 800a - 43{,}600$ **b)** $8{,}000   **c)** 69
d) The slopes 500, 667, and 800 indicate the additional amount per year received beyond the basic amount in each category.

Making Connections Chapters 1–3
1. 128   **2.** 64   **3.** 49   **4.** −29   **5.** −5   **6.** −5
7. $12t^2$ **8.** $7t$ **9.** $x + 2$ **10.** $7y$ **11.** $7x - 32$
12. $-21x^2 + 8x$ **13.** $\{27\}$ **14.** $\{200\}$ **15.** $\left\{\frac{7}{3}\right\}$
16. $\left\{\frac{4}{3}, \frac{10}{3}\right\}$ **17.** $\varnothing$ **18.** $\left\{0, \frac{14}{3}\right\}$

19.

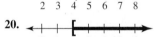

20.

21.

22.

23.

24.

25.

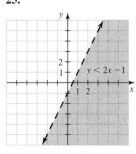

$y < 2x - 1$

26.

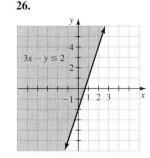

$3x - y \le 2$

Chapter 4

Section 4.1 Warm-ups T F F T T T T T T
1. The intersection point of the graphs is the solution to an independent system.
3. The graphing method can be very inaccurate.
5. If the equation you get after substituting turns out to be incorrect, such as $0 = 9$, then the system has no solution.
7. $\{(1, 2)\}$ **9.** $\{(0, -1)\}$ **11.** $\{(2, -1)\}$ **13.** $\varnothing$
15. $\{(x, y)\} \mid x + 2y = 8\}$ **17.** $\{(-1, 2)\}$ **19.** $\varnothing$ **21.** c
23. b   **25.** $\{(8, 3)\}$, independent
27. $\{(-3, 2)\}$, independent   **29.** $\{(20, 10)\}$, independent
31. $\varnothing$, inconsistent   **33.** $\{(x, y) \mid y = 2x - 5\}$, dependent
35. $\{(5, -1)\}$, independent   **37.** $\{(7, 7)\}$, independent
39. $\{(15, 25)\}$, independent   **41.** $\left\{\left(\frac{11}{4}, \frac{9}{2}\right)\right\}$, independent
43. $\{(0, 0)\}$, independent   **45.** $\left\{\left(\frac{9}{2}, -\frac{1}{2}\right)\right\}$, independent
47. $\{(x, y) \mid 3y - 2x = -3\}$, dependent
49. $\varnothing$, inconsistent
51. $\{(0.8, 0.7)\}$, independent
53. Width 13 feet, length 28 feet
55. $14{,}000 at 5%, $16{,}000 at 10%
57. −12 and 14
59. 94 toasters, 6 vacation coupons
61. State tax $3{,}553, federal tax $28{,}934
63. $20{,}000
65. a) $500{,}000   **b)** $300{,}000   **c)** 20,000   **d)** $400{,}000
67. a
69. a) $(2.8, 2.6)$ **b)** $(1.0, -0.2)$

Section 4.2 Warm-ups T F T T F T T F T T
1. In this section we learned the addition method.
3. In some cases we multiply one or both of the equations on each side to change the coefficients of the variable we are trying to eliminate.
5. If an identity, such as $0 = 0$, results from addition of the equations, then the equations are dependent.
7. $\{(8, -1)\}$ **9.** $\{(5, -7)\}$

11. $\left\{\left(\dfrac{3}{8}, -\dfrac{31}{8}\right)\right\}$ **13.** $\{(-1, 3)\}$ **15.** $\left\{\left(\dfrac{7}{9}, \dfrac{2}{3}\right)\right\}$

17. $\{(-1, -3)\}$ **19.** $\{(-2, -5)\}$ **21.** $\{(22, 26)\}$

23. $\varnothing$, inconsistent   **25.** $\{(x, y) \mid 5x - y = 1\}$, dependent

27. $\left\{\left(\dfrac{5}{2}, 0\right)\right\}$, independent   **29.** $\{(12, 6)\}$ **31.** $\{(-8, 6)\}$

33. $\{(16, 12)\}$ **35.** $\left\{\left(\dfrac{1}{2}, \dfrac{1}{3}\right)\right\}$ **37.** $\{(12, 7)\}$

39. $\{(400, 800)\}$ **41.** $\{(1.5, 1.25)\}$ **43.** $\left\{\left(\dfrac{3}{4}, \dfrac{2}{3}\right)\right\}$

45. $\{(5, 6)\}$ **47.** $\{(2, -17)\}$ **49.** $\{(0, 1)\}$

51. $\{(3, 4)\}$ **53.** $\left\{\left(\dfrac{1}{2}, \dfrac{1}{3}\right)\right\}$ **55.** $\varnothing$ **57.** $\{(x, y) \mid y = x\}$

59. $1.40   **61.** 1380 students   **63.** 31 dimes, 4 nickels

65. a) $(20, 30)$

     b) 20 pounds chocolate, 30 pounds peanut butter

67. 4 hours   **69.** 80%

71. Width 150 meters, length 200 meters

Section 4.3 Warm-ups F F T F F T T F F F

1. A linear equation in three variables is an equation of the form $Ax + By + Cz = D$, where A, B, and C cannot all be zero.

3. A solution to a system of linear equations in three variables is an ordered triple that satisfies all of the equations in the system.

5. The graph of a linear equation in three variables is a plane in a three-dimensional coordinate system.

7. $\{(1, 2, -1)\}$ **9.** $\{(1, 3, 2)\}$ **11.** $\{(1, -5, 3)\}$

13. $\{(-1, 2, -1)\}$ **15.** $\{(-1, -2, 4)\}$

17. $\{(1, 3, 5)\}$ **19.** $\{(3, 4, 5)\}$ **21.** $\varnothing$

23. $\{(x, y, z) \mid 3x - y + z = 5\}$ **25.** $\varnothing$

27. $\{(x, y, z) \mid 5x + 4y - 2z = 150\}$ **29.** $\{(0.1, 0.3, 2)\}$

31. Chevrolet $20,000, Ford $22,000, Toyota $24,000

33. First 10 hr, second 12 hr, third 14 hr

35. $1500 stocks, $4500 bonds, $6000 mutual fund

37. Anna 108 pounds, Bob 118 pounds, Chris 92 pounds

39. 3 nickels, 6 dimes, 4 quarters

41. $24,000 teaching, $18,000 painting, $6,000 royalties

43. Edwin 24, father 51, grandfather 84

Section 4.4 Warm-ups T T T F T F F F T F

1. A matrix is a rectangular array of numbers.

3. The order of a matrix is the number of rows and columns.

5. An augmented matrix is a matrix where the entries in the first column are the coefficients of x, the entries in the second column are the coefficients of y, and the entries in the third column are the constants from a system of two linear equations in two unknowns.

7. 2×2 **9.** 3×2 **11.** 3×1

13. $\begin{bmatrix} 2 & -3 & | & 9 \\ -3 & 1 & | & -1 \end{bmatrix}$ **15.** $\begin{bmatrix} 1 & -1 & 1 & | & 1 \\ 1 & 1 & -2 & | & 3 \\ 0 & 1 & -3 & | & 4 \end{bmatrix}$

17. $5x + y = -1$
$2x - 3y = 0$

19. $x = 6$
$-x + z = -3$
$x + y = 1$

21. $R_1 \leftrightarrow R_2$ **23.** $\dfrac{1}{5} R_2 \to R_2$ **25.** $\{(1, 2)\}$

27. $\{(4, 5)\}$ **29.** $\{(1, -1)\}$ **31.** $\{(7, 6)\}$ **33.** $\varnothing$

35. $\{(x, y) \mid x + 2y = 1\}$ **37.** $\{(1, 2, 3)\}$ **39.** $\{(1, 1, 1)\}$

41. $\{(1, 2, 0)\}$ **43.** $\{(1, 0, 1)\}$

45. $\{(x, y, z) \mid x - y + z = 1\}$ **47.** $\varnothing$

Section 4.5 Warm-ups T F F T T T T T T T

1. A determinant is a real number associated with a square matrix.

3. Cramer's rule works on systems that have exactly one solution.

5. A minor for an element is obtained by deleting the row and column of the element and finding the determinant of the 2×2 matrix that remains.

7. -1 **9.** -3 **11.** -14 **13.** 0.4 **15.** $\{(1, -3)\}$

17. $\{(1, 1)\}$ **19.** $\left\{\left(\dfrac{23}{13}, \dfrac{9}{13}\right)\right\}$ **21.** $\{(10, 15)\}$

23. $\left\{\left(\dfrac{27}{4}, \dfrac{13}{2}\right)\right\}$ **25.** 11   **27.** 4   **29.** 3   **31.** 1

33. -7 **35.** -1 **37.** 9   **39.** 5   **41.** 22   **43.** 6

45. 70   **47.** 25   **49.** $\{(1, 2, 3)\}$ **51.** $\{(-1, 1, 2)\}$

53. $\{(-3, 2, 1)\}$ **55.** $\left\{\left(\dfrac{3}{2}, \dfrac{1}{2}, 2\right)\right\}$ **57.** $\{(0, 1, -1)\}$

59. a) $(9, 11)$ **b)** 9 servings peas, 11 servings beets

61. Milk $2.40, magazine $2.25

63. 12 singles, 10 doubles   **65.** Gary 39, Harry 34

67. Square 10 feet, triangle $\dfrac{40}{3}$ feet

69. 10 gallons of 10% solution, 20 gallons of 25% solution

71. Mimi 36 pounds, Mitzi 32 pounds, Cassandra 107 pounds

73. $39°, 51°, 90°$ **75.** Use another method.

77. No. These are nonlinear equations.

Section 4.6 Warm-ups F F F F F T F T F T

1. A constraint is an inequality that restricts the values of the variables.

3. Constraints may be limitations on the amount of available supplies, money, or other resources.

5. The maximum or minimum of a linear function subject to linear constraints occurs at a vertex of the region determined by the constraints.

7.

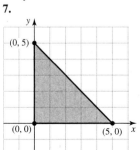

9.

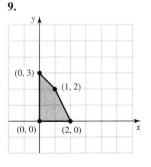

11.

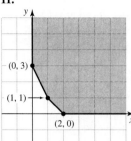

13.

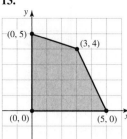

15.

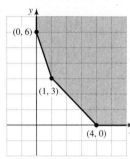

17. a) 0, 320,000, 510,000, 450,000
   b) 30 TV ads and 60 radio ads
19. 6 doubles, 4 triples
21. 0 doubles, 8 triples
23. 1.75 cups Doggie Dinner, 5.5 cups Puppie Power
25. 10 cups Doggie Dinner, 0 cups Puppie Power
27. Laundromat $8,000, carwash $16,000

Chapter 4 Wrap-Up

Enriching Your Mathematical Word Power
1. c   **2.** a   **3.** a   **4.** d   **5.** b
6. c   **7.** a   **8.** c   **9.** d   **10.** b
11. a   **12.** d

Review Exercises
1. $\{(1, 1)\}$, independent   **3.** $\{(x, y) \mid x + 2y = 4\}$, dependent
5. $\varnothing$, inconsistent   **7.** $\{(-3, 2)\}$, independent
9. $\varnothing$, inconsistent   **11.** $\{(x, y) \mid 2x - y = 3\}$, dependent
13. $\{(30, 12)\}$, independent   **15.** $\left\{\left(\dfrac{1}{5}, \dfrac{2}{5}\right)\right\}$, independent
17. $\{(-1, 5)\}$, independent
19. $\{(x, y) \mid 3x - 2y = 12\}$, dependent
21. $\varnothing$, inconsistent   **23.** $\left\{\left(2, -\dfrac{1}{3}\right)\right\}$, independent
25. $\{(20, 60)\}$, independent   **27.** $\{(2, 4, 6)\}$
29. $\{(1, -3, 2)\}$ **31.** $\varnothing$ **33.** $\{(3, 4)\}$
35. $\{(2, -4)\}$ **37.** $\{(1, 1, 2)\}$ **39.** 2
41. -0.2 **43.** $\{(-1, -2)\}$
45. $\{(2, 1)\}$ **47.** 58   **49.** -30
51. $\{(1, 2, -3)\}$

53.

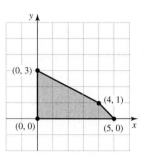

55. 30   **57.** 78   **59.** 36 minutes
61. 4 liters of A, 8 liters of B, 8 liters of C
63. Three servings of each

Chapter 4 Test
1. $\{(1, 3)\}$ **2.** $\left\{\left(\dfrac{5}{2}, -3\right)\right\}$ **3.** $\{(x, y) \mid y = x - 5\}$
4. $\{(-1, 3)\}$ **5.** $\varnothing$ **6.** Inconsistent   **7.** Dependent
8. Independent   **9.** $\{(1, -2, -3)\}$
10. $\{(2, 5)\}$ **11.** $\{(3, 1, 1)\}$ **12.** -18 **13.** -2
14. $\{(-1, 2)\}$ **15.** $\{(2, -2, 1)\}$
16. Singles $18, doubles $25
17. Jill 17 hours, Karen 14 hours, Betsy 62 hours   **18.** 44

Making Connections Chapters 1–4
1. -81 **2.** 7   **3.** 73   **4.** 5.94   **5.** $-t - 3$
6. $-0.9x + 0.9$ **7.** $3x^2 + 2x - 1$ **8.** y
9. $y = \dfrac{3}{5}x - \dfrac{7}{5}$ **10.** $y = \dfrac{C}{D}x - \dfrac{W}{D}$ **11.** $y = \dfrac{K}{W - C}$
12. $y = \dfrac{bw - 2A}{b}$ **13.** $\{(4, -1)\}$ **14.** $\{(500, 700)\}$
15. $\{(x, y) \mid x + 17 = 5y\}$ **16.** $\varnothing$ **17.** $y = \dfrac{5}{9}x + 55$
18. $y = -\dfrac{11}{6}x + \dfrac{2}{3}$ **19.** $y = 5x + 26$ **20.** $y = \dfrac{1}{2}x + 5$
21. $y = 5$ **22.** $x = -7$
23. a) Machine A
   b) Machine B $0.04 per copy, machine A $0.03 per copy
   c) The slopes 0.04 and 0.03 are the per copy cost for each machine.
   d) B: $y = 0.04x + 2000$, A: $y = 0.03x + 4000$
   e) 200,000

Chapter 5

Section 5.1 Warm-ups T F F F T F T T T F
1. An exponential expression is an expression of the form a^n.
3. The product rule states that $a^m a^n = a^{m+n}$.
5. To convert a number in scientific notation to standard notation, move the decimal point n places to the left if the exponent on 10 is $-n$ or move the decimal point n places to the right if the exponent on 10 is n, assuming that n is a positive integer.

7. $4, -4, 4, \dfrac{1}{4}, -\dfrac{1}{4}, \dfrac{1}{4}$ **9.** $8, -8, -8, \dfrac{1}{8}, -\dfrac{1}{8}, -\dfrac{1}{8}$

11. $\dfrac{1}{25}, -\dfrac{1}{25}, \dfrac{1}{25}, 25, -25, 25$ **13.** $7, -7, -7, \dfrac{1}{7}, -\dfrac{1}{7}, -\dfrac{1}{7}$

15. $\dfrac{1}{4}, \dfrac{1}{4}, -\dfrac{1}{4}, 4, 4, -4$ **17.** $\dfrac{8}{27}, -\dfrac{8}{27}, -\dfrac{8}{27}, \dfrac{27}{8}, -\dfrac{27}{8}, -\dfrac{27}{8}$

19. 2^{17} **21.** $-\dfrac{6}{x^6}$ **23.** $\dfrac{21}{b^{10}}$ **25.** $1, -1, 1, -1$

27. $1, 2, 1$ **29.** $3s, 3, 1$ **31.** 2 **33.** 32 **35.** $\dfrac{100}{3}$

37. $\dfrac{8y^2}{5x^2}$ **39.** $\dfrac{1}{48x^2}$ **41.** x^2 **43.** 3^8 **45.** $\dfrac{1}{3a^3}$

47. $\dfrac{-3}{w^8}$ **49.** $3^8 w^6$ **51.** $\dfrac{xy}{2}$ **53.** 9 **55.** -14

57. $\dfrac{1}{16}$ **59.** $\dfrac{3}{8}$ **61.** $\dfrac{4}{9}$ **63.** $-15a^4$ **65.** $8a^3$ **67.** a

69. $\dfrac{-2x^2y^4}{3}$ **71.** $\dfrac{5}{3}$ **73.** 3 **75.** -2 **77.** -4

79. -3 **81.** $486,000,000$ **83.** 0.00000237

85. $4,000,000$ **87.** 0.000005 **89.** 3.2×10^5

91. 7.1×10^{-7} **93.** 7.03×10^{-5} **95.** 2.05×10^7

97. 6×10^3 **99.** 7.5×10^{-1} **101.** 3×10^{22}

103. -1.2×10^{13} **105.** 1.578×10^5

107. 9.187×10^{-5} **109.** 3.828×10^{30}

111. 4.910×10^{11} ft **113.** 3.83×10^7 seconds

115. 2.6 lb/person/day

Section 5.2 Warm-ups F T T F F F T T T T
1. The power of a power rule states that $(a^m)^n = a^{mn}$.
3. The power of a quotient rule states that $(a/b)^m = a^m/b^m$.
5. To compute the amount A when interest is compounded annually use $A = P(1 + i)^n$, where P is the principal, i is the annual interest rate, and n is the number of years.

7. 64 **9.** y^{10} **11.** $\dfrac{1}{x^8}$ **13.** m^{18} **15.** 1 **17.** $\dfrac{1}{x^2}$

19. $81y^2$ **21.** $25w^6$ **23.** $\dfrac{x^9}{y^6}$ **25.** $\dfrac{b^2}{9a^2}$ **27.** $\dfrac{6x^3}{y}$

29. $\dfrac{1}{8a^3 b^4}$ **31.** $\dfrac{w^3}{8}$ **33.** $-\dfrac{27a^3}{64}$ **35.** $\dfrac{x^2 y^2}{4}$ **37.** $\dfrac{y^2}{9x^6}$

39. $\dfrac{25}{4}$ **41.** 4 **43.** $-\dfrac{27}{8x^3}$ **45.** $\dfrac{27y^3}{8x^6}$ **47.** 5^{6t}

49. 2^{6w^2} **51.** 7^{m+3} **53.** 8^{5a+11} **55.** $6x^9$ **57.** $-8x^6$

59. $\dfrac{3z}{x^2 y}$ **61.** $-\dfrac{3}{2}$ **63.** $\dfrac{4x^6}{9}$ **65.** $-\dfrac{x^2}{2}$ **67.** $\dfrac{y^3}{8x^3}$

69. $\dfrac{b^{14}}{5a^7}$ **71.** $\dfrac{x^6}{16y^8}$ **73.** $3ac^8$ **75.** 2^{11} **77.** 2^{-4}

79. 2^{6n} **81.** 2^{4m^2} **83.** 25 **85.** 0.75 **87.** 850.559

89. 1.533 **91.** $\$56,197.12$ **93.** $\$2,958.64$

95. a) 75.1 yr **b)** 81.4 yr **99.** d

101. a) 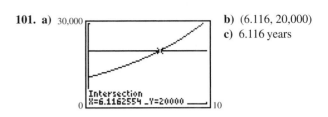 **b)** (6.116, 20,000) **c)** 6.116 years

Section 5.3 Warm-ups F F F T F T F T T F
1. A term of a polynomial is a single number or the product of a number and one or more variables raised to whole number powers.
3. A constant is simply a number.
5. The degree of a polynomial in one variable is the highest power of the variable in the polynomial.
7. Yes **9.** No **11.** Yes **13.** No
15. $4, -8$, binomial **17.** $0, 0$, monomial
19. $7, 0$, monomial **21.** $6, 1$, trinomial
23. 80 **25.** -29 **27.** 0 **29.** $3a + 2$ **31.** $5xy + 25$
33. $2x - 9$ **35.** $2x^3 - x^2 - 2x - 8$
37. $11x^2 - 2x - 9$ **39.** $x + 5$ **41.** $-6x^2 + 5x + 2$
43. $2x$ **45.** $-15x^6$ **47.** $-3x + 2$
49. $15x^4 y^4 - 20x^3 y^3$ **51.** $x^2 - 4$ **53.** $2x^3 - x^2 + x - 6$
55. $-10x^2 + 15x$ **57.** $x^2 + 10x + 25$
59. $2x^2 + 9x - 18$ **61.** $x^3 - y^3$ **63.** $2x - 5$
65. $4a^2 - 11a - 4$ **67.** $4w^2 - 8w - 7$ **69.** $x^3 - 8$
71. $xz - wz + 2xw - 2w^2$ **73.** $x^4 - x^2 + 4x - 4$
75. $14.4375x^2 - 29.592x - 9.72$
77. $15.369x^2 + 1.88x - 0.866$
79. $\dfrac{3}{4}x + \dfrac{3}{2}$ **81.** $-\dfrac{1}{2}x^2 + x$
83. $3x^2 - 21x + 1$ **85.** $-4x^2 - 62x - 168$
87. $x^4 - m^2 - 4m - 4$ **89.** $-6x^3 - 53x^2 - 8x$
91. $-4a^{2m} - 4a^m + 5$ **93.** $x^{2n} + 2x^n - 3$
95. $5z^{3w} - z^{1+w}$ **97.** $x^{6r} + y^3$ **99.** $\$75$
101. $\$49.35, \$15.61$
103. a) 6.2 years **b)** no **c)** 2037

Section 5.4 Warm-ups T T F T F T T T F F
1. The distributive property is used to multiply binomials.
3. FOIL quickly gives us the product of two binomials.
5. The square of a difference is the square of the first term minus twice the product of the two terms plus the square of the last term.
7. In general $(a + b)^2 = a^2 + 2ab + b^2$.
9. $x^2 + 2x - 8$ **11.** $2x^2 + 7x + 3$ **13.** $2a^2 - 7a - 15$
15. $4x^4 - 49$ **17.** $2x^6 + 7x^3 - 4$ **19.** $w^2 + 5wz - 6z^2$
21. $9k^2 + 6kt - 8t^2$ **23.** $xy - 3y + xw - 3w$
25. $m^2 + 6m + 9$ **27.** $a^2 - 8a + 16$
29. $4w^2 + 4w + 1$ **31.** $9t^2 - 30tu + 25u^2$
33. $x^2 + 2x + 1$ **35.** $a^2 - 6ay^3 + 9y^6$
37. $w^2 - 81$ **39.** $w^6 - y^2$ **41.** $49 - 4x^2$
43. $9x^4 - 4$ **45.** $25a^6 - 4b^2$ **47.** $m^2 + 2mt + t^2 - 25$

49. $y^2 - r^2 - 10r - 25$
51. $4y^2 - 4yt + t^2 + 12y - 6t + 9$
53. $9h^2 + 6hk - 6h + k^2 - 2k + 1$
55. $x^2 + 3x - 54$ **57.** $25 - x^2$
59. $6x^2 + 7ax - 20a^2$ **61.** $2t^2 + 2tw - 3t - 3w$
63. $9x^4 + 12x^2y^3 + 4y^6$ **65.** $6y^2 - 4y - 10$
67. $4m^2 - 28m + 49$ **69.** $49x^2 + 42x + 9$
71. $36y^3 + 12y^2 + y$ **73.** $2ah + h^2$
75. $x^3 + 6x^2 + 12x + 8$ **77.** $y^3 + 9y^2 + 27y + 27$
79. $-3x^2 + 34x - 75$ **81.** $16.32x^2 - 10.47x - 17.55$
83. $12.96y^2 + 31.68y + 19.36$ **85.** $x^{3m} + 2x^{2m} + 3x^m + 6$
87. $a^{3n+1} + a^{2n+1} - 3a^{n+1}$ **89.** $a^{2m} + 2a^{m+n} + a^{2n}$
91. $15y^{3m} + 24y^{2m}z^k + 20y^mz^{3-k} + 32z^3$
93. $x^2 + 4x + 3$ **95.** $4x^2 - 36x + 80, 66.24 \text{ km}^2$
97. $4x^3 - 20x^2 + 24x, 5.9 \text{ ft}^3$

Section 5.5 Warm-ups T T T T F F F T F F

1. A prime number is a natural number greater than 1 that has no factors other than itself and 1.
3. The greatest common factor for the terms of a polynomial is a monomial that includes every number or variable that is a factor of all terms of the polynomial.
5. A linear polynomial is a polynomial of the form $ax + b$ with $a \neq 0$.
7. A prime polynomial is a polynomial that cannot be factored.
9. 12   **11.** 3   **13.** $6xy$ **15.** $x(x^2 - 5)$
17. $12w(4x + 3y)$ **19.** $2x(x^2 - 2x + 3)$
21. $12a^3b^2(3b^4 - 2a + 5a^2b)$ **23.** $(x - 6)(a + b)$
25. $(y - 1)^2(y + z)$ **27.** $2(x - y), -2(-x + y)$
29. $3x(2x - 1), -3x(-2x + 1)$
31. $w^2(-w + 3), -w^2(w - 3)$
33. $a(-a^2 + a - 7), -a(a^2 - a + 7)$
35. $(x + y)(a + 3)$ **37.** $(x - 3)(y + 1)$
39. $(a - b)(4 - c)$ **41.** $(x - 1)(y - 6)$
43. $(x - 10)(x + 10)$ **45.** $(2y - 7)(2y + 7)$
47. $(3x - 5a)(3x + 5a)$ **49.** $(12wz - h)(12wz + h)$
51. $(x - 10)^2$ **53.** $(2m - 1)^2$ **55.** $(w - t)^2$
57. $(a - 1)(a^2 + a + 1)$ **59.** $(w + 3)(w^2 - 3w + 9)$
61. $(2x - 1)(4x^2 + 2x + 1)$
63. $(4x + 5)(16x^2 - 20x + 25)$
65. $(2a - 3b)(4a^2 + 6ab + 9b^2)$
67. $2(x + 2)(x - 2)$ **69.** $x(x + 5)^2$ **71.** $(2x + 1)^2$
73. $(x + 3)(x + 7)$ **75.** $3y(2y + 1)$ **77.** $(2x - 5)^2$
79. $2m(m - n)(m^2 + mn + n^2)$ **81.** $(2x - 3)(x - 2)$
83. $a(3a + w)(3a - w)$ **85.** $-5(a - 3)^2$
87. $2(2 - 3x)(4 + 6x + 9x^2)$ **89.** $-3y(y + 3)^2$
91. $-7(ab + 1)(ab - 1)$ **93.** $(x - h)(7 - h)$
95. $(x + 3)(a - 2)(a + 2)$ **97.** 9   **99.** 20   **101.** 16
103. 100   **105. a)** $b - 3$ **b)** 4050 in.^3 **c)** 30 in.

Section 5.6 Warm-ups T F F F T F F F T T

1. To factor $x^2 + bx + c$, find two integers whose sum is b and whose product is c.
3. Trial and error means simply to write down possible factors and then use FOIL to check until you get the correct factors.

5. $(x + 1)(x + 3)$ **7.** $(a + 10)(a + 5)$
9. $(y - 7)(y + 2)$ **11.** $(x - 2)(x - 4)$
13. $(a - 9)(a - 3)$ **15.** $(a + 10)(a - 3)$
17. $(3w + 1)(2w + 1)$ **19.** $(2x + 1)(x - 3)$
21. $(2x + 5)(2x + 3)$ **23.** $(2x - 1)(3x - 1)$
25. $(3y + 1)(4y - 1)$ **27.** $(6a - 5)(a + 1)$
29. $(2x - 1)(x + 8)$ **31.** $(3b + 5)(b - 7)$
33. $(3w - 4)(2w + 3)$ **35.** $(4x - 1)(x - 1)$
37. $(5m - 2)(m + 3)$ **39.** $(3y + 4)(2y - 5)$
41. $(x^5 - 3)(x^5 + 3)$ **43.** $(z^6 - 3)^2$ **45.** $2x(x^3 + 2)^2$
47. $x(2x^2 + 1)^2$ **49.** $(x^2 - 2)(x^4 + 2x^2 + 4)$
51. $(a^n - 1)(a^n + 1)$ **53.** $(a^r + 3)^2$
55. $(x^m - 2)(x^{2m} + 2x^m + 4)$
57. $(a^m - b)(a^{2m} + a^mb + b^2)$ **59.** $k(k^w - 5)^2$
61. $(x^3 + 5)(x^3 - 7)$ **63.** $(a^{10} - 10)^2$
65. $-2a(3a^2 + 1)(2a^2 + 1)$ **67.** $(x^a + 5)(x^a - 3)$
69. $(x^a - y^b)(x^a + y^b)$ **71.** $(x^4 - 3)(x^4 + 2)$
73. $x^a(x - 1)(x + 1)$ **75.** $(x^a + 3)^2$ **77.** $2(x + 5)^2$
79. $a(a - 6)(a + 6)$ **81.** $5(2a - 1)(a + 6)$
83. $2(x + 8y)(x - 8y)$ **85.** $-3(3x + 1)(x - 4)$
87. $m^3(m + 10)^2$ **89.** $(3x + 4)(2x + 5)$
91. $y(3y - 4)^2$ **93.** $(r - 4s)(r - 2s)$
95. $m(m + 1)(m + 2)$ **97.** $m(2m + n)(3m - 2n)$
99. $(3m - 5n)(3m + 5n)$ **101.** $5(a + 6)(a - 2)$
103. $-2(w - 10)(w + 1)$ **105.** $x^2(w + 10)(w - 10)$
107. $9(3x + 1)(3x - 1)$ **109.** $(4x + 5)(2x - 3)$
111. $3m(m - 2)(m^2 + 2m + 4)$ **113.** a and b
115. a) $(x + 5)^2$ **b)** $(x - 5)^2$ **c)** $(x + 25)(x + 1)$
     d) $(x + 5)(x - 5)$ **e)** Not factorable

Section 5.7 Warm-ups F T T F F T F T T F

1. Always factor out the greatest common factor first.
3. In factoring a trinomial, look for the perfect square trinomials.
5. Prime   **7.** Not prime   **9.** Not prime   **11.** Prime
13. Prime   **15.** Prime   **17.** $(a^2 - 5)^2$
19. $(x^2 - 2)(x - 2)(x + 2)$ **21.** $3(x - 2)(3x - 4)$
23. $2(y - 2)(y^2 + 2y + 4)(y + 2)(y^2 - 2y + 4)$
25. $2(4a^2 + 3)(4a^2 - 3)$ **27.** $(x + 3)(x - 2)(x^2 - x + 6)$
29. $(m + 5)(m + 1)$ **31.** $(3y - 7)(y + 4)$
33. $(y - 3)(y + 3)(y - 1)(y + 1)$
35. $(x - 2)(x + b)$ **37.** $(x - y)(x + a)$
39. $(x + 1 - a)(x + 1 + a)$ **41.** $(x - 2 - w)(x - 2 + w)$
43. $(x + 2 - z)(x + 2 + z)$ **45.** $(3x - 4)^2$
47. $(3x - 1)(4x - 3)$ **49.** $3a(a + 3)(a^2 - 3a + 9)$
51. $2(x^2 + 16)$ **53.** Prime   **55.** $(x + y - 1)(x + y + 1)$
57. $ab(a - b)(a + b)$ **59.** $(x + 2)(x - 2)(x^2 + 2x + 4)$
61. $n(m + n)^2$ **63.** $(m + n)(2 + w)$
65. $(2w + 3)(2w - 1)$ **67.** $(t^2 + 7)(t^2 - 3)$
69. $-a(a + 10)(a - 3)$ **71.** $(y + 2)(y + 6)$
73. $-2(w - 5)(w + 5)(w^2 + 25)$ **75.** $4(a^2 + 4)$
77. $8a(a^2 + 1)$ **79.** $(w + 2)(w + 8)$ **81.** $a(2w - 3)^2$
83. $(x - 3y)^2$ **85.** $3x^2(x - 5)(x + 5)$

87. $n(m - 1)(m^2 + m + 1)$ **89.** $2(3x + 5)(2x - 3)$
91. $2(a^3 - 16)$ **93.** $(a^m - 1)(a^{2m} + a^m + 1)$
95. $(a^w - b^{2n})(a^{2w} + a^w b^{2n} + b^{4n})$
97. $(t^n - 2)(t^n + 2)(t^{2n} + 4)$
99. $a(a^n - 5)(a^n + 3)$ **101.** $(a^n - 3)(a^n + b)$

Section 5.8 Warm-ups F T T F T F T T F F
1. The zero factor property says that if $a \cdot b = 0$, then either $a = 0$ or $b = 0$.
3. The hypotenuse of a right triangle is the side opposite the right angle.
5. The Pythagorean theorem says that a triangle is a right triangle if and only if the sum of the squares of the legs is equal to the square of the hypotenuse.

7. $\{-4, 5\}$ **9.** $\left\{\dfrac{5}{2}, -\dfrac{4}{3}\right\}$ **11.** $\{-5, 2\}$ **13.** $\{-5, 0, 5\}$

15. $\{-7, 2\}$ **17.** $\{0, 7\}$ **19.** $\{-4, 5\}$ **21.** $\left\{-5, \dfrac{3}{2}\right\}$

23. $\left\{-4, \dfrac{1}{5}\right\}$ **25.** $\{-3, 4\}$ **27.** $\left\{-4, \dfrac{5}{2}\right\}$ **29.** $\{-2, 0, 2\}$

31. $\left\{-1, 0, \dfrac{1}{4}\right\}$ **33.** $\{-5, -4, 5\}$ **35.** $\{-1, 1, 2\}$

37. $\{-3, -1, 1, 3\}$ **39.** $\{-8, -6, 4, 6\}$ **41.** $\{-4, -2, 0\}$

43. $\{-7, -3, 1\}$ **45.** $\left\{-\dfrac{3}{2}, 2\right\}$ **47.** $\{-6, -3, -2, 1\}$

49. $\{-6, 1\}$ **51.** $\{-5, 2\}$ **53.** $\{-5, -4, 0\}$

55. $\{-3, 0, 3\}$ **57.** $\left\{-3, \dfrac{1}{2}, 3\right\}$ **59.** $\left\{-\dfrac{1}{3}, \dfrac{1}{4}, \dfrac{1}{2}\right\}$

61. $\left\{\dfrac{3}{2}\right\}$ **63.** $\{0, -b\}$ **65.** $\left\{-\dfrac{b}{a}, \dfrac{b}{a}\right\}$ **67.** $\left\{-\dfrac{b}{2}\right\}$

69. $\left\{-\dfrac{3}{a}, 1\right\}$ **71.** Width 4 inches, length 6 inches

73. 4 and 9   **75.** Length 43 inches, width 22 inches
77. a) 4 seconds   **b)** 4 seconds   **c)** 64 feet   **d)** 2 seconds
79. a) 1225 ft   **b)** 20.3125 sec
81. 3 sec   **83.** Width 5 feet, length 12 feet
85. Width 5 feet, length 12 feet   **87.** 12 ft   **89.** -3 or 4
91. 3 and 4, or -4 and -3
93. Length 20 feet, width 12 feet

Chapter 5 Wrap-up

Enriching Your Mathematical Word Power
1. d   **2.** b   **3.** c   **4.** d   **5.** b   **6.** a   **7.** c   **8.** a
9. a   **10.** d   **11.** c   **12.** a   **13.** c   **14.** b   **15.** c
16. a   **17.** c

Review Exercises
1. 2   **3.** 36   **5.** $-\dfrac{1}{27}$ **7.** 1   **9.** $\dfrac{8}{x^3}$ **11.** $\dfrac{1}{y^2}$

13. a^7 **15.** $\dfrac{2}{x^4}$ **17.** 8,360,000   **19.** 0.00057

21. 8.07×10^6 **23.** 7.09×10^{-4} **25.** 1×10^2

27. $\dfrac{1}{a}$ **29.** $\dfrac{n^2}{m^{16}}$ **31.** $\dfrac{81}{16}$ **33.** $\dfrac{25}{36}$ **35.** $-\dfrac{4}{3ab}$

37. $\dfrac{b^{14}}{a^7}$ **39.** 5^{6w-1} **41.** 7^{15a-40} **43.** $8w + 2$

45. $-6x + 3$ **47.** $x^3 - 4x^2 + 8x - 8$ **49.** $-4xy + 22z$
51. $5m^5 - m^3 + 2m^2$ **53.** $x^2 + 4x - 21$ **55.** $z^2 - 25y^2$
57. $m^2 + 16m + 64$ **59.** $w^2 - 10xw + 24x^2$
61. $k^2 - 6k + 9$ **63.** $m^4 - 25$ **65.** $3(x - 2)$
67. $-4(-a + 5)$ **69.** $-w(w - 3)$
71. $(y - 9)(y + 9)$ **73.** $(2x + 7)^2$ **75.** $(t - 9)^2$
77. $(t - 5)(t^2 + 5t + 25)$ **79.** $(x - 10)(x + 3)$
81. $(w - 7)(w + 4)$ **83.** $(2m + 7)(m - 1)$
85. $m(m^3 - 5)(m^3 + 2)$ **87.** $5(x + 2)(x^2 - 2x + 4)$
89. $(3x + 2)(3x + 1)$ **91.** $(x + 1)^2(x - 1)$
93. $-y(x - 4)(x + 4)$ **95.** $-ab^2(a - 1)^2$
97. $(x - 1)(x^2 + 9)$ **99.** $(x - 2)(x + 2)(x^2 + 3)$
101. $a^3(a - 1)(a^2 + a + 1)$ **103.** $-2(2m + 3)^2$
105. $(2x - 7)(2x + 1)$
107. $(x + 2)(x^2 - 2x + 4)(x - 1)(x^2 + x + 1)$
109. $(a^2 - 11)(a^2 - 12)$ **111.** $(x^k - 7)(x^k + 7)$
113. $(m^a - 3)(m^a + 1)$ **115.** $(3z^k - 2)^2$
117. $(y^a - b)(y^a + c)$ **119.** $\{0, 5\}$ **121.** $\{0, 5\}$
123. $\left\{-\dfrac{1}{2}, 5\right\}$ **125.** $\{-5, -1, 1\}$ **127.** $\{-3, -1, 1, 3\}$
129. 6 feet   **131.** 7 m by 9 m   **133.** 7 in. by 24 in.
135. a) 68.7 yr   **b)** 6.5 yr   **137. a)** 15%   **b)** $12,196.46

Chapter 5 Test

1. $\dfrac{1}{9}$ **2.** 36   **3.** 8   **4.** $12x^7$ **5.** $4y^{12}$ **6.** $64a^6 b^3$

7. $\dfrac{27}{x^6}$ **8.** $\dfrac{2a^3}{b^3}$ **9.** 3,240,000,000   **10.** 0.0008673

11. 2.4×10^{-5} **12.** 2×10^{-13} **13.** $3x^3 + 3x^2 - 2x + 3$
14. $-2x^2 - 8x - 3$ **15.** $x^3 - 5x^2 + 13x - 14$
16. $x^3 - 6x^2 + 12x - 8$ **17.** $2x^2 - 11x - 21$
18. $x^2 - 12x + 36$ **19.** $4x^2 + 20x + 25$
20. $9y^4 - 25$ **21.** $(a - 6)(a + 4)$ **22.** $(2x + 7)^2$
23. $3(m - 2)(m^2 + 2m + 4)$ **24.** $2y(x - 4)(x + 4)$
25. $(2m + 3)(6m + 5)$ **26.** $(2x^5 - 3)(x^5 + 4)$
27. $(2x + 3)(a - 5)$ **28.** $(x - 1)(x + 1)(x^2 + 4)$

29. $\left\{-5, \dfrac{3}{2}\right\}$ **30.** $\{-2, 0, 2\}$ **31.** $\{-4, -3, 2, 3\}$

32. Width 8 inches, height 6 inches
33. 38.0, 10.8, 7.9
34. a) 96 ft, 96 ft   **b)** 5 sec   **35.** 20 ft by 24 ft

Making Connections Chapters 1–5

1. 16   **2.** -8 **3.** $\dfrac{1}{16}$ **4.** 2   **5.** 1   **6.** $\dfrac{1}{6}$ **7.** $\dfrac{1}{12}$

8. 49   **9.** 64   **10.** 8   **11.** -29 **12.** $\dfrac{11}{30}$ **13.** $\{200\}$

14. $\left\{\dfrac{9}{5}\right\}$ **15.** $\left\{-9, \dfrac{3}{2}\right\}$ **16.** $\left\{-\dfrac{15}{2}, 0\right\}$ **17.** $\left\{2, \dfrac{8}{5}\right\}$

18. $\left\{\dfrac{9}{5}\right\}$ **19.** $\varnothing$ **20.** $\{-3, -2, 1, 2\}$ **21.** $\left\{-5, \dfrac{1}{2}\right\}$

22. $\left[-\frac{2}{3}, \frac{4}{3}\right]$ **23.** 5×10^{10} **24.** 2.05×10^5

25. a) $20,000   **b)** $2,500   **c)** $(20,000, 20,000)$ **d)** $0

Chapter 6

Section 6.1 Warm-ups T T F T F F F T T F
1. A rational expression is a ratio of two polynomials with the denominator not equal to zero.
3. The basic principle of rational numbers states that $(ab)/(ac) = b/c$, provided a and c are not zero.
5. We build up the denominator by multiplying the numerator and denominator by the same expression.
7. $(-\infty, 1) \cup (1, \infty)$ **9.** $(-\infty, 0) \cup (0, \infty)$
11. $(-\infty, -2) \cup (-2, 2) \cup (2, \infty)$
13. $(-\infty, -3) \cup (-3, -2) \cup (-2, \infty)$
15. $(-\infty, \infty)$ **17.** $(-\infty, -3) \cup (-3, 0) \cup (0, 2) \cup (2, \infty)$
19. $\frac{2}{19}$ **21.** $\frac{1}{5}$ **23.** $\frac{x+1}{2}$ **25.** $-\frac{3}{5}$ **27.** $\frac{b}{a^2}$
29. $\frac{-w}{3x^2y}$ **31.** $\frac{b^2}{1+a}$ **33.** $-\frac{1}{2}$ **35.** $\frac{x+2}{x}$
37. $a^2 + ab + b^2$ **39.** $\frac{x^2-1}{x^2+1}$ **41.** $\frac{6x+2}{2x+5}$
43. $\frac{x^2+7x-4}{x^2-16}$ **45.** $\frac{a+y}{b-5}$ **47.** $\frac{2x-6}{x+5}$
49. $\frac{a+b}{2a+3b}$ **51.** $\frac{10}{50}$ **53.** $\frac{3xy^2}{3x^2y^3}$ **55.** $\frac{5x-5}{x^2-2x+1}$
57. $\frac{6x+15}{4x^2-25}$ **59.** $\frac{-3}{-6x-6}$ **61.** $\frac{5a}{a}$ **63.** $\frac{x^2+x-2}{x^2+2x-3}$
65. $\frac{-7}{1-x}$ **67.** $\frac{3x^2-6x+12}{x^3+8}$ **69.** $\frac{2x^2+9x+10}{6x^2+13x-5}$
71. $\frac{4}{7}$ **73.** $\frac{1}{10}$ **75.** Undefined   **77.** $\frac{7}{21}$ **79.** $\frac{10}{2}$
81. $\frac{3a}{a^2}$ **83.** $\frac{-2}{b-a}$ **85.** $\frac{2x+2}{x^2-1}$ **87.** $\frac{-2}{3-w}$
89. $\frac{x+2}{3}$ **91.** $\frac{a+1}{a}$ **93.** $\frac{x^2+x+1}{x^3-1}$ **95.** $x^a - 2$
97. $\frac{1+w}{x^a-m}$ **99.** $\frac{x^{2b}+x^b+1}{x^b+1}$ **101.** $\frac{250}{x}$ mph
103. a) $A(n) = \dfrac{0.50n+45}{n}$ dollars   **b)** 7.5 cents
   c) Decreases   **d)** Increases
105. a) $p(n) = \dfrac{0.053n^2 - 0.64n + 6.71}{3.43n + 87.24}$
   b) 7.7%, 18.5%, 41.4%
107. The value of $R(x)$ gets closer and closer to $\frac{1}{2}$.

Section 6.2 Warm-ups F F T F T T T T T F
1. To multiply rational numbers, multiply the numerators and the denominators.
3. The expressions $a - b$ and $b - a$ are opposites.
5. $\frac{5}{11}$ **7.** $\frac{ab}{4}$ **9.** $\frac{1}{2}$ **11.** $\frac{x+1}{x^2+1}$ **13.** $\frac{1}{a-b}$

15. $\frac{a+2}{2}$ **17.** $-\frac{2}{3}$ **19.** $-7a - 14$ **21.** $6x^2 - x - 1$
23. $\frac{3}{2}$ **25.** $\frac{63}{5}$ **27.** $\frac{6b}{5c^8}$ **29.** $\frac{w}{w-1}$ **31.** $\frac{2}{x-y}$
33. $\frac{2}{x}$ **35.** $2x - 2y$ **37.** $2x + 10$ **39.** $\frac{a-b}{6}$
41. $3a - 3b$ **43.** $\frac{5x}{6}$ **45.** 3   **47.** $\frac{1}{12}$ **49.** $\frac{2x}{3}$
51. -1 **53.** -2 **55.** $\frac{a+b}{a}$ **57.** $\frac{x-9}{2}$ **59.** -2
61. $2a + 2b$ **63.** $\frac{3x}{5y}$ **65.** $\frac{3a}{10b}$ **67.** $\frac{7x^2}{3x+2}$
69. $\frac{-a^6b^2}{8c^2}$ **71.** $\frac{2m^8n^2}{3}$ **73.** $\frac{2x-3}{8x-4}$ **75.** $\frac{h-3}{5h+1}$
77. $\frac{-3a-1}{2}$ **79.** $\frac{k+m}{m-k}$ **81.** $\frac{y^b}{x^a}$ **83.** $\frac{x^a-1}{x^a+2}$
85. $\frac{m^k+1}{m^k+2}$ **87.** 7.1%   **89.** $\frac{75}{x}$ miles   **91.** e

Section 6.3 Warm-ups F F T F F F T T T F
1. The sum of a/b and c/b is $(a+c)/b$.
3. The least common multiple (LCM) of some numbers is the smallest number that is a multiple of all of the numbers.
5. To add rational expressions with different denominators, you must build up the expressions to equivalent expressions with the same denominator.
7. $4x$ **9.** $\frac{-x+1}{x}$ **11.** $\frac{5}{2}$ **13.** $\frac{2}{x-3}$
15. $\frac{3x-5}{x+3}$ **17.** 120   **19.** $30x^3y$ **21.** $a^3b^5c^2$
23. $x(x+2)(x-2)$ **25.** $12a + 24$ **27.** $(x-1)(x+1)^2$
29. $x(x-4)(x+4)(x+2)$
31. $(2x+3)(3x+4)(3x-4)$
33. $\frac{17}{140}$ **35.** $\frac{1}{144}$ **37.** $\frac{3w+5z}{w^2z^2}$ **39.** $\frac{2x-1}{24}$
41. $\frac{11x}{10a}$ **43.** $\frac{9-4xy}{4y}$ **45.** $\frac{-2a-14}{a(a+2)}$
47. $\frac{3a-b}{(a-b)(a+b)}$ **49.** $\frac{4x+9}{(x+3)(x-3)}$ **51.** 0
53. $\frac{11}{2x-4}$ **55.** $\frac{-x+3}{(x-1)(x+2)(x+3)}$
57. $\frac{3x^2+5x-3}{(x+1)(2x-1)(3x-1)}$ **59.** $\frac{8x-2}{x(x-1)(x+2)}$
61. $\frac{7}{12}$ **63.** $-\frac{19}{40}$ **65.** $\frac{5x}{6}$ **67.** $\frac{3a-2b}{3b}$ **69.** $\frac{3a+2}{3}$
71. $\frac{a+3}{a}$ **73.** $\frac{3}{x}$ **75.** $\frac{8x+3}{12x}$ **77.** -3
79. $\frac{-13}{15(x-2)}$ **81.** $\frac{-4x}{(x+1)(x-1)(2x+1)}$
83. b **85.** $\frac{x^2+10x}{(5x-2)^2}$ **87.** $\frac{4x^2+9}{x(2x-3)}$

89. $\dfrac{-w^2 + 2w + 8}{(w + 3)(w^2 - 3w + 9)}$ **91.** $\dfrac{a - 3}{a^2 + 2a + 4}$

93. $\dfrac{-w^3 - 2w^2 - 5w + 6}{(w - 2)(w + 2)(w^2 + 2w + 4)}$

95. $\dfrac{x^3 + x^2 + 2x + 1}{(x - 1)(x + 1)(x^2 + x + 1)}$

97. $\dfrac{16x + 8}{x^2 + x}$ **99.** $\dfrac{3x + 60}{x}$ **101.** $\dfrac{300x + 500}{x^2 + 5x}$ hours

Section 6.4 Warm-ups   F T T T F F F F T T

1. A complex fraction is a fraction that contains fractions in the numerator, denominator, or both.

3. $\dfrac{10}{3}$ **5.** -8 **7.** $\dfrac{a^2 + ab}{a - b}$ **9.** $\dfrac{a^2b + 3a}{a + b^2}$

11. $\dfrac{x - 3y}{x + y}$ **13.** $\dfrac{60m - 3m^2}{8m + 36}$ **15.** $\dfrac{a^2 - ab}{b^2}$

17. $\dfrac{xy + x^2}{y^2 - x^2y^2}$ **19.** $\dfrac{x + 2}{x - 2}$ **21.** $\dfrac{y^2 - y - 2}{(y - 1)(3y + 4)}$

23. $\dfrac{4x - 10}{x - 4}$ **25.** $\dfrac{6w - 3}{2w^2 + w - 4}$ **27.** $\dfrac{2b - a}{a - 3b}$

29. $\dfrac{-y^2 - 12}{y^2 - 3}$ **31.** $\dfrac{3a - 7}{5a - 2}$ **33.** $\dfrac{3m^2 - 12m + 12}{(m - 3)(2m - 1)}$

35. $\dfrac{2x^2 + 4x + 5}{4x^2 - 2x - 6}$ **37.** $\dfrac{yz + wz}{wy + wz}$ **39.** $\dfrac{x}{x + 1}$

41. $\dfrac{a^2 + b^2}{ab^3}$ **43.** $\dfrac{a - 1}{a}$ **45.** $\dfrac{1}{x^2 - x + 1}$ **47.** $2m - 3$

49. $-\dfrac{1}{ab}$ **51.** $-x^3y^3$ **53.** $x - 2$ **55.** $\dfrac{xy}{x + y}$

57. $-1.7333,\ -\dfrac{26}{15}$ **59.** $0.1667,\ \dfrac{1}{6}$ **61.** 47.4%

63. 49.5 mph   **67.** $\dfrac{2x + 1}{3x + 2}, x = 0, -1, -\dfrac{1}{2}, -\dfrac{2}{3}$

Section 6.5 Warm-ups   F F T T T F F T T T

1. If $a \div b = c$, then the divisor is b, the dividend is a, and the quotient is c.

3. If the term x^n is missing in the dividend, insert the term $0 \cdot x^n$ for the missing term.

5. Synthetic division is used only for dividing by a binomial of the form $x - c$.

7. $12x^4$ **9.** -2 **11.** $2b - 3$ **13.** $x + 1$

15. $-5x^2 + 4x - 3$ **17.** $\dfrac{7}{2}x^2 - 2x$

19. $2, -3$ **21.** $\dfrac{2}{3}x + \dfrac{1}{3}, 4x - 3$

23. $2x^2 + x, -6x - 7$ **25.** $x + 5, -2$

27. $x - 4, 8$ **29.** $x^2 - 2x + 4, 0$

31. $a^2 + 2a + 8, 11$ **33.** $x^2 - 2x + 3, -6$

35. $x^3 + 3x^2 + 6x + 11, 21$

37. $-3x^2 - 1, x - 4$ **39.** $3x + 5, -1$

41. $2b - 5, -2$ **43.** $x^2 + x - 2, 0$ **45.** $x - 5, 0$

47. $2 + \dfrac{10}{x - 5}$ **49.** $x - 1 + \dfrac{1}{2x + 1}$

51. $x^2 - 2x + 4 + \dfrac{-8}{x + 2}$ **53.** $x + \dfrac{2}{x}$

55. $x - 6 + \dfrac{2}{2x + 1}$ **57.** $3x^2 - x - 1 + \dfrac{6}{x - 1}$

59. $6x^2 + 12x + 20 + \dfrac{45}{x - 2}$ **61.** $x^2 - x + 2 + \dfrac{-2}{x + 1}$

63. $x^2 - 3x, -3$ **65.** $2x - 6, 11$

67. $3x^3 + 9x^2 + 12x + 43, 120$

69. $x^4 + x^3 + x^2 + x + 1, 0$ **71.** $x^2 - 2x - 1, 8$

73. $x^2 + 2x + 10, 55$ **75.** No   **77.** Yes, $(x - 4)(x - 2)$

79. Yes, $(w - 3)(w^2 + 3w + 9)$ **81.** No

83. Yes, $(y - 2)(y^2 - 2y + 2)$ **85.** -15 **87.** 9   **89.** 28

91. a) $AC(x) = 0.03x + 300$ **b)** No   **c)** Because $AC(x)$ is very close to 300 for x less than 15, the graph looks horizontal.

93. $x - 1$ ft   **95.** 6,333.3 m^3

Section 6.6 Warm-ups   T F F T F T F F F T

1. The first step is to multiply each side of the equation by the LCD.

3. A proportion is an equation expressing equality of two rational expressions.

5. In $a/b = c/d$ the extremes are a and d.

7. $\{-24\}$ **9.** $\left\{\dfrac{22}{15}\right\}$ **11.** $\{5\}$ **13.** $\{1, 6\}$ **15.** $\{20, 25\}$

17. $\varnothing$ **19.** $\{-2\}$ **21.** $\varnothing$ **23.** $\{-5, 1\}$ **25.** $\left\{\dfrac{8}{3}\right\}$

27. $\left\{-\dfrac{3}{4}\right\}$ **29.** $\left\{-\dfrac{14}{5}\right\}$ **31.** $\{20\}$ **33.** $\{-3, 3\}$

35. $\{-5, 6\}$ **37.** $\varnothing$ **39.** $\left\{\dfrac{11}{2}\right\}$ **41.** $\{0\}$

43. $\{-6, 6\}$ **45.** $\{8\}$ **47.** $\{2, 4\}$

49. $\{-1\}$ **51.** $\{5\}$ **53.** $\{-3, 3\}$ **55.** $\{8\}$ **57.** $\left\{\dfrac{25}{2}\right\}$

59. $\varnothing$ **61.** $\{4\}$ **63.** $\{-5, 2\}$ **65.** $\left\{\dfrac{16}{3}\right\}$

67. $\dfrac{3x + 16}{4x}$ **69.** $\left\{\dfrac{8}{5}\right\}$ **71.** $\dfrac{-5x + 8}{4x}$ **73.** \$166,666.67

75. 138   **77.** Width 132 cm, length 154 cm

79. 20%, 96%   **81. a)** \$17,142.86   **b)** \$57,142.86

83. To solve the equation, multiply each side by the LCD. To find the sum, build up each rational expression so that its denominator is the LCD.

Section 6.7 Warm-ups   F T F T T T F T F F

1. $y = 5x - 7$ **3.** $y = -\dfrac{1}{3}x + 1$

5. $y = mx - bm + a$ **7.** $y = -\dfrac{7}{3}x - \dfrac{29}{3}$

9. $f = \dfrac{F}{M}$ **11.** $D^2 = \dfrac{4A}{\pi}$ **13.** $m_1 = \dfrac{Fr^2}{km_2}$

15. $q = \dfrac{pf}{p - f}$ **17.** $a^2 = \dfrac{b^2}{1 - e^2}$ **19.** $T_1 = \dfrac{P_1 V_1 T_2}{P_2 V_2}$

21. $h = \dfrac{3V}{4\pi r^2}$ **23.** $\dfrac{1}{2}$ **25.** 24 **27.** $\dfrac{32}{3}$

29. -6.517 **31.** 19.899 **33.** 1.910 **35.** 4 mph

37. Patrick 24 min, Guy 36 min, 100 mph, no

39. 10 mph **41.** 6 hours **43.** 60 minutes

45. 30 minutes **47.** 10 pounds apples, 12 pounds oranges

49. 6 ohms **51. a)** 80 **b)** $C(n) = \dfrac{24{,}000}{n}$

53. 25.255 days

Chapter 6 Wrap-Up

Enriching Your Mathematical Word Power

1. b **2.** d **3.** b **4.** d **5.** b **6.** a **7.** a **8.** d
9. a **10.** b **11.** d **12.** d **13.** a **14.** c **15.** d

Review Exercises

1. $(-\infty, 1) \cup (1, \infty)$ **3.** $(-\infty, -1) \cup (-1, 2) \cup (2, \infty)$

5. $\dfrac{c^2}{a^2 b}$ **7.** $\dfrac{4x^2}{3y}$ **9.** $-a$ **11.** $\dfrac{3}{2}$ **13.** $6x(x - 2)$

15. $12a^5 b^3$ **17.** $\dfrac{3x + 11}{2(x - 3)(x + 3)}$ **19.** $\dfrac{aw - 5b}{a^2 b^2}$

21. $\dfrac{21}{10x - 60}$ **23.** $\dfrac{7 - 3y}{4y - 3}$ **25.** $\dfrac{b^3 - a^2}{ab}$

27. $x^2 + 3x - 5, 0$ **29.** $m^3 - m^2 + m - 1, 0$

31. $a^6 + 2a^3 + 4, 0$ **33.** $m^2 + 2m - 6, 0$

35. $x + 1 + \dfrac{-4}{x - 1}$ **37.** $3 + \dfrac{6}{x - 2}$ **39.** Yes

41. Yes **43.** No **45.** Yes **47.** $\left\{-\dfrac{16}{3}\right\}$

49. $\varnothing$ **51.** $\{10\}$ **53.** $y = mx + b$ **55.** $m = \dfrac{Fr}{v^2}$

57. $r = \dfrac{3A}{2\pi h}$ **59.** $y = 2x - 17$ **61.** $\dfrac{10 + 7y}{6xy}$

63. $\dfrac{8a + 10}{(a - 5)(a + 5)}$ **65.** $\{-8, 8\}$ **67.** $-\dfrac{3}{2}$ **69.** $\{-9, 9\}$

71. $\dfrac{1}{x - m}$ **73.** $\dfrac{8a + 20}{(a - 5)(a + 5)(a + 1)}$

75. $\dfrac{-15a + 10}{2(a + 2)(a + 3)(a - 3)}$ **77.** $\{2\}$

79. $\left\{-\dfrac{5}{2}\right\}$ **81.** $-\dfrac{1}{3}$ **83.** $\dfrac{x - 2}{3x + 3}$ **85.** $\dfrac{3a^2 + 7a + 16}{a^3 - 8}$

87. $\dfrac{3 - x}{(x + 1)(x + 3)}$ **89.** $\dfrac{a + w}{a + 4}$ **91.** $\{-6, 8\}$

93. $\dfrac{18}{3x}$ **95.** $\dfrac{-3}{b - a}$ **97.** $\dfrac{4x}{x}$ **99.** $10x$ **101.** $\dfrac{1}{3}$

103. $\dfrac{1}{a + 3}$ **105.** $\dfrac{3}{10}$ **107.** $\dfrac{5a}{6}$ **109.** 28,000

111. 10 hours **113.** 400 hours

Chapter 6 Test

1. $(-\infty, 4/3) \cup (4/3, \infty)$ **2.** $(-\infty, -3) \cup (-3, 3) \cup (3, \infty)$

3. $(-\infty, \infty)$ **4.** $\dfrac{3a^3}{2b}$ **5.** $\dfrac{-x - y}{2x - 2y}$ **6.** $-\dfrac{1}{36}$

7. $\dfrac{7y^2 + 3}{y}$ **8.** $\dfrac{5}{a - 9}$ **9.** $\dfrac{4a + 3b}{24a^2 b^2}$ **10.** $\dfrac{a^3}{30b^2}$

11. $-\dfrac{3}{a + b}$ **12.** $\dfrac{1}{x^2 - 1}$ **13.** $\dfrac{-4x + 2}{(x + 2)(x - 2)(x - 5)}$

14. $\dfrac{m + 1}{3}$ **15.** $\left\{\dfrac{12}{7}\right\}$ **16.** $\{4, 10\}$ **17.** $\{-2, 2\}$

18. $t = \dfrac{a^2}{W}$ **19.** $b = \dfrac{2a}{a - 2}$ **20.** $\dfrac{16}{9 - 6x}$ **21.** $w - m$

22. $\dfrac{3a^2}{2}$ **23.** $3x + 2, -8$ **24.** $-1, 0$ **25.** $5 + \dfrac{-15}{x + 3}$

26. $x + 5 + \dfrac{4}{x - 2}$ **27.** 24 minutes **28.** 30 miles **29.** 9

Making Connections Chapters 1–6

1. $\left\{\dfrac{15}{4}\right\}$ **2.** $\{-4, 4\}$ **3.** $\left\{\dfrac{12}{5}\right\}$ **4.** $\{-6, 3\}$ **5.** $\left\{\dfrac{1}{4}\right\}$

6. $\{6\}$ **7.** $\left\{\dfrac{1}{2}\right\}$ **8.** $\left\{\dfrac{3}{2}\right\}$ **9.** $\{-3, 3\}$ **10.** $\{-8, 3\}$

11. $\left\{\dfrac{1}{3}, \dfrac{2}{3}\right\}$ **12.** $\{-3, 9\}$ **13.** $\left\{-\dfrac{9}{2}, \dfrac{1}{2}\right\}$ **14.** $\varnothing$

15. $y = \dfrac{C - Ax}{B}$ **16.** $y = -\dfrac{1}{3}x + \dfrac{4}{3}$ **17.** $y = \dfrac{C}{A - B}$

18. $y = A$ or $y = -A$ **19.** $y = 2A - 2B$

20. $y = \dfrac{2AC}{2B + C}$ **21.** $y = \dfrac{3}{4}x - \dfrac{3}{2}$ **22.** $y = A$ or $y = 2$

23. $y = \dfrac{2A - BC}{B}$ **24.** $y = B$ or $y = -C$ **25.** $12x^{13}$

26. $3x^5 + 15x^8$ **27.** $25x^{12}$ **28.** $27a^9 b^6$ **29.** $-4a^6 b^6$

30. $\dfrac{1}{32x^{10}}$ **31.** $\dfrac{27x^{12} y^{15}}{8}$ **32.** $\dfrac{a^2}{4b^6 c^2}$

33. $\dfrac{ab + a^2 b^4}{b + a^2}$ **34.** $a + b$

35. a) 2188 calories **b)** increases
c) $B = 9.56W + 918.7$ **d)** $B = 2328 - 4.68A$

Chapter 7

Section 7.1 Warm-ups T F T F T F F F T T
1. If $b^n = a$, then b is an nth root of a.
3. If $b^n = a$, then b is an even root of a provided n is even or an odd root of a provided n is odd.
5. The product rule for radicals states that $\sqrt[n]{a} \cdot \sqrt[n]{b} = \sqrt[n]{ab}$ provided all of the roots are real.
7. 6 **9.** 10 **11.** -3 **13.** 2 **15.** -2 **17.** 2
19. 10 **21.** Not a real number **23.** -2 **25.** m
27. x^8 **29.** y^3 **31.** y^5 **33.** m **35.** w^3 **37.** $3\sqrt{y}$
39. $2a$ **41.** $x^2 y$ **43.** $m^6 \sqrt{5}$ **45.** $2\sqrt[3]{y}$
47. $a^2 \sqrt[3]{3}$ **49.** $2\sqrt{5}$ **51.** $5\sqrt{2}$ **53.** $6\sqrt{2}$ **55.** $2\sqrt[3]{5}$
57. $3\sqrt[3]{3}$ **59.** $2\sqrt[4]{3}$ **61.** $2\sqrt[3]{3}$ **63.** $a\sqrt{a}$
65. $3a^3 \sqrt{2}$ **67.** $2x^2 \sqrt{5xy}$ **69.** $2m\sqrt[3]{3m}$
71. $2a\sqrt[4]{2a}$ **73.** $2x\sqrt[3]{2x}$ **75.** $4xy^4 z^3 \sqrt{3xz}$

77. $\dfrac{\sqrt{t}}{2}$ **79.** $\dfrac{25}{4}$ **81.** $\sqrt{10}$ **83.** $\dfrac{\sqrt[3]{t}}{2}$ **85.** $\dfrac{-2x^2}{y}$

87. $\dfrac{2a^3}{3}$ **89.** $\dfrac{2\sqrt{3}}{5}$ **91.** $\dfrac{3\sqrt{3}}{4}$

93. $\dfrac{a\sqrt[3]{a}}{5}$ **95.** $\dfrac{3\sqrt[3]{3}}{2b}$ **97.** $\dfrac{x\sqrt[3]{x^3}}{y^2}$ **99.** $\dfrac{a\sqrt[4]{a}}{2b^3}$

101. $1, [2, \infty)$ **103.** $\sqrt{14}, [-4, \infty)$ **105.** No $f(3), (-\infty, 1]$

107. $-4°F, -10°F$ **109. a)** $t = \dfrac{\sqrt{h}}{4}$ **b)** $\dfrac{\sqrt{10}}{2}$ sec

c) 100 ft **111.** 5.8 knots **113.** 114.1 ft/sec, 77.8 mph

115. a) Yes **b)** No **c)** Yes **d)** Yes
117. Arithmetic mean

Section 7.2 Warm-ups T F F T T T T F T T
1. The nth root of a is $a^{1/n}$.
3. The expression $a^{-m/n}$ means $\dfrac{1}{a^{m/n}}$.
5. The operations can be performed in any order, but the easiest is usually root, power, and then reciprocal.
7. $7^{1/4}$ **9.** $(5x)^{1/2}$ **11.** $\sqrt[5]{9}$ **13.** $\sqrt{a}$ **15.** 5
17. -5 **19.** 2 **21.** Not a real number
23. $w^{7/3}$ **25.** $2^{-10/3}$ **27.** $\sqrt[4]{\dfrac{1}{w^3}}$ **29.** $\sqrt{(ab)^3}$

31. 25 **33.** 125 **35.** $\dfrac{1}{81}$ **37.** $\dfrac{1}{64}$ **39.** $-\dfrac{1}{3}$

41. Not a real number **43.** $3^{7/12}$ **45.** 1 **47.** $\dfrac{1}{2}$

49. 2 **51.** 6 **53.** 4 **55.** 81 **57.** $\dfrac{1}{4}$ **59.** $\dfrac{9}{8}$

61. $|x|$ **63.** a^4 **65.** y **67.** $|3x^3y|$ **69.** $\left|\dfrac{3x^3}{y^5}\right|$

71. $x^{3/4}$ **73.** $\dfrac{y^{3/2}}{x^{1/4}}$ **75.** $\dfrac{1}{w^{8/3}}$ **77.** $12x^8$ **79.** $\dfrac{a^2}{b}$

81. $8w^{13/4}$ **83.** $\dfrac{h^{1/6}}{3k^{1/2}}$ **85.** 9 **87.** $-\dfrac{1}{8}$ **89.** $\dfrac{1}{625}$

91. $2^{1/4}$ **93.** 3 **95.** 3 **97.** $\dfrac{4}{9}$ **99.** Not a real number

101. $\dfrac{4}{3}$ **103.** $-\dfrac{216}{125}$ **105.** $3x^{9/2}$ **107.** $\dfrac{a^2}{27}$ **109.** $a^{5/4}b$

111. $k^{9/2}m^4$ **113.** 1.2599 **115.** -1.4142 **117.** 2
119. 2.5 **121.** $a^{3m/4}$ **123.** $a^{2m/15}$ **125.** a^nb^m
127. $a^{4m}b^{2n}$ **129.** 13 inches **131.** 274.96 m²
133. 26.3% **135.** 6.1% **137.** Second is incorrect.

Section 7.3 Warm-ups F T F F T F T F F T
1. Like radical are radicals with the same index and same radicand.
3. In the product rule the radicals must have the same index, but do not have to have the same radicand.
5. $-\sqrt{3}$ **7.** $9\sqrt{7x}$ **9.** $5\sqrt[3]{2}$ **11.** $4\sqrt{3} - 2\sqrt{5}$
13. $5\sqrt[3]{x}$ **15.** $2\sqrt[3]{x} - \sqrt{2x}$ **17.** $2\sqrt{2} + 2\sqrt{7}$
19. $5\sqrt{2}$ **21.** 0 **23.** $-\sqrt{2}$ **25.** $x\sqrt{5x} + 2x\sqrt{2}$
27. $7\sqrt[3]{3}$ **29.** $-4\sqrt[4]{3}$ **31.** $ty\sqrt[3]{2t}$

33. $\sqrt{15}$ **35.** $30\sqrt{2}$ **37.** $6a\sqrt{14}$ **39.** $3\sqrt[4]{3}$
41. 12 **43.** $6\sqrt{2} + 18$ **45.** $5\sqrt{2} - 2\sqrt{5}$
47. $3\sqrt[3]{t^2} - t\sqrt[3]{3}$ **49.** $-7 - 3\sqrt{3}$ **51.** 2
53. $-8 - 6\sqrt{5}$ **55.** $-6 + 9\sqrt{2}$ **57.** $\sqrt[6]{3^5}$ **59.** $\sqrt[12]{5^7}$
61. $\sqrt[6]{500}$ **63.** $\sqrt[12]{432}$ **65.** -1 **67.** 3 **69.** 19
71. 13 **73.** $25 - 9x$ **75.** $11\sqrt{3}$ **77.** $10\sqrt{30}$
79. $8 - \sqrt{7}$ **81.** $16w$ **83.** $3x^2\sqrt{2x}$
85. $28 + \sqrt{10}$ **87.** $\dfrac{8\sqrt{2}}{15}$ **89.** 17

91. $9 + 6\sqrt{x} + x$ **93.** $25x - 30\sqrt{x} + 9$
95. $x + 3 + 2\sqrt{x + 2}$ **97.** $-\sqrt{w}$ **99.** $a\sqrt{a}$
101. $3x^2\sqrt[3]{x}$ **103.** $13x\sqrt[3]{2x}$ **105.** $\sqrt[6]{32x^5}$

107. $3\sqrt{2}$ ft² **109.** $\dfrac{9\sqrt{2}}{2}$ ft² **111.** No

113. a) $(y - \sqrt{3})(y + \sqrt{3}), (\sqrt{2}a - \sqrt{7})(\sqrt{2}a + \sqrt{7})$
b) $\{\pm 2\sqrt{2}\}$ **c)** $\{\pm\sqrt{a}\}$

Section 7.4 Warm-ups T T F T F T F T T T

1. $\dfrac{2\sqrt{5}}{5}$ **3.** $\dfrac{\sqrt{21}}{7}$ **5.** $\dfrac{\sqrt[3]{2}}{2}$

7. $\dfrac{\sqrt[3]{150}}{5}$ **9.** $\dfrac{\sqrt{15}}{6}$ **11.** $\dfrac{1}{2}$ **13.** $\dfrac{\sqrt{2}}{2}$ **15.** $\dfrac{\sqrt[3]{18}}{3}$

17. $\dfrac{\sqrt[3]{14}}{2}$ **19.** $\dfrac{\sqrt{xy}}{y}$ **21.** $\dfrac{a\sqrt{ab}}{b^4}$ **23.** $\dfrac{\sqrt{3ab}}{3b}$

25. $\dfrac{\sqrt[3]{ab^2}}{b}$ **27.** $\dfrac{\sqrt[3]{20b}}{2b}$ **29.** $\sqrt{3}$ **31.** $\dfrac{\sqrt{15}}{5}$

33. $\dfrac{3\sqrt{2}}{10}$ **35.** $\dfrac{\sqrt{2}}{3}$ **37.** $\dfrac{\sqrt{3a}}{3}$ **39.** $\sqrt[3]{10}$ **41.** 2

43. $\dfrac{2}{w}$ **45.** $2 + \sqrt{5}$ **47.** $1 - \sqrt{3}$ **49.** $2\sqrt{2} - 2$

51. $\dfrac{\sqrt{11} + \sqrt{5}}{2}$ **53.** $\dfrac{1 + \sqrt{6} + \sqrt{2} + \sqrt{3}}{2}$

55. $\dfrac{2\sqrt{3} - \sqrt{6}}{3}$ **57.** $\dfrac{6\sqrt{6} + 2\sqrt{15}}{13}$

59. $128\sqrt{2}$ **61.** $x^2\sqrt{x}$ **63.** $-27x^4\sqrt{x}$ **65.** $8x^5$

67. $4\sqrt[3]{25}$ **69.** x^4 **71.** $\dfrac{\sqrt{6} + 2\sqrt{2}}{2}$ **73.** $2\sqrt{6}$

75. $\dfrac{\sqrt{2}}{2}$ **77.** $\dfrac{2}{3}$ **79.** $\dfrac{2 - \sqrt{2}}{5}$ **81.** $\dfrac{1 + \sqrt{3}}{2}$

83. $a - 3\sqrt{a}$ **85.** $4a\sqrt{a} + 4a$ **87.** $12m$ **89.** $4xy^2z$
91. $m - m^2$ **93.** $5x\sqrt[3]{x}$ **95.** $8m^4\sqrt[4]{8m^2}$ **97.** $\sqrt{x} + 3$

99. $\dfrac{3k - 3\sqrt{7k}}{k - 7}$ **101.** $2 + 8\sqrt{2}$ **103.** $\dfrac{3\sqrt{2} + 2\sqrt{3}}{6}$

105. $7\sqrt{2} - 1$ **107.** $\dfrac{4x + 4\sqrt{x}}{x - 4}$ **109.** $\dfrac{x + \sqrt{x}}{x - x^2}$

111. a) $x^3 - 2$ **b)** $(x + \sqrt[3]{5})(x^2 - \sqrt[3]{5}x + \sqrt[3]{25})$ **c)** 3
d) $(\sqrt[3]{a} + \sqrt[3]{b})(\sqrt[3]{a^2} - \sqrt[3]{ab} + \sqrt[3]{b^2})$,
$(\sqrt[3]{a} - \sqrt[3]{b})(\sqrt[3]{a^2} + \sqrt[3]{ab} + \sqrt[3]{b^2})$

Section 7.5 Warm-ups F T F F T F F T T T

1. The odd-root property states that if n is an odd positive integer, then $x^n = k$ is equivalent to $x = \sqrt[n]{k}$ for any real number k.

3. An extraneous solution is a solution that appears when solving an equation but does not satisfy the original equation.

5. $\{-10\}$ 7. $\left\{\dfrac{1}{2}\right\}$ 9. $\{1\}$ 11. $\{-2\}$ 13. $\{-5, 5\}$

15. $\{-2\sqrt{5}, 2\sqrt{5}\}$ 17. No real solution   19. $\{-1, 7\}$

21. $\{-1 - 2\sqrt{2}, -1 + 2\sqrt{2}\}$ 23. $\{-\sqrt{10}, \sqrt{10}\}$

25. $\{3\}$ 27. $\{-2, 2\}$ 29. $\{52\}$ 31. $\left\{\dfrac{9}{4}\right\}$ 33. $\{9\}$

35. $\{3\}$ 37. $\{3\}$ 39. $\{-5, 3\}$ 41. $\{1\}$ 43. $\varnothing$

45. $\{4\}$ 47. $\{2\}$ 49. $\{6\}$ 51. $\{7\}$ 53. $\{-5\}$

55. $\varnothing$ 57. $\{0\}$ 59. $\{-3\sqrt{3}, 3\sqrt{3}\}$

61. $\left\{-\dfrac{1}{27}, \dfrac{1}{27}\right\}$ 63. $\{512\}$ 65. $\left\{\dfrac{1}{81}\right\}$ 67. $\left\{0, \dfrac{2}{3}\right\}$

69. $\left\{\dfrac{4 - \sqrt{2}}{4}, \dfrac{4 + \sqrt{2}}{4}\right\}$ 71. No real solution

73. $\{-\sqrt{2}, \sqrt{2}\}$ 75. $\{-5\}$ 77. No real solution

79. $\{-9\}$ 81. $\left\{\dfrac{5}{4}\right\}$ 83. $\varnothing$ 85. $\left\{-\dfrac{2}{3}, 2\right\}$

87. $\{-2 - 2\sqrt[4]{2}, -2 + 2\sqrt[4]{2}\}$ 89. $\{0\}$ 91. $\left\{\dfrac{1}{2}\right\}$

93. $4\sqrt{2}$ feet   95. $5\sqrt{2}$ feet   97. 50 feet

99. a) 1.89   b) $d = \dfrac{64b^3}{C^3}$ c) $d > 19{,}683$ pounds

101. $\sqrt[6]{32}$ meters   103. $\sqrt{73}$ km

105. $S = P(1 + r)^n$, $P = S(1 + r)^{-n}$ 107. 9.5 AU

109. $\{-1.8, 1.8\}$ 111. $\{4.993\}$ 113. $\{-26.372, 26.372\}$

Section 7.6 Warm-ups T F F T T T T F T F

1. A complex number is a number of the form $a + bi$, where a and b are real numbers.

3. The union of the real numbers and the imaginary numbers is the set of complex numbers.

5. The conjugate of $a + bi$ is $a - bi$.

7. $-2 + 8i$ 9. $-4 + 4i$ 11. -2 13. $-8 - 2i$

15. $6 + 15i$ 17. $-2 - 10i$ 19. $-4 - 12i$

21. $-10 + 24i$ 23. $-1 + 3i$ 25. $-5i$

27. 29   29. 2   31. 20   33. -9 35. -25

37. 16   39. i 41. 34   43. 5   45. 5

47. 7   49. $\dfrac{12}{17} - \dfrac{3}{17}i$ 51. $\dfrac{4}{13} + \dfrac{7}{13}i$ 53. $3 - 4i$

55. $1 + 3i$ 57. $\dfrac{1}{13} - \dfrac{5}{13}i$ 59. $-2i$ 61. $2 + 2i$

63. $5 + 6i$ 65. $7 - i\sqrt{6}$ 67. $5i\sqrt{2}$ 69. $1 + i\sqrt{3}$

71. $-1 - \dfrac{1}{2}i\sqrt{6}$ 73. $-2\sqrt{3}$ 75. -9 77. $-i\sqrt{2}$

79. $\{\pm 6i\}$ 81. $\{\pm 2i\sqrt{3}\}$ 83. $\left\{\pm\dfrac{i\sqrt{10}}{2}\right\}$ 85. $\{\pm i\sqrt{2}\}$

87. $18 - i$ 89. $5 + i$ 91. $-\dfrac{6}{25} - \dfrac{17}{25}i$ 93. $3 + 2i$

95. -9 97. $3i\sqrt{3}$ 99. $-5 - 12i$ 101. $-2 + 2i\sqrt{2}$

Chapter 7 Wrap-Up

Enriching Your Mathematical Word Power

1. d   2. b   3. b   4. b   5. d   6. b   7. c   8. a
9. d   10. c   11. a   12. c   13. d   14. b

Review Exercises

1. 2   3. 10   5. $6\sqrt{2}$ 7. x^6 9. x^2 11. $x^4\sqrt{2x}$

13. $2w^2\sqrt{2w}$ 15. $2x\sqrt[3]{2x}$ 17. $a^2b\sqrt[4]{ab}$ 19. $\dfrac{x\sqrt{x}}{4}$

21. $\dfrac{1}{9}$ 23. 4   25. $\dfrac{1}{1000}$ 27. $27x^{1/2}$ 29. $a^{7/2}b^{7/2}$

31. $x^{3/4}y^{5/4}$ 33. 13   35. $3\sqrt{5} - 2\sqrt{3}$

37. $30 - 21\sqrt{6}$ 39. $6 - 3\sqrt{3} + 2\sqrt{2} - \sqrt{6}$

41. $\dfrac{5\sqrt{2}}{2}$ 43. $\dfrac{\sqrt{10}}{5}$ 45. $\dfrac{\sqrt[3]{18}}{3}$ 47. $\dfrac{2\sqrt{3x}}{3x}$

49. $\dfrac{y\sqrt{15y}}{3}$ 51. $\dfrac{3\sqrt[3]{4a^2}}{2a}$ 53. $\dfrac{5\sqrt[4]{27x^2}}{3x}$ 55. 9

57. $1 - \sqrt{2}$ 59. $\dfrac{-\sqrt{6} - 3\sqrt{2}}{2}$ 61. $\dfrac{3\sqrt{2} + 2}{7}$

63. $256w^{10}$ 65. $\{-4, 4\}$ 67. $\{3, 7\}$

69. $\{-1 - \sqrt{5}, -1 + \sqrt{5}\}$ 71. No real solution

73. $\{10\}$ 75. $\{9\}$ 77. $\{-8, 8\}$ 79. $\{124\}$ 81. $\{7\}$

83. $\{2, 3\}$ 85. $\{9\}$ 87. $\{4\}$ 89. $5 + 25i$ 91. $7 - 3i$

93. $-1 + 2i$ 95. $2 + i$ 97. $2 - i\sqrt{3}$ 99. $\dfrac{5}{17} - \dfrac{14}{17}i$

101. $\{\pm 10i\}$ 103. $\left\{\pm\dfrac{3i\sqrt{2}}{2}\right\}$ 105. False

107. True   109. True   111. False   113. False
115. False   117. False   119. True   121. False
123. True   125. False   127. False   129. True
131. True   133. $5\sqrt{30}$ seconds   135. $10\sqrt{7}$ feet
137. $200\sqrt{2}$ feet   139. $26.4\sqrt[3]{25}$ ft^2

141. a) 4.9%   b) \$1600 billion   143. $V = \dfrac{29\sqrt{LCS}}{CS}$

Chapter 7 Test

1. 4   2. $\dfrac{1}{8}$ 3. $\sqrt{3}$ 4. 30   5. $3\sqrt{5}$ 6. $\dfrac{6\sqrt{5}}{5}$

7. 2   8. $6\sqrt{2}$ 9. $\dfrac{\sqrt{15}}{6}$ 10. $\dfrac{2 + \sqrt{2}}{2}$ 11. $4 - 3\sqrt{3}$

12. $2ay^2\sqrt[4]{2a}$ 13. $\dfrac{\sqrt[3]{4x}}{2x}$ 14. $\dfrac{2a^4\sqrt{2ab}}{b^2}$ 15. $-3x^3$

16. $2m\sqrt{5m}$ 17. $x^{3/4}$ 18. $3y^2x^{1/4}$ 19. $2x^2\sqrt[3]{5x}$

20. $19 + 8\sqrt{3}$ 21. $\dfrac{5 + \sqrt{3}}{11}$ 22. $\dfrac{6\sqrt{2} - \sqrt{3}}{23}$

23. $22 + 7i$ 24. $1 - i$ 25. $\dfrac{1}{5} - \dfrac{7}{5}i$ 26. $-\dfrac{3}{4} + \dfrac{1}{4}i\sqrt{3}$

27. $\{-5, 9\}$ 28. $\left\{-\dfrac{7}{4}\right\}$ 29. $\{-8, 8\}$ 30. $\left\{\pm\dfrac{4}{3}i\right\}$

31. $\{3\}$ 32. $\{5\}$ 33. $\dfrac{3\sqrt{2}}{2}$ feet   34. 25 and 36

35. Length 6 ft, width 4 ft   36. 39.53 AU, 164.97 years

Making Connections Chapters 1–7

1. $\left\{-\dfrac{4}{7}\right\}$ 2. $\left\{\dfrac{3}{2}\right\}$

3. $(-\infty, -3) \cup (-2, \infty)$

$$-5\ -4\ -3\ -2\ -1\ \ 0$$

4. $\left\{\dfrac{3}{2}\right\}$ 5. $(-\infty, 1)$

$$-3\ -2\ -1\ \ 0\ \ 1\ \ 2\ \ 3$$

6. $\varnothing$ 7. $\{9\}$ 8. $\varnothing$ 9. $\{-12, -2\}$ 10. $\left\{\dfrac{1}{16}\right\}$

11. $(-6, \infty)$

$$-8\ -7\ -6\ -5\ -4\ -3\ -2$$

12. $\left\{-\dfrac{1}{64}, \dfrac{1}{64}\right\}$ 13. $\left\{-\dfrac{\sqrt{3}}{3}, \dfrac{\sqrt{3}}{3}\right\}$ 14. R

15. $\left(-\dfrac{1}{3}, 3\right)$

$$-2\ -1\ \ 0\ \ 1\ \ 2\ \ 3\ \ 4$$

16. $\left\{\dfrac{1}{3}\right\}$ 17. $\{82\}$ 18. $\left\{\dfrac{6}{5}, \dfrac{12}{5}\right\}$ 19. $\{100\}$ 20. R

21. $\{4\sqrt{30}\}$ 22. $\{400\}$ 23. $\left\{\dfrac{13 + 9\sqrt{2}}{3}\right\}$

24. $\{-3\sqrt{2}, 3\sqrt{2}\}$ 25. $\{5\}$ 26. $\{7 + 3\sqrt{6}\}$

27. $\{-2, 3\}$ 28. $\{-5, 2\}$ 29. $\{-2, 3\}$ 30. $\left\{\dfrac{1}{2}, 3\right\}$

31. 3 32. -2 33. $\dfrac{1}{2}$ 34. $\dfrac{1}{3}$

35. a) $48.5\ \text{cm}^3$ b) 14% c) $56\ \text{cm}^3$

Chapter 8

Section 8.1 Warm-ups F F F F T F F T F F

1. In this section quadratic equations are solved by factoring, the even-root property, and completing the square.

3. The last term is the square of one-half the coefficient of the middle term.

5. $\{-2, 3\}$ 7. $\{-5, 3\}$ 9. $\left\{-1, \dfrac{3}{2}\right\}$ 11. $\{-7\}$

13. $\{-4, 4\}$ 15. $\{-9, 9\}$ 17. $\left\{-\dfrac{4}{3}, \dfrac{4}{3}\right\}$ 19. $\{-1, 7\}$

21. $\{-1 - \sqrt{5}, -1 + \sqrt{5}\}$ 23. $\left\{\dfrac{3 - \sqrt{7}}{2}, \dfrac{3 + \sqrt{7}}{2}\right\}$

25. $x^2 + 2x + 1$ 27. $x^2 - 3x + \dfrac{9}{4}$ 29. $y^2 + \dfrac{1}{4}y + \dfrac{1}{64}$

31. $x^2 + \dfrac{2}{3}x + \dfrac{1}{9}$ 33. $(x + 4)^2$ 35. $\left(y - \dfrac{5}{2}\right)^2$

37. $\left(z - \dfrac{2}{7}\right)^2$ 39. $\left(t + \dfrac{3}{10}\right)^2$ 41. $\{-3, 5\}$ 43. $\{-5, 7\}$

45. $\{-4, 5\}$ 47. $\{-7, 2\}$ 49. $\left\{-1, \dfrac{3}{2}\right\}$

51. $\{-2 - \sqrt{10}, -2 + \sqrt{10}\}$

53. $\{-4 - 2\sqrt{5}, -4 + 2\sqrt{5}\}$ 55. $\left\{\dfrac{1 \pm \sqrt{2}}{2}\right\}$

57. $\left\{\dfrac{-3 \pm \sqrt{41}}{4}\right\}$ 59. $\{4\}$ 61. $\left\{\dfrac{1 + \sqrt{17}}{8}\right\}$

63. $\{1, 6\}$ 65. $\{-2 - \sqrt{2}, -2 + \sqrt{2}\}$

67. $\{-1 - 2i, -1 + 2i\}$ 69. $\{3 + i\sqrt{2}, 3 - i\sqrt{2}\}$

71. $\left\{\pm\dfrac{i\sqrt{2}}{2}\right\}$ 73. $\{-2i\sqrt{3}, 2i\sqrt{3}\}$ 75. $\left\{\dfrac{2 \pm i}{5}\right\}$

77. $\{\pm 11i\}$ 79. $\left\{-\dfrac{5}{2}i, \dfrac{5}{2}i\right\}$ 81. $\{-2, 1\}$

83. $\left\{\dfrac{-2 - \sqrt{19}}{5}, \dfrac{-2 + \sqrt{19}}{5}\right\}$ 85. $\{-6, 4\}$

87. $\{2 \pm 3i\}$ 89. $\{-2, 3\}$ 91. $\{3 - i, 3 + i\}$ 93. $\{6\}$

95. $\left\{\dfrac{9 - \sqrt{65}}{2}, \dfrac{9 + \sqrt{65}}{2}\right\}$ 101. $136.9\ \text{ft/sec}$ 103. 12

105. c   109. $\{4.56, 2.74\}$ 111. $\{3.53\}$

Section 8.2 Warm-ups T F T F T T T T F F

1. The quadratic formula can be used to solve any quadratic equation.

3. Factoring is used when the quadratic polynomial is simple enough to factor.

5. The discriminant is $b^2 - 4ac$.   7. $\{-3, -2\}$

9. $\{-3, 2\}$ 11. $\left\{-\dfrac{1}{3}, \dfrac{3}{2}\right\}$ 13. $\left\{\dfrac{1}{2}\right\}$ 15. $\left\{\dfrac{1}{3}\right\}$ 17. $\left\{-\dfrac{3}{4}\right\}$

19. $\{-4 \pm \sqrt{10}\}$ 21. $\left\{\dfrac{-5 \pm \sqrt{29}}{2}\right\}$ 23. $\left\{\dfrac{3 \pm \sqrt{7}}{2}\right\}$

25. $\left\{\dfrac{3 \pm i}{2}\right\}$ 27. $\left\{\dfrac{3 \pm i\sqrt{39}}{4}\right\}$ 29. $\{5 \pm i\}$ 31. $28, 2$

33. $-23, 0$ 35. $0, 1$ 37. $-\dfrac{3}{4}, 0$ 39. $97, 2$ 41. $0, 1$

43. $140, 2$ 45. $1, 2$ 47. $\{-2 \pm 2\sqrt{2}\}$ 49. $\left\{-2, \dfrac{1}{2}\right\}$

51. $\left\{\dfrac{-1 \pm \sqrt{13}}{3}\right\}$ 53. $\{0\}$ 55. $\left\{\dfrac{13}{9}, \dfrac{17}{9}\right\}$

57. $\{\pm 5\sqrt{3}\}$ 59. $\{4 \pm 2i\}$ 61. $\{2 \pm i\sqrt{6}\}$

63. $\left\{-\dfrac{3}{4}, \dfrac{5}{2}\right\}$ 65. $\{-4.474, 1.274\}$ 67. $\{3.7\}$

69. $\{-2.979, -0.653\}$ 71. $\{-4792.983, -0.017\}$

73. $\{-0.079, 0.078\}$

75. $\dfrac{1 + \sqrt{65}}{2}$ and $\dfrac{-1 + \sqrt{65}}{2}$, or 4.5 and 3.5

77. $3 + \sqrt{5}$ and $3 - \sqrt{5}$, or 5.2 and 0.8

79. $W = \dfrac{-1 + \sqrt{5}}{2} \approx 0.6\ \text{ft}$, $L = \dfrac{1 + \sqrt{5}}{2} \approx 1.6\ \text{ft}$

81. $W = -2 + \sqrt{14} \approx 1.7\ \text{ft}$, $L = 2 + \sqrt{14} \approx 5.7\ \text{ft}$

83. $3\ \text{sec}$ 85. $7.0\ \text{sec}$ 87. $4\ \text{in.}$ 89. 4

95. 2 97. 0 99. 0

Section 8.3 Warm-ups T F T T F T T T T F

1. A quadratic function is a function of the form $f(x) = ax^2 + bx + c$ with $a \ne 0$.

3. If $a > 0$ then the parabola opens upward. If $a < 0$ then the parabola opens downward.

5. The vertex is the highest point on a parabola that opens downward or the lowest point on a parabola that opens upward.

7. $(3, -6), (4, 0), (-3, 0)$ **9.** $(4, -128), (0, 0), (2, 0)$

11. Domain $(-\infty, \infty)$, range $[2, \infty)$

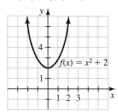

13. Domain $(-\infty, \infty)$, range $[-4, \infty)$

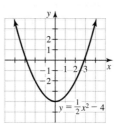

15. Domain $(-\infty, \infty)$, range $(-\infty, 5]$

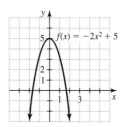

17. Domain $(-\infty, \infty)$, range $(-\infty, 5]$

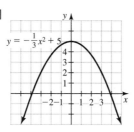

19. Domain $(-\infty, \infty)$, range $[0, \infty)$

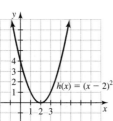

21. Vertex $\left(\dfrac{1}{2}, -\dfrac{9}{4}\right)$, intercepts $(0, -2), (-1, 0), (2, 0)$,

domain $(-\infty, \infty)$, range $\left[-\dfrac{9}{4}, \infty\right)$

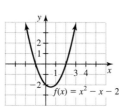

23. Vertex $(-1, -9)$, intercepts $(0, -8), (-4, 0), (2, 0)$, domain $(-\infty, \infty)$, range $[-9, \infty)$

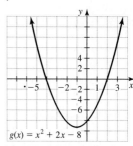

25. Vertex $(-2, 1)$, intercepts $(0, -3), (-1, 0), (-3, 0)$, domain $(-\infty, \infty)$, range $(-\infty, 1]$

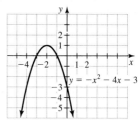

27. Vertex $\left(\dfrac{3}{2}, \dfrac{25}{4}\right)$, intercepts $(0, 4), (4, 0), (-1, 0)$, domain

$(-\infty, \infty)$, range $\left(-\infty, \dfrac{25}{4}\right]$

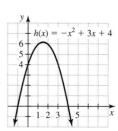

29. Vertex $(3, -25)$, intercepts $(0, -16), (8, 0), (-2, 0)$, domain $(-\infty, \infty)$, range $[-25, \infty)$

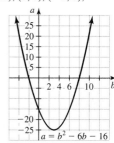

31. Minimum -8 **33.** Maximum 14

35. Minimum 2   **37.** Maximum 2

39. Maximum 64 feet

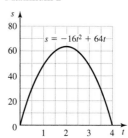

41. 100   **43.** 625 square meters

45. 2 P.M.   **47.** 15 meters, 25 meters

49. The graph of $y = kx^2$ gets narrower as k gets larger.

51. The graph of $y = x^2$ has the same shape as $x = y^2$.

53. a) Vertex $(0.84, -0.68)$, domain $(-\infty, \infty)$,
range $[-0.68, \infty)$, $(1.30, 0)$, $(0.38, 0)$

    b) Vertex $(5.96, 46.26)$, domain $(-\infty, \infty)$,
range $(-\infty, 46.26]$, $(12.48, 0)$, $(-0.55, 0)$

Section 8.4 Warm-ups T F F T F F F T F F

1. If the coefficients are integers and the discriminant is a perfect square, then the quadratic polynomial can be factored.

3. If the solutions are a and b, then the quadratic equation $(x - a)(x - b) = 0$ has those solutions.

5. Prime   **7.** Prime   **9.** $(3x - 4)(2x + 9)$ **11.** Prime

13. $(4x - 15)(2x + 3)$ **15.** $x^2 + 4x - 21 = 0$

17. $x^2 - 5x + 4 = 0$ **19.** $x^2 - 5 = 0$ **21.** $x^2 + 16 = 0$

23. $x^2 + 2 = 0$ **25.** $6x^2 - 5x + 1 = 0$ **27.** $\left\{-\dfrac{3}{2}, \dfrac{3}{2}\right\}$

29. $\left\{\dfrac{-3 \pm \sqrt{5}}{2}\right\}$ **31.** $\{\pm\sqrt{5}, \pm 3\}$ **33.** $\{-2, 1\}$

35. $\{-1 \pm \sqrt{5}, -3, 1\}$ **37.** $\{-3, -2, 1, 2\}$ **39.** $\{16, 81\}$

41. $\{9\}$ **43.** $\left\{-\dfrac{1}{3}, \dfrac{1}{2}\right\}$ **45.** $\{64\}$ **47.** $\left\{\dfrac{2}{3}, \dfrac{3}{2}\right\}$

49. $\left\{\pm\dfrac{\sqrt{14}}{2}, \pm\dfrac{\sqrt{38}}{2}\right\}$ **51.** $\{-1 + \sqrt{2}, -1 - \sqrt{2}\}$

53. 2:00 P.M.

55. Before $-5 + \sqrt{265}$ or 11.3 mph, after $-9 + \sqrt{265}$ or 7.3 mph

57. Andrew $\dfrac{13 + \sqrt{265}}{2}$ or 14.6 hr, John $\dfrac{19 + \sqrt{265}}{2}$ or 17.6 hr

59. Length $5 + 5\sqrt{41}$ or 37.02 ft, width $-5 + 5\sqrt{41}$ or 27.02 ft

61. $14 + 2\sqrt{58}$ or 29.2 hr   **63.** $-5 + 5\sqrt{5}$ or 6.2 meters

65. a) $x^2 - 6x + 4 = 0$ **b)** $x^2 - 8x + 20 = 0$
    c) $x^2 - x + 1 = 0$

67. $\{-10, -4, 4, 10\}$ **69.** $\{4.27\}$

Section 8.5 Warm-ups F F F F T T T T T F

1. A quadratic inequality has the form $ax^2 + bx + c > 0$. In place of $>$ we can also use $<$, $\leq$, or $\geq$.

3. A rational inequality is an inequality involving a rational expression.

5. $(-3, 2)$

<!-- number line -->
$-4\,-3\,-2\,-1\ \ 0\ \ 1\ \ 2\ \ 3$

7. $(-\infty, -2) \cup (2, \infty)$

<!-- number line -->
$-4\,-3\,-2\,-1\ \ 0\ \ 1\ \ 2\ \ 3\ \ 4$

9. $(-\infty, -4] \cup \left[\dfrac{3}{2}, \infty\right)$

<!-- number line -->
$-6\,-5\,-4\,-3\,-2\,-1\ \ 0\ \ 1\ \ 2\ \ 3\ \ 4$

11. $(-\infty, 0] \cup [2, \infty)$

<!-- number line -->
$-2\,-1\ \ 0\ \ 1\ \ 2\ \ 3\ \ 4$

13. $(-\infty, 0) \cup \left(\dfrac{1}{2}, \infty\right)$

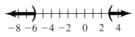
$-3\,-2\,-1\ \ 0\ \ 1\ \ 2\ \ 3$

15. $(-\infty, \infty)$

17. $(-\infty, 0) \cup (3, \infty)$

<!-- number line -->
$-2\,-1\ \ 0\ \ 1\ \ 2\ \ 3\ \ 4\ \ 5$

19. $[-2, 0)$

<!-- number line -->
$-4\,-3\,-2\,-1\ \ 0\ \ 1\ \ 2$

21. $(-\infty, -6) \cup (3, \infty)$

<!-- number line -->
$-8\,-6\,-4\,-2\ \ 0\ \ 2\ \ 4$

23. $(-\infty, -2) \cup (-1, \infty)$

<!-- number line -->
$-4\,-3\,-2\,-1\ \ 0\ \ 1$

25. $(-13, -4) \cup (5, \infty)$

<!-- number line -->
$-13\,-9\,-5\,-1\ 1\ 3\ 5\ 7$

27. $(-\infty, -5) \cup (1, 3) \cup (5, \infty)$

<!-- number line -->
$-7\,-5\,-3\,-1\ \ 1\ \ 3\ \ 5\ \ 7$

29. $[-6, 3) \cup [4, 6)$

<!-- number line -->
$-6\,-4\,-2\ \ 0\ \ 2\ \ 4\ \ 6$

31. $(-\infty, 1 - \sqrt{5}) \cup (1 + \sqrt{5}, \infty)$

$1 - \sqrt{5} \qquad 1 + \sqrt{5}$

33. $\left(-\infty, \dfrac{3 - \sqrt{3}}{2}\right] \cup \left[\dfrac{3 + \sqrt{3}}{2}, \infty\right)$

<!-- number line -->
$\dfrac{3 - \sqrt{3}}{2} \qquad \dfrac{3 + \sqrt{3}}{2}$

35. $\left[\dfrac{3 - 3\sqrt{5}}{2}, \dfrac{3 + 3\sqrt{5}}{2}\right]$

<!-- number line -->
$\dfrac{3 - 3\sqrt{5}}{2} \qquad \dfrac{3 + 3\sqrt{5}}{2}$

37. $[-3, 3]$ **39.** $(-4, 4)$ **41.** $(-\infty, 0] \cup [4, \infty)$

43. $\left(-\dfrac{3}{2}, \dfrac{5}{3}\right)$ **45.** $(-\infty, -2] \cup [6, \infty)$

47. $(-\infty, -3) \cup (5, \infty)$ **49.** $(-\infty, -4] \cup [2, \infty)$

51. $(-3, 4]$ **53.** $[-1, 2] \cup [5, \infty)$

55. $(-\infty, -3) \cup (-1, 1)$ **57.** $(-27.58, -0.68)$

59. $(-\infty, -2 - \sqrt{6}) \cup (-3, -2 + \sqrt{6}) \cup (2, \infty)$

61. 6, 7, 8, . . .   **63.** 4 seconds

65. a) 900 ft   **b)** 3 sec   **c)** 3 sec

67. a) (h, k) **b)** $(-\infty, h) \cup (k, \infty)$
    c) $(-k, -h)$ **d)** $(-\infty, -k] \cup [-h, \infty)$
    e) $(-\infty, h] \cup (k, \infty)$ **f)** $(-k, -h]$

69. c   **71.** b

Chapter 8 Wrap-up

Enriching Your Mathematical Word Power

1. b   **2.** a   **3.** d   **4.** c   **5.** b   **6.** c

7. c   **8.** a   **9.** c   **10.** a   **11.** c

Review Exercises

1. $\{-3, 5\}$ **3.** $\left\{-3, \dfrac{5}{2}\right\}$ **5.** $\{-5, 5\}$ **7.** $\left\{\dfrac{3}{2}\right\}$

9. $\{\pm 2\sqrt{3}\}$ **11.** $\{-2, 4\}$ **13.** $\left\{\dfrac{4 \pm \sqrt{3}}{2}\right\}$ **15.** $\left\{\pm \dfrac{3}{2}\right\}$

17. $\{2, 4\}$ **19.** $\{2, 3\}$ **21.** $\left\{\dfrac{1}{2}, 3\right\}$ **23.** $\{-2 \pm \sqrt{3}\}$

25. $\{-2, 5\}$ **27.** $\left\{-\dfrac{1}{3}, \dfrac{3}{2}\right\}$ **29.** $\{-2 \pm \sqrt{2}\}$

31. $\left\{\dfrac{5 \pm \sqrt{13}}{6}\right\}$ **33.** $0, 1$ **35.** $-19, 0$ **37.** $17, 2$

39. $\left\{\dfrac{2 \pm i\sqrt{2}}{2}\right\}$ **41.** $\left\{\dfrac{3 \pm i\sqrt{15}}{4}\right\}$ **43.** $\left\{\dfrac{-1 \pm i\sqrt{5}}{3}\right\}$

45. $\{-3 \pm i\sqrt{7}\}$

47. Vertex $(3, -9)$, intercepts $(0, 0)$, $(6, 0)$

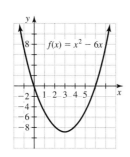

49. Vertex $(2, -16)$, intercepts $(0, -12)$, $(-2, 0)$, $(6, 0)$

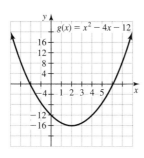

51. Vertex $(2, 8)$, intercepts $(0, 0)$, $(4, 0)$

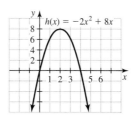

53. Vertex $(1, 4)$, intercepts $(0, 3)$, $(-1, 0)$, $(3, 0)$

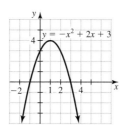

55. Domain $(-\infty, \infty)$, range $[-3, \infty)$

57. Domain $(-\infty, \infty)$, range $(-\infty, 4.125]$

59. $(4x + 1)(2x - 3)$ **61.** Prime   **63.** $(4y - 5)(2y + 5)$

65. $x^2 + 9x + 18 = 0$ **67.** $x^2 - 50 = 0$

69. $\{-2, 1\}$ **71.** $\{\pm 2, \pm 3\}$ **73.** $\{-6, -5, 2, 3\}$

75. $\{-2, 8\}$ **77.** $\left\{-\dfrac{1}{9}, \dfrac{1}{4}\right\}$ **79.** $\{16, 81\}$

81. $(-\infty, -3) \cup (2, \infty)$

83. $[-4, 5]$

85. $(0, 1)$

87. $(-\infty, -2) \cup [4, \infty)$

89. $(-3, \infty)$

91. $(-2, -1) \cup \left(-\dfrac{1}{2}, \infty\right)$

93. $\left\{\dfrac{5}{12}\right\}$ **95.** $\left\{\dfrac{-3 \pm \sqrt{5}}{2}\right\}$ **97.** $\left\{\dfrac{4 \pm 2i}{3}\right\}$ **99.** $\left\{\dfrac{5}{2}\right\}$

101. $\left\{-2, -\dfrac{1}{4}\right\}$ **103.** $\{625, 10{,}000\}$

105. $-2 + 2\sqrt{2}$ and $2 + 2\sqrt{2}$, or 0.83 and 4.83

107. Width $\dfrac{4 + \sqrt{706}}{2}$ or 15.3 inches, height $\dfrac{-4 + \sqrt{706}}{2}$ or 11.3 inches

109. 2 inches   **111.** Width 5 ft, length 9 ft

113. \$20.40, 400   **115.** 0.5 sec and 1.5 sec

Chapter 8 Test

1. $-7, 0$ **2.** $13, 2$ **3.** $0, 1$ **4.** $\left\{-3, \dfrac{1}{2}\right\}$

5. $\{-3 \pm \sqrt{3}\}$ **6.** $\{-5\}$ **7.** $\left\{-2, \dfrac{3}{2}\right\}$ **8.** $\{-4, 3\}$

9. $\{\pm 1, \pm 2\}$ **10.** $\{11, 27\}$ **11.** $\{\pm 6i\}$ **12.** $\{-3 \pm i\}$

13. $\left\{\dfrac{1 \pm i\sqrt{11}}{6}\right\}$

14. Domain $(-\infty, \infty)$, range $(-\infty, 16]$

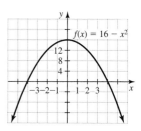

15. Domain $(-\infty, \infty)$, range $\left[-\dfrac{9}{4}, \infty\right)$

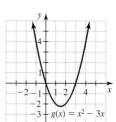

16. $x^2 - 2x - 24 = 0$ **17.** $x^2 + 25 = 0$

18. $(-6, 3)$

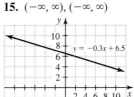

19. $(-1, 2) \cup (8, \infty)$

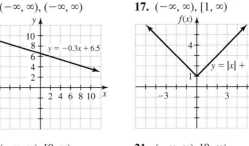

20. Width $-1 + \sqrt{17}$ feet, length $1 + \sqrt{17}$ feet

21. $\dfrac{5 + \sqrt{37}}{2}$ or 5.5 hr   **22.** $(1, 0), (5, 0)$

23. 36 feet

Making Connections Chapters 1–8

1. $\left\{\dfrac{15}{2}\right\}$ **2.** $\left\{\pm\dfrac{\sqrt{30}}{2}\right\}$ **3.** $\left\{-3, \dfrac{5}{2}\right\}$ **4.** $\left\{\dfrac{-2 \pm \sqrt{34}}{2}\right\}$

5. $\left\{-\dfrac{7}{2}, -2\right\}$ **6.** $\left\{-3, \dfrac{1}{4}, \dfrac{-11 \pm \sqrt{73}}{8}\right\}$ **7.** $\{9\}$

8. $\left\{-\dfrac{3}{2}, \dfrac{13}{2}\right\}$ **9.** $(-4, \infty)$ **10.** $\left[\dfrac{1}{2}, 5\right]$ **11.** $\left[\dfrac{1}{2}, 5\right)$

12. $(2, 8)$ **13.** $[-3, 2)$ **14.** $(-\infty, \infty)$ **15.** $y = \dfrac{2}{3}x - 3$

16. $y = -\dfrac{1}{2}x + 2$ **17.** $y = \dfrac{-c \pm \sqrt{c^2 - 12d}}{6}$

18. $y = \dfrac{n \pm \sqrt{n^2 + 4mw}}{2m}$ **19.** $y = \dfrac{5}{6}x - \dfrac{25}{12}$

20. $y = -\dfrac{2}{3}x + \dfrac{17}{3}$ **21.** $\dfrac{4}{3}$ **22.** $-\dfrac{11}{7}$ **23.** -2

24. $\dfrac{58}{5}$ **25.** 40,000, 38,000, \$32.50

26. \$800,000, \$950,000, \$40 or \$80, \$60

Chapter 9

Section 9.1 Warm-ups T T T T T F T T F T

1. A linear function is a function of the form $f(x) = mx + b$, where m and b are real numbers with $m \neq 0$.

3. The graph of a constant function is a horizontal line.

5. The graph of a quadratic function is a parabola.

7. $(-\infty, \infty), \{-2\}$

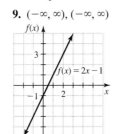

9. $(-\infty, \infty), (-\infty, \infty)$

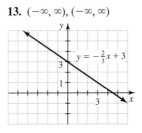

11. $(-\infty, \infty), (-\infty, \infty)$

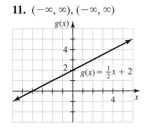

13. $(-\infty, \infty), (-\infty, \infty)$

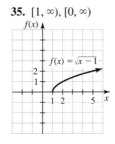

15. $(-\infty, \infty), (-\infty, \infty)$

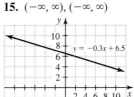

17. $(-\infty, \infty), [1, \infty)$

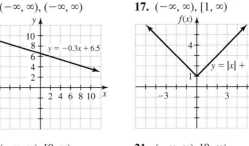

19. $(-\infty, \infty), [0, \infty)$

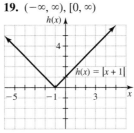

21. $(-\infty, \infty), [0, \infty)$

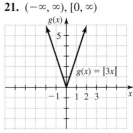

23. $(-\infty, \infty), [0, \infty)$

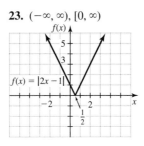

25. $(-\infty, \infty), [1, \infty)$

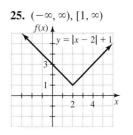

27. $(-\infty, \infty), [2, \infty)$

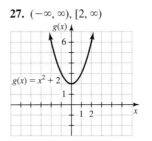

29. $(-\infty, \infty), [0, \infty)$

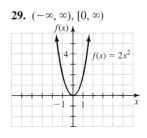

31. $(-\infty, \infty), (-\infty, 6]$

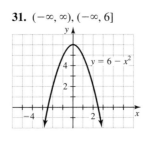

33. $[0, \infty), [0, \infty)$

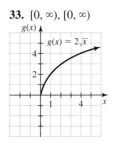

35. $[1, \infty), [0, \infty)$

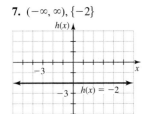

37. $[0, \infty), (-\infty, 0]$

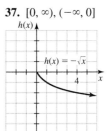

39. $[0, \infty)$, $[2, \infty)$

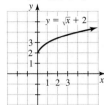

41. $[0, \infty)$, $(-\infty, \infty)$

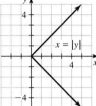

43. $(-\infty, 0]$, $(-\infty, \infty)$

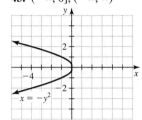

45. $\{5\}$, $(-\infty, \infty)$

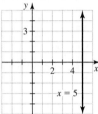

47. $[-9, \infty)$, $(-\infty, \infty)$

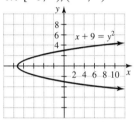

49. $[0, \infty)$, $[0, \infty)$

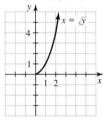

51. $[0, \infty)$, $(-\infty, \infty)$

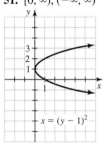

53. $(-\infty, \infty)$, $(-\infty, 1]$

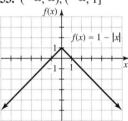

55. $(-\infty, \infty)$, $[-1, \infty)$

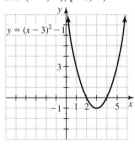

57. $(-\infty, \infty)$, $[1, \infty)$

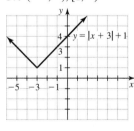

59. $[0, \infty)$, $[-3, \infty)$

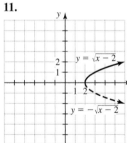

61. $(-\infty, \infty)$, $(-\infty, \infty)$

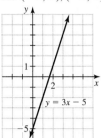

63. $(-\infty, \infty)$, $(-\infty, 0]$

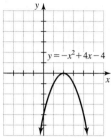

65. The graph of $f(x) = \sqrt{x^2}$ is the same as the graph of $f(x) = |x|$.

67. For large values of k the graph gets narrower and for smaller values of k the graph gets broader.

69. The graph of $y = (x - k)^2$ moves to the right for $k > 0$ and to the left for $k < 0$.

71. The graph of $y = f(x - k)$ lies to the right of the graph of $y = f(x)$ when $k > 0$.

Section 9.2 Warm-ups F T T F T T F T T F

1. The graph of $y = -f(x)$ is a reflection in the x-axis of the graph of $y = f(x)$.

3. The graph of $y = f(x) + k$ for $k < 0$ is a downward translation of $y = f(x)$.

5. The graph of $y = f(x + k)$ for $k > 0$ is a translation to the left of $y = f(x)$.

7.

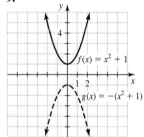

9.

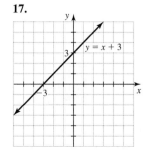

11.

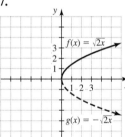

13.

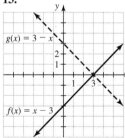

15.

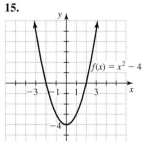

17.

19.

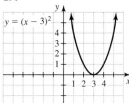

$y = (x - 3)^2$

21.

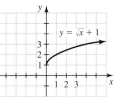

$y = \sqrt{x} + 1$

23.

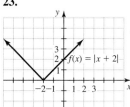

$f(x) = |x + 2|$

25.

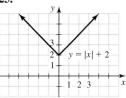

$y = |x| + 2$

27.

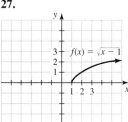

$f(x) = \sqrt{x} - 1$

29.

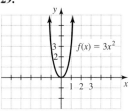

$f(x) = 3x^2$

31.

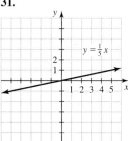

$y = \frac{1}{5}x$

33.

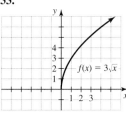

$f(x) = 3\sqrt{x}$

35.

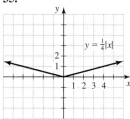

$y = \frac{1}{4}|x|$

37.

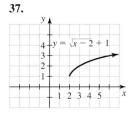

$y = \sqrt{x - 2} + 1$

39.

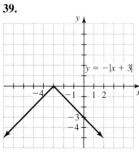

$y = -|x + 3|$

41.

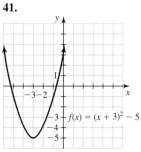

$f(x) = (x + 3)^2 - 5$

43.

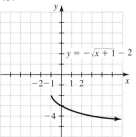

$y = -\sqrt{x + 1} - 2$

45.

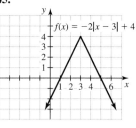

$f(x) = -2|x - 3| + 4$

47.

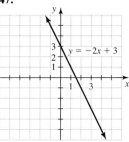

$y = -2x + 3$

49.

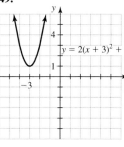

$y = 2(x + 3)^2 + 1$

51.

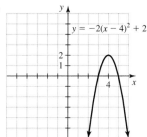

$y = -2(x - 4)^2 + 2$

53.

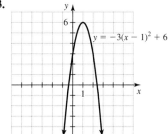

$y = -3(x - 1)^2 + 6$

55. d   **57.** e   **59.** h   **61.** c   **63.** $y = x^2 + 8$
65. $y = \sqrt{x + 5}$ **67.** $y = |x + 3| + 5$
69. Move f to the right 20 units and upward 30 units.

Section 9.3 Warm-ups T T F F F F T T T T
1. The basic operations of functions are addition, subtraction, multiplication, and division.
3. In the composition function the second function is evaluated on the result of the first function.
5. $x^2 + 2x - 3$ **7.** $4x^3 - 11x^2 + 6x$ **9.** 12   **11.** -30
13. -21 **15.** $\frac{13}{8}$ **17.** $y = 6x - 20$ **19.** $y = x + 2$
21. $y = x^2 + 2x$ **23.** $y = x$ **25.** -2 **27.** 5   **29.** 7
31. 5   **33.** 5   **35.** 4   **37.** 22.2992   **39.** $4x^2 - 6x$

41. $2x^2 + 6x - 3$ **43.** x **45.** $4x - 9$ **47.** $\dfrac{x + 9}{4}$

49. $F = f \circ h$ **51.** $G = g \circ h$ **53.** $H = h \circ g$

55. $J = h \circ h$ **57.** $K = g \circ g$ **67. a)** 50 ft^2 **b)** $A = \dfrac{d^2}{2}$

69. $P(x) = -x^2 + 20x - 170$ **71.** $J = 0.025I$

73. a) 397.8 **b)** $D = \dfrac{1.116 \times 10^7}{L^3}$ **c)** Decreases

75. $[0, \infty), [0, \infty), [16, \infty)$ **77.** $[0, \infty), [0, \infty)$

Section 9.4 Warm-ups   F F F T T T F T T T F
1. The inverse of a function is a function with the same ordered pairs except that the coordinates are reversed.
3. The range of f^{-1} is the domain of f.
5. A function is one-to-one if no two ordered pairs have the same second coordinate with different first coordinates.
7. The switch-and-solve strategy is used for finding a formula for an inverse function.
9. No   **11.** Yes, $\{(4, 16), (3, 9), (0, 0)\}$ **13.** No
15. Yes, $\{(0, 0), (2, 2), (9, 9)\}$ **17.** No   **19.** Yes
21. Yes   **23.** Yes   **25.** Yes   **27.** No

29. $f^{-1}(x) = \dfrac{x}{5}$ **31.** $g^{-1}(x) = x + 9$ **33.** $k^{-1}(x) = \dfrac{x + 9}{5}$

35. $m^{-1}(x) = \dfrac{2}{x}$ **37.** $f^{-1}(x) = x^3 + 4$ **39.** $f^{-1}(x) = \dfrac{3}{x} + 4$

41. $f^{-1}(x) = \dfrac{x^3 - 7}{3}$ **43.** $f^{-1}(x) = \dfrac{2x + 1}{x - 1}$

45. $f^{-1}(x) = \dfrac{1 + 4x}{3x - 1}$ **47.** $p^{-1}(x) = x^4$ for $x \geq 0$

49. $f^{-1}(x) = 2 + \sqrt{x}$ **51.** $f^{-1}(x) = \sqrt{x - 3}$
53. $f^{-1}(x) = x^2 - 2$ for $x \geq 0$

55. $f^{-1}(x) = \dfrac{1}{2}x - \dfrac{3}{2}$ **57.** $f^{-1}(x) = \sqrt{x + 1}$

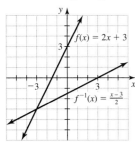
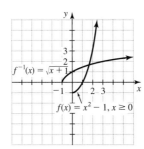

59. $f^{-1}(x) = \dfrac{x}{5}$ **61.** $f^{-1}(x) = \sqrt[3]{x}$

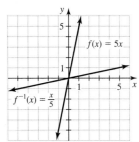
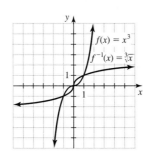

63. $f^{-1}(x) = x^2 + 2$ for $x \geq 0$

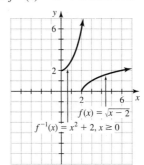

65. $(f^{-1} \circ f)(x) = x$ **67.** $(f^{-1} \circ f)(x) = x$
69. $(f^{-1} \circ f)(x) = x$ **71.** $(f^{-1} \circ f)(x) = x$

73. a) 33.5 mph **b)** Decreases   **c)** $L = \dfrac{S^2}{30}$

75. $T(x) = 1.09x + 125,\ T^{-1}(x) = \dfrac{x - 125}{1.09}$

77. An odd positive integer   **79.** Not inverses

Section 9.5 Warm-ups   T F F T F T F F F T
1. If y varies directly as x, then $y = kx$ for some constant k.
3. If y is inversely proportional to x, then $y = k/x$.
5. If y is jointly proportional to x and z, then $y = kxz$ for some constant k.
7. $a = km$ **9.** $d = k/e$ **11.** $I = krt$ **13.** $m = kp^2$

15. $B = k\sqrt[3]{w}$ **17.** $t = \dfrac{k}{x^2}$ **19.** $v = \dfrac{km}{n}$ **21.** $y = \dfrac{3}{2}x$

23. $A = \dfrac{30}{B}$ **25.** $m = \dfrac{36}{\sqrt{p}}$ **27.** $A = \dfrac{2}{5}tu$

29. $y = \dfrac{1.067x}{z}$ **31.** $-\dfrac{21}{5}$ **33.** $-\dfrac{3}{2}$ **35.** $\dfrac{1}{2}$

37. 3.293 **39.** Inverse   **41.** Direct
43. Combined   **45.** Joint   **47.** $420
49. 9 cm^3 **51.** $360   **53.** $18.90
55. a) $d = 16t^2$ **b)** 4 feet   **c)** 2.5 sec
57. 400 pounds   **59.** 7.2 days

61. a) $G = \dfrac{Nd}{c}$ **b)** 84   **c)** 23, 20, 17, 15, 13

     d) Decreases

63. $(1, 1)$, y_1 increasing, y_2 decreasing, y_1 direct variation, y_2 inverse variation

Chapter 9 Wrap-up

Enriching Your Mathematical Word Power
1. a   **2.** b   **3.** d   **4.** d
5. a   **6.** b   **7.** d
8. c   **9.** d   **10.** b
11. a   **12.** d

Review Exercises

1. $(-\infty, \infty)$, $(-\infty, \infty)$

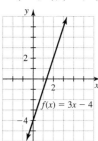

3. $(-\infty, \infty)$, $[-2, \infty)$

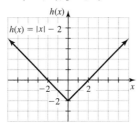

5. $(-\infty, \infty)$, $[0, \infty)$

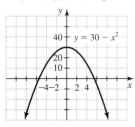

7. $[0, \infty)$, $[2, \infty)$

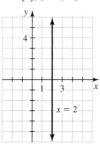

9. $(-\infty, \infty)$, $(-\infty, 30]$

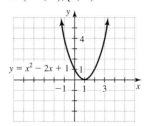

11. $\{2\}$, $(-\infty, \infty)$

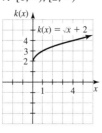

13. $[1, \infty)$, $(-\infty, \infty)$

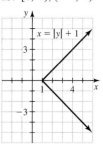

15.

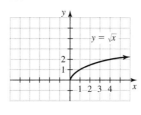

17.

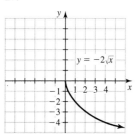

19.

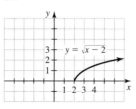

21.

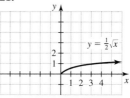

23.

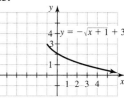

25. -4 **27.** $\sqrt{2}$ **29.** 99   **31.** 17

33. $3x^3 - x^2 - 10x$ **35.** 20   **37.** $F = f \circ g$ **39.** $H = g \circ h$

41. $I = g \circ g$ **43.** No   **45.** Yes, $f^{-1}(x) = x/8$

47. Yes, $g^{-1}(x) = \dfrac{x + 6}{13}$ **49.** Yes, $j^{-1}(x) = \dfrac{x + 1}{x - 1}$ **51.** No

53. $f^{-1}(x) = \dfrac{1}{3}x + \dfrac{1}{3}$ **55.** $f^{-1}(x) = \sqrt[3]{2x}$

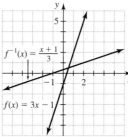 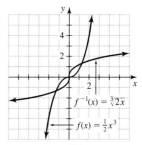

57. 24   **59.** -16 **61.** 256 ft   **63.** $B = \dfrac{2A}{\pi}$

65. $a = 15w - 16$ **67.** $A = s^2$, $s = \sqrt{A}$

Chapter 9 Test

1.

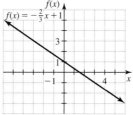

2.

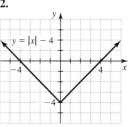

3.

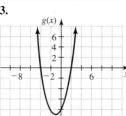

4.

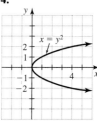

5.

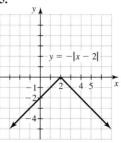

6.

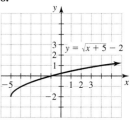

7. 11 **8.** 125 **9.** -3 **10.** $\dfrac{x-5}{-2}$

11. $x^2 - 2x + 9$ **12.** 15 **13.** 1776 **14.** $\dfrac{1}{8}$

15. $-2x^2 - 3$ **16.** $4x^2 - 20x + 29$ **17.** $H = f \circ g$
18. $W = g \circ f$ **19.** Not invertible **20.** $f^{-1}(x) = (x-9)^3$

21. $(-\infty, \infty),\ [0, \infty)$ **22.** $f^{-1}(x) = \dfrac{x+1}{x-2}$ **23.** $\dfrac{32\pi}{3}$ ft^3

24. $\dfrac{36}{7}$ **25.** \$5076

Making Connections Chapters 1–9

1. $\dfrac{1}{25}$ **2.** $\dfrac{3}{2}$ **3.** $\sqrt{2}$ **4.** x^8 **5.** 2 **6.** x^9

7. $\{\pm 3\}$ **8.** $\{\pm 2\sqrt{2}\}$ **9.** $\{0, 1\}$ **10.** $\{2 \pm \sqrt{10}\}$

11. $\{81\}$ **12.** $\varnothing$ **13.** $\{\pm 8\}$ **14.** $\left\{-\dfrac{17}{5}, 5\right\}$

15. $\{2\}$ **16.** $\left\{\dfrac{5}{3}\right\}$ **17.** $\{42\}$ **18.** $\{11\}$

19.

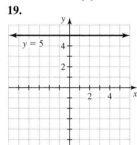

20.

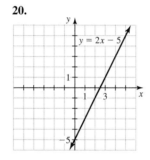

21.

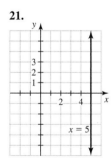

22.

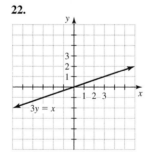

23.

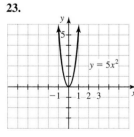

24.

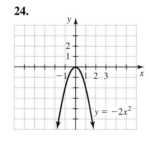

25. $(2, 4), (3, 8), (1, 2), (4, 16)$
26. $\left(\dfrac{1}{2}, 2\right), \left(-1, \dfrac{1}{4}\right), (2, 16), (0, 1)$
27. $[0, \infty)$ **28.** $(-\infty, 3]$ **29.** $(-\infty, \infty)$
30. $(-\infty, 1) \cup (1, 9) \cup (9, \infty)$
31. a) $C = 0.12x + 3000$ **b)** $P = 1 \times 10^{-6}x + 0.15$

32. a) \$0.44, \$0.40, \$0.39
b)

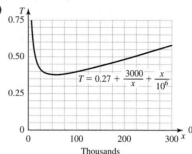

c) 60,000 miles **d)** $[50,000, 60,000]$

Chapter 10

Section 10.1 Warm-ups T T F T T T T T T T
1. A zero of the function f is a number a such that $f(a) = 0$.
3. Two statements are equivalent means that they are either both true or both false.
5. If the remainder is zero when $P(x)$ is divided by $x - c$, then $P(c) = 0$.
7. Yes **9.** Yes **11.** No **13.** Yes **15.** No **17.** Yes
19. Yes **21.** $(x - 3)(x^2 + 3x + 3)$
23. $(x + 5)(x + 3)(x + 1)$ **25.** No
27. $(x + 1)(x - 2)(x^2 + 2x + 4)$
29. $(2x - 1)(x - 3)(x + 2)$

31. $\{-4, 1, 3\}$ **33.** $\left\{-\dfrac{1}{2}, 2, 3\right\}$ **35.** $\left\{-4, -\dfrac{1}{2}, 6\right\}$

37. $\{-3, 1\}$ **39.** $\{-1, 1, 2\}$
41. a) $f(x) = x + 2$ **b)** $f(x) = x^2 - 25$
   c) $f(x) = (x - 1)(x + 3)(x - 4)$
   d) Yes. The degree is the same as the number of zeros.

43. a) $\{-2, 1, 5\}$ **b)** $\left\{-\dfrac{3}{2}, \dfrac{3}{2}, \dfrac{5}{2}\right\}$

Section 10.2 Warm-ups F F T T F T F T F F
1. A polynomial function is a function for which the value of the dependent variable is determined by a polynomial.
3. A zero of a function $f(x)$ is a number c such that $f(c) = 0$.
5. The rational root theorem states that if a rational number p/q (in lowest terms) is a zero of a polynomial, then its p is a factor of the constant term and q is a factor of the leading coefficient.
7. 0 **9.** 15 **11.** 3 **13.** -15 **15.** 0 **17.** 17

19. Yes **21.** No **23.** Yes **25.** No **27.** $\dfrac{9}{5}$

29. $2, 3$ **31.** $3i, -3i$ **33.** $-2i, 2i, 3$ **35.** $-\dfrac{1}{2}, 0, 3$

37. $-1, \pm\sqrt{7}$ **39.** $\dfrac{-1 \pm i\sqrt{3}}{2}, 1$ **41.** $\pm 1, \pm 2, \pm\dfrac{1}{2}$

43. $\pm 1, \pm 2, \pm 3, \pm 4, \pm 6, \pm 8, \pm 12, \pm 24$

45. $\pm 1, \pm 2, \pm 3, \pm 6$ **47.** $-\dfrac{1}{2}, 1, 2$ **49.** $-4, -3, -2$

51. $-3 - \sqrt{3}, -3 + \sqrt{3}, 1$ **53.** $-2 \pm 2i, 2$ **55.** $\dfrac{1}{2}, \dfrac{1}{3}, \dfrac{1}{4}$

57. \$1000, 0 or 20 **59.** $-0.2, 0.1, 0.3$ **61.** 10, 20, 30

Section 10.3 Warm-ups F T T F F T F F T T

1. Multiplicity of a root c is the number of times that $x - c$ occurs as a factor.

3. The conjugate pairs theorem states that for a polynomial equation with real coefficients if $a + bi$ $(b \neq 0)$ is a root, then $a - bi$ is also a root.

5. If there are no roots greater than c, then c is an upper bound for the roots.

7. Degree 5, $-2, 2, 0$ multiplicity 3

9. Degree 4, 0 multiplicity 2, -1 multiplicity 2

11. Degree 4, $-\sqrt{3}$ multiplicity 2, $\sqrt{3}$ multiplicity 2

13. Degree 4, 1 multiplicity 2, -2 multiplicity 2

15. Degree 4, -1 multiplicity 2, 1 multiplicity 2

17. $x^3 - 7x^2 + 17x - 15 = 0$

19. $x^3 + 2x^2 + x + 2 = 0$ **21.** $x^3 + 2x = 0$

23. $x^4 - 2x^3 + 3x^2 - 2x + 2 = 0$

25. $x^2 - 3x + 2 = 0$ **27.** $x^3 - 4x^2 + x + 6 = 0$

29. 3 negative, or 1 negative and 2 imaginary

31. 1 positive and 2 negative, or 1 positive and 2 imaginary

33. 4 positive, or 2 positive and 2 imaginary, or 4 imaginary

35. no positive, no negative, 4 imaginary

37. 1 positive and 2 imaginary   **39.** 4 imaginary and 0

41. Between -3 and 3   **43.** Between -1 and 3

45. Between -5 and 4   **47.** Between -1 and 7

49. $-2, 1 \pm 2i$ **51.** $\dfrac{1}{2}, 1 \pm \sqrt{5}$ **53.** $-\dfrac{1}{2}, \dfrac{2 \pm \sqrt{2}}{2}$

55. $-1, 1, 2, 3$ **57.** $1, 2, 3$ **59.** $0, 1, \pm i\sqrt{5}, \pm\sqrt{3}$

61. 6 feet **63.** $\dfrac{1}{2}$ in. **65.** $3.3315, 0.9492, -0.9492, -3.3315$

67. $-2.4495, -1.4142, -1, 1, 1.4142, 2.4495$

Section 10.4 Warm-ups F F F F T T F F T F

1. The graph of $y = f(x)$ is symmetric about the y-axis if $f(x) = f(-x)$ for all x in the domain of the function.

3. An x-intercept is a point at which a graph intersects the x-axis.

5. Symmetric about y-axis   **7.** Neither symmetry

9. Neither symmetry   **11.** Neither symmetry

13. Symmetric about y-axis   **15.** Symmetric about origin

17. Does not cross at $(5, 0)$ **19.** Crosses at $(4, 0)$ and $(-1, 0)$

21. Does not cross at $(0, 0)$

23. Crosses at $(-5, 0)$, does not cross at $(3, 0)$

25. Crosses at $(1, 0)$, does not cross at $(0, 0)$

27. Crosses at $\left(\dfrac{1}{2}, 0\right)$, does not cross at $(-1, 0)$

29. d   **31.** a   **33.** c   **35.** e

37.

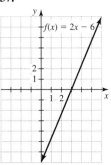

39.

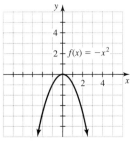

41.

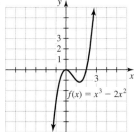

43.

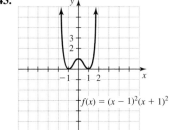

45.

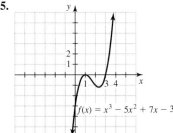

47.

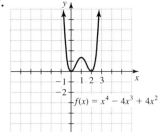

49.

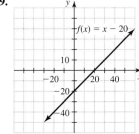

51.

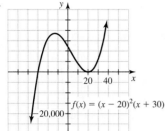

$f(x) = (x - 20)^2(x + 30)$

53.

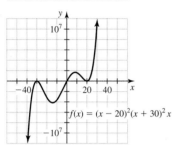

$f(x) = (x - 20)^2(x + 30)^2 x$

Section 10.5 Warm-ups F F F F T F T F T T

1. A rational function is of the form $f(x) = P(x)/Q(x)$, where $P(x)$ and $Q(x)$ are polynomials with no common factor and $Q(x) \neq 0$.

3. A vertical asymptote is a vertical line that is approached by the graph of a rational function.

5. An oblique asymptote is a nonhorizontal, nonvertical line that is approached by the graph of a rational function.

7. $(-\infty, 1) \cup (1, \infty)$ **9.** $(-\infty, 0) \cup (0, \infty)$

11. $(-\infty, -4) \cup (-4, 4) \cup (4, \infty)$

13. Vertical: $x = -4$; horizontal: x-axis

15. Vertical: $x = 4, x = -4$; horizontal: x-axis

17. Vertical: $x = 7$; horizontal: $y = 5$

19. Vertical: $x = 3$; oblique: $y = 2x + 6$

21. c   **23.** b   **25.** g   **27.** f

29. $x = -4$, x-axis   **31.** $x = 3, x = -3$, x-axis

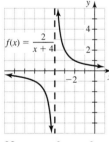

$f(x) = \frac{2}{x + 4}$

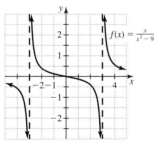

$f(x) = \frac{x}{x^2 - 9}$

33. $x = -3, y = 2$ **35.** y-axis, $y = x - 3$

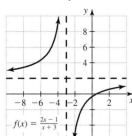

$f(x) = \frac{2x - 1}{x + 3}$

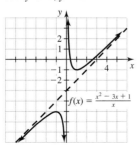

$f(x) = \frac{x^2 - 3x + 1}{x}$

37. $x = 1, y = 3x + 1$

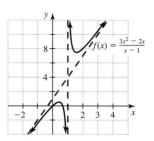

$f(x) = \frac{3x^2 - 2x}{x - 1}$

39. $x = 0, y = 0$

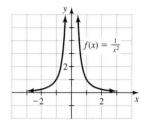

$f(x) = \frac{1}{x^2}$

41. $x = -3, x = 2,$
$y = 0, \left(0, \frac{1}{2}\right), \left(\frac{3}{2}, 0\right)$

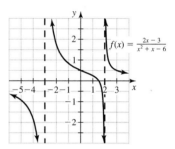

$f(x) = \frac{2x - 3}{x^2 + x - 6}$

43. $x = 0, y = 0, (-1, 0)$

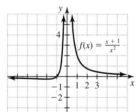

$f(x) = \frac{x + 1}{x^2}$

45. $x = 0, x = \pm 3,$
$y = 0, \left(\frac{1}{2}, 0\right)$

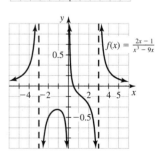

$f(x) = \frac{2x - 1}{x^3 - 9x}$

47. $x = \pm 1, y = 0, (0, 0)$

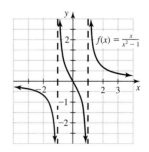

$f(x) = \frac{x}{x^2 - 1}$

49. $y = 0, (0, 2)$

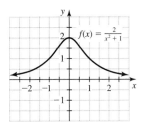

51. $x = -1, y = x - 1, (0, 0)$

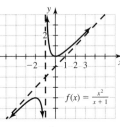

53. $f(20) = \$2.35,$
$f(30) = \$1.46,$
average approaches 0

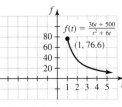

55. a) $y = 25,000$ **b)** $\$39,000$ **c)** $140,000$

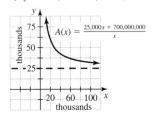

57. The graph of $f(x)$ is an asymptote for the graph of $g(x)$.
59. The graph of $f(x)$ is an asymptote for the graph of $g(x)$.
61. The graph of $f(x)$ is an asymptote for the graph of $g(x)$.

Chapter 10 Wrap-up

Enriching Your Mathematical Word Power
1. c **2.** b **3.** a **4.** d **5.** a **6.** a **7.** d
8. d **9.** a **10.** b **11.** a

Review Exercises
1. $\{-3, 2, 5\}$ **3.** $\{-2, 3, 4\}$ **5.** $(x - 3)(x + 2)(x + 5)$

7. No **9.** $-45, \dfrac{5}{2}$ **11.** $\pm 1, \pm 2, \pm 4, \pm\dfrac{1}{3}, \pm\dfrac{2}{3}, \pm\dfrac{4}{3}$

13. $\pm 1, \pm 3, \pm\dfrac{1}{2}, \pm\dfrac{3}{2}, \pm\dfrac{1}{4}, \pm\dfrac{3}{4}$ **15.** $\dfrac{3}{2}$ **17.** ± 10

19. $4, -2 \pm 2i\sqrt{3}$ **21.** $\pm 2\sqrt{2}, \pm 2i\sqrt{2}$

23. $\dfrac{1}{3}, \pm\dfrac{1}{2}$ **25.** $2x^2 - 5x + 2 = 0$ **27.** $x^2 - 10x + 29 = 0$

29. $x^3 - 5x^2 + 16x - 30 = 0$
31. 4 imaginary and 0 with multiplicity 2
33. 3 positive, or 1 positive and 2 imaginary
35. Between -2 and 4 **37.** Between -2 and 5

39. $\dfrac{1}{2}, 4, 5$ **41.** $-\dfrac{3}{2}, \dfrac{1}{2}, \dfrac{5}{2}$ **43.** $5, \dfrac{1}{2} \pm i$

45. 3 with multiplicity 2, $\dfrac{1 \pm \sqrt{2}}{2}$ **47.** 1 with multiplicity 3

49. Symmetric about y-axis **51.** Symmetric about origin
53. $(1, 0), (-2, 0), (0, 2)$

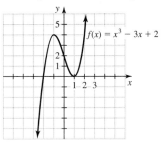

55. $(1, 0), (-1, 0), (0, -1)$

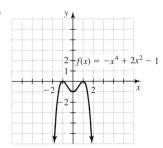

57. $(0, 0), (2, 0), (-2, 0)$

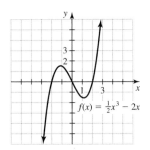

59. $\left(-\infty, -\dfrac{3}{2}\right) \cup \left(-\dfrac{3}{2}, \infty\right)$ **61.** $(-\infty, \infty)$

63. $x = 3$, x-axis **65.** $x = 2$, $x = -2$, x-axis

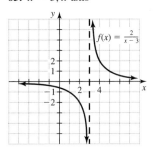 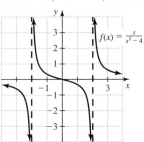

67. $x = 1, y = 2$ **69.** $x = 2, y = x$

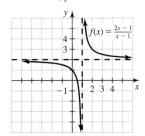 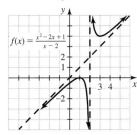

71.

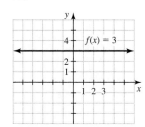

73.

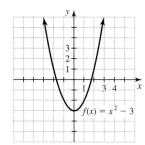

75.

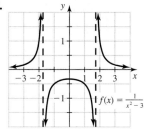

77.

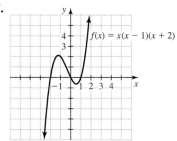

79. 3 in.

Chapter 10 Test

1. 52   **2.** 7   **3.** $\pm 1, \pm 2, \pm 3, \pm 6$ **4.** $\pm 1, \pm 3, \pm \dfrac{1}{2}, \pm \dfrac{3}{2}$

5. $-4, 1, 3$ **6.** $\dfrac{1}{2}, 2 \pm i$ **7.** $x^3 - 2x^2 - x + 2 = 0$

8. $x^3 - 8x^2 + 22x - 20 = 0$ **9.** Yes
10. $(x - 3)(x - 4)(x - 5)$
11. 3 positive, or 1 positive and 2 imaginary
12. 4 imaginary roots and 0   **13.** Between -2 and 3
14. Between -2 and 3   **15.** Symmetry about origin
16. Symmetry about y-axis
17.

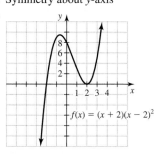

18.

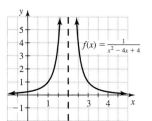

19.

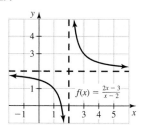

20.

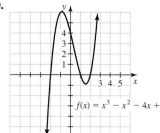

Making Connections Chapters 1–10

1. -2 **2.** $\dfrac{3}{2}, 5$ **3.** $\dfrac{3}{2}$ **4.** $\pm \dfrac{\sqrt{6}}{2}$ **5.** -9

6. $\pm \dfrac{\sqrt{6}}{2}, \pm i\sqrt{5}$ **7.** $-5, 2$ **8.** $-\dfrac{1}{3}, -\dfrac{1}{5}, \dfrac{3}{2}$

9.

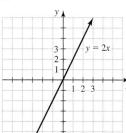

10.

11.

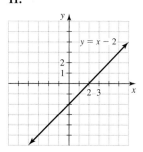

12.

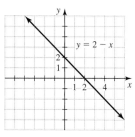

13.

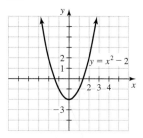

14.

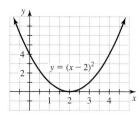

15.

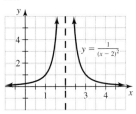

16.

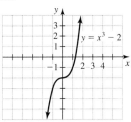

35.

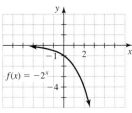

37.

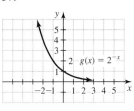

17.

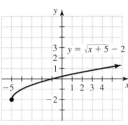

18.

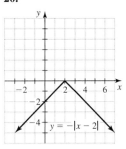

39.

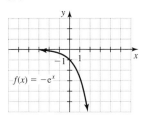

41.

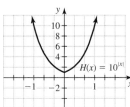

19.

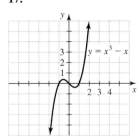

20.

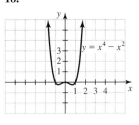

43.

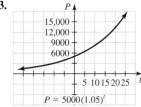

45. $\{6\}$ **47.** $\{-3\}$ **49.** $\{-2\}$ **51.** $\{-1\}$ **53.** $\{-2\}$

55. $\{-2\}$ **57.** $\{-3, 3\}$ **59.** 2   **61.** $\dfrac{4}{3}$ **63.** -2

65. 0   **67.** $\dfrac{3}{2}$ **69.** $\dfrac{1}{2}$ **71.** \$9861.72

73. a) \$53,277.30 **b)** 2010   **75.** \$45, \$12.92

77. \$616.84   **79.** \$6230.73

81. 300 grams, 90.4 grams, 12 years, no

83. 2.66666667, 0.0516, 2.8×10^{-5}

85. The graph of $y = 3^{x-k}$ lies k units to the right of $y = 3^x$ when $k > 0$ and $|k|$ units to the left of $y = 3^x$ when $k < 0$.

Chapter 11

Section 11.1 Warm-ups F T F T T F T F T F

1. An exponential function has the form $f(x) = a^x$, where $a > 0$ and $a \neq 1$.

3. The two most popular bases are e and 10.

5. The compound interest formula is $A = P(1 + i)^n$.

7. 16   **9.** 2   **11.** 3   **13.** $\dfrac{1}{3}$ **15.** -1 **17.** $-\dfrac{1}{4}$

19. 1   **21.** 100   **23.** 2.718   **25.** 0.135

27.

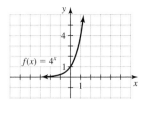

29.

Section 11.2 Warm-ups T F T T F F F F T T

1. If $f(x) = 2^x$, then $f^{-1}(x) = \log_2(x)$.

3. The common logarithm uses the base 10 and the natural logarithm uses base e.

5. The one-to-one property for logarithmic functions states that if $\log_a(m) = \log_a(n)$, then $m = n$.

7. $2^3 = 8$ **9.** $\log(100) = 2$ **11.** $5^y = x$ **13.** $\log_2(b) = a$

15. $3^{10} = x$ **17.** $\ln(x) = 3$ **19.** 2   **21.** 4   **23.** 6

25. 3   **27.** -2 **29.** 2   **31.** -2 **33.** 1   **35.** -3

37. $\dfrac{1}{2}$ **39.** 2   **41.** 0.6990   **43.** 1.8307

31.

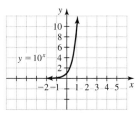

33.

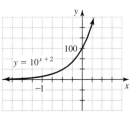

45.

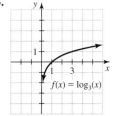

47.

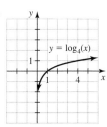

49.

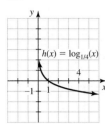

51.

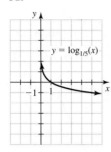

53. $f^{-1}(x) = \log_6(x)$ **55.** $f^{-1}(x) = e^x$

57. $f^{-1}(x) = \left(\dfrac{1}{2}\right)^x$ **59.** $\{4\}$ **61.** $\left\{\dfrac{1}{2}\right\}$ **63.** $\{0.001\}$

65. $\{6\}$ **67.** $\left\{\dfrac{1}{5}\right\}$ **69.** $\{\pm3\}$ **71.** $\{0.4771\}$

73. $\{-0.3010\}$ **75.** $\{1.9741\}$ **77.** 5.776 years

79. 1.9269 years   **81. a)** 14.58%   **b)** \$66,576.60

83. 4.1   **85.** 6.8   **87.** 90 db

89. $f^{-1}(x) = 2^{x-5} + 3$, $(-\infty, \infty)$, $(3, \infty)$

91. $y = \ln(e^x) = x$ for $-\infty < x < \infty$, $y = e^{\ln(x)} = x$ for $0 < x < \infty$

Section 11.3 Warm-ups T F T T F T F F F T

1. The product rule for logarithms states that $\log_a(MN) = \log_a(M) + \log_a(N)$.

3. The power rule for logarithms states that $\log_a(M^N) = N \cdot \log_a(M)$.

5. Since $\log_a(M)$ is the exponent you would use on a to obtain M, using $\log_a(M)$ as the exponent produces M: $a^{\log_a(M)} = M$.

7. $\log(21)$ **9.** $\log_3(\sqrt{5x})$ **11.** $\log(x^5)$ **13.** $\ln(30)$

15. $\log(x^2 + 3x)$ **17.** $\log_2(x^2 - x - 6)$ **19.** $\log(4)$

21. $\log_2(x^4)$ **23.** $\log(\sqrt{5})$ **25.** $\ln(h - 2)$

27. $\log_2(w - 2)$ **29.** $\ln(x - 2)$ **31.** $3\log(3)$

33. $\dfrac{1}{2}\log(3)$ **35.** $x\log(3)$ **37.** 10   **39.** 19   **41.** 8

43. 4.3   **45.** $\log(3) + \log(5)$ **47.** $\log(5) - \log(3)$

49. $2\log(5)$ **51.** $2 \cdot \log(5) + \log(3)$ **53.** $-\log(3)$

55. $-\log(5)$ **57.** $\log(x) + \log(y) + \log(z)$

59. $3 + \log_2(x)$ **61.** $\ln(x) - \ln(y)$ **63.** $1 + 2 \cdot \log(x)$

65. $2\log_5(x - 3) - \dfrac{1}{2}\log_5(w)$

67. $\ln(y) + \ln(z) + \dfrac{1}{2}\ln(x) - \ln(w)$ **69.** $\log(x^2 - x)$

71. $\ln(3)$ **73.** $\ln\left(\dfrac{xz}{w}\right)$ **75.** $\ln\left(\dfrac{x^2y^3}{w}\right)$ **77.** $\log\left(\dfrac{(x - 3)^{1/2}}{(x + 1)^{2/3}}\right)$

79. $\log_2\left(\dfrac{(x - 1)^{2/3}}{(x + 2)^{1/4}}\right)$ **81.** False   **83.** True   **85.** True

87. False   **89.** True   **91.** True   **93.** True   **95.** False

97. $r = \log(I/I_0)$, $r = 2$ **99.** b

101. The graphs are the same because
$$\ln(\sqrt{x}) = \ln(x^{1/2}) = \dfrac{1}{2}\ln(x).$$

103. The graph is a straight line because $\log(e^x) = x \log(e) \approx 0.434x$. The slope is $\log(e)$ or approximately 0.434.

Section 11.4 Warm-ups T T T F T T T F T F

1. The exponential equation $a^y = x$ is equivalent to $\log_a(x) = y$.

3. $\{7\}$ **5.** $\{31\}$ **7.** $\{e\}$ **9.** $\{2\}$ **11.** $\{3\}$ **13.** $\varnothing$

15. $\{6\}$ **17.** $\{3\}$ **19.** $\{2\}$ **21.** $\{4\}$ **23.** $\{\log_3(7)\}$

25. $\left\{\dfrac{\ln(7)}{2}\right\}$ **27.** $\{-6\}$ **29.** $\left\{-\dfrac{1}{2}\right\}$

31. $\dfrac{5\ln(3)}{\ln(2) - \ln(3)}$, -13.548 **33.** $\dfrac{4 + 2\log(5)}{1 - \log(5)}$, 17.932

35. $\dfrac{\ln(9)}{\ln(9) - \ln(8)}$, 18.655   **37.** 1.5850   **39.** -0.6309

41. -2.2016 **43.** 1.5229   **45.** $\dfrac{\ln(7)}{\ln(2)}$, 2.807

47. $\dfrac{1}{3 - \ln(2)}$, 0.433   **49.** $\dfrac{\ln(5)}{\ln(3)}$, 1.465

51. $1 + \dfrac{\ln(9)}{\ln(2)}$, 4.170   **53.** $\log_3(20)$, 2.727   **55.** $\dfrac{3}{5}$ **57.** $\dfrac{1}{2}$

59. 41 months   **61.** 594 days

63. 10 g, 9163 years ago   **65.** 7524 ft³/sec   **67.** 7.1 years

69. 16.8 years   **71.** 2.0×10^{-4} **73.** 0.9183

75. 2.2894   **77.** (2.71, 6.54)   **79.** (1.03, 0.04), (4.73, 2.24)

Chapter 11 Wrap-up

Enriching Your Mathematical Word Power

1. a   **2.** d   **3.** b   **4.** d   **5.** d   **6.** b   **7.** a

8. b   **9.** b   **10.** c

Review Exercises

1. $\dfrac{1}{25}$ **3.** 125   **5.** 1   **7.** $\dfrac{1}{10}$ **9.** 4   **11.** $\dfrac{1}{2}$ **13.** 2

15. 4   **17.** $-\dfrac{5}{2}$ **19.** 2   **21.** 8.6421   **23.** 177.828

25. 0.02005   **27.** 0.1408

29.

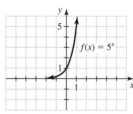

31.

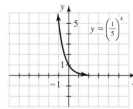

33.

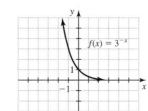

35.

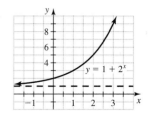

37. $\log(n) = m$ **39.** $k^h = t$ **41.** -3 **43.** -1 **45.** 2

47. 0   **49.** 256   **51.** 6.267   **53.** -5.083 **55.** 5.560

57. $f^{-1}(x) = \log(x)$　　**59.** $f^{-1}(x) = \ln(x)$

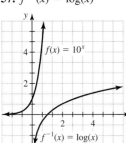

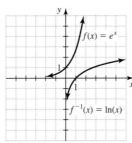

61. $2\log(x) + \log(y)$　　**63.** $4\ln(2)$　　**65.** $-\log_5(x)$

67. $\log\left(\dfrac{\sqrt{x+2}}{(x-1)^2}\right)$　　**69.** $\{256\}$　　**71.** $\{3\}$　　**73.** $\{2\}$

75. $\{3\}$　　**77.** $\left\{\dfrac{\ln(7)}{\ln(3)-1}\right\}$　　**79.** $\left\{\dfrac{\ln(5)}{\ln(5)-\ln(3)}\right\}$

81. $\left\{\dfrac{1}{3}\right\}$　　**83.** $\{22\}$　　**85.** $\left\{\dfrac{200}{99}\right\}$　　**87.** $\{1.3869\}$

89. $\{0.4650\}$　　**91.** \$51,182.68　　**93.** 161.5 grams

95. 5 years　　**97.** 4347.5 ft³/sec

Chapter 11 Test

1. 25　　**2.** $\dfrac{1}{5}$　　**3.** 1　　**4.** 3　　**5.** 0　　**6.** -1

7.

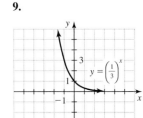

8.

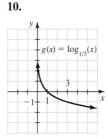

9.

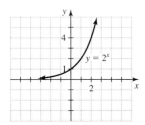

10.

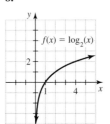

11. 10　　**12.** 8　　**13.** $\dfrac{3}{2}$　　**14.** 15　　**15.** -4

16. $\{\log_3(12)\}$　　**17.** $\{\sqrt{3}\}$　　**18.** $\left\{\dfrac{\ln(8)}{\ln(8)-\ln(5)}\right\}$

19. $\{5\}$　　**20.** $\{3\}$　　**21.** $\{0.5372\}$　　**22.** $\{20.5156\}$

23. 10; 147,648　　**24.** 1.733 hours

Making Connections Chapters 1–11

1. $\{3 \pm 2\sqrt{2}\}$　　**2.** $\{259\}$　　**3.** $\{6\}$　　**4.** $\left\{\dfrac{11}{2}\right\}$

5. $\{-5, 11\}$　　**6.** $\{67\}$　　**7.** $\{6\}$　　**8.** $\{4\}$　　**9.** $\left\{-\dfrac{52}{15}\right\}$

10. $\left\{\dfrac{3 \pm \sqrt{3}}{3}\right\}$　　**11.** $f^{-1}(x) = 3x$　　**12.** $g^{-1}(x) = 3^x$

13. $f^{-1}(x) = \dfrac{x+4}{2}$　　**14.** $h^{-1}(x) = x^2$ for $x \geq 0$

15. $j^{-1}(x) = \dfrac{1}{x}$　　**16.** $k^{-1}(x) = \log_5(x)$

17. $m^{-1}(x) = 1 + \ln(x)$　　**18.** $n^{-1}(x) = e^x$

19.

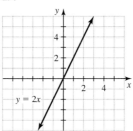

20.

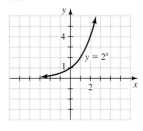

21.

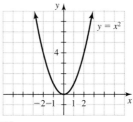

22.

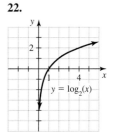

23.

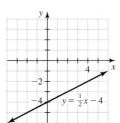

24.

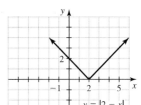

25.

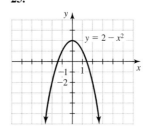

26.

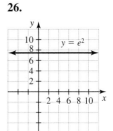

27. a)

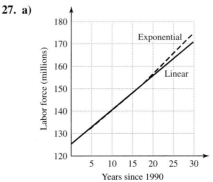

b) Linear 155.7 million, exponential 156.5 million

28. a) $d_1 = 0.135v$　**b)** $d_2 = 0.216v$　**c)** $d_1 = 200.2$ m

Chapter 12

Section 12.1 Warm-ups T F F T F T T T T T

1. If the graph of an equation is not a straight line, then it is called nonlinear.

3. Graphing is not an accurate method for solving a system and the graphs might be difficult to draw.

5. $\{(2, 4), (-3, 9)\}$ **7.** $\{(-2, 2), (6, 6)\}$

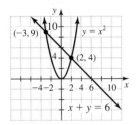

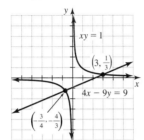

9. $\{(8, 4)\}$ **11.** $\left\{\left(-\dfrac{3}{4}, -\dfrac{4}{3}\right), \left(3, \dfrac{1}{3}\right)\right\}$

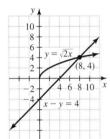

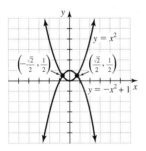

13. $\left\{\left(\dfrac{\sqrt{2}}{2}, \dfrac{1}{2}\right), \left(-\dfrac{\sqrt{2}}{2}, \dfrac{1}{2}\right)\right\}$

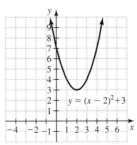

15. $\{(0, -5), (3, 4), (-3, 4)\}$ **17.** $\{(4, 5), (-2, -1)\}$

19. $\left\{\left(-3, -\dfrac{5}{3}\right)\right\}$

21. $\{(\sqrt{5}, \sqrt{3}), (\sqrt{5}, -\sqrt{3}), (-\sqrt{5}, \sqrt{3}), (-\sqrt{5}, -\sqrt{3})\}$

23. $\{(\sqrt{2}, \sqrt{3}), (\sqrt{2}, -\sqrt{3}), (-\sqrt{2}, \sqrt{3}), (-\sqrt{2}, -\sqrt{3})\}$

25. $\left\{\left(\dfrac{3}{2}, -\dfrac{3}{13}\right)\right\}$ **27.** $\{(3, 4)\}$ **29.** $\left\{\left(-\dfrac{5}{3}, \dfrac{36}{5}\right), (2, 5)\right\}$

31. $\{(2, 5), (19, -12)\}$

33. $\{(\sqrt{2}, 2), (-\sqrt{2}, 2), (1, 1), (-1, 1)\}$

35. $\{(3, 1)\}$ **37.** $\varnothing$ **39.** $\{(-6, 4^{-7})\}$

41. $\sqrt{3}$ feet and $2\sqrt{3}$ feet

43. Height $5\sqrt{10}$ inches, base $20\sqrt{10}$ inches

45. Pump A 24 hours, pump B 8 hours

47. 40 minutes   **49.** 8 feet by 9 feet   **51.** $4 - 2i$ and $4 + 2i$

53. Side of square 8 feet, height of triangle 2 feet

55. a) $(1.71, 1.55), (-2.98, -3.95)$ **b)** $(1, 1), (0.40, 0.16)$
  c) $(1.17, 1.62), (-1.17, -1.62)$

Section 12.2 Warm-ups F T T F F T T T T T

1. A parabola is the set of all points in a plane that are equidistant from a given line and a fixed point not on the line.

3. A parabola can be written in the forms $y = ax^2 + bx + c$ or $y = a(x - h)^2 + k$.

5. We use completing the square to convert $y = ax^2 + bx + c$ into $y = a(x - h)^2 + k$.

7. $\sqrt{13}$ **9.** $2\sqrt{17}$ **11.** $\sqrt{65}$

13. Vertex $(0, 0)$, focus $\left(0, \dfrac{1}{8}\right)$, directrix $y = -\dfrac{1}{8}$

15. Vertex $(0, 0)$, focus $(0, -1)$, directrix $y = 1$

17. Vertex $(3, 2)$, focus $(3, 2.5)$, directrix $y = 1.5$

19. Vertex $(-1, 6)$, focus $(-1, 5.75)$, directrix $y = 6.25$

21. $y = \dfrac{1}{8}x^2$ **23.** $y = -\dfrac{1}{2}x^2$ **25.** $y = \dfrac{1}{2}x^2 - 3x + 6$

27. $y = -\dfrac{1}{8}x^2 + \dfrac{1}{4}x - \dfrac{1}{8}$ **29.** $y = x^2 + 6x + 10$

31. $y = (x - 3)^2 - 8$, vertex $(3, -8)$, focus $(3, -7.75)$, directrix $y = -8.25$, axis $x = 3$

33. $y = 2(x + 3)^2 - 13$, vertex $(-3, -13)$, focus $(-3, -12.875)$, directrix $y = -13.125$, axis $x = -3$

35. $y = -2(x - 4)^2 + 33$, vertex $(4, 33)$, focus $\left(4, 32\dfrac{7}{8}\right)$, directrix $y = 33\dfrac{1}{8}$, axis $x = 4$

37. $y = 5(x + 4)^2 - 80$, vertex $(-4, -80)$, focus $\left(-4, -79\dfrac{19}{20}\right)$, directrix $y = -80\dfrac{1}{20}$, axis $x = -4$

39. Vertex $(2, -3)$, focus $\left(2, -2\dfrac{3}{4}\right)$, directrix $y = -3\dfrac{1}{4}$, $x = 2$, upward

41. Vertex $(1, -2)$, focus $\left(1, -2\dfrac{1}{4}\right)$, directrix $y = -1\dfrac{3}{4}$, $x = 1$, downward

43. Vertex $(1, -2)$, focus $\left(1, -1\dfrac{11}{12}\right)$, directrix $y = -2\dfrac{1}{12}$, $x = 1$, upward

45. Vertex $\left(-\dfrac{3}{2}, \dfrac{17}{4}\right)$, focus $\left(-\dfrac{3}{2}, 4\right)$, directrix $y = \dfrac{9}{2}$, $x = -\dfrac{3}{2}$, downward

47. Vertex $(0, 5)$, focus $\left(0, 5\dfrac{1}{12}\right)$, directrix $y = 4\dfrac{11}{12}$, $x = 0$, upward

49. $(3, 2), \left(\dfrac{13}{4}, 2\right), x = \dfrac{11}{4}$

51. $(-2, 1), (-1, 1), x = -3$ **53.** $(4, 2), \left(\dfrac{7}{2}, 2\right), x = \dfrac{9}{2}$

55.

57.

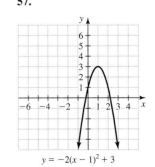

59.

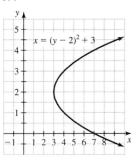

61.

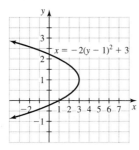

3. $x^2 + (y - 3)^2 = 25$ **5.** $(x - 1)^2 + (y + 2)^2 = 81$

7. $x^2 + y^2 = 3$ **9.** $(x + 6)^2 + (y + 3)^2 = \dfrac{1}{4}$

11. $\left(x - \dfrac{1}{2}\right)^2 + \left(y - \dfrac{1}{3}\right)^2 = 0.01$ **13.** $(3, 5), \sqrt{2}$

15. $\left(0, \dfrac{1}{2}\right), \dfrac{\sqrt{2}}{2}$ **17.** $(0, 0), \dfrac{3}{2}$ **19.** $(2, 0), \sqrt{3}$

21.

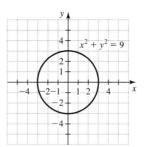

23.

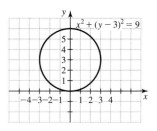

63. $y = \dfrac{1}{60} x^2$

65. $\{(-1, 2), (1, 2)\}$ **67.** $\{(1, -1)\}$

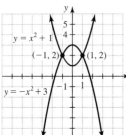

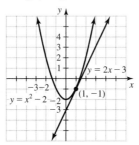

69. $\left\{\left(\dfrac{3}{2}, \dfrac{11}{4}\right), (-4, 0)\right\}$

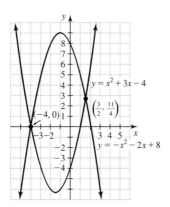

25.

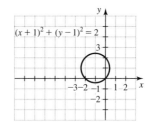

27.

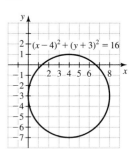

71. $\{(-3, -4), (2, 6)\}$

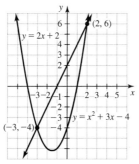

29.

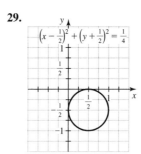

31. $(x + 2)^2 + (y + 3)^2 = 13, (-2, -3), \sqrt{13}$
33. $(x - 1)^2 + (y - 2)^2 = 8, (1, 2), 2\sqrt{2}$
35. $(x - 5)^2 + (y - 4)^2 = 9, (5, 4), 3$

73. $(3, 0), (-1, 0)$ **75.** $(20, 4), (-20, 4)$ **77.** $(0, 0), (1, 1)$
81. The graphs have identical shapes.

37. $\left(x - \dfrac{1}{2}\right)^2 + \left(y + \dfrac{1}{2}\right)^2 = \dfrac{1}{2}, \left(\dfrac{1}{2}, -\dfrac{1}{2}\right), \dfrac{\sqrt{2}}{2}$

Section 12.3 Warm-ups F F T F F F T F T F
1. A circle is the set of all points in a plane that lie at a fixed distance from a fixed point.

39. $\left(x - \dfrac{3}{2}\right)^2 + \left(y - \dfrac{1}{2}\right)^2 = \dfrac{7}{2}, \left(\dfrac{3}{2}, \dfrac{1}{2}\right), \dfrac{\sqrt{14}}{2}$

41. $\left(x - \dfrac{1}{3}\right)^2 + \left(y + \dfrac{3}{4}\right)^2 = \dfrac{97}{144}, \left(\dfrac{1}{3}, -\dfrac{3}{4}\right), \dfrac{\sqrt{97}}{12}$

43. $\{(1, 3), (-1, -3)\}$ **45.** $\{(0, -3), (\sqrt{5}, 2), (-\sqrt{5}, 2)\}$

9.

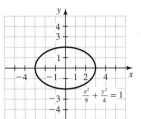

11.

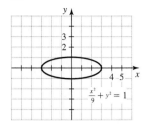

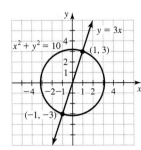

47. $\{(0, -3), (2, -1)\}$ **49.** $(0, 2 + \sqrt{3})$ and $(0, 2 - \sqrt{3})$

13.

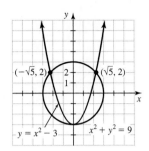

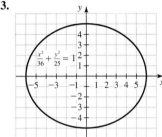

51. $\sqrt{29}$ **53.** $(x - 2)^2 + (y - 3)^2 = 32$

55. $\left(\dfrac{5}{2}, -\dfrac{\sqrt{11}}{2}\right)$ and $\left(\dfrac{5}{2}, \dfrac{\sqrt{11}}{2}\right)$ **57.** 755,903 mm^3

15.

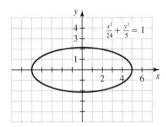

17.

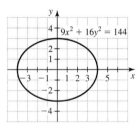

59. $(0, 0)$ only   **61.**

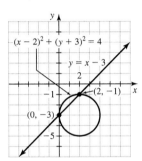

19.

21.

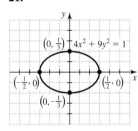

63. B and D can be any real numbers, but A must equal C, and $4AE + B^2 + D^2 > 0$. No ordered pairs satisfy $x^2 + y^2 = -9$.

65. $y = \pm\sqrt{4 - x^2}$ **67.** $y = \pm\sqrt{x}$ **69.** $y = -1 \pm\sqrt{x}$

23.

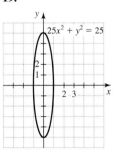

25.

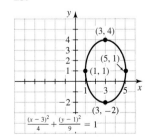

Section 12.4 Warm-ups F F T T T F F T T T

1. An ellipse is the set of all points in a plane such that the sum of their distances from two fixed points is constant.

3. The center of an ellipse is the point that is midway between the foci.

5. The equation of an ellipse centered at (h, k) is
$$\dfrac{(x - h)^2}{a^2} + \dfrac{(y - k)^2}{b^2} = 1.$$

7. The asymptotes of a hyperbola are the extended diagonals of the fundamental rectangle.

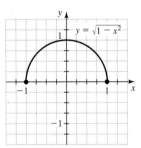
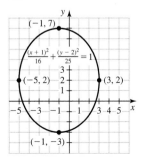
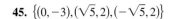

27.

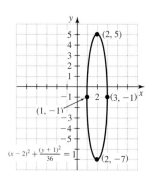

29. $y = \pm\dfrac{3}{2}x$

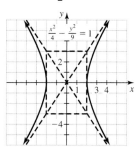

43.

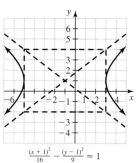

$\dfrac{(x+1)^2}{16} - \dfrac{(y-1)^2}{9} = 1$

45.

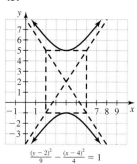

$\dfrac{(y-2)^2}{9} - \dfrac{(x-4)^2}{4} = 1$

47. $\left(\dfrac{2\sqrt{10}}{5}, \dfrac{3\sqrt{15}}{5}\right), \left(\dfrac{2\sqrt{10}}{5}, -\dfrac{3\sqrt{15}}{5}\right),$

$\left(-\dfrac{2\sqrt{10}}{5}, \dfrac{3\sqrt{15}}{5}\right), \left(-\dfrac{2\sqrt{10}}{5}, -\dfrac{3\sqrt{15}}{5}\right)$

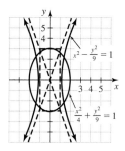

31. $y = \pm\dfrac{2}{5}x$

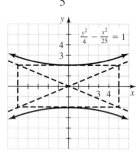

33. $y = \pm\dfrac{1}{5}x$

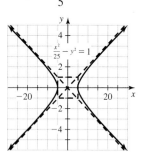

35. $y = \pm5x$

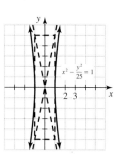

37. $y = \pm\dfrac{3}{4}x$

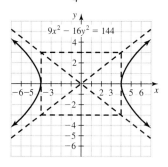

49. No points of intersection

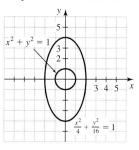

51. $\left(\dfrac{\sqrt{10}}{2}, \dfrac{\sqrt{6}}{2}\right), \left(\dfrac{\sqrt{10}}{2}, -\dfrac{\sqrt{6}}{2}\right),$

$\left(-\dfrac{\sqrt{10}}{2}, \dfrac{\sqrt{6}}{2}\right), \left(-\dfrac{\sqrt{10}}{2}, -\dfrac{\sqrt{6}}{2}\right)$

39. $y = \pm x$

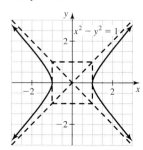

41.

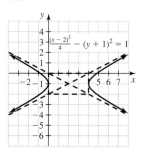

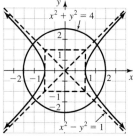

53. $\left(\dfrac{3\sqrt{6}}{4}, \dfrac{\sqrt{10}}{4}\right), \left(\dfrac{3\sqrt{6}}{4}, -\dfrac{\sqrt{10}}{4}\right),$
$\left(-\dfrac{3\sqrt{6}}{4}, \dfrac{\sqrt{10}}{4}\right), \left(-\dfrac{3\sqrt{6}}{4}, -\dfrac{\sqrt{10}}{4}\right)$

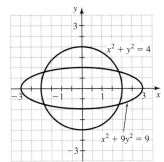

55. $\left(\dfrac{\sqrt{17}}{3}, \dfrac{8}{9}\right), \left(-\dfrac{\sqrt{17}}{3}, \dfrac{8}{9}\right), (0, -1)$

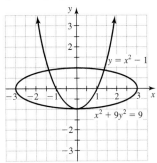

57. $(2, 0), \left(-\dfrac{5}{2}, -\dfrac{9}{4}\right)$

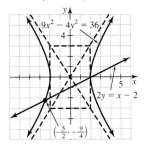

59. a) $(2.5, 1.5)$ **b)** $(\sqrt{7}, \sqrt{2})$

Section 12.5 Warm-ups F T T T F F F T T T
1.

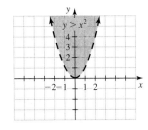

3.

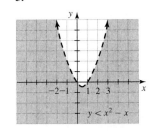

5.

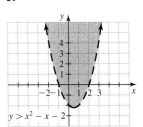

7.

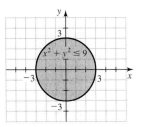

9.

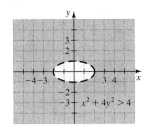

11.

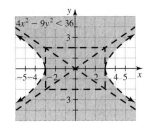

13.

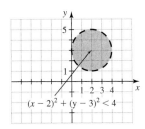

15.

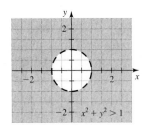

17.

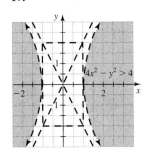

19.

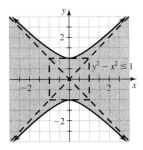

21.

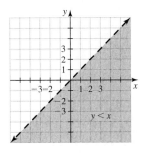

23.

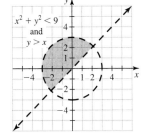

25.

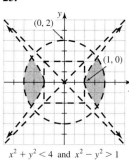

$x^2 + y^2 < 4$ and $x^2 - y^2 > 1$

27.

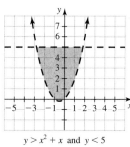

$y > x^2 + x$ and $y < 5$

41.

$x^2 + y^2 < 1$ and $y < x^2$

43.

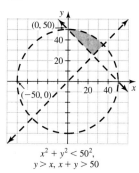

$x^2 + y^2 < 50^2$, $y > x$, $x + y > 50$

45. No solution

Chapter 12 Wrap-up

Enriching Your Mathematical Word Power

1. c   **2.** a   **3.** d   **4.** a   **5.** c   **6.** d   **7.** b   **8.** d
9. c   **10.** a

Review Exercises

1. $\{(3, 9), (-5, 25)\}$

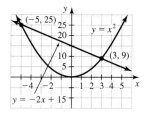

29.

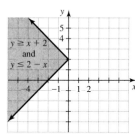

$y \geq x + 2$ and $y \leq 2 - x$

31.

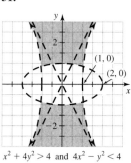

$x^2 + 4y^2 > 4$ and $4x^2 - y^2 < 4$

3. $\left\{\left(\dfrac{\sqrt{3}}{3}, \sqrt{3}\right), \left(-\dfrac{\sqrt{3}}{3}, -\sqrt{3}\right)\right\}$

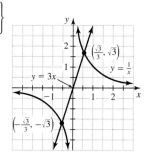

33.

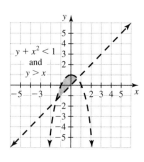

$y + x^2 < 1$ and $y > x$

35.

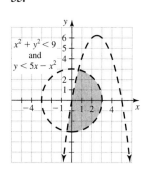

$x^2 + y^2 < 9$ and $y < 5x - x^2$

5. $\{(\sqrt{3}, 1), (-\sqrt{3}, 1)\}$ **7.** $\{(-5, -3), (3, 5)\}$

9. $\{(5, \log(2))\}$ **11.** $\{(2, 4), (-2, 4)\}$ **13.** $2\sqrt{2}$ **15.** $2\sqrt{58}$

17. Vertex $\left(-\dfrac{3}{2}, -\dfrac{81}{4}\right)$, axis of symmetry $x = -\dfrac{3}{2}$, focus
$\left(-\dfrac{3}{2}, -20\right)$, directrix $y = -\dfrac{41}{2}$

19. Vertex $\left(-\dfrac{3}{2}, -\dfrac{1}{4}\right)$, axis of symmetry $x = -\dfrac{3}{2}$, focus $\left(-\dfrac{3}{2}, 0\right)$,
directrix $y = -\dfrac{1}{2}$

21. Vertex $(2, 3)$ axis of symmetry $x = 2$, focus $\left(2, \dfrac{5}{2}\right)$,
directrix $y = \dfrac{7}{2}$

23. $y = 2(x - 2)^2 - 7$, $(2, -7)$

25. $y = -\dfrac{1}{2}(x + 1)^2 + 1$, $(-1, 1)$

37.

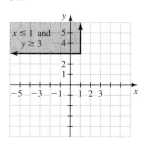

$x \leq 1$ and $y \geq 3$

39.

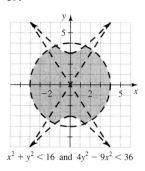

$x^2 + y^2 < 16$ and $4y^2 - 9x^2 < 36$

27. $(0, 0)$, 10

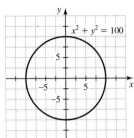

29. $(2, -3)$, 9

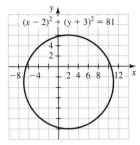

31. $(0, 0)$, $\dfrac{2}{3}$

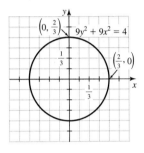

33. $x^2 + (y - 3)^2 = 36$ **35.** $(x - 2)^2 + (y + 7)^2 = 25$

37.

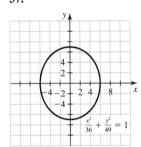

39.

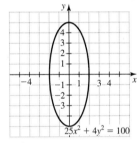

41.

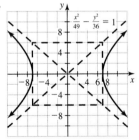

43.

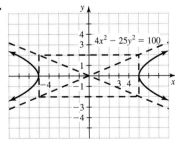

45.

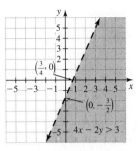

47.

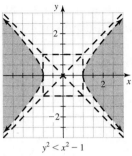

49.

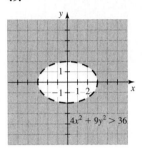

51.

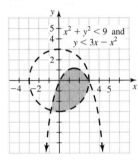

53.

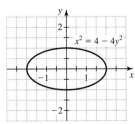

55. Hyperbola **57.** Circle **59.** Circle **61.** Circle
63. Hyperbola **65.** Hyperbola

67.

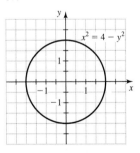

69.

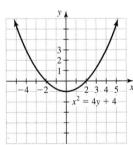

71.

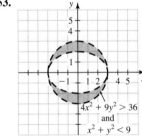

73.

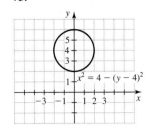

75. $x^2 + y^2 = 25$ **77.** $(x + 1)^2 + (y - 5)^2 = 36$

79. $y = \frac{1}{4}(x - 1)^2 + 3$ **81.** $y = x^2$ **83.** $y = \frac{2}{9}x^2$

85. $\{(4, -3), (-3, 4)\}$ **87.** $\varnothing$ **89.** 6 ft, 2 ft

Chapter 12 Test

1.

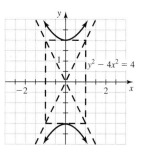

2.

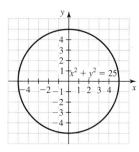

3.

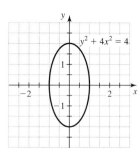

4.

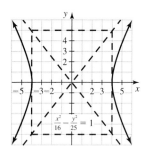

5.

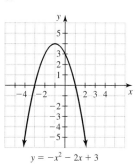

6.

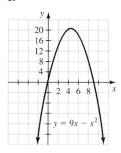

7.

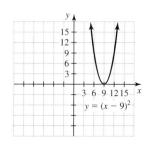

8.

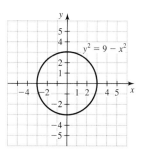

9.

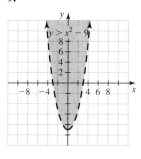

10.

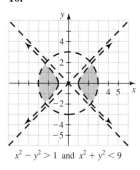

$x^2 - y^2 > 1$ and $x^2 + y^2 < 9$

11.

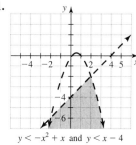

$y < -x^2 + x$ and $y < x - 4$

12. $\{(-5, 27), (3, -5)\}$ **13.** $\{(\sqrt{3}, 3), (-\sqrt{3}, 3)\}$

14. $2\sqrt{2}$ **15.** $(-1, -5), 6$

16. Vertex $\left(-\frac{1}{2}, \frac{11}{4}\right)$, focus $\left(-\frac{1}{2}, 3\right)$, directrix $y = \frac{5}{2}$, axis of symmetry $x = -\frac{1}{2}$, upward

17. $y = \frac{1}{2}(x - 3)^2 - 5$ **18.** $(x + 1)^2 + (y - 3)^2 = 13$

19. 12 ft, 9 ft

Making Connections Chapters 1–12

1.

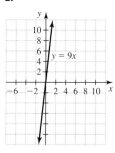

2.

(See graph)

3.

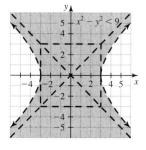

4.

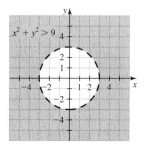

5.

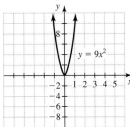

6.

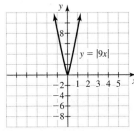

7.

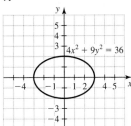

8.

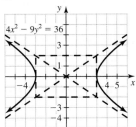

9.

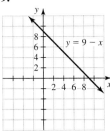

10.

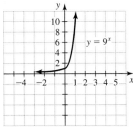

11. $x^2 + 4xy + 4y^2$ **12.** $x^3 + 3x^2y + 3xy^2 + y^3$
13. $a^3 + 3a^2b + 3ab^2 + b^3$ **14.** $a^2 - 6ab + 9b^2$
15. $6a^2 - 7a - 5$ **16.** $x^3 - y^3$ **17.** $\{(1, 2)\}$
18. $\{(3, 4), (4, 3)\}$ **19.** $\{(1, -2, 3)\}$ **20.** $\{(-1, 1), (3, 9)\}$

21. $x = -\dfrac{b}{a}$ **22.** $x = \dfrac{-d \pm \sqrt{d^2 - 4wm}}{2w}$

23. $B = \dfrac{2A - bh}{h}$ **24.** $x = \dfrac{2y}{y - 2}$ **25.** $m = \dfrac{L}{1 + xt}$

26. $t = \dfrac{y^2}{9a^2}$ **27.** $y = -\dfrac{2}{3}x - \dfrac{5}{3}$ **28.** $y = -2x$

29. $(x - 2)^2 + (y - 5)^2 = 45$ **30.** $\left(-\dfrac{3}{2}, 3\right), \dfrac{3\sqrt{5}}{2}$

31. $-10 + 6i$ **32.** -1 **33.** $3 - 5i$ **34.** $7 + 6i\sqrt{2}$

35. $-8 - 27i$ **36.** $-3 + 3i$ **37.** 29 **38.** $-\dfrac{3}{2} - i$

39. $-\dfrac{1}{2} + \dfrac{9}{2}i$ **40.** $2 - i\sqrt{2}$

41. a) $q = -500x + 400$ **b)** $R = -500x^2 + 400x$
c)   **d)** \$0.40 per pound
                                e) \$80

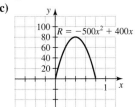

Chapter 13

Section 13.1 Warm-ups T T T F F F T F T T
1. A sequence is a list of numbers.
3. A finite sequence is a function whose domain is the set of positive integers less than or equal to some fixed positive integer.
5. 1, 4, 9, 16, 25, 36, 49, 64
7. $-1, \dfrac{1}{2}, -\dfrac{1}{3}, \dfrac{1}{4}, -\dfrac{1}{5}, \dfrac{1}{6}, -\dfrac{1}{7}, \dfrac{1}{8}, -\dfrac{1}{9}, \dfrac{1}{10}$

9. $1, -2, 4, -8, 16$ **11.** $\dfrac{1}{2}, \dfrac{1}{4}, \dfrac{1}{8}, \dfrac{1}{16}, \dfrac{1}{32}, \dfrac{1}{64}$

13. $-1, 1, 3, 5, 7, 9, 11$ **15.** $1, \dfrac{\sqrt{2}}{2}, \dfrac{\sqrt{3}}{3}, \dfrac{1}{2}, \dfrac{\sqrt{5}}{5}$

17. $\dfrac{1}{2}, \dfrac{1}{6}, \dfrac{1}{12}, \dfrac{1}{20}$ **19.** $-\dfrac{1}{3}, -1, 1, \dfrac{1}{3}$ **21.** $-1, 0, -1, 4$

23. $1, \dfrac{1}{4}, \dfrac{1}{9}, \dfrac{1}{16}$ **25.** $a_n = 2n - 1$

27. $a_n = (-1)^{n+1}$ **29.** $a_n = 2n - 2$ **31.** $a_n = 3n$
33. $a_n = 3n + 1$ **35.** $a_n = (-1)^n 2^{n-1}$

37. $a_n = (n - 1)^2$ **39.** $4, 2, 1, \dfrac{1}{2}, \dfrac{1}{4}$ yard line

41. \$36,687, \$38,521, \$40,447, \$42,470, \$44,593, \$46,823
43. \$1,000,000, \$800,000, \$640,000, \$512,000
45. 27 in., 13.5 in., 9 in., 6.75 in., 5.4 in.
47. 137,438,953,500, larger
51. a) 0.9048, 0.3677, 0.00004517   **b)** a_n goes to zero

Section 13.2 Warm-ups T F F F F T T T T F
1. Summation notation provides a way to write a sum without writing out all of the terms.
3. A series is the indicated sum of the terms of a sequence.

5. 30 **7.** 24 **9.** $\dfrac{31}{32}$ **11.** 50 **13.** -7 **15.** 0

17. $\displaystyle\sum_{i=1}^{6} i$ **19.** $\displaystyle\sum_{i=1}^{6} (-1)^i (2i - 1)$ **21.** $\displaystyle\sum_{i=1}^{6} i^2$ **23.** $\displaystyle\sum_{i=1}^{4} \dfrac{1}{2 + i}$

25. $\displaystyle\sum_{i=1}^{3} \ln(i + 1)$ **27.** $\displaystyle\sum_{i=1}^{4} a_i$ **29.** $\displaystyle\sum_{i=1}^{48} x_{i+2}$ **31.** $\displaystyle\sum_{i=1}^{n} w_i$

33. $\displaystyle\sum_{j=0}^{4} (j + 1)^2$ **35.** $\displaystyle\sum_{j=1}^{13} (2j - 3)$ **37.** $\displaystyle\sum_{j=1}^{5} \dfrac{1}{j + 3}$

39. $\displaystyle\sum_{j=0}^{3} x^{2j+5}$ **41.** $\displaystyle\sum_{j=0}^{n-1} x^{j+1}$

43. $x + x^2 + x^3 + x^4 + x^5 + x^6$ **45.** $x_0 - x_1 + x_2 - x_3$

47. $x + 2x^2 + 3x^3$ **49.** $\displaystyle\sum_{i=1}^{9} 2^{-i}$ **51.** $\displaystyle\sum_{i=1}^{4} 1,000,000(0.8)^{i-1}$

53. A sequence is basically a list of numbers. A series is the indicated sum of the terms of a sequence.

Section 13.3 Warm-ups F F F F F F T T T F
1. An arithmetic sequence is one in which each term after the first is obtained by adding a fixed amount to the previous term.
3. An arithmetic series is an indicated sum of an arithmetic sequence.

5. $a_n = 6n - 6$ **7.** $a_n = 5n + 2$
9. $a_n = 2n - 6$ **11.** $a_n = -4n + 9$
13. $a_n = -7n + 5$ **15.** $a_n = 0.5n - 3.5$
17. $a_n = -0.5n - 5.5$ **19.** 9, 13, 17, 21, 25
21. 7, 5, 3, 1, −1   **23.** −4, −1, 2, 5, 8
25. −2, −5, −8, −11, −14
27. −7, −11, −15, −19, −23   **29.** 4.5, 5, 5.5, 6, 6.5
31. 1020, 1040, 1060, 1080, 1100
33. 51   **35.** 4   **37.** 26   **39.** 17   **41.** 1176
43. 330   **45.** −481   **47.** 435   **49.** −540   **51.** 150
53. −308   **55.** $25,000   **57.** 1085   **59.** b

Section 13.4 Warm-ups F F T T T T F F T F

1. A geometric sequence is one in which each term after the first is obtained by multiplying the preceding term by a constant.
3. A geometric series is an indicated sum of a geometric sequence.
5. The approximate value of r^n when n is large and $|r| < 1$ is 0.
7. $a_n = \frac{1}{3}(3)^{n-1}$ **9.** $a_n = 64\left(\frac{1}{8}\right)^{n-1}$ **11.** $a_n = 8\left(-\frac{1}{2}\right)^{n-1}$
13. $a_n = 2(-2)^{n-1}$ **15.** $a_n = -\frac{1}{3}\left(\frac{3}{4}\right)^{n-1}$ **17.** $2, \frac{2}{3}, \frac{2}{9}, \frac{2}{27}, \frac{2}{81}$
19. 1, −2, 4, −8, 16   **21.** $\frac{1}{2}, \frac{1}{4}, \frac{1}{8}, \frac{1}{16}, \frac{1}{32}$
23. 0.78, 0.6084, 0.4746, 0.3702, 0.2887
25. 5   **27.** $\frac{1}{3}$ **29.** $-\frac{1}{9}$ **31.** $\frac{511}{512}$ **33.** $\frac{11}{32}$
35. $\frac{63,050}{729}$ **37.** 5115   **39.** 0.111111   **41.** 42.8259
43. $\frac{1}{4}$ **45.** 9   **47.** $\frac{8}{3}$ **49.** $\frac{3}{7}$ **51.** 6   **53.** $\frac{1}{3}$
55. $\frac{4}{33}$ **57.** $3,042,435.27   **59.** $21,474,836.47
61. $5,000,000   **63.** d   **65.** $\frac{8}{33}$

Section 13.5 Warm-ups F F F T T T T T T T

1. The sum obtained for a power of a binomial is called a binomial expansion.
3. The expression $n!$ is the product of the positive integers from 1 through n.
5. 10   **7.** 56
9. $r^5 + 5r^4t + 10r^3t^2 + 10r^2t^3 + 5rt^4 + t^5$
11. $m^3 - 3m^2n + 3mn^2 - n^3$
13. $x^3 + 6ax^2 + 12a^2x + 8a^3$
15. $x^8 - 8x^6 + 24x^4 - 32x^2 + 16$
17. $x^7 - 7x^6 + 21x^5 - 35x^4 + 35x^3 - 21x^2 + 7x - 1$
19. $a^{12} - 36a^{11}b + 594a^{10}b^2 - 5940a^9b^3$
21. $x^{18} + 45x^{16} + 900x^{14} + 10,500x^{12}$
23. $x^{22} - 22x^{21} + 231x^{20} - 1540x^{19}$
25. $\frac{x^{10}}{1024} + \frac{5x^9y}{768} + \frac{5x^8y^2}{256} + \frac{5x^7y^3}{144}$
27. $1287a^8w^5$ **29.** $-11,440m^9n^7$ **31.** $448x^5y^3$

33. $635,043,840a^{28}b^6$ **35.** $\sum_{i=0}^{8} \frac{8!}{(8-i)!\,i!}a^{8-i}m^i$
37. $\sum_{i=0}^{5} \frac{5!(-2)^i}{(5-i)!\,i!}a^{5-i}x^i$
39. $a^3 + b^3 + c^3 + 3a^2b + 3a^2c + 3ab^2 + 3ac^2$
$+ 3b^2c + 3bc^2 + 6abc$

Chapter 13 Wrap-up

Enriching Your Mathematical Word Power

1. a   **2.** d   **3.** c   **4.** b   **5.** a   **6.** c   **7.** d   **8.** b
9. d   **10.** a

Review Exercises

1. 1, 8, 27, 64, 125   **3.** 1, 1, −3, 5, −7, 9   **5.** $-1, -\frac{1}{2}, -\frac{1}{3}$
7. $\frac{1}{3}, \frac{1}{5}, \frac{1}{7}$ **9.** 4, 5, 6   **11.** 36   **13.** 40   **15.** $\sum_{i=1}^{\infty} \frac{1}{2(i+1)}$
17. $\sum_{i=1}^{\infty} (i-1)^2$ **19.** $\sum_{i=1}^{\infty} (-1)^{i+1}x_i$ **21.** 6, 11, 16, 21
23. −20, −22, −24, −26   **25.** 3000, 4000, 5000, 6000
27. $a_n = \frac{n}{3}$ **29.** $a_n = 2n$ **31.** 300   **33.** $\frac{289}{6}$ **35.** 35
37. $3, \frac{3}{2}, \frac{3}{4}, \frac{3}{8}$ **39.** $1, \frac{1}{2}, \frac{1}{4}, \frac{1}{8}$
41. 0.23, 0.0023, 0.000023, 0.00000023
43. $a_n = \frac{1}{2}(6)^{n-1}$ **45.** $a_n = 0.7(0.1)^{n-1}$ **47.** $\frac{40}{81}$
49. 0.3333333333   **51.** $\frac{3}{8}$ **53.** 54
55. $m^5 + 5m^4n + 10m^3n^2 + 10m^2n^3 + 5mn^4 + n^5$
57. $a^6 - 9a^4b + 27a^2b^2 - 27b^3$
59. $495x^8y^4$ **61.** $372,736a^{12}b^2$ **63.** $\sum_{i=0}^{7} \frac{7!}{(7-i)!\,i!}a^{7-i}w^i$
65. Neither   **67.** Arithmetic   **69.** Arithmetic
71. $\frac{1}{\sqrt[3]{180}}$ **73.** $-1 + \frac{1}{2} - \frac{1}{6} + \frac{1}{24} - \frac{1}{120}$
75. $a^5 + 5a^4b + 10a^3b^2 + 10a^2b^3 + 5ab^4 + b^5$
77. 26   **79.** $118,634.11   **81.** $13,784.92

Chapter 13 Test

1. −10, −4, 2, 8   **2.** 5, 0.5, 0.05, 0.005
3. $-1, \frac{1}{2}, -\frac{1}{6}, \frac{1}{24}$ **4.** $1, \frac{3}{4}, \frac{5}{9}, \frac{7}{16}$ **5.** $a_n = 10 - 3n$
6. $a_n = -25\left(-\frac{1}{5}\right)^{n-1}$ **7.** $a_n = (-1)^{n-1}2n$ **8.** $a_n = n^2$
9. 5 + 7 + 9 + 11 + 13
10. 5 + 10 + 20 + 40 + 80 + 160
11. $m^4 + 4m^3q + 6m^2q^2 + 4mq^3 + q^4$
12. 750   **13.** $\frac{155}{8}$ **14.** 5   **15.** 10,100
16. $\frac{1}{2}$ **17.** $\frac{511}{128}$ **18.** ±2   **19.** 11   **20.** $1365r^{11}t^4$
21. $-448a^{10}b^3$ **22.** $86,545.41

Making Connections Chapters 1–13

1. 6   **2.** $n^2 - 3$

3. $x^2 + 2xh + h^2 - 3$ **4.** $x^2 - 2x - 2$ **5.** 11

6. 6   **7.** 4   **8.** 32   **9.** $\frac{1}{2}$ **10.** 3   **11.** 1

12. x **13.** $-\frac{27}{2}$ **14.** $-\frac{8}{3}$ **15.** $-\frac{128}{9}$ **16.** 16

17.

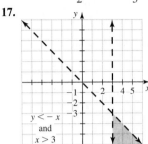

18.

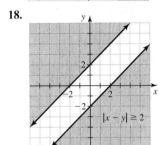

19.

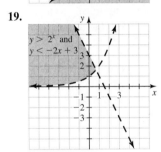

20.

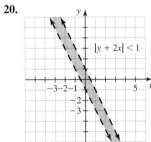

21.

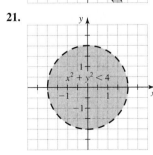

22.

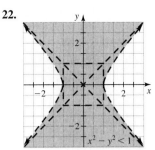

23.

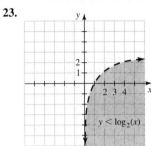

24.

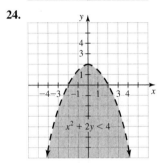

25.

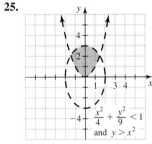

26. $\frac{a^2 + b^2}{ab}$ **27.** $\frac{y - 3}{y}$ **28.** $\frac{10}{(x - 3)(x + 3)(x + 1)}$

29. $\frac{2(x^3 - 64)}{x^3 - 16}$ **30.** $\frac{a^7}{b^4}$ **31.** 1   **32.** 4   **33.** $\frac{1}{32}$

34. -2 **35.** $\frac{1}{9}$ **36.** $-\frac{1}{8}$ **37.** $\frac{1}{4}$ **38.** $\frac{1}{5}$ **39.** 25

40. a) 105.8 cm or 41.7 in.   **c)** 1.3 years

Chapter 14

Section 14.1 Warm-ups F F T T T F T T F T

1. A tree diagram shows the number of different ways that a sequence of events can occur.

3. A permutation is an ordering or arrangement of distinct objects in a linear manner.

5. 12   **7.** 1024   **9.** 8   **11.** 120   **13.** 1320
15. 35,904   **17.** 1.0995×10^{12} **19.** 1.01989×10^{46}
21. 180   **23.** 9,000,000   **25.** 5040
27. 26,000,000, 156,000,000   **29.** 8   **31.** 1×10^{10}
33. 24   **35.** 336   **37.** 1   **39.** 210   **41.** 220
43. 364   **45.** 152,096

Section 14.2 Warm-ups T T F F F T T F T T
1. A combination of n things taken r at a time is a subset of size r taken from a set of n elements.
3. In a labeling problem we want the number of ways of labeling n objects with n labels, where some of the labels are identical.
5. 2,598,960   **7.** 10   **9.** 15,504   **11.** 13,983,816
13. 35   **15.** 120   **17.** 56   **19.** 479,001,600
21. 591,600,030   **23.** 3, 6, 10, $C(n, 2)$ **25.** 36   **27.** 8
29. $C(n, r) = \dfrac{n!}{(n - r)!r!}$ and $C(n, n - r) = \dfrac{n!}{r!(n - r)!}$
31. 60   **33.** 21,162,960   **35.** 576   **37.** 960,960
39. 5.36447×10^{28}, larger   **41.** 180, 2,520, 50,400
43. 698,377,680   **45.** 630   **47.** 2520   **49.** 56

Section 14.3 Warm-ups F F T T F F T F F F
1. An experiment is a process for which the outcomes are uncertain.
3. An event is a subset of a sample space.
5. The addition rule says that if A and B are events in a sample space, then $P(A \cup B) = P(A) + P(B) - P(A \cap B)$.
7. $\dfrac{1}{2}, \dfrac{5}{6}, \dfrac{5}{6}$, 0, 1   **9.** $\dfrac{1}{4}, \dfrac{3}{4}, \dfrac{1}{4}, \dfrac{3}{4}$ **11.** $\dfrac{1}{36}, \dfrac{11}{36}, \dfrac{6}{36}$, 1, 0
13. $\dfrac{1}{4}, \dfrac{2}{3}, \dfrac{2}{3}, \dfrac{1}{3}$ **15.** $\dfrac{1}{90}, \dfrac{1}{45}, \dfrac{2}{45}$ **17.** $\dfrac{1}{2,598,960}, \dfrac{1,024}{2,598,960}$
19. 0.79   **21.** $\dfrac{1}{4}$ **23.** $\dfrac{4}{13}$ **25.** 0.995   **27.** $\dfrac{1}{36}, \dfrac{35}{36}, \dfrac{35}{36}$
29. 3 to 2   **31.** 3 to 2, 2 to 3   **33.** 1 to 3, $\dfrac{3}{4}$ **35.** 3 to 5
37. 5 to 31   **39.** 1 to 999,999   **41.** $\dfrac{1}{32}$
43. $\dfrac{1}{7,059,052}, \dfrac{7,059,051}{7,059,052}$, 1 to 7,059,051

Chapter 14 Wrap-up

Enriching Your Mathematical Word Power
1. c   **2.** a   **3.** b   **4.** d   **5.** b   **6.** a   **7.** d   **8.** b
9. d   **10.** a

Review Exercises
1. 14,348,907   **3.** 120   **5.** 144   **7.** 70   **9.** 126, 5, 60
11. 120   **13.** 4620   **15.** 3360, 120   **17.** 64
19. $\dfrac{1}{4096}, \dfrac{1}{4096}$ **21.** $\dfrac{5}{14}, \dfrac{9}{14}$, 0, 1   **23.** 1 to 7   **25.** 3 to 2
27. 0.9   **29.** 40,320   **31.** 20   **33.** 1680   **35.** 28
37. 1680   **39.** 8

Chapter 14 Test
1. 72   **2.** 6840   **3.** 10   **4.** 1848   **5.** 495   **6.** 165
7. 2,522,520   **8.** 120   **9.** $\dfrac{3}{4}$ **10.** 1   **11.** 1 to 3
12. 7 to 1   **13.** 20 to 1, $\dfrac{1}{21}, \dfrac{20}{21}$ **14.** $\dfrac{11}{36}, \dfrac{1}{6}, \dfrac{1}{18}, \dfrac{5}{12}$
15. 4950   **16.** 7,880,400   **17.** 4200

Appendix A

Geometry Review Exercises
1. 12 in.   **2.** 24 ft^2 **3.** 60°   **4.** 6 ft   **5.** 20 cm
6. 144 cm^2 **7.** 24 ft^2 **8.** 13 ft   **9.** 30 cm   **10.** No
11. 84 yd^2 **12.** 30 in.   **13.** 32 ft^2 **14.** 20 km
15. 7 ft, 3 ft^2 **16.** 22 yd   **17.** 50.3 ft^2 **18.** 37.7 ft
19. 150.80 cm^3 **20.** 879.29 ft^2 **21.** 288 in.^{3}, 288 in.^{2}
22. 4 cm   **23.** 100 mi^2, 40 mi   **24.** 20 km
25. 42.25 cm^2 **26.** 33.510 ft^3, 50.265 ft^2
27. 75.4 in.^{3}, 100.5 in.^{2} **28.** 56°   **29.** 5 cm
30. 15 in. and 20 in.   **31.** 149°
32. 12 km   **33.** 10 yd

INDEX

DEFINITIONS, RULES, AND FORMULAS

Subsets of the Real Numbers

Natural Numbers = $\{1, 2, 3, \ldots\}$

Whole Numbers = $\{0, 1, 2, 3, \ldots\}$

Integers = $\{\ldots -3, -2, -1, 0, 1, 2, 3, \ldots\}$

Rational = $\left\{ \dfrac{a}{b} \,\middle|\, a \text{ and } b \text{ are integers with } b \neq 0 \right\}$

Irrational = $\{x \mid x \text{ is not rational}\}$

Properties of the Real Numbers

For all real numbers a, b, and c

$a + b = b + a; \; a \cdot b = b \cdot a$ Commutative

$(a + b) + c = a + (b + c); \; (ab)c = a(bc)$ Associative

$a(b + c) = ab + ac; \; a(b - c) = ab - ac$ Distributive

$a + 0 = a; \; 1 \cdot a = a$ Identity

$a + (-a) = 0; \; a \cdot \dfrac{1}{a} = 1 \; (a \neq 0)$ Inverse

$a \cdot 0 = 0$ Multiplication property of 0

Absolute Value

$|a| = \begin{cases} a & \text{for } a \geq 0 \\ -a & \text{for } a < 0 \end{cases}$

$\sqrt{x^2} = |x|$ for any real number x.

$|x| = k \leftrightarrow x = k \text{ or } x = -k \quad (k > 0)$

$|x| < k \leftrightarrow -k < x < k \quad (k > 0)$

$|x| > k \leftrightarrow x < -k \text{ or } x > k \quad (k > 0)$

(The symbol $\leftrightarrow$ means "if and only if.")

Interval Notation

$(a, b) = \{x \mid a < x < b\}$ $[a, b] = \{x \mid a \leq x \leq b\}$

$(a, b] = \{x \mid a < x \leq b\}$ $[a, b) = \{x \mid a \leq x < b\}$

$(-\infty, a) = \{x \mid x < a\}$ $(a, \infty) = \{x \mid x > a\}$

$(-\infty, a] = \{x \mid x \leq a\}$ $[a, \infty) = \{x \mid x \geq a\}$

Exponents

$a^0 = 1$ $a^{-1} = \dfrac{1}{a}$

$a^{-r} = \dfrac{1}{a^r} = \left(\dfrac{1}{a}\right)^r$ $\dfrac{1}{a^{-r}} = a^r$

$a^r a^s = a^{r+s}$ $\dfrac{a^r}{a^s} = a^{r-s}$

$(a^r)^s = a^{rs}$ $(ab)^r = a^r b^r$

$\left(\dfrac{a}{b}\right)^r = \dfrac{a^r}{b^r}$ $\left(\dfrac{a}{b}\right)^{-r} = \left(\dfrac{b}{a}\right)^r$

Roots and Radicals

$a^{1/n} = \sqrt[n]{a}$ $a^{m/n} = \left(\sqrt[n]{a}\right)^m = \sqrt[n]{a^m}$

$\sqrt[n]{ab} = \sqrt[n]{a} \cdot \sqrt[n]{b}$ $\sqrt[n]{\dfrac{a}{b}} = \dfrac{\sqrt[n]{a}}{\sqrt[n]{b}}$

Factoring

$a^2 + 2ab + b^2 = (a + b)^2$

$a^2 - 2ab + b^2 = (a - b)^2$

$a^2 - b^2 = (a + b)(a - b)$

$a^3 - b^3 = (a - b)(a^2 + ab + b^2)$

$a^3 + b^3 = (a + b)(a^2 - ab + b^2)$

Rational Expressions

$\dfrac{a}{b} + \dfrac{c}{b} = \dfrac{a + c}{b}$ $\dfrac{a}{b} - \dfrac{c}{b} = \dfrac{a - c}{b}$

$\dfrac{ac}{bc} = \dfrac{a}{b}$ $\dfrac{a}{b} + \dfrac{c}{d} = \dfrac{ad + bc}{bd}$

$\dfrac{a}{b} \cdot \dfrac{c}{d} = \dfrac{ac}{bd}$ $\dfrac{a}{b} \div \dfrac{c}{d} = \dfrac{a}{b} \cdot \dfrac{d}{c}$

If $\dfrac{a}{b} = \dfrac{c}{d}$, then $ad = bc$.

Quadratic Formula

The solutions to $ax^2 + bx + c = 0$ with $a \neq 0$ are

$$x = \dfrac{-b \pm \sqrt{b^2 - 4ac}}{2a}.$$

Distance Formula

The distance from (x_1, y_1) to (x_2, y_2), is

$$\sqrt{(x_2 - x_1)^2 + (y_2 - y_1)^2}.$$

Midpoint Formula

The midpoint of the line segment with endpoints (x_1, y_1) and (x_2, y_2) is

$$\left(\dfrac{x_1 + x_2}{2}, \dfrac{y_1 + y_2}{2}\right).$$

Slope Formula

The slope of the line through (x_1, y_1) and (x_2, y_2) is

$$\dfrac{y_2 - y_1}{x_2 - x_1} \quad (\text{for } x_1 \neq x_2).$$

Linear Function

$f(x) = mx + b$ with $m \neq 0$

Graph is a line with slope m.

A constant function
$f(x) = 2$

The identity function
$f(x) = x$

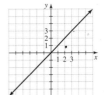

Absolute Value Function

$f(x) = |x|$

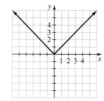

Quadratic Function

$f(x) = ax^2 + bx + c$ with $a \neq 0$

Graph is a parabola.

$f(x) = x^2$ (the squaring function)

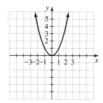

Square-Root Function

$f(x) = \sqrt{x}$

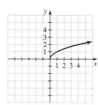

Exponential Function

$f(x) = a^x$ for $a > 0$ and $a \neq 1$

One-to-one property: $a^m = a^n \leftrightarrow m = n$

$f(x) = a^x$ for $a > 1$ $\qquad$ $f(x) = a^x$ for $0 < a < 1$

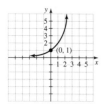 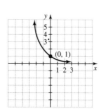

Logarithmic Function

$f(x) = \log_a(x)$ for $a > 0$ and $a \neq 1$

One-to-one property: $\log_a(m) = \log_a(n) \leftrightarrow m = n$

Base-a logarithm: $y = \log_a(x) \leftrightarrow a^y = x$

Natural logarithm: $y = \ln(x) \leftrightarrow e^y = x$

Common logarithm: $y = \log(x) \leftrightarrow 10^y = x$

$f(x) = \log_a(x)$ $\qquad$ $f(x) = \log_a(x)$
for $a > 1$ $\qquad\qquad$ for $0 < a < 1$

Properties of Logarithms

$\log_a(a) = 1$ $\qquad\qquad$ $\log_a(1) = 0$

$\log_a(a^M) = M$ $\qquad\qquad$ $a^{\log_a(M)} = M$

$\log_a(MN) = \log_a(M) + \log_a(N)$

$\log_a\left(\dfrac{M}{N}\right) = \log_a(M) - \log_a(N)$

$\log_a(M^N) = N \cdot \log_a(M)$

$\log_a\left(\dfrac{1}{N}\right) = -\log_a(N)$

$\log_a(M) = \dfrac{\log_b(M)}{\log_b(a)} = \dfrac{\ln(M)}{\ln(a)} = \dfrac{\log(M)}{\log(a)}$

Interest Formulas

A = amount and P = principal

Compound interest: $A = P(1 + i)^n$, where n = number of periods and i = interest rate per period

Continuous compounding: $A = Pe^{rt}$, where r = annual interest rate and t = time in years

Variation

Direct: $y = kx$ $\quad (k \neq 0)$

Inverse: $y = \dfrac{k}{x}$ $\quad (k \neq 0)$

Joint: $y = kxz$ $\quad (k \neq 0)$

Straight Line

Slope-intercept form: $y = mx + b$

Slope: m $\qquad$ y-intercept: $(0, b)$

Point-slope form: $y - y_1 = m(x - x_1)$

Slope: m $\qquad$ Point: (x_1, y_1)

Standard form: $Ax + By = C$

Horizontal: $y = k$ $\qquad$ Vertical: $x = k$